ENCYCLOPEDIA OF
FOOD AND
COOKERY

ENCYCLOPEDIA OF
FOOD AND
COOKERY

MARGARET FULTON

FOREWORD BY
PRUE LEITH

B. Mitchell

DEDICATION

While working on this book I continually drew on the support of the other members of my family who share my love of cooking and interest in food – my sister Jean Hatfield and my daughter Suzanne Gibbs, cookbook authors and food writers in their own right, with whom I share a very happy relationship. I look forward to a time when my granddaughters, Kate and Louise Gibbs, will cook from this book. Their fascination of the happenings of the kitchen show their strong inheritance! My only regret is that my mother is not here to see the important role she played in establishing a line of dedicated, fun-loving cooks.

Margaret Fulton

RECIPE NOTES
All spoon measurements are level.
All cup measurements are level.
Use a measuring cup or jug for liquids.
Plain (all-purpose) flour and granulated sugar are
used unless otherwise specified.
Standard eggs of 55 g weight are used, unless
otherwise specified.
All ovens should be preheated to the specified
temperature, particularly for cakes, biscuits and
pastry recipes.

First published 1985 by Octopus Books Ltd, 59 Grosvenor Street, London W1
©1984 Octopus Books Ltd
ISBN 0 7064 2067 5
Printed and bound in Hungary

FOREWORD

Margaret Fulton's Encyclopedia of Food and Cookery is an enviable achievement. It is the sort of practical, accessible and all-encompassing book that every generation needs. It is written in a conversational and encouraging tone, and Mrs. Fulton's experience and informed opinion permeate the book. 'Not recommended', she says firmly of dried abalone. 'An ethereal souffléed dumpling' is her definition of a quenelle.

Mrs. Fulton is interested in, and delighted by, good food, but not obsessed by gourmandise – her pleasure in a simple English Roly-Poly is as great as her enthusiasm for a liqueur-soaked French Savarin. And the proximity of her native Australia to the East has meant the inclusion of Indonesian Satay, Chinese soups and Japanese Sashimi.

I suppose if I had to describe this book in one word, instead of the 500-odd here, I would have to do so with the adjective 'sensible'. The encyclopaedic information, such as the origin of the vanilla bean or the temperature fermenting yogurt, is presented in clear, relaxed phrases. No hint of academia, no whiff of gastro-snobbery here. The recipes, which occur where you would expect to find them (rice puddings and fried rice both under R for Rice: Upside-down-Cake under U) are interspersed with odd bits of information or advice – on the best Chinese rice wine, for example, or the right saucepan for Saffron rice or how to ensure a perfect topping for the Upside-down Cake.

The bulk of the book is for family food. Economic, sensible, achievable by all of us. Mrs. Fulton is not above a flour-thickened 'Memsahib's curry', English style, because she knows it is a useful and delicious recipe for using up left-over roast lamb. But food buffs should not curl a lip. The other eight curries are authentic, careful recipes giving rich moist curry thickened only by their sauces' slow reduction. Mrs. Fulton is a serious food writer. But she's a mother and grandmother too, and that helps.

I have become rather bored of late with exquisite photographs of one perfect langoustine decorating the side of an immaculate thimble-sized fish mousse or two wafer-thin slices of avocado. And also of the 'country-style' farmhouse kitchen bedecked with onion strings, baskets of herbs and bubbling hot-pot. It is a great relief therefore to find drawings that are crystal-clear and tell you something – how to fillet fish, clean a crab or carve a leg of lamb, for example – and photographs that show you what you are trying to produce, with a minimum of designer's dreamtime about them.

To sum up: this is an easy-to-use cookbook, a fascinating browsing book, and a thoroughly reliable reference book. It has given me great pleasure already and I know it will continue to do so as it becomes tacky with age and use. Good cookery books soon lose their coffee-table looks and acquire that well-thumbed, much loved look and exude a faint smell of cinnamon and olive oil. Which is, of course, the only honourable fate for an Encyclopedia of Food and Cookery.

Prue Leith

A

ABALONE

The beautiful single ear-shaped shell of the abalone is lined with mother of pearl, which is used to make buttons. The tough, fleshy mollusc in the shell is the edible part, and has a delicious clam-like flavour. Abalone is considered a great delicacy and is available fresh or canned.

If fresh, it should be cut into thin slices and pounded to tenderize it before sautéeing briefly (45–55 seconds). It will toughen if overcooked. Dried abalone has to be soaked for 4 days before using and is not recommended.

Sautéed Abalone Slice abalone into strips against the grain. If fresh, pound with a meat mallet until soft and limp. Coat with egg and breadcrumbs or flour, and cook very quickly in hot oil or butter until golden. Season with salt and pepper and serve with lemon wedges or Tartare Sauce (see page 205).

ABERDEEN SAUSAGE

A Scottish favourite. Serve cold, with salads.

Aberdeen Sausage

250 g/8 oz bacon, rind removed; 500 g (1 lb) minced (ground) beef; 60 g/2 oz (1 cup) fresh breadcrumbs; 2 tsp Worcestershire sauce; 1 tbsp finely chopped parsley; 1 tsp salt; freshly ground black pepper; $\frac{1}{2}$ tsp nutmeg; grated rind $\frac{1}{2}$ lemon; 1 egg; flour for dusting; fine dry breadcrumbs.

Mince bacon and combine with remaining ingredients, except the flour and dry breadcrumbs. Form into a roll about 8 cm (3 in) wide and dust with flour. Tie securely in a scalded, floured cloth and plunge into a saucepan of boiling water. Boil steadily for 2 hours, replacing water if necessary. Unwrap while hot and roll in dry breadcrumbs. Place on a baking tray and dry in a preheated cool oven (150°C/300°F, Gas Mark 2) for 15 minutes. Serves 6.

AIOLI

A garlic-flavoured sauce from Provence in France. Serve it with hot or cold fish, cold meats, cooked or raw vegetables and hard-boiled (hard-cooked) eggs.

Aïoli

4 fat cloves garlic; salt; 1 egg yolk; 250 ml/ 8 fl oz (1 cup) olive oil; 1 tbsp lemon juice.

Crush garlic to a pulp with $\frac{1}{4}$ tsp salt. Beat in egg yolk, then 3 tbsp olive oil drop by drop, then lemon juice. Beat in remaining oil a little at a time. Mixture should be smooth and thick, like mayonnaise. Taste and adjust seasoning. Makes 300 ml/$\frac{1}{2}$ pint (1$\frac{1}{4}$ cups).

ALLSPICE

A spice which seems to combine the flavours of cinnamon, cloves and nutmeg. The source is the berry of the pimento tree, and allspice is sometimes bought as 'pimento'. Whole berries are used in pickles and preserves. Crushed, they flavour cakes, puddings, biscuits and some meat and fish dishes.

ALMOND

Whole, slivered, chopped, crushed or ground, plain or toasted, almonds are one of the pleasures of the kitchen.

To blanch almonds (remove brown skin): Cover whole almonds with boiling water and leave until skins are wrinkled (about 5 minutes). Drain, pinch off skins and dry, without colouring, in a preheated very cool oven (120°C/250°F, Gas Mark $\frac{1}{2}$).

To sliver or flake almonds: Cover freshly blanched nuts with boiling water and simmer 2–3 minutes; drain. Using a very sharp paring knife, cut almonds horizontally into flakes, or split in 2 and cut each half lengthways into fine slivers. Dry, without colouring, in a preheated very cool oven (120°C/250°F, Gas Mark $\frac{1}{2}$).

To toast almonds: Spread in a single layer on a baking tray and bake in a preheated cool oven (150°C/300°F, Gas Mark 2) turning them frequently until golden.

To grind almonds: Use a special rotary nut mill or process in small batches in a blender or food processor. Use high speed but be careful to stop as soon as the almonds become a dry meal. **See recipes.**

Almond Soup

125 g/4 oz (1 cup) ground almonds; 750 ml/1$\frac{1}{4}$ pints (3 cups) chicken stock; 1 small onion stuck with 2 cloves; 1 bay leaf; 120 ml/4 fl oz ($\frac{1}{2}$ cup) milk; pinch nutmeg; salt and freshly ground black pepper; 30 g/1 oz (2 tbsp) butter; 2 tbsp flour; 250 ml/8 fl oz (1 cup) single (light) cream; slivered toasted almonds to garnish.

Combine ground almonds, stock, onion and bay leaf in a saucepan. Simmer, covered, 30 minutes. Remove onion and bay leaf, pour mixture into a jug and add milk, nutmeg, salt and pepper. Melt butter, add flour and stir on low heat 1 minute. Remove from heat, and blend in stock mixture. Stir over heat until boiling. Simmer 5 minutes. Add cream and reheat but do not boil. Serve hot or cold, with a sprinkle of slivered almonds. Serves 4.

Almond Macaroons
(Amaretti)

2 egg whites; 160 g/5$\frac{1}{3}$ oz (1$\frac{1}{3}$ cups) ground almonds; 250 g/8 oz (1 cup) caster sugar;

2 tbsp icing (confectioners) sugar, sifted; extra sifted icing (confectioners) sugar for dusting.

Beat egg whites to a firm snow and fold in almonds and sugars. Pipe mixture on to squares of greaseproof (waxed) paper in small round or oval shapes. Dust with icing (confectioners) sugar and leave about 4 hours. Bake macaroons in a preheated moderate oven (160°C/325°F, Gas Mark 3) for 15 minutes or until delicately browned. Cool before removing from paper squares. Store in an airtight container. Makes 14–16.

Almond Tart

PASTRY (DOUGH): 125 g/4 oz (1 cup) flour; 2 tbsp sugar; ¼ tsp baking powder; 90 g/3 oz (6 tbsp) butter; 1 egg, lightly beaten; 1 tbsp iced water.
FILLING: 125 g/4 oz (½ cup) butter; 250 g/8 oz (1 cup) caster sugar; 30 g/1 oz (¼ cup) flour, sifted; 4 tbsp single (light) cream; 180 g/6 oz (1½ cups) slivered almonds, toasted.

PASTRY (DOUGH): Sift together flour, sugar and baking powder; rub in butter until mixture resembles fine breadcrumbs. Quickly stir in egg and add enough iced water to form into a ball. Knead very lightly, wrap in plastic wrap and chill for 1 hour. Place dough on a lightly floured surface and roll out to line a 20 cm (8 in) flan ring (loose-bottomed pie pan). Chill for 30 minutes.
FILLING: Cream butter, add sugar and beat until light and fluffy. Stir in flour and cream, mixing well. Add almonds and spoon mixture evenly into tart shell. Bake in a preheated moderately hot oven (200°C/400°F, Gas Mark 6) for 30–40 minutes (the filling will not be quite firm). Remove from oven and cool on a wire rack until filling is firm. Serve cold. Serves 8.

Almond-Chicken Party Salad

750 g/1½ lb (3 cups) cooked, diced chicken; 90 g/3 oz (½ cup) sultanas (golden raisins); 60 g/2 oz (½ cup) slivered almonds, toasted; 3 sticks celery, finely sliced; 6 spring onions (scallions), chopped; 175 ml/6 fl oz (¾ cup) Mayonnaise (page 204); 4 tbsp orange juice; salt and freshly ground black pepper.
GARNISH: lettuce leaves; orange slices; extra toasted almonds.

Combine all ingredients for salad. Spoon into a bowl lined with lettuce and garnish with orange and almonds. Serves 4–6.

ALMOND PASTE

This sweet pale paste, made from ground almonds, is used to cover fruit cakes before they are iced (frosted), as a filling in pastries, as an ingredient in biscuits (cookies), etc.

Almond Paste

430 g/14 oz (3 cups) icing (confectioners) sugar, sifted; 250 g/8 oz (2 cups) ground almonds; 2 tbsp lemon juice; 2 tbsp sweet sherry; 1 egg yolk; 2–3 drops almond essence (extract).

Combine icing (confectioners) sugar and ground almonds. Combine lemon juice, sherry, egg yolk and essence (extract). Mix with sugar-almond mixture to form a firm paste which can be rolled out. If necessary, add a little more sherry. Will cover the tops of 2 × 20 cm (8 in) cakes.

To apply almond paste to the top of a cake: Trim top of cake, if necessary, to give a flat surface, or turn cake upside-down and use the bottom. Brush lightly with lightly beaten egg white or warm, sieved apricot jam. On a board dusted with sifted icing (confectioners) sugar, roll out paste to fit cake, place on top and press gently with a rolling pin. Leave several hours or overnight before icing (frosting) cake.

ANCHOVY

A member of the herring family. Anchovies are often eaten fresh where caught, but are more familiar to most people as salted fillets packed in oil. They are also made into a paste, which is used as a spread for toast, or an essence (extract) to flavour sauces, etc. **See recipes.**

Anchovy Butter

Spread on bread, toast, crisp crackers or croûtons, or slice and place on hot cooked steaks. For a milder flavour, soak anchovies in a little milk for 20 minutes before using.

125 g/4 oz (½ cup) butter; 1 tbsp mashed, drained anchovy fillets; squeeze lemon juice.

Cream butter, then beat in anchovies and lemon juice. Store, covered, in refrigerator.

Fettucine with Butter and Anchovies

500 g/1 lb fettucine (ribbon noodles), freshly cooked and drained; 125 g/4 oz (½ cup) butter; 60 g/2 oz (¼ cup) drained, chopped anchovy fillets; freshly ground white pepper; 125 g/4 oz (1 cup) grated Parmesan cheese.

Place fettucine on a heated serving dish. Heat butter with anchovies, stirring well. Grind white pepper over noodles, sprinkle with half the cheese and pour anchovy butter over. Serve remaining cheese separately. Serves 6.

Anchoiade

This spicy anchovy and garlic spread is delicious served on hot dry toast or crunchy French bread. Small black olives and crisp radish make an interesting addition to the plate.

20 anchovy fillets, rinsed; 2 cloves garlic, crushed; 1 tbsp red wine vinegar or lemon juice; freshly ground black pepper; 4 tbsp olive oil; 6 slices white bread or 12 slices French bread.
GARNISH: lemon wedges, red radish; black olives.

Mash anchovies in a mortar (or use a blender or food processor for this). Add garlic, vinegar and pepper, and drizzle oil in very slowly so sauce does not separate. Sprinkle slices of bread with olive oil, place on a baking tray and toast under a preheated grill (broiler) for 2–3 minutes or until slightly crisp. Turn over, spread with anchovy paste and return to heat for 3–5 minutes. Cut each slice into 4 triangles and serve immediately while piping hot. Arrange on a platter with lemon, radish and black olives. Serves 6.

ANGEL CAKE

A delicate American speciality. Because of its light texture it is not cut, but separated into pieces with 2 forks. You should be able to find an angel cake pan – a high tube pan, often with a removable base – in a good kitchen shop.

Angel Cake

125 g/4 oz (1 cup) flour; 370 g/12 oz (1½ cups) caster sugar; 10 egg whites; ¼ tsp salt; 1½ tsp cream of tartar; 1½ tsp vanilla essence (extract); few drops almond essence (extract).

Sift flour and 180 g/6 oz (¾ cup) sugar together 3 times. Beat egg whites with salt and cream of tartar until soft peaks form. Sprinkle rest of sugar over egg whites 2 tbsp at a time, beating well after each addition. Continue beating until whites stand in stiff peaks, then fold in vanilla and almond essence (extract). Sift about a quarter of the dry ingredients over egg whites and fold in gently. Repeat until all the mixture is used. Pour batter into an ungreased 23 cm (9 in) angle cake pan – if there is a speck of grease on the pan, the cake will not rise. Cut gently through batter with a spatula to remove large air bubbles. Bake in a preheated moderate oven 180°C/350°F, Gas Mark 4) for 45–50 minutes or until crust is golden-brown. Take cake from oven and place tube on a funnel or bottle, so cake hangs upside-down. When cool, use a thin knife to help remove cake from pan. Serve plain or iced. Serves 10–12.

ANGELS ON HORSEBACK

The intriguing name for oysters wrapped in thin rashers (slices) of bacon and grilled (broiled) until bacon is crisp. Serve on small rounds of buttered toast or fried bread. Can be served as an hors d'oeuvre or as a savoury.

ANGELICA

An aromatic herb, which most home cooks know as bright green, candied stalks used to decorate desserts, cakes and biscuits. Keep candied angelica airtight to avoid drying out, and if necessary wash in warm water to remove excess sugar, and dry before using.

ANISE/ANISEED

A tall plant which has a pronounced licorice flavour. It is also known as sweet cumin. The tiny, greyish-brown seeds are dried for use in cooking and are called aniseed. To release the full flavour of the seeds, they may be crushed – but use them with a light hand, especially in savoury dishes, as the flavour can dominate. Aniseed is used in fish dishes, in particular some fish and vegetable curries and mussels. It is also added to cheeses, cakes, breads and confectionery, as well as some alcoholic drinks.

Anise Drop Biscuits

These tiny biscuits (cookies) bake to a puffed top on a soft biscuit base.

3 eggs; 250 g/8 oz (1 cup) caster sugar; ½ tsp vanilla essence (extract); 250 g/8 oz (2 cups) flour; 1 tsp baking powder; 1½ tbsp crushed aniseeds.

Beat eggs until light, then beat in sugar, a little at a time. Mixture should be thick and pale yellow. Add vanilla, then flour and baking powder, sifted together. Add aniseed and beat for 5 minutes. Drop mixture in half-teaspoonfuls, well apart, on a baking tray lined with lightly greased foil. Bake in a preheated moderate oven (160°C/325°F Gas Mark 3) for about 12 minutes or until lightly coloured. Remove from oven, loosen biscuits (cookies) on foil and leave them on it, uncovered and at room temperature, for 18 hours to dry. Store in airtight containers. Makes about 90.

ANTIPASTI

The Italian version of appetizers or hors d'oeuvre. They may be hot or cold and, in Italy, are most often served at the table as a first course. Antipasti may be arranged on one large platter for guests to serve themselves, or on individual plates.

Popular ingredients for cold antipasti (Antipasti Freddi) include crisp raw vegetables, lightly cooked vegetables marinated in dressing, slices of ham, prosciutto and salami, marinated mushrooms, stuffed eggs, caviar, smoked salmon, tuna, herring fillets and sardines. Hot antipasti might include chicken livers on crisp fried bread, grilled (broiled) cheese fingers, dumplings stuffed with spinach or cheese, grilled (broiled) sardines and batter-fried seafood. **See recipes.**

Antipasto Variato Use a large, round platter. In the centre, put a mound of drained tuna. Coat with Mayonnaise (see page 204) and sprinkle with capers. Surround tuna with overlapping slices of prosciutto, then a round of salami. Add a circle of thinly sliced fennel, then a circle of hard-boiled (hard-cooked) eggs, cut into quarters, and topped with strips of anchovy. Arrange celery sticks, radishes and olives round the edge. Serve with salt and freshly ground black pepper, separate jugs of oil and vinegar, fresh crusty bread and butter.

Antipasto Misto On a long dish arrange an assortment of salads – raw peppers, seeded and cut into rings; raw mushrooms, sliced; potato salad; whole small red tomatoes (the plum-shaped, egg tomatoes are ideal); fennel or celery, finely sliced. Sprinkle with a little Vinaigrette Dressing (see page 358), top with hard-boiled (hard-cooked) eggs, cut into quarters, and sprinkle with freshly chopped parsley.

See also *Appetizers* and *Hors d'oeuvre*.

Neapolitan Tomato Salad

6 tomatoes, peeled and sliced; 4 tbsp Vinaigrette Dressing (page 358); 2 cloves garlic, finely chopped; 6–8 leaves fresh basil.

Arrange tomato slices overlapping on a large platter and pour over dressing mixed with the garlic. Scatter with freshly cut ribbons of basil. Serves 6–8.

Green Beans and Tuna

500 g (1 lb) green beans, topped, tailed and stringed if necessary; salt; 4 tbsp olive oil; 1 tsp lemon juice; freshly ground black pepper; 1 × 200 g/6½ oz can tuna in oil.

Drop beans into boiling salted water and cook just until crisp tender; drain. While still hot, sprinkle with oil and lemon juice and season with salt and pepper. Drain tuna, break into large chunks and toss with beans. Cover and chill thoroughly before serving. Serves 4–6.

Stuffed Eggs with Anchovies

Use as part of an antipasto tray, or serve on a bed of finely shredded lettuce as a first course (allow 2 per serving).

6 hard-boiled (hard-cooked) eggs; 5 anchovy fillets, mashed; 30 g/1 oz (2 tbsp) butter; 1 tbsp finely chopped parsley; 2 tbsp Mayonnaise (page 204); freshly ground black pepper.

Shell eggs, cut in half lengthways and remove yolks. Mash yolks with anchovies, butter, parsley, mayonnaise and pepper. Refill whites with mixture. Serve slightly chilled. Makes 12.

Crostini con Gorgonzola

(Gorgonzola on Fried Bread Fingers)

BASE: *6 slices white bread, crusts removed and cut into 4 strips each; 30 g/1 oz (2 tbsp) unsalted butter; 3 tbsp olive oil.*
TOPPING: *60 g/2 oz (½ cup) crumbled Gorgonzola cheese at room temperature; 60 g/2 oz (4 tbsp) unsalted butter, softened; 1 tbsp brandy; 1 tsp paprika; freshly ground white pepper.*

BASE: Fry bread strips in hot butter and oil until golden-brown on both sides. Drain on paper towels.
TOPPING: Cream Gorgonzola and butter, and mix in brandy, paprika and pepper. Spread on fried bread and serve at once. This mixture may also be spread on biscuits or toast. Serves 4–6.

Marinated Mushrooms

500 g/1 lb (4 cups) button mushrooms; 2 tbsp olive oil; 120 ml/4 fl oz (½ cup) Vinaigrette Dressing (page 358); 2 cloves garlic, split in half; finely chopped parsley to garnish.

Lightly brown mushrooms in hot olive oil. Do not overcook – they should stay firm. Turn into a bowl, add dressing and garlic and marinate, covered, in refrigerator for several hours. Bring mushrooms to room temperature to serve, sprinkled with chopped parsley. Serves 4–6.

ANZAC BISCUITS

Crunchy and economical – an Australian favourite, made popular during World War I when there were egg shortages. Sent in food parcels to the troops who became famous as Anzacs (Australia, New Zealand Army Corps).

Anzac Biscuits

125 g/4 oz (½ cup) butter; 1 tbsp golden (light corn) syrup; 2 tbsp boiling water; 1½ tsp bicarbonate of soda (baking soda); 105 g/3½ oz (1 cup) rolled oats; 75 g/2½ oz (¾ cup) desiccated (shredded) coconut; 125 g/4 oz (1 cup) flour; 250 g/8 oz (1 cup) sugar.

Melt butter and syrup over low heat. Add boiling water mixed with soda. Pour into mixed dry ingredients and mix well. Drop teaspoonfuls of mixture on to greased baking trays, leaving room for spreading. Bake in a preheated cool oven (150°C/300°F, Gas Mark 2) for 20 minutes. Cool on trays for a few minutes, then remove to wire racks. Store in airtight containers. Makes about 48.

A

APPETIZERS

The name covers a wide variety of foods served in small portions with drinks before a meal, or as the first course. They may include vegetables with a light dressing, dips, small fancy sandwiches, pâtés, cold meats and fish, skewered foods and tiny, hot pastries. **See recipes**.

See also *Antipasti, Canapé, Hors d'oeuvre,* and *Sandwiches*.

Anchovy Appetizer Turnovers

½ × 375 g/12 oz packet frozen puff pastry (paste), thawed; 2 × 56 g/2 oz cans rolled, stuffed anchovy fillets, drained; 1 egg yolk, lightly beaten.

Roll out thawed packet pastry thinly. Cut out 5 cm (2 in) rounds, wet edges and place an anchovy on one side of each. Fold other sides over, press with a fork to seal and chill 30 minutes. Brush tops with egg yolk and bake in a preheated hot oven (230°C/450°F, Gas Mark 8) for 15 minutes or until turnovers are puffed and golden. Makes about 24.

Chicken Satés

3 chicken fillets (skinless, boneless half-breasts); 1 chilli, halved and seeded; ½ medium onion, chopped; 2 tsp grated fresh ginger; juice ½ lemon; 1 tsp salt; 1 tbsp water; 2 tbsp light soy sauce; 1 tbsp peanut oil; extra oil for brushing.

Cut chicken into 2 cm (¾ in) cubes. Put chilli, onion, ginger, lemon juice, salt, water, soy sauce and oil in a blender and blend until smooth. Pour over chicken, cover and marinate 2 hours in refrigerator. Thread on short skewers, brush with extra oil and cook under a preheated grill (broiler) for 5–8 minutes, turning often, until chicken is crisp and brown. Serves 6.

Ham and Chicken Rolls

4 chicken fillets (skinless, boneless half-breasts); 1 tsp salt; ¼ tsp white pepper; ¼ tsp five-spice powder; 1 clove garlic, crushed; 4 slices cooked ham; 60 g/2 oz (½ cup) flour; 1 egg, lightly beaten; 2 tbsp milk; 4 spring roll wrappers (page 406); oil for deep-frying.

Separate strip of fillet which runs lengthways along each half breast. Pound breast and fillet pieces separately until very thin, being careful not to tear meat. Lay a fillet piece on top of each breast and pound lightly. Spread chicken pieces with combined mixture of salt, pepper, five-spice powder and garlic. Separately roll each slice of ham and place on top of each chicken piece. Roll up firmly, folding ends in securely. Dip chicken rolls in flour, then in egg beaten with milk. Place

chicken roll diagonally across spring roll wrapper, fold in ends and roll up securely. Seal with a little of the egg mixture. Deep-fry rolls in hot oil for 3–5 minutes until golden-brown and cooked through. Do not have the oil too hot or the rolls will brown too much before they are cooked through. Drain on crumpled paper towels. Serve cut into diagonal slices. If serving as a first course, serve accompanied by Sweet and Sour Sauce (see page 422). Serves 6–8.

APPLE

Since the days of the Garden of Eden, apples have been munched with enjoyment at any time of the day in most parts of the world. Although there are many varieties, in general they can be divided into apples for cooking and those for eating, though in many cases they overlap.

Apples grew wild in Britain before the Roman invasion. Settlers took them to America and Australia and today there are thousands of varieties.

In England the most famous dessert apple is probably Cox's Orange Pippin, while Bramleys are most popular for cooking – Americans and South Africans share a penchant for Jonathan apples and York Imperials, and all the world loves the Granny Smith, which was originally bred in New South Wales, Australia, in 1868.

Apples are used in a great number of ways. They can be baked, stewed, puréed, and used to make tarts and puddings; they can be preserved as jam or jelly, in pickles and chutney, or dried. Raw, they feature in salads, can be eaten with cheese, and are used with savoury meats.

Store small quantities of apples in the refrigerator crisper, large quantities in a cool, dark place where plenty of air can circulate. If raw apples are cut up for salads etc., sprinkle with a little lemon juice to prevent discolouring.

☐ **To Cook:** If you want apple pieces to hold their shape, cook them in syrup (125 g/4 oz (½ cup) sugar to 250 ml/8 fl oz (1 cup) water for tart apples, less sugar for sweeter apples). If you want the apples to break up (e.g. for apple sauce), add sugar to taste after cooking in water. For best flavour and colour in apple sauce, slice apples but do not peel or core, and rub through a sieve or put through a food mill after cooking. **See recipes.**

Apple Sauce (Chunky)
Serve with roast or grilled (broiled) pork.

4 large cooking apples, peeled, cored and quartered; 120 ml/4 fl oz (½ cup) water; 60–125 g/2–4 oz (¼–½ cup) sugar; 2 tsp lemon juice; ¼ tsp cinnamon.

Cook apples until soft in covered saucepan,

Sprinkle sliced apples with lemon juice to prevent discoloration

using just enough water to keep them from scorching. Stir occasionally during cooking. Break up apple a little and add sugar to taste. Stir in lemon juice and cinnamon. Makes about 370 g/12 oz (1½ cups).

Apple Sauce (Smooth)
Serve hot or cold with roast duck or pork.

4 cooking apples, quartered; about 120 ml/4 fl oz (½ cup) water; 60–125 g/2–4 oz (¼–½ cup) sugar; 2 tsp lemon juice.

Do not peel or core apples. Cook until soft in covered saucepan, using just enough water to keep them from scorching. Stir occasionally during cooking. Force through a sieve or food mill and stir in sugar to taste and lemon juice. Makes about 370 g/12 oz (1½ cups).

Apple Bavarian Slaw

1 Spanish onion, sliced; 2 red apples, cored and thinly sliced; 340 g/11 oz (4 cups) shredded red cabbage; 60 g/2 oz (½ cup) sliced dill pickles; 120 ml/4 fl oz (½ cup) Vinaigrette Dressing (page 358).

Separate onion into rings. Combine onion, apples, cabbage and pickles. Chill. Just before serving, toss with dressing. Serves 6.

Apple Butter

2 kg (4 lb) well-flavoured apples, quartered; 450 ml/¾ pint (2 cups) cider or water; sugar; 3 tsp cinnamon; 1½ tsp ground cloves; ½ tsp ground allspice.

Cook apples in cider or water until soft. Strain pulp. To each 250 ml/8 fl oz (1 cup) of pulp, add 125 g/4 oz (½ cup) sugar. Stir in spices. Cook over low heat, stirring constantly, until mixture is thick. Pour into hot sterilized jars, cool and seal. Store in a cool dry place. Makes about 5 × 250 g/8 oz (1 cup) jars.

Deep Dish Apple Pie

*3 tbsp quick-cooking tapioca; 180 g/6 oz
(¾ cup) white sugar; 60 g/2 oz (⅓ cup) firmly
packed dark brown sugar; ¼ tsp salt; 1 tsp
cinnamon; ½ tsp nutmeg; 6 tart apples,
peeled, cored and sliced; ½ × 375 g/12 oz
packet frozen shortcrust, puff or flaky pastry
(basic pie dough, puff or flaky paste),
thawed; whipped cream flavoured with a
little sugar and nutmeg to serve (optional).*

Mix all ingredients except pastry (dough) and
whipped cream. Pour into buttered deep
20 cm (8 in) round or square dish. Roll out
pastry (dough) to fit top of dish. Cut several
slits near the centre and lay pastry over apple
mixture. Bake in a preheated hot oven
(220°C/425°F, Gas Mark 7) for about 35
minutes; reduce heat to moderate
(180°C/350°F, Gas Mark 4) and bake for a
further 30 minutes. Serve with whipped
cream if desired. Serves 6.

Apple Crisp

*5 large cooking apples, peeled, cored and
sliced; 4 tbsp water; 125 g/4 oz (½ cup) white
sugar; 90 g/3 oz (½ cup) firmly packed light
brown sugar; ½ tsp nutmeg; ½ tsp cinnamon;
¼ tsp salt; 90 g/3 oz (¾ cup) flour; 125 g/4 oz
(½ cup) butter or margarine.*

Put apples into shallow 1.25 litre/2 pint
(4 cup) ovenproof dish and add water.
Combine sugars, nutmeg, cinnamon, salt
and flour. Cut in butter with pastry blender.
Spoon evenly over apples. Cover and bake
in a preheated moderate oven (180°C/
350°F, Gas Mark 4) for 30 minutes. Uncover
and bake for 30 minutes longer.
Serves 6.

Apple Slices in Brandy and Cream

*6 medium cooking apples, peeled, cored
and thinly sliced; 60 g/2 oz (4 tbsp) unsalted
butter; 3 tbsp brandy; 3 tbsp water;
135 g/4½ oz (¾ cup) firmly packed brown
sugar; 1 tsp nutmeg; 180 g/6 oz (1 cup)
currants or dried mixed fruit; 250 ml/8 fl oz
(1 cup) single (light) cream.*

Place apples in a buttered shallow baking
dish and dot with remaining butter. Stir rest
of ingredients together and spoon over
apples. Bake in a preheated moderate oven
(180°C/350°F, Gas Mark 4) for 30 minutes
or until apples are tender. Serve warm with
crisp biscuits or plain cake. Serves 6–8.

Quick Apple Strudel

An Austrian speciality – paper-thin pastry
(dough) enveloping buttery, spiced apple
slices. This version is simplified by using
commercial puff pastry (paste) rolled as thin
as possible. The same method is used when
making with classic Strudel Pastry (see page
416).

*4 large cooking apples, peeled, cored and
thinly sliced; 2 tbsp brown sugar; 1 tsp vanilla
essence (extract); 250 g/8 oz puff pastry
(paste); 125 g/4 oz (½ cup) unsalted butter;
30 g/1 oz (½ cup) fresh breadcrumbs; 2 tbsp
redcurrant jelly; 60 g/2 oz (½ cup) chopped
almonds; sifted icing (confectioners) sugar.*

Sprinkle apples with brown sugar and
vanilla, toss well to coat apples and stand for
1 hour. Roll out pastry (dough) on a floured
tea-towel to an oblong shape about
35 × 50 cm (14 × 20 in). Melt half the butter
and sauté breadcrumbs until golden. Melt
remaining butter and brush half over pastry
(dough). Sprinkle half the breadcrumbs over
pastry (dough), leaving a 5 cm (2 in) margin
along each side. Spread half apples over
crumbs, dot with 1 tbsp of redcurrant jelly
and sprinkle with half the almonds. Top with
remaining apples, jelly, almonds and
breadcrumbs. Fold in edges of pastry and
brush with remaining melted butter. Roll up
like a Swiss roll (jelly roll) and place strudel,
seam side down, on a greased baking tray,
curving it if necessary to fit. Brush top with
butter and bake in a preheated moderately
hot oven (190°C/375°F, Gas Mark 5) for 45
minutes, brushing again with butter every 10
minutes. Remove from oven and dust
generously with icing (confectioners) sugar.
Serve warm. Serves 6–8.

Baked Apples

*6 large cooking apples, cored; 125 g/4 oz
(½ cup) sugar; 250 ml/8 fl oz (1 cup) water;
1 tsp cinnamon or nutmeg.*

Make a slit around the centre of each apple
to prevent splitting. Arrange close together in
a shallow baking dish. Boil sugar and water
together for 2–3 minutes and stir in spice.
Pour over apples and bake in a preheated
moderate oven (180°C/350°F, Gas Mark 4)
for 50 minutes to 1 hour, basting often with
syrup. Serve warm. Serves 6.
NOTE: Cavities of apples may be filled with
chopped dates or raisins if wished. Brown
sugar may be used instead of white for a
caramel flavour, and grated lemon rind
added to the syrup instead of spice.

Fresh Apple Chutney

*2 medium cooking apples, peeled, cored
and grated; 3 tbsp apricot jam; 1 tbsp
vinegar; 1 tbsp finely chopped fresh mint;
salt; pinch cayenne.*

Mix apples with remaining ingredients,
seasoning to taste with salt and cayenne.
Serve at once with curries or cold meats.
Makes about 180 g/6 oz (2 cups).

Normandy Pork Chops

*6 large pork chops; 60 g/2 oz (4 tbsp) butter;
2 large onions, sliced; 1 clove garlic, crushed;
3 large cooking apples, peeled, cored and
sliced; salt and freshly ground black pepper;
1 tbsp sugar; 450 ml/¾ pint (2 cups) cider.*

Trim excess fat from chops and fry them in
butter until golden-brown on both sides.
Remove to a shallow casserole, arranging
them in a single layer. In the same pan fry
onions, garlic and apple slices until
beginning to soften. Arrange over chops.
Add salt, pepper, sugar and cider to pan and
bring to the boil, stirring to get up brown bits
from bottom. Pour over chops, cover tightly
and bake in a preheated moderate oven
(180°C/350°F, Gas Mark 4) for 45 minutes
or until chops are tender. Serve with noodles
and braised red or green cabbage. Serves 6.

Apple Fritters

*3 large cooking apples, peeled and cored;
125 g/4 oz (½ cup) sugar; 2 tbsp brandy; 2 tsp
grated lemon rind; 180 g/6 oz (1½ cups)
flour, sifted; ½ tsp baking powder; ¼ tsp salt; 2
eggs, lightly beaten; 1 tsp oil; 5 tbsp beer;
oil for deep-frying; sifted icing (confectioners)
sugar (for dessert fritters).*

Cut each apple crossways into 4 rings. Mix
60 g/2 oz (¼ cup) of the sugar with the
brandy and lemon rind, pour over apples
and stand 2–3 hours. Mix remaining sugar
with flour, baking powder, salt, eggs, oil and
beer to make a batter. Let batter stand 1
hour. Drain and dry apple rings. Dip in batter
one at a time and deep-fry in hot oil until
golden-brown and crisp. Drain on crumpled

A

paper towels. Sprinkle fritters with icing (confectioners) sugar. Serve hot. Serves 4.

Apple Pie

Sweet Rich Shortcrust Pastry (Basic Pie Dough) made with 250 g/8 oz (2 cups) flour etc. (page 274); 6 large cooking apples, peeled, cored and thinly sliced; 180 g/6 oz (¾ cup) sugar; 1 tbsp flour; 1 tsp cinnamon; ¼ tsp nutmeg; pinch salt; 30 g/1 oz (2 tbsp) butter; 1 egg white, lightly beaten; extra sugar.

Reserve ⅓ pastry (dough) for lid of pie. Roll out remainder to line a greased 23 cm (9 in) pie plate. Toss apples with sugar, flour, spices and salt. Spread evenly in pastry case (dough shell) and dot with butter. Roll out remaining pastry (dough) to cover top of pie, moisten edges and press firmly together. Press edges with tines of a fork to decorate. Make a few slits in top crust for steam to escape, brush with egg white and sprinkle with extra sugar. Bake in a preheated moderately hot oven (200°C/400°F, Gas Mark 6) for 10 minutes. Lower heat to moderate (160°C/325°F, Gas Mark 3) and bake for a further 45 minutes or until pastry (dough) is golden and apples are tender. Serve warm. Serves 6–8.

Apple Kuchen

250 g/8 oz (2 cups) flour; ½ tsp salt; 15 g/½ oz (1 tbsp) fresh (compressed) yeast, 2 tbsp sugar; 1 egg, beaten; 120 ml/4 fl oz (½ cup) warm milk; 30–60 g/1–2 oz (2–4 tbsp) butter, melted; 45 g/1½ oz (¼ cup) raisins; 1 apple, peeled, cored and sliced; syrup or water; caster sugar; 1 tsp cinnamon.

Sift flour and salt. Cream yeast with sugar. Mix into flour with egg, milk and butter. Beat thoroughly, then leave to rise in a warm place until double its bulk. Turn out on to a floured board and knead lightly. Work raisins into dough. Shape into a large bun with the hand and put into a lightly greased 20 cm (8 in) cake tin (pan). Flatten top with your fist and cover with sliced apple, pressing the sharp edge of the slices into the dough. Brush lightly with a thin syrup (3 tbsp water and 1 tbsp sugar boiled 1 minute) or water, sprinkle thickly with caster sugar mixed with a little cinnamon, and leave to prove 20 minutes. Bake in a preheated moderately hot oven (190°C/375°F, Gas Mark 5) for 40–45 minutes.

German Apple Cake

60 g/2 oz (4 tbsp) butter; 75 g/2½ oz (⅓ cup) sugar; 1 egg; 125 g/4 oz (1 cup) self-raising flour, sifted; 4 tbsp milk; 4 medium apples, peeled, quartered and cored; juice 1 lemon; sugar; cinnamon.

Cream butter with sugar. Add egg and beat well. Add ½ flour and beat to combine. Add milk and remaining flour alternately (this will make a thick mixture). Spread mixture over bottom of greased 23 cm (9 in) loose-bottomed tin (springform pan). Cut quartered apples into thin slices but not all the way through. Put apples as you are preparing them in a bowl and squeeze over lemon juice. Placed drained apples, cored side down, on cake. Bake in a preheated moderate oven (180°C/350°F, Gas Mark 4) for 1 hour. While still warm sprinkle with sugar and cinnamon.

APRICOT

This small, round, golden fruit is a member of the peach family. Keep fresh apricots in the refrigerator in a covered container, or in a plastic bag perforated with a few holes.

☐ **To Cook Fresh Apricots:** Poach gently in a syrup so that they keep their shape. Bring to the boil 250 ml/8 fl oz (1 cup) water; 180 g/6 oz (¾ cup) sugar and 4 cloves or a piece of cinnamon stick. Simmer 5 minutes. Add 12–15 washed apricots, whole or halved and stoned. Simmer 10 minutes or until just tender. Serve warm or chilled. If desired, liquid may be flavoured with lemon rind instead of spice, or you may use half white wine and half water.

☐ **To Cook Dried Apricots:** Simmer in water to cover for 20 minutes or until tender. Sweeten after cooking with sugar or honey. Dried apricots will also become plump and tender without cooking, if soaked overnight in water, fruit juice or cold tea. Keep covered in the refrigerator. **See recipes.**

Apricot Glaze Simply boil 350 g/12 oz (1 cup) apricot jam with 4 tbsp water, stirring frequently until mixture is clear and will just drop from the spoon. Use a pastry brush to apply it. (Redcurrant jelly may be treated and used in the same way).

Fresh Apricot Crumble Pie

1 kg (2 lb) fresh apricots, halved and stoned; 180 g/6 oz (¾ cup) sugar; pinch salt; 1 tbsp grated lemon rind; 2 tbsp lemon juice; 1 tbsp cornflour (cornstarch); 1 × 23 cm (9 in) unbaked Rich Shortcrust (Basic Pie Dough) Pie Shell (page 274).

TOPPING: *60 g/2 oz (⅓ cup) firmly packed brown sugar; 60 g/2 oz (½ cup) flour; 1 tsp cinnamon; 90 g/3 oz (6 tbsp) butter.*

Mix together apricots, sugar, salt, lemon rind and juice and cornflour (cornstarch). Pack into pie shell. For topping, combine sugar, flour and cinnamon and rub in butter to form crumbs. Sprinkle over apricots. Bake in a preheated moderately hot oven (200°C/400°F, Gas Mark 6) for 15 minutes. Reduce heat to moderate (180°C/350°F, Gas Mark 4) and bake 30 minutes longer or until apricots are tender. Serve warm with cream or custard. Serves 6–8.

Apricot Chicken

A recipe that swept the world – a way of turning chicken pieces into an exotic dish with only three ingredients.

1 large roasting chicken, cut into serving pieces; 1 × 43 g/1½ oz packet French onion soup mix; 1 × 250 ml/8 fl oz can apricot nectar; canned apricot halves to garnish (optional).

Arrange chicken pieces in one layer in a casserole. Sprinkle with soup mix and pour nectar over. Cover and bake in a preheated moderate oven (180°C/350°F, Gas Mark 4) for 40 minutes or until chicken is tender, turning the pieces once or twice. If desired, garnish with canned apricots heated in a little syrup from the can. Serves 4.

Dried Apricot Jam

250 g/8 oz (1½ cups) dried apricots; 2 lemons; 900 ml/1½ pints (3¾ cups) water; 1 kg/2 lb (4 cups) sugar; 6 blanched almonds.

Cut each apricot in half. Halve the lemons, squeeze 3 tbsp of the juice and reserve. Gather lemon pips and tie in a muslin bag. Soak apricots and lemon pips in the water for several hours. Put apricots, pips and water into a saucepan and cook slowly until fruit is soft. Remove pips. Warm sugar in a preheated very cool oven (120°C/250°F, Gas Mark ½) for 10 minutes and add to fruit with strained lemon juice. Stir with a wooden spoon until sugar has dissolved.

Boil the fruit mixture quickly until setting point is reached (place a small teaspoon of jam on a saucer and wait 20 seconds, then run a finger through it; if it wrinkles at the edges and stays in 2 separate parts the jam is right for bottling). Cool slightly and stir once to distribute fruit evenly. Ladle into warm dry jars, including 1–2 almonds in each jar to represent kernels. Moisten clear preserve covers with cloth dipped in vinegar and cover, or cover with sterilized screw-on lids. Tie down, then cool. Makes about 1 kg/2 lb (3 cups).

Apricot Crescents

125 g/4 oz ($\frac{1}{2}$ cup) butter or margarine; 90 g/3 oz ($\frac{1}{3}$ cup) cream cheese, softened; 90 g/3 oz ($\frac{3}{4}$ cup) flour, sifted; pinch salt; 1 tbsp cold water; apricot conserve; chopped nuts; sifted icing (confectioners) sugar.

Cut butter and cheese into flour and salt. Add water and mix lightly with fork until blended. Chill until firm, then cut into 24 pieces. Keep dough chilled before rolling. Roll each piece very thin on floured board to form 8 cm (3 in) squares. Spread each with apricot conserve and sprinkle with nuts. Roll up from one corner and bend ends in slightly to form crescents. Put folded side down on ungreased baking trays and bake in a preheated hot oven (230°C/450°F, Gas Mark 8) for about 10 minutes. Dust icing (confectioners) sugar over cooled crescents. Makes 24.

Spiced Apricots

1 × 825 g/1 lb 13 oz can apricots; 8 whole cloves; 1 × 3 cm (1 in) cinnamon stick; 8 whole allspice; 4 tbsp white vinegar; 125 g/4 oz ($\frac{1}{2}$ cup) sugar; 1 small orange, sliced; extra whole cloves (optional).

Drain apricots, reserving 250 ml/8 fl oz (1 cup) syrup. Tie whole cloves, cinnamon and allspice in a piece of muslin or cheesecloth and put into saucepan with reserved apricot syrup, vinegar, sugar and orange slices. Bring to the boil. Add apricot halves and simmer 5 minutes. Cover and allow to cool at room temperature. Remove spice bag. Serve warm or chilled. If liked, stud some apricots with extra whole cloves. Spiced apricots improve on keeping; after 1 week they are at their best. Serve with baked ham, roast pork or cold meats. Serves 8.

Apricot Mousse

500 g/1 lb (3 cups) dried apricots; 125 g/4 oz ($\frac{1}{2}$ cup) sugar; 175 ml/6 fl oz ($\frac{3}{4}$ cup) double (heavy) cream; 1 tsp vanilla essence (extract).
DECORATION: *whipped cream; slivered toasted almonds.*

Simmer apricots in water to cover for 25 minutes. Stir in sugar and cook a further 5 minutes. Rub through a sieve or purée in a blender or food processor. Cool. Whip cream, add vanilla and fold into apricot purée. Spoon into small mousse pots or dessert bowls and chill. Decorate with whipped cream and almonds. Serves 6.

ARROZ CON POLLO (Rice with Chicken)

One of the best known dishes of Spain. Recipes may vary slightly from region to region, but flavourings should always include olive oil, garlic and saffron. **See recipes.**

Arroz con Pollo

1 chicken, about 2 kg (4 lb), cut into serving pieces; 4 tbsp olive oil; 1 × 130 g/4 oz can pimientos, drained and sliced; 1 large onion, chopped; 2 cloves garlic, crushed; 2 large ripe tomatoes, peeled, seeded and chopped; 12 large green olives, stoned and sliced; 180 g/6 oz (1 cup) shelled fresh or frozen peas; 750 ml/1$\frac{1}{4}$ pints (3 cups) chicken stock; $\frac{1}{2}$ tsp saffron threads; 430 g/14 oz (2 cups) long-grain rice; salt and freshly ground black pepper.

Brown chicken pieces on all sides in hot oil. Add pimientos, onion, garlic, tomatoes, olives and peas. Fry together for a few minutes, stirring. Meanwhile, heat chicken stock and soak saffron threads in it for 5 minutes. Add stock to pan, bring to the boil, add rice and stir. Taste, and season with salt and pepper. Simmer, covered, for 30 minutes or until chicken is tender and rice has absorbed the liquid. Serves 4.

Arroz con Pollo Mexicano

(Mexican Rice with Chicken)
Arroz con Pollo travelled from Spain to Mexico, then to Peru, Colombia and Cuba and each country has its own adaptation. In Mexico, oregano and cilantro are used. Cilantro is the Mexican name for coriander.

6 chicken pieces (breasts, thighs, etc.); 120 ml/4 fl oz ($\frac{1}{2}$ cup) olive oil; 1 onion, chopped; 2 cloves garlic, chopped; 310 g/10 oz (1$\frac{1}{2}$ cups) long-grain rice; 1 × 425 g/14 oz can tomatoes, drained; 1 tsp salt; freshly ground black pepper; 1 tbsp chopped fresh oregano; 750 ml/1$\frac{1}{4}$ pints (3 cups) chicken stock.
GARNISH: *1 × 130 g/4 oz can pimientos, drained and sliced; fresh cilantro (coriander or Chinese parsley) or chopped parsley.*

Wipe over chicken and cut into small serving-sized pieces. Heat oil in a large frying pan (skillet) and sauté chicken until just browned. Remove chicken and sauté onion and garlic. Add rice and cook until grains are coated with oil, shaking pan and stirring rice

around. Add tomatoes, salt, pepper, oregano and chicken stock, mixing gently. Return chicken pieces to pan, pushing them down into rice. Simmer, covered (foil will do), until all liquid has been absorbed and chicken and rice are tender. Serves 6.

ARTICHOKE

The Globe or Common Artichoke

The leafy bud of a plant of the thistle family. When buying fresh artichokes, look for solid heads with tightly packed leaves. They should be used as soon as possible after buying. If not cooking the same day, store in a closed container in the refrigerator.

□ **Basic Preparation:** Wash and drain artichokes and trim stems. Pull off any coarse outer leaves (**fig 1**) then cut one-third off the top of the artichokes (**2**) or cut off the thorny tips of the remaining leaves with kitchen scissors. As each artichoke is prepared, drop at once into a bowl of cold water containing lemon juice or vinegar; use about 3 tbsp to each litre/1$\frac{3}{4}$ pints (4 cups) water. This will prevent discoloration. It is possible to remove the hairy choke before cooking (**3**), to form little cups which are pre-boiled and then filled with a savoury sauce or stuffing.

□ **To Cook:** The basic cooking methods are boiling and braising. **See also recipes.**
BOILED ARTICHOKES Bring a large pan of salted water to the boil, add artichokes and boil, uncovered, until they are tender (from 20–45 minutes depending on size and freshness). A leaf will pull away easily when cooked. Drain upside-down and serve hot with melted butter, warmed cream or Hollandaise Sauce, or allow to cool and serve with Vinaigrette Dressing, Mayonnaise or Tartare Sauce (see pages 358 and 204).

To eat: Using fingers, pull off one leaf at a time, and dip the base in butter, cream or sauce. Pull the leaf between the teeth to scrape away the soft fleshy base and discard the rest of the leaf. In the centre of older artichokes you will find the fuzzy portion called the choke. Lift up and discard the choke and eat the soft fond (bottom) underneath. This is the most delicate part, and the one often canned for use in salads and antipasti (as are hearts of artichokes).

Preserved Artichokes Hearts and fonds of artichokes are available canned or bottled in brine or in oil. They are used in the preparation of antipasti and hors d'oeuvre. Artichoke hearts in brine are drained, dressed with Vinaigrette Dressing (see page 358) and chopped parsley and served chilled.

Italian Artichokes in Wine Use young artichokes with slender elongated heads. Cut the artichokes lengthwise into quarters. Put in cold water to cover with some lemon slices as you prepare them. Heat a little olive oil in a heavy pan with a sprig of fresh or a pinch of

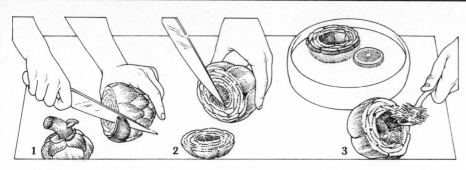

Preparing Globe Artichokes

dried oregano and 1 clove garlic. Add artichokes and cook over a moderate heat tossing the artichokes until burnished and crispy on the outside. Remove garlic clove, add 120 ml/4 fl oz (½ cup) white wine, season with salt and black pepper, cover and simmer gently until artichokes are tender, 10–15 minutes. Serve as a first course.

The Jerusalem Artichoke

Despite the name, this vegetable is quite different from the globe artichoke. The globe is a bud, the Jerusalem artichoke is a tuber. About the size of a small potato, it is creamy-brown with a knobbly shape.

□ **To Cook:** Wash well, peel and cut to the size of pigeons' eggs, then drop into boiling salted water with a squeeze of lemon juice or a little wine added to prevent discoloration. Cook with the lid on for about 5 minutes. Drain, return to pan, add a good knob of butter and cook gently for about 10 minutes or until tender. Season with salt and pepper and, if liked, toss with chopped fresh herbs.

Purée of Jerusalem Artichokes Peel and quarter artichokes and cook as above. Rub through a sieve, return to saucepan and heat gently with a few tbsp of milk or cream and a touch of nutmeg.

Jerusalem Artichoke Soup Prepare Purée of Jerusalem Artichokes (above). Add enough chicken stock or milk to make a cream soup consistency. Swirl with single (light) cream.

Braised Artichokes

Artichokes cooked gently with oil, wine and aromatics are an epicurean treat.

6 globe artichokes; 3 tbsp olive oil; 250 ml/8 fl oz (1 cup) dry white wine; 2 cloves garlic; 1 small onion, finely chopped; 1 tbsp chopped parsley; 2 sprigs fresh oregano, or pinch dried; salt and freshly ground black pepper.

Prepare artichokes (see above). Combine remaining ingredients in a heavy saucepan, add artichokes and cook, covered, for 30–45 minutes or until tender. Add a little more oil and wine if necessary. Serve hot or warm with pan juices poured over. Alternatively, drain and chill and serve with Vinaigrette Dressing (see page 358). Serves 6.

VARIATION

Artichokes à la Grecque: Prepare as for Braised Artichokes, adding 2 peeled, seeded and chopped tomatoes. Serve warm with some of the pan sauce spooned over, or cold, cut into quarters, again with some of the delicious sauce in which they were cooked. Top with chopped parsley. Serves 6.

Artichokes Clamart

Choose very small, young artichokes for this dish. Prepare in a heavy enamelled cast iron pan or flameproof casserole and serve in the same dish.

8 small, young globe artichokes; 75 g/2½ oz (5 tbsp) butter; 1 lettuce, shredded; 370 g/12 oz (2 cups) shelled fresh peas; ½ tsp salt; 1 tsp sugar; 120 ml/4 fl oz (½ cup) chicken stock.

Trim artichokes down to tender hearts. Melt 60 g/2 oz (4 tbsp) butter in a heavy saucepan, add lettuce and place artichokes and peas on top. Add salt and sugar to taste and moisten with stock. Cover and simmer about 30 minutes or until vegetables are tender. Add remaining butter and serve immediately. Serves 4.

VARIATION

Artichokes Crécy: Prepare as for Artichokes Clamart, replacing peas with an equal quantity of small young carrots or larger carrots, diced.

Artichoke Heart Salad

1 × 400 g/13 oz can artichoke hearts; 1 head small firm lettuce, shredded; 180 g (6 oz) small, uncooked cauliflower florets; 1 large tomato, peeled, seeded and diced; 1 tbsp snipped chives; 2 tbsp sliced stuffed olives; 2 tbsp chopped dill pickle; about 120 ml/4 fl oz (½ cup) Vinaigrette Dressing (page 358).

Drain artichokes and chill. Combine with remaining ingredients, adding enough dressing to moisten well. Serve at once as a first course, or as a luncheon salad with cold meat. Serves 6.

Artichoke Halves Greek-Style

6 large globe artichokes; 1 litre/1¾ pints (4 cups) water; 3 lemons; 1 tbsp flour;

2 onions, chopped; 250 ml/8 fl oz (1 cup) olive oil; salt and freshly ground black pepper.

Cut stems off artichokes. Remove bottom leaves and with scissors trim off brown thorny tips of all remaining leaves. Cut off tops and halve each artichoke lengthways. Soak in 900 ml/1½ pints (3¾ cups) water and juice of 2 of the lemons. Meanwhile, sprinkle flour over onions and sauté in olive oil until lightly browned. Arrange artichoke halves, cut sides up, in roasting tin (pan) or heavy frying pan (skillet). Add salt, pepper and juice of remaining lemon to onion and oil, and pour over artichokes. Add remaining water. Cover and simmer over low heat for 35–40 minutes or until artichokes are tender. Serve warm or cold. Serves 6.

Artichokes Roman-Style

Carciofi fritti vecchia Roma, the fried artichokes found on menus in Rome, are a treat. Young, tender artichokes, about 60 g/2 oz in weight, are used for this dish.

6 baby globe artichokes; flour for dredging; 1 large egg, lightly beaten; 125 g/4 oz (2 cups) fresh breadcrumbs; 250 ml/8 fl oz (1 cup) olive oil; 450 ml/¾ pint (2 cups) vegetable oil; salt.

Trim artichoke stems even with their bases and remove any hard exterior leaves. Blanch artichokes in boiling water for 7 minutes or until just tender. Drain in a colander and refresh under cold running water. Spread leaves of artichokes gently outward, flatten them with the side of a large knife, being careful not to crack them, and pat dry. Dredge artichokes lightly in flour, then coat with egg, letting excess drip off. Finally coat with breadcrumbs, and shake off excess. Heat oils in a deep heavy saucepan over moderate heat and fry artichokes, a few at a time, for 3–5 minutes or until leaves are golden. Drain on paper towels. Sprinkle with salt and arrange on a heated platter. Serves 6 as a first course.

ASPARAGUS

This edible member of the lily family with its crisp stalks and closed, tender tips is considered a luxury vegetable throughout the world. Stalks may range from slender and green to thick, white and fleshy. Asparagus is delicious served hot, warm or cold. It may be served as an accompaniment, a first course, with salads, or combined with ingredients such as ham, cheese and eggs in main courses. When served as a separate course, it is best eaten with the fingers. When buying fresh asparagus look for firm, straight stalks with tightly closed, well-formed tips. Allow 6–8 spears per person when serving as a separate course.

Canned asparagus is one of the most

versatile and popular of canned vegetables. It is used to make salads, sandwiches or a lovely mousse (see below), and may be used in any of the ways suggested for hot, boiled asparagus.

☐ **Basic Preparation:** Wash gently in cold, running water. Break off the bottom of the stalks at the point where they will snap easily. If stalks seem woody or scaly, peel them thinly with a vegetable peeler or sharp knife.

☐ **To Cook:** Asparagus is usually boiled, but may also be prepared Chinese-style (see below). **See also recipes**.

BOILED ASPARAGUS Put prepared stalks into a large, shallow pan of boiling, salted water. Cook, uncovered, for 10–12 minutes or until just tender. Lift out of pan and drain on paper towels or a napkin.

CHINESE-STYLE ASPARAGUS Slice prepared stalks in slanted pieces, leaving tips whole. Heat enough butter to cover the bottom of a frying pan (skillet), add asparagus pieces and season with salt and pepper. When steam rises, cover the pan, lower the heat and cook for about 4 minutes until asparagus is tender-crisp.

Ways to Serve Asparagus

Devotees enjoy asparagus in many different ways. See above for preparation and cooking of asparagus. Good canned asparagus may also be treated in the following ways.

Asparagus Flamande Prepare, boil and drain 24–30 asparagus spears, or use drained canned asparagus. Hard-boil (hard-cook) 4 eggs for 8–10 minutes. Melt 90 g/3 oz (6 tbsp) butter. Serve asparagus to each guest with 2 egg halves and melted butter. Each guest mashes the eggs, then adds them to the butter, and dips the asparagus into the mixture. Serves 4.

Asparagus au Gratin Prepare, boil and drain 24–30 asparagus spears, or use drained canned asparagus. Make Mornay Sauce (see page 368), adding 2–3 tsp French (Dijon) mustard. Arrange asparagus in a buttered flameproof dish, spoon sauce over spears, sprinkle with 60 g/2 oz (½ cup) grated Parmesan cheese and 1 tbsp melted butter, and brown under a preheated grill (broiler). Serves 4.

Asparagus Milanese Proceed as in the recipe for Asparagus au Gratin, but omit Mornay Sauce. Serves 4.

Asparagus Hollandaise Prepare, boil and drain 24–30 asparagus spears, or use drained canned asparagus. Keep warm. Make 1 quantity Hollandaise Sauce (see page 369). Serve asparagus with sauce spooned over tips. Serves 4.

Asparagus with Melted Butter Prepare, boil and drain 24–30 asparagus spears, or use drained canned asparagus. Keep warm. Melt 125 g/4 oz (½ cup) butter with a grinding of white pepper and a squeeze of lemon juice. Serve asparagus with melted butter. Serves 4.

Asparagus Polonaise Prepare, boil and drain 24–30 asparagus spears, or use drained canned asparagus. Keep warm. To make Polonaise Butter: Combine 3 hard-boiled (hard-cooked) egg yolks, chopped, with 1 tbsp chopped parsley. Heat 2 tbsp butter and fry 45 g/1½ oz (¾ cup) fresh breadcrumbs until golden. Add egg yolks and parsley. Serve asparagus with Polonaise Butter. Serves 4.

Asparagus Noisette Prepare, boil and drain 24–30 asparagus spears, or use drained canned asparagus. Keep warm. Heat 90 g/3 oz (6 tbsp) butter until a light hazelnut (noisette) colour. Serve asparagus with browned butter. Serves 4.

Asparagus and Ham au Gratin

An excellent dish for a first course or light luncheon.

18 large, cooked asparagus spears (fresh or canned); 18 paper-thin slices cooked ham or prosciutto; 125 g/4 oz (½ cup) butter, melted; 125 g/4 oz (1 cup) grated Parmesan cheese; 6 slices white bread, crusts removed; butter for frying.

Wrap each asparagus spear in a slice of ham. Arrange seam sides down, close together, in a shallow baking dish greased with a little of the butter. Sprinkle with half the remaining butter, then the cheese, then top with rest of butter. Bake in a preheated hot oven (230°C/450°F, Gas Mark 8) for 10 minutes or until topping is golden-brown. Meanwhile, cut bread into triangles and fry on both sides in a little butter until crisp and golden. Serve asparagus garnished with triangles of fried bread. Serves 6.

Cream of Fresh Asparagus Soup

500 g (1 lb) fresh asparagus; salt; 1.25 litres/2¼ pints (5¾ cups) chicken stock; 1 medium onion, finely chopped; 2 sticks celery, finely chopped; 45 g/1½ oz (3 tbsp) butter; 2 tbsp flour; 120 ml/4 fl oz (½ cup) single (light) cream; freshly ground white pepper; paprika; 2 finely chopped hard-boiled (hard-cooked) eggs, to garnish.

Wash asparagus and remove tips. Simmer tips in lightly salted water for 4–6 minutes or until tender. Drain and reserve. Cut stalks into small pieces and place in saucepan with stock, onion and celery. Simmer, covered, for 20 minutes or until vegetables are tender. Drain, reserving liquid, and rub vegetables through a sieve. Melt butter in a large saucepan, stir in flour, then slowly stir in cream over low heat. Add warm asparagus stock and stir until soup thickens. Add vegetable purée and reserved asparagus tips and heat through. Season with salt and pepper. Ladle into heated bowls and top each serving with a sprinkle of paprika and a spoonful of chopped egg. Serves 6.

Asparagus Mousse

A delicately coloured and superbly flavoured first course for a formal dinner. At its best when served very cold.

2 × 440 g/14 oz cans asparagus spears; 2 tbsp gelatine; 6 tbsp water; 350 ml/12 fl oz (1½ cups) double (heavy) cream; salt and freshly ground white pepper; 3 egg whites; few drops green food colouring (optional). GARNISH: extra asparagus spears; canned pimiento strips.

Drain asparagus and rub through a sieve, or purée in a blender then rub through a sieve to remove any stringy stalk. Soften gelatine in water, then stand container in hot water until dissolved. Add to asparagus purée, stirring continuously. Cool, then chill until mixture begins to thicken round edges. Whip cream lightly and gradually stir into asparagus mixture until smooth. Season with salt and pepper. Beat egg whites to a firm snow and fold in with a few drops of green food colouring, if desired. Pour into a 1.75 litre/3 pint (7 cup) mould which has been rinsed with cold water. Chill. To serve, unmould and garnish with extra asparagus spears and pimiento strips. Serve very cold. Serves 8.

Asparagus Rolls

Popular on the afternoon tea tray, or with pre-dinner drinks. Suitable for large receptions.

12 slices sandwich bread, crusts removed; 60 g/2 oz (4 tbsp) butter, softened; 1 × 340 g/11 oz can asparagus spears, drained; salt and freshly ground white pepper.

Butter bread and place 1 asparagus spear diagonally on each slice. Season with salt and pepper, roll up and secure with a toothpick. Store, seam sides down, in shallow containers, covered with a slightly dampened tea-towel, in refrigerator. Take out 15 minutes before serving, and remove toothpicks to serve. Makes 12.

ASPIC

This is a clear, savoury jelly in which cold fish, poultry, meat or vegetables may be served. Aspic is also used to cover food, chopped for a garnish, or mixed with Mayonnaise (see page 204) to coat cold dishes. It is sold in powdered form with instructions for use on the package, or can be made at home.

To make an aspic mould: After preparing aspic, allow it to cool until it is the consistency of unbeaten egg white. Have the mould chilled. Spoon a little aspic into the mould and run it round to cover the inside completely. Keep aspic jelly moving until it sets, to ensure only a thin coating. Allow to set firm. Pour a little aspic into a saucer, dip decorations – hard-boiled (hard-cooked) egg slices, raw or cooked vegetable or fruit pieces etc. – into it and arrange them over base and sides of mould. (Place small decorations on the end of a skewer for dipping and arranging.) When design is completed, put to chill until set firm before adding filling.

To coat food with aspic: Have food well dried and chilled. Place on a rack over a tray. Cool aspic to consistency of unbeaten egg white and spoon over food. Allow to set firm. Pour a little aspic into a saucer, dip decorations into it and arrange on food. Allow to set firm again, then spoon over 2–3 more layers aspic, allowing each to set firm before adding the next. Aspic that runs on to the tray can be warmed and re-used.

Quick aspic: Soften 1½ tbsp powdered gelatine in 4 tbsp cold water, then dissolve by standing container in hot water. Heat the contents of 1 × 440 g/14 oz can consommé, and stir in gelatine mixture and 2 tbsp port, sherry or Madeira. Pour through a scalded cloth into a bowl. Makes about 450 ml/¾ pint (2 cups).

AUBERGINE (Eggplant)

Although there are many varieties of aubergine (also called eggplant or brinjal) ranging from white to almost black, the rich, purple one is the most familiar. Aubergine combines well with other vegetables such as tomatoes, courgettes (zucchini) and peppers. It makes a wonderful pickle. Cooked and mashed with spices, it is served as a dip (see *Baba Ghannouj*). It makes a case for savoury stuffings, and adds distinction to meat dishes and stews. Fried aubergine can be served with eggs, fish, lamb chops, steaks or chicken.

When buying aubergines, look for smooth, firm, shiny vegetables with no blemishes and a fresh, green calyx. Avoid the very large ones as they can be spongy with little taste. Aubergines should be used as soon as possible after buying as they deteriorate quickly. If not using immediately, store, covered, in the refrigerator.

☐ **Basic Preparation:** Aubergines are often 'dégorged' (treated with salt to remove excess liquid) before cooking. This process is aimed at removing any bitterness and also prevents them from becoming soggy when cooked, and from soaking up too much oil if fried.
To dégorge: Remove stem and calyx and cut the aubergine in half lengthways, or cut into slices. Score the surface of the flesh, sprinkle with salt and leave on a tilted plate or in a colander for 30 minutes or so, for liquid to run off. Rinse off excess salt and dry thoroughly with paper towels before proceeding with the recipe.

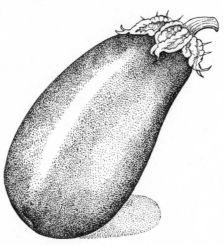

☐ **To Cook:** Aubergine may be grilled (broiled), pan-fried, sautéed or baked. **See also recipes.**
GRILLED AUBERGINE Slice aubergine thickly (do not peel) and dégorge (see above). Brush both sides with oil and season with freshly ground black pepper. Cook under a preheated grill (broiler), turning once, until surface is flecked with brown and flesh is soft. Season with salt after cooking.

Serve with grilled (broiled) meats.
FRIED AUBERGINE Slice aubergine thickly or cut into large dice (do not peel) and dégorge (see above). Dip in flour and fry in olive oil over medium heat until golden-brown. Drain on paper towels and season with salt and freshly ground black pepper. Serve as a hot vegetable, or as a first course with a sauce of chilled plain yogurt, flavoured with garlic and mint.
BAKED AUBERGINE Brush whole, unpeeled aubergines with oil and bake in a preheated moderate oven (180°C/350°F, Gas Mark 4) for 30 minutes or until soft. Halve the aubergines lengthways and scoop the flesh into a bowl. Mash with a little butter, freshly ground black pepper, salt, crushed garlic and chopped fresh herbs such as parsley, basil or mint. Replace in shells, sprinkle with grated cheese or buttered breadcrumbs and reheat in the oven or under a preheated grill (broiler) until golden and bubbling.

Aubergine Pickle

Serve with shish kebab, meatballs, chicken or curry dishes.

2 medium aubergines (eggplant); 250 ml/8 fl oz (1 cup) vinegar; 4 tbsp lemon juice; 2 tsp mustard seeds; 2 tsp coriander seeds, toasted; 1 tsp fennel seeds; 3 cloves garlic; 2 tsp fresh ginger, chopped; pinch chilli powder; salt and freshly ground black pepper.

Pierce aubergines (eggplant) all over with a fork and place on rack in a preheated moderately hot oven (200°C/400°F, Gas Mark 6), with a dish on the shelf below to catch juices. Bake for about 30 minutes or until soft. Halve lengthways, scoop out flesh and chop finely. Mix with 120 ml/4 fl oz (½ cup) vinegar to prevent discolouring. Put lemon juice and remaining vinegar into a blender with mustard, coriander and fennel seeds, garlic and ginger and blend until smooth. Add to aubergine (eggplant) flesh and season to taste with chilli powder, salt and pepper. Spoon into sterilized jars and store, covered, in the refrigerator. Makes 750 g–1 kg/1½–2 lb (3–4 cups).

Aubergine Parmigiana

2 medium aubergines (eggplant), thickly sliced; salt; 1 small onion, finely chopped; 2 cloves garlic, crushed; 120 ml/4 fl oz (½ cup) olive oil; 250 g/8 oz (1 cup) chopped canned tomatoes; freshly ground black pepper; 90 g (3 oz) prosciutto, finely sliced; 60 g/2 oz (½ cup) grated Parmesan cheese; 15 g/½ oz (1 tbsp) butter.

Sprinkle aubergine (eggplant) slices with salt. Toss and let stand for 1 hour. Meanwhile, make sauce. Fry onion and garlic in 1 tbsp oil until soft. Add tomatoes and simmer, covered, for 10 minutes. Season with salt and pepper. Rinse and dry aubergine (eggplant) slices. Fry over fairly high heat in remaining oil until golden-brown on both sides. Drain on paper towels. Arrange slices overlapping in a shallow baking dish, covering each slice with a slice of prosciutto, a spoonful of tomato sauce, a grinding of pepper and a sprinkling of Parmesan. Dot with butter and bake in a preheated moderate oven (180°C/350°F, Gas Mark 4) for 30–40 minutes. Serves 4.

Stuffed Aubergine

2 large aubergines (eggplant); salt; 4 tbsp oil; 1 onion, chopped; 4 tomatoes, peeled and chopped; 1 clove garlic, crushed; 2 tbsp chopped parsley; freshly ground black pepper; 120 ml/4 fl oz (½ cup) beef stock (bouillon); 30 g/1 oz (2 tbsp) butter; 90 g/3 oz (1½ cups) fresh white breadcrumbs; 60 g/2 oz (½ cup) grated Cheddar cheese.

Cut aubergines (eggplant) in half lengthways, slash cut edges, sprinkle with salt and leave to stand upside-down for 1 hour. Drain and dry on paper towels. Heat oil in a frying pan (skillet) and fry aubergine gently for a few minutes, cut sides down. Remove from heat, carefully scoop out flesh, not damaging skins, and chop it finely. Mix together aubergine (eggplant) flesh, onion, tomatoes, garlic, parsley and pepper. Fill aubergine shells and place them in a flameproof gratin dish with stock. Cover with foil and bake in a preheated moderate oven (180°C/350°F, Gas Mark 4) for 30–40 minutes or until aubergine (eggplant) is tender. Melt butter in a small frying pan (skillet) and fry breadcrumbs until crisp and golden. Sprinkle crumbs over cooked aubergine (eggplant), top with cheese and grill (broil) until cheese melts. Serves 4.

Aubergine Mousse

This delicious mousse is wonderfully versatile. Use it to fill halves of tomatoes, or serve it as an appetizer in a brightly coloured bowl with corn crisps (chips) or crusty bread, or sticks of cucumber, courgettes (zucchini) and fennel for dipping. The mousse improves when made a day ahead and left in the refrigerator.

3 large aubergines (eggplant), sliced; salt; 2 tbsp olive oil; 2 onions, very finely chopped; 3 cloves garlic, crushed; 2 anchovies, finely chopped; freshly ground black pepper; 2 tbsp chopped fresh parsley or basil; juice ½ lemon.

Sprinkle aubergine (eggplant) slices with salt. Toss and let stand for 1 hour. Rinse and dry aubergine (eggplant) slices. Sprinkle with olive oil and place in an oiled baking dish. Bake in a preheated moderately hot oven (190°C/375°F, Gas Mark 5) for 1 hour or until soft. Pass aubergine (eggplant) through a food mill or lightly purée in a food processor. Add onions, garlic, anchovies, salt and pepper (it should be highly seasoned). Chill. Before serving, sprinkle on parsley and lemon juice and, if you like, a few drops of olive oil. Makes 450 ml/1¾ pints (2 cups).

Aubergine Provençale

3 medium aubergines (eggplant); 2 tbsp olive oil; 1 medium onion, chopped; 2 cloves garlic, crushed; 1 green pepper, cored, seeded and chopped; 500 g/1 lb (2 cups) minced (ground) steak; 1¼ tsp salt; ¼ tsp black pepper; ½ tsp dried oregano; 60 g/2 oz (½ cup) grated Romano cheese or Parmesan; 30 g/1 oz (¼ cup) dry breadcrumbs; 2 tbsp tomato purée (paste); 1 quantity Basic Tomato Sauce (page 436).

Cook aubergines (eggplant) in boiling water, covered, for 15 minutes. Drain and cut in

half lengthways. Carefully remove flesh, leaving a shell 1 cm (½ in) thick. Chop flesh. Heat oil in a heavy frying pan (skillet), add onion, garlic and green pepper and sauté until just tender. Combine aubergine (eggplant) flesh with sautéed mixture. Add remaining ingredients, except tomato sauce, and mix well. Fill aubergine (eggplant) shells with mixture and place in a greased baking pan. Brush tops with additional oil and bake in a preheated moderate oven (180°C/350°F, Gas Mark 4) for about 45 minutes. Serve with tomato sauce. Serves 6.

AVGOLEMONO

The name indicates an egg-lemon mixture, whipped into stock to make a delicate, creamy sauce. It is famous in Greek cookery and popular throughout the Balkans. The mixture is also used to thicken soup. The sauce is always made from the liquid in which meats or vegetables have been cooked, thickened with beaten egg and fresh lemon juice. Fish may be poached and the liquor used to make an avgolemono sauce. Chicken, lamb, meatballs and dolmas may all be served with this sauce. **See recipes.**

See also *Dolma, Dolmades*.

Soupa Avgolemono

105 g/3½ oz (½ cup) short-grain rice or tiny pasta shapes; 1.25 litres/2¼ pints (5¾ cups) chicken or fish stock; salt and freshly ground white pepper; 3 eggs, separated; 120 ml/ 4 fl oz (½ cup) lemon juice.

Cook rice or pasta in boiling stock until tender. Season with salt and pepper. Beat egg whites to a firm snow, add yolks and lemon juice and beat until creamy. Whisk a large ladleful of soup into egg mixture, then remove soup from heat and gradually add egg mixture. Stir vigorously while adding it, and for 1 minute longer. Serve at once. Serves 6–8.

Avgolemono

250 ml/8 fl oz (1 cup) stock (bouillon); 2 eggs; juice 1 lemon.

Heat stock in a small saucepan. Beat eggs and add lemon juice. Slowly add some of the hot stock to eggs while continuing to beat. Stir egg mixture into remaining stock. Remove from heat. Cover and let stand for 5 minutes to thicken. Serve at once. Do not reheat. Serves 4–6.

Meatballs with Avgolemono

500 g/1 lb (2 cups) lean minced (ground) steak; 1 small onion, chopped; 2 tsp chopped fresh mint; 1 tbsp chopped parsley; 1 tbsp cooked rice; salt and freshly ground black pepper; 350 ml/12 fl oz (1½ cups) beef stock (bouillon); 250 ml/8 fl oz (1 cup) water; 2 egg yolks; juice 1 lemon.

Mix together steak, onion, mint, parsley, rice, salt, pepper and 4 tbsp beef stock (bouillon). Form into balls the size of a walnut. Bring remaining stock (bouillon) and the water to the boil in a saucepan and drop in meatballs. Simmer for 30 minutes. Beat egg yolks with lemon juice. Slowly add some of the hot stock (bouillon), beating constantly. Stir egg yolk mixture into remaining stock in pan, cover and stand for 5 minutes off heat before serving. Serves 4.

Chicken Macerata

1 medium roasting chicken; salt; 2 tbsp olive oil; 60 g/2 oz (4 tbsp) butter; 450 ml/¾ pint (2 cups) chicken stock (cubes may be used); 2 egg yolks; grated rind and juice 1 lemon.

Rub chicken inside and out with salt, and tie into a good shape. Heat oil and butter in a flameproof casserole, preferably an oval one, into which chicken will fit snugly. Add chicken and cook, turning it, until golden-brown all over. Turn chicken breast side up. Add stock – there should be enough to come halfway up bird. Cover casserole with grease-proof (waxed) paper, then lid and cook over a low heat for about 1 hour or until chicken is tender. Remove bird and boil liquid over a high heat to reduce it by about ⅓. Cut the chicken into serving pieces and arrange on a flameproof platter. Keep warm.

Beat egg yolks until well mixed but not frothy. Add lemon rind and juice and salt. Add to liquid in casserole and cook, lightly

beating, over a gentle heat for 1 minute. Do not boil, and be careful not to overcook; keep beating or eggs will set in strands. Allow to stand off heat for a few minutes. Spoon sauce over chicken. Serve with crusty bread to mop up juices. Serves 4.

AVOCADO

Avocados are the fruit of trees native to Central and South America. They are easy to eat, easy to digest and are rich in oils, proteins and vitamins, particularly Vitamin C. They may be pear-shaped or round, and green, purple or blackish-coloured. Some have a thin skin and some a hard, knobbly shell. All have pale, creamy green flesh and are ready to eat when they yield slightly if pressed gently between the hands. Choose fruit that is heavy and even-coloured without cracks, bruises or very soft spots. Avocados that are hard will ripen if kept at room tempe____ for 2–3 days.

□ Ba____ ____ss steel ____ in half ____ halves ____ ne by ____ If you ____ nife if ____ le if ____ d or ____ on ____ly

____
n____
sa____
jui____

As ____
*sauc*____
and ____
of cru____ Crumbled
crisp b____ on top is delicious.
To serve hot: Fill cavities of halved avocados in the shell with hot creamed seafood, ham or chicken. Top with grated cheese or buttered breadcrumbs and bake in a preheated moderate oven (180°C/350°F, Gas Mark 4) for 10 minutes. **See recipes.**

See also *Guacamole.*

Guacamole Salad

2 avocados, peeled, stoned and cut into large dice; 2 medium tomatoes, peeled, seeded and chopped; 2 spring onions (scallions) finely sliced; crisp lettuce leaves; chopped parsley; 2 canned pimientos, drained.
DRESSING: *2 tbsp oil; 1 tbsp vinegar; few drops Tabasco (hot pepper) sauce; juice ½ lemon; salt and freshly ground black pepper.*

DRESSING: Beat all ingredients together in a small bowl until mixture thickens.

Put avocado into a bowl and toss gently with dressing. Add tomatoes and spring onions (scallions). Cover and chill. To serve, line individual plates with lettuce leaves. Place avocado mixture on lettuce. Sprinkle with parsley. Finely dice or sieve pimientos and spoon over. Serves 4.

Avocado Soup

This soup can be served hot or cold.

2 medium avocados, peeled, stoned and sliced; 250 ml/8 fl oz (1 cup) single (light) cream; 900 ml/1½ pints (3¾ cups) chicken stock; salt and freshly ground white pepper; pinch nutmeg; 1 tbsp lemon juice; extra single (light) cream to finish.

Purée avocados with cream in a blender or food processor, or mash together and rub through a sieve. For a cold soup, add purée ____ cold stock, season with salt, pepper, nutmeg and lemon juice and chill. For hot soup, add purée to hot stock and heat to just below boiling point. Season, and serve immediately. Finish hot or cold soup with a swirl of cream on each serving. Serves 6–8.

Avocado Mousse

7 g/¼ oz (1 envelope) gelatine; 250 ml/8 fl oz (1 cup) chicken stock; 2 large avocados, peeled, stoned and mashed; 2 tsp snipped chives; salt and freshly ground white pepper; 2 tbsp lemon juice; 1 tsp Worcestershire sauce; few drops Tabasco (hot pepper) sauce; 120 ml/4 fl oz (½ cup) double (heavy) cream; 175 ml/6 fl oz (¾ cup) Mayonnaise (page 204); 2 egg whites.

Soften gelatine in a little cold stock, then stand container in hot water until dissolved. Add remaining stock, avocados and chives, and beat until smooth. Add salt, pepper, lemon juice, and sauces. Chill until mixture is

consistency of unbeaten egg white. Whip cream and fold in with mayonnaise. Beat egg whites until they hold soft peaks and fold in. Adjust seasoning and pour into a wet 1.5 litre/2½ pint (6 cup) mould. Chill until set. To serve, unmould mousse on to a chilled platter. Serves 8–10.

Avocado and Bacon Salad

This makes a lovely main course salad for 4 or a first course for 8.

2 avocados, peeled, stoned and sliced; 120 ml/4 fl oz (½ cup) Vinaigrette Dressing (page 358); 4 rashers (slices) bacon, rind removed; crisp lettuce leaves; 2 tomatoes, peeled and cut into wedges; 8 black olives; chopped fresh parsley to garnish.

Sprinkle avocado slices with a little of the vinaigrette. Cut each bacon rasher (slice) into 3 and pan-fry; drain on crumpled paper towels. Place lettuce on 4 plates and arrange avocado slices on top and tomato wedges at one side. Strew bacon over avocado, add olives and drizzle with remaining vinaigrette. Sprinkle with parsley. Serves 4 or 8.

Avocado Grand Duc

180 g/6 oz (¾ cup) crabmeat, canned or fresh, picked over well; 2 tbsp Mayonnaise (page 204); 1 tbsp tomato purée (paste); juice ½ lemon; salt and freshly ground black pepper; 1 avocado, halved and stoned; 1 hard-boiled (hard-cooked) egg, chopped; 1 tsp chopped parsley; 1 tsp chopped fresh tarragon; 1 tsp chopped fresh chervil; 2 tsp caviar (optional).

Combine crabmeat, mayonnaise, tomato paste, lemon juice, salt and pepper. Mix lightly and fill avocado halves with mixture. Mix together egg, parsley, tarragon and chervil, and sprinkle over avocado halves. If wished, top each half with a teaspoonful of caviar. Serves 2.

Avocado Sauce

A sauce for cold fish or chicken.

1 large avocado, halved and stoned; 1 tbsp tarragon vinegar; 4 tbsp olive oil; 2 tbsp lemon juice; pinch cayenne; salt and freshly ground black pepper; 1 egg yolk.

Scoop flesh from avocado halves and beat with vinegar, oil, lemon juice, cayenne, salt and pepper. Chill. Just before serving add egg yolk and beat again. Makes about 350 ml/12 fl oz (1½ cups).

Avocado Dressing

Similar to guacamole but smoother and not so hot. Use with chicken or fish salads. May also be added to coleslaw.

1 large avocado, peeled and stoned; 3 tbsp lime or lemon juice; 1 tbsp finely chopped onion; 1 clove garlic; 1 tsp salt; freshly ground black pepper.

Mash avocado to a soft purée. Add lime or lemon juice, onion and garlic which has been finely chopped or crushed with the salt and pepper. Blend ingredients well. Cover dressing. Makes about 300 ml/½ pint (1¼ cups).

Spanish Avocado Salad

This filling salad makes a delicious lunch dish served with chicken or ham.

1 avocado, peeled, stoned and thickly sliced crossways; juice 1 lemon; 1 head lettuce; 4 ripe tomatoes, peeled and thickly sliced; 4 new potatoes, boiled and thickly sliced; 1 green pepper, cored, seeded, blanched and cut into thick strips; 120 ml/4 fl oz (½ cup) Vinaigrette Dressing (page 358); 1 small onion, finely sliced.

Brush avocado slices with lemon juice to preserve colour. Line a salad bowl with lettuce leaves. Toss prepared vegetables lightly in dressing and arrange in lettuce-lined bowl. Pour remaining dressing over salad and garnish with onion rings. Serves 4–6.

Avocado Pimiento Salad

crisp lettuce leaves; 2 avocados, peeled, stoned and sliced; 2 canned pimientos, diced or cut into strips; 8 black olives, halved and stoned; 3 tsp lemon juice; finely chopped parsley.
DRESSING: 2½ tbsp oil; 2 tsp lemon juice; ¼ tsp French (Dijon) mustard; few drops Tabasco (hot pepper) sauce; salt and freshly ground black pepper.

Beat together dressing ingredients or shake them in a jar. Place lettuce leaves on 4 plates and arrange avocados on leaves. Sprinkle with dressing. Add pimiento, olives and lemon juice. Top with parsley. Serves 4.

BABA (AU RHUM)

A delectable French dessert cake made of yeast dough containing currants and soaked in rum-flavoured syrup. Large babas are baked in a tall, cylindrical mould and small ones in individual baba, dariole or castle pudding moulds.

Baba Au Rhum

45 g/1½ oz (¼ cup) currants; 90 g/3 oz (½ cup) sultanas (golden raisins); 4 tbsp dark rum; 15 g/½ oz (1 tbsp) fresh (compressed) yeast; 120 ml/4 fl oz (½ cup) lukewarm milk; 3 tbsp plus pinch sugar; 250 g/8 oz (2 cups) flour; ½ tsp salt; 4 eggs, lightly beaten; 125 g/4 oz (½ cup) butter, softened.
SYRUP: 350 ml/12 fl oz (1½ cups) water; 350 g/12 oz (1½ cups) sugar; 4 tbsp dark rum.
GLAZE: 350 g/12 oz (1 cup) apricot jam; 2 tbsp water; 2 tbsp dark rum.

Soak currants and sultanas (golden raisins) in rum overnight. To make dough, cream yeast with milk and pinch sugar and stand for 10 minutes. Sift flour, remaining sugar and salt into a large warmed bowl, make a well in centre and add yeast mixture. Sprinkle a little flour from sides over liquid, cover with a cloth and leave in a warm place for 20 minutes. Add eggs and butter to flour-yeast mixture and beat vigorously until dough is smooth and elastic. Drain fruit and mix into dough. Cover with greased plastic wrap and a cloth and leave in a warm place to rise for about 1 hour until doubled in bulk.

Pipe or spoon the baba dough into 16–18 buttered individual baba moulds, filling ⅓ full. Let dough rise until it reaches tops of moulds. Place babas in a preheated hot oven (230°C/450°F, Gas Mark 8), then immediately reduce the oven heat to moderately hot (200°C/400°F, Gas Mark 6). Bake for 15 minutes or until well browned. Remove babas from moulds and cool on a wire rack until lukewarm.
SYRUP: Combine water and sugar and cook, stirring, until sugar dissolves. Boil for 10 minutes without stirring, then remove from heat and add rum. Cool until warm. Place rack of babas over a tray and slowly spoon warm syrup over babas so they absorb as much as possible. As syrup collects in tray, re-spoon over babas.
GLAZE: Heat jam and water together, stirring until jam melts. Stir in rum, then rub through a sieve. Brush over babas. Makes 16–18.

BABA GHANNOUJ

This Middle Eastern aubergine (eggplant) purée with tahini is served as a dip with flat bread, or as a salad with meats and fish.

B

Baba Ghannouj

3 medium aubergines (eggplant); 3 cloves garlic, crushed with 1 tsp salt; ½ cup tahini (sesame paste); juice 2 medium lemons; 1 tsp ground cumin.
GARNISH: *2 tbsp finely chopped parsley; black olives; sliced tomato.*

Sear aubergines (eggplant) over a gas flame or under a grill (broiler), turning often. Continue searing until skins are blackened and blistered, and flesh soft. Scrape or peel charred skin from aubergines (eggplant), rinse under cold water and squeeze in a tea-towel to remove as much juice as possible. Mash aubergine (eggplant) flesh with a fork or potato masher. Add garlic and pound to a smooth purée. (This may also be done in a blender or food processor.) Add tahini and lemon juice alternately, beating or blending between each addition. Add cumin and blend. Taste, and add more lemon juice, garlic, tahini or salt if necessary. Mixture should be highly flavoured. Spoon into a bowl or individual serving dishes, sprinkle with parsley, and garnish with olives and tomato slices. Serves 8–12 as a dip.

BACON

This is the fat and lean meat from the side and back of the pig, cured (i.e. preserved) by dry salting or brining. It is frequently smoked as well, for extra flavour and keeping qualities.

Types of Bacon

Streaky bacon has alternate streaks of fat and lean, and is sold in narrow strips. These are known as rashers in Britain; slices in the United States, where it is the most common form of bacon available. It is delicious grilled (broiled), or fried with eggs, tomatoes, kidneys; on grilled (broiled) sandwiches etc. It crumbles easily when cooked, to make a crisp garnish for vegetables, savoury creamed dishes and salads.

Middle cut bacon is lean meat with an edging of fat. If it has a 'tail' of streaky bacon, and is in addition strongly salted and smoked, Americans will know it as Irish bacon.

Back bacon (Canadian bacon) is sugar-cured, smoked pork loin, boned and with the fillet removed. It is very choice and may be eaten hot or cold. Americans can buy it fresh or canned, in which case it is known as Pork loin roll.

Shoulder bacon is lean meat from the shoulder, with little or no fat. Slices are squarish, and usually thicker than other cuts. They are often used in dishes calling for ham.

Gammon of bacon is particularly popular in Britain. In recipes, gammon and ham may often be interchanged. The flavour is not quite the same however, because of the different breed of pig and curing method.

Speck is highly flavoured, cured and smoked pork which contains a very high proportion of fat. It is sold in slabs and is particularly popular in Germany and other European countries where it is used as the basic fat for browning and adding flavour to vegetables, soups, stews, savoury pastries etc. It is easy to cut into slices, squares or dice and, when the fat is rendered, there are delicious crispy bits left to add extra flavour and texture to a dish. When a recipe calls for speck and it is not available, fatty streaky bacon or pickled (salt) belly of pork with a good proportion of fat, may be used instead.

Green bacon has been lightly cured but not smoked. It has a milder flavour than smoked bacon. If a recipe has green bacon in it, you can blanch ordinary bacon by covering with cold water and bringing to the boil. Boil 1 minute and drain. This will remove some of the salty and smoky flavour.

□ **To Cook:** Bacon rashers (slices) may be grilled (broiled), fried or baked. **See also recipes**.

GRILLED (BROILED) BACON Remove rind, if desired. Snip bacon edges with kitchen scissors to prevent curling. Place rashers (slices) on a rack over the grill (broiler) pan and grill (broil) about 10 cm (4 in) from the heat for 2–3 minutes on each side.

FRIED BACON Remove rind, if desired, and snip edges of bacon. Streaky bacon should be placed in a cold frying pan (skillet) without extra fat and cooked over very low heat, turning frequently, until done to your liking. If you want the bacon crisp, pour off fat as it collects. Never allow the fat to smoke or the bacon will have a burnt flavour. For lean bacon, grease the frying pan (skillet) with lard or butter and heat before adding bacon. Cook over medium heat, turning once or twice. Add a little extra fat if necessary to prevent sticking.

BAKED BACON This is a useful method when you have a large quantity of bacon to cook, as it requires less watching and doesn't need turning. Remove rind from bacon, if desired. Arrange bacon rashers (slices) on a wire rack placed over a baking dish, and bake in a preheated moderately hot oven (200°C/400°F, Gas Mark 6) for 10–15 minutes.

Green Salad with Bacon Tear washed and dried, crisp salad greens into bite-sized pieces and place in a bowl. Season with salt and pepper and sprinkle with chopped fresh herbs. Fry streaky bacon rashers (slices), rind removed, until crisp, chop or crumble coarsely and add to salad. To the fat in the pan add a little vinegar to sharpen taste, pour hot over greens, toss lightly and serve at once.

Grilled Cheese and Bacon Toast bread on one side, butter untoasted side and cover with sliced cheese. Arrange bacon rashers (slices) on top and grill (broil) until bacon is crisp and cheese melted.

Warm Bacon, Avocado and Lettuce Salad

1 large or 2 small head lettuce, preferably a soft-leaved variety such as cos; 3 thick rashers (slices) bacon, rind removed; 2 tomatoes, peeled, seeded and cut into wedges; 2 large avocados, peeled, stoned and cut into chunks.
DRESSING: *3 tsp wine vinegar; pinch salt; freshly ground black pepper; 2 tbsp olive oil.*

Rinse and dry lettuce, and crisp in refrigerator. Cut bacon into small strips. Line a bowl with lettuce leaves and add tomatoes.
DRESSING: Whisk ingredients together. Add avocado to dressing and toss to coat. Place in bowl. Toss bacon strips in a frying pan (skillet) over high heat until lightly browned. Pour over salad and serve at once. Serves 6.

Wilted Salad with Bacon

4 tbsp vinegar; 1½ tsp sugar; 1 clove garlic, crushed; ½ tsp pepper; 6 rashers (slices) bacon, rind removed and cut into 2.5 cm (1 in) strips; 1 head cos lettuce, rinsed and dried; 2 large ripe tomatoes, each cut into 4 thick slices; 3–4 spring onions (scallions), finely sliced.

Mix vinegar, sugar, garlic and pepper in a small bowl. Let stand at least 30 minutes. Fry bacon in a large pan until crisp. Remove pan from heat and add lettuce to hot bacon fat. Gently stir for a minute or until lettuce wilts a little. Add vinegar mixture and mix well. Arrange tomato slices on a large plate or individual salad plates, mound the lettuce on top and sprinkle the spring onions (scallions) over before serving. Serves 4.

Bacon Appetizers

Soak 30 small wooden skewers in water to prevent their catching fire during cooking.

500 g (1 lb) chicken livers; 1 × 238 g/7½ oz can water chestnuts, drained; 10–15 rashers (slices) bacon, rind removed.

Cut each liver in 2 or 3 pieces. Halve the water chestnuts. Cut each bacon rasher (slice) in 4 pieces, and wrap a piece around each water chestnut half. On each skewer, thread a piece of liver and a piece of bacon-wrapped water chestnut. Repeat so that each skewer has at least 2 pieces of liver. Cook under a preheated grill (broiler) for 3 minutes each side or until the bacon is lightly browned. Makes 30.

Bacon Muffins

250 g/8 oz (2 cups) flour; 3 tsp baking powder; ½ tsp salt; 1 tbsp sugar; 1 egg, lightly beaten; 250 ml/8 fl oz (1 cup) milk; 60 g/2 oz (4 tbsp) melted butter; 3 rashers (slices) bacon, rind removed, fried and crumbled.

Sift flour, baking powder, salt and sugar into a large bowl. Add egg, milk, butter and bacon, stirring only enough to dampen the flour; the batter should not be smooth. Spoon into buttered muffin pans, filling each cup about ⅔ full. Bake in a preheated moderately hot oven (190°C/375°F, Gas Mark 5) for 20–25 minutes. Makes 12.

Bacon and Scallops en Brochette

750 g (1½ lb) scallops; 120 ml/4 fl oz (½ cup) white wine; 1 tbsp soy sauce; 1 tbsp olive oil; 2 cloves garlic, finely chopped; grated rind; 1 lemon; 20 g/⅔ oz (½ cup) chopped parsley; 250 g/8 oz sliced bacon, rind removed.

Trim off any dark parts from scallops but retain coral. Cover scallops with a mixture of white wine, soy sauce and olive oil. Let them marinate for about 20 minutes, then drain. Mix garlic, lemon rind and parsley. Cut each bacon rasher (slice) into 4 and curl into rolls. Roll each scallop in parsley mixture and thread scallops on to skewers alternately with bacon rolls. Grill (broil), turning skewers frequently, until scallops are just cooked but not dry, about 8–10 minutes. Serve with rice, plain or saffron-flavoured. Serves 6.

Ham Steaks with Pineapple

6 gammon (ham) steaks; 30 g/1 oz (2 tbsp) melted butter; 1 tbsp made mustard; 6 slices fresh or canned pineapple; 2 tbsp brown sugar mixed with 1 tbsp vinegar; 1 tbsp chopped chives or spring onions (scallions).

Cut off the rind and snip the fat around the steaks at 1 cm (½ in) intervals. Brush one side with melted butter and a little mustard and cook under a preheated grill (broiler) for 5 minutes. Turn over, brush with butter and spread with more mustard. Grill (broil) for another 3 minutes. Arrange a pineapple slice on each steak, spread with remaining butter and drizzle over the brown sugar mixture. Grill (broil) for a further 2 minutes, increasing the heat if necessary to lightly glaze and brown the pineapple. Sprinkle with the chives or spring onions (scallions). Serves 6.

Herb and Bacon Bread

250 g (8 oz) streaky bacon; 250 g/8 oz (2 cups) plain (all-purpose) flour; 65 g/2½ oz (⅓ cup) sugar; 1 tbsp baking powder; 1 tsp salt; ½ tsp bicarbonate of soda (baking soda); 3 tbsp chopped mixed fresh herbs; 2 eggs, beaten; 250 ml/8 fl oz (1 cup) sour cream; 5 tbsp milk.

Finely dice the bacon and fry gently until crisp. Drain and then spread on paper towels to cool. Sift the flour, sugar, baking powder, salt and soda into a large bowl. Stir in the herbs. Combine the eggs, sour cream and

milk and pour this into the dry ingredients. Sprinkle the bacon bits over the top and stir lightly with a wooden spoon just enough to moisten the flour. Do not overmix, the mixture will still be lumpy. Turn into a well greased 500 g/1 lb loaf tin (pan) and bake in a preheated moderate oven (180°C/350°F, Gas Mark 4) for 55 minutes or until a fine skewer inserted in the centre comes out clean. Turn the loaf out of the tin to allow the steam to escape. Serve warm with butter. Serves 6–8.

BAGEL

A doughnut-shaped roll which is a distinctive part of Jewish cuisine. It is first cooked in water, then baked, which gives the bagel its characteristic hard, glazed crust. A traditional filling for bagels is cream cheese and lox (smoked salmon).

BAGNA CAUDA

An Italian garlicky sauce served hot as a dip for crisp, raw vegetables.

Bagna Cauda

250 g/8 oz (1 cup) butter; 4 tbsp olive oil; 4 cloves garlic, crushed; 6 anchovy fillets, finely chopped; salt if necessary.

Heat butter and oil together in a shallow pan, add garlic and stir over medium heat until garlic is soft but not brown. Remove pan from heat and add anchovies. Return to low heat and continue cooking, stirring well with a wooden spoon, until anchovies have dissolved to a paste. Taste and season with salt if necessary. Keep hot over a candle warmer or other burner, and serve surrounded by cold, crisp raw vegetables. Serves 6–8.

BAGUETTE (French Bread)

This is the name for the flattened, cylindrical loaf which is the everyday bread of France, bought warm and crisp from the bakery, often twice a day. Baguettes may come in different lengths, but are always distinguished by their shape and crisp crust which is slashed on top.

BAKLAVA

A superb sweet pastry, typical of the luscious pastries of Greece and the Middle East.

Baklava

20 sheets filo (phyllo) pastry (about 1 × 375 g/12 oz packet); 180 g/6 oz (¾ cup) unsalted butter, melted; 180 g/6 oz (1½ cups) finely chopped walnuts; 90 g/3 oz (¾ cup) finely chopped almonds; 60 g/2 oz (¼ cup)

caster sugar; 2 tsp cinnamon; pinch ground cloves.
SYRUP: *500 g/1 lb (2 cups) sugar; 450 ml/¾ pint (2 cups) water; 2 whole cloves; 1 × 8 cm (3 in) cinnamon stick; 1 tbsp lemon juice; thin strip lemon rind; 2 tbsp honey.*

Unwrap filo (phyllo) pastry, spread flat on a tea-towel and cover with a dry tea-towel then a damp one to stop drying out while assembling baklava. Place one sheet of filo (phyllo) in a buttered 33 × 23 × 5 cm (13 × 9 × 2 in) baking dish, brush all over with melted butter and place another sheet on top. Continue adding sheets, buttering in between, until 9 sheets are used. Mix nuts with sugar and spices and sprinkle half over filo (phyllo). Add 2 more sheets, brushing each with butter. Top with remaining nuts and then 9 more sheets of buttered filo (phyllo). Trim edges and brush top layer with butter. With a sharp knife, cut through top few sheets to make a diamond pattern. Sprinkle a little water over surface to keep pastry flat while baking, and bake in centre of a preheated moderate oven (160°C/325°F, Gas Mark 3) for 30 minutes. Move baklava to a shelf placed above centre and bake for a further 30 minutes. If top is browning too much, cover with foil, but do not reduce cooking time.
SYRUP: Place all the ingredients in a saucepan and stir over high heat until sugar dissolves. Bring to the boil and boil over moderate heat for 10 minutes. Strain and cool before using. Spoon syrup over hot baklava as soon as it comes from the oven. Allow to cool, and cut into diamonds to serve. Makes 30.

BAMBOO SHOOTS

The tender, inner part of young shoots of the bamboo tree are used as an ingredient in Chinese, Japanese and other Oriental dishes. Canned bamboo shoots are widely available today. They should be drained and rinsed in cold water before using.

Bamboo Shoots with Broccoli and Mushrooms

500 g (1 lb) broccoli; 8–10 dried Chinese mushrooms; 6 spring onions (scallions); 4 tbsp peanut oil; 250 g/8 oz (1 cup) drained, canned bamboo shoots; 1 tsp salt; 1 tsp sugar; 1 tbsp light soy sauce; 1 tbsp dry sherry or rice wine; hot boiled rice to serve.

Cut thick stems from broccoli and save for another use. Cut flower part into pieces 2.5–5 cm (1–2 in) long. Soak dried mushrooms in warm water for 15 minutes.

Right: Deep Dish Apple Pie (page 10)
Overleaf: Globe Artichokes (page 12)

Drain, reserving 4 tbsp water. Cut each spring onion (scallion) into 3 pieces. Drop broccoli into boiling water. When water boils again, drain and refresh under cold running water. Heat oil in a wok or frying pan (skillet), add mushrooms, bamboo shoots and spring onions (scallions) and stir-fry on high heat 1 minute. Add broccoli, salt, sugar, soy sauce, sherry and soaking water from mushrooms. Toss gently for 2 minutes and serve immediately with hot boiled rice. Serves 4.

BANANA

Buy bananas with smooth, unblemished skins and, if possible, in a bunch rather than separately as they keep better. Slightly green bananas may be used for cooking; for eating, allow to ripen at room temperature. Never store in the refrigerator. If slicing or chopping bananas for fruit salads or to decorate cakes, pies etc., toss with a little lemon or other citrus fruit juice to prevent their turning brown. **See recipes.**

Baked Bananas To cook green bananas as a vegetable, place unpeeled bananas in a baking dish and cook in a preheated moderate oven 180°C/350°F, Gas Mark 4) for about 20 minutes until soft when tested with a fork. Peel when cool enough to handle, and season with salt and pepper. Ripe bananas may be cooked the same way, though cooking time will be less. Serve as a vegetable, or sprinkle with a little brown sugar and lemon juice or rum and serve with ice cream as a dessert.

Banana Custard Slice 1 ripe banana for each person into a heatproof serving bowl, and sprinkle with lemon juice and a little sugar. Make Stirred Custard (page 94), using 500 ml/¾ pint (2 cups) milk for 4 bananas. Pour hot custard over the sliced bananas. Sprinkle with nutmeg and serve warm or chilled.

Banana Fritters

4 medium, firm bananas; 3 tbsp lemon juice; 2 tbsp icing (confectioners) sugar, sifted; 125 g/4 oz (1 cup) flour; pinch salt; 150 ml/¼ pint (⅔ cup) warm water; 2 tbsp oil; 2 egg whites; oil for deep-frying.
TO SERVE: *lemon juice; sifted icing (confectioners) sugar.*

Peel bananas and cut each into 3 chunks. Sprinkle with lemon juice and icing (confectioners) sugar. Let stand 30 minutes.

Preceding Page: Bananas Caribbean (page 25)
Left: Fudge Brownies (page 48), Ginger and Butter Shortbread Biscuits (page 36), Chocolate Cherry Squares and No-Bake Fruit Bars (page 74)

Meanwhile, sift flour and salt into a bowl, make a well in centre and add water and oil. Stir from centre, gradually drawing in flour, and beat until smooth. Cover and stand 30 minutes. Beat egg whites to a firm snow and fold into batter. Dry banana chunks, dip in batter and deep-fry in hot oil until golden-brown. Drain on paper towels. Serve at once, sprinkled with extra lemon juice and icing (confectioners) sugar. Serves 4.

Bananas au Rhum

60 g/2 oz (4 tbsp) butter; 1 tsp grated lemon rind; 1 tbsp lemon juice; 4 firm ripe bananas; 4 tbsp brown sugar; 4 tbsp rum; single (light) cream to serve.

Put the butter and lemon rind and juice in a baking dish and place it in a preheated moderate oven (180°C/350°F, Gas Mark 4) for 2–3 minutes, just long enough to melt the butter. Remove and stir. Put bananas in baking dish, turning so they are coated with butter mixture. Sprinkle brown sugar over them and bake for 15 minutes. Heat rum, pour over bananas and set alight. Spoon burning liquor over bananas until flames die down. Serve hot with cream. Serves 4.

Bananas Caribbean

8 medium, firm bananas; 45 g/1½ oz (¼ cup) firmly packed brown sugar; 120 ml/4 fl oz (½ cup) orange juice; grated rind 1 orange; ¼ tsp cinnamon; ¼ tsp nutmeg; 120 ml/4 fl oz (½ cup) sherry; 30 g/1 oz (2 tbsp) butter; 4 tbsp rum; 30 g/1 oz (⅓ cup) desiccated (shredded) coconut; vanilla ice cream or whipped cream to serve.

Peel bananas and arrange in a buttered, shallow, baking dish. Heat brown sugar, orange juice and rind, spices and sherry together. Pour over bananas and dot butter over top. Bake in a preheated moderately hot oven (190°C/375°F, Gas Mark 5) for 10–15 minutes or until soft, basting now and again. Transfer bananas and sauce to a serving dish. Heat rum, pour over bananas and set alight. Spoon sauce over bananas until flames die down. Sprinkle with coconut and serve with ice cream. Serves 4–6.

Sautéed Bananas

This makes a lovely dessert, and also a fine accompaniment to curry or chicken dishes without the icing (confectioners) sugar.

60 g/2 oz (4 tbsp) butter; 4 firm ripe bananas, halved lengthways; 4 tbsp icing (confectioners) sugar.

Melt butter in a frying pan (skillet). Add bananas. Cook over a moderate heat for 5 minutes, turning once. Remove to a heated dish. Spoon butter from pan over them.

Sift icing (confectioners) sugar on top. Serves 3–4.

Banana Nut Bread

3 ripe bananas, well mashed; 2 eggs, well beaten; 250 g/8 oz (2 cups) flour; 180 g/6 oz (¾ cup) sugar; 1 tsp salt; 1 tsp bicarbonate of soda (baking soda); 60 g/2 oz (½ cup) coarsely chopped walnuts.

Mix bananas and eggs together in a large bowl. Stir in flour, sugar, salt and soda. Add walnuts and blend. Put batter in greased 21 × 11 cm (8½ × 4½ in) loaf tin (pan) and bake in a preheated moderate oven (180°C/350°F, Gas Mark 4) for 1 hour. Serve warm or cooled with butter. Makes 1 loaf.

Delicate Banana Soufflé

5–6 ripe bananas, mashed; grated rind and juice of 1 medium orange; 1 tbsp lemon juice; 125 g/4 oz (½ cup) caster sugar; 1 tbsp slivered almonds or chopped walnuts; 4 egg whites; pinch of salt; pinch of cream of tartar.

Mix the bananas with the orange rind and juice, lemon juice, sugar and nuts. Whisk the egg whites with the salt and cream of tartar until firm peaks form, then gently fold into the banana mixture. Turn at once into a prepared soufflé dish and bake in a preheated moderate oven (180°C/350°F, Gas Mark 4) for 25–30 minutes, or until well risen and golden brown. Remove the paper collar and serve immediately with cream or ice-cream. Serves 4.

BANBURY TART

A sweet pastry from Banbury in Oxfordshire.

Banbury Tarts

1 × 375 g/12 oz packet frozen puff pastry (paste), thawed; 90 g/3 oz (½ cup) each raisins, currants and chopped mixed candied peel; 125 g/4 oz (½ cup) sugar; grated rind and juice 1 large lemon; 1 tsp ground allspice; 120 ml/4 fl oz (½ cup) water; 2 tbsp flour.
GLAZE: *beaten egg; sugar.*

Roll out pastry (dough) thinly and cut into rounds about 8 cm (3 in) in diameter. Combine remaining ingredients (except glaze) in a saucepan and stir over low heat until thick. Allow to cool. Dampen edges of half the pastry (dough) rounds and place about 2 tsp filling in centre of each. Top with remaining rounds. Press edges firmly together and decorate with tines of a fork. Glaze with egg and sprinkle with sugar. Place on baking trays and bake in a preheated hot oven (220°C/425°F, Gas Mark 7) for 15–20 minutes or until golden-brown. Cool on a wire rack. Makes about 12.

BANNOCK

The word bannock comes from the Gaelic for 'cake', and this flat, substantial cake has been part of traditional Scottish fare for centuries.

Oatmeal Bannocks

180 g/6 oz (⅔ cup) medium oatmeal; pinch bicarbonate of soda (baking soda); pinch salt; 2 tsp melted lard, dripping or bacon fat; about 4 tbsp hot water; extra oatmeal.

Place oatmeal in a basin with soda and salt and stir to combine. Make a well in the centre and pour in melted fat. Add enough hot water to bind mixture to a stiff paste. Turn out on to a work surface spread thickly with oatmeal. Roll mixture into a ball, using oatmeal to prevent sticking. Knead a few times, then pat out to a round about 5 cm (¼ in) thick. Sprinkle with a little extra oatmeal, and cut into quarters. Place on a lightly greased hot griddle or frying pan (skillet) and cook over medium heat until the underside is brown and the edges curl slightly. Turn over with a spatula and brown the other side. Serve warm with butter and honey or jam. Makes 4.

BAP

Baps are the breakfast rolls of Scotland – to the Scot, as indispensable as croissants are to the French. They are light, white and soft (not crusty), and delicious eaten hot with butter.

Floury Baps

500 g/1 lb (4 cups) flour; 1 tsp salt; 180 ml/6 fl oz (¾ cup) milk; 120 ml/4 fl oz (½ cup) water; 60 g/2 oz (4 tbsp) butter; 15 g/½ oz (1 tbsp) fresh (compressed) yeast; 1 tsp sugar; little extra milk and flour.

Sift flour with salt into a bowl. Heat milk and water together to blood heat; add butter and remove from heat when butter has melted. Cream yeast with sugar and stir into warm liquid. Make a well in centre of flour and pour in yeast mixture. Stir in a little flour from the sides until yeast mixture is consistency of thick batter. Cover with a folded cloth and place in a warm spot. When yeast mixture has doubled, and bubbles have formed, mix in remaining flour. Turn dough on to a floured board and knead for about 5 minutes until smooth. Place in a clean, greased bowl and turn over so top surface is also lightly greased. Cover with greased plastic wrap and leave in a warm place for 2 hours or until doubled in bulk. Knock (punch) down, and turn on to a floured board. Knead lightly, divide into 12 pieces and shape each into a ball. Place balls of dough on a greased baking tray; cover and allow to rise in a warm place for 20 minutes.

Brush with a little milk and sprinkle lightly with flour. Bake in a preheated moderately hot oven (200°C/400°F, Gas Mark 6) for 15–20 minutes or until very pale golden. Makes 12.

BARBECUE SAUCE

A sauce can add flavour and promote juiciness in barbecued fish, chicken or meat.

Barbecue Basting Sauce

180 ml/6 fl oz (¾ cup) tomato ketchup; 2 tsp celery seeds; 1 clove garlic, crushed; 1 tbsp Worcestershire sauce; 2 tbsp vinegar; 2 tbsp sugar; dash cayenne or black pepper; 3 tbsp oil.

Combine all ingredients in a saucepan, bring to the boil and simmer for 3 minutes. Cool before using. Brush over steak, chops, sausages or hamburgers in the last 5–10 minutes of cooking. Do not use too early or sauce may become bitter or make meat stick. Pass leftover sauce separately. Makes about 250 ml/8 fl oz (1 cup).

Herb and Lemon Marinade

Use for barbecued fish or chicken.

5 tbsp olive oil; 150 ml/¼ pint (⅔ cup) white wine; juice 1 lemon; 1 onion, sliced; 1 carrot, sliced; 1 celery stick, sliced; 1 sprig parsley; 1 bay leaf; 1 tbsp chopped fresh thyme, dill or rosemary, or 1 tsp dried; 6 peppercorns.

Combine all ingredients and marinate fish for 20–30 minutes, chicken for 1 hour or more before barbecuing. Brush remaining marinade over food while cooking. Makes about 250 ml/8 fl oz (1 cup).

BARLEY

Barley is a cereal related to wheat and grows in the same grass-like form. As food prices continue to rise, barley is receiving increased attention from cooks everywhere who appreciate its economy and good nutty flavour. It is excellent in vegetarian dishes, soups and

stews and, in addition to its high carbohydrate content, contains useful amounts of protein, calcium and phosphorus and small amounts of B vitamins.

Pot barley (also called Scotch or hulled barley) is the grain with only the outer husk removed. It requires 2–3 hours cooking.

Pearl barley has had the complete husk removed and is then steamed and polished. This is probably the most familiar type of barley, used for barley water and side dishes, soups and stews. It needs 1½–2 hours cooking to become tender. **See recipes.**

Barley Water

This refreshing drink, very popular in Victorian times, is enjoying a revival today. It keeps well in the refrigerator.

50 g/1¾ oz (¼ cup) pearl barley; 1 litre/ 1½ pints (4 cups) water; thinly peeled rind and juice 2 medium lemons; sugar to taste.

Place barley, water and lemon rind in a saucepan and bring to the boil. Lower heat and simmer as gently as possible, with lid on, for 2 hours. Strain into a container and add lemon juice and sugar to taste. Cool, then chill. Serves 4–6.

Lamb and Barley Casserole

2 breasts of lamb, cut into serving-sized pieces; 2 tbsp oil; salt and freshly ground black pepper; 105 g/3½ oz (½ cup) pearl barley; 4 ripe tomatoes, peeled and chopped; 1 tbsp chopped fresh basil or oregano, or 1 tsp dried; 1 tbsp sugar; ½ medium cabbage, cut into wedges; 20 g/⅔ oz (½ cup) finely chopped parsley to serve.

Trim excess fat from lamb. Heat oil in a heavy frying pan (skillet) and brown lamb on both sides. Season well with salt and pepper, and transfer to a deep saucepan. Add barley and enough water to cover, and simmer with lid on for 1 hour. Skim any fat from top, and add tomatoes, herbs, sugar and cabbage. Simmer, covered, for a further 30 minutes or until barley is tender. Adjust seasoning and sprinkle with parsley to serve. Serves 6.

Scotch Broth
(Barley Broth)

1 kg (2 lb) lamb neck chops, or 4 lamb shanks; 2 litres/3½ pints (8 cups) water; 1 tsp salt; 105 g/3½ oz (½ cup) pearl barley; 2 medium onions, chopped; 2 medium carrots, chopped; 1 medium turnip, chopped; 20 g/⅔ oz (½ cup) finely chopped parsley.

Remove surplus fat from meat and place in a large saucepan with water and salt. Bring slowly to the boil, cover and simmer for 1 hour, removing any scum that comes to the surface. Add remaining ingredients except parsley. Simmer, covered, for a further 1½–2 hours or until tender. Remove meat from pot, and discard bones. Skim any fat from soup. Chop meat into small pieces, return to soup and reheat. Adjust seasoning and stir in parsley just before serving. Serves 6.

BARQUETTES

Made of pastry (dough) and meaning 'little boats', these are filled with hot or cold fillings to serve as hors d'oeuvre. They are shaped in special little boat-shaped tin moulds. For pastry (dough) recipes see *Pastry;* for suitable fillings, see *Hors d'oeuvre.*

To shape barquettes: Place moulds close together, about 6 in a group. Roll out short-crust or flaky pastry (dough) thinly, lift on to rolling pin and lay it over all tins together. Form a small piece of pastry (dough) into a ball, dip it in flour and use it to press pastry (dough) into moulds. Flour rolling pin and roll first one way, then the other, over moulds to remove surplus pastry (dough). Fold trimmings together and roll out again to line more moulds in the same way. Take each mould, press edges lightly up with the thumb and prick bottom before baking.

BASIL

This fragrant, aromatic herb is a member of the mint family and is widely used in Italian cooking. They call it the tomato herb because it goes so well with tomatoes.

It is an annual, so basil is available fresh only during summer, but keeps well packed in oil for winter cooking. Simply snip leaves from the stems, pack in a jar and cover with olive oil. Store tightly covered in the refrigerator and remove leaves as required.

Use fresh basil leaves, cut into thin strips, in all salads, particularly with tomatoes. Add to salad dressings, and blend into butter for sandwiches. Use to add fresh flavour to scrambled eggs and cheese sauces, sprinkle on pizzas before baking and over pasta dishes. Sprinkle lamb chops and liver with chopped basil before cooking, and stir a little

into the pan juices after cooking chicken, meat or fish. For a simple but superb Mediterranean-style salad, alternate slices of fresh tomato and baby Mozzarella cheese on a serving platter and sprinkle with olive oil, salt and fine ribbons of basil.

Just a word of caution – unlike some herbs, the flavour of fresh basil bears little relation to the dried variety. To enjoy the true aromatic taste, it is necessary to grow your own, or patronize a greengrocer who sells fresh herbs in season. **See recipes.**

See also *Pasta Sauces.*

Baked Tomatoes with Basil

6 large ripe tomatoes; salt and freshly ground black pepper; 6 spring onions (scallions), chopped; 8 leaves fresh basil, shredded; 60 g/2 oz (1 cup) fresh breadcrumbs; 15 g/½ oz (1 tbsp) butter.

Cut each tomato in half and remove cores. Season the cut surfaces generously with salt and lightly with pepper, sprinkle with spring onions (scallions) and basil, top with breadcrumbs, and put a generous dot of butter on each half. Arrange in a buttered baking dish, and bake in a preheated moderate oven (180°C/350°F, Gas Mark 4) for 10 minutes. Remove from the oven and brown under a moderate grill (broiler) for about 3 minutes. If the oven is in use, simply grill (broil) under a moderate heat for 10–12 minutes, taking care not to burn. Serves 6.

Stewed Tomatoes with Sweet Basil

4 large ripe tomatoes, peeled, seeded and diced; 25 g/1 oz (2 tbsp) butter; salt and freshly ground black pepper; 10 leaves fresh basil, shredded; 30 g/1 oz (½ cup) fresh breadcrumbs.

Place tomatoes in a saucepan. Add butter, salt and pepper. Cover and stew gently for about 5 minutes, stirring occasionally. Add basil and cook 5 minutes longer. Add crumbs and mix well. Cook until tomatoes are soft. The crumbs will take up the excess liquid. Serves 4.

Tomato Salad

A simple yet striking way to prepare tomatoes. Perfect to serve with grilled (broiled) meats, fish or pasta dishes.

4 firm ripe tomatoes; salt and freshly ground black pepper; 3 tbsp olive oil; 1 tsp lemon juice or wine vinegar; 6–8 spring onions (scallions), finely chopped; 8–10 leaves fresh basil, finely shredded.

Cut tomatoes crossways into thin slices (use serrated-edge knife) and arrange overlapping on a flat dish. Season well with salt and pepper. Mix oil with lemon juice or vinegar and sprinkle over tomatoes. Blanch spring onions (scallions) in boiling water for 30 seconds, refresh under cold water and drain well. Sprinkle tomatoes with basil leaves. Serves 4.

VARIATION

Tomato and Onion Salad: Omit spring onions (scallions). Finely slice 1 onion and break slices into rings. Scatter over tomato slices before adding dressing.

BASMATI

See *Rice.*

BATTER

This is flour and liquid, and usually eggs and other ingredients, that are mixed to a consistency that can be stirred or 'battered'. Batters are used for crêpes, pancakes and fritters, waffles and doughnuts, for coating foods for frying, for making Yorkshire Pudding and baked desserts, and sometimes for making small, crisp cases to hold a filling, in the same way as pastry (dough) cases. In America, the word is also used for cake mixtures, though they may be thicker than the batter used for other foods.

Depending on the purpose of the batter, ingredients and consistency vary. A batter for crêpes contains a high proportion of eggs and milk to flour, and should be the consistency of pouring cream. Coating batters for fish, etc., are often thicker, and may contain beer or soda (carbonated) water for extra lightness and crispness (the gases have this lightening effect). Whisked egg white is also added to some batters to give lightness. Yeast batters are also used for particular recipes (see *Blini*).

Recipes often advise to rest the batter for anything from 20 minutes to 3–4 hours. During this time the starch cells swell and are more easily broken down in cooking, giving better flavour and texture. Batter may thicken slightly while resting, and a little more liquid may have to be added to bring it back to the right consistency.

Before dipping foods in batter be sure they are dried thoroughly or the batter will not cling. **See recipes.**

B

Basic Batter

The method described below is the basic one for mixing most batters when making by hand. Batter may also be made by putting all the ingredients into a blender, liquid ingredients first then dry ones, and blending until smooth, or by putting dry ingredients into a food processor and, with the motor running, adding liquid ingredients through the feed tube.

125 g/4 oz (1 cup) flour; pinch salt; 1 egg; 300 ml/½ pint (1¼ cups) milk.

Sift flour and salt into a large bowl and make a well in centre so that you can see the bottom of the bowl. Put in egg and about ⅓ milk and stir them together with a wooden spatula or spoon. Use a rapid circular motion, gradually extending it to allow flour to wash into liquid little by little. Add more liquid as flour is drawn in. Beat batter until very smooth. Cover and stand at least 30 minutes or up to 3–4 hours. Check consistency before using and stir in a little water, if needed, for the thickness specified in particular recipes.

Use Basic Batter when frying fish, and for Toad-in-the-Hole (see separate entries). For other batter recipes, see *Crêpes, Fritters, Pancakes, Waffles.*

Yorkshire Pudding

1 quantity Basic Batter (above); melted dripping or butter.

Set batter aside for 1 hour. Stir in a little water if necessary to make batter consistency of thick (heavy) cream. Pour into a jug. Brush deep bun tins (muffin pans) generously with beef dripping from roast or melted butter. Place tins (pans) on top shelf of a preheated hot oven (220°C/425°F, Gas Mark 7) for 2–3 minutes or until the fat begins to smoke. Remove from oven, stir batter and pour in quickly to fill each tin (pan) about ⅔ full. Replace on top shelf of oven and bake for 15–20 minutes or until well risen, crisp and golden-brown. Serve immediately as an accompaniment to roast beef. Makes 12.

NOTE: If you prefer, make one large pudding and cut it into squares. In this case, heat 3 tbsp dripping or butter in a 25 × 23 × 5 cm (10 × 9 × 2 in) baking tin (pan), pour in the batter and bake as above but in a preheated moderately hot oven (200°C/400°F, Gas Mark 6) for 30–40 minutes or until puffed around the edges, crisp and golden-brown.

Breakfast Fritters

1 quantity Basic Batter (above); flavouring ingredients chosen from: 250 g/8 oz (1 cup) finely diced corned beef, sausage or other cold cooked meat, mixed with 1 tsp French (Dijon) mustard and 1 tbsp grated onion; 1 × 440 g/15 oz can sweet corn, drained, mixed with 2 rashers (slices) bacon, cooked and crumbled; 180 g/6 oz (1 cup) cooked vegetables (carrots, peas, beans, spinach, cauliflower), diced and mixed with 1 tbsp grated onion, 1 tbsp chopped parsley and 1 rasher (slice) bacon, cooked and crumbled; oil for frying; chutney, Tomato Sauce (page 370) or grilled (broiled) tomato to accompany, if desired.

Mix the batter with the chosen flavouring ingredients. Heat 1 cm (½ in) oil in a frying pan (skillet) until it gives off a slight haze. Drop mixture in large spoonfuls into oil and fry about 2 minutes on each side. Turn heat down and cook 2 minutes more. Drain on crumpled paper towels and serve very hot, with chutney, tomato sauce or grilled (broiled) tomato if desired. Serves 4–6.

BAY

No kitchen should be without bay leaves, which come from the sweet bay or laurel tree. (Do not confuse with varieties of laurel which are poisonous.) If you have a bay tree, use the leaves 3–4 days after picking. To dry them for later use, cut a small twig or branch and hang it for a week or two in a cool, dry place, then pick off the leaves and store in an airtight jar. Use sparingly.

In a supermarket the leaves are usually sold in packets, but avoid the very old, dried leaves which have little flavour.

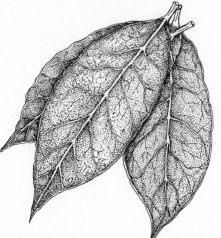

Ways to Use Bay Leaves
● Place a small leaf on top of terrines and meat loaves.
● When making kebabs, secure small pieces of bay between cubes of meat.
● Add a small leaf to the liquid when cooking ham, tongue, corned beef or other boiled meats.
● Always remember to add a small bay leaf to the bouquet garni which is used to flavour marinades, stocks, court bouillon, pickles and many other dishes.
● Add a piece of bay leaf when cooking aubergine (eggplant), cauliflower, carrots, beetroot, tomatoes or onion.
● Transform sauces, sweet custards and rice puddings by infusing a small bay leaf in the milk.
● Add a bay leaf to vegetable and fish soups.

BEANS, BROAD AND LIMA

These are annual plants cultivated mainly for their seeds, which are used both fresh and dried; see also *Pulses: Dried Beans, Peas and Lentils.*

Fresh broad beans, with their large, lumpy pods, are usually shelled immediately before going into the pot. When the seeds are large, it is necessary also to remove the rather tough outer skin before cooking. If the beans are very young, they can be cut up, cooked and eaten, pods and all.

□ **To Cook:** Drop beans into boiling, salted water and cook until just tender. Drain and add a little butter, freshly ground black pepper and salt.

They are also delicious with chopped ham: Heat cooked beans and ham gently together until warmed through. A few spoonfuls of cream with a dash of nutmeg is another delicious dressing for broad beans; heat until cream just begins to thicken. The herb savory is a natural with broad beans; chop and add to cooked beans just before serving.

Lima beans, named after the capital of Peru, are also known as butter beans. Cook as for broad beans.

BEANS, DRIED

See Pulses: Dried Beans, Peas and Lentils.

BEANS, GREEN

'Green Beans' is the general term for beans with edible pods. There is a great variety on the market – they actually come in colours ranging from deep green and purple to pale yellow. The main types are French beans and runner or pole beans. French beans include snap beans, which are fleshy and should snap in half juicily if they are fresh, and yellow wax beans. Runner beans grow on a climbing vine. Often the pods are purple but turn green on cooking.

Buy beans as you need them. Store in the vegetable compartment of the refrigerator and use within 2–3 days while they are still crisp fresh.

□ **Basic Preparation:** Many beans are now stringless but some types still need stringing. Young, small beans are nicest cooked whole; larger beans may be snapped in half or sliced in diagonal lengths.

□ **To Cook:** Wash beans in cold water, then drop into a small amount of boiling, salted

B

water – just enough to cover. Simmer without a lid for 6–15 minutes, depending on size and type, until they are tender but still a little crisp. Be careful not to overcook. Drain in a colander and, if not required immediately, plunge into cold water to stop the cooking process. Beans may then stand for an hour or more before finishing.

To reheat, place them in a large frying pan (skillet) and shake over a moderate heat for a minute or two to heat and rid them of excess moisture. Use as desired. **See also recipes.**

Ways to Serve Beans

Runner beans and French beans of any kind may be used interchangeably in these recipes.

Buttered Green Beans Prepare, cook and drain 750 g (1½ lb) green beans. Place in a large pan and shake over high heat while adding 30 g/1 oz (2 tbsp) butter, bit by bit. Season to taste with salt and freshly ground black pepper. Serves 4–6.

Green Beans Amandine Prepare, cook and drain 750 g (1½ lb) green beans. Melt 30 g/1 oz (2 tbsp) butter in a large pan, add 2 tbsp slivered almonds and toss until golden. Add beans, toss gently together and season to taste with salt and freshly ground black pepper. Serves 4–6.

Green Beans with Onion Prepare, cook and drain 750 g (1½ lb) green beans. Melt 30 g/1 oz (2 tbsp) butter in a large pan, add a finely chopped onion and cook until golden. Add the beans and shake pan over high heat to mix beans and onions. Season with salt and freshly ground black pepper and sprinkle with chopped parsley. Serves 4–6

Green Beans Paysanne Prepare, cook and drain 750 g (1½ lb) green beans. Cook 2 diced rindless rashers (slices) bacon in a large pan. Remove bacon with a slotted spoon, add 30 g/1 oz (2 tbsp) butter and 2 finely chopped onions to the pan and cook until onion is soft. Add 2 peeled, seeded and chopped tomatoes and, if liked, 180 g/6 oz (1 cup) diced potato. Add beans, bacon and 120 ml/4 fl oz (½ cup) water and simmer, covered, about 20 minutes. Season with salt and freshly ground black pepper. Serves 4–6.

Green Beans with Mustard Vinaigrette Prepare, cook and drain 750 g (1½ lb) green beans. Mix 2 tsp French (Dijon) mustard, 2 tbsp olive oil, 2 tsp vinegar, 1 small clove garlic, crushed, and salt and freshly ground black pepper to taste. Toss beans gently in dressing, place in a chilled serving dish and sprinkle with chopped parsley. Serve cold. Serves 4–6.

Green Beans Smitane Prepare, cook and drain 750 g (1½ lb) green beans. Place in a large pan and stir in 175 ml/6 fl oz (¾ cup) thick sour cream mixed with 1 tsp flour and 1 tsp each finely chopped fresh parsley, chives and dill. Heat gently about 5 minutes. Season with salt and freshly ground black pepper. Serves 4–6.

Spiced Green Beans Wash and trim 750 g (1½ lb) green beans, and cut into 4 cm (1½ in) lengths. Combine 1 tsp salt, 2 cloves garlic, crushed, 2 slices fresh ginger and 1 tbsp lemon juice in a small bowl and add cayenne to taste. Heat 5 tbsp oil in a frying pan (skillet), add ½ tsp cumin seeds and fry a few seconds. Add beans and stir 1 minute. Add garlic mixture, cover pan and cook over low heat for 10 minutes or until beans are just tender, stirring occasionally. Remove cover, increase heat and stir constantly until liquid has evaporated. Serves 4–6.

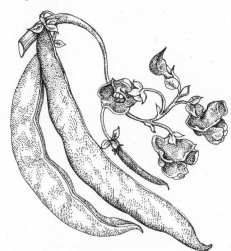

Green Bean Bhaji

2 tbsp oil; 1 tsp black mustard seeds; 1 tsp turmeric; 1 tsp salt; 2 tbsp chopped onion; 500 g (1 lb) green beans, trimmed and cut into 2 cm (¾ in) lengths; 2–4 tbsp water; 30–45 g/1–1½ oz (⅓–½ cup) desiccated (shredded) coconut (optional).

Heat oil in a large, heavy pan. Add mustard seed, cover and allow to brown, but not to burn. Stir in turmeric and salt. Add onion and sauté until softened. Add green beans and water. Turn down the heat and cook until beans are tender, adding a little more water as needed. If you like, stir in coconut a few minutes before beans finish cooking. Good with curries, or grilled (broiled) or barbecued meats. Serves 4.

BEAN SPROUTS

Crunchy, nutritious sprouts are delicious, not only in Asian recipes but in salads and sandwich fillings. Popular types for sprouting include alfalfa, soya beans and tiny, green mung peas. If fresh sprouts are not available, it is easy to grow your own.

To grow your own: Use enough dried soya beans, mung peas or alfalfa seeds to come about ⅙ of the way up a glass jar. Fill the jar with cold water, then drain the water off through a piece of muslin or other fabric, secured tightly over the top with a rubber band. Leave in a cool, dark place until next day. Repeat the watering and draining each day until sprouts are about 2.5 cm (1 in) long. Drain, then keep refrigerated.
NOTE: Sprouts should appear in 2–3 days and will be large enough to eat in 5–6 days.

Bean Sprout and Mushroom Salad

One of the secrets of a good salad is to provide interesting contrasts in textures. The mushrooms in this salad are the perfect foil for the crisp bean sprouts.

125 g/4 oz (2 cups) fresh bean sprouts; 250 g/8 oz (2 cups) mushroom caps, finely sliced; 1 large carrot, grated; 6 spring onions (scallions), chopped; 4 tbsp olive or walnut oil; 1 tbsp wine vinegar; 2 tbsp light soy sauce; 1 tbsp sugar; 1 clove garlic, crushed; 1 tsp finely chopped fresh ginger; 2 tbsp dry sherry.

Place sprouts, mushrooms, carrot and spring onions (scallions) in a bowl. Combine remaining ingredients and toss lightly with vegetables. Serve immediately. Serves 6.

Chinese Noodle Salad

375 g (12 oz) Chinese noodles; salt; 1 tbsp oil; 500 g (1 lb) fresh bean sprouts; 60 g/2 oz (½ cup) sliced spring onions (scallions); toasted sesame seeds to garnish.
SESAME PEANUT SAUCE: *2 tbsp shredded fresh ginger; 1½ tbsp sesame oil; 2½ tsp sugar; 2 tbsp sesame seeds; 1 tbsp peanut oil; 4 tbsp peanut butter; 4 tbsp water; 2 tbsp soy sauce; 2 tsp vinegar; ½ tsp Tabasco (hot pepper) sauce; ½ tsp black pepper.*

Cook noodles in plenty of boiling salted water for about 7 minutes or until tender. Drain, rinse under cold water, drain again and toss lightly with oil to prevent sticking. Place noodles in a serving bowl and top with bean sprouts.
SESAME PEANUT SAUCE: Marinate ginger in ½ tbsp sesame oil mixed with ½ tsp sugar. Leave for 30 minutes. Toast sesame seeds in a dry, heavy frying pan (skillet) over very gentle heat until golden. Place in a bowl and crush lightly with a pestle or end of a rolling pin until aroma of seeds is released. Combine peanut oil and peanut butter with rest of sesame oil and crushed seeds. Add remaining ingredients, stirring until mixed. Pour sauce over bean sprouts, and sprinkle with spring onions (scallions) and sesame seeds. Toss well. Serves 4–6.

Vegetarian Egg Fu Yung

4 dried Chinese mushrooms; 4 eggs, lightly beaten; ¼ tsp salt; ¼ tsp white pepper; 2 spring onions (scallions), finely chopped; 6 water chestnuts, chopped; 60 g/2 oz (1 cup) fresh bean sprouts; 1 tsp light soy sauce; 1 tbsp peanut oil; sliced spring onions (scallions) to garnish.

Soak mushrooms in hot water for 30 minutes; squeeze out excess water and discard stems. Chop mushroom caps. Season eggs with salt and pepper and stir in mushrooms and remaining ingredients except oil. Heat a wok or frying pan (skillet), add 1 tsp oil and swirl to coat bottom of pan. Pour in about $\frac{1}{3}$ of egg mixture and cook on medium heat until lightly browned underneath. Turn and cook until other side is set. Keep warm.

Repeat with remaining mixture to make 2 more omelettes. Stack omelettes on top of each other and garnish with sliced spring onions (scallions). Serves 2–4.

Bean Threads with Bean Sprouts

A simple cold dish that is made easily in minutes. Use the transparent pea-starch noodles and, if liked, vary the bean sprouts – julienne (matchstick) strips of crispy cucumber are ideal. The hot mustard dip makes all the difference.

30 g/1 oz (1 cup) transparent noodles; 180 g/6 oz (3 cups) fresh bean sprouts; 3 spring onions (scallions), thinly bias cut. MARINADE: *4 tbsp vinegar; 2 tsp salt; 2 tsp sesame oil.*

First prepare marinade by combining ingredients in a bowl. Cover noodles with boiling water and soak until soft and transparent, about 15 minutes. Drain and cut into 8 cm (3 in) pieces. Drop bean sprouts into boiling salted water, bring back to the boil, then quickly drain in a colander. While bean sprouts are still hot, toss quickly in marinade. Add shallots and drained noodles and mix well. Refrigerate and serve cold with hot English mustard for dipping. Serves 6.

BEARNAISE SAUCE

A classic French egg and butter sauce. The creamy texture and piquant flavour of Béarnaise Sauce make it the perfect partner for grilled (broiled) steak or roast fillet (tenderloin) of beef. It also goes well with roast or grilled (broiled) chicken.

See page 370 for recipe.

BECHAMEL SAUCE

The French call Béchamel Sauce a *sauce mère* or mother sauce because it is the basic white sauce from which so many others are made. It can be made as a flowing sauce, to serve as a separate accompaniment or as a base for cream soups. Made thicker, it becomes a coating sauce to cover food in the dish in which it is to be served (for instance, in Mornay or creamed dishes). Thicker still, it is called a panada and is used for soufflés, croquettes etc.

See page 368 for recipe.

BEEF

In general, the characteristics of good beef, freshly cut, are a rich red to dark red colour, fairly fine grain, marbling (flecks of fat) through the thicker parts, and firm, smooth fat which is white or yellowish according to the breed of animal, its age and the way it was fed.

See *Meat* for amount to buy, factors determining tenderness, testing meat for doneness etc. **See recipes**.

Roast Beef

There is no standard method for carcase cutting, either in Britain or internationally. In Britain there are regional variations, not only in the butchering of meat but in the names given to the various cuts. Thus shin is known as hough or skink in Scotland, and what Londoners call clod is bosum in the Midlands. To further complicate the issue, Americans use a butchering system which is different again, and have cuts of meat which would not even be recognized in England. It is therefore very difficult to give exact equivalents to British cuts but where possible, American alternatives are given.

☐ **Choice Cuts for Roasting:**

Sirloin: May be boneless or on the bone.
Wing Rib (Standing Rib (bone-in)): The best rib meat is from the fore rib, nearest the loin.
Rolled Rib: Boneless.
Rump: Boneless.
Fillet (Tenderloin): Small, boneless and fatless – the most tender (and expensive) cut of all, though less full-flavoured than the cuts mentioned above.
Eye of Blade (Blade Steak): Boneless, not so tender as fillet (tenderloin) but still a luxury cut.

☐ **To Roast Choice Cuts:** Have the meat at room temperature; tie it into a compact shape if necessary, so that it will cook evenly. Weigh it and place, fatty side up, on a greased rack in a roasting tin (pan). If meat has no fat layer, spread with dripping or butter or brush with oil. Place in the centre of a preheated hot oven (220°C/425°F, Gas Mark 7) for 20 minutes, then reduce heat to moderate (180°C/350°F, Gas Mark 4) and continue to roast, basting with pan juices every 20 minutes. Rest for 15–20 minutes in turned-off oven with door ajar, or other warm place, before carving.

Allow approximately:
15 minutes per 500 g (1 lb) plus 15 minutes for rare meat
20 minutes per 500 g (1 lb) plus 20 minutes for medium-done meat
25 minutes per 500 g (1 lb) plus 25 minutes for well-done meat.

ROAST FILLET (TENDERLOIN) OF BEEF Use this special method. Remove all fat and covering tissue, tie into a neat shape, folding tail under, and brown well in butter in flameproof baking dish on top of the stove. Flame with brandy if desired, place in a preheated moderately hot oven (200°C/400°F, Gas Mark 6) and roast 15 minutes per 500 g/1 lb for rare beef, 20 minutes per 500 g/1 lb for medium-done. Leave in turned-off oven with door ajar, or other warm place, for 15 minutes before carving.

☐ **Economical Cuts for Roasting:** The following cuts are good for roasting if they come from a high-quality, young carcase.
Topside (Top Round): Preferably a corner of topside (top round) which often has a pocket cut in it for a stuffing.
Silverside (Bottom Round) (unsalted): Like topside (top round), a lean, boneless cut.
Blade (Bottom Chuck Roll): Boneless or bone-in.

☐ **To Roast Economical Cuts:** Make sure the meat is at room temperature and, if necessary, tie it into a compact shape for even cooking. Weigh it and place, fatty side up, on a greased rack in a roasting tin (pan). If meat has little or no fat layer, brush with melted butter or dripping. Place in the centre of a preheated moderate oven (160°C/325°F, Gas Mark 3) and roast at this temperature for the whole of cooking time. Baste every 15 minutes with pan juices to which a little stock or wine may be added to promote juiciness. Rest for 15–20 minutes in turned-off oven with door ajar, or other warm place, before carving.

Allow approximately:
20 minutes per 500 g (1 lb) plus 20 minutes for rare meat
25 minutes per 500 g (1 lb) plus 25 minutes for medium-done meat
30 minutes per 500 g (1 lb) plus 30 minutes for well-done meat.

Grilled (Broiled) Steak

Ideally, cut steak thick, about 4 cm ($1\frac{1}{2}$ in).

☐ **Choice Cuts for Grilling (Broiling):**
Fillet (tenderloin), Rump, Sirloin (T-bone, porterhouse, club steak), Wing rib (rib steak).

☐ **To Grill Choice Cuts:** Have the steak at room temperature. If it has been marinated, dry well. If steak is edged with fat, cut right through fat to lean meat in several places to prevent buckling. Season with pepper but do not salt until after cooking. Brush the steak with melted butter or oil and the grill (broiler) rack with oil. Grill (broil) thick steaks close to high heat under a preheated grill (broiler) for a minute or two on each side until seared, then lower heat to moderate or move meat further away and continue to cook, turning once, until cooked as desired. If steak is cut thin, grill (broil) close to high heat for the whole cooking time.

A steak about 4 cm ($1\frac{1}{2}$ in) thick will take 10–15 minutes total cooking time for medium-rare meat; steak 2 cm ($\frac{3}{4}$ in) thick will take 7–10 minutes. Times vary with different cuts and different grills (broilers). To test for doneness, see *Meat*.

B

☐ **Economical Cuts for Grilling:**
Chuck Steak and Topside (Top Round).
These are satisfactory if they come from a high-quality young carcase. Tenderness may be promoted by marinating.

☐ **To Grill (Broil) Economical Cuts:** Follow same procedure as for grilling (broiling) choice cuts, left.

Pan-grilled (broiled) Steak The following method may be used for both the choice cuts and the economical cuts listed above for Grilled (Broiled) Steak.

Steak can be pan-grilled (broiled) for a crusty outside and juicy inside – especially useful if you are not sure of the efficiency of your grill (broiler). Use a thick, heavy pan. Heat on high heat for a few minutes, add just enough oil to coat the base and, when it gives off a slight haze, put in the steak. Cook 30–60 seconds on each side, until seared, then lower heat to moderate and continue to cook, turning once, until cooked as desired. When beads of pink juice appear on surface steak is medium-rare. For other ways to test for doneness, see *Meat.*

Braised and Casseroled Beef
Cuts for casseroling and braising (browning, then simmering with a little liquid) include *Topside (Top Round), Silverside (Bottom Round), Thick Flank (Flank Steak),* and *Chuck.*

Meat may be cut into steaks, then into serving-sized pieces, or smaller pieces, or may be cooked in one large piece – this is called a pot roast. See *Meat.*

Braised Steak and Onions

750 g (1½ lb) braising steak; seasoned flour; 1 tbsp oil; 15 g/½ oz (1 tbsp) butter; 3 onions, sliced; 1 clove garlic, crushed; 350 ml/12 fl oz (1½ cups) beef stock (bouillon); 1 bouquet garni; salt; freshly ground black pepper.

Trim excess fat from beef, cut into serving sized pieces and dredge with seasoned flour. Brown, a few pieces at a time, in hot oil and butter in a heavy saucepan or flameproof casserole. Remove meat. Add onions and garlic and cook gently until beginning to brown. Pour off all but 1 tbsp fat. Add stock (bouillon) and bouquet garni and bring to the boil, stirring once or twice. Add meat, cover tightly and simmer gently on top of the stove or in a preheated moderate oven (160°C/325°F, Gas Mark 3) for 1½–2 hours or until meat is tender. Remove bouquet garni, adjust seasoning and serve. Serves 4.

Braised Steak with Red Wine

1 kg (2 lb) braising steak; seasoned flour; 1 tbsp oil; 30 g/1 oz (2 tbsp) butter; 1 clove garlic, crushed; 2 onions, coarsely chopped; 1 tbsp sugar; 1 tbsp French (Dijon) mustard; 1 tbsp vinegar; 250 ml/8 fl oz (1 cup) red wine;

120 ml/4 fl oz (½ cup) beef stock (bouillon); 1 bouquet garni; salt and freshly ground black pepper.

Trim excess fat from beef, cut into cubes and dredge with seasoned flour. Brown, a few pieces at a time, in hot oil and butter in a heavy saucepan or flameproof casserole. Remove meat. Add garlic and onions and cook gently until beginning to brown. Pour off surplus fat, leaving about 1 tbsp. Add sugar, mustard, vinegar, wine, stock (bouillon) and bouquet garni. Add meat, cover tightly and simmer gently on top of the stove or in a preheated moderate oven (160°C/325°F, Gas Mark 3) for 1½–2 hours or until meat is tender. Remove bouquet garni and adjust seasoning. Serves 4–6.

Old-fashioned Beef Casserole

750 g (1½ lb) braising steak; 30 g/1 oz (2 tbsp) lard or dripping; 1½ tbsp flour; 450 ml/¾ pint (2 cups) warm beef stock (bouillon); 3 onions, sliced; 2 carrots, sliced; 1 turnip, cut into neat chunks; 2 sticks celery, sliced; 1 bouquet garni; salt and freshly ground black pepper.

Trim excess fat from meat and cut into bite-sized pieces. Brown in hot fat in a heavy saucepan or flameproof casserole. Remove meat. Stir flour into fat and cook until browned. Remove from heat, cool a little and add stock (bouillon), stirring until smoothly blended. Stir over heat until boiling. Add vegetables and bouquet garni, and place meat on top. Cover tightly and simmer gently on top of the stove or in a preheated moderate oven (160°C/325°F, Gas Mark 3) for 1½–2 hours or until meat and vegetables are tender. Remove bouquet garni, adjust seasoning and serve. Serves 4.

Beef Pot Roast

1–1.5 kg (2–3 lb) piece braising beef; 1 tbsp oil; 15 g/½ oz (1 tbsp) butter; 2 large carrots, diced; 2 large onions, chopped; 2 sticks celery, chopped; 1 small turnip, diced; 1 bouquet garni; 350 ml/12 fl oz (1½ cups)

beef stock (bouillon) or mixed stock and red wine; salt and freshly ground black pepper.

Brown meat all over in hot oil and butter in a flameproof casserole. Remove meat. Add diced and chopped vegetables, cover and cook gently 5 minutes. Place meat on vegetables, add bouquet garni and stock, (bouillon), and season lightly with salt and pepper. Cover and cook in a preheated moderate oven (160°C/325°F, Gas Mark 3) for 2 hours or until meat is very tender. Remove meat from casserole. Boil down gravy until it is syrupy, then strain it. Slice meat and arrange on a heated platter. Spoon gravy over and surround with vegetables. Serves 4–6.

Stir-Fried Beef with Oyster Sauce

250 g (8 oz) Scotch fillet or flank; 150 ml/¼ pint (⅔ cup) oil; 4 spring onions (scallions), cut into finger lengths (include some green tops); 6 thin slices fresh ginger, finely chopped.

MARINADE: *1 tbsp soy sauce; 1 tsp Chinese rice wine, saké or dry sherry; 5 tbsp water; 2 tsp cornflour (cornstarch); 1 tbsp oil.*

GRAVY: *½ tbsp Chinese rice wine, saké or dry sherry; 1½ tbsp oyster sauce; ½ tsp sugar; ¼ tsp black pepper; ¼ tsp Chinese sesame oil; 1½ tbsp water; 1 tsp cornflour (cornstarch).*

Remove fat or membrane from beef and cut across grain into thinnest possible slices. Mix all ingredients for marinade, pour over beef and allow to stand for 1 hour. Heat 150 ml/¼ pint (⅔ cup) oil in a wok or deep, heavy frying pan (skillet) and stir-fry meat slices for about 20 seconds until they change colour. Drain beef. Pour off all but 2 tbsp oil from wok. Reheat oil, and add spring onions (scallions) and ginger to pan. Stir-fry over medium heat for about 30 seconds, then add beef slices and all ingredients for gravy. Continue cooking, stirring lightly, for about 30 seconds or until gravy thickens and turns translucent. Serves 4–6 as part of a Chinese meal, or 2 as a main course with rice or noodles.

Oriental 'Snakes' of Beef

Thin strips of beef are marinated then threaded in zig-zag or 'snake' fashion on skewers – more interesting and much more economical than serving large steaks to everyone.

750 g/(1½ lb) grilling (broiling) steak, 4 cm (1½ in) thick; 120 ml/4 fl oz (½ cup) soy sauce; 2 tbsp honey; 1 tbsp dry sherry; 2 cloves garlic, crushed; 1 tbsp grated fresh ginger; few drops Chinese sesame oil.

Slice steak across grain into 5 mm (¼ in) strips and place in a bowl. Mix remaining ingredients and pour over. Leave to marinate, covered, at room temperature for 1 hour, turning meat over several times to coat evenly.

Soak the bamboo skewers in hot water for 30 minutes. Remove beef strips from marinade and thread on to skewers, zig-zag or 'snake' fashion. Cook under a preheated very hot grill (broiler) for about 3 minutes, turning once and brushing with marinade. Beef should be rare on the inside. Serve skewers on a bed of rice, or push meat off skewers into Pita with addition of chopped celery, peppers or bean sprouts
Serves 4–6.

Beef and Parsley Vinaigrette

Economical thick flank (flank steak) is used in this salad, which makes a main course for 6 from a relatively small amount of meat.

750 g (1½ lb) thick flank (flank steak); 60 g/2 oz (½ cup) finely chopped spring onions (scallions); 3 sticks tender celery, finely sliced; 2 tbsp drained capers; 1½ tbsp lemon juice; 1½ tbsp wine vinegar; 1 tbsp French (Dijon) mustard; 1½ tsp salt; ½ tsp pepper; 150 ml/¼ pint (⅔ cup) olive oil; 45 g/ 1½ oz (1 cup) finely chopped fresh parsley.
TO SERVE: *lettuce leaves; small (cherry) tomatoes or tomato wedges.*

Score steak lightly on both sides in a diamond pattern, using a very sharp pointed knife. Grill (broil) steak on both sides under a preheated grill (broiler) as close to flame as possible, about 4 minutes each side or until browned but still rare in the middle. When steak is cool, slice it paper thin against the grain, then shred with 2 forks. Place in a bowl. Mix together spring onions (scallions), celery, capers, lemon juice, vinegar, mustard, salt and pepper. Add oil, little by little, whisking until well combined. Add dressing and parsley to steak and toss to combine. Adjust seasoning, adding extra salt and pepper if necessary. Cover and chill for several hours. To serve, line a platter or bowl with lettuce leaves. Allow beef to come to room temperature, spoon into centre of platter and garnish with polished small (cherry) tomatoes or tomato wedges. Serves 6.

Potted Meat

Eat this very cold, accompanied by hot English mustard and vinegar, which points up the flavour of the meat. For a summer meal, serve with cucumber slices, tomatoes and potato salad.

1.5 kg (3 lb) shin of beef (fore shank) on the bone, cut into thick slices; 750 g (1½ lb) pickled (salt) belly pork; 6 black peppercorns; 1 bay leaf; 2 tsp anchovy essence (extract); salt and freshly ground black pepper.

Put beef, pork, peppercorns and bay leaf into a large saucepan and cover with cold water. Bring to the boil and skim. Cover and simmer for 3 hours, or cook in a slow cooker overnight (8 hours) on low. Cool. Remove meat from broth and strain broth. Trim away beef fat and gristle and remove bones from beef and pork. Chop meats finely and return to broth. Boil uncovered for 20 minutes, until broth is reduced. Add anchovy essence (extract) and season with salt and pepper. Boil a further 5 minutes to blend flavours. Put into a 1.5 litre/2½ pint (6 cup) bowl rinsed with cold water. Cover with plastic wrap and chill until firm. Turn out and cut in thick slices to serve. Serves 8–10.

Beef Niçoise

Black (ripe) olives give this special beef dish a traditional Mediterranean touch and interesting smoky flavour.

1–1.5 kg (2–3 lb) shin of beef (fore shank); 2 tbsp oil; 125 g (4 oz) streaky bacon or pickled (salt) pork, rind removed and cut into strips; 3 cloves garlic, crushed; 6 medium carrots, sliced; 6 medium onions, sliced; 6 sprigs parsley, coarsely chopped; 2 tbsp chopped fresh mixed herbs (rosemary, thyme, basil, oregano), or 1 tsp dried; 1 × 425 g/14 oz can tomatoes with their juice; 2 tbsp wine vinegar; salt and freshly ground black pepper; 8–12 stoned (pitted) black (ripe) olives (optional).
GARNISH: *chopped parsley; croûtons.*

Trim fat and sinews from beef and cut into thick slices or cubes. Heat oil in a large flameproof casserole and fry bacon until fat starts to run. Add meat and brown well on both sides. Stir in garlic, carrots, onions, parsley, herbs, tomatoes and vinegar. Season with salt and pepper and stir gently until liquid reaches simmering point. Place lid on casserole and cook in a preheated moderate oven (180°C/350°F, Gas Mark 4) for 2–2½ hours or until meat is tender. During this time, check once or twice to see if the liquid has evaporated too much. If so, add a little water, but finished gravy should be thick. Add olives to casserole and cook for a further 20 minutes, covered, so flavours can blend. Turn into a heated serving dish and garnish with chopped parsley and croûtons. Serves 6–8.
NOTE: Cut round or heart-shaped croûtons from white bread and fry in a little hot oil until golden-brown on both sides.

Sailor's Stew

This traditional stew from Scandinavia is a cousin of Irish stew. The name probably indicates that sailors, when they come ashore, appreciate a change from fish! In Scandinavia, this might be offered with rye bread and butter, dill pickles, and a salad.

750 g (1½ lb) stewing beef; 750 g (1½ lb) old potatoes, peeled and thickly sliced; 2 large onions, thickly sliced; 450 ml/¾ pint (2 cups) boiling water; 1 small bay leaf; 2 tsp salt; 6 black peppercorns; 60 g/2 oz (4 tbsp) butter; chopped parsley to garnish.

Remove excess fat from beef and cut into bite-sized cubes. Place beef, potatoes and onions in a pan with remaining ingredients. Bring to the boil, and remove any scum that comes to surface. Reduce heat to low, cover pan and simmer for 1½–2 hours or until meat is very tender and potatoes are reduced to a mash. Stir well to combine potatoes with gravy. Adjust seasoning, discard bay leaf, and sprinkle with chopped parsley. Serves 4.

Paprika Beef Stew

Use any lean stewing beef for this rich, heart-warming and economical stew.

1 kg (2 lb) stewing beef; 60 g (2 oz) streaky bacon, rind removed and diced; 3 large onions, chopped; 1 tbsp paprika; 1 × 820 g/1 lb 12 oz can tomatoes, drained and chopped; 450–750 ml/¾–1¼ pints (2–3 cups) water; 1 clove garlic, crushed; 1 bay leaf; 2 tbsp flour; 120 ml/4 fl oz (½ cup) sour cream; salt and freshly ground black pepper.

Cut beef into bite-sized cubes. Sauté bacon in a heavy saucepan or flameproof casserole until golden-brown. Add beef cubes, a few at a time, and brown on all sides. Remove meat from pan with a slotted spoon. Add onions and paprika to pan. Cook gently for 4–5 minutes until onions soften a little, stirring so they do not stick. Return meat to pan and add tomatoes with enough water to come halfway up the meat. Stir well and add garlic and bay leaf. Cover and simmer for 1½ hours or until meat is very tender. Stir flour with sour cream, add to stew and simmer for 2–3 minutes until gravy is smooth and thickened. Adjust seasoning, and discard bay leaf. Serves 6.

Roasted Sirloin

Easy to prepare, cook, carve and serve – this is an ideal buffet dish. Take care to trim away any sinews and excess fat from the meat before tieing.

1.5–2.5 kg (3–5 lb) piece sirloin; freshly ground black pepper, or 2 tbsp crushed green peppercorns; 30 g/1 oz (2 tbsp) butter; 2 tbsp oil; 3 tbsp brandy; 2 tbsp each chopped parsley, chives and capers.

Trim sirloin and tie with string to keep a good shape. Season well with freshly ground pepper or press crushed green peppercorns firmly on to meat. Melt butter and oil in a flameproof baking dish and sear meat quickly to brown the surface, turning with 2 spoons. Heat brandy, set alight and pour over meat, shaking dish so that meat burns with the flame. Roast in a preheated hot oven (220°C/425°F, Gas Mark 7) for 10 minutes, then reduce heat to moderately hot (190°C/375°F, Gas Mark 5) and roast for a further 25–35 minutes. Top beef with herbs and capers, pressing them in well, and allow to stand 20 minutes before slicing. Transfer to a board and slice ⅔ of the beef. Arrange uncut beef with sliced meat on a large heated platter and accompany with a choice of mustards and horseradish sauce, if liked. Serves 8.

Piquant Beef Roulades

This makes an interesting dinner party main course, served with buttered noodles and a fresh green or mixed salad.

4 thin slices topside (top round) steak; 1 clove garlic, crushed; salt and freshly ground black pepper; 250 g/8 oz (1 cup) sausage meat; 1 small onion, finely chopped; ¼ tsp dried thyme or oregano; 1 small carrot, quartered; 60 g/2 oz (4 tbsp) butter; 250 ml/8 fl oz (1 cup) red wine; 1 tbsp tomato purée (paste); 1 tbsp Worcestershire sauce; 1 tsp sugar; 2 tbsp chopped parsley or sliced olives.

If steaks are cut very thin, there is no need to pound them. Otherwise, place between 2 sheets of plastic wrap and flatten with a rolling pin, being careful not to tear the meat. Spread a little garlic over each steak and season with salt and pepper. Combine sausage meat with onion and thyme or oregano and spread a layer of sausage meat over each steak. Place a slice of carrot in the middle, then roll up the steaks neatly, tucking in ends to give a good shape. Melt butter in a flameproof casserole and gently brown steak rolls on all sides. Pour in wine and tomato purée (paste) combined with the Worcestershire sauce and sugar, and cover casserole tightly with a lid or foil.

Bake in a preheated moderate oven (180°C/350°F, Gas Mark 4) for about 1 hour, or until the roulades are very tender. Stir in parsley or sliced olives and adjust seasoning. Serve in the casserole, or transfer to a heated platter. Serves 4.
NOTE: The roulades may also be cooked in a saucepan on top of the stove if desired.

Budapest Beef Goulash

60 g/2 oz (4 tbsp) butter; 750 g (1½ lb) onions, coarsely chopped; 1 kg (2 lb) chuck steak, cubed; 1½ tsp salt; 1 tbsp paprika; 3 tbsp tomato purée (paste).

Heat butter in a heavy saucepan, add onions and sauté until golden-brown. Add beef and cook over moderate heat, stirring, until beef loses its bright redness. Add remaining ingredients. Simmer very gently, covered, for 1½–2 hours until beef is tender. If necessary, to prevent meat sticking, 4 tbsp water may be added. If liked, stir in 120 ml/4 fl oz (½ cup) sour cream before serving. Serves 6.

Ragoût of Beef

45 g/1½ oz (3 tbsp) butter; 1 medium onion, chopped; 1 clove garlic; 1 kg (2 lb) shin of beef (fore shank), cut into large cubes; 1 tsp paprika; salt and freshly ground black pepper; 2 large tomatoes, peeled and chopped; 15 g/½ oz (2 tbsp) dried Continental mushrooms; 250 ml/8 fl oz (1 cup) water; 125 g/4 oz (1 cup) diced celery; 3 tbsp Beurre Manié (page 35).

Heat butter in a large frying pan (skillet). Add onion and garlic and sauté until onion is transparent. Discard garlic. Add meat, paprika, salt and pepper. Cook over moderate heat, stirring, until meat is browned. Add tomatoes. Cover and simmer very gently 1 hour. Meanwhile, soak mushrooms in water for 15 minutes. Boil for 3 minutes in their soaking liquid. Add celery to frying pan (skillet) and cook 15 minutes, then add mushrooms and their liquid and simmer gently until meat is tender. The total cooking time is 1½–2 hours. When meat is tender, add beurre manié, bit by bit, stirring constantly until liquid is thickened. Serve with steamed rice, buttered noodles or polenta. Serves 6.

BEEF WELLINGTON

This is the name given to fillet (tenderloin) of beef, topped with a good liver pâté (preferably Pâté de Foie Gras) and sometimes sautéed mushrooms, wrapped in pastry (dough) and baked. A great luxury dish and quite easy to manage for a dinner party. Prepare up to 1 day in advance, except for glazing with egg and baking. Refrigerate if keeping overnight, but take out and leave at room temperature for 2 hours before baking so that timing will be accurate.

Beef Wellington

1.25 kg (2½ lb) piece beef fillet (tenderloin); freshly ground black pepper; 1 tbsp oil; 60 g/2 oz (4 tbsp) butter; 4 tbsp brandy; 60 g/2 oz (½ cup) mushrooms, sliced; 90 g (3 oz) good liver pâté; 1 × 375 g/12 oz packet frozen puff pastry (paste), thawed; 1 egg, lightly beaten; watercress or parsley to garnish.

Trim meat of all fat and gristle, fold tail under and tie into a neat shape. Season with pepper. Brown meat well on all sides in hot oil and butter. Warm brandy, set alight and pour over meat, shaking pan until flames subside. Remove meat to a rack and allow to get quite cold. Sauté mushrooms in the same pan until tender; cool. Spread meat with pâté and top with mushrooms. Roll out

pastry (dough) thinly, trim edges and brush them with beaten egg. Place meat on one half, fold other half over, press edges to seal and tuck under neatly. Cut strips of pastry (dough) from trimmings. Brush pastry around meat with egg, arrange strips lattice-fashion on top and brush with egg. Chill for 30 minutes, then place on a dampened baking tray. Bake in a preheated hot oven (230°C/450°F, Gas Mark 8) for 15 minutes, then reduce heat to moderate (180°C/350°F, Gas Mark 4) and bake 15–20 minutes more or until golden-brown. Serve on a platter, garnished with a bouquet of watercress or parsley. Serves 6.

BEER

Cooking with beer is popular in many countries. The Germans have their beer soup and cook sausages in beer, the Belgians their beef and beer stew; Australians use beer to add extra lightness and crispness to batter for fish, and the Americans like it as a cooking liquid for prawns.

See also Carbonnade de Boeuf, Fish Fried in Batter page 125, and *Welsh Rarebit*.

Sauerkraut with Apples and Beer

1 × 825 g/1 lb 12 oz can sauerkraut; 60 g/2 oz (4 tbsp) butter; 2 rashers (slices) streaky bacon, rind removed and diced; 1 large onion, finely chopped; 1 large tart apple, peeled, cored and diced; 4 juniper berries, crushed; 600 ml/1 pint (2½ cups) beer; 1 large potato, peeled and grated; 2 tbsp sugar; salt and freshly ground black pepper.

Place sauerkraut in a colander, rinse under running hot water and drain well. Heat butter in a large heavy saucepan and fry bacon for 1–2 minutes, then add onion and cook, stirring, until onion is softened. Add sauerkraut, apple and crushed juniper berries and cook over low heat for 15 minutes, stirring frequently. Pour in beer and simmer for 30 minutes, then add potato and simmer another 30 minutes, adding more beer if necessary to keep mixture moist. Season with sugar, salt and black pepper. Excellent with pork and sausage dishes. Serves 6.

BEETROOT

Beetroot (called beet in America) is a root vegetable with a bulbous shape and rich sweet, red flesh of a unique texture. To avoid losing any of the rich red colour, beetroot are not peeled or cut before cooking. Cooked beetroot is delicious sliced and heated with a little chopped onion and garlic, or with a spoonful of chopped horseradish folded through. Diced freshly cooked beetroot, heated through in the juice and grated rind of

an orange, is delicious. Grated raw beetroot, seasoned with salt and freshly ground black pepper and a squeeze of lemon juice is often added to a salad plate.

When buying fresh beetroot, look for those that are smooth and firm to touch and a good, round shape. Choose small to medium sized ones as they are usually more tender. Raw beetroot should stay fresh in the refrigerator for up to a week. Beetroot have always been one of the most popular canned vegetables.

☐ **To Cook:** Beetroot is usually boiled whole, but may also be baked in the oven. **See also recipes.**

BOILED BEETROOT Cut off the tops about 5 cm (2 in) above the beetroot. Wash, but leave whole and do not peel. Place in cold unsalted water to cover and cook, with the lid on, until tender when pierced with a skewer. Very old beetroot may take anything up to 3 hours, although most beetroot will be cooked in 30–40 minutes. When tender, drain (reserving a little of the liquid) and slip off the skins. To serve beetroot hot, leave whole or cut into slices, dice or cut into segments. Reheat gently in reserved liquid, season with salt and freshly ground black pepper and add butter and vinegar or lemon juice as desired.

BAKED BEETROOT Beetroot may be baked in a preheated moderate oven (180°C/350°F, Gas Mark 4) for 1 hour or until tender. Leave whole and unpeeled, as for Boiled Beetroot, above, and peel when cooked.

Cold Beetroot Cook and peel beetroot as above, then slice, dice or quarter. Marinate in vinegar or Vinaigrette Dressing (see page 358), with a little cooking liquid added to preserve the colour, and chill until required. Flavourings such as sugar, shallots or parsley may be added to suit your own taste.

Sautéed Beetroot Peel and dice 3 medium sized beetroot. Melt 60 g/2 oz (4 tbsp) butter in a frying pan (skillet), add beetroot and season lightly with salt and freshly ground black pepper. Stir over medium heat for 1 minute; reduce heat, cover and cook for about 15 minutes, stirring frequently, until tender. Sprinkle with chopped parsley. Serves 4.

Shredded Beetroot Peel 3 medium beetroot and grate coarsely. Melt 60 g/2 oz (4 tbsp) butter in a heavy saucepan, add beetroot and season with salt and freshly ground black pepper. Stir over low heat for 2–3 minutes until beetroot is well coated with butter, then add 2 tbsp water, cover and cook for 7–10 minutes, stirring frequently, until crisp-tender. Remove from heat and toss with 1 tbsp lemon juice, 2 tsp chopped parsley and chives and ½ tsp chopped fresh tarragon or a pinch of dried. Serves 4.

Beetroot with Orange Glaze Boil 3 medium beetroot as above; peel and dice and set aside. Melt 30 g/1 oz (2 tbsp) butter in a heavy saucepan, stir in 2 tbsp brown sugar and 2 tsp flour and cook on low heat for 1 minute. Blend in 175 ml/6 fl oz (¾ cup) orange juice and stir until boiling. Season with salt and freshly ground black pepper. Add beetroot and heat, stirring gently, until beetroot is heated through. Serves 4.

Glazed Beetroot

1 × 825 g/1 lb 12 oz can whole baby beetroot, or 370 g/12 oz (2 cups) peeled, diced, cooked beetroot; 60 g/2 oz (4 tbsp) butter; 2 tbsp sugar; salt and freshly ground black pepper.

Drain beetroot. Heat butter in a heavy frying pan (skillet), add beetroot and shake pan to coat with butter. Cook over medium heat for 3 minutes. Sprinkle with sugar and continue shaking pan gently until beetroot are glazed. Season with salt and pepper. Serves 4.

Finnish Beetroot Salad

4 medium beetroot, freshly cooked and peeled; 1 tsp coarse sea salt; 1 tbsp grated fresh horseradish or prepared horseradish (not creamed type); 120 ml/4 fl oz (½ cup) sour cream; 1 tbsp grated orange rind.

Cut beetroot into julienne (matchstick) strips. Combine remaining ingredients and toss with beetroot. Cover and chill for at least 1–2 hours to blend flavours. Serves 4–6.

Beetroot and Herring Salad

370 g/12 oz (2 cups) peeled, diced, cooked beetroot; 180 g/6 oz (1 cup) peeled, diced, cooked potatoes; 180 g/6 oz (1 cup) diced, cooked carrots; 90 g/3 oz (½ cup) diced dill pickles or gherkins; 1 large tart apple, peeled, cored, diced and moistened with lemon juice; 1 medium onion, finely chopped; 1 tsp coarse sea salt; freshly ground black pepper; 1 tbsp snipped fresh dill, or 1 tsp dried dill weed; 2–3 herring fillets (matjes), cut into strips, to garnish. DRESSING: 120 ml/4 fl oz (½ cup) double (heavy) cream; 1 tbsp wine vinegar; 2 tsp sugar.

Combine salad ingredients, cover and chill. Just before serving, whip cream with vinegar and sugar until stiff. Serve salad, dressing and herring strips separately, each diner combining them to suit his own taste. Serves 6–8.

Beetroot Smitane

6 beetroot, freshly cooked and peeled; 350 ml/12 fl oz (1½ cups) sour cream 15 g/½ oz (1 tbsp) butter; salt and freshly ground black pepper; cayenne.

Mash or grate beetroot (this can be done in a food processor). Gently heat sour cream with butter, salt, pepper and a dash of cayenne. Beat sauce until it is light and creamy, and mix with beetroot. Serves 6.

BEIGNETS SOUFFLES (French Fritters)

Light and fluffy fritters of deep-fried choux pastry (paste) appear in several cuisines. The French *Beignets Soufflés* and German *Crullers* are shaped with a spoon; Spanish *Churros* and German *Strauben* are piped directly into the hot oil (see *Churros*).

Beignets Soufflés

1 quantity Choux Pastry (page 276); oil for deep-frying; sifted icing (confectioners) sugar; Quick Apricot Sauce (page 373).

Prepare choux pastry (paste). Heat oil for deep-frying. With a dessertspoon or large teaspoon, take up portions of pastry (paste). Dip another spoon in hot oil, then mould off pieces of choux pastry (paste) the size of a walnut into the hot oil. Cook 5–6 at a time, turning them over in oil from time to time. When golden (about 5–6 minutes), drain on crumpled paper towels. Dredge well with icing (confectioners) sugar and serve with apricot sauce. Makes 15–20.
NOTE: If liked, the beignets may be twice-fried. Fry the quantity you want to serve until pale golden, drain, then just before serving return to hot oil for a few minutes. Twice-frying helps when you want to serve a large quantity for a dinner party.
Crullers: Prepare in the same way as Beignets Soufflés, above, but shape with 2 small teaspoons. Crullers are usually served as a snack with coffee.

BEURRE MANIE

A mixture of flour and butter blended to a paste, and used to thicken stews, sauces, casseroles etc., at the end of cooking. Use 15 g/½ oz (1 tbsp) butter to 1 tbsp flour. Have butter at room temperature and work in the flour with a fork or your fingers until smooth.

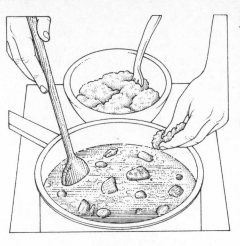

Whisk beurre manié, a little at a time, into the simmering liquid until thickened as desired.

BIGARADE, SAUCE

An orange sauce served with roast duck. In the original French recipe, bitter Seville oranges are used. If they are not available, look for oranges that are not too sweet. The duck is roasted in the usual way (see *Duck*), then served with the sauce.

Sauce Bigarade

250 ml/8 fl oz (1 cup) rich chicken stock; 1 tsp arrowroot or cornflour (cornstarch); 2 tbsp wine vinegar; 2 tbsp sugar; 2 tbsp finely shredded, blanched orange rind; 120 ml/4 fl oz (½ cup) hot, fresh orange juice; 1 tsp lemon juice; 2 tbsp Curaçao (optional); salt and freshly ground white pepper; peeled orange sections to garnish.

When duck is cooked, remove to a serving platter and keep warm. Pour off fat from roasting tin (pan) and add stock. Bring to the boil, stirring well, and thicken with arrowroot or cornflour (cornstarch) mixed to a cream with a little water. Remove from heat. In a saucepan, cook vinegar and sugar together over low heat until a light brown colour. Add liquid from roasting tin (pan) and simmer 4–5 minutes. Stir in orange rind, juices and Curaçao, if using. Bring to the boil and season with salt and pepper. Pour a little sauce over duck to glaze (carve first, if desired). Garnish platter with orange sections and serve remaining sauce separately. Serves 2–4, depending on size of duck.

BIRYANI (Biviani)

A great and traditional Mogul dish from India, consisting of layers of delicately perfumed pilau rice and lamb in spiced gravy. A biryani is a festive dish, ideal for a party, and can be made ahead and reheated. Serve with chutneys, sambals and pappadams.

Lamb Biryani

LAMB: *1.5–2 kg (3–4 lb) boned leg of lamb; 125 g/4 oz (½ cup) ghee or 120 ml/4 fl oz (½ cup) oil; 3 large onions, sliced; 5–6 cloves garlic, finely chopped; 5 cm (2 in) piece fresh ginger, finely chopped; 6 tbsp curry powder; 1 tsp chilli powder (optional); 4 tsp salt; 2 tbsp vinegar; 2 tsp Garam Masala (page 139); 2 fresh hot chillies; 20 g/⅔ oz (½ cup) chopped fresh mint; 2 large ripe tomatoes, peeled, seeded and chopped.*
PILAU: *1 kg/2 lb (4½ cups) long-grain rice, preferably Basmati; 125 g/4 oz (½ cup) ghee; 1 cinnamon stick; 10 cardamom pods; 5 cloves; 2 onions, sliced; ½ tsp saffron threads, crumbled and soaked in 2 tsp hot water; 1.75 litres/3 pints (7½ cups) boiling chicken stock; salt.*
GARNISH: *180 g/6 oz (1 cup) sultanas (golden raisins); 60 g/2 oz (½ cup) blanched almonds; 1 onion, sliced; little ghee; 180 g/6 oz (1 cup) cooked peas.*

LAMB: Trim excess fat from lamb and cut into 2.5 cm (1 in) cubes. Heat ghee or oil in a large pan and fry onions, garlic and ginger until soft and golden. Add curry and chilli powder (if using) and fry 1 minute longer, then add salt and vinegar. Add lamb and stir until well coated with curry mixture. Add garam masala, whole chillies, mint and tomatoes. Cover and cook, stirring from time to time, on very low heat for 1 hour or until lamb is tender and gravy thick. Add a little water if mixture is dry. Remove chillies.
PILAU: While lamb is cooking, wash rice under running water and drain well. Melt ghee in a large pan and add cinnamon stick broken into pieces, cardamom, cloves and onions. Fry until onions are golden. Add rice and fry, stirring, until grains are well coated with ghee. Add saffron and boiling stock, season with salt and stir until boiling. Turn heat very low, cover tightly and cook without uncovering for 10–15 minutes or until rice is tender and liquid absorbed. Remove lid, turn off heat and fluff up rice with a fork.

Put a generous layer of cooked rice in a large, buttered ovenproof casserole and cover with a layer of lamb mixture. Repeat these layers, ending with a layer of rice. Depending on the size of the dish, there should be about 3 layers of rice and 2 of lamb. Cover with foil, then a lid, and reheat over low heat on top of the stove or in a preheated moderate oven (160°C/325°F, Gas Mark 3) for 40–50 minutes.
GARNISH: Fry sultanas (golden raisins), almonds and onion in a little ghee. Leave biryani in casserole or turn it out into a heap on a serving dish. Garnish with sultanas (golden raisins), almonds, onion rings and peas. Serves 10–12.
NOTE: The biryani can be prepared ahead, except for final reheating and garnishing.

BISCUITS

The first biscuits (cookies) were small, flat cakes which were baked twice to make them crisp. The word now covers an infinite variety of crunchy, crisp, chewy or brittle baked goods, from the plain water biscuit (cracker) to the sweetest confections. **See recipes.**

Cherry Wink Cookies

210 g/7 oz (1¾ cups) flour; 2 tsp baking powder; pinch salt; 125 g/4 oz (½ cup) butter or margarine; 125 g/4 oz (½ cup) caster sugar; 1½ tsp vanilla essence (extract); 2 tbsp honey; 1 egg; 60 g/2 oz (2 cups) cornflakes, lightly crushed; 125 g/4 oz (½ cup) glacé (candied) cherries, halved.

Sift flour, baking powder and salt. Cream butter or margarine with sugar and vanilla. Add honey and egg and beat well. Fold in dry ingredients, a little at a time, alternating with milk. Drop teaspoonfuls of mixture into lightly crushed cornflakes and toss gently to coat. Place on greased baking trays and press a halved glacé (candied) cherry in centre of each. Bake in a preheated moderately hot oven (200°C/400°F, Gas Mark 6) for 10 minutes. Makes about 36.

Cinnamon Crinkles

125 g/4 oz (½ cup) butter; 180 g/6 oz (¾ cup) sugar; 1 egg; 165 g/5½ oz (1⅓ cups) self-raising flour; extra 2 tbsp sugar; 2 tbsp cinnamon.

Cream butter with 180 g/6 oz (¾ cup) sugar, add egg and beat well. Sift flour and add to creamed mixture. Mix well. Form into small balls and roll in combined extra sugar and cinnamon. Place on ungreased baking trays and bake in a preheated moderate oven (180°C/350°F, Gas Mark 4) for 15 minutes or until golden. Cool on trays until biscuits are crisp. Makes about 36.

French Fingers

125 g/4 oz (½ cup) butter; 125 g/4 oz (½ cup) caster sugar; ½ tsp vanilla essence (extract); 1 egg; 180 g/6 oz (1½ cups) self-raising flour; 130 g/2¼ oz (½ cup) cornflour (cornstarch).

Cream butter with sugar and vanilla until light and fluffy. Add egg and beat well. Mix in sifted dry ingredients. Spoon or pipe mixture, using a large rose nozzle, in 5 cm (2 in) lengths on greased baking trays. Bake in a preheated moderate oven (180°C/350°F, Gas Mark 4) for about 15 minutes. Cool on trays. Makes about 46.

Almond Biscuits

125 g/4 oz (½ cup) butter; 60 g/2 oz (¼ cup) sugar; 1 tsp vanilla essence (extract); 1 egg yolk; 250 g/8 oz (2 cups) self-raising flour; pinch salt; 1 egg white; 140 g/4½ oz (1 cup) icing (confectioners) sugar, sifted; finely chopped blanched almonds.

Cream butter with sugar and vanilla, add egg yolk and beat well. Mix in sifted flour and salt to form a firm dough. Place dough on floured surface and roll out to 5 mm (¼ in) thickness. Beat egg white until stiff, add icing (confectioners) sugar gradually and beat until smooth. Spread icing over prepared biscuit (cookie) mixture. Sprinkle with almonds and cut into shapes. Place on greased baking trays. Bake in a preheated moderately hot oven (190°C/375°F, Gas Mark 5) for 10–12 minutes. Makes about 60.

Ginger Shortbread Biscuits

250 g/8 oz (1 cup) butter, softened; 125 g/4 oz (½ cup) caster sugar; 250 g/8 oz (2 cups) flour; 2 tsp ground ginger; caster sugar for sprinkling.

Cream together butter and sugar until light and fluffy. Sift together flour and ginger and gradually work into butter mixture. Knead lightly then roll out on a lightly floured surface until 5 mm (¼ in) thick. Cut into round or star shapes using a biscuit (cookie) cutter. Transfer to a baking tray and bake in a preheated moderate oven (160°C/325°F, Gas Mark 3) until golden. Sprinkle with caster sugar while warm. Makes about 40.
VARIATIONS
Spiced Biscuits: Omit ginger but sift 1 tsp ground cinnamon and 1 tsp ground mace with the flour.

Orange and Lemon Shortbread

180 g/6 oz (¾ cup) butter; 125 g/4 oz (½ cup) sugar; 2 tsp each finely grated lemon and orange rind; 250 g/8 oz (2 cups) flour; pinch salt; extra 2 tbsp sugar.

Cream butter with sugar until fluffy. Mix in fruit rinds and flour sifted with salt. Divide dough in half and mould each portion into a sausage shape. Wrap dough in plastic wrap and chill for 1–2 hours. Cut into 5 mm (¼ in) thick slices and arrange on greased baking trays. Sprinkle with extra sugar and bake in a preheated moderate oven (180°C/350°F, Gas Mark 4) for 20 minutes or until golden-brown. Cool on a wire rack, and store in an airtight container. Makes about 30.

Butter Wafers

A good basic biscuit (cookie) recipe. Vary the flavour by using brown sugar instead of white, adding poppy or sesame seeds, etc., or a little instant coffee powder. For chocolate butter wafers add a little (unsweetened) cocoa but reduce flour in proportion.

125 g/4 oz (½ cup) butter; 75 g/2½ oz (⅓ cup) sugar; 1 egg; 1 tsp vanilla essence (extract); 90 g/3 oz (¾ cup) flour, sifted; pinch salt.

Cream butter with sugar, then beat in egg and vanilla. Stir in flour and salt together. Drop teaspoonfuls of mixture on to greased baking trays, spacing well apart. Bake in a preheated moderately hot oven (190°C/375°F, Gas Mark 5) for 10 minutes or until biscuits (cookies) are golden-brown around the edges. Makes about 36.

Coconut Drops

180 g/6 oz (1½ cups) self-raising flour; pinch salt; 250 g/8 oz (1 cup) sugar; 1 egg, lightly beaten; 1 tsp vanilla essence (extract); few drops almond essence (extract); 125 g/4 oz (½ cup) butter, melted; 135 g/4½ oz (1½ cups) desiccated (shredded) coconut.

Sift flour and salt into a bowl and stir in sugar. Add remaining ingredients, except coconut, and combine. Form mixture into small balls about the size of a marble and roll in coconut. Arrange on greased baking trays, spacing well apart. Bake in a preheated moderate oven (180°C/350°F, Gas Mark 4) for 15 minutes or until golden. Cool on a wire rack. Makes about 30.

Highland Oatmeal Cookies

250 g/8 oz (1 cup) butter; 180 g/6 oz (1 cup) firmly packed brown sugar; 125 g/4 oz (½ cup) white sugar; 1 egg; 2 tsp vanilla essence (extract); 4 tbsp water; 250 g/8 oz (2 cups) flour; ½ tsp salt; ½ tsp bicarbonate of soda (baking soda); 1 tsp cinnamon;

B

60 g/2 oz (½ cup) chopped nuts; 180 g/6 oz (1 cup) raisins; 270 g/8¾ oz (2½ cups) rolled oats; walnuts or glacé (candied) cherries to decorate.

Cream butter with sugars, egg and vanilla until light and fluffy. Beat in the water. Sift dry ingredients and stir in with nuts, raisins and oats. Drop heaped teaspoonfuls of mixture, about 5 cm (2 in) apart, on to greased baking trays. Press a walnut or cherry into the top of each biscuit. Bake in a preheated moderately hot oven (190°C/375°F, Gas Mark 5) for 12–15 minutes or until lightly browned. Cool on a wire rack. Makes about 60.

Refrigerator Biscuits

180 g/6 oz (¾ cup) butter; 180 g/6 oz (1 cup) firmly packed brown sugar; 1 egg; 1 tsp vanilla essence (extract); 280 g/9 oz (2¼ cups) flour; ½ tsp salt; ½ tsp baking powder.

Cream butter with brown sugar. Add egg and vanilla and beat well. Sift flour with salt and baking powder. Stir into creamed mixture. Shape into long rolls about 5 cm (2 in) in diameter. Wrap in plastic wrap or foil and freeze until needed. Slice thinly, put on a baking tray and bake in a preheated moderate oven (180°C/350°F, Gas Mark 4) for 7–10 minutes. If wished, store in a refrigerator, wrapped in foil, for up to 2 weeks. Makes 6 dozen.

Drop Biscuits

Drop biscuits vary in texture. Some fall easily from the spoon and flatten into wafers when baking. Stiffer doughs need a push with the finger or the use of a second spoon to release them.

210 g/7 oz (1¾ cups) flour; 2 tsp baking powder; pinch salt; 125 g/4 oz (½ cup) butter; 90 g/3 oz (½ cup) firmly packed brown sugar; 2 tbsp golden (light corn) syrup; 1 egg; 1½ tsp vanilla essence (extract); 3–4 tbsp milk.

Sift flour, baking powder and salt together. Cream butter with sugar until fluffy. Add syrup, egg and vanilla and beat well. Blend in sifted dry ingredients a little at a time alternately with milk until you have a stiff dough. Drop teaspoonfuls of the mixture on to greased baking trays and bake in a preheated moderately hot oven (200°C/400°F, Gas Mark 6) for 10–12 minutes or until golden. Cool on a wire rack and store in an airtight container. Makes 36.

VARIATIONS

Chocolate Drop Biscuits: Add 60 g/2 oz (⅓ cup) cooled, melted cooking chocolate to creamed mixture. Bake as directed.

Cherry Drop Biscuits: Add 60 g/2 oz (¼ cup) chopped glacé (candied) cherries with the flour and milk. Bake as directed.

BISCUIT TORTONI

A rich Italian iced dessert made from cream and crushed macaroons, spooned into small custard cups, or soufflé dishes, decorated with fruit, chocolate and nuts then frozen.

Biscuit Tortoni

90 g/3 oz (¾ cup) crushed macaroons, home-made or purchased; 400 ml/14 fl oz (1¾ cups) double (heavy) cream; 30 g/1 oz (¼ cup) icing (confectioners) sugar, sifted; tiny pinch salt; 1 tsp vanilla essence (extract).
DECORATION: *halved maraschino cherries; grated chocolate; chopped, toasted almonds; shreds candied angelica.*

Combine macaroons, 175 ml/6 fl oz (¾ cup) cream, the icing (confectioners) sugar and salt. Allow to stand for 1 hour. Whip remaining cream until thick enough to stand in soft peaks (but not stiff) and fold into macaroon mixture with vanilla. Spoon into 8–10 small custard cups or soufflé dishes arranged in a shallow tray that will fit in freezer. Decorate tops with cherries, chocolate, almonds and angelica and freeze overnight or until firm. Serves 8–10.

BISHOP'S CAKE

An old English fruit cake that got its name from the stained-glass window appearance of each slice.

Bishop's Cake

500 g/1 lb (4 cups) whole, shelled Brazil nuts; 12 dates, stoned (pitted); 250 g/8 oz (1 cup) glacé (candied) cherries, red and green mixed; 90 g/3 oz (¾ cup) flour; ½ tsp baking powder; ½ tsp salt; 180 g/6 oz (¾ cup) caster sugar; 3 eggs, beaten; 1 tsp vanilla essence (extract).

Grease a 21 × 11 cm (8½ × 4¼ in) loaf tin (pan). Line base and sides with greased greaseproof (waxed) paper. Put whole nuts, whole dates and whole glacé (candied) cherries into a large mixing bowl. Sift dry ingredients over and mix thoroughly. Pour in eggs and vanilla. Stir well and spoon into the prepared tin (pan). Bake in a preheated cool oven (150°C/300°F, Gas Mark 2) for about 1¾ hours or until a skewer inserted in centre comes out clean. Remove from tin (pan), peel away paper and cool completely on a wire rack. Wrap in foil and store in the refrigerator. It will keep for up to 3 weeks.

BISQUE

This French term describes a particular type of cream soup, frequently made of seafood and enriched with cream or egg yolks or both. Bisques may be served hot or cold. **See recipes**.

Oyster Bisque

90 g/3 oz (6 tbsp) butter; 2 tsp grated onion; 350 ml/12 fl oz (1½ cups) milk; 120 ml/4 fl oz (½ cup) single (light) cream; salt and freshly ground white pepper; 2 egg yolks, beaten; 450 ml/¾ pint (1½ cups) oysters and their liquor (bottled or from the shell).

Place butter and onion in top half of a double saucepan (double boiler) over hot water. Melt butter, add milk and cream. Season with salt and pepper. Increase heat so water in lower half of saucepan boils. When milk is just about to boil, remove from heat and pour a little over beaten egg yolks. Mix well, then return to the pan. Add oysters and liquor. Heat but do not boil. Serves 4.

Mushroom Bisque

500 g (1 lb) young mushroom caps, stems, removed and reserved; 900 ml/1½ pints (3¾ cups) chicken stock; 1 medium onion, chopped; 90 g/3 oz (6 tbsp) butter; 4 tbsp flour; 750 ml/1¼ pints (3 cups) milk; 250 ml/8 fl oz (1 cup) single (light) cream; 1 tsp salt; freshly ground white pepper; Tabasco (hot pepper) sauce; 2 tbsp sherry.

Slice 6 mushroom caps and reserve. Chop remaining caps and stems. Simmer chopped mushrooms, covered, in stock with onion for 30 minutes. Sauté reserved sliced mushrooms in 15 g/½ oz (1 tbsp) butter and reserve for garnish. Melt remaining butter in a saucepan, add flour and stir with a wire whisk until blended. Meanwhile, bring milk to the boil. Add milk all at once to butter-flour mixture, stirring vigorously with whisk until sauce is thickened and smooth. Stir in cream. Combine mushroom-broth mixture with sauce and season with salt, pepper and Tabasco (hot pepper) sauce. Reheat, add sherry and mushrooms. Serves 6–8.

BLACKBERRY

A large luscious berry that is cultivated and also grows wild. Blackberries are delicious eaten fresh or stewed, or in jams (see page 166), pies and tarts.

Blackberry Pie

Rich Shortcrust Pastry (Basic Pie Dough) for a 2-crust, 23 cm (9 in) pie (page 274); 500 g/1 lb (4 cups) fresh or frozen blackberries, or 370 g/12 oz (3 cups) drained, canned blackberries; 180 g/6 oz (¾ cup) sugar; 1½ tbsp cornflour (cornstarch); 2 tbsp lemon juice.

Roll out just over half the pastry (dough) and use to line a greased 23 cm (9 in) pie plate. If using fresh blackberries, toss gently with 180 g/6 oz (¾ cup) sugar, the cornflour (cornstarch) and lemon juice. For sweetened, frozen blackberries or for canned blackberries, use less sugar. Spoon into pie shell. Dampen edges and roll out remaining pastry (dough) to make lid. Press into place, trim and crimp edges and make a few slashes in the top for steam to escape. Bake in a preheated moderately hot oven (200°C/400°F, Gas Mark 6) for 10 minutes, then reduce the oven heat to moderate (180°C/350°F, Gas Mark 4) and bake for a further 25 minutes or until pastry (dough) is cooked and golden-brown. Serve warm with cream, ice cream or custard. Serves 6.

BLACK BUN, SCOTTISH

Not a bun in the usual sense but a rich fruit mixture enclosed in pastry (dough).

Scottish Black Bun

1 quantity Plain Shortcrust Pastry (Basic Pie Dough) (page 274); 250 g/8 oz (2 cups) flour; ½ tsp baking powder; ¼ tsp black pepper; 1 tsp ground ginger; 1 tsp ground cloves; 90 g/3 oz (½ cup) firmly packed brown sugar; 500 g/1 lb (3 cups) raisins; 500 g/1 lb (3 cups) currants; 60 g/2 oz (⅓ cup) chopped mixed candied peel; 60 g/2 oz (½ cup) blanched almonds, chopped; 1 apple, peeled, cored and grated; 2 eggs, beaten.

Roll out ⅔ pastry (dough) thinly and use to line a greased and lined 20 cm (8 in) cake tin (pan). Sift flour, baking powder, pepper and spices into a bowl and stir in sugar, fruit, peel, nuts and grated apple. Add eggs and mix thoroughly. Turn into tin. Roll out remaining pastry (dough) for lid and place on top, pinching edges together. Make 4 holes right through to bottom with a skewer. Bake in a preheated moderate oven (180°C/350°F, Gas Mark 4) for 3 hours. Turn out carefully and cool. When completely cold, store in an airtight tin. Serve cut into thin fingers.

BLACK FOREST CHERRY TORTE

This famous German torte originated in Swabia in the Black Forest region.

Black Forest Cherry Torte

CAKE: *90 g/3 oz (3 squares) dark chocolate; 1 tbsp water or black coffee; 4 eggs; 180 g/6 oz (¾ cup) caster sugar; 90 g/3 oz (¾ cup) self-raising flour; 1 tsp vanilla essence (extract); grated rind ½ lemon; 45 g/1½ oz (3 tbsp) butter, melted and cooled.*
TOPPING AND FILLING: *280 g/9 oz (1½ cups) milk chocolate, at room temperature; 1 × 700 g/1 lb 7 oz jar German sour cherries; 3 tbsp Kirsch; 450 ml/¾ pint (2 cups) double (heavy) cream.*

CAKE: Place chocolate and water or coffee in a heatproof basin and melt over hot water. Beat eggs with sugar until very light and fluffy. Sift in flour and fold into egg mixture with vanilla, lemon rind, melted butter and chocolate mixture. Turn into a greased, lined and floured 23 cm (9 in) springform tin (pan). Bake in a preheated moderate oven (180°C/350°F, Gas Mark 4) for 1 hour. Cool with the spring released.
TOPPING AND FILLING: Shave thin curls from side of block of chocolate with a swivel-bladed vegetable peeler. Chill. Drain syrup from cherries and mix syrup with Kirsch. Halve cherries, leaving a few whole to decorate cake. Cut cake into 2 layers and prick bottom layer with a fork. Place bottom layer on a serving plate and soak with half Kirsch-flavoured syrup. Whip cream until it just holds its shape and pile about ⅓ over bottom cake layer. Spoon over half the halved cherries. Place top cake layer in position, prick with a fork and spoon remaining syrup over. Arrange remaining cherry halves on top. Cover cake with remaining cream, piling most of it on top. Press chocolate curls around side of cake and sprinkle some on top. Decorate with reserved whole cherries and chill for 1–2 hours before serving. Serves 10–12.

BLACKCURRANT

A small black, juicy berry. Fresh, it is used to make jam (see page 166), tarts, mousses, and other desserts, and to flavour syrup, cordial, and the delicious liqueur called Cassis. Black-currants are also available frozen and canned.

BLANCMANGE

A white pudding made of milk, flavourings and cornflour (cornstarch) and set in a mould.

Blancmange

450 ml/¾ pint (2 cups) milk; 2 thin strips lemon rind; 4 tbsp cornflour (cornstarch); 2 tbsp sugar.

Put all but 4 tbsp milk into a saucepan with lemon rind and bring slowly to the boil. Remove rind. Mix cornflour (cornstarch) and sugar to a smooth paste with remaining milk. Slowly pour boiling milk into cornflour (cornstarch) paste, stirring constantly, then return mixture to saucepan. Simmer for 5 minutes, stirring. Pour into a dampened mould. Cool, then chill until set. To serve, dip mould into hot water 2–3 seconds, wipe mould, shake and unmould on to a serving dish. Serves 4.

BLANQUETTE

A blanquette is a French-inspired stew made of lamb, chicken, veal or sweetbreads. It differs from other stews in that the meat is not browned before cooking, and the addition of cream and egg yolks to the cooking liquid results in a white sauce.

Blanquette de Veau
(White Veal Stew)

1.5 kg (3 lb) boneless veal, cut into large cubes; salt and freshly ground white pepper; 1 large onion, studded with 1 clove; 1 large carrot, coarsely chopped; 1 stick celery, sliced; 1 bouquet garni; 1.2 litres/2 pints (5 cups) veal or chicken stock; 20 small white onions, blanched; 125 g/4 oz (1 cup) button mushrooms; 2 tbsp flour; 30 g/1 oz (2 tbsp) butter; 3 egg yolks, beaten with 120 ml/4 fl oz (½ cup) single (light) cream; 2 tbsp lemon juice.
GARNISH: *chopped parsley; croûtons.*

Blanch veal for 2 minutes in boiling salted water; drain and rinse under cold running water. Place meat in a deep, heavy saucepan with whole onion, carrot, celery and bouquet garni. Pour stock over, bring to the boil, then cover and simmer 1½ hours or until veal is very tender. Remove vegetables and bouquet garni with a slotted spoon. Add small onions and mushrooms to the saucepan. Simmer 10 minutes. Blend flour and butter together, and whisk a little at a time into simmering liquid. Simmer another 10 minutes, then remove pan from heat. Stir 2 tbsp of liquid into egg and cream mixture. Add this mixture to pan with lemon juice and reheat gently but do not boil. Adjust seasoning with salt and pepper. Serve in a heated serving bowl, sprinkled with chopped parsley and croûtons. Serves 6.

BLINI

Blini (bliny) are small Russian yeast pancakes made with buckwheat flour. The classic topping is sour cream and caviar. For dessert, blini may be topped with sour cream and jam.

Blini

30 g/1 oz (1 cake) fresh (compressed) yeast; 450 ml/¾ pint (2 cups) milk, scalded and cooled to lukewarm; 180 g/6 oz (1½ cups) each plain (all-purpose) flour and buckwheat flour, sifted together; 2 tbsp sugar; 3 eggs, separated; 125 g/4 oz (½ cup) butter, melted; 1 tsp salt; little melted butter for cooking.

Dissolve yeast in warm milk, then stir in 180 g/6 oz (1½ cups) flour and the sugar. Cover with greased plastic wrap and a cloth and stand in a warm place for 1½ hours or until covered with bubbles. Beat egg yolks in another bowl, combine with melted butter and salt and stir in remaining flour. Beat this mixture into yeast mixture, cover as before and stand in a warm place for another 1½ hours or until almost doubled in bulk. Beat egg whites until they form soft peaks and fold into batter. Stand 10 minutes. Without stirring batter again, drop a tablespoonful at a time on to a heated greased griddle or heavy frying pan (skillet). When undersides are brown, sprinkle a little melted butter over the tops, turn over and cook other side. Stack on a heated serving platter and keep covered with a warm cloth until all are cooked. Makes about 24.

BLINTZ

Blintzes are one of the many joys of Jewish cooking – tender pancakes filled with cottage cheese, then fried.

Blintzes

PANCAKES: *90 g/3 oz (¾ cup) flour, sifted; ½ tsp salt; 1 tsp baking powder; 2 tbsp caster sugar; 2 eggs; 150 ml/¼ pint (⅔ cup) milk; 5 tbsp water; ½ tsp vanilla essence (extract); oil for cooking.*
FILLING: *370 g/12 oz (1½ cups) cottage cheese; 1 egg yolk; 1 tsp softened butter; 2 tsp sugar; 1 tsp grated lemon rind.*
TO FINISH: *oil and butter for frying; sugar; cinnamon; sour cream.*

PANCAKES: Sift flour, salt, baking powder and sugar into a bowl. Beat eggs with milk, water and vanilla. Make a well in the centre of the dry ingredients, add liquid mixture and combine very quickly and lightly. Batter will still be lumpy and must not be overbeaten. Heat a pancake pan, about 13 cm (5 in) in diameter, and grease with a few drops of oil. Pour in just enough batter to cover bottom of pan and cook over moderate heat until golden-brown underneath. Remove without cooking other side and repeat with remaining batter. Stack pancakes on a dampened tea-towel, cooked side up, with squares of greaseproof (waxed) paper between them, and cover with ends of towel.
FILLING: Mix all ingredients well together.
TO FINISH: Place about 2 tbsp filling in middle of each pancake on cooked side. Turn edges in and roll up like a cigar. Heat about 2 tsp each oil and butter in a large, heavy frying pan (skillet) and put in several blintzes, seam sides down. Fry over medium heat until golden-brown on each side. Add more oil and butter to pan and continue cooking blintzes until all are browned. Serve hot, sprinkled with sugar and cinnamon, and pass a bowl of sour cream. Makes about 14.

BOMBE

A frozen dessert set in a mould. The name comes from the spherical moulds traditionally used to shape the dessert. In the absence of a special mould, a bombe can be made in a pudding basin (mold) or soufflé dish. It usually consists of an outer layer of ice cream or sherbet and a softer, inner layer of custard, mousse, fruit purée or cream. Using the following recipe as a starting point, it is easy to experiment with variations. **See recipes**.

Strawberry Bombe

500 g (1 lb) strawberries; 250 ml/8 fl oz (1 cup) double (heavy) cream; 30 g/1 oz (¼ cup) icing (confectioners) sugar, sifted; 2 tbsp Kirsch or other fruit liqueur; 1 litre/1¾ pints (4 cups) strawberry or vanilla ice cream, slightly softened; extra whipped cream to decorate.

Grill a 2 litre/3½ pint (8 cup) mould in the freezer. Hull and purée enough strawberries to make 250 ml/8 fl oz (1 cup). Whip cream with icing (confectioners) sugar until stiff, then fold in Kirsch and puréed strawberries. Remove mould from freezer and quickly line it with ice cream. Fill centre with strawberry cream, cover with foil and freeze until firm. Unmould to serve, decorated with remaining strawberries and whipped cream. Serves 6.

Bombe Alaska (Baked Alaska)

A spectacular dessert. For a party, set a broken egg shell in the meringue, put a sugar lump soaked in brandy in the shell, and flame; it then becomes Bombe Vesuvius.

1 × 23 cm (9 in) round or square Genoise cake layer (see page 143); 1 litre/1¾ pints (4 cups) ice cream; 4 egg whites; ½ tsp cream of tartar; 6 tbsp caster sugar.

Place sponge on a wooden board and top with ice cream, leaving a small margin of cake uncovered round the edge. Freeze until ice cream is very hard. Beat egg whites with cream of tartar until soft peaks form, then gradually beat in sugar until meringue is stiff and glossy. Swirl meringue over cake and ice cream to cover completely. Bake in a preheated hot oven (230°C/450°F, Gas Mark 8) for 2–3 minutes until just lightly tinted. Serve at once. Serves 6.

BORAGE

This large herb has greyish-green leaves, which may be cooked and eaten like spinach or added to salads. With their faint cucumber flavour, they are also one of the traditional ingredients in Pimms, the long, refreshing alcoholic drink that is popular in Britain.

BOREK

A savoury pastry from Turkey, served hot. Feather-light pastry (dough) is wrapped around fillings made from spinach and eggs, pumpkin, cheese, meat or fruit. Borek vary in size from small, cigar-shaped mouthfuls to cushion-shapes to serve 3 or 4, or enormous ones baked on a tray for parties.

Meat Borek

This simplified recipe is made with filo (phyllo) pastry.

375 g/12 oz (1½ cups) minced (ground) lean beef or lamb; 2 tbsp olive oil; 1 clove garlic, crushed; 1 large onion, finely chopped; 2 tbsp finely chopped parsley; salt and freshly ground black pepper; 1 egg, beaten; 125 g/4 oz (6 sheets) filo (phyllo) pastry; 60 g/2 oz (4 tbsp) butter, melted.

Brown meat in olive oil, stirring with a fork to break up any lumps. Add garlic and onion and continue to cook and stir until onion is soft. Stir in parsley and season well with salt and pepper. Allow to cool, then stir in beaten egg. Layer 3 sheets of filo (phyllo) in a greased 28 × 19 cm (11 × 7½ in) tin (pan), brushing generously with melted butter between layers. Spread meat filling over and cover with 3 more buttered sheets of filo (phyllo). Press edges together. Pour any remaining butter over top. Bake in a preheated moderate oven (180°C/350°F, Gas Mark 4) for about 25 minutes or until filo (phyllo) is crisp and golden-brown. Serve hot or cold, cut into squares. Serves 18 as an appetizer, 4 as a lunch dish.

VARIATION

Cocktail Borekler: Small cigar-shaped borekler are made by folding a buttered sheet of filo (phyllo) into 4. Brush with butter, put a spoonful of meat filling in a cigar shape on the centre, fold in ends and roll up. Repeat with remaining ingredients. Place rolls seam sides down, on a baking tray, brush with butter and bake in a preheated moderately hot oven (190°C/375°F, Gas Mark 5) for 20 minutes or until golden. Makes 24.

BORSCH (BORTSCH)

A basic soup of Russia and Poland, mainly characterized by its use of beetroot, which gives the soup a lovely wine-red colour. There are thick and thin versions as well as hot and cold. All borschs are served with a sour cream garnish. **See recipes.**

Borsch

This recipe is for hearty borsch from Russia – a meal in itself.

750 g (1½ lb) stewing beef in one piece; 1.6 litres/2¾ pints (7 cups) beef stock (bouillon); 1 bay leaf; 90 g/3 oz (6 tbsp) butter; 1 large onion, chopped; 2 carrots, sliced; ½ medium cabbage, shredded; 2 medium potatoes, peeled and sliced; 10 g/⅓ oz (¼ cup) chopped parsley, including stalks; 165 g/5½ oz (⅔ cup) tomato purée (paste); 1 tbsp vinegar; 3 medium raw beetroot, peeled and grated; salt and freshly ground black pepper; 4 tbsp fresh beetroot juice (while grating beetroot, sieve a little to give juice).

GARNISH: *lemon slices; sour cream.*

Place beef in a large saucepan with stock and bay leaf and bring to the boil. Skim, then lower heat and simmer, covered, for 1½ hours or until beef is almost tender. Heat butter in another saucepan and gently fry onion, carrots, cabbage and potatoes for 2–3 minutes, stirring to coat with butter. Add vegetables to soup pot and simmer, covered, until beef and vegetables are very tender, another 30–40 minutes. Stir in parsley, tomato purée (paste), vinegar and beetroot and simmer uncovered a further 5 minutes.

Taste and season well with salt and pepper. Remove beef from pot, cut into slices and divide among 6 large bowls. Stir beetroot juice into soup and ladle into bowls. Garnish each bowl with a slice of lemon and a spoonful of sour cream. Serves 6.

Iced Borsch

900 ml/1½ pints (3¾ cups) strong beef stock (bouillon); 4 raw beetroot, peeled and grated; 120 ml/4 fl oz (½ cup) red wine; 2 tbsp tomato purée (paste); 2 bay leaves; 3 egg whites, stiffly beaten; grated rind 1 lemon; salt; cayenne; 5 tbsp sour cream.

Put stock (bouillon) in a large pan. Add beetroot, wine, tomato purée (paste), bay leaves and egg whites. Beat over moderate heat until borsch comes to the boil, then draw off heat and leave for 10 minutes. Pour through a fine damp cloth and place in refrigerator until cold. Add grated lemon rind, salt and cayenne to sour cream and serve separately. Serves 4–6.

BOUCHEES

Tiny mouthful-sized cases for sweet or savoury food, made of choux pastry (paste) or puff pastry (paste). Choux pastry (paste) bouchées are shaped in the same way as Cream Puffs and puff pastry bouchées in the same way as Vol-au-Vent.

See Pastry (Dough), Cream Puffs and Vol-au-Vent.

BOUILLABAISSE

The superb fish stew of the French Mediterranean coast. It is made with a rich assortment of fish and seafood peculiar to the region, cooked in a highly flavoured stock with olive oil, spices and herbs. Saffron adds the authentic golden colour and flavour to the broth.

See page 396 for recipe.

BOUILLON

The word comes from the French *bouillir* (to boil) and refers to a broth made by simmering meat, chicken, fish or vegetables in water. When the flavour is extracted the liquid is strained and seasoned, and may be served as it is or with rice, pasta or vegetables added.

See Soups.

BOUQUET GARNI

A bundle or 'faggot' of herbs and aromatics for flavouring soups, stocks and casseroles. The classic combination is bay leaf, parsley stalks, thyme and celery, but the ingredients may be varied. A bouquet garni is tied in a bundle, or in muslin if dried herbs are used, with a string long enough to tie to the handle of the pan for easy removal.

BOURGUIGNONNE, BOEUF A LA

The famous beef-in-red-wine dish from the French province of Burgundy.

Boeuf à la Bourguignonne

1.5 kg (3 lb) shin (fore shank) of beef or chuck steak; 125 g (4 oz) pickled (salt) pork, diced; 2 tbsp olive oil; 60 g/2 oz (4 tbsp) butter; 18 small onions, peeled; 4 tbsp brandy; 1 tbsp flour; 250 ml/8 fl oz (1 cup) red wine; 250 ml/8 fl oz (1 cup) beef stock (bouillon); 1 bouquet garni containing 1 clove garlic; salt and freshly ground black pepper; 250 g/8 oz (2 cups) button mushrooms.

TO SERVE: *boiled rice; chopped parsley.*

Cut beef into 5 cm (2 in) cubes. Brown pork in oil and half the butter in a heavy flameproof casserole. Remove pork and brown onions. Remove onions and brown beef. Warm brandy, set alight and pour over beef. Stir in flour, then wine. Simmer 1 minute, then add stock (bouillon), bouquet garni, garlic and salt and pepper. Cover and cook in a preheated cool oven (150°C/300°F, Gas Mark 2) for 3–3½ hours or until beef is very tender. Sauté mushrooms in remaining butter. Add to beef with reserved pork and onions, cover and cook 30 minutes more. Remove bouquet garni and serve with boiled rice sprinkled with parsley. Serves 8.

BOURRIDE

A creamy Provençal fish stew with Aïoli (garlic sauce). Some recipes include a chopped tomato, and a little dried orange peel and saffron in addition to the ingredients given below.

Bourride

500 g (1 lb) mixed small white fish; 1.2 litres/ 2 pints (5 cups) fish stock; 1 bay leaf; 1 sprig fresh thyme, or pinch dried; 1 onion, chopped; salt; 6 black peppercorns; 250 ml/8 fl oz (1 cup) single (light) cream; sliced French bread, crisped in oven; 250 ml/8 fl oz (1 cup) Aïoli (page 6).

Place fish in saucepan with stock, bay leaf, thyme, onion, salt and peppercorns. Simmer gently 15–25 minutes or until fish is cooked. Remove fish and keep hot. Add cream to pan and simmer a few moments. Arrange bread in a heated soup tureen and add fish. Strain cooking liquid into aïoli, stir to blend and pour over bread and fish. Serve immediately. Serves 6.

Right: Cabbage Rolls (page 51)

BRAINS

Lamb and calf brains are considered a delicacy. They are very perishable and should be used as soon as possible after buying. Allow one set of lamb brains per person, or one set of calf brains for 2 people. If buying frozen brains, make sure they are completely frozen. Unlike most other frozen foods, brains are best thawed quickly by plunging them into hot water.

☐ **Basic Preparation:** Soak brains in lightly salted cold water for 2 hours, changing the water every 30 minutes. Drain them, carefully peel off the membrane with a sharp knife and soak in tepid water to remove any blood. Place brains in a saucepan and cover with water, add salt and a little lemon juice or white vinegar. Bring just to simmering point and simmer over very gentle heat for 15 minutes for lamb brains, 20 minutes for calf brains. Allow to cool in liquid, then drain and dry on paper towels.

NOTE: If not using brains immediately, do not drain from cooking liquid but cool in the liquid, cover and then keep in refrigerator for up to 24 hours. **See recipes.**

Brain Fritters

2 sets lamb brains; 1 tbsp lemon juice; 4 shallots, finely chopped; freshly ground white pepper; oil for frying.
BATTER: 125 g/4 oz (1 cup) flour; 1 tsp baking powder; $\frac{1}{4}$ tsp salt; 2 eggs; 250 ml/8 fl oz (1 cup) milk.

Prepare brains as described above and cut into pieces (not too small). Mix gently with lemon juice, shallots and pepper.
BATTER: Sift flour, baking powder and salt into a bowl and make a well in centre. Beat eggs and milk together, pour into well and gradually stir in flour. Beat until batter is smooth. Cover and stand 20 minutes. Fold brains into batter. Drop by tablespoonfuls into hot oil about 1 cm ($\frac{1}{2}$ in) deep. When fritters are crisp and golden on the bottom, turn with a spatula and cook other side. Drain on paper towels and serve very hot. Serves 4.

Brains in Black Butter

2 sets lamb brains, or 1 set calf brains; 90 g/3 oz (6 tbsp) butter; 1 tbsp finely chopped parsley; 1 tbsp chopped capers; 1 tbsp vinegar.

Prepare and cook brains as described above and slice. Heat gently in a little of the butter, place on a heated serving plate and keep

Left: Vienna Cakes and Chocolate Toffee Cake (page 55)

warm. Heat remaining butter slowly in a small frying pan (skillet) until it is nut-brown (not black). Add parsley and capers, stir quickly and pour at once over brains. Add vinegar to pan, swirl it round and pour over brains. Serve immediately. Serves 2.

BRAN

This is the outer layer or husk of cereal grains and is a major source of fibre, the dietary component vital in ensuring that food passes efficiently through the digestive system. Bran is missing from refined white flour but is wholly or partly retained in wholewheat and wholegrain flours.

Bran is also available in unprocessed form and in some dry breakfast cereals. It can be sprinkled on other cereals, fruit or other foods, added to drinks, mixed with crumbs or cheese to top au gratin dishes or added to biscuits (cookies), cakes, casseroles and other dishes during preparation.

Bran Muffins

A marvellous recipe for busy households. The batter will keep for up to one month, covered, in the refrigerator. Delicious served with butter and honey or with ham or bacon.

750 g/1$\frac{1}{2}$ lb (6 cups) flour; 5 tsp bicarbonate of soda (baking soda); 1 tsp salt; 370 g/12 oz (2 cups) firmly packed brown sugar; 370 g/12 oz (2 cups) raisins; 280 g/9 oz (3 cups) All-Bran; 3 eggs; 250 ml/8 fl oz (1 cup) vegetable oil; 90 g/3 oz ($\frac{1}{4}$ cup) molasses; 1 litre/1$\frac{3}{4}$ pints (4$\frac{1}{4}$ cups) buttermilk, or fresh milk soured with 4 tbsp white vinegar; 350 ml/12 fl oz (1$\frac{1}{2}$ cups) water.

Sift flour, soda and salt into a large bowl. Stir in brown sugar, raisins and All-Bran. Beat eggs with oil and molasses and mix in buttermilk and water. Pour into dry mixture and stir well. Cover with plastic wrap and refrigerate for at least 1 day (or up to 1 month). Stir mixture lightly, then pour into greased deep bun tins (muffin pans), filling $\frac{3}{4}$ full. Bake in a preheated moderately hot oven (200°C/400°F, Gas Mark 6) for 20 minutes. Serve warm. Makes about 70.

BRANDADE

A thick, creamy fish purée which may be served warm or cold as a first course, as a main dish for a casual meal, or on croûtes as an hors d'oeuvre.

Brandade de Morue
(Cream of Salt Cod)

500 g (1 lb) salt cod; 2 cloves garlic, chopped; 120 ml/4 fl oz ($\frac{1}{2}$ cup) single (light) cream; 120 ml/4 fl oz ($\frac{1}{2}$ cup) olive oil; 1–2 potatoes, peeled and cooked (optional);

grated rind and juice 1 lemon; freshly ground black pepper; nutmeg; triangular croûtes of bread to serve.

Soak cod overnight in cold water. Drain, cover with fresh cold water and bring to the boil. Drain, cover again with cold water and bring to the boil. Remove from heat and leave to soak in hot water 10 minutes. Drain cod, remove skin and bones and flake flesh coarsely. Place in a food processor or blender, add garlic and a little cream or oil and process, adding remaining cream and oil gradually as if making mayonnaise. If making by hand, work mixture constantly with a pestle and mortar or a wooden spoon in a bowl while adding cream and oil gradually. Blend in potato, if using (you may need it to reduce saltiness). Beat in lemon rind and juice, pepper and nutmeg. Serve warm or cold, mounded in a dish and surrounded by croûtes. Serves 4–6 as a first course.

Oeufs Bénédictine: Top warm Brandade de Morue with hot poached eggs and cover the eggs with warm Hollandaise Sauce (page 369). A good brunch or luncheon dish.

BRANDY

A spirit distilled principally from grape wine but also from the fermented juice of other fruits. Grape brandy is widely used in cooking, especially French cooking.

Ways to Use Brandy
With fruit: Sprinkle a little brandy, lemon juice and sugar over summer fruits such as strawberries, peaches or apricots. By the time you have prepared the rest of the meal, they will have formed their own brandy-flavoured syrup.
With cheese: Grate leftover pieces of cheese, place in a bowl or food processor and work in some freshly ground black pepper, softened butter and brandy to make a soft paste. Stir in some chopped nuts and store, covered, in the refrigerator for a few days to mellow. Serve at room temperature with biscuits or French bread.
With pan juices: After sautéeing steak, chops, hamburgers or vegetables, deglaze the pan with single (light) cream and a spoonful of brandy for a delectable sauce to serve on the food.
In savoury dishes: A spoonful of brandy, added just before serving, makes all the difference to French Onion Soup (see page 400). Add a sprinkle of brandy to the butter in which Carrots Vichy (see page 58) are glazed.
Brandied Fruit Use one kind of fruit or add different fruits as they come into season. Suitable fruits are strawberries, raspberries, gooseberries, peeled peaches, apricots, grapes and plums, peeled and sliced pineapple. Fruits such as peaches and apricots may be left whole or halved.

Choose a large crock or jar with a well-fitting lid and scald with boiling water. Put in prepared fruit, brandy and sugar in equal quantities – 250 g/8 oz (1 cup) sugar and 250 ml/8 fl oz (1 cup) brandy for every 150 g/5 oz (1 cup) fruit – and cover. Stir gently every day until the last of the fruit has been added, securing the lid after each addition, and store for at least a month or two in a cool place before using. The mixture will keep indefinitely and can be added to as you wish. Serve the drained brandied fruit as a dessert, and enjoy the liqueur with after-dinner coffee.

□ **Cooking with Brandy:** This is not as extravagant as it sounds – the French have been cooking with brandy for centuries, but always with discretion.

Brandy is perhaps the main spirit used in cooking, certainly it is the most traditional, but most good cooks like to vary the spirit, or use a fortified wine. Prawns (shrimp) may be flamed in brandy, but Pernod or whisky may also be used.

Pâtés and terrines are flavoured with brandy, and brandy can lift a consommé or hearty soup like French Onion. Brandy, and other spirits, can be added at different stages of cooking; it is often flamed, whether added half-way through or at the last minute. When you flame food with spirits (all the alcohol in it is burnt away, leaving just the flavour), you also burn off some of the fatty bits on the food; this singeing the surface of the food gives it a distinctive taste.

To get a flame, it is necessary to warm the spirit first; sometimes just adding it to the hot pan is enough. When flaming the Christmas pudding, dip a sugar cube in the spirit (brandy, whisky or rum) and place it on top of the pudding, then warm the spirit, ignite and carefully pour it over the pudding. **See recipes**.

Sweet Potatoes with Brandy Layer parboiled, thickly sliced, sweet potatoes in a shallow baking dish, dotting each layer with butter and sprinkling with salt, freshly ground black pepper, brown sugar and brandy. Dot top with butter. Cover and bake in a pre-heated moderate oven (180°C/350°F, Gas Mark 4) for 20 minutes, then remove cover and baste with juices from dish. Return to oven and bake, uncovered, for a further 10 minutes until top is golden.

Brandy Sauces

Brandy flavours two simple but delicious dessert sauces that are especially associated with Christmas.

Brandy Custard Sauce Stir brandy into Crème Anglaise (see page 97) in the proportion of 1 tbsp per 250 ml/8 fl oz (1 cup), or to taste. Serve Brandy Custard Sauce warm or cold with Christmas pudding.

Brandy Hard Sauce (Brandy Butter) see page 154 for recipe.

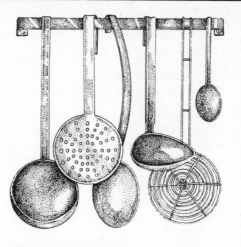

Flambéed Peaches

1 × 825 g/1 lb 13 oz can peach halves; 1 cinnamon stick; 2 tsp arrowroot; 4 tbsp brandy; 60 g/2 oz (½ cup) slivered, toasted almonds.

Pour 175 ml/6 fl oz (¾ cup) syrup from can of peaches into a large pan, add cinnamon stick and bring to the boil. Blend arrowroot with a little cold water, stir into peach syrup and stir until slightly thickened. Add peaches and baste with sauce until they are heated through. Warm brandy, set alight and pour over peaches. Top with almonds and serve with ice cream and crisp sweet biscuits (cookies). Serves 6.

Ice Cream with Mincemeat Flambé

1 litre/1¾ pints (4½ cups) vanilla ice cream; 1 × 275 g/9 oz jar mincemeat; 120 ml/4 fl oz (½ cup) brandy.

At serving time, pile scoops of ice cream into a serving bowl. Gently heat mincemeat and spoon over ice cream. Warm brandy in a small pan, ignite, and pour flaming over mincemeat. Serve immediately. Serves 6.

Brandied Chicken Sauté

This is the basic sauté method for poultry or small, tender cuts of meat. You can do veal steaks and lamb noisettes (loin chops) or cutlets in the same way.

4 half-breasts of chicken; 1 tbsp olive oil; 30 g/1 oz (2 tbsp) butter; 6–8 mushrooms; 8 button onions, peeled; 3 tbsp brandy; salt and freshly ground black pepper; 1 clove garlic, crushed; 4 tbsp white wine; 120 ml/4 fl oz (½ cup) chicken stock; extra nut of butter.

Trim chicken neatly and dry with paper towels. Heat oil and butter and sauté mushrooms and onions on high heat until lightly browned. Remove vegetables with a slotted spoon. Add chicken to pan and brown all over. Warm brandy and pour over chicken. Set alight and shake pan until

flames subside. Season with salt and pepper and add garlic, wine, stock and fried vegetables. When liquid boils lower heat, cover pan and simmer gently for 10 minutes or until chicken is tender. Place chicken and vegetables on a heated serving dish. Boil sauce rapidly until slightly reduced, swirl in extra butter off heat and pour over chicken. Serves 4.

Brandy Snaps

These crisp, lacy, rolled wafers are elegant for afternoon tea or to accompany a fruit dessert.

60 g/2 oz (4 tbsp) butter; 60 g/2 oz (⅓ cup) lightly packed brown sugar; 125 g/4 oz (⅓ cup) golden (light corn) syrup; 60 g/2 oz (½ cup) flour; 1 tsp ground ginger; grated rind ½ lemon.
TO SERVE: 250 ml/8 fl oz (1 cup) double (heavy) cream; 1 tbsp brandy.

Heat butter, brown sugar and syrup together until butter melts. Cool, then add flour sifted with ginger. Stir in lemon rind. Drop teaspoonfuls on to buttered baking trays, spacing at least 15 cm (6 in) apart and allowing only 2 biscuits to each tray. Bake one tray at a time in a preheated moderate oven (180°C/350°F, Gas Mark 4) for about 10 minutes or until golden-brown. Remove from oven, allow to set for a few seconds, then ease biscuits off tray with a palette knife and wrap loosely round handle of a wooden spoon, lacy side out. When crisp, remove from spoon. As soon as completely cold, store in an airtight container unless using immediately. To serve, whip cream, fold in brandy and pipe into both ends of each rolled biscuit. Makes about 12.

BRAWN

A preparation of meat stewed with spices and seasonings until soft. The meat is boned, chopped and set in moulds with some of the cooking liquor. Brawn is served cold and thinly sliced, with mustard and vinegar.

Brawn

500 g (1 lb) pickled (salt) pork; 1 kg (2 lb) shin of beef (fore shank) on the bone, sawn in half; 2 veal knuckles, each cut into 4; 1 bay leaf; 1 large onion, halved; 6 black peppercorns; 1 bouquet garni; freshly ground black pepper; salt; nutmeg.

Put all meat into a large saucepan, cover with cold water, bring to the boil and drain. Add fresh water barely to cover meat. Add remaining ingredients except pepper, salt and nutmeg. Cover and simmer about 2 hours, skimming occasionally, until meat comes off bones. Lift out meat and strain stock (bouillon). Skim stock and return to rinsed-out saucepan. Bring to the boil while cutting meat into 2.5 cm (1 in) pieces. Strain stock (bouillon) through 2 thicknesses of butter muslin (cheesecloth) to clear. Layer meat in a 23 × 12 cm (9 × 5 in) loaf tin (pan), grinding pepper liberally over each layer. Season stock (bouillon) to taste with salt and nutmeg and spoon into tin (pan) to come just level with meat. Cover with foil or plastic wrap and top with weighted lid or another loaf tin (pan) filled with heavy weights. Chill until set. Turn out to serve. Serves 8.

BRAZIL NUT

Hard-shelled, angular seed of the fruit of a large tree native to Brazil. They are particularly rich in oil. Brazil nuts may be chopped or thinly shaved and used in place of almonds with fish or vegetables.

To shave Brazil nuts: Cover the shelled nuts with cold water, bring slowly to the boil and simmer 5 minutes. Drain and slice thinly lengthways with a sharp knife or shave off layers with a vegetable peeler. The slices may be toasted in a preheated moderate oven (180°C/350°F, Gas Mark 4) for about 12 minutes until pale brown.

Butterscotch Brazils Make Butterscotch Toffee (see page 50). Have ready about 250 g/8 oz (2 cups) shelled Brazil nuts, a large, greased darning needle, a buttered knife and a buttered baking tray or marble slab. Impale each nut on the needle, dip into hot toffee, let drip a moment and push off on to the tray. When cool, store in airtight jars.

BREAD

The products we call breads today are an agreed group of preparations rather than a rigidly defined category. The group may differ somewhat from place to place and from time to time. The Germans and Austrians specialize in black bread and rye breads, or bread flavoured with caraway seeds and poppy seeds. The Scandinavians have a large array of dark breads and crispbreads, Ireland has its soda bread. *Pita* (*peda*) bread from the Middle East, and *Chapati*, *Puri*, *Paratha* and *Nan* from India, are now enjoyed in the West.

However, it can be said that the main ingredient of all bread is flour of some kind and that 'bread' always means a wholesome and sustaining food.

Bread containing yeast as the raising agent is the basic bread of the Western World. Baking bread offers the home cook one of the most satisfying pleasures of the kitchen. It is not difficult to achieve a good result at the first attempt, and one of the joys of breadmaking is that you get better and better as you repeat a recipe. **See recipes**.

See also *Yeast Cookery*.

Breadmaking Ingredients

Yeast: A living plant which grows when given moisture and food, and in the process produces the gas which causes bread to rise. It grows best in warm conditions but will also do its work of leavening, though more slowly, in cool conditions.

Fresh (compressed) yeast is available from many cake shops and health food stores. It should be fresh smelling, even coloured and easily crumbled. It can be kept for several days, well wrapped, in the refrigerator or can be frozen. (Thaw in the refrigerator before using.)

Dried yeast (active dry yeast) is usually sold by supermarkets. It takes a little longer to dissolve and needs warm rather than lukewarm water for this; the dough may also take a little longer to rise. Dried yeast will keep for a year or more in an airtight container in a cool place. For use follow directions on packet.

Flour: The basic ingredient of all bread. Special bread flour, called strong flour or baker's flour, is best for most breadmaking as it is high in gluten and gives the bread its characteristic chewy texture. For brown bread, use a mixture of wholewheat and white flour or all wholewheat, if you like a more dense and solid loaf. Bread flours are available from health food shops.

Rising Times for Bread Recipes usually say that yeast dough should be allowed to rise in a warm place, but if it suits you better, you can allow it to rise more slowly in a cool place or even in the refrigerator. A dough will take 30–60 minutes to double in bulk in a warm place, about 2 hours at normal room temperature, or up to 12 hours in a cold room or refrigerator. Keep the bowl covered with oiled plastic wrap and a cloth, or place the dough in a plastic bag, large enough to allow for expansion, loosely tie the mouth. A slow rise is considered by many experts to give bread a better texture and flavour than a quickly risen loaf.

Breadcrumbs

Fresh Breadcrumbs: Use bread that is 1 or 2 days old. Rub through a wire sieve, or process in a food processor, using the metal chopping

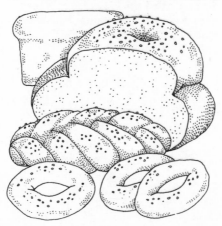

blade, or drop a few pieces at a time through the hole in the lid of a blender while motor is running at high speed.

Dried Breadcrumbs: Use whole slices of bread, with crusts removed, and spread on baking trays. Bake in a moderate oven (160°C/325°F, Gas Mark 3) until golden. Remove from oven and process to very fine crumbs in a food processor or blender, crush with a rolling pin, or rub through a sieve. Store in airtight containers. About 6 slices make 125 g/4 oz (1 cup) fine dry crumbs.

To coat food with egg and breadcrumbs: Food to be coated must be quite dry – pat meat, chicken, fish, cut vegetables etc., with paper towels. Dip in flour, shake off the surplus, dip in beaten egg and allow excess to drip off. Place in fresh or dried breadcrumbs and turn about to coat well, patting crumbs on with your fingers. Shake off excess crumbs, press coating lightly with a spatula and chill the food in the refrigerator for 20 minutes, to allow the egg to harden, before cooking.

Basic Bread

575 g/1¼ lb (5 cups) strong white flour (bread flour), or for wholewheat bread a mixture of half strong white flour (bread flour) and half plain wholewheat flour; 1½ tsp salt; 30 g/1 oz (1 cake) fresh (compressed) yeast, or 2½ tsp dried (active dry) yeast; 350–450 ml/12 fl oz – ¾ pint (1½–2 cups) lukewarm water (or warm for dry yeast); 60 g/2 oz (4 tbsp) butter or margarine, melted; oil for greasing bowl.

Sift flour and salt into a large warmed bowl, then take out 60 g/2 oz (½ cup) and sift it on to work surface. Mix yeast with 4 tbsp of the water in a small bowl, stirring to dissolve. Run your fingers through flour in large bowl and make a well in the centre. Pour yeast mixture into well and add butter or margarine (which should be warm, not hot) and 350 ml/12 fl oz (1½ cups) water. Mix flour and liquid ingredients with the fingers, then beat with your hand, adding a little more water if necessary to make a firm dough. With your hand, fold and slap dough against sides of bowl until it begins to feel elastic and leaves the sides (**Fig 1 overleaf**).

Turn the dough out of the bowl on to the floured work surface and knead by folding the far edge towards you, then pushing it firmly away with the heel of the hand (**2**). Turn dough a little and repeat. Continue kneading until dough is smooth and elastic and springs back when you make a dent with your finger. Place dough in a clean, warm, oiled bowl, turn it so that it is lightly oiled all over, and cover with oiled plastic wrap and a cloth (**3**). Leave to rise in a warm place for 30 minutes to 1 hour (or in a cool place for longer – see Rising Times for Bread, left).

Test by pushing a finger into the dough. If the indentation remains, it is ready. Knock back (punch down) dough by punching with your fist several times, squeezing out any large bubbles. Turn the dough out on to a lightly floured surface and knead 3 or 4 times (**4**).

For tin (pan) loaves, divide dough equally and pat each piece into a round, then fold sides under to form a neat oblong (**5**). Press together to seal and place in lightly oiled 12 × 23 cm (5 × 9 in) bread tins (pans). Cover loosely with oiled plastic wrap and a cloth and leave in a warm place until risen to the tops of the tins (**6**). The dough may also be formed into any shape such as plaits (braids), twists, cottage rounds or crescents and baked on a greased baking tray. Bake in a preheated hot oven (230°C/450°F, Gas Mark 8) for 15 minutes, then turn tins (pans) round, reduce heat to moderate (180°C/350°F, Gas Mark 4) and bake for a further 20–25 minutes. If you want a crisp crust all over, take bread out of tins (pans) and bake directly on oven bars for last 10 minutes. Bread is cooked if it sounds hollow when underside is knocked with the knuckles. If not, return to the oven for more baking. Turn bread out of tins (pans) as soon as it comes from oven, and cool on a wire rack. Makes 2 loaves.

VARIATION

Bread Rolls: Pat dough out into a rectangle, cut into 24 equal parts and shape each into a thick round. Turn under all round to make balls, pressing edges together underneath to seal. Place on greased baking trays, cover loosely with oiled plastic wrap and leave in a warm place until almost doubled in bulk. Bake in a preheated moderately hot oven (200°C/400°F, Gas Mark 6) for about 25 minutes, turning trays round halfway through baking time.

Toppings: These may be varied. For a crisp crust, brush dough with cold water and repeat several times during baking. For a golden shiny crust, brush with a little beaten egg; for a cottage loaf, dust the bread lightly with flour and for a rich crust, brush with melted butter. Coarse salt, poppy, sesame or caraway seeds,

Preparing Basic Bread

or coarse wheat can be sprinkled over the bread before baking for an attractive loaf with good flavour.

Farmhouse Bread

750 g/1½ lb (6 cups) wholewheat flour; 2 tsp salt; 1 tbsp sugar; 30 g/1 oz (1 cake) fresh (compressed) yeast, or 2½ tsp dried (active dry) yeast; 400 ml/⅔ pint (1⅔ cups) lukewarm water; 1 tbsp oil; beaten egg to glaze.

Mix the flour, salt and sugar in a warmed bowl. Blend the yeast with a little of the water, then stir into the remaining water and add to the dry ingredients with the oil. Mix to a soft dough. Turn out on to a lightly floured surface and knead for 10 minutes, until dough is smooth and does not stick to the fingers. Place dough in a lightly oiled plastic bag, and leave in a warm place for 1 hour or until doubled in size.

Knock back (punch down) firmly with the knuckles to remove air bubbles, then turn out on to a floured surface and knead again for 5 minutes. Divide dough into two pieces. Pat each one out to a rectangle, then fold into three and place in 2 greased 500 g/1 lb loaf tins (pans). Cover with a damp cloth and leave in a warm place for 30–40 minutes, until dough has risen to tops of tins (pans). Brush the tops with beaten egg and bake in a preheated hot oven (230°C/450°F, Gas Mark 8) for 40 minutes, or until well risen, brown, and hollow when tapped on the bottom. Cool on a wire rack. Makes 2 × 500 g (1 lb) loaves.

Bread Sauce

The traditional English sauce to serve with roast chicken, turkey and pheasant.

300 ml/½ pint (1¼ cups) milk; 1 onion stuck with 2 cloves; 1 small bay leaf; 30 g/1 oz (2 tbsp) butter; 1 slice stale white bread about 2 cm (¾ in) thick, crusts removed; salt and freshly ground white pepper; extra milk if needed; 1 tbsp fresh breadcrumbs, fried in butter (optional).

Put milk, onion, bay leaf, butter and bread, torn into large pieces, in a small saucepan. Season with salt and pepper. Place on very

low heat half covered with a lid. As milk heats, break bread down with a fork, then beat until consistency is porridge-like but free of lumps. Simmer, stirring gently, for 5 minutes, then cover and stand off the heat for 30 minutes or longer. Remove onion and bay leaf. Reheat gently, adding a little milk if necessary to give a thick consistency. Adjust seasoning and serve in a heated bowl, sprinkled with crisp fried breadcrumbs, if liked. Serves 4.

Bread and Butter Custard

6 thin slices buttered stale white or fruit bread, crusts removed; sugar; 2 tbsp currants or sultanas (golden raisins) or a mixture of both; 2 tsp chopped mixed candied peel.
CUSTARD: *2 eggs; 1 egg yolk; 1 tbsp sugar; ½ tsp vanilla essence (extract); 350 ml/12 fl oz (1½ cups) milk.*

Cut bread into triangles and layer in a buttered pie dish, sprinkling each layer with sugar, fruit and peel.
CUSTARD: Beat eggs and yolk together. Heat sugar, vanilla and milk together, stir into eggs and strain into dish. Stand 30 minutes. Bake in a preheated moderate oven (180°C/350°F, Gas Mark 4) for about 45 minutes or until pudding is set and puffy with a firm crusty top. Serve hot from the dish. Serves 4.

Bread Pudding

9 slices day-old bread; 180 g/6 oz (1 cup) mixed dried fruit; 90 g/3 oz (½ cup) firmly packed brown sugar; 2 tsp mixed spice (ground allspice); grated rind 1 lemon; 60 g/2 oz (4 tbsp) butter, softened; white sugar for sprinkling.

Soak bread in cold water to cover for 30 minutes, then squeeze out excess water and beat with a fork until smooth. Stir in fruit, sugar, spice and lemon rind and beat in butter in small pieces. Put mixture into a soufflé dish or deep ovenproof dish and bake in a preheated moderately hot oven (190°C/375°F, Gas Mark 5) for 1½ hours. Sprinkle surface generously with sugar before serving, accompanied by custard or cream. Serves 6.

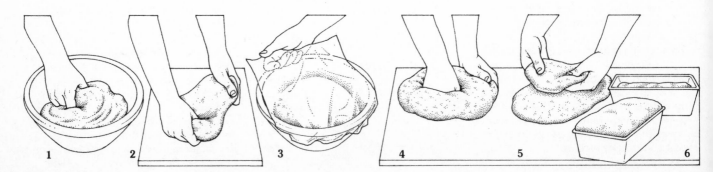

1   2   3   4   5   6

BRIOCHE

A little topknot-shaped yeast bread which, along with croissants, spells breakfast to millions in France. Eat brioches warm with chilled butter, preferably unsalted, and fruit conserve. They are also delicious toasted, or may be hollowed out and used as a case for cooked savoury food such as seafood, pâté or mushrooms. **See recipes**.

See also *Yeast Cookery*.

Brioche

15 g/½ oz (½ cake) fresh (compressed) yeast; 4 tbsp lukewarm water; 500 g/1 lb (4 cups) flour; pinch salt; 2 tbsp sugar; 3 eggs, lightly beaten; 175 ml/6 fl oz (¾ cup) lukewarm milk; 105 g/3½ oz (7 tbsp) butter, softened; beaten egg to glaze.

Dissolve yeast in water. Sift flour and salt into a large bowl. Take out 60 g/2 oz (½ cup) flour and work gradually into dissolved yeast to form a soft dough. Form dough into a ball and cut a cross in the top. Place ball in a bowl of warm water and leave for about 5 minutes or until it doubles in bulk (it will rise to the surface when ready). Meanwhile, make a well in centre of remaining flour, put in sugar, eggs and milk and stir them together. Drain yeast sponge, place it in the well and combine with egg mixture. Stir in flour gradually to form a soft dough. Beat dough vigorously with the hand until thoroughly mixed, then beat in butter.

Place the dough in a greased bowl, sprinkle lightly with flour, cover bowl with plastic wrap and let rise in refrigerator overnight or for at least 6 hours. Remove from refrigerator, punch dough down, and turn on to a floured board. Knead lightly, then divide into pieces the size of an egg. Cut off ⅓ of each piece; roll remainder of each piece into a ball and put into greased brioche moulds (deep fluted molds). Roll small pieces of dough into little 'tadpole'-shaped tops with tails. Cut a cross in top of each brioche, open a little and push tops in, tail down. Leave to rise 10–15 minutes in a warm place. Brush with beaten egg and bake in a preheated hot oven (220°C/425°F, Gas Mark 7) about 15 minutes or until golden-brown. Makes 12.

BRISLING

Small herring which may be smoked or canned. Also known as sprats (smelts) or sild, but canned under the name 'brisling' by Norwegian canners.

BROCCOLI

A member of the cabbage and cauliflower family. Choose broccoli with tight heads

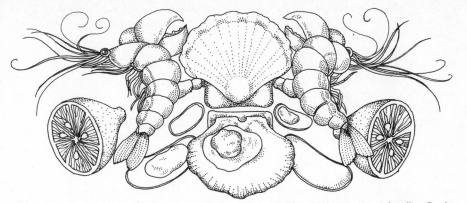

which look fresh and are dark green with no hint of yellow.

☐ **Basic Preparation:** Cut off most of the stalks, leaving 5–8 cm (2–3 in) attached to flower heads.

☐ **To Cook:** Drop into boiling salted water and cook, uncovered, about 8 minutes until just tender. Drain and serve immediately or refresh under cold running water to be served cold, or reheated later according to recipe instructions. **See recipes**.

Ways to Serve Broccoli

● Serve hot with melted butter and lemon juice or with Hollandaise Sauce (see page 369).

● Cover partially cooked broccoli in cheese sauce, sprinkle with grated cheese and bake in a preheated moderate oven (180°C/350°F, Gas Mark 4) for 20 minutes.

● Serve cooked broccoli cold, coated with Mayonnaise (see page 204).

Broccoli Parmesan

2 bunches broccoli, lightly cooked; 60 g/2 oz (4 tbsp) butter; 60 g/2 oz (½ cup) grated Parmesan or Romano cheese.

Sauté broccoli in butter until heated through. Arrange on heated platter and sprinkle with cheese. Serve very hot. Serves 4.

Broccoli Florentine

2 bunches broccoli, lightly cooked; 2–3 cloves garlic, chopped; 120 ml/4 fl oz (½ cup) olive oil; salt and freshly ground black pepper.

Cut broccoli into large pieces. Lightly sauté garlic in oil; do not allow to brown. Add broccoli and sauté until tender and heated through, turning pieces frequently. Season with salt and pepper. Serve as a separate course or as an accompaniment to a meat dish. Serves 4.

Broccoli Amandine

2 large bunches broccoli; 90 g/3 oz (6 tbsp) butter; 30 g/1 oz (¼ cup) slivered blanched almonds; 1 tbsp lemon juice.

Wash broccoli, pull off large, coarse leaves

and cut off tough lower parts of stalks. Cook in rapidly boiling water until just tender, about 15 minutes. Drain and arrange on heated serving platter. Melt butter and fry almonds until golden. Add lemon juice and pour over broccoli. Serves 4.

BROCHE, BROCHETTE

Broche is the French word for a spit or skewer, *brochette* is a little skewer, and foods *en broche* or *en brochette* are the French version of skewer cookery. **See recipes**.

Coquilles St. Jacques en Brochette

16 scallops; 2 tbsp olive oil; 1 tbsp lemon juice; 1 tsp chopped fresh basil, or ¼ tsp dried; 16 button mushrooms; 30 g/1 oz (2 tbsp) melted butter; salt and freshly ground black pepper; fresh breadcrumbs; lemon wedges.

Marinate scallops for 1 hour in olive oil, lemon juice and basil. Thread 4 skewers with scallops and mushrooms, alternating them. Brush with melted butter, season with salt and pepper and roll in breadcrumbs. Grill (broil) gently until crumbs are browned, about 2 minutes each side. Serve with lemon wedges. Serves 4 as a first course.

Broche Provençale

500 g (1 lb) lean lamb from the leg; 4 tbsp white wine; 2 tbsp olive oil; 1 tbsp chopped mixed fresh herbs, or 2 tsp dried mixed herbs chopped with 2 tbsp fresh parsley; 1 clove garlic, crushed; bay leaves; 250 g (8 oz) fatty belly pork (fresh pork sides); salt and freshly ground black pepper.

Trim skin and any gristle from lamb and cut it into 3 cm (1¼ in) cubes. Marinate for several hours, or overnight, in wine, oil, herbs and garlic. Cut bay leaves in half if large. Cut pork into 2.5 cm (1 in) pieces, about 1 cm (½ in) thick. Thread 4 skewers with lamb, bay leaf and pork, in that order, not pushing pieces too tightly together. Season with salt and pepper. Grill (broil) close to a preheated very hot grill (broiler) for 3–4 minutes on each side or until meats are well-browned but lamb cubes are still a little pink inside. Serves 4.

BROWNIES

These are American – a delicious cross between a cake and a biscuit (cookie). There are 2 basic types. One is very moist and chewy and called a 'fudge-type' brownie. The other is lighter and fluffier, more like a cake. They keep well in an airtight container, and carry well in lunch-boxes. **See recipes.**

Fudge Brownies

250 g/8 oz (1 cup) butter, softened; 500 g/1 lb (2 cups) sugar; 3 eggs; 1 tsp vanilla essence (extract); 125 g/4 oz (⅔ cup) dark chocolate, broken into pieces; 125 g/4 oz (1 cup) flour, sifted; ½ tsp salt; 125 g/4 oz (1 cup) chopped walnuts, almonds or pecans.

Cream half the butter with sugar until light and fluffy. Add eggs, one at a time, and beat until light. Stir in vanilla. Place remaining butter and chocolate in a heatproof basin over hot water and stir until melted. Cool, then combine well with creamed butter and sugar mixture. Stir in flour, salt and nuts. Pour into a greased shallow cake tin (pan) about 32 × 23 cm (13 × 9 in). Bake in a preheated moderate oven (180°C/350°F, Gas Mark 4) for 45 minutes or until a skewer inserted in centre comes out clean. Allow brownie mixture to cool in the tin (pan). Cut into small squares to serve. Makes about 48.

Two-Tone Brownies

(Cake Type)

250 g/8 oz (1 cup) butter, softened; 1 tsp vanilla essence (extract); ¼ tsp almond essence (extract); 500 g/1 lb (2 cups) sugar; 4 eggs; 250 g/8 oz (2 cups) flour, sifted with ½ tsp salt; 250 g/8 oz (2 cups) chopped almonds, pecans, walnuts or Brazil nuts; 60 g/2 oz (⅓ cup) dark chocolate, broken into pieces.
CHOCOLATE ICING (FROSTING): *210 g/7 oz (1½ cups) icing (confectioners) sugar, sifted; 1 tbsp (unsweetened) cocoa; ½ tsp vanilla essence (extract); ½ tsp cinnamon; 1 tsp butter, softened; about 1 tbsp hot water.*

Cream butter with essences and sugar until light and fluffy. Add eggs one at a time, beating well after each addition. Stir in flour and nuts, mixing well. Divide mixture in half. Melt chocolate in a heatproof basin placed over hot water. Stir melted chocolate into one half of batter. Drop alternate teaspoonfuls of dark and white batter into a greased 32 × 23 cm (13 × 9 in) cake tin (pan). Cut through batter several times, down and across, to give a marbled effect. Bake in a preheated moderate oven (180°C/ 350°F, Gas Mark 4) for 45 minutes or until a skewer inserted in centre comes out clean. Turn out on to a wire rack and cool.

ICING (FROSTING): Combine icing (confectioners) sugar, cocoa, vanilla, cinnamon and butter. Stir in hot water little by little to give a good spreading consistency. Ice (frost) brownie cake when cold, and cut into bars to serve. Makes 24.

BROWN SAUCE

See page 368 for recipe.

BRUSSELS SPROUTS

These look like tiny cabbages. The smaller they are, the better the flavour and texture. They are an excellent vegetable cooked until tender but not too soft and finished off with a little butter and pepper. Choose small, tight, bright green heads with no trace of yellow. Use them soon after buying as they fade quickly. Store, covered, in the refrigerator for a few days only.
☐ **Basic Preparation:** Remove any faded leaves and trim stems level with base of leaves. Unless sprouts are very tiny, cut a cross in the end of each stem to speed cooking. Rinse in cold water.
☐ **To Cook:** Drop into boiling salted water, cover and cook until tender but still firm (test a stem with a knife), 6–12 minutes depending on size. Drain and serve immediately with butter, freshly ground black pepper and a few drops of lemon juice. Breadcrumbs, fried in butter and tossed through, give a contrast in texture. **See recipes.**
Butter-braised Sprouts This recipe is an exception to the basic cooking method for Brussels Sprouts, but it is too delicious to omit. When chestnuts are added, the dish is a traditional accompaniment to roast turkey or goose.

Partially cook sprouts in boiling, salted water. Drain and dry. Heat 60 g/2 oz (4 tbsp) butter in a shallow flameproof dish, add sprouts and turn them to coat evenly with butter. Cover with buttered paper and bake in a preheated moderate oven (180°C/350°F, Gas Mark 4) for about 20 minutes. Cooked or canned chestnuts may be baked in the butter with the sprouts. A little cream is a nice addition, or the sprouts may be covered with buttered breadcrumbs and grated cheese and the top browned under a preheated grill (broiler).

Brussels Sprouts à la Crème

500–750 g (1–1½ lb) baby Brussels sprouts; 150 ml/¼ pint (⅔ cup) single (light) cream; nut of butter; salt; freshly ground white pepper.

Cook sprouts in boiling salted water for 7 minutes. Drain thoroughly. It is important that the sprouts are absolutely dry when added to the cream. Care must therefore be taken not to overcook them and to allow

time for draining. Meanwhile, put cream in the pan and bring to the boil. Add sprouts, butter, salt and pepper. Cover pan and shake well to mix the contents thoroughly. Set on a very low heat and simmer for a few minutes to allow flavour of cream to mix with that of sprouts and for cream to reduce and thicken. Serves 4–6.

Brussels Sprouts with Croûtons

500–750 g (1–1½ lb) Brussels sprouts; 30 g/1 oz (2 tbsp) butter; 1 shallot, chopped; ½ clove garlic, crushed; salt and freshly ground black pepper; lemon juice.
GARNISH: *125 g/4 oz (1 cup) croûtons (bread cubes fried in oil until crisp).*

Cook sprouts in boiling water, drain well and chop. Heat butter in a frying pan (skillet), add shallot and garlic and cook gently without browning too much. Add sprouts, season well with salt and pepper, and add a good squeeze of lemon juice. Serve garnished with croûtons. Serves 4–6.

Brussels Sprouts with Celery

500–750 g (1–1½ lb) Brussels sprouts; 2 sticks celery, sliced; 45 g/1½ oz (3 tbsp) butter; 1 onion, chopped; 1 tbsp flour; 350 ml/12 fl oz (1½ cups) milk; salt and freshly ground black pepper.
TOPPING: *melted butter; breadcrumbs.*

Cook sprouts in boiling water until tender and drain well. Blanch celery for 1 minute and drain. Melt butter and soften onion and celery for a few minutes. Sprinkle in flour, add milk and stir until blended. Add sprouts, season with salt and pepper and continue cooking for a few minutes to blend the whole, then turn into a flameproof dish. Sprinkle with melted butter and crumbs and brown in a preheated hot oven (220°C/425°F, Gas Mark 7) or under a preheated hot grill (broiler). Serves 4–6.

BUBBLE AND SQUEAK

Surely one of the most charming names given to any dish. It is believed to have sprung from the sound effects made by the ingredients as they sizzle in the pan.
To make Bubble and Squeak: Simply combine equal amounts of cold mashed potato and chopped, cooked cabbage (well drained). Season well and brown both sides in a little hot fat. It is good for breakfast with grilled (broiled) bacon, sausages or tomatoes.

BUN

Buns are usually made from a yeast dough, like bread, but are soft on top instead of having a crisp crust. They come in great variety – sweet, savoury, steamed or baked. The

B

name 'bun' is also given to some small cakes that don't contain yeast, and to the famous Scottish delicacy, Black Bun, a rich fruit filling enclosed in pastry (dough) (see page 38).

See also Hot Cross Buns and Chelsea Buns (page 477).

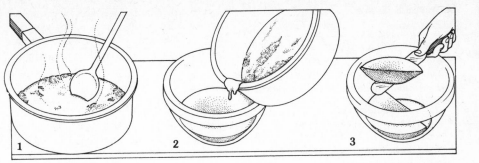

BUTTER

The delicate flavour and enriching qualities of butter are important to the cooking of many nations. It is used as a spread, as a dressing, as a cooking medium and as an ingredient in a great range of recipes from sauces to cakes. Butter should be stored in the refrigerator, in its original protective wrapping or container, or in a covered container kept especially for it. It may also be stored in the freezer for up to 6 months, with a moisture-proof wrapping over the original wrapping.

Salted or Unsalted Butter: Salting improves the keeping quality of butter. It is a matter of preference which to use as a spread, but be sure to use unsalted butter if it is specified in a recipe – the flavour of some Continental cakes and biscuits depends on it, and some foods are less inclined to stick if fried in unsalted rather than salted butter.

Clarified Butter: This has had the water and non-fat solids removed. It is sold as *ghee* (its name in Indian and other Asian cooking where it is extensively used), or you can make it yourself. Cut salted or unsalted butter into pieces, melt and heat slowly, without browning **(fig 1)**. Remove from heat and allow to stand for a few minutes: a milky residue will sink to the bottom and the clear yellow liquid above it is the clarified butter **(2)**. Pour off the butter and allow to solidify **(3)**. The residue may be added to soups or sauces to enrich them.

Savoury Butters

Butter creamed with flavourings such as mustard, curry powder, nuts, garlic, capers, herbs or cheese, can be used as a spread for sandwiches or canapés, or chilled and cut into slices to melt on top of steak, fish and other foods.

Maître d'Hôtel Butter Cream 125 g/4 oz (½ cup) butter with 2 tbsp finely chopped parsley, freshly ground white pepper and 1 tbsp lemon juice, beaten in little by little. Add salt to taste, form into a roll about 2.5 cm (1 in) in diameter, wrap in plastic wrap and chill until firm. Serve in slices on grilled (broiled) steak, chops, liver or fish.

Mustard Butter Cream 125 g/4 oz (½ cup) butter with 2 tbsp French (Dijon) mustard and 1 tbsp chopped parsley. Add salt and freshly ground white pepper to taste. Use as a spread for ham or roast beef sandwiches or canapés, or form into a chilled roll as for Maître d'Hôtel Butter, above, and serve on grilled (broiled) or fried steak, grilled (broiled) kidneys or liver.

Preparing Clarified Butter

Tarragon Butter Cream 125 g/4 oz (½ cup) butter with 2 tbsp chopped fresh tarragon, or 2 tsp dried tarragon chopped with 2 tbsp parsley. Beat in 1 tbsp lemon juice, little by little, and add salt and freshly ground white pepper to taste. Use as a spread for chicken sandwiches or canapés, or form into a chilled roll as for Maître d'Hôtel Butter, above, and serve on grilled (broiled) or roast chicken or grilled (broiled) fish.

Marchand de Vin Butter Boil 5 tbsp red wine and 5 tbsp beef stock (bouillon) with 2 tbsp chopped shallots and freshly ground black pepper until reduced to about 2 tbsp. Cool. Cream 125 g/4 oz (½ cup) butter and, little by little, beat in wine mixture. Add 1 tbsp chopped parsley and salt and pepper to taste. Form into a chilled roll as for Maître d'Hôtel Butter, above, and serve on steak, hamburgers or calf's liver, or stir into gravies, casseroles and pan sauces to enrich them.

See also *Anchovy Butter*.

Sweet Butters

Sweet butters are excellent for topping waffles, crumpets, pancakes, toast and muffins. Cream unsalted butter and beat in, a little at a time, clear or creamed honey, golden (light corn) syrup or maple syrup, brown sugar and cinnamon.

BUTTERMILK

Traditionally, the thin liquid left after butter has been churned from milk. Nowadays, the term usually refers to a different product, made commercially by adding a culture to skim milk to give a slightly acid-flavoured beverage. Chilled buttermilk is refreshing alone, mixed with equal parts of orange juice or blended with soft fruit such as strawberries. Buttermilk adds lightness and flavour to pancakes, scones, muffins and cakes, and is a good low-kilojoule (low-calorie) substitute for oil or cream in salad dressings. **See recipes**.

Buttermilk Date Cream

The combination of buttermilk and orange juice always gives a marvellous flavour, and the addition of fresh dates puts this superb dessert in the dinner party class.

180 g/6 oz (¾ cup) sugar; 120 ml/4 fl oz (½ cup) water; 1½ tbsp gelatine; extra 5 tbsp water; 250 ml/8 fl oz (1 cup) buttermilk; 150 ml/¼ pint (⅔ cup) orange juice; pinch salt; 250 ml/8 fl oz (1 cup) double (heavy) cream; 275 g/9 oz (1½ cups) fresh dates, stoned and cut into slivers.
DECORATION (optional, see method):
1 orange; 120 ml/4 fl oz (½ cup) water; 1 tbsp sugar.

Heat sugar with 120 ml/4 fl oz (½ cup) water, stirring until sugar has dissolved. Bring to the boil and remove from heat. Soften gelatine in the 5 tbsp of cold water for 10 minutes. Stir gelatine mixture into sugar syrup until dissolved, then combine with buttermilk, orange juice and salt. Chill mixture until it thickens to the consistency of unbeaten egg white, but do not let it set. Whip cream until it holds soft peaks and fold it into buttermilk mixture together with slivered dates. Pour into a serving bowl. Cover and chill until set.
OPTIONAL DECORATION: For special occasions decorate this dessert with strips of rind from orange, using a vegetable peeler (the rind is the orange part of the skin, not including white pith). Cut rind into fine matchstick lengths and cook gently in water with sugar for about 5 minutes or until the rind becomes clear. Peel white pith from orange and cut between the dividing membranes to take out skinless segments. Arrange on the dessert and strew with rind. Serves 8.

Buttermilk Scones

250 g/8 oz (2 cups) self-raising flour; 1 tsp salt; 1 tsp sugar; ½ tsp bicarbonate of soda (baking soda); 60 g/2 oz (4 tbsp) butter; 150–175 ml/¼ pint – 6 fl oz (⅔–¾ cup) buttermilk.

Sift all dry ingredients into a mixing bowl. Rub (cut) in butter until mixture resembles breadcrumbs. Add enough buttermilk to make a fairly soft dough. Turn out on to a floured board. Knead lightly, then pat or roll the dough to about 1 cm (½ in) thickness. Cut into rounds with a 5 cm (2 in) cutter. Place on ungreased baking trays and bake in a preheated hot oven (230°C/450°F, Gas Mark 8) for 10–12 minutes or until golden. Makes about 16 scones.

Buttermilk Bread

A Canadian recipe for quick-bread.

310 g/10 oz (2½ cups) flour; ¼ tsp bicarbonate of soda (baking soda); 1 tsp salt; 175 ml/6 fl oz (¾ cup) buttermilk; 90 g/3 oz (6 tbsp) butter, melted; 1 tbsp black treacle (molasses) or golden (light corn) syrup.

Sift flour, soda and salt into a bowl. Stir in buttermilk, 60 g/2 oz (4 tbsp) butter and the black treacle (molasses) or syrup to form a soft dough. Transfer dough to a floured surface and knead for 5 minutes or until smooth and elastic. Pat into a round loaf about 15 cm (6 in) in diameter. With a sharp knife, score loaf to make 6 wedges, cutting about 1 cm (½ in) into dough. Place on a baking tray. Bake in a preheated moderately hot oven (190°C/375°F, Gas Mark 5) for 30 minutes or until a skewer inserted in centre comes out clean. Brush hot loaf with remaining melted butter and cool on a wire rack. Serve cut into wedges. Serves 6.

BUTTERNUT PUMPKIN/SQUASH

A member of the gourd family, with a smooth, tender yellow skin which gives it its name. The flavour is similar to that of the hard-skinned pumpkin – perhaps a little sweeter – and the texture is lighter and less mealy. Butternut is excellent baked or steamed and mashed, like other pumpkin. It may also be stuffed for a main course.

Stuffed Butternut Pumpkin

1 small butternut pumpkin (squash); 4 tbsp water; 30 g/1 oz (2 tbsp) butter; 1 onion, finely chopped; 1 rasher (slice) streaky bacon, rind removed and chopped; 180 g/6 oz (¾ cup, firmly packed) minced (ground) cooked or uncooked beef, pork, veal or lamb, or 125 g/4 oz (1 cup) grated cheese; 1 large, ripe tomato, peeled, seeded and chopped; 1 tbsp chopped mixed fresh herbs, or 1 tsp dried herbs mixed with 1 tbsp chopped fresh parsley; 60 g/2 oz (1 cup) fresh breadcrumbs; salt and freshly ground black pepper.

Cut pumpkin (squash) in half lengthways and scoop out seeds and fibres. Place cut sides down in a baking dish, add water and bake in a preheated moderate oven (180°C/350°F, Gas Mark 4) for about 30 minutes until just tender. Meanwhile, heat butter and cook onion and bacon gently until onion is soft. If using uncooked meat, add it and cook, stirring and breaking down lumps with a fork, until lightly browned. Otherwise, mix onion with meat or cheese off the heat. Add tomato, herbs, half the breadcrumbs and salt and pepper. Scoop out flesh from pumpkin, leaving a thin wall. Dice flesh, add to stuffing mixture and fill pumpkin shells. Sprinkle with remaining breadcrumbs. Return to oven and bake for 15–20 minutes or until topping is brown and crisp. Serves 4.

BUTTERSCOTCH

The name of a hard toffee made from butter, sugar and water, and of a popular flavouring for cakes, biscuits, sauces, icing (frosting) and puddings. Butterscotch Sauce is delicious over ice cream and waffles. **See recipes**.

Easy Butterscotch Sauce

60 g/2 oz (4 tbsp) butter; 90 g/3 oz (½ cup) firmly packed brown sugar; 2 tbsp cold water; 1 egg yolk, beaten; 4 tbsp double (heavy) cream, whipped; ½ tsp vanilla essence (extract).

Melt butter over low heat, add brown sugar and cook 2 minutes, stirring. Add cold water and egg yolk and continue cooking gently, stirring, until mixture thickens. Do not allow to boil. Remove from heat and cool, then chill. Fold in whipped cream and vanilla just before serving. Serves 4.

Butterscotch Filling

45 g/1½ oz (3 tbsp) butter; 90 g/3 oz (½ cup) firmly packed brown sugar; 250 ml/8 fl oz (1 cup) milk; 3 tbsp flour; ½ tsp salt; 2 eggs, lightly beaten; ½ tsp vanilla essence (extract).

Mix butter and sugar in a heavy saucepan and heat gently, stirring, until melted. Stir in 120 ml/4 fl oz (½ cup) milk and cook for 2 minutes. Blend flour, salt and remaining milk together, stir into hot mixture and cook, stirring, until boiling. Stir a little of this mixture into beaten eggs, pour back into saucepan and stir over low heat until thickened a little more. Do not allow to boil. Stir in vanilla. Cool and use as a cake or pie filling. Makes about 450 ml/¾ pint (2 cups).

Butterscotch Toffee

120 ml/4 fl oz (½ cup) water; pinch salt; 750 g/1½ lb (3 cups) sugar; ½ tsp cream of tartar; 60 g/2 oz (4 tbsp) butter.

Bring water to the boil in a large, heavy saucepan. Remove from heat, add salt and sugar and stir until dissolved. Return to fairly high heat, cover and return to the boil. Add cream of tartar mixed with a little water and boil, covered, 2 minutes. Remove lid and boil without stirring until mixture reaches hard-crack stage (155°C/315°F or when a little dropped in cold water will break). Remove from heat and stir in butter. Pour into buttered shallow tins (pans) and mark into squares or bars when almost set, or drop teaspoonfuls on to a buttered marble slab or foil. Makes about 60 small pieces.

CABBAGE

There are many varieties of cabbage: the tightly-packed round cabbage, the striking red cabbage and the crinkly Savoy are the most familiar.

There is also a relative called Chinese cabbage (bok choy), pale green and slender, which is milder in flavour than other cabbage. Cabbage is an economical vegetable and is popular cooked, pickled (as in sauerkraut), or raw in salads.

□ **Basic Preparation:** It is usually cut into wedges or shredded for cooking. Trim heavy stem and inside ribs from wedges. To shred, cut a head downward, into quarters. Hold each quarter by the stem, with the top pressed firmly on a board, and use a sharp knife to cut thin slices from the side. Discard heavy ribs and stems.

□ **To Cook:** The old way to cook cabbage is to boil it for hours. The new way is to steam it until just crisp-tender, or for quite a different effect, gently braise in stock with added flavourings. **See also recipes.**

STEAMED CABBAGE Shred cabbage or cut into wedges. Wash in a colander under cold running water. Melt a knob of butter in a heavy saucepan and add cabbage. Season with salt and pepper, plus a grating of nutmeg if desired. Cover tightly and steam on brisk heat until cabbage is just tender, with a slight crunch – about 5 minutes for shredded cabbage, 8–10 minutes for wedges. Shake pan frequently to toss cabbage with butter and to prevent scorching.

BRAISED CABBAGE Shred half a small red or green cabbage. Heat enough butter to cover the bottom of a heavy flameproof casserole, and toss cabbage until coated in butter. Season with salt and pepper and add enough stock to come to top of cabbage, plus a spoonful of vinegar for red cabbage. Cover tightly and bake in a preheated moderate oven (160°C/325°F, Gas Mark 3) or cook over a gentle heat for about 1 hour or until cabbage is very tender and stock absorbed. If desired, aniseed, nutmeg, caraway seeds or other flavourings may be added to the cabbage. Serves 4.

Cabbage Cooked Chinese-Style

2 tbsp peanut oil; 1 clove garlic, crushed; 2 spring onions (scallions), cut into short lengths; 4 thin slices fresh ginger, finely chopped; ½ cabbage, finely shredded; salt and freshly ground black pepper.

Heat oil in a wok or heavy frying pan (skillet) with garlic, spring onions (scallions) and ginger. Add cabbage, toss to coat with oil, cover pan and steam for 5 minutes, tossing once or twice. Cabbage should be still a little crisp to the bite. Season with salt and pepper if necessary and serve immediately. Serves 4.

Cabbage Rolls
(Dolmas)

8 cabbage leaves; 500 g/1 lb (2 cups) minced (ground) beef or pork and veal mince; 1 small onion, finely chopped; 2 tbsp finely chopped parsley; 1 clove garlic, crushed; ½ tsp dried thyme; 1 tsp salt; pinch cayenne; 2 tbsp vinegar; 3 tbsp brown sugar; 2 tsp chopped capers; 1 egg, beaten; 30 g/1 oz (2 tbsp) butter; 1 × 425 g/14 oz can tomatoes, chopped.

Blanch cabbage leaves in boiling salted water for 2 minutes, then drain and plunge into cold water. Drain again and pat dry with paper towels. Combine all remaining ingredients except butter and tomato juice. Divide into 8 portions and place one portion on the stem end of each cabbage leaf. Fold sides over filling and roll up into a cylinder. Place stuffed rolls close together in a buttered casserole dish, seam sides down. Dot with butter and pour tomatoes over. Cover tightly and bake in a preheated moderate oven (180°C/350°F, Gas Mark 4) for 1 hour or until tender. Serves 4.

Sweet and Sour Red Cabbage

1 small red cabbage, shredded; 90 g/3 oz (6 tbsp) butter; 1 large onion, finely chopped; 2 large cooking apples, cored and thinly sliced; pinch caraway seeds; 2 tbsp honey; 2 tbsp vinegar; salt and freshly ground black pepper.

Soak cabbage in cold water to cover for 15 minutes. Heat butter in a wide heavy saucepan or deep frying pan (skillet) and fry onion gently until soft. Lift cabbage from water with hands, leaving it moist, and add to pan with remaining ingredients. Stir to combine, then cover and simmer very gently for 1½ hours. By this time, cabbage should be very tender and all liquid absorbed. (If necessary, add a little boiling water during cooking to prevent cabbage from sticking.) Adjust seasoning, and spoon into a heated serving dish. Serves 4.

Baked Cabbage with Cream

½ cabbage, shredded; 175 ml/6 fl oz (¾ cup) single (light) cream; 1 tbsp sugar; ½ tsp salt; ½ tsp paprika; 60 g/2 oz (½ cup) chopped nuts; 30 g/1 oz (½ cup) fresh breadcrumbs; 45 g/1½ oz (⅓ cup) grated mature (sharp) cheese.

Steam cabbage as described left. Place in a buttered casserole dish. Combine cream, sugar, salt, paprika and nuts and pour over cabbage. Sprinkle with breadcrumbs and bake in a preheated moderate oven (160°C/325°F, Gas Mark 3) for 30 minutes or until cabbage is very tender. Sprinkle with cheese and place under a preheated grill (broiler) until cheese melts. Serves 4.

Cabbage au Gratin

1 medium cabbage, quartered; 350 ml/12 fl oz (1½ cups) Béchamel Sauce (page 368); salt and freshly ground black pepper; pinch nutmeg; 60 g/2 oz (½ cup) grated Gruyère cheese.
TOPPING: Fresh white breadcrumbs; melted butter.

Cook cabbage in plenty of boiling salted water until just tender. Drain, refresh and press well to remove water. Remove core and chop moderately finely. Mix with the sauce, using sufficient to give a creamy mixture. Season well with salt and pepper, add a little nutmeg, and cook gently for 10 minutes. Stir in grated cheese, reserving a little for the top. Put mixture in flameproof dish and sprinkle with reserved cheese mixed with crumbs and melted butter. Brown in a hot oven or under a preheated grill (broiler). Serves 6.

Cabbage Lorraine

1 cabbage, quartered; 2 onions, sliced; 1 tbsp oil or butter; 2 large tomatoes, peeled, seeded and chopped; 1 tbsp flour; 175 ml/6 fl oz (¾ cup chicken stock; salt and freshly ground black pepper; finely chopped parsley; 3–4 tbsp sour cream.

Blanch cabbage in boiling water for 5–10 minutes. Drain well, pressing gently to remove water. Arrange in a baking dish. Soften onions in oil or butter. Lift from fat, draining well, and spoon over cabbage. Put tomatoes into fat in which onions were fried, dust in flour, add stock and bring to the boil, stirring continuously. Season with salt and pepper, add parsley and spoon over cabbage. Cook in a preheated moderate oven (180°C/350°F, Gas Mark 4), basting occasionally, for about 1 hour. Fifteen minutes before serving, spoon over sour cream. Serves 6.

CABINET PUDDING

A traditional English pudding made of cubed bread or cake, dried fruit and custard.

Steamed Cabinet Pudding

30 g/1 oz (2 tbsp) butter; 2 tbsp sugar; 4 slices white bread, crusts removed and diced; 90 g/3 oz (½ cup) sultanas (golden raisins), raisins or mixed dried fruit; 2 eggs; 250 ml/8 fl oz (1 cup) milk; pinch salt; ½ tsp vanilla essence (extract).

Use all the butter to grease a 1 litre/2 pint (4 cup) pudding basin (mold). Sprinkle with 1 tbsp sugar. Put bread into a bowl with fruit. Beat eggs, add remaining ingredients, including remaining sugar, and pour over bread. Allow to soak for 30 minutes, then

spoon into prepared basin (mold). Cover with greased greaseproof (waxed) paper and a snap-on lid, or tie down with 2 layers of foil. Place in a saucepan with boiling water to come halfway up sides of basin (mold), cover with lid. Steam for 1 hour. Replenish boiling water as necessary. Unmould and serve with custard, cream or ice cream. Serves 4.
NOTE: Cabinet pudding may be baked. Grease a 1 litre/2 pint (4 cup) ovenproof dish. Follow recipe instructions and spoon mixture into prepared dish. Cover with greased foil and bake in a preheated moderate oven (180°C/350°F, Gas Mark 4) for 35–40 minutes or until set.

CAESAR SALAD

One of the world's great salads, created by chef Alexander Cardini, working at the San Diego race track, in honour of his brother Caesar – also a chef, working in England.

Caesar Salad

1 head Cos (romaine) lettuce; 4 anchovy fillets; 1 clove garlic, crushed; 30 g/1 oz (2 tbsp) butter; 8 slices French bread; 1 egg; salt and freshly ground black pepper; 1 tbsp lemon juice; 3 tbsp olive oil; 1 tsp Worcestershire sauce; 3 tbsp grated Parmesan cheese.

Wash and dry lettuce leaves and crisp in refrigerator. Mash anchovies with garlic and butter, and spread on bread. Bake bread in a preheated cool oven (150°C/300°F, Gas Mark 2) for 25–30 minutes or until crisp. Allow to cool. Place egg in boiling water for 50 seconds and remove. Place lettuce in a large bowl, season with salt and pepper and break egg over. Beat the lemon juice, oil and Worcestershire sauce together and pour over lettuce. Add bread slices and cheese and very gently roll lettuce in the dressing. Serve at once. Serves 2 as a main course, 4 as a side salad or first course.

CAFE AU LAIT

French for coffee with milk. In France and most European countries it means coffee and hot milk in equal proportions.

CAKES

Most cakes fall into one of four main categories – Butter Cakes, Sponge Cakes, Quick-mix Cakes and rich Continental Cakes, which are often served for dessert with coffee. They are classified according to the proportion of fat, sugar and eggs they contain and the method by which they are made.

Very young children take great pleasure from novelty cakes decorated for special party occasions.

BUTTER CAKES

One of the most popular categories of cakes, having the fine flavour that butter can give. They are enjoyed, too, for their own particular taste, whether it be the basic butter mixture or flavoured with vanilla, lemon, orange, ginger or chocolate, etc. They can stand on their own, unadorned, or can be dressed up with various icings (frostings) and fillings. Butter cakes keep well because of the high proportion of butter to flour. Cooking margarines may replace the butter, if liked. You will, however, trade the distinctive flavour for a measure of economy, a spongier texture and a somewhat greater volume.

Basic Butter Cake

125 g/4 oz (½ cup) butter; 180 g/6 oz (¾ cup) caster sugar; 1 tsp vanilla essence (extract); 2 eggs, lightly beaten; 250 g/8 oz (2 cups) self-raising flour; pinch salt; 120 ml/4 fl oz (½ cup) milk.

Cream butter with sugar and vanilla until light and fluffy. Gradually beat in eggs (if using an electric mixer, add eggs one at a time and beat well after each). Sift flour and salt together 3 times and fold into creamed mixture alternately with milk, beginning and ending with flour. Pour into 2 greased and bottom-lined 20 cm (8 in) sandwich tins (layer pans). Lightly smooth tops and bake in a preheated moderate oven (180°C/350°F, Gas Mark 4) for 25–30 minutes or until a fine skewer inserted in centre comes out clean. Cool on a wire rack and fill and ice (frost) as desired.
NOTE: The cake may also be baked in a deep 20 cm (8 in) square or round tin (pan). It will then take 45–50 minutes to bake.
VARIATIONS
Lemon Cake: Add grated rind 1 lemon and 2 tsp lemon juice. Omit vanilla.
Cherry Cake: Add 125 g/4 oz (½ cup) glacé (candied) cherries (dusted with flour to prevent them sinking).
Seed Cake: Add 1 tbsp caraway seeds to batter and sprinkle 1 tsp on top before baking.
Fruit Squares: Add 90 g/3 oz (½ cup) mixed fruit and bake in a 28 × 19 cm (11 × 7½ in) tin (pan).

Cup Cakes

125 g/4 oz (½ cup) butter; 180 g/6 oz (¾ cup) sugar; 1 tsp vanilla essence (extract); 2 eggs, lightly beaten; 250 g/8 oz (2 cups) self-raising flour; pinch salt; 150 ml/¼ pint (⅔ cup) milk; Glacé Icing (page 164).
DECORATION: *nuts, glacé (candied) cherries, candied angelica etc.*

Cream butter with sugar until light and fluffy. Add vanilla, then beat in eggs a little at a time. Sift flour and salt 3 times and fold into creamed mixture alternately with milk, beginning and ending with flour. Spoon into patty cases set in muffin tins (pans). Bake in a preheated moderately hot oven (190°C/375°F, Gas Mark 5) for 15 minutes or until golden and when a skewer inserted in centre comes out clean. Cool on a wire rack, then ice. Makes about 20.
VARIATIONS
Butterfly Cakes: Use the same mixture as for Cup Cakes, but increase oven temperature to moderately hot (200°C/400°F, Gas Mark 6), and bake cakes in hottest part of the oven. The tops of the cakes will rise in a peak. When cool, cut a slice from the top of each cake and reserve. Top cakes with a peak of sweetened whipped cream. Cut cake slices in half and arrange on top of cream to form 'wings'.
Sultana Cup Cakes: Omit vanilla and add 1 tsp grated lemon rind. Fold 90 g/3 oz (½ cup) sultanas (golden raisins) into creamed mixture with flour.
Cherry Cup Cakes: Fold 125 g/4 oz (½ cup) glacé (candied) cherries into creamed mixture with flour.

Orange Cake

125 g/4 oz (½ cup) butter or soft margarine; grated rind and juice 1 medium orange; 180 g/6 oz (¾ cup) caster sugar; 2 eggs, separated; 250 g/8 oz (2 cups) self-raising flour; pinch salt; 2–3 tbsp milk; sifted icing (confectioners) sugar.

Cream butter with orange rind and sugar until light and fluffy. Add egg yolks one at a time and beat well after each. Sift flour with salt and fold into creamed mixture alternately with strained orange juice and milk, beginning and ending with flour. Beat egg whites until stiff peaks form and gently fold in. Spoon into 20 cm (8 in) round or square tin (pan), or 21 × 11 cm (8½ × 4½ in) loaf tin (pan) that has been greased with melted butter, bottom-lined with greased greaseproof (waxed) paper and dusted with flour. Bake in a preheated moderate oven (180°C/350°F, Gas Mark 4) for 35–40 minutes or until a skewer inserted in centre comes out clean. Turn out on to a wire rack and when cool dust with sifted icing (confectioners) sugar.

C

Chocolate Sandwich Cake

This sandwich (layer) cake has the special flavour of raspberry jam.

2 tbsp (unsweetened) cocoa powder; 2 tbsp raspberry jam; 125 g/4 oz (½ cup) butter; 180 g/6 oz (¾ cup) caster sugar; 1 tsp vanilla essence (extract); 2 large eggs, lightly beaten; 250 g/8 oz (2 cups) self-raising flour, sifted; extra raspberry jam for filling; icing (confectioners) sugar, sifted or Chocolate Glaze (page 73).

Mix cocoa to a smooth thin paste with a little boiling water. Add jam and mix in sufficient boiling water to make 175 ml/6 fl oz (¾ cup). Allow to cool. Cream butter with sugar until light and fluffy. Beat in vanilla then gradually add eggs, mixing well after each addition. Fold in flour alternately with cocoa and jam mixture. Spread evenly in 2 greased and bottom-lined 18 cm (7 in) sandwich tins (layer pans). Bake in a preheated moderate oven (180°C/350°F, Gas Mark 4) for 25–30 minutes or until cakes spring back when lightly touched with the finger. Turn out on to wire racks to cool. Sandwich together with raspberry jam and top with sifted icing (confectioners) sugar or with chocolate glaze.

SPONGE CAKES

There are two ways of making a sponge cake. The first method is to beat whole eggs with sugar until thick and light, then fold in the flour – this is called a Whisked Sponge. The second way is to separate the eggs, make a meringue of the whites and sugar, then add beaten yolks and flour. This is called a Sponge Sandwich (Layer Cake).

The French, however, make a slightly different version called *Génoise* (see page 143). Swiss Rolls (see page 423) also belong to the sponge family.

Whisked Sponge

3 eggs; 180 g/6 oz (¾ cup) caster sugar; grated rind ¼ lemon; 125 g/4 oz (1 cup) self-raising flour; pinch salt; 1 tsp melted butter; 2 tbsp hot water.
FILLING AND TOPPING: *250 ml/8 fl oz (1 cup) double (heavy) cream; few drops vanilla essence (extract); 1–2 tsp sugar; pulp 2 passionfruit; 180 g (6 oz) sliced strawberries, or 2 sliced bananas tossed with a little lemon juice; 1 tbsp icing (confectioners) sugar, sifted.*

Combine eggs, sugar and lemon rind in a heatproof bowl and place it over a saucepan containing simmering water. Whisk for 10 minutes or until a little of the mixture when lifted on the whisk falls in a smooth, steady ribbon on to mixture in the bowl. Remove from heat and continue whisking for about 5 minutes until cool. Sift flour and salt and, using a metal spoon, gently fold

flour into egg mixture, alternately with combined butter and hot water. Turn into 2 × 18 cm (7 in) sandwich tins (layer pans) that have been greased, bottom-lined with greased greaseproof (waxed) paper and dusted with a mixture of 1 tsp each flour and sugar. Bake cakes in a preheated moderate oven (180°C/350°F, Gas Mark 4) for 20–25 minutes or until cakes spring back when touched lightly with the finger. Immediately turn out on to a wire rack to cool.
FILLING AND TOPPING: Whip cream with vanilla and sugar until stiff. Combine half the cream with selected fruit and use to sandwich cake together. Decorate top with whipped cream and dust with icing (confectioners) sugar.

Sponge Sandwich

3 eggs, separated; 180 g/6 oz (¾ cup) caster sugar; 125 g/4 oz (1 cup) self-raising flour; pinch salt; 1 tsp melted butter; 3 tbsp hot water.
TO FINISH: *jam, whipped cream.*

Beat egg whites until stiff. Gradually add sugar and continue whisking until thick and glossy. Add egg yolks all at once and whisk only until combined. Sift flour and salt together twice. Sift flour again directly over egg mixture, and fold in lightly and evenly. Sprinkle melted butter and hot water over top, and fold in quickly and lightly. Pour into 2 greased and floured 18 cm (7 in) sandwich tins (layer pans). Bake in a preheated moderate oven (180°C/350°F, Gas Mark 4) for 20 minutes. Turn out and cool on a wire rack. When cold, sandwich together with jam and decorate with whipped cream.

Blowaway Sponge

4 eggs, separated; 125 g/4 oz (½ cup) caster sugar; generous 60 g/2 oz (½ cup) arrowroot; 1 tbsp flour; 1 tsp cream of tartar; ½ tsp bicarbonate of soda (baking soda); 1 tsp vanilla essence (extract).
FILLING AND DECORATION: *sweetened whipped cream; sifted icing (confectioners) sugar.*

Beat egg whites until stiff. Gradually add sugar and continue whisking until thick and glossy. Add egg yolks all at once and whisk only until combined. Sift together arrowroot, flour, cream of tartar and bicarbonate of soda (baking soda) and fold lightly into egg mixture with vanilla. Gently pour mixture at once into 2 greased and floured 20 cm (8 in) sandwich tins (layer pans). Bake in a preheated moderate oven (180°C/350°F, Gas Mark 4) for 25 minutes or until cakes have shrunk slightly from sides of tins (pans) and centres spring back when touched with a finger. Cool on wire racks. Sandwich together with whipped cream and dust top of cake with icing (confectioners) sugar.

Australian Chocolate Cake

90 g/3 oz (½ cup) cooking chocolate; 2 tbsp water or coffee; 5 eggs; 150 g/5 oz (⅔ cup) caster sugar; 180 g/6 oz (⅔ cup) self-raising flour, sifted; 1 tsp vanilla essence (extract); grated rind 1 lemon; 60 g/2 oz (4 tbsp) butter, melted.
FILLING AND ICING (FROSTING): *180 g/6 oz (1 cup) cooking chocolate; 250 ml/8 fl oz (1 cup) double (heavy) cream; 2 tbsp icing (confectioners) sugar, sifted; 1 tbsp rum.*

Melt chocolate in a heatproof basin over gently simmering water. Stir in water or coffee and cool slightly. Beat eggs until light and frothy. Add sugar and beat until very thick and mousse-like. Fold flour into egg mixture with vanilla, lemon rind, butter and chocolate mixture. Pour into a greased, lined and floured 23 cm (9 in) loose-bottomed tin (springform pan). Bake in a preheated moderate oven (180°C/350°F, Gas Mark 4) for 45–50 minutes or until cake springs back when lightly pressed in the centre. Cool with the spring released.
FILLING AND ICING (FROSTING): Melt chocolate and cool. Whip cream, fold in icing (confectioners) sugar and rum. Reserve a little melted chocolate and fold remainder through cream to create a ripple effect. When cold, split cake in half and sandwich together with half the mixture. Spread remainder over top of cake and drizzle melted chocolate over.

QUICK-MIX CAKES

These are also sometimes referred to as 'one bowl' cakes, because they are made by mixing all the ingredients simultaneously in one bowl. To make mixing easy, the fat type specified is often melted butter, but can be oil or sour cream.

Don't try to adapt ordinary recipes to this method, but use those especially created for quick mixing. **See recipes.**

Boiled Fruit Cake

An economical and easy cake that keeps well.

750 g/1½ lb (4 cups) mixed dried fruit; 180 g/ 6 oz (¾ cup) butter or margarine; 225 g/ 7½ oz (1¼ cups) firmly packed brown sugar; 1 tbsp grated lemon rind; 2 tsp mixed spice (ground allspice); 250 ml/8 fl oz (1 cup) water; 2 tbsp rum or sherry; 125 g/4 oz (1 cup) plain (all-purpose) flour; 180 g/6 oz (1½ cups) self-raising flour; ¼ tsp salt; 3 eggs; ¼ tsp bicarbonate of soda (baking soda).

Place fruit, butter, sugar, lemon rind, spice, water and rum or sherry in a saucepan and bring slowly to the boil. Reduce heat and simmer for 5 minutes, then remove from heat and leave until lukewarm. Sift flours and salt together. Beat eggs with bicarbonate of soda (baking soda). Stir flour and beaten eggs alternately into fruit mixture. Pour into a deep 20 cm (8 in) cake tin (pan) that has been greased and lined with 2 layers of greaseproof (waxed) paper. Bake in a preheated moderate oven (180°C/350°F, Gas Mark 4) for 45 minutes, then reduce heat to moderate (160°C/325°F, Gas Mark 3) and bake for a further 45 minutes or until a skewer inserted in centre comes out clean. Turn out of tin (pan) and cool on a wire rack before removing paper. Store in an airtight container for up to 2 weeks.

Melt and Mix Chocolate Cake

1 tbsp white vinegar; 250 ml/8 fl oz (1 cup) evaporated milk; 180 g/6 oz (1½ cups) flour; pinch salt; 60 g/2 oz (½ cup) cocoa powder (unsweetened); 1½ tsp bicarbonate of soda (baking soda); 350 g/12 oz (1½ cups) caster sugar; 150 g/5 oz (½ cup plus 2 tbsp butter, melted; 1 tsp vanilla essence (extract); 2 eggs. TO FINISH: raspberry jam or whipped cream; Rich Chocolate Icing (Frosting) (page 164) or sifted icing (confectioners) sugar.

Mix vinegar with evaporated milk. Sift flour, salt, cocoa, soda and sugar into a bowl. Add butter to dry ingredients with soured milk, vanilla and eggs. Beat vigorously until smooth, about 2 minutes. Pour into 2 greased and bottom-lined 20 cm (8 in) sandwich tins (layer pans). Bake in a preheated moderate oven (180°C/350°F, Gas Mark 4) for 30–35 minutes or until a

skewer inserted in centre comes out clean. Cool on a wire rack. Sandwich together with raspberry jam or whipped cream and top with chocolate icing (frosting) or dust with icing (confectioners) sugar.

Caramel Nut Cake

210 g/7 oz (1¾ cups) flour; pinch salt; 1¾ tsp baking powder; 180 g/6 oz (1 cup) firmly packed brown sugar; 125 g/4 oz (½ cup) butter, softened (or soft margarine); 2 eggs; 120 ml/4 fl oz (½ cup) milk; 1 tsp vanilla essence (extract); 90 g/3 oz (¾ cup) chopped walnuts, almonds or pecans; sifted icing (confectioners) sugar.

Sift flour, salt, baking powder and sugar into a bowl. Add butter, eggs, milk and vanilla and beat vigorously until well blended. Fold in nuts. Spoon into a greased and bottom-lined 23 × 33 cm (9 × 13 in) cake tin (pan). Bake cake in a preheated moderate oven (180°C/350°F, Gas Mark 4) for 30–35 minutes or until a skewer inserted in centre comes out clean. Cool on a wire rack, then dust with icing (confectioners) sugar. Cut into squares to serve.

CONTINENTAL CAKES

Europe has given us a heritage of superb cakes. Generally speaking, Continental cakes have a richer, closer texture than butter, sponge or quick-mix cakes. When they contain a high proportion of ground nuts instead of flour they are often referred to as *tortes*, and when they are split into many layers and decorated they may be called *gâteaux*. Rich butter-cream fillings are used, and different types of liqueurs, chocolate or coffee are favourite flavourings. Nuts and fruit are used as decorations, and frequently the cake is chilled before serving.

Springform tins (pans) make it easy to turn out the richer mixtures, and the interestingly-shaped *gugelhopf, bundt* and ring tins (pans) give authentic shapes to Continental cakes. **See recipes.**

See also *Gâteau.*

Bienenstich

210 g/7 oz (1¾ cups) flour; 2 tsp baking powder; pinch salt; 75 g/2½ oz (5 tbsp) butter; 75 g/2½ oz (⅓ cup) caster sugar; 2 tbsp milk; 1 egg.
TOPPING: 75 g/2½ oz (5 tbsp) butter; 125 g/4 oz (½ cup) sugar; 125 g/4 oz (1 cup) blanched, slivered almonds; 1 tsp vanilla essence (extract).
FILLING: 250 g/8 oz (1 cup) butter; 4 tbsp caster sugar; 250 ml/8 fl oz (1 cup) thick cold egg custard (dairy custard from the supermarket may be used); 2 tsp vanilla essence (extract).

Sift together flour, baking powder and salt. Cream butter with sugar until light and fluffy. Combine milk and egg and gradually add to creamed mixture. Work in dry ingredients to make a soft dough. Press dough evenly over bottom of greased 20 cm (8 in) loose-bottomed tin (springform pan).
TOPPING: Melt butter in a saucepan over low heat, add sugar and stir until combined. Remove from heat, stir in almonds and vanilla and allow to cool. Spread over dough. Bake in a preheated moderately hot oven (190°C/375°F, Gas Mark 5) for 40 minutes. Release spring and cool on a wire rack.
FILLING: Cream butter and sugar together until light and fluffy, then gradually beat in cold custard and vanilla. When cold split cake into 2 layers and sandwich together with filling.

Finnish Sour Cream Cake

2 eggs, beaten; 450 ml/¾ pint (2 cups) sour cream; 500 g/1 lb (2 cups) caster sugar; 3 drops almond essence (extract); 350 g/12 oz (3 cups) flour; 1 tsp bicarbonate of soda (baking soda); ½ tsp salt; 1 tsp cinnamon; 1 tsp ground cardamom.

Place eggs, sour cream, sugar and almond essence (extract) in a bowl and mix until combined. Sift flour with soda, salt and spices and add gradually to egg mixture, beating until batter is smooth. Pour into greased 23 cm (9 in) gugelhopf, bundt or ring tin (pan) that has been dusted with sugar. Bake in a preheated moderate oven (180°C/350°F, Gas Mark 4) for 1¼ hours or until a skewer inserted in centre comes out clean. Leave in tin (pan) for 10 minutes before turning out to cool on a wire rack.

Mocha Nut Cake

5 eggs, separated; 250 g/8 oz (1 cup) caster sugar; 1 tbsp instant coffee powder; 60 g/2 oz (½ cup) flour, sifted; 60 g/2 oz (½ cup) finely ground hazelnuts or walnuts; sifted icing (confectioners) sugar. FILLING: 450 ml/¾ pint (2 cups) double (heavy) cream; 2 tbsp icing (confectioners) sugar, sifted; 1 tbsp instant coffee powder dissolved in 1 tbsp brandy.

Beat egg whites until soft peaks form. Gradually beat in sugar until mixture stands in stiff peaks. Beat egg yolks separately until thick and light, then fold into whites. Mix coffee, flour and nuts together and fold into egg mixture gently but thoroughly until no white streaks remain. Spoon into greased and floured 23 cm (9 in) ring or loose-bottomed tin (springform pan). Bake in a preheated moderate oven (160°C/325°F, Gas Mark 3) for 50–55 minutes or until cake springs back when lightly pressed with a finger. Cool on a wire rack.

FILLING: Whip cream until thick, then fold in sugar and coffee dissolved in brandy. Split cake into 4 layers. Just before serving, sandwich together with filling and sprinkle icing (confectioners) sugar on top.

Chocolate Toffee Cake

125 g/4 oz (½ cup) butter; 125 g/4 oz (⅔ cup) firmly packed brown sugar; 2 eggs; 60 g/2 oz (½ cup) self-raising flour; 60 g/2 oz (½ cup) ground almonds; 75 g/2½ oz (2½ squares) cooking chocolate, grated; extra grated chocolate (optional).
TOFFEE ICING (FROSTING): 60 g/2 oz (4 tbsp) butter; 125 g/4 oz (⅔ cup) firmly packed brown sugar; 2 tbsp golden (light corn) syrup; 120 ml/4 fl oz (½ cup) single (light) cream; sifted icing (confectioners) sugar (optional).

Cream butter with sugar until light and fluffy. Beat in eggs one at a time, then fold in flour and ground almonds. Add chocolate and mix well. Pour into a greased and lined 20 cm (8 in) cake tin (pan). Bake in a preheated moderate oven (180°C/350°F, Gas Mark 4) for 1¼ hours or until firm to a light touch. Leave in the tin (pan) for 5 minutes, then turn carefully on to a wire rack to cool.

TOFFEE ICING (FROSTING): Put butter, sugar and syrup into a saucepan. Stir over a gentle heat until sugar has dissolved. Bring to the boil, reduce heat immediately and simmer, without stirring, for 5 minutes. Remove from the heat and slowly pour in cream in a steady stream, beating well with a wooden spoon. Leave to cool and thicken. If you prefer a thicker icing (frosting), add sufficient icing (confectioners) sugar to give the desired consistency. Spread over cake and swirl surface with a spoon. Decorate with extra grated chocolate, if wished.

Vienna Cakes

180 g/6 oz (¾ cup) butter, softened; ½ tsp vanilla essence (extract); 68 g/2¼ oz (½ cup)

icing (confectioners) sugar, sifted; 210 g/7 oz (1¾ cups) flour; extra sifted icing (confectioners) sugar; raspberry jam.

Cream butter with vanilla and sugar until light and fluffy. Fold in flour. Pipe or spoon mixture into paper patty cases set in tartlet pans and make a slight dent in the top of each cake. Bake in a preheated moderately hot oven (190°C/375°F, Gas Mark 5) for 10–12 minutes. Leave to cool. Sift extra icing (confectioners) sugar over each cake and drop a little raspberry jam into the centres. Makes 12.

CHILDREN'S CAKES

Plain cakes are best when the party is for tiny children. **See recipes.**

Little Bear Maypole Cake

2 × 20 cm (8 in) Basic Butter Cakes (page 52); 1½ quantities Butter Cream (page 164); 90 g/3 oz (¼ cup) raspberry jam; 2 packets chocolate-coated finger biscuits; 2–3 drops green food colouring; 90 g/3 oz (1 cup) desiccated (shredded) coconut; stick and narrow ribbons for maypole; 5 or 6 small model bears; artificial or sugar flowers.

Sandwich cakes together with a little of the butter cream and some of the raspberry jam. Place cake on a board or tray covered with foil and spread a thin layer of butter cream around sides of cake. Stick chocolate-coated finger biscuits all around sides of cake with the tops just showing above edge to represent a fence. Add food colouring to coconut and mix through with your fingertips to distribute evenly. You may need to add more colour according to the shade desired. Brush top of cake with remaining jam and cover it with an even layer of coconut. Make maypole with a long thin stick covered with foil, with one of the ribbons wound around it. Position the maypole in the centre of the cake, pushing the stick through until it reaches the board. Stand the little model bears around edge of cake. Attach several ribbons to top of maypole with a drawing pin (thumb tack), cover pin with a rosette of butter cream and arrange the ribbons over the cake, taking them out to the bears. The maypole and the edge of the cake may be decorated with artificial or sugar flowers, if you wish. Use remaining butter cream to decorate the biscuit fence.

Winifred White Mouse

1 packet butter cake mix, or 1 quantity Basic Butter Cake mixture (page 52); 1 quantity Butter Cream (page 164); 135 g/4½ oz (1½ cups) desiccated (shredded) coconut; 1 licorice stick; 2 pink marshmallows; 4 white pipe cleaners.

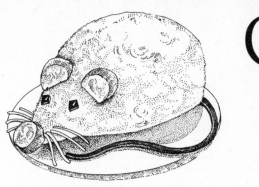

Make cake mixture according to directions on the packet, or follow the recipe. Pour into a well greased 1.25 litre/2 pint (4 cup) ovenproof pudding basin (mold) and bake in a preheated moderate oven (180°C/350°F, Gas Mark 4) for 1 hour or until a skewer inserted in centre comes out clean. Turn on to wire rack to cool. Cover a board with foil. Trim flat top of cake so the mouse will sit evenly and invert cake on the board. Cut the cake into a mouse shape by trimming away one side from top to base so that it is narrower and slopes more, and trimming base of this slope into a slight point for the nose. Cover cake evenly with butter cream and sprinkle thickly with coconut, pressing on firmly. Position a long piece of licorice at the broad end of the mouse to form a tail and cut 2 small pieces of licorice to make the eyes. Halve one of the marshmallows and use for the ears; use the whole marshmallow for the nose. Halve pipe cleaners and place on each side of the nose for the whiskers.

CALAMARI

The Italian name for squid. Found in many parts of the world, and prized for their sweet, tender flesh. See Squid.

CAMOMILE

A plant which resembles a daisy, and is cultivated for the pleasantly aromatic flavour and scent of its flower heads. Dried, they are used for camomile tea, in aperitifs and hair rinses.

CANAPE

A French word meaning 'couch', which is used to describe bite-sized pieces of bread, toast, biscuits (crackers) or pastry (dough) topped with savoury food. Canapés may be hot or cold, simple or elaborate, but should be decorative.

Canapé Bases

White or wholewheat toast, cut into strips, squares or circles; crispbreads; Melba toast; pumpernickel and rye breads; plain or flavoured savoury biscuits (crackers); fried bread (croûtes); pastry (dough) rounds; sliced French bread, bread sticks or rolls; home-made quick breads; tiny split hot scones or pancakes.

Canapé Butters

Use these alone, or garnish as desired; the garnish may be a dab of the flavouring – caviar, sardine, olive, etc.

Sardine Butter Soften 125 g/4 oz (½ cup) butter and combine with 125 g/4 oz can mashed sardines, 1 tsp Worcestershire sauce, 1 tbsp tomato ketchup, 1 tbsp lemon juice and salt and freshly ground black pepper to taste.

Caviar Butter Soften 60 g/2 oz (4 tbsp) butter and combine with 2 tbsp caviar or lumpfish roe, 1 tsp grated onion, 1 tsp lemon juice and salt and freshly ground black pepper to taste.

Olive Butter Soften 60 g/2 oz (4 tbsp) butter and combine with 2 tbsp finely chopped stuffed olives and 1 tsp grated onion.

Canapé Toppings

Blend all ingredients well together.

Liverwurst and Bacon 90 g/3 oz (½ cup) good liverwurst (Latvian, chicken etc.); 2 bacon rashers (slices), rind removed, grilled (broiled) and crumbled; few drops Tabasco (hot pepper) sauce or chilli sauce; 1 tbsp lemon juice.

Roquefort 90 g/3 oz (6 tbsp) cream cheese; 30 g/1 oz (¼ cup) Roquefort cheese; 4 tbsp single (light) cream; salt and freshly ground black pepper to taste.

Cheese and Ham 90 g/3 oz (¾ cup) grated mature (sharp) Cheddar cheese; 125 g/4 oz (½ cup) devilled ham spread; 1 tsp Worcestershire sauce; 4 tbsp single (light) cream.

Egg and walnut 4 hard-boiled (hard-cooked) eggs, finely chopped; 30 g/1 oz (¼ cup) finely chopped walnuts; 1 tbsp finely chopped shallot; Mayonnaise (page 204) to bind.

Camembert Canapés A make-your-own canapé plate – this is a German favourite, great with beer. On individual plates place a wedge of Camembert, a small mound of finely chopped onion and smaller mounds of finely chopped anchovies and canned pimientos. Salt shakers, pepper mills and oil and vinegar cruets should be on the table, with platters of thickly buttered rye and pumpernickel bread. Each person mixes his own canapé topping according to taste.

Hot Canapés

Snails Use any of the canapé toppings suggested. Roll out Plain Shortcrust Pastry (page 274) into an oblong shape, spread generously with chosen filling and roll up like a Swiss (jelly) roll. Chill for 1 hour, then cut into 1 cm (½ in) slices and arrange on greased baking trays. Bake in a preheated moderately hot oven (200°C/400°F, Gas Mark 6) until golden. Serve hot.

Rarebit Puffs Beat 2 egg whites until they form soft peaks. Fold in 125 g/4 oz (1 cup) grated mature (sharp) Cheddar cheese, 1 tsp Worcestershire sauce, 1 tsp paprika, ½ tsp dry mustard, salt and ground black pepper. Spread over round cracker biscuits. Place under a hot grill (broiler) until topping is puffed and brown. Makes 24.

Hot Crabmeat Canapés Flake 1 × 185 g/6 oz can drained crabmeat and mix in 1 tbsp chopped onion, 1 tsp chilli sauce, 3 tbsp mayonnaise. Spread on crustless toast triangles, going right to the edges. Place under a hot grill (broiler) until browned. Makes 24.

CANNELLONI

Meaning 'big pipes', these are an Italian speciality – tubes of pasta which are filled with a savoury stuffing. The pasta is usually cooked first and, after filling, the cannelloni are sprinkled with melted butter and grated cheese or with a sauce, and browned in the oven.

Cannelloni are usually bought as dried pasta, already formed into tubes. If you prefer, you can make your own fresh pasta dough, cut it into squares and roll round the filling (in some areas, you may be able to buy fresh pasta). Thin crêpes, fried on one side only, may be used instead of pasta dough. For cannelloni recipes see page 270.

CANTALOUP

See Melon.

CAPER

The small, olive-green bud of a bush native to the Mediterranean and North Africa. Capers are hand-picked, salted and pickled in vinegar. Their piquant flavour adds zest to white sauces, mayonnaise, salads, creamed foods and fish dishes; they also make an excellent garnish for open sandwiches.

Caper Sauce The traditional sauce for boiled mutton and lamb. Add drained capers to Velouté or Béchamel Sauce (page 368) in the proportion of 1 tbsp per 250 ml/8 fl oz (1 cup) of sauce, or according to taste.

Egg and Caper Sauce Add 1 chopped hard-boiled (hard-cooked) egg per 250 ml/8 fl oz (1 cup) Caper Sauce, above, and serve on poached or steamed fish, smoked fish, vegetables or hot corned beef.

CAPSICUM

See Pepper.

CARAMEL

The familiar flavour of caramel results when sugar is cooked long enough to form a rich golden-brown syrup. It is used in cakes, sauces and puddings, to line moulds for creams and custards, and to colour Parisian Essence (Extract).

To caramelize: This means to dissolve sugar slowly and boil steadily without stirring until a dark brown colour. Put 250 g/8 oz (1 cup) sugar and 120 ml/4 fl oz (½ cup) water in a small saucepan and stir over gentle heat, until sugar dissolves. Bring to the boil and cook quickly without stirring, until golden-brown. Dip pan in cold water (it will make a loud hissing noise but there's no need for alarm) to prevent caramel from getting darker. **See recipes.**

Caramel Syrup This syrup, used to flavour cakes and biscuits (cookies) keeps indefinitely if stored in a covered container in the refrigerator. Gently melt 250 g/8 oz (1 cup) sugar in a heavy based pan until golden. When bubbles appear over the whole surface, remove from heat and very slowly pour in 250 ml/8 fl oz (1 cup) boiling water. Cool. Makes 350 ml/12 fl oz (1½ cups).

Creamy Caramel Sauce

125 g/4 oz (½ cup) butter; 180 g/6 oz (1 cup) firmly packed brown sugar; 1 × 225 g/7½ oz can cream.

Melt butter in a heavy saucepan, add sugar and stir over low heat until dissolved. Increase heat and boil for 3 minutes. Remove from heat and when bubbles subside, carefully stir in cream. Makes about 350 ml/12 fl oz (1½ cups).

Butter Caramels

Caramels should be soft and chewy; the longer you cook them, the harder they become, so be sure to stop when they are the colour of milky coffee.

C

125 g/4 oz (½ cup) butter; 2 tbsp golden (light corn) syrup; 350 g/12 oz (1½ cups) sugar; 1 × 400 g/13 oz can sweetened condensed milk; 120 ml/4 fl oz (½ cup) water; large pinch cream of tartar; 1 tsp vanilla essence (extract).

Place all ingredients except vanilla in a heavy saucepan and stir constantly over fairly low heat until mixture is pale brown – a little dropped into cold water should form a firm but pliable ball. Remove from heat. Stir in vanilla and pour into a buttered 15 cm (6 in) square tin (pan). When nearly set, mark into squares. Wrap squares in wax paper or cellophane when cold. Makes about 36.

CARAWAY

Tiny pungent seeds used in many popular sweet and savoury dishes in Europe, which add flavour to cheeses and cakes, rye breads, casseroles, salads, sauerkraut and potatoes. In Europe the root of the plant is boiled and eaten with parsley sauce.

CARBONNADE DE BOEUF
(Carbonnade Flamande)

A traditional dish from Belgium with a rich sauce based on beer.

Carbonnade de Boeuf

750 g (1½ lb) chuck steak, cubed; 2 tbsp dripping; 2 onions, sliced; 1 tbsp flour; 250 ml/8 fl oz (1 cup) beer; 250 ml/8 fl oz (1 cup) hot beef stock (bouillon); 1 clove garlic, crushed; 1 bouquet garni; salt and freshly ground black pepper; ½ tsp nutmeg; ½ tsp sugar; 1 tsp vinegar; 8 slices French bread, 5 mm (¼ in) thick; French (Dijon) mustard.

Brown meat in hot dripping in flameproof casserole, then lower heat and add onions. Cook for 2 minutes. Sprinkle with flour, pour on beer and hot stock (bouillon) and stir until boiling. Add garlic, bouquet garni, salt, pepper, nutmeg, sugar and vinegar. Cover and cook in a preheated moderate oven (160°C/325°F, Gas Mark 3) for 2 hours or until meat is tender. Remove casserole from oven, remove bouquet garni, skim off fat and spoon it over bread slices. Spread bread thickly with mustard. Arrange on top of casserole, pushing bread well into gravy (it will float again to the top). Cook uncovered for a further 30 minutes or until bread forms a good brown crust. Serves 4–6.

CARDAMOM

The dried seed pods and the little aromatic dark brown seeds of cardamom are used in curry, pickles, pilau and sweet dishes. There are several varieties – green, white and black –

and it is best to buy the seed pods and grind the seeds as needed. **See recipes.**

Cardamom Chicken

6 chicken legs; 1 clove garlic, crushed; ½ tsp salt; 1 tsp chopped fresh ginger; 1 tsp ground cardamom; ½ tsp nutmeg; ½ tsp black pepper; 1 tsp chilli powder; 1 tbsp butter; 2 tbsp oil; 60 g/2 oz (½ cup) toasted almonds; 120 ml/4 fl oz (½ cup) water.
GARNISH: *1 hard-boiled (hard-cooked) egg, sliced; 2 tomatoes, sliced.*

Dry chicken legs on paper towels. Combine garlic, salt, ginger, cardamom, nutmeg, pepper and chilli and rub over chicken legs. Allow to stand for 1 hour. Heat butter and oil in frying pan (skillet) and fry chicken until golden-brown. Add almonds and cook for 2 minutes. Stir in water, cover and simmer over low heat for about 15–20 minutes or until chicken is cooked. Serve chicken on a bed of boiled rice, garnished with egg and tomato slices. Serves 4–6.

Cardamom Creams

180 g/6 oz (2 cups) desiccated (shredded) coconut; 450 ml/¾ pint (2 cups) milk; 6 whole cardamom pods; 4 eggs; 60 g/2 oz (¼ cup) caster sugar; 1 tsp freshly ground cardamom; 250 ml/8 fl oz (1 cup) single (light) cream.

To make cardamom coconut milk, place coconut, milk and cadamom pods in a heavy saucepan. Bring to the boil slowly, then reduce heat and simmer for 5 minutes to extract flavour from cardamom pods. Cool slightly. Strain through a sieve and squeeze out as much of the milk as possible from coconut. Beat eggs, sugar and freshly ground cardamom until well blended. Add cardamom coconut milk (this should measure 250 ml/8 fl oz (1 cup) and cream and mix well. Strain custard mixture into 6–8 individual moulds or mousse custard pots and set in a roasting tin (pan) of hot water. Bake in a preheated moderate oven (160°C/325°F, Gas Mark 3) for 35 minutes or until custard is set and a knife inserted

near centre comes out clean. Allow to cool, then chill for several hours or overnight. Unmould on to serving dish or plates, or leave in mousse pots. Serves 6–8.

Rice Blancmange

750 ml/1¼ pints (3 cups) milk; 3 tbsp rice flour; 3 tbsp sugar; ½ tsp ground cardamom; ¼ tsp nutmeg; 1 tsp vanilla essence (extract); 2 tbsp blanched, slivered almonds.

Mix 120 ml/4 fl oz (½ cup) of the milk with flour to make a smooth paste. Add sugar to remaining milk and bring to the boil. Remove from heat, stir in milk and flour mixture, return to heat and stir constantly until mixture boils and thickens. Boil, stirring, for 3–5 minutes. Remove from heat and stir in cardamom, nutmeg, vanilla and half the almonds. Pour into 6 individual little pots or a 750 ml/1¼ pint (3 cup) dish and chill. Sprinkle with remaining nuts. Serves 6.

CARPETBAG STEAK

Claimed as an Australian contribution to gastronomy. A thick cut of steak becomes a 'carpetbag' when it has a pocket cut into it and is filled with oysters.

Carpetbag Steak

250 g (8 oz) rump, boned sirloin or fillet (tenderloin) steak, cut 2.5 cm (1 in) thick; 4 canned oysters, drained; freshly ground black pepper; parsley to garnish.

Trim excess fat and any gristle from steak and cut a deep pocket in it, about halfway through. Fill pocket with oysters, season with pepper and close opening with wooden toothpicks or poultry pins. Place steak under a preheated very hot grill (broiler), and cook on each side for about 5 minutes for medium-rare. Serve garnished with parsley. Steak may also be pan-fried. Use a thick frying pan (skillet), oil bottom lightly and cook steak over high heat for 1 minute each side or until a brown crust forms. Lower heat to moderate and continue cooking 3–4 minutes each side. Serves 1.

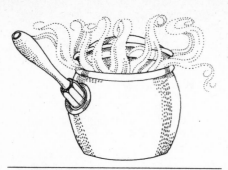

CARROT

Carrots are one of the three great aromatic vegetables, the others being onion and celery. They are used constantly in casseroles, soups and stews and they are the traditional accompaniment to boiled beef. There is also an excellent carrot soup, Potage Crécy (see page 395).

☐ **Basic Preparation:** Young carrots need only be lightly scraped and, if they are tiny, cooked whole. They are delicious cooked in a very little water and a little butter, in a tightly-closed pan that permits them to steam until they are just tender. A little sugar or honey added to the water brings out the natural sweetness of the carrots.

Older carrots should be scraped or skins peeled with a swivel-bladed vegetable peeler, and sliced or cut into strips or dice and lightly boiled.

☐ **To Boil:** Cook, with lid on, in boiling salted water until tender. Young whole carrots will take about 15–20 minutes, older carrots, cut in thick slices, will take 15 minutes. Drain, glaze with butter and toss in chopped parsley or coat with a creamy white sauce. **See also recipes.**

Golden Carrots Scrape 500 g (1 lb) young carrots and slice thinly. Drop into a small saucepan containing 3–4 tbsp boiling chicken stock, cover and simmer 3 minutes or until tender but still crisp. Sprinkle with salt and, if liked, add a dab of butter. Serves 4.

Carrots Vichy Scrape 500 g (1 lb) young carrots and cut into slices. Melt 60 g/2 oz (4 tbsp) butter in a heavy saucepan, add carrots, 2 tbsp water and 2 tsp sugar. Cover and cook gently until almost tender, then remove lid and continue cooking until water evaporates leaving a light syrup. Toss carrots to glaze and sprinkle with salt and chopped parsley. Serves 4.

Carrots Julienne Scrape 500 g (1 lb) carrots and cut into julienne (matchstick) strips. Put into a saucepan with 2 tbsp each of butter and water and cook, covered, for 6–7 minutes or until tender. Drain off any remaining liquid; add salt, freshly ground black pepper and 5–6 mint leaves, cut into fine strips. Toss over low heat for 1 minute and serve immediately. Serves 4–6.

Dilled Carrots Scrape 500 g (1 lb) young carrots and cut lengthways into quarters.

Place in a saucepan with 175 ml/6 fl oz (¾ cup) dill-pickle juice and simmer, covered, 10–15 minutes until crisp-tender. Cool, then chill overnight in the liquid. Drain carrots and toss them with 1½ tbsp each snipped fresh dill and chives and 175 ml/6 fl oz (¾ cup) sour cream. Serve with fish or other salads. Serves 4–6.

Lemon-glazed Carrots Scrape 500 g (1 lb) young carrots and cut lengthways into quarters, or leave whole if very small. Simmer, covered, in salted water for 10–15 minutes or until crisp-tender; drain. Melt 60 g/2 oz (4 tbsp) butter in a frying pan (skillet), add 1 tbsp sugar, 2 tsp chopped parsley and 1½ tbsp lemon juice and heat gently. Add carrots and toss over medium heat until glazed. Serves 4.

Carrot Cake

350 g/12 oz (3 cups) flour; 500 g/1 lb (2 cups) caster sugar; 1 tsp salt; 1½ tsp bicarbonate of soda (baking soda); 180 g/6 oz (1 cup) undrained canned crushed pineapple; 250 g/8 oz (2 cups) grated carrot; 4 eggs; 350 ml/12 fl oz (1½ cups) salad oil; 1 tsp vanilla essence (extract); 125 g/4 oz (1 cup) chopped walnuts.

Sift flour, sugar, salt and soda together into a large mixing bowl. Add pineapple, carrot, eggs, oil and vanilla and beat until combined. Stir in chopped nuts. Spoon batter into a well greased bundt tin (pan) or 2 deep 20 cm (8 in) ring tins (pans). Bake in a preheated moderate oven (180°C/350°F, Gas Mark 4) for 1 hour or until a skewer inserted in centre comes out clean.

CASHEW

The nut of a tree indigenous to Brazil but now grown in many tropical countries. Cashews are sold raw or roasted, salted or unsalted. They are delicious as a snack food or made into a butter like peanut butter. They are also used as an ingredient for sweet and savoury dishes in both Western and Eastern cuisines.

Chinese Chicken with Cashews

1 egg white; 2 tbsp dry sherry; 1 tsp salt; pinch white pepper; 1 tsp cornflour (cornstarch); 2 half-breasts of chicken, skinned and boned; 120 ml/4 fl oz (½ cup) peanut oil; 125 g/4 oz (1 cup) shelled roasted cashews; 1 spring onion (scallion), chopped; 1 green or red pepper, seeded and cut into 1 cm (½ in) squares; 250 g/8 oz (1 cup) canned sliced bamboo shoots; 1 tbsp soy sauce; 1 tsp sugar; 1 extra tsp cornflour (cornstarch) mixed with 1 tbsp water; hot boiled rice to serve.

Beat egg white lightly with a fork and mix in 1 tbsp sherry, the salt, pepper and cornflour

(cornstarch). Slice chicken into 2.5 cm (1 in) slices, add to egg white mixture and turn pieces to coat them. Heat 3 tbsp oil in a wok or frying pan (skillet) over high heat. Add chicken and stir-fry until golden. Remove from heat. In another pan, heat 3 tbsp oil and fry cashews gently until golden-brown. Remove with a slotted spoon and drain on paper towels. Add remaining oil to pan, heat and stir-fry spring onion (scallion), green pepper and bamboo shoots for 1 minute. Add remaining sherry with soy sauce, sugar and cornflour (cornstarch) mixed with water. Stir until thickened. Add chicken, turn to coat with sauce and heat through. Sprinkle with cashews and serve hot with boiled rice. Serves 3–4.

CASSATA

Meaning 'in a case or chest', *cassata* is the name of two famous Italian desserts. As the name suggests, both were traditionally made in the form of a case with a filling, but they are often made in layers instead.

Cassata Gelata Line a mould with softened ice cream, fill centre with lightly sweetened, whipped cream, mixed with chopped glacé (candied) fruit and chopped sugared almonds, and freeze until firm. If preferred, ice cream and whipped cream mixture can be arranged in layers.

Cassata Siciliana

500 g/1 lb (2 cups) Ricotta cheese; 250 g/8 oz (1 cup) caster sugar; pinch cinnamon; 60 g/2 oz (⅓ cup) dark chocolate, grated; 2 tbsp sweet liqueur; 2 tbsp chopped pistachios or pine nuts; 3 tbsp chopped glacé (candied) fruit; 1 × 20 cm (8 in) round or square sponge cake (page 53).
DECORATION: *sifted icing (confectioners) sugar; extra glacé (candied) fruit.*

Beat Ricotta and sugar together until fluffy. Reserve half for topping. Add cinnamon, chocolate and liqueur to remaining mixture and mix well. Fold in nuts and fruit. Line bottom of a 1.2 litre/2 pint (5 cup) bowl or mould with greaseproof (waxed) paper. Cut cake into 1 cm (½ in) slices and use about ¾ of them to line mould. Fill centre with Ricotta mixture, cover with remaining slices of cake and chill, covered, for several hours or overnight. Turn out of mould, coat with reserved topping, dust with icing (confectioners) sugar and decorate with glacé (candied) fruit. Alternatively the cake may be split into 3 or 4 layers and filled with the Ricotta mixture. Chill, coat with topping, and decorate as described. Serves 8–10.

Right: Basic Bread (page 45), Ring Doughnuts (page 481)

CAULIFLOWER

A fresh head of cauliflower has very white, closely-packed florets, and surrounding leaves still fresh and green. Before cooking, all the dark outside leaves should be broken off. Boiled cauliflower needs a sauce of some kind; cauliflower and cheese have an affinity. Raw sprigs are often served as part of a dish of *crudités* with garlic mayonnaise.

□ **To Cook:** Separate florets, leaving no more than about 2.5 cm (1 in) of stem. Drop into boiling salted water and cook, uncovered, for about 5 minutes. Drain.

Boiled Whole Cauliflower Cut off thick stem and make deep incisions with a sharp knife in remaining smaller stems, so that heat will penetrate them more easily. Sometimes tender young leaves are left on; when lightly cooked they enhance the look of the dish.

Boil head of cauliflower, stem down, in a large pan of lightly salted water, uncovered, for about 15–20 minutes. When stems can be easily pierced with a fork, it is fully cooked. Drain it carefully without breaking off any florets and place on a heated serving platter. Pour on melted butter, Mornay Sauce (see page 368) or fried crumbs. **See recipes.**

Cauliflower Parmigiana

1 large cauliflower, trimmed into florets; salt; 45 g/1½ oz (3 tbsp) butter; 125 g/4 oz (2 cups) fresh breadcrumbs; 60 g/2 oz (½ cup) grated Parmesan cheese; 2 tbsp chopped parsley.

Cook florets in boiling salted water for about 8 minutes or until tender. Drain carefully in a colander. Melt butter and fry breadcrumbs until golden. Butter a shallow baking dish, sprinkle with a little grated Parmesan cheese and arrange florets in dish. Sprinkle with breadcrumbs mixed with remaining Parmesan cheese. Bake in a preheated hot oven (230°C/450°F, Gas Mark 8) for about 5 minutes or until golden. Remove from oven and sprinkle parsley over. Serves 6.

Cauliflower au Gratin

1 cauliflower, trimmed into florets; salt; 250 ml/8 fl oz (1 cup) Mornay Sauce (page 368); 60 g/2 oz (½ cup) grated Parmesan cheese; 30 g/1 oz (2 tbsp) butter, melted.

Cook florets in boiling salted water for about 8 minutes or until tender. Drain. Arrange stem side down in a baking dish, cover with mornay sauce, sprinkle with cheese, and then with melted butter. Bake in a preheated moderately hot oven (200°C/400°F, Gas Mark 6) for 5–6 minutes or until the surface is golden. Serves 6.

Left: Little Bear Maypole Cake (page 55)

CAVIAR

The salted roe of the sturgeon, which is considered a great delicacy. The caviar from Russia, and from the Beluga sturgeon in particular, is thought by many people to be the finest. Caviar varies in colour from grey to shiny, jet black, and in size from tiny eggs the size of a pin head to eggs the size of seed pearls.

Iced champagne or vodka usually accompany caviar.

Ways to Serve Caviar

● Well chilled, with small, neat triangles of hot toast, fresh unsalted butter and thin slices of lemon.

● In a dish surrounded with crushed ice, accompanied by Melba toast, finely chopped onion, sour cream and freshly ground black pepper.

● Accompanied by very finely chopped egg white and egg yolk, with hot toast.

● Spread savoury butters on canapés and top with caviar.

● As an accompaniment to Blini, which are small buckwheat pancakes made with yeast (see page 39).

CAYENNE PEPPER

This hot, pungent spice is a member of the pepper family and is sold as a powder, ground from dried red chillies. Cayenne is used sparingly to flavour curry and chilli and to season sauces, cheese and fish dishes. Just a pinch of cayenne can add sufficient piquancy to a dish – it should be used sparingly.

CELERIAC

The edible turnip-like root of a variety of celery, and with a similar flavour. The root is peeled, the flesh sliced or diced and cooked in boiling salted water for 20–30 minutes or until tender. It is drained and served with a good white sauce, or melted butter and pepper.

Celeriac is often used raw in salad. The flesh is grated or cut in julienne (matchstick) strips and dressed with Vinaigrette Dressing (see page 358). Raw celeriac discolours quickly, so the minute it is exposed to air and cut, it should be put into a bowl of acidulated water until required.

CELERY

This features in many salads and is a favourite flavouring for soups and stews. It is excellent served in its own right as a special dish or accompaniment to meats.

□ **Basic Preparation** (this is always the same): The root ends should be trimmed off and the top leaves removed (these may be reserved for the stock pot). Trim a whole bunch down to about 18 cm (7 in) long and cut in 2. The tough, fibrous strings on the outer stalks should be scraped off, or if using large bunches, the outer stalks may be removed and reserved for the stock pot. Wash the stalks under running cold water.

□ **To Cook:** Drop into a small quantity of lightly salted boiling water and boil, uncovered, for 10 minutes. Drain, return to pan, heat gently to dry off any moisture. Add 1 tsp butter, pepper, salt, a little grated cheese and chopped parsley to enhance flavour. **See recipes.**

Celery Poulette

1 bunch celery; 1 tbsp chopped onion; salt and freshly ground black pepper; 30 g/1 oz (2 tbsp) butter; 2 tsp flour; 4 tbsp single (light) cream; 350 ml/12 fl oz (¾ cup) chicken stock.

Prepare celery as described above, cutting it into roughly 8 cm (3 in) lengths. Place celery onion, salt and pepper in a saucepan with a tight-fitting lid. Cook slowly, shaking pan often, until celery is almost tender, about 10 minutes. If the lid does not fit tightly, it will be necessary to add a little water, but celery should be almost dry at end of cooking time. Place in a heated serving dish. Melt butter, blend in flour and gradually add cream and chicken stock. Bring to the boil, stirring, then reduce heat and simmer for 3 minutes. Spoon over celery. Serves 6.

VARIATION

Scalloped Celery in Cheese Sauce: Prepare Celery Poulette and add 90 g/3 oz (¾ cup) grated cheese to the sauce. Stir until cheese has melted. Place celery in a casserole, pour over sauce and sprinkle top with additional grated cheese. Brown under a preheated grill (broiler) or in a preheated moderate oven (180°C/350°F, Gas Mark 4).

Celery and Mushroom Salad

1 bunch celery, trimmed and sliced diagonally; 250 g/8 oz (2 cups) mushrooms, finely sliced; 1 large canned pimiento, drained and sliced; 2 spring onions (scallions), sliced; 2 tbsp chopped parsley; 4 tbsp red wine vinegar; 2 tbsp French (Dijon) mustard; 4 tbsp olive oil; 4 tbsp vegetable oil; juice 1 lemon; salt and freshly ground black pepper.

Combine celery and mushrooms in a salad bowl, cover and chill. Place pimiento in blender or food processor, add spring onions (scallions), parsley, vinegar and mustard, and purée; or place in a small bowl and pound with a pestle or the end of a rolling pin. Gradually add oils, then mix in lemon juice, salt and pepper. Pour over celery and mushrooms, toss well. Cover and chill for 2 hours. Serves 4–6.

CEREALS

Cereals are cultivated grasses essential for good health. The seeds and grain obtained from them contain protein, vitamins and minerals and provide a cheap source of energy in the form of carbohydrate. Wholegrain cereals are the most nutritious and add fibre to the diet.

See also *Barley; Cornmeal; Muesli; Oatmeal; Polenta; Porridge; Rice; Semolina.*

CEVICHE

The name given to marinated raw fish, which is very popular in South America and the South Pacific. The fish fillets are cut into pieces, then 'cooked' or marinated in lemon or lime juice until the flesh becomes opaque. From here on the treatment varies from one place to another: the excess lemon or lime is squeezed from the fish and the fish is dressed in a sauce like Vinaigrette Dressing (see page 358) or coconut milk, and may be mixed with salad vegetables, onion rings, tomato cubes or wedges, chopped chilli, green or red peppers. In Mexico avocado is added, while in the Pacific Islands coconut milk is used. While raw fish fillets are mostly used, raw scallops or fresh green prawns (shrimp, unshelled), may be treated in the same way. **See recipes**.

Ceviche

(Tahitian Fish Salad)

1 kg (2 lb) firm-fleshed fish fillets; juice 5–6 lemons or limes; 1 green or red pepper, seeded and diced; 3 sticks celery, cut into strips; 4 spring onions (scallions), chopped; 3 hard-boiled (hard-cooked) eggs, chopped; salt and freshly ground black pepper; 120–175 ml/4–6 fl oz ($\frac{1}{2}$–$\frac{3}{4}$ cup) Coconut Milk (page 80).

Remove skin and bones from fish, then cut into thin strips. Place in a glass or plastic container and pour lemon or lime juice over. Cover and chill at least 3 hours, turning with a wooden spoon from time to time. (Do not use a metal spoon.) The juice will turn fish white and opaque and it will look cooked. Squeeze out all juice from the fish by placing fish in a plastic colander and pressing with a wooden spoon. Put into a clean bowl and add vegetables, eggs, salt and pepper. Stir in coconut milk and toss to coat well. Place fish salad in large serving dish or shell and chill. Alternatively, serve in small individual dishes or shells. Serves 8.

Ceviche of Scallops

The combination of ceviche made with scallops and avocado is perfect to serve as a dinner party starter or at a light luncheon followed by a green salad.

350 g (12 oz) scallops; juice 1 lemon; 1 stick celery, diced; 1 small onion, sliced; 4 scallop shells; chopped parsley or snipped chives; lemon wedges to serve.
DRESSING: *1 tbsp lemon juice; 1 small clove garlic, crushed with little salt; 1 tbsp olive oil; salt and freshly ground black pepper; dash Tabasco (hot pepper) sauce.*

Wash scallops and trim off any brown bits. Place in a bowl, add lemon juice and marinate for 2–3 hours. Squeeze out excess lemon juice. Mix all ingredients for dressing in a small bowl and pour over scallops. Add celery and onion. Cover and chill for at least 1 hour. Spoon marinated seafood into each scallop shell and sprinkle with parsley or chives. Serve with lemon wedges. Serves 4.
VARIATION

Ceviche of Scallops with Avocado: Halve 2 chilled avocados and remove stones. Scoop out some of the flesh and add to above seafood mixture. Mix lightly and spoon into avocado shells.

CHAMPIGNON

The French name for mushroom, but particularly associated with button mushrooms.
See *Mushroom*.

CHAPATI

An Indian unleavened bread made from wholewheat or *atta* flour. Chapatis are eaten with curries and all Indian savoury dishes. Break off a piece of bread and use to scoop up the food.

Chapatis

250 g/8 oz (2 cups) fine wholewheat or atta flour; 1 tsp salt; 1 tbsp ghee or peanut oil; 250 ml/8 fl oz (1 cup) lukewarm water.

Place 210 g/7 oz (1$\frac{3}{4}$ cups) flour in a bowl. Add salt and rub in ghee or add oil. Make a well in the centre and add water all at once. Mix with one hand to form a dough and knead for at least 10 minutes. Wrap dough and chill for at least 1 hour. (It is preferable to chill the dough overnight for lighter chapatis.)

Shape dough into 12–14 small balls about the size of large walnuts. Roll out each one on a board, sprinkled with remaining flour, to a 13 cm (5 in) round. Heat a heavy frying pan (skillet) until a drop of water spits when dropped on pan. Place chapatis in pan and press edge with a folded tea-towel to encourage bubbles to form and make chapatis light. Cook for 1 minute, then turn to cook other side. Wrap each chapati in a tea-towel as soon as it is cooked. Serve hot to accompany curries or vegetable dishes. Makes 12–14.

CHARLOTTE

A name given to two entirely different desserts. One is cold: a mould is lined with sponge fingers or sponge cake and filled with a creamy mousse or Bavarian Cream (*Bavarois*), fruit- or nut-flavoured. The other is hot: the mould is often lined with buttered bread fingers, and usually filled with apples then baked.

The traditional charlotte mould is made of tin, with sloping sides, and has 2 lugs on either side. A charlotte may, however, be made in a loaf tin (pan) or a soufflé dish. **See recipes**.

Strawberry Charlotte

1 kg (2 lb) strawberries; 180 g/6 oz ($\frac{3}{4}$ cup) caster sugar; 2$\frac{1}{2}$ tbsp Kirsch; 16–18 sponge fingers (lady fingers); 120 ml/4 fl oz ($\frac{1}{2}$ cup) sherry; 350 ml/12 fl oz (1$\frac{1}{2}$ cups) double (heavy) cream.

Hull strawberries and cut them in half. Put in a bowl with half the sugar and the Kirsch. Moisten sponge fingers (lady fingers) with sherry (dip in and out quickly) and use some to line bottom and sides of a charlotte mould. Whip cream with remaining sugar. Put a layer of strawberries in mould, then whipped cream and cover with moistened sponge fingers (lady fingers). Continue layering ingredients, finishing with sponge fingers (lady fingers). Chill at least 4 hours. Unmould. Serves 8.
VARIATION

Chocolate Charlotte: Prepare and line charlotte mould as described in Strawberry Charlotte. Make Chocolate Mousse (see page 74). Fill the mould with alternate layers of mousse and sponge fingers. Chill for 4 hours. Unmould and serve in slices with whipped cream.

Apple Charlotte

1 loaf white bread, sliced; 2 eggs, beaten; 125 g/4 oz (2 cups) fresh white bread-crumbs.
FILLING: *60 g/2 oz (4 tbsp) butter; 5 large apples, peeled, cored and sliced; 2 tbsp caster sugar; $\frac{1}{4}$ tsp cinnamon; $\frac{1}{2}$ tsp grated lemon rind; 3–4 tbsp apricot jam.*

Remove crusts from bread and cut each slice into 2 strips. Dip into beaten eggs, then coat with breadcrumbs. Arrange around the sides of a greased 1.2–1.5 litre/2–2$\frac{1}{2}$ pint (5–6 cup) charlotte mould or soufflé dish, overlapping slightly. Line bottom of mould, keeping a few slices to cover top.
FILLING: Melt butter in a saucepan, add apples, sugar, cinnamon and lemon rind and cook over a high heat, stirring continuously. When apples are reduced to a thick purée, stir in jam. Spoon into prepared mould and top with reserved bread slices. Bake in a

preheated moderate oven (180°C/350°F, Gas Mark 4) for 35–40 minutes. Allow charlotte to stand for a few minutes before turning out on to a heated dish. Serves 6.

CHATEAUBRIAND

This is a large piece of steak, cut from the thick part of the fillet (tenderloin), usually 5–8 cm (2–3 in) thick, and weighing 500–750 g (1–1½ lb). It usually appears on menus as a serving for 2.

☐ **To Cook:** Trim meat, sprinkle both sides with salt, spread with a little butter and grill (broil) meat under a preheated grill (broiler) for about 6 minutes on each side. Transfer meat to a hot frying pan (skillet), spread it with additional butter and continue to cook over medium heat, about 10 minutes for rare, 15 minutes for medium-rare. To test: if you look carefully, you will notice that when meat reaches medium-rare stage, tiny drops of pink juice appear on the surface. Touch meat at this stage with the first and second fingers; it will be firm but still retain a noticeable springiness. If it feels soft it is not done; if it is quite firm, it is well done.

Serve with Béarnaise Sauce (see page 370) or Maître d'Hôtel Butter (see page 49), watercress and French Fried Potatoes (see page 308).

CHEESE

There are hundreds of varieties of cheese, and it is infinitely versatile. It can appear on the menu at any time of day and in any course; it makes a splendid snack and is one of the most useful 'emergency' foods; it is a good companion to drinks from coffee and beer to fine wine. Cheese is remarkable in its ability to complement other foods.

Types of Cheese

All natural cheeses, no matter how they may vary in individual character, can be divided into four basic types: soft unripened, soft ripened, firm, and hard. Processed cheeses are usually treated to resemble one of these types, and can be used in the same way.

Soft Unripened Cheeses: These include fresh Cottage Cheese and Ricotta and processed Creamed Cottage Cheese, all low in fat. Cream Cheese and Neufchâtel, usually in processed form, are rich and smooth. Fresh Mascarpone is luscious and creamy.

Store these cheeses, closely covered, in the refrigerator. Use fresh varieties within a day or two of purchase, processed varieties within a week or two. They are used in salads, for savouries and desserts, as spreads, and in cooking both savoury and sweet dishes.

Salty Feta, though firm in texture, is classified in this group because of its high moisture content. Store in a covered container in the refrigerator and use within a week or so. Feta is sliced or diced and served with black olives as an appetizer, or in a salad.

Soft Ripened Cheeses: These vary from richly flowing Camembert and Brie to the great blue cheeses, namely, Stilton, Roquefort, Gorgonzola and Dolcelatte and buttery Danish Blues. Tangy Port Salut, mild Bel Paese and Chèvre (made with goat's milk) are others. America produces the rich and creamy Liederkranz. Mozzarella, an Italian soft cheese, melts readily in cooking and is used in many Italian dishes.

Many manufacturers produce soft cheeses combined with walnuts, Kirsch, pepper, herbs and other flavourings.

Serve these cheeses as part of the cheese board on biscuits (crackers) or bread as a snack or with drinks, or with fruit or nuts for dessert. Small whole Camemberts may be dipped in egg and breadcrumbs and quickly crisped in hot oil for the 'Fried Camembert' featured in some top restaurants as a first course.

Store soft cheeses, loosely wrapped in foil, in the refrigerator and use within a week or so of purchase. If you are lucky enough to have a whole Stilton, give it special care. Store it, covered with a damp cloth wrung out in salt water, in the refrigerator. If it is going to be used fairly quickly, the cheese may be cut in half horizontally, one half wrapped round with a napkin and scooped from the centre to serve. There is a tradition of pouring a little port into the centre, but purists disapprove of this. If the cheese is to be used slowly, cut slices across the face as this lessens the risk of drying out.

Firm Cheeses: These are the all-rounders, and every cheese-making country has its specialities. Cheddar, originally from the West of England, is probably the most famous of all; Cheddar-style cheeses are now made in many countries. American varieties include Monterey Jack, Colby, Herkimer, Vermont and Wisconsin. Salty Cheshire, Leicester, Sage Derby (so-named because it is flecked with sage) and sharp, white Caerphilly from Wales or Somerset, are other well known British cheeses.

Holland produces smooth-bodied Gouda (shaped like a yellow wheel) and Edam (shaped like a red ball); Denmark makes mild Havarti (formerly called Tilsit) and fuller-flavoured Samsöe. Swiss Emmenthal (smooth and nutty, with large holes) and Gruyère (stronger, with smaller holes) are the originals on which Swiss cheeses around the world are styled.

Firm cheeses are excellent for snacks, savouries, sandwiches, for toasting, for the cheese board and cooking. Store them in the refrigerator in a covered container, cut sides covered with foil, and use within a few weeks of purchase.

Hard Cheeses: These are strong-flavoured and dry, perfect for grating over pasta, rice, vegetables or soups, or for cooking with. For best flavour, buy in the piece and grate off as you need it. This is practical as these cheeses, low in moisture, do not need refrigeration and keep for a long time provided they have good air circulation. Cheese sellers simply hang them from hooks in a cool, airy place. The great names in hard cheeses are Parmesan, Pecorino and Romano, all originally produced in Italy but now much-copied elsewhere.

☐ **Serving Cheese:** Always bring cheese to room temperature before serving so that it can release its full flavour. Cheese which should be buttery or melting-soft may be hard or rubbery if served too cold.

Put flowing cheeses, such as Brie and Camembert, on to the board uncut if possible. French bread, water biscuits (crackers) or other crisp, thin crackers, crispbreads or oatcakes (Scottish or Irish) are good accompaniments. Serve with butter, if liked.

Serve cheese, as the French do, after the main course so that diners can finish their red wine with it, or serve at the end of the meal.

There is no need to serve a great variety of types on a cheese board or platter. One beautiful Brie, or 2 generous wedges of different types, are far more tempting than an array of little pieces.

☐ **Cooking with Cheese:** Cooking for too long or at too high a heat makes cheese tough and stringy. Always add it at the end of cooking and heat gently for no longer than it takes to melt. Grate hard cheese finely so that it will melt readily; shred firm or soft cheese, or chop it finely. **See recipes.**

Cheese and Bacon Rolls

Serve with pre-dinner drinks.

250 g/8 oz (2 cups) Cheddar cheese; 4 rashers (slices) streaky bacon, rinds removed.

Cut cheese into 2.5 cm (1 in) cubes. Cut bacon into strips and wrap round the cheese, securing with wooden toothpicks. Grill (broil), turning once, under a preheated very hot grill (broiler) so that bacon is crisp before cheese melts. Serve immediately. Makes 24.

Cheese Feathers

120 ml/4 fl oz (½ cup) cold water; 15 g/½ oz (1 tbsp) butter; 60 g/2 oz (½ cup) flour; 6 tbsp grated mature (sharp) cheese; 2 eggs, beaten; freshly ground black pepper; oil for deep-frying.

Put water and butter into a small, heavy saucepan and bring slowly to the boil. Add flour, stirring all the time. Remove from heat and beat in cheese, then eggs, a little at a time. Season with black pepper. Drop teaspoonfuls into hot oil and fry until pale brown. Drain on crumpled paper towels and serve as an hors d'oeuvre with drinks or as an accompaniment to soup. Makes 60–70.

Devilled Cheese

60 g/2 oz (½ cup) grated mature (sharp) cheese; 1 tsp chopped mixed pickle; 1 tsp curry powder; butter; 2 slices toast.

Mix cheese, pickle and curry powder together. Butter toast lightly and spread with cheese mixture. Place slices side by side on a buttered baking tray. Bake in a preheated moderately hot oven (200°C/400°F, Gas Mark 6) for about 4 minutes or grill (broil) under a preheated grill (broiler) until browned. Serves 1–2.

Cheese and Almond Fingers

3 tbsp chopped blanched almonds; 60 g/2 oz (4 tbsp) butter; 3 tbsp single (light) cream; 6 tbsp grated mature (sharp) cheese; salt and freshly ground black pepper; toast fingers.

Fry almonds in about ⅓ of the butter until pale gold. Mix remaining ingredients except toast and spread mixture on toast. Sprinkle with almonds and place under a preheated grill (broiler) to heat through. Serve at once. Makes 15–18.

Edam Tea Ring

250 g/8 oz (2 cups) flour; 4 tsp baking powder; 1 tsp salt; 1 tsp paprika; 180 g/6 oz (1½ cups) grated Edam cheese; 4 tbsp piccalilli pickle, chopped; 1 egg; 150 ml/ ¼ pint (⅔ cup) milk.

Sift the flour, baking powder, salt and paprika. Stir in cheese and piccalilli. Beat together egg and milk. Pour into flour mixture to make a soft dough, reserving a little milk for glazing. Knead dough very lightly and divide into 6 pieces. Form each into a roll and place on a greased baking tray to form a circle with rolls just touching each other. Brush with reserved milk and egg mixture. Bake in a preheated hot oven (220°C/425°F, Gas Mark 7) for 25 minutes or until golden-brown. Cool on a wire rack. Separate rolls and serve split and buttered, either hot or cold. Serves 6.

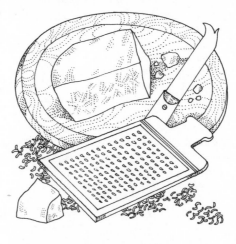

Bacon and Onion Roly-Poly

250 g/8 oz (2 cups) self-raising flour; 1 tsp baking powder; 125 g (4 oz) grated suet; 1 tbsp oil; 3 medium onions, finely sliced; 4 rashers (slices) bacon, rind removed and chopped; 180 g/6 oz (1½ cups) grated Cheddar cheese; 1 tsp chopped fresh sage or ¼ tsp dried; beaten egg to glaze.

Sift flour, baking powder and salt into a mixing bowl, stir in suet and add sufficient water to make a fairly stiff dough. Knead lightly and quickly. Roll dough out into a 30 × 15 cm (12 × 6 in) oblong on a floured board. Heat oil in a pan and fry onions and bacon until just cooked. Allow to cool and spoon over dough, leaving edges clear. Sprinkle cheese over onion mixture and top with sage. Brush edges of dough with beaten egg, roll up and seal ends. Make 4 diagonal cuts in top of roll, glaze with beaten egg and put on a greased baking tray. Bake in a preheated moderately hot oven (190°C/375°F, Gas Mark 5) for 45 minutes or until golden-brown. Serves 4 as a luncheon dish, or 8 as a snack.

CHEESECAKE

Most cheesecakes are made from fresh, unripened cheeses such as cream cheese, cottage cheese or Neufchâtel cream cheese, available in bulk from most delicatessens and cheese counters.

All cottage cheeses should be rubbed through a sieve or puréed in a blender before using to give a smooth texture to the finished cheesecake. Ricotta cheese is very white and creamy and may be substituted for any other kind, as well as being used in recipes specifically needing it. It is a low-fat cheese, blends easily and is sold in bulk or in pre-wrapped packages. **See recipes.**

Lindy's Cheesecake

(Bistro Cheesecake)

CRUST: *250 g/8 oz (3 cups) plain sweet biscuits (graham crackers), crushed; 1 tbsp sugar; ½ tsp mixed spice (ground allspice); 90 g/3 oz (6 tbsp) butter, melted.*
FILLING: *750 g/1½ lb (3 cups) cream cheese; 125 g/4 oz (½ cup) caster sugar; 1 tsp vanilla essence (extract); grated rind 1 lemon; 1 tbsp lemon juice; 4 eggs, separated; 250 ml/8 fl oz (1 cup) single (light) cream; 1 tbsp flour, sifted.*
TOPPING: *250 ml/8 fl oz (1 cup) chilled double (heavy) cream, whipped; nutmeg.*

Combine all ingredients for crust and press on sides and bottom of greased 23 cm (9 in) loose-bottomed tin (springform pan). Chill. FILLING: Beat cheese until soft, then add sugar, vanilla and lemon rind and juice and beat until creamy. Beat in egg yolks one at a time, then cream. Fold in flour. Beat egg whites until stiff and fold in. Pour into crust and bake in a preheated moderate oven (160°C/325°F, Gas Mark 3) for 1 hour 10 minutes. Turn off heat and leave cake in oven until cold. Release spring and remove sides of tin (pan). Chill. Serve topped with whipped cream and nutmeg. Serves 10–12.

Sultana Cheese Slice

PASTRY (DOUGH): *250 g/8 oz (2 cups) flour; 125 g/4 oz (½ cup) butter; 1 egg yolk, beaten; egg beaten with water to glaze.*
FILLING: *250 g/8 oz (1 cup) cream cheese; 60 g/2 oz (4 tbsp) butter; 60 g/2 oz (¼ cup) caster sugar; 1 tbsp flour; 2 tbsp single (light) cream; 3 eggs, separated; 90 g/3 oz (½ cup) sultanas (golden raisins).*

PASTRY (DOUGH): Sift flour into a bowl. Rub (cut) in butter until mixture resembles fine breadcrumbs. Add egg yolk and enough iced water to make a firm dough. Chill for 1 hour. Roll out ⅔ of dough thinly and use to line a greased 28 × 19 cm (11 × 7 in) tin (pan). Chill thoroughly.

FILLING: Combine cheese, butter and sugar, beating well. Add flour, cream and egg yolks, then sultanas (golden raisins). Beat egg whites until they form stiff peaks. Fold into cheese mixture. Pour into prepared tin (pan). Roll out remaining dough and cut into 1 cm ($\frac{1}{2}$ in) wide strips. Use to decorate the top. Join strips with egg glaze if too short. Brush dough with egg glaze. Bake in a preheated moderately hot oven (200°C/400°F, Gas Mark 6) for 10–15 minutes, then reduce oven heat to 190°C/375°F, Gas Mark 5 and bake for a further 15–20 minutes. Cool and cut into squares. Makes about 16.

Manhattan Cheesecake

500 g/1 lb (2 cups) cream cheese; 500 g/1 lb (2 cups) Ricotta cheese; 350 g/12 oz (1$\frac{1}{2}$ cups) caster sugar; 4 large eggs; 60 g/2 oz (4 tbsp) butter, melted; 3 tbsp each flour and cornflour (cornstarch), sifted together; 2$\frac{1}{2}$ tsp vanilla essence (extract); 450 ml/$\frac{3}{4}$ pint (2 cups) sour cream.
DECORATION: 250 ml/8 fl oz (1 cup) double (heavy) cream, whipped; cherries or other fresh fruit; cinnamon or nutmeg.

Combine cheeses and beat well until creamy. Gradually add sugar, then beat in eggs one at a time. Stir in melted butter, flour, cornflour (cornstarch) and vanilla. Fold in sour cream. Spoon mixture into an ungreased 23 cm (9 in) loose-bottomed tin (springform pan). Bake in centre of a pre-heated moderate oven (160°C/325°F, Gas Mark 3) for 1 hour (cake will still be soft in centre). Turn off heat and leave cake in oven for 2 hours. Remove and cool completely in tin (pan), standing on a wire rack. Chill for at least 2 hours before removing sides of tin (pan). Decorate with cream, fruit, cinnamon or nutmeg. Serves 10–12.

Torta di Ricotta

PASTRY (DOUGH): 250 g/8 oz (2 cups) flour; 125 g/4 oz ($\frac{1}{2}$ cup) butter; 1 egg yolk, beaten.
FILLING: 750 g/1$\frac{1}{2}$ lb (3 cups) Ricotta cheese; 125 g/4 oz ($\frac{1}{2}$ cup) caster sugar; 60 g/2 oz ($\frac{1}{2}$ cup) ground almonds; grated rind 1 lemon; $\frac{1}{2}$ tsp vanilla essence (extract); 4 eggs.

PASTRY (DOUGH): Sift flour into bowl and rub (cut) in butter until mixture resembles fine breadcrumbs. Add egg yolk and enough iced water to make a firm dough. Chill for 1 hour. Roll out dough and use to line a greased 23 cm (9 in) pie plate. Chill for 1 hour.
FILLING: Combine Ricotta, sugar, almonds and lemon rind. Beat in vanilla and eggs, one at a time. Pour into chilled pastry (dough) case and bake in a preheated hot oven (220°C/425°F, Gas Mark 7) for 5 minutes, then reduce heat to moderate (180°C/350°F, Gas Mark 4) and bake for a further 30 minutes. Cool and chill. Serves 8.

Country Cheesecake

CRUST: 2 tbsp finely ground unblanched almonds; 125 g/4 oz (1$\frac{1}{2}$ cups) plain sweet biscuit (graham cracker) crumbs; 2 tbsp sugar; 75 g/2$\frac{1}{2}$ oz (5 tbsp) butter, melted.
FILLING: 350 g/12 oz (1$\frac{1}{2}$ cups) cream cheese; 2 eggs, beaten; 140 g/4$\frac{1}{2}$ oz ($\frac{1}{2}$ cup plus 1 tbsp) caster sugar; 1 tsp lemon juice; salt; 350 ml/12 fl oz (1$\frac{1}{2}$ cups) sour cream; $\frac{1}{2}$ tsp vanilla essence (extract).
DECORATION (optional): whipped cream; toasted slivered almonds.

Combine almonds, crumbs and sugar. Pour in melted butter and mix well. Press into bottom and sides of a greased 20 cm (8 in) loose-bottomed tin (springform pan). Bake in a preheated moderately hot oven (190°C/375°F, Gas Mark 5) for 10 minutes. Allow to cool thoroughly.

FILLING: Beat cream cheese, eggs, 125 g/4 oz ($\frac{1}{2}$ cup) sugar, lemon juice and $\frac{1}{2}$ tsp salt until smooth and creamy. Put into prepared crust and bake in oven for about 20 minutes, or until just set. Turn off heat and allow cake to cool in oven. Combine sour cream, remaining sugar, the vanilla and pinch salt. Pour over filling and bake in a preheated hot oven (230°C/450°F, Gas Mark 8) for 10 minutes. Allow to cool in oven as before. Chill before serving and decorate, if liked, with a thin layer of whipped cream and almonds. Serves 8.

Semolina Cheesecake

CRUST: 180 g/6 oz (1$\frac{1}{2}$ cups) flour; pinch salt; 90 g/3 oz (6 tbsp) butter; 1 tsp caster sugar; 1 egg yolk, beaten.
FILLING: 60 g/2 oz (4 tbsp) butter; 125 g/4 oz ($\frac{1}{2}$ cup) caster sugar; 2 eggs, separated; grated rind and juice 1 lemon; 30 g/1 oz ($\frac{1}{4}$ cup) ground almonds; 250 g/8 oz (1 cup) cottage cheese, sieved; 2 tbsp semolina; 90 g/3 oz ($\frac{1}{2}$ cup) raisins, chopped.

Sift flour and salt into a bowl and rub (cut) in butter until mixture resembles fine

breadcrumbs. Add sugar and mix to a firm dough with egg yolk. If necessary, add a little water. Roll out on a lightly floured board and line a 20 cm (8 in) loose-bottomed tin (springform pan), pressing the pastry 4 cm (1$\frac{1}{2}$ in) up sides of tin (pan). Press down well to remove any air bubbles and trim edges neatly.
FILLING: Cream butter and sugar together until light and fluffy. Lightly beat egg yolks with lemon rind and juice, ground almonds, cottage cheese, semolina and raisins. Mix into creamed butter and sugar. Stiffly beat egg whites and fold in. Turn filling into prepared tin (pan) and bake in a preheated moderate oven (160°C/325°F, Gas Mark 3) for 50–60 minutes or until pastry (dough) is golden and filling is set. Remove side of tin (pan) and allow cake to cool on base. Chill before serving. Serves 8.

CHELSEA BUN

See page 477 for recipe.

CHERRY

Cherries are delicious fruit eaten fresh or stewed 5–10 minutes in sugar syrup, flavoured with a piece of cinnamon stick, lemon peel, and with a little brandy stirred in before they cool. They have a very short season and are worth preserving so you can enjoy them later in the year. One of the best ways to do this is by preserving them in brandy, when they can be used over ice cream, and the brandy syrup folded through whipped cream or stirred into fruit salads or fruit desserts to give a rich flavour. **See recipes.**

Rancin Line an ovenproof dish with thinly sliced white bread and butter. Fill nearly to top with cherries which have been stoned and cooked for a few minutes with plenty of sugar. Do not add any of the syrup. Cover with a second layer of bread and butter, and sprinkle with sugar. Bake in a preheated moderately hot oven (200°C/400°F, Gas Mark 6) for about 20 minutes or until the top is golden and crisp. Dust with caster or sifted icing (confectioners) sugar and serve warm with cream.

Brandied Cherries

180 g/6 oz ($\frac{3}{4}$ cup) sugar; 250 ml/8 fl oz (1 cup) water; 1 strip lemon peel; 1.5 kg (3 lb) dark cherries, stoned; brandy.

Place sugar, water and lemon peel in a saucepan and heat, stirring to dissolve sugar. Bring to the boil and boil for 10 minutes. Add cherries and simmer for 5 minutes more. Pack cherries into warm sterilized jars, half fill with brandy and top up with syrup. Seal and store in a cool, dark place for at least 1 month before using.

CHERVIL

One of the classic French *fines herbes* (the others are parsley, tarragon and chive), used to flavour Omelette aux Fines Herbes (see page 249) and to sprinkle on salads. Chervil is good in all egg dishes and with fish and shellfish. Its leaves are lacy, like those of parsley, but a softer and a more delicate green. The flavour is light and distinctive with a hint of anise. It is also available dried.

CHESTNUT

The edible nut is available fresh in winter, and also in cans (whole or puréed) and dried (soak overnight in water, then use as fresh). The kernel is sweet and slightly floury. Chestnuts roasted in the shell are a traditional cold-weather snack; chestnut kernels may be simmered in stock and served as a vegetable or chopped for stuffings; sweetened chestnut purée makes the Italian dessert, *Monte Bianco* (or French, *Mont Blanc*). *Marrons glacés* (glazed chestnuts) are luxurious sweetmeats, served in paper cases or used to decorate cakes.

To shell chestnuts: With a small, sharp knife, cut gashes in the shape of a cross on flat side of brown outer shell. Put nuts in a pan of cold water, bring quickly to the boil and boil 1 minute. Turn off heat. Remove one nut at a time, peel off shell and rub off inner skin. Any nut which resists peeling may be returned to the hot water for a few minutes.

To roast chestnuts: Cut a cross in outer shells as described above. Place in a pan with an ovenproof handle. Add 1 tbsp oil for each 500 g (1 lb) nuts. Shake over moderate heat until sizzling, then place in a preheated moderate oven (180°C/350°F, Gas Mark 4) for about 30 minutes, when shells and skins will come off easily. **See recipes.**

Monte Bianco

(Mont Blanc)
Prepare as close to serving time as possible to achieve the best effect.

60 g/2 oz (¼ cup) sugar; 5 tbsp milk; 1 × 440 g/14 oz can unsweetened chestnut purée; 250 ml/8 fl oz (1 cup) double (heavy) cream; 1 tbsp rum; grated chocolate to decorate.

Dissolve sugar in milk over a gentle heat. Add chestnut purée and stir until smooth. Cool, then chill. Whip cream and fold half into chestnut mixture with rum. Fill a greaseproof (waxed) paper funnel with chestnut cream and pipe so that it falls loosely into cone shape on 6 individual serving plates. Top with remaining cream and sprinkle with grated chocolate. Serves 6.

Chestnut Soup

45 g/1½ oz (3 tbsp) butter; 2 onions, chopped; 1 rasher (slice) bacon, rind removed and finely chopped; 1 carrot, diced; 1 stick celery, chopped; 1 × 440 g/14 oz can unsweetened chestnut purée; salt and freshly ground black pepper; 1.25 litres/2¼ pints (6 cups) chicken stock; Croûtons (page 90) to garnish.

Melt butter in a heavy saucepan, add onion, bacon, carrot and celery and cook until softened. Stir in chestnut purée, salt, pepper and stock. Simmer for about 30 minutes. Put soup through a sieve or purée in a blender or food processor. Reheat and serve garnished with croûtons. Serves 6.

Chestnut Stuffing

250 g/8 oz (1 cup) butter; 2 large onions, very finely chopped; 1 tsp dried thyme; 1 tsp dried sage; 1½ tsp salt; ½ tsp pepper; 15 g/½ oz (⅓ cup) chopped parsley; 90 g/3 oz (¾ cup) chopped celery; 250 g/8 oz (4 cups) fresh breadcrumbs; 500 g (1 lb) chestnuts, cooked, shelled, skinned and chopped.

Melt butter in a frying pan (skillet) and add all ingredients except breadcrumbs and chestnuts. Cook for 5 minutes, then add crumbs and chestnuts. Cook, stirring, until crumbs are crisp. Use as a stuffing for turkey. Makes about 1.5 kg/3 lb (8 cups).
NOTE: Canned whole chestnuts may be used in this recipe.

Whole Braised Chestnuts

500 g (1 lb) chestnuts, shelled and skinned; 250 ml/8 fl oz (1 cup) chicken stock; 3 tsp cornflour (cornstarch); 2 tbsp dry sherry; salt and freshly ground black pepper; 60 g/2 oz (4 tbsp) butter.

Place chestnuts in a heavy saucepan. Cover with stock to a depth of 1 cm (½ in). Mix cornflour (cornstarch) and sherry to a smooth paste, pour over chestnuts, add salt and pepper and dot with butter. Simmer, covered, over lowest possible heat for 50

minutes or until chestnuts are tender. Serve as a separate dish or mix with red cabbage or Brussels sprouts as an accompaniment to turkey.
NOTE: Canned whole chestnuts may be used in this recipe, but simmer for 10 minutes.

Frozen Chestnut Soufflé

210 g/7 oz (1½ cups) icing (confectioners) sugar, sifted; 6 egg yolks; 450 ml/¾ pint (2 cups) milk; 450 ml/¾ pint (2 cups) double (heavy) cream; 1 × 440 g/14 oz can unsweetened chestnut purée; 1 quantity Crème Anglaise (page 97) to serve.

Whisk sugar and egg yolks together in a heatproof bowl until very light and fluffy. Scald milk and gradually add to egg yolk mixture in a steady stream, beating slowly. Place bowl over simmering water and cook custard until it is thickened. Strain, cool and chill for 1 hour, stirring occasionally. Whip cream until it holds soft peaks and fold it gently but thoroughly into chestnut purée. Combine chestnut mixture with custard. Freeze, covered, for 24 hours. Soften a little before serving with well-chilled crème anglaise and crisp biscuits. Serves 8–10.

CHICKEN

Modern poultry-raising has put chicken on everyone's table at a reasonable price. The wide availability of chicken pieces and special cuts such as chicken fillets (skinless, boneless half-breasts) or suprêmes (see *Supreme of Chicken*) makes it one of the most convenient meats.

You can be reasonably confident that packaged chicken will be tender. In unpackaged chicken, check that the end of the breastbone will bend readily when pressed – the sign of a young bird.

To truss a chicken: Shape the bird neatly with your hands, tucking the neck flap underneath. Take a piece of string and place its centre below the breastbone at the neck end. Bring the ends of the string down over the wings to cross underneath, then up to tie the legs and parson's nose together.

To joint a chicken: See **figs 1** and **2 opposite**.

☐ **To Cook:** Chicken may be cooked in any of the following ways. **See also recipes.**

ROAST CHICKEN Put a little butter and a piece of lemon or a few herbs inside chicken; or if using stuffing, spoon it loosely into cavity. Truss bird and lay it on its side on a greased rack in a roasting tin (pan). Spread chicken with a little butter and place in a preheated moderately hot oven (200°C/400°F, Gas Mark 6) for 10 minutes. Turn chicken over and continue cooking, turning and basting every 15 minutes. Turn chicken on its back for last 20 minutes of cooking. Allow about 25 minutes cooking time per 500 g (1 lb).

C

Chicken is done when juices run clear if a skewer is inserted in thickest part of thigh near body. Allow chicken to rest in a warm place for 20 minutes before carving. Make Clear Gravy or Thickened Gravy to accompany the chicken if desired (see *Gravy*).

FRENCH ROAST CHICKEN This method of roasting gives a beautifully moist chicken, and the skin crisps to a golden-brown in the last 15–20 minutes of cooking. Put a few strips of orange peel, a few tarragon or parsley stalks and a little salt and freshly ground black pepper inside the chicken.

Truss and roast as for Roast Chicken, above, but add 175 ml/6 fl oz ($\frac{3}{4}$ cup) chicken stock to the pan at the start of cooking and baste bird with pan juices every 15 minutes. Add more stock if it dries up.

FRIED CHICKEN Dust pieces with flour and coat with egg and breadcrumbs. Chill 20 minutes to firm crumbs. Shallow-fry in oil and butter over moderate heat, turning once, until golden-brown and cooked through. Breasts will take about 15 minutes, thicker pieces up to 25 minutes. Drain on crumpled paper towels.

POACHED CHICKEN Place chicken on its back in a heavy saucepan and add water to come to top of thighs (or just to cover chicken pieces). Add salt, pepper, a few slices of carrot, celery and onion, and a few herbs. Cover and simmer gently just until thigh meat feels tender when tested with a skewer – about 30 minutes for a young bird. Cool in the liquid.

BRAISED CHICKEN (CHICKEN CASSEROLE) Use pieces or a whole, trussed bird. Brown all over in a little butter in a heavy saucepan or flameproof casserole. Remove chicken, add a little sliced carrot, celery and onion to pan and fry until golden. Place chicken on top of vegetables, add a few herbs, salt and freshly ground black pepper and 450 ml/$\frac{3}{4}$ pint (2 cups) water or stock, with a little wine if liked. Cover and simmer on top of stove or in a preheated moderate oven (160°C/325°F, Gas Mark 3) until juices run clear when tested with a skewer in the thickest part. Chicken pieces will take about 30 minutes, a whole bird 1 hour or more. Thicken liquid, if liked, with Beurre Manié (see page 35) at the end of cooking.

SAUTEED CHICKEN Heat a little oil and butter in a heavy frying pan (skillet). Add well-dried chicken pieces, a few at a time, and sauté on brisk heat until golden on both sides. Replace leg and thigh pieces in pan, cover and cook on low heat 8 minutes. Add breast and wing pieces, cover and cook 15 minutes more. Turn and baste several times during cooking.

GRILLED (BROILED) CHICKEN Use very small chickens, or chicken pieces. For whole birds, split in half and cut away back and rib bones. Arrange chicken, skin side down, on a greased rack under a preheated grill (broiler). Brush with melted butter and grill (broil) at moderate heat, turning once and basting with butter several times. Chicken halves will take 25–30 minutes, pieces 10–15 minutes.

Poached Chicken Breasts

Store in the poaching liquor in a covered bowl to keep them moist and fresh-tasting. Good for any recipe calling for cooked chicken, salads, sandwiches etc.

900 ml/1$\frac{1}{2}$ pints (3$\frac{3}{4}$ cups) water; $\frac{1}{2}$ carrot, sliced; 2 slices onion; small piece celery; 4 black peppercorns; 2 parsley stalks; 1 sprig fresh thyme, or pinch dried; 1 tsp salt; 6 half-breasts of chicken.

Put all ingredients except chicken into a large saucepan and bring to the boil. Place chicken in pan, skin side up, turn heat to low, cover and simmer very gently for 10–15 minutes or until meat is tender when tested with a fine skewer. Place chicken breasts in a refrigerator container and strain liquor over. Cool then refrigerate, covered. If you prefer dark to white meat, use chicken thighs and poach according to this recipe.

Chicken Pie

1 large roasting chicken; 1 carrot, sliced; 1 onion, sliced; 1 bay leaf; 1 tsp salt; 6 black peppercorns; 90 g/3 oz (6 tbsp) butter; 6 mushrooms, halved or quartered; 2 tbsp flour; 120 ml/4 fl oz ($\frac{1}{2}$ cup) single (light) cream; freshly ground black pepper; 1 × 375 g/12 oz packet frozen puff pastry (paste), thawed; beaten egg yolk to glaze.

Put chicken in a large pan. Add carrot, onion, bay leaf, salt and peppercorns. Cover with hot water to top of thighs and bring to the boil, skimming occasionally. Simmer gently for 20 minutes. Allow chicken to cool in stock for about 1 hour, then remove to a dish. Joint chicken and remove all flesh from bones. Skin and cut into large chunky pieces.

Place chicken meat in pie dish and cover with a little stock to keep flesh moist. Return

Jointing a chicken: Cut off legs at the joints (Fig 1). Cut either side of backbone and remove. Turn bird over and cut either side of breastbone, discard. Cut each side of chicken in half, removing wings if liked (2).

bones to stock and boil for 10–15 minutes to reduce it. Strain and leave to cool. Measure 450 ml/$\frac{3}{4}$ pint (2 cups) of stock and chill so that fat will rise to the surface and settle for easy removal. (The remaining stock can be used as a base for soups or sauces.)

Melt 1 tbsp of the butter in a small frying pan (skillet) and fry mushrooms over high heat for a few minutes. Remove and add to chicken. Melt remaining butter in a saucepan and blend in flour. Add reserved 450 ml/$\frac{3}{4}$ pint (2 cups) stock, stirring to make a smooth sauce. Stir in cream and season with salt and pepper. Spoon sauce over chicken and mushrooms and mix gently. If you have a pie funnel, place it in centre. Roll out pastry (dough) to size which fits pie dish. From remaining pastry (dough), make strip long enough to go around top rim of pie dish. Moisten rim of dish and attach strip to it. Moisten strip and press lid of pastry (dough) into place. Cut small leaves of pastry (dough) from trimmings and arrange on top. Brush top with beaten egg yolk. Bake in a preheated moderately hot oven (200°C/ 400°F, Gas Mark 6) for 10 minutes, then reduce heat to moderate (180°C/ 350°F, Gas Mark 4) and bake for a further 20 minutes. Serve with green vegetables or salad. Serves 4–6.

Chicken Kebabs

4 chicken fillets (skinless, boneless half-breasts); 1 tbsp soy sauce; 1 tbsp French (Dijon) mustard; 1 tbsp brown sugar; 1 tbsp sherry or whisky; 1 tbsp oil; 1 red or green pepper.

Cut chicken breasts into cubes, about 2 cm ($\frac{3}{4}$ in). Combine remaining ingredients, except pepper, in a shallow dish (not metal). Add chicken and marinate, covered, for at least 2 hours. Cut pepper into squares, same size as chicken. Drain chicken, reserving marinade. Thread pieces of pepper and chicken alternately on 8 metal skewers. Grill (broil) kebabs under a preheated grill (broiler) about 13 cm (5 in) from heat, turning and basting with reserved marinade, for 5 minutes or until cooked to taste. Serve with hot buttered rice and, if liked, halved tomatoes, seasoned and cooked with kebabs.

For a more informal meal serve a split round of flat Lebanese bread on each plate. The chicken may be slipped off skewers into bread pocket and eaten in hand. Serves 4.

Chicken Schnitzels

The schnitzels are not crumbed in this recipe, but dipped in egg only and then quickly fried.

4 chicken fillets (skinless, boneless half-breasts); salt and freshly ground black pepper; about 60 g/2 oz (½ cup) flour; 2 eggs, beaten; 60 g/2 oz (4 tbsp) butter; 3 tbsp oil. GARNISH: *4 thin slices lemon; 8 anchovy fillets; capers.*

Place chicken fillets between 2 sheets of plastic wrap and flatten them out slightly with a rolling pin. Trim off any very ragged edges with a sharp knife. Season fillets well with salt and pepper and dust lightly with flour. Have beaten eggs in a shallow dish beside stove, and floured fillets on a plate. Heat butter and oil together in a large, heavy frying pan (skillet) over medium heat. When foam subsides, quickly dip fillets into egg, then place them at once in pan. Cook until underside is crisp and golden, about 2 minutes, then turn fillets with a spatula and cook other side for 2–3 minutes. Serve at once on heated plates, garnishing each fillet with a thin slice of lemon, 2 drained anchovy fillets arranged criss-cross fashion on the lemon, and a few capers. Serves 4.

Fried Chicken Florentine

1 × 1.5 kg (3 lb) chicken, or 4–6 chicken pieces; 3 tbsp olive oil; 2 tbsp lemon juice; ½ tsp salt; freshly ground black pepper; 1 tbsp chopped parsley; flour for coating; oil for frying; 1 egg, beaten. TO SERVE: *lemon wedges; Fried Parsley (page 265).*

Cut whole chicken into serving pieces. Combine oil, lemon juice, salt, pepper and parsley and marinate chicken in this mixture for 2 hours, turning pieces occasionally. Dry chicken thoroughly, and coat well with flour. Heat enough oil in a heavy frying pan (skillet) to come about halfway up sides of chicken pieces. When oil is hot, dip chicken pieces in egg then place at once in oil. Cook

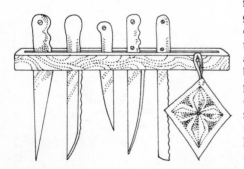

over medium heat, turning several times, until chicken is golden and crusty outside and juices run clear when flesh is pierced with a skewer. This will take about 15 minutes. Drain on paper towels, and serve with wedges of lemon and fried parsley. Serves 4.

Roast Chicken with Honey and Orange Sauce

60 g/2 oz (4 tbsp) butter; 3 tbsp honey; salt; 1 tsp paprika; 1 × 1.5 kg (3 lb) chicken; 300 ml/½ pint (1¼ cups) orange juice; 4 shallots, chopped; 1 green pepper, seeded and diced; ½ tsp ground ginger; 1 tsp prepared horseradish; 2 tsp cornflour (cornstarch); orange slices to garnish.

Melt half the butter in a saucepan, remove from heat and blend in honey, salt and paprika. Place chicken in a roasting tin (pan) and brush with honey mixture. Pour over 120 ml/4 fl oz (½ cup) orange juice. Roast in a preheated moderately hot oven (190°C/375°F, Gas Mark 5) for 1–1½ hours or until juices run clear when pierced with a skewer. Baste every 15 minutes. About 10 minutes before chicken is ready, make sauce. Melt remaining butter and gently cook shallots and green pepper. Add remaining orange juice, the ginger, horseradish and salt and bring slowly to the boil. Simmer for 3–5 minutes. Transfer chicken to a heated platter. Pour pan juices into sauce. Blend cornflour (cornstarch) with a little cold water, then stir briskly into sauce. Stir over low heat until thickened. Pour into a heated sauceboat and serve with chicken. Garnish chicken with orange slices. Serves 6.

Chicken Pilaf

4 half-breasts of chicken, or 6 thighs; 2 onions, sliced; 90 g/3 oz (6 tbsp) butter; 210 g/7 oz (1 cup) long-grain rice; 90 g/3 oz (½ cup) raisins; 1 tsp turmeric; 900 ml/1½ pints (3¾ cups) water or chicken stock; 2 cardamom pods; 1 bay leaf; ¼ tsp cloves; ¼ tsp cinnamon; salt and freshly ground black pepper.

If using chicken breasts, cut into 2–3 pieces. Fry chicken and onions in butter in a heavy frying pan (skillet) for a few minutes until golden. Add rice, raisins and turmeric, stir to coat with buttery mixture. Remove pan from the heat. Place water or stock in a saucepan and bring to the boil. Add cardamom pods, bay leaf and spices, season with salt and pepper and return to the boil. Pour over chicken and rice and mix lightly. Cover, reduce heat and simmer gently for about 25 minutes or until rice and chicken are tender. Remove cardamom pods and bay leaf and serve. Serves 4.

VARIATION

Barbecued Chicken Pilaf: Thread chicken on to Satay skewers that have been soaked in water and cook over hot coals. Cook rice mixture as above and serve separately.

Roast Chicken Chinese-Style

1 × 1.5 kg (3 lb) chicken; 3 tbsp soy sauce; 1 tbsp honey; ½ tsp ground ginger; 1 tbsp dry sherry; 2 tbsp finely chopped spring onions (scallions); 3 cloves garlic, crushed; 1 tsp five-spice powder; 3 tsp salt.

Remove any loose fat from inside chicken and wipe inside with paper towels. Combine soy sauce, honey, ginger, sherry, spring onions (scallions), garlic and ½ tsp five-spice powder. Brush over chicken and in cavity. Loosen skin of breast and thighs and brush mixture on chicken flesh. Cover and leave in refrigerator for 1–2 hours, turning occasionally. Drain chicken, reserving marinade. Place on rack in roasting tin (pan) containing 2 cm (¾ in) water. Roast in a preheated moderate oven (180°C/350°F, Gas Mark 4) for about 1¼ hours, turning occasionally and brushing frequently with reserved marinade. Chicken is cooked when juices run clear when thickest part of flesh is pierced with a fine skewer. Chop chicken into serving portions and serve with remaining five-spice powder mixed with salt for dipping. Usually accompanied by rice. Serves 4.
NOTE: Five-spice powder is available at Chinese grocery stores.

Smoked Chicken Hunan-Style

In Hunan they have a way of smoking chicken which is superb – moist, tender meat with a rich smoky flavour and glistening skin. If you haven't got a wok with a lid, use a deep, heavy frying pan (skillet) with a tight-fitting lid or an electric frying pan (skillet).

15 g/½ oz (¼ cup) black tea leaves; 2 tbsp brown sugar; 1 cooked White Chicken (Chinese Steamed Chicken, opposite); 1 tbsp Chinese sesame oil.

Line inside of a wok and its lid with heavy-duty foil. Mix tea leaves with brown sugar and place in bottom of wok. Put a rack in wok which will keep chicken about 5 cm (2 in) above tea leaves – a round wire cake rack is ideal. If using a wire cake rack in a frying pan (skillet) you will probably need to rest it on something else to bring it to required height – e.g., 4 metal egg cups, or the outside rim of a loose-bottomed flan tin. Arrange chicken on rack, breast side up. Cover wok tightly and heat over a moderate heat for 5 minutes or until tea mixture begins to smoke. (If using an electric frying pan (skillet) set dial at medium.) Smoke chicken for 10 minutes, then turn it breast side down and smoke for a further 10 minutes. Take wok from heat and allow chicken to stand, with lid on, for 15 minutes. Remove chicken and brush skin all over with sesame oil. Place on a cutting board and, using a sharp chopper, cut through bones into serving pieces. The wings should be cut in 2, thighs in 3–4 portions each, drumsticks in 3, and breast into 6–8 pieces. Serve as an appetizer, or as part of a Chinese meal. Serves 6–8.

Chicken Japonais

Chicken breasts are first coated with a Japanese-style marinade, then grilled (broiled) with a sweet glaze. The crispy golden skin is delicious and the flesh moist and tender. Serve with noodles and a salad.

4 half-breasts of chicken; 120 ml/4 fl oz ($\frac{1}{2}$ cup) dry sherry; 4 tbsp light soy sauce; 1 tsp finely chopped fresh ginger; 1 clove garlic, crushed; 1 tbsp sugar; 2 tbsp honey.

Place chicken breasts in a shallow baking dish. Combine sherry, soy sauce, ginger, garlic and sugar and pour over breasts, turning them so all sides are coated with marinade. Cover dish and chill overnight. Drain breasts, reserving marinade, and arrange in grill (broiler) pan, skin side down. Place under preheated grill (broiler) for 12 minutes. Meanwhile, make glaze by combining honey and 2 tbsp of the marinade. Turn breasts skin side up and continue grilling (broiling) for a further 8 minutes, brushing several times with glaze. Serves 4.

Thai Chicken Curry

There is little that is plain or bland about the cooking of Thailand, which is rich and highly seasoned, happily blending the themes of Indian and Chinese cooking.

6 chicken pieces (breasts or thighs); juice 1 lemon; 60 g/2 oz (4 tbsp) butter; 1 tbsp oil; 2 onions, finely sliced; 1 clove garlic, crushed; 1 cinnamon stick; 4 cardamom pods, crushed; 4 whole cloves; 1$\frac{1}{2}$ tbsp ground coriander; 1$\frac{1}{2}$ tsp turmeric; $\frac{1}{2}$ tsp ground ginger; $\frac{1}{2}$ tsp ground cumin; 1 small red chilli (optional); 250 ml/8 fl oz (1 cup) chicken stock; 6 dried apricots, soaked, drained and cut into strips; salt; coriander (Chinese parsley) to garnish.

Remove skin and bones from chicken and cut meat into 2.5 cm (1 in) strips. Sprinkle chicken with lemon juice. Heat butter and oil in a heavy frying pan (skillet) and stir-fry onions and garlic until onions are soft but not brown. Stir in spices. If a hot curry is desired add chilli – or part of chilli. Cook mixture, stirring, for 4–5 minutes, then add chicken and stir-fry until it is well coated with spices and is just white. Add stock and simmer for about 10 minutes or until chicken

is cooked through. Add apricots with a squeeze of lemon juice and salt to taste. Remove cinnamon and serve in 4 individual dishes. Strew over a few sprigs of coriander and serve with bowls of boiled rice. Serves 4.

Devilled Drumsticks

8 chicken drumsticks; 3 tbsp oil; 2 tsp Worcestershire sauce; 2 tsp finely chopped mango or fruit chutney; 2 tsp cider vinegar; 1 tbsp each English and French (Dijon) mustard; $\frac{1}{4}$ tsp Tabasco (hot pepper) sauce; 1 clove garlic, finely chopped; pinch salt; freshly ground black pepper.

Slash chicken flesh in several places. Mix all remaining ingredients together and spread over chicken, pressing it into slashes. Cover and leave 6 hours, or overnight, in refrigerator, turning pieces over several times. Grill (broil), bony side up, under a preheated moderate grill (broiler) for 10 minutes. Turn, baste with marinade and cook a further 10 minutes or until done. Serves 4–8.

Fried Chicken Legs

6 chicken legs; 2 tbsp soy sauce; 1 tbsp dry sherry; $\frac{1}{2}$ tsp black pepper; 2 tbsp cornflour (cornstarch); 600 ml/1 pint (2$\frac{1}{2}$ cups) oil for deep-frying; 1 tbsp finely chopped spring onions (scallions) to garnish.

Chop each chicken leg into 2–3 pieces, then mix with soy sauce, sherry and pepper. Leave to marinate for about 20 minutes, turning occasionally. Coat each piece of chicken with cornflour (cornstarch). Heat oil to moderate (when a bread cube fries golden-brown in 45 seconds) in a saucepan. Add chicken pieces and turn down heat to low. Fry chicken pieces for 8–10 minutes or until cooked and golden. Remove and drain on paper towels. Serve garnished with spring onions (scallions). Serves 4–6.

Chicken in Silver Foil

This is a variation of the traditional 'paper-wrapped chicken'.

6 chicken breasts, skinned, boned and halved; 3 spring onions (scallions), each sliced into 4 pieces; $\frac{1}{4}$ tsp salt; 1 tbsp soy sauce; 1 tsp sugar; 1 tsp dry sherry; 1 tsp Chinese sesame oil; 4 tbsp oil; extra 4 tbsp oil for frying.
GARNISH: *shredded spring onions (scallions); finely chopped red pepper.*

In a bowl combine chicken and spring onions (scallions) with salt, soy sauce, sugar, sherry and sesame oil. Leave to marinate for 30 minutes. Cut 12 squares of foil each large enough to wrap around a chicken piece 4 times. Brush foil with oil, then place a piece of chicken on each. Top with a piece of

spring onion (scallion), then wrap foil around to make a parcel, making sure no meat is exposed. Heat the extra oil in a wok or frying pan (skillet). Add chicken parcels and fry over moderate heat for about 2 minutes on each side. Remove and leave to drain on a rack for a few minutes. Reheat oil and, when it is very hot, return chicken parcels to pan and fry for 1 minute only. Serve hot in the foil, with spring onions (scallions) and pepper. Serves 6.

Lotus White Chicken

5 egg whites; 120 ml/4 fl oz ($\frac{1}{2}$ cup) chicken stock; 1 tsp salt; 1 tsp dry sherry; 2 tsp cornflour (cornstarch); 125 g/4 oz ($\frac{1}{2}$ cup) chicken breast meat, skinned and finely chopped; oil for deep-frying; 30 g/1 oz (2 tbsp) cooked ham, shredded, to garnish.

Put egg whites in a bowl. Stir in 3 tbsp of the chicken stock, the salt, sherry and half the cornflour (cornstarch). Add chicken and mix well. Heat oil to 180°C/350°F in a wok or deep-fat fryer. Gently pour in about $\frac{1}{3}$ of egg and chicken mixture. Deep-fry for 10 seconds or until mixture begins to rise to surface, then carefully turn over. Fry until golden, then remove from pan with a slotted spoon. Drain and place on a heated serving dish. Keep hot while cooking remaining chicken mixture in same way. Heat remaining stock in a small pan. Mix the rest of the cornflour (cornstarch) to a paste with a little cold water, add to stock and simmer, stirring, until thickened. Pour over chicken. Garnish with ham. Serve hot. Serves 4.

White Chicken

(Chinese Steamed Chicken)
This method is excellent and may be used for any recipes specifying cooked chicken.

1 × 1.5 kg (3 lb) chicken; about 2.75 litres/5 pints (12 cups) water; 1 tsp salt; 2 shallots, chopped; 4 tbsp peanut oil; extra salt.

Place chicken in a large, heavy saucepan and add sufficient water to cover the chicken well. When you have established the amount of water you will need, remove chicken. Add salt and shallots to water and bring to the boil. Lower chicken back into pan, bring back to the boil and simmer for 5 minutes. Cover pan, remove from heat and let chicken cool in the liquid for 2 hours. Remove chicken from pan, rinse under cold water and dry with paper towels. Brush skin all over with peanut oil and sprinkle generously with extra salt. Use as desired for Coriander Chicken (page 83), or for chicken salads, creamed chicken etc. The cooking liquid makes a very good light chicken stock, for light soups, sauces and gravies.

NOTE: When cool and just before serving, chop chicken into 5 × 2 cm (2 × 1 in) pieces and arrange on plate.

Chicken à la King

45 g/1½ oz (3 tbsp) butter; 3 tbsp flour; 350 ml/12 fl oz (1½ cups) chicken stock or single (light) cream; 500 g/1 lb (2 cups) cooked chicken, diced (see Poached Chicken, page 67); 60 g/2 oz (½ cup) sliced mushrooms, sautéed; 30 g/1 oz (¼ cup) canned pimiento, cut into strips; 1 egg yolk, beaten; salt and freshly ground black pepper; 30 g/1 oz (¼ cup) slivered, blanched almonds; 1 tbsp dry sherry.

Melt butter in a heavy saucepan, stir in flour and cook for 2 minutes over low heat. Gradually add chicken stock or cream, stirring until sauce thickens and boils. Add chicken, mushrooms and pimiento. Pour some sauce over egg yolk and mix well, then return to mixture in pan. Cook gently, stirring until thickened slightly. Season with salt and pepper and fold in almonds and sherry. Serve at once with boiled rice or noodles. Serves 4–6.

CHICKEN KIEV

Chicken Kiev at its finest is simply a boned and flattened chicken breast wrapped around chilled butter lightly flavoured with chives. It is then dipped in egg and breadcrumbs and fried golden-crisp. Pierced with a fork, the chicken releases a jet of golden butter (unwary diners should be warned!) and the combination of liquid butter and juicy chicken is perfection, with no further dressing-up needed. If you order chicken Kiev and find it flavoured with garlic, or with mushrooms added to the filling, it is a chef's unnecessary variation. Follow the recipe below, and you will be making it as it was created in Kiev in Russia, and is still served there today.

Chicken Kiev

1 whole chicken breast, cut from a large chicken, with wing attached; 30 g/1 oz

(2 tbsp) butter; salt and freshly ground black pepper; 2 tbsp finely snipped chives; flour for coating; 1 egg, lightly beaten; 60 g/2 oz (1 cup) fresh white breadcrumbs, rubbed through a sieve; oil for deep-frying.

Cut chicken breast in half. With a sharp, pointed knife remove bones from breast, leaving wing joints (including bones) attached. Cut wing off at first joint and scrape meat off bone so it is clean and attached to breast. Peel away skin. Place 2 pieces of breast between 2 sheets of plastic wrap and pound until thin with a mallet. Cut butter into 2 pieces and roll each into a cork shape. Chill. Place a roll of butter at base of each chicken breast, diagonally in line with wing bone. Sprinkle with salt, pepper and chives. Fold chicken flesh over butter, then roll up towards bone, folding sides in as you go to enclose butter completely inside chicken. The flesh will adhere without skewers. Coat each rolled breast lightly with flour, dip in egg and roll in breadcrumbs. Refrigerate for at least 2 hours.

Heat oil in large saucepan, using enough to cover chicken breasts. To test if oil is hot enough, drop a cube of bread into it. The bread should rise to the surface immediately. Gently lower chicken into oil and fry for 4½–5 minutes or until golden-brown. (This is the only tricky part to Chicken Kiev. The oil must be hot enough to brown chicken breast, but not colour it too much before chicken is cooked through.) If chicken starts to brown too quickly during this time, lower the heat. Remove from oil, drain on paper towels and serve immediately, with warm straw potatoes (the packaged variety will do). Serves 2.

CHICKEN WINGS

Many people think the wing is the best part of the chicken. Certainly the wings contain meat that is tender, full of flavour and can be prepared in an endless variety of ways. They make an economical dish to serve a crowd, provide delectable mini-drumsticks to serve with drinks, and are perfect in dishes from China, Italy, Spain or in almost any cuisine imaginable.

Barbecue Chicken Wings

Guests can nibble these while waiting for the main barbecued food.

1 kg (2 lb) chicken wings, tips removed; 2 tbsp tomato purée (paste); 2 tbsp cider or wine vinegar; 2 tbsp oil; 1 tbsp French (Dijon) mustard; 2 cloves garlic, crushed; 1 tbsp salt.

Place wings in a large bowl. Mix together remaining ingredients and spoon over wings. Marinate, covered, for several hours or overnight in refrigerator, turning wings occasionally to coat evenly. Drain wings of marinade, and barbecue or grill (broil) under

a preheated moderate grill (broiler) until crisp and brown on both sides. Or bake in a preheated moderately hot oven (190°C/375°F, Gas Mark 5), turning once. Cooking time will be 10–15 minutes. Serves 4.

Southern Fried Chicken Wings

1 kg (2 lb) chicken wings, tips removed; 750 ml/1¼ pints (3 cups) milk; 125 g/4 oz (1 cup) flour; salt; ¼ tsp white pepper; 250 g/8 oz (1 cup) lard (shortening); 30 g/1 oz (2 tbsp) butter; 3 cloves garlic, unpeeled; 1 onion, finely chopped; ¼ tsp dried sage; extra 4 tsp flour; 250 ml/8 fl oz (1 cup) chicken stock; 4 tbsp single (light) cream; ½ tsp Worcestershire sauce; ¼ tsp cayenne.

Place chicken wings in a bowl, cover with 500 ml/18 fl oz (2 cups) milk and chill for 1 hour; drain. In a plastic bag combine flour, salt and pepper. Shake wings in bag until they are well coated with flour. Shake off excess flour. Heat lard (shortening) in a deep frying pan (skillet) until very hot. Add butter, whole garlic cloves and chicken wings and fry for about 8 minutes or until tender and golden-brown. Drain on crumpled paper towels and keep warm. Pour off all but 2 tbsp fat from pan and discard garlic. Add onion and sage and cook until onion softens. Mix in extra 4 tsp flour and cook, stirring, until golden-brown. Add remaining milk and the stock, stirring until gravy thickens and boils. Stir in the cream, Worcestershire sauce and cayenne, bring to the boil, and strain gravy into a sauceboat. Serve gravy with chicken wings. Serves 4.

Chicken Wings Provençale

1 kg (2 lb) chicken wings, tips removed; 2 tbsp olive oil; 15 g/½ oz (1 tbsp) butter; 1 onion, finely chopped; 2 cloves garlic, crushed; 1 large green pepper, cored, seeded and cut in 2.5 cm (1 in) pieces; 120 ml/4 fl oz (½ cup) dry white wine; 250 ml/8 fl oz (1 cup) chicken stock; 1 × 425 g/14 oz can tomatoes; 1 tsp tomato purée (paste); 2 tsp chopped, fresh marjoram or ½ tsp dried; 2 tsp chopped fresh thyme, or ½ tsp dried; 1 bay leaf; 12 black (ripe) olives; chopped parsley.

Halve wings at joints. Heat olive oil and butter in a frying pan (skillet) and fry chicken wings over moderately high heat until golden-brown. Remove and keep warm. Add onion, garlic and green pepper and cook until onion is softened. Add wine and reduce over high heat for 1 minute. Add chicken wings, stock, tomatoes and juice, tomato purée (paste), marjoram, thyme and bay leaf. Bring to the boil, lower heat and simmer, covered, for 15 minutes. Add olives and cook 5 minutes longer or until chicken wings

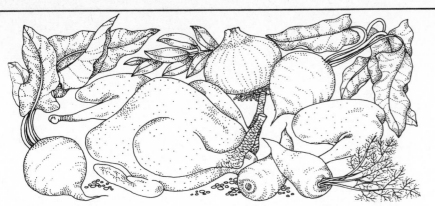

C

are tender. Transfer chicken wings to heated serving platter. Reduce liquid over moderately high heat to about 250 ml/8 fl oz (1 cup), discard bay leaf, and pour over chicken wings. Garnish with chopped parsley. Serves 4.

Chicken Wings Italian-Style

120 ml/4 fl oz ($\frac{1}{2}$ cup) olive oil; juice 1 lemon; 1 tbsp chopped parsley; salt and freshly ground black pepper; 1 kg (2 lb) chicken wings, tips removed; 125 g/4 oz (1 cup) flour; 2 eggs, lightly beaten; oil for deep-frying.

Combine olive oil, lemon juice, parsley, salt and pepper. Add chicken wings, turning to coat thoroughly. Marinate, covered, for 1 hour at room temperature or overnight in refrigerator. Drain chicken and dredge with flour to give a light coating. Dip in beaten egg and deep-fry in hot oil for about 5 minutes or until tender and golden-brown. Drain on crumpled paper towels and serve immediately. Serves 4.

Chicken Wings in Black Bean and Oyster Sauce

1 kg (2 lb) chicken wings, tips removed; 2 tbsp soy sauce; 2 tbsp dry sherry; 1 tbsp peanut oil; 2 tsp cornflour (cornstarch); 1 tsp sugar; 3 tsp very finely chopped fresh ginger; 2 tbsp canned black beans; 2 tbsp very finely chopped spring onions (scallions); 2 cloves garlic, crushed with pinch salt; 120 ml/4 fl oz ($\frac{1}{2}$ cup) chicken stock; 2 tbsp oyster sauce; 2 tsp sesame oil; 30 g/1 oz ($\frac{1}{4}$ cup) sliced spring onions (scallions) to garnish.

Halve wings at joints. Combine soy sauce, sherry, peanut oil, 1 tsp cornflour (cornstarch), the sugar and 1 tsp ginger. Add wings, coat well with marinade and marinate, covered, at room temperature for 1 hour. Rinse, drain and chop beans. Combine with spring onions (scallions), remaining ginger, garlic. Preheat a wok or frying pan (skillet), add black bean mixture and stir-fry for 30 seconds. Add wings and marinade and stir-fry for 3 minutes or until wings are browned lightly. Stir in remaining cornflour (cornstarch) dissolved in stock and simmer,

covered, for 15 minutes or until wings are tender. Cook uncovered, over high heat, tossing wings until they are glazed and sauce thickened. Stir in oyster sauce and sesame oil and cook mixture, tossing it, for 1 minute. Serve on a heated platter, sprinkled with sliced spring onions (scallions). Serves 4.
NOTE: Buy canned black beans, oyster sauce and sesame oil from Chinese grocery stores, health food shops, delicatessens and most supermarkets.

Spiced Chicken Wings with Chick Peas

1 kg (2 lb) chicken wings, tips removed; salt; $\frac{1}{2}$ tsp ground ginger; 120 ml/4 fl oz ($\frac{1}{2}$ cup) oil; 2 large onions, finely chopped; 2 cloves garlic, crushed; 2 tsp ground coriander; 2 tsp ground cumin; 1 tsp cinnamon; pinch cayenne; 500 ml/18 fl oz (2 cups) chicken stock; freshly ground black pepper; 350 g/12 oz (2 cups) canned chick peas (garbanzos), drained.

Sprinkle wings with salt and ginger. Heat oil in a large frying pan (skillet) and brown wings over moderately high heat. Transfer to a casserole dish. Add onions and garlic to frying pan (skillet) and cook until onions soften. Stir in spices and cook for 1 minute, then add chicken stock, salt and pepper. Arrange drained chick peas over chicken wings and pour stock mixture over. Cover and cook in a preheated moderate oven (180°C/350°F, Gas Mark 4) for 25 minutes. Remove lid and bake 5 minutes longer. Serve with plenty of crusty bread and a salad. Serves 4–6.

CHICK PEA

See Pulses: Dried Beans, Peas and Lentils.

CHICORY

A group of plants cultivated for their leaves. Chicory was first grown in Belgium, where it is called *witloof*. Its elongated yellowish leaves, with pale green tips, are tightly bunched together. Sliced across, with leaves separated, it makes a lovely salad, dressed with a little lemon juice and olive or walnut oil. It can be mixed with julienne (matchstick) strips of

cooked beetroot or slices of orange.
BRAISED CHICORY (ENDIVE) Blanch whole heads in a little boiling salted water, drain, then cook in a little melted butter and stock. In this way it is particularly good with veal, chicken or ham. **See recipes.**
NOTE: There is some confusion between the use of the names chicory and endive. In the U.S.A. and France, what we (in the U.K.) refer to as chicory or witloof is called endive or Belgian endive, while our curly endive is called chicory in the U.S.A. and France.

Creamed Chicory

6 heads chicory (endive); 90 g/3 oz (6 tbsp) butter; salt and freshly ground white pepper; pinch nutmeg; 120 ml/4 fl oz ($\frac{1}{2}$ cup) single (light) cream.

Cook chicory (endive) in boiling salted water for 10–15 minutes. Drain, pressing well to remove as much water as possible. Heat butter in a frying pan (skillet), add chicory (endive), salt, pepper and nutmeg and sauté over brisk heat for about 3 minutes. Add cream and bring to the boil, shaking pan until cream thickens a little. Serves 4–6.
VARIATION
Purée of Chicory: Prepare 6 heads chicory (endive) as above. When cooked, purée in a food processor fitted with steel blade or in a blender. Reheat before serving. Good with roast beef, pork or duckling. Serves 4–6.

Chicory Flamande

A version of braised chicory served as a first course or as a vegetable accompaniment.

6 heads chicory (endive); 60 g/2 oz (4 tbsp) butter; juice 1 lemon; 150 ml/$\frac{1}{4}$ pint ($\frac{2}{3}$ cup) chicken stock; 1 tsp salt; 1 tsp sugar; freshly ground white pepper; paprika or chopped parsley to garnish.

Arrange chicory (endive) in a buttered ovenproof dish. Melt butter with lemon juice, stock, salt, sugar and pepper and pour over chicory (endive). Cover with lid or a piece of buttered greaseproof (waxed) paper and cook in preheated moderate oven (180°C/350°F, Gas Mark 4) for 35–40 minutes. Remove lid and brown top under a preheated grill (broiler). Sprinkle with paprika or chopped parsley. Serves 6.

Chicory and Walnut Salad

2 tbsp red wine vinegar; 1 tsp French (Dijon) mustard; 2 tsp salt; 5 tbsp olive oil; 1 tsp black pepper; 60 g/2 oz ($\frac{1}{2}$ cup) coarsely chopped walnuts; 4 firm heads chicory (endive), quartered lengthways; 125 g/4 oz (2 cups) watercress sprigs.

Mix together vinegar, mustard and salt in a bowl, then add olive oil, pepper, and walnuts. Wrap chicory (endive) and watercress in a tea-towel and refrigerate to chill and crisp them. When ready to serve, put greens in a salad bowl, pour dressing over them, and toss gently. Serves 4.

CHILLIES

These small, fiery members of the pepper family are essential to Latin American, Indian and much of South East Asian cuisine. They are used in cooking, as condiments and garnishes and as a flavouring for vinegar and pickles. Unripe (green or yellow) chillies are juicier, with more flavour; ripe (red) chillies, either fresh or dried, are hotter. The dried ones give brighter colour but are less fragrant than the fresh ones. The heat of chillies also differs from one variety to another – the tiny bird's-eye chilli is particularly fiery.

To handle whole chillies: Working under cold, running water, make a slit down the side of the chilli and scrape out the seeds with the point of a knife. Take care not to touch your nose or eyes as the juice will burn them, and always wash your hands well after handling chillies. Before chopping or grinding dried chillies, tear each one into 3–4 pieces and soak in hot water for 10 minutes. Drain and squeeze out excess moisture before using as required.

Other ways to add chilli flavour: Chilli powder is made from ground, dried chilli flesh. Asian-style powder is hotter than Mexican-style powder, which contains cumin and other spices as well as chilli. Sambal ulek (or oelek) is a paste of fresh chillies ground with salt. Chilli sauce combines chillies with other aromatics and comes in various degrees of heat.

See also *Tabasco Sauce.*

CHILLI CON CARNE

A Texan dish of beans and beef in a chilli sauce, now popular all over the U.S.A. and in other parts of the world. The meat may be diced or minced (ground), and the amount of chilli depends on the cook – though the original version was fiery.

Chilli Con Carne

30 g/1 oz (2 tbsp) bacon dripping or butter; 1 large onion, finely chopped; 1 large clove garlic, finely chopped; 750 g (1½ lb) stewing beef, minced (ground) or diced; 1 × 425 g/ 14 oz can tomatoes; 2 × 310 g/10 oz cans kidney beans, drained; ½ bay leaf; 2 tsp–2 tbsp chilli powder (to taste); salt; pinch brown sugar.

Melt fat in a large, heavy saucepan and cook onion and garlic gently until golden. Add beef and brown lightly. Chop tomatoes and add with their juice, the beans, bay leaf, chilli powder, salt and brown sugar. Stir, cover tightly and simmer very gently for about 1 hour for minced (ground) meat, 1½ hours or until tender for diced meat. Discard bay leaf. Serve with Tortillas or Corn Bread (see pages 441 and 84). Serves 8.

CHINESE PARSLEY

See *Coriander.*

CHIPOLATA

Chipolatas are especially small sausages, often pan-fried or grilled (broiled) and served with cocktail sticks (toothpicks) and a sauce for dunking. Chipolatas are also used to garnish roast chicken or the Christmas turkey, in which case they are not separated, but cooked in a string and draped around the festive bird like a necklace.

CHIVES

A member of the onion family. Chives grow in clumps of slender green tubular leaves. With their delicate flavour and bright green colour, chives go particularly well with cheese, eggs and potatoes – especially baked potatoes, split open and piled with sour cream.

Chives grow easily in the garden or in pots; they need plenty of sun and the more you cut them the more they grow. Chives are usually cut up small with scissors to prevent their bruising, and added to foods just before serving.

CHOCOLATE

Chocolate and cocoa are made from the bean of the cacao tree. Chocolate was first enjoyed as a hot drink, later it was used for baking, then a great development took place in Switzerland when someone thought of combining milk and chocolate for eating.

Chocolate is more than a delicacy; it is good solid food and nourishment and is considered as such by many nations. Chocolate is part of army rations in times of stress. Mountaineers carry it with them as a matter of course. French children eat it on bread instead of butter and jam, and the comfort derived from a bar of chocolate when one is feeling tired is not to be underestimated.

Chocolate is also used in baking – chocolate cake is an international favourite. It is essential to some of the world's most delicious cakes and sweets – truffles, éclairs, chocolate mousse. Chocolate sauce is superb with ice creams or spooned over profiteroles. **See recipes.**

See also *Cocoa.*

Types of Chocolate and Their Uses

Dark chocolate is semi-sweet (the less sugar that is added to chocolate, the stronger its flavour) and ideal for cooking. Use for icing (frosting), mousse, sauces etc.; it has a high fat content so is easy to melt and the sugar in it helps to produce a good sheen.

Milk chocolate, available in bars, has dried milk added to the formula. It is lighter and milder than chocolate without milk added, and is used primarily as an eating chocolate.

Chocolate chips are made from semi-sweet dark chocolate. They retain their shape to some extent in baking, and are especially adapted to biscuit (cookie) making – see Tollhouse Cookies, opposite.

Powdered or drinking chocolate was introduced before eating chocolate; use in hot or cold milk drinks.

Cooking chocolate is a semi-sweet dark chocolate. Cheap cooking chocolate compounds are available and are suitable for use in cakes.

To melt chocolate: It burns so easily it is best to melt it on a plate or in a bowl over a pan of hot water – if chocolate is overheated it scorches. Break up or grate chocolate so it melts evenly and quickly.

To make chocolate curls: or thin chocolate shavings for topping pies, ice cream or desserts, use a swivel-bladed vegetable parer. Have chocolate at room temperature and pare little curls of chocolate from edge of block. Store in refrigerator until required.

To make chocolate caraque: This is the classic chocolate decoration for cakes and many desserts. It takes practice and skill to make, but is well worth the trouble. Shred or grate 90 g/3 oz (½ cup) good dark chocolate and melt it on a plate over a pan of hot water.

Do not allow the plate to get too hot and work chocolate with a palette knife. Spread it thinly on a marble slab. When just on point of setting, curl it off with a thin knife – the chocolate will form long scrolls or flakes. Place these on greaseproof (waxed) paper and chill in refrigerator; handle carefully. Keep in an airtight container if necessary.

Chocolate Glaze Melt together 60 g/2 oz (4 tbsp) butter and 60 g/2 oz (⅓ cup) dark chocolate in a bowl over a pan of hot water. Gradually beat in 2 tbsp boiling water, 140 g/4½ oz (1 cup) icing (confectioners) sugar, sifted, a pinch of salt and ¼ tsp vanilla essence (extract). Use as a glaze over chocolate cake.

Rum Chocolate Frosting Melt 90 g/3 oz (½ cup) dark chocolate with 120 ml/4 fl oz (½ cup) rum over a low heat. Add 560 g/ 1 lb 2 oz (4 cups) icing (confectioners) sugar, sifted, 140 g/4½ oz (1 cup) at a time, beating well after each addition. Beat in 60 g/2 oz (4 tbsp) soft butter. Add a little more rum, if necessary, to make frosting of spreading consistency. Use to frost and fill chocolate cakes or gâteaux.

Chocolate Mint Sauce This is one of the easiest recipes for chocolate sauce. Put 12 chocolate peppermint creams in a small bowl that will fit over a pan of boiling water. Melt creams, then stir in 120 ml/4 fl oz (½ cup) single (light) cream. Serve warm or cool, over ice cream or poached pears. Serves 4.

Mexican Chocolate This is especially prepared for making into drinks, and is strongly flavoured with cinnamon. You can get the same effect by melting 30 g/1 oz (2–3 tbsp) grated dark chocolate in a mug of hot milk, with ¼–½ tsp cinnamon added. Beat with a whisk until foamy, adding a little brown sugar if you prefer it sweeter.

Chocolate Cake

(For a crowd)

60 g/2 oz (½ cup) cocoa powder (unsweetened); 120 ml/4 fl oz (½ cup) boiling water; 180 g/6 oz (¾ cup) butter; 350 g/12 oz (1½ cups) caster sugar; 1 tsp vanilla essence (extract); 3 eggs, beaten; 250 g/8 oz (2 cups) self-raising flour; pinch salt; ¼ tsp bicarbonate of soda (baking soda); 175 ml/6 fl oz (¾ cup) milk.

TO SERVE: raspberry jam; whipped cream.

Blend cocoa with boiling water and cool. Cream butter with sugar until light and fluffy. Beat in vanilla and eggs. Gradually mix in cooled cocoa mixture. Sift flour, salt and bicarbonate of soda (baking soda) and fold into creamed mixture alternately with milk. Spoon into a greased and floured 28 × 19 × 4 cm (11 × 7½ × 1½ in) tin (pan). Bake in a preheated moderate oven (180°C/350°F, Gas Mark 4) for 30–35 minutes or until a fine skewer inserted in the

centre comes out clean. Leave to stand in the tin (pan) for a few minutes, then turn out on to a wire rack to cool. Cut into squares and serve with raspberry jam and a bowl of whipped cream. Makes 24 pieces.

Honey Chocolate Cake

180 g/6 oz (¾ cup) butter; 180 g/6 oz (1 cup) lightly packed brown sugar; 125 g/4 oz (⅓ cup) honey; 2 eggs, beaten; 3 tsp rum; ½ tsp vanilla essence (extract); 2 tbsp (unsweetened) cocoa powder; 210 g/7 oz (1¾ cups) self-raising flour; pinch salt; 120 ml/4 fl oz (½ cup) sweet sherry.
TO FINISH: whipped cream; almond essence (extract); icing (confectioners) sugar or Chocolate Glaze (left).

Cream butter with brown sugar and honey until light and fluffy. Add eggs one at a time, beating well after each addition. Add rum and vanilla. Sift cocoa, flour and salt together 3 times. Fold into creamed mixture alternately with sherry. Spoon into a greased and bottom-lined 23 cm (9 in) round cake tin (pan). Bake in a preheated moderate oven (180°C/350°F, Gas Mark 4) for 45 minutes or until a skewer inserted in the centre comes out clean. Cool in tin (pan) for 5 minutes, then turn out on to a wire rack. When cold, split cake into 2 layers and fill with whipped cream flavoured with a few drops of almond essence (extract). Dust top with sifted icing (confectioners) sugar or top with chocolate glaze.

Chocolate Syrup

Serve over ice cream, pancakes, steamed puddings or use to flavour milk drinks.

180 g/6 oz (1 cup) dark chocolate, melted, or 125 g/4 oz (1 cup) cocoa powder (unsweetened); nut of butter (optional); 350 g/12 oz (1½ cups) sugar; ¼ tsp salt; 250 ml/8 fl oz (1 cup) boiling water; 1 tsp vanilla essence (extract).

Blend melted chocolate or cocoa with sugar and salt. Add butter, if liked, for a richer syrup. Place in a saucepan with boiling water and cook over medium heat for 5 minutes, stirring constantly. Cool, then stir in vanilla. Makes 450 ml/¾ pint (2 cups).

Chocolate Sauce

60 g/2 oz (½ cup) drinking chocolate powder; 250 ml/8 fl oz (1 cup) evaporated milk; 1 tbsp golden (light corn) syrup; ½ tsp vanilla essence (extract); 2 tsp butter.

Combine drinking chocolate with evaporated milk and golden syrup in a saucepan. Bring to the boil, stirring constantly, then simmer for 5 minutes. Remove from heat and add vanilla and butter. Makes 300 ml/½ pint (1¼ cups).

Tollhouse Cookies

150 g/5 oz (1¼ cups) flour; ¼ tsp bicarbonate of soda (baking soda); ½ tsp salt; 125 g/4 oz (½ cup) butter; 45 g/1½ oz (¼ cup) firmly packed brown sugar; 125 g/4 oz (½ cup) white sugar; 1 egg, beaten; 1 tsp vanilla essence (extract); 1 × 100 g/3½ oz packet chocolate chips.

Sift flour, soda and salt together. Cream butter with sugars until light and fluffy. Add egg and vanilla and beat well. Stir in sifted dry ingredients and chocolate chips. Drop teaspoonfuls on to greased baking trays, leaving room for spreading. Bake in a preheated moderate oven (180°C/350°F, Gas Mark 4), for 10 minutes. Cool on wire racks. Makes about 36.

Chocolate Roll

A lovely, light-as-air chocolate roll with very little flour.

60 g/2 oz (½ cup) flour; ¼ tsp salt; ½ tsp baking powder; 60 g/2 oz (⅓ cup) cooking chocolate, broken up; 4 eggs; 180 g/6 oz (¾ cup) caster sugar; 1 tsp vanilla essence (extract); 2 tbsp cold water; ½ tsp bicarbonate of soda (baking soda); sifted icing (confectioners) sugar.

Sift together flour, salt and baking powder. Melt chocolate gently in a heatproof bowl over hot water. Allow to cool slightly. Beat eggs with caster sugar until very light and thick. Fold flour mixture and vanilla all at once into egg mixture. Add water and soda to chocolate, stirring until smooth. Fold quickly and lightly into egg and flour mixture. Turn mixture into a greased and lined 38 × 25 × 2.5 cm (15 × 10 × 1 in) Swiss roll tin (jelly roll pan), or a paper case (see page 74). Bake in a preheated moderately hot oven (200°C/400°F, Gas Mark 6) for about 15 minutes or until cake springs back when centre is gently pressed. Loosen edges and turn cake out on to a tea-towel generously dredged with icing (confectioners) sugar. Peel off lining paper and trim edges of cake with a sharp knife. Roll immediately in towel, first folding hem of towel over edge of cake, and rolling towel in the cake to prevent sticking. After cake is rolled, cool on a wire rack for at least 1 hour.

Before serving, carefully unroll cake and quickly spread with whipped cream sweetened with a little sugar and flavoured with vanilla or brandy, then sprinkle with sliced strawberries if you wish. Re-roll cake, using tea-towel to help, and dust with more icing (confectioners) sugar. The cake can be decorated with rosettes of whipped cream and the rosettes topped with chocolate caraque (see page 72) or whole strawberries, if liked.

To make a paper baking case: Choose a fairly thick greaseproof (waxed) paper or non-stick paper. Take a piece 30 × 43 cm (12 × 17 in) and fold over ends and sides to form a border about 2.5 cm (1 in). Cut a slit at each corner and fold one cut piece over the other to mitre corner. Fasten each corner with a paper clip so borders stand up. Slide case on to a baking tray before filling with mixture.

Hot Chocolate Soufflés

125 g/4 oz (⅔ cup) dark chocolate; 3 tbsp brandy or coffee; 5 eggs, separated; 4 tbsp sugar; 250 ml/8 fl oz (1 cup) double (heavy) cream, whipped, to serve.

Melt chocolate with brandy or coffee in a heatproof bowl placed over hot water. Beat egg yolks with sugar until very pale and thick. Beat in chocolate mixture. Beat egg whites until firm but not dry and fold in egg yolk mixture with a large metal spoon. Spoon into individual soufflé dishes that have been greased with unsalted butter, filling them about ¾ full. Place on a baking tray, arranging so the dishes do not touch each other. Bake on the bottom shelf of a preheated moderately hot oven (190°C/375°F, Gas Mark 5) for 15–18 minutes. Serve immediately on heated plates. Pass whipped cream: each guest makes a hole in the centre of the soufflé and fills it with a dollop of whipped cream. Serves 4–6.

Chocolate Cherry Squares

180 g/6 oz (1 cup) dark chocolate; 60 g/2 oz (4 tbsp) butter; 210 g/7 oz (2½ cups) crushed digestive biscuits (graham crackers); grated rind 1 orange; 90 g/3 oz (½ cup) sultanas (golden raisins); 60 g/2 oz (¼ cup) chopped glacé (candied) cherries; glacé (candied) cherries to decorate.

Melt chocolate and butter in a bowl over a pan of hot water. Remove the pan from heat. Add crushed biscuits (crackers) with orange rind, sultanas (golden raisins) and cherries. Mix well and press into a greased 18 cm (7 in) square tin (pan). Mark into 9 squares and decorate with halved cherries. Chill before cutting into squares to serve. Makes 9.

No Bake Fruit Bars

150 g/5 oz (1¼ cups) crushed sweet biscuits (graham crackers); 60 g/2 oz (½ cup) chopped walnuts; 90 g/3 oz (½ cup) sultanas (golden raisins); 2 tbsp golden (light corn) syrup; 75 g/2½ oz (5 tbsp) butter; 60 g/2 oz (⅓ cup) dark chocolate.

Grease a shallow 18 cm (7 in) square tin (pan). Mix biscuits (crackers) with walnuts and sultanas (golden raisins). Heat syrup, butter and chocolate in a bowl over a pan of hot water. When hot, pour into biscuit (cracker) mixture and mix well. Spoon into the prepared tin (pan) and smooth surface with a palette knife. Chill until set, then cut into small bars. Makes 14.

Chocolate Mousse

125 g/4 oz (⅔ cup) dark chocolate, broken up; 2 tsp instant coffee powder, dissolved in 1 tbsp hot water; 4 eggs, separated; 2 tsp rum or brandy; cream to serve.

Place chocolate and coffee in a small heatproof bowl placed over hot water and stir until chocolate is smooth and melted. Remove from heat and blend in egg yolks one at a time, stirring until thoroughly combined. Beat egg whites until stiff and gently fold into chocolate mixture with rum or brandy. Spoon into 6 mousse pots and chill for 4 hours or overnight. Serve with pouring or whipped cream, or pipe a swirl of whipped cream on top and finish off with chocolate curls or caraque (see page 72) or candied violets. Serves 6.

CHOKO

A delicate pale green, pear-shaped vegetable which makes its first appearance at the end of summer and continues on until early winter. It is one of the most attractive and delicious of vegetables. The choko, which is related to the gourd family, originally came from Mexico, where it is still considered a great delicacy. In Mexico it is known as chayote.

When you buy chokos, look for young, tender ones, with a pale green, almost translucent skin. The spikes on the skin should be short and soft. Older chokos have a lighter coloured, opaque skin, and the spikes are quite brittle.

□ **Basic Preparation:** Cut choko into quarters along the natural grooves, peel and remove the centre core. It is best to do this under cold running water, as the choko exudes a sticky liquid which stains the hands. Very young chokos need not be peeled, just halved – the skin is quite tender.

□ **To Cook:** Drop choko quarters into boiling salted water and simmer for 5–8 minutes until just tender. Drain and toss in butter and chopped fresh herbs.

CHOP SUEY

The name literally means 'bits and pieces' and is a Chinese way of dealing with leftovers or small quantities of food. It originated in the U.S.A., and is served over steamed rice.

Chop Suey

2 tbsp peanut oil; 250 g (8 oz) pork fillet (tenderloin), very finely sliced; ½ Chinese cabbage, shredded; 125 g (4 oz) green beans, sliced diagonally; 2 onions, halved and sliced lengthways; 3 sticks celery, sliced diagonally; 2 tsp cornflour (cornstarch); 250 ml/8 fl oz (1 cup) chicken stock; 1 tbsp soy sauce; 250 g (8 oz) cooked White Chicken (Chinese Steamed Chicken, page 69); 250 g (8 oz) prawns (shrimp), shelled and deveined; 250 g/8 oz (1 cup) sliced bamboo shoots.

Heat oil in a wok or large frying pan (skillet), add pork and cook until well browned, about 5 minutes. Add cabbage, beans, onions and celery and toss until all ingredients are well combined. Stir-fry a further 3 minutes. Mix cornflour (cornstarch) with a little stock and add to remaining stock with soy sauce. Pour into wok and stir until sauce boils and thickens. Add chicken, prawns (shrimp) and bamboo shoots and cook 3 minutes or until prawns (shrimp) are cooked. Serves 4.

CHORIZO

A spicy, coarse-textured sausage very popular in Spain.

Chicken Catalonia

4 tbsp olive oil; 1 kg (2 lb) chicken pieces; 125 g (4 oz) chorizo sausage, finely sliced; 125 g (4 oz) boned pork leg or loin, cubed; 125 g/4 oz (½ cup) cooked ham, cubed; 1 large onion, chopped; 1 tomato, chopped; 1 green pepper, cored, seeded and sliced; 280 g/9 oz (1¼ cups) long-grain rice; 600 ml/1 pint (2½ cups) boiling stock; ¼ tsp saffron, crumbled; 125 g (4 oz) sliced green beans; 1 tsp salt; ½ tsp black pepper; 90 g/3 oz (½ cup) frozen or shelled fresh peas; 1 canned pimiento, sliced; chopped parsley to garnish.

Heat oil in a large frying pan (skillet) or paella dish. Brown chicken on both sides, then transfer to a plate. Add sausage, pork and ham, brown lightly and remove to a plate. Put onion in pan and brown lightly over gentle heat. Add tomato and green pepper, and cook for 2 minutes. Stir in rice and cook, stirring, for 3 minutes. Add stock, saffron, beans, sausage, pork, ham and chicken and bring back to the boil. Season with salt and pepper. Cook over gentle heat for 25–30 minutes or until rice and chicken are tender and liquid is absorbed. It may be necessary to add more stock or water during cooking to prevent dish becoming too dry. Stir in peas and pimiento for last 10 minutes of cooking. Sprinkle with chopped parsley before serving. Serves 6–8.

CHOWDER

A thick fish or seafood soup to which salt pork or bacon and diced vegetables are added, cream or milk making up part of the stock. It takes its name from the French word for pot or cauldron, *chaudière*, but is now more associated with New England and Newfoundland.

Old-Fashioned Fish Chowder

This recipe may also be made with smoked fish. Poach the fish to remove excess salt, then flake and use as for fresh fish.

125 g (4 oz) pickled (salt) pork, diced, or 4 rashers (slices) bacon, rind removed and diced; 2 onions, finely sliced; 3 potatoes, peeled and diced; 2 tbsp flour; 900 ml/1½ pints (3¾ cups) Fish Stock (page 414); 1 kg (2 lb) cod or any firm white fish fillet, cut in chunks; 500 ml/18 fl oz (2 cups) hot single (light) cream or milk; 2 tbsp butter; salt and freshly ground white pepper; 2 tbsp chopped parsley.

Cook pork or bacon very gently in a heavy saucepan, until fat has melted and meat is brown. Remove and reserve pork or bacon. Add onions to fat in pan and cook over low heat until golden. Stir in potatoes and flour, and toss until coated. Add fish stock and cook about 10 minutes. Add fish chunks and simmer, partially covered, until fish is tender, about 10 minutes. Stir in hot, but not boiling,

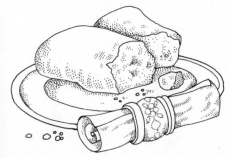

cream or milk and heat very slowly, without boiling. Add pork or bacon and butter, then season with salt and pepper and stir in parsley. Serves 6.

NOTE: Use head and bones from filleted fish to make fish stock. A good brand of packaged fish soup may be used in place of the home-made stock.

CHOW MEIN

Food with noodles is the literal translation. Diced chicken, pork or seafood is stir-fried in oil with Chinese vegetables, then finished with a sauce and served with fried noodles.

Chow Mein with Seafood

3½ tbsp oil; 1 onion, sliced; 2 rashers (slices) bacon, rind removed and chopped; 1 × 185 g/6 oz can crabmeat, drained; 3 tbsp soy sauce; 350 g (12 oz) Chinese noodles, cooked in boiling water and drained well; 2½ tbsp butter; 3 slices fresh ginger, chopped; 3 cloves garlic, crushed; 1 small red pepper, seeded and shredded; 6 oysters; 250 g (8 oz) prawns (shrimp), shelled and deveined; 3 spring onions (scallions), sliced; salt and freshly ground white pepper; 1 tsp sugar; 2 tbsp dry sherry.

Heat oil, add onion and bacon and stir-fry for 1 minute. Add crabmeat and 2 tbsp soy sauce, and stir-fry for 1 minute. Mix in noodles and remaining soy sauce and stir-fry for 1 minute. Reduce heat to low and simmer gently 3–4 minutes. Heat butter in a separate small frying pan (skillet) over medium heat, add ginger, garlic, red pepper, oysters and prawns (shrimp). Stir-fry for 1 minute. Sprinkle with spring onions (scallions), salt, pepper, sugar and sherry. Stir-fry for a further 1 minute. Spoon the noodles mixture into a large serving bowl and spoon prawn (shrimp) mixture over. Serves 2–4.

CHRISTMAS CAKE

The rich and spicy fruit cake of England, made a few months before 25th December so that it will mature into a truly festive cake, is one of the joys of Christmas. It may be topped with halved almonds before baking, and finished off with a sprig of holly. Some prefer a more elaborate iced (frosted) version: a coating of almond paste, then an icing (frosting). A few Christmas decorations, a fir tree, a toy Santa Claus, Christmas bells or an appropriate greeting may be used to give a dash of colour.

Christmas Cake

1 Rich Fruit Cake (page 136); ½ quantity Almond Paste (page 7).

GLAZE: *3 tbsp apricot jam; 2 tbsp water; 1 tsp lemon juice.*
ICING (FROSTING): *2 egg whites; 500 g/1 lb (3½ cups) pure icing (confectioners) sugar, sifted; 1–2 tsp lemon juice.*

Make cake 2 months before Christmas, and store in an airtight tin until required.
GLAZE: Bring apricot jam and water to the boil and boil for 4 minutes. Push through a sieve, return to saucepan with lemon juice and heat through. Brush hot glaze over top of cake. Roll out almond paste into a round to fit top of cake. Place on cake and gently press with edge of rolling pin. Leave at least 24 hours before icing (frosting).
ICING (FROSTING): Whisk egg whites to a light froth and gradually add icing (confectioners) sugar, beating well. Stir in lemon juice and continue beating until icing (frosting) stands in soft peaks. Spread icing (frosting) over top and sides of cake. Rough up icing (frosting) around sides and edge of cake to resemble drifting snow. Decorate with any suitable Christmas decoration. A little of the icing (frosting) may be set aside, coloured, and used to write Merry Christmas on the cake. Leave icing (frosting) to set overnight.

CHRISTMAS PUDDING

The Christmas pudding, stuck with a piece of holly, flaming with lighted brandy or rum, served with brandy or rum butter or with a rich custard or cream, is one of the highlights of an English Christmas dinner. Plum or Christmas puddings always improve with keeping, which allows the mixture to mature.

Rich Christmas Pudding

250 g/8 oz (1⅓ cups) raisins, chopped; 60 g/2 oz (⅓ cup) chopped mixed candied peel; 250 g/8 oz (1⅓ cups) currants; 250 g/8 oz (1⅓ cups) sultanas (golden raisins); 3 tbsp rum or brandy; 250 g/8 oz (1 cup) butter; 250 g/8 oz (1⅓ cups) firmly packed brown sugar; grated rind 1 orange and 1 lemon; 4 eggs, lightly beaten; 60 g/2 oz (½ cup) blanched almonds, chopped; 125 g/4 oz (1 cup) flour, sifted; ½ tsp each salt, mixed spice (ground allspice), nutmeg, ground ginger, cinnamon and bicarbonate of soda (baking soda); 125 g/4 oz (2 cups) fresh breadcrumbs; extra rum or brandy to serve.

The day before, mix raisins, candied peel, currants and sultanas, sprinkle with rum or brandy and leave overnight. The next day, cream butter with sugar and fruit rinds until light and fluffy. Add eggs a little at a time, then stir in fruit and almonds alternately with dry ingredients and breadcrumbs. Put into a large well-buttered 1.5 litre/2½ pint (6 cup) heatproof mixing bowl, bottom-lined with a round of greased greaseproof (waxed) paper. Cover with another round of greased greaseproof (waxed) paper (to fit over the top of the bowl), then with a pudding cloth which has been scalded, wrung out and floured lightly, or use a large sheet of foil. Tie firmly with string. Steam, covered, in a saucepan with boiling water to come halfway up the sides of the bowl, for 6 hours. Add more boiling water as necessary. Remove from water and when cold cover with fresh greaseproof (waxed) paper. On Christmas Day put pudding into a saucepan of boiling water and steam as described above and steam for $2\frac{1}{2}$ hours. Turn hot pudding on to a heated serving plate. Warm a little rum or brandy in a soup ladle or small saucepan, set alight and pour over pudding at the table. Serve immediately. Serves 8.

CHURRO

This golden choux pastry (paste) fritter is a Spanish favourite. Churros make a lovely dessert, though in Spain they are usually served with a mug of hot chocolate as a recklessly fattening snack.

Churros

oil for deep-frying; 1 quantity Choux Pastry (page 276), sweetened; sifted icing (confectioners) sugar.

Heat 10–13 cm (4–5 in) oil in a large, deep saucepan until it gives off a slight haze. Using a piping (pastry) bag fitted with an 8 mm ($\frac{3}{8}$ in) star nozzle, pipe 13 cm (5 in) lengths of choux pastry (paste) into the oil. Hold bag high so that pastry (paste) falls in thin strips, and cut off with a knife as each churro is formed. Fry for 3–5 minutes or until golden-brown all over, rolling with a spoon to brown evenly. As churros are cooked, lift out with a slotted spoon and drain on crumpled paper towels. Dredge generously with icing (confectioners) sugar while still warm. Serve immediately. Makes about 12.

VARIATION

Strauben (Ruffles): The German equivalent of churros. Prepare in the same way, but cut pastry (paste) in 5 cm (2 in) lengths as it is piped into the hot oil.

CHUTNEY

This word, of Hindustani origin, describes a well-seasoned relish or pickle that originated in India. Chutney is the standard accompaniment to curried dishes. It may be made from a mixture of chopped fruits, spices, acids and sugar, cooked slowly until thick, while some chutneys are a combination of fresh fruits, chopped, seasoned and served uncooked. Chutney can also be served with cold meat, cheese, or as a sandwich filling. **See recipes.**

Mango Chutney

500 ml/18 fl oz (2 cups) cider vinegar; 560 g/1 lb 2 oz ($2\frac{1}{4}$ cups) sugar; 2 large firm mangoes, peeled and sliced; 180 g/6 oz ($\frac{3}{4}$ cup) preserved ginger, chopped; 2 cloves garlic; 1 tsp mustard seeds; $\frac{1}{2}$ tsp salt; 90 g/3 oz ($\frac{1}{2}$ cup) raisins; 90 g/3 oz ($\frac{1}{2}$ cup) sultanas (golden raisins).

Combine vinegar and sugar in a heavy saucepan and bring to the boil. Add remaining ingredients and cook for 8–10 minutes or until mango slices are almost tender. Remove fruit with a slotted spoon. Bring syrup back to the boil and continue cooking until reduced to half original volume and quite thick, about 15 minutes. Remove from heat. Return fruit to syrup, return to the boil and pour into hot sterilized jars. Seal. Makes about 1.5 litres/$2\frac{1}{2}$ pints (6 cups).

Pineapple Chutney

6 small dried hot red chillies; 2 × 425 g/14 oz cans pineapple chunks; 750 ml/$1\frac{1}{4}$ pints (3 cups) white vinegar; 350 g/12 oz (2 cups) firmly packed brown sugar; 2 tsp salt; 180 g/6 oz (1 cup) raisins; 2 tbsp finely chopped preserved ginger; 3 cloves garlic, crushed; 125 g/4 oz (1 cup) chopped blanched almonds.

Soak chillies in cold water for 30 minutes, then drain and remove seeds. Chop chillies. Drain syrup from pineapple into heavy saucepan. Add chillies, vinegar, sugar, salt, raisins, ginger and garlic. Bring to the boil, reduce heat and simmer for 10 minutes. Add fruit and simmer for 45 minutes longer or until thick. Add almonds. Pour into hot sterilized jars and seal. Makes 1.5 litres/$2\frac{1}{2}$ pints (6 cups).

Tomato Chutney

1 kg (2 lb) ripe tomatoes, peeled; 350 g/12 oz ($1\frac{1}{2}$ cups) sugar; 250 ml/8 fl oz (1 cup) cider vinegar; 1 tsp chopped garlic; 1 tsp salt; $\frac{1}{4}$ tsp cayenne; 1 tsp ground ginger.

Cut tomatoes into eighths. Combine with sugar, vinegar, garlic, salt and cayenne in a saucepan. Cook until syrup thickens and tomatoes are soft, about 45 minutes. Add ginger and cook for 5 minutes more. Pour into hot sterilized jars. Cool and seal. Makes about 600 ml/1 pint ($2\frac{1}{2}$ cups).

Apple Chutney

4 large cooking apples, peeled, cored and chopped; 140 g/$4\frac{1}{2}$ oz ($\frac{3}{4}$ cup) sultanas (golden raisins); 4 medium onions, finely chopped; 1 clove garlic, chopped; 125 g/4 oz ($\frac{1}{2}$ cup) sugar; 1 tsp salt; 2 tsp ground ginger; 2 tsp dry mustard; $\frac{1}{4}$ tsp cayenne; 60 g/2 oz ($\frac{1}{3}$ cup) chopped dates; 75 g/$2\frac{1}{2}$ oz ($\frac{1}{3}$ cup) chopped preserved ginger.

SPICED VINEGAR: 500 ml/18 fl oz (2 cups) white vinegar; 2 tsp black peppercorns; 1 tsp mustard seeds; 1 tsp whole allspice; 2 tsp brown sugar.

SPICED VINEGAR: Place ingredients in an enamel-lined saucepan, bring to the boil, remove from heat and leave until cold. Strain. Combine with ingredients for chutney in enamel-lined saucepan and simmer gently for about $1\frac{1}{2}$ hours or until thick. Spoon into sterilized jars. Cool and seal. Makes 1.5 litres/$2\frac{1}{2}$ pints (6 cups).

Apple and Plum Chutney

5 large cooking apples, peeled, cored and chopped; 12 small dark plums, stoned and sliced; 2 large onions, chopped; 250 g/8 oz (1 cup) sugar; 140 g/$4\frac{1}{2}$ oz ($\frac{3}{4}$ cup) sultanas (golden raisins); 2 tsp dry mustard; 2 tsp salt; 2 tsp ground ginger; $\frac{1}{4}$ tsp cayenne; 500 ml/ 18 fl oz (2 cups) white vinegar.

Combine ingredients in an enamel-lined saucepan, and simmer very gently for about 2 hours, until thick. Spoon into hot sterilized jars. Cool and seal. Makes about 1.5 litres/$2\frac{1}{2}$ pints (6 cups).

Apricot Chutney

250 g/8 oz ($1\frac{1}{2}$ cups) dried apricots, soaked overnight in water to cover; 4 chillies, seeded and chopped; 280 g/9 oz ($1\frac{1}{2}$ cups) firmly packed brown sugar; $1\frac{1}{2}$ tsp salt; 1 tbsp chopped fresh ginger; 500 ml/18 fl oz (2 cups) brown vinegar.

Combine apricots and soaking water with remaining ingredients in an enamel-lined saucepan and simmer gently for about 1 hour or until mixture is thick. Spoon into sterilized jars. Cool and seal. Makes 750 ml/$1\frac{1}{4}$ pints (3 cups).

Bengal Chutney

3 cloves garlic, chopped; 4 medium onions, finely chopped; 7 cooking apples, peeled, cored and chopped; 750 ml/$1\frac{1}{4}$ pints (3 cups) brown vinegar; 140 g/$4\frac{1}{2}$ oz ($\frac{3}{4}$ cup) firmly packed brown sugar; 2 tsp salt; $\frac{1}{2}$ tsp cayenne; 1 tbsp chopped fresh ginger; 1 tbsp black mustard seeds; 140 g/$4\frac{1}{2}$ oz ($\frac{3}{4}$ cup) raisins.

Combine garlic, onions, apples and vinegar in an enamel-lined saucepan. Simmer about 15 minutes or until onions and apples are soft. Cool, then add remaining ingredients and bring back to the boil. Simmer for about 30 minutes or until thick. Spoon into hot sterilized jars. Cool and seal. Makes 1.5 litres/$2\frac{1}{2}$ pints (6 cups).

Right: Basic Bread Rolls (page 46), Floury Baps (page 26), Cherry Cake and Fruit Squares (page 52)

C

CIDER

The juice of apples that have been ground to a pulp and pressed to extract their juice; the juice is then fermented to make alcoholic cider or processed without fermenting to make non-alcoholic cider. Sparkling cider, made sparkling by a number of processes, is a great favourite of the British.

Cider is enjoyed mainly as a drink but is also used, like beer, in batters, casseroles or in baking. Unless otherwise stated, alcoholic and non-alcoholic ciders are interchangeable in cooking. **See recipes.**

Cider Muffins

250 g/8 oz (2 cups) flour; 2 tsp baking powder; ⅓ tsp salt; 90 g/3 oz (½ cup) sultanas (golden raisins); 250 ml/8 fl oz (1 cup) apple cider; 90 g/3 oz (6 tbsp) butter, melted; 1 egg, lightly beaten.
TOPPING: *60 g/2 oz (¼ cup) sugar; 1½ tsp cinnamon.*

Sift flour, baking powder and salt into a bowl. Add sultanas (golden raisins) and toss to coat evenly with flour. Combine cider, butter and egg, then pour over flour mixture, stirring until just blended. The batter will be lumpy. Spoon into well-greased muffin pans, filling ⅔ full. Combine sugar and cinnamon, and sprinkle over muffins. Bake in a preheated moderately hot oven (200°C/400°F, Gas Mark 6) for 20–25 minutes or until browned and risen. Makes 12.

Apple Cider Cup

2 dessert apples, peeled, cored and thinly sliced; thinly pared rind and juice 1 lemon; 8 cloves; 4 tbsp sugar; 900 ml/1½ pints (3¾) cups cider; 500 ml/18 fl oz (2 cups) soda (carbonated) water.

Put apples into a bowl with lemon rind and juice and cloves. Heat the sugar and 250 ml/8 fl oz (1 cup) cider until boiling, then pour over ingredients in bowl and leave to cool. When cold add rest of cider and soda (carbonated) water. Makes 1.6 litres/2¾ pints (7 cups).

CIGARETTE RUSSE

The name means 'Russian cigarette'. These crisp, rolled biscuits (cookies) are a classic accompaniment to creamy or fruit desserts.

Cigarettes Russes

2 egg whites; 125 g/4 oz (½ cup) caster sugar; 90 g/3 oz (6 tbsp) butter, melted; 2–3 drops

Left: Ceviche of Scallops (page 62)

vanilla essence (extract); 60 g/2 oz (½ cup) flour, sifted.

Beat egg whites and sugar with a fork until smooth. Stir in melted butter, vanilla and flour. Place 1 small teaspoonful of mixture on one half of a buttered and floured baking tray and, using a metal spatula, spread to an oblong shape about 13 × 8 cm (5 × 3 in) in size. Spread out another teaspoonful of mixture on other half of tray, spacing well apart. Bake in a preheated moderately hot oven (190°C/375°F, Gas Mark 5) for 5–6 minutes or until golden. Remove immediately from oven and cool 1–2 minutes, then lift from tray with a thin-bladed knife and place upside-down on the table. Quickly wind each biscuit (cookie) round the handle of a wooden spoon. Remove at once, and cool. Bake the remaining biscuits (cookies) in the same way. Makes 15–20.
NOTE: To test mixture is of the correct consistency, bake 1 biscuit (cookie) first. If it is too firm and hard to remove from tray, add an extra 1–2 tsp melted butter. If too soft and difficult to handle, add 1–2 tsp flour.

CINNAMON

With its sweet, spicy smell, cinnamon gives an indefinable, delicious haunting quality to many foods. It is the bark of a tropical tree, trimmed from the thin branches and dried in the sun to form curled-up 'quills'. The finest quality is pale yellow-buff in colour and looks like a roll of dried paper.

Whole cinnamon, in sticks, is used when cooking corned beef or smoked pork, for the court bouillon for fish or in curry dishes and in many rice dishes like Pilau or Pilaff (*see Rice*). It is also used in pickling, in the cooking of many dried pea, bean and lentil dishes, and pears and apples poached with a piece of cinnamon are delicious.

Ground cinnamon is widely used in baking and in flavouring fruits and desserts, also rice custard, custard and eggnog. In Middle Eastern, Oriental and South American cooking, ground cinnamon is used in meat, seafood and sauce cookery. **See recipes.**

Cinnamon Sticks

Apple sauce and whipped cream are good to serve with cinnamon sticks.

4 very thick slices fresh white bread, crusts removed; 45 g/1½ oz (3 tbsp) butter, softened; 4 tbsp caster sugar; 2 tsp cinnamon.

Cut each slice of bread into 3 sticks, spread with butter and roll in a mixture of sugar and cinnamon. Place on greased baking tray and bake in a preheated moderately hot oven (200°C/400°F, Gas Mark 6) for about 8 minutes. Makes 12.

Cinnamon Toast

4 thick slices fresh white bread; 30 g/1 oz (2 tbsp) butter; 2 tbsp sugar; 1 tsp cinnamon.

Toast bread under a preheated hot grill (broiler). Butter each slice, then sprinkle with mixture of sugar and cinnamon. Return to grill (broiler) until topping bubbles. Remove crusts and cut into fingers Serves 2–4.

Cinnamon Tea Cake

1 egg, separated; 125 g/4 oz (½ cup) sugar; 120 ml/4 fl oz (½ cup) milk; ½ tsp vanilla essence (extract); 125 g/4 oz (1 cup) self-raising flour, sifted; 30 g/1 oz (2 tbsp) butter, melted.
TOPPING: *butter for brushing; ½ tsp cinnamon; 1 tbsp sugar.*

Beat egg white until stiff. Add egg yolk, and gradually beat in sugar, beating well between additions. Mix milk and vanilla, and add a little at a time. Gently stir in flour and melted butter. Pour into a greased 18 cm (7 in) sandwich tin (layer pan). Bake in a preheated moderately hot oven (190°C/375°F, Gas Mark 5) for 20–25 minutes. While still hot, brush with melted butter and sprinkle with a mixture of sugar and cinnamon. Serve warm or cold.

Cinnamon-Ricotta Mousse

250 g/8 oz (1 cup) Ricotta cheese; 1 tsp grated lemon rind; 2 egg yolks; 60 g/2 oz (¼ cup) caster sugar; 1 tsp cinnamon; 2 tbsp dark rum; 90 g/3 oz (½ cup) grated chocolate; strawberries or grated chocolate to decorate.

Beat Ricotta and lemon rind until very smooth and creamy. In a separate bowl, beat egg yolks until light, then add sugar, cinnamon and rum and beat for 2 minutes. Combine the 2 mixtures and fold in chocolate. Spoon into 4 glass bowls or tall glasses, and chill for 1 hour. Top with fresh strawberries or grated chocolate to serve. Serves 4.

CLAM

There are many different kinds of saltwater bivalves called clams, the word being an American term for a shell that closes tightly. North America is the place to appreciate clams. But there are similar and equally fine varieties of clam to be found elsewhere in the world. In France, you may be offered *clovisses, palourdes* or *praires*; in Italy, *vongole, tartufi di mare*; in Spain, *almejas* or *margaritas*; while in Britain cockles are to be found on the seashore and in fish markets.

Clams are available fresh all the year round; they can also be bought canned or bottled in a liquid brine.

Fresh clams are best eaten raw with just a squeeze of lemon juice, like oysters. The Italians use tiny clams as a sauce with pasta, the Japanese eat them raw and in soups; and American clam chowder is an international dish. They are a good addition to risotto, fritters or they can be stewed in their own juices in a thick tomato sauce for serving with pasta.

Clams are opened much like mussels or oysters – a flat knife is inserted between the 2 shells in front of the muscle that holds them together; then they are rinsed in water. They may also be steamed open.

CLOVE

One of the best known and loved of all spices. The little brown clove buds shaped like nails vary in size, depending on their age and where they come from. Cloves should be bought whole, not ground. If a little is needed in powder form, the central 'bobble' can easily be crushed.

Cloves are often stuck in an onion and put in the stock pot, into ham, or used to flavour milk for white or cream sauces and bread sauce. They are also used with stewed apple, in mincemeat, and a single clove will do wonders for a beef stew. In the East cloves go into many types of curry and they are also used in pickles.

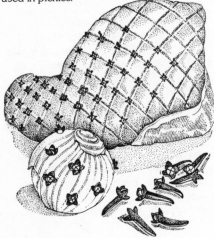

Kourambiedes

These little morsels pierced with a clove and coated with icing sugar are sometimes known as Greek shortbreads.

250 g/8 oz (1 cup) butter, softened; 75 g/2½ oz (⅓ cup) caster sugar; 1 egg yolk; 350 g/12 oz (3 cups) flour, sifted; 60 g/2 oz (½ cup) finely chopped almonds; whole cloves; sifted icing (confectioners) sugar.

Cream butter with sugar until light and fluffy. Add egg yolk and beat well. Stir in flour alternately with almonds. Knead mixture lightly and form into a ball. Roll small pieces of dough into balls the size of hazelnuts, and press a whole clove into centre of each.

Place on greased baking trays and bake in a preheated cool oven (150°C/300°F, Gas Mark 2) for 25–30 minutes. While still warm, toss in icing (confectioners) sugar and place on wire racks to cool. Serve in tiny paper patty cases, if you wish. Makes about 70.

COCK-A-LEEKIE

Nourishing soups are a great tradition of Scottish cooking. You can serve cock-a-leekie with the chicken in it, or serve the broth first and the chicken as the main course. Some recipes include chopped bacon and a few prunes.

Cock-a-Leekie

1 large chicken with its giblets; 2.25 litres/ 4 pints (10 cups) water; 2 tsp salt; 6 leeks, shredded; 1 onion, chopped; 2 tbsp long-grain rice; good pinch white pepper; 1 tbsp chopped parsley.

Truss chicken and put it into a large saucepan with water, salt and giblets. Bring slowly to the boil and skim well. Cover and simmer gently for 1 hour. Add leeks, onion and rice and continue to simmer until chicken is tender. Remove chicken and giblets, and skim off any excess fat from top of soup. If serving chicken in the soup, remove meat from bones and cut it into chunks. Cut giblets into pieces and return with chicken meat to the pot. Add pepper, parsley and more salt if required, and reheat soup. Serves 6–8.

COCOA

A product of the cacao bean which, when fermented, roasted, hulled and ground, produces a rich, reddish-brown liquid which contains about 50 per cent of a fat called cocoa butter. It is at this stage that cocoa and chocolate undergo their separate processes. To make cocoa a proportion of the cocoa butter is removed; the remaining liquid sets rock hard and is then pulverized. This needs to be sweetened before it becomes palatable. Unlike cocoa, chocolate retains all the natural cocoa butter found in the liquid extracted from the beans, so is a richer product than cocoa.

When using cocoa to make a hot drink, it should be mixed to a paste with a little cold milk or water before being added to the hot milk, otherwise it will be lumpy. To improve the flavour of drinking cocoa, let it simmer a minute or two, then whisk it to a froth before serving.

Instant cocoa, known as drinking chocolate, is pre-cooked cocoa to which sugar and flavourings have been added. It mixes into hot milk easily and does not require cooking.

Cocoa powder is used in flavouring cakes,

biscuits (cookies) and desserts. Some people prefer cocoa to chocolate for a chocolate cake or sauce.

See also *Chocolate.*

COCONUT

The fruit of the coconut palm, which is one of the most important trees of the tropics. The hard, brown, hairy shell, with 3 basal pores commonly known as 'eyes', protects a layer of white, sweet, edible flesh, and the coconut juice, which can be extracted by puncturing 2 of the eyes. Chilled, it makes a refreshing drink or it can be used to make coconut milk (see below). The flesh of the coconut can be grated or shredded and eaten as is or used for cooking.

□ **Basic Preparation:** Pierce eyes with a screwdriver or ice pick. Drain juice and reserve for drinking or cooking. Tap all over shell with a hammer, then break open. To grate white flesh, use grater or work pieces in a blender. **See recipes.**

Coconut Milk It may be made with fresh or desiccated (shredded) coconut. For 250 ml/ 8 fl oz (1 cup) coconut milk, combine in a saucepan 140 g/4½ oz (1½ cups) flaked, grated or desiccated (shredded) coconut and 300 ml/½ pint (1½ cups) milk. Simmer over low heat, stirring once or twice, about 2 minutes. Strain, pressing mixture well to extract milk. Use in a curry sauce or other recipes that call for coconut milk, or chill and serve as a drink.

Coconut cream is made by chilling coconut milk; the 'cream' that rises to the top is skimmed off. Used in curries or desserts.

To toast coconut: Spread desiccated (shredded) coconut on a baking tray. Bake in a preheated moderate oven (180°C/350°F, Gas Mark 4) for about 15 minutes until light brown, stirring frequently, or toast under a hot grill (broiler).

To tint coconut: Mix a few drops of food colouring into desiccated (shredded) coconut and toss lightly until evenly coloured.

Coconut Raspberry Slices

125 g/4 oz (½ cup) butter; 250 g/8 oz (1 cup) caster sugar; 2 eggs; 180 g/6 oz (1½ cups) self-raising flour, sifted; pinch salt; raspberry jam; 90 g/3 oz (1 cup) desiccated (shredded) coconut.

Cream butter with 125 g/4 oz (½ cup) sugar until light and fluffy. Add 1 egg. Mix in flour and salt. Spread in a well-greased or lined 35 × 25 × 2 cm (14 × 10 × ¾ in) tin (pan). Spread with raspberry jam. Beat remaining egg and sugar together, add coconut, and spread mixture over jam. Bake in a preheated moderate oven (180°C/350°F, Gas Mark 4) for about 20 minutes. When cold, cut into thin slices. Makes 24.

Coconut Pyramids

pinch salt; 2 egg whites; 250 g/8 oz (1 cup) caster sugar; 1 tsp vanilla essence (extract); 140 g/4½ oz (1½ cups) desiccated (shredded) coconut.

Add salt to egg whites and whisk until stiff. Fold in sugar, vanilla and coconut using a metal spoon. Pile in small pyramids on a baking tray lined with buttered foil or rice paper and press into neat shapes. Bake in a preheated cool oven (140°C/275°F, Gas Mark 1) for 45 minutes or until pale fawn. Cool on trays. Makes about 14.

Coconut Cones

½ × 400 g/13 oz can sweetened condensed milk; 1 tsp vanilla essence (extract); 250 g/8 oz (2⅔ cups) desiccated (shredded) coconut.

Put condensed milk, vanilla and coconut in a bowl and mix well. Scoop out in small portions, about the size of a walnut, and shape into cones. Place on greased baking trays (lined with rice paper, if liked). Bake in a preheated moderate oven (180°C/350°F, Gas Mark 4) for about 10 minutes or until lightly tinted. Cool on trays. Makes about 18.

Coconut Tarts

1 quantity Biscuit Pastry (page 274); 12 tsp jam; 90 g/3 oz (1 cup) desiccated (shredded) coconut; 125 g/4 oz (½ cup) sugar; 1 egg, beaten.

Roll out dough and use to line 12 small tart tins (pans), about 8 cm (3 in) in diameter. Place 1 tsp jam in bottom of each case. Combine coconut and sugar and beat in egg. Place spoonfuls in cases on top of jam. Bake the tarts in a preheated moderate oven (180°C/350°F, Gas Mark 4) for about 20 minutes or until golden-brown. Stand in tins (pans) for a few minutes, then transfer to a wire rack to cool. Makes 12.

Coconut Ice

500 g/1 lb (3½ cups) icing (confectioners) sugar; 250 g/8 oz (2⅔ cups) desiccated (shredded) coconut; 2 egg whites, lightly beaten; 1 tsp vanilla essence (extract); 125 g/4 oz (½ cup) solid white vegetable fat (shortening), melted and cooled; pink food colouring.

Sift icing (confectioners) sugar into a bowl and stir in coconut. Make a well in the centre and add egg whites and vanilla. Add fat (shortening) and stir thoroughly into sugar mixture. Divide mixture in half and tint one half pink with food colouring. Press white half evenly over bottom of greased and foil-lined 8 × 25 cm (3 × 10 in) tin (pan). Press pink half evenly over white. Allow to set, then cut into pieces. Makes about 30 pieces.

COEUR A LA CREME

One of the simple, pastoral, sweet dishes of France.

Coeur à la Crème

250 g/8 oz (1 cup) cream cheese; 300 ml/½ pint (1¼ cups) single (light) cream; 1 tbsp caster sugar; 2 egg whites; extra 250 ml/8 fl oz (1 cup) single (light) cream to serve.

Press cheese through a fine wire sieve, then beat in cream and sugar. Beat egg whites until they hold soft peaks and lightly but thoroughly fold them into cheese mixture. Turn into a muslin-lined mould, see note below, place over a bowl and leave in refrigerator to drain overnight. When ready to serve, unmould on to a serving dish, remove muslin and pour cream over. Surround with strawberries, or serve with other fresh lightly poached fruits or with redcurrant jelly. Serves 4.

NOTE: The classic coeur à la crème mould is a little heart-shaped basket or perforated porcelain mould. You can improvise by piercing holes in a cream or cottage cheese carton, or simply use a round sieve.

COFFEE

Coffee is not only a beverage without which many of us would find life impossible, but one of the great flavours in cooking. Its distinctive fragrance enhances cakes, meringues, icings (frostings) and fillings, and desserts both hot and cold. Whole coffee beans are used to flavour one of the most superb of ice creams and instant coffee granules are the secret of a brilliant 'instant' ice cream dessert. **See recipes.**

Ice Cream, Coffee and Scotch

2 scoops best quality vanilla ice cream; 1–2 tsp instant coffee granules; 1 tbsp Scotch whisky.

Spoon ice cream into an individual bowl, sprinkle over coffee and pour over whisky. Serve immediately. Serves 1.

Coffee Ice Cream

500 ml/18 fl oz (2 cups) double (heavy) cream; 4 egg yolks, beaten; 60 g/2 oz (1 cup) freshly roasted coffee beans, cracked; 180 g/6 oz (¾ cup) sugar.

Stir cream into egg yolks, add coffee beans and cook in a heatproof bowl over simmering water, stirring constantly, until thickened. Remove from heat and add sugar, stirring until dissolved. Stand custard for several hours to develop a good coffee flavour, then strain through a nylon sieve into ice cream trays. Cover tightly with foil

and freeze until it forms a solid rim about 2.5 cm (1 in) wide. Transfer to a chilled bowl and beat vigorously with an electric or rotary beater. Return to trays and freeze until firm and creamy. Place in refrigerator for 30 minutes before serving to soften a little. Serve each portion with a crisp biscuit (cookie). Serves 6.

Coffee Almond Layer Cake

CAKE: 125 g/4 oz (½ cup) unsalted butter; 125 g/4 oz (½ cup) caster sugar; 90 g/3 oz (¾ cup) flour; 1 tsp baking powder; 2 tsp instant coffee powder; pinch salt; 2 eggs, lightly beaten; 60 g/2 oz (½ cup) ground almonds; slivered almonds to decorate.
ICING (FROSTING): 180 g/6 oz (¾ cup) butter; 280 g/9 oz (2 cups) icing (confectioners) sugar, sifted; 2 tsp instant coffee powder, dissolved in 2 tsp hot water.

CAKE: Cream butter with sugar. Sift together flour, baking powder, coffee and salt, and stir into creamed mixture alternately with eggs. Stir in ground almonds. Divide mixture evenly between 2 greased and bottom-lined 18 cm (7 in) sandwich tins (layer pans). Bake in a preheated moderately hot oven (190°C/375°F, Gas Mark 5) for about 25 minutes or until a skewer inserted in the centre comes out clean. Turn cakes out and cool on a wire rack.
ICING (FROSTING): Cream butter with sugar until light and fluffy, then beat in coffee. Use to sandwich cake layers and to cover top and sides. Press flaked almonds lightly into top and sides to decorate.

Coffee Kisses

250 ml/8 fl oz (1 cup) very strong black coffee; 250 ml/8 fl oz (1 cup) water; 500 g/1 lb (2 cups) sugar; 5 egg whites; pinch salt; whipped cream to serve.

Heat coffee, water and sugar together, stirring until sugar has dissolved, then boil without stirring to make a thick syrup. Beat egg whites in a heatproof bowl until foamy, add salt and beat whites to a firm snow. Pour on the syrup in a steady stream, beating all the time. Place bowl over simmering water and beat 5 minutes. Drop the meringue from a teaspoon in small peaked mounds on to a baking tray lined with cooking parchment or foil, spacing the mounds a little apart. Bake in a preheated cool oven (150°C/300°F, Gas Mark 2) for 40 minutes or until lightly browned at the top and firm to the touch. Cool. Store meringues in an airtight container. To serve, join together in pairs with whipped cream. Makes about 24.

COLCANNON

The splendid Irish relation of Bubble and Squeak (see page 48).

Colcannon

4 medium, old potatoes, peeled and quartered; salt and freshly ground black pepper; 1 medium onion, finely chopped; 175 ml/6 fl oz (¾ cup) milk; 60 g/2 oz (4 tbsp) butter; 180 g/6 oz (2 cups) lightly cooked, finely chopped cabbage; finely chopped parsley to garnish.

Cook potatoes in boiling water until tender. Drain them, return to saucepan and shake over low heat until they are dry and mealy. Mash them and season well. Put chopped onion and milk into a saucepan and bring to the boil; beat into potatoes until they are soft and light. Melt butter and toss cabbage in it. Fold into potato mixture and check seasoning. Transfer to a heated serving dish and sprinkle with parsley. Serves 4–6.
NOTE: Colcannon is often served with bacon rashers (slices), or a little cooked bacon can be chopped and added with the cabbage. If desired, colcannon can be fried. Press it in an even layer into a frying pan (skillet), containing a little hot bacon fat or butter. Cook until brown and crusty underneath, then cut into pieces and turn over to make a fresh layer. Repeat until you have a cake with crisp brown bits through it.

COLESLAW

An American invention, Coleslaw derives from the Dutch words 'kool sla', meaning cabbage salad. It can be hot or cold, crisp or wilted, and is an excellent accompaniment to sausages and cold or barbecued meats.

Choose green, red, Savoy or Chinese cabbage and shred fine (see directions under *Cabbage*). Put cabbage into iced water and leave 30 minutes. Drain and dry well. For a crisp slaw, refrigerate in a plastic bag and mix with dressing shortly before serving. For wilted slaw, mix immediately with dressing, cover and refrigerate until needed. **See recipes**.

See also *Salad*.

Walnut Coleslaw with Watercress

350 g/12 oz (4 cups) shredded, crisped green cabbage; 3 sticks celery, finely sliced; 175 ml/6 fl oz (¾ cup) Mayonnaise (page 204); 2 tsp honey; 1 tbsp lemon juice; 2 tsp French (Dijon) mustard; 60 g/2 oz (½ cup) walnut pieces; 90 g/3 oz (1 cup) watercress sprigs

Put cabbage and celery into a bowl. Mix mayonnaise, honey, lemon juice and mustard, add to vegetables and toss. Fold walnuts through. Transfer to a serving bowl and surround with watercress. Serves 4–6.

Apple and Caraway Coleslaw

Caraway seeds sharpen the flavour of coleslaw.

120 ml/4 fl oz (½ cup) sour cream; 2 tbsp caraway seeds; 1 large red apple, cored and thinly sliced; 1 tbsp lemon juice; ½ medium green or red cabbage, shredded and crisped; salt and freshly ground black pepper; 1 small onion, finely chopped.

Mix sour cream and caraway seeds and chill 30 minutes. Sprinkle apple with lemon juice. Sprinkle cabbage with salt and pepper, mix in onion and apple and toss gently with sour cream mixture. Serves 4–6.

COMPOTE

A dish of fresh, canned or dried fruits, cooked gently in a syrup. A compote may be served hot or cold.

Compote of Fresh Fruit

500–750 g (1–1½ lb) fresh fruit (plums, peaches, apricots, cherries, apples, pears, rhubarb); 250 g/8 oz (1 cup) sugar; 500 ml/18 fl oz (2 cups) water; flavouring (see right).
TO SERVE: *cream or Crème Anglaise (page 97); crisp biscuits (cookies) or Pain Perdu (page 129).*

First prepare fruit: cover plums or peaches with boiling water, stand 3 minutes, drain and slip skins off; wash, halve and stone apricots; remove stems from cherries; peel apples or pears; trim rhubarb and cut into short lengths. Stir sugar, water and chosen flavouring in a wide saucepan over moderate heat until sugar has dissolved, then simmer 3 minutes. Place fruit in syrup, one kind at a time, and poach just below simmering point until tender but still firm. Spoon syrup over fruit frequently and turn fruit over once or twice with 2 wooden spoons while cooking. Remove fruit to a serving bowl, arranging it carefully. Boil syrup down a little and strain over fruit. A little strained lemon juice to sharpen flavour or 1–2 tbsp brandy, rum, Kirsch or other liqueur may be added to

syrup if desired. Serve hot or chilled, with cream or crème anglaise and crisp biscuits (cookies) or pain perdu. Serves 4–6.
NOTE: For flavourings, choose from: 2 strips orange rind and ½ vanilla pod (bean); 2 strips lemon rind; ½ tsp cinnamon, nutmeg or ginger, 3 cloves, or a mixture of spices, with 120 ml/4 fl oz (½ cup) red or white wine.

CONFECTIONERY

See *Butterscotch, Caramel, Coconut,* etc.

CONSERVE

A kind of jam with whole or sliced fruit which is unbroken and retains its original shape. It is pleasant to make a few pots of conserve of a fruit whose season is short, such as cherry. **See recipes**.

Cherry Conserve

1 kg (2 lb) halved and stoned cherries; 875 g/1¾ lb (3½ cups) sugar; 2 tbsp lemon juice; finely sliced peel, including white pith, 1 lemon.

Layer cherries and sugar in a large bowl, cover and leave 24 hours for sugar to extract juice. Place in large, heavy saucepan with lemon juice, and peel in a muslin bag tied to saucepan handle (pith provides extra pectin to aid setting). Bring to a rapid boil and boil until setting point is reached (when a little of the liquid dropped on to a cold plate and cooled appears stiff and wrinkled if pushed with the finger). Remove from heat, remove bag of peel and allow to cool slightly. Stir gently to distribute fruit evenly and pour into hot sterilized jars. Cool and seal. Makes 4 × 500 g (1 lb) jars.

Strawberry Conserve

1 kg (2 lb) small strawberries, hulled; 1 kg/2 lb (4 cups) sugar; 2 tbsp lemon juice; finely sliced peel, including white pith, 1 lemon.

Layer strawberries and sugar in a large bowl, cover and leave 24 hours for sugar to extract juice. Place in a large heavy saucepan with lemon juice, and peel in a muslin bag tied to saucepan handle. Bring to a rapid boil and boil 5 minutes. Remove bag of peel, reserving it and return conserve mixture to bowl. Cover and leave 8 hours, then replace in saucepan with bag of peel and boil until setting point is reached (see *Cherry Conserve*). Remove from heat, remove bag of peel and allow to cool slightly. Stir gently to distribute fruit evenly and pour into hot sterilized jars. Cool and seal. Makes 4 × 500 g (1 lb) jars.

CONSOMME

See Soup.

COQ AU VIN

A robust Burgundian dish of chicken cooked in red wine with onions, mushrooms and diced bacon.

Coq Au Vin

1 × 1.5 kg (3 lb) chicken; 500 ml/18 fl oz (2 cups) red wine; 2 bay leaves; 1 sprig fresh thyme; 1 clove garlic, crushed; 250 g/8 oz (2 cups) button mushrooms, stalks trimmed; 125 g (4 oz) slipper of bacon (smoked picnic shoulder), diced; 60 g/2 oz (4 tbsp) butter; 2 tbsp olive oil; 12 button onions, peeled; 4 tbsp brandy; 1 bouquet garni; 1 extra clove garlic, peeled; salt and freshly ground black pepper; 2 tbsp flour.
CHICKEN STOCK: *giblets from chicken; 1 onion, halved; 1 carrot, cut into chunks; 1 bouquet garni; 500 ml/18 fl oz (2 cups) water; pinch salt.*
GARNISH: *chopped parsley; triangular Croûtes of bread (page 90) fried in oil.*

Cut chicken into quarters. Make stock by simmering all ingredients together for 1 hour, then strain. Place red wine in a saucepan with bay leaves, thyme, crushed garlic and chicken stock. Boil until reduced to about 300 ml/½ pint (1¼ cups), adding mushrooms about 5 minutes before reduction is complete. Remove mushrooms with a slotted spoon, strain wine mixture and set aside. Fry bacon in half the butter and all the oil until fat runs. Add onions and fry until golden-brown. Dry chicken well, add to pan and fry until golden. Warm brandy, set alight and pour over chicken, shaking pan until flames die. Add bouquet garni, extra garlic clove and wine mixture. Bring to simmering point, season, and cook very gently, covered, for 40 minutes or until chicken is tender. Add mushrooms and cook 5 minutes more. Transfer chicken, mushrooms, onions and bacon to a heated serving dish. Mix remaining butter with flour to a paste and whisk, a small piece at a time, into the simmering sauce until it thickens. Adjust seasoning, discard bouquet garni, and spoon sauce over chicken. Sprinkle with parsley and serve garnished with fried bread croûtes. Serves 4.

COQUILLE ST. JACQUES

The French name for scallop, so-called because the scallop shell is the emblem of St. James of Compostela. The name is often also applied to a recipe in which scallops are the main feature.
See Scallop.

CORIANDER (Chinese Parsley)

In talking about coriander, a distinction must be made between the green leaf and the seed, as their taste and uses are quite different.
Green coriander can be recognized by its refreshing smell. The lower leaves are fan-like, the upper leaves are feathery, and it is often sold with the roots still attached. This is known also as Chinese parsley. In Spain and Mexico it is called *cilantro*, and in India *dhania*, and throughout these countries and the Middle East, its odour and taste are much treasured. It adds a great deal to many curries and, ground with coconut, green chilli, salt, a squeeze of lemon and sometimes a little yogurt, is the basis for a delicious and very common Indian chutney.
Coriander seeds taste sweet, aromatic and vaguely like orange peel. Because of their mild flavour, they are used in large quantities in curry making. In France the seeds are used to flavour a delicious mushroom dish and are almost always used in dishes cooked *à la grecque*.
  The seeds are also used in the spicing of some sausages. Roughly powdered, they are the flavouring for roast pork, lamb or kid or spicy meat dishes of many kinds from North Africa and Lebanon, and are a most important spice in Arab cooking. Use ground seeds in cakes, biscuits (cookies) and chutneys.
  You can easily germinate coriander seeds and grow your own green coriander. Sow the seeds in rich soil and full sun. Sow thinly where they are to mature and thin them out as they grow, removing each plant complete with root. In a warm climate, they mature in 4–6 weeks. **See recipes.**

Mushrooms Coriander

juice ½ lemon; 500 g/1 lb (4 cups) button mushrooms, quartered or left whole; 1 tbsp coriander seeds; 4 tbsp olive oil; 2 bay leaves; salt and freshly ground black pepper.

Squeeze lemon juice over mushrooms.

Crush coriander lightly in a mortar or use end of a rolling pin. Heat olive oil in a heavy frying pan (skillet), add coriander seeds and cook for 10–15 seconds. Add mushrooms, bay leaves, salt and pepper. Cook 3–4 minutes, tossing mushrooms to cook lightly. Cool. Remove bay leaves and serve in individual bowls with crusty French bread to mop up juices. Serves 4.

Coriander Chicken

1 cooked White Chicken (Chinese Steamed Chicken, page 69); 6–8 spring onions (scallions), shredded; 1 tbsp finely shredded fresh ginger; 2–3 tbsp toasted sesame seeds; 40 g/1⅓ oz (1 cup) coriander sprigs; 2 tbsp peanut oil; 2 tbsp light soy sauce; 1 tsp sesame oil.

Arrange chopped cooked chicken on a plate. Top with spring onions (scallions) and shredded ginger. (The shreds should be very fine and free from fibres.) Add sesame seeds and coriander. Just before serving heat peanut oil, soy sauce and sesame oil, and pour over chicken. Serves 6.

Coriander Chutney

A bright herby green chutney to accompany Indian samosas or pakoras, little meatballs or dried fish. Makes a good dip for crudités, too. You will need a good 20 g/⅔ oz (½ cup) chopped fresh coriander and 10 g/⅓ oz (¼ cup) mint.

2 bunches fresh coriander, stalks removed; 1 small bunch fresh mint, stalks removed; 6 shallots, chopped; 1 tbsp grated fresh ginger; 1 clove garlic, crushed; 1 tsp salt; 1 tsp sugar; 1 tbsp lemon juice; 120 ml/4 fl oz (½ cup) plain yogurt.

Put all ingredients, except yogurt, into a blender or food processor fitted with a steel blade. Blend until finely chopped. If you don't have a blender, then chop everything finely. Add yogurt and whirl in blender only long enough to mix through. Serve in a small bowl. Makes about 250 ml/8 fl oz (1 cup).

Steamed Fish Coriander

1 whole fish weighing about 1 kg (2 lb); salt; 2 spring onions (scallions), sliced; 2 slices fresh ginger; fresh coriander; 4–6 extra spring onions (scallions), green parts only, shredded; 2 extra slices fresh ginger, shredded.
GARNISH: *4 spring onions (scallions), white parts only, shredded lengthways; 20 g/⅔ oz (½ cup) fresh coriander; 2 slices fresh ginger, finely shredded; 2 tsp sesame oil; 2 tbsp peanut oil; 2 tsp soy sauce.*

Clean, scale and remove head from fish. Slash in thickest part and lightly salt inside and out. Place sliced spring onions (scallions), 2 slices ginger and fresh coriander in cavity. Lay shredded green ends of extra spring onions (scallions), extra shredded ginger and more fresh coriander in top part of a steamer. Place fish on herb bed and steam for 15–20 minutes or until fish flesh is opaque and flakes when tested with a fine skewer.
GARNISH: Remove to a heated serving platter and garnish with white ends of spring onions (scallions), coriander and ginger. Warm sesame and peanut oils, pour over fish and sprinkle with soy sauce. Serve immediately. Serves 2–4.

CORN (Sweetcorn)

Choose corn with fresh, dark green husks and plump yellow kernels. Fresh corn looks moist and has a sweet taste. Old corn looks hard and shrunken and tastes floury. Corn deteriorates quickly after picking, so ideally it should be cooked as soon as possible. If storing corn before cooking, refrigerate with husks left on.
□ **To Cook:** Remove husks and silk tassels from corn. Put in a deep saucepan with enough boiling water to cover cobs. 1 tsp sugar can be added to water, but do not add salt – it toughens corn. Return water to the boil and boil for 8 minutes. Overcooking will toughen, not soften, kernels. Serve with butter, salt and freshly ground black pepper, or serve a butter sauce to which has been added fresh or dried tarragon.
Barbecued Corn on the Cob Remove husks and silk tassels. Rub cobs generously with butter, salt and freshly ground black pepper and wrap each cob in foil, folding in ends to seal it well. Place on grid of barbecue over hot coals. Cook about 15 minutes, depending on the size of the cob, turning frequently. A dash of soy sauce may be added to each cob with the butter before wrapping in foil.

Cobs can also be boiled for 5 minutes, removed from water and drained, brushed generously with melted butter, then barbecued on a grid for 10 minutes. Brush occasionally with melted butter.

Corn Kernels

These can be used in soufflés, omelettes, and quiches, or added to cream soups, stuffings, macaroni cheese, or mixed with cream or butter and served as an accompaniment to other dishes.
□ **To Cook Kernels:** Cut kernels from cob, place in a saucepan, cover and simmer in their juice and a little butter for several minutes until tender. Season and moisten with milk or cream.
Creamed Sweetcorn Combine 350 g/12 oz (2 cups) sweetcorn kernels (whole kernel corn) with 250 ml/8 fl oz (1 cup) Béchamel Sauce (see page 368) or single (light) cream, ½ tsp salt and freshly ground black pepper. Simmer 5 minutes. Serves 4–6.
Creole Sweetcorn Cook 1 chopped onion and ½ chopped green pepper in 45–60 g/1½–2 oz (3–4 tbsp) butter until lightly browned. Add 575 g/1 lb 4 oz (2½ cups) peeled, chopped tomatoes, 1 tsp sugar, 1 tsp salt, ¼ tsp black pepper and 500 g/1 lb (2⅔ cups) cooked or canned sweetcorn kernels (whole kernel corn). Simmer 10 minutes. Serves 6.

Corn Bread or Muffins

60 g/2 oz (4 tbsp) melted butter or bacon dripping; 60 g/2 oz (½ cup) flour; 2½ tsp baking powder; 1 tbsp sugar; ½ tsp salt; 250 g/8 oz (1½ cups) yellow cornmeal; 1 egg; 175 ml/6 fl oz (¾ cup) milk.

Use 1½ tbsp melted fat to grease a shallow 29 × 18 cm (11 × 7 in) cake tin (pan) or 12 × 8 cm (3 in) muffin tins (pans). Place in top half of a preheated hot oven (220°C/425°F, Gas Mark 7) until sizzling hot. Have all other ingredients at room temperature. Sift flour, baking powder, sugar and salt into a bowl and stir in cornmeal. Beat together egg, milk and remaining butter or bacon dripping, pour into dry ingredients and combine with a few rapid strokes; batter will be lumpy. Turn batter into hot tin (pan) or muffin tins (pans) and bake in oven for about 25 minutes or until well-risen and browned. Serve immediately, cutting bread into squares. Makes 12.

CORNED BEEF

Beef is corned (the old name for salting) by soaking and injecting it with brine, plus a little sodium nitrite to make it pink. The cuts usually used are silverside (bottom round), solid lean meat with a layer of fat on one side, and brisket, alternating layers of fat and lean meat – this is often rolled and tied. Corned beef is excellent hot, served with vegetables, which may be cooked with it – carrots and cabbage are the classic choice – or cold, with salads.

Corned Beef

1 × 1.5–2 kg (3–4 lb) joint corned beef, either silverside (bottom round) or rolled brisket; 1 large onion, peeled and studded with 6 cloves; 1 tbsp vinegar; 12 black peppercorns; 1 blade mace; 1 stick celery, cut into several pieces; 1 bay leaf; 1 bouquet garni; 2 tbsp brown sugar; 1 carrot, cut into chunks.

Put all ingredients into a large saucepan and cover with cold water. Simmer, covered, until tender – about 30 minutes per 500 g (1 lb) after liquid reaches simmering point. Beef is done when a fine skewer inserted through thick part comes out easily. If serving hot, allow beef to rest in liquid for 30 minutes after cooking, then remove and carve it in thick slices. If serving cold, allow to cool completely in liquid before removing and slicing thinly. Serves 6–8 hot, 8–10 cold.

CORNISH PASTY

A Cornish pasty is the sturdy pastry-enclosed meal which was the standard food carried to work by 19th-century tin miners in Cornwall, England. Pasties sometimes contained a savoury filling at one end and sweetened apple at the other, separated by a wall of pastry (dough). Nowadays the filling is usually meat and vegetables. It is cooked in the pastry (dough) so that it forms its own gravy; a little kidney should be included to make the gravy richer. The pasty's traditional long shape was designed to fit in a workman's deep pocket.

Cornish Pasties

double quantity Plain Shortcrust Pastry (page 274); 250 g (8 oz) braising beef, cut into thin slivers; 90 g/3 oz (⅓ cup) kidney, finely chopped; 1 large onion, finely chopped; 1 large potato, diced; 1 large carrot, diced; 1 small turnip, diced; salt and freshly ground black pepper; 30 g/1 oz (2 tbsp) butter; beaten egg to glaze.

Divide pastry (dough) into 4 equal pieces and roll out each to an 18 cm (7 in) round. Mix beef and kidney together; mix vegetables together. Season both mixtures with salt and pepper. Put a layer of vegetables on one side of each pastry (dough) round, leaving edge uncovered. Put meat in a layer on top of vegetables. Dot with butter and sprinkle lightly with water. Dampen edges of pastry (dough) and fold uncovered half over filling. Press edges of pastry (dough) together and pinch firmly, turning edge over like a hem, to seal well. This makes a flat pasty – if preferred, filling can be placed down centre of pastry (dough) and sides brought up to make a high pasty with a ridge across the centre. Chill pasties 20 minutes, then place on a baking tray and brush with beaten egg. Bake in a preheated moderately hot oven (200°C/400°F, Gas Mark 6) for 20 minutes, then reduce heat to cool (150°C/500°F, Gas Mark 2) and bake a further 35 minutes. If pastry is browning too much, cover tops loosely with dampened greaseproof (waxed) paper. Makes 4.

CORNMEAL

Cornmeal is important in the cooking of the southern U.S.A. and of northern Italy, where it is called *polenta*. The meal may be yellow or white, and is processed in one of two ways: old-style stone-ground, in which some skin and most of the germ are retained, and modern-style steel-milled, in which skin and germ are almost entirely removed.

Stone-ground cornmeal is softer in texture and is superior in nutrition and flavour, but does not keep so well. It should be stored in the refrigerator. Steel-milled cornmeal can be kept on a shelf in an airtight container.

See also *Polenta*.

COULIBIAC

A Russian delicacy which is a larger relation of Pirog and Piroshki. Coulibiac is a plump savoury turnover filled with layers of salmon, rice (or rice vermicelli) and eggs. In Russia it would be made with fresh salmon but it is delicious made with a good quality canned salmon. The pastry (dough) can be a cream cheese pastry (dough) or puff pastry (paste). Coulibiac can be served warm or cold.

Coulibiac

1 × 375 g/12 oz packet frozen puff pastry (paste), thawed; beaten egg to glaze.
FILLING: *1 × 220 g/7½ oz can red salmon, drained; 30 g/1 oz (2 tbsp) butter; 1 small onion, chopped; 6–8 mushrooms, sliced; 125 g/4 oz (1 cup) boiled rice; 1 tbsp chopped parsley; 2 hard-boiled (hard-cooked) eggs, sliced; salt and freshly ground black pepper.*
TO SERVE: *120 ml/4 fl oz (½ cup) melted butter mixed with juice ½ lemon or 250 ml/8 fl oz (1 cup) sour cream (optional).*

FILLING: Flake drained salmon coarsely, discarding skin and bones. Melt about half

butter in a frying pan (skillet), add onion and cook gently until soft. Add mushrooms, toss a few moments and remove pan from heat.

Roll out about ¾ of the thawed puff pastry (dough) on a lightly floured surface to a neat rectangle about 18 × 30 cm (7 × 12 in). Place pastry (paste) on a baking tray and trim edges neatly, reserving trimmings. Leaving a clear border of 2.5 cm (1 in) all round, place filling ingredients in layers on pastry (dough). Begin with a layer of rice, sprinkled with parsley and dotted with a little butter. Cover with a layer of salmon, then a layer of onion and mushroom mixture, then sliced eggs. Season each layer with salt and pepper.

Roll out remaining pastry (dough) to a rectangle that will cover the filling, and place it on top. Brush uncovered border with a little beaten egg and fold up to overlap the covering piece of dough. Press edges together to seal. Make 2 slits in top and decorate coulibiac with fish or other shapes made from trimmings. Secure decorations with beaten egg. Chill for at least 30 minutes.

Brush with beaten egg and bake in centre of a preheated moderately hot oven (200°C/400°F, Gas Mark 6) for 30 minutes. Remove from oven and pour a little melted butter through slits in top – or serve coulibiac with a melted butter and lemon sauce or sour cream. Serves 6.

COURGETTE

See *Zucchini*.

COURT BOUILLON

Court bouillon is a flavoured, acidulated liquid used for cooking shellfish and whole or large pieces of fish. It may be based on water with a little vinegar or lemon juice added, or on a mixture of water and wine, with the addition of aromatic vegetables and herbs.

The purpose of Court Bouillon is to add flavour and to keep the flesh of the fish a good colour. Court bouillon is prepared ahead, strained and sometimes cooled before the fish is placed in it.

Court Bouillon

1.5 litres/2½ pints (6¼ cups) water; 4 tbsp lemon juice or white vinegar; 2 tsp salt; ½ bay leaf; 1 carrot; ½ stick celery; 1 onion, sliced; 6 parsley stalks; 3–4 sprigs fresh tarragon, dill or chervil (optional); 6 black peppercorns.

Put all ingredients except peppercorns into a covered saucepan (not aluminium). Simmer 45 minutes, then add peppercorns and simmer 10 minutes more. Strain before using. It will keep, refrigerated, about 1 week. Makes 1.25–1.5 litres/2¼–2½ pints (5–6 cups).

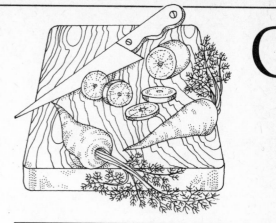

COUSCOUS

The cereal dish of North Africa, consisting of fine semolina combined with flour, salt and water into tiny, pasta-like pellets.

□ **To Cook:** Cover couscous with cold water, stir with the fingers and drain. Stand 15 minutes to allow couscous to swell. Turn couscous into a fine sieve or muslin-lined colander, which will fit snugly over a deep saucepan. For 500 g/1 lb (3 cups) couscous, put 1 litre/1¾ pints (4 cups) water or stock into saucepan, bring to the boil and place container over it (container must not touch liquid). Drape a tea-towel over the top, fit the lid on tightly and bring ends of cloth up over lid. Steam 15 minutes, then turn couscous into a bowl. Fork over, breaking up any lumps, and sprinkle with 2 tbsp cold water. Replenish water in saucepan if necessary and return couscous to steaming container. Steam as before for 30 minutes. Turn into a bowl, fork over again and toss with 125 g/4 oz (½ cup) melted butter. Use as an accompaniment to stews, etc., or (for couscous cooked over plain water only) sprinkle with icing (confectioners) sugar and peanuts or almonds and serve as a dessert.

CRAB

This edible crustacean is popular with gourmets the world over. Most of the delicately flavoured meat comes from the large claws – these yield white meat while the body cavities yield only a little dark, moist meat.

Probably the most famous of all crabs is the huge Alaskan King crab, which rivals the Giant Tasmanian and the very large spider crabs caught off the coast of Japan. The type we see most often is the blue Atlantic crab. A 1 kg (2 lb) crab will yield about 350 g (12 oz) meat, enough for 2 people. Miniature crabs include oyster and hermit crabs, which are sometimes treated like whitebait.

Americans differentiate between hard-shell and soft-shell crabs. Crabs moult fairly frequently but the new carapace is soft and pliable for only a few days. Crabs caught in this condition are known as soft-shell crabs and are considered a delicacy.

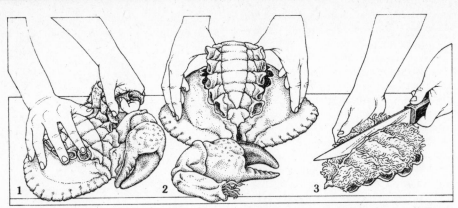

'Preparing a cooked crab for eating'

Crab is very popular in England, where roadside stalls in summer sell such favourites as Cromer crab. Crabs are usually sold ready boiled. British fishmongers also sell dressed crabs: the meat has been shredded and seasoned with salt and pepper, then mixed with mustard, oil and vinegar. It is then returned to the shell and decorated with hard-boiled (hard-cooked) egg yolk and chopped parsley. Serve dressed crab with mayonnaise.

If you do buy a crab fresh from the sea, make sure it is not only alive but lively. It should be heavy for its size and smell fresh and sweet with no hint of ammonia.

☐ **To Cook:** First drown the crab (or crabs) in fresh water. Bring a large saucepan of fresh seawater (or salted water) to the boil, drop in a bouquet garni; 1 sliced carrot; 1 onion, halved; 2 sticks celery, sliced, and simmer gently for 10–15 minutes. Drop the crab (or crabs) into the water, bring to the boil and cook for 5–8 minutes, depending on the size. The crabs will turn red. Remove the crabs.

To prepare a cooked crab for eating: At all times work with a cloth to protect the hands. Remove the big claws and set aside, twist off the legs (**Fig 1 above**). Remove the undershell by using thumbs to prise out round body section from underside (**2**). Remove and discard the beige, spongy gills lying flat against inner side of body shell. Cut the undershell body in 2 (**3**). You now have 2 semi-circles, each semi-circle is divided inside by thin shell partitions, into 4 segments. Split through the semi-circle horizontally, then you can scoop out the meat from between the partitions with a small spoon. Place the flesh in a bowl and discard the rest.

To crack the claws: Fold double newspaper over them, crack with a hammer, then pull out the meat. Sometimes the claws and legs are cracked and served with a fork, the diner extracting the flesh.

To crack crabs: Remove claws and legs, crack with a hammer. Remove the undershell, discarding spongy gills. Cut undershell in two, then cut each semi-circle horizontally (see *To prepare a cooked crab for eating*, and **Fig 1, 2** and **3** above).

NOTE: There is a mustardy curd present in all crustacea – its presence in abundance indicates not only freshness but quality. This curd is often added to a little cream or mayonnaise and served with the crab. **See recipes.**

Hot Crabs with Butter Cook crabs as above, crack them open, and arrange on large plate.

Melt 125 g/4 oz ($\frac{1}{2}$ cup) butter with 120 ml/4 fl oz ($\frac{1}{2}$ cup) white wine, 3 tbsp chopped parsley, 1 tsp chopped fresh thyme and 30 g/1 oz ($\frac{1}{4}$ cup) chopped shallot; pour butter mixture over cracked crabs. The meat is extracted, then dipped in butter. Place plenty of paper napkins nearby, and a finger bowl.

Dressed Crab (Crab Salad) Prepare crab as above. The flesh may be returned to cleaned and washed crab shell or set on a bed of shredded lettuce. Surround with cracked claws and legs. Send to table with freshly-made mustard, the curd from the crab, mixed with cream or mayonnaise, some good mild vinegar and brown bread and butter.

NOTE: Mustard enhances the flavour of crab and should always be used in crab sandwiches.

Chilli Crab

1 large crab; 120 ml/4 fl oz ($\frac{1}{2}$ cup) peanut oil; 6 thin slices fresh ginger, cut in strips; 3 cloves garlic, finely chopped; 1–2 fresh chillies, seeded and chopped; 5 tbsp chilli sauce (Malaysian); 1 tbsp soy sauce; 1 tbsp sugar; 1 tsp salt.

Remove large claws from crab and crack. Remove undershell and discard gills. Cut body of crab in 2 or 3 pieces, then crack legs. Heat a wok or frying pan (skillet), add oil and when hot, fry crab pieces until they change colour, turning so they cook on all sides. Remove to a plate. Turn heat to low, add ginger, garlic and chillies and fry for 1 minute. Add sauces, sugar and salt and bring to the boil. Return crab and cook gently, turning crab, in sauce to cook and flavour. Rice may accompany crab. Serve with finger bowls and napkins. Serves 2–3.

Crab in Black Bean Sauce

1 large crab; 120 ml/4 fl oz ($\frac{1}{2}$ cup) peanut oil; 6 thin slices fresh ginger, cut in strips; 2 cloves garlic, crushed; 2 tbsp canned black beans; 2 tsp soy sauce; 150 ml/$\frac{1}{4}$ pint ($\frac{2}{3}$ cup) hot chicken stock; 1 tsp cornflour (cornstarch), blended with a little water.

Remove large claws from crab and crack. Remove undershell and discard gills. Cut body in 2 or 3 pieces, depending on size. Crack legs. Heat oil in a wok or frying pan (skillet), add ginger, garlic and beans and fry, crushing beans with back of a spoon. Add crab and cook over a fairly high heat, tossing and turning until crab changes colour. Add soy sauce, stock and cornflour (cornstarch). Cook for 2–3 minutes. Serve crab and sauce with boiled rice and finger bowls and large napkins. Serves 2–3.

Stir-Fried Crab

In the Chinese province of Hunan, small crabs are cut up and stir-fried. Provide finger bowls and large napkins when serving.

3–4 small, or 1 large crab; 3 tbsp cornflour (cornstarch); 3 tbsp light soy sauce; 2 tbsp Chinese rice wine or sherry; 1 tbsp sugar; 1$\frac{1}{2}$ tbsp vinegar; 1 tbsp chopped spring onion (scallion); 1 tsp chopped fresh ginger; 4 tbsp water; 4 tbsp peanut oil; 2 tsp sesame oil.

Remove large claws and shell from crabs and crack. Remove undershell and discard gills. Cut bodies into 4 or more pieces. Crack legs. Coat crab pieces with cornflour (cornstarch). Combine remaining ingredients except peanut and sesame oil. Heat a wok or large frying pan (skillet), add peanut oil and when hot, fry crab pieces until they change colour, stirring well. Add flavouring mixture and cook over low heat, stirring, for about 5 minutes. Place crab on heated platter and sprinkle with sesame oil. Serves 2–3.

Devilled Crab

45 g/1$\frac{1}{2}$ oz (3 tbsp) butter; 1 tbsp flour; 175 ml/6 fl oz ($\frac{3}{4}$ cup) milk or single (light) cream; 2 hard-boiled (hard cooked) eggs, chopped; 1 tbsp French (Dijon) mustard; pinch cayenne; 350 g/12 oz (1$\frac{1}{2}$ cups) canned, frozen or fresh crabmeat, picked over; 60 g/2 oz (1 cup) fresh breadcrumbs.

Melt 30 g/1 oz (2 tbsp) butter in a saucepan, blend in flour and stir in milk or cream. Bring to the boil, stirring. Fold in eggs, mustard, cayenne and crabmeat and heat gently. Put mixture into 4 buttered ramekins or crab or scallop shells. Top with breadcrumbs and dot with remaining butter. Place in a preheated moderately hot oven (200°C/400°F, Gas Mark 6) or under a preheated grill (broiler) until brown. Serves 4.

Crab Egg Fu Yung

Delicious omelettes, a speciality of Canton.

250 g/8 oz (1 cup) canned, frozen or cooked fresh crabmeat, picked over; 180 g/6 oz (1 cup) cooked peas; 1 tsp sherry; 2 spring onions (scallions), sliced; 3 slices fresh ginger, finely chopped; 125 g/4 oz (½ cup) sliced water chestnuts; 1 tsp salt; pinch freshly ground black pepper; 6 eggs, beaten; 4 tbsp vegetable oil.

Combine crabmeat with peas, sherry, spring onions (scallions), ginger, water chestnuts, salt and pepper. Add eggs. Heat oil in a frying pan (skillet) and fry large spoonfuls of omelette mixture, turning once, until golden-brown on both sides. Serve with soy sauce. Makes 6.

Crab Bisque

90 g/3 oz (6 tbsp) butter; 2 tbsp grated onion; 2 tsp flour; 500 g/1 lb (2 cups) canned, frozen or fresh crabmeat, picked over; 750 ml/1¼ pints (3 cups) warm milk; 250 ml/8 fl oz (1 cup) single (light) cream; salt and freshly ground white pepper; pinch nutmeg; 3 tbsp sherry; 2 tbsp chopped parsley or chives.

Melt butter in a saucepan, add onion and cook gently for 2 minutes. Stir in flour. Add crabmeat and heat through, then stir in warm milk. Heat through but do not boil. Add cream, salt, pepper, nutmeg, sherry and parsley or chives. Serves 6.

CRABAPPLE

Crabapple trees are grown mainly for their beauty, but the small, sour fruits make excellent preserves and jelly.

Crabapple Jelly is made in the same way as Quince Jelly (see page 171).

Spiced Crabapples

500 g (1 lb) crabapples; 750 ml/1¼ pints (3 cups) boiling water; 2 strips lemon peel; 350 g/12 oz (1½ cups) sugar; 6 cloves; 4 whole allspice; 1 × 5 cm (2 in) cinnamon stick; 4 black peppercorns; ½ tsp salt; 2 tbsp wine vinegar.

Simmer crabapples, water and lemon peel together in a covered saucepan until crabapples are barely tender. Lift out fruit and discard lemon peel. Add sugar, spices tied in a bag, salt and vinegar to pan and stir until sugar has dissolved, then boil without stirring for 5 minutes. Replace crabapples in liquid and simmer 35–45 minutes, or until liquid is syrupy, removing spice bag after 30 minutes. Put the crabapples into sterilized jars and strain syrup over. Cool and seal. Serve with pork, ham, goose or duck. Makes about 400 ml/14 fl oz (1¾ cups).

CRANBERRY

A tart fruit cultivated in North America and used in jellies, tarts, poultry glazes and pies. Cranberry Sauce is a thick fruity sauce, the traditional accompaniment for roast turkey at Christmas and, in America, at Thanksgiving feasts. You can buy it ready-made from good food stores.

CRAYFISH

See *Lobster.*

CREAM

The fatty part of whole milk which rises to the surface on standing, or it can be separated from the milk during processing. There are few dishes which do not improve with the addition of cream. It adds richness and smoothness to sauces, soups and casseroles. It is often used to decorate and fill cakes, and as an ingredient in flavoured creams and custards. Cream is served with puddings, fruits and many desserts.

The following terms are used throughout this book:

Single (Light) Cream: This is fairly thin and contains not less than 18 per cent butterfat (milkfat). It is lower in kilojoules (calories) than other creams but because of its lower fat content, it cannot be whipped successfully.

Double (Heavy) Cream: This can be whipped until it holds a shape and contains a minimum of 48 per cent (36 to 40 per cent in America) butterfat (milkfat).

Sour Cream: This is cream with a culture added to give it a sharp tangy flavour. Its thick consistency means it can be swirled through hot or chilled soups. It is used to accompany paprikas and goulash; or use with chopped spring onions (scallions) and crumbled fried bacon in potato salad. Serve sour cream in a separate bowl with smoked fish such as mackerel and trout. It is the traditional accompaniment with caviar for the buckwheat pancakes called *Blini* (see page 39), and is used as a topping for Idaho potatoes baked in their skins.

Canned Creams: These are heat treated to last without refrigeration. Treat as fresh cream and refrigerate after opening.

UHT Creams: These are subjected to ultra-high heat treatment, which gives them a long shelf life. Once opened they should be refrigerated. They usually whip successfully.

Ways to Use Cream

Pan Sauces: Add 2–3 tbsp single (light) cream with 4 tbsp stock or wine to pan after sautéeing fillet (tenderloin) steaks, chicken breasts, fish fillets or pork chops. Stir rapidly and continuously until thickened, scraping up pan juices. Season as desired and pour over previously cooked meat, fish or poultry.

Pan gravy for roast chicken may be made in the same way. Remove chicken and all but 1 tbsp fat from the pan, then proceed as above, using more cream and stock.

Whipped Cream: For best and fastest results, chill cream and bowl first. If it is a hot day, place bowl of chilled cream over ice. Whip with a whisk, rotary or electric beater until it reaches the consistency desired. Be careful not to overbeat, as the cream will turn to butter. Whip until soft peaks form and hold their shape. Stop beating immediately if the colour darkens and cream clings heavily to the beaters.

You may whip 250 ml/8 fl oz (1 cup) double (heavy) cream with 1 egg white if you want to use the cream for piping. This helps to stabilize the cream and it holds its shape better. It is best to add flavour to cream after whipping by folding through quickly and lightly. Avoid using sugar if possible, as the cream can separate and does not retain its freshness for as long as plain whipped cream. Flavour whipped cream with liqueurs, wines such as sherry or port, essences (extracts) or sweet spices. If making Crème Chantilly (see page 88), which is sweetened, use as soon as possible.

Ice Cream Cream is essential to all true ice creams. This is a rich, quickly-made ice cream. Beat 4 egg whites with 4 tbsp caster sugar until stiff and glossy. Beat in 4 egg yolks, with 1 tbsp brandy, 2 tbsp strong black coffee or 1 tsp vanilla essence (extract). Fold 250 ml/8 fl oz (1 cup) whipped cream through egg mixture. Pour into ice cream trays, cover and freeze 4 hours or overnight. Serves 6–8.

See also *Ice Cream.*

Frozen Fruit Cream Whip 500 ml/18 fl oz (2 cups) double (heavy) cream and fold through 250 ml/8 fl oz (1 cup) sweetened fruit purée. Freeze until beginning to set around edges, remove and beat well. Replace in freezer and allow to freeze about 4 hours. This cream is served slightly soft. Place container in refrigerator for 30 minutes before serving, if it has been frozen for longer than 4 hours. Serves 6–8.

CREAM PUFF

This is a delectable little puff of feather-light choux pastry (see page 276), filled with sweetened whipped cream or Crème Pâtissière (see page 165). Poached or fresh fruit can also be added if liked.

See *Profiterole.*

CREME BRULEE

A beautiful rich French custard, with a glaze of hard, caramelized sugar.

See page 97 for recipe.

CREME CARAMEL

See page 97 for recipe.

CREME CHANTILLY

The French name for sweetened whipped cream. It is particularly delicious with fresh fruits, but can also be used as a cake filling or icing (frosting), and as an accompaniment for many desserts.

Crème Chantilly

(Sweetened Whipped Cream)

250 ml/8 fl oz (1 cup) double (heavy) cream; 1 tbsp icing (confectioners) sugar, sifted; ½ tsp vanilla essence (extract).

Whip cream until soft peaks form, then fold in sugar and vanilla. Makes about 350 ml/ 12 fl oz (1½ cups).

VARIATIONS

Jamaican Cream: Fold into Crème Chantilly 45 g/1½ oz (½ cup) toasted desiccated (shredded) coconut and 1 tbsp dark rum.

Coffee-Nut Cream: Fold into Crème Chantilly 1 tsp instant coffee powder and 90 g/3 oz (¾ cup) crushed peanut or almond brittle.

Raspberry Cream: Fold into Crème Chantilly 175 g/6 oz (½ cup) raspberry jam.

CREME FRAICHE

In France, the cream called crème fraîche is treated with a special culture which helps it to stay fresh longer, makes it thick and gives it a delicious, slight tang. It is an important ingredient in the light style of cooking called nouvelle cuisine, where it is used in sauces, soups and with fresh fruits. The original crème fraîche is not available in other countries but a good substitute can be made. **See recipes**.

To whip crème fraîche: Measure crème fraîche to calculate ⅓ of its volume. Then add this calculated amount of cold milk, water or chipped ice and a little sugar to taste, and whip until thick.

Ways to Use Crème Fraîche

● Use instead of cream with fresh fruits and fruit desserts.

● Use to enrich sauces such as Velouté and Béchamel (see *Sauces*).

● Swirl on top of individual bowls of cream soups such as Vichyssoise, Asparagus, Pumpkin or Spinach (see *Soups*).

● Use with creamy salad dressings and fold through chicken salads and potato salads.

Crème Fraîche

150 ml/¼ pint (⅔ cup) single (light) cream; 1 tbsp plain yogurt.

Stir cream and yogurt together in a jar. Cover and keep warm overnight or for 8

Preparing Basic Crêpes

hours. One method of doing this is to put jar into an electric frying pan (skillet) on lowest temperature and with a few centimetres of warm water in it. Another method is to keep container well wrapped and leave it above – not in – an oven on lowest possible setting. Chill cream well before using; it will thicken as it chills. Makes about 250 ml/8 fl oz (1 cup).

CREME PATISSIERE

A classic French cream used for cakes, tarts, flans and pastries.

See page 165 for recipe.

CREPES

These light and lacy pancakes of France can be enjoyed simply with a squeeze of lemon juice and a sprinkling of sugar, or they can be folded around savoury or sweet fillings and topped with sauces, creams, fruit syrups or liqueurs. They are used to make that most evocative dessert, Crêpes Suzette.

To store crêpes: They can be made freshly each time they are required but they also freeze well. Stack the crêpes in groups of 8 or 10 (depending on how many you intend serving at one time), separating each with a square of greaseproof (waxed) paper. Wrap in foil and place in freezer bags, then store in the freezer.

Crêpe pans are made of cast-iron and should not be used for any purpose other than cooking crêpes. They should not be washed after use but wiped out with a paper towel. If a pan becomes sticky, rub it with salt, then finish with an oiled cloth.

To season a new pan: Fill with oil and bring to smoking point. Remove from heat at once, then stand 24 hours. Pour off the oil, wipe well with paper towels. **See recipes**.

See also *Pancakes*.

Basic Crêpes

150 g/5 oz (1¼ cups) flour; pinch salt; 3 eggs,

beaten; 350 ml/12 fl oz (1½ cups) milk; 1 tbsp brandy; 2 tsp melted butter; extra butter for frying.

Sift flour and salt into a bowl. Make a well in centre and add eggs and milk (**Fig 1 above**). Using a wooden spoon, mix well, drawing in flour from sides. Beat well, then stir in brandy and melted butter (**2**). Cover and stand 1 hour. Strain as the batter must be free of lumps.

To make crêpes, heat a little butter in a crêpe pan and pour off excess. Use a jug and pour about 1 tbsp batter into an 18 cm (7 in) pan (**3**). Rotate pan quickly to coat bottom thinly and evenly, then pour off any excess batter. Heat gently and when small bubbles appear (after about 1 minute) use a spatula to flip crêpe over (**4**). Cook for 1 minute on other side. Makes 20–24.

Seafood Crêpes

6 shallots, finely chopped; 60 g/2 oz (4 tbsp) butter; 125 g/4 oz (⅔ cup) shelled prawns (shrimp); 125 g/4 oz (⅔ cup) shelled mussels; 6–8 scallops, poached for 1 minute; 6–8 oysters (optional); 1 egg yolk; 2 tsp dry sherry; 3 hard-boiled (hard-cooked) eggs, chopped; 2 tbsp whipped cream; slivered, toasted almonds to garnish.

CREAM SAUCE: *500 ml/18 fl oz (2 cups) milk; 1 bay leaf; ½ onion, chopped; 5 black peppercorns; 60 g/2 oz (4 tbsp) butter; 4 tbsp flour; 120 ml/4 fl oz (½ cup) single (light) cream; salt and white pepper.*

CREAM SAUCE: Heat milk slowly in a saucepan over low heat with bay leaf, onion and peppercorns. When bubbles form around edge, remove from heat, cover and stand for 10 minutes. Melt butter over low heat, stir in flour and cook, stirring, for 1 minute. Remove from heat, cool a little, then strain in warm milk and cream. Stir until smoothly blended, then return to heat and stir until boiling. Season.

Cook the shallots gently in butter until softened. Add prawns (shrimp), mussels, scallops and oysters. Set aside 4 tbsp cream sauce and fold egg yolk, sherry, chopped eggs, chives and crab mixture into the remainder. Spread on crêpes, roll up and arrange in one layer in a buttered, ovenproof serving dish. Cover dish with foil and warm in a preheated moderate oven (180°C/350°F, Gas Mark 4) for 15 minutes. Fold cream into reserved 4 tbsp sauce. Uncover crêpes and spoon sauce along centre of dish. Return to oven and bake, uncovered, for 5 minutes. Garnish with toasted almonds and serve immediately. Serves 4–6.

Spinach and Ricotta Crêpes

1 kg (2 lb) spinach; 45 g/1½ oz (3 tbsp) butter; 350 g/12 oz (1½ cups) Ricotta cheese; 3 egg yolks; 125 g/4 oz (1 cup) grated Parmesan cheese; pinch nutmeg; 1 tsp salt; ¼ tsp black pepper; 10–12 crêpes (left); 120 ml/4 fl oz (½ cup) sour cream.

Cook spinach, covered, in a large saucepan in a little water for 10 minutes over a moderate heat. Drain thoroughly, squeezing the leaves in your hands to remove all moisture. Chop and purée in a blender with 1 tbsp butter. Press Ricotta cheese through a sieve. Add it to cooled spinach with beaten egg yolks, half of the Parmesan cheese, the nutmeg, salt and pepper. Blend to a smooth paste. Fill crêpes with this stuffing. Roll up and place in a greased ovenproof dish. Dot with remaining butter. Cover with foil and cook in a preheated moderate oven (180°C/350°F, Gas Mark 4) for 20–25 minutes or until well heated through. Remove foil, spoon over sour cream and sprinkle with remaining Parmesan cheese. Return to oven and cook a further 10 minutes. Serves 5–6.

Hungarian Pancakes

60 g/2 oz (4 tbsp) butter; 1 small onion, finely chopped; 1 tbsp paprika; 250 ml/8 fl oz (1 cup) Béchamel Sauce (page 368); 125 g/4 oz (1 cup) mushrooms, sliced; 1 × 185 g/6 oz can crabmeat, drained and flaked; 175 ml/6 fl oz (¾ cup) single (light) cream; salt and freshly ground black pepper; 4 tbsp brandy; 8 crêpes (left); 30 g/1 oz (¼ cup) grated Parmesan cheese.

Melt half the butter in a saucepan, add onion and cook gently for 10 minutes or until soft. Stir in paprika and cook gently for 2 minutes, then add béchamel sauce and continue cooking over a low heat for 5 minutes. Allow mixture to cool slightly. Sauté mushrooms in remaining butter and add half of them to paprika sauce with the crab, half the cream, salt, pepper and 2 tsp of the brandy. Fill crêpes with this mixture, roll them up and arrange in a buttered ovenproof dish. Warm

remaining brandy, set alight and pour over remaining mushrooms. Shake over heat until flames die out, then add remaining cream. Cook, stirring, until sauce thickens slightly, then spoon over crêpes. Sprinkle with cheese and bake in a preheated moderate oven (180°C/350°F, Gas Mark 4) for 10–15 minutes or until glazed. Serves 8 as a first course, 4 as a main course.

Crêpes Suzette

8 crêpes (left); 30 g/1 oz (2 tbsp) butter, melted; 4 cubes sugar; 2 oranges; extra 60 g/2 oz (4 tbsp) butter, softened; 2 tbsp Grand Marnier, Cointreau or Curaçao; sifted icing (confectioners) sugar for dusting; 3 tbsp brandy.

Brush cooked crêpes with melted butter and keep warm in oven. Rub each sugar cube over skin of oranges to remove zest or oil. This process saturates sugar with oil from the orange rind and the oranges will look as though their rinds have been grated. Crush sugar and work in softened butter and liqueur. Spread each warm crêpe with orange butter and fold into a triangle. Arrange crêpes overlapping down centre of a heated serving dish and dust with icing (confectioners) sugar. Heat brandy in a small saucepan, set alight and pour over the crêpes. Serves 4.

Soufflé in a Crêpe

The crêpes can be made ahead and the soufflé up to the point of adding the beaten egg whites. Then, just as you are finishing the main course, add the whites to the mixture, spoon into the crêpes and bake.

3 tbsp flour; 3 tbsp caster sugar; pinch salt; 175 ml/6 fl oz (¾ cup) milk; 3 eggs, separated; few drops vanilla essence (extract); about 12 crêpes (left); icing (confectioners) sugar; 4 tbsp Grand Marnier or other orange-flavoured liqueur.

Mix flour, sugar and salt in a saucepan and stir in milk. Cook over a gentle heat, stirring constantly, until thickened, and simmer for 2 minutes. Remove from heat and beat in egg yolks. Whisk egg whites until stiff and fold into yolk mixture with vanilla. Put a good tablespoon of this soufflé mixture in centre of each crêpe. Fold crêpes loosely in quarters and arrange in a buttered ovenproof serving dish. Bake in a preheated moderately hot oven (200°C/400°F, Gas Mark 6) for 5–8 minutes. Sift over icing (confectioners) sugar, sprinkle with Grand Marnier and serve immediately. Serves 6.

Apricot Pancakes

10–12 crêpes (left); apricot conserve; lemon juice; finely chopped walnuts; sifted icing (confectioners) sugar; whipped cream to serve.

Spread each crêpe with apricot conserve mixed with a few drops of lemon juice. Roll them up loosely and arrange in a greased ovenproof dish. Heat in a preheated very cool oven (110°C/225°F, Gas Mark ¼) for 10 minutes. Serve sprinkled with nuts and icing (confectioners) sugar, with a bowl of whipped cream. Serves 5–6.

CRESS

Mustard and Cress: Mustard seeds and cress seeds are planted together. Cress is sown 2 or 3 days before the mustard. Use while they are still seedlings about 2.5–5 cm (1–2 in) high. Strew freshly snipped mustard and cress over hard-boiled (hard-cooked) egg slices, salmon salads, Cheddar cheese and tomato slices.
Watercress: Small sprigs of dark green watercress leaves make a beautiful garnish for roast lamb or chicken, grilled (broiled) lamb cutlets or kidneys, and green or orange salads. When buying watercress choose bunches with very dark green, quite large leaves. Try to use it as soon as possible after purchase or store tied in small bunches in the refrigerator in sealed plastic bags. The bunches can be put in a vase of water and stored in a cool place or submerged in a bowl of water.

Watercress and Walnut Salad Discard any yellowing leaves or thick stems from a bunch of watercress. Wash quickly, drain and dry. Put 125 g/4 oz (2 cups) watercress and 60 g/2 oz (½ cup) halved walnuts in salad bowl. When ready to serve, toss with a dressing made with 1 tbsp olive or walnut oil and a squeeze of lemon juice. Serve with chicken or pork. Serves 6.

Watercress Sauce Make 250 ml/8 fl oz (1 cup) Béchamel Sauce (see page 368). Fold in 120 ml/4 fl oz (½ cup) watercress purée (see below). Season with salt, freshly ground black pepper and lemon juice. Use with lamb, chicken or fish dishes.

Watercress Purée Blanch 125 g/4 oz (2 cups) watercress in 120 ml/4 fl oz (½ cup) boiling water for 2 minutes. Purée in blender or rub through a sieve. Stir in 15 g/½ oz (1 tbsp) butter.

Watercress Soup See page 395.

CROISSANT

Croissants are crescent-shaped rolls which make breakfast for millions of people in France and the Continent. The classic croissant is made of a yeast milk dough that has been rolled, spread with butter and folded several times. It is light, flaky and buttery, and is served warm either on its own or with jam.
Jam Croissant: A type of croissant using puff pastry (paste). A little jam is placed along the base of a triangle of puff pastry (paste), which is then rolled into a crescent. After baking they are sprinkled with caster sugar, and served warm.

CROQUE MONSIEUR

This French favourite is virtually a toasted cheese sandwich with ham added and is sold in nearly every pavement and open-air café. Delicious with a glass of wine or hot coffee. Use crusty French bread or a sandwich loaf.

Croque Monsieur

8 slices white bread; butter; 4 slices lean cooked ham; 125 g/4 oz (1 cup) grated Emmenthal or Gruyère cheese; freshly ground black pepper.

Spread bread generously with butter and make into sandwiches with ham, cheese and a grinding of black pepper. Press firmly together and trim crusts if liked. Fry in butter until golden-brown on both sides. Drain on crumpled paper towels. Serve hot. Serves 4.
VARIATION
Prepare Croque Monsieur as above, but before frying dip in a mixture of 2 eggs beaten with 120 ml/4 fl oz ($\frac{1}{2}$ cup) milk.

CROQUEMBOUCHE
(Croque-en-bouche)

The French *croque-en-bouche* translated means 'crunch and crumble in the mouth'. Croquembouche is usually made with little choux puffs filled with cream, toffee-glazed and arranged in a pyramid shape on a circular base. When the pyramid is decorated with spun sugar and crystallized fruit or flowers, it becomes the traditional French wedding cake. Other croquembouche can be made with tiny, crisp meringues filled with cream, or even with orange segments, dipped in sugar syrup and arranged on a base of pastry (dough).

CROQUETTE

A mixture of chopped savoury food, bound with sauce, formed into a small cork or cylinder shape, then dipped in egg, crumbed and fried. Well-made croquettes make a delicious entrée or luncheon dish. Their texture should be such that the creamy inside contrasts deliciously with the crisp crumb covering. They can be made with freshly-cooked ingredients but are also an attractive way of using leftover food.

Chicken Croquettes

2 tsp lemon juice; 1 egg yolk; 250 ml/8 fl oz (1 cup) panada-thickness Béchamel Sauce (page 368); 500 g/1 lb (2 cups) finely chopped cooked chicken; 1 tbsp each finely chopped chives and parsley; pinch nutmeg; little melted butter; flour; 1 egg; 1 tsp oil; pinch salt; dry white breadcrumbs; oil for deep-frying; parsley sprigs to garnish.

Beat lemon juice and egg yolk into hot sauce, then mix in chicken, chives, parsley and nutmeg, combining thoroughly. Cover surface with plastic wrap and leave in pan until cool. Turn mixture out on to a buttered baking tray and shape to a rectangle about 2 cm ($\frac{3}{4}$ in) thick. Brush surface with melted butter and chill well. Divide into 8 equal parts. Working on a lightly-floured surface with floured hands, form into cork shapes, rolling with the side of the hand and flattening ends. Beat egg with oil and salt. Flour croquettes lightly, then coat with egg mixture and breadcrumbs. Chill 30 minutes. Deep-fry, a few at a time, in hot oil (temperature is right when a bread cube fries golden-brown in 20 seconds). Drain on paper towels and seve hot, garnished with parsley. Serves 4.

CROUSTADE

A bread case made to hold a savoury filling, usually of sauced mixtures based on ham, poultry, seafood or vegetables.

Use one-day-old bread, cut into 5 cm (2 in) slices, and remove the crust. Scoop out the centre, leaving a rim 1 cm ($\frac{1}{2}$ in) thick around the sides and base. Brush inside and out with melted butter and bake in a preheated moderate oven (180°C/350°F, Gas Mark 4) for about 30 minutes or until crisp and golden-brown.

You can make one large croustade by using a whole loaf of white bread. Remove crusts, do not slice and proceed as above.

CROUTE AND CROUTON

Croûtes can be small triangles, heart shapes or rounds of bread, varying from 2.5 cm (1 in) to 7.5 cm (3 in) in diameter. They are fried in oil, butter or a mixture of these, and used as a base on which to set Tournedos (see page 441), as a base for Canapés (see page 56) and to accompany mornays or other dishes.
Croûtons are tiny cubes of bread that have been fried to golden crispness in oil, butter, or a mixture of these. They are used as a garnish for soups, fricassées and vegetable purées, or in salads.
Garlic Croûtons Fry 1–2 cloves sliced garlic in oil or butter and remove before bread cubes are added.
Oven Baked Croûtes Remove crusts from sliced bread and cut each slice into 4. Brush with oil and bake in a cool oven until golden-brown and crisp.

CROWN ROAST

This is made with 2 racks of lamb, bent round and sewn together at each end, with bones on the outside and the meat on the inside. Each rack consists of 7 or 8 cutlets (Frenched rib chops), and is chined – the bone cut through between each cutlet (chop) – and trimmed of all the skin and some of the fat, and the meat is cleaned away from the bones to about 4 cm (1½ in) from the ends.

Your butcher will prepare a crown roast for you if you ask him a day or two ahead. Order it by the number of cutlets (chops) according to how many people you wish to serve; allow 2–3 cutlets (chops) per person.
☐ **To Roast:** Cover ends of bones with foil and stand prepared crown roast in a baking dish. Roast in a preheated moderately hot oven (200°C/400°F, Gas Mark 6) for about 1 hour or until meat juice runs clear when tested with a skewer. If desired, the centre may be filled with a stuffing after first 30 minutes cooking (see *Stuffings*). Remove from oven and allow meat to stand for 15 minutes in a warm place while making gravy. When ready to serve, cover ends of each cutlet (chop) bone with a paper frill, and slice meat into double cutlets (chops) for serving.

CRUDITES (Raw Vegetables)

A favourite hors d'oeuvre of provincial France. Prepare a variety of fresh, crisp, young raw vegetables and arrange decoratively on a large platter. You might have carrot, celery or pepper sticks; cauliflower florets, courgette (zucchini) chunks, tiny tomatoes, button mushrooms, etc.

Serve with a dip or sauce for dunking, such as Mayonnaise, Aïoli (see pages 204 and 6), or plain yogurt flavoured with herbs and crushed garlic.

CUCUMBER

This member of the gourd family is usually eaten as a salad vegetable, but its delicate and distinctive flavour is very good in soups and hot vegetable dishes too. Hot or cold, it makes an attractive container for other foods; its refreshing coolness makes it important as a curry accompaniment; it makes the most elegant of tea sandwiches, and an outstandingly good and easily-prepared pickle.

Store cucumbers in the refrigerator crisper and use within a week.

□ **Basic Preparation:** Green cucumbers may be left unpeeled, scored lengthways with a fork and sliced into thin rounds, or may be lightly peeled so that some of the green remains, and cut into slices, sticks or cubes. Seeds may be scooped out or not, as preferred. Raw cucumber may be dégorged to make it more digestible and make the flavour milder (this also wilts it). To dégorge, sprinkle slices with salt and leave to drain in a colander for 30 minutes. Rinse and dry before using. **See recipes.**

Hot Cucumbers with Basil and Tomatoes

A superb accompaniment to grilled (broiled) chicken or fish.

2 medium green cucumbers; salt; 30 g/1 oz (2 tbsp) butter; 2 spring onions (scallions), including green tops; 120 ml/4 fl oz ($\frac{1}{2}$ cup) Crème Fraîche (page 88); freshly ground black pepper; 1 tbsp fresh basil leaves; 3 medium tomatoes, peeled, seeded and diced.

Peel cucumbers thinly, halve lengthways and scoop out seeds. Cut crossways into crescents about 5 mm ($\frac{1}{4}$ in) thick. Sprinkle with salt and leave to drain in a colander for 20 minutes. Rinse and dry well. Heat butter, add cucumber and cook on high heat 2–3 minutes, turning pieces over to seal them. Cut spring onions (scallions) into long slivers and add to pan with crème fraîche. Season with salt and pepper and cook gently 5 minutes. Cut basil leaves into thin ribbons and stir in, reserving some for garnish. Add tomatoes and cook, stirring several times, 5 minutes more. Serve at once, scattered with reserved basil. Serves 6.

Chilled Cucumber Yogurt Soup

Quick, light and healthy, with a pleasant tang.

1 green cucumber, lightly peeled, seeded and chopped; 2 spring onions (scallions), including some green part, cut into short lengths; 1 tsp chopped fresh mint; 350 ml/12 fl oz (1$\frac{1}{2}$ cups) plain yogurt; salt and freshly ground white pepper; paper-thin cucumber slices to garnish.

Purée vegetables, mint and yogurt in a food processor or blender. Season with salt and pepper and chill. Serve in chilled bowls with a slice of cucumber floated on each serving. Serves 4.

Cucumber Pickles

These crisp pickles can be eaten after 8 hours. They are lovely with sandwiches or with hot or cold corned beef or other meats.

12 green cucumbers, 13–15 cm (5–6 in) long; 1 tbsp salt; 1 large clove garlic, quartered; 4 tiny onions (pickling onions), peeled and halved; 8 bay leaves; 4 small cinnamon sticks; 4 tsp mustard seeds; 2 tsp prepared horseradish; 175 ml/6 fl oz ($\frac{3}{4}$ cup) white vinegar; 125 g/4 oz ($\frac{1}{2}$ cup) sugar; 120 ml/4 fl oz ($\frac{1}{2}$ cup) water.

Peel cucumbers, slice lengthways into quarters and remove seeds. Place in a bowl, sprinkle with salt and leave 2 hours. Lift cucumber out but do not rinse, and pack quarters lengthways into warm, sterilized 600 ml/1 pint (2$\frac{1}{2}$ cup) jars, allowing 3 cucumbers per jar. Into each jar tuck $\frac{1}{4}$ garlic clove, 2 onion halves, 2 bay leaves, 1 cinnamon stick, 1 tsp mustard seeds and $\frac{1}{2}$ tsp horseradish. Heat vinegar, sugar and water together, stirring until sugar has dissolved. Bring to the boil and pour into jars. Seal at once. Makes 4 × 600 ml/1 pint (2$\frac{1}{2}$ cup) jars.

Cucumber Appetizer

1 medium green cucumber, lightly peeled and finely sliced; salt; 1 tbsp wine vinegar; 2 tsp sugar; 3 tbsp olive oil; 1 tbsp chopped fresh dill or mint; freshly ground black pepper; 60 g/2 oz ($\frac{1}{4}$ cup) cream cheese, at room temperature; 3 tbsp sour cream; 1 tbsp lemon juice; 1 small clove garlic, crushed; sprigs fresh dill or mint to garnish.

Sprinkle cucumber with salt and leave to drain in a colander for 20 minutes. Place

vinegar, sugar, oil and chopped herbs in a screwtop jar and shake until emulsified. Season with salt and pepper. Beat cream cheese until soft, then gradually beat in sour cream, lemon juice, garlic, salt and pepper. Rinse cucumber and dry well. Toss with oil and vinegar dressing, and divide evenly among 4 individual serving plates. Spoon cream cheese mixture on top and garnish with a sprig of dill or mint and serve with crusty French bread. Serves 4.

CUMBERLAND SAUCE

This is an excellent fruity sauce served cold as an accompaniment to hot or cold ham, lamb or game.

Cumberland Sauce

3 tbsp redcurrant jelly; 1 tbsp lemon juice; 1 tbsp orange marmalade; 2 tbsp port; 1 tsp prepared English mustard, or 2 tsp French (Dijon) mustard.

Combine all ingredients in a bowl and mix together thoroughly. Makes 120 ml/4 fl oz ($\frac{1}{2}$ cup).

CUMIN

Spicy, aromatic seeds, used whole or ground, but in common with most spices, cumin is best ground as needed to retain its peak. It is used to spice chicken, rice, lamb and vegetables such as aubergine (eggplant) in Middle Eastern and North African dishes and it is an essential ingredient in most curry powders used throughout India.

Although cumin looks similar to aniseed and caraway seeds, its aroma is quite different, and you cannot substitute one for the other without changing the dish.

Lamb and Aubergine Stew

An Iranian dish beautifully scented with cumin.

2 small aubergine (eggplant); salt; 4 tbsp oil; 1 large onion, sliced; 750 g–1 kg (1½–2 lb) lamb shoulder, boned and cubed; 2 tbsp chopped fresh mint, or 2 tsp dried; ½ tsp white pepper; 3 tomatoes, peeled and chopped; 1 clove garlic, crushed; 2 tsp ground cumin; chopped fresh mint to garnish; boiled rice to serve.

Cut aubergine (eggplant) into small cubes, place in a colander, sprinkle with 1 tbsp salt and leave for 1 hour to allow bitter juices to drain away. Dry on paper towels. Heat oil in a heavy pan and sauté onion until golden. Add lamb, mint, salt and pepper and fry until lamb is well browned, stirring frequently to brown on all sides. Remove lamb and onion from pan and keep warm. Add aubergine (eggplant) cubes to pan, cover and fry gently for 10 minutes, stirring occasionally. Return lamb and onion to pan and add tomatoes, garlic and cumin. Cover pan and simmer very gently for 1 hour or until lamb is very tender. Serve sprinkled with extra chopped mint and a dish of boiled rice. Serves 4–6.

CUMQUAT

The cumquat tree has small, decorative citrus fruits resembling tiny oranges. Cumquats are extremely bitter. They are delicious when preserved in a sugar syrup, sometimes with brandy added, or glazed in a syrup reduction.
Glacé (Candied) Cumquats Use about 12–18 fresh cumquats for this delicious recipe. Using a fine skewer, pierce skin of each cumquat about 8 times. Place in a bowl with cold water to cover and add 1 tbsp salt. Leave overnight, then drain. Put into a pan with fresh water to cover, bring to the boil and simmer until tender, about 30 minutes. Drain and place in a heavy syrup to cover – 500 g/1 lb (2 cups) sugar to every 600 ml/1 pint (2½ cups) water. Simmer cumquats in the syrup until they are clear and transparent. Put

in a bowl and stand overnight. Next day, drain syrup into a saucepan, add 60 g/2 oz (¼ cup) sugar, bring to the boil and pour back over cumquats. Leave for 4 hours. Repeat this process once more, adding another 60 g/2 oz (¼ cup) sugar and leaving a further 4 hours. Lastly, drain cumquats from syrup, roll in crystal sugar and place on a wire rack to dry, preferably in a very cool oven. Store in an airtight container in a cool place. Serve in small paper cases or use to flavour ice cream, decorate creamy desserts, or serve with after-dinner coffee.

Cumquats in Brandy See Brandy: Brandied Fruit.

CUP CAKE

See page 52 for recipe.

CURRANT

See Fruits, Dried and Candied.

CURRY

A good curry meal, with its accompaniments and bowls of steaming rice, is something we all look forward to. A curry meal may consist of a meat, chicken or fish curry, several vegetable dishes, a lentil and a rice dish. Some curries are very rich, the palate being refreshed with yogurt or a salad. Fiery curries are balanced by cooling, bland accompaniments (see right). There should be a dry dish and a moist dish, a rich dish and a light one. These dishes are all put on the table at the same time; each person then makes a selection to suit personal taste and palate.

A variety of accompaniments may be served with curry. They include cucumber or sliced banana, chutneys, pickles and fresh sambals (see right). You might like to make Chapatis or Puris (see pages 62 and 322), the flat Indian breads that are used to scoop up the curry and its delicious gravy.

Curries are eaten with a spoon and fork. Each spoonful is mixed separately and should consist of rice, curry and a different accompaniment.

Curry Powder: This is probably the world's earliest spice blend. In India housewives daily grind or bruise their curry spices on a 'curry stone', and throughout the world, enthusiasts are now blending their own spices.

Thanks to certain spices, all curry powders have a characteristic flavour. Turmeric, fenugreek, cumin, coriander and chilli are the basic spices. Beyond that, curry powder may include allspice, cinnamon, cardamom, cloves, fennel and ginger; the various combinations and amounts determine the flavour of the curry.

If you prefer to rely on a favourite brand of curry powder or curry paste, you will know by experience it is better to purchase it in small amounts and use it as quickly as possible. **See recipes.**

SAMBALS AND ACCOMPANIMENTS

Accompaniments are an essential part of every curry meal. They are easy to make and provide intriguing contrasts in flavour and texture which are most enjoyable. Sambals can be red or white, that is heating or cooling. Red sambals are made by grinding together chillies with ingredients like onion, dried fish, or grated (shredded) coconut. When the amount of chillies is reduced, the sambal is white or cooling.

Serve one or two of the following sambals, plus a few commercially-made chutneys and nuts with your choice of curried food.
Banana Sambal Peel and slice bananas at the last moment and sprinkle with a little lemon juice.
Coconut Sambal Blend 45 g/1½ oz (½ cup) desiccated (shredded) coconut with 1 tbsp finely chopped onion, ¼ tsp chilli powder or a little finely chopped chilli, add salt and lemon juice to taste.
Cucumber Sambal Dice or finely slice 1 peeled cucumber. If seeds are large, cut cucumber in 2 and remove seeds before slicing. Crush 1 clove garlic with a good pinch salt. Beat 120 ml/4 fl oz (½ cup) plain yogurt with a fork, add cucumber and garlic. Blend well.
Fruit Sambal Sour apples, firm plums, green mangoes or any firm fruit in season may be used. Cut fruit into small dice, mix with a little finely chopped red chilli, salt and lemon juice to taste.
Potato Sambal Boil 2 medium potatoes, peel and cut into dice. Lightly mix with a little finely chopped green chilli and 2 tbsp finely chopped onion. Sprinkle over a little olive oil, add salt and lemon juice to taste.
Tomato Sambal Combine 2 tomatoes, cut into thin slices, 1 finely sliced small onion, and a little green chilli, finely chopped. Mix lightly with a squeeze of lemon juice and season with salt and freshly ground black pepper. A little desiccated (shredded) coconut may be sprinkled over top.
Pappadums These spicy lentil wafers are fried in about 1 cm (¾ in) hot oil for only 3–4 seconds. They increase in size and become crispy and golden.
Bombay Duck This is actually fish, which is salted and dried. Fry in hot oil or grill (broil) until crisp. Crumble over curry.

See also Chapati, Dhal, Lassi and Puri.

Curry Powder

A simple recipe: use about 1 tbsp for every 500 g (1 lb) meat, fish or poultry, substituting it for the spices, curry powder or paste in a recipe.

60 g/2 oz (⅓ cup) cardamom seeds; 6 large cinnamon sticks; 1 tbsp whole cloves; 1½ tbsp

cumin seeds; large pinch each ground mace and nutmeg.

Grind all ingredients in a blender or coffee grinder. Pass mixture through a sieve and store in an airtight jar, preferably in the refrigerator. Will keep fresh and aromatic for 4–5 weeks.

Madras-Style Curry Paste

Use about 1 tbsp of this paste for each 500 g (1 lb) meat, fish or poultry, substituting it for garlic, ginger and spices in a recipe.

90 g/3 oz (½ cup) coriander seeds; 2 tbsp cumin seeds; 1 tsp each black peppercorns, turmeric, black mustard seeds, chilli powder and salt; 3 cloves garlic, peeled; 1 knob fresh ginger (about walnut-size), grated; 1 tbsp vinegar; 5 tbsp oil.

Combine spices, garlic, ginger and vinegar in food processor or coffee grinder and grind until a paste, adding more vinegar if needed. Heat oil in small saucepan and when very hot add spice mixture. Reduce heat and cook gently, stirring, for a few minutes or until oil separates from spices. Cool and pour into an airtight jar. Store in the refrigerator and use as required.

Lamb with Cashew Nut Curry
(Korma)

MASALA SAUCE: *3 dried red chillies, seeded; 2.5 cm (1 in) piece fresh ginger, peeled and quartered; 60 g/2 oz (½ cup) unsalted cashew nuts; 175 ml/6 fl oz (¾ cup) water; 2 large cloves garlic; ½ tsp cinnamon; ½ tsp cardamom seeds; 3 whole cloves; 2½ tsp coriander seeds; 1 tsp cumin seeds.*
LAMB: *½ tsp saffron threads, crumbled; 3 tbsp boiling water; 90 g/3 oz (6 tbsp) ghee; 2 medium onions, finely chopped; 1½ tsp salt; 120 ml/4 fl oz (½ cup) plain yogurt; 750 g (1½ lb) boned lamb shoulder, cubed; 1½ tbsp chopped fresh coriander; juice ½ lemon.*

MASALA SAUCE: Purée chillies, ginger and cashew nuts in blender with water until smooth. Peel garlic cloves and add to cashew nut purée with remaining masala ingredients. Blend again until mixture is completely ground. Set aside. Soak saffron in boiling water for about 10 minutes. Heat ghee and cook onions slowly until soft and golden-brown, about 10 minutes. Stir in salt and masala, then add yogurt. Cook over a gentle heat, stirring, until ghee covers the surface. Add lamb and stir gently. Cover and cook gently for about 20 minutes. Sprinkle 1 tbsp coriander over lamb and continue cooking for 10 minutes more or until lamb is tender. To serve, transfer to a heated serving dish and sprinkle top with lemon juice and remaining coriander. Serve with boiled rice and accompaniments. Serves 4–6.

Prawn Curry

500 g/1 lb (2½ cups) shelled prawns (shrimp); 30 g/1 oz (2 tbsp) ghee or butter; 10 curry leaves; 1 large onion, finely chopped; 3 cloves garlic, crushed; 5 cm (2 in) piece fresh ginger, peeled and grated; 2 tbsp curry powder or paste; ½–1 red chilli, seeded and chopped; 250 ml/8 fl oz (1 cup) Coconut Milk (page 80); 2 tsp ground rice; 1 cinnamon stick; juice 1 lemon; 1 tsp salt.

Devein prawns (shrimp). Heat ghee in pan, add curry leaves, onion, garlic and ginger and fry over gentle heat until golden. Add curry powder and chilli, and fry for 1 minute. Stir in coconut milk, ground rice (mixed with a little coconut milk), cinnamon, lemon juice and salt. Cover and simmer gently for 15 minutes. Add prawns (shrimp), stir well, then cover and simmer gently for 10 minutes. Serves 4.
NOTE: If using cooked prawns (shrimp), it is only necessary to heat gently, about 5 minutes.
VARIATION
Chicken Curry: Prepare as for Prawn Curry but use 750 g (1½ lb) chicken fillets, each fillet cut into 3, in place of prawns (shrimp). Add to curry sauce and simmer gently for 20 minutes or until tender.

Lamb Almond Curry

Many good curries are cooked by this method of gently braising the meat and spices, adding more water as the meat browns and cooks. The result is tender, excellent meat with a rich brown gravy.

45 g/1½ oz (3 tbsp) ghee or butter; 2 medium onions, finely sliced; 1 kg (2 lb) boneless lamb, cut into large cubes; 1 tbsp finely sliced fresh ginger; 4–5 cardamom pods; 2 tsp salt; 2–3 red chillies, seeded and ground to a paste; 2 bay leaves; 4 cloves garlic, chopped; 1 onion, finely chopped; 350 ml/12 fl oz (1½ cups) hot water; 250 ml/8 fl oz (1 cup) plain yogurt; 12 almonds, blanched and halved.

Heat ghee in a heavy saucepan and sauté sliced onions until tender. Add meat, ginger, cardamom, salt, ground chilli paste, bay leaves and half the garlic. Cook, stirring, for

10 minutes. Add chopped onion and remaining garlic. Cover and when simmering add some of the hot water. Stir and cover again. When simmering again add more water. Repeat process 3 or 4 times. Add 2 tbsp yogurt and more hot water and cook until meat is tender, adding more hot water when necessary. Add remaining yogurt and blanched almonds. Simmer for 5–7 minutes or until gravy is well blended and rich golden-brown. Remove bay leaves. Serve with boiled rice and accompaniments. Serves 4–6.

Fish Curry with Tomato

500 g (1 lb) fish steaks; 30 g/1 oz (2 tbsp) ghee; 1 onion, finely chopped; 2 cloves garlic, crushed; 2 tbsp chopped fresh mint or coriander; 1 tsp ground cumin; 1 tsp ground turmeric; ½ tsp chilli powder; 1 tomato, chopped; 1 tsp salt; ½ tsp black pepper; juice ½ lemon.

Cut fish into serving pieces. Heat ghee in a heavy saucepan and fry onion and garlic over low heat until translucent. Mix in mint or coriander, cumin, turmeric and chilli powder, and stir for 2 minutes. Add tomato, salt and pepper, and cook until tomato becomes soft and pulpy. Add lemon juice and fish pieces, and spoon sauce over fish. Cover pan and simmer gently for 10 minutes or until fish flakes easily when tested with a fine skewer. Serve with boiled rice and lemon wedges. Serves 4.

Memsahib's Lamb Curry

An English-style curry quickly made with lamb left over from the weekend roast.

60 g/2 oz (4 tbsp) butter; 2 onions, finely chopped; 125 g/4 oz (1 cup) diced celery; 1 clove garlic, crushed; 1–2 tbsp curry powder; 2 tsp flour; 500 ml/18 fl oz (2 cups) chicken stock; 1 green apple, peeled and diced; 500 g/1 lb (2 cups) diced cooked lamb.

Melt butter in frying pan (skillet) and sauté onions, celery and garlic until soft. Stir in curry powder and flour and cook, stirring, for 2 minutes. Remove from heat and stir in stock. Bring to the boil, add apple and lamb and simmer, covered, 30 minutes. Serves 4.

Vegetable Curry

120 ml/4 fl oz (½ cup) oil or melted ghee; 1 tsp mustard seeds; 6–8 curry leaves (optional); 1 tsp turmeric; 2 cloves garlic, crushed; 2 cm (¾ in) piece fresh ginger, peeled and grated; ½ red chilli, seeded and chopped; ½ cauliflower, broken into florets; 1 carrot, sliced; 250 g (8 oz) green beans, strung and chopped; 180 g/6 oz (1 cup) shelled green peas; salt.

Heat oil in large saucepan, add mustard seeds, curry leaves, turmeric, garlic, ginger and chilli and fry for 1–2 minutes. Add vegetables and fry over a medium heat, stirring, for 10–12 minutes or until vegetables are almost tender but still a little crisp. Add salt, cover and simmer for 2–3 minutes. Serve at once. Serves 4.
NOTE: You may vary the vegetables for this dish, using diced potato, Brussels sprouts, cabbage, green peppers, spinach etc.

Chicken Curry

2 medium onions, finely chopped; 1 clove garlic, crushed; 2 cm (1 in) piece fresh ginger, peeled and grated; 60 g/2 oz (4 tbsp) ghee; 1 tbsp curry powder; 2 large tomatoes, peeled, seeded and diced; 2 tsp paprika; 2 whole cloves; 8 cm (3 in) cinnamon stick; 450 ml/¾ pint (2 cups) Coconut Milk (page 80); 2 tsp salt; 2 green peppers, seeded and shredded; 1 × 1.5 kg (3 lb) chicken; 2 tbsp single (light) cream; 1 tbsp chopped fresh mint.

Cook onions, garlic and ginger gently in hot ghee until beginning to turn golden. Add curry powder and cook 3–4 minutes. Add tomatoes, paprika, cloves, cinnamon, coconut milk, salt and green peppers. Simmer, covered, for about 15 minutes, then add chicken, cut into serving pieces, and simmer 30–40 minutes, until chicken is tender. Add cream and fresh, chopped mint. Heat curry through and serve with boiled rice. Serves 4.

Burma Beef Curry

1 medium onion, finely chopped; 1 clove garlic, crushed; 30 g/1 oz (2 tbsp) butter or ghee; 1 tbsp curry powder; 2 ripe tomatoes, peeled and diced; 500 g (1 lb) stewing steak, cubed; 120 ml/4 fl oz (½ cup) milk; 2 tsp lemon juice; salt and freshly ground black pepper; 2 tsp sugar.

Fry onion with garlic in butter or ghee for 3–4 minutes. Add curry powder and fry for a further 2 minutes. Add tomatoes and meat with just enough water barely to cover meat. Simmer very gently for about 1½ hours or until meat is tender. Stir in milk and lemon juice, season to taste and add sugar. Serve with boiled rice. Serves 4.

Pork Vindaloo

1 kg (2 lb) pork; 350 ml/12 fl oz (1½ cups) boiling water; 60 g/2 oz (¼ cup) tamarind pulp; 4 tbsp mustard oil; 12 whole peppercorns; 2–3 bay leaves.
MARINADE: *3 large cloves garlic, crushed; 1 tbsp ground ginger; 1 tsp ground chilli; 1 tbsp curry powder; ½ tsp ground cloves; ½ tsp ground cardamom; 1 tsp cinnamon; ½ tsp salt; 120 ml/4 fl oz (½ cup) malt vinegar.*

Combine all the ingredients for the marinade in a bowl. Cut the pork into large cubes and add to the marinade. Leave for 18–24 hours. Pour the boiling water over tamarind pulp and cool. When cold, push through a sieve and reserve the liquid. Heat the oil in a frying pan (skillet), add the meat, marinade, peppercorns, bay leaves and tamarind juice. Simmer gently 2 hours or until meat is tender. Serves 4.

Singaras

500 g (1 lb) potatoes; 2 tsp curry powder; 2 tsp salt; 1 tsp cumin seeds; 1 tsp fennel seeds; ½ tsp black mustard seeds; 30 g/1 oz (2 tbsp) ghee or butter; 500 g/1 lb (4 cups) flour; 300 ml/½ pint (1¼ cups) water; oil for deep frying.

Boil potatoes in their skins and when cooked, but still firm, peel and cut into 6 mm (¼ in) dice. Sprinkle curry powder, salt and seeds evenly over and mix lightly. Rub soft ghee or butter into flour. Make a well in the centre, then add all the water at once to make a soft dough. Knead well until smooth and elastic. Divide into 32 pieces and roll each into a ball. Roll out each one thinly on a floured board, with a lightly floured rolling pin, to a circle about 10 cm (4 in) across. Cut each circle in 2 with a sharp knife. Moisten edges of each half circle and put a spoonful of potato mixture on each. Fold over and press edges well together. From each circle, you will get 2 triangular-shaped pastries. Fry in deep hot oil until puffed and golden. Drain and serve hot or cold. Makes 64.

CUSTARD

Whether or not a custard is a simple, baked one flavoured with nutmeg or an elegant Crème Brûlée (see page 97) with soft cream covered with a brittle crust of burnt sugar, the custard base is milk and/or single (light) cream and eggs or egg yolks. Gentle cooking is essential to ensure the perfect smoothness of texture necessary for any custard.

There are two basic kinds of custard: stirred custard, cooked on top of the stove, and baked custard, cooked in the oven. Once these have been mastered a great many variations can be made, such as Crème Pâtissière (see page 165), which is used to fill French tarts, tartlets, éclairs and profiteroles, or such classic custards as Crème Caramel or Petits Pots de Crème. **See recipes.**

Baked Custard

500 ml/18 fl oz (2 cups) milk; 2 eggs; 1 egg yolk; 2 tbsp sugar; pinch salt; ½ tsp vanilla essence (extract) or nutmeg.

Heat milk in heavy saucepan over low heat. Mix together eggs, egg yolk, sugar, salt and vanilla or nutmeg. Mix well, but do not beat. When small bubbles appear around edge of milk pan, pour about ⅓ into egg mixture and mix until well blended. Add this mixture to remaining milk and mix again. Put 6 buttered custard cups or 1 large ovenproof dish in a baking tin (pan), and fill with strained custard. Carefully pour hot water into baking tin (pan) to halfway up sides of cups or dish. Bake in a preheated moderate oven (160°C/325°F, Gas Mark 3) for 20 minutes (30 minutes for large dish) or until a knife inserted in centre of custard comes out clean. Remove custard cups or dish from water. Cool. Serves 6.

Stirred Custard

This is the simple custard sauce that accompanies many English steamed puddings and poached fruit.

250 ml/8 fl oz (1 cup) milk; 1 tsp cornflour (cornstarch); 1 egg; 1 tbsp sugar; vanilla essence (extract) to taste.

Heat most of the milk in the top of a double saucepan (double boiler). Blend cornflour (cornstarch) with remaining cold milk. Blend in a little of the hot milk, then return to saucepan and cook for 1 minute. Allow to cool. Add egg and sugar beaten together. Stand pan over boiling water and cook, stirring until custard coats spoon. Stir in vanilla. Makes 250 ml/8 fl oz (1 cup).

Right: A selection of cheeses (page 63)

Crème Anglaise

125 g/4 oz (½ cup) sugar; 4 large or 5 small egg yolks; 1 tsp cornflour (cornstarch); 500 ml/18 fl oz (2 cups) milk; 1 vanilla pod (bean).

Beat sugar into egg yolks gradually and continue to beat for 2–3 minutes until pale yellow. Beat in cornflour (cornstarch); then gradually stir in milk, scalded with vanilla bean (see page 215). Pour mixture into top part of double saucepan (double boiler), place over hot water and stir slowly and continuously until custard thickens sufficiently to coat back of spoon. Keep custard well under simmering point. Remove from heat and stir for 1–2 minutes to cool slightly. Strain. Serve warm or cold. If serving cold, cover surface with damp greaseproof (waxed) paper to prevent skin forming on top, and chill. Serves 6–8.

Crème Brûlée

Make as for Crème Anglaise, using only 60 g/2 oz (¼ cup) sugar and substituting single (light) cream for milk. Pour into 4 individual or 1 larger serving dish and chill well. Just before serving, stand custard in shallow baking dish surrounded with ice to keep custard chilled. Sprinkle white or brown sugar in a 3 mm (⅛ in) layer over top and put under preheated grill (broiler) until sugar melts and forms a toffee glaze. Serve immediately. Serves 4.

Petits Pots de Crème

These rich custard creams can be flavoured with vanilla essence (extract), coffee or chocolate. Offer a choice of flavours or make all the Pots de Crème in one flavour.

600 ml/1 pint (2½ cups) milk; 1 vanilla pod (bean) or ½ tsp vanilla essence (extract); 60 g/2 oz (¼ cup) caster sugar; 4 egg yolks; 1 whole egg; 1 tsp instant coffee powder; 1 tbsp warm water; 2–3 tbsp cooking chocolate, grated.

Scald milk with vanilla bean and sugar (see page 215). Remove bean. Lightly beat egg yolks with whole egg. Add milk and vanilla if vanilla bean is not being used. Strain custard and divide into 3 equal parts. Flavour one part with coffee dissolved in the warm water; one with chocolate melted on a plate over hot water; and leave the third plain. Pour carefully into 9–10 little pots. Stand these in a shallow baking tin (pan) and half fill tin (pan) with hot water to surround pots. Cover pots and bake in a preheated moderate oven (180°C/350°F, Gas Mark 4) for 12–20 minutes or until set depending on your oven and thickness of pots. Cool and serve with crisp dessert biscuits (cookies). Serves 6.

Left: Cassata Siciliana (page 58)

Oeufs à la Neige

600 ml/1 pint (2½ cups) milk; 1 vanilla pod (bean); 1 tbsp sugar or vanilla sugar; 1 quantity Crème Anglaise (left); 2 tbsp slivered, toasted almonds, to decorate.
MERINGUE: *4 egg whites; 250 g/8 oz (1 cup) caster sugar.*

MERINGUE: Whisk egg whites until peaks form. Gradually beat in sugar 1 tbsp at a time until stiff peaks form and hold their shape.

Put milk, vanilla bean and sugar into shallow pan and bring to simmering point. Poach tablespoons of meringue in the milk, turning to cook evenly, for 3–5 minutes or until set. Lift out carefully with slotted spoon, drain and put on top of custard (crème anglaise) in a glass or china bowl. Serve decorated with almonds. Serves 6–8.

Crème Caramel

CARAMEL: *120 ml/4 fl oz (½ cup) water; 250 g/8 oz (1 cup) sugar.*
CUSTARD: *250 ml/8 fl oz (1 cup) single (light) cream; 250 ml/8 fl oz (1 cup) milk; ½ tsp vanilla essence (extract); 3 whole eggs; 2 egg yolks; 125 g/4 oz (½ cup) sugar.*

CARAMEL: Put water and sugar in a small saucepan over low heat and stir until sugar dissolves. Boil, without stirring, until golden-brown. Pour into 6 individual 120 ml/4 fl oz (½ cup) moulds, turning moulds to coat bottom and sides.
CUSTARD: Warm cream and milk together, remove from heat and add vanilla. Beat whole eggs, egg yolks and sugar, and stir into warmed cream and milk. Strain, then pour into prepared moulds. Set in a baking tin (pan) of hot water and bake in a preheated moderate oven (160°C/325°F, Gas Mark 3) for 25 minutes or until custard is set and a knife inserted in centre comes out clean. Cool and chill overnight. Unmould on to serving plates. Serves 6.
NOTE: Custard may be baked in a 750 ml/ 1¼ pint (3 cup) mould lined with caramel, if desired. Bake for 45 minutes or until the custard is set.

Ile Flottante aux Praline
(Floating Island)
This classic dish with its 'island' of baked, toffee-coated meringue in a lake of rich custard is one of the greats of the dessert world.

125 g/4 oz (½ cup) sugar; 2 tbsp water; pinch cream of tartar; 45 g/1½ oz (⅓ cup) crushed Praline (page 310); 1 quantity Crème Anglaise (left), very well chilled.
MERINGUE: *4 egg whites; pinch cream of tartar; pinch salt; 150 g/5 oz (⅔ cup) caster sugar; ½ tsp vanilla essence (extract).*

In a heavy saucepan combine sugar, water and cream of tartar. Heat gently, stirring, until sugar has dissolved. Wash sugar crystals frequently from sides of pan with a brush dipped in water. Cook over moderate heat, without stirring, until mixture caramelizes and turns a deep golden-brown. Pour caramel carefully into a 1.25 litre/2 pint (5 cup) ovenproof mould, tilting it to coat bottom and sides. Set aside.
MERINGUE: Whisk egg whites with cream of tartar and salt until they form soft peaks. Beat in sugar, a little at a time, and vanilla, and continue beating until mixture holds stiff glossy peaks.

Spoon half meringue into caramel lined mould, sprinkle with crushed praline and spoon in remaining meringue. Smooth top with a spatula. Place mould in a baking tin (pan) and add enough hot water to reach halfway up sides of mould. Bake in centre of a preheated cool oven (140°C/275°F, Gas Mark 1) for 40 minutes or until a skewer inserted in the centre comes out clean. Invert meringue on to a serving dish, surround with crème anglaise and hand remaining crème anglaise separately. Serves 4.

Maple Syrup Custard

Creamy custard with a subtle maple flavour, baked in individual pots or one large dish.

4 eggs; 500 ml/18 fl oz (2 cups) milk; 120 ml/4 fl oz (½ cup) maple syrup; pinch salt.
TO SERVE: *whipped cream; maple syrup.*

Beat eggs, then add milk, maple syrup and salt and combine well. Pour into 6 buttered custard cups or a buttered 1 litre/1¾ pint (4 cup) casserole. Set container in a baking tin (pan) with enough warm water to come halfway up sides of container. Bake in a preheated moderate oven (180°C/350°F, Gas Mark 4) for about 30 minutes for individual cups, or 45–50 minutes for larger dish, or until set. Serve warm, with cream and a drizzle of maple syrup. Serves 6.

CUSTARD APPLE

The fleshy, round or heart-shaped fruit of the Anona tree, found in the tropics. The fruit is cut open and the creamy white flesh is spooned out of the knobbly green shell. The flesh is soft, sweet, aromatic and custard-flavoured; the shiny black seeds should be discarded.

CUTTLEFISH

A saltwater mollusc, closely related to squid. Like squid, the eyes, long central bone, sac of ink and yellowish deposit under the head must be removed. More tender than octopus and squid, cuttlefish can be cooked in the same way as squid.
See Squid.

DANISH OPEN SANDWICHES
(Smørrebrød)

Smørrebrød means 'buttered bread', but Danish open sandwiches are very much more than that. They are special to the Danes and have been copied throughout the world as one of the great Danish inspirations. They are made with thin slices of any type of rye bread, crusty French bread, toasted or plain, or crispbreads. These are spread with butter, or fat such as spiced pork dripping, right to the edge of the bread to prevent any moisture from the topping making the bread soggy. The fat helps to hold everything in place.

The generous toppings turn the sandwiches into a meal; they are eaten at lunch, and always with a knife and fork.

Toppings are generally made up from foods found in the household pantry or refrigerator. Cold roast meats or poultry; canned or spiced fish; potato salad; cheese; mayonnaise; cold scrambled or hard-boiled (hard-cooked) eggs. The delicatessen supplies salami, smoked pork and beef, ham, liver sausage, smoked salmon or mackerel, along with capers, horseradish, gherkins and pickles.

Fresh vegetables play an important role – tomatoes, cucumber, lettuce, onions – and herbs, such as chives, dill, parsley and cress, are all used.

Toppings for Danish Open Sandwiches

Egg with Anchovy and Capers Place flat anchovy fillets in parallel rows on a piece of buttered rye bread. Hard-boil (hard-cook) and finely chop an egg before arranging it between the rows. Garnish with capers.

Sardine with Sliced Tomato Place tomato on buttered rye or French bread in overlapping slices; on these put a whole sardine or several small ones. Garnish with a twist of lemon and a sprig of parsley.

Roast Beef with Potato Salad and Chives Place thin, furled slices of roast beef on buttered bread and heap a generous mound of potato salad in the centre. Sprinkle with chives.

Bacon and Kidney with Tomato Fry rindless streaky bacon rashers (slices) until crisp; drain and cool. Place bacon on buttered rye bread and top with a slice of tomato. Place chopped grilled (broiled) kidney over tomato and garnish with a parsley sprig.

Smoked Mussels Place mussels on buttered French bread or crispbread; garnish with dill sprays and a sliver of lemon zest.

Smoked Salmon with Scrambled Egg Place a slice of smoked salmon on buttered French or rye bread and across it spread a strip of scrambled egg. Garnish with sour cream.

Spiced Herring with Onion Rings Place herrings on buttered dark rye bread, top with overlapping raw onion rings and garnish with capers or cress.

Roast Pork and Beetroot Place slices of roast pork on buttered light rye bread or crispbread; garnish with a slice of cooked beetroot.

Ham with Vegetable Salad Make vegetable salad with equal quantities of chopped cooked beetroot and apple, and a little chopped gherkin. Add some stiff Mayonnaise (see page 204) to bind. Place ham slice on buttered dark or light rye bread, French bread or crispbread. Mound salad neatly on top and garnish with watercress sprigs.

Salami with Potato and Chives Spread rye or French bread or crispbread with spiced lard (see below) and place slices of salami on it; arrange slightly overlapping slices of boiled new potato on top and sprinkle with chives.

Spiced Lard Melt some pure lard (shortening) or gently fry some fat pork or fat bacon dice until the fat runs. Add a little finely chopped onion and a few leaves of thyme and fry until onion is softened. Allow fat to solidify before using on bread for *smørrebrød*.

DANISH PASTRY

Light-as-air Danish pastries are made from a rich, buttery, yeast dough with a variety of toppings and fillings. The pastries may be filled with preserves, dried fruit, nuts or Crème pâtissière (see page 165); glazed with icing (frosting), sprinkled with spices, coarse sugar or ground nuts and then shaped into knots, twists or little parcels.

They are served with steaming hot cups of coffee but are sometimes eaten after the main course at lunch. Most people buy their favourite Danish pastries from good pastry shops; even in Denmark, the housewife considers they require the special skills of a pastry cook but here is a basic recipe for almond flavoured squares for those cooks brave enough to try making their own Danish Pastries.

Almond Danish Pastries

250 g/8 oz (2 cups) plain (all-purpose) flour; pinch salt; 150 g/5 oz (⅔ cup) butter; 1½ tsp dried yeast (active dry yeast); 1 tbsp sugar; 5 tbsp warm milk; 2 eggs; 250 g (8 oz) Almond Paste (page 7); 1 quantity Glacé Icing (page 164).

Sift flour and salt into a warm mixing bowl and rub in 30 g/1 oz (2 tbsp) of the butter. Blend yeast with sugar and milk and leave to stand in a warm place until it begins to froth, about 10 minutes. Stir into the flour with one beaten egg and mix to a soft dough. Cover and leave in a warm place until doubled in bulk. Knock back (punch down) and turn out on to a lightly floured board. Roll dough into a rectangle about 1 cm/½ in thick. Cut remaining butter into walnut-sized pieces and place half on the top ⅔ of the dough.

Bring up the bottom ⅓ of the dough and fold down the top ⅓ (see Flaky Pastry page 275). Seal the edges with the rolling pin and give the dough a quarter turn. Roll out again and repeat the folding process using the remaining butter. Cover and refrigerate for 15 minutes then repeat the rolling and folding process twice more. Refrigerate well before shaping.
SHAPING: Roll dough thinly and cut into 12 × 10 cm/4 in squares. Roll almond paste into 12 walnut-sized balls. Place one in the centre of each square and brush with a little of the remaining egg, beaten. Draw up the corners to the centre like an envelope and seal with beaten egg. Place pastries on a baking tray, cover and leave in a warm place for about 20 minutes or until puffy. Brush with beaten egg and bake in a preheated moderately hot oven (200°C/400°F, Gas Mark 6) for 15–20 minutes or until crisp and golden. Transfer to a wire rack and brush with glacé icing while still warm. Makes 12.

DATE

Dates grow in huge, hanging bunches, often weighing up to 15 kg (33 lb), on the date palm, and are eaten either fresh or dried. The best dried dates are soft and juicy, packed whole in small boxes. These can be eaten as they are or used in recipes for stuffed dates. The hard, dry variety comes in blocks and is good for cooking.

Fresh dates can be bought from many greengrocers and should be purchased when their skins are a smooth, shiny brown and the fruit is plump and not sticky.

Ways to Use Dates
Whole Dried Dates: Remove the stones and stuff with any of the following – marzipan; whole or ground nuts; flavoured fondant; cream cheese, sweetened with vanilla sugar; glacé (candied) fruits such as cherries or pineapple; or very thick crème pâtissière (see page 165), flavoured with Kirsch and sprinkled with sugar. Serve in frilly paper sweet cases as petits fours.
Dried Dates Sold in Blocks: Use, finely chopped, in puddings, cakes, breads, scones or sandwiches.
Fresh Dates: Serve with a bowl of thick, creamy plain yogurt; Ricotta cheese, flavoured with grated lemon or orange rind; in a fruit salad or simply enjoy them on their own. They also make a good addition to a cheese board. **See recipes**.

Date Bars

125 g/4 oz (1 cup) flour; 180 g/6 oz (1¾ cups) rolled oats (plain or quick-cooking); 250 g/8 oz (1 cup) butter or firm margarine.
FILLING: *180 g/6 oz (1 cup) chopped, stoned dates; 1 tbsp lemon juice; 2 tbsp rum or water; 2 tsp grated lemon rind; 45 g/1½ oz (¼ cup) firmly packed brown sugar; 1 tsp cinnamon or allspice.*

FILLING: Place dates in a saucepan with remaining filling ingredients and simmer 20 minutes, stirring often, or until dates are soft. Cool. Sift flour into a bowl. Add oats and rub (cut) in butter or margarine until well blended. Divide mixture in half and press one portion into a greased 18 cm (7 in) square cake tin (pan). Smooth date mixture evenly on top, then sprinkle with remaining rolled oats mixture and press it into place to cover filling. Bake in a preheated moderate oven (180°C/350°F, Gas Mark 4) for 25 minutes. Cut into bars and allow to cool in tin (pan). Makes 12–14.

Frosted Date Bars

These nutty, economical fruit bars stay moist for weeks. Make them 2–3 weeks ahead if liked, but don't roll in icing (confectioners) sugar until you serve them.

175 ml/6 fl oz (¾ cup) evaporated milk; 180 g/6 oz (1 cup) chopped dates; 125 g/4 oz (1 cup) self-raising flour; ½ tsp salt; 125 g/4 oz (½ cup) butter; 125 g/4 oz (½ cup) caster sugar; 1 egg, beaten; 1 tsp vanilla essence (extract); 60 g/2 oz (½ cup) chopped walnuts; sifted icing (confectioners) sugar.

Place evaporated milk in a small saucepan and heat until small bubbles appear at edge of saucepan. Pour over dates and allow to cool. Sift flour and salt together. Cream butter with sugar until light and fluffy. Add egg and vanilla and beat well. Fold in sifted flour alternately with milk and date mixture. Stir in nuts. Spoon mixture into a greased 23 cm (9 in) square cake tin (pan). Bake in a preheated moderate oven (180°C/350°F, Gas Mark 4) for 30–35 minutes or until a skewer inserted in the centre comes out clean. Turn out and cool on a wire rack. Cut into bars and toss in icing (confectioners) sugar. Makes 24.

Date and Nut Rolls

180 g/6 oz (1 cup) chopped dates; 140 g/4½ oz (¾ cup) firmly packed brown sugar; 1 tsp bicarbonate of soda (baking soda); 60 g/2 oz (4 tbsp) butter; 1 tsp grated lemon rind; 250 ml/8 fl oz (1 cup) boiling water; 250 g/8 oz (2 cups) self-raising flour; 1 tsp mixed spice (ground allspice); 1 egg, beaten; 60 g/2 oz (½ cup) chopped walnuts.

Put dates in a large mixing bowl with brown sugar, soda, butter and lemon rind. Pour boiling water over and stir until butter has melted. Leave to cool. Sift flour and spice together and add to cooled date mixture alternately with egg and walnuts. Stir well, spoon into 2 well-greased 21 × 11 cm (8¼ × 4½ in) tins and bake in a preheated moderate oven (180°C/350°F, Gas Mark 4) for 45 minutes. Cool in tins (pans) for 5 minutes before turning out. Makes 2.

Date and Nut Cake

250 g/8 oz (1⅔ cups) stoned dates; 250 ml/8 fl oz (1 cup) boiling water; 90 g/3 oz (6 tbsp) butter, softened; 250 g/8 oz (1 cup) sugar; 1 tsp vanilla essence (extract); 1 egg, beaten; 180 g/6 oz (1½ cups) self-raising flour; 1 tsp bicarbonate of soda (baking soda); 1 tsp cinnamon; ¼ tsp salt; 60 g/2 oz (½ cup) chopped walnuts.

Place dates in a large bowl and pour boiling water over. Leave for 2–3 minutes or until they soften. Add butter and sugar and beat well until combined. Blend in vanilla and egg. Sift flour with soda, and fold in with cinnamon and salt. Stir in the nuts. Turn into a greased and lined 21 × 11 cm (8½ × 4½ in) loaf tin (pan), or a 20 cm (8 in) round or square cake tin (pan). Bake in a preheated moderate oven (180°C/350°F, Gas Mark 4) for 25–30 minutes or until cooked when tested with a skewer. Leave in the tin (pan) for 2 minutes, then turn on to a wire rack to cool. Serve warm as a dessert accompanied by whipped cream, or store in an airtight container and serve sliced with butter.

DESSERTS AND PUDDINGS

The name for the sweet course of a meal varies from country to country and even from family to family – 'dessert' and 'pudding' are both widely used to mean sweet dishes ranging from substantial hot pies and steamed puddings to such cold sweets as jellies, soufflés, moulds, sweet rice dishes and fruits. Here we have elected to call our 'just desserts' pudding (part of the author's Scottish heritage).

Desserts and puddings fall into one of the following categories:
Baked Puddings: This large class includes baked fruit pies, flans and tarts, such as Lemon Meringue Pie (see page 185); cake and yeast mixtures such as Babas and savarins; scone mixtures like Fruit Crumble (see page 330); and bread puddings.
Milk Puddings: These are made with milk and cereals such as rice, sago or semolina, and either cooked on top of the stove or in the oven. They can be served hot or cold. Junkets are an example of cold milk puddings (see page 172).
Steamed Puddings: These may be made with a cake-like batter, sponge mixtures, custard or breadcrumb mixtures, and may be light or rich with fruit and nuts like Sultana Pudding, Steamed Pineapple Pudding, Chocolate Pudding (see page 103) and Rich Christmas Pudding (see page 75).

Batter Puddings: Those made with a thin mixture of eggs, flour and milk, which may be fried like fritters, cooked on a griddle like pancakes, or cooked in special irons like waffles (see individual recipes).

Jellies, Creams, Mousses and Moulds: Innumerable cold sweets come into this category. They are usually set with jelly, sago or cornflour (cornstarch), can be made in a mould and turned out or served in a glass bowl or sundae glasses etc.; e.g. jellies, Bavarian creams, mousses and cold soufflés (see individual recipes).

Iced Sweet Puddings: These include ice creams, water ices, sorbets, sherbets and sundaes (see individual recipes).

Fruit Sweet Puddings: Fruits make lovely puddings; e.g. Baked Apples, Poached Pears, fruit fools, Fruit Trifle, Strawberries Romanoff, Apricots in Brandy and Bananas Flambé (see individual recipes).

Egg Puddings: These include puddings where eggs are the main ingredients; e.g. Crème Caramel, Queen of Puddings, sweet or soufflé omelettes, soufflés, meringues and meringue-based sweets. **See recipes.**

BAKED PUDDINGS

Butter the dish, tin (pan) or mould well, so that the pudding is easily turned out or served. Wipe round edges of container before baking. The pudding is easier to handle if it is placed on a baking tray while cooking.

Spiced Apple Charlotte

4 apples, peeled, cored and finely diced; 180 g/6 oz (¾ cup) sugar; ¼ tsp salt; ½ tsp ground cloves; ½ tsp grated lemon rind; 120 ml/4 fl oz (½ cup) orange juice; 3 tbsp sherry; 60 g/2 oz (4 tbsp) butter, melted; 180 g/6 oz (3 cups) fresh breadcrumbs.

Mix apples with sugar, salt, cloves, lemon rind, orange juice and sherry. Set aside. Combine melted butter and breadcrumbs, mixing well. Fill a buttered 1.2 litre/2 pint

(5 cup) charlotte mould or casserole with alternate layers of breadcrumbs and the apple mixture, beginning and ending with breadcrumbs. Cover pudding and bake in a preheated moderate oven (180°C/350°F, Gas Mark 4) for 30 minutes. Remove cover and bake for about 15 minutes longer or until crumbs are brown and apples are tender. Serve warm, with single (light) cream. Serves 6.

Apple and Date Crisp

180 g/6 oz (1 cup) dates, stoned; 120 ml/4 fl oz (½ cup) water; 1 tsp grated lemon rind; 150 g/5 oz (⅔ cup) sugar; juice ½ lemon; 180 g/6 oz (1½ cups) self-raising flour; ½ tsp cinnamon; 125 g/4 oz (½ cup) butter; 105 g/3½ oz (1 cup) rolled oats; 2 large cooking apples, peeled, cored and thinly sliced.

Combine dates, water, lemon rind and 2 tbsp sugar in a saucepan and cook 2–3 minutes or until dates are soft. Remove from heat, add lemon juice and beat with a wooden spoon until smooth. Allow to cool. Sift flour and cinnamon into a bowl. Rub (cut) in butter and mix in remaining sugar and oats. Press about ⅔ oat mixture into a greased and lined 19 cm (7½ in) square cake tin (pan). Spread this with date mixture. Arrange apple slices on top. Place remaining oat mixture on top of apples and press down. Bake in a preheated moderate oven (180°C/350°F, Gas Mark 4) for 45 minutes. Serve with cream or ice cream. Serves 6.

Wholewheat Apple Crisp

3 cooking apples, peeled, cored and sliced; 350 g/12 oz (1 cup) honey; 1 tbsp lemon juice; 60 g/2 oz (½ cup) wholewheat flour; 60 g/2 oz (4 tbsp) butter; 45 g/1½ oz (¼ cup) firmly packed brown sugar; 1 tsp grated lemon rind; 2 tsp cinnamon.

Place apples in a well-greased pie dish. Heat honey, add lemon juice and pour over apples. Put flour in a bowl and rub (cut) in butter until mixture resembles dry breadcrumbs. Add sugar and lemon rind and spread over apples. Sprinkle with cinnamon. Bake in a preheated moderately hot oven (190°C/375°F, Gas Mark 5) for 30–40 minutes, or until apples are tender and the topping crispy brown. Serves 4–6.

Almond Castles

90 g/3 oz (6 tbsp) butter; 75 g/2½ oz (⅓ cup) caster sugar; 3 eggs, separated; 3 tbsp single (light) cream or milk; 1 tbsp brandy (optional); 180 g/6 oz (1½ cups) ground almonds.

Cream together butter and sugar. Stir in egg yolks, cream or milk, brandy, if used, and

almonds. Whisk egg whites to a stiff froth and fold lightly into almond mixture. Spoon into 8 greased dariole moulds, filling them ¾ full. Bake in a preheated moderate oven (160°C/325°F, Gas Mark 3) for 20–25 minutes or until the puddings are firm in the centre and golden-brown. Turn out and serve with custard. If liked, the puddings may be steamed – cover with greased greaseproof (waxed) paper and steam 40–50 minutes or until firm. Serves 8.

Pineapple Delicious Pudding

30 g/1 oz (¼ cup) self-raising flour; ¼ tsp salt; 125 g/4 oz (½ cup) sugar; 2 eggs, separated; 120 ml/4 fl oz (½ cup) milk; 1 tbsp lemon juice; 45 g/1½ oz (¼ cup) crushed, drained pineapple; 4 tbsp pineapple juice.

Sift flour, salt and sugar into a bowl. Beat egg yolks and add to flour mixture with milk, lemon juice and crushed pineapple and juice, and mix well. Fold in stiffly beaten egg whites. Pour into ovenproof dish and stand dish in a roasting tin (pan) of water. Bake in a preheated moderate oven (180°C/350°F, Gas Mark 4) for 45–50 minutes or until set. Serve with cream or ice cream. Serves 4.

Sultana Bread Pudding

875 ml/1 pint 9 fl oz (3½ cups) milk; 1 piece vanilla pod (bean) or 1 tsp vanilla essence (extract); 60 g/2 oz (4 tbsp) butter, softened; 8 slices French bread (centre portion, not the crusty end); 90 g/3 oz (½ cup) sultanas (golden raisins); 3 eggs, or 5 yolks; 75 g/2½ oz (⅓ cup) sugar; pinch salt; nutmeg.

Scald milk (see page 215), then add vanilla bean, if used. Simmer 15 minutes. Cool. Discard vanilla bean, if used, or add vanilla. Butter one side of each slice of bread. Arrange slices in a 1.5 litre/2½ pint (6 cup) casserole, buttered sides down, sprinkling the sultanas (golden raisins) between the layers. Beat eggs or yolks with sugar and salt and add the scalded milk, stirring. Pour over the bread. Let stand 30 minutes. Sprinkle with nutmeg. Set casserole in a roasting tin (pan) of hot water and bake in a preheated moderate oven (180°C/350°F, Gas Mark 4) for about 1 hour or until a knife inserted in the centre comes out clean. Serve warm. Serves 6–8.

Orange Bread Pudding

3 slices bread, cubed; 250 ml/8 fl oz (1 cup) milk, scalded (see page 215); 175 ml/ 6 fl oz (¾ cup) orange juice; grated rind 1 orange; 4 egg yolks, beaten; 125 g/4 oz (½ cup) sugar; pinch salt; butter; whipped cream to serve.

Soak bread cubes in milk for 10 minutes. Add orange juice and rind, egg yolks, sugar

D

and salt. Stir until sugar has dissolved. Pour into 4 well-buttered individual moulds, dot with butter and place in a roasting tin (pan) of hot water. Bake in a preheated moderately hot oven (190°C/375°F, Gas Mark 5) for 30 minutes or until the tip of a knife inserted 2.5 cm (1 in) from the outside edge comes away clean. Chill. Unmould and serve with whipped cream. Serves 4.

New England Bread Pudding

875 ml/1 pint 9 fl oz (3½ cups) milk; 60 g/2 oz (4 tbsp) butter; 180 g/6 oz (3 cups) stale bread cubes; 125 g/4 oz (½ cup) sugar; 2 eggs, lightly beaten; 120 ml/4 fl oz (½ cup) sherry; 1 tsp cinnamon; 1 tsp nutmeg; 180 g/6 oz (1 cup) seedless raisins; 90 g/3 oz (½ cup) chopped mixed candied peel.

Heat milk, add butter and pour hot liquid over bread cubes. Soak about 5 minutes, then stir in sugar, eggs, sherry and spices. Add raisins and peel. Pour mixture into a buttered baking dish. Set dish in a roasting tin (pan) of hot water and bake in a preheated moderately hot oven (190°C/375°F, Gas Mark 5) for about 1 hour or until a knife inserted in the centre comes out clean. Serves 6.

Fruit Sponge

500 g (1 lb) fresh fruit (e.g. apricots, peaches, apples); sugar; 90 g/3 oz (6 tbsp) butter; 2 eggs, beaten; 125 g/4 oz (1 cup) self-raising flour.

Prepare fruit according to kind and arrange in a greased 1 litre/1¾ pint (4 cup) pie dish. Sprinkle with sugar to taste and add a little water if required. Cream together butter and 125 g/4 oz (½ cup) sugar. Add eggs gradually, beating well between each addition – if there is sign of curdling, add some flour. Sift flour and stir lightly into creamed mixture. Spread mixture over fruit. Bake in the middle of a preheated moderate oven (180°C/350°F, Gas Mark 4) for 35–40 minutes. Serve hot or cold with cream or custard. Serves 6.
NOTE: This can be made with drained canned fruit, if liked.

Winter Fruit Brown Betty

180 g/6 oz (1 cup) dried apricots; 350 g/12 oz (2 cups) dried apples; 125 g/4 oz (2 cups) fresh breadcrumbs; 60 g/2 oz (4 tbsp) butter, melted; 45 g/1½ oz (⅓ cup) chopped blanched almonds; grated rind 1 orange; 90 g/3 oz (½ cup) firmly packed brown sugar; 15 g/½ oz (1 tbsp) butter.

Soak apricots and apples overnight in plenty of water to cover. Drain and chop roughly. Toss breadcrumbs in melted butter. Spread a thin layer of crumbs in bottom of baking or

soufflé dish. Cover with a little of the chopped fruit. Sprinkle over a little of the almonds, orange rind and sugar. Repeat layers until dish is full, finishing with a layer of crumbs. Dot with butter and sprinkle with any remaining sugar. Bake in a preheated moderately hot oven (200°C/400°F, Gas Mark 6) for 30 minutes or until golden and crisp. Serve very hot with cream. Serves 6.

Baked Apple Roly-Poly

PASTRY (DOUGH): *180 g/6 oz (1½ cups) flour; ½ tsp bicarbonate of soda (baking soda); 1 tsp cream of tartar; 15 g/½ oz (1 tbsp) butter; about 4 tbsp iced water.*
FILLING: *3 cooking apples, peeled, cored and sliced.*
SYRUP: *180 g/6 oz (¾ cup) sugar; 60 g/2 oz (4 tbsp) butter; 250 ml/8 fl oz (1 cup) boiling water.*

To make pastry (dough), sift dry ingredients together, rub (cut) in butter with fingertips and mix in enough water to make a soft dough. Roll out to a rectangle. Spread apples over pastry (dough) and roll up like a Swiss (jelly) roll. Lift roly-poly into a greased shallow ovenproof dish, seam side down. Mix sugar, butter and boiling water and pour over. Bake in a preheated moderate oven (180°C/350°F, Gas Mark 4) for 1 hour, basting roly-poly every 10 minutes with syrup. Serve hot, cut into slices, with custard or cream. Serves 6.
VARIATION
Jam or Syrup Roly-Poly: Follow recipe for Apple Roly-Poly, but substitute jam or syrup for apples. Roll out pastry (dough) fairly thin.

BATTER PUDDINGS

Batters are made from a basic mixture of flour, milk and egg. The flour is worked to a very soft consistency with the eggs and some of the liquid, so that it can be beaten more easily until smooth. The rest of the liquid is then stirred in. The mixture is left to stand for 30 minutes before use.

The lightness of a batter depends on the quick formation of steam within the mixture and quick cooking. A baked batter therefore needs to be cooked in a preheated hot oven (220°C/425°F, Gas Mark 7), and the

temperature can be reduced when the flour is almost cooked. It is best to put the batter at the top of the oven to begin with, then to move it to a lower shelf at reduced heat to finish cooking.

See also *Fritters and Pancakes.*

Batter Pudding

250 g/8 oz (2 cups) flour; ¼ tsp salt; 2 eggs; 600 ml/1 pint (2½ cups) milk; 1 tbsp cooking fat.

Sift flour and salt into a bowl. Make a well in the centre of the flour and break eggs into this. Add about 120 ml/4 fl oz (½ cup) of the milk. Stir, gradually working flour down from sides and adding more milk as required to make a stiff batter consistency. Beat well for about 5 minutes. Add rest of the milk. Cover and leave to stand for 30 minutes. Put fat into a Yorkshire pudding tin (pan) about 20 × 25 cm (8 × 10 in) and heat in a preheated hot oven (220°C/425°F, Gas Mark 7). The fat should just be beginning to smoke. Quickly pour in the batter and return to the oven, placing the tin (pan) at the top of the oven. Bake for 25 minutes or until nicely browned. Reduce heat to moderately hot (190°C/375°F, Gas Mark 5) and continue baking for 10–15 minutes. Serve with wine, syrup or jam sauce. Serves 6.

MILK PUDDINGS

These are basically made with a farinaceous ingredient, sugar and milk. Eggs may be added, if liked, or any other suitable flavouring such as grated lemon or orange rind, nutmeg, cinnamon, vanilla or other flavouring essences (extracts).

The addition of egg to a milk pudding increases the nutritive value, and the pudding is made much lighter if the whites are whisked before being added. The egg must not be added until the rice, macaroni or other grain is fully cooked, otherwise the long cooking necessary to cook the grain would overcook the eggs and cause them to curdle. Baking for about 30 minutes in a preheated moderate oven (160°C/325°F, Gas Mark 3) is usually long enough to cook the eggs and brown the top of a 450–750 ml/¾–1¼ pint (2–3 cup) pudding.

The correct consistency of a boiled or baked milk pudding is such that it will just flow over the plate when served. This result is achieved by using the correct quantities of ingredients and slow cooking to prevent excessive evaporation.

GENERAL POINTS: Heavy saucepans are ideal. Avoid using thin saucepans. Rinse out the saucepan with cold water before using, or lightly grease with butter to lessen the risk of burning.

In puddings where eggs are included, the mixture must be cooled slightly before the egg yolks are added.

Sago Fluff

3 tbsp sago; 750 ml/1¼ pints (3 cups) milk; 2 eggs, separated; 3 tbsp sugar; pinch salt; 1 tsp vanilla essence (extract); stewed dried apricots or prunes.

Cook sago in 500 ml/18 fl oz (2 cups) of the milk until all grains disappear, being careful it does not burn. Beat egg yolks with sugar, salt and remaining milk. Add to sago, stirring until thick. Remove from heat. When cool, fold in stiffly beaten egg whites and vanilla. Pile into a serving dish when cold. Arrange apricots or prunes around edge. Serves 6.

Coconut Meringue Custard

750 ml/1¼ pints (3 cups) milk; 3 eggs, separated; 3 tbsp sugar; 4 tbsp desiccated (shredded) coconut; 2 tbsp glacé (candied) cherries; 2 tbsp plum jam; 2 tbsp caster sugar.

Scald milk (see page 215) in a heavy saucepan. Beat egg yolks and sugar together and add to milk, stirring all the time. Scatter 2 tbsp coconut over bottom of a greased pie dish and strain custard over this. Leave for 30 minutes. Add glacé (candied) cherries (leaving a few for decoration) and stir through. Stand dish in a roasting tin (pan) of cold water and bake in the coolest part of a preheated moderate oven (160°C/325°F, Gas Mark 3) for 1 hour, or until mixture is set. Remove from oven and spread jam over top of custard. Beat egg whites until stiff and fold in caster sugar. Pile this on to custard. Top with rest of coconut and cherries and return to the oven. Bake for 20 minutes longer. Serve hot with cream. Serves 6.

Cloud Custard

350 ml/12 fl oz (1½ cups) milk; 2 tsp cornflour (cornstarch); 1 large egg, separated; pinch salt; ½ tsp vanilla essence (extract); 4 tsp sugar.

Place milk (reserving about 1 tbsp) in a small saucepan and bring to the boil. Meanwhile, mix cornflour (cornstarch) to a smooth paste with reserved milk, and blend in egg yolk, salt, vanilla and 2 tsp of the sugar. When milk boils, pour a little on to cornflour (cornstarch) mixture, stir well and return to saucepan. Stir over low heat for 3–4 minutes until custard is smooth and thick. Remove from heat and cool. Beat egg white until stiff, then beat in remaining sugar. Spoon custard into bowl with meringue, and lightly fold together for a pretty yellow and white effect. Chill until serving time. Serves 4.

Creamy Rice Pudding

4 tbsp short-grain rice; 1 tbsp sugar; 900 ml/1½ pints (3½ cups) milk; 15 g/½ oz (1 tbsp) butter; nutmeg; 1 tbsp single (light) cream.

Place rice in buttered pie dish. Add sugar and milk and stir well. Add butter in small pieces and top with nutmeg. Bake in a preheated moderate oven (160°C/325°F, Gas Mark 3) for 1½ hours, stirring every 30 minutes. Stir well, then add the cream and leave to cook a further 30 minutes or until brown. Serve with cream or jam. Serves 6.

Geneva Pudding

105 g/3½ oz (½ cup) short-grain rice; 1 litre/ 1¾ pints (4 cups) milk; pinch salt; 1 kg (2 lb) cooking apples, roughly chopped; 30 g/1 oz (2 tbsp) butter; ¼ tsp cinnamon; 3 tbsp water; 75 g/2½ oz (⅓ cup) sugar.

Simmer rice in milk, with salt, until tender. Meanwhile, put apples in a saucepan with butter, cinnamon and water. Simmer very gently until tender, then rub the mixture through a fine sieve. Stir 1 tbsp sugar into rice and add rest to apple purée. Arrange rice and apple purée in alternate layers in a well-buttered pie dish, with rice forming bottom and top layers. Bake in a preheated moderate oven (180°C/350°F, Gas Mark 4) for about 1¼ hours or until brown. Serves 6.

Swedish Rice

400 g/14 oz (2 cups) short-grain rice; salt; 750 g (1½ lb) cooking apples, peeled, cored and thinly sliced; 500 ml/18 fl oz (2 cups) milk; pared rind 1 lemon; 75 g/2½ oz (⅓ cup) sugar; pinch cinnamon; 120 ml/4 fl oz (½ cup) sherry; 140 g/4½ oz (¾ cup) seedless raisins, roughly chopped.

Add rice to a pan of salted boiling water. Boil for 3 minutes, then drain off the water. Add

apples, milk and lemon rind to rice and cook until tender. Remove lemon rind. Add sugar, cinnamon, sherry and raisins and mix well. Cook for 3–4 minutes longer. Serve with cream. Serves 6.

Tapioca Cream Pudding

90 g/3 oz (½ cup) tapioca; 1 litre/1¾ pints (4 cups) milk; pinch salt; 15 g/½ oz (1 tbsp) butter; 2 tbsp sugar; ¼ tsp almond essence (extract); 3 eggs, separated; 6 coconut macaroons, crushed.

Soak tapioca in milk, with salt, for 1–2 hours, then tip mixture into a saucepan. Bring to the boil and simmer until tapioca is cooked. Add butter, sugar and almond essence (extract) and mix well. Cool slightly, then add egg yolks. Pour into a well-buttered pie dish and bake pudding in a preheated moderate oven (180°C/350°F, Gas Mark 4) until just set. Whisk egg whites stiffly and fold in crushed macaroons lightly. Pile on top of tapioca pudding. Reduce oven temperature to cool (150°C/300°F, Gas Mark 2) and bake for a further 30 minutes or until a pale golden-brown on top. Serves 6.

STEAMED PUDDINGS

The mould or basin in which a pudding is steamed should be well-greased with fresh butter. Always prepare the steamer, the mould or basin, and the covering before the pudding is mixed.

There should be plenty of boiling water in the steamer. If a steamer is not available, the pudding can be partly steamed by standing it on an old plate, saucer or pastry cutter (to prevent direct contact with the source of heat) in a saucepan, with just enough water to reach halfway up the mould or basin. Put a tightly-fitting lid on the saucepan and simmer gently. If the water boils down, add more boiling water to replace it. Do not let pan boil dry.

Where gentle steaming is indicated in the recipe, the water below the steamer should only simmer. The basin or mould should not be more than ¾ full.

Always cover the pudding with greased paper before steaming; this acts as a waterproof cover against condensing steam. Use a piece of strong paper, such as greaseproof (waxed), grease it well, make a pleat down the centre and place it, greased side down, over the top of the basin. Turn the edges of the paper under and twist them securely below the rim of the basin. If liked, tie with string, looping it to make a handle for easy removal of the basin.

After taking the pudding out of the steamer, leave it for a minute or two to allow it time to shrink slightly from the sides of the mould or basin, before turning it out on to a warm serving plate.

Madeira Pudding

*4 slices bread, diced; 75 g/2½ oz (⅓ cup)
caster sugar; 1 tsp grated lemon rind;
500 ml/18 fl oz (2 cups) milk; 3 eggs, beaten;
120 ml/4 fl oz (½ cup) sherry or Madeira.*

Mix together bread, sugar and lemon rind.
Heat milk to about blood heat and pour it on
to eggs, stirring well. Add sherry or Madeira
and pour over bread mixture. Leave to soak
for 15–20 minutes. Pour into a well-buttered
mould or pudding basin, cover with greased
greaseproof (waxed) paper and steam very
gently for 2 hours. Serve with custard, wine
or jam sauce. Serves 6.

Windsor Pudding

*2½ tbsp short-grain rice; 500 ml/18 fl oz
(2 cups) milk; 1 kg (2 lb) cooking apples,
cored and roughly chopped; 60 g/2 oz
(¼ cup) caster sugar; grated rind and juice
½ lemon; 3–4 egg whites.*

Simmer rice in milk until tender and all the
milk has been absorbed. Meanwhile, cook
apples in as little water as possible, until soft.
Sieve or purée in a blender, then stir in
sugar, rice, and lemon rind and juice. Whisk
egg whites stiffly and fold lightly into the
mixture. Put into greased mould or pudding
basin, cover with greased greaseproof
(waxed) paper and steam very gently for
about 40 minutes. Serve with custard sauce
made from the egg yolks. Serves 6.

Chocolate Puddings

Cook these little puddings in your electric
frying pan (skillet), or use any large
flameproof dish with foil fitted over to make
a good cover.

*3 tbsp (unsweetened) cocoa powder; 7 tbsp
boiling water; 90 g/3 oz (6 tbsp) butter;
125 g/4 oz (½ cup) caster sugar; 1 egg; ½ tsp
vanilla essence (extract); 180 g/6 oz
(1½ cups) self-raising flour; pinch salt; 6 tsp
raspberry jam.*

Put cocoa into a small bowl, add boiling
water and mix together until blended. Cool.
Cream butter with sugar, then add egg and
vanilla and beat in thoroughly. Sift in flour
and salt. Add cocoa mixture and combine
thoroughly. Put 1 tsp jam in bottom of each
of 6 greased individual moulds. Divide
chocolate mixture between moulds. Have
frying pan (skillet) heated, with water to a
depth of about 2 cm (¾ in). Place moulds in
pan, cover with pan lid and simmer for 20
minutes. Turn out and serve hot with cream
or custard sauce. Serves 6.

Chocolate Sauce Pudding

*30 g/1 oz (2 tbsp) butter; 125 g/4 oz (½ cup)
caster sugar; ½ tsp vanilla essence (extract);*
*1 egg; 125 g/4 oz (1 cup) self-raising flour;
2 tsp (unsweetened) cocoa powder; ½ tsp salt;
120 ml/4 fl oz (½ cup) milk.*
SAUCE: *125 g/4 oz (½ cup) sugar; 2 tsp
(unsweetened) cocoa powder; 350 ml/
12 fl oz (1½ cups) hot water.*

Cream butter with sugar and vanilla. Add
egg and beat well until creamy. Fold in sifted
flour, cocoa and salt alternately with milk.
Pour into greased 1–1.2 litre/1¾–2 pint (4–5
cup) mould or pudding basin. For sauce, mix
sugar and cocoa and sprinkle over sponge
mixture. Lastly pour over hot water. Cover
basin with greased greaseproof (waxed)
paper and steam for 1–1½ hours. Serves 4.

Light Cottage Pudding

*60 g/2 oz (4 tbsp) butter; 60 g/2 oz (¼ cup)
sugar; 1 egg; ½ tsp vanilla essence (extract);
125 g/4 oz (1 cup) self-raising flour; 3 tbsp
milk.*

Cream butter with sugar. Beat in egg and
vanilla. Stir in sifted flour and milk. Turn into
greased mould or pudding basin, cover with
greased greaseproof (waxed) paper and
steam 1¼ hours. Serve with jam, golden (light
corn) syrup or sweet sauce. Serves 4.

Sultana Pudding

*180 g/6 oz (1½ cups) self-raising flour; pinch
salt; 125 g/4 oz (½ cup) butter; 125 g/4 oz
⅔ cup) firmly packed brown sugar; 2 eggs,
lightly beaten; ½ tsp vanilla essence (extract);
60 g/2 oz (⅓ cup) sultanas (golden raisins);
4 tbsp milk.*

Sift flour with salt. Cream butter with sugar
until light, then gradually beat in eggs and
vanilla. (Add a little flour with the last few
additions.) Fold in remaining flour, sultanas
(golden raisins) and milk. Spoon into a well-
buttered mould or pudding basin, cover with
double thickness of greased greaseproof
(waxed) paper and steam 2 hours. Serve with
stirred custard or cream. Serves 6.

Steamed Pineapple Pudding

*3 – 4 slices canned pineapple; 6–8 glacé
(candied) cherries.*
BUTTERSCOTCH: *75 g/2½ oz (5 tbsp) butter;
280 g/9 oz (1½ cups) firmly packed brown
sugar.*
PUDDING: *125 g/4 oz (1 cup) self-raising
flour; pinch salt; 90 g/3 oz (6 tbsp) butter;
125 g/4 oz (½ cup) caster sugar; 1 tsp vanilla
essence (extract); 2 eggs; 4 tbsp milk.*

Cut pineapple slices in half to make 6–8 thin
circles. Make butterscotch by creaming butter
and sugar together. Spread over bottom and
sides of a greased 1 litre/1¾ pints (4 cup)
pudding basin or charlotte mould. Arrange
pineapple circles on top and decorate with
cherries. Sift flour and salt. Cream butter
with sugar and vanilla until light. Beat in eggs

one at a time, then fold in milk alternately
with flour. Spoon into basin. Cover with 2
thicknesses of pleated greased greaseproof
(waxed) paper and steam for 1½ hours. Serve
with cream or custard sauce. Serves 6.

Steamed Ginger Pudding

*310 g/10 oz (2½ cups) flour; 1 tsp ground
ginger; pinch mixed spice (ground allspice);
1 tsp bicarbonate of soda (baking soda);
150 g/5 oz (1 cup) finely grated suet; 1 egg;
250 g/8 oz (¾ cup) golden (light corn) syrup;
175 ml/6 fl oz (¾ cup) warmed milk; 3 tbsp
finely chopped preserved ginger.*

Sift flour, spices and soda into a bowl. Add
suet. Make a well in the centre and pour in
beaten egg mixed with syrup and milk. Stir
well to a batter that will fall easily from spoon.
Spoon preserved ginger over bottom of
greased 1.2 litre/2 pint (5 cup) pudding
basin or mould. Pour in mixture, cover basin
with a pleated piece of greased greaseproof
(waxed) paper and steam for 2½–3 hours.
Serve with warmed golden (light corn) syrup
or custard. Serves 4–6.

Sago Plum Pudding

*2 tbsp sago; 250 ml/8 fl oz (1 cup) milk;
60 g/2 oz (4 tbsp) butter; 250 g/8 oz (1 cup)
sugar; 1 tsp bicarbonate of soda (baking
soda); pinch salt; 60 g/2 oz (1 cup) fresh
breadcrumbs; 180 g/6 oz (1 cup) sultanas
(golden raisins) or mixed dried fruit; 1 tbsp
chopped mixed candied peel; ½ tsp mixed
spice (ground allspice).*

Soak sago overnight in the milk. Beat butter
and sugar together, then beat in soaked sago
and milk, soda and salt. Add breadcrumbs,
fruit, peel and spice. Mix well and turn into a
well-greased pudding basin or mould. Cover
top with greased greaseproof (waxed) paper
and steam for 2 hours. Serve with custard or
cream. Serves 6.

NOTE: The pudding mixture may be divided
between 6 individual moulds and steamed
for 1 hour, if preferred.

Desserts and Puddings –

Quick Steamed Pudding

Easy, inexpensive and good.

1 egg; 2 tbsp sugar; ½ tsp vanilla essence (extract); 125 g/4 oz (1 cup) self-raising flour; 120 ml/4 fl oz (½ cup) milk; 1 tbsp melted butter; 2 tbsp jam or golden (light corn) syrup.

Place all ingredients except jam or syrup in a bowl and beat until smooth. Put jam or syrup into bottom of a greased 1 litre/1¾ pint (4 cup) mould or pudding basin, add mixture and cover with greased greaseproof (waxed) paper. Steam for 40 minutes. Serve with custard, sweet white sauce or cream. Serves 4–6.

ICED SWEET PUDDINGS

Ices may be broadly divided into 2 categories: water ices, sorbets, sherbets, etc., and ice creams. But there is also a large selection of iced sweet puddings. These include frozen soufflés; creamy cake-like concoctions and layered ice cream and fruit combinations.

See also *Ice Cream; Ices, Sorbets, Granite and Sherbets* and *Cassata.*

Vanilla Soufflé Glacé

(Frozen Vanilla Soufflé)

250 ml/8 fl oz (1 cup) milk; 250 ml/8 fl oz (1 cup) single (light) cream; 1 vanilla pod (bean) or 1 tsp vanilla essence (extract); 4 egg yolks; 125 g/4 oz (½ cup) sugar; 500 ml/18 fl oz (2 cups) double (heavy) cream, whipped; 1 tbsp (unsweetened) cocoa powder.

Heat milk, cream and vanilla bean in a heavy saucepan to boiling. Meanwhile, beat egg yolks with sugar until thick and light coloured. Discard vanilla bean from liquid, if used, or stir in vanilla. Beat some of the hot liquid into the egg mixture, then mix into remainder in pan and heat, stirring, until mixture coats the back of the spoon. Strain through a fine sieve and cool to room temperature. Fold in whipped cream. Pour into a 1.2 litre/2 pint (5 cup) soufflé dish fitted with a lightly greased greaseproof (waxed) paper collar. Freeze until firm. Before serving, remove paper collar and sprinkle top with sifted cocoa. Serves 6.

Frozen Soufflé with Glacé Fruit

To make this dessert it is best to have both a portable electric beater and a standard electric beater with a good motor.

5 egg yolks; 5 whole eggs; 350 g/12 oz (1½ cups) sugar; 140 g/4½ oz (¾ cup) chopped candied fruit (cherries, apricots, angelica); 4 tbsp Kirsch or Cognac; 500 ml/18 fl oz (2 cups) double (heavy) cream.

Put egg yolks and whole eggs in the heatproof mixing bowl of an electric beater.

Set bowl in a saucepan containing hot water and set over low heat. Start beating using a portable beater and gradually add sugar. The egg yolk mixture should become thick and like a soft meringue, several times the original volume (10–15 minutes). Remove mixing bowl from saucepan and set in place in the standard beater. Beat until the egg yolk mixture reaches room temperature. Meanwhile, soak fruit in Kirsch or Cognac. Fold fruit and liqueur into egg yolk mixture. Whip cream until stiff and fold into mixture. Pour into a 1.75 litre/3 pint (7 cup) soufflé dish fitted with a greaseproof (waxed) paper or foil collar. Place in the freezer and freeze until fairly solid. Remove collar before serving. Serves 8–10.

Frozen Lemon Creams

250 ml/8 fl oz (1 cup) milk; 250 ml/8 fl oz (1 cup) single (light) cream; 250 g/8 oz (1 cup) sugar; grated rind and juice 2 lemons; 6 large lemons.

Combine milk, cream and sugar, stirring until sugar has thoroughly dissolved. Pour into an ice cream tray and freeze until mushy. Add lemon rind and juice and beat mixture well with a rotary beater. Freeze again for 2 hours. Beat mixture again thoroughly, return to the freezer and freeze until solid. (Alternatively, use a sorbetière; see To Freeze Ice Cream, page 161.) Slice off tops of lemons and remove all the pulp. (Discard the pulp or save it for another use.) Cut a thin slice from the bottom of each lemon shell so that it will stand upright. Fill shells with frozen mixture, piling it high. Serve decorated with a green lemon leaf or other green leaf. Serves 6.

Pavé au Chocolat

180 g/6 oz (1 cup) unsweetened chocolate; 125 g/4 oz (½ cup) butter, softened; 180 g/6 oz (¾ cup) sugar; 4 egg yolks; 4 tbsp brandy; 175 ml/6 fl oz (¾ cup) water; 2 × 90 g/3 oz packets sponge fingers (30 lady fingers).

Melt chocolate over hot, not boiling, water. Cream butter with sugar until smooth. Add egg yolks, one at a time, and stir them in thoroughly. Add melted chocolate and mix well. Combine brandy with water in a shallow pan. Dip sponge fingers (lady fingers) quickly into liquid to moisten, then arrange ⅓ side by side down an oblong platter. Cover with a coating of the chocolate mixture (allow ⅓ of the mixture for between the layers and use the remainder for the top and sides). Build up 2 more layers of sponge fingers (lady fingers) with chocolate mixture between them. Ice the top and sides of loaf with chocolate mixture and refrigerate 3 hours. Serves 8.

Velvet Ice Cream

1 × 410 g/13 oz can evaporated milk, chilled; 2 tsp vinegar; 300 ml/½ pint (1¼ cups) double (heavy) cream; 1 × 400 g/13 oz can condensed milk; 250 ml/8 fl oz (1 cup) fresh milk; 1 tsp vanilla essence (extract).

Beat together evaporated milk and vinegar until frothy. Add cream slowly. Add condensed milk, fresh milk and vanilla. Pour into an ice cream tray and freeze 1 hour or until mushy. Beat 5 minutes, then return to freezer and freeze until firm. Makes about 2 litres/3½ pints (9 cups).

JELLIES, CREAMS, MOUSSES AND MOULDS

Jellies are usually fruit juices or wines jelled with dissolved gelatine but they can also be made from milk or custard. They may be set in bowls or in jelly moulds and turned out when set (see *Gelatine* and *Jelly, Sweet and Savoury*).

Creams are also set in gelatine; those known as Bavarian creams are compounds of custard, cream and flavouring. These may be set in bowls or in moulds and turned out.

A mousse is a light creamy dish; it may be hot or cold, sweet or savoury. A cold mousse can be frozen, but when a gelatine mixture is used, it is merely chilled. Sweet mousses can be flavoured with puréed fruit, liqueur, coffee or chocolate, one of the world's favourite mousses. (See *Chocolate*).

Amor Frio

1 tbsp gelatine; 2 tbsp water; 175 ml/6 fl oz (¾ cup) orange juice; 4 tbsp sherry; 1 × 410 g/13 oz can evaporated milk, well chilled; 125 g/4 oz (½ cup) sugar.

Soften gelatine in water, then place over simmering water until dissolved. Remove from heat, add orange juice and sherry and mix together. Beat milk with sugar for a few minutes, then add orange mixture and beat until thick and fluffy. Place in a serving bowl and chill until set. Serves 6.

Apricot Marshmallow

60 g/2 oz (¼ cup) sugar; 250 ml/8 fl oz (1 cup) water; 500 g (1 lb) apricots, halved and stoned; 1 tbsp lemon juice; 1 tbsp gelatine; whipped cream to decorate.

Dissolve sugar in water and bring to the boil. Add apricots and poach gently until fruit is soft. Measure 4 tbsp of fruit pulp and syrup, add lemon juice and set aside to cool. Dissolve gelatine in 500 ml/18 fl oz (2 cups) remaining hot syrup. Add to cooled apricots and stir well. Leave until mixture is almost on setting point, then beat until very thick. Spoon into parfait glasses. Chill. Decorate with whipped cream. Serves 6.

104

D

Vanilla Bavarian Cream

This is a basic recipe for Bavarian cream.

350 ml/12 fl oz (1½ cups) milk; 4 egg yolks; 180 g/6 oz (¾ cup) caster sugar; pinch salt; 1 tbsp gelatine softened in 4 tbsp cold water; 2 tsp vanilla essence (extract); 350 ml/12 fl oz (1½ cups) double (heavy) cream.
DECORATION: *strawberries or other fruit, grated chocolate, toasted almonds etc.*
TO SERVE: *Fruit, Creamy Caramel or Chocolate Sauce (pages 56 and 73).*

Scald milk (see page 215) and cool. Beat egg yolks with sugar and salt until thick and lemon-coloured. Place in a heavy saucepan with milk and stir over low heat until mixture coats spoon. Add softened gelatine, stir until dissolved, then add vanilla. Cool, then chill until mixture is beginning to set. Whip cream until stiff and fold in. Pour into a 1.5 litre/2½ pint (6 cup) mould rinsed with cold water and chill for at least 5 hours. Unmould carefully on to a chilled serving plate. Decorate as desired and serve with a fruit, caramel or chocolate sauce. Serves 6.
VARIATIONS
Chocolate Bavarian Cream: Add 60 g/2 oz (⅓ cup) chocolate, roughly chopped, to the hot milk and stir until melted, then proceed with recipe.
Orange Bavarian Cream: Add grated rind of 1 orange to the hot milk, then proceed with recipe.

Berry Bavarian Cream

180 g/6 oz (1½ cups) berries, fresh or frozen and thawed; 125 g/4 oz (½ cup) sugar; 3 tsp gelatine; 6 tbsp water; 1 tbsp lemon juice; 150 ml/¼ pint (⅔ cup) double (heavy) cream, whipped.

Crush berries and add sugar. Leave to stand for 30 minutes. Meanwhile, soften gelatine in water, then place over simmering water until dissolved. Stir into berries. Add lemon juice and refrigerate until thickened slightly. Lightly fold in whipped cream and pour into a bowl. Chill. Serves 4–6.

Coffee Bavarian Cream

3 tsp gelatine; 4 tbsp cold water; 2 eggs, separated; 125 g/4 oz (½ cup) sugar; ¼ tsp salt; 120 ml/4 fl oz (½ cup) milk; ½ tsp vanilla essence (extract); 120 ml/4 fl oz (½ cup) strong black coffee; 250 ml/8 fl oz (1 cup) double (heavy) cream.

Sprinkle gelatine over the water and allow to soften. Beat egg yolks in top part of a double saucepan (double boiler) and add 60 g/2 oz (¼ cup) sugar and the salt. Gradually add milk. Cook over hot water, stirring constantly, until slightly thickened. Add gelatine mixture and stir until dissolved. Stir in vanilla and coffee and chill until slightly thickened. Beat egg whites until stiff. Gradually add remaining sugar, beating constantly. Whip cream until slightly stiff. Fold into gelatine mixture with the egg whites. Pour mixture into a rinsed 1.2 litre/ 2 pint (5 cup) mould and chill until firm. Unmould and serve. Serves 4–6.

Chestnut Mousse

1½ tbsp gelatine; 4 tbsp water; 1 × 500 g/1 lb can unsweetened chestnut purée; 500 ml/18 fl oz (2 cups) milk; 180 g/6 oz (¾ cup) sugar; ½ tsp vanilla essence (extract); 6 egg yolks; 2 tbsp dark rum or Grand Marnier; 250 ml/8 fl oz (1 cup) double (heavy) cream.

Soften gelatine in water. Blend chestnut purée with milk in a saucepan and stir in sugar. Beat with an electric beater until smooth. Add gelatine mixture, bring almost to the boil, stirring to dissolve gelatine. Stir in vanilla. Beat egg yolks in a mixing bowl. Beat in a little of the hot chestnut mixture, then stir into the remaining mixture in the pan. Cook, stirring, until mixture thickens slightly. Do not boil. Stir in rum or Grand Marnier. Sieve mixture into a mixing bowl. Allow to cool, but do not let it start to set. Whip cream and fold into the chestnut mixture. Pour into a lightly oiled 1.75 litre/2½ pint (7 cup) mould and refrigerate until firm. Serves 6–8.

Caramel Cream

1 tbsp gelatine; 4 tbsp water; 600 ml/1 pint 2½ cups) milk; 1 tbsp sugar; 2 eggs, beaten; 120 ml/4 fl oz (½ cup) double (heavy) cream, whipped.
CARAMEL: *3 tbsp sugar; 1 tbsp lemon juice; 2 tbsp water.*

Soften gelatine in water. Meanwhile, heat milk with sugar in a heavy saucepan, stirring until sugar has dissolved. Add eggs and cook gently, stirring, until custard thickens enough to coat back of spoon. Add gelatine mixture and stir until dissolved. Cool. For caramel, put sugar and lemon juice into a saucepan and cook until brown, taking care it does not burn. Add water, then stir into custard mixture. When cold and beginning to set, fold in whipped cream. Pour into a mould and chill until set. Serves 6.

Hazelnut Cream

You can buy ground hazelnuts at good health food shops and delicatessens. Better still, for the best flavour, grind your own (nut mills are available at kitchen shops). Toast hazelnuts, rub off the skins, then grind.

250 g/8 oz (2 cups) hazelnuts, ground; 600 ml/1 pint (2½ cups) milk; 6 egg yolks; 250 g/8 oz (1 cup) caster sugar; 1 tbsp gelatine; 2 tbsp water; 2 tsp vanilla essence (extract); 500 ml/18 fl oz (2 cups) double (heavy) cream.
DECORATION: *whipped cream, whole hazelnuts.*

Combine ground hazelnuts and milk in a heavy saucepan and bring to the boil. Cool. Beat egg yolks and sugar together until pale and thick. Pour on milk mixture, stirring constantly. Place in the top of a double saucepan (double boiler) and cook, stirring, until custard has thickened. Cool. Soften gelatine in water for 5 minutes, then dissolve over hot water. Stir into custard with vanilla. Cool until mixture has the consistency of unbeaten egg white. Whip cream and fold into mixture. Pour into 8 individual serving dishes and chill until firm. Decorate with whipped cream and hazelnuts. Serves 8.

Raspberry Mousse

1 × 425 g/14 oz can raspberries; 3 tsp gelatine; 150 ml/¼ pint (⅔ cup) double (heavy) cream; 1 egg white.

Drain raspberries, reserving 120 ml/4 fl oz (½ cup) can syrup. Place syrup in a pan, sprinkle over gelatine and let soften; then heat, stirring, until gelatine has dissolved. Pour over berries and stir thoroughly. Chill until beginning to thicken. Whip cream and fold into berry mixture. Whisk egg white stiffly and fold in. Pour into a dish or 6 individual dishes and chill. Serves 6.

Egg Nog Rum Cream

5 eggs, separated; 150 g/5 oz (⅔ cup) caster sugar; 120 ml/4 fl oz (½ cup) rum; 1 tbsp gelatine; 4 tbsp water; 500 ml/18 fl oz (2 cups) double (heavy) cream; Clear Raspberry Sauce (page 329) to serve.
DECORATION: *175 ml/6 fl oz (¾ cup) double (heavy) cream, whipped; 6–8 glacé (candied) cherries; few strips angelica; nutmeg.*

Beat egg yolks with sugar until thick and foaming. Stir in rum. Soften gelatine in water, then dissolve over simmering water. Whip cream until it holds its shape. Beat egg whites until stiff. Fold cream and gelatine into egg yolk mixture, then fold in egg whites. Pour into a large glass bowl or other pretty dessert bowl and leave to set. Decorate with piped rosettes of whipped cream, or pile cream around the edge. Sprinkle with chopped cherries, angelica and nutmeg. Serve with sauce. Serves 6–8.

Puréed Fruit Mould

125 g/4 oz (½ cup) sugar; 250 ml/8 fl oz (1 cup) water; 750 g (1½ lb) apricots or red plums, halved and stoned; blanched almonds; 3 tsp gelatine.

Dissolve sugar in water, then bring to the boil. Add fruit to syrup and poach gently for 10 minutes. Lift fruit out of syrup and pick out a few of the best halves. Place half a blanched almond in each of these reserved halves and arrange them rounded side up in a 20–23 cm (8–9 in) sandwich tin (layer pan). Allow to cool, then place in refrigerator. Sieve remaining poached fruit and make resulting purée up to 400 ml/⅔ pint (1⅔ cups) with the cooking syrup. Heat an extra 120 ml/4 fl oz (½ cup) syrup and stir in gelatine briskly until dissolved. Add to fruit purée, stir well and allow to cool. When purée is almost on the point of setting, pour carefully over fruit halves arranged in tin (pan). Chill until set. Turn out, and serve with whipped cream. Serves 4–6.

Pineapple Mist

3½ tsp gelatine; 120 ml/4 fl oz (½ cup) water; 60 g/2 oz (¼ cup) sugar; 175 ml/6 fl oz (¾ cup) canned pineapple juice; 2 tsp lemon juice; 2 egg whites.

Soften gelatine in water, then place over simmering water until dissolved. Add sugar, stirring until dissolved. Stir in pineapple and lemon juices. Refrigerate until slightly thickened. Beat mixture until thick, adding the stiffly beaten egg whites. When quite thick, spoon into a serving bowl or 6 individual dishes. Serve with crisp biscuits (cookies) or sponge fingers (lady fingers). Serves 6.

Maple Mousse

1 tbsp gelatine; 1 tbsp cold water; 120 ml/4 fl oz (½ cup) maple syrup; 3 egg yolks; 30 g/1 oz (¼ cup) slivered almonds; 600 ml/1 pint (2½ cups) double (heavy) cream; 2 tsp rum.

Soften gelatine in water, then dissolve over simmering water. Heat maple syrup in a heavy saucepan and stir in gelatine mixture. Beat egg yolks until very light. Add a little of the hot syrup mixture to them, then add remaining syrup mixture, stirring constantly. Cool maple mixture in the refrigerator for 30 minutes or until the consistency of unbeaten egg whites. Fold in the almonds. Whip 500 ml/18 fl oz (2 cups) cream and fold into maple mixture. Place in a large serving dish or individual serving dishes and chill until set. Whip remaining cream and flavour with rum. Serve with the maple mousse. Serves 4–6.

FRUIT SWEET PUDDINGS

Fruits make lovely desserts. In summer months set them in a bowl of ice cubes, and enjoy them lightly chilled.

Discover light, airy fools and snows, fruit mousses and soufflés (see individual recipes), enjoy fruits baked, poached in wine, flambéed with spirits or marinated in fruit juice or liqueurs.

Apple Snow

4–6 cooking apples, cored and thickly sliced; 250 g/8 oz (1 cup) caster sugar; juice ½ lemon; 2 egg whites.
DECORATION: *whipped cream; toasted slivered almonds.*

Put apples in a saucepan with very little water. Cover and cook until soft. Drain. Sieve or purée in a blender and measure 250 ml/8 fl oz (1 cup) purée (applesauce). Add sugar and lemon juice and cool. Whisk egg whites until stiff, fold in apple mixture and continue whisking until fluffy. Pile into tall glasses and decorate with whipped cream and toasted almonds. Serves 6.

Apples and Sago

600 ml/1 pint (2½ cups) water; 45 g/1½ oz (¼ cup) fine sago; 6 cooking apples, peeled and cored; 125 g/4 oz (½ cup) sugar; pared rind and juice ½ lemon; few drops red food colouring.

Bring water to the boil in a large saucepan. Sprinkle in sago and cook until mixture is clear, about 15 minutes. Add apples, sugar, and lemon rind and juice to the sago. Cover and simmer very gently 10–20 minutes or until apples are tender. Lift apples out on to a heated serving dish. Remove lemon rind from sago mixture and add a few drops of food colouring. Pour it over and around the apples. Serves 6.

Bananas Brazilian

6 bananas, cut in half lengthways; 120 ml/4 fl oz (½ cup) fresh orange juice; 1 tbsp fresh lemon juice; 45 g/1½ oz (¼ cup) firmly packed brown sugar; pinch salt; 60 g/2 oz (4 tbsp) butter; 90 g/3 oz (1 cup) grated fresh or desiccated (shredded) coconut.

Place bananas in a buttered casserole. Combine orange and lemon juices, sugar and salt and pour over bananas. Dot with butter. Bake in a preheated moderately hot oven (200°C/400°F, Gas Mark 6) for 10–15 minutes. Sprinkle bananas with coconut and serve immediately. Serves 6.

Cherries Jubilee

250 g/8 oz (1 cup) sugar; 500 ml/18 fl oz (2 cups) water; pinch salt; 750 g (1½ lb) fresh cherries, stoned (pitted); 1 tbsp cornflour (cornstarch); 120 ml/4 fl oz (½ cup) cognac, warmed; French Vanilla Ice Cream (page 161) to serve.

Place sugar, water and salt in a saucepan and bring to the boil, stirring to dissolve sugar. Add cherries, reduce heat and simmer until tender. Drain cherries, reserving 250 ml/8 fl oz (1 cup) of the syrup. Combine cornflour (cornstarch) with reserved syrup in a saucepan, bring to the boil and simmer 3 minutes, stirring constantly. Add cherries. Pour cognac into cherries and ignite. Spoon juices over cherries and serve, flaming, over French vanilla ice cream. Serves 6.

Baked Figs

Orange liqueur and cloves enhance the flavour of fresh figs in this recipe.

12–18 ripe figs; 90 g/3 oz (½ cup) firmly packed brown sugar; 175 ml/6 fl oz (¾ cup) water; ½ tsp ground cloves; 2 tbsp Cointreau or Grand Marnier.

Prick figs with fork. Place in an ovenproof dish and sprinkle with brown sugar. Add

D

water. Bake in a preheated cool oven (150°C/300°F, Gas Mark 2) for about 30 minutes, basting occasionally with syrup in dish. Drain figs. Dust with cloves and sprinkle over liqueur. Serve warm with whipped cream or ice cream. Serves 6.

Melon with White Grapes and Grand Marnier

Use seedless white sultana grapes, or big white grapes, halved and seeded, or canned grapes for this recipe.

1 large cantaloup melon, peeled, seeded and cubed; 1 large bunch grapes; 120 ml/4 fl oz ($\frac{1}{2}$ cup) Grand Marnier.

Place melon cubes in a crystal bowl. Cover with a layer of grapes. Pour Grand Marnier over. Cover bowl with foil to keep in all the fragrance of the Grand Marnier. Chill thoroughly. Serve with crisp, dainty biscuits (cookies) or small sponge fingers (lady fingers). Serves 6–8.

Melon Compote

1 honeydew melon; 1 cantaloup melon; 2–3 pieces preserved ginger, chopped; 2 tsp ginger syrup; 250 ml/8 fl oz (1 cup) water; 120 ml/4 fl oz ($\frac{1}{2}$ cup) white wine or dry sherry; 180 g/6 oz ($\frac{3}{4}$ cup) sugar.

Halve melons, remove seeds and scoop out flesh in dessertspoon-sized pieces. Put melon into earthenware bowl with preserved ginger and ginger syrup. Make a syrup by simmering together water, wine or sherry and sugar. Pour boiling syrup over melon. Cool and chill well before serving. Serves 6.

Pears in Port Wine

6 firm, ripe pears; juice $\frac{1}{2}$ lemon; 500 ml/18 fl oz (2 cups) water; 250 ml/8 fl oz (1 cup) port wine; 300 g/10 oz (1$\frac{1}{4}$ cups) sugar; 1 cinnamon stick; pared rind $\frac{1}{2}$ orange; strip lemon rind.

Peel pears and drop them into a bowl of cold water, with lemon juice added. This will keep them from darkening. Combine the water with remaining ingredients in a saucepan and bring to the boil, stirring until sugar has dissolved. Add drained pears and simmer until fruit is tender. Do not overcook. Let pears cool in the syrup, then chill before serving. Serves 6.

Pineapple Flambé

60 g/2 oz ($\frac{1}{4}$ cup) sugar; 120 ml/4 fl oz ($\frac{1}{2}$ cup) sherry; 120 ml/4 fl oz ($\frac{1}{2}$ cup) water; 1 ripe pineapple, peeled, cored and sliced; 460 g/15 oz (1$\frac{1}{2}$ cups) redcurrant jelly; 120 ml/4 fl oz ($\frac{1}{2}$ cup) Cognac or Kirsch.
TO SERVE: *French Vanilla Ice Cream (page 161); 8–10 macaroons, crumbled.*

Combine sugar, sherry and water in a saucepan and bring to the boil. Add pineapple slices and poach for about 5 minutes. Drain. Melt currant jelly in a frying pan (skillet) over low heat. Add pineapple slices and simmer, spooning syrup over fruit, for 5 minutes. Add Cognac or Kirsch directly into centre of fruit mixture and let it heat for several minutes without stirring. When well warmed, light Cognac or Kirsch and spoon over fruit while flaming. Serve fruit over ice cream and top with macaroon crumbs. Serves 6.

Italian Fruits in Marsala

250 g/8 oz (1 cup) sugar; 120 ml/4 fl oz ($\frac{1}{2}$ cup) water; juice 1 lemon; 120 ml/4 fl oz ($\frac{1}{2}$ cup) Marsala; 4–6 small peaches, skinned; 1 small pineapple, peeled, cored and thickly sliced; 250 g (8 oz) strawberries, hulled.

Dissolve sugar in water with lemon juice, and boil to form a heavy syrup. Allow to cool. Stir in Marsala and leave to become quite cold. Immerse peaches, pineapple and strawberries in the syrup. Chill thoroughly in the refrigerator before serving with crisp sweet biscuits (cookies) or sponge fingers (lady fingers). Serves 6.

Oranges with Grand Marnier Syrup

6 large navel oranges; 120 ml/4 fl oz ($\frac{1}{2}$ cup) water; 350 g/12 oz (1$\frac{1}{2}$ cups) sugar; 4 tbsp orange juice; 4 tbsp Grand Marnier.

Thinly pare rind from 3 of the oranges and cut into very thin julienne (matchstick) strips. Place rind strips in a small saucepan, barely cover with water, bring to the boil and simmer 10 minutes. Drain and run cold water over rind. Place the water and the sugar in another saucepan. Heat, stirring, until sugar dissolves. Bring to the boil and boil until syrup thickens and turns a pale straw colour. Immediately remove from the heat, add blanched orange rind strips and

stir gently. Let the rind soak in the syrup for 30 minutes, then stir in orange juice and Grand Marnier. Remove peel and pith from all of the oranges. Slice each orange into 3 or more slices and place in a shallow serving dish. Top with the glazed rind and spoon syrup over oranges. Chill well before serving, spooning syrup over oranges occasionally. Serves 6.

Strawberries in Liqueur

500 g/1 lb (3 cups) strawberries, hulled and sliced; 60 g/2 oz ($\frac{1}{2}$ cup) icing (confectioners) sugar; 1 tbsp Cointreau; 1 tbsp Kirsch; 2 tbsp brandy or Cognac; 6 sponge fingers (lady fingers).

Sprinkle strawberries with icing (confectioners) sugar and mix gently. Pour liqueurs over berries and mix carefully. Cover and let stand at room temperature for 1 hour, then refrigerate for 3–4 hours. Serve with sponge fingers (lady fingers). Serves 6.

Pineapple Romanoff

1 large pineapple, peeled, cored and diced; 6 tbsp icing (confectioners) sugar; 4 tbsp Cointreau; 2 tbsp rum; 250 ml/8 fl oz (1 cup) double (heavy) cream; 2 tbsp Kirsch; grated rind 1 orange.

Toss pineapple in a bowl with 2 tbsp icing (confectioners) sugar. Pour over Cointreau and rum. Cover and chill for several hours. Whip cream, add remaining icing (confectioners) sugar and flavour with Kirsch. Add whipped cream to marinated pineapple and toss until every piece is coated with creamy liqueur mixture. Spoon into a glass bowl or 6 individual dishes and sprinkle with orange rind. Chill. Serves 6.

Rhubarb and Ginger Compote

An unusual combination, but rhubarb, spices and gin complement each other beautifully.

250 g/8 oz (1 cup) sugar; 120 ml/4 fl oz ($\frac{1}{2}$ cup) water; 1 kg (2 lb) rhubarb, chopped; 1 tbsp finely grated orange rind; $\frac{1}{4}$ tsp nutmeg; $\frac{1}{2}$ tsp ground ginger; 120 ml/4 fl oz ($\frac{1}{2}$ cup) gin; 1 tbsp finely chopped preserved ginger.

Dissolve sugar in water in a large saucepan over low heat. Increase the heat and bring to the boil, without stirring. Add rhubarb, orange rind, nutmeg and ground ginger and reduce heat to low. Simmer for 5 minutes or until rhubarb is tender. Using a slotted spoon, transfer rhubarb to a serving dish. Increase heat to high and bring cooking liquid to the boil. Boil for 10–12 minutes or until liquid has reduced by about $\frac{1}{3}$. Remove pan from heat, add gin and pour over rhubarb. Sprinkle chopped preserved ginger over the top, cover and chill for at least 30 minutes. Serves 6.

Pineapple Ambrosia

2 bananas, sliced; juice ½ large lemon; 1 ripe pineapple, peeled, cored and diced; 2 oranges, peeled and sliced; 250 g (8 oz) strawberries, hulled; 60 g/2 oz (½ cup) icing (confectioners) sugar; 90 g/3 oz (1 cup) grated fresh or desiccated (shredded) coconut.

Toss banana slices in lemon juice to prevent discolouring. Layer fruit in a glass bowl, sifting a little icing (confectioners) sugar to taste between each layer. Sprinkle with coconut and chill. Serve with whipped cream. Serves 6.

Cardamom Pears

6 pears, peeled, cored and sliced; 2 tbsp soft brown sugar; 175 ml/6 fl oz (¾ cup) water; 2 tsp ground cardamom; 120 ml/4 fl oz (½ cup) Grand Marnier or Cointreau; 250 ml/8 fl oz (1 cup) double (heavy) cream, whipped, to serve.

Arrange pears in a shallow ovenproof dish and sprinkle over sugar. Pour water over top, then sprinkle over cardamom. Bake in a preheated moderate oven (180°C/350°F, Gas Mark 4) for 40 minutes or until pear slices are tender. Transfer pear mixture to a serving bowl, add liqueur, cover and set aside to cool completely. Serve well chilled, with whipped cream. Serves 6.

Rhubarb Cream

1 × 450 g (1 lb) can rhubarb; 1 tbsp cornflour (cornstarch), dissolved in 2 tbsp water; grated rind and juice 1 orange; little red food colouring (optional).

Heat undrained rhubarb in a saucepan. Add a few spoonfuls of hot rhubarb juice to cornflour (cornstarch) mixture, then add to rhubarb in saucepan and stir over gentle heat until thickened. Add orange rind and juice and cook gently for 5 minutes. Tint with a little food colouring, if desired. Turn into a serving bowl or 4 individual dishes and leave until cold. Serve with cream and crisp biscuits (cookies). Serves 4.

Oranges with Liqueurs

8 large oranges; 60 g/2 oz (½ cup) icing (confectioners) sugar; 2 tbsp brandy; 3 tbsp Grand Marnier; 3 tbsp Kirsch.

Peel oranges, removing all white membrane. Segment them by running a sharp knife on either side of the connecting tissues between the flesh. Keep segments intact. Squeeze juice from peel on to the orange segments. Sprinkle segments with icing (confectioners) sugar and refrigerate for 1 hour or longer. Sprinkle with liqueurs and toss lightly with a fork and spoon. Serve on chilled dessert plates. Serves 6.

Strawberries in Orange Juice

500 g (1 lb) strawberries, hulled; juice of 2 oranges, strained; 2 tsp grated orange rind; sifted icing (confectioners) sugar; whipped cream (optional).

Choose small strawberries. Toss with orange juice and rind and icing (confectioners) sugar to taste. Chill for at least 1 hour. Serve in individual bowls, garnished with a little whipped cream, if liked. Serves 6.

DEVILS ON HORSEBACK

The name given to one of the classic savouries, now most often served as appetizers. Poach some prunes in red wine until they are plump. Drain, stone and stuff with an almond and anchovy fillet and wrap in bacon. Cook quickly under a preheated grill (broiler) or in a hot oven (220°C/425°F, Gas Mark 7) for 4–5 minutes. Serve on hot buttered toast. Allow 3 per person.

DHAL

Dhal is a lentil purée served with curry meals, boiled rice or Indian breads.
    See *Pulses: Beans, Peas and Lentils.*

DILL

Dark green, feathery dill has a delicate flavour somewhere between parsley and fennel; it is one of the most beautiful herbs for garnishing. It is much used in Scandinavian, Russian and Balkan cooking, especially with cucumbers and fish, and in combination with yogurt and sour cream. Dill seeds are a favourite flavouring in sauerkraut and in pickled cucumbers (in the U.S.A. these are known as dill pickles). Fresh dill tends to lose its aroma during cooking, so it is usually added toward the end of cooking time.

Sprinkle chopped fresh dill on potato salads or hot new potatoes; add a little to mayonnaise to be served with cold fish or shellfish, or stir it into a cream sauce to serve with hot fish; add stalks and seeds to cooking water for lobster or prawns (shrimp); add chopped dill and a little vinegar to melted butter for a sauce to pour over freshly-cooked beetroot. **See recipes.**

Dill Pickles

These fresh-tasting pickles are quick and easy to make and are ready to use after a week. As they do not keep well, make just a jar or two at a time.

500 g (1 lb) small green cucumbers; 250 ml/8 fl oz (1 cup) white vinegar; 250 ml/8 fl oz (1 cup) water; 1 tbsp salt; 2 tbsp dill seeds; 6 peppercorns.

Wash cucumbers thoroughly and cut in half lengthways unless very small. Pack into warm sterilized jars. Bring vinegar, water and salt to the boil and pour into jars. Add dill seeds and peppercorns, and cover immediately. Use after a week. Makes about 1.5 litres/2½ pints (6¼ cups).

Dilled Herring Pâté

This is one of those magically easy recipes that produce surprising results. Guests find it difficult to identify the taste but are always appreciative.

1 × 200 g/6½ oz can herring in tomato sauce; 125 g/4 oz (½ cup) butter, softened; lemon juice; chopped fresh dill leaves or dill seeds; chopped fresh lemon balm, lemon thyme, or grated lemon rind.

Purée herring with their sauce in a blender or food processor. With motor running, add butter, a little at a time, and lemon juice to taste, then just a little chopped dill or dill seeds – keep tasting. Transfer to a bowl and stir in a little chopped lemon balm or lemon thyme, or grated lemon rind. Chill before using. Serve with fingers of hot wholewheat toast. Makes about 175 ml/6 fl oz (¾ cup).

DIPS

People of many lands enjoy scooping up a savoury mixture with pieces of food for relaxed nibbling. Some dips are famous – Mexico's Guacamole, Middle Eastern Baba

Ghannouj and Hummus, Italy's Bagna Cauda, Provence's Aïoli, Greek Tzatziki (see separate entries).

The dipping idea gains new interest with crisp, chilled pieces of vegetables or fruit, cold seafood, flat Lebanese (pita) bread, spears of ham or sausage, pumpernickel or fingers of home-made pastry (dough) as a change from biscuits (crackers) or potato crisps (chips) for the dipping food. **See recipes.**

Brandied Cheese Dip for Fruit

125 g/4 oz (1 cup) blue cheese; 125 g/4 oz (½ cup) cream cheese; 1 tbsp single (light) cream; 2 tbsp brandy.

Mash blue cheese, add cream cheese and cream and beat until smooth. Stir in brandy. Serve at room temperature with chilled wedges of apple, pear or melon. Makes about 250 ml/8 fl oz (1 cup).

Tuna and Green Peppercorn Dip

1 × 200 g/6½ oz can tuna in oil, drained; 120 ml/4 fl oz (½ cup) Mayonnaise (page 204); ½ tsp green peppercorns, crushed; salt.

Mash tuna and blend with remaining ingredients, adding salt to taste. Spoon into a bowl and chill. Serve with small rounds of pumpernickel. Makes about 300 ml/½ pint (1¼ cups).

Hot Clam Dip

2 × 100 g/3½ oz cans minced clams; 60 g/2 oz (4 tbsp) butter; 60 g/2 oz (¾ cup) cracker biscuit crumbs; 1 small onion, finely chopped; 1 tsp lemon juice; dash Tabasco (hot pepper) sauce.

Drain juice from 1 can of clams. Melt butter, add drained clams and other can of clams with juice. Stir in remaining ingredients. Pour into an ovenproof serving dish and bake in a preheated moderate oven (180°C/350°F, Gas Mark 4) for 30 minutes. Place in centre of a platter and surround with chilled celery or cucumber sticks, tiny crisp lettuce leaves, cauliflower florets or cooked shelled prawns (shrimp) for dipping. Makes about 500 ml/ 18 fl oz (2 cups).

Refried Bean Dip

2 × 310 g/10 oz cans red kidney beans; 1 onion, finely chopped; 1 clove garlic, crushed; 1 small red chilli, seeded and chopped, or 1 tsp Mexican chilli powder (or to taste); 4 tbsp bacon dripping or oil; 125 g/4 oz (1 cup) grated cheese; salt.

Drain beans, reserving liquid. Gently fry onion, garlic and chilli or chilli powder in fat until onion is soft. Add beans a little at a time, mashing them into mixture. Add 120 ml/4 fl oz (½ cup) bean liquid, mix well

and stir in cheese. Remove from heat as soon as cheese melts. Taste and add a little salt if necessary. Serve hot with corn crisps (chips) or crackers. If mixture gets too stiff for dipping, add a little more hot bean liquid or water. Makes about 750 ml/1¼ pints (3 cups).

DOLMA, DOLMADES

A dolma is any dish prepared by stuffing a vine, fig, cabbage or other edible leaf with a savoury mixture and braising the packages.

Dolmades – stuffed vine leaves – are a speciality throughout Greece and Turkey. They may be served hot with a sauce or cold as an appetizer. The stuffing is based on rice and herbs, often with minced (ground) lamb, or pine nuts and currants. Dolmades freeze well so it is worth making a good batch at a time. If making dolmades to serve as an appetizer, use the following recipe but do not make the sauce. Arrange cooked dolmades in an oiled dish, sprinkle with a little olive oil and store, covered, in the refrigerator until required. Serve with lemon wedges and, if liked, squares of feta cheese. **See recipes.**

See also *Cabbage.*

Dolmades with Avgolemono

about 80 young fresh vine leaves, or 500 g (1 lb) preserved vine leaves (available in bulk from Continental delicatessens); 2 onions, finely chopped; 175 ml/6 fl oz (¾ cup) olive oil; 3 tbsp short-grain rice; 500 g/1 lb (2 cups) minced (ground) lamb; 1 tbsp finely chopped fresh mint; 10 g/⅓ oz (¼ cup) finely chopped parsley; 2 tbsp currants; salt and freshly ground black pepper; 250 ml/8 fl oz (1 cup) lamb, beef or chicken stock; 4 tbsp dry white wine.
SAUCE: *4 egg yolks; juice 1 lemon.*

Rinse fresh or preserved vine leaves and drop into boiling water, a few at a time. Blanch for 3 minutes. Remove to a bowl of cold water, then drain. Cook onions gently in 2 tbsp oil until soft. Add rice and stir 2 minutes. Put meat into a bowl, add mint, parsley, currants, onion mixture, salt and pepper, and blend well.

Place a vine leaf, shiny side down, on a flat surface and put a heaped teaspoonful of stuffing in centre. Fold stem end and sides over, then roll up tightly toward the point. Repeat with remaining stuffing and leaves, reserving about 10 leaves. Line a heavy saucepan with a few reserved leaves and pack rolls in, seam sides down, close together in layers, sprinkling each layer with remaining oil. Pour stock and wine over and cover top of rolls with remaining leaves. Weight with a heavy plate, cover saucepan tightly and simmer gently 1 hour.

Remove dolmades and lining leaves to a heated platter and keep warm. For sauce, add water if necessary to liquid in saucepan

to make 250 ml/8 fl oz (1 cup) and bring to the boil. Beat egg yolks and add lemon juice, then hot liquid, beating constantly. Pour over dolmades and serve immediately. Makes about 70, to serve 15–20 as an appetizer or as part of a buffet.

Stuffed Grape Vine Leaves
(Dolmathakia Latheres)

about 80 young fresh vine leaves, or 500 g (1 lb) preserved vine leaves (available in bulk from Continental delicatessens); 2 large onions, finely chopped; 175 ml/6 fl oz (¾ cup) olive oil; 210 g/7 oz (1 cup) short-grain rice; 3 tbsp pine nuts; 3 tbsp chopped parsley; 2 tsp chopped fresh mint; 2 tsp chopped fresh dill; 3 tbsp currants; salt and freshly ground black pepper; 500 ml/18 fl oz (2 cups) water; juice 1 lemon.

Rinse fresh or preserved vine leaves and blanch in boiling water for 3 minutes, a few at a time. Put in a bowl of cold water, drain and cut off stems. Gently fry onions in 120 ml/ 4 fl oz (½ cup) olive oil until translucent. Add rice and pine nuts and stir over heat for 2 minutes. Stir in herbs, currants, salt, pepper and 250 ml/8 fl oz (1 cup) water. Cover tightly and cook over low heat for 15 minutes until water is absorbed.

Place a vine leaf, shiny side down, on flat surface and put a heaped teaspoon of stuffing in centre. Fold stem end and sides over stuffing and roll up tightly toward point. Repeat with remaining stuffing and leaves, reserving about 12 leaves. Line a heavy-based saucepan with half reserved vine leaves. Pack rolls close together, seam sides down, in layers in pan. Sprinkle each layer with remaining oil and the lemon juice. Add remaining 250 ml/8 fl oz (1 cup) of water and cover top of rolls with rest of leaves. Invert a plate on top to keep rolls in shape during cooking. Cover saucepan tightly, bring to the boil and simmer gently for 1 hour. Remove from heat and leave for 1–2 hours until liquid is absorbed. Lift rolls out carefully into a dish and chill for several hours before serving. Garnish with lemon slices and serve with a bowl of chilled plain yogurt. Makes about 70.

DRIED FRUIT

See *Fruit, Dried and Candied.*

DUCHESS POTATOES
(Pommes Duchesse)

A rich potato and egg mixture that is piped into decorative borders or rosettes, then browned under a grill (broiler) or in a hot oven. It is one of the few potato recipes that can be prepared ahead.

See page 310 for recipe.

DUCK

A bird prized by gourmets for its rich flavour and succulence; it can be prepared in a great variety of ways. A duck has more fat, a larger frame and less meat than a chicken of the same weight, so allow about 370–500 g (12 oz–1 lb) raw weight per person. For a dinner party, it is pleasant (and certainly very convenient for the carver) to serve half a small duckling for each person. A good young duck has creamy skin and a plump breast, with a pliable breastbone.

To truss a duck: Truss in the same way as chicken. Shape the bird neatly with your hands, tucking the neck flap underneath. Take a piece of string and place its centre below the breastbone at the neck end. Bring the ends of the string down over the wings to cross underneath, then up to tie the legs and tail together.

ROAST DUCK Pull out loose fat around neck and inside body. Press the 2 little oil glands near base of tail to empty them. Wipe bird inside and out with damp paper towels. If using stuffing, spoon it loosely into the body cavity. Or, instead of stuffing, a few lemon slices or a quartered green apple, with some sliced onion and a little sage or other herbs, may be placed inside duck to flavour it. Truss bird and place it, breast side up, on a rack set in a roasting tin (pan).

Roast in the centre of a preheated moderately hot oven (190°C/375°F, Gas Mark 5) for 15 minutes, then reduce heat to moderate (180°C/350°F, Gas Mark 4) and continue roasting, allowing about 25 minutes per 500 g (1 lb). Very small birds will take a little less and very large ones a little more than this time. Baste with pan juices every 15 minutes and, 20 minutes before end of cooking time, prick breast all over to allow excess fat to escape and make skin crisp.

Test for doneness by inserting a fine skewer into thickest part of the thigh near the body; juices should run clear with no tinge of pink. Allow duck to rest in a warm place for 20 minutes before carving.

Make Clear Gravy or Thickened Gravy to accompany duck, if desired (see *Gravy*). A little orange or lemon juice may be added to gravy.

Roast duck may also be served with apple sauce or another tart sauce such as Sauce Bigarade (see page 35). Young green peas, braised celery, glazed turnips and onions are classic accompaniments. A crisp green salad is a good alternative.

NOTE: If you have any doubt about the tenderness of a duck, it is advisable to braise it instead of roasting it. The slower, longer cooking ensures moist tender flesh, and you can still achieve a crisp skin if you uncover the bird for the last 15 minutes of cooking. **See recipes**.

Braised Duck with Glazed Turnips

1 × 1.5 kg (3 lb) duckling; 30 g/1 oz (2 tbsp) butter; 1 carrot, chopped; 1 stick celery, chopped; 1 onion, chopped; 250 ml/8 fl oz (1 cup) dry white wine; 1 bouquet garni; salt and freshly ground black pepper; 2 tsp cornflour (cornstarch).
VEGETABLES: *1 kg (2 lb) small white turnips, peeled and quartered; 1 kg (2 lb) small white onions, peeled; 2 tbsp sugar; 60 g/2 oz (4 tbsp) butter; 250 ml/8 fl oz (1 cup) water.*

Remove excess fat from duck, empty oil glands near tail and truss bird. Heat butter in a flameproof casserole to fit the duck, put bird in and brown all over. Lift duck out and discard all but 1 tbsp fat from casserole. Add carrot, celery and onion and cook gently until golden. Replace duck on top of vegetables and add wine, bouquet garni, salt and pepper. Cover and cook in a preheated moderately hot oven (190°C/375°F, Gas Mark 5) for 1½ hours. Meanwhile, trim turnips to pigeon's egg shapes, if desired. Place turnips and onions in a heavy saucepan with sugar, butter and water. Cover and cook until just tender, then remove lid and cook until liquid is reduced to a glaze, rolling vegetables to glaze them. Remove duck to a heated serving dish, remove trussing string and keep warm. Strain liquid from casserole into a saucepan, spoon fat from top and bring to the boil. Stir in cornflour (cornstarch) mixed with a little water and, when sauce is thickened, adjust seasoning. Pour into a heated gravy boat. Surround duck with glazed turnips and onions, and serve sauce separately. Serves 4.

Grilled Duckling with Mandarin and Green Peppercorn Sauce

1 × 1.5 kg (3 lb) duckling, quartered; 120 ml/4 fl oz (½ cup) lemon juice; 1 small onion, thinly sliced; salt; 1 tsp cracked black peppercorns; 120 ml/4 fl oz (½ cup) oil; 30 g/1 oz (2 tbsp) butter, melted; 2 small mandarins, thinly sliced.
SAUCE: *1½ tbsp sugar; 1 tbsp red wine vinegar; 150 ml/¼ pint (⅔ cup) duck stock or canned chicken stock; 5 tbsp orange juice; 2 tbsp lemon juice, or to taste; 1½ tsp arrowroot; 1 tbsp water; 1½ tbsp drained green peppercorns, crushed; salt.*

Remove backbone from duck, trim pieces neatly and cut off wing tips. Use trimmings, with giblets, if these were included with duck, to make duck stock for the sauce (see page 413). Remove visible fat from inside duck and wipe all over with damp paper towels. Mix lemon juice, onion, 1 tsp salt, cracked peppercorns and oil in a bowl. Add duck and turn pieces about so that they are coated with marinade. Cover, and refrigerate overnight, turning pieces occasionally.

Drain duck, pat pieces dry with paper towels and prick skin all over with a skewer. Brush duck all over with melted butter and place, skin side down, on a grill (broiler) rack. Cook under a preheated grill (broiler), about 13 cm (5 in) from heat, for 20 minutes, basting pieces with pan juices after 10 minutes. Turn duck skin side up, brush with melted butter again and sprinkle with salt. Grill (broil), basting frequently with pan juices, for 15–20 minutes more or until the skin is crisp and juices run clear when fatty part of thigh is pricked with a skewer. If necessary, prop up legs with crumpled foil to achieve even browning; also reduce heat to prevent duck browning too quickly.
SAUCE: In a small heavy saucepan mix sugar and vinegar and bring to the boil over moderate heat, stirring until sugar dissolves. Cook, watching carefully, until vinegar evaporates and sugar is slightly caramelized. Remove saucepan from heat, cool slightly, then pour stock into caramel and stir until caramel has dissolved. Place back on heat and boil until reduced to about 120 ml/4 fl oz (½ cup). Add orange and lemon juice and simmer, stirring, for 1 minute. Mix arrowroot with water and stir into the sauce. Simmer, stirring, until thickened. Add green peppercorns and salt, and simmer for 1 minute.

Arrange duck on heated platter with mandarin slices. Serve sauce separately. Serves 4.

Duckling Casserole

1 × 1.5 kg (3 lb) duckling, quartered; salt and freshly ground black pepper; 1 stick celery, chopped; 2 carrots, chopped; 1 onion, sliced; 6 tbsp Cognac or brandy; 1 strip lemon peel; 250 ml/8 fl oz (1 cup) red wine; 1 rasher (slice) bacon, cut thick, rind removed and diced; 2 tbsp olive oil; 120 ml/4 fl oz (½ cup) rich duck stock, made with trimmings and giblets (see page 413); 1 bouquet garni; 2 cloves garlic.
GARNISH: *12 small new potatoes, boiled; 250 g/8 oz (2 cups) sliced mushrooms; butter; lemon juice.*

Remove backbone from duck pieces and place in a porcelain or earthenware bowl. Add salt, pepper, celery, carrots, onion, Cognac, lemon peel and red wine, and marinate duck in this mixture overnight. Remove duck pieces from marinade and dry with paper towels. Reserve marinade. Sauté bacon in olive oil in flameproof casserole until golden. Remove bacon and brown duck pieces in bacon fat. Return bacon to casserole and cook, covered, over a moderate heat for 20 minutes. Add reserved marinade, stock, bouquet garni and garlic. Cook over a low heat for 1½ hours or until duck is tender. Remove bouquet garni, skim fat and adjust seasoning. Remove duck pieces and bacon to a heated serving platter. Strain over sauce and garnish with boiled potatoes and sliced mushrooms which have been cooked quickly in butter and lemon juice. Serve immediately. Serves 4.

Sauté of Duck with Burgundy

1 × 1.5 kg (3 lb) duckling; 1 tbsp oil; 1 onion, finely sliced; 15 g/½ oz (1 tbsp) butter; 180–250 g/6–8 oz (1½–2 cups) button mushrooms; 175 ml/6 fl oz (¾ cup) red Burgundy; 120 ml/4 fl oz (½ cup) duck stock; salt and freshly ground black pepper; 4 tsp Beurre Manié (page 35).

Quickly brown duck all over in oil in a large pan. Remove from pan and leave to cool a little, then quarter: first cut down through breastbone with kitchen scissors and then on either side of backbone through rib cage. Cut each half into 2 just above the leg, and set aside. (The backbone can be used for stock for a stew.) Add onion to pan in which there should be about 1–2 tbsp of duck fat. Brown onion slightly, then add butter and mushrooms, whole or sliced according to size, and sauté briskly for 2–3 minutes. Heat wine in a small saucepan, then add to pan with stock. Stir until it boils. Season with salt and pepper. Put in pieces of duck, cover and simmer for 20 minutes. The duck should still be slightly pink. When ready to serve, trim duck pieces with scissors or poultry shears if necessary to remove any ugly bones, and arrange in a heated serving dish. Thicken sauce slightly with beurre manié, boil again and spoon over duck.

Caneton à l'Orange

(Duckling with Orange)

2 × 1.5 kg (3 lb) ducklings; salt; 90 g/3 oz (6 tbsp) butter; 2 large oranges; 1 tbsp brandy; watercress to garnish.
ORANGE SAUCE: *1 tsp sugar; 1 tbsp flour; 250 ml/8 fl oz (1 cup) duck stock or water; 120 ml/4 fl oz (½ cup) dry white wine; juice 2 oranges; salt and freshly ground black pepper; 3 tbsp port wine (optional).*

Season ducklings with salt, rub all over with butter and place a few strips of orange rind inside each bird. Put in baking dish. Place in a preheated moderately hot oven (200°C/ 400°F, Gas Mark 6) and roast for 15 minutes, then reduce heat to moderate (180°C/350°F, Gas Mark 4) and continue roasting until tender, 1½–2 hours. Baste frequently with butter while cooking. Peel remaining rind from oranges very thinly, using a potato peeler, and cut rind into very fine shreds. Cover with hot water, simmer 3 minutes, then drain. Cool and reserve for garnish. Remove pith from oranges and cut into sections. Sprinkle with brandy and leave

until required. Remove duck from pan and keep warm on heated serving dish. Pour off all but 2 tbsp butter and drippings from baking dish. Add sugar and cook until caramelized a pale golden colour. Stir in flour and cook a few minutes until light brown. Stir in stock (this should be made with ducks' feet, neck, etc – see page 413) or water and cook gently until thickened. Strain into saucepan. Add wine, orange juice, salt and pepper. Cook gently for 5–10 minutes. Add a few of the blanched shreds of orange rind and the port wine, if liked. Garnish duck with orange sections, orange rind and watercress, and serve with sauce. Serves 6.

DUMPLING

Light, fluffy and flavoursome – that's what good dumplings should be. They are a treasured part of home cooking in many countries from China to Central Europe and the British Isles.

Dumplings come in a great variety of shapes, textures and flavours; they may be made with flour, semolina, cornmeal, potato, soft cheese or even stiffly-beaten egg whites, and contain ingredients such as salt, butter, yeast, spices, herbs or fruit. Some dumplings are steamed on top of a stew or casserole, some are simmered in stock or, for sweet dumplings, in a syrup, and others are baked.

When making dumplings, if they are too soft and fall apart, add a little more flour; if too heavy, add a little liquid. Dumplings made with a raising agent are always cooked with the lid on the pot.

Test dough by cooking one small dumpling ahead of the rest. The kind of stew and amount of liquid can make a difference.

Cook dumplings just before serving. The dough can be made ahead and refrigerated until needed. **See recipes.**

Fluffy Dumplings

Superb light and tender dumplings to cook on top of a stew.

125 g/4 oz (1 cup) flour; 1 tsp baking powder; ½ tsp salt; pinch nutmeg; 30 g/1 oz (2 tbsp) butter; 4–5 tbsp milk.

Sift dry ingredients into a bowl and rub (cut) in butter. Add milk, blending with a fork until a fairly wet dough is formed. Shape with wet hands or between 2 wet tablespoons (or whatever size you like) and drop on top of a simmering stew 15 minutes before the end of cooking time, making sure dumplings sit on meat and do not sink into gravy. Cover and simmer 15 minutes without lifting lid. Serve dumplings with stew. Makes about 12.
VARIATIONS
Bacon Dumplings: Follow the recipe for Fluffy Dumplings, adding 2 tbsp crisp-fried and crumbled bacon – about 1 large rasher (slice) – to flour-butter mixture.
Caraway Dumplings: Follow the recipe for Fluffy Dumplings, adding 1 tsp caraway seeds to the dry ingredients.
Cheese Dumplings: Follow the recipe for Fluffy Dumplings, adding 2 tbsp grated cheese, ½ tsp dry mustard and a pinch cayenne to the dry ingredients.
Herb Dumplings: Follow the recipe for Fluffy Dumplings, omitting nutmeg and adding 1½ tbsp chopped parsley or other fresh herbs to flour-butter mixture.

DUNDEE CAKE

Many a Scottish housewife makes this traditional light fruit cake every week so that there is always some on hand for family and visitors.

Dundee Cake

250 g/8 oz (1 cup) butter; 250 g/8 oz (1 cup) caster sugar; grated rind 2 oranges; 5 eggs, beaten; 310 g/10 oz (2½ cups) flour; 1 tsp baking powder; pinch salt; 30 g/1 oz (¼ cup) chopped blanched almonds; 180 g/6 oz (1 cup) sultanas (golden raisins); 180 g/6 oz (1 cup) currants; 90 g/3 oz (½ cup) chopped mixed candied peel; 1 tbsp orange juice; extra blanched almonds to decorate.

Cream butter with sugar and orange rind until light and fluffy. Gradually beat in eggs. Sift flour, baking powder and salt. Mix in chopped almonds, fruit and peel. Stir into creamed mixture with strained orange juice. Turn into a greased 20 cm (8 in) round deep cake tin (pan) lined with greased brown and greaseproof (waxed) papers. Smooth surface and arrange extra almonds in pattern on top. Bake cake in a preheated cool oven (150°C/300°F, Gas Mark 2) for 2–2½ hours or until a skewer inserted in centre comes out clean. Allow to cool in tin (pan).

DUXELLES

French name for mushrooms finely chopped and sautéed in butter, used for many kinds of stuffings and quick mushroom sauces.

See page 231 for recipe.

ECCLES CAKES

These little English pastries, filled with fruit and spices, were once part of the Eccles Wakes. These festival holidays were held 300 years ago in the Lancashire town of Eccles to celebrate the dedication of the local parish church.

Eccles Cakes

30 g/1 oz (2 tbsp) butter, softened; 2 tbsp brown sugar; 2 tbsp finely chopped mixed candied peel; 60 g/2 oz ($\frac{1}{3}$ cup) currants; $\frac{1}{4}$ tsp mixed spice (ground allspice); 1 × 375 g/12 oz packet frozen puff pastry (paste), thawed; 1 egg white, lightly beaten; 60 g/2 oz ($\frac{1}{4}$ cup) caster sugar.

Mix together butter, brown sugar, peel, currants and mixed spice (ground allspice). Roll out pastry (paste) dough thinly and cut into 8 cm (3 in) rounds. Place a spoonful of fruit mixture in centre of each round. Moisten edges of rounds with water and draw up edges of each round to meet in the centre and completely enclose filling. Press well together and turn over so join is underneath. Roll out lightly until currants just show through dough and cake is about 8 mm ($\frac{1}{3}$ in) thick. Place on greased baking trays and leave in a cool place for 10 minutes. Make 3 slits in top of each cake, then brush with lightly beaten egg white and dredge with caster sugar. Bake in a preheated hot oven (230°C/450°F, Gas Mark 8) for about 15 minutes or until golden-brown and crisp. Remove from baking tray and cool on a wire rack. Makes about 12.

ECLAIR

A finger-shaped puff of choux pastry (paste). Eclairs make one of the most delicate confections for afternoon tea or dessert or, filled with a savoury mixture, are served as a first course or as party savouries.

The shells for savoury éclairs are made from unsweetened choux pastry (paste), shaped and baked in the same way as sweet éclairs. They may be filled with a hot or cold savoury mixture.

For filling suggestions see *Profiterole* (page 313).

Party Eclairs For miniature éclairs to serve as party savouries, place 1 quantity savoury Choux Pastry (see page 276) in a piping (pastry) bag with a 1 cm ($\frac{1}{2}$ in) plain nozzle. Pipe into 4 cm (1$\frac{1}{2}$ in) lengths about 5 cm (2 in) apart on lightly greased baking trays. Bake in a preheated hot oven (230°C/450°F, Gas Mark 8) for 10 minutes, then reduce the heat to moderate (180°C/350°F, Gas Mark 4) and bake for a further 10 minutes or until golden-brown, firm and light in the hand. Slit each éclair along the side and dry out in the turned-off oven for 20 minutes. Fill with hot or cold savoury mixture of your choice. Makes about 24.

Chocolate Eclairs

1 quantity sweetened Choux Pastry (page 276); 250 ml/8 fl oz (1 cup) double (heavy) cream; 1 tsp caster sugar.
GLOSSY CHOCOLATE ICING (FROSTING): *2 tbsp (unsweetened) cocoa powder, sifted; 1$\frac{1}{2}$ tbsp sugar; 3 tbsp water; 140 g/4$\frac{1}{2}$ oz (1 cup) icing (confectioners) sugar, sifted; few drops vanilla essence (extract).*

Spoon choux pastry (paste) into a large piping (pastry) bag fitted with a 1 cm ($\frac{1}{2}$ in) plain nozzle. Pipe mixture in 8 cm (3 in) lengths about 5 cm (2 in) apart on 2 lightly greased baking trays. Bake in a preheated hot oven (230°C/450°F, Gas Mark 8) for 12 minutes, then reduce heat to moderate (180°C/350°F, Gas Mark 4) and bake for 15–20 minutes more or until golden-brown, firm and light in the hand. Slit each éclair along the side, turn off the oven and leave éclairs in the oven to cool for 20 minutes with the door half open. Remove and cool completely on a wire rack. When cold, whip cream with sugar and fill the éclairs.
GLOSSY CHOCOLATE ICING (FROSTING): Stir cocoa, sugar and water over low heat until sugar has dissolved, then bring to the boil without stirring. Remove from the heat and stir in icing (confectioners) sugar and vanilla. Add a little boiling water if necessary to make a coating consistency. Spread icing (frosting) over tops of éclairs and leave to set. Makes about 12.

Raspberry or Strawberry Eclairs: Make as for Chocolate Eclairs but fill with whole raspberries or sliced strawberries and whipped cream. Ice with Lemon Glacé Icing (see page 164) tinted pink.

EEL

Fresh eel is firm and delicately flavoured; its high oil content makes it rich eating. Smoked eel makes a luxury first course or canapé topping.

□ **Basic Preparation:** Fresh eel is cleaned in the same way as other fish, and is always skinned before cooking. Cut it, on the diagonal, into 5–8 cm (2–3 in) pieces and peel off the skin, then proceed according to the recipe.

Smoked eel is ready to eat. Simply remove the skin and lift fillets off the bone. Serve as a first course with lemon wedges and brown bread and butter.

Right: Bacon and Onion Roly-Poly (page 64) and Welsh Rarebits (page 468)

Sautéed Eel Provençale

750 g (1½ lb) eel; seasoned flour; 2 tbsp olive oil; 60 g/2 oz (4 tbsp) butter; 6 shallots, finely chopped; 2 cloves garlic, crushed; 30 g/1 oz (½ cup) fresh breadcrumbs; 2 tbsp chopped parsley; salt and freshly ground black pepper; lemon wedges to serve.

Cut eel into pieces and skin as described in the section on Basic Preparation. Cut fillets from bones, roll in seasoned flour and sauté in the oil and half the butter until golden-brown. Remove from pan and keep warm. Add remaining butter to pan and sauté shallots, garlic and breadcrumbs until crumbs are crisp. Stir in parsley, season with salt and pepper and spoon over eel. Serve with lemon wedges. Serves 4.

EGG

An egg is a remarkably efficient package of nutrition, being rich in protein, vitamins and minerals. Eggs are indispensable in the kitchen. They are used to thicken, as in custards or puddings; to leaven, as in soufflés, cakes and puffy omelettes; to emulsify, as in mayonnaise. A beaten egg stirred into hot, not boiling, liquid will thicken and enrich soups or sauces. Use a beaten egg to bind mixtures for croquettes, meatballs and stuffings, and if you want to fry foods, a coating of egg will protect the food and keep the outer coating of breadcrumbs in place. Beaten egg gives a beautiful shiny glaze when brushed over pastry (dough) before baking.

To buy and store: In England, as in all EEC countries, eggs are graded by weight, ranging from Size 1 eggs (over 70 g/2½ oz) to Size 7 (below 45 g/1½ oz). Most popular is the Size 3 egg (60–65 g/2–2¼ oz), which is equivalent to an American 'large' egg. A fresh egg when broken into a saucer, should be quite highly domed, with the white thick and compact.

Never wash eggs before storing as this will destroy the natural protective film over the shells; store them in the refrigerator away from highly flavoured foods as the shells are porous and absorb odours. Place the pointed ends down to allow the air space at the rounded end to 'breathe'.

Egg whites can be stored for 2–3 weeks in an airtight container in the refrigerator. To use: measure 1½ tbsp for each egg white. Egg yolks may be covered with water, and re-frigerated. Use within 5 days.

For best results in cooking, remove eggs from the refrigerator a few hours before using. Eggs used at room temperature mix with other ingredients more readily and the whites whisk to a greater volume.

Left: Chicken in Silver Foil, Fried Chicken Legs and Lotus White Chicken (page 69)

To whisk egg whites: These can be beaten by hand, with a whisk or rotary beater, or with an electric mixer. The bowl and beater should be very clean, and the whites have no trace of yolk.

Start beating slowly until a soft foam forms, then add a pinch of salt and ¼ tsp cream of tartar for 4 egg whites. Gradually increase the beating speed and circulate the beaters right round the bowl, to incorporate all the egg white and beat in as much air as possible. Beat until the whites are glossy and creamy. Their volume by now should be 7 times greater than when you started beating and should hold a soft peak when the beater is raised. Stop beating before the whites form very stiff peaks as they become dry and brittle and will not mix well with other ingredients.

☐ **To Cook:** Eggs can be baked, boiled, coddled, fried, poached, scrambled and made into an omelette. **See also recipes.**

BAKED EGGS Butter small ramekins and break an egg into each. Season with salt and freshly ground white pepper, cover with 1 tsp warm single (light) cream or melted butter, and bake in a preheated moderate oven (180°C/350°F, Gas Mark 4) for 8–10 minutes until the white is set and the yolk still runny.

Diced bacon, ham, salami or chopped spinach may be placed in the bottom of each ramekin before adding the egg if you wish. Cheese can be sprinkled over the egg before adding the cream or butter.

BOILED EGGS Boil enough water to cover the eggs, lower one at a time into the water, reboil, then simmer for the required time: 3 minutes for soft-boiled (soft-cooked), 4 minutes for medium-boiled (medium-cooked) and 10 minutes for hard-boiled (hard-cooked). Cool hard-boiled (hard-cooked) eggs rapidly under cold running water and tap gently all over to crack the shell and prevent an unsightly dark ring forming around the yolk.

CODDLED EGGS Butter inside of egg coddler lightly and drop in 1–2 eggs. Add a tiny piece of butter and season with salt and pepper. Screw on the lid and cook for 10 minutes in a saucepan of boiling water. The yolks should be soft, the whites just set.

FRIED EGGS Melt enough bacon fat or butter to cover the bottom of a frying pan (skillet). When it begins to sizzle break the eggs, one at a time, into a cup and slide them into the pan. Fry gently, basting from time to time with the fat, until the eggs are cooked with firm whites and soft yolks or as you like them. Remove with an egg slice and serve at once.

OMELETTES For 1–2 people, beat 3 eggs lightly with 1 tbsp water, season with salt and freshly ground white pepper. Melt 15 g/½ oz (1 tsp) butter in a small frying pan (skillet) and, when the foam subsides, pour in the eggs. Lift the cooked egg from the edges

towards the centre – the uncooked egg will run underneath. Repeat until mixture has set underneath but is still moist on top. Fold ⅓ of the omelette towards the centre and roll out on to a heated plate, tilting the pan so that the omelette folds over again. Serve at once.

To fill omelettes: Heat the filling and spoon it across the centre just before the omelette is folded over. Use about 3 tbsp of any of the following fillings: chopped cooked mushrooms; chopped fresh herbs; chopped cooked bacon and onion; warm asparagus tips; grated cheese; salmon or crab mixed with a little cream.

POACHED EGGS Use very fresh eggs, straight from the refrigerator, as they hold their shape better. Half fill a shallow pan with water, add ¼ tsp vinegar and bring to the boil. Break each egg into a cup, slide it into the water, cover the pan, remove from the heat and leave for 3½ minutes for soft eggs or 4 minutes for firmer ones. Remove, using an egg slice, drain and serve at once.

SCRAMBLED EGGS For one person, beat together 2 eggs, 1 tbsp milk or single (light) cream, salt and freshly ground pepper. Melt 2 tsp butter in a pan, pour in the eggs and cook over low heat, stirring gently until the eggs are creamy and soft. Serve immediately.

Eggs Florentine

340 g/11 oz (1½ cups) cooked, chopped spinach, well drained; 2 tbsp single (light) cream; salt and freshly ground black pepper; 4 eggs, poached and kept hot; 4 slices Gruyère or Emmenthal cheese; 4 black (ripe) olives to garnish (optional).

Combine spinach, cream, salt and pepper and put into a gratin dish or 4 individual ramekins. Arrange eggs on spinach purée. Place a slice of cheese on each egg and put into a preheated moderately hot oven (200°C/400°F, Gas Mark 6) or under a preheated hot grill (broiler) until cheese melts and turns golden. Garnish with olives if liked and serve immediately. Serves 4.

Eggs New Orleans

3 tomatoes, peeled, seeded and chopped; 1 green pepper, cored, seeded and chopped; 1 onion, chopped; 2 sticks celery, chopped; 3 tbsp tomato purée (paste); 1 tsp sugar; ½ tsp salt; ¼ tsp black pepper; 1 bay leaf; 60 g/2 oz (1 cup) fresh breadcrumbs; 4 eggs; 60 g/2 oz (½ cup) grated cheese.

In a saucepan combine all ingredients except breadcrumbs, eggs and cheese. Simmer, stirring occasionally, for 10 minutes. Remove bay leaf, then stir in breadcrumbs. Place mixture in a shallow ovenproof dish. Make 4 depressions on surface and break an egg into each. Sprinkle with grated cheese and bake in a preheated moderate oven

(180°C/350°F, Gas Mark 4) for 15–20 minutes or until cheese has melted and the eggs are firm. Serves 4.

Eggs with Watercress Mayonnaise

180 g/6 oz (3 cups) watercress sprigs; 120 ml/4 fl oz (½ cup) thick Mayonnaise (page 204); squeeze lemon juice; cayenne or Tabasco (hot pepper) sauce; 4 tbsp Vinaigrette Dressing (page 358); 4–5 hard-boiled (hard-cooked) eggs, halved.

Boil 60 g/2 oz (1 cup) watercress sprigs in water for 2 minutes. Drain well and purée in a blender or push through a sieve. Add to mayonnaise with lemon juice and cayenne or Tabasco (hot pepper) sauce. Toss remaining cress through vinaigrette dressing and arrange down centre of a platter. Place eggs on top. Coat with mayonnaise. Serves 4.

Salmon-Stuffed Eggs

16 flat anchovy fillets (2 × 50 g/1⅔ oz cans); milk; 8 hard-boiled (hard-cooked) eggs, halved; 90 g/3 oz smoked salmon, chopped; 120 ml/4 fl oz (½ cup) Mayonnaise (page 204); freshly ground black pepper; capers; 1 tbsp snipped fresh dill or chives; watercress or shredded lettuce.

Drain oil from anchovies and put fillets in a shallow dish with a little milk to cover. Remove yolks carefully from the egg halves and mash with smoked salmon, mayonnaise and pepper. Spoon mixture back into egg whites, mounding it. Drain anchovies, pat dry and cut each fillet lengthways into 2 strips. Garnish each egg with 2 strips of anchovy, crossed in the centre. Place a caper on each yolk quarter and sprinkle with herbs. Arrange on cress or lettuce. Serves 8.

Tea Eggs
(Marbled Eggs)
In China eggs are often pickled, (known in the West as Thousand Year Old Eggs), or

Separating eggs: Slip yolk from one shell half to the other until white drains away.

preserved by salting. The Chinese also braise eggs in this mixture of tea and soy sauce.

6 eggs; 2 tbsp Indian tea leaves; 600 ml/ 1 pint (2½ cups) water; 2 tbsp soy sauce.

Place eggs in a saucepan, cover with cold water and bring gently to the boil. Simmer for 10 minutes. Drain eggs and crack shells all over with a spoon without removing any shell. Boil tea leaves in the 600 ml/1 pint (2½ cups) water for 5–6 minutes until liquid is strong and dark. Add soy sauce and stir. Remove from heat. Put eggs into liquid and leave for at least 1 hour or until liquid is quite cool. To serve, remove shells. You will find that some of the tea mixture has seeped through the cracks in shells to form a marble-like pattern on whites. Makes 6.

Eggs Mornay

250 g/8 oz (2 cups) macaroni; 90 g/3 oz (6 tbsp) butter; 3 tbsp flour; 600 ml/1 pint (2½ cups) milk; 90 g/3 oz (¾ cups) Cheddar cheese, grated; salt and freshly ground black pepper; pinch nutmeg; 6 hard-boiled (hard-cooked) eggs, halved; parsley to garnish.

Bring a large saucepan of salted water to the boil. Add macaroni and cook rapidly for 15–20 minutes, or until tender. Meanwhile, melt 60 g/2 oz (4 tbsp) butter in a saucepan, stir in flour and cook, stirring, for 2 minutes. Add milk and stir until sauce boils and thickens. Beat in 60 g/2 oz (½ cup) cheese, and season with salt, pepper and nutmeg. Do not allow sauce to boil once cheese has been added. Drain macaroni and toss with remaining butter. Spoon hot macaroni into flameproof serving dish, top with eggs and spoon sauce over. Sprinkle with remaining cheese and put under preheated hot grill (broiler) until cheese melts and browns. Garnish with parsley and serve immediately. Serves 6.

Egg Croquettes

60 g/2 oz (4 tbsp) butter; 3 tbsp flour; 250 ml/8 fl oz (1 cup) milk; 1 tbsp chopped parsley; 4 hard-boiled (hard-cooked) eggs, chopped; 2 eggs; salt and freshly ground black pepper; pinch nutmeg; flour; dry breadcrumbs; oil or dripping for deep-frying; parsley to garnish.

Melt butter in small saucepan, add flour and cook for 2 minutes. Add milk and cook until thick, stirring constantly. Remove from heat and, while sauce is still hot, stir in parsley, hard-boiled (hard-cooked) eggs, and 1 beaten egg. Season well with salt, pepper and nutmeg. Turn into a shallow dish or tin and smooth over with palette knife. Chill until ready to use (several hours if possible). Turn croquette mixture on to a floured board and cut into small sausage shapes. Dip

into flour, then into second egg, beaten with ½ tsp salt. Roll in breadcrumbs. Deep-fry in hot fat until golden-brown. Drain on paper towels and serve immediately, garnished with parsley. Serves 4.

Curried Eggs

45 g/1½ oz (3 tbsp) butter; 1 small onion, finely chopped; ½ cooking apple, peeled, cored and finely chopped; 2 tbsp curry powder; 2 tbsp flour; 600 ml/1 pint (2½ cups) stock or water; 1 tsp curry paste (optional); 1 tbsp chopped mango chutney; 1 tbsp brown sugar; juice ½ lemon; ½ tsp salt; 30 g/1 oz (2 tbsp) sultanas (golden raisins); 8 hard-boiled (hard-cooked) eggs, halved.

Melt butter in a heavy saucepan, add onion and apple and cook gently for 5–6 minutes. Stir in curry powder and flour, then gradually stir in stock or water and bring to the boil. Add remaining ingredients (except eggs), cover and simmer for 20–30 minutes. Arrange eggs in a heated serving dish. Pour over sauce, and serve with boiled rice and chutney. Serves 4–6.

Straciatella alla Romana
(Egg and Cheese Soup)

3 eggs; 1½ tbsp grated Parmesan cheese; 1 tbsp chopped parsley; 1.5 litres/2½ pints (6 cups) chicken stock.

Beat eggs until frothy. Add cheese and parsley. Bring stock to a rolling boil. Pour egg mixture into it, stirring all the time until eggs are set. Serve immediately. Serves 6.

Stuffed Eggs

8 hard-boiled (hard-cooked) eggs, halved; 60 g/2 oz (4 tbsp) butter; 2 tbsp single (light) cream; ½ tsp dry mustard; salt and freshly ground black pepper; paprika.

Remove yolks from eggs, mash and mix with butter, cream, mustard, salt and pepper. Stuff egg whites with the mixture, sprinkle with paprika and chill before serving. Serves 4–8.
VARIATIONS
Stuffed Eggs with Liver Pâté: Use Stuffed Egg recipe, adding 2 tbsp chopped pickle relish and 90 g/3 oz (½ cup) liver pâté to egg yolks.
Stuffed Eggs with Anchovies: Use Stuffed Egg recipe, adding 1 × 50 g/1⅔ oz can anchovy fillets, drained and crushed, or 1 tbsp anchovy paste to egg yolks. Garnish with capers.
Stuffed Eggs with Devilled Ham: Use Stuffed Egg recipe, adding 2 or more tbsp devilled ham to egg yolks. Garnish with chopped parsley.
Stuffed Eggs with Olives: Use Stuffed Egg recipe, adding 2 tbsp chopped stuffed green or black (ripe) olives to egg yolks.

Stuffed Eggs with Mushrooms: Use Stuffed Egg recipe, adding 2–3 tbsp chopped sautéed or raw mushrooms to egg yolks. Garnish with a bit of canned pimiento.

Stuffed Eggs with Caviar: Use Stuffed Egg recipe, adding 2 or more tbsp caviar to egg yolks. Garnish with chutney.

Curried Stuffed Eggs: Use Stuffed Egg recipe, adding 1 tsp curry powder to egg yolks. Garnish with chutney.

Stuffed Eggs with Herbs: Use Stuffed Egg recipe, adding chopped fresh chives, chervil, parsley, savory or other herbs to egg yolks.

EGG FLIP

A nutritious meal-in-a-glass which should be in everyone's repertoire.

Egg Flip

1 egg; 1 tsp sugar; ½ tsp vanilla essence (extract), or 1 tsp brandy or sherry; 250 ml/8 fl oz (1 cup) hot or cold milk.

Beat egg, sugar and vanilla, brandy or sherry thoroughly together. Add milk and beat until frothy. Pour into a glass and serve immediately. Serves 1.

EGG NOG

A smooth but potent blend of eggs, cream and brandy, rum or whisky. Egg nog is a festive drink, associated especially with Christmas.

Egg Nog

6 eggs, separated; 125 g/4 oz (½ cup) caster sugar; 500 ml/18 fl oz (2 cups) brandy, rum or whisky; 1 litre/1¾ pints (4¼ cups) single (light) cream; pinch salt; freshly grated nutmeg.

Beat egg yolks with sugar until thick. Beat in spirit and cream. Beat egg whites with salt until they form soft peaks, then fold into cream mixture. Serve in small punch cups or coffee cups, sprinkled with grated nutmeg. Serves 10–12.

EGGPLANT

See Aubergine.

EMPANADAS

These spicy meat turnovers are popular in several Latin American countries. Fillings vary from region to region, and the empanadas may be baked or deep-fried.

Empanadas

PASTRY (DOUGH): *500 g/1 lb (4 cups) flour; 2 tsp paprika; ½ tsp salt; 180 g/6 oz (¾ cup) butter or lard; cold water.*

FILLING: *120 ml/4 fl oz (½ cup) oil; 1 onion, finely chopped; 1 tomato, peeled, seeded and chopped; 1 tsp paprika; 1 kg (2 lb) lean stewing beef, trimmed and cut into 5 mm (¼ in) dice; 2 tsp flour; 120 ml/4 fl oz (½ cup) beef stock (bouillon); ½ tsp ground cumin; salt; ½ tsp chilli powder; 1 hard-boiled (hard-cooked) egg, chopped; 45 g/1½ oz (¼ cup) chopped green olives; 60 g/2 oz (⅓ cup) sultanas (golden raisins).*

To make pastry (dough), sift flour, paprika and salt together, and rub (cut) in fat. Using a knife, stir in enough water to make a fairly stiff dough. Knead lightly, wrap in plastic wrap and chill.

To prepare filling: heat oil in a large frying pan (skillet), add onion and fry gently until golden-brown. Add tomato and paprika and cook slowly until soft. Add meat, flour, stock (bouillon), cumin, salt to taste and chilli. Stir until mixture comes to the boil. Cover and simmer for 15 minutes, then remove lid and cook rapidly for 5–10 minutes to reduce liquid by half. Cool mixture.

Divide pastry (dough) into pieces about the size of an egg. Roll each piece thin to form an 18 cm (7 in) circle. Put 2 tbsp meat filling, 1 tsp chopped egg, ½ tsp chopped olives and a few sultanas (golden raisins) in the centre of each pastry (dough) circle.

Spread filling over half the circle, leaving a 2 cm (¾ in) margin. Moisten edges of pastry (dough) and fold over to make turnovers, pressing edges firmly together. Pinch edge between thumb and finger and fold pinched part over on to unpinched part, or fold circle to within 1 cm (½ in) of opposite edge, fold lower half over the upper and crimp. Chill empanadas for 20 minutes, then bake in a preheated moderately hot oven (200°C/400°F, Gas Mark 6) for 15 minutes. Alternatively, deep-fry in oil until golden-brown and drain on crumpled paper towels. Makes 18.

ENCHILADAS

Spicy enchiladas are a Mexican dish made of flat, soft tortillas (see *Tortilla*) dipped in a chilli- and cumin-flavoured sauce, rolled around a filling and topped with more sauce. Traditionally they are sprinkled with grated cheese and garnished with hard-boiled (hard-cooked) egg, radish and lettuce.

Enchiladas de Pollo
(Chicken-Stuffed Tortillas in Sauce)

2 eggs, beaten; 2 tbsp water; ¼ tsp cinnamon; 12 Tortillas, about 13 cm (5 in) in diameter (page 441); oil for frying.
SAUCE: *2 tbsp olive oil; 6 tomatoes, peeled, seeded and chopped; 1 onion, chopped; 1 green or red pepper, seeded and chopped;*

½ tsp ground cumin; ½ tsp chilli powder; salt and freshly ground black pepper.
FILLING: *250 g/8 oz (1 cup) cooked chicken meat, chopped; 45 g/1½ oz (¼ cup) raisins; 60 g/2 oz (½ cup) chopped blanched almonds; 2 tbsp chopped green olives.*
GARNISH: *½ small head lettuce, shredded; 3 radishes, finely sliced; 1 Spanish onion, finely sliced into rings; 1 hard-boiled (hard-cooked) egg, sliced.*

SAUCE: Heat the oil in a frying pan (skillet) and sauté tomatoes, onion and green or red pepper until tender. Add cumin, chilli powder, salt and pepper. Remove from heat and keep warm.

Combine all the filling ingredients and mix well. Beat eggs with water and cinnamon until frothy, then dip each tortilla into this mixture to coat. Place some of the filling in centre of each tortilla, roll up and secure with wooden toothpicks. Heat oil in a frying pan (skillet) and sauté enchiladas for about 2 minutes on each side or until golden-brown. Drain on paper towels. Place on a heated serving dish, pour sauce over and arrange garnish around edge. Serves 4–6.

ENDIVE, CURLY

A member of the chicory family (and known as chicory in America). The decorative, curly-fringed leaves and pleasantly bitter taste make it a good partner to other greens, fruit or other robust-flavoured ingredients in a salad.
□ **Basic Preparation:** Discard tough outer green leaves and break tender leaves off tough stalks. Wash leaves in cold water, dry in a salad dryer or on a tea-towel and store in a closed plastic bag in the refrigerator to crisp. **See recipes.**

Endive, Apple and Walnut Salad
Serve with grilled (broiled) chicken.

½ bunch curly endive (chicory), trimmed and crisped; 1 red and 1 green apple, cored and cut into thin wedges; 2 tsp lemon juice; 30 g/1 oz (¼ cup) walnut pieces.

DRESSING: *2 tsp lemon juice; salt and freshly ground black pepper; 2 tbsp walnut or olive oil; 2 tbsp sour cream.*

Place endive (chicory) in a salad bowl. Toss apples with lemon juice and add to bowl. Make dressing: mix lemon juice with a little salt and pepper, beat in oil a little at a time, then sour cream. Pour over salad and toss lightly. Add walnuts, toss again and serve immediately. Serves 6.

Ensalada Sevillana
(Seville Winter Salad)

1 bunch curly endive (chicory), trimmed and crisped; 1 red pepper, cored, seeded and sliced; 2 small onions, finely sliced into rings; 16 black (ripe) olives, stoned (pitted); 2 oranges, peeled and finely sliced into rounds.
DRESSING: *4 tbsp olive oil; 1 tbsp white wine vinegar; 1 clove garlic, crushed; $\frac{1}{2}$ tsp salt; $\frac{1}{4}$ tsp sugar; little fresh or dried tarragon.*

Mix all salad ingredients together in a salad bowl. Combine ingredients for dressing in a screw-top jar, shake well and pour over salad just before serving. Serves 4–6.

ENTRECOTE

Meaning 'between the ribs', entrecôte was originally the French name for a beef steak from the rib section, but the term is now widely used on menus to denote any fine steak dish. The dish is named after its sauce or garnish, e.g., Entrecôte Chasseur is a grilled (broiled) or pan-fried steak with Sauce Chasseur (see page 369).

Entrecôtes Vert-Pré

4 rib, sirloin or rump (top round) steaks, cut 2.5–4 cm (1–1$\frac{1}{2}$ in) thick, each weighing about 200 g (7 oz); Straw Potatoes (page 308); watercress; Maître d'Hôtel Butter (page 49).

Grill (broil) or pan-fry steaks until rare or medium, as desired. Put each steak on to a heated plate and garnish with a portion of straw potatoes and a small bouquet of watercress. Place a slice of maître d'hôtel butter on each steak and serve immediately. Serves 4.

ENTREE

Today, an entrée describes a made-up dish, served as a first course or as a light supper or luncheon dish – it may even be the main dish of a meal.

The French word *entrée* means 'way in' or 'entrance'. At a formal dinner, these dishes follow the soup and fish course and come before the main meat course. It is amusing to go through the menus of old-fashioned books – one cannot help but wonder how they did it. Today, much simpler menus are in favour and the separate hors d'oeuvre, soup, fish and entrée courses have practically combined into a first or starter course, and any one of these courses may be served.

Since entrées are usually 'dressed' or 'made' dishes, they are considered the first course to show the cook's skill to the full. Attractive presentation is vital and, luckily, by their nature these small portions of meat, fish and so on, and their accompaniments, can be arranged in myriad different ways; in a pretty pastry case (dough shell), *en brochette*, in individual ramekins or shells. They may also be individual feather-light soufflés, golden croquettes, fritters, filled crêpes or bouchées, dainty portions of Beef Stroganoff (see page 416), or sautéed calf's liver (see *Liver*).

ESCABECHE (Escovitch)

This dish is a form of pickled fish; the sauce preserves the fish with or without refrigeration for 2 days. It is served throughout the West Indies, but in Jamaica it is called Escovitch.

Escabeche

1 kg (2 lb) fish fillets; flour for coating; 1 quantity Basic Fritter Batter (page 129); olive oil for deep-frying.
SAUCE: *250 ml/8 fl oz (1 cup) dry white wine; 250 ml/8 fl oz (1 cup) white wine vinegar; 250 ml/8 fl oz (1 cup) olive oil; 1 tsp salt; 6 black peppercorns.*
PICKLES: *350 g (12 oz) finely sliced mixed vegetables (carrots, turnips, onions and green beans); 1 red pepper, seeded and sliced; 1 green pepper, seeded and sliced; 2 cloves garlic, sliced; 1 chilli, seeded and finely chopped (optional); 250 ml/8 fl oz (1 cup) white vinegar; 1 tbsp sugar.*

Cut fish into bite-sized strips or cubes. Roll in flour, dip into batter and fry in oil until golden-brown. Drain on paper towels and cool. Mix together ingredients for sauce and set aside. Cover pickle vegetables with vinegar, add sugar and boil for 3 minutes. Cool. Place fish in an earthenware bowl, cover with sauce and pickles and marinate for 24 hours. Drain before serving with a salad. Serves 8.

ESCALOPE

Escalope is a French word which may mean any thin, boneless and skinless slice of meat or fish, but it is mainly used for fine slices of veal, beaten thin. The same delicate slices feature in the cuisines of various countries and take different names accordingly. The French escalope becomes *scaloppine* (plural, *scaloppini*) or sometimes *costolette* (cutlet) in Italian; the German name is *schnitzel;* in England, as in America, it is a scallop or simply a veal steak. You may find it under any of these names in butchers' shops. Classically, escalopes are cut from the top of the leg, across the grain. Thin veal steaks from other sections are often sold as escalopes, schnitzel etc., and they may also be satisfactory cooked in the same way as escalopes.

□ **Basic Preparation:** If you buy large veal steaks which separate into natural divisions, divide them. Snip round the edges so that escalopes will cook without curling. If not already beaten out, place each one between 2 sheets of greaseproof (waxed) paper and beat gently with a cutlet bat, rolling pin or the flat side of a meat mallet (not the knobbly side which would tear the meat) to a thickness of 5 mm ($\frac{1}{4}$ in).

See also *Scaloppine* and *Schnitzel*.

Escalopes de Veau au Beurre
(Veal with Butter Sauce)

6 large or 12 small veal escalopes, beaten thin; seasoned flour; 60 g/2 oz (4 tbsp) clarified butter; 4 tbsp white wine; finely chopped parsley.

Coat escalopes lightly with flour, patting off excess. Heat butter in a large, heavy frying pan (skillet), add escalopes just as it begins to brown and sauté on fairly high heat until golden-brown on both sides (do this in 2 batches if necessary). Remove them to a heated serving dish and pour the butter over them. Add wine to pan and boil 1–2 minutes, stirring in all the brown bits. Pour over meat, sprinkle with chopped parsley and serve at once. Serves 6.
VARIATIONS
Escalopes de Veau à la Crème: Sauté the escalopes as described in Escalopes de Veau au Beurre. Remove them to a heated serving dish. Pour out fat from sauté pan, add 1 tbsp dry sherry and 4 tbsp single (light) cream and boil for 1–2 minutes, stirring in all the brown bits. Pour sauce over meat and serve at once.
Escalopes de Veau à la Crème et Champignons: Follow the recipe for Escalopes de Veau à la Crème, but do not pour off fat from pan after removing the escalopes. Sauté 90 g/3 oz ($\frac{3}{4}$ cup) sliced button mushrooms in the fat before adding sherry and cream.

ESCAROLE (Batavian Endive)

Escarole has broad, crinkled leaves and comes from the same group of green-leaved vegetables as curly endive (chicory). It is used in salads and should be prepared in the same way as curly endive (chicory).
See *Endive*.

F

FENNEL

Both the herb and vegetable varieties of fennel are of ancient origin. The herb plant is tall, with green stalks and feathery leaves, and the vegetable, known as Florence fennel, is a bulbous root that looks somewhat like celery. The flavour depends on the variety and ranges from bitter to sweet, tasting quite strongly of anise.

Fennel as a Vegetable: Use the bulb raw, sliced into a tomato or green salad or on its own dressed with Vinaigrette Dressing (see page 358). The distinctive flavour lends itself well as a salad accompaniment to fish, pork or lamb. The bulbs can also be used and prepared in the same way as celery.

Fennel as a Herb: The feathery leaves, so often used in the South of France, lend a delicate flavour to fish, fish soups or cream sauces to accompany seafood. In Italy the stalks and leaves are used, chopped with garlic, to make a stuffing for roast pork.

Fennel Seeds: These are aromatic and are used to flavour foods such as pickles, biscuits (cookies), pastries and fish. **See recipes.**

Fennel Smoked Fish

1 × 1.25 kg (2½ lb) whole fish, scaled and cleaned; 6 short pieces dried fennel; olive oil; 1 large bunch dried fennel branches; 120 ml/4 fl oz (½ cup) brandy.

Cut 3 incisions on each side of fish. Put a piece of fennel in each incision and brush fish with oil. Place in a barbecue grid and grill (broil) fish for 7–10 minutes on each side. Lay dried fennel branches on a large flameproof dish and place fish in grid on top. Warm brandy, set alight and pour flaming over dried fennel branches which catch alight and give out a strong scent to flavour the fish. When flames die down, remove fish from grid to a heated serving plate. Serves 2. NOTE: Any white-fleshed fish is suitable for this dish. Salt or fresh water fish may be used and small fish can be prepared this way.

Fennel with Butter and Cheese

4 bulbs fennel, trimmed and cut into segments; 1 tbsp olive oil; 1 clove garlic; 1 slice lemon; 1 tsp salt; 30 g/1 oz (2 tbsp) butter; 2 tbsp grated Parmesan cheese; freshly ground black pepper.

Put fennel into a saucepan containing enough boiling water to cover. Add oil, garlic, lemon and salt. Bring back to the boil, reduce heat, cover and simmer for 30–35 minutes or until just tender. Melt butter in a shallow gratin dish. Drain fennel well, put into dish and turn gently to coat with butter. Sprinkle with cheese and pepper. Brown lightly under a preheated grill (broiler) before serving. Serves 4.

Fennel and Tomatoes with Dill

oil for frying; 4 bulbs fennel, trimmed and finely sliced lengthways; salt and freshly ground black pepper; 4 ripe tomatoes, peeled and sliced; 3 tbsp chopped fresh dill.

Heat enough oil to cover bottom of a heavy pan and stew fennel gently, stirring often, until almost soft. Add salt, pepper and tomatoes and continue to cook gently for 5 minutes, stirring occasionally with a spatula to avoid breaking up tomatoes. Remove from heat, stir in dill and turn into a serving dish. Serve cold but not chilled. Serves 4–6.

Braised Fennel

A French way with this anise-scented vegetable, gently braised, to complement fish or lamb dishes.

4 bulbs fennel, trimmed; 2 tbsp olive oil; 1 tsp salt; 120 ml/4 fl oz (½ cup) water, stock or dry white wine.

Halve or quarter fennel lengthways, depending on size. Heat olive oil in a frying pan (skillet) or heavy flameproof casserole, add fennel and salt and cook gently, turning vegetable, for about 10 minutes. Add water, stock or wine, cover and cook over low heat for about 25 minutes or until tender. Serves 4.

FENUGREEK

Both the leaves and seeds of fenugreek are used in Indian cooking. The small flat, beige-coloured seeds are ground and used in curry powders and are especially good in fish curries. The hard seeds should be lightly roasted before they are ground, but don't roast them for too long or a bitter flavour will develop. The fresh leaves can be used to give a distinctive tang to salads. Fenugreek seeds are also used to give a maple flavour to sweets and candies.

Sour Fish Curry

1 tbsp tamarind pulp; 120 ml/4 fl oz (½ cup) hot water; 1 medium onion, chopped; 3 cloves garlic, crushed; 1 tsp chopped fresh ginger; 1 tbsp ground coriander; 2 tsp ground cumin; 1 tsp turmeric; 1 tsp chilli powder; ½ tsp ground fenugreek; 3 tbsp oil; 1 tbsp vinegar or lemon juice; 1½ tsp salt; 500 g (1 lb) fish fillets or steaks, cut into serving pieces.

Soak tamarind pulp in hot water for 10 minutes, then rub pulp off seeds and soften it in the water. Strain and discard seeds and fibres. Purée onion, garlic, ginger and 1 tbsp tamarind liquid in a blender or food processor, or pound in a mortar with a pestle. Mix in spices. Heat oil in a saucepan and fry spice mixture, stirring, until it thickens and darkens. Add rest of tamarind liquid, the vinegar or lemon juice, salt and enough hot water just to cover fish. When this comes to the boil put in fish and simmer very gently for 10–15 minutes or until it flakes easily when tested with a fine skewer. Serves 4.

FETTUCINE

See Pasta.

FIG

Fresh figs are sweet and luscious eaten raw when they are very soft and ripe. Figs should be eaten at room temperature; if they are too cold their delicate flavour is lost. Dried figs are extremely sweet and can be used in cakes and puddings or stewed.

Ways to Use Figs

Fig Salad Slice fresh figs, sprinkle with brandy and serve with cream, or sprinkle with sweet white wine and serve with plain yogurt.

Prosciutto and Figs Halve figs and arrange paper-thin slices of prosciutto around them.

Figs with Orange Juice Cut stalks from 4 fresh figs, quarter them and place in a serving bowl. Pour over them the freshly squeezed juice of 1 large orange and set aside for an hour before eating. Serves 2.

Baked Figs In an ovenproof dish arrange 5–6 slightly under-ripe whole figs. Pour in 4 tbsp water, sprinkle with 60 g/2 oz ($\frac{1}{4}$ cup) sugar and bake in a preheated moderate oven (180°C/350°F, Gas Mark 4) for 20 minutes. Serve chilled with cream. Serves 2–3.

See also *Fruit, Dried and Candied*.

Rich Fig Pudding

240 g/7$\frac{1}{2}$ oz (1$\frac{1}{4}$ cups) chopped dried figs; 140 g/4$\frac{1}{2}$ oz ($\frac{3}{4}$ cup) raisins; 250 g/8 oz (1$\frac{1}{2}$ cups) chopped stoned dates; 45 g/1$\frac{1}{2}$ oz ($\frac{1}{4}$ cup) chopped preserved ginger, drained; 2–3 tbsp brandy or rum; 180 g/6 oz (3 cups) fresh breadcrumbs; 250 g/8 oz (2 cups) self-raising flour; 150 g/5 oz (1 cup) shredded suet; pinch salt; 3 eggs; grated rind and juice 1 lemon; 4 tbsp milk.

Combine figs, raisins, dates and ginger. Sprinkle with brandy or rum, cover and leave for 1 hour. Mix together breadcrumbs, flour, suet and salt. Beat eggs to a froth and mix into dry ingredients with lemon rind and juice and prepared fruit. Mix thoroughly, adding milk to bring mixture to dropping consistency. Spoon mixture into greased 1.2 litre/2 pint (5 cup) pudding basin or mould, cover with 2 thicknesses buttered greaseproof (waxed) paper and tie securely. Place in a large saucepan with enough water to come halfway up sides of basin or mould. Cover and steam for 4 hours. Serve in wedges with cream or custard. Serves 6.

FILET MIGNON

A small, choice steak cut from the narrow (tail) end of a fillet (tenderloin) of beef, which should be trimmed of all fat and surrounding filament. A *filet mignon* should be about 4 cm (1$\frac{1}{2}$ in) thick when it is ready for cooking, but as the tail of fillet (tenderloin) may be very narrow, the fillet (tenderloin) is often cut thicker and beaten gently with the flat of a cleaver or large knife to the required thickness. Shape it with your hands into a neat circular shape, and tie string round it to keep the shape before cooking it.

It can be prepared in any of the ways described for *Tournedos* (see page 441), or in the classic way, Filets Mignons Henri IV.

Filets Mignons Henri IV

4 filets mignons; 1 tbsp oil; 30 g/1 oz (2 tbsp) butter; 4 round croûtes white bread sautéed in clarified butter (page 49); Straw Potatoes (page 308); artichoke hearts or asparagus tips sautéed in butter, or watercress sprigs; 1 quantity Béarnaise Sauce (page 370).

Sauté filets mignons in oil and butter, heated until just turning brown, for 3–4 minutes on each side for rare, or a few minutes longer for medium-rare. Remove strings from filets and place each on a hot croûte set on a heated plate. Garnish plates with straw potatoes and artichoke hearts, asparagus tips or watercress. Serve immediately with béarnaise sauce. Serves 4.

FILO PASTRY (Phyllo)

A very light, thin and delicate pastry widely used in cookery of the Middle East, for both sweet and savoury dishes. Filo is available either fresh or frozen. You will find the pastry ready to use, separated into thin sheets. Despite its delicate texture, filo is one of the easiest of all pastries to use.

☐ **To Use:** The main point to remember is that filo dries very quickly and becomes brittle when exposed to the air. Spread a dry tea-towel on your work surface, remove the filo sheets from their plastic pack and unfold on to the tea-towel. Do not separate the sheets. Cover with another dry tea-towel and cover that with a lightly dampened tea-towel. Remove each sheet as you need it, making sure you keep the remainder covered. Brush each sheet lightly with melted butter or oil before using.

Filo pastries freeze well and are ideal for entertaining. They may be baked from the frozen state at the temperature given in the recipe, although they may need extra cooking time. A sprinkling of cold water on the top layer of the pastry will help to make it crisp. **See Recipes.**

Tiropitakia

(Greek Cheese Pastries)

2 onions, finely chopped; 30 g/1 oz (2 tbsp) butter; 500 g/1 lb (4 cups) feta cheese, crumbled; 375 g/12 oz (1$\frac{1}{2}$ cups) Ricotta cheese; 3 eggs; 20 g/$\frac{2}{3}$ oz ($\frac{1}{2}$ cup) finely chopped parsley; salt and freshly ground black pepper; 1 tsp nutmeg; 500 g/1 lb (24 sheets) filo pastry; 250 g/8 oz (1 cup) butter, melted.

Cook onions gently in 30 g/1 oz (2 tbsp) butter until soft. Turn them on to a plate to cool a little. Mix feta and Ricotta cheeses. Add eggs, beat thoroughly and fold in onions and parsley. Season with salt, pepper and nutmeg. Unfold filo pastry and, leaving it stacked, cut lengthways in three strips. Stack strips between 2 dry tea-towels with a dampened towel on top. Lay 1 strip on work surface. Brush lightly with melted butter, fold lengthways in half and brush again with butter. Place a teaspoon of cheese filling on one end of pastry strip. Fold corner of pastry over filling until it meets the folded edge of pastry to form a triangle. Continue to fold pastry over in triangles until you come to end of strip. Brush top with melted butter and place, seam side down, on a lightly greased baking tray. Repeat with remaining filling and pastry. Bake Tiropitakia in a preheated moderately hot oven (190°C/375°F, Gas Mark 5) 15–20 minutes or until puffed and golden-brown. Serve hot. Makes about 72.
NOTE: Tiropitakia can be prepared and frozen unbaked until required. Bake straight from the freezer, allowing 10 more minutes' cooking time.

Spanakopita

(Greek Spinach Pie)

1 kg (2 lb) spinach, finely chopped; 12 shallots, chopped; 20 g/$\frac{2}{3}$ oz ($\frac{1}{2}$ cup) chopped parsley; 120 ml/4 fl oz ($\frac{1}{2}$ cup) vegetable oil; 1 onion, chopped; 4 eggs, beaten; 250 g/ 8 oz (2 cups) feta cheese, crumbled; 250 g/ 8 oz (2 cups) Cheddar cheese, grated; $\frac{1}{4}$ tsp cinnamon; $\frac{1}{4}$ tsp nutmeg; $\frac{1}{4}$ tsp salt; freshly ground black pepper; 20 sheets filo pastry.

Combine spinach, shallots and parsley in a large bowl. Heat 2 tbsp of the oil and gently fry onion until soft. Add to spinach mixture with eggs, feta and Cheddar cheeses, cinnamon, nutmeg, salt and pepper and mix well. Stack filo sheets between 2 dry tea-towels with a dampened towel on top. Lightly brush 1 sheet of filo pastry with oil and place in a greased baking dish, about 33 × 23 cm (13 × 9 in). Repeat until 10 sheets of filo have been used, brushing each with oil. Spread spinach mixture over filo. Cover with remaining sheets of filo pastry, brushing each with oil. Sprinkle water over

F

op sheet of filo. Bake in a preheated moderate oven (180°C/350°F, Gas Mark 4) for 45 minutes or until golden-brown. Cut into diamond shapes. Serves 6–8.

Lamb Filo Pie

2 tbsp olive oil; 2 onions, chopped; 1.25 kg/ 2½ lb (5 cups) minced (ground) lamb; 10 g/⅓ oz (¼ cup) chopped fresh mint; 1 tsp cinnamon; ¼ tsp nutmeg; salt; 90 g/3 oz (¾ cup) pine nuts; 500 g/1 lb (24 sheets) filo pastry; 250 g/8 oz (1 cup) butter, melted.

Heat oil in a large frying pan (skillet), add onions and cook until softened. Add lamb and sauté until browned. Drain off excess fat. Stir in mint, cinnamon, nutmeg, salt and pine nuts. Set aside. Stack filo sheets between 2 dry tea-towels with a dampened towel on top. Line a buttered 33 × 23 cm (13 × 9 in) baking dish with 4 sheets of filo, brushing each lightly with butter, and allowing ends to hang over sides of dish. Spread ¼ of lamb mixture over filo and top with 4 more filo sheets, each lightly brushed with butter. Continue layering filo and lamb mixture, reserving 4 sheets of filo and ending with lamb mixture. Fold overhanging ends of filo over lamb mixture in dish. Top with remaining 4 sheets of filo, each brushed with butter, and tuck ends down inside edge of dish to enclose filling completely. Bake in a preheated moderately hot oven (190°C/375°F, Gas Mark 5) for 45 minutes or until top is golden. Serve hot, cut into diamond shapes. Serves 10–12.

Ricotta and Artichoke Pie

olive oil; 3 shallots, chopped; 500 g/1 lb (2 cups) Ricotta cheese; 125 g/4 oz (1 cup) grated Gruyère cheese; 90 g/3 oz (¾ cup) grated Parmesan cheese; 120 ml/4 fl oz (½ cup) sour cream; 4 eggs, beaten; ½ tsp dried tarragon; 1 × 400 g/13 oz can artichoke hearts, drained and quartered; salt and freshly ground black pepper; 500 g/1 lb (24 sheets) filo pastry.

Heat 1 tbsp olive oil in a small frying pan (skillet), add shallots and cook until softened. Set aside. Place Ricotta, Gruyère and Parmesan cheeses in a large bowl and add sour cream, eggs and tarragon. Mix until thoroughly combined. Stir in shallots, artichoke hearts, salt and pepper. Stack sheets of filo between 2 dry tea-towels with a dampened towel on top. Brush a 25 cm (10 in) springform tin (pan) with olive oil. Line tin (pan) with 5 sheets of filo pastry, each brushed lightly with olive oil, overlapping them and allowing ends to hang over sides of tin (pan). Spread half cheese mixture over filo. Top with 5 more sheets of filo, brushed with oil. Add remaining cheese mixture, spreading evenly, fold in overhanging pastry

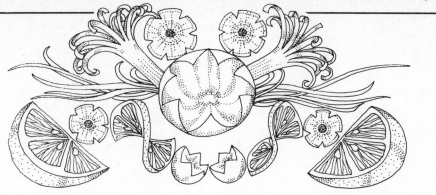

and then top with remaining filo sheets, each lightly brushed with oil. Tuck overhanging ends down inside tin (pan), enclosing filling completely. Bake in a preheated moderately hot oven (200°C/400°F, Gas Mark 6) for 40–45 minutes or until top is golden. Let pie cool completely in tin (pan). Serves 8–10.

Indian Beef Triangles

150 g/5 oz (½ cup plus 2 tbsp) butter; 1 large onion, chopped; 2 cloves garlic, crushed; 2 tbsp curry powder; 1½ tsp grated fresh ginger; 1½ tsp salt; 1 tsp sugar; ¼ tsp cayenne; 750 g/1½ lb (3 cups) minced (ground) beef; 500 g/1 lb (24 sheets) filo pastry.

Melt 30 g/1 oz (2 tbsp) butter in a large, heavy frying pan (skillet). Add onion and garlic and cook until onion has softened. Stir in curry powder, ginger, salt, sugar and cayenne and cook for 1 minute. Add beef and cook until browned and crumbly. Set aside. Melt remaining butter and cool slightly. Stack sheets of filo between 2 dry tea-towels with a dampened towel on top. Brush 1 sheet of filo with melted butter, cut in half lengthways, and fold each half in half lengthways. Brush halves with butter. Place 1½ tsp of meat mixture in corner of one end of each half. Fold filo over filling, enclosing it to form a triangle. Continue to fold pastry over in triangles until you come to the end of strip. Make triangles with remaining filo and meat filling. Place on a buttered baking tray and brush with melted butter. Bake in a preheated moderately hot oven (190°C/375°F, Gas Mark 5) for 20–25 minutes or until golden. Makes 48.

Greek Custard Pie

1 litre/1¾ pints (4 cups) milk; 180 g/6 oz (¾ cup) sugar; 140 g/4½ oz (¾ cup) fine semolina; 1 cinnamon stick; 1 tsp grated lemon rind; pinch salt; 5 eggs, lightly beaten; 1 tsp vanilla essence (extract); 250 g/8 oz (12 sheets) filo pastry; 180 g/6 oz (¾ cup) unsalted butter, melted.
SYRUP: 250 ml/8 fl oz (1 cup) water; 250 g/8 oz (1 cup) sugar; 1 cinnamon stick; 1 tbsp lemon juice; 1 strip lemon rind.

Mix milk, sugar, semolina, cinnamon, lemon and salt in a heavy saucepan and stir over

low heat until thickened. Simmer 5 minutes, then remove from heat. Discard cinnamon stick. Cover surface of mixture with plastic wrap to prevent a skin from forming, and cool. When cool, add eggs and vanilla and mix thoroughly. Stack sheets of filo between 2 dry tea-towels with a dampened towel on top. Place 1 sheet of filo in a greased 33 × 23 cm (13 × 9 in) ovenproof dish and brush it with melted butter. Repeat until you have used half the filo. Pour in custard mixture and top with remaining filo, brushing each sheet with butter.

Trim edges of filo to fit dish and brush top with remaining butter. With a sharp knife, cut through top 3 sheets of filo in a diamond pattern. Bake in a preheated moderate oven (180°C/350°F, Gas Mark 4) for 45 minutes or until pastry is golden-brown and a thin knife inserted into custard comes out clean. Remove from oven and cool in dish.
SYRUP: Place all ingredients in a saucepan and bring to the boil, stirring until sugar has dissolved. Boil over moderate heat 10 minutes, then strain and cool to lukewarm. When pie is cold, pour over lukewarm syrup and leave to cool completely before serving. Serves 10–12.

Cream Cheese Slices

250 g/8 oz (1 cup) cream cheese or Ricotta cheese; 2 eggs; 125 g/4 oz (½ cup) sugar; 1 tbsp lemon juice; 90 g/3 oz (½ cup) sultanas (golden raisins); 125 g/4 oz (6 sheets) filo pastry, cut in half; 125 g/4 oz (½ cup) butter, melted.

Place cheese, eggs, sugar and lemon juice in a mixing bowl and beat well until smooth. Stir in sultanas (golden raisins). Stack filo between 2 dry tea-towels with a dampened towel on top. Place 1 sheet of filo in a greased 28 × 18 cm (11 × 7 in) baking dish, first brushing sheet with melted butter. Repeat until you have used half the filo. Spoon over cheese filling, and continue adding remaining filo sheets, brushing each with butter. Using a sharp knife, mark top filo layers into diamond shapes 6 × 4 cm (2½ × 1¾ in). Bake in a preheated moderate oven (180°C/350°F, Gas Mark 4) 20–30 minutes or until golden and filling is set. Serve cold. Makes about 18.

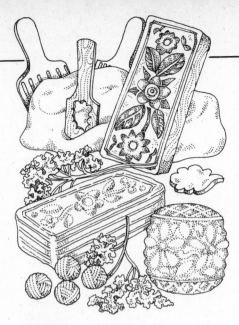

Nut Rolls

90 g/3 oz (¾ cup) finely chopped walnuts; 60 g/2 oz (½ cup) finely chopped almonds; 1 tsp sugar; ¼ tsp cinnamon; pinch nutmeg; 10 sheets filo pastry; 250 g/8 oz (1 cup) butter, melted.
CINNAMON HONEY SYRUP: *250 g/8 oz (1 cup) sugar; 150 ml/¼ pint (⅔ cup) water; 90 g/3 oz (¼ cup) honey; 1 small cinnamon stick; 1 tsp fresh lemon juice.*

Mix together nuts, sugar and spices. Stack filo between 2 dry tea-towels with a dampened towel on top. Brush half of a sheet of filo with melted butter, fold other half over and brush with butter so that you have a piece of filo 18 × 30 cm (7 × 12 in). Sprinkle with 1 tbsp of nut mixture. Beginning at one end, roll filo as you would a jam (jelly) roll. Cut in 3. Place on greased baking tray with smooth side of pastry rolls up and brush with melted butter. Repeat with remaining filo and nut filling. Bake in a preheated moderate oven (180°C/350°F, Gas Mark 4) for 20 minutes or until golden-brown.
CINNAMON HONEY SYRUP: Mix all ingredients together and simmer for 30 minutes. Cook only until light brown. Dip hot nut rolls into warm syrup. Makes 30.

FINNAN HADDIE

The smoked haddock of Scotland, which is split, flattened and smoked to a beautiful pale gold. The flavour is light and delicate and mixes well with cream, eggs, rice or potatoes.
□ **To Cook:** Finnan Haddie can be grilled (broiled), poached or baked. **See also recipes.**
GRILLED (BROILED) FINNAN HADDIE Rub with butter, place skin side down on a greased grill (broiler) tray and cook under a preheated moderate grill (broiler) on one side only for about 7 minutes. Serve with extra melted butter.
POACHED FINNAN HADDIE Place skin side down

in a shallow flameproof dish, cover with water, milk or a combination of both, and simmer very gently for 5–7 minutes or until flesh flakes. Drain well and remove skin and bones. Serve with melted butter or a Béchamel Sauce (see page 368), garnished with sliced hard-boiled (hard-cooked) eggs.
BAKED FINNAN HADDIE Place skin side down in a baking dish, dot with butter and add 250 ml/8 fl oz (1 cup) water. Bake uncovered, in a preheated moderate oven (180°C/350°F, Gas Mark 4) for 15 minutes or until flesh flakes. Remove fish, take off skin and bones and serve garnished with fresh dill, or accompany with Mushroom Sauce (see page 373) or a fresh Tomato Sauce (see page 370).

Creamed Finnan Haddie

500 g (1 lb) smoked haddock, cooked in half water, half milk; 22 g/¾ oz (1½ tbsp) butter; 1½ tbsp flour; 250 ml/8 fl oz (1 cup) single (light) cream; 250 ml/8 fl oz (1 cup) fish stock; freshly ground black pepper; ¼ tsp nutmeg.
GARNISH: *triangles of bread; butter for frying; 1 tbsp chopped parsley.*

Skin, bone and flake haddock and set aside. Melt butter in a saucepan, add flour and stir until smooth. Add cream and fish stock, stirring constantly until boiling. Simmer for 3 minutes. Season with pepper and nutmeg. Fry bread triangles in butter until golden-brown and drain on paper towels. Fold fish through cream sauce, reheat gently and pile into a heated serving dish. Serve surrounded with bread triangles and sprinkled with parsley. Serves 2–4.

Far Eastern Kedgeree

250 g (8 oz) smoked haddock, cooked, skinned, boned and flaked; 250 g/8 oz (2 cups) warm freshly boiled long-grain rice; 60 g/2 oz (4 tbsp) butter, melted; freshly ground black pepper; 2 tbsp oil; 60 g/2 oz (¼ cup) raw peanuts, shelled and skinned; 2 tbsp sultanas (golden raisins); 2 hard-boiled (hard-cooked) eggs, 1 chopped and 1 sliced; 2–3 tbsp single (light) cream (optional); chopped parsley.

Fork fish into warm rice, add butter and pepper and keep warm. Heat oil and fry peanuts until they are pale gold. Add sultanas (golden raisins) and continue frying for a few seconds until they are plump. Add these to fish and rice together with chopped egg and cream, if using. Pile on a heated dish, garnish with slices of hard-boiled (hard-cooked) egg and sprinkle with chopped parsley. Serves 4.

Omelette Arnold Bennett

This is an elegant dish, created for the writer Arnold Bennett by the Savoy Grill in London.

60 g/2 oz (4 tbsp) butter; 120 ml/4 fl oz (½ cup) single (light) cream; 4 tbsp cooked, skinned, boned and flaked smoked haddock; 4 eggs, separated; 3 tbsp grated Parmesan cheese; salt and freshly ground white pepper.

Melt 30 g/1 oz (2 tbsp) butter and 2 tbsp cream in a frying pan (skillet) over medium heat, add haddock and stir for 2–3 minutes. Leave to cool. Beat egg yolks with 1 tbsp cream. Whisk egg whites to form very soft peaks and fold into yolks with haddock and half the cheese. Season with salt and pepper. Melt rest of butter in the pan, pour in omelette mixture and cook until golden and set underneath. Do not fold omelette but slide on to a heated flameproof serving dish. Sprinkle on rest of cheese and pour remaining cream over it. Brown quickly under a preheated hot grill (broiler) and serve at once. Serves 2.

FISH

Fish is the gourmet's joy, the hurried cook's friend, a boon to weight-watchers and the cholesterol-conscious, being highly nutritious, digestible and always tender. Select fish carefully, use it promptly and cook it briefly and it will reward you with fine eating.

Freshness is all-important. A fish which has been kept a day too long in the shop or in your refrigerator may still be perfectly edible, but the best of its pure and delicate flavour will have disappeared. When buying a whole fish, check for full, bright eyes, flat gills, which are red underneath, and a clenched mouth. It should feel slippery not tacky, and should smell 'of the sea' – fishy but fresh.

When buying fish steaks or fillets, be especially careful. Sometimes stale fish are filleted and labelled 'fresh fillets'. Again, they should smell fishy but fresh, and have a sheen, not a dull surface. If pressed, the flesh should feel springy and the indentation should quickly disappear. If the flesh oozes and the indentation fills with moisture, then the steak or fillet has been frozen and thawed and should not be offered as fresh fish.

Buy fish on the day you will eat it, if possible. If you must keep it overnight, store it, loosely covered in foil, in the coldest part of the refrigerator.

Fish can be divided into 2 types, fat and lean.
Fat Fish includes mullet and all those which are commercially canned or smoked – salmon, trout, herring, sardines, tuna, mackerel, and so on. These are technically classified as 'oily' fish, though they come in many variations of texture and fat content. In general, dark-fleshed fish are the oiliest.

Fat fish are a good choice for grilling (broiling), baking, barbecuing or hot-plate griddling: the more delicate ones are also good pan-fried or poached.

Lean (white) Fish includes cod, plaice, haddock, whiting, bream, John Dory, snapper, sole, flounder and perch. They are a good choice for pan-frying, deep-frying or poaching. If baked or grilled (broiled), they should be protected from drying out by basting; a stuffing also helps to keep the flesh moist.

□ **Basic Preparation:** If you are buying fish, ask the fishmonger to clean and scale it for you. He will also skin, fillet or cut it into steaks if you ask. If you have caught it or been given it, you can prepare it at home.

To scale a fish: Working on plenty of newspaper, grasp the tail and scrape firmly from the tail towards the head with a small rigid knife or a serrated, fish-scaling knife. Repeat on the other side.

To clean a fish: Cut open along the belly from the vent (near the tail) to the head, and pull out the entrails. Wash the fish inside and out under cold running water. With a small knife, remove any dark stomach lining or dark vein inside under the backbone. Wash again and dry the fish well.

To fillet round fish: Place fish on a board and grasp firmly. With a sharp, flexible knife, remove head and cut along the backbone to the tail (**Fig 1 below**). Starting at the head end, slide the knife closely along the backbone, cutting away the fillet all the way to the tail (**2**). Turn the fish over and repeat on the other side, cutting off the tail (**3**).

To fillet flat fish: These fish yield 4 fillets – 2 on each side. Place fish on a board and grasp the head firmly. Cut round behind the head and down the backbone from head to tail. Using a sharp, flexible knife slide the blade closely down the backbone to the tail on one side, cutting away the fillet. Remove the second fillet in the same way. Turn fish over and repeat on the other side.

To skin a fish fillet: Place the fillet, skin side down, on a board with the tail towards you. Make a small cut through the flesh at the tail end. Dip the fingers of one hand in salt and hold the tail firmly, while with the other hand

Filleting a round fish

ease a sharp, flexible knife between flesh and skin, pushing the flesh off the skin.

□ **To Cook:** Fish should be moist and juicy when served, and must not be cooked beyond the moment when the flesh turns from translucent to opaque. This usually takes minutes only. If cooking a whole fish, start testing halfway through the recommended cooking time by pushing a fine skewer into the thickest part near the bone. When it slides in easily and you can push the flesh away from the bone just a little, the fish is cooked. **See recipes.**

PAN-FRIED FISH Use clarified butter (see page 49) or a mixture of oil and butter, enough to cover the base of the pan. When sizzling well, place fish in and cook quickly. Before frying, the fish may be coated with seasoned flour or with egg and breadcrumbs.

FISH MEUNIERE Skin fillets of white fish, dust with seasoned flour and pan-fry as above. Remove to a heated plate when done. Add a little more butter to the pan and while it is foaming, add the strained juice of a lemon, chopped parsley, salt and freshly ground black pepper. Pour over the fish, garnish with lemon and serve at once.

DEEP-FRIED FISH Coat fish with egg and breadcrumbs or with batter; very small fish such as whitebait may simply be dipped in milk and seasoned flour. Deep-fry in very hot oil (190°C/375°F) or test oil with a bread cube: if it browns in 30 seconds the oil is hot enough. Drain on crumpled paper towels.

POACHED FISH Use Court Bouillon (see page 85), water acidulated with vinegar or lemon juice or a mixture of wine and water – there should be just enough to cover fish. Cover dish with buttered greaseproof (waxed) paper and cook very gently so that the liquid barely shivers, never bubbles, on top of the stove, or in a preheated moderate oven (160°C/325°F, Gas Mark 3). The poaching liquor is often used for a sauce to accompany the fish.

GRILLED (BROILED) FISH Preheat the grill (broiler) so that fish will cook as fast as possible. For fillets and small steaks, line the grill (broiler) pan with foil, melt a little butter in it and grill (broil) the fish on one side only –

the heat of the pan will cook the underside. Baste once or twice with pan juices.

Large steaks and small whole fish can be grilled (broiled) in the same way, but turn them halfway through cooking. Slash whole fish in the thickest part so that heat can penetrate.

BARBECUED FISH Place fish in an oiled, hinged grill for ease of turning. Cook close to very hot coals, brushing several times with oil or melted butter.

BAKED FISH Brush fish with oil or melted butter, place in a well-greased ovenproof dish and season with salt, freshly ground black pepper and a sprinkling of lemon juice or white wine. Cover loosely with buttered foil or greaseproof (waxed) paper and bake in a preheated moderately hot oven (200°C/400°F, Gas Mark 6), allowing 6–10 minutes (depending on thickness of the fish) per 500 g (1 lb), plus 6–10 minutes over. Uncover and brush once or twice with pan juices during cooking.

Ways to Use Preserved Fish

SMOKED FISH See *Finnan Haddie* and use the same methods for grilling (broiling), poaching or baking any smoked fish.

PICKLED FISH Pickling is an excellent way of preserving oily-fleshed fish such as herring. Pickled herring are available packed in jars.

Pickled rollmops are boned, halved herrings, rolled around peppercorns and onion slices. Try them on black bread spread with unsalted butter and accompany with a salad of baby beetroot.

DRIED FISH Fish such as cod and haddock can be dried to a flatness and hardness resembling hide. It is reconstituted by soaking in water for at least 12 hours. Change the water several times during this period.

SALTED FISH Use salt cod to make *Brandade de Morue* (see page 43), a deliciously light dish from Provence, which is almost a fish purée.

Grilled (Broiled) Sardines Grilled (broiled) or barbecued fresh sardines make a memorable first course. Rub off scales with a cloth or soft paper. Leave sardines whole or butterfly them. If leaving whole, there is no need to gut them – eat flesh off bone in same way as you would eat corn on the cob.

To butterfly them, cut the head almost through from backbone; pull, and as head comes off the gut will come with it. Slit fish along belly and lift out backbone, cutting it off with scissors close to the tail (leave tail on).

Rinse and dry sardines; turn them in seasoned flour, brush with oil and arrange side by side in an oiled, hinged grill. Grill (broil) or barbecue close to high heat, brushing several times with oil, for 2–3 minutes each side. Serve with lemon wedges and crusty bread. Allow 500 g (1 lb) sardines to serve 4 as a first course.

See also *Anchovy* and *Tuna*.

Whiting or John Dory Fillets with Vermouth Sauce

90 g/3 oz (6 tbsp) butter, melted; 8 whiting or John Dory fillets, skinned; 4 tbsp dry vermouth; 1 tbsp lemon juice; 1 tsp tomato purée (paste); salt and freshly ground black pepper; 120 ml/4 fl oz (½ cup) single (light) cream; chopped parsley; puff pastry fleurons (page 126) to garnish.

Brush a large, flameproof baking dish generously with some of the butter and lay fillets in it side by side. Blend remaining butter with vermouth, lemon juice and tomato purée (paste). Pour over fish, season with salt and pepper and place over high heat. Cook, basting fish with pan juices, until flesh turns white. Lift fish on to a heated serving dish. Add cream to baking dish and stir until sauce thickens a little. Pour over fish, sprinkle with parsley and serve immediately, garnished with fleurons. Serves 4.

Oven-fried Fillets Niçoise

2 tsp salt; 250 ml/8 fl oz (1 cup) milk; 90 g/3 oz (1½ cups) fresh breadcrumbs; 3 tbsp chopped parsley; 2 cloves garlic, finely chopped; 1 tsp grated lemon rind; 1 tsp chopped fresh thyme, or ¼ tsp dried; 6 white fish fillets (plaice, sole, cod), skinned; 90 g/3 oz (6 tbsp) butter, melted; paprika; lemon wedges to garnish.

Mix salt and milk. Mix breadcrumbs, parsley, garlic, lemon rind and thyme. Dip fillets in milk, then in breadcrumb mixture. Arrange side by side in a well-buttered baking dish and drizzle melted butter over. Bake on the top shelf of a preheated hot oven (230°C/450°F, Gas Mark 8) for about 12 minutes or until the fish flakes easily when tested with a fine skewer. Sprinkle with a little paprika and serve immediately, garnished with lemon wedges. Serves 4–6.

Fish Steaks Baked in Cream

4 thick fish steaks (cod, haddock); salt and freshly ground black pepper; 250 ml/8 fl oz (1 cup) single (light) cream; 1 tbsp lemon juice; 1 tbsp French (Dijon) mustard; 1 tsp Worcestershire sauce; fresh coriander leaves or chopped parsley.

Arrange fish steaks side by side in a buttered, shallow flameproof dish. Season with salt and pepper. Blend cream with lemon juice, mustard and Worcestershire sauce and pour over fish. Cover dish with buttered greaseproof (waxed) paper and bake in a preheated moderate oven (160°C/325°F, Gas Mark 3) for 20 minutes or until fish flakes easily when tested with a fine skewer. Lift steaks on to a heated serving platter and keep warm. Place flameproof dish over high heat and boil liquid, stirring, until it is slightly

reduced and thickened. Adjust seasoning and spoon over fish. Scatter with coriander leaves or chopped parsley and serve immediately. Serves 4.

Mediterranean Mullet

45 g/1½ oz (3 tbsp) butter; 2 tomatoes, peeled and sliced; 1 small green pepper, cored, seeded and sliced; 125 g/4 oz (1 cup) mushrooms, sliced; salt and freshly ground black pepper; 4 red mullet, whiting or other small whole fish, scaled and cleaned; 4 tbsp red wine; 2 tbsp chopped chives.

Melt 30 g/1 oz (2 tbsp) butter in a shallow flameproof casserole or gratin dish. Add vegetables and cook gently for 5 minutes, stirring occasionally. Season with salt and pepper. Place fish side by side on top of vegetables and pour over wine. Sprinkle with chives and dot with remaining butter. Cover and bake in a preheated moderate oven (180°C/350°F, Gas Mark 4) for 20–30 minutes or until the fish flakes easily when tested with a fine skewer. Serves 4.

Sardinian-Style Tuna

4 tuna or halibut steaks, 2.5 cm (1 in) thick; salt and freshly ground black pepper; flour for dusting; 3 tbsp olive oil; 1 small onion, chopped; 1 clove garlic, crushed; 750 g (1½ lb) tomatoes, peeled; 2 tbsp chopped parsley; 1 bay leaf; 4 anchovy fillets, mashed; few black (ripe) olives.

Season fish with salt and pepper and dust with flour. Heat 2 tbsp oil in a large shallow pan and fry fish quickly until golden on each side. Transfer to a plate. Add remaining oil to pan and fry onion and garlic gently for 5 minutes. Press tomatoes through a coarse sieve or purée in a blender. Add parsley, bay leaf and anchovy to pan and stir for a few seconds. Add tomatoes, bring to the boil and continue boiling until mixture has reduced to a thin sauce consistency. Season with pepper. Replace fish and simmer gently for 15 minutes, turning fish steaks once during cooking. Turn off heat, add olives and leave for 5 minutes. Remove bay leaf and serve with a crisp green salad. Serves 4.

Deep-Fried Szechuan Fish

1 × 750 g (1½ lb) whole fish (plaice, flounder, sole or bream), scaled and cleaned; 1 tsp grated fresh ginger; 3 shallots, chopped; 2 tsp salt; 2 tbsp dry sherry; oil for deep-frying; 1 tsp ground Szechuan pepper or black pepper; 2 tbsp sesame oil; lemon slices to garnish.

Dry fish on paper towels and score each side diagonally to make a diamond pattern. Place ginger, shallots, 1 tsp salt and the sherry in a dish. Add fish, spoon marinade over and

leave for 30 minutes. Drain fish and dry on paper towels. Heat oil to medium, and deep-fry fish until golden-brown, about 7–10 minutes depending on thickness of fish. Remove and drain on crumpled paper towels. Sprinkle with pepper and remaining salt. Heat sesame oil to moderately hot, pour over fish and serve immediately, garnished with lemon slices. Serves 2–4.

Fried Marinated Fish

Marinating fish after frying is a good way of adding flavour to fresh water fish or eel.

500 g (1 lb) filleted fresh water fish (perch, mullet or eel), cut into 2.5 cm (1 in) wide strips; 2 tbsp milk; seasoned flour for coating; oil for frying.
MARINADE: *2 tbsp oil; 1 small onion, finely sliced; 1 large clove garlic, crushed; 1 yellow or green pepper, grilled (broiled) skinned, cored and seeded; 4 tbsp dry white wine; 2 tbsp wine vinegar; 3 leaves fresh sage; 1 tsp sugar; salt and freshly ground black pepper.*

Dip fish strips in milk, drain and then coat in seasoned flour. Heat enough oil in a shallow frying pan (skillet) to give a depth of about 5 mm (¼ in). Fry fish until crisp and golden on both sides and cooked through. Drain on paper towels and arrange, closely packed, in a shallow serving dish.
MARINADE: Heat oil in a saucepan and fry onion and garlic very gently for about 8 minutes or until soft and golden. Cut pepper into fine strips, add to pan and fry for 3–4 minutes. Stir in wine, vinegar, sage leaves, sugar, salt and pepper. Bring to the boil and simmer for 1–2 minutes, then pour over fish. Cover and leave in a cold place overnight. Serve cold as antipasto. Serves 4.

Soused Fish

1 onion, sliced; 6 small mullet, herring or mackerel, filleted; 2 bay leaves; 1 clove; 4 whole allspice or black peppercorns; 1 tsp salt; 120 ml/4 fl oz (½ cup) vinegar.

Place slices of onion on the centre of each fillet and roll up, skin side out, from head to tail, securing with a wooden toothpick if necessary. Place fish in a flameproof casserole with bay leaves, clove, allspice or

peppercorns and salt. Pour over vinegar and just cover with water. Cover casserole and heat very gently until simmering point is reached. Transfer dish to a preheated moderate oven (160°C/325°F, Gas Mark 3) and cook for about 1 hour or until fish flakes easily when tested with a fine skewer. Transfer fish to a serving dish, deep enough so that the rolls can be covered with liquid. Strain over sufficient cooking liquid to cover. Cool, then chill. Serves 6.
NOTE: This dish will keep for up to 2 weeks in the refrigerator.

Fish Fried in Batter

For the classic fish-and-chip shop style, use Basic Batter mixture to coat the fish. For a light, crisp coating use Crisp Fritter Batter (page 130).

4 large or 6 small white fish fillets; flour for coating; 1 quantity Basic Batter (page 28); oil for frying.

Check that fillets are well scaled and remove as many bones as possible (long-nose pliers or strong tweezers are a help). Coat fillets with flour and pat off excess. Dip each into batter, holding by the tail and allowing surplus batter to drip back into bowl. Have 1 cm (½ in) hot oil ready in a frying pan (skillet) – oil is hot enough when a slight haze rises from it. Place fillets in oil, skinless side down first, and fry 3–4 minutes on each side. Do not crowd pan; fry fish in batches if necessary, adding a little more oil as required. Drain on crumpled paper towels. Keep cooked fish hot on paper towels in a warm oven until all are done, then serve immediately. Serves 4–6.

Baked Fish with Oysters and Herbs

1 × 1.5–2 kg (3–4 lb) whole fish; 60 g/2 oz (4 tbsp) butter, melted; 125 g/4 oz (2 cups) fresh white breadcrumbs; 1 tsp dried marjoram; 2 tbsp chopped parsley; salt and freshly ground black pepper; cayenne; 2 thin rashers (slices) bacon; 300 ml/½ pint (1 cup) oysters.

Have fish cleaned and scaled but leave head and tail intact. Heat butter in a frying pan (skillet) and lightly brown crumbs. Add marjoram, parsley, salt, pepper and cayenne and mix well. Stuff fish loosely with herb mixture and close with skewers and string. Place fish in baking pan lined with greased foil and arrange bacon on top. Bake, uncovered, in a preheated moderate oven (180°C/350°F, Gas Mark 4) for 30–40 minutes or until fish flakes easily when tested with a fine skewer. Using foil as handles, transfer fish to a heated platter. Discard bacon. Garnish with oysters that have been simmered in their juices for 1 minute. Serves 6–8.

Fish Cakes

60 g/2 oz (4 tbsp) butter; 4 tsp finely chopped onion or chives; 500 g/1 lb (2 cups) mashed potatoes; 1 × 250 g/8 oz can tuna in oil or salmon, drained and flaked; squeeze lemon juice; salt and freshly ground black pepper; 1 egg, beaten; 125 g/4 oz (1 cup) dry breadcrumbs; oil or butter for frying.

Beat butter and onion into mashed potatoes. Add tuna or salmon and season with lemon juice, salt and pepper. Form into 6 small cakes. Dip in beaten egg, then in breadcrumbs. Fry in a little oil or butter until nicely browned. Serve with Sauce Tartare (page 205) or dill mayonnaise made by combining 120 ml/4 fl oz (½ cup) Mayonnaise (page 204) with 1 tbsp chopped fresh dill or 1 tsp dried dill. Serves 3.

Skate with Black Butter Sauce

1 × 750 g–1 kg (1½–2 lb) wing skate, scaled and cleaned; 3 tbsp vinegar; 3 tsp salt; 1 bay leaf; 1 onion, sliced; 4 black peppercorns; few stalks parsley; 3 tsp finely chopped parsley; 3 tsp chopped capers; 60 g/2 oz (4 tbsp) butter.

Place skate in a pan sufficiently wide for fish to lie flat while cooking. Cover with cold water, add 1 tbsp vinegar, the salt, bay leaf, onion, peppercorns and parsley stalks and bring gently to the boil. Simmer very gently for 20–25 minutes, depending on thickness of fish. Lift with a fish slice on to a board or clean folded tea-towel. Scrape away the skin from both sides and remove flesh from the large bone. Transfer to a heated serving dish, sprinkle with chopped parsley and capers and keep hot. Heat butter in a small frying pan (skillet) until it turns brown but not in the least burnt. Pour quickly over fish. Add remaining 2 tbsp vinegar to pan and boil to reduce by half. Pour over fish and serve immediately. Serves 4.

Fish à la Grecque

1 × 1.5 kg (3 lb) whole fish (red snapper or bream), scaled and cleaned; salt and freshly ground black pepper; lemon juice; 1 onion, chopped; 1 clove garlic, crushed; 1 tbsp finely chopped parsley; 1 tbsp olive oil; 3 tomatoes, peeled, seeded and chopped; 120 ml/4 fl oz (½ cup) dry white wine; lemon wedges to garnish.

Sprinkle fish inside and out with salt, pepper and lemon juice and place in a baking dish lined with greased foil. Sauté onion and garlic with parsley in olive oil until soft. Add tomatoes to onion mixture. Fry gently for a few minutes, then add a little water and simmer a few minutes longer. Spoon this mixture over fish. Pour wine over and around fish. Cook in a preheated moderate

oven (180°C/350°F, Gas Mark 4) for about 40 minutes or until fish flakes easily when tested with a fine skewer. Garnish with lemon. Serves 4.

FLAN

An open round pastry case (dough shell) filled with fruit, cream or a savoury mixture. A *flan case* is a pastry (dough) shell which is either baked blind (*see Pastry*), or with the required filling. Use 1 quantity of Pâte Brisée for a savoury flan or 1 quantity of Pâte Sucrée for a sweet flan to line a 20 cm (8 in) flan ring (*see Pastry*). Ease the uncooked dough in from the edge of the flan ring before baking to help prevent pastry (dough) from sticking.

Flan tins (pans) have a moveable base so you can easily remove the tin (pan) from the sides of the pastry (dough). When flan is baked, sit it on a jar, carefully ease the sides away from the pastry (dough) and let outer ring fall on to the table, leaving the pastry (dough) sides exposed. Carefully slide the flan off the metal base, using a spatula, and place on a serving platter. **See recipes.**

See also *Quiche* and *Tarts and Tartlets.*

Glazed Strawberry Flan

1 quantity Pâte Sucrée (page 276).
FILLING: *250 g/8 oz (1 cup) cream cheese; 125 g/4 oz (½ cup) sugar; 1 tsp grated lemon rind; 1 tbsp orange juice; 1 tbsp single (light) cream; 250 g (8 oz) strawberries, hulled.*
GLAZE: *180 g/6 oz (½ cup) redcurrant jelly; 1 tbsp water; 2 tsp Cointreau or Grand Marnier, or 2 tbsp orange juice.*

Roll out pastry (dough) thinly and use to line a 20 cm (8 in) flan ring. Chill for at least 30 minutes. Prick bottom all over with a fork, then bake blind in a preheated moderately hot oven (190°C/375°F, Gas Mark 5) for about 20 minutes or until pastry (dough) is a pale biscuit colour. Allow to cool.
FILLING: Cream together all ingredients except strawberries and chill.
GLAZE: Heat jelly and water in a small saucepan, stirring until smooth. Cool slightly. Stir in liqueur or orange juice.
TO ASSEMBLE: Put cream cheese filling in flan case and smooth surface with a spatula. Carefully decorate with strawberries. Spoon glaze over them and chill. Serves 6.

French Apple Flan

*1 quantity Pâte Sucrée (page 276); 1 kg
(2 lb) cooking (tart) apples, peeled, cored
and sliced; 60 g/2 oz (4 tbsp) butter; 2 tbsp
sugar; caster sugar for sprinkling.
APRICOT GLAZE: 180 g/6 oz (½ cup) apricot
jam; 1 tbsp water; 2 tbsp orange juice.*

Roll out pastry (dough) thinly and use to line
a 20 cm (8 in) flan ring. Chill for at least 30
minutes. Prick bottom all over with a fork.
Put apple slices in a frying pan (skillet) with
butter and sugar, and cook over a low heat
for about 3 minutes. Fill pastry (dough) case
with apples, reserving best slices for the top.
Arrange them in overlapping circles, by
starting at the edge of the pastry (dough)
and forming smaller and smaller circles until
apples underneath are completely covered.
Brush top with a little of the butter in which
apples were cooked and sprinkle with caster
sugar. Bake in a preheated moderately hot
oven (190°C/375°F, Gas Mark 5) for 20–25
minutes or until the edges of apple slices are
tinged a golden-brown.
APRICOT GLAZE: Heat jam and water in a
small saucepan, stirring until blended. Rub
through a sieve and cool a little. Stir in
orange juice and keep warm. Remove flan
from oven and, while still warm, brush with
apricot glaze. Serves 8.

Flan aux Pruneaux
(Prune Tart)

*1 tsp tea leaves; 500 g (1 lb) large dessert
prunes; 1 quantity Rich Shortcrust Pastry
(page 274); 1 egg; 120 ml/4 fl oz (½ cup)
single (light) cream; 1 tsp cornflour
(cornstarch); 60 g/2 oz (¼ cup) caster sugar;
2 tbsp Cointreau or Grand Marnier;
30 g/1 oz (2 tbsp) butter.*

Make a weak tea, strain and pour over
prunes. Soak for 4 hours. Roll out pastry
(dough) and use to line a greased 20 cm
(8 in) flan ring. Drain and stone prunes, then
spread out in pastry (dough) case. Bake in
a preheated moderately hot oven.
(200°C/400°F, Gas Mark 6) for about 20
minutes. Meanwhile, beat egg with cream,
cornflour (cornstarch), sugar and liqueur.
Remove tart from oven, pour custard
mixture over and dot with butter. Return to
oven and bake for further 10–15 minutes to
set custard. Cool on wire rack. Serves 6–8.

FLAPJACK

A favourite breakfast all over North America
consists of a stack of thick pancakes with
butter and maple syrup accompanied by
bacon, ham or sausage. The pancakes are
large, but tender and light. They are known by
many names – griddle cakes, hot cakes,
flannel cakes, wheat cakes and flapjacks.

Flapjacks

*250 g/8 oz (2 cups) self-raising flour; ½ tsp
salt; 2 tsp sugar; 3 eggs; 400 ml/⅔ pint (1⅔
cups) milk; 60 g/2 oz (4 tbsp) butter, melted.*

Sift flour and salt together into a bowl and
sprinkle sugar over. Beat eggs with milk and
pour over flour. Stir just until all the flour is
moistened – batter will be lumpy. Lightly stir
in melted butter. Heat a heavy, greased
frying pan (skillet) or griddle until a drop of
cold water, flicked on to the surface, bounces
and sputters. Pour batter on to make
pancakes spaced a little apart, using a
1-tablespoon ladle for small pancakes or a
larger measure for larger ones. Cook until
pancakes are full of bubbles on top and
undersides are browned, then turn and cook
other sides. Serve in a stack with butter in
between. Makes 12–15 × 15 cm (6 in)
flapjacks.

FLEURONS

Small ovals, diamonds or crescents of puff
pastry (paste), which are used to garnish
certain dishes finished with a rich sauce, or
are served with elegant soups.
To make fleurons: Roll out trimmings of puff
pastry (paste) thinly, brush the surface with
beaten egg and cut shapes 6–8 cm (2½–3 in)
in length. Bake in a preheated hot oven
(230°C/450°F, Gas Mark 8) for 6–8 minutes
until golden. Serve 1–2 with each portion.

FLOATING ISLAND (Ile Flottante)

See page 97 for recipe.

FLORENTINES

These great European favourites are
flavoured with fruit and nuts, and spread with
chocolate after baking.

Florentines

*90 g/3 oz (6 tbsp) butter; 125 g/4 oz (½ cup)
sugar; 125 g/4 oz (1 cup) roughly chopped,
blanched almonds; 3 tbsp chopped raisins;
45 g/1½ oz (¼ cup) chopped mixed candied
peel; 60 g/2 oz (¼ cup) chopped glacé
(candied) cherries; 2 tbsp double (heavy)
cream, whipped; finely grated rind ¼ lemon;
180 g/6 oz (1 cup) plain (semi-sweet)
chocolate, broken in pieces.*

Melt butter and sugar in a saucepan and boil
for 1 minute. Remove from heat and stir in
all remaining ingredients except the
chocolate. Leave to cool. Put teaspoons of
the mixture on greased, foil-lined baking
trays in heaps well apart – 4 or 5 per tray.
Bake in the centre of a preheated moderate
oven (180°C/350°F, Gas Mark 4) for 10–12
minutes or until golden-brown. Remove and
cool until just firm, pressing edges back to a
neat shape. Remove carefully to a wire rack
and leave until cold. Melt chocolate in a
heatproof bowl over a saucepan of hot
water. Spread chocolate over smooth side of
each florentine; as chocolate sets, mark into
wavy lines with a fork. Leave to harden. The
florentines can be stored (without chocolate)
for about a week in an airtight container with
greaseproof (waxed) paper separating them.
Makes 24.

FLOUR

The indispensable item in store cupboards,
milled from grains or cereals such as rye,
wheat, rice and corn. Wheat flour is most
used in cooking and is classified according to
the type of wheat milled, which varies
through hard to soft. Wheat flours can be
highly refined white or coarse ground
wholewheat.

Types of Flour

All-purpose flour is used for all types of
cooking in the U.S.A.; it has no raising agent.
It is milled from a blend of medium to strong
wheats.
Atta flour is a fine ground wholewheat flour
used to make Indian flatbreads.
Arrowroot is an excellent thickening agent,
especially for fruit sauces or pie fillings as it
becomes clear when cooked. Do not overcook arrowroot as it has a tendency to
become thin again.
Buckwheat flour is also known as saracen
corn or beechwheat. It is used to make Blini
(see page 39), the traditional little yeast
pancakes of Russia which are eaten with
caviar and sour cream. It is also used for some
crêpes, and added to other flours in
breadmaking.
Chick pea (Besan) flour is used for batters,
especially for *pakoras*, little Indian fritters, or
to thicken soups, stews and gravies.
Cornflour (cornstarch) is used as a thickening
agent; also in shortbreads and biscuits
(cookies) when a particularly short texture is
needed and in cakes and puddings for extra
lightness. Pure cornflour (cornstarch) is

made from the heart of the maize kernel which is ground to a very fine, silky powder. Some cornflour (cornstarch) is made from wheat, and this is stated on the packet.

Plain flour is produced from soft wheat grain that is refined and bleached to give the familiar fine white flour. The low gluten content gives a light, short texture which makes it excellent for baking cakes, biscuits (cookies), pastries and scones. Plain flour can be substituted for self-raising flour by adding 30 g/1 oz (2 tbsp) baking powder to each 500 g/1 lb (4 cups) flour. Sift together 3 times before using.

Potato flour has much the same qualities as arrowroot and can be used in the same way.

Rice flour is made from very finely ground, polished rice grains. It is used as a thickening agent, and if you wish to freeze a dish, rice flour will help prevent the sauce separating during reheating.

Roti flour has a granular texture and is cream in colour. It is made from part of the wheat grain and is used for unleavened breads.

Rye flour is used for breads and crispbreads. Coarsely ground whole rye flour is used in pumpernickel, more finely ground in black bread, and a blend of rye and wheat flours is used in lightly coloured rye breads.

Self-raising (self-rising) flour is plain flour with the addition of baking powder as the raising agent. It is used to make standard butter cakes, sponge cakes, scones etc.

Strong plain white flour is a mixture of soft and hard wheat with a higher gluten content than plain flour. Strong flour is the one to use when baking breads, buns and pizzas as the gluten strands stretch and become flexible and elastic during kneading.

Wholewheat flour is milled from whole wheat grains, retaining most of their original vitamins, minerals, salts and fibre. Breads made from wholewheat taste delicious and produce loaves with a more dense texture than those made with plain white flour.

If you prefer a lighter loaf, use a mixture of half wholewheat flour and half strong flour. For wholewheat pastry (dough), sift the flour and use the fine part to make the dough. Retain the particles of grain and roll the dough in them before shaping. Do not buy more wholewheat flour than you need at one time and store in a very cool dry place.

FLUMMERY

The charming name of a very good old-fashioned, fluffy fruit dessert.

Passionfruit Flummery

1 tbsp gelatine; 120 ml/4 fl oz (½ cup) cold water; 2 tbsp flour; 250 g/8 oz (1 cup) sugar; 120 ml/4 fl oz (½ cup) orange juice; 250 ml/8 fl oz (1 cup) hot water; 1 tbsp lemon juice; 125 g/4 oz (½ cup) passionfruit pulp; cream or ice cream to serve.

Soak gelatine in cold water. Mix flour and sugar in a saucepan, blend to a smooth paste with a little orange juice, then stir in remaining orange juice and hot water. Stir over medium heat until mixture boils. Remove from heat, add soaked gelatine and stir until dissolved. Turn into a mixing bowl and chill until mixture is starting to thicken. Beat until very thick and at least doubled in volume. Add lemon juice and passionfruit, and chill until set. Serve with cream or ice cream. Serves 6.

FOIE GRAS

A great delicacy, made from the liver of especially fattened geese or from the livers of ducks or chickens. The finest *foie gras* comes from Alsace-Lorraine and Toulouse in France. *Pâté de foie gras* is a subtle mixture of goose liver, finely chopped veal and truffles enveloped in a rich pastry (dough).

A slice of *foie gras* basted with Madeira and stock (bouillon) is an essential part of the classic French dish Tournedos Rossini. The steaks are placed on warm artichoke bottoms, covered with a slice of *foie gras*, topped with slivers of truffles and served with a spoonful of Madeira Sauce (see page 369).

See also *Tournedos*.

FONDANT

See page 164 for recipes.

FONDUE

This means 'melted' in French, and the name now applies to a number of dishes. It is the name of a cheese dish, melted in wine, which originally came from Switzerland; under the same name comes a beef fondue from France, and a dessert fondue. Certain vegetable preparations are also called fondue. The vegetables in question are cooked for a very long time, often in butter, until they are reduced to pulp. Tomato Fondue is used in many other dishes. **See recipes.**

Fondue Utensils: Fondues are cooked and served in one communal pot. Each person is given a fork and spears a cube of bread, meat or fruit for dunking before eating.

The traditional fondue pot for cheese is made of earthenware and is wide and shallow, though cast-iron pots can also be used. Those for beef fondue are of metal – copper or stainless steel. Spirit burners, used for cheese and meat fondues, should be sturdy and easily regulated. For dessert fondues, use decorative ceramic pots kept warm over the gentle heat of a candle.

Fondue Bourguignonne Pieces of tender steak are speared and cooked in melted butter or a mixture of oil and butter for a minute or so until done to the guest's taste. The meat is then dipped into one of several sauces before it is eaten. The sauces may be tomato, curry, Béarnaise or soy, and it is traditional to try all the sauces on the table.

Dessert Fondue Made with hot chocolate melted in cream and flavoured with a liqueur. Squares of cake, marshmallows or fruit are dipped first into the sauce, then into dishes of desiccated (shredded) coconut or finely chopped mixed nuts.

Tomato Fondue

This recipe can be used as a garnish for eggs, vegetables or grilled (broiled) meats, fish or poultry or as an ingredient in dishes called provençale, portugaise, or madrilène.

60 g/2 oz (4 tbsp) butter, or 30 g/1 oz (2 tbsp) butter and 2 tbsp oil; 1 onion, chopped; 6–8 tomatoes, peeled, seeded and chopped; salt and freshly ground black pepper; 1 clove garlic, crushed; 1 tbsp chopped parsley.

Melt butter, or butter and oil, in a heavy saucepan and gently cook onion until golden. Add tomatoes, salt, pepper and garlic. Cover and simmer very gently for about 1 hour or until tomatoes have reduced to a thick pulp and liquid has almost disappeared. Stir in parsley. Makes about 350 ml/12 fl oz (1½ cups).

Swiss Fondue

A delicious dish for a small informal dinner party.

1 clove garlic, halved; 370 g/12 oz (3 cups) Emmenthal cheese, grated; 370 g/12 oz (3 cups) Gruyère cheese, grated; 2 tsp flour; 350 ml/12 fl oz (1½ cups) dry white wine; 1 tsp lemon juice; 1 tbsp Kirsch; ¼ tsp nutmeg; ¼ tsp black pepper; French bread cubes.

Rub inside of a deep flameproof casserole with garlic. Mix cheeses with flour and place in casserole with wine, lemon juice, Kirsch, nutmeg and pepper. Cook over a very low heat, stirring occasionally (the fondue should be a creamy consistency). Keep mixture hot over a table spirit burner and serve with cubes of bread. Guests spear the bread and dip it into cheese mixture. Serves 8.

FOOL

Fruit fool is a superbly simple, delicate dessert made with sweetened puréed fruit, thick cream and sometimes custard.

Fool

150 ml/¼ pint (⅔ cup) double (heavy) cream or 120 ml/4 fl oz (½ cup) double (heavy) cream and 5 tbsp thick custard; 400 ml/⅔ pint (1⅔ cups) fruit purée, sweetened to taste (choose fresh, frozen or canned strawberries, raspberries, rhubarb, apricots, blackcurrants or gooseberries (see below); sponge fingers (lady fingers) to serve.

Whip cream and fold into fruit. If using cream and custard, beat custard into fruit purée before folding in whipped cream. Pile into individual serving dishes. Chill and serve with sponge fingers (lady fingers). Decorate with additional cream if liked. Serves 4.
NOTE: Purée fresh strawberries and raspberries; lightly poach fresh rhubarb, apricots, blackcurrants or gooseberries and drain before puréeing; thaw and drain frozen fruits before puréeing; drain canned fruits before puréeing. The purée should be the consistency of thick cream and may be sweetened to taste.

FORCEMEAT

See Stuffings.

FOUR SPICES (Quatre Epices)

A blend of ground white pepper, cloves, nutmeg and ginger, sold everywhere in France and used in making pâtés, pies, sausages and brawns.

To make your own Four Spices, grind 30 g/1 oz (1 tbsp) white peppercorns and 1 tbsp whole cloves, coarsely chopped, to a fine powder in a blender. Mix with 1 tbsp freshly grated nutmeg and 1 scant tbsp ground ginger. Store in an airtight jar in a cool, preferably dark place.

Pâté de Campagne
(Country-style Pâté)

370 g (12 oz) chicken livers; 250 g (8 oz) streaky bacon; 250 g (8 oz) stewing veal; 2 cloves garlic, crushed; 8 juniper berries, crushed; ¼ tsp cracked black peppercorns; 120 ml/4 fl oz (½ cup) dry white wine; 2 tsp brandy; 1 large egg; 60 g/2 oz (1 cup) fresh white breadcrumbs; 1 tsp dried sage; 1 tsp dried thyme; ½ tsp Quatre Epices; 1 small onion, chopped; 60 g/2 oz (4 tbsp) butter; 1½ tsp salt; 1 thin slice pork back fat, beaten flat with side of a cleaver (ask butcher to do this) or 2 extra rashers (slices) streaky bacon.

Trim chicken livers, removing membranes and any discoloured parts. Chop fine and place in a bowl. Cover bacon with boiling water, stand 5 minutes, drain and remove rind. Mince (grind) bacon and veal coarsely, or chop in a food processor. Add to livers with garlic, juniper berries, cracked peppercorns, wine, brandy, egg, breadcrumbs, herbs and quatre épices. Mix well. Cover and leave 2–3 hours. Cook onion gently in butter until soft and add to meat mixture with salt. Press mixture into a greased terrine. Cut pork fat or extra bacon into strips and arrange in a lattice over top of pâté. Cover terrine with a lid of foil. Place terrine in a baking tin (pan) of warm water and bake in a preheated moderate oven (180°C/350°F, Gas Mark 4) for 2 hours. Remove from oven, remove terrine lid and place a light weight on top of pâté (e.g. a plate with a couple of cans of food on it). Leave pâté in refrigerator for 2 days before serving, cut into slices. Serves 6 as a lunch dish with salad.

FRANKFURTERS

Frankfurters are sausages, usually made from spiced beef and pork (kosher frankfurters are all beef) and lightly smoked. Manufacturers usually call their more lightly spiced varieties 'Continental' or 'Vienna' frankfurters.

They are fully cooked when bought and need only heating through. Frankfurters are good poached, grilled (broiled), barbecued, baked in a sauce or added to baked beans or to pea or potato soup. Serve them with hot or cold potato salad, creamy mashed potatoes, braised red cabbage, sauerkraut or coleslaw, and such condiments as mustard, dill pickles, tomato ketchup or chutney. **See recipes.**
POACHED FRANKFURTERS Place in hot water to cover and heat through at just below boiling point. Do not boil or the frankfurters may split.
GRILLED (BROILED) OR BARBECUED FRANKFURTERS Cut 2 or 3 diagonal slashes in the frankfurters and grill (broil) or barbecue at high heat until lightly browned. Baste with barbecue sauce if you wish.
BAKED FRANKFURTERS IN A SAUCE Pour 250 ml/8 fl oz (1 cup) of a well-flavoured sauce such as Barbecue Basting or Tomato Sauce (see pages 26 and 370) over 6 frankfurters arranged in a shallow ovenproof dish. Bake, uncovered, in a preheated moderate oven (180°C/350°F, Gas Mark 4) for about 20 minutes until heated through.

Frankfurter Kebabs

6 frankfurters; 120 ml/4 fl oz (½ cup) garlic-flavoured Vinaigrette Dressing (page 358); 2 thick rashers (slices) bacon, rind removed and cut into squares; 2 small onions, quartered and separated into layers; 1 small green pepper, cored, seeded and cut into squares; 18 cherry tomatoes, or 3–4 small firm tomatoes, cut into wedges; hot buttered rice to serve.

Cut frankfurters into short lengths and marinate 30 minutes in Vinaigrette dressing. Thread pieces on to skewers, alternating with bacon and vegetables. Brush all over with dressing and grill (broil) or barbecue, turning once or twice and brushing again with dressing, until meats are lightly browned. Serve on hot buttered rice. Serves 6.

Piglets in Blankets

4–5 Vienna frankfurters; ½ quantity Sour Cream Pastry (page 274); French (Dijon) or German (mild) mustard; 1 egg, beaten.

Poach frankfurters for 5 minutes, cool and skin. Roll out half the pastry (dough) into a rectangular sheet and place a frankfurter on one end. Spread frankfurter with a little mustard, then turn pastry (dough) over to enclose frankfurter as if making a sausage roll and cut off excess pastry (dough). Brush edges with beaten egg and press to seal. Repeat with remaining frankfurters and pastry (dough). Brush pastry (dough) tops with beaten egg and cut each 'pig in a blanket' into 4 or 5 'piglets'. Cut pastry (dough) scraps into little leaves or fancy shapes and use to decorate piglets, securing and brushing decorations with egg. Place on a buttered baking tray, keeping each frankfurter in shape (so that ends do not dry out). Bake in a preheated moderately hot oven (200°C/400°F, Gas Mark 6) for 15–20 minutes or until pastry (dough) is golden. Makes 16–25.

FRAPPE

The French word for 'iced', or 'chilled'. A frappé is made from sweetened fruit juice, frozen until mushy and served as a refreshing finish to a rich meal. It looks very pretty topped with whipped cream and served in parfait or sherbet glasses. A frappé can also be an iced drink. Various liqueurs are served over shaved ice in a cocktail glass and sipped through a short straw as the ice melts. Crème de Menthe, Tia Maria and Cointreau make delicious liqueur frappés.

FRENCH FRIES

For recipe see page 308.

FRENCH TOAST

Home cooks of many countries have had the same excellent idea – to transform bread into a delectable, comforting breakfast or dessert by dipping it into an egg-and-milk mixture and frying it in butter. It is variously called French Toast, German Toast or Nun's Toast. In Austria it is *Arme Ritter* (Poor Knights), in England, Poor Knights of Windsor. Spanish Toast, *Pain Perdu* and Orange French Toast are variations.

French Toast

2 eggs; pinch salt; 1 tbsp sugar (optional); 150 ml/¼ pint (⅔ cup) milk; 6 slices day-old bread, crusts removed; about 60 g/2 oz (4 tbsp) butter; sugar and cinnamon, jam, maple syrup or bacon etc. to serve.

Beat eggs with salt and sugar, if using, and mix with milk. Cut bread into triangles or strips. Heat a little butter in a frying pan (skillet). Dip bread, a few pieces at a time, into egg mixture and fry in butter until golden-brown on both sides. Add more butter to pan as needed. Serve French toast very hot, as a dessert, with sugar and cinnamon or warmed jam, or (omitting sugar from dipping mixture) with maple syrup and grilled (broiled) bacon for breakfast. Serves 3–6.
VARIATIONS
Pain Perdu: Follow recipe for French Toast but use half milk and half cream in the dipping mixture, and flavour it with a dash of vanilla essence (extract). Serve Pain Perdu

sprinkled with sugar and cinnamon, alone or as an accompaniment to poached fruit.
Spanish Toast: Follow recipe for French Toast but substitute 120 ml/4 fl oz (½ cup) sweet sherry for the milk. Fry toast until crisp and serve dusted with sifted icing (confectioners) sugar and cinnamon.

FRIKADELLER

Danish meat patties, very light and moist. They can be made according to various recipes; the pork and veal version is a favourite.

Frikadeller

500 g/1 lb (2 cups) minced (ground) pork and veal; 30 g/1 oz (½ cup) fresh white breadcrumbs; 120 ml/4 fl oz (½ cup) milk; 1 medium onion, grated; 1 egg; 1 tsp nutmeg; ½ tsp salt; ½ tsp white pepper; seasoned flour; 30 g/1 oz (2 tbsp) butter; 2 tbsp oil.
GARNISH: *sour cream; beetroot or dill pickles.*

Place meat in a large bowl. Soak breadcrumbs in milk and beat, a little at a time, into meat. Beat in onion, egg, nutmeg, salt and pepper. Mixture should be light and fluffy. Cover and chill 1 hour to firm. Shape into small, thick round or oblong patties and coat in seasoned flour. Heat butter and oil; when foam subsides, add frikadeller and fry 8–10 minutes on each side. Serve very hot, garnished with sour cream and beetroot or dill pickles. Boiled or mashed potatoes, cucumber salad and red cabbage are traditional accompaniments. Serves 4.

FRITTERS

Deep- or shallow-fried delicacies, either sweet or savoury, made by encasing slices of food in a special batter, or mixing chopped food through a batter before frying. Well-made and perfectly fried fritters should be light, crisp and golden outside, soft and creamy inside and served as soon as they are cooked.

Tiny bite-sized fritters can be served as appetizers. Larger ones make perfect lunches, served with a crisp green salad and fresh fruit. Sweet fritters are delicious finales to have as dessert at dinner.

The French also make a type of fritter called *beignets* using choux pastry (paste), sometimes mixed with cheese, which are deep-fried and served as hors d'oeuvre. Sweet ones are filled with cream, custard or jam after deep-frying (see *Beignets Soufflés*). In Vienna fritters can be made with a light pastry or rich yeast dough (see *Yeast Cookery*), shaped into little buns with a filling of cream, custard, jam or fruit and deep-fried. There are also the Spanish churros (see page 76), which are made with choux pastry (paste). **See recipes.**

□ **To Deep-Fry Fritters:** Use an electric frying pan (skillet), a deep-fryer or deep wide saucepan. Pour in vegetable oil to reach halfway up the sides of the frying utensil, making certain it is at least 8 cm (3 in) deep. Heat oil to moderate (185°C/360°F), test with a thermometer or by immersing a cube of bread in the hot oil. It is ready to use when the bread turns pale brown in 45 seconds. Place 5–6 pieces of food into hot oil, fry for 2–3 minutes until golden. Lift out the fritters and drain on crumpled paper towels, keep warm and fry the remaining batches in the same way. Serve immediately. Use a slotted spoon or tongs to lower the food into the oil and remove it when cooked.
□ **To Shallow-Fry Fritters:** Put equal quantities of oil and butter into a heavy frying pan (skillet) to a depth of not more than 5 mm (¼ in). Heat the fat and cook fritters 2–3 minutes each side or until golden-brown. Drain on paper towels and serve at once.

Basic Fritter Batter

Use for fish, vegetables and meat.

125 g/4 oz (1 cup) flour; 1½ tsp baking powder; ½ tsp salt; 2 eggs; 150 ml/¼ pint (⅔ cup) milk.

Sift flour, baking powder and salt into a bowl. Beat eggs with milk. Make a well in centre of flour. Add egg mixture in a steady pouring stream, stirring in flour gradually, and beat to a smooth batter. Stand for several hours before using. Makes about 500 ml/18 fl oz (2 cups).

Fluffy Fritter Batter

Use for small seafood fritters, for fruit or for chopped cooked meats.

165 g/5½ oz (1⅓ cups) flour; ½ tsp salt; 1 tbsp melted butter; 2 eggs, separated; 175 ml/6 fl oz (¾ cup) flat beer or soda (carbonated) water.

Sift flour and salt into a bowl. Make a well in centre and add melted butter, egg yolks and beer. Gradually work in flour and beat to a smooth batter. Allow to stand several hours. Just before using whisk egg whites until stiff and fold into batter. Makes about 500 ml/18 fl oz (2 cups).

Crisp Fritter Batter

Use to coat fish for frying.

125 g/4 oz (1 cup) flour; pinch salt; 1 whole egg; 1 egg, separated; 60 g/2 oz (4 tbsp) butter or margarine, melted; 250 ml/8 fl oz (1 cup) beer or soda (carbonated) water.

Sift flour with salt into a bowl and make a well in centre. Beat 1 whole egg and 1 egg yolk (keep second white for later) and pour into well with melted butter or margarine. Stir, incorporating flour gradually and adding beer or soda (carbonated) water little by little, until mixture is smooth. Cover and stand 1 hour. Just before using, whisk remaining egg white to a firm snow and fold into batter. Makes enough batter for 4 thick fish fillets.

Sweet Fritter Batter

Use for fruit fritters.

2 eggs, separated; 150 ml/¼ pint (⅔ cup) milk; 1 tbsp melted butter; 125 g/4 oz (1 cup) flour; 1 tbsp caster sugar.

Beat together egg yolks, milk and melted butter. Sift flour and sugar into a bowl, make a well in centre and stir in egg mixture. Gradually work in flour, beating to a smooth batter. Allow to stand several hours. Just before using, whisk egg whites until stiff and fold into batter. Makes about 500 ml/18 fl oz (2 cups).

Cooked Vegetable Fritters

350 g/12 oz (2 cups) cooked, chopped vegetables; 1 quantity Basic Fritter Batter (page 129); oil and butter for frying.

Add chopped vegetables to prepared batter. Heat oil and butter in a frying pan (skillet) (see To Shallow-Fry Fritters, page 129). Drop vegetable mixture in tablespoonfuls into hot fat and fry on both sides until golden and crisp. Do not crowd the pan. Drain the fritters on crumpled paper towels and serve hot. Serves 4.

Cooked Meat Fritters

Cooked lamb, beef, veal or chicken meat, chopped and fried in fritter batter makes a delicious lunch or supper dish.

500 g/1 lb (2 cups) chopped, cooked meat; 1 tbsp finely chopped onion; salt and freshly ground black pepper; 1 quantity Basic Fritter Batter (page 129); oil and butter for frying.

Combine chopped meat and onion, season with salt and pepper and fold into batter. Heat oil and butter in a frying pan (skillet) (see To Shallow-Fry Fritters, page 129). Drop meat mixture in large tablespoonfuls into hot fat and fry on both sides until golden and crisp. Drain on crumpled paper towels. Serve hot. Serves 4.

Sweetcorn Fritters

2 eggs, beaten; 175 ml/6 fl oz (¾ cup) milk; 1 tsp grated onion; 1 tbsp chopped parsley; 300 g/10 oz (2½ cups) flour; 2 tsp baking powder; 1 tsp salt; 2 tbsp melted butter; 1 × 450 g/16 oz can cream-style sweetcorn (whole kernel corn); oil for deep-frying.

Combine eggs, milk, onion and parsley. Add sifted dry ingredients, butter and corn; mix well. Heat oil in a deep fryer or saucepan to 185°C/360°F (see To Deep-Fry Fritters, page 129). Drop batter in tablespoonfuls into hot oil and fry for 3–4 minutes or until golden-brown. Drain on paper towels and serve hot. Makes about 24.
NOTE: Fritter batter may be dropped in tablespoonfuls into 2 tbsp hot oil in a frying pan (skillet) and shallow-fried on each side until golden-brown.

Seafood Fritters

Use whole fresh scallops, bearded and dried; green prawns (shrimp), shelled and deveined; strips of fish fillets; whole oysters; sliced squid or mussels. Make certain the food is well dried before coating with batter otherwise the batter will not stick.

1 kg (2 lb) seafood (see above); 1 quantity Fluffy Fritter Batter (page 129); oil for deep-frying; lemon wedges to serve.

Heat oil in deep fryer or saucepan to 185°C/360°F (see To Deep-Fry Fritters, page 129). Dip pieces of seafood into batter and allow excess batter to drain off; a sharp bamboo or metal skewer is good for this job. Drop into oil, 4 or 5 pieces at a time, and fry for 2–3 minutes or until golden-brown. Drain on crumpled paper towels. Serve hot with lemon wedges and, if liked, Sauce Tartare (see page 205). Serves 4.

Fruity Rice Fritters

An unusual Danish speciality.

500 g/8 oz (2 cups) cold boiled rice; 2 eggs, lightly beaten; pinch salt; 1 tbsp grated lemon or orange rind; 90 g/3 oz (½ cup) chopped raisins or sultanas (golden raisins); 30 g/1 oz (¼ cup) chopped blanched almonds; 2 tbsp flour; 60 g/2 oz (4 tbsp) butter.
TO SERVE: *sifted icing (confectioners) sugar; jam; double (heavy) cream (optional).*

Mix together rice, eggs, salt, lemon or orange rind, raisins or sultanas (golden raisins), nuts and flour. Heat butter in a large frying pan (skillet) and drop mixture into the pan in large spoonfuls. Cook fritters until golden on both sides and cooked through, turning once, about 3 minutes each side. Drain on paper towels. If serving as a dessert, sprinkle with icing (confectioners) sugar and serve hot with apricot or raspberry jam and double (heavy) cream. Serves 4.

Banana Fritters

4–6 firm ripe bananas; juice 1 lemon; caster sugar; oil for deep-frying; 1 quantity Sweet Fritter Batter (left).

Peel bananas and slice each into 3 diagonal pieces. Sprinkle with lemon juice and caster sugar. Heat oil in a deep-fryer or saucepan to 185°C/360°F (see To Deep-Fry Fritters, page 129). Use enough oil to come at least 8 cm (3 in) up sides of pan. Pat fruit dry, dip each piece in batter, place in hot oil and cook 2–3 minutes or until golden-brown. Drain on crumpled paper towels, sprinkle with caster sugar and serve immediately, with a bowl of lightly whipped cream. Serves 4.

Fresh Fruit Fritters

Sliced fruit such as apples, pears and bananas as well as whole berry fruit, and strawberries, may be frittered. Keep apple, pear and pineapple slices about 1.2 cm (½ in) thick; bananas may be cut in 3 diagonal slices. Apricots and plums may be halved and stoned.

oil for deep-frying; 250–350 g (8–12 oz) or 4 portions prepared fruit; 1 quantity Sweet Fritter Batter (left); sifted icing (confectioners) sugar (optional).

Heat oil in deep-fryer or saucepan to 185°C/360°F (see To Deep-Fry Fritters, page 129). Coat fruit with batter. Drop into hot oil, 3 or 4 pieces at a time, and fry until crisp and golden. Drain on crumpled paper towels. Sprinkle with icing (confectioners) sugar, if liked, and serve hot with whipped cream or a sauce like Sabayon (see page 343). Serves 4.

Fresh Vegetable Fritters

Use the freshest possible vegetables: sliced mushrooms or whole button mushrooms, blanched and dried slices of courgettes (zucchini), salted and dried thin slices of aubergine (eggplant), red or green peppers or onion rings, tiny sprigs of cauliflower or broccoli.

250 g (8 oz) sliced or prepared vegetables (see above); oil for deep-frying; 1 quantity Basic Fritter Batter (page 129).

Prepare vegetables. Heat oil in a deep-fryer or saucepan to 185°C/360°F (see To Deep-Fry Fritters, page 129). Dip sliced vegetables into batter, allow excess batter to drain off, and drop into oil, 4 or 5 pieces at a time. Fry for 2–3 minutes or until golden-brown. Drain on crumpled paper towels and serve hot. Serves 4.

Right: White Chicken (page 69)

FRITTO MISTO

A Fritto Misto, or 'mixed fry', is an Italian dish of small pieces of tender meats, young fresh vegetables or succulent seafood encased in a light, fluffy batter which are quickly deep-fried. Fritto misto, like all fried food in batter, must be eaten as soon as it is cooked to be at the peak of perfection. Choose the freshest possible ingredients, small slices of courgette (zucchini), aubergine (eggplant), artichoke hearts, mushrooms or tiny cauliflower florets, or very thin slices of veal escalope (scallop) or lamb's brains. Dip them in batter (see *Fritters*) and deep-fry for 2–3 minutes until golden.

Fritto Misto di Mare, the famous Italian fisherman's fish fry, can include small whole fish or strips of fillet, calamari, prawns (shrimp), or scallops – whatever combination of seafood is best and freshest on the day.

Fritto Misto di Mare

1 kg (2 lb) fish (a mixture of very small whole fish, fish fillets, prawns (shrimp), scallops, calamari); juice 1 lemon; oil for deep-frying; flour for coating.
BATTER: *125 g/4 oz (1 cup) self-raising flour; ¼ tsp salt; 1 tbsp brandy; 1 tbsp oil; 175 ml/ 6 fl oz (¾ cup) warm water; 1 egg white.*
TO SERVE: *lemon wedges; 350 ml/12 fl oz (1½ cups) Mayonnaise (page 204); 1 tbsp chopped capers; 1 tbsp chopped parsley; 1 tbsp chopped canned pimiento (optional).*

Remove heads of small whole fish, open out and remove backbone (see *Fish:* Grilled Sardines for method). Cut fillets into 5 cm (2 in) strips. Shell prawns (shrimp), leaving tails on, and devein. Discard any dark beards from scallops. Wash and clean calamari (see *Squid*) and cut into rings. Dry all seafood on paper towels and sprinkle with lemon juice.
BATTER: Sift flour and salt into a bowl, make a well in centre and add brandy and oil. Gradually add water, stirring from centre until mixed, then beat batter until smooth. Leave 30 minutes. Just before cooking seafood, whisk egg white until it stands in soft peaks and fold gently into batter.

Heat oil in a deep fryer or saucepan (a cube of bread should brown in 30 seconds). Toss seafood in flour and dip in batter. Deep-fry a few pieces at a time, for 1–2 minutes or until golden. To prevent toughness, do not overcook. Drain on crumpled paper towels and keep hot in a cool oven until all pieces are fried. Arrange on a heated serving platter and serve immediately with lemon wedges, and mayonnaise mixed with capers, parsley and pimiento, if using. Serves 4.

Left: Chicken Pilaf (page 68) and Devilled Drumsticks (page 69)

FROMAGE BLANC (White Cheese)

This refreshingly tangy, versatile cheese is one of the main ingredients in sauces of the *Cuisine Minceur* for meat, poultry, fish and vegetables. Try it, too, mixed with puréed vegetables, with crisp green salads, as a topping on fresh tomato slices or as a dipping sauce to accompany a platter of crudités (see page 90). It is also delicious served with fresh fruits, especially berry fruits.

In France fromage blanc is made from skimmed milk soured with a culture, but you can make an excellent substitute at home by blending together cottage cheese, plain yogurt and lemon juice.

Fromage Blanc

100 g/3⅓ oz (scant ½ cup) cottage cheese; plain yogurt; 3 tsp lemon juice.

Place all ingredients in a food processor or blender, and blend thoroughly until mixture is smooth, shiny and as thick as whipped cream. Cover and store in refrigerator for 12 hours before using. You may use a food mill if you wish, beating mixture thoroughly after pushing through mill. Makes about 250 ml/8 fl oz (1 cup).

FROSTING

See Icings, Frostings and Fillings.

FRUIT

Fruit is such a pleasure to look at and to eat, it seems a pure bonus that it's so good for us as well. Every bite contains vitamins, minerals and fibre, that most important food component for a healthy digestive system. Eat the peel when possible for the best investment in good health.

Keep fruit at room temperature until fully ripened; the process can be hastened by leaving it in a paper bag with the top closed. Once ripe, most fruits should be refrigerated to slow further changes. The exceptions are bananas, which blacken under refrigeration, and citrus fruits that will be used within a week or two – citrus does not ripen further after picking, and will stay in good condition at room temperature for some time before beginning to deteriorate.

Ways to Use Fruit
Of course, a piece of choice fruit is a splendid way to finish a meal. Fresh fruit is also a favourite food to nibble or munch between meals. Fruit can be poached, baked, sautéed, deep-fried, grilled or barbecued. It combines with other ingredients for hundreds of lovely desserts, cakes, pies and tarts. Don't forget how well fruit goes with savoury foods, too – fried apples with sausage or pork chops, apricots with lamb, pears with cheese, green grapes with fish, melon or figs with prosciutto, orange with duck, apple with pork, and pineapple with ham or cheese are some of the best known combinations.

Fruit and vegetable salads, fruit stuffings for meat, fruit relishes, sauces and soups add verve to the first or main course. Ideas such as quinces stuffed with a savoury meat mixture; cherries simmered in red wine and orange juice and served with ham or poultry; an apple and mint water ice to accompany roast lamb or game birds; hot curried fruit or chilled pears with tarragon cream dressing served as a first course, are more unusual ways to add a happy surprise to a meal. **See also recipes.**
Fresh Fruit Salad The nicest fruit salads have the fruit left in fairly big pieces – about 2–2.5 cm (¾–1 in) so that their beautiful appearance and contrasting textures are not lost. Leave skin on where practicable. Two or three good fruits are often better than a big variety. Sprinkle salad with sugar and lemon juice, cover and leave to chill and develop flavours for 30 minutes or more before serving. Fruits which darken quickly after cutting (peaches, bananas, apples, pears) should be turned in a little lemon juice and added only a short time before serving.

Add interest to fresh fruit salads with the addition of a little white wine or liqueur or just a sprinkling of rum or brandy. Crème Fraîche (see page 88), sour cream lightly sweetened with brown sugar, or double (heavy) cream half-whipped with a few drops of liqueur, rum or brandy, are good fruit salad toppings. Serve with Tuiles, Cigarettes Russes (see pages 447 and 79) or other crisp delicate biscuits (cookies).

Honeyed Apricots with Brandy

18 ripe apricots, halved and stoned; 250 ml/8 fl oz (1 cup) honey; 4 tbsp lemon juice; 4 tbsp water; 4 tbsp brandy.

Simmer apricots in honey, lemon juice and water over very low heat for 8–10 minutes or until tender. Cool apricots in syrup, then stir in brandy. Chill and serve with whipped cream. Serves 6.
NOTE: When fresh apricots are not in season, use canned fruit. Add 4 tbsp of the syrup instead of water and reduce amount of honey to 175 ml/6 fl oz (¾ cup).

Strawberries with Marsala and Pernod

750 g (1½ lb) ripe strawberries, hulled and halved; juice 1 lemon; 6 tbsp Marsala; 3 tbsp Pernod; sugar.

Sprinkle strawberries with lemon juice, Marsala and Pernod. Toss well and add sugar to taste. Chill until ready to serve. Serves 6.

Tropical Cream

*4 ripe bananas, mashed; pulp of
2 passionfruit; 60 g/2 oz (¼ cup) sugar; pinch
salt; 150 ml/¼ pint (⅔ cup) pineapple juice;
2 tbsp lemon juice; 250 ml/8 fl oz (1 cup)
double (heavy) or whipping cream, whipped;
4 tbsp chopped walnuts.*

Mix bananas with passionfruit, sugar, salt and
fruit juices. Fold in cream. Spoon into a
freezer tray and freeze until firm, about 3
hours. Break up with a fork then, using an
electric mixer, beat until frothy. Fold in
walnuts and freeze, covered, until firm.
Serves 6–8.

Champagne Fruit Salad

*1 medium ripe pineapple; 4 pears; 2 tbsp
lemon juice; 4 medium oranges; 250 g (8 oz)
strawberries; 500 g (1 lb) seedless grapes;
50 g/2 oz (½ cup) icing (confectioners) sugar;
120 ml/4 fl oz (½ cup) Kirsch or brandy;
½ bottle champagne.*

Peel and core pineapple and cut into
wedges, reserving the frond. Peel, core and
slice pears and toss in lemon juice. Peel and
slice oranges. Wash and hull strawberries
and wash grapes.

Combine all fruit in a large serving bowl
with icing (confectioners) sugar and Kirsch
or brandy. Just before serving place an
upturned glass or small dish in the middle of
the serving bowl and place pineapple frond
on it. Pour the champagne around the fruits
and serve. Serves 8.

Grape Salad

*250 ml/8 fl oz (1 cup) orange juice; 1 tbsp
chopped fresh chervil, or 1 tsp dried; 500 g
(1 lb) seedless green grapes, halved; 1–2 tbsp
orange liqueur.*

Combine orange juice and chervil, and allow
mixture to stand for 1 hour. Add grapes and
liqueur and chill, covered, for at least 3 hours
or overnight. Serve salad alone or topped
with plain yogurt or ice cream. Serves 4.

Fruit Salad with Honey and Wine

You can use your own choice of fruit for this
salad; fresh cubed pineapple, melons or any
ripe berries. Do not use citrus fruit – the acid
is too strong for the wine.

*175 ml/6 fl oz (¾ cup) white wine; 2 tbsp
honey; 4 tbsp chopped mixed nuts; 1 large
apple; 1 large ripe pear; 2 ripe peaches;
3 ripe apricots; 250 g (8 oz) strawberries.*

Mix wine with honey and stir in nuts. Wash,
peel, core and stone fruit as necessary and
cut into thin slices. Combine all fruit in a
large glass serving bowl and pour honey
sauce over. Toss gently with a wooden
spoon until thoroughly mixed. Chill.
Serves 4–6.

FRUIT BOTTLING (Canning)

Bottled fruits retain their natural flavour,
colour and texture and are ideal for serving
chilled with their own syrup or in pies and
tarts or in favourite dessert recipes. Included
as fruit are tomatoes.

Successful fruit bottling depends on efficient sterilization – by this is meant that
anything that will cause the fruit to ferment or
turn mouldy must be killed by heat. This can
be done in an oven. It is most important to
have good preserving jars, and there is a wide
choice. Take care of them, particularly when
opening jars; don't probe them unduly with
knives or sharp instruments, any chip will
render the jars useless for later processing.

Choice of Fruit

All fruits are suitable for bottling, but because
of their short season stone and berry fruits are
particular favourites.

Fruit should be prepared as for stewing. All
stone fruits are halved and the stones (pits)
removed. To remove skins of peaches,

Approximate times for processing fruit by the boiling water bath method

Fruit	Style of Pack	Syrup Recommended	Processing times at boiling point at 0–1000 feet	
			500 ml/18 fl oz (2 cups)	1 litre /1¾ pints (4 cups)
Apples	Cold pack	Water or light syrup	20 minutes	25 minutes
	Steam or boil to wilt		15 minutes	20 minutes
	Bake or boil whole hot pack*		15 minutes	15 minutes
	Apple sauce, hot pack*		10 minutes	10 minutes
Berries				
Blackberries,	Pack raw; cover with boiling syrup	Medium	20 minutes	25 minutes
Loganberries, Mulberries,	Boil 3–4 minutes with equal weight sugar, stand overnight; hot pack*	In own syrup	10 minutes	15 minutes
Raspberries, Gooseberries	Pack raw; cover with boiling syrup; hot pack*	Medium	15 minutes	20 minutes
Cherries	Pack raw; cover with boiling syrup	Medium	15 minutes	20 minutes
	Precook; hot pack*	Medium	10 minutes	15 minutes
Grapes	Wash, stem, pack; cover with boiling syrup	Light	15 minutes	20 minutes
Oranges	Immerse 4 minutes in boiling water then in cold, Peel, remove pith, quarter, drop or pack in jars. Cover with boiling syrup	Heavy	30 minutes	35 minutes
Pears	Pack raw; cover with boiling syrup	Medium	25 minutes	30 minutes
	Precook 6 minutes; hot pack*	Medium	20 minutes	25 minutes
Plums	Pack raw; cover with boiling syrup	Medium	25 minutes	30 minutes
	Precook; hot pack*	In own juice	10 minutes	15 minutes
Quinces	Precook 3 minutes; pack	Medium	25 minutes	30 minutes
Rhubarb	Precook; hot pack* (not necessary to use sugar)	In own juice	10 minutes	15 minutes

*Fruits referred to on timetable as 'hot pack'
should be put into a pan and brought to a gentle
boil in syrup, or a little water (which may be
poured into the jar with the fruit). Small soft fruits
should be simmered approximately 2 minutes,
large or firm fruits approximately 2–4 minutes,
depending on ripeness and maturity. This cuts
down the processing time as fruits have been
heated prior to being packed into the sterilized
preserving jars.

plunge into boiling water, count to 10, then cool in iced water and the skins should slip off easily. Pears are peeled and halved, pineapples are trimmed and sliced. Berry fruits are washed lightly and drained, and so on. Tomatoes are left whole.

Basic rules
- Preserve only choice and sound fruit.
- Prepare small quantities at a time.
- Ensure that jars and rubbers are sterile, wash in hot soapy water, rinse in boiling water.
- Check all jars to be used, to make sure these are free from flaws.
- Use only new rubber rings, not old ones.

Testing of seal
24 hours after bottling, the lids should be tested to make sure the vacuum has formed and the lid is firmly sealed. To test clip-type jars: remove the clip and lift the jar gently by the lid. If the jar is a screw-band type, remove the band and tilt until the weight of the liquid is against the lid. Make the same test for jars sealed with rubber solution. If the seals have not formed, the jars should be reprocessed, or the contents eaten the same day.

If lids are secure, label the jars, mark the date of preserving on each and store in a cool, dark places. If preserves are subjected to bright light, the colour of the fruit in the jars will fade.

Steps to Oven Bottling

The procedure of sterilizing bottled fruit in the oven is one of the simplest of all methods. The oven method is convenient when only small quantities of fruit are to be processed. For this and other reasons, the berry fruits or just a few jars of cherries or special stone fruits may be preserved for use later in the year.

1. Preheat the oven to 120°C/250°F, Gas Mark ½. Slow cooking is required. If the fruit cooks too quickly it will burst, go pulpy and lose its shape.

2. Pack prepared fruit (see Choice of Fruit above) into the bottles. The fruit will shrink during cooking, so jars must be well filled.

3. Stand the bottles on a baking sheet on a shelf in the lower half of the oven. Jars must not touch each other. Put on lids of jars, without rubber rings, and do not seal.

4. Leave the fruit in the oven until it looks cooked, has shrunk and changed colour slightly. This normally takes 45 minutes to 1 hour. Pears need 1½ hours in the oven.

5. Prepare the syrup (see right) and when required, bring back to boiling point. Remove one bottle from the oven and stand on a double thickness of paper towel or tea-towel.

6. Have rubber rings soaking in water, place rubber ring on the lid of the jar. Add boiling syrup to fill the jar, until it just overflows. Clip jar tightly.

7. Allow jar to cool and repeat step 6 with the remaining jars. The procedure is the same for

tomatoes except that salted water or tomato juice replaces the syrup.

8. The next day test the seal, see above.

NOTE: It is very important to perform the steps as quickly as possible, and with one jar only at a time.

Sugar Syrup

The syrup should be made while the fruit is heating in the oven. 120–175 ml/4–6 fl oz (½–¾ cup) syrup will be needed for each 500 ml/18 fl oz (2 cup) jar. The strength of the syrup is largely a matter of personal taste, but a guide to quantities is:

Light Syrup: 250 g/8 oz (1 cup) sugar to 750 ml/1¼ pints (3 cups) water

Medium Syrup: 500 g/1 lb (2 cups) sugar to 750 ml/1¼ pints (3 cups) water

Heavy Syrup: 750 g/1½ lb (3 cups) sugar to 750 ml/1¼ pints (3 cups) water

Apples are better done in a light syrup, but for most fruits use a medium syrup.

Boiling Water Bath Method

Use suitable preserving jars and a lidded cooker or boiler, deep enough for the jars to be covered by at least 5 cm (2 in) boiling water. The jars of fruit being preserved must be covered completely by 5 cm (2 in) water, they must also stand in the cooker on a rack so that the water flow freely under them; an ordinary cake rack will do.

Except when preserving grapefruit, it is not necessary to use a thermometer, because the temperature required for preserving by this boiling water bath method is reached when the water boils.

Thoroughly clean jars, rubbers and lids in hot water, and make the syrup. The fruit to be preserved should be sorted and simultaneously blanched and peeled by scalding, see Choice of Fruit, above.

Packing and Processing: Pack fruit into jars

Bottling by Boiling Water Bath Method

(Fig 1 above). Before adding the syrup, run water gently in and out of the jars to remove any particles of fruit and keep the syrup clear. The syrup, which should be boiling, will be clearer if strained through a cloth. Fill only to within 1 cm (½ in) of the top of 500 ml (2 cup) jars **(2)**, and wipe the rim of the jar with a moist cloth before sealing. A skewer worked gently between the fruit and the jar will release air bubbles **(3)**. If the screw-band type of jar is used, do not seal tightly.

Lower jars into the boiling water in the cooker or boiler with tongs, or by holding the top of the jar with a cloth **(4)**. Count the processing time from the time the water returns to the boil. As soon as the water is seen to be boiling, put the lid on the cooker and process according to the times given in the table on page 134.

Remove jars from cooker after processing and place on a wooden surface or a folded cloth, away from draughts. Hot jars may break if placed on marble or other cold materials. Tightly seal screw-bound jars immediately on removal from cooker. Test seal after 24 hours, see above.

VARIATIONS

Brandied Fruit: For special occasions, brandied fruit is really superb. Fill jars of fruit 3 parts full or more with syrup, top up with brandy, cover and clamp to seal.

Bottling in Water: Home-bottled fruit is excellent for diabetic people and dieters. Simply use boiling water instead of syrup. The best size to use are 500 ml/18 fl oz (2 cup) jars. The fruit may be sweetened before serving with artificial sweeteners.

Rhubarb is considered particularly good for diabetics and dieters. Peaches, pears, apricots, pineapples, plums, figs and quinces are also very suitable for bottling in water.

FRUIT CAKE

The ich aroma of fruit cake-baking conjures up memories of Christmas, birthdays or exciting special occasions in every household. Rich fruit cake keeps for months wrapped and stored in a cool dry place and is best made well ahead to allow the flavour to ripen before cutting. Light fruit cakes are ideal for any occasion and many people prefer them to the very rich ones. They keep well for up to 3 weeks when stored wrapped in an airtight container.

Boiled Fruit Cake (see page 54) is mixed using a particularly easy method and is excellent for families who love to have fruit cake at any time. It may be kept for 2 weeks in an airtight container. **See recipes**.

For more fruit cakes, see Sultana Cake (page 420), *Dundee Cake* and *Bishop's Cake*.

Light Fruit Cake

250 g/8 oz (1⅓ cups) sultanas (golden raisins); 60 g/2 oz (⅓ cup) currants; 60 g/2 oz (⅓ cup) raisins; 60 g/2 oz (⅓ cup) chopped mixed candied peel; 90 g/3 oz (⅓ cup) roughly chopped glacé (candied) cherries; grated rind ½ lemon or orange; 250 g/8 oz (1 cup) butter; 150 g/5 oz (⅔ cup) caster sugar; 125 g/4 oz (⅔ cup) firmly packed brown sugar; 310 g/10 oz (2½ cups) plain (all-purpose) flour; 60 g/2 oz (½ cup) self-raising flour; 5 eggs; 1–2 tbsp lemon juice.

Combine dried fruit with peel, cherries and lemon or orange rind. Cream butter with sugars until very light and fluffy. Sift flours together. Beat eggs into creamed mixture one at a time, following each with 1 tbsp flour. Fold in remaining flour, then fruit. Add lemon juice. Turn into a greased and lined 20 cm (8 in) round or square deep cake tin (pan). Bake cake in a preheated cool oven (150°C/300°F, Gas Mark 2) for 2½ hours or until a skewer inserted in centre comes out clean. Turn out on to a wire rack and leave to cool. When cold, remove paper lining and store in an airtight tin.
NOTE: Spices can be sifted with the flour if liked. Use ½ tsp cinnamon, 1 tsp mixed spice (ground allspice) and ¼ tsp nutmeg.

Rich Fruit Cake

FRUIT: *250 g/8 oz (1⅓ cups) raisins, chopped; 250 g/8 oz (1⅓ cups) sultanas (golden raisins); 250 g/8 oz (1⅓ cups) currants; 180 g/6 oz (1 cup) mixed candied peel, finely chopped; 60 g/2 oz (¼ cup) glacé (candied) cherries, diced; 60 g/2 oz (¼ cup) glacé (candied) apricots, diced; 6 tbsp brandy or rum; 2 tbsp sherry.*
CAKE MIXTURE: *250 g/8 oz (1 cup) butter; 250 g/8 oz (1⅓ cups) firmly packed brown sugar; grated rind 1 lemon; 2 tbsp marmalade; 5 eggs; 310 g/10 oz (2½ cups) flour; 1 tsp mixed spice (ground allspice); 1 tsp cinnamon; ¼ tsp salt; 125 g/4 oz (1 cup) blanched almonds chopped, extra blanched almonds (optional); 1 tbsp extra brandy.*

FRUIT: Put all fruit into a bowl and sprinkle with brandy or rum and sherry. Leave overnight.
CAKE MIXTURE: Beat butter and brown sugar with lemon rind until light and creamy. Add marmalade and beat well. Add eggs one at a time, beating well after each addition. Add 1 tbsp flour with the last egg. Sift together remaining flour, mixed spice (ground allspice), cinnamon and salt, and stir into creamed mixture alternately with fruit and chopped almonds. Turn mixture into a 20 cm (8 in) round or square deep cake tin (pan) lined with 1 layer of brown paper and 2 layers of greased greaseproof (waxed) paper. If not covering cake with almond paste and royal icing, decorate with whole almonds arranged in a pattern on top. Bake in a preheated cool oven (150°C/300°F, Gas Mark 2) for 3–3½ hours or until a skewer inserted in centre comes out clean. Remove from oven and immediately sprinkle with about 1 tbsp extra brandy. Remove cake from tin (pan), leaving paper on cake. Wrap in a tea-towel and leave on a wire rack until cool. Store in an airtight tin.

FRUIT COCKTAIL

A first-course fruit cocktail should delight the eye and refresh the palate. Avoid formless canned fruit, pieces cut too small, and over-sweetening. Use just one fruit, or 2 or 3 which contrast in colour and texture; melon and grapes, grapefruit and cherries, orange and strawberries, pineapple with pawpaw and kiwi fruit.

Leave fruit in good-sized chunks. Macerate in a little lemon juice and just a touch of honey or sugar, plus, if you wish, ground or grated fresh ginger, or mint leaves, cut into thin ribbons. Serve in stemmed, clear glass bowls and garnish each with a sprig of mint, a Maraschino cherry or fine slivers of orange or lemon rind.

FRUIT CUP

This is a deliciously refreshing drink based on fresh fruit and fruit juices. You can mix the fruit with iced water, soda (carbonated) water or mineral water and sweeten to taste. Some fruit cups use orangeade, lemonade or ginger ale to add some fizz. All fruit cups look inviting served in long glasses, decorated with slices of fruit or sprigs of mint. **See recipes**.

Festive Fruit Cup

350 g/12 oz (1½ cups) sugar; 1 litre/1¾ pints (4 cups) water; 1 pineapple; juice 6 lemons; juice 6 oranges; pulp 6 passionfruit; 1 × 1.25 l/2 pint bottle (5 cups) lemonade; 1 × 1.25 l/2 pint bottle (5 cups) orangeade.

Heat sugar and water together, stirring until sugar has dissolved. Boil without stirring for 5 minutes. Cool, then chill. Peel, core and grate pineapple (or use a food processor if you have one). Mix sugar syrup, pineapple, fruit juices and passionfruit pulp and chill well. Two hours before serving, stir in lemonade and orangeade. Serve chilled. Makes 5–6 litres/8–10 pints (20–25 cups).

Citrus Grape Cooler

3 tbsp caster sugar; 250 ml/8 fl oz (1 cup) orange juice; 120 ml/4 fl oz (½ cup) lemon juice; 120 ml/4 fl oz (½ cup) grape juice; 500 ml/18 fl oz (2 cups) water; ice cubes; orange slices to decorate.

Combine sugar and fruit juices and stir until sugar dissolves. Add water and ice and mix well. Serve in tall glasses, each decorated with a twist of orange. Serves 4–5.

FRUIT, DRIED AND CANDIED

Dried Fruit

The preservation of fruits by drying gives us a sweet, nourishing food available all year round. Dried fruits have a high concentration of sugar for a quick boost of energy, and contain valuable minerals and vitamin A. Many kinds of fruit are dried, from larger ones such as peaches, pears, apples, bananas and apricots, to dates and all the grape family: raisins, sultanas (golden raisins) and currants, or a mixture of these with peel and cherries ready to use in baking.

When buying dried fruits, choose clean, well-washed fruit, which has no musty smell, and store, tightly covered, in a cool, dry, airy place. Buy only as much as you use within 6–8 weeks.

Dried fruits make marvellous snacks on their own, so are ideal to carry outdoors or for busy mothers when children arrive home from school feeling hungry. Add dried fruits to cakes, puddings, breads, buns, biscuits (cookies) and pastries. They are especially

F

good with rice in pilaffs and in rice-based stuffings flavoured with spices, herbs and nuts for meats, poultry or vegetables.

To reconstitute dried fruit: The very best quality dried fruits are graded as 'dessert'. Such fruit as prunes, dates, apricots, figs, peaches and pears can be purchased in this grade and reconstituted without cooking, by soaking in water (or cold tea for prunes) for 3 hours. They can also be stewed without prior soaking.

To plump raisins, sultanas (golden raisins) or currants, cover with boiling water or tea; leave 10 minutes then drain. They can also be plumped by washing briefly and then heating, closely covered, in a preheated moderate oven (180°C/350°F, Gas Mark 4) until they puff up.

To stew dried fruit: Place the fruit in a saucepan and cover with cold water. Simmer, covered, until the fruit is soft and plump.

To retain whole fruit, add sugar to water before cooking. Most fruit will take 60 g/2 oz (¼ cup) sugar to 180–250 g/6–8 oz (1 cup) fruit, but this depends on your taste and which fruit you are cooking; some are more tart than others. Flavour apricots with a piece of cinnamon stick, pears with a little ground or fresh ginger, and prunes with a whole clove. Serve with thick whipped cream or custard.

If fruit is very hard and dry, soak overnight in cold water to cover before cooking it in the same water. Sweeten after cooking.

Candied Fruit

Glacé Fruit: The word refers to the glossy coating found on candied fruits such as cherries, apricots, peaches, pineapple rings and whole baby figs, small oranges or mandarin oranges.

Glacé fruits are eaten as a sweetmeat – lovely with after dinner coffee – and are also used as an ingredient in sweet dishes or as a decoration. One of the prettiest ways to use the fruits is in the traditional Bishop's Cake (see page 37). When the cake is cut the slices look like stained glass windows.

Crystallized Fruit: Candied fruit with a coating of granulated sugar. Candied peel and angelica may not have the addition of a sugar coating; both are used to decorate cakes, puddings, custards, breads and biscuits (cookies), while mixed candied peel is used in fruit cakes, loaves, and breads, puddings and sweet cheese desserts. **See recipes.**

Grilled Stuffed Figs Soak dried figs in sherry or port for 36 hours. Split and fill with nuts or cream cheese, or a combination of both, or with Cheddar cheese. Wrap with partially cooked bacon strips and secure with a wooden toothpick. Grill (broil) until bacon is crisp and figs are heated through.

Savoury Stuffed Dates Fill dates with whole or chopped nuts, cream cheese and peanut butter, or a stuffing made by combining cream cheese with a little mayonnaise, finely chopped celery and onion, pepper and salt to taste.

Prune Snow To 350 g/12 oz (1½ cups) sieved cooked prunes add 1 tbsp lemon juice, 1 tsp grated lemon rind, pinch cinnamon. Fold in 2 egg whites, beaten until stiff, with 1–2 tbsp sugar. Spoon into serving dishes, top with single (light) cream. Serves 3–4.

Macerated Prunes, Apricots and Figs Macerate dried fruit in large sealed jars. Prunes can be macerated in sherry or red wine, apricots in sherry or brandy; figs in brandy. Allow to macerate for at least 1 week before using and use the liquid left in the jars for making another batch. Serve prunes on their own or with a sprinkling of chopped nuts as a dessert, or as an accompaniment to curry. Figs are delicious served with coffee after dinner.

See also *Fruit Cake, Dundee Cake, Eccles Cakes, Christmas Cake, etc.*

Apricot Sauce

250 g/8 oz (1⅓ cups) dried apricots; 1 cinnamon stick; 125 g/4 oz (½ cup) sugar; 1 tsp grated orange rind; 1 tbsp Grand Marnier (optional).

Soak apricots in water to cover for several hours. Bring to the boil with cinnamon stick and simmer until soft. Remove cinnamon stick. Rub apricots through a sieve or purée in a food processor or blender, then add sugar. Return to saucepan and cook until sugar has dissolved. A little more water may be added if sauce is too thick. Stir in orange rind and Grand Marnier, if using. Allow to cool before serving. Serve with vanilla ice cream; fold through whipped cream for a pavlova filling; or serve with tiny meringues sandwiched together with Crème Chantilly (see page 88) as a dessert. Makes 350 ml/12 fl oz (1½ cups).

Apricot Soufflé

90 g/3 oz (½ cup) dried apricots; 120 ml/4 fl oz (½ cup) water; 5 tbsp sugar; 2 tbsp orange juice or Grand Marnier; grated rind ½ orange; 3 egg whites.

Soak apricots in water to cover for 3 hours. Drain and place in a saucepan with the 120 ml/4 fl oz (½ cup) water. Cook over very gentle heat until tender. Drain again and add 2 tbsp sugar. Push apricots through a sieve or purée in a blender. Stir in orange juice or liqueur and orange rind. Whisk egg whites until stiff, then gradually beat in remaining sugar. Fold gently into cooled apricot purée. Turn into a buttered 18 cm (7 in) soufflé dish which has been lightly sprinkled with sugar. Bake soufflé in a preheated moderately hot oven (200°C/400°F, Gas Mark 6) for about 20 minutes. Serve immediately. Serves 4.

Gingered Figs

500 g (1 lb) dried figs; 1 tsp ground ginger; 3 tbsp sugar; 1 large orange; 3 slices lemon.

Wash figs and clip off stems. Put into a saucepan with cold water to cover, add ginger and bring to the boil. Simmer until figs are plump and soft, 30–35 minutes. Drain, reserving liquid. Place figs in a serving dish. Measure liquid and return 250 ml/8 fl oz (1 cup) to saucepan. Add sugar and cook gently about 5 minutes. Peel rind thinly from orange and cut into julienne (matchstick) strips. Remove white pith and cut orange flesh into segments or thin slices. Add to syrup with orange strips and lemon slices. Pour syrup over figs, chill and serve, with plain yogurt or sour cream flavoured with finely chopped ginger in syrup. Serves 6.

Date and Raisin Crunch

125 g/4 oz (⅔ cup) dates, chopped; 60 g/2 oz (⅓ cup) raisins; grated rind and juice 2 oranges; 265 g/8½ oz (2½ cups) rolled oats; 45 g/1½ oz (⅓ cup) flour; 180 g/6 oz (¾ cup) butter; 75 g/2½ oz (⅓ cup) sugar.

Combine dates and raisins in a saucepan. Make up orange juice to 250 ml/8 fl oz (1 cup) liquid with water. Add liquid to dates and raisins and cook gently until fruit is a thick pulp. Remove from heat and cool. Mix rolled oats and flour, rub (cut) in butter and add sugar and orange rind. Press half the date mixture into a greased 28 × 19 cm (11 × 7½ in) tin (pan). Spread with fruit filling and sprinkle rest of oat mixture on top. Press down lightly. Bake in a preheated moderately hot oven (190°C/375°F, Gas Mark 5) for 45 minutes. Serve warm as a dessert or cut in wedges when cold and serve as a biscuit (cookie) bar for tea. Serves 6–8 as a dessert or makes 30 pieces.

Fruit, Nut and Rice Casserole

180 g/6 oz (1 cup) dried apricots; 90 g/3 oz (½ cup) sultanas (golden raisins); 210 g/7 oz (1 cup) long-grain rice; 60 g/2 oz (4 tbsp) butter; 2 onions, chopped; 1 small green pepper, cored, seeded and chopped; ½ tsp curry powder; 60 g/2 oz (½ cup) toasted almonds, chopped.

Cover apricots and sultanas (golden raisins) with water and soak for 2 hours. Drain and chop apricots. Boil rice until tender, drain and set aside. Melt butter in a frying pan (skillet) and sauté onions, green pepper and curry powder over gentle heat until onion is beginning to soften. Add almonds, apricots, sultanas (golden raisins) and rice. Pile into a greased baking dish and bake in a preheated moderate oven (180°C/350°F, Gas Mark 4) for about 20 minutes. Serve with roast or grilled (broiled) chicken or lamb. Serves 6.

Plumped Prunes with Oranges

370 g/12 oz (2 cups) dessert prunes; 2 large oranges, peeled and cut into segments; 500 ml/18 fl oz (2 cups) boiling water.

Toss prunes and oranges in a bowl. Pour in boiling water to cover fruit, seal with plastic wrap and refrigerate overnight. If liked, add 1 tbsp Grand Marnier before serving, with whipped cream or sour cream. Serves 4.

Riesling Rice

Rice flavoured with white wine, spices and currants is an elegant accompaniment to grilled (broiled) chicken, fish or lamb.

310 g/10 oz (1½ cups) long-grain rice; 750 ml/1¼ pints (3 cups) boiling water; 90 g/3 oz (½ cup) currants; 60 g/2 oz (4 tbsp) butter; 250 ml/8 fl oz (1 cup) riesling or other dry white wine; 2 tsp salt; ¼ tsp white pepper; ¼ tsp nutmeg; ¼ tsp ground allspice; 1 tsp sugar.

Wash rice under cold running water and drain well. Pour 250 ml/8 fl oz (1 cup) boiling water over currants and soak for 10 minutes, then drain and set aside. Melt butter in a large saucepan, add rice and stir over medium heat for 5 minutes. Add rest of boiling water and remaining ingredients. Boil until liquid is absorbed and steam holes appear in rice. Turn heat very low, cover tightly and steam 10 minutes or until rice is just tender. Remove from heat, add currants and fork through. Serves 6.

FUDGE

A soft, creamy sweet or candy made with sugar and milk or cream to which are added various flavourings and other ingredients. Fudge makes a lovely gift at Christmas time. Wrap the pieces in coloured cellophane and pack in a pretty box or basket, or serve with black coffee after dinner.

Chocolate Fudge

350 g/12 oz (1½ cups) sugar; 5 tbsp evaporated milk; 125 g/4 oz (½ cup) cream cheese, softened and mashed; 75 g/2½ oz (1¼ cups) chopped marshmallows; 90 g/3 oz (½ cup) milk chocolate, chopped; 90 g/3 oz (½ cup) dark chocolate, chopped; 60 g/2 oz (½ cup) chopped walnuts; ½ tsp vanilla essence (extract) or 1 tbsp brandy.

Combine sugar and milk in a heavy saucepan. Stir over medium heat until boiling. Add cheese and marshmallows and cook, stirring, for 5 minutes. Remove from heat and stir in chocolate, walnuts and vanilla or brandy. Pour into an oiled 18 cm (7 in) square cake tin (pan). Cool, cut into squares and store in refrigerator. Makes about 24 large pieces.

GALETTE

A galette is a flat cake traditionally made with flaky pastry (dough) or yeast dough. It is the symbolic cake eaten on Twelfth Night in France. A more elaborate version can consist of meringue, fruit and nuts. Savoury galettes made with vegetables, served hot or cold cut into wedges are also delicious. **See recipes.**

Almond and Hazelnut Galette

4 egg whites; 1½ tbsp flour; 45 g/1½ oz (⅓ cup) ground hazelnuts; 75 g/2½ oz (½ cup) ground almonds; 125 g/4 oz (½ cup) caster sugar; 45 g/1½ oz (3 tbsp) butter, melted; 350 ml/12 fl oz (1½ cups) double (heavy) cream; ½ tsp vanilla essence (extract); 350 g/12 oz (1½ cups) sliced peaches, fresh or drained canned; sifted icing (confectioners) sugar.

Cut out 3 rounds of greaseproof (waxed) paper 20 cm (8 in) in diameter. Spray with non-stick cooking spray, and place on baking trays. Whisk egg whites until very stiff peaks form. Sift flour, nuts and sugar into egg whites, add melted butter and fold together gently using a metal spoon. Divide the mixture into 3 and spread out on each paper round. Bake in a preheated moderate oven (180°C/350°F, Gas Mark 4) for 25–30 minutes or until pale gold. Place on wire racks to cool and remove paper bases when cold. Whip cream and flavour with vanilla. Place one meringue round on a serving platter, spoon ⅓ of the cream over and arrange sliced peaches on cream. Cover with second meringue round. Repeat layering with cream and peaches and place last meringue round on top. Dust with icing (confectioners) sugar and decorate with remaining ⅓ whipped cream. Serves 8.

Potato Galette

500 g (1 lb) potatoes, cooked; 30 g/1 oz (2 tbsp) butter; 1 medium onion, chopped; 2 eggs, beaten; 4 tbsp hot milk; salt and freshly ground black pepper; ¼ tsp nutmeg.

Push potatoes through a sieve or purée in a blender or food processor. Melt butter in a saucepan and soften onions over low heat. Remove from heat and beat in potatoes, eggs, hot milk, salt, pepper and nutmeg. Turn into a greased 20 cm (8 in) sandwich tin (layer pan). Smooth top with a spatula and bake in a preheated moderate oven (180°C/350°F, Gas Mark 4) for 1 hour. Turn out cake and serve cut into wedges. Serves 8.

Galette Normandy

PASTRY (DOUGH): *250 g/8 oz (2 cups) flour; 150 g/5 oz (½ cup plus 2 tbsp) butter; 5 tbsp icing (confectioners) sugar, sifted; 2 egg*

yolks; $\frac{1}{4}$ tsp vanilla essence (extract).
FILLING: 30 g/1 oz (2 tbsp) butter; 1 kg (2 lb) cooking apples, peeled, cored and quartered; grated rind and juice $\frac{1}{2}$ lemon; 125 g/4 oz ($\frac{1}{2}$ cup) sugar.
TO FINISH: Glacé Icing (page 164); 1 tbsp redcurrant jelly (optional).

PASTRY (DOUGH): Sift flour on to a board, make a well in the centre and put in butter, sugar, egg yolks and vanilla. Work together into a smooth paste. Divide into 3 portions and chill for 30 minutes.
FILLING: Melt butter in a heavy saucepan, add apples and lemon rind and juice, cover and cook gently until soft and pulpy. Mix in sugar and purée in a food processor or blender or push through a sieve. Roll out pastry (dough) into 3 equal-sized rounds about 20 cm (8 in) diameter. Bake on baking trays in a preheated moderate oven (180°C/350°F, Gas Mark 4) for about 15 minutes or until a pale golden colour. When pastry (dough) is cold sandwich layers together with apple mixture. Cover the top with a thin layer of glacé icing and marble with redcurrant jelly, if using. Serves 8.

GAME

For culinary purposes, 'game' means the meat of wild animals and birds or of traditional game species which are now farmed for the table.

Game is prized for its rich flavours and textures. The powerful aroma and taste referred to as 'gamey' develop with lengthy hanging – a necessity with much wild game in order to tenderize it, but less necessary for the farmed kind.

Most game tends to be dry, so game is often marinated or barded or larded with fat before cooking to promote juiciness.
To bard game: Cover the breast of the bird with fat bacon or pork fat before roasting; toward the end of cooking the covering is removed and the breast dredged with flour and basted. This is called 'frothing' and is done to brown the breast.
To lard game: Cut strips of pork fat and thread or insert through the flesh, using a larding needle.

Roasting is the best way to cook good, young game, but if you have any doubts about tenderness, it is advisable to casserole it to ensure moist, tender meat. Game also makes a luxurious soup or pie. Small game birds are often roasted on a piece of toast and are served on the toast. **See recipes.**
Accompaniments for Game: Game Chips (see page 308), wild rice and browned breadcrumbs (see page 45) are classic accompaniments to game. Other accompaniments should be robustly flavoured, e.g. braised celery, Brussels sprouts and chestnuts, glazed onions or turnips; spiced fruit or orange salad.

See also *Pheasant, Quail, Rabbit* and *Venison.*

Game Pie

1 pheasant or 2–3 smaller game birds; 2 slices each onion, carrot and celery; 1 bouquet garni; 500 ml/18 fl oz (2 cups) water; 250 g (8 oz) skinless belly pork (fresh pork sides), diced; 125 g (4 oz) cooked ham, diced; 1 onion, finely chopped; 1 tbsp chopped parsley; 1 tsp chopped fresh thyme, or $\frac{1}{2}$ tsp dried; 1 leaf fresh sage, finely chopped, or pinch dried; 4 juniper berries, crushed; $\frac{1}{4}$ tsp ground mace; 120 ml/4 fl oz ($\frac{1}{2}$ cup) port; 2 tbsp brandy; 1 tsp salt; freshly ground black pepper; 90 g/3 oz ($\frac{3}{4}$ cup) mushrooms, sliced; 30 g/1 oz (2 tbsp) butter; 1 tbsp flour; 250 g (8 oz) frozen puff pastry (paste), thawed; 1 egg yolk, beaten.

Cut meat off pheasant or other birds. Put carcase into a saucepan with slices of onion, carrot and celery, bouquet garni and water and simmer, covered, for $1\frac{1}{2}$ hours. Strain, chill and remove fat from surface. Cut pheasant meat into bite-sized pieces and place in a bowl with pork, ham, chopped onion, herbs, berries, mace, port, brandy, salt and pepper. Cover and leave 6–8 hours, turning over occasionally. Put meat mixture into a pie dish just big enough to hold it. Sauté mushrooms in butter and place them on top of meat mixture. Add flour to fat in sauté pan and stir until golden, then add 250 ml/8 fl oz (1 cup) stock from carcase and stir until boiling. Season with salt and pepper and pour over pie filling. Cool completely. Cover dish with puff pastry (paste), make a hole in the centre and decorate with pastry (dough) leaves. Brush with egg yolk and bake in a preheated hot oven (230°C/450°F, Gas Mark 8) for 15 minutes or until pastry is well-risen, then reduce heat to moderately hot (190°C/375°F, Gas Mark 5) and bake for a further $1\frac{1}{2}$ hours or until meat is tender (test with a skewer through hole in crust). If crust is browning too much, cover loosely with foil. Serves 4–6.

Game Soup

2–3 game bird carcases, cooked or raw; 1.5 litres/2$\frac{1}{2}$ pints (6 cups) good beef stock (bouillon); 2 tsp chopped mixed fresh herbs, or $\frac{1}{2}$ tsp dried; 3 juniper berries, crushed; 60 g/2 oz (4 tbsp) butter; 60 g (2 oz) cooked ham, diced; 1 onion, diced; 1 small carrot, diced; 1 tender stick celery, diced; 60 g/2 oz ($\frac{1}{2}$ cup) mushrooms, sliced; 3 tbsp flour; salt and freshly ground black pepper; 4 tbsp port or sherry; 60–90 g (2–3 oz) cooked game bird meat, cut into small strips.

Simmer carcases, stock, herbs and juniper berries together for $1\frac{1}{2}$ hours. Strain into a bowl and wash out saucepan. In same saucepan, melt butter and brown ham and vegetables. Stir in flour and cook 2 minutes. Remove from heat, cool a little, then add 1.2 litres/2 pints (5 cups) warm stock and stir until smoothly blended. Return to heat and stir until boiling. Season with salt and pepper and add port or sherry and the meat. Cover and simmer 20–30 minutes or until vegetables are tender. Serves 6.

GARAM MASALA

A fragrant blend of spices used in curries. There are dry masalas in powder form and wet masalas ground into a paste with water, oil or vinegar. The spices are roasted to bring out the flavour and make it easier to grind to a fine powder.

There are many versions of garam masala, and most cooks use their own favourite combinations of spices according to their preference. Some use hot spices such as pepper, while others use only the fragrant aromatic ones. Always use good quality spices, and buy them from a store that has a rapid turnover to ensure freshness. Store in an airtight jar in a cool, dry place.

Garam masala is sometimes added to recipes with other spices at the frying stage, but it is more often used during the last few minutes of cooking when it is sprinkled over the food. **See recipes.**

Garam Masala

4 tbsp coriander seeds; 2 tbsp cumin seeds; 1 tbsp black peppercorns; 2 tsp cardamom seeds; 4 × 8 cm (3 in) cinnamon sticks; 1 tsp whole cloves; 1 whole nutmeg, finely grated.

Over medium heat in a small pan roast separately first coriander, then cumin, peppercorns, cardamom, cinnamon and lastly cloves. Remove each spice from the pan as it begins to smell fragrant and cool it on a plate. Put all into a blender and blend to a fine powder or pound using a mortar and pestle. Mix in nutmeg and store in an airtight jar. Will keep several months. Makes 90 g/3 oz ($\frac{3}{4}$ cup).

Fragrant Garam Masala

3 × 8 cm (3 in) cinnamon sticks; 2 tsp cardamom seeds; 1 tsp whole cloves; ½ nutmeg, grated.

Over medium heat in a small pan roast separately first cinnamon, then cardamom, then cloves. Remove each spice from the pan when it begins to smell fragrant and cool on a plate. When all are roasted and cooled, blend to a fine powder in a blender or pound using a mortar and pestle. Finally add nutmeg. Makes 30 g/1 oz (¼ cup).

GARLIC

The distinctive taste of garlic makes it one of the best-known herbs. A perennial plant of the onion family, it is the small bulbous root that is used for flavouring. When fully grown, the bulb is made up of a number of small sections, known as cloves. One clove is usually sufficient to bring out the flavours in a savoury dish, although there is a famous chicken dish that calls for 40 cloves of garlic – yet the flavour is surprisingly gentle (see opposite).

Garlic is an essential ingredient in the cuisines of France, Spain and Italy, the Middle East and Far Eastern countries. In the south of France and in Spain, garlic is used lavishly – in sauces, salads, meat and fish dishes, as a vegetable, or crushed and spread on crusty bread which has been liberally sprinkled with fruity olive oil. In Italy, on the other hand, its use is generally more discreet. The garlic clove is added whole and then removed from the dish before serving. In the south of Italy, however, a more lusty flavour is enjoyed.

For some, garlic's odour is a deterrent to its enjoyment, but for those who love garlic there are ways to render it inoffensive. The aroma of a garlic-flavoured meal is less offensive when accompanied by salad greens, providing garlic is not used in the dressing. Fresh parsley neutralizes garlic on the breath most effectively. If a whole clove of garlic is cooked peeled but not cut, a much milder flavour results. The smell of garlic can be removed from the hands by sprinkling them with salt, then rinsing with cold water.

Ways to Use Garlic

● Garlic is an essential ingredient in curries.
● It perks up otherwise bland dishes such as yogurt, soups and some side salads. Try sliced cucumber in sour cream and see what a difference a little garlic makes (good as an accompaniment to curries).
● Crushed and lightly fried with some butter, garlic gives boiled vegetables a delicious flavour – try it with spinach, beans or courgettes (zucchini).
● One clove, blended with 30 g/1 oz (2 tbsp) butter, makes the butter for garlic bread that everyone loves (see below).
● A whole peeled clove, steeped in Vinaigrette Dressing (see page 358) for a few hours makes a difference to green salads.
● It is a basic ingredient of many rich casseroles and seafood soups.
● Its robust flavour turns mayonnaise into Aïoli (see page 6). **See recipes**.

To crush garlic: Garlic may be crushed in a garlic press but by far the easiest method is to crush it with salt.

Take an unpeeled garlic clove. Place it on a board. Place the flat part of the knife blade on top and give the blade a sharp crack with the side of the palm. This flattens the garlic clove and makes the skin easy to remove. Remove the thin papery skin of the garlic. Sprinkle the garlic with 1 tsp salt. Using the flat edge of the knife blade, work the garlic and salt to a pulp.

Garlic Bread Cut a loaf of Italian or French bread into thin diagonal slices, *almost* through to bottom crust but so loaf still holds together. Spread cut surfaces with Garlic Butter (see below). Wrap bread in foil. Bake in a preheated moderately hot oven (190°C/375°F, Gas Mark 5) for 15 minutes, loosen foil and bake for a further 5 minutes to make crust crispy. Serve hot.

Garlic Butter Cream 125 g/4 oz (½ cup) butter. Crush 1 or more garlic cloves (to taste), and blend into butter. Use to make Garlic Bread, or use on snails, mussels, over boiled fish or vegetables.

Garlic Chapons This is the name given, in the south-west of France, to crusts of bread or slices of crusty French bread which have been rubbed with raw garlic, seasoned with oil, vinegar, salt and pepper and added to green salad, especially to curly endive (chicory). Sometimes seasoned chapons are put into a preheated cool oven (150°C/300°F, Gas Mark 2) for 15–20 minutes to allow them to dry out and become crispy.

Garlic Oil Use for seasoning salads. Peel 10 garlic cloves, drop into boiling salted water for 3–4 minutes. Drain them, then pound in a mortar to a fine paste. Add 250 ml/8 fl oz (1 cup) good olive oil, then push through a muslin cloth or sieve.

Garlic and Oil Sauce Cook 2–3 finely chopped garlic cloves gently in 4 tbsp olive oil. Season with salt and pepper to taste and serve at once over well-drained hot pasta or boiled potatoes.

Tomatoes Provençale

2 medium tomatoes, halved; salt and freshly ground black pepper; 15 g/½ oz (¼ cup) fresh breadcrumbs; 2 tsp melted butter; 1 clove garlic, crushed.

Season tomatoes with salt and pepper. Mix breadcrumbs with butter and garlic and season with salt and pepper. Spoon on to tomato halves. Grill (broil) under a preheated moderate grill (broiler) until crumbs have browned and tomatoes heated through, or bake in a preheated moderately hot oven (190°C/375°F, Gas Mark 5) for 15 minutes. Serves 4.

Garlic Prawns

500 g (1 lb) large prawns (shrimp); 175 ml/6 fl oz (¾ cup) olive oil; 4 cloves garlic, finely chopped; ½ tsp chopped red chilli, or pinch chilli powder; 2 tsp salt; 1 tbsp chopped parsley and 1 tbsp snipped chives (optional).

Shell and devein prawns or leave whole, unshelled. Place in covered container with 120 ml/4 fl oz (½ cup) olive oil, the garlic, chilli and salt. Cover and refrigerate for at least 2 hours. When ready to serve, heat remaining oil in 4 flameproof dishes. Drain prawns, reserving marinade. Divide prawns between dishes and cook for 3–4 minutes or until prawns turn pink. Pour reserved marinade over, add parsley and chives and cook for further 1 minute. Serve with crusty French bread. Serves 4.

Lamb Aillade

Leg of lamb cooked with garlic, anchovies, rosemary and thyme is a speciality of Provence. It is traditionally served at Easter.

1 leg of lamb, about 2 kg (4 lb); 12 cloves garlic, 6 whole and 6 slivered; 12 anchovy fillets, chopped; 3 tbsp olive oil; 1 tsp chopped fresh rosemary; 1 tsp chopped fresh thyme; salt and freshly ground black pepper; 120 ml/4 fl oz (½ cup) dry white wine; 2 tbsp chopped parsley or mint.

Make slits in lamb and insert a sliver of garlic and a piece of anchovy in each incision. Rub lamb with 2 tbsp of the olive oil, the rosemary, thyme, salt and pepper. Let it stand for 1–2 hours. Place meat on a rack in a roasting tin (pan) and roast in a preheated moderately hot oven (200°C/400°F, Gas Mark 6) for 20 minutes. Reduce heat to moderate (180°C/350°F, Gas Mark 4) and cook for a further 1–1¼ hours. Heat remaining 1 tbsp olive oil in a frying pan (skillet) and cook whole garlic cloves slowly for about 10 minutes or until they are soft (do not let edges become crisp). Set aside in a small bowl. Remove lamb from roasting pan and pour off excess fat. Pour wine into pan, scrape up brown bits and boil wine over high heat to reduce it by half. Add reduced liquid to garlic cloves. Mash well with a fork and add salt and pepper. Slice lamb and sprinkle with pepper. Spoon sauce over it and sprinkle with parsley or mint. Serves 6–8.

Chicken with 40 Cloves of Garlic

A dish from the French provincial area of Dauphine. Don't be startled by the quantity of garlic in this recipe. The chicken will emerge golden, meltingly tender and with the most wonderful aroma of herbs and garlic. Serve with plenty of thick slices of crusty bread.

1 × 1.75 kg (3½ lb) chicken; salt and freshly ground black pepper; small bouquet fresh parsley, thyme, rosemary and tarragon; 175 ml/6 fl oz (¾ cup) olive oil; 40 unpeeled garlic cloves; bunch fresh rosemary, thyme, sage, bay leaf, parsley and celery leaves; 125 g/4 oz (1 cup) flour mixed to a thick paste with 4 tbsp water.

Season chicken inside and out with salt and pepper. Place bouquet of fresh herbs inside. Pour oil into a flameproof casserole just large enough to hold chicken and add unpeeled garlic cloves. Place the larger bunch of fresh herbs on top of garlic. Gently warm oil, then add chicken and turn to coat all over. Cover dish and seal lid to base with flour and water paste. Bake in a preheated moderate oven (180°C/350°F, Gas Mark 4) for 1½ hours. Break pastry seal, clean seal from the edge and serve in the dish with crusty bread. Serves 4–6.

GATEAU

The French word for cake of all types – plain or decorated, large or small, used for dessert, with coffee or at celebrations and parties. In other parts of the world the word 'gâteau' is synonymous with a rich, highly-decorated

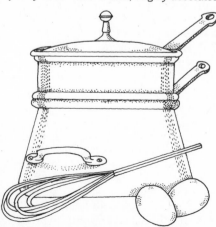

cake, often layered with cream or butter cream, flavoured with liqueur, and decorated with cream, chocolate, nuts or fruits. **See recipes.**

See also *Cakes.*

Gâteau Caraque

75 g/2½ oz (scant ½ cup) unsweetened chocolate, broken into small pieces; 2 tbsp coffee; 3 eggs; 140 g/4½ oz (½ cup plus 1 tbsp) caster sugar; 65 g/2¼ oz (½ cup plus 1 tbsp) flour; 1 quantity Chocolate Crème au Beurre (page 165); Chocolate Caraque or Curls (page 72).

Melt chocolate with coffee over warm water. Set aside to cool. Whisk eggs with sugar until very thick and pale. This will take 8–10 minutes. Sift in flour and fold it in quickly and carefully with the melted chocolate. Turn mixture into a 20 cm (8 in) cake tin (pan) that has been greased, bottom-lined with greased greaseproof (waxed) paper, and floured. Bake in a preheated moderate oven (180°C/350°F, Gas Mark 4) for 30–40 minutes or until a skewer inserted in centre comes out clean. Cool on a wire rack. When cold, split cake into 2 layers and sandwich with ⅓ of the chocolate crème au beurre. Spread sides and top with rest of crème au beurre and cover with chocolate caraque or curls. Serves 8.

Gâteau Rolla

4 egg whites; pinch cream of tartar; 350 g/12 oz (1½ cups) caster sugar; 45 g/1½ oz (⅓ cup) ground almonds; sifted icing (confectioners) sugar.
MOCHA CREME AU BEURRE: 2 egg yolks; 125 g/4 oz (½ cup) sugar; 120 ml/4 fl oz (½ cup) warm milk; 2 tbsp (unsweetened) cocoa powder; 125 g/4 oz (⅔ cup) chocolate, chopped; 250 g/8 oz (1 cup) butter.

Beat egg whites with cream of tartar until they stand in stiff peaks. Add 2 tbsp sugar and continue to beat for a few minutes longer. Fold in remaining sugar and ground almonds with a metal spoon. Cut out 4 rounds of greaseproof (waxed) paper 20 cm (8 in) diameter. Spray with non-stick cooking spray. Place on baking trays. Spread each round with meringue and bake in a preheated cool oven (150°C/300°F, Gas Mark 2) for 15 minutes or until meringue is dry. Turn layers over, peel off paper, and continue to dry for 5 minutes. Turn oven off and leave to cool completely in oven with door open.
MOCHA CREME AU BEURRE: Put egg yolks and sugar in a heatproof bowl and place over hot, but not boiling, water. Beat until very thick and pale lemon coloured. Gradually add milk and cocoa. Add chocolate and blend in to soften, then beat well. Cool. Cream butter until light and fluffy and

resembling whipped cream. Gradually beat in cooled chocolate custard mixture. Sandwich meringue layers together with mocha crème au beurre. Make a lattice of 2.5 cm (1 in) wide strips of paper on top of cake and dust with icing (confectioners) sugar. Remove paper. Refrigerate for at least 24 hours. Serves 8.

Gâteau St Honoré

This is the traditional French birthday cake.

½ quantity Pâte Sucrée (page 276); 1 egg, beaten, to glaze; 1 quantity Choux Pastry (page 276).
CREME ST HONORE: 1 egg, separated; 1 egg yolk; 60 g/2 oz (¼ cup) caster sugar; 2 tbsp flour; 1 tbsp cornflour (cornstarch); 300 ml/½ pint (1¼ cups) milk; 1 vanilla pod (bean); 120 ml/4 fl oz (½ cup) double (heavy) cream.
TO FINISH: 120 ml/4 fl oz (½ cup) double (heavy) cream; vanilla essence (extract); 250 g/8 oz (1 cup) sugar; 120 ml/4 fl oz (½ cup) water.

Roll out pâte sucrée to a 20 cm (8 in) round and place on a greased baking tray. Prick well with a fork, and brush edge with beaten egg. Fill a piping (pastry) bag with a 1 cm (½ in) plain nozzle with choux pastry (paste). Make border around edge of pastry round, 1 cm (½ in) in from outside to allow for spreading. Brush with beaten egg. Pipe remaining choux on to a greased baking tray in 15 small rounds the size of a walnut. Brush with beaten egg. Bake all the pastry in a preheated moderately hot oven (200°C/400°F, Gas Mark 6) for 25 minutes for the choux puffs and 35 minutes for the base or until crisp and golden. Remove from oven. Prick base of each choux puff 2 or 3 times to allow steam to escape and cool on a wire rack. While choux puffs and choux ring are cooling, prepare crème St Honoré.
CREME ST HONORE: Beat 2 egg yolks with sugar until creamy and very light in colour. Mix flour and cornflour (cornstarch) with a little cold milk to make a smooth paste and add to egg yolk mixture. Scald remaining milk (see page 215) with vanilla bean, strain on to egg yolk mixture, blend and return to saucepan. Stir over a gentle heat until mixture boils. Whisk egg white until peaks form, add a little of the hot custard, mix thoroughly and pour back into pan. Stir gently over low heat for 2–3 minutes. Chill. Whip cream and fold through just before serving.

To finish, whip cream, flavour with vanilla and put in a piping (pastry) bag. Cut a tiny hole in the side of each puff with the point of a knife and force in cream through the hole. In a small heavy saucepan heat sugar with water until dissolved. Bring to the boil and boil, without stirring, until golden. Spoon a little syrup on to choux pastry rim and fix.

choux puffs on top. Fill centre of gâteau with crème St Honoré. Return caramel to the heat and cook until a rich amber colour. Immediately put saucepan into cold water to prevent further cooking. Spoon over the puffs. For a spectacular effect, dip 2 spoons into caramel, then pull and spin caramel strands around the gâteau. Serve immediately. Serves 8.

NOTE: The gâteau may be prepared ahead if desired. Make pâte sucrée 2 days ahead, wrap and store in refrigerator.

The day before: Make choux pastry. Roll out pâte sucrée and pipe on choux pastry border. Bake. Prepare and bake puffs. When cool, store base and individual puffs in an airtight tin. Make basic custard but do not fold in whipped cream. Store, covered, in refrigerator.

A few hours before assembling: Place case and puffs in a preheated moderate oven (180°C/350°F, Gas Mark 4) for 10 minutes until crisp. Cool completely.

Just before assembling and serving: Whip cream and fold into basic custard. Fill puffs with vanilla-flavoured cream and continue as directed in recipe.

GAZPACHO

The refreshing, spicy, chilled soup-salad which is served in almost every Spanish home and restaurant. It is a favourite alfresco dish and, accompanied by separate bowls of garnishes, is almost a meal in itself.

Gazpacho

6 ripe, red tomatoes, peeled, or 1 × 425 g/ 14 oz can tomatoes, drained, plus 2 fresh tomatoes, peeled; 250 ml/8 fl oz (1 cup) white wine or chicken stock; 2 cloves garlic, crushed; ½ tsp ground cumin; salt and freshly ground black pepper; 90 g/3 oz (1½ cups) fresh breadcrumbs; 5 tbsp olive oil; 4 tbsp wine vinegar; 750 ml/1¼ pints (3 cups) tomato juice; 1 large onion, diced; 1 green pepper, cored, seeded and diced; 1 cucumber, peeled seeded and diced;

12–16 ice cubes; 3 hard-boiled (hard-cooked) eggs, chopped; 125 g/4 oz (1 cup) small garlic croûtons (page 90).

Seed 6 fresh or the canned tomatoes. Coarsely chop half the fresh or all the canned tomatoes and simmer 5 minutes with wine or stock. Purée in a blender or rub through a sieve. Set aside. Cut remaining tomatoes into small dice. Mix garlic, cumin, salt and pepper. Mix in breadcrumbs, then very gradually beat in oil to form a thick paste. Stir in vinegar little by little, then puréed tomatoes and tomato juice. Combine with half the diced vegetables. Adjust seasoning and chill 2–3 hours before serving. Place 2–3 ice cubes in each bowl, then ladle gazpacho over. Serve remaining vegetables, chopped hard-boiled (hard-cooked) egg and garlic croûtons in separate bowls for each diner to add his own choice of garnish. Serves 6–8.

GELATINE (Gelatin)

An extract of the animal protein, collagen, gelatine makes possible a great range of culinary triumphs both sweet and savoury – a delicate Bavarois (Bavarian Cream, page 105), an airy cold soufflé, a beautifully shaped salmon or vegetable mousse, a sparkling aspic – as well as dozens of family dishes from simple jellies and whips to cake and pie fillings, smooth and economical ice cream, home-made confectionery and appetizing moulds of meat, fish and vegetables. It is sold in powdered form, often in individual envelopes.

Gelatine can be used with almost any food except uncooked pineapple and pawpaw, which contain an enzyme that prevents jelling. As the enzyme is inactivated by heat, cooked or canned pineapple or pawpaw present no problem.

Do not boil gelatine mixtures, as this will weaken the jelling power, nor freeze them unless their fat content is very high, as in ice creams.

Amount to use: Proportions of gelatine to liquid may vary from recipe to recipe, depending on other ingredients. As a general guide, 1 envelope or 3 tsp gelatine will set 500 ml/18 fl oz (2 cups) liquid into jelly. If the jelly is to be unmoulded, use 1 tbsp gelatine to 500 ml/18 fl oz (2 cups) liquid to give a slightly firmer texture.

To add gelatine to a mixture: Sprinkle gelatine over cold water or some of the liquid used in the recipe, using about 3 times the volume of liquid to gelatine. Do not stir but leave the liquid to absorb the gelatine, undisturbed. If gelatine is to be added to a hot mixture, add it and stir until dissolved. If gelatine is to be added to a cold mixture, soften it first. Place the gelatine container in

hot water on gentle heat, and leave until mixture is clear. Stir or fold into the cold mixture, and continue to stir or fold carefully until mixture is on the point of setting (when it has the consistency of unbeaten egg whites), before turning into a mould or dish to set.

To unmould a gelatine mixture: This is not difficult if you don't try to rush it. Have ready a chilled, dampened serving plate and a sink or pan of comfortably hand-warm water, deep enough to come up to the rim of the mould. Remove mould from refrigerator and, with your fingers, gently pull the edge of the gelatine away from the mould all round. Dip the mould into warm water for 4 seconds if it is metal, 8 seconds if it is china or glass.

Lift out and invert the serving plate on top. Hold mould and plate firmly together, turn over and shake gently up and down until the gelatine slips from the mould on to the plate. If it doesn't, repeat the process. Centre the gelatine on the dampened plate, then wipe the edges dry. **See recipes.**

Jambon Persillé
(Cold Parsleyed Ham)

1 kg (2 lb) cooked or canned ham, cut into 2.5 cm (1 in) cubes; 350 ml/12 fl oz (1½ cups) well-flavoured chicken stock; 120 ml/4 fl oz (½ cup) dry white wine; freshly ground black pepper; nutmeg; 40 g/1⅓ oz (1 cup) finely chopped parsley; 2 tbsp gelatine; 120 ml/4 fl oz (½ cup) cold water; 1–2 tbsp tarragon vinegar.

Simmer ham in stock and white wine, seasoned with pepper and nutmeg, for 5 minutes. Drain, reserving liquid. Put ham into a bowl or loaf tin (pan) which has been rinsed out with cold water and lightly dusted with parsley. Soften gelatine in water, then stir in hot liquid. When gelatine has dissolved, add remaining parsley and tarragon vinegar to taste. Allow to cool and, when syrupy, pour over the ham. Chill in refrigerator until well set, then unmould. Serves 8–10.

Fresh Orange Jelly

thinly peeled rind 1 orange; thinly peeled rind and juice ½ lemon; 75 g/2½ oz (⅓ cup) sugar; 300 ml/½ pint (1¼ cups) hot water; 2 tbsp plus 3 tsp gelatine; 600 ml/1 pint (2½ cups) freshly squeezed orange juice, strained; extra sugar or lemon juice; single (light) cream to serve.

Put orange and lemon rind, lemon juice, sugar and half the water into a saucepan and warm on low heat for 10 minutes to infuse. Dissolve gelatine in remaining hot water. Stir into ingredients in saucepan, strain and cool. Stir in orange juice, taste and add a little more sugar or lemon juice, if needed. Pour into a mould or glass bowl. Chill until set. Serve with cream. Serves 6–8.

GENOISE CAKE (Genoese)

A sponge cake used for filled cakes, sponge fingers (lady fingers), petits fours or Bombe Alaska. The eggs and sugar are beaten with a balloon whisk over gentle heat until they are warm, thick and pale lemon-coloured, and the beating continues at room temperature until the mixture is cool and even thicker. These 2 steps can be done using a hand-held electric mixer, with or without the use of heat, although the volume of the cake will not be quite as great as it would when hand-mixed with a balloon whisk. Flour and melted butter are then mixed in very quickly and lightly to preserve the masses of air bubbles formed through whisking.

To make filled, layered cakes, use whipped cream or Butter Cream (see page 163) flavoured with liqueur, and decorate with fruit or nuts.

Top single cakes with Butter Icing (Frosting) flavoured to your taste (see Icings, Frostings and Fillings).

Genoise Cake

4 eggs; 125 g/4 oz ($\frac{1}{2}$ cup) caster sugar; $\frac{1}{2}$ tsp vanilla essence (extract); 125 g/4 oz (1 cup) flour, sifted; 60 g/2 oz (4 tbsp) butter, melted and cooled.

Put eggs, sugar and vanilla in a heatproof bowl, place over warm water over a gentle heat and whisk until the mixture is pale lemon-coloured, thick and doubled in bulk. This will take about 7 minutes. Remove bowl from heat and beat a further 3–4 minutes or until cool and very thick. Fold in flour, then add butter. Mix as lightly and rapidly as possible. Turn at once into 2 greased 20 cm (8 in) round or 18 cm (7 in) square tins (pans) that have been bottom-lined with greased greaseproof (waxed) paper. Bake in a preheated moderate oven (180°C/350°F, Gas Mark 4) for 20–30 minutes or until cooked. To test, gently press centre with finger – if cake springs back it is cooked. If impression remains, leave cake for further 5 minutes and test again. Cool on a wire rack. This recipe will make 2 × 20 cm (8 in) round cakes or 2 × 18 cm (7 in) squares.

GHEE

See Butter

GHERKIN (Cornichon)

Gherkins or cornichons ('little horns') are very small cucumbers which are grown for pickling. The best are about 3 cm (1$\frac{1}{2}$ in) long. Serve pickled gherkins with hot boiled beef, corned beef or frankfurters, or with cold meats or cheese. They are also part of the

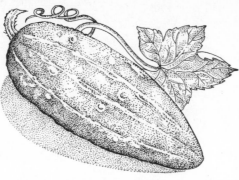

flavouring for Tartare, Gribiche and Rémoulade Sauces (see pages 151 and 205).

Gherkins

1 kg (2 lb) firm gherkins; 310 g/10 oz (1 cup) salt; 1 litre/1$\frac{3}{4}$ pints (4 cups) water; 1 tbsp whole cloves; 1 tbsp white peppercorns; 1 tbsp blade mace; 1 tbsp whole allspice; 1 × 8 cm (3 in) cinnamon stick; 2 slices fresh ginger; 1 litre/1$\frac{3}{4}$ pints (4 cups) white vinegar; grape leaves (optional).

Place gherkins in a large bowl. Dissolve salt in water and pour over gherkins. Cover and leave 3 days. Meantime, tie spices and flavourings in a muslin bag, place in vinegar and bring to the boil. Cool, with spice bag in vinegar, for 2 hours, then remove bag. After 3 days, drain, rinse and dry gherkins. Pack them into scalded wide-mouthed jars. Bring vinegar to the boil, pour over gherkins, cover tightly and leave 24 hours. Pour off vinegar into a saucepan, bring to the boil again, pour over gherkins and leave as before. Repeat this process once more. Add a few grape leaves to each jar, if desired, to help keep gherkins crisp. Cover tightly and leave 6 weeks. Makes 2 × 500 g (1 lb) jars.

GIBLETS

The name for the neck, heart, gizzard and liver of poultry (though livers may or may not be included in giblets that you buy). If giblets are sold with a bird, they are packaged and placed in the body cavity, so always be sure to check before cooking. If they are there, use them to enrich the gravy to be served with the bird. Giblets are also sold separately. They make excellent soup or can be served in a sauce made from their cooking liquid.

□ **Basic Preparation:** Remove all fat and membrane from giblets and cut off any discoloured or dark parts from liver. Clean all grit from gizzard and scrape the lining well. Wash giblets under cold running water.

Giblet Gravy Put all giblets, except liver, into a saucepan and add a slice each of onion and carrot, a small piece of celery and a few fresh herbs if you have them. Cover with cold water and simmer 45 minutes or until giblets are tender. It is best to cook liver separately

because of its strong flavour. If you are roasting a bird, cook liver under it for 5–10 minutes; otherwise sauté it in a little butter.

Strain liquid from the pan of giblets and reserve, and discard neck. Finely dice the heart, gizzard and cooked liver. Use reserved liquid when making gravy and add diced giblets at the end.

GINGER

A bold perennial, with the most heavenly scented flower. The 'root', which is known as the 'hand' (it looks rather like a hand with plump, deformed fingers) is the edible part of the plant. Whole, fresh ginger should be smooth-skinned and kept dry. Also see 'To keep fresh ginger' (below).

Fresh Ginger: It can be peeled and grated or ground to a pulp and used in many types of curries. (See Prawn Curry and Lamb with Cashew Nut Curry, page 93). In Chinese dishes, a slice of fresh ginger is added to oil and sautéed for a minute to give its distinctive but delicate flavour to the oil. Peeled and cut into fine strips, it is often used in Chinese and Japanese dishes (see Coriander Chicken and Steamed Fish Coriander, pages 83 and 84). Peeled and sliced, it can be rubbed over chicken, fish or duck, as you would garlic.

Dried Ginger: The root is often dried. To use, cut into pieces and soak in cold water for several hours. Dried ginger is also ground to a powder, and is a popular spice for flavouring cakes, biscuits (cookies) and puddings.

Preserved Ginger: The peeled root is often preserved in syrup and eaten as a sweetmeat. Preserved ginger is used in fruit and cream desserts and steamed puddings. The syrup may be poured over ice cream, etc.

Candied Ginger: This is another popular treatment; chopped or sliced it is used in baking or as a sweetmeat.

Finally, ginger is widely used for flavouring ginger ale and ginger beer.

To keep fresh ginger: Juicy young roots that have not become too fibrous may be peeled and cut into small knobs. Place in a clean glass jar and cover with dry sherry. Keep, covered, in refrigerator and use as for fresh ginger. **See recipes.**

Gingered Honeydew Melon Peel and slice a ripe chilled honeydew melon. Discard seeds and arrange slices in an overlapping design on a chilled platter. Sprinkle them with a mixture of 1 tbsp icing (confectioners) sugar, sifted, and $\frac{1}{2}$ tsp ground ginger. Serve as a first course or dessert with ice cream.

Ginger Ice Cream Take 500 ml/18 fl oz (2 cups) vanilla ice cream from freezer and allow to soften slightly. Swirl in 2 tbsp finely chopped, preserved ginger and return to freezer. Serve with a crisp sweet biscuit (cookie). Good with poached pears, peaches or sliced fresh melon.

Oriental Chicken Wings

A popular starter for barbecues or casual entertaining. Best eaten in your fingers.

1 kg (2 lb) chicken wings; 4 tbsp soy sauce; 2 tbsp lemon juice; 1 tbsp grated fresh ginger, or ½ tsp ground ginger; 2 tsp honey; 2 tbsp tomato ketchup.

Cut tips off wings. Mix remaining ingredients together, add wings and turn to coat. Leave to marinate, covered, for several hours in refrigerator. Drain and arrange wings on a greased grill (broiler) rack. Cook under a preheated grill (broiler) for about 10 minutes, then turn, brush with marinade, and grill (broil) for a further 10 minutes. Serve hot with plenty of paper napkins. Serves 6.

Ginger Marinade

1 tbsp grated fresh ginger; 2 tbsp soy sauce; 1 tbsp lemon juice; 2 tbsp oil.

Combine ingredients. Use to marinate 500 g (1 lb) shelled prawns (shrimp) or scallops, diced chicken or pork, fish fillets or chicken pieces. Marinate, covered, about 30 minutes to 2 hours. Thread marinated food on skewers or place fish fillets or chicken joints on grill (broiler) rack. Cook under preheated grill (broiler) turning several times and brushing with extra marinade during cooking.

Chinese Gingered Roast Chicken

3 tbsp soy sauce; 1 tbsp honey; 2.5 cm (1 in) piece fresh ginger, grated, or ½ tsp ground ginger; 3 cloves garlic, crushed; 1½ tsp five-spice powder; 1 × 1.5 kg (3 lb) roasting chicken; 3 tbsp salt.

Combine soy sauce, honey, ginger, garlic and ½ tsp five-spice powder, and rub over chicken and in cavity. Cover and refrigerate 1–2 hours, turning occasionally. Drain chicken, reserving marinade. Put on a rack in roasting pan containing a little water (to prevent drippings from burning). Roast in a preheated moderate oven (180°C/350°F, Gas Mark 4) for 1¼ hours, brushing 3 or 4 times with reserved marinade and turning chicken occasionally. Chop chicken through skin and bones into bite-sized pieces. Arrange on a heated serving dish. Serve remaining five-spice powder mixed with salt for dipping. Serves 6.
NOTE: Five-spice powder is available from oriental grocery shops or oriental sections at supermarkets.

Rich Ginger Cake

A marvellously rich, moist cake with excellent keeping qualities; an old family favourite that is splendid for picnics, lunch-boxes and morning and afternoon snacks.

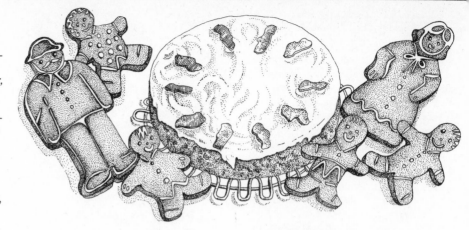

125 g/4 oz (½ cup) butter; 140 g/4½ oz (¾ cup) firmly packed brown sugar; 250 g/8 oz (2 cups) flour; 1 tsp ground ginger; pinch salt; 2 eggs; 350 g/12 oz (1 cup) treacle; 60 g/2 oz (⅓ cup) sultanas (golden raisins); 60 g/2 oz (⅓ cup) sliced, preserved ginger; 4 tbsp milk; ½ tsp bicarbonate of soda (baking soda).

Cream butter with sugar until light and fluffy. Sift flour with ground ginger and salt. Beat eggs into creamed butter mixture one at a time, sprinkling mixture each time with 2 tsp flour. Stir in treacle, sultanas (golden raisins), preserved ginger and remaining flour. Warm milk, add soda and stir at once into cake mixture. Turn into a greased and floured 18 cm (7 in) round deep cake tin (pan) or 21 × 11 × 6 cm (8½ × 4½ × 2½ in) loaf tin (pan). Bake cake in a preheated moderate oven (180°C/350°F, Gas Mark 4) for 1 hour, then reduce heat to 160°C/325°F, Gas Mark 3 and bake for a further 30 minutes. If cake begins to brown too much on top, cover loosely with a piece of greaseproof (waxed) paper. Cool for 5 minutes before turning out.

Crystal Prawns

Soaking prawns (shrimp) in water with bicarbonate of soda (baking soda) gives the prawn (shrimp) meat a clear colour – thus the name. It also slightly changes the texture of the meat.

1½ tbsp bicarbonate of soda (baking soda); 575 ml/19 fl oz (2¼ cups) water; 500 g (1 lb) Dublin Bay prawns (jumbo shrimp), shelled and deveined; 1½ tbsp cornflour (cornstarch); ½ tsp salt; ½ tsp sugar; 2 tbsp shredded fresh ginger; 2 tbsp shredded red pepper; 30 g (1 oz) sliced spring onions (scallions).

Dissolve soda in 500 ml/18 fl oz (2 cups) water, add prawns (shrimp) and soak for 2 hours. Drain and rinse well under cold running water, then soak again in fresh cold water to cover for a further 1 hour. Drain. Blanch in boiling water for 2 minutes, drain well and dry. Combine remaining 4 tbsp water, the cornflour (cornstarch), salt and sugar and heat in a wok or frying pan (skillet), stirring, until boiling. Add prawns (shrimp) and toss until well coated and heated through. Place ginger and vegetables on a heated serving platter, spoon prawns (shrimp) on top and toss through. Serves 4.

GINGER BEER

Home-made ginger beer is one of the joys of childhood. It is made by fermenting a simple syrup with a yeast, ginger and sugar mixture (called 'plant'). As fermentation causes strong pressure inside bottles, be sure to use sturdy bottles, seal them with patent clip-on bottle seals or screw-tops and store them in a cool place where a burst bottle will do no harm.

Ginger Beer

GINGER BEER PLANT: *1 tsp fresh (compressed) yeast or ½ tsp dried (active dry) yeast; 9 tsp sugar; 250 ml/8 fl oz (1 cup) warm water; 9 tsp ground ginger.*
SYRUP: *1 kg/2 lb (4 cups) sugar; 6 litres/10½ pints (24 cups) warm water; 120 ml/4 fl oz (½ cup) strained lemon juice.*

PLANT: Mix yeast and ½ tsp sugar in a large jar and add water – lukewarm for fresh (compressed) yeast, comfortably hand-warm for dry yeast – and ½ tsp ginger. Cover jar with muslin and leave 8 days, adding ½ tsp each of ginger and sugar every day.
SYRUP: Heat sugar and 1.5 litres/2½ pints (6 cups) water, stirring, until sugar dissolves. Remove from heat, add remaining water and lemon juice. Strain yeast mixture through 2 thicknesses of muslin. Reserve sediment. Add strained liquid to syrup. Stir well. Pour into bottles, filling only to base of necks, and seal. Leave about 5 days before drinking.

To make further batches of ginger beer, halve plant left on muslin and place in 2 jars with 1 tsp ground ginger, 1 tsp sugar and 250 ml/8 fl oz (1 cup) water in each (no more yeast is added). Repeat process as before, adding sugar and ginger daily. Makes 8 × 750 ml/1¼ pint (3 cup) bottles.

G

GINGERBREAD AND GINGER-BREAD MEN

These lovely old favourites are easy to make, keep well and are immensely popular with all members of the family. **See recipes.**

Gingerbread

180 g/6 oz (1½ cups) flour; 2 tsp baking powder; 1 tsp ground ginger; ½ tsp mixed spice (ground allspice); pinch salt; 60 g/2 oz (4 tbsp) butter; 2 tbsp treacle (molasses); 90 g/3 oz (½ cup) loosely packed brown sugar; 2 eggs, beaten; 175 ml/6 fl oz (¾ cup) milk; 1 tsp bicarbonate of soda (baking soda); Lemon Glacé Icing (page 164).

Sift flour, baking powder, ginger, spice and salt. Cream butter with treacle (molasses) and sugar until light. Stir in flour mixture, eggs and milk in which soda has been dissolved. Beat vigorously until surface of batter is covered with bubbles. Pour into a greased 20 cm (8 in) round or square cake tin (pan) that has been bottom-lined with greased greaseproof (waxed) paper. Bake in a preheated moderate oven (180°C/350°F, Gas Mark 4) for 30–35 minutes. Keep cake airtight for 1–2 days before cutting, to develop flavours. Top with lemon glacé icing (frosting).

Nutty Gingerbread

310 g/10 oz (2½ cups) flour; ½ tsp bicarbonate of soda (baking soda); ½ tsp salt; 1½ tsp cinnamon; 1½ tsp ground ginger; 125 g/4 oz (⅔ cup) sultanas (golden raisins); 45 g/1½ oz (⅓ cup) chopped almonds; 125 g/4 oz (⅔ cup) firmly packed brown sugar; 180 g/6 oz (½ cup) treacle (molasses); 90 g/3 oz (¼ cup) golden (light corn) syrup; 180 g/6 oz (¾ cup) butter; 2 large eggs, beaten.
TO FINISH: *lemon or orange Vienna Icing (page 163); glacé (candied) ginger (optional).*

Sift flour, soda, salt, cinnamon and ginger, and stir in sultanas (golden raisins) and almonds. Put sugar, treacle (molasses), syrup and butter in a pan and heat gently until butter melts. Add to flour mixture. Mix in eggs and beat well. Pour into a greased 28 × 19 cm (11 × 7½ in) cake tin (pan) that has been bottom-lined with greased grease-proof (waxed) paper. Bake in a preheated moderate oven (180°C/350°F, Gas Mark 4) for 30–35 minutes or until a skewer inserted in centre comes out clean. Allow to cool, then ice (frost) with lemon or orange Vienna icing (frosting) and decorate with slices of glacé (candied) ginger, if using.

Gingerbread Men

125 g/4 oz (½ cup) butter; 75 g/2½ oz (⅓ cup) sugar; 125 g/4 oz (⅓ cup) golden (light corn) syrup; 350 g/12 oz (3 cups) flour; ½ tsp ground ginger; 1 tsp cinnamon; 3 tsp bicarbonate of soda (baking soda); 1 egg; 2 tsp vanilla essence (extract).
DECORATION: *currants; glacé (candied) cherries.*

Put butter, sugar and syrup in a saucepan and heat gently, stirring occasionally, until butter melts. Allow to cool. Sift flour, ginger and cinnamon. Add soda to cooled butter mixture and pour on to flour mixture. Add egg and vanilla, and mix to a soft dough. Roll out to a thickness of 5 mm (¼ in) and cut out shapes with a gingerbread man cutter or a sharp knife. Place on greased baking trays. Put currants in place for eyes and buttons, and cherries cut into strips for mouths. Bake in a preheated moderate oven (180°C/350°F, Gas Mark 4) for 10 minutes. Cool on a wire rack. Makes about 20 small gingerbread men.

GINGERNUT BISCUITS

These hard, crunchy biscuits (cookies) have a wonderfully spicy flavour.

Gingernuts

125 g/4 oz (1 cup) flour; 2 tbsp sugar; 1 tsp bicarbonate of soda (baking soda); 1 tsp mixed spice (ground allspice); 1 tsp cinnamon; 1 tsp ground ginger; 60 g/2 oz (4 tbsp) butter; 2 tbsp golden (light corn) syrup; extra 60 g/2 oz (¼ cup) sugar (optional).

Sift dry ingredients. Melt butter with syrup and pour into flour mixture. Mix well and roll into balls the size of a walnut. If liked, roll the balls in extra sugar before baking for super crunchiness. Place on greased baking trays and press lightly. Bake in a preheated hot oven (230°C/450°F, Gas Mark 8) for 5 minutes, then reduce the oven heat to moderate (180°C/350°F, Gas Mark 4) and bake for a further 7–10 minutes. Cool on trays. Makes about 20.

GNOCCHI

The delectable little savoury dumplings or cakes of Italy are mostly made from mixtures containing semolina or polenta (see page 300), mashed potatoes or Ricotta cheese and spinach. They are served with a variety of sauces or simply with melted butter and grated cheese, and hold the same place as pasta in a meal. They can also make a satisfying meal when served alone with salad, or can accompany grilled (broiled) meats or roast chicken. Gnocchi can be shaped like little dumplings and poached in lightly salted water, or cut into cakes and baked in the oven. **See recipes.**

Gnocchi alla Romana

(Semolina Gnocchi)

1 medium onion, halved; 1 bay leaf; 900 ml/1½ pints (3¾ cups) milk; 140 g/4½ oz (¾ cup) semolina or polenta; 1½ tsp salt; freshly ground white pepper; 90 g/3 oz (¾ cup) grated Parmesan cheese; 60 g/2 oz (4 tbsp) butter; ½ tsp dry mustard.

Put onion halves in a saucepan with bay leaf and milk. Bring slowly to the boil. Remove onion and bay leaf, and add semolina or polenta, salt and pepper. Cook, stirring, over a low heat for 15–20 minutes or until very thick. Remove from heat and stir in half the cheese, 15 g/½ oz (1 tbsp) butter and the mustard. Spread on an oiled baking tray to about 1 cm (½ in) thick. Cool. When cold, cut into rounds with a 5 cm (2 in) cutter or into squares with a knife. Arrange in rings, slightly overlapping, in a well-oiled shallow ovenproof dish. Sprinkle with remaining cheese. Melt remaining butter and sprinkle over top. Bake in a preheated moderate oven (180°C/350°F, Gas Mark 4) for 15 minutes, then place under a preheated hot grill (broiler) until top is brown and crisp. Serve immediately. Serves 4.

Potato Gnocchi

2 kg (4 lb) potatoes, cooked, mashed and kept warm; 2 tsp salt; 2 eggs, beaten; 350 g/12 oz (3 cups) flour, sifted; 1 quantity Bolognese Sauce (page 272); grated Parmesan cheese.

Make dough for potato gnocchi just before cooking as it becomes damp if allowed to stand. Mix together warm mashed potatoes, salt and eggs. Work in enough flour to make a firm but soft dough. Divide dough into pieces and roll in well-floured hands to thick pencil shapes about 1 cm (½ in) diameter. Cut into 2.5 cm (1 in) lengths and pinch centre of each one lightly between finger and thumb.

Place gnocchi on a lightly floured tea-towel, making sure they do not touch each other and stick together. Bring a large

saucepan of salted water to a simmer and drop in gnocchi, a few at a time. Do not crowd pan. As soon as gnocchi float to surface, remove with a slotted spoon. When all are cooked and drained, stir into hot sauce and serve topped with grated Parmesan cheese. Serves 6.

Herb Gnocchi

250 g (8 oz) fresh or frozen spinach; 125 g (4 oz) fresh sorrel leaves (if not available substitute same amount of extra spinach); 60 g/2 oz (1 cup) watercress sprigs; 40 g/1⅓ oz (1 cup) parsley sprigs; 1 tbsp chopped fresh chervil; 1 tbsp chopped fresh tarragon; 1 tbsp chopped fresh dill; 180 g/6 oz (¾ cup) Ricotta cheese; 30 g/1 oz (2 tbsp) butter, cut into small pieces; salt and freshly ground black pepper; 90 g/3 oz (¾ cup) grated Parmesan cheese; 2 eggs, beaten; 2½ tbsp flour; melted butter to serve (optional).

Wash and drain spinach, sorrel, watercress and parsley (if using frozen spinach, allow to thaw and do not wash). Boil 120 ml/4 fl oz (½ cup) water in a large saucepan, add spinach, sorrel, watercress and parsley and boil for 4 minutes. Drain well, squeezing out as much water as possible, and chop finely. Add chervil, tarragon and dill. Stir mixture in a saucepan over a low heat for several minutes to dry out as much as possible. This gives a good dry mixture for shaping gnocchi. Beat Ricotta cheese until smooth and add to green mixture with butter, salt and pepper. Stir in ⅓ of the Parmesan cheese. Remove pan from heat. Beat in eggs and flour until smooth. Pour into a shallow dish and leave, uncovered, in refrigerator overnight.

After chilling, mixture should be firm enough to handle; if it is not, add a little more sifted flour but not too much or gnocchi will be heavy. Heat a large pan of salted water to just below simmering point. Form mixture into egg-shaped gnocchi by using 2 teaspoons and rolling very lightly on a floured board. Drop gnocchi in batches into water, making certain they do not stick together. When they float to the surface, after 4–5 minutes, lift them out with a slotted spoon and drain on a clean cloth. Test one to make sure they are cooked enough. Keep drained gnocchi warm in a heated serving dish while you cook remainder.

Sprinkle gnocchi with a little Parmesan cheese and serve with remaining Parmesan and a jug of melted butter. Serves 4.

GOAT'S MILK

This is more easily digestible than cow's milk, and is excellent for people who are allergic to cow's milk. Goat's milk cheeses are delicious, velvet-textured and fresh. They are found all over France and in countries around the Mediterranean. Goat's cheeses vary in flavour according to the region and the length of time taken for ripening, but most taste nutty and sweet. Garlic, chives and herbs can be used as flavourings.

GOLDEN SYRUP

This light, pale golden syrup is a by-product of sugar refining. In America, where it is not well known, light corn syrup is often used as a substitute. It is used in cakes, puddings, sweet sauces, confectionery, tart fillings and ginger-breads. **See recipes**.

See also *Treacle*.

Golden Syrup Dumplings

250 g/8 oz (2 cups) self-raising flour; pinch salt; 45 g/1½oz (3 tbsp) butter; 2 eggs, beaten; little milk.
SYRUP: 500 ml/18 fl oz (2 cups) water; 75 g/2½ oz (⅓ cup) sugar; 2 tbsp golden (light corn) syrup; 30 g/1 oz (2 tbsp) butter.

Sift flour and salt and rub (cut) in butter. Add eggs and stir in with a knife, adding enough milk to make a soft dough. Divide dough into 12 pieces and roll into balls. In a large saucepan, heat water with sugar and syrup, stirring until sugar dissolves. Add butter and bring to the boil. Place dumplings in syrup, cover and simmer for 20 minutes without lifting lid. Serve dumplings at once, with syrup spooned over them. Serve with custard or cream. Serves 6.

Golden Sponge Pudding

125 g/4 oz (½ cup) butter; 125 g/4 oz (½ cup) caster sugar; 2 eggs; 125 g/4 oz (1 cup) self-raising flour; 2–3 tbsp milk; 6–8 tbsp golden (light corn) syrup.

Cream butter with sugar. Beat in eggs and stir in flour. Add sufficient milk to lighten mixture, which should be soft enough to drop lightly from a spoon. Put syrup in bottom of greased 1 litre/1¾ pint (4 cup) pudding basin (mold). Spoon mixture into basin (mold), cover and steam for 2 hours. Turn out on to a heated serving dish and serve with double (heavy) cream and more hot syrup if you wish. Serves 6.

GOOSE

A festive bird, which is traditionally eaten at Christmas, Michaelmas (29th September) or Martinmas (11th November).

A young roast goose makes succulent eating, though if there is any doubt about tenderness it is better to braise the bird in the same manner as duck. The meat is rich and goose releases quite a lot of fat during cooking, so roast goose is usually stuffed with a sharp sage-and-onion or fruit stuffing.

A pliable breastbone is the sign of a young goose, and a good bird should have a plump breast and a creamy colour. As the bird has a large, bony frame, allow 500–750 g (1–1½ lb) uncooked weight per serving. A 3.5 kg (8 lb) goose will serve 6; a 4.5 kg (10 lb) one will serve 8.

Roast Goose

1 young goose; salt and freshly ground black pepper; 2 apples, halved; 1 onion, halved; 3–4 fresh leaves sage, or ¼ tsp dried; 1 tbsp oil; 2 tbsp flour; 4 tbsp brandy.

Remove excess fat from inside goose and press or cut oil sacs at base of tail to empty them. Wipe bird inside and out with a damp towel and rub inside and out with salt and pepper. Place apples, onion and sage in cavity; sew up opening or close with poultry pins laced with string. Truss goose: tuck wing tips under back, pull loose skin of neck to back and fasten these with small skewers. Tie ends of legs together with string, drawing them close to tail. Prick breast all over with a skewer and dry bird well. Brush a roasting tin (pan) with the oil and place over high heat. Dust goose with flour and place in tin (pan), turning to sear all over. Warm brandy, set alight and pour over bird. (This adds flavour and also sears off any remaining pin feathers.)

Place goose, breast up, on a rack in the tin (pan), cover loosely with foil and roast in a preheated moderate oven (180°C/350°F, Gas Mark 4) for 25 minutes per 500 g (1 lb) or until juice runs clear when a fine skewer is inserted between top of leg and body. Remove fat with a spoon or bulb baster as it accumulates, and remove foil for last 30 minutes to give goose a good golden colour. For a crisp skin, increase heat to hot (220°C/425°F, Gas Mark 7) 10 minutes before end of cooking time, and flick a little ice water over breast once or twice during this time. Leave goose on a heated platter in a warm place for 20 minutes before carving. Serves 6.
NOTE: The goose may be loosely stuffed with a mixture such as Apple, Prune and Nut Stuffing (see page 418), or stuffing may be baked separately with some of the fat that runs from goose. Any leftover fat, lifted from the chilled pan juice, is delicious spread on bread or used for frying potatoes.

GOOSEBERRY

A summer fruit that can have red, yellow or green berries that are either sweet or tart. Gooseberries are grown in cool climates and are widely used in the northern countries of Europe. In English home-cooking, goose-berries are used in tarts, desserts, jams, jellies

G

and sauces, or poached in syrup flavoured with elderflower. Gooseberry Sauce is traditionally served with mackerel, but is good with any oily-fleshed fish, and with roast duck or roast pork. Gooseberry Fool (see page 128) is also a delicious favourite for dessert.

Gooseberry Sauce

250 g (8 oz) fresh gooseberries, or 310 g/10 oz (2 cups) drained canned gooseberries; 2 tsp caster sugar; 60 g/2 oz (4 tbsp) butter; 1 tbsp flour; 250 ml/8 fl oz (1 cup) hot water; ½ tsp ground ginger; salt and freshly ground white pepper; ¼ tsp nutmeg.

If using fresh gooseberries, top and tail (clean) them, cover with cold water and simmer gently until tender. Purée drained fresh or canned gooseberries and sweeten with sugar. Melt half the butter in a small saucepan, stir in flour and pour on hot water. Stir until boiling and simmer for 2 minutes. Remove from heat, stir in remaining butter and then gooseberry purée. Finish with ground ginger, salt, pepper and nutmeg. Makes about 175 ml/6 fl oz (¾ cup).

GOUGERE

A gougère is a savoury choux pastry (paste) ring which may be served in slices with drinks or to accompany soup, or may have the centre filled with a well-flavoured meat or chicken mixture for a luncheon dish or entrée.

Gougère

120 ml/4 fl oz (½ cup) water; 60 g/2 oz (4 tbsp) butter, cut into pieces; 125 g/4 oz (1 cup) flour; 1 tsp salt; ¼ tsp pepper; ½ tsp dry mustard; 2 large eggs; 125 g/4 oz (1 cup) grated Gruyère cheese; beaten egg to glaze.

Put water and butter into a saucepan. Sift flour, salt, pepper and mustard on to a square of greaseproof (waxed) paper. Heat water and butter until butter has melted, then bring to a brisk boil. Tip flour mixture all at once into saucepan and beat briskly with a

wooden spoon over heat until mixture leaves sides of saucepan and begins to film the bottom. Remove from heat, cool slightly and beat in eggs one at a time. Beat in all but 1 tbsp cheese. Put into a piping (pastry) bag with a 1 cm (½ in) plain nozzle. Grease and flour a baking tray, and mark a circle on it with a saucepan lid. Pipe a circle of pastry (paste) on the tray, following outline, then pipe another circle on top of the first. Brush with beaten egg, sprinkle with remaining cheese and bake in centre of a preheated moderately hot oven (200°C/400°F, Gas Mark 6) for 30 minutes or until well risen, crisp and golden-brown. Serve warm, cut into thin slices. For a luncheon dish, fill centre with Chicken à la King (see page 70), creamed seafood or any savoury mixture desired, and cut gougère in wedges to serve. Serves 4.

GOULASH (Gulyas)

The Hungarian word *gulyas* means 'herdsman's stew'. Goulash is popular all over the world, and in Hungary is regarded as the national meat dish. It is an enticingly rich stew that always contains meat, usually beef or veal, onions and sweet or spicy paprika. Goulash should never be thickened except with the use of a diced potato. The meat is best cut into large pieces, about 5 cm (2 in), to prevent breaking up during the long slow cooking process, and the paprika should not be cooked over high heat without liquid as the heat turns it bitter. Sour cream should be served in a bowl on the table for the diners to help themselves.

Hungarian Goulash

2 tbsp lard (shortening); 4 onions, finely chopped; 2 cloves garlic, finely chopped; 1.5 kg (3 lb) veal neck chops or stewing veal, cut into 5 cm (2 in) cubes; 1 tbsp paprika; 2 green peppers, cored, seeded and chopped; 2 tomatoes, peeled and chopped; salt and freshly ground black pepper.
TO SERVE: *noodles; sour cream.*

Heat lard (shortening) in a flameproof casserole and add onions and garlic. Cover and cook gently about 10 minutes until soft and translucent, stirring occasionally. Add veal cubes and sauté until golden. Reduce heat, sprinkle with paprika and cook very gently for about 10 minutes. Add green peppers and tomatoes. Bring to the boil, cover and cook goulash in a preheated cool oven (150°C/300°F, Gas Mark 2) for about 2 hours or until the meat is tender. Season with salt and pepper. Serve with buttered noodles and a bowl of sour cream handed separately. Serves 6–8.

GRANITA (Granite)

Granita and *spumone* are the Italian names for the soft, water ices which are also called sorbets or sherbets elsewhere, though they are unlike some sorbets. Granita should have a slightly granular texture; it can be made from sweetened fruit juices, fruit or coffee.

See also *Ices, Sorbets, Granite and Sherberts.*

Granita di Caffé
(Coffee Water Ice)

150 g/5 oz (1⅔ cups) freshly ground Continental roast coffee; 6 tbsp sugar; 1 litre/1¾ pints (4 cups) boiling water.
TO SERVE: *whipped cream; extra ground coffee (optional).*

Put coffee and sugar into a warmed earthenware jug and pour boiling water over. Cover jug, stand in a saucepan of boiling water and leave to infuse off the heat for 20–30 minutes. Cool. When cold, strain through a filter paper. Pour into a shallow ice cream tray and freeze, without stirring, until frozen to a granular but solid mush. Serve in tall glasses, topped with whipped cream and a sprinkling of ground coffee. Serves 4–6.

GRAPES

Grapes from the vine have been celebrated down the centuries as much for their decorative qualities as for the pleasure of eating them. A fine bunch, served at the end of a meal with creamy cheese or, in the Italian way, on ice, has an air of luxury and refreshes the eye as well as the palate.

When buying grapes, look for those which are fully ripe, but still fresh. Dark grapes should have lost any tinge of green, and white grapes should be just beginning to show an amber tone. All varieties should be plump, with a bloom on the skin, and be firmly attached to the stem. Stems should not be withered, though they should be showing some brown. Store grapes unwashed on a plate, loosely covered with plastic wrap, in the refrigerator.

147

Canned grapes are also available and make an attractive addition to many sweet or savoury dishes.

Ways to Use Grapes

● Chilled grapes are a perfect picnic dessert – carry them in a covered container with a few ice cubes.

● Use grapes in fruit salads, bowls and platters; serve them on ice or with creamy cheese at the end of a meal.

● Grapes combine well with poultry, ham or crab in main course salads, and with ingredients such as apples, pears, watercress, hearts of palm, melon, celery, cottage cheese, walnuts or endive (chicory) in first-course or side salads.

● They also make a good garnish or sauce for hot ham, tongue or game birds and for fish, particularly sole. A grape garnish gives the name *véronique* to a dish.

To peel grapes: Most grapes can be peeled easily with the fingers or a small knife. If they prove difficult, dip them in boiling water while you count to 4, before peeling.

To seed grapes: The seeds are easily flipped out with the point of a knife if grapes are halved. If you want to keep grapes whole, push the prongs of a hair grip (bobby pin) into a cork and use the other end to hook out seeds through the stem end of the grapes.

Frosted Grapes: One of the prettiest decorations for a cake, dessert or fruit bowl. Beat 1 egg white just until frothy and brush over a bunch of grapes, coating each fruit. Dredge with caster sugar, turning to cover all over, shake off excess and dry on a wire rack.

See recipes.

Grape Jelly

under-ripe grapes; sugar.

Put grapes into a heavy saucepan with just enough water to prevent scorching. Stir and crush. Stew over gentle heat until juice runs freely, then strain through a colander lined with several layers of cheesecloth and set over a bowl. Do not press grapes, just allow juice to drip through slowly. Chill juice, then measure it. Do not use sediment. Transfer juice to a saucepan. Add 180 g/6 oz (¾ cup) sugar for every 250 ml/8 fl oz (1 cup) of juice. Stir over heat until sugar has dissolved, then boil rapidly until a few drops of the mixture, dropped on to a chilled plate, will jell as they cool. Pour into clean, warm jars and seal.

Grape Ice Cream

A simple and delicate ice cream, the colour of lilacs.

600 ml/1 pint (2½ cups) double (heavy) cream; 300 ml/½ pint (1¼ cups) unsweetened grape juice; 75 g/2½ oz (⅓ cup) caster sugar; little fresh lemon or lime juice.

Mix cream, grape juice and sugar together and stir until sugar has dissolved. Add lemon or lime juice to taste. Freeze in an electric ice cream maker or sorbetière (see *Ice Cream*). Serves 6.

Grapes Brûlée

370 g/12 oz (3 cups) seedless white grapes; 350 ml/12 fl oz (1½ cups) sour cream; ¼ tsp vanilla essence (extract); 140 g/4½ oz (¾ cup) firmly packed brown sugar.

Arrange grapes in an even layer in a 23 cm (9 in) heatproof glass pie plate or other shallow dish. Mix sour cream and vanilla, and spread over grapes, covering them. Chill for at least 2 hours. Cover with a layer of brown sugar so that none of the cream shows through, then place dish under a preheated very hot grill (broiler) until sugar melts – watch carefully and remove before it blackens. Cool, then refrigerate for several hours before serving. Serves 6–8.

GRAVLAX (Marinated Salmon)

A dish synonymous with Scandinavia, fresh fish, traditionally salmon, is cured for 3 days before serving. It is often accompanied by Mustard and Dill Sauce (page 234), or mustard-flavoured sour cream.

Gravlax

(Marinated Salmon)

750 g (1½ lb) fillets fresh salmon, salmon trout or large trout; 60 g/2 oz (¼ cup) sugar; 90 g/3 oz (¼ cup) coarse salt; 1 tsp white peppercorns, cracked; 1 large bunch fresh dill; 4 tbsp Cognac or brandy; 4 tbsp dry white wine.

Place 1 fillet skin side down on a plate, sprinkle thickly with sugar, salt and white pepper, cover with plenty of dill sprigs and press seasonings on to fish. Cover with second fillet of fish, skin side uppermost. Sandwich remaining fillets in the same way. Select a ceramic or glass dish just large enough to hold the fish, pour in Cognac or brandy and white wine and place fillets in it, with seasonings sandwiched between them. Cover with plastic wrap, weight with a 1 kg (2 lb) weight, and let marinate in refrigerator for 3 days. Turn fish every 12 hours, basting with marinade and separating fillets a little to baste fish inside. After 3 days remove weight and plastic wrap. Transfer with a slotted spoon to a cutting board. Separate fillets, scrape off dill, and cut fish horizontally into 5 mm (¼ in) slices, cutting it off without the skin. Place slices on black bread, top with a swirl of sour cream mixed with mustard and a sprig of dill, or serve with Mustard and Dill Sauce (see page 234). Serves 6–8 as an appetizer.

GRAVY

A sauce made in the pan from the browned coagulated juices left after meat is roasted or pan-fried. It is made by deglazing, that is by adding liquid to the pan and scraping and stirring the flavoursome bits into it as it boils. The liquid used may be vegetable cooking water, stock, wine, cream or a mixture of these.

A good gravy should be well-flavoured and light-bodied so that it 'shows the meat'. It is usually rather scant since the rich meat flavours are lost if too much liquid is added. A thin or clear gravy (in French, *jus*), achieves its body by reduction and perhaps a little butter swirled in at the end.

Purists frown on the use of flour to thicken a gravy, but since a great many people like gravy made this way, and since it is, after all, simply a roux-based sauce like many respected classics, it seems unreasonable to decry it. The points to watch are that the flour is browned slowly to give good flavour and colour and that you use just enough to give body, without making the gravy heavy and blanketing.

For a gravy which is lightly thickened but still clear, make *jus lié* by thickening clear gravy with a little arrowroot, or add body with two or three spoonfuls of vegetable purée (see opposite).

Clear Gravy Put a few slices of onion or carrot under meat in roasting pan if desired, to strengthen flavour of the juices. After meat is cooked, transfer it to a heated platter and keep warm. Heat pan gently on top of stove, allowing juices and sediment to colour without burning. Pour fat off slowly without disturbing sediment.

Off the heat, add 250–500 ml/8–18 fl oz (1–2 cups) hot vegetable water or stock and stir thoroughly, scraping up sediment. Return to heat and boil until reduced by about ¼, stirring and scraping several more times. Add any juices that have escaped from meat. Season, strain and serve very hot. If desired, a walnut of butter may be swirled into the gravy, off the heat, at the last moment.

Wine Gravy Follow recipe for Clear Gravy, above, using half vegetable water or stock and half red or white wine as the liquid. Or make clear gravy, using all stock and add a glass of dry sherry before reducing gravy.

Cream Gravy Follow recipe for Clear Gravy, above, using cream or a mixture of cream and stock or vegetable water as the liquid.

Jus Lié Follow recipe for Clear Gravy, above. Mix a little arrowroot to a cream with cold water, using 2 tsp arrowroot per 250 ml/ 8 fl oz (1 cup) of gravy. Pour into boiling

Right: Dhal Soup (page 397)

gravy, stirring until it is clear and lightly thickened. A spoonful of Madeira, port or brandy may be added per 250 ml/8 fl oz (1 cup) gravy, simmer for a few minutes longer before serving.

Vegetable-thickened Gravy To make a thickened gravy without starch, follow recipe for Clear Gravy, opposite, stir in some vegetable purée at the end. Use 2–3 tbsp purée per 250 ml/8 fl oz (1 cup) of gravy. For the purée, choose a mixture from mushrooms, cauliflower, spinach, onions, carrots, celery and canned or fresh tomatoes. Simmer in a little stock, or water and a stock cube, with a few fresh herbs or a pinch of dried herbs, and drain well. Purée in a blender or food processor, then sieve. Any leftover purée may be frozen in small portions for future use.

Thickened Gravy Put a few slices of onion or carrot under meat in roasting pan if desired, to strengthen flavour of the juices. After meat is cooked, transfer it to a heated platter and keep warm. Slowly pour off all but 2 tbsp fat from pan, leaving sediment undisturbed. Off the heat, sprinkle 1 tbsp flour into pan and blend well with fat. Place over low heat, stirring constantly, until mixture is nut-brown. Slowly pour in 250–350 ml/8–12 fl oz (1–1½ cups) vegetable water or stock, stirring constantly until smooth. Stir until boiling, then add any juices that have escaped from meat and simmer 5 minutes. Season, strain to remove lumps and serve very hot.

Thickened Wine Gravy or Cream Gravy Prepare by varying liquid used, in the same way as for the Wine and Cream variations of Clear Gravy.

Onion Gravy After meat is cooked, pour off all but 2 tbsp fat, add 1 onion, finely chopped, and sauté until softened. Add 1 tbsp flour and 1 tsp dry mustard, stir on low heat until browned. Stir in 175 ml/6 fl oz (¾ cup) beef stock, 120 ml/4 fl oz (½ cup) flat beer, ½ tsp sugar and 1 tsp chopped fresh thyme, or ¼ tsp dried. Stir until boiling, simmer 5 minutes and season to taste with salt and freshly ground black pepper.

Mushroom Gravy Follow recipe for Thickened Gravy, above, but pour off all fat from pan, add 30 g/1 oz (2 tbsp) butter and sauté 125 g/4 oz (1 cup) sliced mushrooms before blending in flour. Use cream or a mixture of cream and stock or vegetable water as the liquid. Use for beef steaks, pork or veal chops, meat loaves or hamburgers.

GREEN GODDESS DRESSING

A salad dressing with a subtle piquancy which complements seafood. Try serving Green Goddess Dressing with prawns (shrimp), lobster or crabmeat arranged on a bed of watercress.

Left: Seafood Crêpes (page 88)

Green Goddess Dressing

250 ml/8 fl oz (1 cup) Mayonnaise (page 204); 120 ml/4 fl oz (½ cup) sour cream; 15 g/½ oz (⅓ cup) chopped parsley; 2 tbsp snipped chives; 1 tbsp lemon juice; 2 tbsp anchovy paste; 2 tbsp tarragon vinegar; salt and freshly ground black pepper.

Combine mayonnaise and sour cream, then add remaining ingredients and mix well. Makes about 500 ml/18 fl oz (2 cups).

GREEN PEPPER

See *Pepper (Sweet)*.

GRIBICHE SAUCE

Use this lovely hard-boiled (hard-cooked) egg mayonnaise with fish or cold meats.

Gribiche Sauce

3 hard-boiled (hard-cooked) eggs, halved; ½ tsp salt; ¼ tsp white pepper; 1 tsp French (Dijon) mustard; 350 ml/12 fl oz (1½ cups) olive oil; 120 ml/4 fl oz (½ cup) vinegar; 60 g/ 2 oz (½ cup) finely chopped sour gherkins and capers, mixed together and drained; 2 tbsp finely chopped mixed fresh parsley, chives, tarragon and chervil.

Separate egg yolks from whites; cut whites in julienne (matchstick) strips and set aside. Mash egg yolks and add salt, pepper and mustard. Add, very gradually and while beating constantly, the olive oil and vinegar. Stir in egg white, gherkins, capers and herbs. Makes about 750 ml/1¼ pints (3 cups).

GRIDDLE CAKES (Girdle Cakes)

These little flat cakes were originally cooked on the griddle or girdle irons which gave them their names. Today, they are cooked on a griddle iron, a hotplate or in a frying pan (skillet). Griddle cakes can be sweet or savoury and eaten at any meal or as a snack during the day. They are usually based on a batter mixture of varying thickness, according to the type of griddle cake being made.

There are as many varieties of griddle cakes as there are different types of flour or meal – Russian Blini (see page 39), are made with buckwheat flour, Scottish Oatmeal Bannocks (see page 26), and Australian Pikelets (see page 294), with refined wheat flour.

When you cook griddle cakes, make sure the iron, hotplate or frying pan (skillet) is hot enough. Test by sprinkling the heated surface with a few drops of water; if the drops dance, the heat is right, and if they splatter and break up, it is too hot. The iron can be greased or not, depending on recipe and batter mixture. **See recipes**.

See also *Pancakes* and *Flapjacks*.

Irish Potato Cakes

500 g (1 lb) old potatoes, cooked, mashed and kept warm; 60 g/2 oz (4 tbsp) butter; salt and freshly ground black pepper; about 125 g/4 oz (1 cup) flour; butter to serve.

Beat potatoes with butter. Season with salt and pepper, and work in enough flour to bind into a dough. Divide dough in half. Place on a floured surface and pat out into 2 rounds, about 1 cm (½ in) thick. Cut each round into 8 triangles. Grease and heat a griddle, hotplate or frying pan (skillet) and cook potato cakes for about 5 minutes on each side until brown. Split in 2 and spread with butter. For breakfast, serve very hot with sausages, bacon, grilled (broiled) tomatoes or fried eggs. Makes 16.

Wholewheat Griddle Cakes

An American breakfast favourite.

90 g/3 oz (¾ cup) self-raising flour; 90 g/3 oz (¾ cup) wholewheat flour; 1½ tsp baking powder; 1 tsp salt; 2 tbsp sugar; 2 eggs, separated; 250 ml/8 fl oz (1 cup) milk; 30 g/1 oz (2 tbsp) butter, melted.

Sift flours with baking powder, salt and sugar. Beat egg yolks with milk and melted butter. Whisk egg whites until they stand in peaks. Stir milk mixture into flour, then fold in egg whites. Grease and heat a griddle, hotplate or frying pan (skillet). Place tablespoonfuls of mixture on pan and cook for about 3 minutes on each side or until brown. Serve hot at breakfast with butter, maple syrup and grilled (broiled) sausages or bacon. Makes about 14.

NOTE: In America, these are served in stacks, with butter melting in between.

Crisp Corn Griddle Cakes

60 g/2 oz (½ cup) plain (all-purpose) flour; 105 g/3½ oz (¾ cup) yellow cornmeal (polenta); 1 tsp salt; ½ tsp bicarbonate of soda (baking soda); 1 tsp baking powder; 30 g/1 oz (¼ cup) self-raising flour; 60 g/2 oz (4 tbsp) butter, melted; 500 ml/18 fl oz (2 cups) buttermilk; 1 egg, beaten.

Sift together plain flour, cornmeal, salt, soda, baking powder and self-raising flour. Blend together the butter, buttermilk and egg. Make a well in the centre of the cornmeal mixture and pour in the liquid. Stir from the centre with a wooden spoon until dry ingredients have been moistened and you have a smooth batter. Do not overmix. Drop spoonfuls of batter on to a hot preheated griddle or frying pan (skillet), making cakes about 10 cm (4 in) in diameter. When undersides are brown, turn over and cook the other sides. If batter thickens while cakes are cooking, stir in a little extra buttermilk. Serve straight from the pan. Makes about 10.

GUACAMOLE

A savoury dip or spread of Mexican origin now famous throughout the world. The superb combination of creamy avocado laced with lemon and chilli is at its best with hot corn crisps (chips) or crackers.

Guacamole

2 ripe avocados, peeled and stoned; 1 clove garlic, crushed; ¼ tsp salt; 1 small onion, finely chopped; 2 tsp lemon or lime juice; 1 small fresh chilli, seeded and chopped, or few drops Tabasco (hot pepper) sauce.

Cut avocado flesh into chunks and blend at high speed until smooth or push through a nylon sieve. Add garlic, salt, onion, lemon or lime juice and chilli or Tabasco (hot pepper) sauce, and blend a further 30 seconds. Transfer to a serving dish. Makes about 250 ml/8 fl oz (1 cup).

NOTE: If you prepare guacamole a few hours before it is needed, leave an avocado stone in mixture to prevent browning, cover and refrigerate. Remove stone before serving.

GUAVA

A tropical fruit with a thick rind and soft flesh, embedded with a mass of seeds. It is green when under-ripe, yellow or pink-flushed when ripe. There is also a red variety. The flavour is light, sweet, a little musky. Guavas can be eaten fresh with sugar and cream, stewed or made into jam or a jelly.

Guava Jelly

slightly under-ripe guavas, cut up; rind and pith 1 lime or lemon; sugar; lime or lemon juice.

Put guavas, lime or lemon rind and pith into a saucepan with enough water to cover. Boil until fruit is very soft. Strain through a colander lined with 2 thicknesses of cheesecloth and set over a bowl. Do not squeeze or press fruit, just allow juice to drip through slowly. Measure juice and add 250 g/8 oz (1 cup) of sugar for each 250 ml/8 fl oz (1 cup) of juice, and juice of 1 lime or lemon for each 1 litre/1¾ pints (4 cups) of juice. Bring to the boil, stirring until sugar has dissolved, then boil until a few drops of the mixture, dropped on to a chilled plate, will jell as they cool. Pour into clean, hot jars and seal.

GUGELHOPF (Kugelhupf)

The yeast cake of Alsace from which babas and savarins were developed. Gugelhopf is studded with rum-soaked currants and is cooked in a distinctive fluted ring mould.

Gugelhopf

45 g/1½ oz (⅓ cup) slivered almonds; 90 g/3 oz (½ cup) currants; 90 g/3 oz (½ cup) raisins; 3 tbsp rum; 175 ml/6 fl oz (¾ cup) milk; 30 g/1 oz (2 tbsp) fresh (compressed) yeast; 350 g/12 oz (3 cups) flour; pinch salt; 1½ tbsp caster sugar; 3 eggs, lightly beaten; 125 g/4 oz (½ cup) butter, melted and slightly cooled; sifted icing (confectioners) sugar.

Generously butter a 20 cm (8 in) gugelhopf tin (pan) or fluted ring tin (pan) and press slivered almonds into butter. Refrigerate until needed. Soak currants and raisins in rum. Warm milk to blood heat, pour on to yeast and stir until dissolved. Sift flour and salt into a warm bowl. Make a well in centre and add milk mixture, sugar, eggs and melted butter. Beat well and add soaked fruits. Pour well mixed batter into prepared pan, which should be ¾ full.

Cover with a damp cloth and stand in a warm place for 20–30 minutes or until mixture has risen to 2.5 cm (1 in) below the top. Bake in a preheated moderately hot oven (190°C/375°F, Gas Mark 5) for 50–60 minutes or until a fine skewer inserted in centre comes out clean. Stand a few minutes, then turn out on to a wire rack to cool. Dust with icing (confectioners) sugar.

GUMBO

Creole cookery, centred on New Orleans in the U.S.A., is a blend of Spanish, French, Negro and Indian influences. A gumbo is a Creole soup-stew which uses okra for flavouring and thickening – the word 'gumbo' comes from an African word for okra. A gumbo may be based on chicken, pork or ham or seafood but it will always have the typical satin-smooth texture which okra's jelly-like juice provides.

Chicken and Oyster Gumbo

1 × 1.5 kg (3 lb) chicken, cut into 8 pieces; 45 g/1½ oz (3 tbsp) bacon fat or butter; 1 onion, chopped; 250 g (8 oz) smoked ham, diced; 500 g/1 lb (4 cups) sliced okra; 4 large ripe tomatoes, peeled and chopped, or 1 × 425 g/14 oz can tomatoes, chopped, with their juice; 1 bay leaf; 750 ml/1¼ pints (3 cups) boiling water; salt and freshly ground black pepper; dash cayenne; 12 large oysters; hot boiled rice to serve.

Brown chicken pieces all over in bacon fat or butter. Remove chicken from pan and set aside. Add onion, ham and okra, and stir over medium heat 5 minutes. Add tomatoes, bay leaf, water, salt, pepper and cayenne. Return chicken to pan, cover and simmer 45 minutes or until chicken is tender. Adjust seasoning, add oysters and simmer 1 minute. Serve at once with rice. Serves 6.

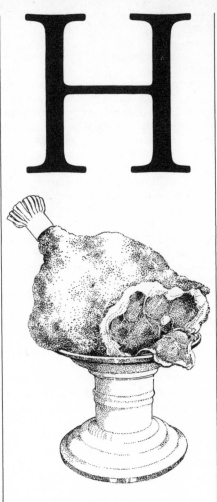

HAM

The cured meat of the hind leg of the pig, ham is extremely versatile. It runs the gamut from being sliced for a filling in a sandwich to a whole ham leg, beautifully glazed, holding pride of place on any celebration table. There are many different types of ham throughout the world depending on the method of curing, the breed of pig and the feed they eat.

Ham can be purchased as a whole leg on the bone, in smaller cuts with or without the bone, or sliced. It is also canned, or pressed into long boneless rounds or rectangles for slicing.

Types of Ham

Coppa is the cured, raw shoulder and neck part of the pig. It is fattier and less expensive than prosciutto, and is excellent in recipes calling for raw ham.

Double-smoked ham has a particularly rich smoky flavour as the name implies, from extra smoking.

Ham steaks are popular pan-fried or grilled (broiled) on the family barbecue and served with pineapple slices and fruit chutneys.

Parma ham or prosciutto is a delicate raw ham which can be purchased at specialist delicatessens. It is served as an entrée, sliced paper-thin, with fresh melon slices, fresh figs or simply with a pat of country butter.

Shoulder (picnic shoulder), loin or forehock meat can be cured in a similar way to ham, which gives it a similar flavour. It can be used in recipes specifying chopped, diced, minced or sliced ham.

Wiltshire ham or gammon is cured as part of the whole pig before being divided into cuts.

Ways to Use Leftover Ham

● In *Croquettes, Rissoles, Fritters* (see separate entries for recipes).

● Serve slices of ham with fried, poached or scrambled eggs.

● Mash hard-boiled (hard-cooked) egg yolks with sour cream and minced (ground) ham, and pile into egg white halves for stuffed eggs.

● As fillings for *Vol-au-vent, Croustades* or *Tartlets*. Add 125 g/4 oz (½ cup) finely diced ham to 250 ml/8 fl oz (1 cup) Mornay or Béchamel Sauce (see page 368); stir in 1 tbsp finely chopped parsley and season with pepper. Pile into selected bread or pastry (dough) cases and warm in a preheated moderate oven (180°C/350°F, Gas Mark 4) for about 15 minutes. Makes sufficient filling for 15 small individual cases.

● Add ham strips to chicken, pasta, potato or rice salads with Mayonnaise dressing (see page 204).

● Mince (grind) ham with a little onion and season with fruit, chutney or mustard. Spread on buttered bread or in bread rolls.

● Add small chunks of ham to pea, potato, pumpkin or lentil soups, and chicken or corn chowder. **See recipes**. See also *Prosciutto*.

Baked Glazed Ham

A traditional recipe for baked ham.

1 × 7 kg (14 lb) cured leg of ham.
GLAZE: *280 g/9 oz (1½ cups) firmly packed brown sugar; 2 tsp dry mustard; 280 g/9 oz (¾ cup) clear honey; whole cloves; 120 ml/4 fl oz (½ cup) orange juice.*

Cut a scallop pattern around thick end of ham shank and ease skin away from fat. Turn ham over and ease away rest of skin, which should come off in one piece. Place ham, fat side uppermost, on a rack in a roasting tin (pan) containing 3.5 cm (1½ in) of water. Cover tin (pan) with foil, making it as airtight as possible, and bake in a preheated moderate oven (160°C/325°F, Gas Mark 3) for 2½ hours. Remove from oven and pour off liquid in tin (pan). Using a sharp knife, score fat with 5 mm (¼ in) deep diagonal cuts, first one way, then opposite way to form a diamond pattern.

GLAZE: Mix sugar, mustard and honey together and using a brush spread half the mixture over ham. Stud each diamond with a clove. Mix remaining glaze with orange juice. Increase oven temperature to moderately hot (200°C/400°F, Gas Mark 6) and bake ham for a further 30–40 minutes, basting it every 10 minutes with remaining glaze. Serve hot or cold. Serves 20–25.
VARIATIONS
Apply any one of the following glazes in the same way as in the preceding recipe.
Cider Glaze: Combine 180 g/6 oz (1 cup) firmly packed brown sugar with 250 ml/8 fl oz (1 cup) apple cider and spread over ham. Use extra 120 ml/4 fl oz (½ cup) apple cider for basting.
Apple Sauce Glaze: Combine 250 g/8 oz (1 cup) apple purée (applesauce) with 2 tbsp prepared mustard and 180 g/6 oz (½ cup) honey, and spread over ham. Use 120 ml/4 fl oz (½ cup) apple juice for basting.
Marmalade Glaze: Combine 370 g/12 oz (1 cup) orange marmalade with 4 tbsp cider vinegar and ¼ tsp nutmeg and spread over ham. Use 120 ml/4 fl oz (½ cup) orange juice for basting.

Ham au gratin

8 slices cooked ham; 2 tbsp white wine; 250 ml/8 fl oz (1 cup) Béchamel Sauce (page 368); 1 tsp French (Dijon) mustard; 2 tbsp grated Parmesan cheese; 1 tbsp dry breadcrumbs.

Place ham in a buttered ovenproof dish, overlapping slices. Moisten with white wine. Season béchamel sauce with mustard and 1 tbsp of the cheese and spoon over ham. Mix remaining cheese and crumbs and scatter over the top. Bake in a preheated moderate oven (180°C/350°F, Gas Mark 4) for 30 minutes. Serves 4.

Croissants with Ham and Cheese

These are ideal for a picnic.

4 croissants, fresh or frozen; 4 thin slices cooked ham, or 8 slices prosciutto; 4 slices Emmenthal, Gruyère or Jarlsberg cheese.

Warm and crisp croissants in a preheated moderate oven (180°C/350°F, Gas Mark 4). Using a serrated knife, slice through each croissant from the outer curve, but don't cut right through. Layer ham and cheese slices in the warm croissants, wrap in a clean tea-towel and then wrap tightly in several sheets of newspaper to retain warmth. They should keep warm for about 3 hours. Serves 2–4.

Baked Ginger Ham with Sweet Potato

1 small sweet potato, peeled and thickly sliced; 2 ham steaks; 1 tsp butter; 1 tsp brown sugar; ¼ tsp ground ginger; 4 tbsp fruit juice (orange, pineapple).

Cook sweet potato in lightly salted boiling water until tender, about 10 minutes. Drain well. Place ham steaks in a flat casserole or pie dish and arrange sweet potato slices around them. Mix together butter, brown sugar and ginger, and spread over ham. Pour fruit juice around ham. Bake in a preheated moderately hot oven (200°C/400°F, Gas Mark 6) for 15 minutes, basting several times with juice. Serve with a green salad. Serves 2.

Ham with Orange and Chicory Salad

8–10 slices cooked ham; 3 heads chicory (endive), sliced; 3 large oranges, peeled and sliced; 1 medium onion, finely sliced; 120 ml/4 fl oz (½ cup) Vinaigrette Dressing (page 358); chopped parsley; 6–8 black (ripe) olives to garnish.

Arrange sliced ham around edge of serving platter. Lightly toss chicory (endive), orange and onion slices in vinaigrette and pile in centre. Sprinkle with chopped parsley and garnish with olives. Serves 4–6.

HAMBURGER

A first-rate hamburger can stand comparison with its grand relation, a fine steak. Like steak, a good hamburger is juicy within, crusty outside and full of flavour. The first secret of success is to build flavour and moistness into the mixture, the second is to handle it lightly when shaping so that it holds together without compacting. If you want the inside rare, make the patties about 4 cm (1½ in) thick; for a well-cooked interior, make patties 2–2.5 cm (¾–1 in) thick. Cook a hamburger as you would a steak: whether pan-frying or grilling (broiling), sear the outside at high heat, then turn heat down to medium to finish cooking.

Basic Hamburgers

4 slices bread, crusts removed; 175 ml/6 fl oz (¾ cup) evaporated milk; 1 kg/2 lb (4 cups) best quality minced (ground) steak; 2 tsp salt; freshly ground black pepper; ½ tsp dry mustard; ¼ tsp Worcestershire sauce; 1 small onion, grated; 2 eggs.

Tear bread into pieces and soak in evaporated milk 10 minutes, then beat with a fork. Lightly mix together all ingredients except eggs, then stir in eggs with a fork. With wet hands, shape into 8 equal-sized patties. Heat grill (broiler) or pan, brush hamburgers with oil or butter and cook at high heat to sear the outsides, then turn down heat to medium and finish cooking. Pan-fry for a total of 4–6 minutes on each side, or grill (broil) for 7–10 minutes on each side for medium done. Serve, on buns or toast if desired, with a selection of garnishes or sauce of your choice. Serves 8.

VARIATIONS

Herbed Hamburgers: Add 1 tbsp chopped fresh dill, thyme or other herbs, or 1 tsp dried, to Basic Hamburger mixture.

Garlic Hamburgers: Add 1 fat clove garlic, crushed, and 2 tbsp chopped parsley to Basic Hamburger mixture.

Devilled Hamburgers: Add 2 tbsp tomato ketchup, 1½ tsp prepared English mustard, 2 tsp lemon juice and a dash of Tabasco (hot pepper) sauce to Basic Hamburger mixture.

Stuffed Hamburgers: Shape Basic Hamburger mixture into 16 thin patties. On 8 of the patties place one of the following: 1 tbsp chopped, sautéed mushrooms, bacon or onion; small piece Cheddar, Swiss, Camembert or blue cheese; 1 tbsp chopped, mixed apple, celery and walnuts; 1 canned anchovy fillet chopped with a few capers. Top with remaining patties and press edges to join.

HAMBURGER TOPPINGS

Top each freshly cooked hamburger with one of the following:

● A thick slice of sautéed tomato and 2–3 sautéed mushrooms threaded on a toothpick.

● 1 tsp sour cream or plain yogurt, seasoned with salt and pepper and sprinkled with snipped chives.

● A slice of Maître d'Hôtel, Anchovy or other flavoured butter (*see* pages 49 and 7).

SAUCES FOR HAMBURGERS

Red Wine Sauce: Pan-fry hamburgers, remove and keep warm. Add 2 tbsp chopped shallots to pan and sauté 1 minute, then add 120 ml/4 fl oz (½ cup) red wine. Boil rapidly 2 minutes, season with salt and pepper, remove from heat and swirl in 30 g/1 oz (2 tbsp) butter. Pour over hamburgers and serve immediately.

Stroganoff Sauce: Pan-fry hamburgers, remove and keep warm. Add 1 small onion,

finely chopped, to pan and sauté, stirring 2 minutes. Add 125 g/4 oz (1 cup) sliced mushrooms and cook, stirring, until limp. Stir in 120 ml/4 fl oz (½ cup) sour cream. Season with salt and pepper, heat through and spoon over hamburgers. Sprinkle with paprika and serve immediately.

HARD SAUCE (Brandy or Rum butter)

A traditional accompaniment to Christmas Pudding and Mince Pies. It is also good with other steamed puddings and with baked apples. As the name suggests, it becomes firm when chilled.

Hard Sauce

90 g/3 oz (6 tbsp) unsalted butter; 140 g/4½ oz (1 cup) icing (confectioners) sugar, sifted; 1 tbsp brandy, rum, Grand Marnier or Cointreau, or more to taste; 1 egg white (optional).

Beat butter until creamy, then add sugar a little at a time, beating until white and fluffy. Add liquor gradually, beating constantly. If using egg white, beat until soft peaks form and fold in. Pile sauce into a bowl and chill. Makes about 500 ml/18 fl oz (2 cups).

HARE

Hare is akin to rabbit in flavour, though it is darker and more gamey. It is often first marinated for a day or so before cooking as it tends to be dry, and is then roasted in the same way as rabbit. However, if there is any doubt about tenderness, hare is best casseroled or used for a pie.

The most famous hare dish, Jugged Hare (immortalized by Mrs. Beeton with the purported advice 'first you must catch your hare'), used to be made by putting hare pieces, vegetables, herbs and port into a pot or jug and standing it in boiling water to cook. It was then thickened with the hare's blood. Nowadays it is more usual to braise hare.

Casserole of Hare

1 hare, jointed; seasoned flour; 1 tbsp oil; 15 g/½ oz (1 tbsp) butter; 125 g (4 oz) streaky bacon, rind removed and diced; 12 small onions; 1 stick celery, sliced; 2 carrots, sliced; 1 bouquet garni; 4 tbsp port; 250 ml/8 fl oz (1 cup) beef or game stock; juice 1 lemon; salt and freshly ground black pepper; 1–2 tbsp Beurre Manié (page 35); 1–2 tbsp redcurrant jelly; fried croûtons to serve (page 90).
MARINADE: *250 ml/8 fl oz (1 cup) red wine; 2 tbsp oil; 1 onion, finely chopped; 1 bay leaf; 3 cloves; 4–5 juniper berries, crushed; freshly ground black pepper.*

Combine marinade ingredients, bring to the boil, cool and pour over hare. Marinate 12 hours, turning pieces occasionally. Remove hare; strain marinade and reserve liquid. Dry hare, dust with seasoned flour and brown in hot oil and butter in a flameproof casserole. Remove hare. Add bacon and vegetables to casserole and sauté until onions are coloured. Place hare on top of vegetables and add bouquet garni, port, stock, lemon juice and strained marinade. Season lightly with salt and pepper, bring to simmering point, cover tightly and bake in a preheated cool oven (150°C/300°F, Gas Mark 2) for 2–3 hours or until hare is tender. Transfer hare, bacon and vegetables to a heated serving dish. Skim fat from liquid in casserole, discard bouquet garni and thicken a little with beurre manié. Stir in redcurrant jelly to taste, adjust seasoning and pour over hare. Garnish with croûtons and serve. Serves 6.

HARICOT (of Mutton or Lamb)

Despite the name, haricots (beans) are not a traditional ingredient in this ancient dish. The word 'haricot' here is thought to have come from the Old French word *halicoter*, to cut into morsels. The dish is a casserole of mutton or lamb with potatoes, turnips and onions.

Haricot of Mutton or Lamb

125 g (4 oz) fatty pork, diced; 750 g (1½ lb) lean stewing mutton or lamb, cut into bite-sized cubes; 1 medium onion, sliced; pinch sugar; 2 tbsp flour; 1 clove garlic, crushed; 1 litre/1¾ pints (4 cups) mutton or beef stock; 2 tbsp tomato purée (paste); 1 bouquet garni; salt and freshly ground black pepper; 4 medium potatoes, quartered; 2 small turnips, quartered; 24 tiny onions.

Put diced pork into a flameproof casserole and fry until fat runs and dice are browned. Remove pork with a slotted spoon. Add mutton or lamb and sliced onion to casserole and brown. Add sugar and allow it to caramelize, then sprinkle in the flour and stir until well mixed. Add garlic, then stock a little at a time, stirring until smoothly blended. Add tomato purée (paste) and bouquet garni, season lightly, cover and place casserole in a preheated moderate oven (180°C/350°F, Gas Mark 4). Cook for 1 hour. Add vegetables and pork dice, and cook another hour or until meat is tender. Adjust seasoning, discard bouquet garni and serve. Serves 6.

HARICOT BEAN

See *Pulses: Dried Beans, Peas and Lentils.*

HASH

A dish made from a mixture of diced and usually cooked food; it is a marvellous way of using up leftovers. Vegetables, meats, poultry or fish are mixed with sufficient sauce, gravy or cream to moisten, seasoned well and heated through. Serve hash on buttered toast, in a pastry (dough) shell, over rice or noodles, with creamy mashed potatoes or on its own.

Heavenly Hash is a sweet variation made using canned fruits. It is a superbly simple dessert to prepare and is always popular with children. **See recipes.**

Corned Beef and Potato Hash

30 g/1 oz (2 tbsp) butter; 1 large onion, chopped; 2 sticks celery, chopped; 1 small green pepper, cored, seeded and diced; 750 g/1½ lb (3 cups) minced (ground) corned beef; 350 g/12 oz (2 cups) diced cooked potatoes; 1 tbsp Worcestershire sauce; 2 tbsp chopped parsley or chives; salt and freshly ground black pepper; 75–150 ml/5 tbsp–¼ pint (⅓–⅔ cup) stock or single (light) cream; 6 hot poached eggs (optional).

Melt butter in a large saucepan, add onion, celery and green pepper and simmer very gently until tender. Stir in corned beef, potatoes, Worcestershire sauce, parsley or chives, salt and pepper. Stir over medium heat while gradually adding stock or cream. Cook until well blended and thoroughly heated. Place on a heated platter and serve topped with poached eggs, if using. Alternatively, sauté hash on a greased griddle or in a shallow-sided frying pan (skillet) until well browned underneath. Remove carefully, folding like an omelette and roll on to a heated serving platter. Serves 6.

Heavenly Hash

1 × 310 g/10 oz can mandarin segments; 1 × 280 g/9 oz jar maraschino cherries; 1 × 425 g/14 oz can pineapple pieces; 2 × 100 g/3½ oz packets marshmallows, one

pink and one white; 300 ml/½ pint (1¼ cups) single (light) cream; 1 tbsp lemon juice; ¼ tsp ground cardamom; ¼ tsp ground ginger; 1 tsp grated orange rind; 1 tbsp Cointreau or Grand Marnier (optional).

Drain fruit. Halve marshmallows and toss carefully with fruit. Whip cream with remaining ingredients. Fold cream mixture through fruit and marshmallows. Chill for about 2 hours. Serves 6.

HAZELNUT (Cobnut or Filbert)

The shiny brown shell of the hazelnut encloses a juicy, milky kernel much used in puddings, cakes and ice creams, especially in European cookery. The mealy texture of the nuts makes them perfect for use in Continental tortes (see *Tortes*), in which the ground nuts take the place of flour.

Hazelnuts can be eaten on their own, roasted or freshly shelled, and their texture should be crisp and brittle. They are delicious in mushroom sauce, or tossed through a watercress salad, and as an extra bonus are highly nutritious, being rich in protein, fat, iron and thiamine.

To skin hazelnuts: Place kernels on a baking tray in a preheated moderate oven (180°C/350°F, Gas Mark 4) for 5–6 minutes, turning once. Put the warm nuts in a paper bag or a clean cloth and rub against one another to break the skin fibres, and remove the skins from the kernels.

To roast hazelnuts: Spread skinned kernels on a baking tray and roast in a preheated moderately hot oven (200°C/400°F, Gas Mark 6) for 7–10 minutes, stirring frequently to prevent scorching.

To grind hazelnuts: Remove skins first and use a special nut grinder or a blender.
To salt hazelnuts: Skin kernels if desired. Roast as above and add 1 tsp salt to 165 g/5½ oz (1 cup) kernels while still warm. **See recipes.**
See also *Galette.*

Hazelnut and Mushroom Sauce

60 g/2 oz (4 tbsp) butter; 75 g/2½ oz (½ cup) halved hazelnuts; 1 small onion, finely chopped; 6 mushroom caps, finely sliced; 2 tbsp flour; 500 ml/18 fl oz (2 cups) chicken stock; salt and freshly ground black pepper.

Melt butter and add hazelnuts, onion and mushrooms. Stir over gentle heat until just browned. Remove from pan with a slotted spoon. Mix flour into butter remaining in pan, then add stock and stir over gentle heat until thickened. Return hazelnut mixture, season with salt and pepper and serve with grilled (broiled) chicken breasts, roast chicken or sautéed veal steaks. Makes 600 ml/1 pint (2½ cups).

Hazelnut Meringue

4 egg whites; 250 g/8 oz (1 cup) caster sugar; ¼ tsp vanilla essence (extract); ½ tsp vinegar; 165 g/5½ oz (1 cup) ground hazelnuts, roasted in oven for 5 minutes; 250 ml/8 fl oz (1 cup) double (heavy) cream, whipped; 250 g (8 oz) strawberries, hulled; sifted icing (confectioners) sugar.

Whisk egg whites until they stand in soft peaks, then gradually whisk in caster sugar a tablespoonful at a time. Continue beating until mixture is very stiff and standing in peaks. Whisk in vanilla and vinegar, then fold in nuts with a metal spoon. Divide mixture between 2 greased and floured 20 cm (8 in) sandwich tins (layer pans) that have been bottom-lined with greased greaseproof (waxed) paper. Bake in a preheated moderately hot oven (190°C/375°F, Gas Mark 5) for 35–40 minutes. Turn out on to wire racks to cool. When cool, sandwich together with whipped cream and strawberries and dust top with icing (confectioners) sugar. Serves 8.
NOTE: Always fill the meringues at least 3 hours before serving to prevent their splintering when cut into portions.

Hazelnut Ice Cream

1 litre/1¾ pints (4 cups) vanilla ice cream, preferably home-made (page 161); 165 g/5½ oz (1 cup) chopped toasted hazelnuts; 1 tbsp coffee liqueur.

Soften frozen ice cream to a partially frozen state and fold chopped hazelnuts through. Stir in coffee liqueur and refreeze. Serves 8.
VARIATIONS
Chocolate Hazelnut Ice Cream: Substitute chocolate ice cream for vanilla ice cream and proceed as for Hazelnut Ice Cream.
Hazelnut Orange Ice Cream: Use recipe for Hazelnut Ice Cream, substituting 1 tbsp Curaçao and 1 tbsp chopped candied orange peel for coffee liqueur.

Hazelnut and Chocolate Roulade

*3 eggs, separated; 2 tsp water; 180 g/6 oz
($\frac{3}{4}$ cup) caster sugar; 125 g/4 oz (1 cup) flour;
1 tsp baking powder; pinch salt; 165 g/5½ oz
(1 cup) ground hazelnuts; 2 tbsp icing
(confectioners) sugar, sifted.*
FILLING: *250 g (8 oz) strawberries, hulled;
3 tbsp icing (confectioners) sugar, sifted;
180 g/6 oz (1 cup) dark chocolate; 1 tbsp
water; 2 egg yolks; 90 g/3 oz (6 tbsp)
unsalted butter, at room temperature.*

Whisk egg whites with water to a firm snow,
then add sugar a spoonful at a time and
continue beating until stiff. Beat in egg yolks.
Sift flour with baking powder and salt, mix
with hazelnuts and fold gently into egg
mixture. Turn into a greased and lined
30 × 25 cm (12 × 10 in) Swiss roll tin (jelly
roll pan) and level the top with a palette
knife. Bake in a preheated moderately hot
oven (200°C/400°F, Gas Mark 6) for 12–15
minutes or until firm to the touch. Turn
roulade out quickly on to a sugared sheet of
greaseproof (waxed) paper and roll up with
greaseproof (waxed) paper on the inside.
Leave to cool.
FILLING: Purée strawberries and stir in icing
(confectioners) sugar. Melt chocolate with
water in a heatproof bowl placed over hot
water. Remove from heat and add egg yolks
one at a time. Beat well, then gradually mix
in butter. Tip into a bowl and blend in
strawberry purée. Uncurl sponge roll very
carefully and remove paper. Spread with
filling and re-roll. Dust with icing
(confectioners) sugar before serving.
Serves 6–8.

Hazelnut Cookies

*250 g/8 oz (1½ cups) toasted, ground
hazelnuts; 250 g/8 oz (2 cups) flour; pinch
salt; 75 g/2½ oz (⅓ cup) caster sugar;
250 g/8 oz (1 cup) butter; 140 g/4½ oz
(1 cup) icing (confectioners) sugar, sifted;
1 tbsp hot water; chopped hazelnuts or
pistachios to decorate.*

Put ground nuts into a bowl. Sift flour with
salt and add to bowl with caster sugar. Rub
(cut) in butter and combine well until
smooth. Form into a ball, wrap in plastic
wrap and chill for 1 hour. Roll out dough
thin and cut into rounds with a plain or
fluted 4 cm (1½ in) cutter. Place rounds on
greased baking trays and bake in a
preheated moderate oven (180°C/350°F,
Gas Mark 4) for about 15 minutes. Allow to
cool for 1 minute on trays, then transfer to a
wire rack to cool completely. Combine icing
(confectioners) sugar with hot water to make
a stiff icing (frosting) and spread a little on
top of each biscuit (cookie). Sprinkle over
chopped nuts. Makes about 80.

HEART

Heart has a mild flavour somewhat like liver,
although not so pronounced in taste. The
flesh is lean and dry with a close texture. The
most tender hearts are those from lambs, pigs
and calves, while ox (beef) heart needs
longer, slower cooking. Hearts can be stuffed
and baked, casseroled or sautéed.

☐ **Basic Preparation:** Cut away the veins
and arteries with a sharp pair of scissors and
trim off the fat. Wash well in cold running
water. Cover with warm water with the addition of 1 tbsp vinegar to 500 ml/18 fl oz (2
cups) water. Soak for at least 3 hours, or
overnight if using ox (beef) heart. Change the
water several times. Drain, rinse and dry
before proceeding with recipe.

Baked Stuffed Heart Use 4 lambs' hearts or 1
ox (beef) heart prepared as above. Make
Apple, Prune and Nut Stuffing (see page
418), fill heart cavities and sew up with a
needle and thread. Put hearts in a baking dish
with 250 ml/8 fl oz (1 cup) beef stock. Cover
with buttered foil and bake in a preheated
moderate oven (180°C/350°F, Gas Mark 4)
for 1½–2 hours for lambs' hearts and 2–2½
hours for ox (beef) heart, basting often with
juices and extra 250 ml/8 fl oz (1 cup) stock.
When cooked, make a gravy with pan juices,
thickened with flour (see page 148). Serves 4.

Sautéed Heart Prepare 4 lambs' hearts as
above. Cut into 1 cm (½ in) slices and sauté in
45 g/1½ oz (3 tbsp) butter and 1 tbsp oil. Add
2 tsp chopped fresh rosemary or 1 tsp dried,
salt and freshly ground black pepper. Cook
over gentle heat, stirring, for 10–12 minutes
Remove from heat, place on a warm platter
and sprinkle with 60 g/2 oz (1 cup) buttered
breadcrumbs. Serves 4–6.

Lambs' Hearts with Orange Sauce

*4 prepared lambs' hearts; 60 g/2 oz (4 tbsp)
butter; 1 tbsp oil; 2 onions, chopped;
2 rashers (slices) bacon, rind removed and
chopped; 2 tbsp flour; 500 ml/18 fl oz
(2 cups) stock; 120 ml/4 fl oz (½ cup) red or
white wine; 1 clove garlic, crushed; salt and
freshly ground black pepper; 2 tbsp bitter
marmalade; grated rind and juice 1 large
orange; 4 tbsp Grand Marnier or Cointreau;
finely chopped parsley.*

Brown hearts in butter and oil in a heavy
frying pan (skillet) together with onion and
bacon. Remove hearts, onion and bacon and
place in a flameproof casserole. Stir flour
into oil and butter in frying pan (skillet), then
add stock and wine. Cook over low heat,
stirring, until thickened. Add garlic, salt,
pepper and marmalade. Pour sauce into
casserole and simmer gently until hearts are
done, about 1½ hours. Remove hearts, slice
them thin and arrange in a shallow
ovenproof dish. Skim fat off sauce, and boil
for 4–5 minutes if necessary to reduce and
thicken. Stir in orange rind, juice and
liqueur. Cover hearts with half the sauce,
keeping the rest warm in a sauce boat to
hand separately. Warm hearts through in a
preheated moderate oven (180°C/350°F,
Gas Mark 4), then sprinkle with chopped
parsley. Serve with boiled new potatoes and
an orange and tomato salad. Serves 4–6.

HERBS

The generous but discriminating use of herbs
is one of the easiest ways of adding flavour to
food. Herbs owe their flavouring qualities to
essential oils which quickly permeate the
foods with which they are mixed. Sometimes
the seeds of the plant are the seasoning
agent, sometimes it is the foliage. You will
find that most herbs are at their best when
home-grown and plucked fresh for use – so
do start a small herb garden.

Herbs are easy to cultivate – in a backyard
garden, in pots or in a box on the kitchen
window-sill – preferring a light, moderately
rich soil and a sunny exposure. Few garden-
ing efforts are less troublesome or more
rewarding than growing herbs of one's own,
for nothing adds such interest and flavour to
cooking as a snip or two of a favourite herb.

Discover the joy of cooking with herbs by
starting with the major ones. Parsley, thyme,
sage, mint, marjoram, basil, chives, oregano
and bay leaf (see separate entries) are the
ones most often used.

H

With fresh parsley and mint we are on familiar ground. To cook without parsley is almost unthinkable. The curly, attractive, bright green leaves can be chopped and sprinkled over dishes before serving to give flavour, colour and nutrition to soups, casseroles, grills (broils), sautés and salads.

A sprig or stalk goes into flavouring many savoury dishes. The new flat-leaf Italian parsley is also good in flavour, and Chinese parsley is becoming popular (see Coriander).

Mint sauce is a favourite with lamb and mint goes well with green peas and carrots.

Thyme, marjoram and sage are used in stuffings; sprigs or a few little chopped leaves are added to roasts, casseroles, meat loaves and sausages.

Chives and garlic, those well-known members of the onion family long used in Mediterranean countries, are now becoming more acceptable throughout the world. Garlic bread is an international favourite. Chives snipped over omelettes and salads, or jacket potatoes with butter or sour cream and snipped chives are all a great treat.

No kitchen should be without bay leaves – the foundation of bouquet garni, bay flavours stocks, soups and stews. And an infusion of bay leaf and milk transforms rice puddings and many cream sauces.

Fresh or Dried? Fresh is almost always best. Parsley, chives, mint and basil should always be fresh. Thyme, marjoram and oregano can be used both fresh and dried. Bay leaves should not be absolutely fresh; they are picked and kept for 3 or 4 days to allow them to lose their bitterness. Or they may be purchased dried. Good quality tarragon is often dried.

Use 1 tsp dried herbs for every tbsp fresh herbs. Crumble dried herbs before using, to release their odour. If using dried herbs, it helps to chop the herbs along with some fresh parsley, it gives a nice look and fresh flavour to the otherwise colourless herbs.

When buying dried and rubbed herbs, the rougher looking ones are usually the best. With very fine or powdered herbs the flavour seems to get lost. Do not expect dried herbs to last forever; buy in small quantities, keep them airtight and in a cool dark place.

See separate entries for individual herbs.

Fines Herbes

A mixture of fresh parsley, tarragon, chives and chervil, all finely chopped, is called *Fines Herbes* in classical French cooking. This is virtually the bouquet garni of uncooked or briefly cooked dishes. Nowadays, the term is commonly applied to other combinations of fresh herbs which may include only one or more of the original fines herbes. They are used in the following traditional ways.

Omelettes: The best-known use for this delicate herb mixture. Stir 1 tbsp fines herbes into a 2-egg omelette mixture before cooking, and garnish the omelette with a fresh herb sprig. Other fresh herbs, or parsley alone, may be used if fines herbes are not available.

Other egg dishes: Flavour scrambled eggs or soufflés with fines herbes; shell soft-boiled (soft-cooked) eggs and serve in little dishes, with a mixture of melted butter and fines herbes poured over them.

With Chicken or Veal: Mix fines herbes with melted butter and a squeeze of lemon for a simple sauce to spoon over grilled (broiled) or roast chicken, veal escalopes or veal cutlets.

Sauces: Mix fines herbes into Mayonnaise or Tartare Sauce (see pages 204 and 205), or Hollandaise or Béarnaise Sauce (see pages 369 and 370), to serve with fish, shellfish, vegetables or eggs.

Salads: Sprinkle fines herbes over a green, potato or pasta salad.

HERMITS

Little cookies from America with raisins, nuts and spices in the mixture.

Hermits

45 g/1½ oz (¼ cup) raisins; 30 g/1 oz (¼ cup) chopped nuts; 250 g/8 oz (2 cups) flour; 60 g/2 oz (4 tbsp) butter; 125 g/4 oz (½ cup) caster sugar; ½ tsp salt; 2 eggs; 180 g/6 oz (½ cup) treacle (molasses); ½ tsp bicarbonate of soda (baking soda); ¼ tsp cream of tartar; 1 tsp cinnamon; ½ tsp ground cloves; ¼ tsp mace; ¼ tsp nutmeg.

Toss raisins and nuts in 30 g/1 oz (¼ cup) of the flour and set aside. Cream butter with sugar until light and fluffy. Add salt, eggs and treacle (molasses) and beat well. Mix together remaining flour, the soda, cream of tartar, cinnamon, cloves, mace and nutmeg and add to creamed mixture. Beat thoroughly, then stir in raisin and nut mixture. Spread in a greased 25 × 30 cm (10 × 12 in) Swiss roll tin (jelly roll pan) or drop in teaspoonfuls on greased baking trays. Bake in a preheated moderate oven (180°C/350°F, Gas Mark 4) for 15–20 minutes if using Swiss roll tin (jelly roll pan) for 8–10 minutes for drop cookies. In each case when baked the tops should be firm and golden and centres chewy. Cut mixture in Swiss roll tin (jelly roll pan) into 5 cm (2 in) squares while still warm. Makes about 30 squares or 60 drops.

VARIATION

Concord Hermits: Substitute 180 g/6 oz (1 cup) firmly packed brown sugar for white sugar and treacle (molasses) and add 120 ml/4 fl oz (½ cup) sour cream.

HERRING

One of the richest and most succulent of the fat fish (see Fish). Herring is pickled, dried

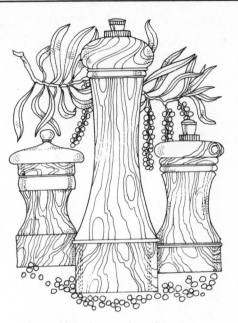

and cured by salting and smoking in a great variety of ways, some of the most famous being kippers, bloaters, salts, rollmops, Bismarck herring and red herring. Fresh or frozen herring can be cooked in any of the ways suitable for fat fish, or in the traditional Scots way with oatmeal, a marvellous breakfast dish.

In Scandinavia and Germany, where herring is a favourite food, Schnapps, Aquavit, or Russian vodka are often served ice-cold with herring, sometimes followed by a cold Pilsener chaser.

See also *Kippers*.

Herring, Canned and Salted

In addition to the many prepared herring and herring salads available in delicatessens, there are dozens of versions in jars and cans. You can do a lot to these preparations by adding, as needed, sour cream, vinegar or sugar if the herring is too sweet or too sour, fresh snipped dill or slivers of onions, a pinch of curry powder or a dab of prepared mustard, a slice of lemon or a few spoonfuls of white wine.

All of the herring sold in barrels for preparation at home is cured in brine and must be kept soaking in the refrigerator in several changes of cold water before you can proceed with a recipe. Salt herring is a firm fish which, as you might expect from its name, is extremely salty.

Matjes denotes a reddish, salt-cured herring that has not yet spawned. It is quite salty and richly flavoured, very tender and delicate in texture. It is almost always sold in fillets and is at its best chilled on ice and served with sprays of dill and hot boiled new potatoes; it may be soaked first in milk or buttermilk.

Bismarck is a sharply-flavoured herring, pickled whole in a spicy mixture of vinegar, onions, spices and lots of dried red chillies. **See recipes.**

Matjes Rolls

6 herring fillets (matjes); milk or buttermilk;
6 thick slices apple, cored; 120 ml/4 fl oz
($\frac{1}{2}$ cup) white wine; 6 tbsp Horseradish
Cream (page 160); 3 tbsp snipped chives.
GARNISH: *pickled baby beetroot; pickled*
gherkins.

Rinse herring, cover with milk or buttermilk
and soak for 2 hours, changing milk several
times for a milder flavour. Let apple slices
marinate in white wine 30 minutes – 1 hour.
Remove herring fillets from milk and drain
on paper towels. Put 1 tbsp horseradish
cream into the centre of each fillet. Roll up
and fasten rolled fillets with a toothpick.
Sprinkle top with snipped chives. Set each
roll on an apple slice that has been drained
on paper towels. Serve on individual plates
garnished with a few pickled baby beetroot
and gherkins. Serves 6.

Crispy Herring in Oatmeal

4 herring; milk; medium oatmeal (from
health food shops); 180 g/6 oz ($\frac{3}{4}$ cup)
butter.
GARNISH: *lemon wedges; parsley sprigs.*

Check that fish is well scaled and cleaned.
Slit each down belly to tail. Cut off head, tail
and fins. Open out flat and place skin side up
on a board. With thumb and forefinger
dipped in salt, hold tail firmly. Press down
with knuckles of other hand along backbone
to loosen it. Turn the herring over and
carefully ease out backbone with point of a
knife. Pull out as many small bones are
possible (a pair of long-nose pliers or
tweezers helps). Wipe fish with damp paper
towels, dip in milk and then in oatmeal. Fry
in hot butter, skinless side first, until outside
is crisp. Drain on crumpled paper towels and
serve very hot, garnished with lemon wedges
and parsley sprigs. Serves 4.
NOTE: If the herring has roe, coat it with milk
and oatmeal, fry separately and place down
centre of each fish.

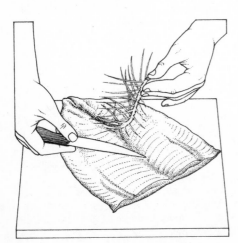

Pickled Herring Salad

Serve as a first-course salad, or as part of a
buffet.

8 herring fillets (matjes would be ideal); milk
or buttermilk; 2 beetroot, cooked, peeled
and diced; 3 potatoes, cooked and diced; 4
hard-boiled (hard-cooked) eggs, chopped; 2
sour pickled cucumbers, chopped; $\frac{1}{2}$ red
salad onion or 4 shallots, chopped.
DRESSING: *175 ml/6 fl oz ($\frac{3}{4}$ cup) sour cream;*
1 tbsp wine vinegar; 2 tsp dry mustard; 1 tsp
salt; 2 tsp lemon juice.
GARNISH: *sour cream; snipped chives.*

Rinse herring, cover with milk or buttermilk
and allow to soak for 2 hours, changing milk
several times. Drain, pat dry with paper
towels and cut into bite-sized pieces.
Combine beetroot, potatoes, eggs,
cucumbers, onion and herring in a salad
bowl. In a small bowl combine dressing
ingredients and fold through salad, tossing
lightly to combine. Chill salad, covered with
plastic wrap, for 1 hour. Garnish salad with a
dollop of sour cream and snipped chives.
Serves 6.

HOLLANDAISE SAUCE

See page 369 for recipe.

HONEY

The natural, unrefined substance bees make
from flower nectar. It varies greatly in colour,
flavour and consistency, depending on the
kind of blossom from which the nectar is
gathered. In general, the honey lightest in
colour will have the mildest flavour.
Honeycomb gives us honey as it is made and
stored by the bees. The honey is sealed in the
cells capped with wax. It is sold by some
specialist health food shops and should be
served cut into small squares.
Cut honeycomb is honeycomb cut into bars,
wrapped separately and sold in health food
stores.
Liquid honey is obtained by uncapping the
comb and extracting the honey. It is usually
sold in jars and heat-treated to prevent
crystallization during storage.
Candied, creamed or solid honey is granulated honey from which some of the moisture
has been removed.

Ways to Use Honey

● Substitute honey for sugar on hot
porridge.
● Sweeten whipped cream with honey for
cakes and desserts.
● Serve fresh fruit for dessert with 90 g/3 oz
($\frac{1}{4}$ cup) honey stirred into 175 ml/6 fl oz
($\frac{3}{4}$ cup) sour cream.
● Top chocolate, vanilla or coffee ice cream
with honey and sprinkle with chopped nuts.

● Mix half honey and half butter to spread
on hot toast, crumpets, muffins or scones.
● Top sautéed apple rings, pineapple or
banana slices with honey, cinnamon and a
little grated orange rind; cook a few moments
longer to glaze.
● Mix honey with Ricotta or cream cheese,
nuts and chopped dried fruit to fill baked
tartlet shells, or serve with plain sweet biscuits
(cookies).
● Make a hot syrup of 280 g/9 oz ($\frac{3}{4}$ cup)
honey and 4 tbsp lemon juice and pour
over a freshly baked nut and fruit loaf.
Prick the loaf first before using the syrup.
● Glaze carrots, turnips, onions or new
potatoes with honey. Cook vegetables, covered, in a very little salted water with a
tablespoonful each of butter and honey.
Remove lid when vegetables are almost
cooked and continue cooking until water has
evaporated leaving a golden glaze. Tilt saucepan to roll vegetables in the glaze before
serving. **See recipes**.

Honey-Ginger Glazed Shoulder of Lamb

1 shoulder of lamb, boned and rolled;
180 g/6 oz ($\frac{1}{2}$ cup) warmed honey; 2 tbsp
lemon juice; 1 tbsp soy sauce; pinch ground
cloves; 1 tsp ground ginger; 120 ml/4 fl oz
($\frac{1}{2}$ cup) hot chicken or veal stock.

Place lamb on a rack in a roasting tin (pan)
and roast in a preheated moderately hot
oven (200°C/400°F, Gas Mark 6) for 15
minutes. Reduce heat to moderate
(180°C/350°F, Gas Mark 4) and roast for a
further 30 minutes. Mix together honey,
lemon juice, soy sauce and spices, and brush
lamb with this mixture. Continue to roast,
brushing with glaze every 10 minutes,
allowing in total 20 minutes per 500 g (1 lb),
plus 20 minutes, for lamb that is pink inside,
or 25 minutes per 500 g (1 lb), plus 25
minutes, for well-done lamb. When cooked,
leave for 15 minutes before carving.
Meantime, skim fat from pan juices, add
stock and stir until boiling. Pour gravy into a
sauce boat and serve with the lamb. Serves 6.

Honey Prawns

750 g (1$\frac{1}{2}$ lb) Dublin Bay prawns (jumbo
shrimp), shelled and deveined; 30 g/1 oz
($\frac{1}{4}$ cup) cornflour (cornstarch); 125 g/4 oz
(1 cup) self-raising flour; $\frac{1}{2}$ tsp salt; $\frac{1}{4}$ tsp white
pepper; 300 ml/$\frac{1}{2}$ pint (1$\frac{1}{4}$ cups) water; 1 egg,
beaten; oil for frying; 2 tbsp honey; 2 tbsp
sesame seeds.

Dust prawns (shrimp) lightly with cornflour
(cornstarch). Sift flour, salt and pepper into a
bowl, make a well in centre and gradually
add water and egg, mixing to a smooth batter
free of lumps. Put 3 or 4 prawns (shrimp) in
a bowl, pour over a small amount of batter to

H

coat and remove. Repeat with remaining prawns (shrimp). Heat oil in a large frying pan (skillet) or wok, add prawns (shrimp) a few at a time and fry for 3 minutes or until prawns (shrimp) are golden and cooked through. Drain and keep warm. Remove oil from pan and wipe clean. Heat 1 tbsp fresh oil in pan, add honey and stir over gentle heat until warm. Add prawns (shrimp), toss quickly, remove and sprinkle with sesame seeds. Serve immediately. Serves 4–6.

Honey Buns

125 g/4 oz (½ cup) butter; 90 g/3 oz (½ cup) firmly packed brown sugar; 1 egg, beaten; 2 tbsp honey; 210 g/7 oz (1¾ cups) self-raising flour; pinch salt; creamed honey for spreading.

Cream butter with brown sugar. Beat in egg and honey. Sift flour with salt and work into mixture until it forms a soft dough. Chill until firm. Shape dough into small balls the size of a walnut and place well apart on greased baking trays. Bake in a preheated moderate oven (180°C/350°F, Gas Mark 4) for 12 minutes or until risen and golden. Cool and sandwich in pairs with creamed honey. Makes 10–12.

Honey Cheesecake

1 quantity Rich Shortcrust Pastry (page 274); lightly beaten egg white to glaze; 500 g/1 lb (2 cups) Ricotta cheese; 125 g/4 oz (½ cup) sugar; 250 g/8 oz (⅔ cup) honey; 4 eggs; 2 tsp cinnamon.

Roll out pastry (dough) to line a greased 20 cm (8 in) square cake tin (pan). Brush pastry (dough) with a little egg white, prick bottom and sides well and bake blind in a preheated moderately hot oven (190°C/375°F, Gas Mark 5) for 10 minutes. Remove and cool while preparing filling. Beat together cheese, sugar and honey, add eggs and beat until combined. Pour into cooled pastry (dough) shell. Reduce oven temperature to moderate (180°C/350°F, Gas Mark 4) and bake cheesecake for 45–50 minutes or until top is golden-brown. Turn off heat and allow to cool in oven. Sprinkle with cinnamon and cut into squares or diamond shapes to serve. Makes about 16.

Honey Rum Chocolate Cake

180 g/6 oz (¾ cup) butter; 180 g/6 oz (1 cup) lightly packed brown sugar; 125 g/4 oz (⅓ cup) honey; 2 eggs; 1 tbsp rum; ½ tsp vanilla essence (extract); 2 tbsp (unsweetened) cocoa powder; 210 g/7 oz (1¾ cups) self-raising flour; pinch salt; 120 ml/4 fl oz (½ cup) sweet sherry; 250 ml/8 fl oz (1 cup) double (heavy) cream, whipped; sifted icing (confectioners) sugar.

Cream butter with brown sugar, add honey and beat until light and fluffy. Beat in eggs one at a time, then stir in rum and vanilla. Sift cocoa, flour and salt and fold into the creamed mixture alternately with sherry, beginning and ending with flour. Turn into a greased and lined 23 cm (9 in) round cake tin (pan). Bake in a preheated moderate oven (180°C/350°F, Gas Mark 4) for 45 minutes or until a fine skewer inserted in centre comes out clean. Allow to cool in the tin for a few minutes, then turn out on to a wire rack to finish cooling. Split cake into 2 layers, fill with whipped cream and dust the top with icing (confectioners) sugar. Serves 8–10.

HONEYDEW MELON

The flesh of honeydew melon, pale green, crisp and delicately fragrant, is superb alone or in combination with other foods both sweet and savoury. It is perhaps the best melon to serve with prosciutto, and can be used in any of the ways suitable for other melons.

See also *Ginger, Melon* and *Prosciutto*.

HORS D'OEUVRE

Hors d'oeuvre means 'outside the main body of work', that is, outside the main part of the meal. The term is the French equivalent of appetizers. In English-speaking countries hors d'oeuvre are usually associated with a party or special occasion. But in France, the midday meal almost invariably begins with a slice of pâté, egg or fish mayonnaise, cold meat dressed with a piquant vinaigrette or *les hors d'oeuvre variés* – the plate of mixed hors d'oeuvre which displays the skill of the French housewife at transforming small quantities of food, including leftovers, into a delicious and thrifty first course.

Serving Hors d'oeuvre

The function of hors d'oeuvre is to delight and invite the diner, and their appearance is very important.
● Slice meats thin and overlap them neatly;

very thin slices of meat such as prosciutto can be rolled or folded loosely into triangles.
● Cut salad ingredients into uniform pieces or shreds.
● Arrange hot pastries geometrically on a tray or pile them into a napkin-lined basket.
● Sprinkle chopped herbs in a narrow strip down the centre of the dish or in a border round the edge, or scatter them lightly over the surface – never in damp clumps.
● Add colour and pattern with canned pimiento or anchovy strips, neatly crossed or arranged trellis-fashion.
● Consider the balance of colour, texture and flavour: juicy red tomato, crisp green pepper, black (ripe) olives; rich golden mayonnaise topped with piquant capers; a slice of pâté with a bright radish, still retaining some of its green leaves, and a few tiny gherkins (cornichons).

Hors d'oeuvre variés

These cold hors d'oeuvre can be a mixture of little salads which you have prepared yourself, such as those given below, and other foods from the kitchen cupboard or delicatessen – smoked fish such as eel or mackerel; good canned or pickled fish; meats such as salami, ham, sausage, liverwurst; fresh, pickled or canned vegetables; eggs; feta and other cheeses. Leftovers of meat, fish or vegetables can be combined with Vinaigrette Dressing (see page 358) or Mayonnaise (see page 204) to add to the platter. Garnish with olives, capers, chopped herbs or fresh herb sprays, watercress or tiny lettuce leaves, canned pimiento, cherry tomatoes or tomato wedges, sieved hard-boiled (hard-cooked) egg, lemon slices or wedges. Serve with fresh crusty bread and butter.

Egg Mayonnaise Halve hard-boiled (hard-cooked) eggs lengthways and arrange, rounded sides up, on a serving platter. Coat with Mayonnaise (see page 204) and garnish with drained canned pimiento, cut into strips and arranged trellis-fashion, and with a stoned half of black (ripe) olive in each square. Scatter with parsley and serve at room temperature.

Fish Mayonnaise Follow recipe for Egg Mayonnaise but substitute about 60 g/2 oz

($\frac{1}{3}$ cup) poached or canned fish, skin and bones removed and broken into large flakes for each egg, and capers for black (ripe) olives.

Salade de Boeuf (Beef Salad) Very lightly mix together equal quantities of diced, cooked beef and diced, cooked new potatoes. Add a little finely chopped onion and peeled, seeded and diced tomato. Moisten with Mustard Vinaigrette (see page 358), season with salt and freshly ground black pepper, cover and chill lightly. Dress neatly in a shallow dish and sprinkle generously with chopped parsley just before serving.

Vegetables à la Grecque Follow recipe for Courgette (Zucchini) à la Grecque, using a selection of young vegetables (see page 486).

Hot Filled Hors d'oeuvre
Ahead of time, prepare miniature tartlet or barquette cases in short or flaky pastry (dough), puff pastry (paste) Bouchées or choux pastry (paste) Profiteroles or Eclairs (see separate entries). Also prepare a savoury filling such as those which follow. Just before serving, put cases into a preheated cool oven (150°C/300°F, Gas Mark 2) to warm, and reheat filling over low heat or by standing the container in boiling water. Fill cases with hot filling and serve immediately, or finish as directed.

Cape Cod Filling Poach quartered scallops in a little dry white wine for 2 minutes. Cook sliced button mushrooms in a little water with a few drops of lemon juice for 5 minutes. Drain each and combine the cooking liquors. Boil until reduced to about 1 tbsp and combine with hot thick Cream Sauce (see page 368) – use a quantity of sauce equal to the amount of cooked filling you have.

Remove from heat, season with salt, pepper and a little lemon juice, and fold in scallops and mushrooms. Small oysters or halved large ones may be added, if desired. Fill cases and sprinkle with finely chopped parsley or chives.

Chicken Filling To 250 g/8 oz (1 cup) finely chopped, cooked chicken, add 1 tbsp each finely chopped celery and shallot. Mix with 300 ml/$\frac{1}{2}$ pint (1$\frac{1}{4}$ cups) hot, thick Cream Sauce (see page 368) and season with salt, pepper and a dash of Worcestershire sauce. Reheat gently, fill cases and sprinkle with paprika.

Florentine Filling Chop 210 g (7 oz) spinach. Cook, covered, with 1 tbsp butter until soft, then uncover, season with salt, freshly ground black pepper and nutmeg and cook, stirring and watching carefully, until moisture evaporates. Add 3–4 tbsp hot thick Béchamel Sauce (see page 368) and 2 tbsp grated Parmesan cheese. Fill cases, sprinkle with more cheese and return to oven until cheese melts.

See also *Antipasti, Appetizers, Canapés* and *Sandwiches*.

HORSERADISH

The thick taproot of the horseradish plant is ground or grated to give the hot stinging flavour of the traditional sauce which accompanies roast beef of old England. In Germany the root is grated and mixed with vinegar as a sauce for fish or mixed with mayonnaise as a dressing for hard-boiled (hard-cooked) eggs. Some specialist greengrocers stock fresh horseradish roots in season. Grated horseradish may be purchased preserved or as a relish from good delicatessens. Manufacturers use it in horseradish cream.

NOTE: Preserved horseradish or relish may be used instead of fresh in the recipes below, in which case use half the quantity of fresh specified in each recipe. **See recipes.**

Horseradish Butter

125 g/4 oz ($\frac{1}{2}$ cup) butter; 1 tbsp chopped parsley; juice $\frac{1}{2}$ lemon; 2 tbsp grated horseradish; $\frac{1}{2}$ tsp French (Dijon) mustard; 1 tbsp wine vinegar.

Mix ingredients together well and refrigerate. Use sliced, on grilled (broiled) steak, chops, kidneys or fried fish. Serves 8.

Horseradish Cream

150 ml/$\frac{1}{4}$ pint ($\frac{2}{3}$ cup) double (heavy) cream; squeeze lemon juice; 2 tbsp grated horseradish; $\frac{1}{2}$ tsp salt; freshly ground black pepper; pinch sugar.

Whip cream. Add lemon juice, horseradish, salt, pepper and sugar, and fold in lightly. If using bottled horseradish, press out moisture before using. Serves 6–8.

Horseradish Sauce

3 tbsp grated horseradish; 120 ml/4 fl oz ($\frac{1}{2}$ cup) double (heavy) cream; 1 tsp French (Dijon) mustard; 1 tbsp white wine vinegar; pinch sugar.

Whisk ingredients together until thick. Taste and add more vinegar or an extra pinch of sugar if necessary. Serve with hot or cold roast beef. For a milder flavour omit vinegar and add a little more sugar. Serves 4.

HOT WATER CRUST

See page 275 for recipe.

HUEVOS RANCHEROS (Ranch-Style Eggs)

A Latin-American dish which makes a splendid weekend breakfast or lunch. These are several versions; the eggs can be poached or fried separately or cooked in the sauce as in the following recipe.

Huevos Rancheros

3 tbsp olive oil; 1 small onion, chopped; 1 clove garlic, crushed; 1 small green pepper, cored, seeded and chopped; 2 ripe tomatoes, peeled, seeded and chopped; salt and freshly ground black pepper; dash Tabasco (hot pepper) sauce; 1 tbsp chopped fresh coriander, or $\frac{1}{4}$ tsp ground cumin; 4 eggs; 4 Tortillas (page 441); coriander sprigs to garnish.

Heat half the oil in a frying pan (skillet) and cook onion, garlic and green pepper gently until soft. Add tomatoes and simmer until thick. Season with salt, pepper, Tabasco (hot pepper) sauce and coriander or cumin. Make 4 depressions in the sauce and break an egg into each. Cover pan and cook 3–4 minutes or until eggs are set. Meantime, heat remaining oil and fry tortillas 30 seconds on each side or until crispy. Place tortillas on 2 heated plates. Use an egg slice to lift 2 eggs and surrounding sauce on to each tortilla. Garnish with coriander. Serves 2.

HUMMUS BI TAHINI (Chick Pea and Sesame Purée)

Chick pea purée or dip is one of the most widely known and appreciated of all the Middle Eastern dishes. Tahini is a paste made from sesame seeds. Hummus should have the consistency of thick mayonnaise and be well seasoned, but neither the flavour of garlic nor that of lemon juice should predominate.

Hummus bi Tahini

500 g/1 lb (2$\frac{1}{3}$ cups) dried chick peas; juice 2–3 lemons; 2–3 cloves garlic; salt; 175 ml/6 fl oz ($\frac{3}{4}$ cup) tahini; 1 tbsp olive oil; 1 tsp paprika; 1 tbsp finely chopped parsley to garnish.

Soak chick peas overnight in cold water to cover. Next day drain and place in a saucepan with fresh water to cover. Bring to the boil, then reduce heat to low and cook, covered, for 2–3 hours or until tender. Drain peas, reserving 120 ml/4 fl oz ($\frac{1}{2}$ cup) liquid. Set aside 105 g/3$\frac{1}{2}$ oz ($\frac{1}{2}$ cup) whole chick peas and purée remainder, adding a little of reserved cooking liquid or lemon juice if necessary. Crush garlic with salt and add to purée. Gradually mix in tahini paste with lemon juice and beat vigorously. Add more cooking liquid to give the consistency of thick mayonnaise. Check seasoning. Hummus is traditionally served spread on a flat plate. Make a shallow depression in the centre and pour in olive oil, then sprinkle with paprika, or mix paprika with oil and drizzle over surface. Garnish with chopped parsley and reserved whole chick peas. Serve as a dip with flat Lebanese (pita) bread. Makes about 1 litre/1$\frac{3}{4}$ pints (4 cups).

I

ICE CREAM

Ice cream just has to be one of the world's favourite desserts. While fine commercial ice creams are available, good, home-made ice cream, made from pure cream and eggs and carefully churned, is the richest, best-textured and finest ice cream of all.

There are many types of ice cream, from the French Vanilla, rich Italian to the economical ones. You can use milk and eggs or half milk and half cream and eggs, evaporated milk or full-cream, powdered milk, Each has its merit. The custard-based ice creams are rich, creamy and smooth. Those based on whipped evaporated milk are inexpensive to make, and the powdered milk base, also inexpensive, brings ice cream to remote areas where fresh milk or cream is unavailable (see *Milk*).

The way to achieve a smooth texture in home-made ice cream is to churn it, which prevents ice crystals from forming as the mixture is freezing. You can do this by freezing the mixture in metal ice cream trays and beating the partially-frozen cream with a rotary or electric mixer, or by using one of the excellent small electric sorbetières or ice cream-makers, complete with paddles, that constantly churn the mixture until it is the right consistency. These small machines make approximately 1 litre/1¾ pints (4 cups) of ice cream at a time. Larger ice cream makers are also available; these require salt and crushed ice and may be hand or electrically driven.

☐ To Freeze Ice Cream and Ices

IN FREEZING COMPARTMENT Turn freezing compartment to maximum or coldest setting about 1 hour before the mixture is prepared. Place prepared mixture in metal ice cream trays and put the trays back into the freezing compartment. Allow the mixture to semifreeze. Transfer the mixture to a mixing bowl, whisk it thoroughly with a rotary or electric mixer, replace it in the ice cream trays, cover with foil and freeze again for 1–4 hours until frozen hard. Store in freezing compartment at normal setting. The beating process may be repeated when the ice cream is just firming.

IN AN ELECTRIC ICE CREAM MAKER OR SORBETIERE Turn freezing compartment to maximum or coldest setting about an hour before the mixture is prepared. Read instruction booklet that usually accompanies these machines – as a general guide: make the ice cream mixture, pour it into the sorbetière and put it in the freezer, preferably in the coldest part, making sure the sorbetière stands level.

The sorbetière has a flat cord which passes under the freezer door and is plugged in to the nearest power point. The ice cream (or water ice if making) is constantly churned by paddles, and when it reaches the right consistency (after about 1–1½ hours), the paddles

lift up automatically. Remove paddles, smooth over surface of ice cream, cover and allow to freeze until hard. Store in freezer compartment at normal setting.

When ice cream is frozen, return freezer control to normal. Home-made ice creams and ices tend to freeze harder than the commercial ones. They reach the peak of flavour and texture after ripening (mellowing) for 2–6 hours and are best eaten within 48 hours of being made. Allow hard ice cream or ices to soften in the refrigerator for about 30–60 minutes before serving. **See recipes**.

Rich Vanilla Ice Cream
(Custard base)

250 ml/8 fl oz (1 cup) milk; 350 ml/12 fl oz (1½ cups) single (light) cream; ½ vanilla pod (bean), or 1 tsp vanilla essence (extract); 2 eggs; 2 egg yolks; 125 g/4 oz (½ cup) sugar; ¼ tsp salt.

Scald milk, cream and vanilla bean, if using, in a heavy saucepan over a low heat, (see page 215). Remove vanilla bean, or add vanilla. Beat the eggs and egg yolks, sugar and salt together in a heatproof bowl until thick and mousse-like. Stir in some of the scalded liquid. Place bowl over a saucepan of boiling water, add remaining scalded liquid and cook, stirring, until thick (the mixture should coat a metal spoon). Remove from heat and cool quickly over cold water, stirring occasionally. Pour mixture into container of a sorbetière or metal ice cream trays. Cover, place in freezer and process as directed (see *To Freeze Ice Cream and Ices*). Makes about 900 ml/1½ pints (3½ cups). Serves 6.

French Vanilla Ice Cream
(Mousse base)

400 ml/⅔ pint (1⅔ cups) single (light) cream; ½ vanilla pod (bean), or 1 tsp vanilla essence (extract); 60 g/2 oz (¼ cup) sugar; 120 ml/4 fl oz (½ cup) water; 3 egg yolks.

Place cream and vanilla bean, if using, in a heavy saucepan and heat gently, without boiling, for 5 minutes. Set aside and add vanilla, if using. Place the sugar and water in a small saucepan, dissolve sugar, then bring to the boil. Boil for 5 minutes without stirring. Allow to cool for 30 seconds. Beat egg yolks until pale and frothy. Pour hot sugar syrup over yolks, whisking constantly until thick. Strain cream, add to egg mixture and whisk until frothy. Pour into container of a sorbetière or metal ice cream trays. Cover, place in freezer and process as directed (see *To Freeze Ice Cream and Ices*). Makes about 750 ml/1¼ pints (3 cups). Serves 5–6.

VARIATIONS

Chocolate Ice Cream: Use French or Rich Vanilla Ice Cream, but melt 125 g/4 oz

(⅔ cup) cooking chocolate in the warm cream or milk and cream.

Coffee Ice Cream: Use French or Rich Vanilla Ice Cream, but add 1 tbsp instant coffee powder to the cream or milk and cream.

Coconut Ice Cream: Use French or Rich Vanilla Ice Cream, but add 90 g/3 oz (1 cup) desiccated (shredded) coconut to cream or milk and cream and heat gently to infuse. Push mixture through a sieve, squeezing out as much of the coconut-flavoured creamy milk as possible. Discard the coconut.

Almond Ice Cream: Use French or Rich Vanilla Ice Cream, but add 60 g/2 oz (½ cup) ground almonds to the cream or milk and cream and heat gently to infuse. Push mixture through a sieve, squeezing out as much almond-flavoured milk as possible. Discard meal.

Burnt Almond Ice Cream: Use French or Rich Vanilla Ice Cream, but add ¾ tsp almond essence (extract) instead of vanilla. When frozen, stir in 60 g/2 oz (½ cup) slivered almonds which have been toasted to a golden colour. Cover and return to freezer with temperature control set at normal and allow to ripen 2–6 hours (see *To Freeze Ice Cream and Ices*).

Strawberry Ice Cream

250 g (8 oz) strawberries, hulled; 3 egg yolks; 180 g/6 oz (¾ cup) sugar; 300 ml/½ pint (1¼ cups) double (heavy) cream, lightly whipped; almond essence (extract).

Place strawberries in bowl of a blender or food processor and purée. Beat egg yolks and sugar until pale and light. Mix in strawberry purée, then fold in whipped cream. Add a few drops of almond essence (extract) to taste. Pour into container of a sorbetière or metal ice cream trays. Cover, place in freezer and process as directed (see *To Freeze Ice Cream and Ices*). Makes about 1 litre/1¾ pints (4 cups). Serves 8.

Italian Apricot Ice Cream

180 g/6 oz (1 cup) dried apricots; 500 ml/18 fl oz (2 cups) single (light) cream; 6 egg yolks; 75 g/2½ oz (⅓ cup) sugar.

Cook apricots in a little water until they are tender. Drain and push fruit through a sieve to make a thick purée. In the top of a double saucepan (double boiler), gradually stir cream into beaten egg yolks and cook gently over simmering water, stirring occasionally, until thickened. Remove custard from heat and add sugar immediately, adding more to taste if necessary. Stir until dissolved. Cool custard, then stir in apricot purée. Pour into container of a sorbetière or metal ice cream trays. Cover, place in freezer and process as directed (see *To Freeze Ice Cream and Ices*). Makes about 1 litre/1¾ pints (4 cups).

ICES, SORBETS, GRANITE AND SHERBETS

Freshly-made water ices are among the most delectable of frozen ices – whether called sorbets as in France, sherbets as in the U.S.A. or granite as in Italy. Sorbets are generally accepted to be fruit juices, sweetened and frozen. However, they may also be made with tea, coffee, champagne or a spirit. Granite are softened fruit purées frozen until granular in texture; sherbet is the American version of a granita. For a finer-grained ice, a lightly beaten egg white or softened gelatine may be folded into the mixture to be frozen. Buttermilk or milk is often added to the fruit mixture.

Ices combine magnificently with a scoop of ice cream, or with fresh fruit. They may be served in fruit shells – scooped-out oranges or lemons, half a poached pear, half a small melon – and garnished with fresh garden leaves. Meringues are often shaped into containers for ices, and pretty crystal or glass plates and goblets can be enhanced with the delicate colours of fruit ices.

Sorbets may be served before the main course to refresh the palate or with other creams or fruit as a dessert. Three-star restaurants all over the world are featuring sorbets and ices on their menus, and offer different flavoured sorbets on a plate, together with the fresh fruits from which they were made.

☐ **To Freeze Ices:** Follow the directions, above and also see *To Freeze Ice Cream and Ices* (page 161). **See recipes.**

Lemon Sorbet (1)

125 g/4 oz (½ cup) cube sugar; 4 lemons; 400 ml/⅔ pint (1⅔ cups) water; 1 small egg white.

Rub sugar cubes over rind of 2 lemons until cubes are impregnated with lemon oils (zest). Place in saucepan with water and stir over low heat until sugar dissolves. Bring to the boil and boil 6 minutes. Cool. Squeeze juice

from all 4 lemons and strain. Add to sugar syrup and mix well. Beat egg white with a few tbsp of the lemon syrup. Fold into remaining syrup. Pour mixture into metal ice cream trays or container of sorbetière. Cover, place in freezer and process as directed (see *To Freeze Ice Cream and Ices*). The sorbet may be transferred to a separate dish or mould, depending on how you want to serve or store it. Makes 1 litre/1¾ pints (4 cups). Serves 6–8.

Lemon Sorbet (2)

175 ml/6 fl oz (¾ cup) lemon juice; juice 1 orange, strained; grated rind 2 lemons; 250 g/8 oz (1 cup) sugar; 350 ml/12 fl oz (1½ cups) water.

Mix lemon and orange juice with grated rind. Put sugar and 250 ml/8 fl oz (1 cup) water in a small saucepan and bring to the boil. Boil for 5 minutes. Remove from heat and cool, then add remaining water and fruit juices. Chill. Pour mixture into metal ice cream trays or container of a sorbetière. Cover, place in freezer and process as directed (see *To Freeze Ice Cream and Ices*). Makes about 1 litre/1¾ pints (4 cups). Serves 6–8.

NOTE: If a fine-grained sorbet is desired beat an egg white until soft but fluffy and stir into the mixture before freezing.

VARIATION

Lime Sorbet: Make as for Lemon Sorbet (2) but replace ½ the lemon juice with the same amount of lime juice.

Orange Sorbet (1)

juice 6 oranges; juice 1 lemon; 140 g/4½ oz (1 cup) icing (confectioners) sugar, sifted.

Mix the orange and lemon juices and measure. If necessary squeeze more oranges to make 500 ml/18 fl oz (2 cups) juice. Stir in sugar, whisking thoroughly until it dissolves. Transfer to an ice cream maker or metal ice cream tray, cover with foil and freeze to a slush. Purée in a food processor or blender or beat with a rotary beater until the slush becomes very light and fine grained. Transfer to a 750 ml/1¼ pint (3 cup) freezerproof soufflé dish or mould and freeze. Take sorbet out of freezer 30–45 minutes before serving and leave to soften in refrigerator. Makes 750 ml/1¼ pints (3 cups). Serves 4–6.

Orange Sorbet (2)

350 ml/12 fl oz (1½ cups) orange juice; grated rind 1 orange; 250 g/8 oz (1 cup) sugar; 175 ml/6 fl oz (¾ cup) water; juice 2 lemons, strained; 1 egg white.

Mix orange juice with grated rind. Place sugar and water in a saucepan, dissolve sugar over a gentle heat and bring to the boil. Boil for 5 minutes, then cool. Add orange and lemon juices and mix well. Beat egg white with 2–3 tbsp of the orange mixture, then fold through remaining orange mixture. Pour into metal ice cream trays or container of a sorbetière. Cover, place in freezer and process as directed (see *To Freeze Ice Cream and Ices*). Makes about 1 litre/1¾ pints (4 cups). Serves 6–8.

VARIATIONS

Orange Rum Sorbet: Make Orange Sorbet, using 120 ml/4 fl oz (½ cup) white rum for 120 ml/4 fl oz (½ cup) of the water.

Grapefruit Sorbet: Make as for Orange Sorbet, replacing orange juice and rind with grapefruit.

Earl Grey Sorbet

750 ml/1¼ pints (3 cups) water; 150 g/5 oz (⅔ cup) sugar; 1 tbsp Earl Grey tea; juice 1 orange; lemon slices to serve.

Combine 500 ml/18 fl oz (2 cups) water with the sugar, bring to the boil and boil for 5 minutes. Bring remaining water to the boil, add tea leaves and leave to infuse. Add strained tea infusion to sugar syrup with orange juice to taste; see that the mixture has a good tea taste. Cool. Pour into metal ice cream trays or container of a sorbetière. Cover, place in freezer and process as directed (see *To Freeze Ice Cream and Ices*). Serve with lemon slices. Makes about 900 ml/1½ pints (3½ cups).

Apricot Buttermilk Sherbet

12 ripe apricots to yield 250 g/8 oz (1 cup) puréed fruit; about 60 g/2 oz (¼ cup) sugar; 2 tbsp lemon juice; pinch salt; 350 ml/12 fl oz (1½ cups) buttermilk.

Combine fruit purée, sugar, lemon juice, salt and buttermilk, stirring well until sugar has dissolved. (This can be done in a blender or food processor fitted with a steel blade, in which case the fruit need not be puréed first.) Taste and add more sugar if necessary. The flavour should be sharp, not sweet. Pour into metal ice cream trays or container of a sorbetière. Cover, place in freezer and process as directed (see *To Freeze Ice Cream and Ices*). Makes about 750 ml/1¼ pints (3 cups). Serves 4–6.

VARIATIONS

Mango Buttermilk Sherbet: Prepare as for Apricot Buttermilk Sherbet, replacing 250 g/8 oz (1 cup) apricot purée with puréed fresh or canned mangoes.

Peach Buttermilk Sherbet: Prepare as for Apricot Buttermilk Sherbet, replacing 250 g/8 oz (1 cup) apricot purée with puréed fresh or canned peaches.

Strawberry Buttermilk Sherbet: Prepare as for Apricot Buttermilk Sherbet, replacing 250 g/8 oz (1 cup) apricot purée with puréed strawberries. Sieve purée before using.

Watermelon Ice

350 g/12 oz (4 cups) watermelon, without seeds; 125 g/4 oz (½ cup) sugar; juice 1 lemon, strained; sprigs fresh mint to decorate.

Place watermelon in a blender and blend at medium speed for 30 seconds, or crush with a potato masher and push through a coarse sieve. Combine sugar and lemon juice and stir well. Add to watermelon purée. Pour into container of a sorbetière or metal ice cream trays. Cover, place in freezer and process as directed (see *To Freeze Ice Cream and Ices*). Makes about 900 ml/1½ pints (3½ cups). Serves 4–6.

Strawberry Sherbet

Replace the strawberries in this recipe with any other soft fruit of your choice.

1 kg (2 lb) strawberries, hulled; juice 1 orange; juice 1 lemon; 430 g/14 oz (1¾ cups) sugar; 120 ml/4 fl oz (½ cup) water.

Blend or purée fruit and push through a sieve. Add fruit juices. Combine sugar and water in a small saucepan, bring slowly to the boil to dissolve sugar and boil for 2–3 minutes. Combine fruit pulp and sugar syrup. Pour into container of a sorbetière or metal ice cream trays. Cover, place in freezer and process as directed (see *To Freeze Ice Cream and Ices*). Makes about 1 litre/1¾ pints (4 cups). Serves 6–8.

VARIATIONS

Melon Sorbet: Prepare as for Strawberry Sherbet using 1 ripe, well-flavoured melon weighing about 1 kg (2 lb), or 2 smaller melons. Halve melon, scoop out seeds and remove flesh. Purée as for strawberries. You should have about 500 g/1 lb (2 cups) purée.

Apricot or Peach Sherbet: Prepare as for Strawberry Sherbet using 1 kg (2 lb) ripe peaches or apricots. Drop fruit into boiling water for 5 minutes, then chill and peel fruit. Halve and remove stones, then purée flesh as for strawberries. You should have about 500 g/1 lb (2 cups) purée.

ICINGS, FROSTINGS AND FILLINGS

Icing

The sweet coating that goes on the outside of a cake. Icings add flavour to cakes, give texture contrast, help them stay fresh and moist and, of course, add to their appearance.

Popular icings include the following:
Almond Paste: For coating and moulding into fruits, flowers, etc. (see page 7).
Butter Cream Icing: For coating and piping.
Glacé Icing: For coating and simple decoration.
Royal Icing: For coating and elaborate decoration.

Plastic Fondant Icing: For covering and modelling.
Frosting
What Americans call icing; use for coating.
Fillings
The range of cake fillings seems almost endless, but there are some universal favourites. Sponges are popular with a simple jam filling or whipped cream and fruit. Lemon Curd (Cheese) transforms a plain butter cake or sponge sandwich. The smooth butter cream called *Crème au Beurre* in France is often sandwiched between many layers of cake to make a Continental gâteau. Cream cheese and Ricotta cheese are the basis of other European cake fillings. Dried fruits, nuts, rum, chocolate, ginger and other flavourings are often added to a rich custard cream (Crème Pâtissière) for luscious dessert cakes. **See recipes**.

See also *Mock Cream*.

Butter Cream Icing

(Vienna Icing)

A soft and creamy icing (frosting) that can be swirled into decorative shapes and also used for piping.

125 g/4 oz (½ cup) butter; 210 g/7 oz (1½ cups) pure icing (confectioners) sugar, sifted; 1 tbsp sherry; few drops vanilla essence (extract).

Beat butter until light and creamy, then gradually beat in half the icing (confectioners) sugar. Beat in sherry alternately with remaining sugar. Stir in vanilla. Sufficient to fill a Swiss roll (jelly roll) or top a 20 cm (8 in) cake.

VARIATIONS

Chocolate Butter Cream Icing: Sift 1 tbsp (unsweetened) cocoa powder with icing (confectioners) sugar.

Orange or Lemon Butter Cream Icing: Add 1 tsp grated orange or lemon rind to icing (confectioners) sugar, and use 1 tbsp orange or lemon juice in place of sherry.

Liqueur Butter Cream Icing: Use 1 tbsp Grand Marnier, Crème de Menthe, Crème de Cacao etc., in place of sherry.

Glacé or Warm Icing

A quickly mixed, easily flavoured icing (frosting) that sets firmly to a decorative glaze. Decorations should be added quickly before the icing sets.

180 g/6 oz (1¼ cups) pure icing (confectioners) sugar; 1 tbsp boiling water; few drops flavouring essence (extract); food colouring as desired.

Sift icing (confectioners) sugar into a small, heatproof bowl. Add boiling water gradually, mixing to a smooth, thick paste that will coat the back of the spoon. Place bowl over a small amount of boiling water and stir icing for 1 minute. Add flavouring and colouring as desired. Pour icing quickly over cake and smooth surface with a spatula or knife dipped in hot water. Sufficient to cover top of a 20 cm (8 in) cake.

VARIATIONS

Chocolate Glacé Icing: Sift 1 tbsp (unsweetened) cocoa powder with icing (confectioners) sugar. Melt 1 tsp butter in boiling water before adding to icing (confectioners) sugar.

Coffee Glacé Icing: Add 1 tsp instant coffee powder dissolved in 1 tbsp boiling water to icing (confectioners) sugar.

Lemon Glacé Icing: Use 1 tbsp lemon juice instead of boiling water.

Royal Icing

2 egg whites; 560 g/1 lb 2 oz (4 cups) pure icing (confectioners) sugar, sifted; 1 tsp lemon juice; food colouring as desired.

Place egg white in a bowl and beat lightly. Add icing (confectioners) sugar 1 tbsp at a time, beating continuously until mixture is very stiff and stands in peaks. Blend in lemon juice and food colouring. Keep icing covered with a damp cloth to prevent it hardening too quickly. This will cover a 20 cm (8 in) cake and can be used for piped decorations, lettering, etc.

Plastic Fondant Icing

A roll-out type of icing (frosting) used to cover rich fruit cakes. It gives a very smooth surface for decoration.

500 g/1 lb (3½ cups) pure icing (confectioners) sugar, sifted; ¼ tsp gelatine; 1 tbsp cold water; 2 tsp glycerine; 90 g/3 oz (4 tbsp) liquid glucose; flavouring and food colouring as desired; cornflour (cornstarch) for dusting.

Sift icing (confectioners) sugar into a bowl. Soften gelatine in cold water, then place over hot water and stir until dissolved. Remove from heat and add glycerine and glucose, stirring well. Add to icing (confectioners) sugar with flavouring, kneading with the hands until mixture forms a firm dough-like paste. Remove to a board sprinkled with

cornflour (cornstarch) and knead until smooth and pliable. Food colouring may be added, if desired, and kneaded through. Roll out until large enough to cover top and sides of cake **(Fig 1 opposite)**. Fit carefully over cake, smoothing with hands dusted with cornflour (cornstarch) **(2)**. Plastic icing may be kept in an airtight container until needed, but do not store in refrigerator as this will cause it to harden. Sufficient to cover top and sides of a 20 cm (8 in) cake. Use Modelling Fondant for moulded decorations **(3)**.

Modelling Fondant

Excellent for moulded decorations such as fruits and flowers.

½ tsp gelatine; 1 tbsp cold water; 3 tsp liquid glucose; 500 g/1 lb (3½ cups) pure icing (confectioners) sugar, sifted; cornflour (cornstarch) for dusting; food colouring as desired.

Soften gelatine in water, then place over hot water and stir until dissolved. Remove from heat and stir in glucose. Add to icing (confectioners) sugar, kneading well until all sugar has been absorbed. Put on a board dusted with cornflour (cornstarch) and knead until pliable, adding colouring if desired. Keep mixture well wrapped in an airtight container until ready to use. Makes about 500 g/1 lb (2 cups).

NOTE: If the mixture is too dry add a little boiled water, and if too moist add extra sifted icing (confectioners) sugar.

Rich Chocolate Icing

180 g/6 oz (1 cup) dark chocolate, roughly chopped; 4 tbsp dark rum; ½ tsp vanilla essence (extract); 280 g/9 oz (2 cups) icing (confectioners) sugar, sifted; 30 g/1 oz (2 tbsp) butter, softened; 1 tbsp hot milk.

Melt chocolate in a heatproof bowl set over simmering water. Stir in dark rum and vanilla. Add icing (confectioners) sugar, butter and milk. Stir vigorously over the hot water until icing is smooth and glossy. If too thick, add a little more milk. Spread at once over cake. Sufficient to cover top of a 23 cm (9 in) square cake.

Economical Chocolate Icing

210 g/7 oz (1½ cups) icing (confectioners) sugar, sifted; ½ tsp cinnamon; 1 tbsp (unsweetened) cocoa powder; 30 g/1 oz (2 tbsp) butter; 1 tbsp hot water.

Mix icing (confectioners) sugar, cinnamon and cocoa in a bowl, then stir in softened butter and water. Mix to a smooth paste, adding a little more hot water if necessary. Sufficient to cover top of a 20 cm (8 in) round cake.

Seven Minute Frosting

250 g/8 oz (1 cup) sugar; ½ tsp cream of tartar; 1 egg white; 2 tbsp water; ¼ tsp vanilla essence (extract).

Place sugar, cream of tartar, egg white and water in the top of a double saucepan (double boiler) or in a heatproof bowl placed over simmering water (do not allow bottom of bowl to touch water). Beat with an electric beater on slow, or with a rotary beater, until mixture is thick enough to hold its shape. This takes about 7 minutes, which gives the frosting its name. Cool a little, then stir in vanilla or other desired flavourings and spread roughly over cake. Sufficient to cover a bar cake or an 18 cm (7 in) round cake.

NOTE: Quantities may be doubled for larger cakes, in which case the frosting takes about 10 minutes to make.

VARIATIONS

Peppermint Seven Minute Frosting: Add 2–3 drops peppermint essence (extract) instead of vanilla and a little pink or green food colouring.

Marshmallow Seven Minute Frosting: When mixture is thick, after cooking for 7 minutes, stir in 60 g/2 oz (1 cup) chopped marshmallows. Stir until melted.

Chocolate Seven Minute Frosting: Stir in 90 g/3 oz (½ cup) melted dark chocolate after cooking for 7 minutes.

Chocolate Cream Cheese Frosting

90 g/3 oz (½ cup) dark chocolate, roughly chopped; 90 g/3 oz (scant ½ cup) cream cheese, softened; 4 tbsp milk; 560 g/1 lb 2 oz (4 cups) icing (confectioners) sugar, sifted; ½ tsp salt.

Melt chocolate in a heatproof bowl over hot water. Remove bowl from heat, and gradually beat in cream cheese and milk. Add icing (confectioners) sugar and salt, beating until mixture is smooth and spreadable. Add a little more milk if necessary. Sufficient to cover tops of two 23 cm (9 in) cakes.

Crème au Beurre

(Butter Cream)

2 egg yolks; 60 g/2 oz (¼ cup) sugar; 120 ml/4 fl oz (½ cup) milk; 250 g/8 oz (1 cup) unsalted butter; ½ tsp vanilla essence (extract).

Beat egg yolks with half the sugar until light and creamy. Place remaining sugar and the milk in a heavy saucepan and bring to the boil, stirring to dissolve sugar. Pour milk on to yolk mixture and blend well. Return to pan and stir over gentle heat until custard coats the back of the spoon. Do not allow to boil. Strain and cool. Cream butter and when soft add cooled custard little by little. Flavour with

Using Plastic Fondant Icing

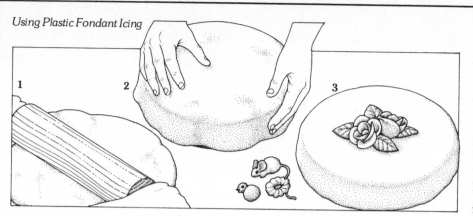

vanilla. Makes about 500 ml/18 fl oz (2 cups).
VARIATIONS
Coffee Crème au Beurre: Stir 2 tsp instant coffee powder into hot custard. Omit vanilla.
Chocolate Crème au Beurre: Melt 60 g/2 oz (⅓ cup) chopped dark chocolate over hot water. Beat into creamed butter with custard.

Ricotta Rum Filling

250 g/8 oz (1 cup) Ricotta cheese; 125 g/4 oz (½ cup) sugar; ½ tsp vanilla essence (extract); 2 tbsp dark rum; 2 tbsp grated dark chocolate; 1 tbsp chopped glacé (candied) fruit (ginger, apricots, pineapple etc).

Combine Ricotta, sugar, vanilla and rum and beat until light and fluffy. Fold in chocolate and fruit. Fill sponge or layer cake, wrap in foil, and leave in refrigerator for 2–3 hours before serving. Makes about 500 ml/18 fl oz (2 cups).

Crème Pâtissière

(Custard Cream Filling)
This filling is good for éclairs and cream puffs as well as sponges, cakes and pastries.

350 ml/12 fl oz (1½ cups) milk; 1 vanilla pod (bean); 125 g/4 oz (½ cup) sugar; 30 g/1 oz (¼ cup) flour; 2 eggs; 2 egg yolks.

Bring milk to the boil with vanilla bean. Put aside. Mix sugar and flour together, add eggs and egg yolks and beat until light. Remove vanilla bean from milk and gradually pour milk into egg mixture, stirring until well blended. Return to pan and cook over gentle heat, stirring constantly, just until boiling point. Remove from heat and continue stirring for a few minutes to release steam. Turn into a bowl to cool, then chill, covered, until ready to use. Makes about 500 ml/ 18 fl oz (2 cups).
Rich Crème Pâtissière: After cooling, fold in 175 ml/6 fl oz (¾ cup) whipped cream.

Lemon Curd Filling

Delicious as a filling for sponges and cakes, or spread on hot, buttered toast.

60 g/2 oz (4 tbsp) butter; grated rind and juice 2 medium lemons; 2 large egg yolks; 125 g/4 oz (½ cup) sugar.

Melt butter in top of double saucepan (double boiler) or heatproof bowl set over hot water. Add lemon rind and juice, egg yolks and sugar and stir with a wooden spoon over simmering water until mixture thickens. Allow to cool before using. Mixture may be made in double quantities and will keep well in a covered jar in the refrigerator. Makes 250 ml/8 fl oz (1 cup).

IRISH COFFEE

The success of this famous coffee depends entirely on the use of the finest ingredients – true Irish whiskey, fresh roasted, freshly-brewed coffee, and cream, lightly whipped so that it floats on top of the hot coffee. An excellent end to a meal.

Irish coffee is served in tall coffee cups or heatproof glasses. An enterprising manufacturer has made a small burner to take a special Irish Coffee glass. This is used to heat the whiskey in the glass, and it ensures that the coffee is piping hot – part of the charm is to sip the hot whiskey-laced coffee through the layer of cold cream.

Irish Coffee

8 tbsp Irish whiskey; sugar; 750 ml/1¼ pints (3 cups) very hot, freshly brewed strong coffee; 250 ml/8 fl oz (1 cup) double (heavy) cream, lightly whipped until it holds soft peaks.

Set out 4 heated Irish Coffee glasses or cups. In each glass stir together 2 tbsp whiskey (heated over a burner for preference) and 1½ tsp sugar. Add hot, strong black coffee, and stir until sugar is dissolved. Spoon cream gently on top. Serves 4.

IRISH SODA BREAD

Irish soda bread is one of the specialities of that country, and is baked in countless farmhouses and homes all over Ireland.

White Soda Bread

750 g/1½ lb (6 cups) flour; 1 tsp bicarbonate of soda (baking soda); 1 tsp salt; 250 ml/8 fl oz (1 cup) buttermilk or sour milk.

Sift dry ingredients into a bowl and make a well in the centre. Add buttermilk in a steady pouring stream, working in flour with a large fork. The dough should be slack but not wet and the mixing done lightly and quickly. Add a little more milk if dough seems too stiff. With floured hands, put dough on to a lightly floured surface and flatten into a round about 4 cm (1½ in) thick. Put on to a baking tray and make a large cross on top with a floured knife. (This is to ensure even distribution of heat.) Bake in a preheated moderately hot oven (190°C/375°F, Gas Mark 5) for about 40 minutes. Test centre with a skewer before removing from oven. To keep bread soft, wrap in a clean tea-towel. Makes 1 large loaf or 2 small ones.
NOTE: If buttermilk or sour milk is not available, 250 ml/8 fl oz (1 cup) fresh milk may be used, in which case add 1 tsp cream of tartar to the dry ingredients.
VARIATION
Brown Soda Bread: Make as for White Soda Bread, using 500 g/1 lb (4 cups) wholewheat flour and 250 g/8 oz (2 cups) white flour. A little more milk will be needed to mix the dough. If a brittle texture is required, add 15 g/½ oz (1 tbsp) melted butter. The bread should not be cut until it is quite cold. Leave for 4–6 hours before serving.

IRISH STEW

Authentic Irish stew uses 1 kg (2 lb) potatoes and 250 g (8 oz) onions to each 500 g (1 lb) of meat. It may be adapted by using equal quantities of meat and potatoes, but the gravy may need to be slightly thickened before serving. It was originally made with either mutton or kid.

Irish Stew

1 kg (2 lb) lamb neck chops; 2 kg (4 lb) potatoes, peeled; 500 g (1 lb) onions, thickly sliced; salt and freshly ground black pepper; 500 ml/18 fl oz (2 cups) water; 1 bouquet garni; 2 bay leaves.

Trim excess fat from chops. Slice a few of the potatoes and halve the rest. Put sliced potatoes into a deep saucepan, then add meat, then halved potatoes and then all the other ingredients. Cover tightly and simmer gently for 2–2½ hours. Shake pan from time to time to prevent stew sticking. This stew should not be thin. It should be thick, well seasoned and creamy. Remove bouquet garni and bay leaves before serving.
Serves 6–8.

J

JAM

Though few of us now want to devote a day to jam-making, a new generation of cooks is discovering the pleasure of making just a few pots when a favourite fruit is in season. Jam is made by boiling fruit with sugar (firm fruits are first cooked without sugar until tender) until the mixture is pulpy and will set, when cool, to a soft jelly-like consistency. It is perfectly practical to make a small quantity and does not take long providing you understand a few basic points.

Pectin: The substance in fruit which, with the right balance of acid and sugar, causes jam to set. The fruit used should be firm-ripe as it contains more pectin than when fully ripe. When making jam with fruits that are low in pectin, such as cherries, apricots and strawberries, the setting can be helped by adding some high-pectin fruit (apple, plum, quince, black- or redcurrants) or a bag of lemon peel, including the high-pectin white pith. Commercial pectin is also available.

Setting Point: The fruit is usually simmered until soft, then sugar is added and the jam is boiled vigorously until setting point is reached. Test for this by the spoon method or the saucer method.

The spoon method: Dip a clean wooden spoon into the jam and remove a spoonful. Allow to cool for a few moments, then turn spoon over gently. If jam breaks distinctly from the spoon in heavy, jelly-like drops or flakes, it is ready.

The saucer method: Place a small teaspoonful of jam on a cold saucer, cool for 20 seconds, then run a finger through it. If it wrinkles at the edges and stays in two separate sections, it is ready.

Potting and Sealing: Wash jars in hot water, drain thoroughly and heat in a low oven before filling. Remove jam from heat, cool slightly and stir gently to distribute the fruit evenly. Use a clean, hot jug or cup and fill to within 3 mm ($\frac{1}{8}$ in) of the top of jar. Cover surface of hot jam with a greaseproof (waxed) paper disc, and seal with screw-top lids or cellophane covers with rubber bands (moisten outside of cellophane first to ensure a tight fit). Label and store in a cool, dark, dry place. **See recipes**.

Plum Jam

1 kg (2 lb) firm plums, halved; butter; 120 ml/4 fl oz ($\frac{1}{2}$ cup) water; 1 kg/2 lb (4 cups) sugar, warmed.

Remove stones from plums, crack a few and remove kernels. Butter a large heavy saucepan, add plums and water and cook gently until tender, 15–20 minutes. Add warm sugar and heat until sugar dissolves, stirring occasionally. Add kernels, bring to the boil rapidly and boil vigorously about 20 minutes or until setting point is reached. Remove pan from heat immediately, cool a little, stir gently and pour into hot sterilized jars. Cover and seal. Makes 3–4 × 500 g (1 lb) jars.

Blackberry Jam

1.5 kg (3 lb) firm blackberries, including a few red ones; 4 tbsp water; 2 tbsp lemon juice; sliced peel (including white pith) 1 lemon; 1.5 kg/3 lb (6 cups) sugar, warmed.

Place blackberries in a large, heavy, buttered saucepan. Add water, lemon juice and peel tied in a muslin bag. Press berries with a wooden spoon to release juice. Bring slowly to boiling point and simmer 30 minutes. Remove bag of peel. Add sugar gradually to berries, stirring until dissolved, then boil quickly until setting point is reached. Remove pan from heat immediately and cool jam a little. Stir gently and pour into hot sterilized jars. Cover and seal. Makes 4–5 × 500 g (1 lb) jars.

Tomato Jam

butter; 1.5 kg (3 lb) very firm, red tomatoes, peeled and thickly sliced; 1.5 kg/3 lb (6 cups) sugar; 3 tbsp lemon juice; sliced peel (including white pith) 1 lemon; pinch salt.

Butter a large heavy saucepan and add tomatoes and sugar. Bring to the boil slowly, stirring until sugar has dissolved, then add lemon juice and peel tied in a muslin bag. Boil quickly until setting point is reached. Stir in salt and remove pan from heat immediately. Remove bag of peel, cool jam a little and pour into hot sterilized jars. Cover and seal. Makes 4–5 × 500 g (1 lb) jars.

Raspberry and Rhubarb Jam

500 g (1 lb) rhubarb; 500 g (1 lb) raspberries; 1 kg/2 lb (4 cups) sugar.

Wipe rhubarb and cut into chunks. Put in a large saucepan with a little water and cook gently until rhubarb softens. Add raspberries and bring to the boil. Cook for a further 5 minutes. Add sugar and stir until dissolved. Boil rapidly for about 10 minutes until setting point is reached. Cool jam a little and pour into hot sterilized jars. Cover and seal. Makes 3–4 × 500 g (1 lb) jars.

JELLY, PRESERVE

Jelly preserves are made from the pure juice of fruit cleared of all other matter, to which

Right: Thousand Year Old Eggs, Salted Eggs and Tea Eggs (page 116)
Overleaf: Rich Christmas Pudding (page 75) and Trifle (page 442)

Chef's Salad

Chef's salads vary according to the ingredients available and the chef's inspiration, but all start with a bed of crisp lettuce.

2 small heads cos lettuce, or 1 firm iceberg lettuce; 1 half-breast of chicken, lightly poached and cooled; 1 thick slice cooked ham; 60 g (2 oz) Swiss cheese; 2 spring onions (scallions) 1 small stick celery; 2 hard-boiled (hard-cooked) eggs, quartered; 5 tbsp Garlic or Herb Vinaigrette Dressing (page 358).

Remove coarse outer leaves of lettuce, cut out cores and rinse under running water without separating leaves. Wrap in a tea-towel and place in refrigerator 1 hour or longer to drain thoroughly and crisp. Cut cos lengthways into halves, iceberg into 4 wedges or 4 thick slices from top to bottom. Arrange on serving platter. Remove skin and bone from chicken. Cut chicken, ham and cheese into julienne (matchstick) strips. Shred spring onions (scallions) and celery to about the same size. Pile these ingredients lightly on lettuce, criss-cross fashion. Use eggs to garnish platter. Serve dressing separately at the table. Serves 4.

LIMA BEAN

See Beans, Broad and Lima.

LIME

This citrus fruit can be pale or dark green and has a tart, greenish flesh; it can be treated as a lemon. Limes make a delicious marmalade and are used commercially to make a marvellous cordial. In India they are used to make pickles, and slices or wedges are used as an accompaniment to many curried dishes. Limes are also used in Mexican and Creole cooking. The limed fish of Tahiti and Acapulco is delicious. The rind and juice of limes may be used in the same way as the rind and juice of lemons.

Limes, with their delicious sharpness, make the most refreshing drinks. Gimlets, Margheritas, Daiquiris and tequilas are not the same without limes. Long cool gin or rum drinks are better for a dash of lime juice. **See recipes.**

See also Lemons and Ceviche.

Cocktails and Long Drinks

A jigger is the traditional bar measure of 45 ml/1½ fl oz. A jigger measure is available at most bottle stores. A simple sugar syrup is a useful ingredient when mixing drinks. Boil

Preceding Page: Sardinian-Style Tuna (page 124)
Left: Mediterranean Mullet (page 124)

250 g/8 oz (1 cup) sugar with 120 ml/4 fl oz (½ cup) water for about 5 minutes. Cool, keep in a bottle in the refrigerator, and use as needed. If you do not possess a cocktail shaker, stir ingredients in a jug or whirl for a few seconds in a blender. Strain the drinks into chilled glasses. When making long drinks the base is mixed and ice added followed by the 'mixer', usually a carbonated water – soda, Vichy, ginger ale – which should be well chilled.

Daiquiri Shake well with 175 ml/6 fl oz (¾ cup) cracked ice; ½ jigger sugar syrup; 1½ jiggers lime juice; 6 jiggers rum. Strain into chilled glasses. Makes 4.

Cubana Shake well with 175 ml/6 fl oz (¾ cup) cracked ice: 1½ jiggers lime juice; 1½ jiggers Bénédictine; 5½ jiggers rum. Strain into chilled glasses. Makes 4.

Gimlet Shake well with 175 ml/6 fl oz (¾ cup) cracked ice: 1 tbsp sugar syrup; 1½ jiggers lime juice; 5 jiggers gin. Strain into tall chilled glasses. Makes 4.

Substituting orange juice for half the lime juice changes a Gimlet into an Orange Blossom. Vodka is becoming increasingly popular and may replace gin in both cocktails.

Margherita Shake well with 175 ml/6 fl oz (¾ cup) cracked ice: 5 jiggers tequila; 1½ jiggers lime juice; ¼ jigger triple sec (white Curaçao). Strain into glasses, the rims of which have been rubbed with citrus rind then spun in salt. Serves 4.

Gin and Tonic Place 3 ice cubes in a tall glass, add 1 large jigger gin (or vodka) and fill glass with tonic (quinine water). Add lime or lemon juice to taste. Makes 1.

Tahitian Limed Fish

There are many ways of making this famous raw fish salad.

500 g (1 lb) firm-fleshed fish fillets; 2 limes; 1 tbsp olive oil; salt and freshly ground black pepper; 6 spring onions (scallions) sliced; 2 tsp green peppercorns, lightly crushed; 1 head cos lettuce; 2 canned pimientos, diced; 2 tomatoes, peeled and quartered, to garnish.

With a sharp knife cut fish into very thin slices which are almost transparent. Pare rind thinly from limes and reserve. Squeeze juice from limes. Spread out fish on a chilled plate and drizzle over lime juice. Combine oil, salt, pepper, spring onions (scallions) and peppercorns. Sprinkle over fish and marinate 1 hour. Cut lime rind into julienne (matchstick) strips, about the thickness of pine needles. Drop into boiling water and blanch for 1 minute. Drain. Make a bed of lettuce leaves on 4 plates and arrange slices of marinated fish on top with any of the marinade left over. Scatter blanched lime rind and pimientos over fish and garnish

with tomato quarters. Serves 4.
VARIATION
Acapulco Limed Fish: Prepare Tahitian Limed Fish. Peel, stone and mash 1 avocado. Season with salt, freshly ground black pepper, a dash of Tabasco (hot pepper) sauce and a squeeze of lime juice. Spoon avocado mixture over fish salad.

Nutbread with Lime Butter

310 g/10 oz (2½ cups) flour; 1 tbsp baking powder; ½ tsp salt; 125 g/4 oz (1 cup) chopped walnuts; 60 g/2 oz (4 tbsp) butter; 140 g/4½ oz (¾ cup) firmly packed brown sugar; 1 egg; 175 ml/6 fl oz (¾ cup) plus 2 tbsp milk.
LIME BUTTER: 60 g/2 oz (4 tbsp) butter; grated rind 1 lime; 1 tbsp lime juice; salt.

Sift flour with baking powder and salt, then add walnuts. Cream butter with sugar until light and fluffy, then beat in egg and milk. Fold in flour mixture 125 g/4 oz (1 cup) at a time. Allow to stand, covered with plastic wrap, for 40 minutes. Spoon into a buttered 21 × 11 cm (8½ × 4½ in) loaf tin (pan) that has been lined on the bottom and long sides with greased greaseproof (waxed) paper. Bake in a preheated moderate oven (180°C/350°F, Gas Mark 4) for 1 hour 10 minutes or until a skewer inserted in centre comes out clean. Cool in tin (pan) for 15 minutes before turning out on to a wire rack.
LIME BUTTER: Cream butter with lime rind and juice. Add salt to taste. Serve with sliced nutbread.

Lime Meringue Pie

3 tbsp cornflour (cornstarch); 310 g/10 oz (1¼ cups) plus 6 tbsp sugar; 120 ml/4 fl oz (½ cup) lime juice; 1 tbsp grated lime rind; 3 eggs, separated; 350 ml/12 fl oz (1½ cups) boiling water; 1 × 23 cm (9 in) Shortcrust Pastry Tart Shell, baked (page 274).

Combine cornflour (cornstarch), 310 g/10 oz (1¼ cups) sugar, and lime juice and rind in a saucepan. Beat the egg yolks until thick and fluffy and add to lime juice mixture. Gradually add boiling water. Heat to simmering over very gentle heat, stirring constantly until thickened. Simmer 2–3 minutes. Pour into pastry shell (pie shell) and leave to cool.

Beat egg whites until stiff but not dry and gradually beat in remaining sugar. Spread meringue over top of pie, carefully sealing in all the filling and being sure to touch edge of pastry (pie) shell all round. Bake in a preheated moderately hot oven (200°C/400°F, Gas Mark 6) for about 5 minutes or until very pale brown. Cool and serve with whipped cream. Serves 8.
VARIATION
Lemon Meringue Pie: Use lemon rind and juice in place of lime rind and juice.

LINZER TORTE (Linz Jam Tart)

Linzer Torte, named after the town of Linz on the River Danube, is made in many parts of Austria. It is distinguished by its unique pastry (dough) made with ground nuts, either almonds or hazelnuts, and spices. This pastry is arranged in lattice strips over a jam filling, either plum or raspberry. Serve Linzer Torte plain or dusted with icing (confectioners) sugar.

Linzer Torte

125 g/4 oz (1 cup) flour; 60 g/2 oz ($\frac{1}{4}$ cup) caster sugar; 2 tsp (unsweetened) cocoa powder; $\frac{1}{2}$ tsp cinnamon; pinch ground cloves; $\frac{1}{2}$ tsp baking powder; pinch salt; 125 g/4 oz (1 cup) ground almonds; 125 g/4 oz ($\frac{1}{2}$ cup) butter; milk or Kirsch; 550 g/1 lb 2 oz (1$\frac{1}{2}$ cups) raspberry or plum jam; beaten egg to glaze; sifted icing (confectioners) sugar (optional).

Sift flour, sugar, cocoa, cinnamon, cloves, baking powder and salt into a mixing bowl. Add ground almonds. Rub (cut) in butter, which has been cut into small pieces, and mix lightly with fingertips to a dry dough, adding milk or Kirsch if necessary. Wrap dough in foil and chill for at least 30 minutes. Divide dough; roll out $\frac{2}{3}$ and press on to bottom of a greased 18 cm (7 in) loose-bottomed tin (springform pan). Spread jam on top. Roll out remaining dough, cut into 1 cm ($\frac{1}{2}$ in) wide strips and arrange in lattice fashion on top, using the last one as an edging around the tart. Press down lightly and chill for 30 minutes. Remove tart from refrigerator, brush with beaten egg and bake in a preheated moderately hot oven (190°C/375°F, Gas Mark 5) for 35–40 minutes. Allow to cool in tin (pan). Dust with icing (confectioners) sugar if desired. Serve with whipped cream. Serves 8–10.

LIVER

Liver has outstanding nutritional properties, and, when properly prepared, is delicious. Ox (beef), calf, lamb, pig (pork) and poultry livers are used in the cookery of many nations. Liver and bacon is a natural combination enjoyed in Britain, U.S.A. and Australia. Lamb, beef or calf livers are all used for this dish. Goose liver is made into the famous pâtés and terrines of France and Hungary. Chicken livers are used in some of the risottos of Italy, in pâté, which is easy to make and a treat, or can be sautéed to make a quick meal.

Ox (beef), calf, lamb, pig (pork) livers are all generally available from butchers. Calf's or lamb's liver is best enjoyed cut in thin slices and quickly pan-fried, and served with a flavoursome accompaniment, such as onions, bacon, etc. Ox (beef) liver is less

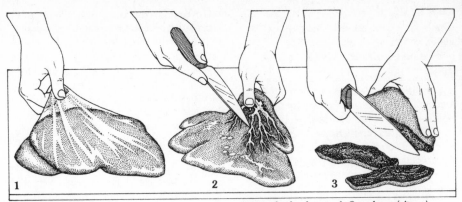

Preparing liver

tender than calf's or lamb's liver and has a more pronounced flavour; it is often braised with onions. Pig's (pork) liver has a strong flavour and is less tender than the other kinds; it is not good for frying but makes excellent pâté, or it may be braised whole with vegetables. Poultry livers are tender and mild in flavour, and are usually available from speciality poultry shops.

□ **Basic Preparation:** Pull thin veil of membrane away from liver **(Fig 1 above)**. Cut away any fat and gristle, and cut out veins, using a small, sharp-pointed knife **(2)**. Cut into thin slices **(3)** or leave whole, depending on recipe.

□ **To Cook:** Liver can be pan-fried, grilled (broiled) or braised. **See also recipes.**

PAN-FRIED OR SAUTÉED LIVER Calf, lamb and good pig (pork) livers are cut into thin slices, seasoned with salt and pepper and lightly dusted on each side with flour. Chicken livers are left whole. Heat a small amount of fat in a frying pan (skillet) – butter, oil or half butter and half oil. Using tongs, put slices in pan. Cook quickly, turning once, until crisp on both sides but pink inside, about 4 minutes in all. Cook pig's (pork) liver a little longer.

GRILLED (BROILED) LIVER Calf, lamb and poultry livers can be grilled (broiled). Have calf's or lamb's livers cut 1 cm ($\frac{1}{2}$ in) thick. Heat the grill (broiler). Put liver on greased grill (broiler) rack and brush with melted butter. Grill (broil) 8–10 cm (3–4 in) from heat, turning once, until done, 4–8 minutes in all.

BRAISED LIVER All livers can be braised. Have ox (beef), calf, lamb or pig (pork) livers cut 1 cm ($\frac{1}{2}$ in) thick. Sprinkle with flour seasoned with salt and freshly ground black pepper. Brown liver quickly on both sides in hot fat (half butter and half oil is ideal), then add 120 ml/4 fl oz ($\frac{1}{2}$ cup) stock and seasonings as desired (fresh herbs, diced bacon, sliced mushrooms, sliced onions) and simmer, covered, until tender.

Liver and Bacon

375–500 g (12 oz–1 lb) calf's or lamb's liver, cut into 1 cm ($\frac{1}{2}$ in) thick slices; salt and freshly ground black pepper; flour; butter or

bacon fat for frying; 4–8 rashers (slices) bacon, rind removed; 2–3 thin slices onion; hot water or stock; lemon juice; chopped parsley.

Season liver slices with salt and pepper and dip in flour. Heat butter or bacon fat in a frying pan (skillet) and fry liver 2–3 minutes on each side. Put on a heated dish. Fry bacon until crisp and arrange over liver. Put onion into the hot fat and cook until golden-brown. Remove, drain and arrange on the dish. Season with salt and pepper. Add a few tbsp of hot water or stock to the pan to make a little brown gravy. Sprinkle liver with lemon juice, gravy and parsley and serve. Serves 4.

Liver Bonne Femme

bacon fat or butter; 500–750 g (1–1$\frac{1}{2}$ lb) lamb's or calf's liver; 3 rashers (slices) lean bacon, rind removed, or cooked ham, cut into strips; 2–3 potatoes, peeled and cut into olive shapes, or 6–8 tiny new potatoes; 2 mushrooms, quartered; 12 small onions; 1 tbsp flour; 150 ml/$\frac{1}{4}$ pint ($\frac{2}{3}$ cup) white wine or cider; 250 ml/8 fl oz (1 cup) beef stock; salt and freshly ground black pepper; 1 bouquet garni.

Heat fat or butter in a heavy pan or flameproof casserole, put in the piece of liver whole and sauté it quickly on all sides for about 5 minutes. Remove liver from casserole and put in bacon or ham, potatoes, mushrooms and onions. Fry them lightly, then scatter over flour and mix. Pour on wine or cider and stock. Bring liquid to the boil, season with salt and pepper and add bouquet garni. Return liver to pan and simmer on top of stove or braise in a preheated moderate oven (180°C/350°F, Gas Mark 4) for 40–50 minutes. Carve liver in thin slices and arrange on a heated serving dish with bacon and vegetables. Boil up sauce, discard bouquet garni and spoon sauce carefully over the liver. Serves 6.

Swiss Liver

750 g (1$\frac{1}{2}$ lb) calf's liver, cut into thin strips; seasoned flour; 60 g/2 oz (4 tbsp) butter;

4 tbsp oil; 3 tbsp chopped onion; 3 tbsp chopped parsley; salt and freshly ground black pepper; 250 ml/8 fl oz (1 cup) single (light) cream; 1 tbsp lemon juice.

Dust liver strips with seasoned flour. Heat butter and oil in a frying pan (skillet). When hot and bubbly, add onion, parsley and liver strips. Sauté quickly, turning liver strips to brown on all sides. Do not overcook. Strips should be pink in centre. Season and add cream and lemon juice. Heat through, but do not boil. Serve on fried bread. Serves 4.

Venetian Liver with Onions

The way liver is prepared in Venice, with lots of onions and the surprising touch of lemon rind, is one of the nicest.

2 tbsp oil; 2 large onions, finely sliced; 2 tbsp water; 1 tsp grated lemon rind; 500 g (1 lb) calf's or lamb's liver, very finely sliced; salt and freshly ground black pepper.

Heat oil in a large frying pan (skillet), add onions, toss to coat with oil and add water. Cover and cook over gentle heat for about 20 minutes. Add lemon rind and mix well. Push onions to one side of pan. Add a little more oil, then the liver and season with salt and pepper. Stir well, cover and cook for 2–3 minutes. If you like a thicker gravy, toss slices of liver in seasoned flour before adding to pan. Serve with mashed potatoes, polenta or fluffy boiled rice. Serves 4.

Devilled Liver on Croustades

A delicious light luncheon or supper dish.

120 ml/4 fl oz (½ cup) oil; 4 slices bread, cut 2 cm (¾ in) thick; 60 g/2 oz (4 tbsp) butter; 2 onions, sliced; 500 g (1 lb) ox (beef), pig's (pork), calf's or lamb's liver, diced; 2 tbsp flour; 2 tsp dry mustard; 250 ml/8 fl oz (1 cup) hot water; ½ tsp salt; freshly ground black pepper; 120 ml/4 fl oz (½ cup) single (light) cream; 1 tsp lemon juice.

First make the croustades. Heat oil in a frying pan (skillet) and fry bread until golden and crisp. Drain on crumpled paper towels and keep hot until required. Pour oil from pan and add half the butter. When melted, add onions and fry until browned. Push onions to side of pan and add remaining butter. Coat liver in flour and brown in the butter, adding more butter if needed. Add mustard, water, salt and pepper. Heat gently until sauce thickens, stirring constantly. Add cream and lemon juice. Serve on croustades. Serves 4.

Sautéed Liver with Basil

500 g (1 lb) calf's or lamb's liver, sliced; seasoned flour; 1 tbsp oil; 60 g/2 oz (4 tbsp) butter; 2 tbsp fresh basil cut into thin strips.

Turn liver slices in seasoned flour and pat off excess. Sauté in the oil and half the butter, then remove to a heated dish. Add remaining butter and basil to pan and heat for a few moments. Pour over liver and serve at once, with grilled (broiled) or sautéed tomatoes. Serves 4.

Flambéed Liver with Cream

500 g (1 lb) calf's liver, sliced; seasoned flour; 1 tbsp oil; 30 g/1 oz (2 tbsp) butter; 1 tbsp lemon juice; 4 tbsp brandy or whisky; 120 ml/4 fl oz (½ cup) single (light) cream; salt and freshly ground black pepper.

Turn liver slices in seasoned flour and pat off excess. Sauté liver in oil and butter for 1 minute, turn and sauté other side for 2 minutes. Pour over lemon juice and brandy or whisky, and set alight. Shake pan until flames die down, stir in cream, season to taste and serve immediately. Serves 4.

Smothered Liver and Onions

5 medium onions, sliced; 60 g/2 oz (4 tbsp) butter; 4 tbsp oil; 500 g (1 lb) calf's or lamb's liver, finely sliced; 2 tbsp flour; 1 tsp salt; freshly ground black pepper; 175 ml/6 fl oz (¾ cup) water.

Cook onions in half the butter and oil in a frying pan (skillet) until golden-brown; remove. Dredge liver slices with flour seasoned with salt and pepper. Fry in remaining butter and oil until browned on both sides. Return onions to pan with water, cover and simmer all together for just 3–4 minutes. Do not overcook or liver will toughen. Serves 4.

Chicken Liver Pâté

One of the simplest but best ways to make a pâté. The chopped hard-boiled (hard-cooked) egg improves the texture.

250 g (8 oz) chicken livers; 300 ml/½ pint (1¼ cups) chicken stock; 60 g/2 oz (½ cup) chopped onion; 45 g/1½ oz (3 tbsp) butter; 2 hard-boiled (hard-cooked) eggs, finely chopped; salt and freshly ground black pepper; 30 g/1 oz (2 tbsp) butter, melted, to seal.

Simmer livers in stock until done, 8–10 minutes. Drain, reserving stock. Remove veins from livers. Purée livers with a little of the stock in a food processor or blender. Brown onion lightly in butter and blend with liver purée and eggs to make a paste. Season with salt and pepper. If desired, season further with a pinch of curry powder or a dash of Cognac. Put in a small dish or 4 individual ramekins. Spoon melted butter over surface to seal pâté and refrigerate several hours. Serve with buttered toast fingers. Serves 4.

Chicken Livers Marsala

75 g/2½ oz (5 tbsp) butter; 500 g (1 lb) chicken livers, halved; ½ tsp salt; ¼ tsp black pepper; 6 leaves fresh sage, chopped; 2 slices prosciutto or cooked ham, diced; 8 bread triangles, sautéed; 4 tbsp Marsala.

Melt 60 g/2 oz (4 tbsp) butter in a frying pan (skillet) and add livers, salt, pepper, sage and prosciutto or ham. Cook 5 minutes. Remove livers from pan and place on sautéed bread triangles. Add Marsala to pan, stir well and cook 3 minutes. Add remaining butter, mix well and pour over livers. Serves 4.

Chicken Liver Risotto

60 g/2 oz (4 tbsp) butter; 6 chicken livers, quartered; 60 g/2 oz (½ cup) chopped onion; 60 g/2 oz (½ cup) finely chopped mushrooms; 210 g/7 oz (1 cup) long-grain rice; 600 ml/1 pint (2½ cups) boiling chicken stock; 2 tbsp chopped parsley; salt and freshly ground black pepper.

Melt butter in a large heavy saucepan and brown chicken livers. Remove livers and keep hot. Add onion to pan and cook until transparent. Add mushrooms and cook 3 minutes longer. Add rice and cook, stirring constantly, 2 minutes. Stir in stock. Cover and simmer over low heat until stock is absorbed and rice is tender but still firm, about 20 minutes. If stock is absorbed and rice is not tender, add a little more stock and cook longer. Stir livers and parsley into rice, season with salt and pepper and serve at once with grated Parmesan cheese. Serves 4.

Risotto with Chicken Livers and Mushrooms

60 g/2 oz (4 tbsp) butter; 1 onion, chopped; 430 g/14 oz (2 cups) long-grain rice; 4 tbsp Marsala; 2 litres/3½ pints (8 cups) hot chicken stock.
SAUCE: 60 g/2 oz (4 tbsp) butter; 1 onion, finely sliced; 1 thin slice prosciutto, cut into julienne (matchsticks); 3 leaves fresh sage, or ½ tsp dried; 1 bay leaf; 6 chicken livers, chopped; 6–8 mushrooms, sliced; salt and freshly ground black pepper; 1 tbsp Marsala; 250 ml/8 fl oz (1 cup) chicken stock.

Melt butter in a heavy saucepan, add onion and sauté until brown. Stir in rice and cook, stirring, until each grain is golden in colour. Add Marsala and cook gently until it is absorbed into rice. Add chicken stock, 500 ml/18 fl oz (2 cups) at a time, each time covering pan until liquid is simmering. Allow risotto to cook very slowly, without stirring, until rice has absorbed all the liquid. When done, rice should be fairly dry but not too soft.

SAUCE: Melt butter in a saucepan and sauté onion, ham, sage and bay leaf until mixture takes on a little colour. Add chicken livers and mushrooms and stir well. Add salt, pepper, Marsala and stock. Simmer 10 minutes. Remove bay leaf. Stir half the sauce into the risotto. To serve, place risotto in a heated bowl. Serve the remaining sauce separately. Serves 6.

Liver Dumplings in Soup

125 g (4 oz) ox (beef) calf's, lamb's, pig's (pork) or chicken liver; $\frac{1}{2}$ small onion; 1 egg yolk; $\frac{1}{4}$ tsp salt; pinch freshly ground black pepper; pinch dried thyme; pinch nutmeg; 1$\frac{1}{2}$ tbsp chopped parsley; 1$\frac{1}{2}$ slices bread, crusts removed; milk or water; about 60 g/2 oz ($\frac{1}{2}$ cup) flour; 2 litres/3$\frac{1}{2}$ pints (8 cups) soup stock.

Mince (grind) or finely chop liver with onion. Add egg yolk, salt, pepper, thyme, nutmeg and parsley. Soak bread in milk or water to moisten and squeeze out excess liquid. Add to liver mixture with enough flour to make a soft dough. Bring soup stock to the boil. Dip a teaspoon in the soup, then fill it with liver dough and drop into soup. Re-dip spoon in soup before shaping each dumpling. Cover pan and simmer 10–15 minutes, depending on size of dumplings. Serves 6–8.

Chicken Liver Toasts

These small savouries are equally good served as an antipasto or as light snacks.

45 g/1$\frac{1}{2}$ oz (3 tbsp) butter; 1 shallot, finely chopped; 3–4 leaves fresh sage; 250 g (8 oz) chicken livers, finely chopped; freshly ground black pepper; 8 slices French bread, halved, or 8 slices sandwich loaf, cut into triangles; extra butter for frying; 2 tsp lemon juice; 1 tbsp chopped parsley.

Melt 45 g/1$\frac{1}{2}$ oz (3 tbsp) butter in a pan and sauté shallot and sage leaves for about 5 minutes. Discard sage leaves. Add livers and pepper and cook gently, stirring, for about 6 minutes or until livers are lightly coloured but still slightly pink. Fry bread pieces in butter until crisp and golden on both sides; drain on paper towels. Stir lemon juice into liver mixture, check seasoning, spread over fried bread and sprinkle with parsley. Serve immediately. Serves 8.

LOBSTER

The European lobster or French *homard* from northern seas has large pincer claws, containing much of the juicy meat, and a smooth shiny carapace.

Its big brother, the American or Northern lobster, is very similar but larger. Both varieties are found in the United States, from Maine to the Carolinas.

America also plays host to the Spiny Rock Lobster or langouste. This has extra long antennae, and most of the meat is found in the tail. The meat is particularly sweet and firm textured. The frozen tails are now widely available.

Allow $\frac{1}{2}$ large or 1 small lobster per serving. They may be bought live or ready cooked. When buying cooked lobster, make certain the tail is tightly curled into the body and snaps back when straightened, and that the lobster is heavy for its size. The smell should be sweet and fresh. A 1–1.5 kg (2–3 lb) lobster is ideal, larger ones tend to be rather tough so are best avoided.

☐ **To Boil Lobster:** If a recipe calls for green (uncooked) lobster, it should be killed immediately before cooking. This can be done by leaving it head first in a bucket of cold fresh water for at least 1 hour, or in the following manner.

Take a heavy, sharp, short-bladed knife. Place lobster on a board, underside up. Hold the lobster with a towel and make a firm incision with the point of the knife where the tail joins the body. This will sever the spinal cord and kill the lobster immediately. Any movement of legs or tail after the lobster is killed is due to reflex muscle spasms.

Alternatively, put the live lobster into the freezer and leave 30 minutes for each 500 g (1 lb) weight, to stun it.

To boil, place the lobster in a large saucepan of fresh cold water and bring slowly to simmering point. Simmer for 10 minutes for the first 500 g (1 lb) weight and 7 minutes for each 500 g (1 lb) over. Remove from water and allow to cool.

You may use frozen green (uncooked) lobster tails instead, if you prefer.

To clean lobster: Use a heavy sharp knife. Cut the lobster in half lengthways. Insert the point of the knife at the tail, cut towards the head and slit the underside. Remove the intestinal vein that runs the length of the lobster, and all the soft matter in the body and at the top of the head. Retain any orange or pink roe and the thick, dark brown liquid which is the mustard or tomalley. The roe can be gently poached; the mustard can be used in a sauce or butter for the lobster, or can be placed in a small bowl and cooked in a water bath, to be served separately as an accompaniment or used as a spread for canapés.

To remove meat from shell: Prise the meat from the tail and body with a sharp knife and cut into pieces. The meat may be extracted from the legs by breaking them at the joints and carefully pulling the meat out. Rinse carapace and dry well. It can then be used as a container in which to serve the meat. **See recipes**.

Grilled Lobster with Lemon Butter

1 green (uncooked) lobster or lobster tail; 125 g/4 oz ($\frac{1}{2}$ cup) butter, melted; juice $\frac{1}{2}$ lemon.

Halve lobster or lobster tail and clean if necessary. Mix butter and lemon juice and brush over lobster meat. Place, cut sides down, on oiled grill (broiler) rack and cook under preheated hot grill (broiler) for 2 minutes. Turn cut sides up. Reduce heat to moderate and cook for a further 8–12 minutes (depending on size), brushing frequently with lemon butter, until flesh is white and firm. Loosen flesh from carapace, and serve in the shell with extra melted butter and lemon wedges. Serves 2.

Lobster Mornay

1 cooked lobster, halved and flesh cut into bite-sized pieces; 250 ml/8 fl oz (1 cup) Mornay Sauce (page 368); 60 g/2 oz ($\frac{1}{2}$ cup) grated cheese; fried breadcrumbs (optional).

Fold lobster meat through hot sauce and reheat gently. Pile into shells. Top with grated cheese and cook under a preheated

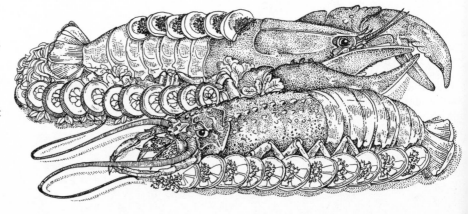

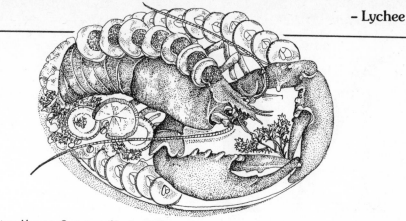

medium hot grill (broiler) for 1–2 minutes to melt cheese. If liked, sprinkle with fried breadcrumbs. Serves 2.

Lobster Mayonnaise

120 ml/4 fl oz (½ cup) Mayonnaise (page 204); 2 tsp chopped mixed fresh herbs (parsley, thyme, chives); ½ tsp French (Dijon) mustard; 1 cooked lobster, halved and flesh cubed; lettuce leaves.
GARNISH: *hard-boiled (hard-cooked) egg slices; tomato wedges; cucumber slices; sprig fresh dill or lemon balm.*

Flavour mayonnaise with chopped herbs and mustard. Spoon over lobster meat in shells. Serve chilled on crisp lettuce leaves, garnished with egg slices, tomato wedges, paper-thin cucumber slices and a sprig of fresh dill or lemon balm. Serves 2.

Lobster Cocktail Salad

125 g/4 oz (1 cup) diced celery; 2 tbsp Mayonnaise (page 204); 2 tbsp tomato purée (paste); 1 tbsp chopped fresh tarragon, or 1 tsp dried; 2 tbsp finely chopped parsley; 2 tbsp gin; 1 tbsp brandy; salt and freshly ground black pepper; 375 g (12 oz) cooked lobster meat, cut into large dice; lettuce leaves; celery strips to garnish.

Blanch celery in boiling water for 1 minute, drain and refresh. Combine celery, mayonnaise, tomato purée (paste), herbs, gin, brandy, salt and pepper. Fold in lobster meat and chill, covered, for at least 2 hours or overnight. Line 4–6 salad plates with lettuce, spoon lobster mixture into a mound on top and garnish with celery strips. Serves 4–6.

Lobster Tails Lucullus

2 small live lobsters; 120 ml/4 fl oz (½ cup) dry white wine.
SAUCE: *mirepoix of ½ small carrot, ½ small onion, ½ small stick celery, all finely chopped; 250 g/8 oz (1 cup) butter; 150 ml/¼ pint (⅔ cup) white wine; bouquet of 1 sprig thyme, 1 sprig marjoram and 1 small piece bay leaf; 150 ml/¼ pint (⅔ cup) single (light) cream; salt; white pepper.*

Prepare lobsters by plunging head first into fresh water or by severing spinal cords as described opposite, then separate tails from bodies and cut tails lengthways in half. Set tails aside while making the sauce.

Clean lobster bodies (retaining mustard and any roe for another use). Smash bodies and sauté with the mirepoix in 60 g/2 oz (4 tbsp) butter. Add wine, boil over high heat until reduced by half, add herb bouquet and cream and boil until liquid is syrupy. Strain and return liquid to rinsed-out saucepan. Cut remaining butter into about 8 pieces. Bring liquid to simmering point, remove

from heat and beat in 2 pieces of butter with a wire whisk. Return to low heat and beat in remaining butter, piece by piece; sauce will thicken to consistency of pouring cream. Season and turn off heat.

Arrange halved tails, meat side upward, in one layer in a baking dish, pour 120 ml/ 4 fl oz (½ cup) white wine around them and cover the dish. Place in a preheated moderately hot oven (200°C/400°F, Gas Mark 6) and steam for 8–10 minutes or until meat turns white. Holding each half tail in a cloth, prise meat from shells.

Reheat sauce on low heat whisking constantly; do not allow to boil. Spoon some sauce on to 4 heated plates, place tail meat on top and spoon more sauce over. Serves 4.

Lobster with Basil Sauce and Mangoes

Court Bouillon (page 85); 2 green (uncooked) lobster tails; 2 large, ripe mangoes.
SAUCE: *2 tbsp good wine vinegar; 6 tbsp olive oil; 1 small clove garlic, peeled; 30 fresh basil leaves; salt and freshly ground black pepper.*

Bring the court bouillon to the boil in a large saucepan. Add lobster tails and simmer for 6–8 minutes or until shells turn red. Remove lobster tails from pan and when cool enough to handle, remove shells and cut flesh into slices, 1 cm (½ in) thick. Meanwhile, make the sauce. Place vinegar, oil, garlic and basil leaves in a blender or food processor and process until smooth. Season to taste.

With a sharp knife, make a slit lengthways around the mangoes and peel off the skin. Cut the flesh into very thin slices.

Assemble the ingredients on 4 large, individual plates. First make a circle of mango slices on each plate, leaving a space in the centre. Heap lobster in the space and spoon the sauce in a ribbon around the outside of the mango slices. Serves 4.

LOGANBERRY

A cross between the blackberry and the raspberry, and its flavour is a blend of these fruits. Ripe loganberries are dark, purplish-red. Fresh loganberries are only occasionally

seen in the shops, but they are available commercially frozen and canned. They are excellent for dessert, and loganberries can be substituted for other berries in many recipes.

LOQUAT (Japanese Medlar)

The fruit of an Oriental tree related to the rose. Loquats are glossy, orange-coloured fruit about the size of a small plum, with juicy tart-sweet flesh. They are eaten raw or made into jams and jellies.

LYCHEE (Litchi, Lichee)

A small fruit native to South China, with translucent white flesh; the flavour and texture are distinctive but somewhat reminiscent of a luscious grape. Canned lychees are more familiar than fresh ones, but the latter in their knobbly, plum-brown shells appear sometimes in good greengrocers' shops.

Lychees make a refreshing dessert at the end of a Chinese meal. They are excellent in a fruit salad, and are also used in Chinese pork or duck dishes, rather as apples and oranges are used in European cooking.

Almond Jelly with Lychees

600 ml/1 pint (2½ cups) water; 3 tsp agar agar powder (see Note); 125 g/4 oz (½ cup) sugar; 250 ml/8 fl oz (1 cup) evaporated milk; ¼ tsp almond essence (extract); 1 × 565 g/1 lb 2 oz can lychees in syrup, chilled; 6 maraschino cherries, to decorate.

Place water in a saucepan and sprinkle agar agar powder over the top. Bring to the boil, then simmer for 5 minutes. Add sugar and milk and heat gently, stirring all the time, until sugar dissolves. Add almond essence (extract) drop by drop, to suit your taste. Pour into a cake tin (pan) or mould, and chill for 1 hour or until set. To serve, cut jelly into squares or diamond shapes. Drain lychees and reserve 250 ml/8 fl oz (1 cup) syrup. Arrange jelly pieces and lychees in 6 individual bowls, pour a little syrup over and decorate each with a cherry. Serves 6.
NOTE: Agar agar powder is a setting agent, like gelatine and is obtainable from Asian and Oriental food stores. If not available use 3 tsp gelatine.

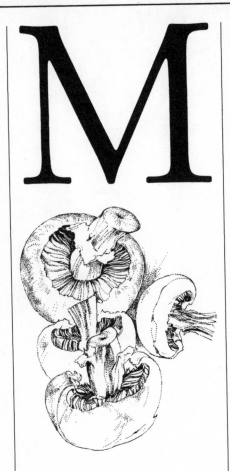

MACADAMIA NUT

This nut is native to Australia – but it is also grown in Hawaii and southern U.S.A. Macadamias are expensive but delicious – crisp, sweet and butter-flavoured. They are about the size of a hazelnut with a round, shiny shell which is so hard that it resists most efforts to crack it at home. Macadamias are sold shelled and usually roasted and salted, in cans or packages. They are excellent served with drinks or as a dessert nut; they can be sliced or chopped for nut breads, cakes, biscuits, ice cream and other desserts, or used in the same way as almonds in a butter sauce to serve with fish. **See recipes**.

Fish Steaks with Macadamias

2 tbsp lemon juice; 4 white fish steaks or fillets; 60 g/2 oz (4 tbsp) ghee or butter, melted; 2 tbsp finely chopped shallots; 3 tbsp chopped macadamia nuts; freshly ground black pepper; lemon wedges to garnish.

Brush lemon juice over fish and leave 10 minutes. Brush fish with 30 g/1 oz (2 tbsp) ghee or butter and grill (broil). Meantime, heat remaining ghee or butter in a small pan and gently fry shallots and nuts until golden. Pour over fish and serve garnished with lemon. Serves 4.

Macadamia Ice Cream

400 ml/⅔ pint (1⅔ cups) milk; 2 eggs, separated; 350 g/12 oz (1½ cups) sugar; 1 tsp vanilla essence (extract); 250 ml/8 fl oz (1 cup) double (heavy) cream; 180 g/6 oz (1½ cups) salted macadamia nuts, finely chopped; 3 tbsp rum or brandy.

Heat milk in top of a double saucepan (double boiler) over simmering water. Beat egg yolks with sugar, stir in a little of the hot milk, then stir this mixture back into milk. Cook, stirring constantly, until slightly thickened. Cool and add vanilla, unbeaten egg whites and cream, stirring until well combined. Pour into container of sorbetière or metal ice cream trays and freeze until just setting, then stir in about half the nuts and the rum or brandy. Freeze until firm and allow to ripen (mellow) for 24 hours. Transfer from freezer to refrigerator about 30 minutes before serving so that ice cream softens slightly. Serve sprinkled with remaining nuts. Serves 6.

MACARONI

See *Pasta*.

MACAROONS

See page 6 for recipe.

MACE

The lacy outer covering of the nutmeg. It is made up of frond-like tendrils; one tendril, left whole, is called a blade of mace. Mace is also sold ground. Its flavour is similar to that of nutmeg. Mace is the indispensable seasoning for English potted meats and shrimp. It is part of the classic combination of aromatics which flavours the milk for Béchamel Sauce (see page 368), and enhances the flavour of fish sauces, pies or creamed dishes, and of mashed or scalloped potatoes. A blade of mace is particularly useful for flavouring dishes where grated nutmeg would spoil the appearance.

Potted Tongue

250 g (8 oz) cooked salted ox (beef) tongue; 150 g/5 oz (½ cup plus 2 tbsp) ghee or butter; ¼ tsp ground mace; freshly ground black or white pepper; extra ghee for sealing.

Remove any skin and bones from tongue and cut meat into pieces. Place in a food processor fitted with the steel blade, add the 150 g (5 oz) ghee and process until smooth. Beat in mace and a little pepper, then pack into a pot or pots and smooth top. Chill until firm. Melt extra ghee and pour over surface to cover and seal. Cover pots with foil and store in refrigerator. Serve chilled with hot toast as a first course, or with crusty bread and crisp raw vegetables for a summer lunch. Makes about 350 g/12 oz (2 cups).

MACKEREL

The mackerel is a rich, oily fish, highly versatile and extremely tasty.

It is vital that mackerel be completely fresh when cooked – the blue-striped skin should be bright and iridescent. Fortunately the fish freezes well and is now freely available, and it is equally tasty when canned or smoked.

Scandinavian smoked mackerel is known around the world as a delicacy to rival smoked trout. It may be skinned and eaten with brown bread, lemon and pepper, or made into a delicious pâté.

Fresh mackerel is often served with a sharp sauce such as mustard, horseradish or gooseberry.

Smoked Mackerel Pâté

1 smoked mackerel, weighing about 500 g (1 lb); 180 g/6 oz (¾ cup) butter; 1½ tbsp lemon juice; freshly ground black pepper; pinch paprika; 2 tbsp single (light) cream.

Remove skin and bones from mackerel and flake flesh. Cream butter, add mackerel flesh (which is soft) and beat well. Add lemon juice and season with pepper and paprika. Beat in cream until just combined. Pack into a pot or pots and chill. Serve with hot toast or Melba toast as a first course or with drinks. Makes about 350 g/12 oz (2 cups).

MADEIRA CAKE

This traditional British cake has the refreshing tang of lemon and orange and is usually baked with a slice of candied citron peel on top. Serve with a glass of Madeira as did the people of Victorian England.

Madeira Cake

250 g/8 oz (1 cup) butter; 250 g/8 oz (1 cup) caster sugar; finely grated rind 1 lemon and 1 orange; ½ tsp cinnamon; 5 eggs; 180 g/6 oz (1½ cups) plain (all-purpose) flour; 60 g/2 oz (½ cup) self-raising flour; ½ tsp salt; 1 tbsp milk; 1 tbsp diced mixed candied peel, or 1 slice glacé (candied) orange.

Cream butter with sugar, fruit rinds and cinnamon. When pale and creamy, add eggs one at a time, beating well after each addition. Sift flours with salt. Fold half the flour into creamed mixture and when thoroughly incorporated, mix in milk. Fold in remaining flour. Turn into a greased and lined deep 20 cm (8 in) round cake tin (pan). Bake in a preheated moderate oven (160°C/325°F, Gas Mark 3) for 45 minutes. Sprinkle top of cake with peel, or press on the glacé (candied) orange slice. Bake for a further 40–45 minutes or until cake has shrunk away from sides of tin (pan) and a fine skewer inserted in centre comes out clean. Remove cake from tin (pan) and cool on a wire rack.

MADELEINES

These very light little French tea cakes are usually baked in shallow, scallop-shaped moulds which give them their distinctive shell-like appearance. They are served dusted with icing (confectioners) sugar. English Madeleines are a slightly more elaborate version baked in dariole moulds, glazed, coated with coconut and topped with a cherry.

Madeleines

2 eggs, lightly beaten; 250 g/8 oz (1 cup) sugar; 125 g/4 oz (1 cup) flour, sifted; 180 g/6 oz (¾ cup) butter, melted and cooled; 1 tbsp rum; 1 tsp vanilla essence (extract); sifted icing (confectioners) sugar.

Place eggs and sugar in the top of a double saucepan (double boiler) and heat, stirring constantly, until just lukewarm. Remove from heat and beat for about 10 minutes or until thick but light and creamy, incorporating as much air as possible. Gradually fold in sifted flour, then add

butter, rum and vanilla. Spoon carefully into greased madeleine moulds. Bake in a preheated moderately hot oven (190°C/375°F, Gas mark 5) for 10–15 minutes or until very pale golden. Remove from moulds, cool on a wire rack and dust with icing (confectioners) sugar. Makes about 15.

NOTE: Dariole moulds or muffin pans can be used if madeleine moulds are not available.

VARIATION

English Madeleines: Make Madeleines according to recipe above but bake in dariole moulds. After baking and when cold, level tops with a sharp knife to give a flat base when inverted. Turn out upside-down and brush with warm Apricot or Redcurrant Glaze (see page 11). Roll immediately in desiccated (shredded) coconut and top each with ½ glacé (candied) cherry.

MADRILENE

See *Spiced Tomato Consommé* (page 393).

MAITRE D'HOTEL BUTTER

See page 49 for recipe.

MALT

This is produced from grain – usually barley – which has been soaked, sprouted, dried and ground, a process resulting in the conversion of the grain starch into a sugar called maltose. Malt extract comes in dried and syrup form, and is a nutritious addition to drinks, bread, cakes and puddings. It also imparts a distinctive flavour and, in baked goods, a rather moist texture. Malted milk powder, prepared with dried milk and malt extracts, can be stirred into hot or cold milk for a nourishing drink or whipped with milk, ice cream and flavouring.

Malt Bread

500 g/1 lb (4 cups) plain wholewheat flour; 250 g/8 oz (2 cups) plain (all-purpose) flour; pinch salt; 30 g/1 oz (2 tbsp) fresh (compressed) yeast; 400 ml/⅔ pint (1⅔ cups) lukewarm water; 2 tbsp black treacle (molasses); 2 tbsp syrup-type malt extract; 60 g/2 oz (⅓ cup) sultanas (golden raisins), optional; 60 g/2 oz (4 tbsp) butter, melted.

SYRUP: *2 tbsp milk; 2 tbsp sugar.*

Put flours and salt into a large warmed mixing bowl. Cream yeast with a little of the water. Make a well in flour mixture. Pour in yeast mixture, treacle (molasses) and malt extract. Add sultanas (golden raisins), if using, and beat vigorously with your hand, mixing in butter and remaining water little by little, to form a soft dough. Turn on to a floured board and knead 5–10 minutes until dough

is even-textured and well blended. Place in a greased bowl and turn greased side of dough up. Cover with greased plastic wrap and a damp cloth and leave in a warm place to rise until dough has doubled in bulk, about 2 hours. Knock (punch) down dough, divide in half and put each half into a greased 500 g (1 lb) loaf tin (pan), pressing down well. Cover and allow to rise again for about 45 minutes or until dough has doubled in bulk. Bake in a preheated moderate oven (180°C/350°F, Gas Mark 4) for about 40 minutes, turning tins (pans) round after first 25 minutes of cooking time.

For syrup, heat milk and sugar, stirring until sugar has dissolved. Brush tops of loaves with syrup and bake a further 5 minutes. When cooked, loaves will sound hollow when undersides are knocked with knuckles. Remove from tins (pans) and cool on a wire rack. Makes 2 loaves.

MANDARIN AND TANGERINE

A small, very sweet type of orange, with a skin that is easily removed and flesh that separates easily into segments. A variety of North African mandarin, grown in Tangiers, is responsible for the name Tangerine. Canned segments are known as mandarins.

Mandarins may be enjoyed as a fruit but may also be used in the making of fruit salad. The small, brightly coloured segments are useful for decorating sweets and gâteaux.

To remove the white pith: Dip segments quickly into boiling water and scrape with a knife.

Glazed Mandarins

3 mandarins, peeled and broken into segments; 250 g/8 oz (1 cup) sugar; 4 tbsp water; ½ tsp cream of tartar.

Remove white pith and large pips from mandarin segments, taking care not to cut or tear the skin too much. Lightly grease a marble slab or baking tray. Put sugar, water and cream of tartar in a small heavy saucepan and stir over low heat until sugar dissolves. Bring to the boil without stirring. Brush sides of pan with a brush dipped in boiling water to remove any sugar crystals. Boil to hard crack stage (155°C/310°F), or

M

test by dropping a little syrup into cold water: it should immediately become crisp and brittle. Tilt pan and allow bubbles to subside. Secure mandarin segments, one at a time, on end of fine skewer and swirl quickly around in syrup until coated. Put on oiled slab and leave to set, about 5 minutes. Serve in small confectionery paper or waxed paper cases. Serve within 1 hour of making. Makes about 24.

MANGE-TOUT

See Snow Peas.

MANGO

This exotic fruit, with its heady perfume, is now cultivated in many tropical countries. As mangoes do not travel well they are often picked green. Allow the fruit to ripen to a rosy orange-yellow to enjoy its unrivalled flavour, likened to a blend of ripe melon, mixed with peach and a tang of apricots. The choicest fruit should have a firm flesh and smooth texture free of any fibres.

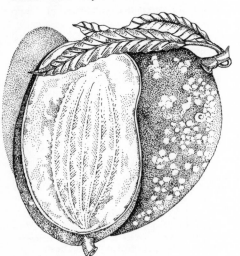

Mango slices are put into curries, made into pickles with salt, oil and chillies, made into chutneys and desserts, or they can be dried to make amchur powder, an important ingredient in some curries.

Like many good fruits, the presentation of a mango contributes greatly to one's pleasure in eating it. It should be neatly skinned, sliced off the stone, laid in small smooth portions, the right size to be picked up and popped in the mouth with a fruit fork. It is best served a little chilled. Alternatively, each side is cut off the stone, turned flesh side up and scored into diamonds or cubes without cutting through the skin. A little pressure on the underside of the skin and the flesh opens like an exotic flower ready for eating.

Mangoes are also available canned in slices or as a pulp, also as nectar or as chutney. **See recipes**.

Mango Mousse

1 tbsp gelatine; 120 ml/4 fl oz (½ cup) water; 250 g/8 oz (2 cups) mango pulp, fresh or canned; 120 ml/4 fl oz (½ cup) orange juice; 2 tbsp rum; 2 egg whites; 2 tbsp sugar; 120 ml/4 fl oz (½ cup) double (heavy) cream.
DECORATION: *120 ml/4 fl oz (½ cup) double (heavy) cream, whipped; 1 orange or mandarin, peeled and cut into segments.*

Sprinkle gelatine over water and leave for 5 minutes to soften, then stir over simmering water until dissolved. Combine mango pulp, orange juice and rum in a bowl. Stir in dissolved gelatine and chill until mixture is on the point of setting. Beat egg whites until stiff peaks form, then add sugar gradually, beating until thick and glossy. Whip chilled cream until soft peaks form. Fold cream into mango mixture, then fold in egg whites. Turn into a serving bowl and chill. Decorate with whipped cream and orange or mandarin segments. Serves 6–8.

Mango Rum Sundae

1 large ripe mango, peeled, stoned and thinly sliced; 60 g/2 oz (¼ cup) caster sugar; 5 tbsp rum; vanilla ice cream.

Put mango slices in a shallow dish and sprinkle with sugar and rum. Chill, covered, for 1 hour. Put ice cream into 4 serving dishes and top with mango slices and juice. Serves 4.

Mango Sorbet

2 tsp gelatine; 2 tbsp water; 250 g/8 oz (2 cups) mango pulp, fresh or canned; juice ½ medium lemon; 1 tbsp rum; 1 egg white.

Soften gelatine in water, then stir over simmering water until dissolved. Stir into mango pulp with lemon juice and rum. Turn the freezer to maximum temperature. Place mango mixture in an ice cream tray, cover with foil and freeze until mushy. Remove sorbet to a bowl and beat with a rotary beater until smooth but not melted. Fold in stiffly beaten egg white. Return to ice cream tray, turn freezer temperature to normal and freeze sorbet until firm. Leave to ripen (mellow) for 2–6 hours. Allow sorbet to stand at room temperature for a few minutes before serving. Serves 6.

Spiced Mango Chicken

Chicken breasts are baked until golden and tender in yogurt flavoured with spices and topped with mango slices. It takes little cooking and the preparation can be done in advance, making this a marvellous party dish.

8 half-breasts of chicken; 125 g/4 oz (½ cup) ghee or butter; 2 small onions, finely chopped; 8 cardamom pods; 2 cinnamon sticks; 250 ml/8 fl oz (1 cup) water; 16 slices fresh or canned mango.
MARINADE: *350 ml/12 fl oz (1½ cups) plain yogurt; 2 tbsp ground coriander; 2 tsp finely chopped fresh ginger; 2 tsp salt; 2 tsp turmeric; ½ tsp black pepper.*

Remove all the tiny rib bones from the chicken breasts, leaving the main breastbone. Combine all ingredients for marinade in a large bowl, add chicken pieces and stir to coat well. Marinate in refrigerator for at least 2 hours or overnight. Melt 60 g/2 oz (4 tbsp) ghee or butter in a large frying pan (skillet). Sauté onions, cardamom pods and cinnamon sticks for 5 minutes or until onions are soft and golden. Add water and stir well. Remove as much marinade as possible from chicken breasts and reserve. Place chicken in a baking dish and spoon a little of the onion mixture on top of each breast. Top each breast with 2 slices mango. Dot with remaining ghee or butter and bake in a preheated moderately hot oven (200°C/400°F, Gas Mark 6) for 10 minutes. Spoon reserved marinade over chicken. Continue cooking until chicken is tender, about 10 minutes longer. Place chicken on a heated serving dish and keep warm. Remove cardamom pods and cinnamon sticks from sauce, bring to the boil and spoon over chicken to serve.

Serve Spiced Mango Chicken with plain boiled or saffron rice or a pilaf and interesting sambals (see *Curry*). Serves 8.

MANGOSTEEN

A tropical fruit with a shiny purple skin and a delicate creamy white flesh with a sweet-sour taste. It is served skinned and segmented and is delicious either at room temperature or well iced.

MAPLE SYRUP

As its name implies, maple syrup is a product of the sap extracted from various species of the maple tree. Maple syrup has a distinctive but delicate flavour and is used over pancakes, popovers, ice cream and other desserts. It may flavour custard, creams, moulds, ice creams or fillings and icings (frostings) for cakes or biscuits (cookies).

There are different grades of maple syrup, the best being light in colour. Once opened, maple syrup should be stored in the refrigerator. **See recipes**.

Maple Jelly

1½ tsp gelatine; 5 tbsp water; 340 g/11 oz (1 cup) maple syrup, heated; 250 ml/8 fl oz (1 cup) double (heavy) cream, whipped.

M

Soften gelatine in cold water for 5 minutes, then add to hot maple syrup and stir until completely dissolved. Chill until slightly set, to the consistency of unbeaten egg whites. Fold in cream and turn into a serving dish. Chill for 2 hours. Serves 4–6.

Frozen Maple Cream

3 egg yolks; 250 g/8 oz (¾ cup) maple syrup; 250 ml/8 fl oz (1 cup) double (heavy) cream; 2 egg whites.

Beat egg yolks in top of a double saucepan (double boiler) until light and lemon-coloured. Add syrup and 4 tbsp cream and cook, stirring, over hot water until thick. Cool. Beat egg whites until stiff but not dry. Fold into custard mixture. Pour into ice cream tray and freeze until mushy. Remove to a bowl and beat with a rotary beater until smooth but not completely thawed. Whip remaining cream until stiff and fold into partially frozen mixture. Return ice cream to tray and freeze until firm. Serves 4–6.

Baked Apples with Maple Syrup

4 cooking apples; maple syrup.

Prepare apples by peeling top halves and coring. Place apples in a shallow baking dish and fill centres with maple syrup. Add water to cover bottom of dish. Bake in preheated moderate oven (180°C/350°F, Gas Mark 4) for 30–40 minutes or until apples are tender. Spoon pan juices over apples several times during cooking. Serves 4.

Maple Parfait

6 egg yolks; 210 g/7 oz (⅔ cup) maple syrup; pinch salt; 500 ml/18 fl oz (2 cups) double (heavy) cream, whipped.

Beat egg yolks and syrup together in top of a double saucepan (double boiler). Add salt and cook over simmering water until slightly thickened, stirring constantly. Cool. Fold in whipped cream. Pour into ice cream tray and freeze until firm. Serves 6.

Maple Freeze

165 g/5½ oz (½ cup) maple syrup; 2 egg whites; 250 ml/8 fl oz (1 cup) undiluted evaporated milk, well chilled.

Boil syrup to soft-ball stage (112°C/238°F). Beat egg whites until stiff but not dry. Add syrup slowly, beating constantly, and continue beating until mixture is cool. Whip milk until thick and fold egg white and syrup mixture into it. Pour into ice cream tray and freeze until firm. Serves 8.

NOTE: If you do not have a sugar thermometer, test syrup by dropping a small quantity into iced water. It should form a ball which will hold its shape.

MARASCHINO

A liqueur made from a small, sour, black cherry known as marasca, grown in Dalmatia, Yugoslavia. The cherry kernels are distilled together with the leaves, giving a bitter tang to an otherwise sweet drink.

Maraschino is used to flavour sweets, punches and cocktails etc. Maraschino cherries are a sweet cherry bleached, then preserved in maraschino syrup. They are used as a decoration on some pastries and drinks, confectionery, biscuits (cookies), cakes and in sauces.

Maraschino cherries are available red in syrup, with or without stems. Or they may be candied or glacéed in red, green or yellow variations, generally used for holiday cooking at Christmas or Easter.

MARBLE CAKE

This is one of the prettiest of all cakes. The mixture is divided into three different colours, pink, white and chocolate, and marbled using a knife to make intriguing colour patterns which are seen when the cake is sliced. Children are especially fond of Marble Cake and it is most popular for birthday parties.

Marble Cake

125 g/4 oz (½ cup) butter; 250 g/8 oz (1 cup) caster sugar; 1 tsp vanilla essence (extract); 2 eggs, beaten; 250 g/8 oz (2 cups) self-raising flour; ½ tsp salt; 175 ml/6 fl oz (¾ cup) milk; 2 tbsp (unsweetened) cocoa powder; 2 tbsp boiling water; red food colouring.

Cream butter with sugar and vanilla until light and fluffy. Gradually beat in eggs. Sift flour with salt and fold into creamed mixture alternating with milk. Divide mixture into 3 portions. Sift cocoa and dissolve in boiling water. Stir into one portion of cake mixture. To another portion add red food colouring, to tint it pink. Leave third portion white. Drop mixtures by tablespoons into a well-greased deep 20 cm (8 in) round cake tin (pan), alternating pink, white and chocolate. Run a knife through to marble mixture. Bake

in a preheated moderate oven (180°C/350°F, Gas Mark 4) for 50–60 minutes. Turn out on a wire rack and, when cool, ice (frost) and decorate marble cake as desired.

MARENGO

The battle of Marengo in 1800 was a victory for Napoleon's army. It marked another victory – for the little General's chef created a dish, fit for the conquering hero, from food found in the surrounding fields and looted gardens. He took a chicken, a head of garlic, a few tomatoes, some bay, parsley and thyme; and a few field mushrooms. These were sautéed in the oil and finished with the wine that travelled with the French army. A few fresh water crayfish were added, a fried egg and some crisp fried bread. Today, these last three ingredients may be omitted.

Napoleon enjoyed the dish, claiming, it is said: 'It has been a glorious day, my children. I am well pleased with you.'

Chicken Marengo

2 kg (4 lb) chicken pieces; salt and freshly ground black pepper; flour; 1 tbsp oil; 1 tbsp butter; 2 cloves garlic, crushed; 1 bouquet garni (parsley, thyme, bay leaf); 250 ml/8 fl oz (1 cup) white wine; 4 tbsp brandy; 2 large tomatoes, peeled and quartered; 12 mushrooms; chopped parsley.

Sprinkle chicken pieces with salt and pepper and coat lightly with flour. Heat oil and butter in a frying pan (skillet). Brown chicken over high heat until golden on all sides, turning frequently. Transfer to a flameproof casserole and add garlic, bouquet garni, white wine, brandy and tomatoes. Cover casserole tightly and cook gently for 30 minutes, turning chicken pieces several times with wooden spoon. Add mushrooms and cook for 10 minutes longer or until chicken is tender. Adjust seasoning and discard bouquet garni. Serve in casserole, sprinkled with chopped parsley. The dish may be garnished with heart-shaped croûtes of bread fried in butter, a fried egg for each serving, and cooked crayfish. Serves 6.

MARGARINE

This is available as Polyunsaturated Table Margarine, Table Margarine, or Cooking Margarine. It is a smooth-textured product, made from vegetable oils only or a combination of both animal fats and vegetable oils, used in varying amounts. The ratio of saturated to unsaturated fats in table margarine is strictly controlled by law and the type of margarine must be specified clearly on the label with other components such as milk products, vitamins, flavouring agents, salt and emulsifiers.

Margarine and butter are both fats and each has the same number of kilojoules or kilocalories (1 tbsp has 578 kilojoules/138 kilocalories), providing the same units of energy. The exception is 'whipped' margarine, which may contain slightly fewer kilojoules (kilocalories) since the volume is increased by the air incorporated during the whipping process.

Polyunsaturated Table Margarine: High in polyunsaturated fats in proportion to saturated fats, and made from vegetable oils. It is often recommended for people on low cholesterol diets because the high level of polyunsaturated fats makes it suitable for people who need to restrict their intake of saturated fats. In this case, the margarine to choose is the one with the highest percentage of polyunsaturated fats.

Table Margarine: This has a higher saturated fat content than polyunsaturated table margarine. It is made from vegetable oils and has a smooth easy-spreading consistency, although not quite as soft as polyunsaturated table margarine.

Cooking Margarine: Best for cooking only. It contains saturated animal fats and vegetable oils and is usually sold in solid blocks.

Margarine in Cooking

Margarine can be used instead of butter quite successfully in most baking. When using, substitute the same quantity of margarine for butter as specified in a recipe. It is particularly good for recipes using the quick-mix method (see *Cakes*), because margarine mixes very easily and quickly with other ingredients. Use also in sauces, steamed puddings, shortcrust pastry (basic pie dough) – see *Pastry (Dough)* – or cake-type desserts. Table margarine is usually quite successful for shallow-frying as well.

MARINADE

A seasoned liquid used to 'marinate' food before or after cooking in order that it will absorb flavour and/or become more tender. The term 'to marinate' is used for meats, game, poultry, fish and vegetables; for fruits, the term 'macerate' is used when steeping in sugar, liqueurs or spirits.

The first marinades were simple brines, used for preserving fish – the word stems from the same root as the word 'maritime'. In modern usage a marinade consists of oil, an acid (lemon juice, wine or vinegar) and spices or aromatics. As the food stands in the marinade, the oil and aromatics impart flavour and the acid tenderizes.

A marinade may be cooked or uncooked, and is used with a large cut of meat for dishes like sauerbraten, or cubes of meat or poultry or tender steaks for grilling (broiling) or pan-frying.

As a marinade usually contains an acid, it and the foods it serves should be kept in a dish made of glass or glazed china. Never use aluminium or porous containers such as some pottery. Use a wooden spoon for stirring or turning the food. Marinate food in containers just large enough to hold the food and cover them with the marinade. Keep marinating foods well covered and under refrigeration if they are to steep for more than 1 hour.

Higher temperatures hasten marinating but care has to be taken in very hot climates as high temperatures also hasten bacterial action. A marinade is powerful – do not marinate foods too long or use too many herbs and spices or you may destroy the food's own flavour. Frequent basting or turning the food in the marinade assures equal distribution and penetration of flavours and aids the tenderizing process. As a general rule, a whole piece of meat may be marinated for 2–3 days for a 'gamey' taste, but otherwise marinate overnight. Cubes of food or small steaks or cutlets need only be steeped 2–3 hours.

Cooking with Marinades

After food has been marinated, drain it and dry with paper towels. Keep marinade as it may be used in the cooking. Stews and pot roasts are often cooked with some of the marinade – it is a good idea to dilute it with stock or water before adding it to the meat.

Part of a marinade may also be used to baste marinated meat during roasting or grilling (broiling), or a spoonful may be added to a gravy or sauce. **See recipes.**

Cooked Marinade

For meats and game to be roasted, pot roasted, grilled (broiled), etc.

4 tbsp oil; 60 g/2 oz (½ cup) chopped onions; 60 g/2 oz (½ cup) chopped celery; 90 g/3 oz (½ cup) chopped carrot; 20 g/⅔ oz (½ cup) chopped parsley; 4 cloves garlic, crushed; 500 ml/18 fl oz (2 cups) cider vinegar; 500 ml/18 fl oz (2 cups) dry red or white wine; 500 ml/18 fl oz (2 cups) water; 2 bay leaves; 1 sprig thyme; tiny sprig rosemary; 1 tsp peppercorns; 5 whole cloves; 5 whole juniper berries, crushed.

Heat oil in deep saucepan. Cook onions, celery, carrot, parsley and garlic in oil over medium heat for 5 minutes or until onions are soft but still white. Do not brown. Add remaining ingredients. Simmer, covered, over low heat for 45–60 minutes, stirring occasionally. Strain and cool before using. Makes about 1 litre/1¾ pints (4 cups) marinade, or enough for about 3 kg (6 lb) meat.

Uncooked Marinade

For shellfish, prawns (shrimp), lobster, to be pan-fried, grilled (broiled), etc.

175 ml/6 fl oz (¾ cup) brandy, dry sherry or dry white wine; ½ tsp salt; ½ tsp black pepper; ½ tsp crushed dried rosemary, basil or thyme, or 1½ tsp fresh.

Combine all ingredients and put in deep bowl. Marinate seafood in mixture for 1–3 hours. Makes about 175 ml/6 fl oz (¾ cup), or enough for 30 prawns (shrimp) or 1 × 500 g (1 lb) lobster.

Uncooked Marinade

For all meats.

250 ml/8 fl oz (1 cup) water; 250 ml/8 fl oz (1 cup) wine; 6 peppercorns; 1 bay leaf; 8 whole cloves; 1 medium onion, finely sliced; 1 tsp crushed dried rosemary, thyme or marjoram, or 1 tbsp fresh.

Combine all ingredients. Makes 500 ml/18 fl oz (2 cups), or enough for 2.5 kg (5 lb) meat.

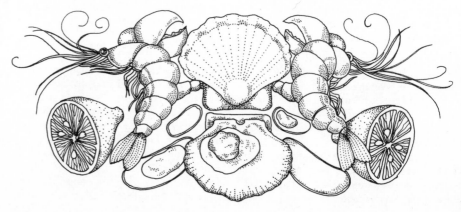

Beer Marinade

For beef, game or prawns (shrimp).

350 ml/12 fl oz (1½ cups) beer; 120 ml/4 fl oz (½ cup) salad oil; 1 small onion, finely sliced; 1 clove garlic, crushed; 2 tbsp lemon juice; 1 tsp salt; ½ tsp black pepper; 1 tsp dry mustard.

Combine all ingredients and blend thoroughly. Makes about 500 ml/18 fl oz (2 cups), or enough for 1–1.5 kg (2–3 lb) meat or prawns (shrimp).

Larded Braised Beef

1 × 2 kg (4 lb) topside (top round) of beef; Uncooked Marinade for meats (see opposite); 250 g (8 oz) pickled (salt) pork, cut into long thin strips; 2 tbsp oil; 1 tbsp tomato purée (paste); 3 tbsp brandy; 250 ml/8 oz (1 cup) stock; salt and freshly ground black pepper; 2 tbsp Beurre Manié (page 35, optional).

Place meat in a large bowl, add marinade and let stand in refrigerator 24 hours, turning occasionally. Remove meat and dry thoroughly with paper towels. Strain marinade and reserve 250 ml/8 fl oz (1 cup).

To lard beef, thread a larding needle by placing a strip of pork in the open end. Insert pointed end of needle into beef at right angles to grain. Push, then pull needle through beef. Trim off the pork flush with the beef. If you do not have a larding needle, holes may be made in meat and strips of pork pushed in, using a finger or handle of wooden spoon.

Heat oil with tomato purée (paste) in a Dutch oven or flameproof casserole. Stir in brandy, stock, reserved marinade, salt and pepper and bring to the boil. Add meat. Cover, reduce heat and simmer for 2–2½ hours. Carve enough beef for one meal in thin slices (saving the remainder for another meal) and place on a heated serving platter. Thicken gravy, if liked, with beurre manié and spoon a little over meat. Serve rest of gravy separately. Serves 6–8.

Lamb Kebabs

1.5 kg (3 lb) lamb leg chops, cut thick; 1 clove garlic, crushed; 5 tbsp oil; 1 tbsp lemon juice; 2 tsp chopped fresh marjoram, or 1 tsp dried; 1 tbsp finely chopped onion; salt and freshly ground black pepper; 250 g/8 oz (2 cups) small, even-sized mushrooms; 3 firm tomatoes, quartered; 1 medium green pepper, cored, seeded and cut into squares; cooked rice to serve.

Trim excess fat from meat and cut into 4 cm (1½ in) cubes. Put into a bowl. Combine garlic, oil, lemon juice, marjoram, onion, salt and pepper and pour over lamb cubes. Let marinate in refrigerator for 4 hours, stirring occasionally. Cut mushroom stalks level with caps. Thread mushrooms on to skewers, alternating with tomato quarters and pepper squares. Drain lamb cubes, reserving marinade, and thread on to separate skewers. Put lamb skewers under a preheated grill (broiler) and grill (broil) for 7 minutes. Brush vegetable skewers with some of the marinade and put under the grill (broiler). Cook, brushing lamb and vegetable skewers with marinade and turning frequently, for 10–12 minutes or until meat is done to your liking. Spoon hot rice on to a heated serving platter and arrange skewers on top. Serves 4.

Lemon-Ginger Chops

4 tbsp oil; 1 tsp grated lemon rind; 1 tbsp lemon juice; 1 tbsp brown sugar; 1 tsp grated fresh ginger; salt and freshly ground black pepper; 4 large lamb chump chops.

Mix together oil, lemon rind and juice, brown sugar, ginger, salt and pepper. Put chops in a shallow dish, in a single layer and pour marinade over. Cover and marinate in refrigerator for at least 8 hours. Drain chops, reserving marinade. Grill (broil) under preheated grill (broiler) for 10–15 minutes or until tender, turning occasionally and basting with marinade. Serves 4.

Marinated Steak

1 × 750 g (1½ lb) slice middle cut rump (top round) steak, cut 4 cm (1½ in) thick; 175 ml/6 fl oz (¾ cup) dry red wine; 4 tbsp oil; 1 onion, sliced; 1 bay leaf, crumbled; 4 stalks parsley; ½ tsp dried tarragon or thyme; salt and freshly ground black pepper.

Trim any fat from steak. Place in a rectangular glass or ceramic dish. Mix remaining ingredients, except salt, and pour over steak. Cover and leave to marinate in refrigerator for several hours, turning steak occasionally. Lift out steak and place on grill (broiler) rack. Cook under a preheated high grill (broiler) for 3 minutes each side until sealed, then reduce heat to medium and cook until done to taste. Total cooking time: rare – 15 minutes; medium – 20–25 minutes; well-done – 30–35 minutes. Baste with marinade during cooking and turn steak with tongs so that juices will not escape. To serve, sprinkle with salt and carve in thin slices. Serves 4–6.

Beef Stew with Wine and Herbs

1 kg (2 lb) stewing beef, cubed; 250 ml/8 fl oz (1 cup) red wine; 1 bay leaf; 1 clove garlic, sliced; 1 tsp salt; ½ tsp black pepper; few sprigs parsley; 4 sprigs fresh thyme; 2 tbsp bacon dripping or other fat; 350 ml/12 fl oz (1½ cups) stock; 1 stick celery with leaves, diced; 1 onion, sliced; 4 cloves; 1 piece fresh ginger; cornflour (cornstarch).

Place meat in a large bowl and add wine, bay leaf, garlic, salt, pepper, all but 2 sprigs parsley, and 2 sprigs of thyme. Marinate, covered, in refrigerator several hours, turning frequently. Remove meat and dry thoroughly with paper towels. Reserve marinade. Heat dripping in a Dutch oven or heavy flameproof casserole, add meat and brown on all sides. Do this in several batches. Meanwhile, place reserved marinade and stock in a saucepan and add celery, onion, remaining herbs and spices tied together in cheesecloth or muslin. Bring to the boil and simmer 10 minutes. Add liquid to meat, cover and simmer until tender, 2–3 hours. Add water if necessary. If desired, when meat is just tender, vegetables such as peas, carrots and onions may be added. Cook until vegetables are tender. Discard herb bag and remove meat to a heated platter. Thicken gravy with cornflour (cornstarch) dissolved in a little cold water, using ½ tbsp cornflour (cornstarch) for each 250 ml/8 fl oz (1 cup) of broth. Boil, stirring, 2 minutes. Pour gravy over meat, with vegetables, if used, arranged around it. Serves 4.

Brochette of Scallops

750 g (1½ lb) fresh scallops; 120 ml/4 fl oz (½ cup) dry vermouth; 120 ml/4 fl oz (½ cup) olive oil; 1 clove garlic, crushed; 2 tbsp chopped parsley.

Remove any brown bits from scallops, then place in a bowl. Add remaining ingredients and turn gently to mix. Marinate, covered, for several hours in refrigerator. Drain scallops, reserving marinade. Thread scallops on to 4 large or 8 small skewers and grill (broil) under preheated grill (broiler) for 5–6 minutes, turning occasionally and brushing with marinade. Serve with fluffy boiled rice or crusty bread. Serves 6.

MARJORAM

A strongly perfumed herb, which is one of the most important of all kitchen herbs. There are three types of marjoram – sweet, pot and wild (known also as oregano) – but sweet marjoram is the one found growing in most gardens and it is the most delicate of the three.

Marjoram and thyme team exceptionally well together, and marjoram can be used in almost any dish that is flavoured with thyme. Marjoram, thyme and sage are the favourite combination for old-fashioned poultry seasoning. There are many more dishes in which marjoram is a good flavouring. It goes particularly well with veal, poultry, pork or beef; for flavouring meat loaves and sausages; in liver dishes, and in most stews. Some fish dishes such as baked fish, salmon croquettes or creamed shellfish are enhanced by the addition of marjoram.

Many vegetables are complemented by the flavour of marjoram. Try adding it to mushroom dishes, green beans and peas, potato dishes, broccoli, Brussels sprouts, aubergines (eggplant), asparagus, carrots, spinach, courgettes (zucchini), or onions.

In salads, try adding chopped marjoram to greens tossed in Vinaigrette Dressing (see page 358); with sliced green peppers; coleslaw; stirred through cottage cheese and cream cheese. A little chopped fresh marjoram gives piquancy to tomato juice, chicken noodle soup, turtle or onion soups.

Veal Chops with Marjoram

4 veal chops; salt and freshly ground black pepper; 2 tsp chopped fresh marjoram; seasoned flour; 30 g/1 oz (2 tbsp) butter; 2 tbsp oil; 120 ml/4 fl oz ($\frac{1}{2}$ cup) stock.

Season veal chops with salt and pepper. Press marjoram into both sides of chops, place on a plate, cover and leave for 1 hour for flavours to penetrate. Coat chops very lightly with seasoned flour and cook in butter and oil over gentle heat until meat is done, about 10–15 minutes, turning once. Remove chops to heated dish and keep warm. Add stock to pan and simmer, stirring in brown bits, to make a gravy. Season and spoon over chops. Serves 4.

MARMALADE

Few British breakfasts are complete without some hot buttered toast and marmalade. Beautifully coloured and flavoured, most marmalades are soft transparent jellies with small pieces of fruit or fruit peel suspended in the jelly.

Marmalades may be made from one, two, three or more fruits, one of which is nearly always a citrus fruit. Orange marmalade is, perhaps, the favourite and can be made from sweet oranges or bitter Seville oranges. These bitter oranges have a short season and are not always easy to come by.

Marmalades need slightly longer cooking and use less sugar than jams. The peel should be soaked first or cooked in water to help soften it before sugar, warmed for 7 minutes in a preheated very cool oven (120°C/250°F, Gas Mark $\frac{1}{2}$) is added, otherwise it will remain hard. Prolonged boiling after the sugar is added will not soften the peel but darken the colour of the marmalade and break down the pectin, causing it to lose its jelling properties. Pectin is contained in the pith and pips, which are cooked with the marmalade, usually in a muslin bag.

To test for setting point: Place 1 tsp marmalade on a chilled saucer, wait 20 seconds, then run a finger through it. If the marmalade crinkles at the edges and stays in 2 separate portions, it is ready for bottling. Pack the warm marmalade into warm, dry, sterile jars, cover and seal. **See recipes**.

See also *Jam.*

Seville Orange Marmalade

If you cannot get bitter oranges use sweet ones instead. These will of course give a sweeter flavour to the marmalade.

1.5 kg (3 lb) Seville oranges; 2 lemons; 3 litres/5$\frac{1}{4}$ pints (12 cups) water; about 3 kg/6 lb (12 cups) sugar, warmed.

Scrub fruit, peel and cut peel into fairly coarse strips. Chop fruit pulp, removing pips and any pith. Tie pips and pith in a muslin bag (they contain the pectin that sets the marmalade). Put peel and flesh in a pan with bag of pips, add water and bring to the boil. Simmer gently until volume has reduced by about $\frac{1}{3}$. Squeeze bag of pips to press out all the juice and discard bag. Measure cooked pulp and return it to pan with 500 g/1 lb (2 cups) sugar to each 500 g/1 lb (2$\frac{1}{2}$ cups) pulp. Stir over a gentle heat until sugar has dissolved, then boil until setting point is reached, 15–20 minutes. Cool a little and ladle into warm, dry, sterilized jars. Cover and seal. Makes about 10 × 500 g (1 lb) jars.

Three-Fruit Marmalade

allow 750 g (1$\frac{1}{2}$ lb) mixed fruit – 2 lemons, 1 large orange, 1 grapefruit; 1.75 litres/3 pints (7$\frac{1}{2}$ cups) water; about 1.5 kg/3 lb (6 cups) sugar, warmed.

Scrub and dry fruit. Slice lemons and orange finely and put pips in a muslin bag. Peel rind thinly from grapefruit with a vegetable peeler. Shred and add to sliced fruit in a large bowl. Peel pith from grapefruit. Chop pith finely and add to pips in muslin bag. Slice grapefruit flesh and put in bowl with other fruit and water. Tie muslin bag closed at top, put in bowl, weight with a plate on top to keep fruit immersed in water and leave overnight. Next day, empty contents of bowl into a pan and cook gently for about 1$\frac{1}{2}$ hours or until fruit is soft and half the liquid has evaporated. Remove muslin bag, squeezing out as much liquid as possible. Measure pulp and return it to pan with 250 g/8 oz (1 cup) sugar to each 180 g/6 oz (1 cup) of pulp. Stir until sugar has dissolved, then bring to the boil and cook rapidly until setting point is reached, about 15–20 minutes. Remove pan from heat and cool marmalade for about 15 minutes. Ladle into warm, dry, sterilized jars. Cover and seal. Makes about 5–6 × 500 g (1 lb) jars.

Apple and Ginger Marmalade

370 g (12 oz) fresh ginger, peeled; 1.5 kg (3 lb) tart green cooking apples, quartered and cored; 1.5 litres/2$\frac{1}{2}$ pints (6 cups) water; 4 tbsp strained lemon juice; 750 g/1$\frac{1}{2}$ lb (3 cups) sugar, warmed.

Slice ginger into very thin julienne (matchstick) strips. Place strips in a saucepan and cover with boiling water. Boil for 30 minutes. Drain ginger in a colander and refresh under cold running water. Place ginger in a bowl, cover with fresh water and chill, covered, for at least 12 hours. Drain and pat dry with paper towels. Place apples and the 1.5 litres/2$\frac{1}{2}$ pints (6 cups) water in a large saucepan and bring to the boil. Boil for 40 minutes, stirring occasionally to mash apples with back of spoon. Pour into a colander lined with 4 layers of boiled, rinsed and squeezed-out cheesecloth. Set colander over a heavy saucepan and allow apple pulp to drip through without squeezing. Do not disturb or press fruit in any way. The following day, measure juice. If there is more than 1.2 litres/2 pints (4$\frac{3}{4}$ cups) of apple juice, reduce by boiling until it measures 1.2 litres/2 pints (4$\frac{3}{4}$ cups). Place apple juice in pan with lemon juice and ginger, gradually add sugar

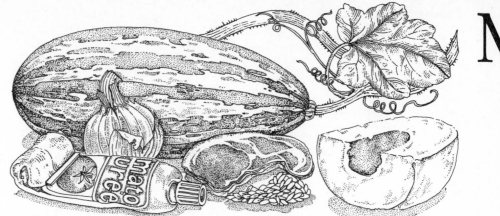

and stir until sugar has dissolved. Bring to the boil and boil rapidly for 15 minutes or until setting point is reached. Remove from heat, skim off froth and stir gently for 5 minutes to prevent ginger from floating to surface. Pour into warm, dry, sterilized jars. Cover and seal. Store for at least a week before using to allow flavours to mellow. Makes 5 × 500 g (1 lb) jars.

Old-Fashioned Marmalade

1 kg (2 lb) oranges; 2.5 litres/4½ pints (10 cups) water; 1.75 kg/4 lb (8 cups) sugar, warmed; juice 1 lemon.

Scrub oranges and put them whole into a saucepan with the water. Simmer gently until fruit is tender, 1½–2 hours. Test by inserting a skewer. If it penetrates the fruit it is ready. Lift fruit from pan and reserve liquid. Halve cooled fruit and remove pips. Return pips to pan of reserved liquid and simmer gently 15 minutes. Strain liquid to remove pips and set aside. Chop oranges into strips. Make up to 2 litres/3½ pints (8 cups) with strained liquid. If there is not enough liquid, make up with extra water. Pour into pan, add sugar and lemon juice and stir until sugar has dissolved. Bring to the boil and cook rapidly until setting point is reached, 15–20 minutes. Remove from heat and cool for about 15 minutes. Ladle into warm, dry, sterilized jars. Cover and seal. Makes about 6–8 × 500 g (1 lb) jars.

MARROW (Squash)

This large, sausage-shaped member of the gourd family is best eaten when it is young, with tender flesh. Marrow, called squash in America, is used as a vegetable – at its best if its bland taste is enhanced by a well-flavoured sauce or stuffing – and for jams or chutneys. It can also be used as a pie filling in much the same way as apple, though again the bland flavour of marrow needs lifting with brown sugar, lemon juice, raisins and spices.

When buying marrow, look for a small, smooth, unblemished one which feels heavy for its size. Store in a cool place and use within a week or two.

☐ **Basic Preparation:** Peel and halve marrow, scoop out seeds with a metal spoon and cut flesh into cubes or fingers. For rounds, cut peeled or unpeeled marrow across into thick slices and stamp out seeds with a cutter. Whole or halved marrow may be baked with a stuffing. For whole marrow, cut off stalk end and scrape out seeds from centre with a metal spoon. Peel marrow completely or remove strips of peel to give a striped effect. For halves, cut unpeeled marrow lengthways in half and scoop out seeds and some of the flesh, leaving a shell about 2.5 cm (1 in) thick. The scooped-out

flesh is usually chopped and used in the stuffing.

☐ **To Cook:** As it has a high water content, marrow is best steamed, baked, fried or stewed gently in its own juices with a little butter. Boiling in water is not advisable. (See also *Minced (Ground) Meat*.) **See recipes**.

BAKED MARROW Prepare a whole marrow, halves or slices as described above. Fill centre with a well-flavoured stuffing, preferably based on rice rather than breadcrumbs, which may become too wet. If using a whole marrow, tie the end piece back in place with string. Place in a greased baking dish, brush with oil or melted butter, cover loosely with foil and bake in a preheated moderate oven (180°C/350°F, Gas Mark 4) until tender – 45–60 minutes for whole marrow or halves, 15–20 minutes for slices.

BUTTERED MARROW Put prepared marrow into a saucepan with 15–30 g/½–1 oz (1–2 tbsp) melted butter, salt and pepper and, if liked, a few chopped or dried herbs or a little finely chopped onion. Cover pan and cook gently 7–10 minutes or until tender.

FRIED MARROW Prepare marrow, dry and coat with seasoned flour or with flour, egg and breadcrumbs. Fry over medium heat in oil, butter or a mixture of these.

STEAMED MARROW Place prepared pieces of marrow in a steamer or colander over boiling water. Season with salt and pepper, cover tightly and steam 20 minutes or until tender.

Marrow with Beurre Noisette

750 g (1½ lb) marrow (squash), peeled and seeded; 60 g/2 oz (4 tbsp) butter; 2 tbsp wine vinegar; 2 tbsp chopped parsley; freshly ground black pepper.

Cut marrow (squash) into cubes or fingers and steam or cook with butter as described above. Heat the butter in a small frying pan (skillet) on moderate heat, shaking occasionally to ensure even colour, until it is a light nut-brown. Stir in vinegar, parsley and pepper and pour while still frothing over hot marrow (squash). Serve immediately. Serves 4–6.

Stuffed Marrow

A simple but delicious dish that is as interesting as it is inexpensive.

1 small marrow (squash); 2 tbsp oil; 1 onion, chopped; 2 thick rashers (slices) streaky bacon, rind removed and coarsely chopped; 250 g/8 oz (1 cup) minced (ground) beef; 180 g/6 oz (1½ cups) cooked long-grain rice; 1 tbsp grated Parmesan cheese; salt and freshly ground black pepper; chopped parsley; 500 ml/18 fl oz (2 cups) Fresh Tomato Sauce (page 271) or Tomato Sauce Neopolitan (page 272).

Cut marrow (squash) in half, remove seeds and scoop out flesh as described left. Chop scooped-out flesh coarsely and reserve. Heat 1 tbsp oil in a frying pan (skillet) and cook onion and bacon gently 5 minutes. Add beef and cook, stirring and breaking up lumps with 2 forks, until lightly browned. Stir in rice, cheese and chopped marrow (squash) and season with salt and pepper. Divide mixture between marrow (squash) halves. Place in a greased baking dish. Brush marrow (squash) with remaining oil, cover loosely with foil and bake in a preheated moderate oven (180°C/350°F, Gas Mark 4) for 45 minutes to 1 hour or until marrow (squash) is tender. Sprinkle with chopped parsley and serve with hot tomato sauce. Serves 4–6.
NOTE: If desired, minced (ground) pork, veal or sausage meat may be used instead of beef.

MARSHMALLOW FROSTING

Marshmallow is a whipped confection resulting in a creamy, stiff mixture with a spongy texture. The name comes from the marshmallow plant; a gum formerly used in the cooking was obtained from its roots. Marshmallow makes a delicious icing (frosting) for butter cakes and looks most decorative for special occasions when swirled into rough peaks. Marshmallow can also be used to top mugs of hot chocolate. For best results use an electric mixer to beat the mixture.

Marshmallow Frosting

2 tsp gelatine; 350 ml/12 fl oz (1½ cups) boiling water; 500 g/1 lb (2 cups) sugar; ½ tsp vanilla essence (extract).

Dissolve gelatine in half the boiling water in a saucepan, add remainder of water and mix with sugar. Heat gently, stirring, until boiling, then boil without stirring over medium heat for 15 minutes. Remove from heat, cool slightly and beat until mixture doubles in bulk and becomes thick. Fold in vanilla. Spread quickly over cake with a warm dry spatula or knife, swirling the top into little peaks for a decorative effect. Sufficient to ice (frost) a 20 cm (8 in) butter cake.

MARSHMALLOWS

These little puffy pillows of marshmallow are among the most popular sweets (candies) found at the confectioner's. They can be coloured pink or white, coated with icing (confectioners) sugar, tinted or toasted coconut, or hundreds and thousands (colored sprinkles). They make delicious fillings when dipped in melted chocolate. Home-made or commercial marshmallows are also used as an ingredient in other sweets, to make sauces for ice creams or in desserts. **See recipes**.

Marshmallows

350 g/12 oz (1½ cups) caster sugar; 120 ml/4 fl oz (½ cup) cold water; 4 tsp gelatine; 120 ml/4 fl oz (½ cup) hot water; 1 tsp vanilla essence (extract); 45 g/1½ oz (½ cup) toasted or tinted desiccated (shredded) coconut, or 30 g/1 oz (¼ cup) cornflour (cornstarch) and 30 g/1 oz (¼ cup) icing (confectioners) sugar, sifted together.

Place sugar and cold water in a large bowl and, using an electric mixer, beat for 3–4 minutes. Dissolve gelatine in hot water and, while still hot, add to sugar mixture. Beat until thick and white. Add vanilla. Pour into a lightly greased 28 × 19 × 4 cm (11 × 7½ × 1½ in) tin (pan). Leave at room temperature until firm. Cut marshmallow into squares or other shapes with a warm, dry knife. Place coconut, or cornflour (cornstarch) and icing (confectioners) sugar mixture, in a plastic bag and toss the marshmallow pieces to coat thoroughly. Makes about 24.

VARIATION
Marshmallow Cones: Prepare marshmallow mixture. After adding vanilla, spoon immediately into 15 ice cream cones and sprinkle tops with hundreds and thousands. Makes 15.

Coffee Marshmallow Cream

500 g (1 lb) marshmallows, chopped; 250 ml/8 fl oz (1 cup) very strong black

coffee; 500 ml/18 fl oz (2 cups) double (heavy) cream, whipped; slivered toasted almonds, Brazil nuts or crushed Nut Brittle (page 240).

Place marshmallows in a heatproof bowl over hot water. Add coffee and heat, stirring frequently, until marshmallows are melted. Chill mixture until it is about to set, then fold in whipped cream. Pour into an oiled 1.5 litre/2½ pint (6 cup) ring mould. Chill until set. Invert on to a serving platter and cover the top with nuts or nut brittle. Serves 6.

Marshmallow Sauce

180 g/6 oz (¾ cup) sugar; 1 tbsp golden (light corn) syrup; 4 tbsp milk; 250 g (8 oz) marshmallows, chopped; 2 tbsp water; 1 tsp vanilla essence (extract).

Combine sugar, syrup and milk in a heavy saucepan. Stir over low heat until sugar has dissolved. Bring to the boil, then simmer gently for 5 minutes. Place marshmallows and water in top of a double saucepan (double boiler) and heat, stirring frequently, until melted. Pour sugar mixture over marshmallows, beating well. Add vanilla. Serve sauce hot or cold over ice cream, baked apples, poached pears or peaches or with fresh fruit salad. Makes about 500 ml/18 fl oz (2 cups).

MARZIPAN

Another name for *Almond Paste*. Marzipan is often modelled into edible cake and dessert decorations.

MAYONNAISE

The delicately flavoured, uniquely light and smooth mixture of oil, egg yolks and lemon juice is perhaps the most popular of the cold sauces.

Deservedly or not, Cardinal Richelieu is credited with the invention of this sauce in the seventeenth century, and it is interesting that it is still made exactly the same way today, except that one may, using great care, combine the emulsion with an electric beater or food processor instead of a wire whisk.

Making mayonnaise presents only one problem: it may curdle or separate. For consistent success, have the egg yolks and oil at room temperature, and beat the oil into the egg yolks very gradually, drop by drop at first then finally in a thin stream, until the emulsion of the egg and oil forms a smooth sauce. If anything goes wrong and the mayonnaise separates, you can restore the emulsion as follows: wash the beater; in another bowl beat another egg yolk with ½ tsp salt and ½ tsp vinegar; then gradually beat in the curdled mayonnaise a teaspoonful at a time at first, then more quickly until emulsified.

Mayonnaise should be stored in a cool place, not in the refrigerator. It will keep for several weeks – the oil is a preservative. Mayonnaise has dozens of uses, can be varied endlessly and will transform such simple ingredients as hard-boiled (hard-cooked) eggs, fresh cooked or canned fish, poached chicken or diced cooked vegetables into elegant dishes. There are many lovely mayonnaise variations. Some of the classics are Sauce Rémoulade, Sauce Tartare, Sauce Niçoise, Aïoli Sauce, Sauce Russe and Sauce à la Ritz. **See recipes**.

See also *Aïoli*.

Mayonnaise

2 egg yolks; ½ tsp salt; pinch white pepper; ½ tsp dry mustard; 2 tsp vinegar or lemon juice; 250 ml/8 fl oz (1 cup) olive or salad oil.

Have all the ingredients at room temperature. Warm the eggs and oil in hot water if they are cold. Rinse out a mixing bowl with hot water and wrap a damp cloth round the base to keep it steady. Place egg yolks, seasonings and 1 tsp vinegar or lemon juice in bowl and beat with a wire whisk to combine. When thick, begin to add oil, drop by drop, from a teaspoon, whisking constantly and incorporating each addition thoroughly before adding the next. As mixture thickens, oil flow can be increased to a steady thin stream but keep beating constantly. Stop pouring every now and then to check that oil is well blended. If mayonnaise should show signs of breaking up or curdling beat in 1–2 tsp boiling water before adding more oil. When all oil is incorporated, beat in remaining vinegar or lemon juice. Makes about 250 ml/8 fl oz (1 cup).

NOTE: For a lighter mayonnaise, add 1 tbsp of very hot water just before using.

VARIATIONS

Food Processor or Blender Mayonnaise: Place egg yolks, seasonings and 1 tsp vinegar or lemon juice in bowl and blend for a few seconds. With motor running, pour oil in very gradually, ensuring that each addition has been absorbed before adding more. When all the oil has been incorporated, add remaining vinegar or lemon juice.

Mayonnaise Dijonnaise: Make Mayonnaise, using 1 tbsp French (Dijon) mustard instead of dry mustard.

Sauce Verte: Rinse 60 g/2 oz (1 cup) watercress sprigs and 8 sprigs parsley, stripped from the stems. Cover with boiling water and let stand 5–6 minutes. Drain greens, plunge into cold water, and drain again, pressing out all surplus water. Rub greens through a sieve, then combine with finished Mayonnaise. Serve with cold lobster, salmon, poached fish or other fish and shellfish. Good also for vegetable salads.

Sauce Russe: Add 3 tbsp chilli sauce, 1 tbsp finely chopped canned pimiento and 1 tsp chopped chives to finished Mayonnaise and mix well. Use for cold eggs and vegetables and for shellfish.

Sauce à la Ritz: Add 1 tbsp chilli sauce, $\frac{1}{2}$ tsp Worcestershire sauce, 1 tomato, peeled, seeded and chopped, and 1 tsp each chopped chives and parsley to the finished Mayonnaise and mix well. Use for seafood cocktails.

Sauce Rémoulade: Press all moisture from 3 tbsp finely chopped sour pickles and 1 tbsp chopped capers. Add pickles and capers to the finished Mayonnaise with 1 tsp French (Dijon) mustard and 1 tbsp chopped mixed fresh parsley, tarragon and chervil. Use with fried or cold poached fish and shellfish.

Sauce Tartare: Add 6 green olives, chopped, and 1 tsp chopped chives to Sauce Rémoulade. Use for fried fish and shellfish.

Sauce Niçoise: Add 1 tbsp tomato purée (paste), 3 tbsp chopped red pepper and 1 tsp chopped mixed fresh tarragon and chives to Mayonnaise. Use with cold poached fish or shellfish.

Mustard Mayonnaise: Combine 120 ml/4 fl oz ($\frac{1}{2}$ cup) Mayonnaise, 3 tbsp single (light) cream, 2 tbsp French (Dijon) mustard, 1 clove garlic, crushed; 1 tbsp lemon juice, salt and freshly ground black pepper, pinch cayenne.

Thousand Island Dressing

5 tbsp Mayonnaise (opposite); 2 tsp tomato ketchup; dash Tabasco (hot pepper) sauce; 1 hard-boiled (hard-cooked) egg, chopped; 2 spring onions (scallions), chopped; 6 green or black (ripe) olives, stoned (pitted) and chopped; salt and freshly ground black pepper.

Mix all ingredients together. Makes about 120 ml/4 fl oz ($\frac{1}{2}$ cup).

MEAT

Meat is usually the star around which the rest of the meal revolves. It is the basis of literally thousands of wonderful dishes. As all meat becomes more expensive, it becomes more and more important to choose meat carefully and to get the best from it. For information on characteristics of good beef, lamb, mutton, pork and veal, specific cuts and methods of cooking them, please see entries under individual names of these meats.

Buying Meat

You can judge meat to some degree by its appearance, but you must rely largely on the skill and integrity of your butcher for first-class meat. Eating is the final test, but for points to help you appraise quality, please see entries for individual meats.

To choose the right cut for the dish: As discussed right under 'Cooking Meat', cuts from different parts of the animal vary greatly in tenderness and, of course, in cost. This does *not* mean that you should buy the most expensive cut you can afford for every dish. The connective tissue which makes cheaper cuts too tough for grilling (broiling) or frying is exactly what gives a rich, melting texture to a dish when it is cooked slowly with moisture and broken down into gelatine. For best results, follow the suggestions for the suitable cuts given in entries for individual meats and in the recipe you are following.

How much to buy: The amount of meat for each serving varies, of course, with appetites and the type of dish.

As a general guide, allow:

125–250 g (4–8 oz) per serving of boneless cuts, such as stewing meat, roasts, steaks and minced (ground) meat.

150–250 g (5–8 oz) of meat with some bone, such as chops, T-bone steaks and roasts on the bone.

370–500 g (12 oz–1 lb) of bony cuts such as spare ribs, lamb shanks and bone-in shoulder.

Storing Meat

As a general rule, the larger the piece of meat and the less surface area it has for its size, the longer it will store. Minced (ground) meat, sausage and offal (variety meats) should be cooked within 24 hours of purchase. Diced meat should be used within 48 hours, steaks and chops within 2–4 days, and roasts within 3–5 days. The bacteria which cause the surface of meat to become slimy thrive in the absence of air, so meat should never be stored tightly wrapped in plastic. Unwrap it, put it on a plate, cover loosely with foil or greaseproof (waxed) paper and store in the coldest part of the refrigerator.

To freeze meat: Freeze it as quickly as possible so, if you want to pack several pieces together, wrap them individually in foil or freezer wrap and freeze in a single layer first. It

is practical to prepare meat ready for cooking by trimming or cutting it up before freezing. Small cuts or diced meat can be stewed or casseroled from frozen, and thin pieces can be fried or grilled (broiled) from frozen; but larger pieces will be overdone on the outside before the inside is fully cooked, so first thaw these completely. It is better to thaw meat in the refrigerator than at room temperature as less juices are lost. Allow 5–6 hours for steak and chops, 6 hours per 500 g (1 lb) for large pieces.

Cooking Meat

Tenderness in meat depends partly on the age and condition of the animal, on how the meat was handled after slaughter and also on the cut. Tender cuts come from those parts of the animal which had the least exercise, such as the loin (lower back) and rump. These cuts respond to dry-heat cooking, so roast, grill (broil), fry or sauté them.

Tougher cuts, from parts of the animal which had more exercise, have developed more connective tissue, which is the main cause of toughness. Slow cooking with moisture changes connective tissue into gelatine, so braise, stew, pot roast or simmer these cuts. In these slow-cooking processes, the liquid should never go above simmering point – when the surface shivers and single bubbles rise slowly. Some meat dishes are traditionally called 'boiled' but this is a misnomer – meat that is cooked at full boiling point loses its juices and becomes tasteless and dry.

Always remove meat from the refrigerator in time for it to reach room temperature right through before cooking it. This ensures that the inside will be cooked as desired before the outside is overdone. Cooking times given in recipes are based on meat at room temperature.

To judge when meat is done: Cooking times given in recipes can be used as a guide, but the shape of the piece, the quality of the meat or the efficiency of your stove can cause variations. Start testing when about $\frac{4}{5}$ of the given cooking time is up.

To test large pieces of meat, a meat thermometer is ideal as it is marked at the correct internal temperatures for different meats. Insert the thermometer into the thickest part of the meat, away from fat or bone, leave for a minute, then read it.

Failing a thermometer, or for smaller cuts such as steak, press the meat with your finger. If it is soft and spongy it is not cooked through. If it is soft but quite springy, it is medium-rare. If it is firm with little resilience, it is well-done.

You can also test by inserting a fine skewer or kitchen needle into the thickest part of the meat and checking the colour of the juice that comes out. If it is red, the meat is rare; if pink, the meat is medium; if clear the meat is well-done.

Carving Meat

The first requisite for good carving is a razor-sharp knife. For meat, it should have a rather long, narrow and slightly flexible blade. The essence of the art is to allow the knife to do the cutting – the carver guides the blade with a long, light, slightly sawing action, rather than driving it. Electric carving knives make the job easier for many people, though purists prefer their traditional tools.

It is easier to carve on a board than on a platter; the board should have a channel to catch the juices. You will also need a fork and a hot plate for the carved meat.

Always allow a cooked joint to rest in a warm place for 15–30 minutes before carving (the larger the piece, the longer the time) so that the juices can settle back into the tissues.

Meat is usually carved across the grain, though some joints may be carved with the grain, parallel to the bone (see diagrams below).

Boneless Rolled Joints (e.g. rib or other cuts of beef; loin or shoulder of lamb, mutton, veal or pork; breast of veal; rolled corned beef): Lay the piece on its side and carve downwards in slices – thinly for beef and veal, more thickly for lamb, mutton and pork.

Other Boneless Joints (e.g. topside (top round), fresh or corned silverside (bottom round) or rump of beef): Carve in slices across the grain, changing the direction of the knife and turning the joint as needed.

Leg of Lamb, Mutton or Pork: This may be carved in two ways. The most economical and easiest way is to carve slices parallel to the surface (with the grain), turning the joint over as needed. The method which gives the juiciest meat, with an edging of the brown outside on each slice, is to start carving in the middle, downward to the bone. Take out a wedge-shaped piece first, then slices, also slightly wedge-shaped, from each side **(Fig 1 below)**. Finally, turn joint over and slice off remaining meat parallel to the surface.

NOTE: Before starting to carve roast leg of pork, remove the crackling, break into pieces. Serve a piece of crackling with each portion.

Ham on the Bone: Carve by either of the methods described for leg of lamb, above (see also **Fig 2**).

Rack of Lamb, Crown Roast of Lamb or Pork, Rib of Pork on the Bone: Carve downwards into single or double cutlets (chops), making sure beforehand that the butcher has chined the joint properly (chopped through the bone where you will be cutting) **(Fig 3)**.

Rib of Beef on the Bone: Cut between meat and bone to separate them, then slice meat at right angles to bone.

Sirloin of Beef on the Bone: First turn the joint over and carve out the fillet (tenderloin) in thick slices. Turn upright again, cut between meat and bone to separate them and push bone down slightly. Slice meat thinly at right angles to the bone **(Fig 4)**.

Shoulder of Lamb or Mutton on the Bone: First hold up the leg end of the joint with the fork, meaty side uppermost, and carve slices parallel to the surface **(Fig 5)**. Next, put joint flat on dish, turn over and carve slices from either side of the shoulder blade **(Fig 6)**.

Saddle of Lamb: There are two ways of carving a saddle. For either method, start by cutting off the skirt pieces that are tucked underneath. These are fatty and are not always served, but may be cut diagonally into small pieces if you want to serve them.

You may now carve lengthways down either side of the central bone to give long flat strips of meat **(Fig 7)**, or cut between bone and meat to separate them, then cut meat across into small thick slices **(Fig 8)**. Lastly, turn the joint over and cut between bone and meat to remove the 2 fillets (tenderloins), then cut these across into small thick slices. Serve a piece from each part of the saddle for each portion.

Sucking Pig: Cut round the outline of shoulder and leg, pull outwards gently and cut off through joints. Carve meat in slices. Remove head and divide meat down centre of back. Cut pig across the middle to separate rib section. Cut through ribs, dividing into chops.

NOTE: The pig will be easier to carve if the skin is first removed. Break the crisp parts (crackling) into pieces and serve some crackling with each portion.

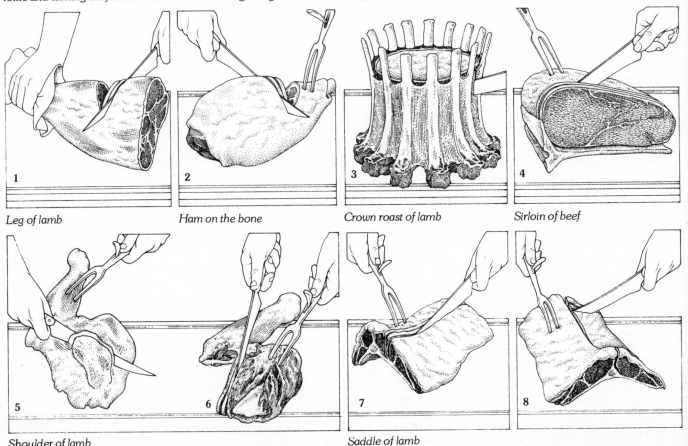

Leg of lamb   Ham on the bone   Crown roast of lamb   Sirloin of beef

Shoulder of lamb   Saddle of lamb

Right: Shoulder of Lamb with Peach and Rosemary Stuffing (page 418)

MEATBALLS

These are made from minced (ground) or very finely chopped or shredded meat and are included in nearly every cuisine of the world. They range from tiny meatballs dropped in soup to much larger ones used as a main course. They can be fried, grilled (broiled), baked, braised or poached; the mixtures are nearly always economical, often incorporating breadcrumbs, rice, vegetables or sometimes a little fruit, to stretch the quantity and improve the flavour.

Meatballs are marvellous for parties. They can be made, cooked ahead and heated when required. Serve them with a dipping sauce when having drinks. Use beef, lamb, pork, or any suitable combinations, such as pork and veal, according to your recipe. Cuts such as beef topside (top round) or round steaks, lamb, veal or pork shoulder are good for mincing (grinding) at home. The meat should be lean and free of gristle and sinew. Buy it ready-minced (ground) from your butcher or mince (grind) the higher-quality cuts at home, using a mincer (grinder) or food processor. It is best to use minced (ground) meat within 24 hours after buying. Store in refrigerator, spread evenly in a dish and loosely covered with foil. **See recipes.**

See also *Frikadeller*.

Onion Soup with Meatballs

60 g/2 oz ($\frac{1}{4}$ cup) barley, soaked overnight and drained; 500 ml/18 fl oz (2 cups) water; 1 litre/1$\frac{3}{4}$ pints (4 cups) beef stock; 250 g/8 oz (1 cup) minced (ground) beef; 1 egg yolk; 1 tbsp minced onion; 1 tbsp chopped parsley; pinch white pepper; 45 g/1$\frac{1}{2}$ oz (3 tbsp) butter; 3 large onions, chopped; $\frac{1}{2}$ tsp Worcestershire sauce; salt and freshly ground black pepper.
GARNISH: *sour cream, chopped parsley.*

Place barley, water and beef stock in a saucepan and bring to the boil. Half cover and simmer until barley is tender, about 1$\frac{1}{2}$ hours. Mix together minced (ground) beef, egg yolk, minced onion, parsley and white pepper and shape into walnut-sized balls. Heat butter in frying pan (skillet) and brown meatballs on all sides. Drain on crumpled paper towels and set aside. Cook chopped onions in fat in frying pan (skillet) until tender and lightly browned. Add meatballs, fried onions and Worcestershire sauce to barley soup and simmer for a further 30 minutes. Season with salt and pepper. Serve with a swirl of sour cream and sprinkled with chopped parsley. Serves 4–6.

Left: Risotto with Prawns (page 337) and Pasta with Garlic and Fresh Herbs (page 268)

Königsberger Klöpse
(Meatballs in Lemon and Caper Sauce)

250 g/8 oz (1 cup) each minced (ground) beef, pork and veal, or 750 g/1$\frac{1}{2}$ lb (3 cups) mixed minced (ground) pork and veal; 3 slices stale white bread; 250 ml/8 fl oz (1 cup) lukewarm water; 1 onion, finely chopped; 5 anchovy fillets, chopped; 2 eggs; 1 tbsp chopped parsley; grated rind 1 lemon; $\frac{1}{2}$ tsp salt; $\frac{1}{4}$ tsp pepper; 750 ml–1 litre/1$\frac{1}{4}$–1$\frac{3}{4}$ pints (3–4 cups) veal or beef stock; 1 small onion; 1 bay leaf.
LEMON AND CAPER SAUCE: *30 g/1 oz (2 tbsp) butter; $\frac{1}{2}$ tsp minced onion; 1$\frac{1}{2}$ tbsp flour; 2 tbsp lemon juice; 2 tbsp capers; 2–3 tbsp sour cream.*

Mix meats together. Cut bread into small pieces and soak in lukewarm water for 15 minutes. Drain, squeeze dry and add to meat with chopped onion and anchovies. Mix well or mince (grind) again in a food processor or mincer (grinder). Add eggs, parsley, lemon rind, salt and pepper and mix thoroughly. With wet hands shape mixture into balls about 5 cm (2 in) in diameter. Place stock (bouillon), onion and bay leaf in a saucepan and bring to the boil. Simmer for 10 minutes, then drop in meatballs. Simmer for 20 minutes longer or until meatballs rise to surface. Using a slotted spoon transfer them to a heated dish and cover. Strain and reserve stock.

LEMON AND CAPER SAUCE: Melt butter in a heavy saucepan, add onion and cook gently until translucent. Stir in flour and allow to brown very slowly. Pour in reserved stock and stir continuously until thickened. Add lemon juice and capers. Add meatballs to sauce and simmer very gently for 15 minutes, stirring occasionally. Stir in sour cream. Serve on a mound of sauerkraut. Serves 4–6.

Swedish Meatballs in Cream Sauce

500 g/1 lb (2 cups) minced (ground) beef; 250 g/8 oz (1 cup) mixed minced (ground) pork and veal; 90 g/3 oz (1$\frac{1}{2}$ cups) fresh white breadcrumbs; 600 ml/1 pint (2$\frac{1}{2}$ cups) single (light) cream; 120 ml/4 fl oz ($\frac{1}{2}$ cup) milk; 1 onion, finely chopped; 90 g/3 oz (6 tbsp) butter; 1 egg, beaten; $\frac{1}{4}$ tsp ground ginger; salt and freshly ground black pepper; pinch nutmeg; 1 tbsp flour; 120 ml/4 fl oz ($\frac{1}{2}$ cup) stock.

Mix meats together. Soak breadcrumbs in a mixture of 120 ml/4 fl oz ($\frac{1}{2}$ cup) cream and the milk. Cook onion in 30 g/1 oz (2 tbsp) butter until tender but not brown. Combine meats, breadcrumbs, egg and onion, and season with ginger, 1$\frac{1}{2}$ tsp salt, pepper and $\frac{1}{4}$ tsp nutmeg. Beat vigorously until very light in texture, then chill. Form into small balls. Melt remaining butter in a large frying pan (skillet)

and lightly brown meatballs on all sides, a few at a time. Remove from pan and keep warm in an ovenproof dish in a preheated cool oven (150°C/300°F, Gas Mark 2) while making the sauce. Stir flour into fat in frying pan (skillet) and cook for 2 minutes, stirring. Remove from heat and add stock and remaining cream. Bring to the boil, stirring constantly. Season with salt, pepper and nutmeg and cook over a low heat for about 10 minutes or until sauce reduces and thickens, stirring frequently. Pour sauce over meatballs and serve with boiled potatoes. Serves 6.
NOTE: The meatballs may be made and cooked the day before and then reheated in the oven, with the sauce poured over just before serving.

Party Meatballs

These meatballs are marvellous for a party. They freeze well, so can be made and stored for 3–4 weeks and reheated as required.

2 large potatoes, peeled and diced; 1 medium tart apple, peeled, cored and diced; 2 large onions, finely chopped; 2 rashers (slices) bacon, rind removed and finely chopped; 2 eggs, beaten; 1 kg/2 lb (4 cups) minced (ground) steak; 500 g/1 lb (2 cups) sausage meat; 2 tsp curry powder; 1 tsp ground ginger; 2 tbsp sugar; $\frac{1}{4}$ tsp dry mustard; $\frac{1}{2}$ tsp salt; $\frac{1}{4}$ tsp pepper; 1 tbsp tomato ketchup; flour; oil for frying.
SPICY TOMATO SAUCE: *250 ml/8 fl oz (1 cup) tomato ketchup; 1 tbsp brown sugar; 1 tbsp Worcestershire sauce; 1 tbsp soy sauce.*

Place potatoes, apple and onions in a saucepan and just cover with water. Bring to the boil, then reduce heat and simmer until very tender. Drain, and mash or purée. Allow to cool. Place all ingredients except flour and oil in a bowl and mix well together. Using floured hands, roll into bite-sized balls. Heat a little oil in a frying pan (skillet) and fry meatballs until golden on all sides. Drain on paper towels and serve hot or cold. The meatballs can also be baked in a preheated moderately hot oven (190°C/375°F, Gas Mark 5) for 15–20 minutes or until golden-brown. For sauce, heat all ingredients together in a saucepan, stirring occasionally. To serve, pour sauce into a bowl on a platter and arrange meatballs around it. Provide a container of toothpicks so guests can spear the meatballs for dunking. Makes about 130–150 small meatballs.

Smoked Chinese Meatballs

The simple meatball transformed with Chinese flavourings then smoked over black tea and fennel seeds makes a stunning first course, especially when taken to the table in the attractive Chinese bamboo steamer.

M

6 dried Chinese mushrooms; $\frac{1}{2} \times 230$ g/$7\frac{1}{2}$ oz can water chestnuts, drained and finely chopped; 250 g/8 oz (1 cup) lean minced (ground) beef; 250 g/8 oz (1 cup) minced (ground) pork; 2 tbsp soy sauce; 2 tbsp cornflour (cornstarch); 1 tbsp finely chopped spring onions (scallions); 1 tbsp finely chopped fresh ginger; 1 tbsp rice wine or dry sherry; 1 tsp Chinese sesame oil.
FOR SMOKING: 2 tbsp brown sugar; 2 tbsp black tea leaves; 2 tbsp fennel seeds.
TO SERVE: 2 tsp sesame oil mixed with 2 tbsp soy sauce; 2 spring onions (scallions), chopped.

Soak mushrooms in hot water to cover for 15 minutes or until soft. Drain, then remove stalks and chop caps finely. Place the mushrooms in a large bowl with remaining ingredients and mix well by hand until mixture is firm and compact. Shape into walnut-sized balls and arrange each on a little square of greaseproof (waxed) paper. Set in one layer on a greased cake rack or in a Chinese bamboo steamer. Cover and steam over boiling water in a wok or deep frying pan (skillet) for 15 minutes. Meanwhile, prepare a container for smoking: use an old frying pan (skillet), wok or other metal container. Line with foil, pressing it well into shape of container. Combine brown sugar, tea leaves and fennel seeds and place in bottom of pan. Set over high heat. When tea mixture starts to smoke, put rack containing meatballs into pan. Cover tightly with a lid or foil and smoke for 5 minutes, then turn heat off and leave for a further 10 minutes, still covered. To serve, brush meatballs with oil and soy sauce and sprinkle with spring onions (scallions). Serves 6–8 as a first course, or 4 as a main course.
NOTE: If using a Chinese bamboo steamer with its own lid, place meatballs in base, cover and place over burning tea mixture.

Curried Koftas
(Indian Meatballs)

500 g/1 lb (2 cups) finely minced (ground) steak; 1 onion, finely chopped; 1–2 chillies, seeded and chopped; 2 tbsp chopped fresh coriander or mint; 1–2 cloves garlic, crushed; $\frac{1}{2}$ tsp salt; 1 tbsp Garam Masala (page 139); 1 tsp chilli powder; flour; oil for frying.
SAUCE: 30 g/1 oz (2 tbsp) butter or ghee; 1 large onion, finely chopped; 1 tbsp chopped fresh ginger; 1 tsp turmeric; $\frac{1}{4}$ tsp salt; 2 tsp Garam Masala; $\frac{1}{4}$ tsp chilli powder; 2 large tomatoes, peeled and chopped; 1 tbsp lemon juice; 120 ml/4 fl oz ($\frac{1}{2}$ cup) water.

Mix steak with onion, chillies, coriander or mint, garlic, salt, garam masala and chilli powder. Knead mixture until stiff and smooth. Roll into walnut-sized balls and dust lightly with flour. Shallow-fry in hot oil until

golden. Drain on paper towels.
SAUCE: Heat butter or ghee in a heavy saucepan and fry onion and ginger until softened. Add turmeric, salt, garam masala and chilli powder and stir for a minute, then add tomatoes. Cook, stirring, for a few minutes. Stir in lemon juice and water. Add meatballs and stir to coat with sauce. Cover and simmer 15–20 minutes or until sauce is thick. Serve with rice, a choice of chutneys, and sambals such as minted chopped tomatoes, sliced bananas, coconut and pappadams. Serves 4.

Polpette
(Italian Meatballs)

500 g/1 lb (2 cups) minced (ground) steak; 2 cloves garlic, sliced; 2 tbsp chopped parsley; 1 strip lemon rind; 1 thick slice white bread; 4 tbsp milk; 2 eggs; $\frac{1}{4}$ tsp salt; $\frac{1}{4}$ tsp pepper; pinch nutmeg; flour; oil for frying.

Put steak, garlic, parsley and lemon rind through a mincer (grinder) or food processor to mince (grind) finely. Soak bread in milk for 15 minutes, then drain and squeeze dry. Stir bread into meat mixture. Beat in eggs and add salt, pepper and nutmeg. Form into little flat cakes and coat lightly in flour. Fry in hot oil and drain on crumpled paper towels before serving. Serves 4.
VARIATION

Italian Meatballs with Tomato Sauce: Make polpette as above and place in an ovenproof dish after frying. Pour in 350 ml/12 fl oz (1$\frac{1}{2}$ cups) Tomato Sauce Neapolitan (see page 272) and bake, covered, in a preheated moderate oven (180°C/350°F, Gas Mark 4) for about 30 minutes or until heated through. Serve with grated Parmesan cheese handed separately. Serves 4.

Moroccan Meatballs

250 g (8 oz) boned shoulder of lamb, trimmed of excess fat and minced (ground); 250 g (8 oz) potatoes, peeled, boiled and mashed; 2 eggs, beaten; 2 tbsp chopped parsley; 2 onions, finely chopped; $\frac{1}{4}$ tsp black pepper; $\frac{1}{2}$ tsp cayenne; salt; 30 g/1 oz ($\frac{1}{4}$ cup) flour; 120 ml/4 fl oz ($\frac{1}{2}$ cup) oil.

Mix together thoroughly all ingredients except flour and oil. Form into balls the size of small eggs. Flatten slightly and roll lightly in flour. Heat oil in a frying pan (skillet) and fry meatballs for 10–15 minutes or until cooked and golden-brown on all sides. Serve very hot. Serves 4.

Porcupines

500 g/1 lb (2 cups) minced (ground) steak; 30 g/1 oz ($\frac{1}{2}$ cup) fresh white breadcrumbs; $\frac{3}{4}$ tsp salt; $\frac{1}{2}$ tsp paprika; $\frac{1}{2}$ green pepper, cored, seeded and diced (optional); 1 egg, beaten; 105 g/3$\frac{1}{2}$ oz ($\frac{1}{2}$ cup) rice; 1 × 310 g/ 10 oz can tomato soup; 120 ml/4 fl oz ($\frac{1}{2}$ cup) water; 180 ml/6 oz (1 cup) frozen peas.

Combine minced (ground) steak, bread-crumbs, salt, paprika, green pepper, if used, and egg. Roll lightly into balls, press into flat cakes and roll in rice. Heat soup and water in a heavy saucepan and add meat cakes. Cover and simmer gently for 40 minutes. Add peas and simmer for a further 5 minutes before serving. Serves 4–6.

Keftethes
(Greek Meat Patties)

500 g/1 lb (2 cups) minced (ground) veal; 250 g/8 oz (1 cup) minced (ground) pork; 3 thick slices stale bread, crusts removed; 1 onion, finely chopped; 1 clove garlic, crushed; 3 tbsp chopped parsley; 1 tsp chopped fresh mint; 1 tsp chopped fresh basil; 1 medium tomato, peeled and chopped; 1 egg; 1 tbsp vinegar; 1 tsp bicarbonate of soda (baking soda); 1$\frac{1}{2}$ tsp salt; freshly ground black pepper; flour; oil for frying.

Combine meats. Soak bread in cold water, drain and squeeze dry. Mix bread with onion, garlic, herbs, tomato, egg and vinegar. Blend in soda, salt and pepper. Add meat and mix in lightly and thoroughly, using hands if necessary. Chill for 1 hour. Roll into balls, dust with flour and flatten into rounds about 5 cm (2 in) in diameter. Shallow-fry in hot oil for 4–5 minutes each side. Patties should puff up. Drain on crumpled paper towels and serve immediately. Serves 5–6.

Courgette and Lamb Patties

500 g/1 lb (4 cups) grated unpeeled courgette (zucchini); salt; 500 g (1 lb) boneless lamb, trimmed of excess fat and minced (ground); ¼ tsp white pepper; 2 tbsp chopped fresh dill; 1 onion, grated; 60 g/2 oz (¼ cup) cream cheese, softened; 2 eggs; 2 tbsp flour; 2 tbsp olive oil.
GARNISH: *1 lemon, cut into 6 wedges; sprigs fresh dill.*

Place grated courgette (zucchini) in a colander, sprinkle with salt and let drain for 30 minutes to extract bitter juices. Squeeze out excess moisture between the palms of your hands and dry courgette (zucchini) on paper towels. Mix with lamb, pepper, dill, onion, cream cheese and eggs. Add flour and form into 12 round patties. Heat oil in a frying pan (skillet) and fry patties over medium heat for about 5 minutes on each side or until golden-brown. Serve hot, garnished with lemon wedges and dill sprigs. Serves 6–8.

MEAT LOAF

A well-made meat loaf should be light, juicy and hold its shape when cut. Handle the meat lightly when mixing so that the final result is not too dense. A small proportion of fat helps to retain juiciness, and the loaves slice best when bound with egg, and not overcooked. Serve meat loaf at lunch with appropriate salads, or hot for dinner with vegetables and a suitable sauce, such as tomato or barbecue. **See recipes.**

Basic Meat Loaf

1 kg/2 lb (4 cups) minced (ground) steak; 1 tsp salt; ¼ tsp black pepper; 60 g/2 oz (1 cup) fresh breadcrumbs; 250 ml/8 fl oz (1 cup) evaporated milk; 1 small onion, finely chopped; 2 tsp chopped fresh herbs, or ½ tsp dried; 2–3 rashers (slices) bacon, rind removed (optional).
GRAVY: *1 tbsp flour; 350 ml/12 fl oz (1½ cups) beef stock.*

Thoroughly combine all ingredients except bacon. Pack lightly into a greased 21 × 15 cm (8½ × 6 in) loaf tin (pan) or shape mixture into a loaf on a shallow baking tray. Top with bacon, if using, and bake in a preheated moderate oven (180°C/350°F, Gas Mark 4) for 1 hour or until loaf shrinks slightly from sides of tin (pan). Pour 2 tbsp fat from tin (pan) into a saucepan. Add flour and stir over medium heat until brown. Add beef stock, stir until boiling and simmer 3 minutes. Strain into a heated sauce boat. Serve meat loaf hot with gravy and vegetables, or cold with a salad. Alternatively, meat loaf may be served hot with Tomato Sauce (see page 370). Serves 6.

VARIATIONS
Crusty Meat Loaf: Make Basic Meat Loaf mixture and shape into a loaf on a baking tray. Omit bacon, score top into diamond shapes with the back of a knife. Bake as left, basting every 15 minutes with 60 g/2 oz (4 tbsp) melted butter mixed with 4 tbsp white wine or stock.
Egg Loaf: Place ¼ Basic Meat Loaf mixture in loaf tin (pan), put 3 shelled hard-boiled (hard-cooked) eggs down the middle and pack remaining meat mixture over and around them. Top with bacon. Bake as above.
Other Seasonings: Add any of the following to Basic Meat Loaf mixture: 1 clove garlic, crushed; 125 g/4 oz (1 cup) grated cheese; 60 g/2 oz (½ cup) sautéed sliced mushrooms; 60 g/2 oz (½ cup) chopped green pepper or celery; 225 g/7½ oz (1 cup) cooked, finely chopped, well-drained spinach; 10 g/⅓ oz (¼ cup) finely chopped parsley and 30 g/1 oz (¼ cup) pine nuts.
Potato Topping: Bake Basic Meat Loaf, omitting bacon, in loaf tin (pan) and drain off fat. Turn out on to baking tray or ovenproof dish. Spread with 500 g/1 lb (2 cups) well-seasoned mashed potatoes and brush with melted butter or sprinkle with grated cheese. Bake in preheated moderately hot oven (200°C/400°F, Gas Mark 6) for 20 minutes.
Pastry (Dough) Crust: Make Basic Meat Loaf, omitting bacon, drain off fat and allow to cool. Roll out 1 × 375 g/12 oz packet frozen puff pastry (paste), thawed, to rectangle about 25 × 35 cm (10 × 14 in). Put cooled meat loaf, top side down, in the centre of the pastry (dough). Fold pastry (dough) completely round loaf, sealing edges with water. Turn right side up on a baking tray and brush with 1 egg lightly mixed with 1 tbsp milk or water. Decorate with pastry (dough) leaves or as desired, attaching decorations with some egg wash. Brush decorations with egg and bake in a preheated moderately hot oven (200°C/400°F, Gas Mark 6) about 15–20 minutes or until nicely browned.

Spicy Meat Loaf with Mustard Sauce

1 egg, beaten; 5 tbsp evaporated milk; 1 tbsp vinegar; 1 tbsp treacle (molasses); 1 tbsp French (Dijon) mustard; 90 g/3 oz (1½ cups) fresh breadcrumbs; 1 small onion, finely chopped; ½ tsp salt; 750 g/1½ lb (3 cups) minced (ground) beef.
SAUCE: *250 ml/8 fl oz (1 cup) beef stock; 2 tsp vinegar; 2 tsp dry mustard; 1 tsp treacle (molasses); 2 tbsp cornflour (cornstarch); 120 ml/4 fl oz (½ cup) cold water.*

Combine egg, evaporated milk, vinegar, treacle (molasses), mustard, breadcrumbs, onion and salt. Mix in beef. Pack mixture lightly into a 21 × 11 cm (8½ × 4½ in) loaf tin (pan). Bake in a preheated moderate oven (180°C/350°F, Gas Mark 4) for 1¼ hours. To make the sauce, combine stock, vinegar, mustard and treacle (molasses) in a saucepan and beat until smooth. Blend together cornflour (cornstarch) and cold water, add to pan and cook, stirring, until thickened and bubbly. Serve with hot meat loaf. Serves 6.

Orange Meat Loaf

750 g/1½ lb (3 cups) minced (ground) steak; 4 tbsp orange juice; 1 egg; 90 g/3 oz (1½ cups) fresh white breadcrumbs; 1 onion, finely chopped; salt; ¼ tsp freshly ground black pepper; 2 tsp chopped parsley; ¼ tsp dried thyme.
TOPPING: *4 tbsp tomato purée (paste); 60 g/2 oz (⅓ cup) firmly packed brown sugar; ¼ tsp dry mustard; ¼ tsp cinnamon; ¼ tsp ground cardamom or cloves; 3 slices orange.*

Combine all meat loaf ingredients and mix well. Lightly pack into a greased 21 × 11 cm (8½ × 4½ in) loaf tin (pan). Bake in a preheated moderate oven (180°C/350°F, Gas mark 4) on the lower shelf, for 30 minutes.
TOPPING: Combine tomato purée (paste), sugar, mustard and spices and mix well. Place halved orange slices on top of meat loaf, spoon spice mixture over and bake for a further 30 minutes. Serves 6.

Meat Loaf with Tahini

750 g/1½ lb (3 cups) minced (ground) lamb or beef; 2 onions, finely chopped; 20 g/⅔ oz (½ cup) chopped parsley; 1 tsp salt; ½ tsp ground allspice.
SAUCE: *3 tbsp tomato purée (paste); 2 tbsp tahini (sesame paste); 3 tbsp white vinegar; salt; ground allspice.*

Place meat in bowl. Add onions, parsley, salt and allspice and knead well. Press meat mixture into a greased 21 × 11 cm (8½ × 4½ in) loaf tin (pan). Bake in a preheated moderately hot oven (200°C/400°F, Gas Mark 6) for 15 minutes or until meat loaf is lightly browned. Meanwhile, prepare sauce by mixing tomato purée (paste), tahini and vinegar. Season with salt and allspice. Add enough water to blend ingredients to a thin but creamy sauce. Pour enough sauce over meat loaf to cover, and return to oven for a further hour, basting with sauce. Serves 6.

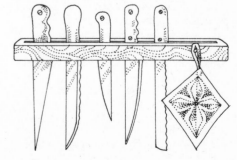

211

Garlic Sausage Meat Loaf

1 onion, finely chopped; 2 cloves garlic, crushed; 2 tbsp oil; 30 g/1 oz (½ cup) fresh breadcrumbs; 1 egg; 1 tsp chopped parsley; ½ tsp salt; ¼ tsp pepper; 750 g/1½ lb (3 cups) sausage meat; 1 tsp dried thyme or rosemary.

Cook onion and garlic in 1 tbsp oil until soft but not brown. Mix together onion, garlic, breadcrumbs, egg, parsley, salt and pepper. Add sausage meat and mix well. Shape into a sausage-shaped loaf, brush with remaining oil and sprinkle with herbs. Wrap in foil and place in an ovenproof dish. Bake the meat loaf in a preheated moderately hot oven (190°C/375°F, Gas Mark 5) for 50 minutes. Serve hot or cold with salad, or use as a filling for sandwiches or bread rolls. Serves 6.

MELBA TOAST

Originally created for the great *diva* Dame Nellie Melba. Melba toast is made with very thin slices of bread. They are baked to golden-brown crispness and make a pleasantly crunchy toast accompaniment – perfect with pâté, and as an accompaniment for creamy soups and other first course dishes. Serve Melba toast while it is still hot.

□ **To Prepare:** Toast bread slices lightly on each side and cut off crusts. Using a very sharp knife, cut each slice through the middle, producing 2 very thin slices. Cut each into 4 triangles and place on an ungreased baking tray, soft side up. Bake in a preheated very cool oven (120°C/250°F, Gas Mark ½) for about 15–20 minutes until crisp and golden. Serve immediately.

MELON

It is hard to say whether the fragrance, the flavour or the cool refreshment of a melon is the most enjoyable thing about it. There are many varieties and two distinct types: Musk melons (such as Ogen, Cantaloup, Tiger and Charentais), delicious and aromatic but soon past their prime, and winter melons (such as Casaba, Persian and Honeydew melons) which have little or no aroma but keep well, and also make good jam. Watermelons, available only in the summer, are in a class of their own. They are very large, usually oval fruit, with dark green lightly striped rind and dark pink succulent flesh. The dark brown or black seeds are very distinctive. The flesh is crisp and thirst-quenching but rapidly becomes pappy so serve watermelon very fresh and well chilled.

In Britain, all the melons available are imported and therefore expensive, so it is particularly important to choose good quality ripe, fresh fruit.

A musk melon should be firm and heavy for its size. A cantaloup should have a clean scar at the stem end; any roughness or stem left on is a sign that the melon was picked before it was mature and will lack flavour. A honeydew should show a slight yellowing of the skin. There should be no moist or soft spots, but if it is fully ripe, the melon will yield slightly if pressed gently between the hands, and will be fragrant.

A watermelon should have a bloom on the skin, and the underside, where it rested on the ground, should be yellowish, not white or green. The melon should sound hollow when tapped. If buying cut melon, the flesh should be deep pink without white streaks, and the seeds very dark.

Store fully-ripe melons in a cool, airy place or, in a tightly-closed plastic bag to avoid scenting other food, in the refrigerator. Keep slightly under-ripe melons in a warm room for a few days before refrigerating. Always remove melon from the refrigerator 30 minutes or so before serving, as it should be only slightly chilled for best flavour.

Ways to Use Melon

An unadorned wedge of ripe melon, eaten in the sun, can hardly be bettered, but melon is wonderfully versatile – an excellent accompaniment to many savoury foods and superb for dessert.

● Use it, alone or with vegetables, for salads; serve it as a sambal with curries; wrap cubes of cantaloup or honeydew in thin strips of ham and serve on toothpicks as a party savoury.

● Serve with a sprinkle of lemon or orange juice and ground ginger or mace for a refreshing breakfast.

● Dice it or cut it into balls and dress with lemon juice and chopped mint for a first course.

● Cut it into thin crescents and serve with prosciutto as a classic and beautiful way to start a meal.

● Garnish chicken, lamb or seafood salad with melon.

● Use small melon halves, scooped out, as containers for ice cream or fruit salad, or a large watermelon shell to hold prepared fruits on a buffet table. Use it in fruit cups and fruit salads.

● Cut a small, deep plug out of a ripe watermelon and pour in a little gin or rum every hour or so for a day; chill overnight and serve next day as a refresher that's definitely not for children.

To cut melon wedges: To serve a melon wedge ready to eat with a fork, scoop out the seeds with a spoon, then use a sharp knife to cut between flesh and rind, from end to end. Cut the flesh across into small blocks and pull these pieces out, alternating to left and right, to extend 2 cm (¾ in) or so beyond the edge of the rind. Decorate with a slice of orange and a maraschino cherry and serve with ground ginger.

To make melon balls: Halve musk melons and remove seeds; cut watermelon into large wedges or slices. Leave melon on shell and, holding it in one hand, press the open side of a melon baller firmly into the flesh until the rounded side touches it. Twist the baller to cut out a neat ball of flesh. Mix melon balls with other fresh fruits for a fruit salad dessert.

To vandyke a melon: Vandyking or cutting a saw-tooth edge is a good finish for melon halves. Mark the equator of the melon with a few toothpicks as a guide, if you wish. Place the point of a small, sharp knife on the equator and, holding the knife on the slant, push it in all the way to the centre. Starting at the bottom of the first cut, make another in the same way but slanting in the opposite direction. Make the third cut from the top of the second one and continue, alternating angles, all the way round. Gently pull and twist the melon apart and remove the seeds. If the halves are to be used as shells to hold food, remove most of the flesh with a sharp spoon, leaving a wall about 1 cm (½ in) thick. Cut a very thin slice from the base to make the melon half stand level on the plate. **See recipes.**

Melon Salad

Very good with duck or ham.

1 cantaloup melon; 1 honeydew melon; freshly ground black pepper; ½ tsp ground ginger; juice 1 lemon or lime.

Halve melons, scoop out seeds and peel. Cut flesh into small cubes and place in a bowl. Add a small grinding of pepper and sprinkle over ginger and lemon or lime juice. Toss melon to coat, then cover and chill. Serves 6–8.

Melon, Chicory and Grape Salad

A fresh combination of textures and flavours. Serve as a light first course.

6 small or 3 large heads chicory (endives), or 2 heads cos lettuce; 1 small cantaloup melon; 125 g/4 oz (1 cup) grapes.

DRESSING: *175 ml/6 fl oz (¾ cup) oil; 4 tbsp lemon juice; 1½ tbsp finely chopped fresh mint; 1 tbsp capers; salt and freshly ground black pepper.*

Cut chicory (endives) in quarters lengthways, then cut across in half if large. Treat lettuce the same way. Peel melon, quarter and remove seeds. Cut each quarter into 6 slices. Chill ingredients in refrigerator, then arrange melon alternately with endive on 6 salad plates. Divide grapes among salads. To make the dressing, add oil slowly to lemon juice in a small bowl, beating with a fork or whisk. Stir in mint and capers and season with salt and pepper. Spoon dressing over salads and serve at once. Serves 6.

Melon Rings with Strawberries

1 small honeydew or cantaloup melon, chilled; 250 g (8 oz) strawberries, chilled; caster sugar; lime or lemon wedges.

Cut melon into 4 thick slices, discarding ends and seeds. Peel slices and place each on an individual serving plate. Choose 4 best strawberries and set aside. Hull remainder, and sprinkle with sugar. Pile strawberries into centres of melon slices, place reserved strawberries on top to decorate and serve with lime or lemon wedges. Serves 4.
NOTE: Fresh raspberries may be substituted for strawberries.

MERINGUE

There are many variations of meringue – all based on egg white and sugar beaten to a stiff froth, then baked. They include small meringues, baked in a very slow oven until light and crisp. Glamorous vacherins, dainty petits fours and mountainous fluffy pie toppings are all favourites. Meringues are usually plain but a flavouring may be added such as chopped or ground nuts, chocolate pieces or coconut.

Meringue mixture can be shaped and used in many different ways. Small buttons or rosettes baked until dry and crisp may be joined together with whipped cream to make a delicious sweet for afternoon tea or dessert. These tiny meringues may also be used as a topping for desserts or cakes. Another popular way is to shape meringue with an oval dessertspoon or tablespoon, and these ovals may be joined with whipped cream to form an egg shape. Meringue is often made into a pie shell or basket – individual baskets are very popular, and these may be filled with fruit, whipped cream or any number of creamy desserts. Small shell meringues make a welcome change from biscuits (cookies) as an accompaniment to soft desserts.

A light meringue is often piled on to a baked, sweet pie or pudding and placed in a moderately hot oven just long enough to tint the meringue. It should be soft and marshmallow-like inside; the crust may be crisp or soft, depending on the treatment. See Lemon Meringue Pie (page 185) and Lime Meringue Pie (page 191).

Another favourite meringue is the Pavlova (see page 277), which, with whipped cream and tart-sweet passionfruit or strawberries, is a dessert sweet-tooths can never resist.

□ **To Prepare Meringue:** Egg whites for meringue should be at room temperature and beaten with a pinch of salt, cream of tartar, or a few drops of lemon juice. This may be done in a copper bowl with a wire whisk or a glass bowl and electric beaters. The slightest trace of yolk in the whites will inhibit their rising (yolks contain fat). The same holds true for bowl and beater, both must be totally free of fat or grease. It is best to wash the bowl and beater with hot water and dry them with a clean, fresh towel before using them to beat egg whites for meringue.

Part of the sugar should be added gradually at first, after the whites become foamy, then the remaining sugar is folded in. The meringue has been sufficiently whipped when the whites form soft peaks and cling to the beater in a mass. You have over-beaten if they look dry and stand in sharp, jagged peaks, and the mixture will probably fall when placed in the oven.

The oven temperature should be as low as possible. The point is to dry the meringue by getting all the moisture out of the mixture, rather than baking it. A temperature of 120°C/250°F, Gas Mark ½, is as high as it should go. Higher than this, the meringues brown too quickly, turn leathery, and collapse. Properly baked, a meringue is crisp, feather-light, the palest bisque in colour, almost white. If liked, meringues may be dusted lightly with caster sugar before baking for extra crispness.

Bake meringues for about 1 hour, although they may be left in the turned-off oven to crisp. Once they are completely cool, meringues keep for a long time in airtight containers. Excess moisture in the air makes them soggy, so it is best not to bake meringues on a very damp or rainy day or have anything steaming on the stove when meringues have been taken out of the oven and left to cool on wire racks.

The baking trays for meringues should either be lightly buttered, dusted with flour, and the excess flour tapped off, or they may be covered with non-stick cooking parchment. Baking trays coated with non-stick surfaces are also excellent.

Meringues

This basic meringue mixture may be used for tiny miniature meringues, joined together with whipped cream and set in paper cases, or used for different kinds of desserts, meringue baskets, swans etc.

3 egg whites; scant ⅛ tsp cream of tartar; 250 g/8 oz (1 cup) caster sugar.

Beat egg whites on very low speed of electric mixer until frothy. Add cream of tartar and beat on highest speed until peaks hold their shape. Gradually beat in 2 tbsp sugar and continue beating for 2–3 minutes. Add all remaining sugar at once and fold in quickly and lightly with a metal spoon. Pipe on to baking trays that have been lightly oiled and floured or lined with non-stick cooking parchment. Or shape meringue mixture with 2 spoons. Bake in a preheated very cool oven (120°C/250°F, Gas Mark ½) for 1 hour. Ease meringues from trays with spatula and leave in oven further 30 minutes or until dry. When cool store in an airtight container. Makes about 36.
VARIATIONS
Meringue Shell: Prepare Meringue mixture as above or Meringue Cuite (page 214). Spread or pipe over bottom and sides of a greased 20–23 cm (8–9 in) pie plate, building it up on the outside edge. Bake in a preheated very cool oven (120°C/250°F, Gas Mark ½) for 1–1½ hours or until surface is set and crusty but only just coloured. Loosen meringue shell from pie plate while still

warm, and cool before filling. The meringue will crisp as it cools. Use for cream pies. If liked the meringue may be shaped on a baking tray lined with non-stick cooking parchment. Mark an 18–20 cm (7–8 in) circle on the paper and use this as a guide, spreading or piping meringue inside circle, building up the outer edge. Bake as above.
Individual Meringue Shells: Prepare basic Meringue (see page 213) or Meringue Cuite (below). Line 2 baking trays with non-stick cooking parchment. Mark 8 cm (3 in) circles on paper, leaving at least 5 cm (2 in) space between circles. Spread or pipe meringue mixture inside circles, building up outer edges. Bake in a preheated very cool oven (120°C/250°F, Gas Mark ½) for 1–2 hours. Turn oven off, turn cases over and allow to cool in oven. Use as shells for fresh fruit salad with whipped cream, fruit fool, or other creamy desserts. Makes 12.

Meringue Cuite
(Cooked Meringue)
Egg whites and sifted icing (confectioners) sugar are beaten over hot water for this meringue. Its advantage is that it will stay thick and firm for some time after it is made. This is a slightly old-fashioned recipe, for with modern, efficient electric beaters it is possible to get the same result without heat. Icing (confectioners) sugar gives a smooth finish but when made in an electric mixer, caster sugar is perfectly satisfactory.

4 egg whites; 180 g/6 oz (1¼ cups) icing (confectioners) sugar or 310 g/10 oz (1¼ cups) caster sugar; pinch salt.

Put ingredients in a copper or heatproof glass bowl. Beat over gentle heat until very thick. Use for tiny meringues, meringue baskets, shells etc.

Meringues Chantilly
These are so called because they are filled with Crème Chantilly (whipped, sweetened, vanilla-flavoured cream, see page 88).

2 large egg whites; 125 g/4 oz (½ cup) caster sugar.
FILLING: *120 ml/4 fl oz (½ cup) double (heavy) cream; 1 tsp caster sugar; few drops vanilla essence (extract); chopped walnuts to finish (optional).*

Using a rotary beater or an electric mixer, beat egg whites until they form soft peaks. Sift 2 tbsp caster sugar over whites and beat again until mixture is stiff and shiny (**Fig 1 above**). Sift half the remaining sugar over whites and, using a large metal spoon, fold it in. To do this, cut gently down through mixture and lift some mixture up and over on to the top, repeating until whites and sugar are lightly mixed. Don't worry about mixing thoroughly; it is important not to overwork

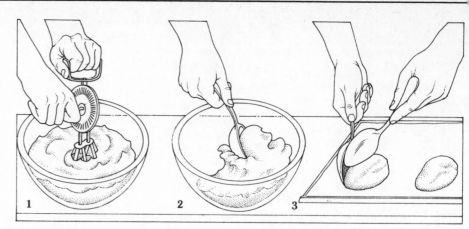

meringue or air bubbles will break down. Shaping meringues will mix whites and sugar a little more. Use 2 damp dessertspoons or tablespoons (depending on size you want meringues) to shape meringues. With one, scoop up a heaped spoonful of mixture (2). With other spoon, scoop meringue out on to a baking tray, that has been lightly greased and floured, or lined with non-stick cooking parchment, to form a half-egg shape (3). Neaten with a knife dipped in cold water. If preferred, meringue can be formed by piping, using a bag fitted with a large plain or rose nozzle.
Dredge with remaining sugar and bake in a preheated very cool oven (120°C/250°F, Gas Mark ½) for about 1 hour or until a delicate beige colour. Peel parchment off meringues, if used, or lift carefully off tray with a thin knife. Gently press base of each meringue, while still warm, to make a hollow. Replace upside-down on tray and return to oven for a further 30 minutes to complete cooking. Cool on a wire rack. An hour or two before required, whip cream with sugar and vanilla until stiff, and use to sandwich meringues together in pairs. The cream may be piped or spread on. Place in refrigerator until serving time. If you wish, sprinkle chopped walnuts on cream just before serving. Makes 12.

Fruit Meringue Pie
Make this with fresh raspberries, strawberries or other fresh or well-drained canned fruit such as plums or apricots.

4 egg whites; 250 g/8 oz (1 cup) caster sugar; 120 ml/4 fl oz (½ cup) double (heavy) cream; 180 g/6 oz (1 cup) sliced fresh or canned peaches; chopped pistachio nuts to decorate.

Line a baking tray with non-stick cooking parchment. Draw on it 2 circles 18 cm (7 in) in diameter. Make meringue mixture, with egg whites and all the sugar, as for Meringues Chantilly. Fit a large plain or rose nozzle into a piping (pastry) bag. Fill it with meringue

Making Meringues Chantilly

mixture. Pipe a ring of meringue round one circle just inside the line. Pipe on to outer edges of paper 8–12 baby rosettes with bases totalling the same width as meringue ring. Pipe remaining meringue mixture inside other circle and spread it evenly into a flat disc. Bake in a preheated very cool oven (120°C/250°F, Gas Mark ½) for 45 minutes to 1 hour or until crisp when tapped. Remove from oven. Lift off rosettes with a thin knife and place on a wire rack. Turn paper upside-down and carefully peel it off meringue ring and disc. (If you try to prise these pieces off the paper, they are likely to splinter.) Lift very carefully and place on a wire rack to cool.
Before serving, whip cream until stiff and fill a piping (pastry) bag fitted with a 1 cm (½ in) rose nozzle. Place meringue disc on a serving plate and pipe a ring of cream round edge. Set meringue ring on top and press down very gently. Arrange peach slices inside ring in concentric circles. Pipe a little cream on base of each rosette and arrange rosettes evenly spaced on the ring, pressing each down gently to secure. Pipe remaining cream round ring to decorate, and top with pistachios. Chill until serving time. Serves 8.

Meringue Pie Topping
3 egg whites; ¼ tsp cream of tartar; 5 tbsp sugar.

Beat egg whites until light and frothy. Add cream of tartar and continue beating until whites are stiff enough to hold a peak. Gradually beat in sugar and beat until meringue is stiff and glossy. Pile meringue lightly on cooled pie filling, spreading it until it touches edges of pastry (dough) to prevent meringue shrinking. Bake in a preheated hot oven (220°C/425°F, Gas Mark 7) until the top is brown, 5–6 minutes. For a more decorative effect, use a piping (pastry) bag with a rose nozzle to pipe rosettes of meringue over pie filling. Sufficient to top a 20–23 cm (8–9 in) pie.

MILK

Whole milk could be regarded as closest to a complete food since it contains all essential nutrients required by the human body, including proteins, vitamins and minerals, especially calcium. Milk or milk foods should be included in the daily diet. Children and adults enjoy drinking milk. There are many lovely milk drinks, but it can be used in forms other than as a drink. Delicious soups, sauces, custards, milk jellies, junkets, scones, cakes and many other dishes use milk as a major ingredient.

Milk should always be heated slowly and cooked at low temperatures.

To scald milk: When a recipe calls for scalded milk, it should be heated to just below boiling point and then removed from the heat. The required temperature is 82°C/180°F, or when tiny bubbles appear on the surface of the milk at the edge of the saucepan.

Types of Milk

Milk is available in many different forms, depending on the method of processing.

Fresh whole milk is available in packages, in bottles or cartons. It has been pasteurized to remove bacteria and is available in various grades.

Ordinary whole milk contains a minimum of 3% butterfat (milkfat).

Homogenized milk has the same percentage of ingredients as whole milk but no cream line, since homogenization breaks down the fat globules and distributes the cream throughout the milk.

Channel Island milk is produced by Guernsey and Jersey breeds and has a very visible cream line, yellow due to its carotene (vitamin A) content. It must have a minimum of 4% butterfat (milkfat).

Sterilized milk Homogenized milk is sterilized by heating at boiling point for 30 minutes. The length of this high temperature treatment causes the milk sugar – lactose – to caramelize, giving the milk its characteristic colour and flavour. Unopened, the milk is legally required to keep for at least 7 days without refrigeration, but several weeks is usual.

Fresh skim milk is packaged in cartons or bottles. It contains little milk fat, having about 0.1% of the total content, and is excellent for use by people on low fat diets. It should not, however, be used for babies except when given under medical advice. Use according to special recipes calling for skim milk. Refrigerate after opening and use within 3–4 days.

Fresh flavoured milk is whole milk that contains added flavouring agents and sugar; the sugar increases the energy content. Refrigerate after opening and use within 3–4 days.

UHT milk (ultra high temperature milk) undergoes a special treatment where very high temperatures are used during pasteurization for a very short time; this preserves proteins and vitamins while destroying bacteria. The milk is packaged in special containers and, unopened, has a long shelf life of about 5–6 months without refrigeration. It is best chilled before serving. Refrigerate after opening and use within 3–4 days. It can also be purchased flavoured and sweetened. Use unsweetened, unflavoured UHT milk in place of whole milk; however, the high temperature treatment alters the protein structure and destroys the enzymes, making UHT milk unsuitable for junket as it will not set.

Evaporated milk is whole milk evaporated to about 40% of its original volume. It is canned and has a very long shelf life. For the equivalent of full cream milk, add 3 parts water to 2 parts evaporated milk. Refrigerate after opening and when reconstituted, and use within 2 days. Use, undiluted, to enrich soups and sauces, or as a binding agent in meat loaves or meatballs. Or use as a topping on desserts and where specified in special recipes calling for evaporated milk.

Sweetened condensed milk is canned milk from which the water content is reduced during processing and about 40% sugar is added. The sugar acts as a preservative, and the milk will keep up to 1 week without refrigeration after opening and up to 3 weeks refrigerated. It is much sweeter than normal milk when reconstituted. Use 5 tbsp with water added to make 250 ml/8 fl oz (1 cup). Use in sweet sauces, pie fillings, and desserts which call for sweetened condensed milk.

Powdered full cream milk has a long shelf life. Reconstitute powder by adding water in the proportion specified on the packet or use 4 tbsp of the milk powder and add water to make up 250 ml/8 fl oz (1 cup). The milk should then be refrigerated and used within 2 days, and the powder stored in a dry airtight container after opening. It can be substituted for fresh whole milk in most recipes, following the proportion given for reconstituting. Refrigerate milk after reconstituting and use within 3–4 days.

Non-fat skim milk powder has a long shelf life. Reconstitute powder by adding water in the proportion as specified on the packet or use 2 tbsp milk powder and add water to make up 250 ml/8 fl oz (1 cup). It is unsuitable for babies except under medical advice, but is excellent for people on low fat diets. It may also be used in recipes calling for skim milk. Store powder in a dry, airtight container. Refrigerate milk after reconstituting, and use within 3–4 days.

Milk substitutes are whiteners used in tea or coffee. They are usually made from vegetable oil, coconut oil, or soya beans. Other additives such as sugar, artificial colour and emulsifiers are often added as well.

See also *Buttermilk*.

Vanilla Milk Shake

Milk shakes can be made using a blender, rotary beater or wire whisk. These help give the drinks a lovely frothy topping.

1 glass (approx 175 ml/6 fl oz/¾ cup) chilled milk; 1 scoop vanilla ice cream; ¼ tsp vanilla essence (extract); nutmeg or cinnamon to decorate (optional).

Combine ingredients and whisk, beat or blend together. Pour into a glass and sprinkle with a little nutmeg or cinnamon, if liked. Serves 1.

VARIATIONS

Chocolate Milk Shake: Substitute 2 tsp chocolate topping or syrup for vanilla; top with grated chocolate.

Strawberry Milk Shake: Use 30 g/1 oz (¼ cup) fresh puréed strawberries or 2 tsp strawberry topping instead of vanilla.

Banana Milk Shake: Substitute 1 mashed banana for vanilla.

Peanut Butter Milk Shake: Substitute 1 tbsp peanut butter for vanilla; sprinkle with nutmeg.

Mocha Milk Shake: Use 2 tsp instant coffee powder and 2 tsp chocolate syrup or topping instead of vanilla. Use coffee or chocolate ice cream instead of vanilla. Top with instant coffee powder.

Lemon Jelly Whip

250 ml/8 fl oz (1 cup) evaporated milk; 1 packet lemon jelly (gelatin) crystals; 250 ml/8 fl oz (1 cup) hot water; 4 tbsp lemon juice; 2 tbsp toasted slivered almonds.

Chill evaporated milk in the freezer for 2–3 hours. Dissolve jelly (gelatin) in hot water and allow to cool but not set. Whip evaporated milk until soft peaks form, then beat in lemon juice followed by jelly, Spoon milk mixture into 6 serving glasses and chill until set. Top with toasted slivered almonds. Serves 6.

M

Basic One Whip Ice Cream

*1 tsp gelatine; 2 tbsp hot water; 15 g/½ oz
(1 tbsp) butter, softened; 4 tbsp caster sugar;
1 tsp vanilla essence (extract); 1 × 375 ml/
12 oz can evaporated milk, chilled; ¼ tsp salt;
1 tbsp lemon juice.*

Soften gelatine in hot water, then stir briskly
over simmering water until thoroughly
dissolved. Add butter and allow to melt. Stir
in sugar and vanilla. Cool. Beat chilled
evaporated milk with salt and lemon juice
until thick. Gradually add cooled gelatine
mixture, beating constantly. Pour into ice
cream trays, cover and freeze. Makes 1.2–1.5
litres/2–2½ pints (5–6 cups).

VARIATIONS

Chocolate One Whip Ice Cream: Add
45 g/1½ oz (¼ cup) chocolate topping to
gelatine mixture.

Coffee Walnut One Whip Ice Cream: Dissolve
3 tsp instant coffee powder in gelatine
mixture. Fold in 30 g/1 oz (¼ cup) chopped
walnuts before freezing.

Vanilla Ice Cream

*1 tsp gelatine; 2 tbsp cold water; 120 ml/
4 fl oz (½ cup) boiling water; 90 g/3 oz (1 cup)
full cream milk powder; 4 tbsp caster sugar;
1 × 110 g/3½ oz can cream; 1 tsp lemon
juice; 1 tsp vanilla essence (extract).*

Soften gelatine by sprinkling on top of cold
water, add boiling water and stir until
dissolved. Whisk in powdered milk and sugar
and add cream, lemon juice and vanilla.
Pour into ice cream trays. Freeze until
beginning to set around the sides, then
remove to a chilled bowl and beat until
doubled in volume. Cover and freeze until
firm. Soften in the refrigerator for 30 minutes
before serving. Serves 6–8.

Whipped Dessert Topping

*45 g/1½ oz (½ cup) non-fat skim milk powder;
120 ml/4 fl oz (½ cup) well-chilled water;
2 tbsp lemon juice; 60 g/2 oz (¼ cup) caster
sugar; ½ tsp vanilla essence (extract).*

Mix together skim milk powder and water.
Beat for 3–4 minutes or until soft peaks
form. Add lemon juice and beat 3–4 minutes

longer or until stiff peaks form. Fold in sugar
and add vanilla. Serve immediately. Makes
about 500 ml/18 fl oz (2 cups).

Fluffy Topping

*1 × 375 ml/12 oz can evaporated milk,
chilled overnight; 1 tsp lemon juice; vanilla
essence (extract); 2 tbsp icing (confectioners)
sugar, sifted (optional).*

Pour milk into a large chilled bowl, add
lemon juice and whip using an electric mixer
or rotary beater until thick and doubled in
volume. Flavour to taste with vanilla and fold
in icing (confectioners) sugar, if using, just
before serving. Use as a topping on cakes or
desserts. Makes about 750 ml/1¼ pints
(3 cups).

MILLE-FEUILLES

The name literally means 'a thousand leaves',
and refers to the many flaky layers of crisp
puff pastry (paste) used to make this beautiful
French pastry. Puff pastry is layered alternately, usually with whipped cream and raspberry or strawberry jam. The top is glazed with
icing (frosting) or dusted with icing (confectioners) sugar and crushed pastry trimmings decorate the sides. Mille-feuilles are
assembled as one whole cake, then cut into
rectangles for serving. Crème Pâtissière (see
page 165) is sometimes used instead of
cream, with a thick fruit purée and a Chocolate Glaze (see page 73).

Savoury mille-feuilles make an elegant and
impressive entrée, and provide an unusual
variation on the traditionally sweet pastry.
Make your own puff pastry (paste), (see page
274), or if you prefer, use commercial frozen
puff pastry (paste). **See recipes.**

Mille-Feuilles

*1 × 375 g (12 oz) packet frozen puff pastry
(paste), thawed, or 1 quantity Puff Pastry
(page 274); 250 ml/8 fl oz (1 cup) double
(heavy) cream; 3 tbsp raspberry or strawberry
jam.*
ICING (FROSTING): *140 g/4½ oz (1 cup) icing
(confectioners) sugar, sifted; 1½ tbsp water;
2–3 drops vanilla essence (extract).*

Roll out pastry (paste) as thin as possible to a
rectangle about the size of a large baking tray.
Lay this over a dampened baking tray,
allowing pastry (paste) to come right up to
the edges. Prick well all over and chill for 15
minutes. Bake in a preheated moderately hot
oven (200°C/400°F, Gas Mark 6) for 5–10
minutes or until pale golden-brown. Using a
palette knife carefully turn pastry (paste) over.
Bake a further 5 minutes. Remove from oven
and cool on a wire rack. When cold, trim
edges and cut into 3 strips about 8 cm (3 in)
wide. Crush trimmings lightly. Whip cream
until it stands in soft peaks. Spread one strip

of pastry (paste) with half the jam then half
the cream. Lay a second strip on top and
press down lightly. Spread with remaining
jam and cream. Top with last pastry (paste)
strip. Press down lightly.
ICING (FROSTING): Mix icing (confectioners)
sugar with enough water to make a creamy
consistency. Add vanilla. Stir over hot water
until icing (frosting) is warm and glossy.
Spread top pastry (paste) layer with warm
icing (frosting) and press crushed pastry
trimmings around sides to decorate. Cut
across into slices 4 cm (1½ in) wide. Makes
about 8.

Savoury Mille-Feuilles

This dish is superb for a buffet party or at a
luncheon. The pastry (paste) may be baked
ahead of time, then reheated in the oven at
the last moment and the scrambled eggs
prepared but not cooked until required.

*1 × 375 g (12 oz) packet frozen puff pastry
(paste), thawed, or 1 quantity Puff Pastry
(page 274), rolled into 2 sheets; 1 egg,
beaten with 2 tsp water and pinch salt.*
FILLING: *8 eggs; salt; ½ tsp white pepper;
45 g/1½ oz (3 tbsp) butter; 250 g/8 oz (1 cup)
smoked fish (any kind), cooked and flaked,
or 125 g (4 oz) smoked salmon; 3 tbsp single
(light) cream; 2 tbsp mayonnaise; 2 tbsp
snipped chives; 1 tsp grated lemon rind.*
GARNISH: *paper-thin slices lemon; sprays of
fresh dill.*

Cut each sheet of ready-rolled puff pastry
(paste) in half, mark halves in a crisscross
pattern and place them on 4 dampened
baking trays. Chill 10 minutes, then brush
with egg wash and bake in a preheated hot
oven (230°C/450°F, Gas Mark 8) for about
12 minutes or until risen and brown. Remove
pastry from baking trays and cool on a wire
rack. If using frozen puff pastry (paste), divide
packet into 4 and roll out each piece into a
rectangle about 25 × 15 cm (10 × 6 in). Chill
for 30 minutes, then brush with egg wash
and bake and cool as above.
FILLING: Beat eggs, season with salt and
pepper and cook gently in butter, stirring
occasionally, until set. Add flaked fish and
allow to cool. Fold in remaining ingredients.
Choose 2 best pieces of pastry (paste) for
tops of mille-feuilles. Spoon egg mixture on
bases and top with pastry to make 2 mille-
feuilles. Garnish tops with lemon slices and
decorate with sprays of dill. Use a very sharp
knife to cut mille-feuilles into slices.
Serves 6–8.

MINCED (GROUND) MEAT

The versatility of minced meat – called
ground meat in America – is well known to
most cooks. Good quality minced meat is a
bargain, being nutritionally sound, full of
flavour and less expensive than many other

M

cuts. Ready-minced meat is available from your butcher or supermarket, or, if you prefer, order a specific cut, such as chuck steak or topside (top round) and mince it at home. Your butcher will also mince special cuts for you if you order ahead.

Beef Mince: Pure beef mince is usually sold graded according to the degree of fat included, and either finely or coarsely ground. Use fine ground, lean beef for meatballs, meat loaves, hamburgers and patties. Coarser ground mince is good for stews, pies and meat sauces. Some fat in mince is essential for flavour and to improve the texture of meat loaves, meatballs and similar dishes.

Hamburger Mince: Usually a combination of finely ground beef, lamb, pork or veal. It can be used for most recipes calling for finely minced meat.

Lamb Mince: Contains lamb meat only and is used in many Middle Eastern dishes.

Veal and Pork Mince: Finely ground veal and pork meat, with some pork fat for flavour. Use where recipes specify.

Always use minced meat within 24 hours of purchase, and store, loosely covered with foil, in the refrigerator. **See recipes.**

See also *Hamburger, Meatballs, Meat Loaf, Pie.*

Savoury Mince

2 onions, finely chopped; 1 tbsp dripping or oil; 500 g/1 lb (2 cups) minced (ground) steak; 1 tbsp flour; 1 tsp salt; freshly ground black pepper; 250 ml/8 fl oz (1 cup) beef stock (bouillon); 2 tsp Worcestershire sauce.

Fry onions in dripping or oil in a frying pan (skillet) until soft. Add minced (ground) steak, press with a fork and fry until browned and crumbly. Add flour, salt and pepper and mix well. Stir in beef stock (bouillon) and Worcestershire sauce and bring to the boil, stirring. Reduce heat, cover and simmer gently for 30 minutes. Serves 4.

Meat and Spinach Pinwheels

1 egg; ½ tsp salt; 30 g/1 oz (2 tbsp) butter, melted; 120 ml/4 fl oz (½ cup) milk; 250 g/8 oz (2 cups) self-raising flour, sifted; extra melted butter for brushing; 225 g/7½ oz (1 cup) cooked, well-drained, chopped spinach; 1 quantity Savoury Mince (above).

Place egg in mixing bowl with salt and beat lightly. Add melted butter and milk and stir in flour with a fork. Turn out on a floured board and knead lightly. The dough should be dry enough for easy handling. Roll out dough thinly to an oblong and brush lightly with a little melted butter. Spread spinach over, then cooled Savoury Mince, leaving a border of 2.5 cm (1 in) clear around edges. Roll dough up loosely, enclosing filling. Moisten

ends with water and pinch together. Using a sharp knife cut roll in slices 2 cm (¾ in) thick. Place in a greased ovenproof serving dish. Brush with melted butter and bake in a preheated moderately hot oven (200°C/400°F, Gas Mark 6) for 15–20 minutes or until golden-brown. Serves 4–6.
NOTE: A scone dough may be used for this recipe, if preferred. The rolls can be prepared in advance and kept, covered, in the refrigerator for a few hours before baking.

Beef and Bean Casserole

30 g/1 oz (2 tbsp) butter; 750 g/1½ lb (3 cups) minced (ground) steak; 1 onion, finely chopped; 1 × 425 g/14 oz can tomatoes, drained and chopped; 250 ml/8 fl oz (1 cup) hot beef stock; 125 g/4 oz (1 cup) pasta shells; ½ tsp dried mixed herbs; 1 tsp chilli powder; 2 tsp Worcestershire sauce; salt and freshly ground black pepper; 1 × 225 g/7½ oz can baked beans; finely chopped parsley to garnish.

Melt butter in a saucepan and brown meat and onion. Stir in all the remaining ingredients except baked beans and parsley. Mix together well and simmer gently for 30 minutes, stirring occasionally. Add more water if necessary. When meat is cooked and pasta is tender, stir in baked beans and heat through. Garnish with chopped parsley. Serves 6.

Swedish Meat Cakes

750 g/1½ lb (3 cups) minced (ground) beef; 1 tbsp capers; 1 egg, lightly beaten; 90 g/3 oz (½ cup) finely chopped, cooked beetroot; 1 small onion, finely chopped; 2 slices white bread, soaked in 1 tbsp milk; ¼ tsp Worcestershire sauce; ½ tsp salt; freshly ground black pepper; oil.

Combine all ingredients, except oil, in a bowl, mixing well with a fork. Form into 8 flat patties, handling lightly. Grease an ovenproof dish with a little oil and place patties in it. Bake in a preheated moderate

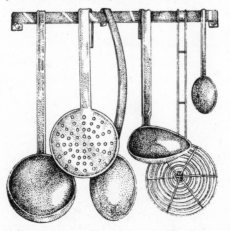

oven (180°C/350°F, Gas Mark 4) for 30 minutes, turning once to brown both sides. Serve with mashed potatoes and a salad or green vegetables. Serves 4.
NOTE: These little cakes may also be pan-fried. Allow 7–8 minutes on each side.

Beef Patties with Horseradish

1 kg/2 lb (4 cups) minced (ground) topside (top round); salt and freshly ground black pepper; 60 g/2 oz (1 cup) fresh breadcrumbs; 60 g/2 oz (4 tbsp) butter, softened; 3 tbsp grated horseradish; 3 tbsp snipped chives; oil; chopped parsley.
SAUCE: *2 tbsp lemon juice; 250 ml/8 fl oz (1 cup) stock; 120 ml/4 fl oz (½ cup) sour cream; salt.*

Season meat with salt and pepper and fork in breadcrumbs. Cream together butter, horseradish and chives and combine with meat. The mixture should be handled lightly; do not compact it too much. Shape into 6 generous patties. Heat a little oil in a heavy frying pan (skillet), just enough oil to grease the bottom, and cook patties over a high heat for about 5 minutes on each side. The centres should still be pink, but the outsides well browned. Transfer to a heated platter and keep warm while sauce is being made. Put lemon juice and stock into frying pan (skillet), and cook over a high heat until reduced to about half. Remove pan from heat and stir in sour cream. Heat gently, stirring in any brown bits. Season with salt. Pour sauce over patties and sprinkle with chopped parsley. Serves 6.

MINCEMEAT

This preserve consists of finely chopped fruit and spices with the addition of brandy, rum or other spirits. It is used as a filling for sweet mince pies which are part of the traditional Christmas fare in Britain. As the name suggests, the original recipes included cooked minced (ground) meat. Today suet is the only part of meat used, but in many recipes this is replaced with butter. There are numerous treasured family recipes, all differing slightly. For example, some contain oranges, others apples, some shredded suet, others butter.

A rich mincemeat is best allowed to mature for a month or two after it is made. The brandy helps preserve the mincemeat. If butter is the fat used, the mincemeat should be stored in a cool place, or in very hot weather in the refrigerator.

Mincemeat is usually made into mince pies or mince tarts. It also makes a delicious topping for ice cream, or it can be used in fruit slices and tea loaves. Make your own mincemeat or use the commercial variety in jars from supermarkets and delicatessens. **See recipes.**

Mincemeat

370 g/12 oz (2 cups) seedless raisins; 250 g/8 oz (1⅓ cups) mixed candied peel; 180 g/6 oz (1 cup) sultanas (golden raisins); 3 medium apples, peeled and cored; 60 g/2 oz (¼ cup) glacé (candied) cherries; 125 g/4 oz (1 cup) blanched almonds; 105 g/3½ oz (⅔ cup) dried apricots; 180 g/ 6 oz (1 cup) currants; 370 g/12 oz (2 cups) firmly packed brown sugar; grated rind and juice 1 lemon; grated rind 1 orange; 2 tsp mixed spice (ground allspice); ½ tsp nutmeg; 125–180 g/4–6 oz (½–¾ cup) butter, melted; 5 tbsp brandy or rum.

Finely chop or mince raisins, mixed peel, half the sultanas (golden raisins), the apples, cherries, almonds and apricots. Add remaining sultanas (golden raisins) and currants. Stir in brown sugar, lemon rind, and juice, orange rind, spices, butter and brandy or rum. Mix well and put into a large jar. Cover and chill. Stir every day for a week. Mincemeat can be kept for a few weeks in the refrigerator. Makes about 1.5 kg/3 lb (6 cups).

NOTE: Brandy can be replaced with the juice of 1 orange, in which case the mixture should not be made in advance.

English Mincemeat

(with suet)

250 g/8 oz (1⅓ cups) each currants, sultanas (golden raisins), seedless raisins and mixed candied peel; 250 g (8 oz) cooking apples, peeled and cored; 125 g/4 oz (1 cup) blanched almonds, chopped; 280 g/9 oz (1½ cups) firmly packed brown sugar; 125 g/4 oz (generous ¾ cup) shredded suet; ½ tsp nutmeg; ½ tsp cinnamon; grated rind and juice 1 lemon; 120 ml/4 fl oz (½ cup) brandy or rum.

Finely chop currants, sultanas (golden raisins), raisins, mixed peel and apples. Add nuts, sugar, suet, spices and lemon rind and juice and mix all ingredients thoroughly. Cover mincemeat and leave to stand for 2 days. Add brandy or rum, stir well and put into jars. Cover and allow to mature for at least 2 weeks before using. Makes about 1.25 kg/2½ lb (5 cups).

Mince Pies

90 g/3 oz (6 tbsp) butter; 60 g/2 oz (¼ cup) caster sugar; 1 egg; 180 g/6 oz (1½ cups) flour; ½ tsp baking powder; beaten egg to glaze; 250 g/8 oz (1 cup) Mincemeat (above); sifted icing (confectioners) sugar.

Cream butter with sugar. Add egg and beat well. Sift flour and baking powder and stir into creamed mixture. Knead lightly on floured board. Wrap pastry (dough) in plastic wrap and chill for 1 hour. Roll out thin and cut into rounds to fit lightly greased patty tins (pans). Cut same number of smaller circles to fit tops of pies. Moisten edges with beaten egg and put 1 heaped teaspoonful mincemeat into each. Make a small slit in each pastry (dough) lid or cut with a small star cutter. Top each filled pie with lid and press edges of pastry (dough) well to seal. Glaze with beaten egg. Bake in a preheated moderate oven (180°C/350°F, Gas Mark 4) for 20–30 minutes or until pale golden-brown. Remove from oven and dust with sifted icing (confectioners) sugar. Makes about 12.

Mincemeat Tea Loaf

This loaf slices beautifully and when wrapped and stored in an airtight container will keep for several weeks. It also freezes well.

250 g/8 oz (2 cups) flour; ½ tsp salt; ½ tsp bicarbonate of soda (baking soda); 1 tsp baking powder; 125 g/4 oz (½ cup) butter; 125 g/4 oz (⅔ cup) firmly packed brown sugar; 2 eggs; 3 tbsp single (light) cream; 1 tsp lemon juice; 250 g/8 oz (1 cup) Mincemeat (left); 60 g/2 oz (½ cup) coarsely chopped walnuts or pecans.

Sift flour, salt, soda and baking powder. Cream butter with sugar until light and fluffy. Add eggs one at a time, beating well. Mix in cream and lemon juice. Gently fold in dry ingredients; do not overmix. The batter should be stiff. Stir in mincemeat and nuts. Spoon into a greased 21 × 15 cm (8½ × 6 in) loaf tin (pan), pressing with the back of a spoon to pack mixture solidly in tin (pan). Bake in a preheated moderate oven (180°C/350°F, Gas Mark 4) for 50–60 minutes or until a skewer inserted in centre comes out clean. Cool on a wire rack before slicing.

Mincemeat Squares

180 g/6 oz (1 cup) firmly packed brown sugar; 150 g/5 oz (1½ cups) rolled oats; 180 g/6 oz (1½ cups) flour, sifted; ½ tsp salt; 180 g/6 oz (¾ cup) butter; 500 g/1 lb (2 cups) Mincemeat (left); 1 egg, beaten.

Combine brown sugar, rolled oats, flour and salt and mix well. Rub (cut) in butter until mixture resembles coarse breadcrumbs. Spread half the mixture in a 28 × 19 cm (11 × 7½ in) Swiss roll tin (jelly roll pan). Cover with mincemeat, spread remaining crumb mixture over the top. Gently brush with beaten egg. Bake in a preheated moderately hot oven (200°C/400°F, Gas Mark 6) for 20–25 minutes. Allow to cool in tin (pan), then cut into squares, bars or diamond shapes. Makes about 20.

Mincemeat Tart

280 g/9 oz (1½ cups) seedless raisins; 3 medium apples, peeled and cored; ½ orange, including rind; ½ lemon, including rind; 120 ml/4 fl oz (½ cup) cider vinegar; 280 g/9 oz (1½ cups) firmly packed brown sugar; ½ tsp salt; ½ tsp cinnamon; ½ tsp nutmeg; ½ tsp ground cloves; 1 × 20 cm (8 in) Rich Shortcrust Pastry Shell, baked (page 274).

TOPPING: *350 ml/12 fl oz (1½ cups) double (heavy) cream; 1 tbsp icing (confectioners) sugar.*

Coarsely chop raisins, apples, orange and lemon. Place in an enamel-lined saucepan, add vinegar and heat to boiling point. Reduce heat and simmer for 10 minutes. Add sugar, salt, cinnamon, nutmeg and cloves and simmer 15 minutes more. Let cool. Fill pastry shell (pie shell) with cooled mincemeat. Whip cream, sweeten with icing (confectioners) sugar and pile over mincemeat filling. Serves 6–8.

NOTE: To serve hot, place filled tart in a preheated moderate oven (180°C/350°F, Gas Mark 4) for 15 minutes and hand whipped cream separately.

MINCE PIES

See recipe on this page.

MINESTRONE

This hearty Italian soup has a fairly broad interpretation since it varies from region to region and cook to cook. In general, the name, *minestrone*, applies to a very thick vegetable soup containing a variety of fresh

and dried vegetables, further thickened with some form of pasta or rice. Minestrone are never thin, watery soups and are sometimes so thick they are eaten rather than drunk. Grated Parmesan cheese is nearly always served with minestrone, and in Genoa, the unique basil sauce Pesto allo Genovese (see page 272) is stirred into the soup just before serving.

Minestrone is almost a meal in itself; serve with plenty of crusty bread, followed with a crisp green salad and fruit. **See recipes.**

Minestrone Genovese

125 g/4 oz (½ cup) dried haricot (navy) beans, soaked overnight and drained; 2 litres/3½ pints (8 cups) water; 2 large aubergines (eggplant), peeled and diced; 500 g/1 lb (2 cups) tomatoes, peeled and chopped; 1 small cabbage, very finely shredded; 2–3 small courgettes (zucchini), diced; 180 g/6 oz (1½ cups) mushrooms, sliced; 2–3 tbsp olive oil; 90 g/3 oz (½ cup) vermicelli; 2 tbsp Pesto alla Genovese (page 272); grated Parmesan cheese to serve.

Put beans in a saucepan, cover with fresh water and bring to the boil. Simmer for about 1 hour or until nearly tender. Drain beans and return to pan with the 2 litres/3½ pints (8 cups) water. Add all the vegetables and the olive oil and bring to the boil. Simmer until vegetables are almost cooked, then add vermicelli and cook a further 5 minutes or until tender. Stir in pesto. Serve with plenty of freshly grated Parmesan cheese handed separately. Serves 6–8.

Minestrone Borghese

90 g/3 oz (6 tbsp) butter; 125 g (4 oz) cooked ham, thinly sliced; 1 onion, finely chopped; 1 clove garlic, crushed; 2 tomatoes, peeled, seeded and chopped; 3 sticks celery, diced; 1 tsp salt; ¼ tsp white pepper; 2 litres/3½ pints (8 cups) chicken stock; 4 potatoes, peeled and diced; 180 g/6 oz (1½ cups) elbow macaroni or other pasta; 4 courgettes (zucchini), peeled and sliced; 2 red peppers, cored, seeded, and sliced; 2 sprigs fresh basil or 1 tsp dried; grated Parmesan cheese to serve.

Melt butter in a saucepan and cook ham gently until golden. Add onion and garlic and cook until translucent. Add tomatoes, cover and simmer for about 10 minutes. Stir in celery and season with salt and pepper. Add stock and bring to the boil, then reduce heat and simmer for 30 minutes. Mix in potatoes and cook for 15 minutes longer. Add pasta. Cook until nearly tender, then add courgettes (zucchini), red peppers and basil and cook for a further 10 minutes. Serve with grated Parmesan cheese. Serves 8.

Minestrone alla Casalinga
(Home-Style Minestrone)

125 g/4 oz (½ cup) dried haricot (navy) beans, soaked overnight and drained; 3 tbsp oil; 2 onions, chopped; 2 cloves garlic, crushed; 2–3 rashers (slices) bacon, rind removed and chopped; 4 tomatoes, peeled, seeded and chopped; 2 litres/3½ pints (8 cups) beef stock; 1 tsp chopped fresh marjoram; ½ tsp chopped fresh thyme; 2 carrots, diced; 2 potatoes, peeled and diced; 1 small turnip, diced; 1–2 sticks celery, finely sliced; 250 g/8 oz (3 cups) shredded cabbage; 60 g/2 oz (½ cup) macaroni pieces or small pasta shells; 2 tbsp chopped fresh parsley; salt and freshly ground black pepper; grated Parmesan cheese.

Put beans in a saucepan, cover with fresh water and bring to the boil. Reduce heat and simmer for 1 hour or until nearly tender. Drain. Heat oil in a large saucepan, add onions, garlic and bacon and sauté for a few minutes. Add tomatoes, drained beans, stock, marjoram and thyme and bring to the boil. Cover, reduce heat and simmer for 2 hours. Stir in carrots and cook 10 minutes, then add potatoes and turnip. Cook for a few more minutes, then add celery, cabbage and pasta. Cook until pasta and all the vegetables are tender. Stir in parsley, salt, pepper and 2–3 tbsp Parmesan cheese. Pass around a bowl of Parmesan cheese when serving soup. Serves 8–10.

MINT

There are over 40 varieties of mint. Peppermint and spearmint are perhaps the best known. The round-leafed common or garden mint, the one found in most gardens, originally grew as a wild mint, and is among the best of culinary mints. Spearmint (the name refers to the arrowhead shape of the leaf) is the most widely grown and is sold commercially.

Mint is one of the easiest herbs to grow; it thrives in most temperate climates, in sun or shade, but likes plenty of water. The leaves can be dried, hung in bunches or laid on a rack, so that the air circulates. Once dried, the leaves should be stripped from the stems and stored in an airtight wrapping or container or in the freezer.

A clean-tasting herb, mint gives a tangy freshness to all dishes in which it is used. It doesn't go well with other herbs or with garlic (although a notable exception is Tabouleh, the lovely parsley and mint salad made with Burghul wheat). However, it does go well with orange – try it in Duckling with Orange (see page 111) or in orange salad – and with lamb or mutton, particularly the fatty cuts. Mint doesn't really do anything for other meats, but it's good with vegetables like fresh beans,

peas and potatoes, lentils, tomatoes, aubergines (eggplant), carrots and mushrooms.

The French rarely, if ever, use mint flavouring, except oil of peppermint in sweets (candies), but in other countries of the old world it is one of the most commonly used herbs. It goes into soups and sauces, omelettes and salads, lentil purées and even tea. In India it is used in some curries (particularly potato or lamb curry). It's also used in the cooling chutneys that accompany hot spicy dishes.

In Middle Eastern cuisine, mint is one of the most frequently used herbs. It flavours salads, such as a cucumber and yogurt salad; soups; the Lebanese kibbeh, and vegetable dishes. The British like to add a sprig of mint to freshly cooked peas or new potatoes, and to serve a mint sauce or jelly with lamb or mutton.

Mint is one herb that can be used in sweet dishes as well – many fruit salads are better for the addition of finely chopped mint. Pineapple, mint and Kirsch make a delightful combination. And you can garnish drinks with leaves of mint, or drop them into iced tea. **See recipes.**

Mint Tea Place fresh or dried mint leaves in a teapot (preferably glass) and pour boiling water over. Leave to infuse 4–5 minutes before serving with a lemon slice and sugar to taste.

Mint Sauce The sharp flavour of mint sauce helped counteract the fattiness of roast mutton in the days when mutton was more easily available than lamb. **See recipes.**

Minted Green Peas

500 ml/18 fl oz (2 cups) water; pinch salt; 2 sprigs fresh mint; 1 tsp sugar; 1 kg/2 lb (6 cups) shelled peas; 30 g/1 oz (2 tbsp) butter; 1 tbsp chopped fresh mint.

Bring water to the boil, add salt, mint sprigs and sugar, and stir in peas. Cook uncovered for 15 minutes or until tender. Drain peas well, refresh under cold water and return to pan with butter and chopped mint. Shake peas over a low heat until butter has completely melted. Serves 6.

Minted Potatoes en Papillote

New potatoes seasoned with butter and mint are cooked sealed in paper to capture the wonderful natural flavours.

1 kg (2 lb) small new potatoes; 60 g/2 oz (4 tbsp) butter; 6–8 leaves fresh mint, finely chopped, or 1 tsp dried chervil; salt.

Scrub potatoes. Fold a large piece of greaseproof (waxed) paper in half, then cut into a heart shape. Place potatoes on one side of paper with the butter and mint or chervil. Season with salt. Fold other side of paper over and seal edges completely by folding edge over and over in a twist. Place on a baking tray and cook in a preheated moderately hot oven (190°C/375°F, Gas Mark 5) for about 40 minutes. Take to the table in the bag. Serves 6.

Mint Julep

A refreshing drink to serve on a hot day.

10–12 sprigs fresh young mint; 1 tsp sugar; 1 tbsp hot water; crushed ice; 4 tbsp brandy, whisky, gin or bourbon; fresh fruit in season.

Crush half the mint with the sugar using a spoon. Add water and mix until all mint flavour is extracted. Take a tumbler or a large balloon wine glass, almost fill with crushed ice and push remaining mint in, stalks downwards. Strain crushed mint mixture into glass and pour in spirit. Decorate top of the ice with small pieces of fruit in season, choosing the most colourful available. Put in a couple of drinking straws and serve. If using brandy you may add just a dash of rum on top. Serves 1.

Cucumber and Mint Refresher

45 g/1½ oz (⅓ cup) seeded and chopped cucumber; 1 tbsp roughly chopped fresh mint leaves; 150 ml/¼ pint (⅔ cup) chilled milk; 150 ml/¼ pint (⅔ cup) plain yogurt; salt and freshly ground black pepper.

Put cucumber and mint into goblet of a blender with enough milk to cover blades. Blend about 30 seconds at high speed. Add remaining ingredients, blend for a few seconds and serve. Serves 2.

Mint Sauce

20 g/⅔ oz (½ cup) fresh mint leaves; 1 tbsp caster sugar; 2 tbsp boiling water; 3 tbsp wine vinegar; pinch salt.

Finely chop the mint leaves with 1 tsp of sugar. Place in sauce boat or bowl and add boiling water. This will set the colour. Stir in remaining sugar, vinegar and salt and let mint sauce stand for 1 hour before serving to let flavours develop. Makes about 120 ml/4 fl oz (½ cup).

MIXED SPICE

Also known as pudding spice, a little jar of this spice-mix is very convenient for those who are addicted to spicy food or make rich fruit cakes or puddings. It is a mixture of the sweet spices used in English cookery – cinnamon, cloves and nutmeg – but it may also contain Jamaica pepper or allspice and sometimes coriander. Americans may substitute apple pie spice or ground allspice.

See *Fruit Cake* and *Christmas Pudding.*

MOCHA

A strongly-flavoured coffee, originally grown in the Yemen.

The word 'mocha' is also used to describe cakes, desserts, biscuits (cookies), etc., flavoured with coffee. It is often applied as well to a mixture of coffee and chocolate, whether it is used as a beverage or flavouring. **See recipes.**

Mocha Chiffon Pie

250 ml/8 fl oz (1 cup) milk; 1 tbsp gelatine; 60 g/2 oz (⅓ cup) semi-sweet chocolate; 180 g/6 oz (¾ cup) sugar; ¼ tsp salt; 4 eggs, separated; 1 tsp vanilla essence (extract); 2 tbsp instant coffee powder; 1 × 23 cm (9 in) Sweet Rich Shortcrust Pastry Shell, baked (page 274).

Put milk in top part of double saucepan (double boiler). Sprinkle gelatine on milk and soften for 5 minutes. Add chocolate and stir over medium heat until melted and gelatine has dissolved. Beat 60 g/2 oz (¼ cup) sugar and the salt with the egg yolks. Beat in chocolate milk and pour back into double saucepan (double boiler). Put over simmering water and cook, stirring constantly, until mixture is thickened and coats a metal spoon. Remove from heat and add vanilla and coffee. Chill until thickened but not firm. Beat egg whites until foamy. Gradually add remaining sugar, beating until stiff but not dry. Fold into gelatine mixture. Pile lightly into pastry (pie) shell and chill until firm. Serve plain, or spread with sweetened whipped cream. If desired, sprinkle with chocolate. Serves 6–8.

Mocha Sundae Sauce

125 g/4 oz (⅔ cup) semi-sweet chocolate; 500 g/1 lb (2 cups) sugar; 1 × 375 ml/ 12 oz can evaporated milk; pinch salt; 2 tbsp instant coffee powder; 1 tsp vanilla essence (extract).

Melt chocolate in double saucepan (double boiler) over boiling water; stir in sugar. Add evaporated milk and salt. Cover and cook very gently over boiling water for 15–20 minutes. Beat until smooth. Stir in coffee and vanilla. Makes 750 ml/1¼ pints (3 cups).

Mocha Chocolate

60 g/2 oz (⅓ cup) semi-sweet chocolate; 175 ml/6 fl oz (¾ cup) water; 75 g/2½ oz (⅓ cup) sugar; 600 ml/1 pint (2½ cups) milk; 175 ml/6 fl oz (¾ cup) double-strength black coffee; 1 tsp vanilla essence (extract).

Put chocolate, water and sugar in saucepan and bring to the boil, stirring until chocolate has melted. Boil for 2 minutes, stirring constantly. Reduce heat and gradually stir in milk. Add coffee and heat to scalding (do not boil). Stir in vanilla. Makes 1 litre/1¾ pints (4 cups).

Frozen Mocha Mousse

125 g/4 oz (⅔ cup) semi-sweet chocolate; 5 tbsp water; 180 g/6 oz (¾ cup) sugar; pinch salt; 3 egg yolks; 1 tbsp instant coffee powder; 1 tsp vanilla essence (extract); 500 ml/18 fl oz (2 cups) double (heavy) cream, whipped.

Put chocolate and water in saucepan. Bring to the boil over low heat, stirring until chocolate has melted. Add sugar and salt, reduce heat and simmer for 3 minutes, stirring. Gradually stir into well-beaten egg yolks. Add coffee and cool. Fold in vanilla and cream. Pour into ice cream trays and freeze until firm. Serves 6.

Mocha Rum Punch

500 ml/18 fl oz (2 cups) hot milk; 250 ml/8 fl oz (1 cup) hot strong black coffee; 4 tbsp drinking chocolate powder; 120 ml/4 fl oz (½ cup) rum; 120 ml/4 fl oz (½ cup) double (heavy) cream, whipped with 1 tbsp sugar.

Beat together milk, coffee, chocolate and rum. Fold in sweetened whipped cream. Serve at once. Serves 6.

MOCK CREAM

A mixture that is similar to fresh cream and can be used as a substitute in certain dishes. Mock cream fillings are especially good for buns and cakes. **See recipes.**

Mock Cream

250 ml/8 fl oz (1 cup) milk; 1 tbsp cornflour (cornstarch); pinch salt; 45 g/1½ oz (3 tbsp) butter; 1 tbsp caster sugar; ½ tsp vanilla essence (extract).

Bring all but 2 tbsp milk to the boil in a heavy saucepan. Mix cornflour (cornstarch) and salt well with reserved cold milk and add to boiling milk. Cook for 3 minutes, stirring, then allow to cool. Beat butter, sugar and vanilla to a cream. Take skin off top of cold milk mixture and add milk a spoonful at a time to butter mixture. Beat well until all is incorporated and mixture is consistency of whipped cream. Makes about 350 ml/ 12 fl oz (1½ cups).

Mock Whipped Cream

1 tsp gelatine; 3 tbsp water; 125 g/4 oz (½ cup) butter; 125 g/4 oz (½ cup) sugar; pinch salt; vanilla or lemon essence (extract); ¼ tsp cream of tartar.

Soften gelatine in 3 tbsp water then stir over simmering water until dissolved. Place butter, sugar, salt and flavouring in a bowl. Beat slightly, then add cream of tartar followed by dissolved gelatine. Whip well for about 10 minutes or until mixture is like whipped cream. Use as a filling for puffs, sponges and buns. Makes about 500 ml/18 fl oz (2 cups).

Washed Mock Cream

125 g/4 oz (½ cup) butter; 125 g/4 oz (½ cup) sugar; vanilla essence (extract).

Cream butter with sugar until light and fluffy (this may be done by hand or with an electric beater). Pour in about 250 ml/8 fl oz (1 cup) cold water, give a light beat, then pour off water. Beat again, pour on more water, beat lightly then pour off water. This is repeated until mixture is light and fluffy and there are no sugar grains left in the cream. Flavour with vanilla. Use to fill cakes, buns, etc. Makes about 350 ml/12 fl oz (1½ cups).

MOLASSES

A dark heavy syrup, called treacle in England, which is a by-product of the various boiling-down processes used to produce sugar finally from sugar cane. There are three main types: light, unsulphured molasses, which is the syrup separated from young sugar canes; dark, sulphured molasses, a direct by-product of sugar manufacture; and blackstrap molasses, a dark, bitter syrup which is the residue of a third boiling process to extract most sugar crystals.

Light molasses, although used in cooking, is more often served over waffles, pancakes, muffins or ice cream as a table syrup. Dark molasses is used as an ingredient in recipes,

while blackstrap molasses is a popular health food.

Molasses is used in making some of the great traditional dishes of the U.S.A., such as Boston Baked Beans (see page 318) and Indian Pudding (below) from New England. Molasses will keep after opening for up to 2 months if tightly covered in the refrigerator. **See recipes.**

Molasses Johnnycake

125 g/4 oz (1 cup) flour, sifted; 3 tsp baking powder; 1 tsp salt; 150 g/5 oz (1 cup) yellow cornmeal (polenta); 1 egg, beaten; 4 tbsp dark treacle (molasses); 250 ml/8 fl oz (1 cup) milk; 60 g/2 oz (4 tbsp) butter, melted.

Sift flour, baking powder and salt into a bowl. Mix in cornmeal. Combine egg, treacle (molasses) and milk, and stir into dry mixture. Blend in melted butter. Pour into greased 20 cm (8 in) square tin (pan). Bake in a preheated hot oven (200°C/400°F, Gas Mark 6) for 25–30 minutes.

Barbecue Sauce

180 g/6 oz (½ cup) dark treacle (molasses); 120 ml/4 fl oz (½ cup) mild prepared mustard; 120 ml/4 fl oz (½ cup) cider vinegar.

Mix ingredients together well and heat gently until just warm. Makes 350 ml/12 fl oz (1½ cups).

Indian Pudding

1–1.2 litres/1¾–2 pints (4–5 cups) milk; 50 g/1⅔ oz (⅓ cup) yellow cornmeal (polenta); 280 g/9 oz (¾ cup) dark treacle (molasses); 125 g/4 oz (½ cup) butter; 1 tsp salt; 1 tsp ground ginger; 3 tbsp sugar; 1 egg, beaten; 90 g/3 oz (½ cup) raisins; ½ tsp cinnamon.

Place 1 litre/1¾ pints (4 cups) of the milk in the top of a double saucepan (double boiler) over direct heat and bring to the boil. Stir in cornmeal. Place over boiling water and cook, stirring, for about 15 minutes. Stir in treacle (molasses) and cook for a further 5 minutes. Remove from heat and mix in butter, salt, ginger, sugar, egg, raisins and cinnamon. Pour batter into a well-greased baking dish. If you would like the pudding to have a soft

centre pour over the remaining milk. Bake in a preheated moderate oven (160°C/325°F, Gas Mark 3) for 1½–2 hours. Serve hot with whipped cream. Serves 8.

Molasses Pancake Sauce

180 g/6 oz (½ cup) dark treacle (molasses); 370 g/12 oz (1 cup) honey; 370 g/12 oz (1 cup) golden (light corn) syrup; 125 g/4 oz (½ cup) butter; ¼ tsp salt; 1 tsp vanilla essence (extract), or 2 tsp lemon juice.

Place all ingredients except vanilla or lemon juice in a heavy saucepan. Heat gently, stirring occasionally, until mixture is well combined and hot but below boiling point. Remove from heat and stir in vanilla or lemon juice. Serve poured over pancakes. Makes about 500 ml/18 fl oz (2 cups).

MOUSSAKA

Moussaka is made in many Mediterranean countries, each with a slight variation. But the main ingredients remain the same – a vegetable, usually aubergine (eggplant), minced (ground) lamb (or beef) and a custard-like topping which can be a Béchamel sauce, sour cream or plain yogurt flavoured with cheese, and egg beaten into the mixture to give the characteristic texture. **See recipes.**

Moussaka

1 large aubergine (eggplant), thickly sliced; salt; 2 tbsp olive oil; 1 large onion, chopped; 1 clove garlic, finely chopped; 500 g/1 lb (2 cups) minced (ground) lamb or beef; 1 tsp flour; 175 ml/6 fl oz (¾ cup) beef stock; freshly ground black pepper; 500 g (1 lb) tomatoes, peeled and sliced, or 1 × 470 g/15 oz can tomatoes, drained and sliced; 2–3 tbsp grated Parmesan cheese.
SAUCE: 30 g/1 oz (2 tbsp) butter; 2 tbsp flour; 300 ml/½ pint (1¼ cups) milk; salt and freshly ground black pepper; 180 g/6 oz (1½ cups) grated Cheddar cheese; 2 egg yolks, beaten.

Score aubergine (eggplant) slices lightly, place in a dish and sprinkle liberally with salt. Cover with a plate and leave for several hours. Heat 1 tbsp oil in frying pan (skillet) and gently fry onion and garlic until golden. Add meat and flour and stir for a few minutes, then pour in stock. Season with salt and pepper. Cook gently for a few minutes, stirring constantly. Turn into a greased ovenproof dish. Place tomatoes on top of meat mixture. Drain aubergine (eggplant) slices, rinse well and dry on paper towels. Heat remaining oil in pan in which meat was cooked and fry aubergine (eggplant) slices until golden on both sides. Drain and place on top of tomato slices.
SAUCE: Melt butter in a saucepan, stir in flour and cook over a gentle heat, stirring, for 2

minutes. Add milk and stir until sauce boils and thickens. Season with salt and pepper, then stir in cheese until melted. Remove from heat and whisk in egg yolks.

Pour sauce over aubergine (eggplant) slices in casserole and sprinkle with the Parmesan. Bake in a preheated moderately hot oven (190°C/375°F, Gas Mark 5) for about 40 minutes or until top is golden. Serves 8–10.

VARIATION

Moussaka with Yogurt Topping: Prepare moussaka as above but replace sauce with the following mixture: beat together 2 eggs, blend in 2 tbsp flour, and whisk in 250 ml/8 fl oz (1 cup) plain yogurt.

Potato Moussaka

A popular Greek variation of moussaka. Good eaten hot or cold.

4 tbsp cooking oil; 750 g (1½ lb) potatoes, peeled and finely sliced; 1 large onion, finely chopped; 1 kg/2 lb (4 cups) minced (ground) beef or lamb; 1 tbsp chopped fresh oregano, or 1 tsp dried; 2 tbsp tomato purée (paste); 1 tsp Worcestershire sauce; 2 cloves garlic, crushed; salt and freshly ground black pepper; 4 tbsp grated Parmesan cheese.
SAUCE: *30 g/1 oz (2 tbsp) butter; 2 tbsp flour; 300 ml/½ pint (1¼ cups) milk; 1 egg, lightly beaten; salt and freshly ground black pepper.*

Heat 3 tbsp of oil in a frying pan (skillet) and cook potatoes for 2 minutes on each side; it will be necessary to cook these in 2 or 3 batches. Heat remaining oil in another frying pan (skillet) or a saucepan and fry onion gently for about 5 minutes. Add meat, oregano, tomato purée (paste), Worcestershire sauce, garlic, salt and pepper to the onion and cook gently for 15 minutes, stirring occasionally. Line a 2 litre/3½ pint (8 cup) casserole with most of potato slices. Put half the meat mixture in the casserole, cover with a layer of remaining potatoes and add rest of meat. Sprinkle over cheese. SAUCE: Melt butter in a saucepan, blend in flour and cook for 1 minute, then add milk gradually, stirring over a moderate heat until sauce thickens. Remove from heat. Add egg and season with salt and pepper.

Pour sauce over contents of casserole and cover with a lid. Cook in a preheated moderate oven (180°C/350°F, Gas Mark 4) for 45 minutes. Serves 8–10.

MOUSSE

The French name for foam or froth. A mousse is a rich, airy mixture which depends on whisked egg white, whipped cream, or both, for its lightness and velvety texture. A mousse can be sweet or savoury; hot, cold or frozen. It can be unmoulded for serving or

served in the individual pots or larger dish in which the mousse is set. **See recipes**.

See also *Apricot Mousse* and *Chocolate Mousse* (pages 12 and 74).

Salmon Mousse

1 tbsp gelatine; 4 tbsp cold water; 2 tsp sugar; 1 tsp salt; 1 tsp dry mustard; 4 tbsp white vinegar; 500 g/1 lb (2 cups) drained, flaked, canned red salmon; 125 g/4 oz (1 cup) finely diced celery; 2 tsp capers; 120 ml/4 fl oz (½ cup) double (heavy) cream, whipped; fresh dill or tiny lettuce leaves to garnish.
SOUR CREAM SAUCE: *120 ml/4 fl oz (½ cup) sour cream; 1 tsp grated onion; ½ tsp salt; freshly ground white pepper; 1 tsp horseradish relish (optional); 2 tsp vinegar; paprika.*

Sprinkle gelatine over water in a small saucepan. Soften for 2 minutes. Add sugar, salt, mustard and vinegar, and stir over low heat until gelatine has dissolved. Remove from heat and chill to consistency of unbeaten egg white. Fold in salmon, celery and capers, then fold in whipped cream. Turn into a wetted 1 litre/1¾ pint (4 cup) mould or individual moulds and chill until firm. Meanwhile, make sauce. Combine all ingredients except paprika and chill well. Sprinkle with paprika just before serving. Unmould mousse on to serving plate and garnish with dill or lettuce. Serve with sauce. Serves 4.

Tomato Mousse

1 kg (2 lb) ripe tomatoes, peeled, seeded and coarsely chopped; 2 tsp tomato purée (paste); salt and freshly ground black pepper; 6 tsp gelatine; 120 ml/4 fl oz (½ cup) water; 175 ml/6 fl oz (¾ cup) double (heavy) cream; 1 tbsp finely chopped fresh basil, or 2 tsp finely chopped fresh mint; sprigs fresh basil or mint, or cherry tomatoes, to garnish.

Place tomatoes in a blender or food processor with tomato purée (paste), salt and pepper and purée until smooth. Sprinkle gelatine over water in a small heatproof bowl and soften, then place bowl

over simmering water and stir until dissolved. Stir gelatine mixture into tomato purée. Lightly whip cream and fold into mixture with chopped basil or mint. Spoon into 6 wetted moulds and refrigerate until set. Unmould on to chilled plates and serve garnished with sprigs of basil, mint, or with cherry tomatoes. Serves 6.

Hot Ham and Chicken Mousse

370 g/12 oz (1½ cups) cooked chicken meat; 250 g/8 oz (1 cup) lean cooked ham; salt and freshly ground black pepper; 1 tbsp grated onion; 1 tbsp French (Dijon) mustard; 3 egg whites; 250 ml/8 fl oz (1 cup) double (heavy) cream, chilled

Place chicken and ham in a food processor fitted with the steel blade, and process until smooth. Add salt, if needed, pepper, onion and mustard. Process until well mixed, then add egg whites and process again until smooth. Turn mixture into a bowl and chill 30 minutes. Whip chilled cream until it forms soft peaks and fold into chicken mixture. Turn into a well-buttered 1.5 litre/2½ pint (6 cup) mould, place in a roasting tin (pan) of warm water and cover with a sheet of buttered greaseproof (waxed) paper. Bake in a preheated moderately hot oven (190°C/375°F, Gas Mark 5) for 40 minutes or until a skewer inserted in centre comes out clean. Unmould on to a heated serving plate and serve with Poulette Sauce or Sauce Suprême (page 368). Serves 6–8.

Tarama and Cream Cheese Mousse

Tarama is salted roe of grey mullet, available from delicatessens. This tangy mousse can be served with sauce as a first course, or with toast points to accompany drinks.

1½ tsp gelatine; 1½ tsp dry sherry; 4 tbsp tarama; 125 g/4 oz (½ cup) cream cheese, softened; 5 tbsp plain yogurt; 120 ml/4 fl oz (½ cup) sour cream; 1 tbsp lemon juice; 1½ tbsp finely chopped fresh dill, or 2 tsp dried; 120 ml/4 fl oz (½ cup) double (heavy) cream; salt and freshly ground black pepper; sprigs fresh dill, lemon twists or red caviar to garnish.

M

SAUCE: *4 tbsp plain yogurt; 5 tbsp single (light) cream; 2 tbsp finely chopped fresh dill or finely chopped cucumber; salt and freshly ground black pepper.*

Sprinkle gelatine over sherry in a heatproof bowl and soften. Place bowl over simmering water and stir until gelatine has dissolved. Beat tarama and cream cheese with an electric mixer or rotary mixer until light and fluffy. Add yogurt, sour cream, gelatine mixture and lemon juice and beat until well combined. Stir in dill. Whip cream until it forms soft peaks and fold into tarama mixture. Season with salt and pepper and turn into a wetted 500 ml/18 fl oz (2 cup) mould or serving dish, or divide among 6 individual moulds or ramekins. Cover and chill until set. Unmould on to chilled plates, or serve in dishes, garnished with dill, lemon twists or caviar. For sauce, combine all ingredients, seasoning with salt and pepper. Serves 6.

Caramel Mousse

CARAMEL: *125 g/4 oz (½ cup) sugar; 5 tbsp water.*

MOUSSE: *1½ tsp gelatine; 2 tbsp water; 5 eggs, separated; 2 tbsp caster sugar; 1 tsp vanilla essence (extract); 300 ml/½ pint (1¼ cups) double (heavy) cream.*

DECORATION: *whipped cream; strawberries.*

To make caramel, combine sugar and 1 tbsp water in a small saucepan and stir until sugar dissolves. Increase heat and cook, rotating pan gently, until a rich brown caramel forms. Remove from heat and, protecting your hand with a cloth, gradually stir in remaining water to dilute caramel. Cool 5 minutes. MOUSSE: Sprinkle gelatine over water and allow to soften, then stir into caramel mixture until dissolved. Beat egg yolks, sugar and vanilla with an electric mixer until thick and lemon coloured. With motor still running, add caramel mixture in a stream, and beat until mixture is thick and fluffy. Whip cream just until it holds firm peaks and fold into caramel mixture. Beat egg whites until they hold soft peaks. Gently but thoroughly fold caramel mixture into whites. Turn mixture into a 1.5–2 litre/2½–3½ pint (6–8 cup) serving dish or 6–8 individual dishes. Cover and chill until set. Serve decorated with whipped cream and strawberries. Serves 6–8.

MOUSSELINE

A French word meaning muslin, which is the name given to various preparations that are as feather-light as the delicate fabric. Mousselines of fish, poultry or meat are small moulds of the main ingredient, beaten with egg whites and cream, and cooked in a bain marie (water bath). Pommes Mousseline are puréed

potatoes beaten with boiling milk to the consistency of lightly whipped cream (see page 307). Some basic sauces which have been lightened by the addition of whipped cream are also described as mousseline, e.g. Mayonnaise Mousseline or Hollandaise Mousseline (the latter often called simply Sauce Mousseline).

See also *Sauces*.

Scallop Mousselines

370 g (12 oz) fresh scallops; salt and freshly ground white pepper; nutmeg; 3 egg whites; 500 ml/18 fl oz (2 cups) single (light) cream, chilled.

Remove any dark beards from scallops. Place them in the bowl of a food processor fitted with the steel blade. Add 1 tsp salt and a pinch each of pepper and nutmeg and process until smooth. Add egg whites and process again until smooth. Add egg whites and process again until smooth. Put bowl in refrigerator and chill 30 minutes. Return bowl to processor, switch on motor and pour chilled cream through feed tube. When cream and scallop mixture are combined, switch off. Adjust seasoning, return container to refrigerator and chill 1 hour.

To make mixture by hand, finely mince (grind) scallops, place in a bowl and add seasonings. Break up egg whites with a fork and add them gradually to scallops, beating vigorously with a wooden spoon to make a smooth, pliable paste. Cover bowl, place in refrigerator and chill thoroughly, then set bowl over ice and add chilled cream a little at a time, beating thoroughly with a wooden spoon. Adjust seasoning.

Fill 6 buttered 120 ml/4 fl oz (½ cup) moulds to brim with mousseline mixture and smooth tops. Place moulds in a large roasting tin (pan) and add enough warm water to come halfway up sides of moulds. Cover with a sheet of buttered greaseproof (waxed) paper and bake in a preheated moderate oven (180°C/350°F, Gas Mark 4) for 10–12 minutes or until a skewer inserted in the centre of a mousseline comes out

clean. Turn mousselines out on to heated plates and serve with a sauce such as Beurre Blanc or Velouté (pages 368 and 370). Serves 6 as a first course.
NOTE: The mousselines may be cooked 24 hours ahead and chilled, covered. To serve, place moulds in a roasting tin (pan) of hot water and cover as before, reheat in a preheated moderately hot oven (200°C/400°F, Gas Mark 6) for 10 minutes.
VARIATION
Chicken Mousselines: Make as above, substituting 500 g (1 lb) boneless breast of chicken for the scallops. After egg whites have been added, work mixture through a sieve to remove small sinews. Place mixture in a bowl over ice, then beat in cream a little at a time, as described.

MUESLI

Muesli is a breakfast enjoyed by millions of people throughout the world. The Bircher-Muesli breakfast, formulated by Dr. Bircher-Benner in his wonderful sanatorium in the Swiss Alps, was an attempt to make a food as perfect as possible. Muesli is based on a mixture containing raw cereal, such as oats, to which is added dried fruit, bran or wheatgerm and sometimes nuts and unrefined sugar. It is eaten with milk or cream and fresh fruit, usually at breakfast. Americans call it granola.

Today, muesli is prepared commercially in many varying forms. It is simple to make, many families developing their own special recipe. **See recipes.**

Muesli

By using the whole apple, skin and all, you increase the minerals in muesli (granola).

6 tbsp whole oats; 6 tbsp water; juice ½ lemon; 2 tbsp single (light) cream; 3 apples, cored; honey.

Soak oats in the water overnight. In the morning add lemon juice and cream and mix well. Shred apples into oats, sweeten with honey to taste and stir. Serve at once. Serves 4.

Swiss Muesli

Also known as Swiss Health Breakfast. Store wheatgerm in the freezer as this is one food that quickly goes rancid. Fresh grapes, peaches, bananas, or any other favourite fruit can be mashed or shredded into the cereal.

1 tbsp fresh wheatgerm; 1 tbsp whole oats; 5 tbsp water; 1 tsp lemon juice; honey; single (light) cream or milk; 1 apple, cored; chopped nuts (optional).

Soak wheatgerm and oats in the water overnight in the refrigerator. Next morning, add lemon juice, honey and cream or milk and mix well. Shred apple into this, stir and serve at once. Scatter a handful of chopped nuts on top if you like – it makes the cereal more nutritious. Serves 1.

Toasted Muesli

250 g/9 oz (3 cups) quick-cooking oats; 90 g/3 oz (½ cup) dried apricots, finely chopped; 90 g/3 oz (½ cup) sultanas (golden raisins); 45 g/1½ oz (¾ cup) fresh wheatgerm; 125 g/4 oz (½ cup) unrefined sugar.
TO SERVE: *apples; milk or single (light) cream.*

Toast oats in a preheated moderate oven (180°C/350°F, Gas Mark 4) for 8–10 minutes. Place oats in a bowl and add apricots, sultanas (golden raisins), wheatgerm and sugar. Mix well. Store in a tightly covered container at room temperature. Serve 3–4 tbsp muesli (granola) in individual cereal bowls, grate 1 apple over each and add milk or cream. Serves 4.

MUFFINS (AMERICAN)

These are one of America's nicest gifts to the culinary world. They are light little quick breads, baked in deep, round tins (pans) and served hot for breakfast, with coffee, or with soups or salads.

It is important to remember when mixing American muffins that the liquid ingredients should be mixed into the dry ones with a few swift strokes, just enough to moisten the flour – the mixture should still be lumpy. Overmixing will produce tough, coarse-textured muffins. Spoon the mixture into each tin (pan) in one large spoonful, pushing it off with the spoon held low, to avoid stretching the elastic gluten strands in the flour. **See recipes.**

Basic American Muffins

250 g/8 oz (2 cups) flour; 1 tbsp baking powder; ¼ tsp salt; 2 tbsp sugar; 1 egg, lightly beaten; 250 ml/8 fl oz (1 cup) milk; 60 g/2 oz (4 tbsp) butter, melted.

Sift dry ingredients into a large bowl. Mix egg, milk and butter together, pour over dry ingredients and mix just until flour is moistened; batter should still be lumpy. Spoon into 12 well-greased muffin tins (pans), filling each one ⅔ full. Bake in a preheated moderately hot oven (200°C/400°F, Gas Mark 6) for 20–25 minutes or until well risen and golden-brown. Makes 12.
VARIATIONS
Nut or Fruit Muffins: Follow recipe for Basic Muffins, but use 60 g/2 oz (¼ cup) sugar and add 60 g/2 oz (½ cup) chopped nuts or 90 g/3 oz (½ cup) dried fruit to the dry ingredients before mixing in liquid. Chopped pecans, walnuts, dried apricots, raisins or mixed dried fruit may be used. After filling muffin tins (pans) sprinkle with sugar.
Wholewheat Muffins: Follow recipe for Basic Muffins, using 125 g/4 oz (1 cup) wholewheat and 125 g/4 oz (1 cup) plain (all-purpose) flour.
Bacon or Ham Muffins: Follow recipe for Basic Muffins, reducing sugar to 1 tbsp and adding 3 rashers (slices) bacon, fried crisp and crumbled, or 125 g/4 oz (½ cup) finely chopped cooked ham to dry ingredients before mixing in liquid.

Buttermilk Corn Muffins

125 g/4 oz (1 cup) flour; 150 g/5 oz (1 cup) yellow cornmeal (polenta); 2 tsp baking powder; 1 tsp bicarbonate of soda (baking soda); 1 tsp salt; 350 ml/12 fl oz (1½ cups) buttermilk; 2 eggs, lightly beaten; 60 g/2 oz (4 tbsp) butter, melted.

Sift dry ingredients into a large bowl. Combine buttermilk, eggs and melted butter, pour over dry ingredients and mix just until flour is moistened; batter should still be lumpy. Spoon into 12 well-greased muffin tins (pans), filling each ⅔ full. Bake in a preheated moderately hot oven (200°C/400°F, Gas Mark 6) for 20–25 minutes or until well risen and golden-brown. Makes 12.

MUFFINS (ENGLISH)

These flat, round, unsweetened yeast cakes were sold for many years in the streets of London and other English towns by the muffin man, with his tray and bell. Now they are available, packaged, at most supermarkets and delicatessens. Muffins are one of the great traditional foods of the English tea. They should be pulled apart (not cut), toasted, buttered and served hot.

They are useful, too, as a base for almost any topping, sweet or savoury. Perhaps their finest hour is as the base for Eggs Benedict, invented at Brennan's Restaurant in New Orleans, U.S.A., as part of the famous 'Breakfast at Brennan's', a leisurely feast which may last most of the day. **See recipes.**

Eggs Benedict

4 slices cooked ham; 2 English muffins; butter; 4 eggs; 1 quantity warm Hollandaise Sauce (page 369).

Trim ham slices to fit muffins. Fry ham in a little butter until lightly browned. Keep warm. Split and toast muffins. Poach eggs. Butter muffins lightly and place 2 halves each on 2 heated plates. Top each muffin half with a slice of ham, then with a hot poached egg. Coat with sauce and serve. Serves 2.

Hamburger Muffins

When hamburger patties are cooked directly on muffins, all the good juices are absorbed.

30 g/1 oz (¼ cup) rolled oats; 4 tbsp evaporated milk; 500 g/1 lb (2 cups) minced (ground) steak; 1 tsp salt; freshly ground black pepper; ¼ tsp dry mustard; 1 small onion, grated; 1 egg, lightly beaten; 3 English muffins; butter; chutney.

To make hamburgers, place rolled oats and milk in a blender or food processor and process until oats are finely chopped (or chop oats by hand and mix thoroughly with milk). Lightly mix oats, meat, salt, pepper, mustard and onion in a large bowl, then stir in egg with a fork. Using wet hands, shape into 6 patties the same diameter as muffins. Split muffins in half and toast both sides under grill (broiler). Spread with butter and chutney. Put a hamburger patty on each muffin and smooth it out to cover top. Pinch it down round edge of muffin so it will not shrink away during cooking. Cook under a preheated medium grill (broiler) for 10–12 minutes. Serve at once. Serves 6.

Cheese and Bacon Muffins

These are splendid for picnics – wrap in foil, then in a tea-towel to keep them warm.

6 English muffins; 3 rashers (slices) bacon, rind removed and chopped; 120 ml/4 fl oz (½ cup) milk; 180 g/6 oz (1½ cups) grated Swiss or other mild cheese; freshly ground black pepper; dash Worcestershire sauce; melted butter.

Split muffins in half and pull out some of the crumb. Fry bacon crisp in frying pan (skillet). Remove pan from heat and stir in muffin crumbs, milk, cheese, pepper and Worcestershire sauce. Fill muffins with mixture, press halves together and secure with wooden toothpicks. Brush tops with melted butter and bake in a preheated moderate oven (180°C/350°F, Gas Mark 4) 15 minutes. Remove toothpicks and serve warm. Serves 6.

Right: Herb Gnocchi (page 146), Green Pancakes with Cream Cheese (page 264)

M

Sunday Breakfast Muffins

4 English muffins; 45 g/1½ oz (3 tbsp) butter, softened; 3 rashers (slices) bacon, rind removed and finely chopped; 3 tbsp peanut butter; 1 tbsp crushed nuts; 2 tbsp honey, golden (light corn) syrup or maple syrup.

Split and toast muffins. Meanwhile, mix all other ingredients together. Spread over muffin halves and cook under a preheated medium grill (broiler) until bacon is crisp and topping brown and bubbly. Serve immediately. Serves 4.

Muffin Pizzas

6 English muffins; 3 tbsp olive oil; 250 g/8 oz (1 cup) minced (ground) steak, sausage meat or finely chopped salami; 1 clove garlic, crushed; 3 tbsp tomato purée (paste); 1 tbsp chopped fresh oregano, or 1 tsp dried; salt and freshly ground black pepper; 12 thin slices Mozzarella or other mild cheese.
GARNISH: *sliced black (ripe) or green olives; halved anchovy fillets; strips of green pepper.*

Split muffins, toast lightly and brush with olive oil. Brown meat and garlic in remaining oil, breaking down lumps in steak or sausage with a fork. Stir in tomato purée (paste) and oregano and season with salt and pepper. Cover each muffin half with meat mixture and top with a slice of cheese. Arrange olives, anchovies or pepper strips on top and bake in a preheated moderately hot oven (190°C/375°F, Gas Mark 5) for 10 minutes or until muffins are heated through and cheese melted. Makes 12.

MULBERRY

A juicy, mild-flavoured berry which grows in many gardens on large, beautiful trees. Unripe mulberries are red, ripe ones purple-black and should be handled with care as the juice is deeply staining. They are good to eat fresh, with a little sugar and lemon juice to bring out the flavour. They also make a splendid pie and can replace other berries in recipes such as Summer Pudding (see page 421). Mulberry jelly is a particularly good preserve. **See recipes.**

Mulberry Jelly

slightly under-ripe mulberries, washed and stalks removed; sugar, warmed.

Put mulberries into a heavy saucepan and cover with cold water. Bring slowly to the boil, mashing down well to extract juice. Simmer gently for about 1 hour or until pulp is very soft. Strain through a colander lined

Left: Beans with Tuna (page 318) and Fennel with Butter and Cheese (page 119)

with several layers of cheesecloth, set over a bowl. Do not press pulp, but allow juice to drip through slowly. Measure juice and transfer it into a saucepan. Do not use sediment. Bring juice to the boil and add 250 g/8 oz (1 cup) sugar for every 250 ml/8 fl oz (1 cup) of juice. Stir until sugar has dissolved, then bring back to the boil and boil until setting point is reached. Pour into clean, warm jars and seal.

Mulberry Pie

875 g/1¾ lb (5 cups) fresh mulberries, stalks removed, or 750 g/1½ lb (4 cups) mulberries and 1 large cooking apple, peeled, cored and finely sliced; 1½ tbsp cornflour (cornstarch); 125 g/4 oz (½ cup) plus 2 tsp caster sugar; 2 tbsp lemon juice; 1 quantity Sweet Rich Shortcrust Pastry (page 274).

Toss fruit gently with cornflour (cornstarch) and 125 g/4 oz (½ cup) sugar, then with lemon juice. Place in a 1 litre/1¾ pint (4 cup) pie dish, mounding it up in the middle. Roll out pastry (dough) to a shape 4 cm (1½ in) larger than top of dish. Cut off a 1 cm (½ in) strip all round, dampen rim of dish and press pastry (dough) strip on rim. Cut off excess and press join together. Brush strip with a little water, then lift remaining pastry (dough) with rolling pin and lay over the top. Press edge down lightly and trim off excess pastry (dough). Seal pastry (dough) by pressing round edge with the back of a knife, then press around with your thumb to make a decorative edge. Sprinkle with remaining sugar. Bake in a preheated moderately hot oven (190°C/375°F, Gas Mark 5) for about 30 minutes or until filling is bubbling and crust is golden-brown. Serve hot with cream. Serves 4–6.

MULLIGATAWNY

A highly-spiced dish, not quite a soup, which is a heritage of the days of the British Raj in India. The name is derived from the Tamil *molegoo tunee*, meaning 'pepper water'. Mulligatawny is usually served in large soup plates with a spoonful of boiled rice in the centre of each plate. Sometimes a bowl of rice is served on the side instead.

Mulligatawny

60 g/2 oz (4 tbsp) butter; 3 medium onions, sliced; 12 curry leaves (optional); 1 tbsp curry powder or curry paste; 2 litres/3½ pints (8 cups) well-flavoured stock (beef, lamb or chicken); 125 g/4 oz (1 cup) finely sliced celery; 370 g/12 oz (1½ cups) diced cooked meat or chicken; 500 ml/18 fl oz (2 cups) Coconut Milk (page 80); salt and freshly ground black pepper; boiled rice; lemon wedges to serve.

Heat butter in a large saucepan and gently fry onions until golden. Add curry leaves and curry powder or paste, and fry, stirring, 1 minute longer. Add stock and celery, bring to the boil, reduce heat and simmer 20 minutes. Add meat or chicken and coconut milk and bring almost to boiling again. Taste and season with salt and pepper. Put a spoonful of rice into each heated soup plate and ladle soup over; alternatively, serve rice in a separate bowl. Serve with lemon wedges which are squeezed over soup just before eating. Serves 6–8.

MUSCATEL

Large, fragrant raisin made from the muscat grape. Muscatels are available loose or in bunches and are attractive served as a dessert or on a cheese board.

MUSHROOM

Many a good cook considers mushrooms almost a kitchen staple which should be always at hand to slice for a garnish, add to a salad, give wonderful flavour to meat, chicken, fish, eggs and vegetables, or to serve as a savoury dish in their own right. Mushrooms are remarkable in their ability to complement both robust and delicate flavours, and their pretty shape can add much to the appearance of a dish.

Not really vegetables but edible fungi, mushrooms were once a luxury but the highly efficient mushroom-growing industry has put them on everyone's table all year round at a reasonable price. They are also found wild; field and wood mushrooms of various types such as *chanterelles, morels* and *cèpes* are prized in European cookery. Most cooks, unless they are expert at identifying wild mushrooms, are happy to stick to the cultivated varieties, or make use of canned or dried mushrooms.

Fresh cultivated mushrooms are supplied in three grades.
Button Mushrooms: Also known by their French name, *champignons*, button mushrooms are completely closed. They are attractive in salads or as a garnish and do not darken when cooked, so are perfect for pale, creamy dishes.
Cup Mushrooms: These have the membrane just breaking to expose the pink gills. They darken a little when cooked but can be kept pale if brushed with lemon juice. They are good for stuffing and for cooking in general.
Flat Mushrooms: These are fully open and are more robust in flavour than buttons or cups. They are excellent grilled (broiled), served on toast or in brown soups and casseroles; because they darken with cooking, they can give a grey cast to pale dishes. Stuffed flat mushrooms make a good starter.

Buy mushrooms in quantities you will use within a few days. Store, lightly covered with damp paper towels or in a paper bag or box, in the refrigerator. Avoid plastic wrap or plastic bags which can cause mushrooms to sweat.

□ **Basic Preparation:** Do not peel cultivated mushrooms. The skin contains much of the flavour and nutritive value; it also helps them to stay in shape during cooking and reduces darkening. Only large, mature wild mushrooms may need peeling; keep the peelings for stock or soup.

Washing or soaking introduces excess water which the mushrooms absorb like a sponge. Cultivated mushrooms need only a wipe with a soft cloth before using. If you must wash wild mushrooms, rinse them quickly and dry well. Do not wipe or cut mushrooms until shortly before using. If they are to be used raw, brush cut surfaces with lemon juice to keep them white.

Trim stems on the diagonal, just beyond the cap, if mushrooms are to be used whole, halved or quartered. Cut stems level with caps if mushrooms are to be sliced downward into little umbrella shapes, or if they are to be stuffed and cooked (the stem helps to keep the shape). Remove stems by twisting, if directed by recipe, but keep all stems and trimmings for stock, soup or sauces.

To prepare dried mushrooms: Soak in hot water to cover 20–30 minutes, depending on size. Remove with a slotted spoon and drain on paper towels, then use as recipe directs. The soaking water is often used in the dish, or may be added to stock or soup.

To make turned or fluted mushrooms: Choose very white mushrooms. Hold rounded side up and with a small, sharp, pointed knife make deep swirling cuts from the centre of the mushroom cap down to the edge. The slivered peeling falls off to reveal the petal-like shape. Use as a garnish for main course dishes.

□ **To Cook:** Mushrooms may be sautéed, grilled (broiled) or added to stews, casseroles and sauces. **See also recipes.**

SAUTEED MUSHROOMS Mushrooms absorb fat in cooking and this can make them soggy. They also release juice and become soft if heat is too low or they are cooked too long. For firm, golden-brown mushrooms, use just enough melted butter, good quality oil or a mixture of both, to cover the bottom of the pan. Heat until it begins to give off a slight haze, add prepared mushrooms and cook briskly without turning, shaking pan gently once or twice, for about 1 minute. Turn and brown on other side, then add a little more butter or oil if necessary and toss mushrooms 1 minute more. Do not crowd the pan, and cook in batches if necessary. Do not cover those mushrooms which are already cooked; when all are done, return them to the pan,

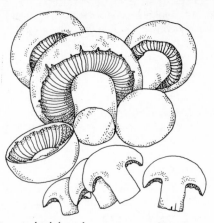

toss on high heat for moments only and serve immediately.

GRILLED (BROILED) MUSHROOMS Wipe with a cloth, wrung out in water with a little lemon juice added. Brush with oil or melted butter and place under a preheated grill (broiler) skin side uppermost. Cook about 2 minutes, turn and brush again with butter or oil, and cook another 2 minutes. Sprinkle with chopped parsley and serve with grilled (broiled) steak, chops, bacon or tomatoes, or on toast.

COOKED IN LIQUID Mushrooms become heavy if cooked too long in liquid, so add to stews or casseroles toward the end of cooking time. Sliced or small whole mushrooms may be simmered for a few minutes in a little acidulated water to make them firm and white before adding to delicate sauces or using as a garnish.

Duxelles

A concentrated mushroom paste that will keep well in the refrigerator – a good way of using up mushrooms that might not keep, or leftover stems and peelings. **See recipes.**

Ways to Use Duxelles

● Add a little to soups, stews and other dishes when a mushroom flavour is wanted.

● Mix with sour cream for an omelette filling or with Béchamel Sauce (see page 368) to stuff crêpes.

● Mix with a little single (light) cream and put some into ramekins when you are baking eggs.

● Mix 60 g/2 oz (½ cup) Duxelles with 90 g/3 oz (⅓ cup) softened cream cheese and enough single (light) cream to make it spreadable. Spoon into baked tartlet shells, sprinkle with grated Parmesan cheese and bake in a preheated moderate oven (180°C/350°F, Gas Mark 4) for 5 minutes.

Stuffed Fresh Mushrooms

Fresh mushroom caps with a savoury stuffing make a healthy light hors d'oeuvre.

20–25 cup mushrooms; chopped parsley, leaves of flat parsley or paprika to garnish.
HERB FILLING: *125 g/4 oz (½ cup) cream cheese; 1 tbsp lemon juice; 4 tbsp chopped parsley; 4 tbsp chopped mixed fresh herbs, or 2 tsp dried herbs mixed with 4 tbsp chopped parsley; salt and freshly ground black pepper.*

Remove mushroom stems and chop fine. Mix ingredients for filling, adding chopped mushroom stems. Fill mushroom caps, mounding mixture up, and garnish each with chopped parsley, a parsley leaf or a sprinkle of paprika. Makes 20–25.
VARIATIONS
Chicken Filling: Mix together 1 boneless, skinless chicken breast, cooked and finely chopped; 4 tbsp Mayonnaise (page 204); 2 tsp chopped parsley or chives; salt and freshly ground black pepper. Use to fill mushroom caps as above.
Nut Filling: Mix together 125 g/4 oz (½ cup) cream cheese; 30 g/1 oz (¼ cup) chopped toasted almonds, walnuts or pecans; 1 tbsp finely snipped chives; salt and freshly ground black pepper. Use to fill mushroom caps as above.

Chilled Mushroom Soup

This superb soup is best made with a good, home-made chicken stock.

180 g (6 oz) flat mushrooms, trimmed; 2 tsp arrowroot; 1 litre/1¾ pints (4 cups) strong chicken stock; 3 egg yolks; 175 ml/6 fl oz (¾ cup) single (light) cream; salt and freshly ground white pepper; snipped chives to garnish.

Put mushrooms through a food mill or purée them in a food processor, then rub through a sieve. Mix arrowroot to a cream with a little of the stock, then bring rest of stock to the boil. Add mushroom purée and simmer 3 minutes. Stir a little of the hot soup into arrowroot mixture, then stir this back into boiling soup. Beat egg yolks with cream, stir in a little of the hot soup, then turn heat down under soup and stir in egg yolk mixture. Stir until soup becomes glossy and thickens slightly but do not allow to boil. Season with salt and pepper. Remove from heat, pour soup into a bowl, cool then chill well. Serve garnished with snipped chives. Serves 6.

Cream of Mushroom Soup

The mushrooms are just heated through to preserve their full flavour.

30 g/1 oz (2 tbsp) butter; 6 shallots or 1 small onion, finely chopped; 1 small clove garlic, crushed (optional); 2 tbsp flour; pinch nutmeg; 750 ml/1¼ pints (3 cups) warm chicken stock; 180 g (6 oz) flat mushrooms, sliced (including stems); 2 egg yolks; 120 ml/4 fl oz (½ cup) single (light) cream; salt and freshly ground black pepper; lemon juice; 3–4 button mushrooms, finely sliced, or snipped chives or fresh tarragon, to garnish.

Melt butter in a heavy saucepan, add shallots or onion and garlic, if using, and cook gently until soft but not coloured. Stir in flour and nutmeg and cook 1 minute, then remove saucepan from heat and cool a little. Add warm stock, stirring until smoothly blended. Return to medium heat and stir until boiling. In several batches, purée soup with sliced flat mushrooms in a blender or food processor. Return to saucepan and heat to just below boiling point. Beat eggs with cream, stir in a little of the hot soup and stir this mixture back into pan. Heat gently, stirring constantly, until soup becomes glossy and thickens a little. Season with salt, pepper and lemon juice and serve garnished with mushroom slices or herbs. Serves 4–5.

Mushroom Frittata

A frittata is a flat omelette. It can be served hot or at room temperature – good for lunch or, cut into small squares, with drinks.

125 g (4 oz) mushrooms; 3 tbsp olive oil; 2 cloves garlic; 1 small onion, finely chopped; ½ small red or green pepper, cored, seeded and diced; 6 eggs; 3 tbsp finely chopped parsley; 30 g/1 oz (¼ cup) grated Swiss cheese; 30 g/1 oz (¼ cup) grated Parmesan cheese; 1 tsp salt; freshly ground black pepper.

Slice mushrooms, cutting first into halves or quarters if they are large. Heat oil in a heavy frying pan (skillet), add garlic, onion, mushrooms and pepper and cook briskly until vegetables are lightly browned. Remove garlic and turn heat low. Beat remaining ingredients together, reserving about 1 tbsp Parmesan cheese. Pour mixture into pan, stir to mix in vegetables and cook slowly until edges shrink a little. Sprinkle with reserved cheese and place under a preheated grill (broiler) until set and lightly browned. Serve hot or cool, cut into wedges or squares. Serves 4 as a main dish.

Baked Mushrooms in Cream

Serve this dish with grilled (broiled) steak, or as part of a leisurely holiday brunch with hot rolls and slices of pan-fried ham.

500 g (1 lb) mushrooms; 60 g/2 oz (4 tbsp) butter, melted; salt and freshly ground black pepper; 2 tbsp snipped chives or chopped spring onions (scallions); 4 tbsp single (light) cream; 3 tbsp grated Parmesan cheese.

Trim mushroom stems level with caps. Arrange caps, stem side down, in a buttered shallow ovenproof dish and brush tops with melted butter. Season well with salt and pepper, sprinkle with chives or spring onions (scallions), and pour cream over. Bake in a preheated hot oven (220°C/425°F, Gas Mark 7) for 10 minutes. Scatter cheese over top and bake 5 minutes more. Serves 4.

Stuffed Grilled Mushrooms

8 large cup mushrooms; 60 g/2 oz (4 tbsp) butter; 4 shallots or ½ small onion, finely chopped; 1 clove garlic, crushed (optional); 180 g/6 oz (¾ cup) finely chopped cooked ham; 2 tsp French (Dijon) mustard; pinch nutmeg; 15 g/½ oz (¼ cup) fresh breadcrumbs; salt and freshly ground black pepper; rounds of hot fried bread or buttered toast to serve; chopped parsley to garnish.

Trim mushroom stems level with caps and chop stems fine. Melt half the butter and fry stems, shallot or onion and garlic, if using, until soft. Stir in ham, mustard, nutmeg, breadcrumbs, salt and pepper. Melt remaining butter, brush skin side of mushrooms and grill (broil) them, skin side up, under a preheated grill (broiler) for 2 minutes. Turn caps over, fill with stuffing and return to grill (broiler). Cook until stuffing is heated through. Place on rounds of fried bread or toast and garnish with parsley. Serve very hot. Serves 4.

Funghi Ripieni

(Stuffed Mushrooms)

12 large mushrooms; 6 tbsp olive oil; 1 onion, finely chopped; 1 clove garlic, crushed; 60 g/2 oz (1 cup) fresh breadcrumbs; 2 tbsp chopped parsley; 60 g/2 oz (¼ cup) finely chopped cooked ham; 2 tbsp grated Parmesan cheese; salt and freshly ground black pepper; extra chopped parsley to garnish.

Remove and chop mushroom stems. Heat 3 tbsp oil in a small saucepan and fry onion and garlic gently for 5 minutes. Stir in breadcrumbs and fry for 2–3 minutes until crisp. Add parsley, mushroom stems, ham, cheese, salt and pepper. Mix well. Lightly oil the bottom of a shallow ovenproof dish and arrange mushrooms, cup sides up, in a single layer in dish. Spoon a little filling into each mushroom and sprinkle liberally with oil. Cover loosely with greaseproof (waxed) paper and bake in a preheated moderately hot oven (190°C/375°F, Gas Mark 5) for 20–30 minutes. Sprinkle with parsley before serving. Serves 4–6.

Poached Eggs Printemps

125 g (4 oz) button or cup mushrooms, sliced; 60 g/2 oz (4 tbsp) butter; 1 small head lettuce, shredded; 4 eggs; 75 g/2½ oz (½ cup) cooked peas; salt and freshly ground black pepper; 60 g/2 oz (½ cup) grated Gruyère cheese.

Fry mushrooms lightly in butter. Add lettuce, cover and cook gently until soft. Meanwhile, poach eggs. Add peas to mushroom mixture, season with salt and pepper and turn into a shallow flameproof dish. Trim eggs neatly. Use a spoon to make 4 hollows in the bed of vegetables and place a poached egg in each. Season lightly, cover with grated cheese and place under a preheated grill (broiler) until cheese is golden and bubbly. Serve at once. Serves 4.

Mushrooms in Pastry Cases

1 quantity Shortcrust Pastry (page 274); 60 g/2 oz (4 tbsp) butter; 500 g (1 lb) open flat mushrooms, sliced; 2 tsp flour; 175 ml/6 fl oz (¾ cup) chicken stock; 175 ml/6 fl oz (¾ cup) sour cream; salt and freshly ground black pepper; lemon juice ½ tbsp chopped parsley; ½ tbsp snipped chives; ½ tbsp chopped fresh tarragon, or ½ tsp dried; 1 egg yolk, beaten.

Line 4 × 8–10 cm (3–4 in) individual pie moulds with pastry (dough). Prick well. Bake pastry (dough) blind in a preheated moderately hot oven (190°C/375°F, Gas Mark 5) for about 15 minutes and leave to cool. Melt 30 g/1 oz (2 tbsp) of the butter in a saucepan. Add mushrooms and cook gently until soft. Drain off juice (use to flavour soup or another sauce) and remove pan from heat. Melt remaining butter in another saucepan and stir in flour. Cook for 1 minute, stirring all the time, then add stock and sour cream and cook, stirring, until thickened and just boiling. Season with salt, pepper and lemon juice and mix in drained mushrooms. Reheat mixture and stir in herbs. Keep hot. Brush pastry cases (pie shells) all over with beaten egg yolk and bake in moderately hot oven for a further 5 minutes. Remove from oven, fill with hot mushroom mixture and serve immediately. Serves 4.

Mushroom Tart

250 g/8 oz (2 cups) button mushrooms, trimmed; 45 g/1½ oz (3 tbsp) butter; 120 ml/4 fl oz (½ cup) single (light) cream; 1 egg yolk; 2 whole eggs; 60 g/2 oz (½ cup) grated Gruyère cheese; 1 tsp salt; freshly ground black pepper; tiny pinch cayenne; small pinch nutmeg; 1 × 20 cm (8 in) Rich Shortcrust Pastry Shell, baked (page 274).

Sauté mushrooms in butter until golden, and remove from heat. Beat cream with egg yolk and eggs, and stir in mushrooms and butter, cheese, salt, pepper, cayenne and nutmeg. Pour into pastry shell (pie crust) and bake in a preheated moderate oven (180°C/350°F, Gas Mark 4) until filling is set and delicately browned. Serve hot or warm with a salad. Serves 4.

Mushrooms on Croûtes

A good first course or light luncheon or supper dish.

180 g/6 oz (1½ cups) button mushrooms; 4 thick slices bread, crusts removed; 90 g/3 oz (6 tbsp) ghee or butter; 3 tbsp finely chopped parsley; 2 cloves garlic, crushed; 1 tsp lemon juice; salt and freshly ground black pepper.

Remove mushroom stems and keep for another dish. Arrange bread slices side by side in a shallow ovenproof dish. Place mushroom caps upside-down on bread. Melt butter, add parsley, garlic and lemon juice and season with salt and pepper. Spoon butter sauce over mushrooms and bread. Bake in a preheated moderately hot oven (190°C/375°F, Gas Mark 5) for 20 minutes. Serve at once. Serves 4.

Mushrooms with Garlic

This delicious way of cooking mushrooms is Italian.

150 ml/¼ pint (⅔ cup) olive oil; 2 cloves garlic; 1 kg (2 lb) mushrooms, thickly sliced; 1 tbsp chopped fresh oregano, or 1 tsp dried; salt and freshly ground black pepper.

Heat a little olive oil in a frying pan (skillet) and add garlic, 1 clove chopped and the other clove whole. When whole clove is brown, remove it from oil and discard it. Add mushrooms in several batches and sauté in remaining oil, as described on page 228. Return all mushrooms to pan, lower heat, sprinkle oregano over and season with salt and pepper. Continue to cook over a gentle heat 3 minutes, stirring occasionally, then turn out on to a heated serving dish. Serves 6–8.

Mushrooms in Cream Sauce

A lovely first course. Serve in individual small bowls or dishes on an entrée plate.

500 g/1 lb (4 cups) button mushrooms; 125 g/4 oz (½ cup) butter; 350 ml/12 fl oz (1½ cups) single light cream; 1 tbsp French (Dijon) mustard; salt and freshly ground black pepper; 40 g/1⅓ oz (1 cup) chopped parsley.

Trim mushroom stems level with caps. Cut caps into halves or quarters depending on size. Sauté mushrooms in butter, in several batches, as described on page 228. Set mushrooms aside. Add cream, mustard, salt and pepper to pan and cook, stirring over moderately high heat, until sauce thickens slightly. Return mushrooms to pan and fold through sauce. Serve hot, topped with a generous sprinkling of parsley. Offer hot crusty bread rolls or French bread to mop up sauce. Serves 6.

Baked Mushrooms with Ham

A good weekend luncheon dish, served with a crisp salad.

250 g (8 oz) medium mushrooms; 60 g/2 oz (4 tbsp) butter; salt and freshly ground black pepper; 125 g/4 oz (½ cup) cooked ham, finely chopped; 4 tbsp sour cream; 2 tsp lemon juice; 4 shallots, finely chopped; black (ripe) olives, to garnish.

Trim mushroom stems level with caps and chop stems fine. Lightly sauté mushroom caps in butter, as described on page 228. Remove to a buttered baking dish just large enough to hold them in one layer and season with salt and pepper. In the same pan, fry chopped mushroom stems until soft. Remove from heat and stir in ham, sour cream, lemon juice and shallots. Season with salt and pepper. Fill caps with mixture and bake in a preheated moderately hot oven (190°C/375°F, Gas Mark 5) for 10 minutes. Garnish with olives to serve. Serves 6.

Farmhouse Mushroom Pie

125 g/4 oz (½ cup) butter; 125 g/4 oz (½ cup) cooked ham or bacon, chopped; 1 large onion, chopped; 2 leaves fresh sage, chopped, or ¼ tsp dried; 1 tsp chopped fresh thyme, or ¼ tsp dried; 500 g (1 lb) mushrooms; salt and freshly ground black pepper; 250 g/8 oz (2 cups) cooked rice; 4 hard-boiled (hard-cooked) eggs, sliced; 1 quantity Flaky Pastry (page 275), or 1 × 375 g/12 oz packet frozen puff pastry (paste), thawed; beaten egg to glaze.

Melt half the butter and fry ham or bacon until golden. Add onion and cook gently until soft. Stir in sage and thyme. Remove from heat and cool a little. Leave mushrooms whole if small; cut into halves or quarters if large. Generously butter a 2 litre/3½ pint (8 cup) pie dish and put in half the mushrooms in one layer. Dot with butter

and season lightly with salt and pepper. Cover with ⅓ of the rice then ⅓ of the onion mixture and half the eggs. Season again. Repeat these layers and top with remaining ⅓ of rice and remaining ⅓ of onion mixture. Roll out pastry (dough) and cover dish. Chill for 30 minutes. Brush with beaten egg and bake in a preheated hot oven (230°C/450°F, Gas Mark 8) for 10–15 minutes or until pastry (dough) is well-risen and lightly coloured, then turn heat down to moderate (180°C/350°F, Gas Mark 4) and bake 20 minutes longer, covering top loosely with foil if browning too much. Serves 6.

Creamed Mushrooms

An excellent quick meal for one.

180 g/6 oz (1½ cups) button mushrooms, sliced; 30 g/1 oz (2 tbsp) butter; 1 tbsp flour; salt and freshly ground black pepper; 175 ml/6 fl oz (¾ cup) milk; 4 tbsp single (light) cream; pinch nutmeg; 2 slices buttered toast; chopped parsley.

Sauté mushrooms in butter. Sprinkle over flour and stir until well blended. Season with salt and pepper. Add milk, cream and nutmeg and bring to the boil, stirring. Serve on freshly buttered toast, topped with parsley. Serves 1 as a main dish or 2 as a snack.

Mushroom Salad

250 g/8 oz (2 cups) small mushrooms, thickly sliced; 5 tbsp Garlic Vinaigrette Dressing (page 358); 10 g/⅓ oz chopped parsley; bouquet of parsley to garnish.

Mix mushrooms with vinaigrette and chopped parsley. Cover and chill. At serving time, put into a pretty bowl. Garnish with a generous bouquet of parsley. Serves 4–6.

Chinese Mushroom Omelette

6 dried Chinese mushrooms; 125 g/4 oz (½ cup) cooked pork or chicken meat, cut into shreds; 2 tsp light soy sauce; ½ tsp grated fresh ginger; 6 eggs; 1 tsp salt; 4 tbsp vegetable oil; 250 g/8 oz (1½ cups) frozen peas, thawed.

Cover mushrooms with hot water and soak 20 minutes. Drain, reserving soaking water, and slice each mushroom into 3 pieces. Place pork or chicken in a bowl, add soy sauce and ginger and turn meat about with chopsticks or 2 forks to coat with sauce.

M

Leave 10 minutes. In a separate bowl, beat eggs lightly with salt. Heat 2 tbsp oil in a heavy frying pan (skillet). When it begins to give off a haze, add meat mixture and stir-fry on high heat 1 minute. Add 2 tbsp soaking water from mushrooms, then add mushrooms and peas. Toss on high heat 2 minutes, turn contents of pan into a bowl and keep warm. Wipe out pan and add remaining oil. Heat until it gives off a haze, then add eggs and cook on high heat, without stirring, until they set underneath into a skin. Lower heat and cook until top is almost set, then spoon meat mixture over half the egg and fold the other half over it. Slide on to a heated platter and serve hot. Serves 4.

Stir-Fried Beef with Mushrooms

60 g (2 oz) dried Chinese mushrooms; 1 egg white; 2½ tbsp soy sauce; 1 tsp cornflour (cornstarch); 500 g (1 lb) lean fillet (tenderloin) or rump (top round) steak, trimmed of all fat and cut against grain into thin shreds; 120 ml/4 fl oz (½ cup) vegetable oil; 125 g/4 oz (½ cup) canned bamboo shoots, drained and shredded; 1 tbsp red wine; 1 tsp sugar; ½ tsp salt; sprigs fresh coriander to garnish.

Cover mushrooms with hot water and soak 20 minutes. Drain. Remove and chop stems and cut caps into fine strips. Mix egg white, soy sauce and cornflour (cornstarch), add shredded beef and marinate 5 minutes. Drain beef, reserving soy sauce mixture. Heat 4 tbsp oil in a wok or frying pan (skillet). When it begins to give off a haze, add beef and stir-fry over high heat until it changes colour. Remove beef and set aside. Add remaining oil to wok and heat. Add bamboo shoots and mushrooms and stir-fry over high heat 1 minute. Return beef to pan and add wine, sugar, salt and reserved soy sauce mixture. Stir-fry 1 minute and serve hot, garnished with sprigs of fresh coriander. Serves 4–6.

Duxelles

Use this mushroom paste in any of the ways described on page 228.

2 tbsp finely chopped shallots; 30 g/1 oz (2 tbsp) butter; 250 g/8 oz (2 cups) mushrooms or mushroom stems and trimmings, finely chopped; salt and freshly ground black pepper; 1 tbsp chopped parsley.

Cook shallots gently in butter until soft. Add mushrooms and cook gently for 5 minutes, then raise heat and cook briskly, stirring, until almost dry. Season with salt and pepper and stir in parsley. Spoon into a jar, press down and cover with foil. Store in refrigerator. If duxelles is to be kept more than a week, run melted butter over the top to seal, or freeze it. Makes 250 g/8 oz (2 cups).

Mushroom and Tarragon Sauce

2 tbsp finely chopped fresh tarragon, or 3 tsp dried; 2 shallots, finely chopped; 1 tbsp red wine vinegar; 125 g/4 oz (1 cup) mushrooms, finely chopped; 120 ml/4 fl oz (½ cup) Madeira or dry sherry; 120 ml/4 fl oz (½ cup) single (light) cream; 60 g/2 oz (4 tbsp) butter; salt and freshly ground black pepper.

In a small pan cook tarragon, shallots and vinegar until reduced by half. Add mushrooms and Madeira or sherry and simmer for 5 minutes. Blend in cream and butter and stir over medium heat a further minute. Season with salt and pepper, and serve. Makes 500 ml/18 fl oz (2 cups).

MUSSEL

A bluish-black edible mollusc, found clumped together on many coastlines and in estuaries, clinging tenaciously to any available support – rocks, poles, piers.

Whether you gather mussels yourself or buy them at the market, the rule is the same as for other shellfish; they must be *alive* when they are cooked. Live mussels hold their shells together so tightly it is difficult to pry them apart. Discard any with open shells.

You will notice that most recipes call for a little wine to be used in the cooking of mussels, and that cooked mussels are often served on the half shell with a sauce made from the cooking liquid. The true devotee will eat the mussels with a fork, then drink the sauce from the shell, the remaining sauce being mopped up with crusty bread.

Mussels are also sold bottled, in a brine solution, or canned – and sometimes smoked.

☐ **Basic Preparation:** Buy at least 500 g (1 lb) mussels for each person. When you get home, rinse the mussels several times in cold running water, then thoroughly scrub each mussel with a clean, stiff brush or pot scourer to remove mud, seaweed or any dirt that may cling to them. Soak for several hours in water with a handful of oatmeal or cornmeal.

Pull away the beard that clings around the edge of the shell and discard any mussel which is not tightly closed; then rinse again in cold running water, and they are ready to cook. All this preparation may sound a little finicky, but the time is well spent.

There are two methods for opening mussels.

To open mussels in the oven: Arrange the cleaned mussels in a single layer in a baking tin (pan) and place the tin (pan) in a preheated hot oven (230°C/450°F, Gas Mark 8) for 7–8 minutes or until the shells have opened. Throw away any unopened mussels.

To steam open mussels: Put the cleaned mussels in a large saucepan with 250 ml/8 fl oz (1 cup) water over high heat and steam the mussels, covered, shaking the pan once or twice, for 5–6 minutes or until the shells have opened. Discard any unopened shells. **See recipes.**

Mussels Marinière

(Moules Marinière)
The beloved moules of France are, of course, mussels. Moules Marinière is the classic and best loved way of enjoying mussels. They are steamed in wine and aromatics – parsley, bay leaf, shallots, etc. – and served with some of the liquor. There are variations which are equally popular throughout the world. Please read instructions on preparation of mussels above and left.

2 kg (4 lb) mussels, prepared; 4 shallots, finely chopped; 4 parsley stalks; 1 bay leaf; sprig fresh thyme; freshly ground black pepper; 60 g/2 oz (4 tbsp) butter; 500 ml/18 fl oz (2 cups) dry white wine; 1 tsp flour; little chopped parsley.

Place mussels in a wide pan with shallots, herbs, pepper, half the butter and the wine. Cover pan and cook over a high heat for 5 minutes, shaking pan occasionally. Remove

mussels as soon as they open, discarding the top of each shell. Discard any mussels that do not open. Arrange mussels in heated soup plates. Strain cooking liquid and return to pan. Mix remaining butter with flour and add to liquid. Boil rapidly, stirring, until slightly thickened. Pour over mussels in each soup bowl and sprinkle with chopped parsley. Serve at once with crusty bread, butter and chilled dry white wine. Serves 4.
VARIATIONS
Mussels with Cream (Moules à la Crème): Replace butter and flour used for thickening with 175 ml/6 fl oz ($\frac{3}{4}$ cup) single (light) cream. Reduce mussel cooking liquid by about $\frac{1}{3}$ by rapid boiling, then stir in cream and cook gently to thicken a little. Pour over mussels and serve.

Mussels in Egg and Cream Sauce (Moules à la Poulette): Steam mussels as described on previous page and keep warm, covered. Strain cooking liquid and reserve 500 ml/18 fl oz (2 cups). Bring liquid to the boil in a stainless steel, enamelled or non-stick saucepan. Reduce to 350 ml/12 fl oz (1$\frac{1}{2}$ cups), then remove from heat. In a bowl whisk together 120 ml/4 fl oz ($\frac{1}{2}$ cup) single (light) cream and 3 egg yolks, gradually whisk in 120 ml/4 fl oz ($\frac{1}{2}$ cup) of the liquid in a steady stream and whisk mixture into remaining liquid. Cook, whisking, over a low heat until thickened slightly. Add 2 tsp lemon juice and 2 tbsp chopped parsley. Divide mussels among 4 heated soup bowls and spoon sauce over mussels.

Baked Buttered Mussels
Serve with crusty bread, to mop up the lovely garlic butter.

1 tbsp oil; 1.5 kg (3 lb) mussels, scrubbed and cleaned (see page 231); 60 g/2 oz (4 tbsp) butter; 2 tbsp chopped parsley; 2 cloves garlic, finely chopped.

Rub a large baking dish with oil and place mussels in it in a single layer. Bake in a preheated hot oven (230°C/450°F, Gas Mark 8) for 5–10 minutes or until the shells open. Do not overcook. Remove upper shell. Melt butter and stir in parsley and garlic. Serve mussels on the lower shell with a little of the butter spooned over and any liquid from the pan. Serves 4.

Mussels in Dilled Cucumber Sauce
1 cucumber, peeled, seeded and chopped, 4 tbsp sour cream; 3 tbsp snipped fresh dill, or 1 tbsp dried; 1 tsp lemon juice; 1 tsp French (Dijon) mustard; 2 drops Tabasco (hot pepper) sauce; salt and freshly ground white pepper; 2 kg (4 lb) mussels, scrubbed, steamed open, shelled, and black rims removed.
GARNISH: *soft-leaved lettuce; cucumber slices; sprigs fresh dill.*

Squeeze cucumber lightly in a tea-towel to remove excess moisture. Combine cucumber, sour cream, dill, lemon juice, mustard, Tabasco (hot pepper) sauce, salt and pepper. Add mussels, and toss the mixture. Serve on chilled salad plates lined with lettuce leaves, garnished with cucumber slices and fresh dill sprigs. Serves 4.

Mussels and Salad Niçoise
250 g (8 oz) potatoes, peeled and sliced; 2 tbsp tomato purée (paste); 500 ml/18 fl oz (2 cups) Mayonnaise (page 204); 1 red pepper, cored, seeded and chopped; $\frac{1}{2}$ tsp chopped fresh tarragon, or pinch dried; $\frac{1}{2}$ tsp snipped fresh or freeze-dried chives; 2 kg (4 lb) mussels, scrubbed, steamed open, shelled, and black rims removed if desired.
GARNISH: *soft-leaved lettuce leaves; 250 g (8 oz) green beans, trimmed, blanched for 1 minute and patted dry; 3 hard-boiled (hard-cooked) eggs, quartered lengthways; stoned (pitted) black (ripe) olives; cherry tomatoes.*

Place potatoes in a saucepan, cover with cold salted water and bring to the boil. Simmer until just tender. Drain potatoes and let them cool. Mix tomato purée (paste) with mayonnaise, red pepper, tarragon and chives. Place mussels in a large bowl, add potatoes and 350 ml/12 fl oz (1$\frac{1}{2}$ cups) of the tomato mayonnaise, or to taste, and toss gently. Serve salad on chilled plates lined with lettuce leaves, garnished with green beans, egg quarters, olives and tomatoes. Serve remaining tomato mayonnaise separately. Serves 6 as a first course or 4 as a main course.

Mussel Salad
1.5 kg (3 lb) mussels, scrubbed and steamed open; 500 g (1 lb) waxy potatoes, peeled, cooked and diced; 180 g (6 oz) green beans or mange tout (snow peas), cooked; 1 stick tender celery, cut into fine strips.
GARNISH: *2 tomatoes, each cut into 6 wedges; 6 spring onions (scallions), finely shredded.*

DRESSING: *3 tbsp olive oil; 1 tbsp wine vinegar; 1 tsp French (Dijon) mustard; salt and freshly ground black pepper; 2 tbsp chopped mixed fresh herbs.*

Reserve 6 mussels in shells for garnishing; remove remaining mussels from shells and discard shells. Mix together dressing ingredients in a salad bowl, add potatoes, beans or mange tout (snow peas), mussels and celery and toss lightly together. Just before serving, garnish with reserved mussels in shells, tomatoes and spring onions (scallions). Serves 4.

Mussel Antipasto
120 ml/4 fl oz ($\frac{1}{2}$ cup) dry white wine or water; 1 kg (2 lb) mussels, scrubbed; 45 g/1$\frac{1}{2}$ oz ($\frac{3}{4}$ cup) fresh white breadcrumbs; 2 large cloves garlic, chopped; 2 tbsp finely chopped parsley; freshly ground black pepper; 4 tbsp olive oil.

Boil wine or water in a large heavy saucepan, add mussels, cover and cook over a high heat for 5–6 minutes, shaking pan frequently, until mussel shells open. Remove from heat. Detach and discard top shells, leaving each mussel in its lower shell. Discard any mussels that have not opened. Arrange side by side in a large shallow gratin dish or in 4 individual gratin dishes. Mix together breadcrumbs, garlic, parsley and pepper and spoon over mussels. Sprinkle oil evenly over the top. Cook in a preheated hot oven (230°C/450°F, Gas Mark 8) for 3–4 minutes or until crumbs are just tinged brown. Take care not to overcook mussels. Serves 4.

Vermicelli with Tomato and Mussel Sauce
1 kg (2 lb) mussels, scrubbed and steamed open; 5 tbsp olive oil; 1 onion, finely chopped; 2 cloves garlic, sliced; 750 g/1$\frac{1}{2}$ lb (3 cups) tomatoes, peeled and chopped; 370 g (12 oz) vermicelli; salt and freshly ground black pepper; 2 tbsp chopped parsley to garnish.

Reserve a few of the mussels in their shells for garnish. Remove remaining mussels from shells and discard shells. Heat 3 tbsp of the oil in a large saucepan and fry onion until soft and golden. Stir in garlic, then tomatoes. Simmer gently for about 30 minutes or until tomatoes have reduced to a pulp. Cook pasta in boiling salted water for about 10 minutes or until tender. Drain, place in a heated serving dish containing remaining oil and toss until lightly coated. Season sauce with salt and pepper, add shelled mussels and heat through for a few minutes, stirring well. Pile sauce over pasta, garnish with chopped parsley and reserved mussels in shell and serve immediately. Serves 4.

MUSTARD

The condiment based on the ground powder of the seeds of the mustard plant. There are three types of mustard seed which may be ground to make mustard – white (*Sinapis alba*), brown (*Brassica juncea*) and black (*Brassica nigra*). Manufactured mustard powder is usually a mixture of one or more varieties of mustard seed.

The pungency of mustard is due to an essential oil, which is not present in the living seed or in dry, ground powder but forms when the crushed dried seed is mixed with water. An enzyme then causes a glucoside (a bitter substance chemically related to sugar) to react with the water and the hot taste of mustard emerges. Mixing with boiling water, as some advocate, kills the enzyme and produces a milder but bitter mustard. Vinegar should not be used to mix mustard either, for salt and vinegar both inhibit the development of the enzyme – unless of course, one prefers a milder but bitter mustard.

Mustard should be mixed with cold water and allowed to stand 10–15 minutes, in which time the essential oils will develop. Once the essential oils have developed, they will not be readily degraded by vinegar or salt or even by heat. To preserve mustard's pungency in cooked dishes, however, add towards end of cooking and cook gently.

Main Types of Mustard

English Mustard: In England mustard is sold in powdered form: it is made from blended seeds of the black mustard seed and yellow-white *alba*, finely ground, and it is a hot yellow in colour. The powder is mixed with water, at home, and is the pungent but perfect partner for the roast beef of England. It is the proper mustard to use with cheese – the toasted Cheddar cheese that Ben Gunn dreamed of in 'Treasure Island' would certainly have had a dash of good English mustard. Welsh rarebits, cheese sauce and cheese soufflés reach their peaks with just the right amount of English mustard. Mixed English mustard is the perfect condiment with ham, roast pork, or pork pie, and beef or pork sausages.

When used in dishes that call for mustard, even English mustard loses much of its pungency if overcooked. In mayonnaise and salad dressings, mustard helps to stabilize the emulsions as well as adding a bite. Mustard is also used in pickles.

Fresh mustard should be mixed every time it is needed. Put a few tablespoons mustard in a small dish, add water a teaspoon at a time and mix to a smooth paste. Allow to stand 10–15 minutes to develop the flavours. To make a milder mustard, with a biting after-taste, mix the mustard with wine vinegar or cider.

Stale, mixed mustard loses much of its essential oils and therefore its pungency. However, as a powder, in its small container (Colmans, the oldest traditional English mustard makers have designed an excellent container), mustard will retain its powers, provided it does not get damp.

French Mustard: While most of the mustard consumed in England is dry, the French, and indeed most of Europe, prefer a mixed mustard. Transportation and travel are changing this as more of the world is introduced to the excellent mixed mustards of France and in particular the mustards of Dijon, in Burgundy.

The two types of mustard used in France are the pale Dijon and the darker Bordeaux mustard. Dijon mustards have a particularly clean taste – sharp and salty, not sweet, and with a strong hot taste of mustard.

Dijon mustard is exceptionally good with steak and anything else in which the taste of the dish should not be masked. Dijon mustard is the one used in French sauces – French cooks prefer it in mayonnaise and vinaigrette and for the delicate creamy sauces that go with kidneys, egg dishes, chicken or fish. Pan gravies are often enhanced with Dijon mustard and cream.

The best-known brands of Dijon mustard include Grey-Poupon, who make dozens of different blends and ship them all over the world, as do Maille, Olida and Amora. There is, of course, the grained French mustard called *Moutarde de Meaux*, an interesting mixture of ground and half-ground seeds, with a grainy texture.

Among the additives to French mustards are tarragon; a mixture of French herbs; green peppercorns, called *Moutarde au Poivres Verts*; and tomato purée (paste) is added to make a mustard that goes well with hamburgers. None, though, really beats the original Dijon mustard of France.

Bordeaux mustard is darker than Dijon (it contains the seed coat). It is sour-sweet with vinegar and sugar, and is heavily flavoured with tarragon and other herbs and spices.

All mixed mustards should be stored, covered, in a cool place and, once opened, they slowly lose their flavour. It is better to buy in small quantities and replace as necessary.

German Mustard: It is of the general type of Bordeaux mustard – dark in colour, sweet-sour and flavoured with herbs and spices. It goes particularly well with German sausage, particularly frankfurters, and *knackwurst*, the Dutch *rookwurst*, and Polish *kielbasa*, etc.

Other Mustards: Manufacturers throughout the world prepare mixed mustards for their local markets. In the U.S.A., a mustard is made from the *alba* seeds, and flavoured with sugar, vinegar or white wine. It is the one you get when you order a hot dog or hamburger in America. Manufacturers emulate the famous mustards of France and Germany, but few match up to the genuine article.

Other Forms of Mustard

Mustard Seeds: Spice shops, Oriental or Chinese groceries and health food shops sell mustard seeds. These find their way into pickles and curries, while some are used for home-made mustards. Again, these home-made mustards never match those from France and Germany.

Mustard Greens: The young green plant of the white mustard (*Sinapis alba*) is the mustard in mustard and cress. In these days rape is sometimes substituted. Trays of mustard and cress are sold, already sprouted, although these may contain only small cress. Snip the tops off and use when making sandwiches, add to egg or chicken dishes and use as a garnish over salads. You can also buy the seeds and sprout your own mustard and cress (see *Cress*).

Mustard Oil: This is obtained by pressing the seeds of field mustard, rape as well as other mustards, and is used to great advantage in Indian cooking, particularly that of Bengal, North India and Pakistan. It has a very distinctive flavour and smell, but is not all that pungent when used in cooking as the essential mustard oil is readily driven off with heat. Mustard oil can be bought in most shops specializing in Indian products. **See recipes**.

White Wine and Mustard Sauce

For sausages, ham steaks or pork chops.

15 g/½ oz (1 tbsp) butter; 2 tbsp chopped shallots; 5 tbsp white wine; 5 tbsp single (light) cream; 1 tbsp French (Dijon) mustard; salt and freshly ground black pepper.

Cook sausages or chops with just enough oil to film pan. Remove meat to a hot dish and slowly pour off fat from pan. Melt butter in pan, add shallots and cook gently 2 minutes. Add wine and bring to the boil, stirring and scraping up brown bits from bottom of pan. Stir in cream and mustard and cook gently 1–2 minutes or until sauce becomes glossy and a little thicker. Season with salt and pepper and spoon over sausages or chops. Serves 4.

Mustard Sauce

To vary the flavour, use some of the many different mustard mixes available now, adapting the amount added to taste.

1 quantity Béchamel Sauce (page 368); 1 tbsp dry mustard; 2 tbsp water; 2 tsp sugar; 1 tbsp vinegar.

Make sauce using all milk or half milk and half stock (veal or chicken). Blend mustard with water and stand for 10 minutes. Blend in sugar and vinegar until smooth and add to hot sauce. Serve with fish. Makes 350 ml/12 fl oz (1½ cups).

Mustard and Dill Sauce

4 tbsp highly seasoned prepared mustard; 1 tsp dry mustard; 3 tbsp sugar; 2 tbsp white vinegar; 5 tbsp vegetable oil; 3 tbsp chopped fresh dill.

Mix mustards, sugar and vinegar to a paste. Using a whisk, gradually beat in oil until it forms a thick emulsion. Stir in dill. Keep refrigerated in a tightly covered container and whisk before using. Sauce will keep for 3–4 days in refrigerator. Makes about 175 ml/6 fl oz (¾ cup).

Chicken Schnitzels Dijonnaise

4 chicken fillets (skinless, boneless half-breasts); salt and freshly ground black pepper; 4 tsp Dijon mustard; about 60 g/2 oz (½ cup) flour; 60 g/2 oz (4 tbsp) butter; 3 tbsp oil; 2 eggs, beaten; 120 ml/4 fl oz (½ cup) single (light) cream.

Place chicken fillets between 2 sheets of plastic wrap and flatten them out slightly with a rolling pin. Trim off any very ragged edges with a sharp knife. Season fillets well with salt and pepper, smear each with ½ tsp mustard and dust lightly with flour. Heat butter and oil together in a large, heavy frying pan (skillet) over medium heat. Have beaten eggs

in a shallow dish beside the stove, and floured fillets on a plate. When foam subsides in pan, quickly dip fillets into egg, then place them at once in pan. Cook until undersides are crisp and golden, about 2 minutes, then turn fillets with a spatula and cook other sides for 2–3 minutes. Remove and keep warm. To pan add cream and remaining mustard, swirling gently over a moderate heat to make a smooth, creamy sauce. Serve chicken topped with sauce. Serves 4.

Dijon Grilled Chicken

6 chicken pieces, breasts or legs, or 2 × 500 g (1 lb) chickens, split; 60 g/2 oz (4 tbsp) butter; 1 tbsp oil; 2–3 tbsp Dijon mustard; 2 tbsp chopped shallots; ¼ tsp dried thyme; salt and freshly ground black pepper; pinch cayenne.

Arrange chicken pieces on grill (broiler) rack, skin side up. Melt butter in a small pan, add oil and brush chicken pieces with some of this mixture. Cook chicken under a preheated grill (broiler) for 10 minutes on each side, brushing or basting frequently with butter and oil. Blend mustard with shallots, thyme, salt, pepper and cayenne and slowly add remaining oil and butter mixture, drop by drop, to thicken it. Turn chicken skin side up again, and spread with some of the mustard mixture. Grill (broil) for a further 10 minutes, reducing heat if necessary, until chicken is golden-brown and tender, basting with mustard mixture from time to time. Small chicken pieces will take less time to cook, 15–20 minutes altogether, so time accordingly. Serves 4.

Mustard Chicken in Yogurt

6–8 chicken joints, breasts, thighs, drumsticks; salt and freshly ground black pepper; 2 tbsp French (Dijon) mustard; 250 ml/8 fl oz (1 cup) plain yogurt, stirred.

Season chicken joints with salt and pepper. Place in a lightly greased shallow ovenproof dish and cover with foil. Bake in a preheated moderately hot oven (200°C/400°F, Gas Mark 6) for 25 minutes. Remove foil and spread each chicken piece with mustard,

then cover with yogurt. Return to oven for about 5 minutes. Serve immediately. Serves 4–6.

Grilled Chicken with Mustard Sauce

2 × 500 g (1 lb) chickens, split and flattened; lemon juice; salt and freshly ground black pepper; 30 g/1 oz (2 tbsp) melted butter; watercress to garnish.
SAUCE: *2 shallots, finely chopped; 1 tbsp dry sherry; 120 ml/4 fl oz (½ cup) chicken stock; 1 tsp tomato purée (paste); 1 tbsp French (Dijon) mustard; few drops Worcestershire sauce; pinch cayenne.*

Season both sides of chickens with lemon juice, salt and pepper. Brush chickens with melted butter and grill (broil) very gently, starting with skin side down, for about 12 minutes, then turn over and continue cooking for 20 minutes, basting occasionally with melted butter. Place chicken on a heated serving dish and keep warm.
SAUCE: Strain pan juices from chicken into a small saucepan, add shallots and fry gently until golden. Add sherry and stock and bring to the boil. Stir in tomato purée (paste), mustard, Worcestershire sauce and cayenne. Garnish chicken with watercress and serve sauce separately. Chicken may also be served on a bed of salad vegetables, to which the chicken gives a delicious taste – the juices from the chicken melt into the salad. Serves 4.

Creamed Onions Dijonnaise

750 g (1½ lb) medium onions, sliced; 120 ml/4 fl oz (½ cup) water; 150 ml/¼ pint (⅔ cup) light (single) cream; 1 tsp lemon juice; 1 tbsp Dijon mustard, ½ tsp or more salt; freshly ground black pepper.

Cook onions in water over a gentle heat, about 10 minutes. Drain and place in a greased ovenproof dish. Mix cream, lemon juice, mustard, salt and pepper and pour over onions. Cover and bake in a preheated moderate oven (180°C/350°F, Gas Mark 4) for 30 minutes. Serve with grilled (broiled) or pan-fried steak or roast beef or lamb. Serves 4–6.

M

Chicken Breasts Dijonnaise

4–6 half-breasts of chicken; salt and freshly ground black pepper; 90 g/3 oz (6 tbsp) butter; 2–3 tbsp brandy, warmed; 120 ml/4 fl oz (½ cup) single (light) cream; 1 tbsp Dijon mustard.

If half-breasts are large, cut each into 2 serving pieces. Season well with salt and pepper. Melt butter in a large frying pan (skillet) and sauté chicken, 3–4 pieces at a time (do not crowd pan), over medium heat. Cook for 15–20 minutes or until golden and juices run clear when chicken is pierced with a fine skewer. Return all chicken to pan. Ignite brandy and pour flaming over chicken. Shake pan until flames subside, then remove chicken to a heated serving dish and keep hot. Add cream to pan along with mustard. Bring to the boil, scraping up any brown bits. Stir until the sauce thickens slightly, and season with salt and pepper. Spoon sauce over chicken. Serve with creamy mashed potatoes or boiled rice and follow with a salad, if liked. Serves 4.

Chicken Breast en Croûte

Mushroom and tarragon sauce is the ideal accompaniment for this chicken dish.

4 large chicken fillets (skinless, boneless half-breasts); 60 g/2 oz (4 tbsp) butter; salt and freshly ground black pepper; squeeze lemon juice; 180 g/6 oz (¾ cup) cooked ham, very finely chopped; 2 tbsp sour cream; 1 tsp English mustard; 1 × 375 g/12 oz packet frozen puff pastry (paste), thawed; beaten egg to glaze; Mushroom and Tarragon Sauce (page 231) to serve.

Fry chicken pieces in butter for 1–2 minutes on each side until colour changes, without browning. Lift from pan and season with salt and pepper. Squeeze a little lemon juice over and put in refrigerator to cool completely. Mix ham with sour cream and mustard. Roll out pastry (paste) very thin and divide into 4, making each piece oblong in shape and large enough to enclose a chicken piece. Place a chicken piece on one edge of each piece of pastry (paste) and spread chicken with ham mixture. Brush edges of pastry (paste) with a little water and fold pastry (paste) over to enclose chicken like an envelope, trimming off any excess pastry (paste) and forming them into neat, attractive shapes. Place seam side down on a baking tray and decorate with some of the trimmings if liked; use a little beaten egg to secure the decorations. Brush pastry (paste) all over with beaten egg. Bake in a preheated moderately hot oven (200°C/400°F, Gas Mark 6) for about 30 minutes or until pastry is golden. Accompany with mushroom and tarragon sauce and buttered green beans, followed by a salad. Serves 4.

Dijon Pork en Croûte

500 g (1 lb) pork fillet (tenderloin) in one piece, or 2 smaller fillets (tenderloins); 2 tbsp brandy; 1 tbsp Dijon mustard; salt and freshly ground black pepper; 30 g/1 oz (2 tbsp) butter; 1 tbsp oil; 2 tsp chopped mixed fresh herbs (chives, parsley, thyme); 1 × 375 g/ 12 oz packet frozen puff pastry (paste), thawed; 1 egg, lightly beaten.

Cut pork fillet (tenderloin) into 4 portions, or cut smaller fillets (tenderloins) in half. Trim edges. Mix together brandy, mustard, salt and pepper in a shallow dish. Marinate pork in this mixture for several hours in refrigerator, turning often. Remove and pat dry. Heat butter and oil in a heavy frying pan (skillet), and quickly fry fillets (tenderloins) until golden on all sides. Sprinkle with herbs. Cool. Roll out pastry (paste) thin and cut into 4 portions. Wrap each piece of fillet (tenderloin) neatly in pastry, sealing joins with a little beaten egg. Use trimmings to make decorative shapes and attach to pastry (paste) with egg. Chill packages for 1 hour. Glaze tops with remaining egg and bake in a preheated moderate oven (180°C/350°F, Gas Mark 4) for 30 minutes. Reduce heat to 160°C/325°F, Gas Mark 3, and bake for a further 15 minutes. A crisp green salad is all that is required to accompany this main course. Serves 4.

Pork Patties

500 g/1 lb (2 cups) minced (ground) pork; salt and freshly ground black pepper; 30 g/ 1 oz (2 tbsp) butter; 1 tbsp French (Dijon) mustard; 120 ml/4 fl oz (½ cup) single (light) cream.

Shape pork into 4 medium patties. Season well with salt and pepper. Heat butter in a frying pan (skillet), add patties, press out flat and cook 3 minutes on each side. Remove to a heated serving plate and keep warm. Add mustard and cream to pan, stir in brown bits from bottom of pan and cook until sauce thickens. Spoon sauce over patties and serve immediately. Serves 4.

Yorkshire Rarebit

A variation on the traditional Welsh rarebit.

15 g/½ oz (1 tbsp) butter; 1 tbsp flour; 2 tbsp milk; 2 tbsp beer; 2 tsp dry mustard mixed with water; large pinch salt; freshly ground black pepper; 125 g/4 oz (1 cup) grated Cheddar cheese; 2 slices hot buttered toast; 2 thick slices lean cooked ham; 2 hot poached eggs.

Melt butter in a saucepan. Remove from heat and stir in flour to make a smooth paste, then stir in milk, beer, mustard, salt and pepper. Return to low heat and stir until thickened. Add cheese and stir just until cheese has melted – about 2 minutes. Place toast on 2 flameproof serving plates. Spoon cheese mixture over toast, top with ham and place under a preheated grill (broiler) until cheese is bubbly and ham lightly browned. Remove from heat and top each serving with a poached egg. Serve immediately. Serves 2.

Sour Cream Coleslaw

½ medium cabbage, finely shredded; 2 tbsp oil; 1 tbsp vinegar; 1 tbsp French (Dijon) mustard; 2 tbsp chopped celery; ½ red pepper, cored, seeded and shredded; ½ green pepper, cored, seeded and shredded; 4 spring onions (scallions), chopped; 120 ml/4 fl oz (½ cup) single (light) cream; 1 tsp lemon juice; 3 tbsp chopped parsley.

Put cabbage in a large salad bowl. Combine oil, vinegar and mustard and beat with a fork until thick. Add to cabbage and mix well. Top with celery, shredded peppers and spring onions (scallions). Chill well. Just before serving, toss in cream and lemon juice, mixing lightly. Top with chopped parsley. Serves 6.

MUTTON

The meat of mature sheep over 2 years of age. Good mutton is brick-red when freshly cut and the bones are dry and white. Although not nearly as tender as lamb, many people prefer mutton's richer flavour.

□ **To Cook:** Mutton can be used in any recipe for pot roasted, casseroled, 'boiled' or stewed lamb, it simply takes longer to cook. The choicest chump or loin chops or cutlets (rib chops) from a top-quality mutton carcase can be pan-fried or grilled (broiled) in the same way as lamb, though they will be less tender. (*See Lamb*).

To roast mutton, use the slow method, in a preheated moderate oven (180°C/350°F, Gas Mark 4) throughout. No fat is needed in the pan. Mutton is best well-cooked – allow 40–45 minutes per 500 g (1 lb). A sliced onion placed on meat before cooking gives it a delicious flavour.

N

NAPOLEONS

French pastries each consisting of three layers of thin crisp puff pastry (paste) rectangles, sandwiched with Crème Pâtissière or whipped cream and topped with white icing (frosting), rippled with lines of chocolate.

Napoleons are similar to the French pastry, Mille Feuilles (see page 216), although in France the name 'Napoleons' is rarely associated with them in any French recipe. Why these pastries were named 'Napoleons' and why the distinctive and decorative icing was used is obscure. The explanation differs from country to country. Probably it was named after *Napolitains*, the imposing, and embellished, layered pastries that used to decorate formal dinner tables.

Napoleons

1 × 375 g/12 oz packet frozen puff pastry (paste), thawed, or 1 quantity Puff Pastry (page 274); 500 ml/18 fl oz (2 cups) Crème Pâtissière (page 165); 1 quantity Glacé Icing (page 164).
CHOCOLATE DECORATION: *60 g/2 oz (⅓ cup) cooking chocolate; 45 g/1½ oz (3 tbsp) butter.*

Roll out pastry (paste) as thin as possible to a rectangle about the size of a large baking tray. Place on dampened baking tray, prick well all over and chill for 15 minutes. Bake in a preheated moderately hot oven (200°C/400°F, Gas Mark 6) for 5–10 minutes or until pale golden, then turn pastry (paste) over carefully and continue baking for a further 5 minutes. Cool on a wire rack. Cut into 3 strips about 8 cm (3 in) wide. Spread one strip of pastry (paste) with half the crème pâtissière. Lay a second pastry (paste) strip on top and spread with remaining crème. Top with last strip. Press down lightly and spread icing over top.
CHOCOLATE DECORATION: Melt chocolate and butter in a double saucepan (double boiler) over warm water and cool slightly. Pipe in thin rows across the icing at 2.5 cm (1 in) intervals. Before chocolate has set use tines of a fork or back of a sharp knife to draw a line down centre of length of pastry (paste). Draw another line in the opposite direction on each side, thus pulling chocolate into a decorative pattern. When chocolate has set, cut strips crossways into pieces about 5 cm (2 in) wide, using a very sharp knife. Best served on the day they are made. Makes about 8.

NASI GORENG

One of the basic dishes of Indonesia, rather similar to fried rice. A variation is popular in Malaysia also. Meats, vegetables or seafood are cut in small chunks and fried separately; the rice is then fried in oil and, towards the end of cooking, all the ingredients are stirred together. The dish can vary from region to region but rice is always the major component. *Bami Goreng* is a similar fried dish, but made with cooked noodles instead of cooked rice. **See recipes.**

Nasi Goreng

3 eggs; salt and freshly ground black pepper; oil for frying; 2 onions, chopped; 2 cloves garlic, crushed; ½ tsp dried shrimp paste (trasi); 500 g (1 lb) pork or lean beef steak; diced; 250 g/8 oz (1⅓ cups) prawns (shrimp), shelled and deveined; 500 g/1 lb (4 cups) cold cooked rice; 6 spring onions (scallions), finely sliced; 2 tbsp light soy sauce; 3 tbsp onion flakes; 1 cucumber, finely sliced.

Beat eggs with salt and pepper. Heat a little oil in a frying pan (skillet) and make an omelette with half the eggs. Turn on to a plate without folding. Make another omelette with the remaining eggs. When cool, place omelettes on top of each other, roll up and cut into strips. Set aside for garnish. Put chopped onions, garlic and shrimp paste in blender and blend to a paste (or chop onions very finely, crush garlic and dissolve paste in a little hot water; combine these 3 ingredients). Heat 3 tbsp oil in frying pan (skillet) or wok and fry blended ingredients for a few minutes. Add meat and fry, stirring, until cooked. Remove meat and keep warm. Fry prawns (shrimp), remove and keep warm. Heat 2 tbsp more oil and stir in rice and spring onions (scallions), mixing thoroughly. Sprinkle with soy sauce and mix evenly. Return meat and prawns (shrimp) to pan and combine with rice. Keep hot. Place onion flakes in a wire strainer and lower them into hot oil for a few seconds or until they turn golden-brown. Drain on paper towels. Pile rice mixture on a heated serving platter and garnish with strips of omelette, fried onion flakes and cucumber slices. Serves 6–8.
NOTE: Dried shrimp paste, or *trasi*, is available from Asian grocery stores. It is also sold as *blachan*.

Nasi Goreng (Malaysia)

750 g/1½ lb (6 cups) cold cooked rice; 2 small brown onions, sliced; 4 tbsp oil; 2 tbsp raisins; 1 egg, lightly beaten; 2 fresh red chillies, seeded and chopped; 2 cloves garlic, chopped; 250 g/8 oz (1⅓ cups) prawns (shrimp), shelled and deveined; 2 spring onions (scallions), finely sliced.

Stir rice to separate grains. Fry one onion gently in oil in a wok or frying pan (skillet) until crisp and golden-brown. Remove with a slotted spoon, drain and set aside for garnish. Fry raisins in same oil for 2 minutes, stirring, then remove and set aside. Pour egg into pan and make a thin omelette. Roll up and slice finely. Reserve for garnish. Blend or pound together chillies, garlic and remaining onion, then fry together gently for 3–4 minutes, adding more oil if necessary. Add prawns (shrimp) and stir-fry until cooked. Stir in rice, increase heat and fry for about 3 minutes. Serve on a large heated platter, garnished with fried onions, raisins, omelette strips and spring onions (scallions). Serves 6–8.

NAVARIN

A French lamb or mutton stew made with a proportion of onions, carrots, turnips and sometimes potatoes, or in spring with peas and young new vegetables, when it becomes *Navarin à la Printanière*.

This substantial dish is best eaten when reheated: first refrigerate overnight to solidify the fat, then remove the fat next day and finish cooking. **See recipes.**

Navarin of Lamb

1 kg (2 lb) lamb neck chops; salt and freshly ground black pepper; 30 g/1 oz (2 tbsp) dripping; 1 tbsp flour; 750 ml/1¼ pints (3 cups) warm water or stock; 1 clove garlic, crushed; 1 tsp tomato purée (paste); 1 bouquet garni; 30 g/1 oz (2 tbsp) butter; 1 tsp sugar; 8 small onions, peeled; 2 large carrots, thickly sliced; 1 turnip, sliced.

Trim chops and season with salt and pepper. Brown in melted dripping in a flameproof casserole. Remove half the fat, then sprinkle chops with flour, turning to coat well. Cook gently until golden-brown. Add water or stock, garlic and tomato purée (paste). Bring to the boil, stirring constantly. Add bouquet garni, cover and simmer gently for 1 hour. Remove meat, strain gravy into a bowl and return meat to gravy. Cover and refrigerate overnight. Next day, remove solidified fat from the surface and place meat and liquid back in casserole. Heat gently. Melt butter and sugar in a frying pan (skillet) and fry vegetables quickly until golden. Add vegetables to meat, cover and simmer very gently for 1 hour or until meat and vegetables are tender. Adjust seasoning. Serve with crusty bread or with creamy mashed potatoes seasoned with nutmeg. Serves 4–6.

Navarin à la Printanière

500 g (1 lb) boned shoulder of lamb, trimmed and cubed; 500 g (1 lb) boned breast of lamb, trimmed and cubed; 60 g/2 oz (4 tbsp) dripping; 500 ml/18 fl oz (2 cups) stock; 2 tbsp tomato purée (paste); 750 g (1½ lb) new potatoes, scraped; 6 baby carrots, scraped; 18 whole baby onions, peeled; 165 g/5½ oz (1 cup) shelled fresh peas, cooked; 250 g/8 oz (1 cup) sliced green beans, cooked; salt and freshly ground black pepper; 20 g/⅔ oz (½ cup) chopped parsley.

Brown meat in melted dripping in a frying pan (skillet). Remove and place in a flameproof casserole. Pour off fat from frying pan (skillet), then deglaze pan with 250 ml/8 fl oz (1 cup) of the stock. Pour this stock into casserole and add remaining stock and tomato purée (paste). Bring to the boil, reduce heat, cover and simmer 1 hour. Cool and refrigerate overnight. Next day, remove solidified fat from surface. Heat meat and liquid gently. Add potatoes, carrots and onions and simmer about 1 hour or until meat and vegetables are tender. Skim any fat from surface, then fold in peas and beans. Season with salt and pepper and simmer 5 minutes longer. Serve sprinkled with parsley. Serves 6–8.

NECTARINE

A superb summer stone fruit of the peach family, with a smooth skin, flushed a pinky red. The flesh is firm and fragrant, and varies from creamy white to quite deep orange. Varieties range from small to large, some with clingstones and some with slipstones, and can be used in most recipes calling for peaches. **See recipes.**

Baked Nectarines

6–8 ripe nectarines, peeled; juice ½ lemon; 370 g/12 oz (1½ cups) sugar; 250 ml/8 fl oz (1 cup) water; 6–8 cloves.

Cover nectarines with cold water and lemon juice to prevent discoloration. Place sugar and water in a saucepan and stir over medium heat until sugar has dissolved. Bring to the boil and boil for 5 minutes without stirring. Remove each nectarine from water, dry and stick with a clove. Arrange in a baking dish and pour syrup over. Bake in a preheated moderate oven (180°C/350°F, Gas Mark 4) for 20 minutes or until tender, basting 2–3 times with syrup. Cool, then chill. Serve with cream. Serves 3–4.

Sugared Nectarines

8 ripe slipstone nectarines; 60 g/2 oz (¼ cup) caster sugar; juice 1 lemon.

Slice nectarines into a glass bowl by making an incision down the natural division of the fruit deep enough to reach stone. Make another incision beside it and slice out section. Continue in this way around fruit to give even slices. Sprinkle sugar over fruit, then lemon juice. Serve immediately. Serves 4–6.

Smetna with Nectarines

A marvellous combination of smetna (the Russian name for sour cream) and brown sugar makes the difference in this dessert. Equally good for peaches.

140 g/4½ oz (¾ cup) firmly packed brown sugar; 350 ml/12 fl oz (1½ cups) single (light) cream; 2 tsp lemon juice; 8 large ripe yellow nectarines, stoned and sliced; toasted slivered almonds to decorate.

Combine brown sugar and cream, soured with lemon juice. Spoon alternate layers of cream and fruit into a dessert bowl or soufflé dish. Cover with plastic wrap and chill for 2 hours. Sprinkle with toasted slivered almonds before serving. Serves 6.

Nectarines in White Wine

A simple yet quite stunning summer dessert.

6 large ripe nectarines, stoned and sliced; 60 g/2 oz (¼ cup) caster sugar; white wine, chilled.

Place nectarines in large wine glasses. Sprinkle with sugar, pour over white wine and refrigerate for 30 minutes. Serves 4. NOTE: Peaches can be used instead of nectarines with equally delicious results.

NESSELRODE PUDDING

Originally this pudding was a very rich frozen confection full of candied fruits, chestnuts and liqueurs. It was invented by the chef to a Russian statesman, Count Nesselrode, who had a taste for lavish living. Today, the pudding is less rich and may be served unfrozen, but is still delicious.

Nesselrode Pudding

3 egg yolks; 180 g/6 oz (¾ cup) sugar; 600 ml/1 pint (2½ cups) single (light) cream; 1 tbsp gelatine softened in 2 tbsp cold water; 90 g/3 oz (½ cup) canned crushed pineapple, drained; 90 g/3 oz (½ cup) raisins; 2 tbsp glacé (candied) cherries, soaked in 2 tbsp rum; 45 g/1½ oz (¼ cup) finely chopped dark chocolate.
DECORATION: *glacé (candied) cherries soaked in rum; dark chocolate, grated.*

Combine egg yolks with sugar in the top of a double saucepan (double boiler). Gradually stir in 350 ml/12 fl oz (1½ cups) of the cream, the softened gelatine and crushed pineapple. Stir over simmering water until custard has thickened slightly. Pour into a chilled ice cream tray and freeze until just firm. Spoon mixture into a chilled bowl and beat with an electric or rotary beater until smooth and creamy. Fold in raisins, cherries and chocolate. Whip remaining cream and fold in. Pour into a decorative freezerproof bowl and return to freezer. Remove to refrigerator 30 minutes before serving to soften slightly. Serve decorated with cherries and chocolate. Serves 8–10.

NICOISE

The word 'Niçoise' conjures up foods ripened by the warm sun of southern France. Dishes à la Niçoise are made from foods of the region around Nice and can be based on fish or vegetables. They are flavoured with garlic and have as their main ingredients tomatoes, black (ripe) olives and olive oil.

Salade Niçoise

Salade Niçoise is a rustic country salad, made with ingredients on hand and in season. Tuna fish can be added, or the lettuce omitted as desired.

1 head lettuce, washed and dried;
1 × 50 g/1⅔ oz can anchovy fillets, drained;
3 tomatoes, peeled and quartered; 3 hard-boiled (hard-cooked) eggs, quartered; 1 cucumber, peeled and sliced; 2 sticks celery, sliced; 1 white onion, sliced; 1 small green or red pepper, cored, seeded and sliced;
90 g/3 oz (½ cup) black (ripe) olives; 1 tbsp capers (optional).
DRESSING: *1 tsp French (Dijon) mustard;*
½ tsp sugar; ½ tsp salt; ¼ tsp black pepper;
1 clove garlic, crushed; 1 tbsp chopped fresh herbs (parsley, chives, oregano); 120 ml/ 4 fl oz (½ cup) olive oil; 2 tbsp wine vinegar; 2 tsp tarragon vinegar; 1 tbsp lemon juice or to taste.

Place lettuce leaves in salad bowl or on a platter. Arrange anchovy fillets, tomatoes, eggs, cucumber, celery and onion slices over lettuce. Garnish with pepper slices, black (ripe) olives and capers if using.
DRESSING: Mix mustard, sugar, salt, pepper, garlic and herbs. Gradually beat in oil and lastly beat in wine and tarragon vinegars. Add lemon juice to taste. Beat again before using. Spoon dressing over salad and serve. Serves 4.

NOCKERL

These Austrian dumplings are usually served in soups, stews and goulashes or as an accompaniment for other dishes. However, Salzburger Nockerl is a wonderfully light fluffy dessert made from puffs of soufflé that bear little resemblance to the general concept of a dumpling. Serve with champagne or a chilled Moselle wine.

Salzburger Nockerl

2 egg yolks; 1 tsp vanilla essence (extract);
½ tsp grated lemon rind; 1 tbsp flour; 4 egg whites; pinch salt; 2 tbsp caster sugar; icing (confectioners) sugar, sifted.

Beat egg yolks lightly and stir in vanilla, lemon rind and flour. In another bowl, beat egg whites with salt until they hold firm peaks. Beat in sugar and continue beating until stiff and glossy. Stir a large spoonful of egg white into egg yolk mixture, then fold quickly and lightly into remaining egg white. Spoon in 4 mounds in a well-buttered 20 × 25 × 5 cm (8 × 10 × 2 in) ovenproof dish; it does not matter if mounds touch each other. Bake in centre of a preheated moderate oven (180°C/350°F, Gas Mark 4) for about 10 minutes or until very pale brown on the outside but still soft and moist on the inside. Sprinkle generously with icing (confectioners) sugar and serve immediately with whipped cream or Crème Anglaise (see page 97). Serves 4.

NOODLES, CHINESE

In China noodles are the *mein* in *Chow Mein*, and differ from other noodles in that the strands are 'thrown' by hand to form the customary long, thin strands or 'strings'; these vary in diameter from that of Italian spaghetti to that of the finest vermicelli. Many large Chinese restaurants throughout the world are beginning to put on displays of noodle-throwing for their delighted clientele.

Chinese noodles can be served in a sauce of meat or vegetables, in soup or fried. Chinese fried noodles get different treatment in different places. Some restaurants (and recipes) call for the noodles to be parboiled, rinsed in cold water, formed into a nest then

fried until crisp; they are then topped with a savoury dish of meat or vegetables in a sauce. In China the noodles are boiled, rinsed, then shallow-fried with meat, vegetables and seasonings or served as a complete dish.
Rice Stick Noodles or Cellophane Noodles: These are also found in Chinese cooking. They are thread-like and clear in colour, and are about the same length as chopsticks. They are sold in Chinese food stores and are used more in southern China.
Commercially-made Noodles: These are sold packaged in fine, medium or wide widths. Some are cut into squares and some fine noodles are shaped into nests. There are also dried soup noodles from Japan, China, Taiwan, Singapore, etc., and packaged noodle dinners. The method of cooking all of these is usually printed on the packet.
□ **To Cook:** The methods of cooking the flat European egg noodles and Chinese noodles differ slightly. Allow 1 bundle Chinese egg noodles for each person. Soak noodles in hot water for about 10 minutes. The strands will separate and enable the noodles to cook evenly. Bring a large saucepan of water to the boil and add a spoonful of peanut oil. Drain the soaked noodles and drop them into the boiling water. When water returns to the boil, cook fine noodles for 2–3 minutes, wide noodles for 3–4 minutes. Do not overcook. Like properly-cooked pasta, noodles should be tender but still firm to the bite.

At end of cooking time, drain noodles in a large colander, then run cold water through the noodles to rinse off excess starch and to cool them so they don't continue to cook in their own heat. Drain thoroughly. Use in soups, or braised noodle dishes – spread noodles out on a damp (not wet) towel, spreading them apart with chopsticks so they dry out a little before using as directed in recipe.
Soft Fried Chinese Noodles Cook noodles as described above and spread out to dry. A little peanut oil may be sprinkled over them to prevent them from sticking.

Heat 2 tbsp each of peanut oil and sesame oil in a wok or frying pan (skillet), and when very hot add a handful of noodles. When golden on one side, turn and fry other side. Repeat with remaining noodles, draining on paper towels before serving at once. It may be necessary to add more oil to the pan if a large quantity of noodles is being fried, but make sure the fresh oil is very hot before adding noodles.

Serve them with beef, pork, poultry or vegetable dishes, or combine with stir-fried ingredients for Chow Mein (see page 75).
Crisp Fried Chinese Noodles These crisp noodles are used mainly as a garnish. Rice vermicelli and cellophane noodles may be fried in deep hot oil straight from the packet. Egg noodles need to be cooked first as for

soft fried noodles. Use a larger amount of peanut oil and deep-fry in handfuls until crisp and golden-brown. Drain on paper towels before serving.

Noodles and Chicken Broth

This is one of the simplest Chinese noodle dishes to prepare and one which is as excellent as it is substantial. It makes an ideal quick luncheon dish.

4 tbsp vegetable oil; 250 g/8 oz (1 cup) shredded cooked chicken meat; 4 tbsp light soy sauce; ¼ onion, finely chopped; ½ tsp grated fresh ginger; 4 tbsp Chinese wine or dry sherry; 250–500 ml/8–18 fl oz (1–2 cups) boiling chicken broth or stock; 250 g (8 oz) Chinese egg noodles; pinch salt.

Heat oil in a wok or deep frying pan (skillet). When very hot, add chicken and stir-fry 3–4 minutes. Add soy sauce, onion, ginger and wine or sherry. Cook for 2 minutes, then add 250 ml/8 fl oz (1 cup) broth or enough to cover noodles completely. When boiling hard, add noodles and salt and cook until done. Serve hot. Serves 4.

Chicken Noodle Soup

125 g (4 oz) cooked Chinese egg noodles; 125 g/4 oz (½ cup) shredded cooked chicken meat; 2 slices cooked ham, shredded; 750 ml/1¼ pints (3 cups) chicken broth or stock; ½ tsp salt; pinch pepper; 2 tsp soy sauce; 4 spring onions (scallions), shredded.

Place cooked noodles in heated serving bowl. Arrange chicken and ham on top of noodles. Heat broth, adding salt, pepper and soy sauce. Pour hot broth over noodles, top with spring onions (scallions) and serve hot. Serves 4.

Braised Noodles with Chicken

4 bundles wide Chinese egg noodles; 1 tbsp soy sauce; 1 tbsp Chinese wine or dry sherry; 4 chicken fillets (skinless, boneless, half-breasts), cubed; ½ Chinese cabbage; 1 tbsp cornflour (cornstarch); 2 tbsp cold water; 1 tbsp oyster sauce; ½ tsp salt; 2 tbsp peanut oil; 2 cloves garlic, crushed; 1 tsp grated fresh ginger; 250 ml/8 fl oz (1 cup) chicken stock; 5 spring onions (scallions), chopped.

Soak noodles in hot water for 10 minutes, then cook as directed on the packet for 3–4 minutes or until tender but still firm. Do not overcook. Drain in a colander and rinse under cold running water to stop cooking. Drain. Pour soy sauce and wine or sherry over chicken. Mix and leave to marinate. Cut stalks of Chinese cabbage into bite-sized pieces. Mix cornflour (cornstarch) with cold water in a small bowl, add oyster sauce and salt, and set aside.

Heat oil in a wok or frying pan (skillet) and gently fry garlic and ginger for a few seconds. Add chicken and stir-fry over high heat for 2 minutes or until colour changes. Add cabbage and fry, stirring, for 1 minute longer. Add stock, bring to the boil, add cornflour (cornstarch) mixture and stir until thick. Add well-drained noodles and heat through, tossing to mix evenly. Garnish with spring onions (scallions). Serves 4–5.

Chinese Chicken and Noodle Salad

4 half-breasts of chicken; salt; 1 bay leaf; 1 slice onion; few black peppercorns; 370 g (12 oz) Chinese egg noodles; 1 tbsp oil; Sesame Peanut Sauce (page 29).
GARNISH: *3 spring onions (scallions), finely sliced; 1 tbsp toasted sesame seeds.*

Place chicken breasts in a saucepan, and add salted water to cover, bay leaf, onion and peppercorns. Simmer gently for 10 minutes. Cool in water. Cook noodles according to packet directions or as opposite. Drain, and rinse under cold running water. Drain thoroughly and toss lightly with oil to prevent sticking. Drain chicken, remove skin and bones, and slice flesh finely. Place noodles in a large heated serving dish, top with chicken and pour sesame peanut sauce over. Garnish with sliced spring onions (scallions) and toasted sesame seeds. Toss salad gently and serve. Serves 6–8.

Fragrant Noodles

20 dried shrimp (from Chinese groceries); 120 ml/4 fl oz (½ cup) peanut oil; 3 medium onions, diced; 1 tbsp light soy sauce; 2 tsp Chinese wine or dry sherry; 500 ml/18 fl oz (2 cups) water; 500 g (1 lb) Chinese egg noodles.

Soak dried shrimp in cold water 10 minutes, then drain and clean. Heat half of the oil in a frying pan (skillet) or wok, add onions and stir-fry 2–3 minutes. Lower heat slightly, add shrimp and cook, stirring, until only residual moisture is left and oil spatters when in contact with moisture. Remove from heat. Heat rest of oil in a small saucepan, add shrimp mixture, soy sauce and wine or sherry and stir-fry 1–2 minutes. Add water and simmer 30 minutes or until water has nearly evaporated. Meanwhile, cook noodles according to packet directions or opposite. Drain, rinse quickly under cold running water and drain again. Reheat all ingredients together and serve. Serves 4.

Prawn Chow Mein

250 g/8 oz (1⅓ cups) Chinese egg noodles; 6 tbsp vegetable oil; 280 g/9 oz (1⅓ cups) small shelled prawns (shrimp), deveined; 3 tbsp soy sauce; 120 ml/4 fl oz (½ cup) Chinese

wine or dry sherry; 2 tsp sugar; 1 tsp salt; ½ tsp grated fresh ginger; vinegar to serve.

Cook noodles according to packet directions or opposite. Drain and rinse under cold running water. Distribute noodles as thinly as possible on a damp (not wet) cloth and place them in a cool, airy place to dry. Place ⅓ of the oil in a wok or frying pan (skillet) and heat. Add prawns (shrimp) and fry until a little over half done (about 3 minutes). Then add half of the soy sauce, Chinese wine or sherry and sugar. Cook another 3 minutes, then remove from pan and keep warm. Put remaining oil into pan and heat. Add noodles, and fry, turning from time to time with a fork or chopsticks, until golden-brown. Add remaining soy sauce, wine and sugar, the salt and ginger. Cook briskly for a further 2 minutes. Return prawns (shrimp) to pan, cook another 2 minutes, and serve immediately. Some people prefer a dash of vinegar on 'Ch'ao Mien' and this should be provided at the table. Serves 4.

Fried Noodles

250 g (8 oz) Chinese egg noodles; 8 tbsp oil; 3 eggs, beaten with ½ tsp salt; 250 g (8 oz) boneless pork, shredded; 2 canned bamboo shoots, shredded; 370 g/12 oz (2 cups) chopped vegetables or 125 g/4 oz (2 cups) bean sprouts; 6 dried mushrooms, soaked in water, drained and shredded; 4 spring onions (scallions), shredded; 1 tbsp Chinese wine or dry sherry; 2 tbsp soy sauce; 120 ml/4 fl oz (½ cup) stock; 1 tsp cornflour (cornstarch); 2 tsp salt.

Cook noodles according to packet directions or as opposite. Drain, rinse under cold running water and drain again. Heat 3 tbsp oil in a frying pan (skillet), add eggs and fry to a thin omelette. Break omelette into small pieces and remove to a plate. Heat a further 3 tbsp oil in pan and fry pork 3–4 minutes. Add bamboo shoots, vegetables or bean sprouts, mushrooms, spring onions (scallions), wine or sherry and soy sauce. Blend stock with cornflour (cornstarch), add to pan and heat, stirring, until thickened. Keep hot. Heat remaining oil in a separate

frying pan (skillet) or wok, add noodles and salt and fry for 6 minutes, stirring constantly. Pat into a pancake shape and allow to brown lightly on both sides. Remove noodles to a large heated plate or bowl, pour over pork mixture, top with omelette pieces and serve hot. Serves 4.

Chilled Noodles with Sauce

370 g (12 oz) Chinese egg noodles; 1 tbsp sesame oil; 1 tbsp vegetable oil; 2 eggs, beaten; 250 g/8 oz (1 cup) shredded cooked chicken or pork; 3 slices cooked ham, shredded; 125 g/4 oz (1 cup) shredded cucumber; 90 g/3 oz (½ cup) cooked shelled prawns (shrimp), deveined.
SAUCE: *1 tbsp sesame seeds; 1 tbsp red pepper oil, or 1 tsp Tabasco (hot pepper) sauce; 2 tbsp soy sauce; 2 tsp vinegar; 500 ml/18 fl oz (2 cups) chicken broth or stock.*

Cook noodles according to packet directions or as on page 238. Drain, mix with sesame oil and chill. Heat vegetable oil in a frying pan (skillet), add eggs and fry into a thin omelette. Shred omelette. Arrange shredded omelette, chicken or pork, ham, cucumber and prawns (shrimp) on top of noodles.
SAUCE: Grind sesame seeds in a mortar. Add remaining sauce ingredients and mix thoroughly. Serve sauce separately in a bowl. Pour sauce over noodles and shredded ingredients just before eating. Serves 4–6.
NOTE: If you cannot buy red pepper oil, make it by heating 2 tbsp sesame oil in a small frying pan (skillet) and frying 2 red chillies until they turn dark. Drain off the oil and discard chillies.

Lamb Shreds with Cellophane Noodles

370 g (12 oz) lamb chump chops, boned; 1 egg white; 1 tsp salt; 1 tsp cornflour (cornstarch); 250 ml/8 fl oz (1 cup) plus 2 tbsp peanut oil; 1 tbsp soy sauce; ¼ tsp red pepper oil or Tabasco (hot pepper) sauce; 30 g (1 oz) cellophane noodles.

Slice lamb into thin, match-like shreds. Mix with egg white, ½ tsp salt and the cornflour (cornstarch). Let stand 5 minutes. Heat 2 tbsp peanut oil in a frying pan (skillet) or wok and stir-fry lamb for about 2 minutes. Add soy sauce and pepper oil or Tabasco (hot pepper) sauce. Mix well and place on a heated platter. Heat remaining peanut oil and deep-fry noodles for 1–2 seconds. Do not burn. Drain on paper towels. Sprinkle with the remaining salt and place at both ends of the lamb shreds. Serves 4.

NOODLES, EGG

A paste made from flour and egg yolks, rolled flat and cut into strips. Egg noodles are a favourite in Germany where they are called *nudeln* or *nockerln,* also in France where they are known as *nouilles.*

Noodles may be cooked and treated in much the same way as spaghetti or other pastas (see *Pasta*).

In Germany noodles are generally boiled, drained and mixed with melted butter or bacon fat. They are seasoned with salt, pepper and nutmeg, paprika, poppyseeds, finely chopped dill or parsley, crumbled cooked bacon or chopped ham – the seasoning added depends on the food being served with the noodles.
☐ **To Cook:** Cook egg noodles in plenty of boiling salted water; keep the water boiling rapidly to prevent noodles sticking together. Drain, use as directed.

See also *Pasta.*

Chicken Noodle Casserole

500 g (1 lb) egg noodles; 1.5 kg (3 lb) chicken joints; salt and freshly ground black pepper; 60 g/2 oz (4 tbsp) butter; 1–2 tbsp oil; 1 onion, finely chopped; pinch dried rosemary; 40 g/1⅓ oz (⅓ cup) flour; 600 ml/1 pint (2½ cups) chicken stock; 120 ml/4 fl oz (½ cup) dry white wine; 120 ml/4 fl oz (½ cup) single (light) cream; 60 g/2 oz (½ cup) chopped walnuts.

Cook noodles in plenty of boiling salted water until tender. Drain and put in bottom

of large shallow ovenproof serving dish. Sprinkle chicken pieces with salt and pepper. Brown in butter in a frying pan (skillet), a few pieces at a time. Place on noodles. Add oil then onion to butter in frying pan (skillet) and cook gently until soft. Stir in rosemary and flour and cook, stirring, 1–2 minutes. Stir in stock gradually, then wine. Bring to the boil, stirring constantly. Add cream and cook gently for 5–10 minutes. Add nuts, then spoon sauce over chicken. Cover dish with lid or foil and bake in a preheated moderate oven (180°C/350°F, Gas Mark 4) for 1 hour. Serves 6.

NUT BRITTLE

Nut brittle is a clear, hard toffee well-flavoured with nuts, either peanuts, pecans, Brazil nuts or some other combination. It is best made with corn syrup, which is available from specialist grocery stores.

Nut Brittle

250 ml/8 fl oz (1 cup) water; 500 g/1 lb (2 cups) sugar; 340 g/11 oz (1 cup) light corn syrup; 310 g/12 oz (2 cups) shelled raw peanuts, pecans or Brazil nuts; 1 tsp salt; 30 g/1 oz (2 tbsp) butter; ¼ tsp bicarbonate of soda (baking soda).

Place water in a large heavy saucepan and bring to the boil. Remove from heat and stir in sugar until dissolved. Stir in corn syrup, nuts and salt. Return to medium heat and cook to hard crack stage (146°C/295°F), stirring occasionally to keep nuts submerged so they cook thoroughly and toffee syrup does not burn. Remove from heat and stir in butter and soda. Pour on to a well-buttered Swiss roll tin (jelly roll pan). When cool, crack into pieces and store in an airtight container. Makes about 1 kg/2 lb (4 cups).
NOTE: To test for hard crack stage without a sugar thermometer, drop ½ tsp of toffee into cold water. It should make brittle threads that stay brittle when removed from water.

NUT BUTTER

This can be smooth or chunky and is made by pounding or grinding a variety of blanched and roasted nuts to a butter-like spread. Probably the best known nut butter is Peanut Butter (see page 281). Nut butters will keep for months if stored in airtight jars in a cool dry place.

Nut Butter

370 g/12 oz (2 cups) toasted, unsalted almonds, pecans, walnuts, cashews or other nuts; 3–6 tbsp safflower or vegetable oil; 1 tsp salt.

Put nuts, half the oil and the salt in a blender or food processor. Purée to desired consistency, adding more oil if necessary. Store in sealed, airtight jars. Makes about 370 g/12 oz (1 cup).

NUTMEG

The large nutmeg tree is native to the Indonesian Islands and the Philippines, and also grows in the West Indies. The ripe plum-like fruit dries and then splits open. The nutmeg seed is encased in a bright red outer covering, which, when dried in the sun, is known as mace (see *Mace*). The seeds are slowly dried in the tropical sun or over slow-burning charcoal fires. They will keep well in an airtight container, sometimes for years.

Nutmeg is at its best when grated fresh into the dish in which it is required as, once grated, it rapidly loses its best flavour.

Beautifully aromatic nutmeg is equally at home in sweet and savoury dishes. The English devotees of the 18th and 19th centuries often travelled with their own, personal nutmeg grater, such was their love of this spice. In English cooking today, nutmeg is mainly used in cakes and sweet dishes, but it is equally important in savoury and meat dishes.

Use it in sausages, terrines, pâtés and potted meats. It is also good in egg dishes, or with mashed potatoes, and it is particularly tasty with spinach. A spinach ravioli filling nearly always contains nutmeg, as does the famous Bolognese Sauce (see page 272). Nutmeg is excellent in white or cheese sauce.

Nutmeg is a frequent ingredient in many Indian spiced foods, and in Garam Masala (see page 139) – that fragrant spice-blend often added at the end of cooking. Nutmeg is also a common flavouring in Middle Eastern cookery, and is good with lamb.

For desserts, nutmeg is a natural partner of rice and other milk puddings, apple pies and spiced fruits. It is often sprinkled over warm milk, punches or drinks to be taken at night, and it is claimed that nutmeg has a slightly soporific effect.

Buy good quality, large nutmegs whole, store in a small jar, then grate freshly each time nutmeg is needed. Small tin nutmeg graters are inexpensive and available from

most kitchen shops; more elaborate mills, rather like pepper mills, are also available. **See recipes**.

Spinach Florentine

1 large bunch spinach, coarsely shredded; 30 g/1 oz (2 tbsp) butter; 1 clove garlic, finely chopped; salt; ¼ tsp nutmeg; 4 tbsp single (light) cream; coarsely grated Parmesan cheese; melted butter.

Place spinach in large saucepan, cover and cook for 5 minutes, tossing occasionally. Drain well, pressing out all excess moisture. Heat butter in a frying pan (skillet), add garlic, salt, nutmeg and cream and stir. Add spinach and toss lightly to heat through. Place in a flameproof serving dish and sprinkle with cheese and melted butter. Brown quickly under a preheated grill (broiler). Serves 4.

Chicken Liver Mousse

180 g/6 oz (1 cup) chicken livers; 2 eggs; 350 ml/12 fl oz (1½ cups) milk; ¼ tsp salt; freshly ground black pepper; nutmeg; 1 clove garlic; 1 tsp chopped parsley.

Remove any veins and sinew from chicken livers. Place in a blender with eggs, milk, salt, pepper, nutmeg, garlic and parsley, and blend to a purée. It may be necessary to do this in 3 batches. Fill 6 small buttered soufflé dishes. Place in a roasting tin (pan) containing enough water to come halfway up sides of dishes. Cover with foil. Bake in a preheated hot oven (220°C/425°F, Gas Mark 7) for 30 minutes or until mixture is set. Loosen sides of mousses from dishes with a knife, invert on to a heated plate and drain off any excess juices. Serve hot with Fresh Tomato Sauce (see page 271). Serves 6.

Cauliflower Cream Soup

½ medium cauliflower, broken into florets; 1 litre/1¾ pints (4 cups) chicken stock; 5 tbsp milk; 30 g/1 oz (2 tbsp) butter; salt and freshly ground black pepper; ¼ tsp nutmeg; 2 egg yolks, 4 tbsp single (light) cream.

Reserve a few cauliflower florets for garnish. Drop remaining cauliflower into boiling salted water and cook until tender, about 10 minutes. Drain and press through a sieve, or purée in a blender or food processor. Place in a saucepan, add stock and bring slowly to the boil. Add milk, butter, salt, pepper and nutmeg. Combine egg yolks with cream, add a little of the hot soup, blend well and stir into remaining soup. Cook gently without boiling until soup thickens. Garnish with sprigs of raw cauliflower and serve immediately, sprinkled with a light fresh grating of nutmeg. Serves 6.

Armenian Nutmeg Cake

370 g/12 oz (2 cups) firmly packed brown sugar; 250 g/8 oz (2 cups) self-raising flour, sifted; 125 g/4 oz (½ cup) butter; 1 tsp bicarbonate of soda (baking soda); 250 ml/8 fl oz (1 cup) milk; 1 egg, beaten; 1 tsp nutmeg; 60 g/2 oz (½ cup) chopped walnuts.

Combine sugar and flour. Rub (cut) in butter until mixture resembles fine breadcrumbs. Press half the mixture into a well-greased 20 cm (8 in) square tin (pan). Dissolve soda in milk, add egg and nutmeg and pour over remaining sugar and flour mixture. Mix well, then spoon into tin (pan) on top of pressed-in mixture. Sprinkle walnuts over. Bake in a preheated moderate oven (180°C/350°F, Gas Mark 4) for 1 hour. Allow to stand for 15 minutes before turning out on to a wire rack to cool.

NUTS

These are one of man's oldest foods and one of the most useful. As well as making sustaining and convenient snacks, they are excellent companions to fruit or cheese for dessert and have dozens of culinary uses from nut butters, salads, savoury dishes, breads, cakes and biscuits (cookies) to desserts, ice creams and confectionery.

For long storage, nuts should be kept unshelled in a cool place or in the freezer. If shelled, buy in quantities you can use up within a few weeks and keep them in an airtight container in a cool, dark, dry place. Larger quantities of shelled nuts are best stored in the freezer.

Salted Nuts Peanuts, cashews, walnuts, almonds, etc., can be salted individually or mixed. Heat about 2 tbsp butter or oil for each 125–180 g/4–6 oz (1 cup) of blanched nuts Spread nuts in a thin, even layer in the pan and cook slowly, stirring continuously, until nuts are a delicate, even brown. Remove from pan, drain on paper towels and sprinkle with salt, allowing approximately ½ tsp per 125–180 g/4–6 oz (1 cup) of nuts. Toss lightly to coat all nuts and serve, or cool and store in an airtight container.

Curried Nuts Follow recipe for Salted Nuts, but add ½ tsp curry powder to salt before sprinkling over. Onion or garlic salt may be substituted for plain salt, to give the nuts added flavour.

Devilled Nuts Follow recipe for Salted Nuts until nuts are browned, then for each 125–180 g/4–6 oz (1 cup) of nuts add 1 tsp Worcestershire sauce, ½ tsp salt and small pinch cayenne to pan. Stir over gentle heat until nuts are evenly coated, remove from pan and drain on paper towels.

See also *Nut Brittle*, *Nut Butter* and the individual entries for nuts.

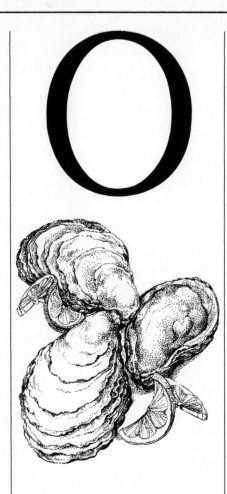

O

OATCAKE

See Bannock.

OATMEAL

Made by grinding hulled oats into flour or meal. Oatmeal is generally prepared in grades according to its texture – coarse, medium or fine; medium is the one most used.

Oatmeal is among the most nutritious of all the grains, and rolled oats have been used to make breakfast porridge for generations of families throughout the world. Oatmeal is also used to give bulk to sausages, to thicken soups and stews or to bake oatcakes, breads, scones, biscuits (cookies) and puddings. The Scots have many splendid dishes containing oatmeal, while Swiss breakfast muesli (granola) contains uncooked rolled or toasted oats. Quick-cooking oatmeal is readily available, and can be used in many recipes as well as for a quick breakfast cereal. **See recipes.**

Ginger Oatmeal Scones

125 g/4 oz (1 cup) flour; 4 tsp baking powder; 2 tsp ground ginger; ½ tsp ground allspice; ½ tsp salt; 60 g/2 oz (1 cup) instant oats; 30 g/1 oz (2 tbsp) butter; 2 tsp honey; 4 tbsp warm water; 5 tbsp milk.

Sift flour, baking powder, spices and salt into a bowl. Add oats and rub (cut) in butter. Mix honey, water and milk, blending thoroughly. Pour into dry ingredients and mix to a soft dough. On a floured surface lightly pat dough into a round about 2.5 cm (1 in) thick. Cut into rounds using a scone cutter or sharp knife. Place on an ungreased baking tray and bake in a preheated hot oven (230°C/450°F, Gas Mark 8) for 10–12 minutes. Serve warm with butter and ginger marmalade or apricot jam. Makes about 12.

Oat and Raisin Bread

1 egg, beaten; 60 g/2 oz (⅓ cup) firmly packed brown sugar; 2 tbsp golden (light corn) syrup, warmed; 300 ml/½ pint (1¼ cups) buttermilk; 60 g/2 oz (4 tbsp) butter, melted; 60 g/2 oz (⅔ cup) rolled oats; 125 g/4 oz (1 cup) wholewheat flour; 2 tsp baking powder; ¾ tsp salt; ¾ tsp bicarbonate of soda (baking soda); 125 g/4 oz (⅔ cup) raisins.

Beat egg with sugar, syrup, buttermilk, butter and rolled oats. Let stand for 5 minutes. Sift flour, baking powder, salt and soda and fold into oat mixture. Stir in raisins lightly. Turn into a greased and lined 20 × 10 cm (8 × 4 in) loaf tin (pan) and spread batter evenly. Bake in a preheated moderate oven (180°C/350°F, Gas Mark 4) for 1 hour or until a skewer inserted in centre comes out clean. Cool on a wire rack. Serve sliced and spread with butter.

Oatmeal Soda Bread

A quick bread made without yeast.

125 g/4 oz (1 cup) wholewheat flour; 125 g/4 oz (1 cup) white flour; 1 tsp baking powder; 1 tsp bicarbonate of soda (baking soda); 1 tsp sugar; 1 tsp salt; 175 g/6 oz (1½ cups) fine oatmeal; 300 ml/½ pint (1¼ cups) buttermilk or sour milk.

Sift flours, baking powder, soda, sugar and salt into a large bowl and mix in oatmeal. Stir in buttermilk or sour milk and mix lightly and quickly to a soft dough. Put on a floured surface, knead once or twice and shape dough lightly into a round. Place on a greased baking tray. Using a sharp knife cut a cross in top of loaf. Bake in a preheated moderately hot oven (190°C/375°F, Gas Mark 5) for about 1 hour or until bread sounds hollow when tapped underneath. Remove from oven and immediately wrap in a clean tea-towel. Serve warm, with plenty of butter.

Cranachan

A marvellous Scottish dessert also known as Cream Crowdie.

4 tbsp medium oatmeal; 300 ml/½ pint (1¼ cups) double (heavy) cream; 1 tbsp icing (confectioners) sugar, sifted; 2 tbsp whisky or 1 tsp vanilla essence (extract).

Spread oatmeal on an ungreased baking tray and lightly toast in a preheated moderate oven (180°C/350°F, Gas Mark 4) for about 15 minutes or until crisp. Cool. Whip cream until it holds soft peaks and fold in icing (confectioners) sugar and whisky or vanilla. Gently stir cooled, toasted oatmeal into cream. Serve on its own or with fresh strawberries or raspberries. Serves 4.

Peanut Butter Biscuits

90 g/3 oz (6 tbsp) butter; 2 tbsp peanut butter; 370 g/12 oz (1½ cups) caster sugar; 90 g/3 oz (½ cup) lightly packed brown sugar; 1 tsp vanilla essence (extract); 1 egg; 180 g/6 oz (1½ cups) self-raising flour, sifted; 1 tsp salt; 45 g/1½ oz (½ cup) rolled oats.

Cream butters, sugars and vanilla. Add egg, beat well, then stir in flour and salt. Mix in oats. Form mixture into 2 rolls about 2.5 cm (1 in) in diameter, wrap in plastic wrap and chill for about 30 minutes. Cut into 5 mm (¼ in) thick slices and arrange on greased baking trays. Bake in a preheated moderate oven (180°C/350°F, Gas Mark 4) about 20 minutes. Cool on baking trays for 3 minutes, then transfer to wire racks. Store in an airtight container. Makes about 36.

Right: Italian Salmon Salad (page 360)

Oatmeal Crunch

90 g/3 oz (1 cup) rolled oats; 90 g/3 oz (1 cup) desiccated (shredded) coconut; 90 g/3 oz (½ cup) demerara or unrefined sugar; ½ tsp vanilla essence (extract); 125 g/4 oz (½ cup) butter, melted; 90 g/3 oz (½ cup) mixed chopped raisins and dried apricots.

Combine oats, coconut, sugar, vanilla and melted butter and mix thoroughly. Stir in chopped fruits. Spread mixture in greased Swiss roll tin (jelly roll pan) and bake in a preheated moderate oven (180°C/350°F, Gas Mark 4) for 20–30 minutes. Cut into squares while still hot. When cool, remove from tin (pan) and store in an airtight container. Makes about 30 squares.

Rolled Oat Biscuits

210 g/7 oz (2¼ cups) rolled oats; 90 g/3 oz (½ cup) demerara or unrefined sugar; 125 g/4 oz (½ cup) butter; 2 tbsp honey; 2 tbsp golden (light corn) syrup; 1 tsp black treacle (molasses) – optional; 1 tbsp sultanas (golden raisins); 2 tbsp chopped dried apricots.

Combine rolled oats and sugar. Melt butter, add honey, syrup and treacle (molasses). Combine thoroughly. Pour over oats and sugar. Add sultanas (golden raisins) and apricots and stir well. Place in a greased Swiss roll tin (jelly roll pan) and smooth top. Bake in a preheated moderate oven (180°C/350°F, Gas Mark 4) for 20–25 minutes. Cut into squares while still warm and remove from tin (pan) when cold. Store in an airtight container. Makes about 20.

Cherry Raisin Drops

90 g/3 oz (1 cup) rolled oats; 250 g/8 oz (1 cup) Ricotta or cottage cheese; 125 g/4 oz (1 cup) self-raising flour, sifted; 125 g/4 oz (½ cup) caster sugar; 45 g/1½ oz (¼ cup) chopped raisins; 60 g/2 oz (¼ cup) chopped glacé (candied) cherries; 125 g/4 oz (½ cup) butter, melted; 5 tbsp milk.

Combine all ingredients and mix well to a stiff batter. Place teaspoonfuls of mixture on greased baking trays, allowing space for spreading. Bake in a preheated moderately hot oven (190°C/375°F, Gas Mark 5) for 15–20 minutes. Makes about 36.

OCTOPUS

A cephalopod, as is squid. The two resemble each other in that they have tentacles but no visible external shell. The best edible octopus is the small variety, with a maximum weight of about 500 g (1 lb).

Left: Swiss Fondue (page 127)

Octopus can be stewed, fried or stuffed and baked like squid (*see Squid*). Little octopuses can be gently fried in olive oil and make a delicious salad, served warm with plenty of lemon juice, garlic and parsley.
☐ **Basic Preparation:** If your recipe calls for only the tentacles, ask the fishmonger to remove the head for you. Otherwise, cut off the tentacles, set aside and clean octopus by pulling out intestines and ink sac, reserving the latter if the octopus is to be cooked in its ink. Using kitchen shears or a very sharp knife, cut out the eyes and beak-like mouth and discard. Rinse well.

If octopus is large, it must be tenderized. After cleaning, pound with a heavy mallet or cleaver then strip off skin by rubbing with salt and rinsing well. Alternatively, simmer in water to cover for 1 hour, then peel off skin and use as required. **See recipes.**

Pickled Octopus

500 g (1 lb) octopus, cleaned, skinned and pounded; 1 clove garlic, crushed; 120 ml/4 fl oz (½ cup) olive oil; 120 ml/4 fl oz (½ cup) vinegar; salt and freshly ground black pepper.
GARNISH: *lemon wedges; chopped parsley.*

Place octopus head and tentacles in a heavy saucepan without any liquid. Cover and cook very gently until octopus turns a deep pink and is tender, about 45 minutes. Drain and, when cool, strip suckers from tentacles if desired. Cut head and tentacles into bite-sized strips and place in a bowl. Add garlic, olive oil, vinegar, salt and pepper. Mix well, cover and leave to marinate in refrigerator for at least 12 hours. Stir occasionally. Drain off marinade, and pile octopus into a serving dish. Garnish with lemon wedges and chopped parsley. Serve with crusty bread. Serves 6.

Octopus Stewed with Onions

500 g (1 lb) octopus, cleaned, skinned and pounded; 5 tbsp olive oil; 3 onions, sliced; 2 cloves garlic, crushed; 1 tsp chopped fresh marjoram, or ½ tsp dried; ½ tsp sugar; 1 bay leaf; 2 tbsp white wine vinegar; 250 ml/8 fl oz (1 cup) red wine; 250 g/8 oz (1 cup) canned tomatoes; 2 tsp tomato purée (paste); salt and freshly ground black pepper; chopped parsley.

Cut octopus into pieces about 5 cm (2 in) long. Heat oil in a deep frying pan (skillet) and sauté onions and garlic until translucent. Add octopus pieces, marjoram, sugar and bay leaf, and cook gently for 5 minutes. Stir in vinegar, wine, tomatoes and tomato purée (paste), cover pan and simmer for 40–45 minutes or until octopus is tender. Remove bay leaf, season with salt and pepper and sprinkle with parsley. Serves 4.

OEUFS A LA NEIGE
(Eggs in the Snow)

See page 97 for recipe.

OFFAL

General term for those parts of an animal left over from cutting up a carcase; in America, they are called variety meats. Some types of offal come from inside the animal (e.g. liver, kidneys, sweetbreads, brains, tripe) while others are external (e.g. tongue, tail, feet, head).

See also entries for individual names.

OIL

Oils are distinguished from fats in that they are liquid at room temperature. Edible oils are processed from many seeds, nuts and fruits including olives, peanuts, sunflower seeds, coconuts, walnuts, pumpkin seeds, grape seeds, avocados, sesame seeds, corn, cotton seeds and soy beans.

There are some edible oils of animal origin, but these are mostly used in manufacturing rather than in the kitchen.

Cold-pressed or unrefined oils have been extracted simply by pressing, and retain their full natural flavour. Refined oils, the majority of those available, have been processed to make them relatively flavourless and odourless, and to keep well. Ideally, buy oil in quantities that you will use within a month or two. Delicate salad oils such as walnut, grape seed or pumpkin seed, and other cold-pressed oils, should be stored in the refrigerator. Cooking oils should be stored, tightly sealed, in a cool place away from light. Do not mix together used and unused oil or the flavour will spoil.

Types of Oil
There are three basic types of oil: poly-unsaturated, mono-unsaturated and saturated. They differ from each other in their chemical structure. There is some controversy about their different effects on health, and it is widely believed that the use of polyunsaturated oils, as well as fats, is preferable to that of saturated ones to help control blood fats (cholesterol and triglycerides), which are a risk factor in heart disease and strokes.

Polyunsaturated oils include sunflower, safflower, maize and soy bean oils.

Mono-unsaturated oils are usually considered fairly neutral in this context. They include olive and peanut oils.

Saturated oils are mostly of animal origin; coconut oil, however, is saturated.

Ways to Use Oils
Salad dressings and sauces: Olive oil is the queen of salad oils and is indispensable for pasta sauces. Its flavour varies in character

245

and strength from one country and from one type of olive to another. A trick for developing a fruity flavour is to keep a few black (ripe) olives in a bottle of oil. The finest oil is virgin oil, from the first cold pressing of the olives. It is sometimes blended with the less expensive, blander oil from later pressings to improve their flavour.

Peanut oil or polyunsaturated all-purpose oils, such as sunflower, safflower, corn or blended oils, can be used in salad dressings and sauces though they will contribute little to the flavour. You may like to mix them half-and-half with olive oil.

Aromatic oils, such as walnut, grape seed, pumpkin seed and avocado, give subtle flavour variations to salad dressings.

Cakes and breads: Oil is used instead of butter or margarine in some cakes and breads, but it cannot be substituted for these in other recipes. All-purpose oils such as the polyunsaturated ones are suitable; the flavour of olive oil is usually too strong though it is occasionally called for.

Frying: The best oils for frying are those which can be heated to fairly high temperatures before beginning to smoke (a sign that the oil is starting to break down and will spoil the flavour of the food; it is also very close to its 'flash' point – when it will burst into flames). Peanut oil (much used in Chinese cooking), corn oil, safflower oil, sunflower and most blended oils are suitable.

So-called 'solid oils' (oils which have been processed to make them solid at room temperature), are much less expensive than polyunsaturated oils; they are recommended by manufacturers for deep-frying and perform particularly well, though the processing makes them more saturated than in their original state.

Olive oil breaks down at high temperatures so can be used for frying only at moderate heat; it is not, therefore, suitable for deep-frying. But its lovely flavour makes it ideal for lightly frying vegetables or for the gentle cooking of onion, which is the first step in so many dishes. It is also used for Ratatouille (see page 329) and other Mediterranean dishes, which are simmered in oil rather than

fried. Mustard seed oil, which has a distinctive flavour, is often used to fry the onions, garlic and spices for a curry.

Heat oil for frying slowly to the correct temperature. If it is not hot enough, too much will be absorbed by the food, and if it is overheated, it will not only spoil the flavour but can be dangerous. If overheated oil should catch alight, smother the flames by sprinkling with flour (don't throw on too much at once as this may cause oil to splash); or cover the pan with a lid and leave so that flames will go out for lack of air. Do not use water as this will only spread the flames. After use, strain oil through a sieve lined with a disposable cloth and store, tightly sealed, in the refrigerator or a very cool place. The 'smoke' point of oil is gradually lowered with use.

Oil that smells burnt or looks dark should be discarded. Solid oil or peanut oil, properly used, should last for about 3–5 fryings. Polyunsaturated oils are less robust and will probably last for only 1–2 fryings.

Sautéeing and browning casserole meat: Use only a little oil, and heat slowly until it just begins to give off a haze, then add food (which should be well-dried or floured) immediately. If you are cooking several batches, wipe pan out quickly with paper towels and use fresh oil for each batch.

Shallow-frying: Usually used for food which is floured or coated with batter or crumbs. Put in enough oil to come halfway up the pieces of food. Be sure the container is deep enough to allow oil to boil up when food is added. Heat slowly until it just begins to give off a haze and add food immediately.

Frying with butter and oil: A mixture of butter and oil is often used for sautéeing and shallow-frying – the butter contributes its distinctive and fine flavour, while the oil with its higher smoking point protects the butter from burning. Heat oil slowly until it just begins to give off a haze, add butter and, as soon as foaming subsides, add food. For sautéeing, use equal quantities of oil and butter unless otherwise instructed. For shallow-frying, use rather more oil and less butter.

Deep-frying: Use a depth of oil sufficient to float the food, but never fill pan more than halfway up as oil will boil up when you add food. Have pieces of food of uniform size so that they cook evenly. A frying basket helps to add and remove food all together so that none is overdone. Heat oil slowly to required temperature – for most deep-frying, this is 180°C/350°F on a kitchen thermometer, or when a cube of day-old bread turns golden and crisp in 1 minute.

OKRA

The rigid green seed pods, elegantly curved and pointed, have a flavour resembling that of aubergines (eggplant) but with a mucilaginous texture. Okra, also called ladies' fingers or gumbo, is used extensively in Creole cooking, particularly in the soup-stew, Gumbo (see page 152). It is also used in Indian curries, and in many Middle Eastern dishes.

Choose crisp, fresh green-coloured pods that are no more than 10 cm (4 in) long. The pods should snap easily and the seeds be firm but not hard. Avoid any pods that are shrivelled, limp, bruised or a dull green.

Okra can also be purchased canned from some supermarkets or delicatessens. Rinse the pods well in cold running water to get rid of the viscous juices before using unless the recipe is for gumbo, curry or meat stew which may need the juices to give the texture required.

☐ **Basic Preparation:** Wash the pods, carefully remove tip and cap – a fringe-like top where the pod meets the stem. Do not cut the pod and expose the seeds and sticky juices inside. This helps prevent the pods splitting and losing shape during cooking when serving whole. **See recipes.**

Buttered Okra Place prepared whole okra pods in lightly salted simmering water. Simmer, uncovered for 8–10 minutes or until tender and still crisp. Drain and serve tossed in butter.

With Fresh Tomato Sauce Prepare as for Buttered Okra, but omit the butter and serve in Fresh Tomato Sauce (see page 271), sprinkled with chopped parsley.

Fried Okra Rings

4 tbsp milk; 1 egg, beaten; 370 g/12 oz (3 cups) okra, trimmed and sliced; 75 g/2½ oz (½ cup) cornmeal or flour; salt and freshly ground black pepper; 60 g/2 oz (4 tbsp) butter.

Beat milk and egg together. Drop in okra, drain then coat lightly with cornmeal or flour seasoned with salt and pepper. Sauté okra in butter until golden, turning once. Drain on paper towels and serve immediately. Serves 3–4.

Okra and Tomatoes

3–4 tbsp olive oil; 3 onions, chopped; 1 clove garlic, chopped; 500 g (1 lb) okra, trimmed; 500 g/1 lb (2 cups) tomatoes, peeled and chopped; juice 1 lemon; salt and freshly ground black pepper; ½ tsp sugar; 1 tbsp water; finely chopped parsley.

Heat oil in a frying pan (skillet), add onions and garlic and cook gently for about 5 minutes or until they soften. Add okra and cook to a light golden colour, turning gently from time to time. Spread out okra in one layer in the pan and put tomatoes on top with lemon juice, salt, pepper and sugar. Sprinkle over water and cook for about 20 minutes or until okra is tender and sauce reduced. Shake pan during cooking but do not stir. Serve warm or cold, sprinkled with parsley. Serves 3–4.

Okra Curry

1 tbsp ghee or oil; 1 large onion, sliced; 2 green chillies, seeded and chopped; 1 clove garlic, chopped; ½ tsp grated fresh ginger; ½ tsp turmeric; 500 g (1 lb) tender okra, trimmed and cut into 5 cm (2 in) lengths; ½ tsp ground coriander; ½ tsp ground cumin; 350 ml/12 fl oz (1½ cups) Coconut Milk (page 80) or buttermilk; 1 tsp salt.

Heat ghee or oil in a saucepan and fry onion and chillies over medium heat until onions are golden. Add garlic, ginger and turmeric and fry, stirring, for 1 minute. Add okra, coriander, cumin, coconut milk or buttermilk and salt. Simmer uncovered until okra is tender, 10–12 minutes. Serve hot with rice. Serves 4–6.

Chicken with Okra

500 g (1 lb) okra, trimmed; 120 ml/4 fl oz (½ cup) vinegar; 180 g/6 oz (¾ cup) butter; 6–8 chicken joints, legs, wings or thighs; 1 onion, finely chopped; 1 clove garlic, crushed; 370 g/12 oz (1½ cups) peeled and chopped tomatoes; 1 tbsp tomato purée (paste); 120 ml/4 fl oz (½ cup) dry white wine; 1 bay leaf; 2 pieces cinnamon stick; ½ tsp sugar; salt and freshly ground black pepper.

Place okra in a bowl, pour over vinegar and toss to coat. Leave 30 minutes, then drain, rinse very well and pat dry. Melt 125 g/4 oz (½ cup) of the butter in a deep frying pan (skillet), add chicken joints and brown on all sides. Remove and keep warm on a plate. Reduce heat and cook onion and garlic in butter in pan until soft. Add tomatoes, tomato purée (paste), wine, bay leaf, cinnamon, sugar, salt and pepper and stir well. Cover and simmer for 20 minutes. Return chicken to pan, cover and simmer for a further 15 minutes. Melt remaining butter in another frying pan (skillet) and cook okra, turning gently, until golden. Add okra to chicken mixture and cook for 20 minutes longer. Remove bay leaf and cinnamon stick. Serve with whole boiled or mashed potatoes. Serves 6.

OLIVE

The fruit of the olive tree, which is a native of the Mediterranean where so many people depend on its oil for a living. So it is only natural that olives and olive oil are the foundation of Mediterranean cooking. The fruit of the olive tree is either black (the ripe fruit) or green (the immature fruit). Black olives are picked ripe and are full-flavoured and mellow, while green ones are picked immature and are firm and tangy. They are often pickled and stuffed with pimiento or anchovy.

Olives are used in sauces, stuffings and salads as well as for garnishes. They add colour to a Neapolitan pizza and flavour to those wondrous Mediterranean stews which simmer away for hours on top of the stove. Stop at any little café or bar around the Mediterranean and you are likely to be offered hors d'oeuvre – black (ripe) and green olives, local salami, cheese and some crisp vegetables. Olives have an interesting salty flavour which seems to complement aperitifs better than anything else. Serve them alone or with cubes of cheese, preferably crumbly Greek feta cheese.

Olives from various countries differ in shape and flavour. In good Continental delicatessens, you can find olives from Greece – mottled, fat and round and stored in olive oil – inky-black Calamata olives, with sharp pointed ends, and green olives, small and very salty. Black (ripe) Spanish olives are large and ripe and their green olives are very firm with large stones. Sometimes you find enormous olives called Spanish or Queen olives, which are excellent for stuffing with a little pimiento mixed with capers, anchovies or almonds.

Olive oil is produced from small olives which are not considered good eating, and its flavour varies with each grove. Some oils are delicate with a pure flavour, others extremely fruity and some so refined they are almost tasteless. It's worth experimenting to find one you're happy with – it can make so much difference to your cooking, salads and mayonnaise.

To store black (ripe) olives: The best way is in a jar with olive oil to cover. A strip of lemon peel, a sprig of oregano or some garlic cloves and a chilli may be placed in the jar as well to give a subtle flavour. **See recipes.**

Herbed Olives Put 1 small red chilli, 1 clove garlic, 1 sprig fresh dill and 2 tbsp olive oil over 500 g/1 lb (3 cups) black (ripe) olives in a jar. Cover and marinate for at least 2 days.

Garlic Olives Put 500 g/1 lb (3 cups) olives into a jar with 2–3 cloves garlic, lightly crushed. Cover with olive oil and allow to stand at least 2 days.

Marinated Olives Put 500 g/1 lb (3 cups) black (ripe) olives into a jar and pour over a mixture of 3 parts olive oil and 1 part vinegar. Add 1 clove garlic and 1 tsp finely chopped fresh oregano and allow to marinate for at least 2 days.

Grecian-Style Olives Place 500 g/1 lb (3 cups) Calamata olives (black, shiny and pointed) in a jar, cover with vinegar and allow to stand for 2 days. Drain, and pack into sterilized jars, arranging the olives alternately with layers of lemon slices and celery. Cover with olive oil and keep in a cool place for at least a week.

Mixed Italian Olives With a sharp knife cut slashes in the flesh of 500 g/1 lb (3 cups) green and black (ripe) olives. Place in a sterilized jar with 1 small green and 1 red pepper, 3 sticks celery and 2 cloves garlic, all finely chopped. Add 4 tbsp each olive oil and vinegar and 1 sprig fresh oregano (or good pinch dried). Let stand at room temperature for at least 2 days. Store in the refrigerator until required. Use as an antipasto.

Preserved Olives Choose fresh black (ripe) olives. Prick them all over with a skewer. Place them on a large cane tray, sprinkle with lots of salt and toss them so that they become well impregnated with salt. Leave for 3–4 days. Continue to toss them 2–3 times a day. On the last day, add a little more salt to replace the salt that has been drained away. When the olives have lost all their bitterness, put them in a jar and pour over some olive oil. Add a few bay leaves and seal the jar. Store in a cool place for 2 months before using, turning the jar occasionally.

Capalatina

A Sicilian aubergine (eggplant) and olive spread or dip. Serve with crudités, cracker biscuits or scoop up with Lebanese bread.

2 large aubergines (eggplant), cut into 2.5 cm (1 in) cubes; salt; 175 ml/6 fl oz (¾ cup) olive oil; 2 large onions, chopped; 3 sticks celery, sliced; 2 × 425 g/14 oz cans Italian-style tomatoes, seeds removed; 165 g/ 5½ oz (1 cup) stoned (pitted) black (ripe) olives; 2 tbsp drained capers; 2 tbsp pine nuts or slivered blanched almonds; 2 tbsp sugar; 4 tbsp wine vinegar; ½ tsp black pepper.

Place aubergine (eggplant) cubes in a colander, sprinkle with salt and leave for 1 hour, turning cubes several times. Press out liquid, rinse and dry with paper towels. Heat oil, add aubergine (eggplant) in batches (do not crowd pan) and brown on all sides. Remove cubes with a slotted spoon as they are browned. Add onions and celery and sauté until lightly browned. Add tomatoes and olives, bring to the boil, then cook over low heat for 10 minutes. Put aubergine (eggplant) back into pan and add remaining ingredients. Cover and simmer gently for 25 minutes, stirring often. Cool, then chill. Makes about 750 g/1½ lb (4–5 cups).

Beef with Olives

1 × 125 g (4 oz) piece speck or bacon, cut into 1 cm (½ in) cubes; 1 × 1.2 kg (2½ lb) piece chuck or topside (top round) beef; 10 small onions, peeled; 2 small carrots, peeled; 1 bouquet garni; salt and freshly ground black pepper; pinch nutmeg; 2 shallots, sliced; 1 clove garlic; 175 ml/6 fl oz (¾ cup) red wine; pinch sugar; 165 g/5½ oz (1 cup) green olives, stoned (pitted); 125 g/4 oz (1 cup) mushrooms, quartered.

Heat speck or bacon slowly in a heavy pan until fat melts. Remove and set aside. Add piece of meat to fat in pan and brown on all sides. Add onions, carrots, bouquet garni, salt, pepper and nutmeg. Reduce heat, cover and cook gently for about 20 minutes, turning meat once. Add shallots, garlic, wine, sugar and cubes of speck or bacon and simmer for 1½ hours. Meanwhile, blanch olives in boiling water in order to extract some of their saltiness. Drain and dry. Add mushrooms and olives to beef and simmer for a further 1 hour. Adjust seasoning, and remove bouquet garni. Place beef on heated serving platter, carve into slices and spoon over a little sauce. Serve with noodles or boiled potatoes. Serves 6.

Beef Stew with Wine and Olives

1.5–2 kg (3–4 lb) braising steak, cut into 2.5 cm (1 in) cubes; 3–4 tbsp flour; 2 tsp salt;

freshly ground black pepper; 4 tbsp oil; 2 onions, chopped; 1 bay leaf; 350 ml/12 fl oz (1½ cups) red wine; ½ onion; 5–6 parsley stalks; 6 black peppercorns; 165 g/5½ oz (1 cup) stuffed green olives.

Coat steak cubes in flour mixed with salt and pepper. Heat oil in a heavy frying pan (skillet). Add beef, a few cubes at a time, and cook over high heat, turning until brown on all sides. Transfer meat to a heavy saucepan. Add onions to frying pan (skillet), and cook gently until golden. Add bay leaf and some of the wine. Bring to the boil, scraping sediment from bottom of pan, then add to saucepan with remaining wine, and onion tied in a muslin bag with parsley stalks and peppercorns. Bring to the boil again, then reduce heat, cover pan and simmer very gently for about 1½ hours or until meat is almost tender when pierced with a skewer or fork. Stir occasionally to prevent sticking. Remove onion and parsley stalks, peppercorns and bay leaf. Stir in olives, and heat through. Serve with crusty bread or creamy, mashed potatoes. Serves 6–8.

Onion and Olive Pizza

Some of the simplest pizzas are the most delicious. This one has no tomatoes or cheese, but just two topping ingredients add up to superb flavour.

1 quantity Pizza Dough (page 299); 6 tbsp olive oil; 6 large onions, finely sliced; salt and freshly ground black pepper; 20 black (ripe) olives, stoned (pitted) and coarsely chopped.

After dough doubles in bulk, knock (punch) down and knead lightly 4 or 5 times. Place in centre of a greased 35 × 30 cm (14 × 12 in) baking tray and pull and push out with the fingers until dough touches all sides of tray. Allow to rise in a warm place for 15 minutes. Heat oil in a large frying pan (skillet), add onions and cook over medium heat until golden-brown and softened. Season with salt and pepper. Spread dough with onions and scatter olives over top, then press topping

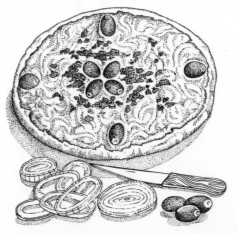

down into dough with the back of a spoon. Bake in a preheated moderately hot oven (190°C/375°F, Gas Mark 5) for 25–30 minutes or until pizza crust is crisp and golden around the edges. Serves 8–10.

Olive Bread

2 eggs; 165 g/5½ oz (1 cup) coarsely chopped stuffed green olives; 2 tbsp olive oil; 250 g/8 oz (2 cups) flour; 1 tbsp sugar; 2 tsp baking powder; ¼ tsp salt; 120 ml/4 fl oz (½ cup) milk.

Beat eggs until frothy. Stir in olives and oil. Sift flour, sugar, baking powder and salt and add to olive mixture with milk. Fold in gently. Pour into a greased and lined 20 × 10 cm (8 × 4 in) loaf tin (pan). Bake in a preheated moderate oven (180°C/350°F, Gas Mark 4) for 1 hour or until bread sounds hollow when tapped on the bottom. Cool the loaf on a wire rack.

OMELETTE

A good French omelette is a smooth, golden oval that is tender, soft and creamy inside. The perfect omelette must be beaten quickly, cooked in less than half a minute and served immediately.

An omelette is one of the greatest instant gourmet meals. Once you master the simple art of making a good omelette, you are well on your way to being a gourmet cook. Learning to make a good omelette is entirely a matter of practice. A few tips: be sure you have everything ready, the pan at hand, egg bowl and beater, spatula for turning the omelette, butter for cooking, the filling or seasoning, heated plates – and don't forget the diner, who should be sitting at the table *before* you start cooking the omelette.

Almost every country has its own omelette in its cuisine, there's a Spanish Potato Omelette and one made with peppers; then there's the famous American omelette, Hangtown Fry, an omelette with oysters, and the Egg Foo Yung of China. The French omelette is a world favourite, and the wonderful thing about learning to make an omelette is that you not only have one dish at your fingertips but nine or ten, for with each different filling you have a new taste sensation.

Dessert Omelettes

Sweet omelettes for dessert can be made the same way as savoury omelettes of the basic type, but more often they are the fluffy kind and are known as soufflé omelettes. Omelettes in soufflé form are closely related to the dessert soufflé proper, but they offer far fewer problems for the cook other than a few minutes absence from the table. As for all light omelettes, basic, savoury or sweet, the soufflé kind must be served immediately it is cooked. For spectacle, the dessert omelette should come to the table enveloped in the blue flames of rum, brandy or a liqueur of some kind, or dusted with sifted icing (confectioners) sugar and burnt in a diamond design. Serve with sweetened whipped cream.

Flaming an omelette: A flamed omelette should be flavoured with the liqueur that will later envelop it in flames. A tablespoon of rum or brandy is sufficient, beaten in with the eggs. If the platter is hot, the omelette straight from the stove, the liqueur heated with a pinch of sugar and ignited as it is poured on, the 'flaming' will be a success. **See recipes.**

Omelette Pans

To produce a really golden omelette you must have a heavy pan. Cast-iron or heavy aluminium are the best because the heat is spread easily; once hot, the pan acts like a hotplate and it is the pan rather than the source of heat that does the cooking. Thinner pans allow the heat to come through, so that the centre of the pan over the flame or element is hotter than the outer part. Don't have your pan bigger than 20–23 cm (8–9 in). This will cook a 3–4-egg omelette nicely and will serve 2; if you are cooking for 4, repeat the recipe.

A new development in pans has been the non-stick silver-stone; this, combined with a heavy aluminium, makes the perfect modern omelette pan. The eggs must be able to slip around freely, and eggs will never stick to a pan that is properly cared for. That is why many people keep a pan especially for omelettes. Certainly you should not pan-fry other foods at high heat in your omelette pan, or you may burn food into the pan and omelettes will stick to it forever after.

Basic French Omelette

3 eggs; 1 tbsp water; ½ tsp salt; freshly ground black pepper; 15 g/½ oz (1 tbsp) butter.

Have eggs at room temperature. Break eggs into a bowl, add water and beat lightly with a fork just to combine white with yolks. It is important not to overbeat as it makes the omelette tough. Add salt and a grinding of pepper. Melt ½ butter in an omelette pan. When foam has subsided pour in eggs **(Fig 1 above)**. Leave for 10–15 seconds until eggs start to set on bottom. Using a fork or a metal spatula pull egg mixture into centre of pan and allow runny mixture to run to outside **(2)**. Do this until eggs have set underneath but the top is still quite moist and soft. If using a filling, spoon across omelette, tilt pan, and using an egg slice flip over ⅓ of the omelette towards the centre **(3)**, then turn over again so that it is folded into 3 as it rolls out on to heated plate. Melt remaining butter in same pan and when it is sizzling pour it over omelette, or smear butter over surface of omelette to give a nice glazed finish. Serve at once. Serves 1.

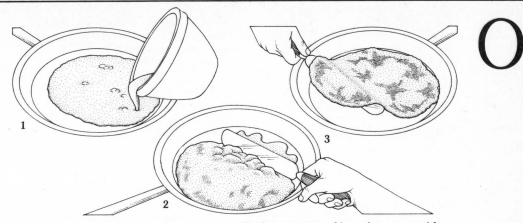

Preparing a Basic French Omelette

VARIATIONS

Asparagus Omelette: Use only the tips of 4–5 cooked fresh or canned asparagus spears. Season with salt and pepper and heat in a little butter. Spoon into centre of a 3-egg omelette and fold over.

Mushroom Omelette: Slice 3–4 small mushrooms, cook lightly in a little butter, and season with salt and pepper. Spoon into centre of a 3-egg omelette and fold over. For an elegant finish, trim stem of 1 mushroom level with cap, slice downward and just colour slices in butter. Lay them, neatly overlapping, along top of finished omelette.

Fines Herbes Omelette: The official fines herbes are parsley, chervil, tarragon and chives. Add any 2 or 3 of these fresh herbs, finely chopped, to the uncooked egg mixture before making the omelette.

Onion Omelette: Cook 1 sliced onion in butter for 5 minutes or until soft. Scatter over omelette, then fold over.

Cheese Omelette: Shred 60 g/2 oz (½ cup) Gruyère, Emmenthal or a tasty Cheddar cheese and strew over 3-egg omelette before folding it.

Bacon and Mushroom Omelette: Fry 1 rasher (slice) bacon, diced, and remove from pan. Add a small nut of butter to bacon fat in pan and cook 2–3 sliced mushrooms until tender. Mix with bacon and use to fill a 3-egg omelette before folding it.

Tomato Omelette: Peel, seed and coarsely chop 2 tomatoes. Heat a nut of butter in a pan, add 2 slices onion, finely chopped, and the tomatoes, season with salt and pepper and heat through. Add a sprinkling of chopped parsley or chives if liked. Use to fill a 3-egg omelette before folding it.

Supper Omelette

A creamy omelette with a crunchy filling.

4 rashers (slices) streaky bacon, rind removed and cut into fine strips; 1 thick slice bread, crusts removed and diced; 4 eggs; salt and freshly ground black pepper; good pinch dry mustard; 2 tsp butter.

Put bacon into a cold omelette pan and fry without additional fat over a low heat until crisp. Remove bacon with a slotted spoon. Add bread to pan and fry in bacon fat until crisp and golden-brown on all sides. Remove bread and keep bacon and bread cubes warm while making omelette. Beat eggs with a little salt and pepper and the mustard. Heat butter in omelette pan, pour in egg mixture and cook fairly briskly, lifting edges of omelette with a spatula to let uncooked egg run underneath. When omelette is just set but top is still creamy, sprinkle bacon and bread cubes along centre. Fold omelette and serve at once. Serves 2.

Neapolitan Omelette

250 g (8 oz) cooked spaghetti; 120 g/4 fl oz (½ cup) fresh tomato purée; 4 eggs, lightly beaten; 1 tbsp chopped parsley; pinch salt; fresh ground black pepper; 1 tbsp grated Parmesan cheese; 1 tbsp olive oil.

Cut spaghetti into short lengths. Add tomato purée, eggs, parsley, salt, pepper and Parmesan cheese and mix very well. Heat oil in pan, pour in spaghetti mixture and cook slowly on both sides. Serves 4.

NOTE: Leftover spaghetti in sauce is often used in this dish.

Spanish Potato Omelette

(Tortilla de Patatas)

Cooked, diced potatoes may be used in this omelette or raw potato fried in the pan before eggs are added.

olive oil for frying; 1 onion, chopped; 2–3 potatoes, peeled and diced; 6 eggs; salt and freshly ground black pepper.

Heat a little oil in an omelette pan, add onion and fry until golden. Remove and set aside. Add more oil to pan and fry potatoes gently until tender but not crisp. Beat eggs well with a few drops of water and season with salt and pepper. Return onion to pan with potatoes and pour eggs over. When set and lightly browned underneath invert carefully or lift on to a large heated plate. Put a little more oil in pan and slide omelette back to cook other side. Cut into wedges and serve immediately. Serves 3–4.

VARIATION

Spanish Pepper Omelette (Tortilla de Pimientos): Fry 1 green or red diced pepper and 1 chopped rasher (slice) of bacon (rind removed) with the onion. Omit potatoes.

Spanish Omelette

(Tortilla Española)

This is often offered in Spanish bars, cut into small squares, as a little something to enjoy with a glass of wine. Also good cold, it is a favourite Spanish picnic dish.

1 tbsp butter or oil; 2 cooked potatoes, peeled and diced; 1 onion, chopped; 2 rashers (slices) bacon, rind removed and diced; 4 eggs; salt and freshly ground black pepper; 1 tomato, sliced; chopped parsley or chives (optional).

Heat butter or oil in a frying pan (skillet), add potatoes, onion and bacon and fry until edges of potato are golden. Beat eggs with salt and pepper and pour into frying pan (skillet). Cook until just set, but no longer. Do not try to fold omelette over – it will be too thick. Serve with sliced tomato and, if liked, a sprinkling of chopped parsley or chives. Serves 4.

Fluffy Omelette

3 eggs, separated; 2 tbsp hot water; salt and freshly ground black pepper; 15 g/½ oz (1 tbsp) butter.

Beat egg yolks and water together until pale yellow. Beat egg whites until they form soft peaks, and fold in yolk mixture. Season with salt and pepper. Heat butter in a small omelette pan. Pour in egg mixture and cook until golden-brown underneath. Place pan under a preheated hot grill (broiler) and cook for a few minutes until golden-brown on top. If using a filling, spoon on to ½ of omelette, fold other half over and slide out of pan on to a heated plate. Serve immediately. Serves 1.

VARIATIONS

Fluffy Bacon Omelette: Make Fluffy Omelette

as left and fill with 2 rashers (slices) bacon, crisply fried and crumbled, before folding.

Fluffy Herb Omelette: Make Fluffy Omelette as above and sprinkle with 2 tbsp finely chopped parsley or other fresh herbs before folding.

Fluffy Salmon Omelette: Make Fluffy Omelette as above and fill with 2 tbsp flaked smoked salmon or smoked fish before folding.

Fluffy Ham and Cheese Omelette: Make Fluffy Omelette as above and fill with 2 tbsp chopped cooked ham, plus 30 g/1 oz (¼ cup) grated cheese, if liked, before folding.

Fluffy Mushroom Omelette: Make Fluffy Omelette as above and fill with 3–4 sliced mushrooms, cooked in a little butter, before folding.

Fluffy Tomato Omelette: Make Fluffy Omelette as above and fill with 1 tomato, peeled, sliced and cooked in a little butter with a few onion slices and chopped fresh herbs, before folding.

Hangtown Fry

15 g/½ oz (1 tbsp) butter; 2 bacon rashers (slices), rind removed; 3–4 fresh oysters; 2 eggs, lightly beaten; salt and freshly ground black pepper.

Heat butter in a frying pan (skillet), add bacon and fry until cooked but not crisp. Place the oysters on top of the bacon and carefully pour the eggs over them. Season with salt and pepper. Cook without stirring until the eggs set. Turn the omelette out upside-down on to a warm plate and serve immediately. Serves 1.

Omelette Soufflé (Sweet)

A last-minute touch makes this delicious soufflé omelette spectacular. A lovely dessert when there are just two for dinner.

3 eggs, separated; 1 tbsp sugar; 2 tsp flour; 1 tbsp single (light) cream; grated lemon rind (optional); pinch salt; 15 g/½ oz (1 tbsp) butter; 2 tbsp good jam; sifted icing (confectioners) sugar.

Place egg whites in a china or copper bowl. Lightly beat egg yolks with sugar, flour, cream and lemon rind, if using. Whisk egg whites with salt until stiff peaks form. Pour in yolk mixture and fold in gently with a large metal spoon. Heat butter in a large omelette pan (if you have it, a heavy cast-iron one) and pour in egg mixture. Place in a preheated moderately hot oven (190°C/375°F, Gas Mark 5) and cook for 12–15 minutes or until golden and risen. Slide on to a heated serving dish and spread with jam. Fold over and serve flamed (see page 249) or sprinkle with sifted icing (confectioners) sugar. For a spectacular look, heat 2 metal skewers over a flame and when

red-hot, use them to mark a lattice over the icing (confectioners) sugar on the omelette; it will caramelize as you lightly press it. Serve immediately. Serves 2.

ONION

The pungent and aromatic onion acts as both a flavouring agent and a vegetable in its own right. It is indispensable in the kitchen and lends its unique qualities to many savoury dishes.

Onions can be used to flavour stocks, soups, stews, sauces, poultry, meat and vegetable dishes. They appear as vegetable accompaniments, as garnishes, either raw or cooked, shaped or whole. Tiny onions can be glazed as a garnish for roast meats or they can be pickled in spicy vinegar – delicious eaten with good Cheddar cheese and fresh white or brown bread.

When buying onions, choose those that are firm, with no bruising or soft spots. The outer skin should be fine and papery. Always store onions in a cool, dry, airy place.

Types of Onion

Brown Onions: Readily available in supermarkets and greengrocers, these onions have a stronger flavour than the white variety, and can be too strong to eat raw. They keep well for some weeks in a cool, dry place. If your eyes water when preparing stronger onions, try peeling them under cold water, but do not let them soak. Dry well before using. Some people say it helps to hold a slice of bread in your mouth while peeling and chopping onions. Use brown onions in most cooked dishes.

Pickling Onions: Tiny brown pickling onions are sometimes available from greengrocers during the winter months. They are used whole in casseroles (see Boeuf à la Bourguignonne on page 40), glazed as a garnish, or fried whole as well as for pickling.

Spanish Onions: These large red-skinned onions have purple-tinted flesh. They are sweet, mild and crisp and delicious sliced in rings in salads, especially those containing fresh oranges and black (ripe) olives.

White Onions: These are readily available in supermarkets and greengrocers through most of the year. White onions are milder than their brown counterparts and do not keep as long. Use in any recipe calling for onions. They can also be sliced into rings and added raw to salads.

□ Basic Preparation:

To dice or chop onions: Cut the onion in half through the root end. Remove the skin and place flat side down on a chopping board. Using a sharp knife, make 3 or 4 slits lengthways through to the board but not through the root end, so the slices are still attached. Then make 3 or 4 horizontal cuts from one side to the other, still leaving the

O

slices attached to the root. Finally, chop into dice by slicing downwards from the stem to the root end.

To make onion rings: Peel the onion, cut off the stem end and slice thinly. Carefully push out the consecutive rings of onion from each slice.

To slice onions: Cut the onion in half from stem to root end. Remove the skin, using a sharp knife; lay flat side down on a chopping board and cut slices to required thickness from the stem to the root end.

To cook whole onions retaining shape: Cut a small slice from the stem end and discard. Remove the skin and scrape the root end, to remove the outer skin and any tiny dried roots remaining. Using a sharp pointed knife, cut a shallow cross through the root base but do not remove or slice off the base.

To extract onion juice: Cut onion in half and squeeze on a lemon squeezer the same way you would squeeze a lemon.

To grate onion: Peel and halve onion. Using short sharp downward strokes, rub it against the medium side of a grater.

☐ **To Cook:** Onions should be cooked over gentle or medium heat; too high a heat may scorch the onions and turn them bitter. **See recipes**.

Fried Onions

Use these fried onions for the old favourite, Steak and Onions.

120 ml/4 fl oz (½ cup) oil; 4 medium onions, sliced; salt and freshly ground black pepper; pinch each paprika and sugar.

Heat oil in a large heavy frying pan (skillet) and add onions. Cook over a gentle heat, stirring often, for 15–20 minutes or until golden-brown and soft. Season with salt, pepper, paprika and sugar. Serve very hot with steak. Serves 4.

VARIATION

Quick Fried Onions: Dice onions. Melt enough butter to cover bottom of a frying pan (skillet) and add onions. Stir until well coated with butter, then barely cover with warm water. Cook over high heat until all the water has evaporated. Reduce heat and continue cooking, stirring and adding more butter if necessary, until golden and tender. Season with salt and pepper.

Onions Baked in their Skins

These are delicious cooked with roasts.

4–6 medium onions; butter; parsley sprigs.

Slice stem ends from onions, scrape root end and make a shallow cross in the root core using a sharp knife. Place onions in baking dish around the meat and bake for about 1 hour or until tender but still firm when pierced with a skewer. Remove from oven, slip off outer skins and place on a

heated serving dish. Top with knobs of butter and sprigs of parsley. Serves 4–6.

NOTE: If you cook onions in boiling water for 10–15 minutes first, the cooking time in the oven will be reduced.

Boiled Onions with Parsley Sauce

6 large onions, peeled; 30 g/1 oz (2 tbsp) butter; 1 tbsp flour; 120 ml/4 fl oz (½ cup) evaporated milk or single (light) cream; salt and freshly ground black pepper; 1 tbsp finely chopped parsley.

Scrape root end of onions and cut a shallow cross in the base of each. Drop onions into boiling water and cook for about 30 minutes or until tender. Drain, reserving 120 ml/4 fl oz (½ cup) cooking liquid. Arrange onions in a heated serving dish and keep warm. Melt butter in a saucepan and blend in flour. Stir in reserved cooking liquid. Cook for 1 minute, stirring, then stir in milk or cream. Heat until boiling, stirring constantly. Season with salt and pepper and stir in parsley. Pour over onions and serve immediately. Serves 4–6.

Crisp Fried Onion Rings

500 ml/18 fl oz (2 cups) milk; ½ tsp salt; 3 large onions, sliced and pushed out into rings; freshly ground black pepper; 1 tsp paprika; 125 g/4 oz (1 cup) flour; oil for deep-frying.

Combine milk with ¼ tsp salt in a shallow dish. Add onion rings and soak for 20 minutes. Combine remaining salt, pepper, paprika and flour in a plastic bag. Shake to mix. Drain a few onion rings at a time and dip in seasoned flour. Shake off excess flour, then deep-fry rings in oil until crisp and brown. Place cooked rings on a baking tray lined with paper towels to drain and keep warm in a preheated very cool oven (120°C/250°F, Gas Mark ½) while frying the remainder. Serves 4–6.

NOTE: To test when oil is hot enough, drop a prepared onion ring into oil. Onion should rise to the surface and turn crisp and golden in about 30 seconds. Take care that the oil does not overheat; the rings should be golden and not dark brown. Use only enough oil to come not more than halfway up sides of frying container to avoid splashing or overflowing.

Glazed Onions

250 g (8 oz) pickling onions, peeled; 30 g/1 oz (2 tbsp) butter; 1 tsp sugar; salt and freshly ground black pepper.

Cut a shallow cross in centre of root end of each onion. Place onions in a saucepan of cold water. Bring to the boil, simmer for 5 minutes and drain well. Put in a heavy saucepan with butter, sugar, salt and pepper.

Cover and cook gently for about 10 minutes or until tender, well glazed and shiny. Shake pan frequently to prevent onions from sticking. Serves 4 (as a garnish).

Braised Onions

120 ml/4 fl oz (½ cup) beef stock; 500 g (1 lb) small onions, peeled; 30 g/1 oz (2 tbsp) butter; salt and freshly ground black pepper.

Bring stock to the boil and add onions and butter. Cover and cook gently for 10 minutes. Remove lid and cook for a further 5 minutes to reduce liquid. Season with salt and pepper. Serves 4.

Creamed Onions

500 g (1 lb) pickling onions or small white onions, peeled; ¼ tsp salt; 250 ml/8 fl oz (1 cup) hot Béchamel or Mornay Sauce (page 368); 1 tbsp chopped parsley (optional).

Drop onions into boiling water and cook for 10 minutes. Drain and return to pan. Add fresh boiling water and continue cooking until tender but still crisp. Just before cooking is completed add salt. Drain onions thoroughly, place in a heated serving dish and pour sauce over them. Sprinkle with chopped parsley, if using. Serves 4–6.

Italian Salad

4 medium oranges; 1 Spanish onion, finely sliced and pushed out into rings; 4 tbsp dry sherry; juice ½ lemon; 1 tbsp olive oil; pinch white pepper; lettuce leaves; 8–10 black (ripe) olives, stoned (pitted).

Peel oranges, removing all white pith. Cut oranges into 5 mm (¼ in) slices. Place in a bowl with onion rings and sherry and marinate 1 hour. Drain, reserving sherry marinade. Blend lemon juice, oil, pepper and sherry marinade. Whisk well. Arrange lettuce leaves in a serving dish. Place orange slices on top, and then olives and onion. Add dressing and toss carefully. Serves 6.

Creamed Onions with Sherry

750 g (1½ lb) medium onions, sliced; 120 ml/4 fl oz (½ cup) water; 5 tbsp single (light) cream; 1 tsp lemon juice; 3 tbsp sherry; ½ tsp salt; freshly ground black pepper.

Cook onions in water over a gentle heat for about 10 minutes. Drain and place in a greased ovenproof dish. Mix cream, lemon juice, sherry, salt and pepper and pour over onions. Cover and bake in a preheated moderate oven (180°C/350°F, Gas Mark 4) for 30 minutes. Serves 4–6.

Onion Sauce

3 medium white onions, finely chopped; 250 ml/8 fl oz (1 cup) hot Béchamel Sauce (page 368); 30 g/1 oz (2 tbsp) butter; pinch cayenne.

Cook onions in boiling water for 5 minutes or until tender. Drain and add to sauce. Reheat gently until simmering. Stir in butter and season with cayenne. Makes 350 ml/ 12 fl oz (1½ cups).

Onion Quiche

30 g/1 oz (2 tbsp) butter; 1 tbsp oil; 4–5 medium onions, finely sliced; ½ tsp ground cumin or nutmeg; ½ tsp salt; 3 egg yolks, beaten; 120 ml/4 fl oz (½ cup) single (light) cream; 1 × 20 cm (8 in) Rich Shortcrust Pastry shell, baked (page 274).

Heat butter and oil in a heavy frying pan (skillet), add onions and cook over a gentle heat for 15–20 minutes or until soft and golden, shaking pan occasionally. Remove from heat, add cumin and salt and stir in egg yolks and cream. Spoon onion mixture into pastry (pie) shell. Bake quiche in preheated moderately hot oven (200°C/400°F, Gas Mark 6) for 10 minutes, then reduce temperature to moderate (180°C/350°F, Gas Mark 4) and bake a further 20 minutes. Serves 4–6.
NOTE: A less rich version can be made using 2 whole eggs instead of 3 yolks, and 4 tbsp each single (light) cream and milk or 120 ml/4 fl oz (½ cup) evaporated milk instead of cream.

Spiced Pickled Onions

1 kg (2 lb) small pickling onions; 90 g/3 oz (⅓ cup) plus 1 tsp salt; 500 ml/18 fl oz (2 cups) white vinegar; 150 ml/¼ pint (⅔ cup) water; 75 g/2½ oz (⅓ cup) sugar; 1 tbsp pickling spice; 1 red chilli (optional).

Soak onions in boiling water to cover in a large bowl for 15 minutes. Drain and peel. Return onions to bowl and soak in fresh water to cover, with 90 g/3 oz (⅓ cup) of the salt, for 48 hours (cover bowl with plastic wrap). Drain and rinse onions. Place vinegar,

the 150 ml/¼ pint (⅔ cup) water, sugar, pickling spice, chilli, if used, and remaining salt in a large heavy saucepan and bring to the boil. Add onions and cook for 5 minutes. Divide onions between sterilized preserving jars and add hot spiced vinegar to cover. Seal jars with lids and let stand in a cool place for at least 2 weeks before serving.

German-style Herring with Onion

8 herring fillets (Matjes); milk or buttermilk; 350 ml/12 fl oz (1½ cups) single (light) cream; 2 tsp lemon juice; 4 tbsp white wine vinegar; 1 tbsp olive oil; 2 large tart apples, peeled, cored and diced; 6 black peppercorns, slightly crushed; 1 bay leaf.
GARNISH: *2 medium Spanish or white onions, finely sliced; parsley or dill sprigs.*

Rinse herring, cover with milk or buttermilk and allow to soak for 2 hours, changing milk several times. Drain, pat dry with paper towels and cut into bite-sized pieces. Place in glass or pottery bowl. Mix together sour cream, vinegar and olive oil and fold remaining ingredients through. Pour over herring. Cover and marinate in refrigerator for at least 24 hours, turning mixture once or twice before serving. Top with onion rings and parsley or dill. Serve with a plate of buttered rye bread. Serves 8.

Onion Buns

Yeast dough buns filled with bacon and onion.

500 g/1 lb (4 cups) flour; 1 tsp salt; 300 ml/½ pint (1¼ cups) mixed milk and water; 60 g/2 oz (4 tbsp) butter; 15 g/½ oz (1 tbsp) fresh (compressed) yeast; 1 tsp sugar; beaten egg to glaze.
FILLING: *4 rashers (slices) streaky bacon, rind removed and finely chopped; 180 g/6 oz (1½ cups) grated onion; freshly ground black pepper.*

Sift flour and salt into a bowl. Warm milk and water, add butter and remove from heat when it has melted. Mash yeast with sugar and stir in warm liquid. Make a well in centre of flour and pour in liquid. Stir in a little flour from edges to make a stiff batter, cover with a cloth and leave in a warm place to sponge. When yeast mixture has doubled and bubbles have formed, mix in all the flour. Turn on to a floured surface and knead until smooth. Place in a clean greased bowl, turn dough over so top surface is lightly greased, cover with a damp cloth and leave to rise in a warm place for about 2 hours or until doubled in bulk. Knock (punch) dough down and knead lightly. Divide into 20 pieces.

Mix filling ingredients, seasoning well with pepper. Place 1 tbsp filling in middle of each piece of dough. Fold edges over to enclose filling, pinching together to seal, and mould

into balls. Arrange buns, seam sides down, on a buttered baking tray and let rise, loosely covered, in a warm place for about 20 minutes. Brush with beaten egg and bake in a preheated moderately hot oven (200°C/400°F, Gas Mark 6) for 15 minutes or until buns are golden and sound hollow when tapped. Serve warm with butter. Makes 20.

Onion Hush Puppies

American fishermen cooked these curiously named buns at their fish fries. Legend says they threw the fatty bits to the dogs at the same time shouting 'Hush puppy'.

225 g/7½ oz (1½ cups) white cornmeal; 30 g/1 oz (¼ cup) flour; 3 tsp baking powder; ½ tsp salt; pinch cayenne; 175 ml/6 fl oz (¾ cup) buttermilk or same amount fresh milk soured with 1 tbsp vinegar; 2 large eggs, lightly beaten; 60 g/2 oz (½ cup) grated onion; 1 clove garlic, crushed; oil for deep-frying; butter to serve.

Combine cornmeal, flour, baking powder, salt and cayenne. In separate bowl beat together buttermilk, eggs, onion and garlic. Stir into cornmeal mixture and allow to stand for 15 minutes. Heat 8 cm (3 in) oil in a deep-fryer and fry tablespoons of batter, 4–6 at a time, for 3 minutes or until golden-brown. Drain on crumpled paper towels and eat while still piping hot, spread with softened butter. Makes about 20.

Stuffed Onions

6 large onions, peeled; 250 g/8 oz (1 cup) minced (ground) cooked ham or 250 g/8 oz (1 cup) minced (ground) veal and 2 rashers (slices) bacon, rind removed and diced; 1 tbsp oil; salt and freshly ground black pepper; cayenne; 120 ml/4 fl oz (½ cup) sour cream; 1 tbsp finely chopped celery; 2 tbsp chopped chives; 2 tbsp chopped parsley; 60 g/2 oz (1 cup) fresh white breadcrumbs; butter; 250 ml/8 fl oz (1 cup) chicken stock.

O

Cook onions in boiling water for 10 minutes. Drain. Scoop out centres and chop fine. Sauté chopped onion centres with ham or veal, and bacon in oil in a frying pan (skillet). Add remaining ingredients, except butter and stock, and mix well. Push stuffing into onion cases. Place in a greased shallow baking dish. Dot with butter, pour stock around onions and bake in a preheated moderately hot oven (200°C/400°F, Gas Mark 6) for 35–45 minutes or until tender and golden-brown. Serves 6.

Dutch Onion Tart

370 g (12 oz) finely sliced onions; 60 g/2 oz (4 tbsp) butter; 500 g/1 lb (2 cups) Ricotta cheese; 4 tbsp single (light) cream; 2 eggs; 1 × 23 cm (9 in) Rich Shortcrust Pastry shell, baked (page 274); salt and freshly ground black pepper; ¼ tsp cayenne.

Fry onions in butter over gentle heat until soft. Moisten cheese with cream, then beat in eggs. Pour into tart shell. Season lightly with salt and pepper. Cover with onions, and sprinkle with cayenne. Bake in a preheated moderately hot oven (200°C/400°F, Gas Mark 6) for 20–25 minutes. Serves 8.

Onion Tartlets

1 quantity Rich Shortcrust Pastry (page 274); 8 medium onions, sliced; 125 g/4 oz (½ cup) butter; salt and freshly ground white pepper; 2 tbsp flour; 500 ml/18 fl oz (2 cups) beef stock; 2 tbsp grated Cheddar cheese; 2–3 tbsp grated Parmesan cheese.

Line 6 × 10 cm (4 in) tartlet tins (pans) with pastry, prick well and bake blind (see *Pastry*). Cook onions gently in half the butter until soft. Increase heat a little and cook until a rich, even brown, stirring occasionally. Season with salt and pepper and remove from heat. Melt remaining butter in a saucepan, stir in flour and cook over medium heat for 5–6 minutes or until flour begins to brown. Gradually add stock and simmer, stirring, for 5 minutes. Mix in onions and spoon mixture into tartlet cases. Mix cheeses together and sprinkle over top of tartlets. Bake in a preheated hot oven (230°C/450°F, Gas Mark 8) for 5–10 minutes, or cook under a preheated hot grill (broiler) until cheese melts and colours slightly. Serves 6.

ORANGE

A golden citrus fruit available all year round. We depend on its refreshing, unique flavour and texture not only as a fresh fruit but also for use in cooking many savoury and sweet dishes.

Orange juice starts the day for many people and fresh squeezed orange juice retains its precious vitamin C.

Valencia oranges have thinner and smoother skins than navels. Seville oranges, which are available for only a short time in winter, are too bitter to eat fresh but make excellent marmalade and are used in the classic Sauce Bigarade (see page 35). Choose oranges with bright shiny skins and no bruising or very soft spots. They should be firm and quite heavy to hold.

To serve whole: Slit the outer skin into 8 segments, cutting from the stem end to base. Carefully peel the skin away from the orange, leaving the skin attached to the base of the fruit. Tuck the skin points underneath the orange.

To segment: Using a sharp knife, remove all the peel and pith then cut each side of each membrane to release segments (see below).

To cut shells: Halve fruit and remove pulp, leaving the shell. Pulp may be chopped and mixed with other fruit before piling back into the shell. If you wish to have a scalloped edge, halve the fruit by cutting diagonal slits into the centre of the fruit. Carefully separate the halves and remove the pulp.

To grate rind: Rub the rind in short light strokes across a grater. Do not grate any of the bitter white pith.

To make orange rind strips: Peel strips of rind from one orange using a vegetable peeler. Do not include any bitter white pith. Cut the rind into fine matchstick lengths and cook gently in 120 ml/4 fl oz (½ cup) water and 1 tbsp sugar for about 5 minutes or until the rind becomes clear. Use to decorate hot or cold puddings, iced desserts, cakes or as specified in recipes.

Ways to Use Oranges

● Squeeze orange juice over strawberries.
● Add grated orange rind to stewed rhubarb.
● Make Orange Butter (mash 125 g/4 oz (½ cup) unsalted butter with 1 tbsp orange juice and 1 tbsp orange rind) and spread on sweet breads, or buns, scones or pikelets.
● Top pineapple rings with a thick orange slice, drizzle warm honey over and serve with yogurt.
● Cook rice in half orange juice and half

Segmenting an orange

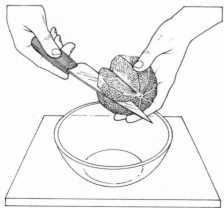

water, add chopped mint to the cooked rice and serve with lamb, or add chopped thyme to orange rice and serve with veal or poultry.
● Add grated orange rind to hot, buttery mashed potatoes and serve with fish or veal. **See recipes.**

Citrus Carrot Soup

1 large onion, finely chopped; 90 g/3 oz (6 tbsp) butter; 8 medium carrots, sliced; 2 potatoes, peeled and sliced; 750 ml/1¼ pints (3 cups) water; salt and freshly ground black pepper; ½ tsp ground cloves; 3 tbsp lemon juice; 500 ml/18 fl oz (2 cups) orange juice.
GARNISH: *chopped fresh mint; sour cream (optional).*

Gently fry onion in butter in a heavy saucepan until golden. Add carrots, potatoes, water, salt, pepper and cloves. Cover and simmer until vegetables are tender, about 20 minutes. Purée soup in a blender until smooth (do this in 2 or 3 batches) or push through a sieve. Add lemon and orange juices. Reheat if soup is to be served hot, or chill for 3–4 hours. Serve sprinkled with chopped mint and add a spoonful of sour cream to each bowl, if desired. Serves 6.

Orange Marinated Steak

500 g (1 lb) rump, topside (top round) or skirt steak.
MARINADE: *120 ml/4 fl oz (½ cup) orange juice; 1 onion, chopped; 1 tbsp ground coriander; 1 tbsp olive oil; 1 clove garlic, crushed.*
GARNISH: *1 orange, peeled and sliced; sprigs fresh coriander or parsley.*

Lightly score steak in a diamond pattern on each side. Combine ingredients for marinade in a glass dish. Add steak, turn to coat, cover and refrigerate for 6–8 hours, turning occasionally. Drain steak, reserving 2 tbsp marinade. Pat steak dry with paper towels. Lightly oil grill (broiler) rack. Grill (broil) steak under a preheated grill (broiler) for 5 minutes on each side for medium-rare meat. Transfer meat to a heated platter. Cut it across grain into thin slices and sprinkle with reserved marinade. Garnish platter with orange slices and sprigs of coriander or parsley. Serves 4.

Chicken in Orange Sauce

8 chicken joints, legs, thighs, wings or breasts; 4 tbsp olive oil; 250 ml/8 fl oz (1 cup) fresh orange juice, strained; 250 ml/8 fl oz (1 cup) dry white wine; 90 g/3 oz (½ cup) raisins; 60 g/2 oz (½ cup) chopped blanched almonds; 1 tbsp sugar; ½ tsp ground ginger; ½ tsp salt; ½ tsp white pepper; 30 g/1 oz (2 tbsp) butter.

Brown chicken joints in hot oil, then place in a shallow baking dish. Combine remaining ingredients, except butter, and pour over chicken. Bake in a preheated moderate oven (180°C/350°F, Gas Mark 4) for about 30 minutes or until tender, basting frequently. Remove chicken to a heated serving platter. Heat sauce, boiling to reduce it if necessary, and swirl in butter. Pour sauce over chicken. Serve with boiled rice and a green salad. Serves 4.

Orange Chicken Salad

1 kg/2 lb (4 cups) diced cooked chicken; 125 g/4 oz (1 cup) finely sliced celery; 60 g/2 oz (½ cup) chopped walnuts; 60 g/2 oz (½ cup) seedless white grapes; 2 oranges, peeled and segmented; lettuce leaves; extra orange segments to garnish (optional).
ORANGE CREAM DRESSING: *3 tbsp thawed frozen concentrated orange juice; 3 tbsp Mayonnaise (page 204); grated rind 1 orange; few drops Tabasco (hot pepper) sauce; 120 ml/4 fl oz (½ cup) double (heavy) cream.*

Combine chicken, celery, walnuts, grapes and oranges and chill, covered, for several hours.
ORANGE CREAM DRESSING: Mix together orange juice, mayonnaise, orange rind and Tabasco (hot pepper) sauce. Whip cream until thick and fold in. Add dressing to chicken mixture and fold through gently. Serve on a bed of lettuce leaves, garnished with orange segments if desired. Serves 4.

Orange Vinaigrette

6 oranges; sprigs fresh mint.
SAUCE: *6 tbsp olive oil; 2 tbsp wine vinegar; 12 black (ripe) olives, halved and stoned (pitted); 1 onion, chopped; 1 tbsp chopped fresh mint; 1 tbsp chopped parsley; 1 tbsp chopped fresh basil; salt and freshly ground black pepper; pinch cayenne.*

Peel oranges, removing all white pith, and slice.
SAUCE: Combine oil, vinegar, olives, onion and herbs. Season with salt, pepper and cayenne and mix well. Toss orange slices in sauce and arrange on a platter with sprigs of mint. Serve as an accompaniment to veal, ham steaks, lamb or poultry. Serves 6–8.
VARIATION
Use a bunch of watercress instead of mint and omit the basil from the dressing.

Beetroot in Orange Sauce

1 tbsp grated orange rind; 1 tbsp lemon juice; 1 tbsp orange juice; ¼ tsp salt; ¼ tsp pepper; ¼ tsp nutmeg; 60 g/2 oz (4 tbsp) butter; 370 g (12 oz) canned baby beetroot, drained; 2 tbsp sour cream; 2 tbsp snipped chives.

Place all ingredients, except sour cream and chives, in a heavy saucepan and heat gently, stirring occasionally. Serve topped with sour cream and chives. Serves 4.

Buttermilk Orange Cream

1 tbsp gelatine; 3 tbsp cold water; 120 ml/4 fl oz (½ cup) orange juice; 1 tbsp lemon juice; 300 ml/½ pint (1¼ cups) buttermilk; 75 g/2½ oz (⅓ cup) caster sugar.
DECORATION: *orange segments; whipped cream.*

Soften gelatine in water, then dissolve over simmering water. Cool. Combine remaining ingredients and stir in cooled gelatine. Spoon into individual serving dishes and chill until set. Decorate with orange segments and whipped cream. Serves 4.
NOTE: Use fresh buttermilk for this recipe, as the longer the buttermilk is stored the more acid-tasting it becomes.

Orange Tea Sticks

A marvellous recipe for those times when the family wants a sweet course and you haven't prepared one. These lovely grilled (broiled) bread sticks are great with ice cream or whipped cream.

8 slices day-old white bread, crusts removed; 180 g/6 oz (¾ cup) sugar; 6 tbsp orange juice; 60 g/2 oz (4 tbsp) butter; 1 tsp grated orange rind.

Cut bread into 2 cm (¾ in) wide strips. Combine sugar, orange juice and butter in a small saucepan and cook over low heat for 5 minutes. Add grated orange rind. Dip each bread stick in syrup, then place side by side on a lightly greased baking tray. Cook under a preheated grill (broiler) until brown on both sides. Serve immediately. Serves 6.

Orange Sherbet

8 oranges; 1 tbsp gelatine; 500 ml/18 fl oz (2 cups) milk; ¼ tsp salt; 125 g/4 oz (½ cup) sugar; 4 tbsp lemon juice; 2 tsp grated orange rind.

Cut tops off oranges and gently squeeze as much juice as possible from them without damaging skins. Scoop out remaining pulp. Reserve shells. Measure 500 ml/18 fl oz (2 cups) orange juice and strain. Soften gelatine in 120 ml/4 fl oz (½ cup) milk in a small heatproof bowl for 5 minutes. Set bowl over simmering water and stir until gelatine has dissolved. Combine remaining ingredients in a separate bowl and stir in gelatine mixture. Pour into an ice cream tray and freeze until mushy. Turn into a chilled bowl and beat well. Return to tray and freeze until firm. Pile into empty orange shells and serve with an Italian type biscuit (cookie) such as amaretti or savoiardi. Serves 8.

Cold Orange Soufflé

600 ml/1 pint (2½ cups) orange juice; 1 tbsp gelatine; 2 tbsp sugar; 2 eggs, separated; fresh fruit to decorate.

Place orange juice in a saucepan. Sprinkle gelatine over and allow to soften for 10 minutes. Add sugar and heat gently, stirring to dissolve sugar and gelatine. As soon as mixture starts to boil, remove from heat and strain over well beaten egg yolks. Stir well to combine and leave until cool and starting to set. Beat egg whites until stiff and fold through orange mixture. Pile into a serving dish and chill until set. Decorate with orange or mandarin segments, strawberries or kiwi fruit. Serves 6.

Oranges in Caramel

8 large seedless oranges.
CARAMEL: *250 g/8 oz (1 cup) sugar; 150 ml/¼ pint (⅔ cup) cold water; 150 ml/¼ pint (⅔ cup) warm water.*

CARAMEL: Put sugar and cold water in a heavy saucepan and heat gently, stirring occasionally, until sugar dissolves. Boil, without stirring, over medium heat until caramel is a rich golden-brown. Remove from heat. Cover hand holding the saucepan with a cloth to prevent possible splashing and scalding and quickly pour in warm water. Heat gently to dissolve caramel in water, then pour into a jug and leave to cool.

Using a swivel-headed vegetable peeler,

thinly pare a little rind from 1 orange and cut into fine shreds. Blanch for 1 minute in boiling water, then drain and dry. Remove all rind and white pith from oranges and cut each orange in thick slices. Re-form each orange, securing slices together with toothpicks, and arrange in a deep glass serving dish. Pour caramel over, sprinkle with shredded rind and chill well. Serve with Brandy Snaps (see page 44) filled with whipped cream. Serves 8.

Moroccan Oranges

This interesting way with fresh oranges couldn't be easier to prepare, but the taste is exotic.

1 large orange for each person; brown sugar; cinnamon; rosewater (obtainable from the chemist); fresh leaves lemon or mint.

Peel each orange carefully, taking care to remove all white pith. Slice across with a sharp knife into very thin slices. Arrange slices on individual plates, overlapping them slightly to form a pretty circular pattern. Sprinkle liberally with brown sugar and cinnamon and then with rosewater. Garnish with fresh lemon or mint leaves, or even a pretty garden leaf, and serve at once.

Oranges in Spiced Red Wine

180 g/6 oz (¾ cup) sugar; 250 ml/8 fl oz (1 cup) dry red wine; 2 cloves; 8 cm (3 in) cinnamon stick; 2 slices lemon; 8 oranges.

Dissolve sugar in water and stir in wine. Add cloves, cinnamon and lemon slices. Bring to the boil and simmer until the mixture is thick and syrupy. Allow to cool a little. Peel oranges, removing all white pith, and cut into 1 cm (½ in) thick slices. Place in a bowl and pour over warm spiced wine. Chill. Serve alone, or with sour cream sweetened with brown sugar. Serves 8.

Soft Orange Cream

juice 5 oranges; juice 1 lemon; 4 egg yolks; 125 g/4 oz (½ cup) caster sugar; 2 tbsp Grand Marnier, orange Curaçao or sweet dessert wine; toasted slivered almonds to decorate.

Strain orange and lemon juices into an enamel-lined saucepan. Whisk together egg yolks and sugar until pale and thick, then add to juice, beating well. Heat very gently, stirring constantly, until mixture thickens enough to adhere to sides of pan. Do not allow to boil. The mixture will not thicken sufficiently to coat spoon. Remove from heat and continue stirring until cool and thickened. Stir in liqueur or wine and pour into 4 custard cups or glasses. Refrigerate overnight. Decorate with toasted slivered almonds and serve with sponge fingers (lady fingers). Serves 4.

Orange and Date Loaf

250 g/8 oz (2 cups) self-raising flour; 125 g/4 oz (½ cup) butter; 125 g/4 oz (½ cup) caster sugar; grated rind 1 orange; 1 egg, beaten; 120 ml/4 fl oz (½ cup) milk; 120 ml/4 fl oz (½ cup) water; 180 g/6 oz (1 cup) chopped dates; 90 g/3 oz (½ cup) chopped candied orange peel.

Sift flour into a bowl and rub (cut) in butter. Stir in sugar and orange rind. Add egg, milk and water and beat well. Stir in dates and candied peel and turn into a greased and base-lined 18 × 10 cm (7 × 4 in) loaf tin (pan). Bake in a preheated moderate oven (180°C/350°F, Gas Mark 4) for 1¼ hours. Cool on a wire rack.

Orange and Walnut Bread

370 g/12 oz (3 cups) self-raising flour; ½ tsp salt; 1 tbsp grated orange rind; 180 g/6 oz (¾ cup) sugar; 1 egg; 4 tbsp orange juice; 300 ml/½ pint (1¼ cups) milk; 30 g/1 oz (2 tbsp) melted butter; 125 g/4 oz (1 cup) chopped walnuts (optional).

Sift flour and salt into a bowl and stir in orange rind and sugar. Beat together egg, orange juice, milk and melted butter and stir in chopped nuts. Pour on to flour mixture and combine ingredients with a few swift strokes, stirring lightly until just blended. Pour into two 20 × 10 cm (8 × 4 in) loaf tins (pans). Bake in a preheated moderate oven (180°C/350°F, Gas Mark 4) for 40–50 minutes or until a skewer inserted in centre comes out clean. Cool on wire racks.

Orange and Almond Cake

75 g/2½ oz (1¼ cups) fine fresh breadcrumbs; grated rind 1 orange; juice 3 large oranges; 125 g/4 oz (1 cup) ground almonds; 1 tbsp orange-flower water; 4 eggs, separated; 125 g/4 oz (½ cup) caster sugar; ½ tsp salt; 250 ml/8 fl oz (1 cup) double (heavy) cream, whipped.

Butter a 20 cm (8 in) square or round cake tin (pan) and sprinkle lightly with 15 g/½ oz (¼ cup) of the breadcrumbs. Mix together remaining breadcrumbs, orange rind and juice, ground almonds and orange-flower water. Beat egg yolks with sugar and salt until very pale and thick and stir into orange mixture. Beat egg whites until they hold stiff peaks and fold into orange mixture. Turn into prepared cake tin (pan). Bake in a preheated moderate oven (180°C/350°F, Gas Mark 4) for about 40 minutes. Allow cake to cool in tin (pan). Turn out and spread whipped cream over top before serving.
NOTE: Orange-flower water can be purchased from health food shops and delicatessens, or in concentrated form from chemists. Use only 2–3 drops if using the concentrate.

Orange Tea Bread

1 tsp Earl Grey tea; 120 ml/4 fl oz (½ cup) boiling water; 60 g/2 oz (4 tbsp) butter; 180 g/6 oz (¾ cup) sugar; 1 egg, lightly beaten; 1 tbsp grated orange rind; 1 tsp grated lemon rind; 370 g/12 oz (3 cups) flour; 1 tsp baking powder; 1 tsp bicarbonate of soda (baking soda); ½ tsp salt; ½ tsp cinnamon; 175 ml/6 fl oz (¾ cup) orange juice; 60 g/2 oz (½ cup) chopped pecans or walnuts.

Mix tea with boiling water. Leave to steep for 3 minutes, then strain. Cream butter with sugar until light and fluffy. Add egg and rinds and beat well. Sift flour, baking powder, soda, salt and cinnamon. Add to butter mixture with juice and tea. Stir gently then mix in nuts. Turn into a greased and lined 21 × 15 cm (8½ × 6 in) loaf tin (pan). Bake in a preheated moderate oven (180°C/350°F, Gas Mark 4) for 45 minutes or until a skewer inserted in centre comes out clean. Cool completely before serving, buttered.

Orange Semolina Cake

This cake will stay moist and light for a week if wrapped in foil and kept in the refrigerator. Allow to stand at room temperature for 30 minutes before serving.

125 g/4 oz (½ cup) butter; 125 g/4 oz (½ cup) caster sugar; 1 tbsp grated orange rind; 2 eggs; 2 tbsp brandy; 180 g/6 oz (1 cup) semolina (semolina flour); 1 tsp baking powder; 150 g/5 oz (1¼ cups) ground almonds.
SYRUP: 125 g/4 oz (½ cup) sugar; 300 ml/ ½ pint (1¼ cups) orange juice.

Cream butter with sugar and orange rind until light and fluffy. Beat in eggs one at a time, beating thoroughly after each addition. Stir in brandy. Combine semolina, baking powder and almonds and fold lightly into creamed mixture. Turn into a greased and lined 20 cm (8 in) round or square cake tin (pan). Place in a preheated moderately hot oven (200°C/400°F, Gas Mark 6), then immediately lower the oven temperature to

255

moderate (180°C/350°F, Gas Mark 4). Bake for 30 minutes or until a skewer inserted in centre comes out clean.

SYRUP: Place sugar and juice in a saucepan, bring to the boil and boil briskly for 5 minutes. Cool slightly. Remove cake from oven, pour syrup over hot cake and allow to cool in tin (pan). Turn on to a serving plate and serve with tea or coffee or as a dessert with whipped cream.

Orange Marmalade Cake

180 g/6 oz (¾ cup) butter; 250 g/8 oz (1 cup) caster sugar; 3 eggs; 3 tbsp orange marmalade; 310 g/10 oz (2½ cups) self-raising flour, sifted; ¼ tsp salt; grated rind 2 oranges; 120 ml/4 fl oz (½ cup) fresh orange juice, strained.

Cream butter with sugar until light and fluffy. Add eggs, one at a time, beating thoroughly. Stir in marmalade. Add flour and salt alternately with orange rind and juice. Spoon into a greased and lined 20 cm (8 in) round deep cake tin (pan). Bake in a preheated moderate oven (180°C/350°F, Gas Mark 4) for 30–40 minutes or until a fine skewer inserted in centre comes out clean. Turn out and cool on a wire rack.

Preserved Orange Rolls

These little confections are a delicacy from Greece. Serve them in liqueur glasses with a teaspoon. Delicious served after dinner with black coffee.

6 large, thick-skinned oranges; 750 g/1½ lb (3 cups) sugar; 750 ml/1¼ pints (3 cups) water; 1 tbsp lemon juice.

Lightly grate entire surface of each orange. Score peel deeply into 6 segments from stem end to base and remove peel from orange. (Use orange flesh in another dish.) Tightly roll up peel segments and, using a needle and thread, pass thread through each roll to keep it tightly rolled. When 12 rolls are threaded, tie the ends together to form a circle of rolls. Continue, to make 3 circles of rolls. Put circles of rolls into a pan of cold water, bring to the boil and drain immediately. Repeat boiling and draining process twice more to remove bitterness from peel. Cover with fresh cold water and let rolls simmer gently until tender. Drain and leave until dry.

In a clean saucepan, bring the sugar and the 750 ml/1¼ pints (3 cups) water to the boil. Add the lemon juice and boil for 5 minutes. Add circles of orange rolls and boil for 10 minutes, skimming off any scum when necessary. Remove from heat, cover and leave overnight. Next day, bring pan contents to the boil and cook gently for 20 minutes or until syrup is thick. To test if syrup is ready, drop a little on to a cold plate. If drops do

not spread, syrup is ready. If you have a sugar thermometer, cook to 105°C/220°F. Cool a little, then remove threads and place rolls and syrup in sterilized jars. Seal and store in a cool place. Makes 36.

ORANGE-FLOWER WATER

This beautiful fragrant liquid, collected from the distillation of oil from the sweet blossoms of the bitter orange tree, is used as a delicate and subtle flavouring in cooking, particularly in Middle East sweet dishes. Orange-flower water is available from Greek and Middle Eastern grocery stores, or in a concentrated form from chemists. The concentrate should be used sparingly in drops, and not spoon measures. **See recipes.**

Moroccan Beetroot Salad

4 beetroot; 2 tsp sugar; 1 tbsp orange-flower water; 1 tsp ground cumin; 1 tbsp chopped fresh coriander or parsley; sprigs fresh coriander or flat parsley to garnish.

Cook beetroot in water to cover for 30–40 minutes or until tender. Drain, slip off skins under cold running water and cut into small cubes. In a bowl combine beetroot with remaining ingredients. Cover and chill for 1 hour. Serve garnished with sprigs of coriander or flat parsley. Serve with barbecued lamb. Serves 4.

Date Pastries

370 g/12 oz (3 cups) flour; 125 g/4 oz (½ cup) caster sugar; 250 g/8 oz (1 cup) unsalted butter; 1 tbsp orange-flower water; 4 tbsp water.
FILLING: *45 g/1½ oz (3 tbsp) butter; 250 g/ 8 oz (1⅓ cups) dates, stoned and chopped.*

Sift flour and sugar into a bowl and rub (cut) in butter until mixture resembles fine breadcrumbs. Mix orange-flower water and water, sprinkle on to flour mixture and mix to a firm dough. Knead lightly, then cover with plastic wrap and set aside for 30 minutes.

FILLING: Melt butter, add dates and stir over gentle heat to soften. Cool. Take about 1 tbsp of dough and roll it into a ball. Push 1 tsp of filling into the centre and mould dough around it. Reshape into a ball. Place on a lightly greased baking tray, flatten slightly and press with tines of a fork around sides and across top to give a slight cone shape. Repeat with remaining dough and filling. Bake in a preheated moderate oven (160°C/325°F, Gas Mark 3) for 30–35 minutes or until pale gold. Cool on baking tray; the pastries will become firm and crisp when cold. Store in an airtight container. Makes about 30.

Khoshaf

Dried fruit salad is prepared throughout the Middle East. Prepare a day or two in advance and make enough to eat over a few days; it gets better every day.

500 g/1 lb (3 cups) dried apricots; 250 g/8 oz (1⅓ cups) prunes; 250 g/8 oz (1⅓ cups) raisins or sultanas (golden raisins); 60 g/2 oz (½ cup) blanched almonds; 30 g/1 oz (⅓ cup) pine nuts; 180 g/6 oz (¾ cup) sugar; 2 tbsp orange flower water or rosewater.

Put all ingredients in a large bowl. Add water to cover, stir, cover and put in refrigerator for 1–2 days. Serve chilled with sour cream that has been sweetened with a little brown sugar. Serves 6.

OREGANO

Also known as wild marjoram, oregano is a more potent herb than its close cousins in the marjoram family. It grows well in the warm climates of sunny countries, particularly those of the Mediterranean. Its scent and flavour are robust, strongly aromatic and flavour many dishes from southern Italy including pizza, tomato and garlic sauces for pasta, seafoods and vegetables, such as aubergines (eggplant), courgettes (zucchini) and mush-rooms.

Oregano also grows in Greece, where it is known as *rigani*, the flavour being even more pungent than in Italy. **See recipes.**

Mushrooms with Oregano

3 tbsp olive oil; 500 g (1 lb) large open mushrooms, thickly sliced; 1 clove garlic, crushed; 1 tsp dried oregano; salt and freshly ground black pepper.

Heat oil in a frying pan (skillet), add mushrooms and cook for 5 minutes, stirring. Add garlic and oregano and season with salt and black pepper. Toss well. Serve as a vegetable accompaniment to meats or poultry, or on hot buttered toast at luncheon or supper. Serves 4–6.

O

Roast Lemon Lamb
(Arni Lemonato)

1 × 1.5 kg (3 lb) leg of lamb; 2–3 cloves garlic, slivered; juice 1 lemon; salt and freshly ground black pepper; 1 tsp dried oregano; 250 ml/8 fl oz (1 cup) hot water; 30 g/1 oz (2 tbsp) butter; 250 ml/8 fl oz (1 cup) stock or water.

Cut small slits in lamb and insert slivers of garlic. Rub skin with lemon juice and season with salt and pepper. Sprinkle with oregano and place in baking dish. Roast in a preheated moderate oven (180°C/350°F, Gas Mark 4) for 30 minutes. Drain off fat and add hot water to dish. Spread butter over lamb and return to oven. Roast a further 45 minutes or until lamb is done to your liking. Turn once to brown evenly. Allow lamb to rest in a warm place for 15 minutes before carving. Meanwhile, skim fat from pan juices and add 250 ml/8 fl oz (1 cup) stock or water, stirring. Boil on top of stove to reduce, if necessary, and serve this sauce separately. Serves 4–6.

NOTE: A nice accompaniment is potatoes, peeled and quartered and cooked with the lamb during the last hour.

Skewered Lamb
(Arni Souvlakia)

1.5–2 kg (3–4 lb) boned leg of lamb, cut into 4 cm (1½ in) cubes; 120 ml/4 fl oz (½ cup) olive oil; 120 ml/4 fl oz (½ cup) dry white wine; juice 1 lemon; 2 tsp dried oregano; 2 cloves garlic, crushed; 8 bay leaves, broken into pieces; salt and freshly ground black pepper.
GARNISH: *parsley; lemon wedges.*

Place lamb cubes in a glass dish. Mix remaining ingredients, reserving about half bay leaves, and add to lamb, turning to coat meat. Cover and refrigerate for 12–24 hours, stirring occasionally. Thread lamb on to metal skewers, with pieces of reserved bay leaf between some cubes of meat. Reserve marinade. Cook under a preheated hot grill (broiler) or over glowing charcoal, turning and basting frequently with marinade, for 15 minutes or until cooked to taste. Place on a platter and garnish with parsley and lemon wedges. Serves 6–8.

Mexican Meatballs

500 g/1 lb (2 cups) minced (ground) steak; 40 g/1⅓ oz (¼ cup) cornmeal; 1 egg; 1 clove garlic, crushed; 1 small onion, finely chopped; 1 tsp dried oregano; ½ tsp salt; ½ tsp pepper.
CHILLI TOMATO SAUCE: *30 g/1 oz (2 tbsp) butter; 1 small onion, chopped; 1 clove garlic, crushed; 2–3 tbsp chilli powder or to taste; 750 ml/1¼ pints (3 cups) tomato juice; 1 tsp dried oregano; salt.*

Combine all ingredients for meatballs and shape into balls about 2.5 cm (1 in) in diameter.
CHILLI TOMATO SAUCE: Melt butter in a large saucepan, add onion and garlic and cook gently until lightly browned. Add chilli powder and stir for a few seconds. Stir in tomato juice, oregano and salt. Simmer for 10 minutes. Drop meatballs into simmering sauce, cover and simmer for 10 minutes longer, or until meatballs are cooked. Serve with rice or Corn Bread (see page 84). Serves 4.
NOTE: Chilli Tomato Sauce can be used with barbecued meats, or as a dipping sauce for cocktail meatballs or sausages. This recipe makes about 750 ml/1¼ pints (3 cups).

OSSO BUCO MILANESE

This dish has spread far beyond Lombardy where it originated, and has become part of international cuisine. Osso Buco is at its best when made with very young, tender veal. It is served sprinkled with Gremolata, a mixture of parsley, garlic and lemon rind.

Osso Buco Milanese
(Stewed Shin of Veal)

1.5 kg (3 lb) shin of veal (veal shank) cut into 5 cm (2 in) pieces; 30 g/1 oz (¼ cup) flour; 60 g/2 oz (4 tbsp) butter; 150 ml/¼ pint (⅔ cup) white wine; 3 medium tomatoes, peeled and chopped; 250 ml/8 fl oz (1 cup) stock; ½ tsp salt; ½ tsp pepper.
GREMOLATA: *20 g/⅔ oz (½ cup) finely chopped parsley; 1 clove garlic, finely chopped; 2 tsp grated lemon rind.*

Dust veal lightly with flour. Melt butter in a large deep pan, add veal, a few pieces at a time, and brown on all sides. Remove browned pieces and keep warm while browning the rest. Return all veal pieces to pan when all are browned, arranging them so they remain upright to prevent the marrow falling out as meat cooks. Pour wine over and simmer for 10 minutes. Add tomatoes and stock and season with salt and pepper. Cover and simmer very gently, basting meat every 15 minutes, for 1½ hours or until meat is tender but not falling off the bones.
GREMOLATA: Mix ingredients together and sprinkle over top of Osso Buco just before serving. Serves 4.

OXTAIL

The tail of a cow or ox. Oxtail soup and stew are among the most comforting dishes of all in winter. The flavour is rich, and the long slow cooking necessary develops the soft gelatinous texture. Oxtail is best cooked the

day before serving and refrigerated overnight. The fat will solidify on the surface which makes it easy to remove before the dish is reheated. Preparation the day ahead also allows the richness to develop fully.

Most butchers stock oxtails during the winter months and they are usually sold ready-jointed. Trim as much fat as possible from joints before using (usually only the upper joints need trimming, see below). One whole oxtail serves two to three people. **See recipes**.

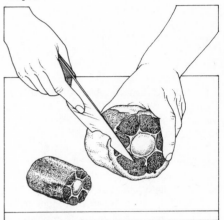

Trimming fat from oxtail

Oxtail Soup

1 oxtail, jointed; 30 g/1 oz (2 tbsp) dripping; 2 carrots, sliced; 1 large onion, sliced; 2 sticks celery, sliced; 1 bouquet garni; 2 rashers (slices) bacon, or 6 bacon rinds; 2 litres/3½ pints (8 cups) beef stock; 2 tsp cornflour (cornstarch); 2 tbsp cold water; juice ½ lemon; salt and freshly ground black pepper; 1 tbsp brandy (optional); finely chopped parsley.

Place oxtail joints in a large saucepan, cover with cold water and bring to the boil. Drain and pat dry. Melt dripping in saucepan, add oxtail pieces and fry until well browned on all sides. Remove and drain on paper towels. Add vegetables to hot dripping and fry until lightly browned. Return oxtail to pan with bouquet garni, bacon rashers (slices) or rinds and beef stock. Bring to the boil, cover and simmer gently for 3–4 hours. Strain off stock and discard bacon, bouquet garni and vegetables.

Refrigerate stock overnight. Next day, remove meat from bones, shred finely and set aside. To finish soup, remove any solidifed fat from surface of stock, pour into pan and bring to the boil. Blend cornflour (cornstarch) with cold water to make a thin paste. Gradually stir this cornflour mixture into stock and simmer, stirring, to thicken slightly. Add reserved meat and lemon juice and season with salt and pepper. Stir in brandy, if using, and sprinkle with chopped parsley. Serves 6.

Braised Oxtail

3 tbsp oil or dripping; 1 large oxtail, jointed; 2 large onions, quartered; 2 large carrots, quartered; 2 sticks celery, cut into 5 cm (2 in) lengths; 1 tbsp flour; 600 ml/1 pint (2½ cups) beef stock; 1 bouquet garni; salt and freshly ground black pepper; finely chopped parsley.

Heat oil or dripping in a flameproof casserole and brown oxtail joints all over. Remove oxtail. Add onions, carrots and celery to casserole and brown lightly over medium heat. Sprinkle flour over and stir well, then remove from heat and pour on beef stock. Heat gently and stir until boiling and thick. Return oxtail with bouquet garni and season with salt and pepper. Cover casserole and cook in a preheated moderate oven (180°C/350°F, Gas Mark 4) for 1½–2 hours or until meat is very tender and comes away from the bone easily. Skim off fat from the surface, discard bouquet garni and serve very hot, sprinkled with chopped parsley. Accompany with creamy mashed potatoes. Serves 4.

NOTE: Cook oxtail a day ahead if you have time and refrigerate overnight to improve the flavour and make the fat easier to remove.

Oxtail with Grapes

2 medium to large oxtails, cut into 5 cm (2 in) pieces; 4 rashers (slices) streaky bacon, rind removed and chopped; 2 large onions, chopped; 2 cloves garlic, crushed; 4 large carrots, sliced; 2 bay leaves; 1 sprig parsley; 1 sprig fresh thyme; salt and freshly ground black pepper; 750 g/1½ lb (6 cups) seedless white grapes.

Remove excess fat from oxtail pieces. Place in a pan, cover with cold water and bring to the boil. Simmer for 10 minutes. Drain and dry well on paper towels. Fry bacon in a large flameproof casserole over a gentle heat until the fat runs. Add onions, garlic and carrots and fry gently, stirring a few times, for about 10 minutes. Add oxtail pieces, bay leaves, parsley, thyme, salt and pepper and cook for a further 20 minutes over gentle heat. Remove stalks from grapes and crush them lightly in a bowl. Add to casserole, cover with a sheet of foil then the lid and transfer to a preheated cool oven (150°C/300°F, Gas Mark 2). Cook for 3–3½ hours or until meat is very tender and comes away easily from the bones. Remove from oven, cool then refrigerate.

The next day remove fat that has risen to top. Take all meat off the bones. Remove carrots and place meat and carrots in a clean saucepan. Remove herbs, place remaining contents of casserole in a blender and blend at high speed for about 30 seconds, or push through a sieve. Pour over meat and carrots and reheat gently on top of stove. Adjust seasoning. Spoon into a heated deep serving dish, garnish with extra grapes if liked and serve with plenty of crusty bread to mop up juices. Serves 8.

OYSTER

A much-prized mollusc; oysters appear on menus throughout the world, their unique flavour and texture being unlike any other mollusc or seafood. Many varieties are extensively cultivated. The best European oysters include the English Whitstable, and the *Belon* and green *Marenne* from France. Most of these are sold raw or sometimes frozen in the half shell; some are bottled in fresh water without preservatives while others can be purchased unopened.

Live rock oysters can survive unopened in the shell for up to 2 weeks if they are stored in a clean damp hessian bag and kept in a cool place. If stored in a plastic bag or in the refrigerator, they will soon die. Always discard oysters with shells that have started to open, or those with an offensive odour.

Select oysters on the half shell from reliable suppliers. They should be plump, creamy and smell of the sea. Opened oysters should always have a fresh sea smell and be eaten on the day of purchase.

Buy fresh bottled oysters only when refrigerated and in clear liquid with no trace of cloudiness. These are excellent for soups and sauces.

Oysters can also be bought canned, smoked, barbecued or natural, either whole or chopped.

☐ **Basic Preparation:** To open oysters, a special flat-bladed knife, with a tough triangular point, is used. Insert the knife point under the smooth lip of the joined shells where there is a gap in the corrugated shell edge (**Fig 1 below**). Push the knife between the upper and lower shells and lever them apart. Gently detach the oyster from the hinge on the upper shell (**2**) and serve in the deeper bottom shell (**3**). It is best to protect your hand with a cloth before grasping the oyster.

Preparing fresh oysters

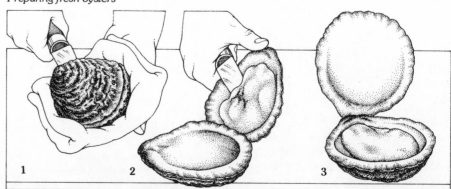

1   2   3

Ways to Use Oysters

They are best eaten raw – *au naturel*, on the half shell, served with lemon wedges and brown bread and butter. There are, however, many other delicious ways to use them.

● Use oysters in beautiful soups and soup stews (see *Gumbo*): serve them hot or cold; baked, grilled (broiled) or fried.

● In many dishes oysters are traditionally served on rock salt, which can be purchased from health food shops and re-used if stored in a covered container. The rock salt is purely for decoration and should not be consumed.

● Add 5 or 6 oysters to Steak and Kidney Pie (see page 412) after mixture is cooked.

● Serve canned smoked oysters on crackers or croûtes, with a sliver of lemon peel and freshly ground black pepper.

● Fill hot vol-au-vent cases or tartlet shells with whole oysters and top with Béchamel or Mornay Sauce (see page 368). **See recipes.**

Oyster Soup

30 g/1 oz (2 tbsp) butter; 2 tbsp flour; 875 ml/1 pint 9 fl oz (3½ cups) Fish Stock (page 414); 120 ml/4 fl oz (½ cup) single (light) cream; 24 bottled or canned oysters, whole or chopped, drained; salt and freshly ground white pepper; snipped chives.

Melt butter in a heavy saucepan. Stir in flour and cook over a gentle heat for about 1 minute. Pour on stock and bring to the boil, stirring constantly. Allow to simmer for 15 minutes, stirring occasionally. Stir in cream. Place oysters in a soup tureen or soup bowls and pour boiling soup over them. Add seasoning and sprinkle with snipped chives. Serves 4.

Oyster Soup Rockefeller

1 bunch spinach; 500 ml/18 fl oz (2 cups) Fish Stock (page 414) or chicken stock; 1 small onion, finely chopped; 500 ml/18 fl oz (2 cups) milk; 36 bottled oysters, drained; salt and freshly ground black pepper; 2 drops Tabasco (hot pepper) sauce; 120 ml/4 fl oz (½ cup) double (heavy) cream, whipped, to garnish.

O

Place spinach in a saucepan with stock and onion and simmer for 5 minutes. Purée in a blender or push through a sieve. Heat milk, add spinach purée and oysters and heat very gently. Season with salt and pepper. Add Tabasco (hot pepper) sauce and serve immediately, garnishing each bowl with a little cream. Serves 6.

Oysters au Naturel

Many people think the delicate flavour is best complemented when oysters are served slightly chilled, with lemon, freshly ground black pepper and thin brown bread and butter. Others enjoy them with a cocktail sauce. Include a small bowl of sauce on each plate.

24–32 fresh oysters on the half shell; rock salt; 2 thin slices buttered brown bread; 1 lemon, quartered.
COCKTAIL SAUCE: *120 g/4 fl oz (½ cup) fresh tomato purée; 2 drops Tabasco (hot pepper) sauce; squeeze lemon juice; 3 tbsp single (light) cream; salt and freshly ground black pepper.*

Chill oysters for 1–2 hours. Place some rock salt on 4 plates and a small bowl for the sauce in the centre of each. Mix sauce ingredients and fill bowls. Remove crusts and cut each slice of bread into 4, arrange bread on a small plate. Arrange 6–8 oysters on each plate on rock salt and place a lemon wedge on each plate. Serves 4.

Oysters Kilpatrick

24 fresh oysters on the half shell; rock salt; 2 tbsp Worcestershire sauce; 30 g/1 oz (2 tbsp) butter; 4 rashers (slices) lean bacon (Canadian bacon), rind removed and finely chopped; freshly ground black pepper.

Arrange oysters on a bed of rock salt in an ovenproof dish, or directly in the grill (broiler) pan. Heat Worcestershire sauce and butter to simmering point. Spoon a little butter mixture over each oyster and sprinkle with bacon. Season with pepper. Place under a preheated grill (broiler) for 3–4 minutes or until oysters are plump and bacon crisp. Serves 2–4.

Oysters Czarina

A marvellously dramatic dish topped with caviar or its close relative, red and black lumpfish roe.

36 fresh oysters on the half shell; 120 ml/4 fl oz (½ cup) single (light) cream; 1 tsp lemon juice; cayenne; 1 small jar each red and black lumpfish roe; rock salt (optional); snipped chives.
TO SERVE: *brown bread and butter sandwiches; lemon wedges.*

Remove oysters from shells and smear a little cream, soured with lemon juice, on bottom

of each shell. Return oysters, put a small dab of sour cream on top and sprinkle with a little cayenne. Mask oysters with red and black lumpfish roe, red on one side, black on the other. Arrange on 6 plates, on a bed of rock salt, if desired. Sprinkle oysters with chives and serve with brown bread and butter sandwiches and lemon wedges. Serves 6.

Oysters Mornay

24 fresh oysters on the half shell; 250 ml/8 fl oz (1 cup) Mornay Sauce (page 368); rock salt; 60 g/2 oz (½ cup) grated cheese.

Remove oysters from shells, smear a little sauce on bottom of each shell and return oysters. Arrange on heatproof plates, on a bed of rock salt. Cover oysters well with sauce. Sprinkle with grated cheese and grill (broil) for 2–3 minutes until lightly browned. Serve immediately. Serves 4.

Soufflé Oysters

24 fresh oysters on the half shell; 3 rashers (slices) bacon, rind removed and finely chopped; 60 g/2 oz (4 tbsp) butter; 1½ tbsp flour; 120 ml/4 fl oz (½ cup) milk; 1 tsp French (Dijon) mustard; salt and freshly ground white pepper; 60 g/2 oz (½ cup) grated Cheddar cheese; 2 eggs, separated.

Put oysters on a baking tray. Fry bacon in an ungreased frying pan (skillet) until crisp and crumbly. Drain and sprinkle over oysters. Melt butter in a saucepan, add flour and stir over medium heat for 1–2 minutes. Remove from heat and gradually stir in milk. Add mustard, salt and pepper. Return pan to low heat and cook, stirring continuously, until sauce boils and thickens. Remove from heat and stir in cheese. Add beaten egg yolks and allow mixture to cool until warm. Beat egg whites until soft peaks form and gently fold into cheese mixture. Spread heaped spoonfuls of the mixture over each oyster. Bake in a preheated moderately hot oven (200°C/400°F, Gas Mark 6) for 5 minutes or until puffed and golden. Serve immediately. Serves 4.

Steak with Oyster Sauce

310 g (10 oz) rump (top round) steak, cut thick; freshly ground black pepper; 30 g/1 oz (2 tbsp) butter, softened.
OYSTER SAUCE: *12 bottled or canned oysters; 30 g/1 oz (2 tbsp) butter; 1 tbsp lemon juice; salt; cayenne; 2 egg yolks; 120 ml/4 fl oz (½ cup) single (light) cream; ½ tsp Worcestershire sauce.*

Snip fat in several places around sides of steak to prevent curling. Sprinkle both sides with pepper and spread with butter. Cook under a preheated grill (broiler) 6–8 minutes

on each side or until cooked as desired.
OYSTER SAUCE: Combine oysters and 120 ml/4 fl oz (½ cup) of their liquid in a saucepan with butter, lemon juice, salt and cayenne. Simmer 30 seconds, then add egg yolks beaten with cream and Worcestershire sauce. Heat through but do not allow to boil or sauce will curdle. Place steak on a heated serving platter and surround with sauce. Garnish with watercress if liked. Serves 2.

Oysters with Garlic Butter

2–3 cloves garlic; ¼ tsp salt; 3 tbsp finely chopped parsley; 90 g/3 oz (6 tbsp) unsalted butter; 24 fresh oysters on the half shell; 60 g/2 oz (1 cup) fine fresh breadcrumbs.

Crush garlic with salt to a smooth paste. Combine garlic, parsley and butter and cream well. Place about ½ tsp of butter on each oyster, top with breadcrumbs and grill (broil) under a preheated hot grill (broiler) for 3 minutes or until golden. Serves 4.

Oyster Brochettes

24 oysters, bottled or fresh; lemon juice; 6 rashers (slices) bacon, rind removed and halved; freshly ground black pepper; 4 slices rye bread; 2 tbsp sour cream; 4 lemon wedges to garnish.

Drain and pat dry bottled oysters, or remove fresh oysters from shell. Squeeze lemon juice over. Wrap 2 oysters in each half rasher (slice) of bacon and carefully thread on to metal skewers. Season with pepper. Place under a preheated grill (broiler) or in a hot, dry frying pan (skillet), and cook 2–3 minutes or until bacon is just cooked. Place brochettes on rye bread spread with sour cream and serve garnished with lemon wedges. Serves 4.

Fried Oysters

24 bottled oysters; 1 egg; fine dry breadcrumbs; oil for deep-frying; freshly ground black pepper.
GARNISH: *1 lemon, quartered; Fried Parsley (page 265).*

Drain oysters over a saucepan, reserving liquid. Bring liquid to the boil, then add oysters and cook for 30 seconds only, just until plump. Cool oysters in the liquid and drain. Beat egg lightly. Dip each oyster in egg then in breadcrumbs, coating well. Heat oil in a deep-fryer until hot enough for a bread cube dropped in the oil to turn golden in 30 seconds. Place oysters in frying basket and fry for 2–3 minutes or until crisp and golden. It is best to fry the oysters in 3–4 batches. Drain on crumpled paper towels, and arrange in bowls on napkins. Grind a little black pepper over before serving. Garnish with lemon and parsley. Serves 4.

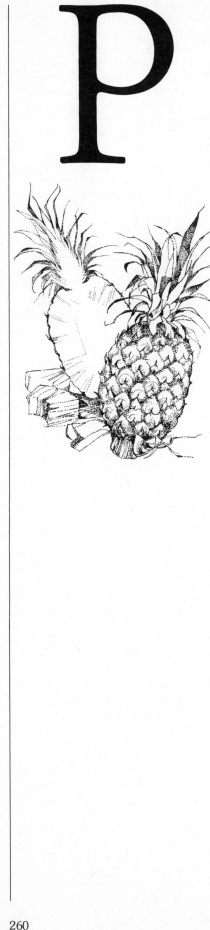

P

PAELLA

A traditional Spanish rice dish that has become famous all over the world. The ingredients, apart from rice flavoured with olive oil, onion, garlic and saffron, vary from region to region and even from family to family. Paella from coastal regions usually contains seafood, poultry and a spicy Spanish sausage such as chorizo. Paella from inland Spain often contains meat, chicken, sausage and vegetables. Paella takes its name from the utensil in which it is cooked – a large two-handled, heavy frying pan (skillet) – but it can be cooked successfully in any large frying pan (skillet).

Paella Valenciana

good pinch saffron, crumbled; 1.2 litres/2 pints (5 cups) chicken stock; 120 ml/4 fl oz (½ cup) olive oil; 6 half-breasts of chicken or 4 small pork chops, cut in two; 2 onions, chopped; 2 cloves garlic, chopped; 2 tomatoes, peeled and chopped; 1 kg/2 lb (4½ cups) rice; salt and freshly ground black pepper; 250 g/8 oz (1½ cups) shelled green peas; 500 g/1 lb (2 cups) cooked prawns (shrimp); 500 g (1 lb) squid, cleaned and sliced; 1 chorizo or peperoni, sliced; ½ green pepper, cored, seeded and sliced; 1 × 130 g/4 oz can pimiento, drained and sliced; 1 cooked crab or crayfish tail (optional); 1 lemon, quartered.

Put saffron and stock into a large saucepan. Bring to the boil and allow stock to take on colour of saffron. Heat oil in either a paella pan or large frying pan (skillet). When very hot sauté chicken breasts or pork until golden-brown. Remove and add onions, garlic and tomatoes. When onions are softened, add rice, combine with other ingredients and fry for 3–5 minutes. Add stock mixture and season with salt and pepper. Spread rice evenly to the edge of the pan and return chicken or pork with peas. Cook on a medium heat until rice has absorbed nearly all the liquid in the pan.

At this stage start decorating paella. Arrange chicken breasts or pork pieces to form a star in the centre. Add prawns (shrimp), squid, slices of peperoni, strips of green pepper and pimiento and lastly crabmeat with legs and cracked claws, or crayfish tail cut in sections, if used. Do not stir at this stage as the decorations are a feature of the paella and must not be disturbed. Continue cooking until rice is tender and other ingredients are cooked. If rice appears too dry or if foods don't appear to be cooking sufficiently add a little more stock. Just before serving garnish with lemon quarters. Serves 8–10.
NOTE: The tiny squid tentacles make a pretty flower-like decoration in the paella.

PALM HEARTS

The pale, tender hearts of the trunks of the cabbage palm. In many tropical climates these are available fresh. For visitors from more temperate climates who have a cabbage palm in the garden at home, it is intriguing to see these little palms cut down for the delicate creamy white hearts that find their way to the table – each palm tree has but one heart!

Canned palm hearts are available in most delicatessens, and may be used as a garnish or in a mixed salad with a variety of salad greens, or as an appetizer salad. They may be served whole, halved lengthways or cut into circles. **See recipes.**

Salad of Palm Hearts Drain canned palm hearts, halved or sliced, toss with Vinaigrette Dressing (see page 358) and chill. Line bowl with washed and dried salad greens, arrange palm hearts on top and pour over dressing. Garnish with fresh herbs, slivers of pimiento, peeled prawns (shrimp) or fine strips of ham.

Palm Hearts and Beetroot Salad with Horseradish Cream

1 head lettuce; 8 canned palm hearts, halved lengthways; 3 small cooked beetroot, peeled, quartered and sliced.
DRESSING: *175 ml/6 fl oz (¾ cup) single (light) cream; 1 tbsp lemon juice; 1 tbsp bottled horseradish, or to taste; salt and freshly ground white pepper; 2 tbsp olive oil.*

Line 4 salad plates with lettuce leaves. Divide palm hearts between plates, arranging them decoratively. Scatter beetroot decoratively over palm hearts.
DRESSING: Whisk together cream, lemon juice, horseradish, salt and pepper for 10 seconds or until mixture is frothy. Add olive oil, drop by drop, whisking, and whisk dressing until it is well combined. Spoon it over the salad. Serves 4.

Hearts of Palm Salad Deluxe

1 × 425 g/14 oz can palm hearts, chilled, drained and cut into matchsticks; 2 tbsp lemon juice; 120 ml/4 fl oz (½ cup) double (heavy) cream, whipped; ¼ tsp celery seeds; ¼ tsp sugar; ½ tsp salt; ¼ tsp white pepper; 60 g/2 oz (½ cup) fresh or canned seedless grapes; 30 g/1 oz (¼ cup) toasted, slivered almonds.

Sprinkle palm hearts with lemon juice. Fold together remaining ingredients, reserving 1 tbsp of almonds. Transfer to a serving bowl and sprinkle with reserved nuts. Serves 4–6.

Right: Herbed Lamb Noisettes and Chutney Chops (page 177), and Spareribs with Spiced Barbecue Sauce (page 304)

PANCAKES

Nearly every country in the world has its own version of pancakes. They are endlessly versatile and range from Chinese Egg Rolls to the sophisticated Crêpes Suzette of France (see *Crêpes*), which many people consider to be the ultimate pancake variation. Pancakes usually have a thick, fluffy texture and can be sweet or savoury. They can be served stacked or rolled, with a sauce, or served flat, with a topping; their thin, lacy relative, crêpes, are usually rolled or folded around a sweet or savoury filling.

Russian Blini made from buckwheat and served with sour cream and caviar (see *Blini*); Jewish Blintzes, with creamy cheese filling, and topped with conserve and sour cream (see *Blintzes*); Griddle Cakes, Flapjacks and Pikelets (see separate entries) are all part of the pancake family.

The pancake pan: Use a heavy, flat pan, preferably made from cast-iron, with sides about 1 cm (½ in) high and about 18 cm (7 in) in diameter. A cast-iron pan should be kept only for making pancakes and their variations. Do not wash after use: simply rub it with paper towels and a few drops of oil. If the pan becomes sticky, rub with salt first and finish with oil.

To season a new pan: Fill with oil and heat to smoking point. Turn off heat and stand 24 hours. Pour off the oil, and wipe well with paper towels.

To toss pancakes: Some people consider the best way to turn over a pancake during cooking is to toss it. Pour the batter from a jug into the pan, tilting the pan to coat the bottom evenly. When bubbles appear on top of the batter and it begins to set, shake the pan to make sure the pancake is not sticking and has browned underneath. Jerk the pan forward quickly until the pancake moves on to the downward sloping part of the pan. Flip the pancake over with a quick movement of the wrist so that the uncooked side is now underneath.

To store pancakes: Store as for Crêpes (see page 88).

To reheat pancakes: Place on a baking tray, cover with foil and warm in a preheated moderate oven (180°C/350°F, Gas Mark 4) for 5 minutes. Or place a stack of 3–4 pancakes on a heatproof plate, cover with another plate and warm over boiling water for 8–10 minutes.

See also *Crêpes.*

Sweet Pancake Toppings Squeeze lemon juice over and sprinkle with sugar; spread with butter and pour on hot maple syrup; top with warm mincemeat (see *Mincemeat*) and a

Left: Herb Marinade for Fish (page 26)

spoonful of whipped cream; spread with lemon cheese and top with whipped cream; spread with apple purée, sprinkle with cinnamon and top with sour cream; spread with sour cream and brown sugar, top with sliced strawberries or pineapple pieces; spread with thick cream and top with warmed apricot, plum or blackberry jam. **See recipes.**

Basic Pancake Batter

125 g/4 oz (1 cup) flour; 1 tsp baking powder; ½ tsp salt; 1 egg; 350 ml/12 fl oz (1½ cups) milk; 15 g/½ oz (1 tbsp) butter, melted; oil for frying.

Sift flour, baking powder and salt into a bowl. Make a well in the centre and add egg, milk and melted butter. Using a wooden spoon, gradually draw in flour. Beat well, cover and leave to stand for 1 hour.

Grease and heat pancake pan. Pour batter into a jug and pour in enough batter while tilting the pan, to coat the bottom. Cook until small bubbles appear on the surface, about 1 minute, then flip over using a metal spatula or toss. Place cooked pancake on a clean tea-towel, fold ends over to cover and continue making pancakes the same way. Drop each directly on top of the last and fold towel over to cover again. Makes 10–12 × 18 cm (7 in) or 14–16 × 15 cm (6 in) pancakes.

Chinese Egg Rolls

125 g/4 oz (1 cup) flour; 2 tbsp cornflour (cornstarch); ½ tsp salt; 2 eggs, lightly beaten; 500 ml/18 fl oz (2 cups) water; oil for deep-frying; 2 spring onions (scallions), sliced, to garnish.
FILLING: 140 g/4½ oz (¾ cup) cooked prawns (shrimp), shelled, deveined and finely chopped; 60 g/2 oz (½ cup) finely diced celery; 90 g/3 oz (⅓ cup) minced (ground) pork; 90 g/3 oz (⅓ cup) finely chopped canned water chestnuts; 90 g/3 oz (⅓ cup) finely chopped canned bamboo shoots; 2 tsp dry sherry; 1 tbsp soy sauce; 1 tbsp grated onion; 1 egg.

Sift flour, cornflour (cornstarch) and salt into a bowl and mix in eggs and water. The batter should be as thin as cream; if it is not add a little more water. Cook pancakes as for Basic Pancakes, cooking on one side only. Cool on a wire rack.

FILLING: Combine all ingredients, using the hands and mixing well. Form into little finger-shaped rolls. Put a roll on the cooked side of each pancake and roll up, tucking in edges to seal in filling. Seal with beaten egg or any leftover batter mixture. Chill for 2–3 hours. Pour enough oil into a deep saucepan to come 5 cm (2 in) up the sides. Heat oil until a bread cube dropped in turns brown in 60 seconds. Deep-fry the rolls in batches until golden-brown, about 5 minutes. Drain on paper towels and serve immediately, garnished with sliced spring onions (scallions) and accompanied by bowls of soy and chilli sauces for dipping. Makes about 20.

Hungarian Pancake Pie

This superb dinner party dessert from Middle Europe consists of pancakes layered with fillings and baked with a coating of meringue. To serve, cut into wedges.

12–14 × 15 cm (6 in) Pancakes (left); 280 g/9 oz (¾ cup) apricot or plum jam; 125 g/4 oz (⅔ cup) dark chocolate, grated; 125 g/4 oz (1 cup) walnuts or pecans, crushed; 180 g/6 oz (1 cup) chopped raisins; 250 ml/8 fl oz (1 cup) double (heavy) cream, whipped; 4 egg whites; 125 g/4 oz (½ cup) sugar.

Place the first pancake on a greased baking tray. Spread with a little jam and sprinkle with chocolate. Place another pancake on top, and sprinkle with crushed nuts, a few raisins, and a spoonful of cream. Continue with these layers until pancakes are used up, leaving the top one plain. Beat egg whites to a froth, then beat in sugar a little at a time until they form firm peaks. Swirl egg white mixture over pancakes, making sure they are completely covered. Bake in a preheated hot oven (220°C/425°F, Gas Mark 7) for 3–4 minutes or until meringue is lightly tipped with brown. Serves 6.

Green Pancakes with Cream Cheese

125 g/4 oz (1 cup) flour; ¼ tsp salt; 1 egg; 175 ml/6 fl oz (¾ cup) milk; 105 g/3½ oz (½ cup) cooked, drained and puréed spinach leaves; butter for frying.
FILLING: 500 g/1 lb (2 cups) cream cheese; salt and freshly ground black pepper; 4 tbsp snipped chives.

Make batter with flour, salt, beaten egg and milk, beating well until smooth. Stir in spinach purée and allow batter to stand for 30 minutes. In a separate bowl, beat cream cheese with salt and pepper, and stir in chives. Melt a little butter in a pancake or crêpe pan and cook pancakes as for Basic Pancakes, page 263. Put 2 tbsp of the cheese filling on each pancake and roll up. Serve warm. Makes about 10 small pancakes or 6 larger ones.

Fluffy Chicken Pancake Peking

Serve this light Chinese pancake as a first course, or with rice and stir-fried vegetables as a main course.

3 egg whites; 2 tsp dry sherry; ¼ tsp salt; freshly ground black pepper; 1 chicken fillet (skinless, boneless half-breast), minced (ground); 3 tbsp peanut oil; ¼ tsp Chinese sesame oil; shredded spring onions (scallions) to garnish.

Beat egg whites until foamy and mix thoroughly with sherry, salt, pepper and chicken. Heat 1½ tbsp peanut oil in a small frying pan (skillet) on a medium heat. When moderately hot, add chicken mixture and tilt pan so that 'pancake' is of even thickness. Cook until top is firm to touch (the underside should be barely coloured). Loosen edges with a metal spatula and slide pancake on to a plate. Add remaining peanut oil to pan and heat. Slide pancake back into pan, cooked side up. Cook 1–2 minutes more, then slide pancake on to a heated platter. Sprinkle with sesame oil and serve immediately, garnished with shredded spring onions (scallions). Serves 2.

Dutch Apple Pancake Cake

60 g/2 oz (4 tbsp) butter; 10 medium apples, peeled, cored and sliced; pared rind 1 lemon; 3 tbsp sugar; 10 × 18 cm (7 in) Pancakes (page 263); Apricot Glaze (page 11); whipped cream; toasted slivered almonds.

Melt 45 g/1½ oz (3 tbsp) of the butter in a saucepan, add apples and lemon rind and cook gently for about 10 minutes or until a thick purée has formed. Stir in sugar, remove lemon rind and rub through a sieve. Place a pancake on a heated serving dish and spread with apple purée. Continue layering pancakes and apple purée, ending with a

pancake. Spread final pancake with a fine layer of apricot glaze. Pipe rosettes of whipped cream around top and decorate these with toasted slivered almonds. Serve pancake cake as soon as possible, cut into wedges. Pass around a bowl of lightly whipped cream separately. Serves 6.

Shrove Tuesday Fritters

This is a beautiful dish of deep-fried pancake strips dusted with icing (confectioners) sugar, served with a bowl of Kirsch-flavoured plum sauce.

8 × 15 cm (6 in) Pancakes (page 263); oil for deep-frying; sifted icing (confectioners) sugar.
PLUM SAUCE: 180 g/6 oz (½ cup) plum jam; 120 ml/4 fl oz (½ cup) water; piece pared lemon rind; juice ½ lemon; 1 tsp arrowroot dissolved in 2 tsp water; 1 tbsp Kirsch.

Roll up each pancake and cut into strips 1 cm (½ in) wide. Heat oil and when very hot put in 1 pancake strip. If oil sizzles immediately, it is hot enough. Add half the pancake strips and toss with a slotted spoon until golden all over. Remove from oil and drain on crumpled paper towels. Keep hot while frying remaining pancake strips. Serve warm, piled on to a dish and dusted with icing (confectioners) sugar. Accompany with plum sauce.
PLUM SAUCE: Place jam, water, and lemon rind and juice in a saucepan and bring slowly to the boil. Thicken with arrowroot mixture and boil, stirring, until clear. Strain, flavour with Kirsch and serve sauce hot or cold. Serves 4–6.

Swedish Pancakes

This is a famous Swedish dish customarily served with loganberries or fruit conserves.

3 eggs; 250 ml/8 fl oz (1 cup) milk; 125 g/4 oz (1 cup) flour, sifted; 175 ml/6 fl oz (¾ cup) single (light) cream; 90 g/3 oz (6 tbsp) unsalted butter, melted; ¼ tsp salt; oil for frying.

Beat eggs with 120 ml/4 fl oz (½ cup) of the milk for 2–3 minutes. Add flour all at once and beat until mixture is thick and smooth. Beat in remaining milk and cream, then stir in melted butter and salt. Cover and allow to stand for at least 2 hours. Very lightly oil a pancake pan, place over a high heat and when very hot, lower heat and drop in batter in small mounds. Immediately sprinkle surface of each pancake with flavouring, if using (see below). When pancakes begin to set and bubbles appear on surface, carefully lift each one and turn it over. Cook for a further 1–2 minutes to brown other side. Serve as soon as possible. Makes about 24.
VARIATIONS
Sprinkle these on to the batter as soon as it is

placed in the pán: chopped mixed candied peel; crushed almond macaroons or amaretti; toasted slivered almonds; chopped dried apricots, soaked; grated eating apple, unpeeled.

PANETONE (Panettone)

An Italian yeast cake, of Milanese origin, enriched with eggs and butter and studded with sultanas (golden raisins) and candied peel. It is very similar to the German Gugel-hopf (see page 152), and is traditionally associated with Christmas.

PANFORTE

See *Siena Cake.*

PAPPADUMS (Pappadoms, Poppadoms, Poddadums)

These thin, lentil-flour rounds are available packaged in Oriental groceries, health food stores and many supermarkets and delicat-essens. When fried, they swell dramatically into crunchy golden wafers to eat with or crumble over curries and other Indian dishes. Packaged pappadums will keep for months in a cool place. Once fried, they will keep crisp for a day or so in an airtight tin; if they soften, crisp them again in a low oven.
☐ **To Fry:** Heat about 2 cm (¾ in) of oil in a wide pan. Have ready a bed of crumpled paper towels on several thicknesses of news-paper. Fry pappadums one at a time, pressing down with a fish slice or 2 spoons so that they will stay fairly flat. Fry only a few seconds on each side, until pappadums are a very pale gold (they will darken more after removing from oil). Drain on paper towels.

PAPRIKA

A spice made from a sweet variety of red pepper, grown widely in Europe. It should be a deep, rich red in colour, with a mild, sweet aroma. The best paprika is said to come from Hungary, where it goes into the characteristic meat dish, Goulash (see page 147).

Paprika is also valued for its colour, which enlivens any pale, creamy-coloured dish. Potato salad, cauliflower au gratin or a dish of

creamed chicken or fish, is all the more appetizing for a light sprinkle of paprika.

Always buy paprika in small quantities, since even the best or 'noble' paprika loses its spicy qualities when stored for very long. For that reason, the quantity of paprika for a recipe is not always specified precisely because it depends on individual tastes and the quality of the paprika. **See recipes.**

Chicken Paprika

1 roast chicken, carved; 1 onion, chopped; 30 g/1 oz (2 tbsp) butter; 1–2 tsp paprika; 1 tbsp flour; 120 ml/4 fl oz (½ cup) chicken stock; 4 ripe tomatoes, peeled, seeded and roughly chopped; salt and freshly ground black pepper; 1 clove garlic; 1 bay leaf; 120 ml/4 fl oz (½ cup) sour cream.

Keep chicken warm in turned-off oven. Cook onion in butter in large saucepan until soft, add paprika and cook 1 minute. Stir in flour, then remove from heat and add stock and tomatoes. Stir well. Return to heat and bring to the boil, stirring. Add salt, pepper, garlic and bay leaf. Simmer until reduced and thickened. Strain sauce and return to pan. Add chicken pieces and simmer 15 minutes. Stir in sour cream just before serving with boiled rice or noodles. Serves 4.

Veal Chops Paprika

6 veal chops; 2 tbsp oil; 2 onions, sliced; 1 clove garlic, crushed; 1 tbsp flour; 1 tbsp paprika, or to taste; 4 ripe tomatoes, peeled and seeded; salt and freshly ground black pepper; 120 ml/4 fl oz (½ cup) sour cream.

Brown chops in oil in a large frying pan (skillet) on both sides, then remove. Add onions and cook until pale brown. Add garlic and return chops. Sprinkle with flour. Stir, then add paprika and cook 2–3 minutes. Add tomatoes, salt and pepper, plus water if necessary just to cover chops. Cover pan and simmer gently until chops are tender, about 1 hour. Just before serving, add sour cream and stir well but do not allow to boil. Serve with steamed potatoes or buttered noodles. Serves 6.

PARFAIT

A French term, meaning 'perfect', which was originally used only for a coffee ice cream, but later came to apply to all kinds of ice creams.

Today, a parfait glass is usually a tall, narrow, short-stemmed glass, and an ice cream parfait is a combination of scoops of ice cream, a sauce such as chocolate, strawberry or caramel, whipped cream and sometimes chopped nuts or fresh fruit for decoration.

A very fine preparation of chicken or goose liver may also be termed a 'parfait'.

PARSLEY

Surely the most popular and most widely-grown herb; indeed, it is one of the essential herbs in the kitchen. Sprigs of parsley are part of a Bouquet Garni; fresh parsley is one of the 'fines herbes' (together with tarragon, chives and chervil); and parsley stalks are used for flavour in a Court Bouillon.

Parsley is a biennial herb, which means that it will yield for two years. It is easily grown from seed, and a parsley patch will be self-perpetuating if some plants are allowed to go to seed each year.

The principal varieties of parsley are the curly-leaved, and flat-leaved or Italian, parsley. The curly-leaved variety makes a most attractive garnish.

Parsley is rich in vitamin C and minerals, and is said to be one of the best natural tonics. It is also said that chewing parsley can get rid of, or at least hide, a garlicky breath.

Small amounts of chopped parsley add flavour interest to mashed potatoes, steamed vegetables, scrambled eggs and omelettes, sauces, stuffings and salads. In large quantities, it goes into Tabouleh and the jellied ham of Burgundy, France, Jambon Persillé (see page 142). **See recipes.**

☐ Basic Preparation

To chop parsley by hand: Wash parsley and dry in a cloth. Use a chopping-board large enough to allow parsley to scatter a bit. Using a good cook's knife, hold blade at both ends and, keeping pointed end on the board, chop with rapid up-and-down movements. Sweep parsley together and repeat until it is chopped to desired fineness. Put parsley into a cloth and wring well to remove excess moisture – this ensures that it will not clump when sprinkled.

To chop parsley in a food processor: The food processor makes it easy to have chopped parsley always on hand – it is a good idea to chop a good-sized bunch at a time and store it ready to give instant colour and added nutrition to many dishes.

Do not wash parsley before chopping. Put into processor, fitted with steel blade, and process by switching rapidly on-off, on-off, until chopped to desired fineness. Wash in a sieve, put into a cloth and wring well to dry. Store as below.

To store parsley: Wash and dry well and store in a screw-top jar or tightly closed plastic bag, with some air left in it, in the refrigerator. Or freeze chopped in plastic bags or tubs, for up to 6 months.

Fried Parsley Garnish Allow 2–3 sprigs per person. Wash and dry parsley sprigs between paper towels. Drop into very hot oil and fry very quickly, about 3 seconds – they should be crisp but not burnt. This is easy to manage if you place parsley in a sieve. Use as a garnish for fried fish and seafood.

Persillade Garnish A mixture of finely chopped parsley, garlic or shallot, added to pan-fried meat, fish or vegetables just before serving. This garnish is typical of southern French cuisine. Mushrooms, courgette (zucchini) rounds, sliced squid, lamb chops, all take well to a persillade treatment.

Parsley Sauce Add very finely chopped parsley to a Béchamel or Velouté sauce (see page 368). Use with salted pork, corned beef or lamb, steamed fish, hard-boiled (hard-cooked) eggs, or chicken.

Parsley and Lemon Stuffing

Use for chicken or turkey – double quantities for a small turkey.

30 g/1 oz (½ cup) dry breadcrumbs; 2 tbsp finely chopped parsley; ¼ tsp dried marjoram; ¼ tsp chopped fresh lemon thyme; grated rind ½ lemon; 2 tsp lemon juice; 1 small egg; 90 g/3 oz (6 tbsp) butter, softened; salt and freshly ground black pepper.

Combine breadcrumbs with parsley, marjoram, lemon thyme, and lemon rind and juice. Beat in egg, then blend in softened butter. Season lightly with salt and pepper. Makes about 150 g/5 oz (¾ cup).

Parsley and Garlic Stuffing

Use to stuff a boned leg or shoulder of lamb for roasting.

20 g/⅔ oz (½ cup) chopped parsley; 1 sprig fresh thyme or rosemary; 2 tbsp finely chopped shallots; 1 clove garlic, crushed; ¼ tsp ground ginger; salt and freshly ground black pepper.

Combine all ingredients (use leaves only of thyme or rosemary). Spread on lamb, roll up, tie and roast as usual. Makes about 90 g/3 oz (¾ cup).

PARSNIP

A carrot-shaped, white root vegetable, most common in winter months. It has a distinctive, slightly sweet and sometimes strong flavour, and makes a good accompaniment to most roast or grilled (broiled) meats.

Parsnip may be added to a mixed vegetable soup or stew, but use only half as much parsnip as carrot. Julienne (matchsticks) of carrot and parsnip, cooked in a little water until tender but still firm, then tossed with butter and finely chopped herbs, is a lovely winter vegetable dish – add the parsnip julienne about a minute after the carrot.

Young parsnips can be mashed like potatoes, with butter and cream, pepper and salt and chopped parsley added. This also makes tasty croquettes, in the same way as potato (see *Potato*). Old parsnips are not always suitable for mashing, as they may have a hard, woody core, which should be cut away before cooking. **See recipes**.

Creamed Parsnips

500 g (1 lb) parsnips, peeled and quartered; 60 g/2 oz (4 tbsp) butter; salt and freshly ground black pepper; 120 ml/4 fl oz (½ cup) single (light) cream; 1–2 tbsp chopped parsley.

Remove core from parsnips if woody, and cut into smaller pieces if desired. Cook until almost tender in boiling salted water. Drain. Return to pan with butter and complete cooking over low heat, shaking pan from time to time. Season with salt and pepper and add cream. Heat through gently and serve, sprinkled with chopped parsley. Serves 4.

Roast Parsnips

4 parsnips, peeled and quartered; dripping or oil if necessary.

Remove core from parsnips if woody. Blanch in boiling water 5 minutes, then drain and pat dry with paper towels. Place parsnips around or under meat in roasting tin (pan) or cook in a separate tin (pan) of dripping or oil, or cook with roast potatoes. Allow about 30–45 minutes in a preheated moderately hot oven (190°/375°F, Gas Mark 5). Serves 4.

PASSIONFRUIT (Grenadilla)

Although a native of Brazil, passionfruit is grown in many other countries where the climate is warm and there is little risk of frost. It is a small, round pulpy fruit with small black edible seeds and a tough purple skin.

Passionfruit are usually considered a summer fruit, although they are available year-round. Passionfruit pulp can be purchased canned.

Passionfruit is a traditional decoration for Pavlova (see page 277), and there are few fruits whose flavour is not enhanced by passionfruit. It goes beautifully with fresh or cooked peaches, nectarines and cantaloup melon; and also with fresh sliced or poached pears. **See recipes**.

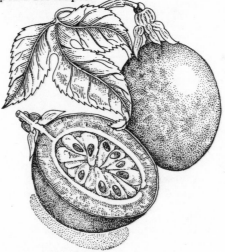

Passionfruit Mousse

180 g/6 oz (¾ cup) passionfruit pulp; 3–4 tbsp caster sugar; 1 tbsp gelatine; 2 tbsp lemon juice; 2 tbsp hot water; 175 ml/6 fl oz (¾ cup) orange juice; 2 egg whites; 250 ml/8 fl oz (1 cup) double (heavy) cream.

Mix passionfruit pulp with caster sugar to taste. Sprinkle gelatine over lemon juice, leave to soften, then add hot water and stir until dissolved. Add to orange juice and chill until just starting to set. Whip juice mixture until frothy. Beat egg whites until stiff. Whip cream until thick. Fold passionfruit pulp into juice mixture, then fold in cream and egg whites. Spoon into a serving bowl and place in refrigerator to set. Serves 6.

Passionfruit Ice Cream

60 g/2 oz (¼ cup) caster sugar; 125 g/4 oz (½ cup) passionfruit pulp; squeeze lemon juice; 175 ml/6 fl oz (¾ cup) double (heavy) cream.

Stir caster sugar into passionfruit pulp until dissolved, then add lemon juice. Place in freezer to chill. Whip cream until thick. Fold cream into passionfruit mixture, pour into container of sorbetière and freeze. Alternatively, pour into ice cream tray, freeze until mushy, then turn out and beat until smooth. Return to ice cream tray and freeze. Serves 6.

Passionfruit Cheese

60 g/2 oz (4 tbsp) butter; 4 passionfruit; 2 egg yolks; 125 g/4 oz (½ cup) sugar.

Melt butter in top of a double saucepan (double boiler) or in a heatproof bowl over simmering water. Add passionfruit, egg yolks

and sugar. Stir over gentle heat until mixture thickens. Cool, pour into sterilized jar and seal. Makes about 250 g/8 oz (1 cup).

PASTA

Spaghetti Caruso, Rigatoni Carbonara, Vermicelli Napolitana, Straw and Grass, Lasagne, Cannelloni – the names conjure up pictures of steaming pasta of different shapes and sizes, each with its own delicious, complementary sauce.

Pasta is as Italian as opera and as varied. There are said to be about 400 different varieties of pasta, from the fine strands of *vermicelli* to the broad, flat *lasagne* and the giant *cannelloni* (large pipes). Pasta comes in different shapes, too: small and large shells; *cornetti* or elbow macaroni; *trivelle* – shaped like a corkscrew. The long thin strands of *spaghetti* are an all-time favourite, but so too is *bucatini* (that's spaghetti with a hole in the middle); and there's *linguine* (flat spaghetti) as well. Some pastas are eaten with a sauce, sometimes just with butter; others like *tortellini* are stuffed with meat or cheese, spices and herbs.

Sauces are important (see *Pasta Sauces*) – contrary to popular belief not all the sauces include tomato, but those that do are legion – the *Ragù alla Bolognese* is, perhaps, the most famous. So too are the fresh tomato sauces that can be made in just a few minutes with fresh or canned tomatoes. And tomato purée (paste) (a concentrated reduction of tomatoes) is added to many sauces to enrich them and give them their lovely natural tomato flavour.

When buying pasta, go for quality. Look also for the pre-cooked varieties, especially *cannelloni* and *lasagne*, which eliminate one whole step – cooking the pasta in boiling water – which can be tricky with these shapes as they have a tendency to stick together. Pre-cooked *spaghetti* is a great boon: it takes only 6 minutes to boil, the strands stay separate and in that time you can make a simple tomato sauce, or simply serve the spaghetti with butter flavoured with a crushed clove of garlic and a grating of Parmesan cheese – it's delicious!

There are three main distinctions to be made with types of Italian pasta. One is called *pasta fatta in casa*, meaning fresh, homemade pasta; another is the mass-produced type, sold dried, in packets, and the third is the pasta made in the fresh pasta shops now occasionally emerging. There is much to be said for all three, but if you have a light hand with pastry (dough), it is well worth trying to make your own pasta. You may even invest in a pasta-making machine. The electric machines actually make the pasta, then roll it out and cut it into a variety of shapes, all automatically. A great toy and if you really love pasta, a joy.

Servings: 500 g/1 lb (4–5 cups) pasta will serve 4 people as a main course, 6 people as a first course.

☐ **To Cook:** Use a large, deep pan with plenty of room for the pasta to cook, without sticking. Allow 3.75 litres/6 pints (15 cups) water for 250 g/8 oz (2 cups) pasta. Add about 1 tsp salt for each litre/1¾ pints (4 cups) of water, and have the water boiling vigorously before adding pasta. A teaspoon of olive oil may be added to water to help prevent pasta sticking together – a good tip, especially for large pasta like *lasagne.*

Drop pasta into water slowly so water does not go off the boil. Stir a few times at start of cooking to prevent pasta sticking, then allow to boil vigorously, uncovered. When cooked, pasta should be tender but still firm to the bite – *al dente,* as the Italians say, which means just firm enough to bite comfortably, but not so soft that it is mushy. Pasta is meant to be chewed. When cooked, remove pan immediately from heat and drain pasta. Pour boiling water through pasta in a colander or sieve, then allow to drain. Toss in hot sauce or melted butter and serve immediately.

Home-made pasta will not take as long to cook as the bought variety, but it is difficult to give exact times as this depends on the thickness of the dough and also the size and shape of the pasta.

Cooking times: There is a guide to cooking times on most packets, but it is best to start tasting and testing pasta, especially fresh pasta, as soon as it rises to the surface of the water. The following are approximate cooking times for dried packaged pasta.

Spaghetti: 12 minutes.

Tagliatelle (long ribbon strips): 8 minutes.

Vermicelli (long thin threads): 8–10 minutes.

Cannelloni and Lasagne (large pipes or squares): 12 minutes.

To combine pasta and sauce: Place drained cooked pasta in a heated serving bowl, add part of the sauce (if desired, sprinkle with grated Parmesan cheese). With 2 forks, or spaghetti tongs, toss gently until pasta is coated with sauce. Top with remaining sauce.

To keep pasta hot: It is best to serve pasta as soon as it is cooked. However, it can be kept hot for a short while. Return drained cooked pasta to the empty cooking pan, add about 60 g/2 oz (4 tbsp) butter, then cover with a lid and keep warm.

Or drain pasta in a colander and set over a pan containing a small amount of simmering water. Coat pasta with 90 g/3 oz (6 tbsp) butter (for 6 servings) to keep it from sticking together. Cover colander. **See recipes.**

Egg Pasta
(Pasta all'Uovo)

250 g/8 oz (2 cups) flour; 2 eggs.

Sift flour into a bowl, make a well in centre and add eggs. Stir with a knife, adding a little cold water (about 3 tbsp) and form into a firm dough with hands. Turn out on to a floured board and knead, turning and pushing with the heel of your hand for about 15 minutes or until dough is smooth and pliable. The dough will be stiff at first but will become more pliable as you knead. Shape into a ball and wrap in plastic wrap. Leave to rest for 20 minutes. Roll out dough to a paper-thin, even sheet on a lightly floured surface. Sprinkle lightly with flour to prevent sticking. Cut into required shapes as described below, and cook in a large saucepan of boiling salted water. Dough can be left for 30 minutes before cooking, but sprinkle with flour to prevent it sticking.

VARIATIONS

Green Pasta (Pasta Verde): Put 1 × 315 g/10 oz packet frozen chopped spinach in a saucepan and stir over a low heat until melted. Or, if using fresh spinach, cook 2 bunches until tender, about 4–5 minutes. Turn into a fine sieve and press with a spoon to extract all liquid. When cool enough to handle, squeeze spinach with hand to extract as much remaining liquid as possible. Chop or process fresh spinach in a blender or food processor. Make pasta as for Egg Pasta, using 310 g/10 oz (2½ cups) flour and 1 egg, and adding spinach purée with egg. It may be necessary to add a little cold water or more flour to make a firm dough.

Ribbon Noodles (Tagliatelle): Roll out Egg or Green Pasta dough to an oblong shape. Starting from the shorter side, roll up dough, then cut across roll into 1 cm (½ in) strips. Unravel each strip and drop into boiling salted water. Cook for about 5 minutes or until pasta is tender. Drain and serve with a sauce or with butter and grated Parmesan cheese.

Lasagne and Cannelloni: Cut rolled out Egg or Green Pasta dough into oblongs about 8 × 10 cm (3 × 4 in). Place on a floured baking tray so they are not touching. Bring a large pan of salted water to the boil and drop in pasta. Cook for about 10 minutes or until tender, then drain and rinse. Spread on a clean cloth, again not touching, and allow to dry. Lasagne and cannelloni can be left 2 hours before cooking. As they are larger than other pasta, they are best cooked in 2–3 lots, or more if your pan is small.

Pasta with Butter
(Pasta al Burro)

500 g (1 lb) pasta, such as ribbon noodles, spaghetti or macaroni; butter; grated Parmesan cheese.

Cook pasta in boiling salted water until 'al dente'. Drain, turn into a heated serving bowl and top generously with butter and grated Parmesan cheese. Stir through pasta until coated. Serve extra butter and cheese at the table. Serves 4.

Ribbon Noodles Alfredo
(Tagliatelle Alfredo)

500 g (1 lb) ribbon noodles; 60 g/2 oz (4 tbsp) butter; 250 ml/8 fl oz (1 cup) single (light) cream; 125 g/4 oz (1 cup) grated Parmesan cheese; freshly ground black pepper.

Cook pasta in boiling salted water until 'al dente'. Drain well in a colander. Melt butter in same saucepan over a low heat. Mix in cream, then toss in noodles. Add cheese and a good grind of pepper. Toss well and serve immediately. Serves 4.

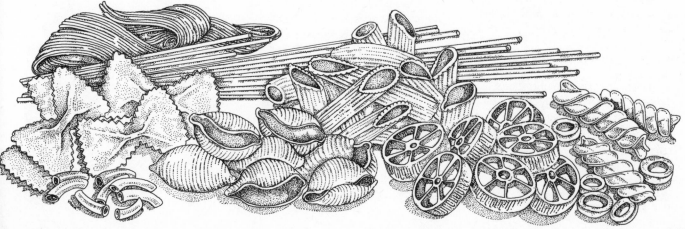

Noodles with Pesto
Pasta con Pesto

500 g (1 lb) fine ribbon noodles; 1 quantity Pesto alla Genovese (page 272); 60 g/2 oz (4 tbsp) butter; grated Pecorino or Parmesan cheese to serve.

Cook pasta in boiling salted water until 'al dente'. Drain and pile into a heated serving bowl. Heap pesto on top with butter and serve. Mix pesto into pasta at the table. Serve with Pecorino or Parmesan cheese. Serves 4.

Spaghetti Bolognese

500 g (1 lb) spaghetti; 1 quantity hot Bolognese Sauce (page 272); grated Parmesan cheese.

Cook spaghetti in boiling salted water until 'al dente'. Drain and turn into a heated serving bowl. Add half the bolognese sauce and toss with 2 forks until each strand is evenly coated. Top with remaining sauce and sprinkle with grated Parmesan cheese. Serve immediately. Serves 4.

Pasta Ammuddicata

Noodles with anchovy sauce accompanied by a bowl of crisp fried crumbs is a speciality from the south of Italy. It is a quick and easy dish but delicious. No cheese is served with this dish.

4–5 canned anchovies; milk; 150 ml/¼ pint (⅔ cup) olive oil; 90 g/3 oz (1½ cups) coarse fresh breadcrumbs; pinch chilli powder; 250 g (8 oz) bucatini or tagliatelle.

Soak anchovies in a little milk for 15–20 minutes, then drain and chop. Heat half the olive oil in a small pan, add anchovies and cook them over lowest possible heat until dissolved to a paste. Heat remaining oil in a frying pan (skillet) and fry breadcrumbs until golden and crispy. Sprinkle with chilli powder and keep warm. Cook pasta in boiling salted water until 'al dente'. Drain and toss with the anchovy sauce. Serve immediately, accompanied by the breadcrumbs in a separate bowl. Serves 3–4.
NOTE: If liked, 2–3 tbsp chopped parsley and 1 tsp chopped fresh oregano may be added to the anchovy sauce.

Pasta with Chunky Tomato Sauce
(Pasta Pizzaiola)
A Neapolitan dish. The tomatoes should just be heated through to retain their fresh flavour. If fresh basil or oregano is not available, add extra chopped parsley.

500 g (1 lb) spaghetti or vermicelli; 90 g/3 oz (¾ cup) grated well-flavoured cheese.
SAUCE: *4 firm ripe tomatoes, peeled, seeded and coarsely chopped; 2 cloves garlic,*
crushed; 3 tbsp olive oil; 1 tsp chopped fresh basil or oregano; 2 tbsp chopped parsley; salt and freshly ground black pepper.

Cook pasta in boiling salted water until 'al dente'.
SAUCE: Meanwhile, cook tomatoes and garlic gently in oil for 5 minutes. Add basil or oregano. Cook 2 minutes longer, then stir in parsley, season with salt and pepper and remove from heat. Drain pasta and place in a heated serving dish. Pour over sauce and serve, passing grated cheese separately. Serves 4.

Pasta with Basil Sauce

500 g (1 lb) fettucini or spaghetti; 20 g/⅔ oz (½ cup) chopped parsley; 20 g/⅔ oz (½ cup) chopped fresh basil; ½ clove garlic, chopped; 120 ml/4 fl oz (½ cup) olive oil; 250 g/8 oz (1 cup) Ricotta cheese; pinch cayenne; grated Parmesan cheese.

Cook pasta in boiling salted water until 'al dente'. Meanwhile, combine parsley, basil and garlic in a mortar. With a pestle pound them into a paste. Gradually work in oil and cheese, then season with cayenne. (This can also be done in a blender or a food processor fitted with a steel blade.) Drain pasta and place in a heated serving dish. Add sauce and gently mix. Serve immediately. Offer some grated Parmesan cheese for topping. Serves 4–6.

Penne with Mushrooms
Tiny, white button mushrooms make a delicious, simple sauce for pasta. Try them with penne or large shells.

4 tbsp olive oil; 1 clove garlic, chopped; 500 g/1 lb (4 cups) button mushrooms, sliced; salt and freshly ground black pepper; 1–2 tbsp chopped parsley; 15 g/½ oz (1 tbsp) butter; 250 g (8 oz) penne or large pasta shells; 4 tbsp grated Parmesan cheese.

Heat oil in a large pan, add garlic and mushrooms and cook until soft, about 6–8 minutes. Add salt, pepper, parsley and butter. Keep warm. Cook pasta in boiling salted water until 'al dente'. Drain well. Pour mushroom mixture over and toss lightly. Turn into heated serving dish and sprinkle with grated Parmesan cheese. If liked, more parsley may also be sprinkled over. Serves 3–4.

Pasta with Garlic and Fresh Herbs
You really need fresh herbs for this dish. In the summer use a mixture of basil, dill, parsley, oregano and coriander which gives a wonderful flavour. In winter, when fewer herbs are growing, use parsley and a little raw grated onion with whatever fresh herbs are available.

500 g (1 lb) noodles, spaghetti, shells, trivelle, or other pasta; 2 tbsp olive oil; 3 cloves garlic, sliced; 60 g/2 oz (4 tbsp) butter; 30 g/1 oz (¾ cup) chopped mixed fresh herbs; ½ tsp salt; freshly ground black pepper; about 150 ml/¼ pint (⅔ cup) milk.

Cook pasta in boiling salted water until 'al dente'. Drain well. Heat oil in a saucepan, add garlic and fry until very light brown (it must not burn or it will be bitter). Add pasta to heat through. Add butter, then using 2 forks toss pasta to mix in butter. Add herbs, salt and pepper and toss again. Add milk slowly, cooking and tossing pasta as you do so. The milk will slowly be absorbed; it should form a little sauce around the pasta. Serve immediately. A green salad makes a good accompaniment. Serves 4.

Spaghetti Caruso
The speciality of the Restaurant Caruso Belvedere, in Italy. This sauce is also good with bucatini, the fine spaghetti with the hole in the middle.

2 cloves garlic, halved; 3 tbsp olive oil; 2 medium onions, chopped; 125 g/4 oz (⅔ cup) chicken livers, trimmed and chopped; 250 g/8 oz (2 cups) mushrooms, sliced; 2 tbsp tomato purée (paste); 120 ml/4 fl oz (½ cup) water; 500 g/1 lb (2 cups) canned tomatoes with juice; 1 tsp chopped fresh thyme, or ¼ tsp dried; 1 tsp chopped fresh basil, or ¼ tsp dried; 1 bay leaf; 1 tsp salt; freshly ground black pepper; 1 tsp sugar; 500 g (1 lb) spaghetti or bucatini; 125 g/4 oz (1 cup) grated Parmesan cheese.

Sauté garlic in olive oil in a frying pan (skillet) for 2 minutes; discard garlic. Add onions and cook gently for 4 minutes, then add chicken livers and mushrooms. Cook, stirring for 5 minutes. Stir in tomato purée (paste) mixed with water, tomatoes and juice, thyme, basil, bay leaf, salt, pepper and sugar. Simmer, covered, 30 minutes. Remove bay leaf. Meanwhile, cook pasta in boiling salted water until 'al dente'. Drain and put on a heated

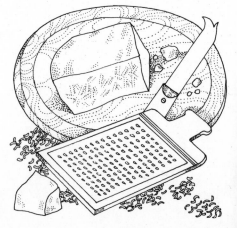

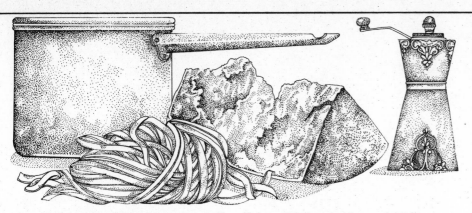

P

platter with half the cheese. Spoon over half the sauce and toss. Pass remaining sauce and Parmesan cheese separately. Serves 4–6.

Spaghetti with Broccoli

This dish is a Calabrian speciality.

1 large head broccoli; 1 tbsp oil; 3 cloves garlic, crushed; 3–4 tomatoes, peeled, seeded and chopped; 1 tsp salt; ¼ tsp pepper; 4 tbsp raisins; 4 tbsp pine nuts; 500 g (1 lb) spaghetti; 1 tbsp chopped parsley; 125 g/4 oz (1 cup) grated Parmesan cheese.

Separate florets from broccoli stalks. Cut stalks into bite-sized pieces. Cook florets and stalks in boiling salted water for 5 minutes. Drain and keep warm in a covered bowl. Put oil and garlic into pan and cook over medium heat until garlic is soft. Add tomatoes, salt and pepper and cook over moderate heat for 10 minutes. Stir in raisins and pine nuts. Keep hot. Cook spaghetti in boiling salted water until 'al dente'. Drain and place in a heated shallow serving bowl. Pour sauce over and top with broccoli and chopped parsley. Mix gently, then serve, with cheese. Serves 6–8.

Spaghetti with Cheese and Green Peppercorns

One of the simplest spaghetti dishes, flavoured with Pecorino cheese and canned green peppercorns.

250 g (8 oz) spaghetti; 60 g/2 oz (½ cup) grated Pecorino cheese; 1 tsp canned green peppercorns, crushed; 45 g/1½ oz (3 tbsp) butter.

Cook spaghetti in boiling salted water until 'al dente'. Drain, reserving a few tablespoons cooking water. Return spaghetti to saucepan and add remaining ingredients with reserved water. Mix gently and serve immediately. Serves 3–4.

Spaghetti con Vongole

If you can get fresh clams, by all means use them for this dish; about 500 g (1 lb) will be required. Scrub and steam open in a little water. Remove clams from shells and rinse out any sand. Canned clams are very good too, and save a visit to the fish market.

3 tbsp oil; 2 cloves garlic, crushed; 3 tomatoes, peeled, seeded and chopped; 1 tbsp tomato purée (paste); 1 × 290 g/9 oz can clams, drained; salt and freshly ground black pepper; 250 g (8 oz) spaghetti; 2 tbsp chopped parsley.

Heat oil in a saucepan and fry garlic a moment, then add tomatoes and tomato purée (paste). Cook over a gentle heat for 20 minutes. Add clams and season with salt and pepper. Heat through gently. Meanwhile, cook spaghetti in boiling salted water until 'al dente'. Drain and place in a heated serving dish. Pour sauce over spaghetti and toss to mix well. Sprinkle with chopped parsley. Serves 3–4.

Tortellini

Stuffed pasta rings that can be served with the stock in which they are cooked or with a Bolognese sauce.

45 g/1½ oz (3 tbsp) butter; 180 g/6 oz (¾ cup) raw turkey breast meat, sliced; 90 g (3 oz) cooked ham; 90 g (3 oz) Italian sausage; 4 tbsp grated Parmesan cheese; 2 eggs, beaten; salt and freshly ground black pepper; 1 quantity Egg Pasta (page 267).
TO SERVE: *1 litre/1¾ pints (4 cups) good quality chicken stock; grated Parmesan cheese.*

Heat butter and fry turkey gently until golden then finely mince (grind) together turkey, ham and sausage. Add cheese, eggs, salt and pepper and mix to form a smooth paste. Cover and refrigerate. Roll pasta dough thinly to form a large rectangle. Dust lightly with a little flour and leave to rest and dry for 15–20 minutes. Cut into about 40 × 3.5 cm (1½ in) squares and place about ½ tsp filling on each square. Fold each square over to form a triangle, press edges firmly to seal and enclose filling. Curve each triangle around your fingertip and press the two ends together. Bring stock to the boil. Drop in tortellini and simmer, stirring occasionally, for 5 minutes. Turn off heat, cover pan and leave to stand for 20–30 minutes. To serve, ladle tortellini into soup plates with a little stock and pass around grated Parmesan. Serves 4.

Rigatoni Carbonara

Try to find rigatoni for this dish; these are the large ribbed noodles or penne, shaped like a pen nib. This is a Roman speciality and translated literally means 'charcoal-burner's style'. Spaghetti is often served this way, but the fat tubes of rigatoni seem better able to collect lovely bits of the egg and bacon sauce.

500 g (1 lb) rigatoni, penne or spaghetti; 1 tbsp oil; 125 g (4 oz) lean (Canadian) bacon or speck, cut into 2.5 cm (1 in) pieces; 4 eggs; 90 g/3 oz (¾ cup) grated Parmesan cheese; 1 tbsp salt; freshly ground black pepper; 4 tbsp single (light) cream; 60 g/2 oz (4 tbsp) butter.

Cook pasta in boiling salted water until 'al dente'. Meanwhile, heat oil in a heavy frying pan (skillet) and fry bacon or speck until crisp and brown. Remove from pan. Beat eggs in a bowl with cheese, salt, pepper and cream. Drain pasta and keep warm. Melt butter in frying pan (skillet), add egg mixture and cook, stirring constantly until it begins to thicken. Add pasta and bacon, mix together quickly and serve at once. Serves 4–6.
NOTE: It is important to drain pasta before cooking the egg mixture and to add it to the eggs just as they are thickening. They must not overcook and should be moist.

Straw and Grass

A Roman dish, which gets its name from the 2 pastas used. This simple sauce calls for strips of ham; use leg ham or the raw prosciutto.

125 g/4 oz (½ cup) butter; 1 clove garlic; 500 g/1 lb (4 cups) button mushrooms, sliced; salt; 250 ml/8 fl oz (1 cup) single (light) cream; 125 g/4 oz (½ cup) cooked ham or prosciutto, cut into strips; 250 g (8 oz) spaghetti; 250 g (8 oz) tagliatelle; 90 g/3 oz (¾ cup) finely grated Parmesan cheese.

Heat butter in a large frying pan (skillet). Add garlic and mushrooms, sprinkle lightly with salt and sauté for 5–8 minutes. Heat cream in the top of a double saucepan (double boiler). Add mushrooms and ham and keep warm. Cook the 2 pastas separately in boiling salted water until 'al dente'. Drain, then toss in mushroom sauce. Serve immediately, topped with grated cheese. Serves 6.

Tagliatelle all'Amatriciana

This recipe is one of the most famous of all pasta dishes. It is said to come from Amatrice, a little village in the Sabine country near Rome. The sauce is based on 'pancetta', a type of bacon (available at some Italian delicatessens) which is diced and mixed with tomatoes, peppers and onions. Purists omit the tomatoes. Try to find the very thin tagliatelle, sometimes called tagliarini, or linguine ribbon noodles. Either bought or home-made noodles may be used in this recipe.

2 tbsp oil; 250 g/8 oz (1 cup) pancetta, bacon or speck, diced; 1 small dried chilli, or pinch cayenne; 1 small onion, chopped; 500 g/1 lb (2 cups) tomatoes, peeled, seeded and chopped; salt and freshly ground black pepper; 500 g (1 lb) tagliatelle or linguine; 60 g/2 oz (½ cup) each grated Pecorino and Parmesan cheese.

Heat oil in a heavy frying pan (skillet). Add bacon and cook until brown and crisp. Remove from pan, drain on paper towels and set aside. Soak dried chilli, if using, in hot water for 5 minutes, then drain, remove seeds and chop finely. Add chilli and onion to the pan and sauté until onion is softened. Stir in tomatoes, season with salt and pepper and add cayenne, if using. Simmer sauce for 10 minutes. While sauce is cooking, cook pasta in boiling salted water until 'al dente'. Drain. Place pasta in a large heated shallow serving dish. Add reserved bacon to sauce and pour over pasta. Sprinkle with grated Pecorino and Parmesan cheese and serve at once. Serves 4–6.

Macaroni with Four Cheeses

This very simply made sauce relies on a combination of different cheeses for its lovely flavour. It is a great favourite with the people of Rome.

500 g/1 lb (4 cups) macaroni (tubular, shell, bow etc.); 60 g/2 oz (4 tbsp) butter; 1 tsp flour; 250 ml/8 fl oz (1 cup) milk; 60 g (2 oz) Gruyère cheese; 60 g (2 oz) Edam or Gouda cheese; 60 g (2 oz) Cheddar cheese; salt and freshly ground black pepper; 60 g/2 oz (½ cup) grated Parmesan cheese.

Cook macaroni in boiling salted water until 'al dente', about 15–18 minutes. Meanwhile, melt half the butter in a heavy saucepan and stir in flour. Cook, stirring, for 30 seconds or so. Gradually stir in milk and simmer sauce for 3 minutes, stirring well. Remove from heat. Cut Gruyère, Edam and Cheddar cheeses into match-sized strips and stir into sauce. Season with salt and pepper. Put pan back on stove over medium heat and stir until cheeses are almost melted (this should take only a minute). Drain macaroni well, place in a heated deep serving dish and toss with remaining butter. Pour sauce at once over macaroni, mix lightly, and serve. The Parmesan cheese may be sprinkled on top of the macaroni or placed in a small bowl and served separately, as preferred. Serves 4–6.

NOTE: This is a substantial dish, full of protein, and needs only a light salad to complete the meal.

Italian Pasta Salad

250 g/8 oz (2 cups) macaroni or fancy pasta; 2 tbsp oil; 250 g/8 oz (1 cup) thickly sliced cooked ham, cubed; 125 g/4 oz (⅔ cup) black (ripe) olives, halved and stoned (pitted); 165 g/5½ oz (1 cup) green peas, cooked; 125–250 ml/4–8 fl oz (½–1 cup) Mayonnaise (page 204); 2 tbsp French (Dijon) mustard; salt and freshly ground black pepper; 2 tomatoes, peeled and quartered.

Cook macaroni in boiling salted water, with 1 tbsp oil added, for 15 minutes or until 'al dente'. Drain and rinse well. Sprinkle remaining oil over and toss well to coat – this will prevent macaroni sticking together. Add ham to macaroni with olives and peas. Combine 120 ml/4 fl oz (½ cup) mayonnaise with mustard and stir through cold macaroni mixture, adding a little more mayonnaise if necessary to give a creamy salad. Season with salt and pepper. Spoon into salad bowl. Place tomatoes around salad. Chill in the refrigerator before serving with cold meats. Serves 4–6.

Cannelloni with Meat Stuffing

The pre-cooked cannelloni tubes eliminate a big step in preparing this dish and you are assured of the pasta being just 'al dente', as it should be.

1 × 130 g/4 oz packet pre-cooked cannelloni tubes; 125 g/4 oz (1 cup) Mozzarella cheese,
SAUCE: *1 onion, chopped; 1 clove garlic, crushed; 4 tbsp oil; 1 tbsp chopped parsley; 1 tsp salt; freshly ground black pepper; 1 × 425 g/14 oz can tomatoes, chopped with juice; 2 tbsp tomato purée (paste); 500 ml/18 fl oz (2 cups) boiling water.*
FILLING: *500 g/1 lb (2 cups) minced (ground) steak; 2 eggs, beaten; 2 tbsp oil; 2 tbsp grated Parmesan cheese; 1 tbsp chopped parsley; 1 tsp chopped fresh oregano or basil, or ¼ tsp dried; 1 tsp salt; freshly ground black pepper.*

If not using pre-cooked cannelloni, cook the tubes in boiling salted water for 5 minutes. Rinse in cold water and drain. Cannelloni should be just flexible enough to handle.
SAUCE: Sauté onion and garlic in oil until brown. Add parsley, salt and pepper. Stir in tomatoes and tomato purée (paste). Gradually stir in the boiling water and simmer gently for 20 minutes.
FILLING: Combine steak, eggs, oil, cheese, parsley and herbs and season with salt and pepper. Pour half the sauce into a shallow baking dish. Fill cannelloni with prepared filling. Arrange side by side in the sauce. Cover with remaining sauce and thin slices of Mozzarella. Bake in a preheated moderate oven (180°C/350°F, Gas Mark 4) for 45–50 minutes. Serves 4–6.

Cannelloni with Cheese and Ham Stuffing

1 × 130 g/4 oz packet pre-cooked cannelloni tubes; oil; 180 g/6 oz (1½ cups) grated Parmesan cheese; extra grated Parmesan cheese to serve.
FILLING: *180 g/6 oz (¾ cup) Ricotta cheese, sieved; 250 g/8 oz (2 cups) Mozzarella cheese, grated; 60 g/2 oz (¼ cup) cooked ham, chopped; 2 eggs; salt and freshly ground black pepper.*
SAUCE: *90 g/3 oz (6 tbsp) butter; 4 large, ripe tomatoes, peeled, seeded and chopped; 1 tbsp chopped fresh basil; ½ tsp salt; ¼ tsp freshly ground black pepper.*

If not using pre-cooked cannelloni, cook in boiling salted water, with a little oil added, for 5 minutes or until tender but firm. Rinse in cold water and drain.
FILLING: Mix all ingredients together and spoon into cannelloni. Arrange cannelloni side by side in a buttered shallow ovenproof dish.
SAUCE: Heat half the butter in a heavy

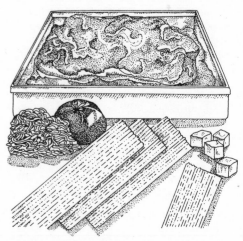

saucepan and add tomatoes, basil, salt and pepper. Simmer, covered, for 15 minutes. Spoon sauce over cannelloni, sprinkle with cheese and dot with remaining butter. Bake in a preheated moderately hot oven (190°C/375°F, Gas Mark 5) for 15 minutes. Serve very hot, and pass a bowl of grated Parmesan cheese separately. Serves 6.

Lasagne with Ricotta

This may be made a day or two ahead and stored in the refrigerator. Reheat in a moderate oven (180°C/350°F, Gas Mark 4) about 30 minutes, and serve cut in squares accompanied by a mixed tossed salad. Good for a crowd.

750 g/1½ lb (3 cups) minced (ground) steak; salt and freshly ground black pepper; 4 tbsp olive oil; 1 quantity Egg Pasta (page 267), or 2 × 250 g/8 oz packets pre-cooked lasagne; 500 g/1 lb (2 cups) Ricotta or cottage cheese; 500 g/1 lb (4 cups) Mozzarella cheese, sliced; 125 g/4 oz (1 cup) grated Parmesan cheese.

TOMATO SAUCE: 3 tbsp olive oil; ½ stick celery, diced; 1 onion, finely chopped; 1 clove garlic, crushed; 750 g/1½ lb (3 cups) ripe tomatoes, chopped, or 2 × 425 g/14 oz cans tomatoes, drained; 3 tbsp tomato purée (paste); 250 ml/8 fl oz (1 cup) white wine; juice from canned tomatoes or water; salt and freshly ground black pepper; 1 bay leaf; 1 bouquet garni.

TOMATO SAUCE: Heat oil in a saucepan, add celery, onion and garlic and brown lightly. Add tomatoes, tomato purée (paste), wine, tomato juice or water. Season with salt and pepper and add bay leaf and bouquet garni. Cook gently for 30 minutes, then remove bay leaf and bouquet garni and rub through a sieve. Set aside.

Season meat with salt and pepper. Shape into balls a little larger than a marble. Heat oil in a frying pan (skillet) and brown meatballs on all sides. Do this in 3 portions so that oil

keeps hot and free from moisture. Place all meatballs back in pan and cook gently for 5 minutes. Drain. If using fresh pasta, divide dough in half and roll out each half thinly to a rectangle, 40 × 45 cm (16 × 18 in). Trim edges and cut dough into 8 × 10 cm (3 × 4 in) oblongs. Drop oblongs, one at a time, into a large pan of boiling salted water and cook for about 10 minutes or until 'al dente'. Cook in at least 2 lots. If using bought pasta that is not pre-cooked, cook it for 15 minutes in boiling salted water. Turn into a colander and rinse with cold water, then place pasta sheets on a clean cloth so they are not touching, and leave to dry.

Butter a large baking dish or ovenproof casserole and spoon about ⅓ of the tomato sauce into it. Arrange half of the pasta sheets on top, then cover with a thin layer of sauce and spoon over ⅓ of the Ricotta. Arrange a layer of ⅓ of the mozzarella cheese on top and sprinkle with ⅓ of the Parmesan cheese.

Spoon over more tomato sauce, then add meatballs, ⅓ of the cheeses and remaining pasta. Coat with remaining tomato sauce, then add remaining cheeses, ending with a layer of Parmesan cheese. Bake in a preheated moderate oven (180°C/350°F, Gas Mark 4) for 45 minutes or until golden. Serves 12–15.

Ravioli

1 quantity Egg Pasta, made with only 180 g/6 oz (1½ cups) flour, 2 eggs and 1 tbsp water (page 267); melted butter; grated Parmesan cheese.

MEAT FILLING: 30 g/1 oz (2 tbsp) butter; 250 g/8 oz (1 cup) minced (ground) steak; 1 small clove garlic, chopped; 1 tbsp finely chopped parsley; 3 tbsp fresh breadcrumbs; 2 tbsp grated Parmesan cheese; good pinch grated nutmeg; salt and freshly ground black pepper; 1 egg.

MEAT FILLING: Heat butter in pan and fry meat, stirring, until beginning to brown. Add garlic and parsley and continue cooking, stirring with a fork, until meat is well browned. Place in a bowl and add breadcrumbs, cheese, grated nutmeg, salt and pepper. Mix all together, then stir in beaten egg. Combine thoroughly and set aside.

The pasta dough should be softer than for other pasta. Halve kneaded dough. Roll out each portion thinly on a floured board to a long oblong shape. Cover first piece with damp paper towel to prevent drying out. Place teaspoonsful of filling in mounds at 5 cm (2 in) intervals in regular lines on second sheet of pasta. Brush between mounds of filling with water, then place second sheet of dough over top. Press firmly between mounds, sealing the 2 sheets of dough together, then, using a pastry wheel, cut into squares. Drop ravioli into a large pan of boiling salted water and cook 15 minutes or until tender (cooking time depends on thinness of dough). Drain and toss in melted butter and grated Parmesan cheese, or in Bolognese Sauce (see page 272). Serve immediately with a selection of salads. Serves 4–6.

NOTE: Meat-filled Ravioli is often served in chicken broth as a soup. Dough for Ravioli can also be cut into 4 cm (1½ in) rounds, then filled and the dough folded over to make half moons. Press edges well together and mark with a fork.

Tortellini Della Nonna

Pasta is often served with cream, Parmesan cheese and a good grinding of black pepper. Here is a famous version made with tortellini (small filled pasta twists), which can be bought frozen from Italian delicatessens and in many supermarket freezer chests. There is no need to thaw before cooking.

1 × 500 g/1 lb packet frozen tortellini; 125 g/4 oz (½ cup) butter; 175 ml/6 fl oz (¾ cup) single (light) cream; 5 thin slices prosciutto, cut into ribbons; 90 g/3 oz (½ cup) cooked peas; 125 g/4 oz (1 cup) grated Parmesan cheese; salt and freshly ground black pepper; extra grated Parmesan cheese to serve.

Plunge tortellini into a large saucepan of boiling salted water and cook for about 25 minutes or until just tender. Drain in a colander. Melt butter in a deep, heavy frying pan (skillet) over a moderately slow heat. Add tortellini and stir until coated with butter. Add cream, prosciutto and peas, and cook mixture until cream thickens slightly. Add Parmesan, and season with salt and pepper. Serve immediately, with a dish of freshly grated Parmesan cheese and a pepper mill for those who would like extra pepper. Serves 6–8.

PASTA SAUCES

Tomato, Pesto and Bolognese are perhaps the most famous of pasta sauces. They are simple to prepare and cook, and have a certain 'freshness' about them.

The pomodoro, or apple of gold as the tomato is often called, sets the stage for many Italian pasta sauces, and tomato sauce is the basis of many regional specialities. Ingredients are added to it as suits local tastes – prosciutto from Bologna, the onion and bacon of the Roman countryside, the clams of Naples, and local fresh cheese and fish.

Flavourings may change, so too may the length of time a sauce is cooked, but this only determines the characteristics of the sauce as it changes from province to province. **See recipes.**

Fresh Tomato Sauce

This light, fresh-tasting sauce is very versatile. Serve it with pasta, roast veal or roast beef and with Chicken Liver Mousse (see page 241), and as an accompaniment to numerous other dishes.

2 tsp olive oil; 1 clove garlic, crushed; 2 shallots, chopped; 4 large tomatoes, peeled, seeded and chopped; 1 tsp tomato purée (paste); pinch sugar; 150 ml/¼ pint (⅔ cup) chicken stock.

Heat oil in a saucepan, add garlic and shallots and cook for 2–3 minutes. Add tomatoes, tomato purée (paste), sugar and stock and cook over gentle heat for 10 minutes, stirring occasionally. Purée sauce in a blender or food processor, or push through a sieve. Check seasoning. If sauce is too thin return to pan and reduce by boiling. Makes 350 ml/12 fl oz (1½ cups), or sufficient for 500 g/1 lb (4 cups) pasta.

Pesto Alla Genovese

(Green Sauce Genovese)
This is the famous sauce which is eaten by the Genoese with all kinds of pasta and gnocchi. It is also added to soups – try a tablespoonful stirred into minestrone or chicken broth at the last minute, or spoon over piping hot baked jacket potatoes.

2–3 cloves garlic, chopped; 4–6 tbsp finely chopped fresh basil; 4 tbsp chopped parsley; 1 tbsp pine nuts or walnuts; 60 g/2 oz ($\frac{1}{2}$ cup) grated Parmesan or Romano cheese; 250 ml/8 fl oz (1 cup) olive oil; freshly ground black pepper.

With a mortar and pestle, pound garlic, basil, parsley, pine nuts or walnuts and cheese together until smooth. Gradually add oil, whisking between additions. Add enough oil, whisking all the time, until sauce is thick and smooth. Season with pepper. Makes sufficient for 750 g/1$\frac{1}{2}$ lb (6 cups) pasta.
NOTE: If made in large quantities, sauce can be made in a blender or food processor. Store in a jar in refrigerator, covered with a layer of olive oil.

Tomato Sauce Neapolitan

Known sometimes as Pizzaiola Sauce, this is often served with roasted or grilled (broiled) chicken or meats. The fresh taste and look of the sauce is preserved by cooking the tomatoes for a relatively short time and by the addition of fresh basil or oregano.

45 g/1$\frac{1}{2}$ oz (3 tbsp) butter; 2 tbsp olive oil; 1 kg/2 lb (4 cups) very ripe Italian egg tomatoes, peeled, seeded and diced; 4 leaves fresh basil, or 8 sprigs fresh oregano; salt and freshly ground black pepper.

Place butter, oil, tomatoes and basil or oregano in a saucepan. Cook over low heat for 10 minutes, stirring occasionally. Season with salt and pepper. Discard herbs before serving. Makes 350 ml/12 fl oz (1$\frac{1}{2}$ cups), or sufficient for 500 g/1 lb (4 cups) pasta.
VARIATION
Pizzaiola Sauce: Prepare Tomato Sauce Neapolitan, but add 2 chopped cloves garlic and a little chopped onion to butter and oil, along with tomatoes. Good also with veal, steak and chicken.

Tomato Sauce, Sicilian-Style

1 small aubergine (eggplant), peeled and diced; salt; 1.25 kg/2$\frac{1}{2}$ lb (5 cups) ripe tomatoes, peeled and chopped; 5 tbsp olive oil; 1 clove garlic; 1 red pepper, seeded, cored and chopped; 4 leaves fresh basil, or pinch dried basil; 4 anchovy fillets, chopped (optional); freshly ground black pepper.

Place aubergine (eggplant) in a bowl, sprinkle with salt and leave at least 30 minutes. Drain well and set aside. Purée tomatoes in a blender, or sieve them. Heat oil in a saucepan and sauté garlic until golden, then discard garlic. Add aubergine (eggplant) and cook for 5 minutes, stirring occasionally. Add tomatoes, red pepper and basil and simmer gently for 40 minutes or until sauce is thick. Add anchovies, if using, and simmer a further 5 minutes. Season with salt and pepper. Makes about 600 ml/1 pint (2$\frac{1}{2}$ cups), or sufficient for 750 g/1$\frac{1}{2}$ lb (6 cups) pasta.

Bolognese Sauce

(Ragù alla Bolognese)
Ragù is the sauce from Bologna that people all over the world love to serve with spaghetti. The true ragù is not just a sauce of tomato-flavoured minced (ground) meat; its ingredients include several kinds of meat, chicken livers and good uncured bacon, pancetta, or better still, prosciutto. Sometimes cream or butter is added to the sauce just before it is tossed with pasta.

250 g (8 oz) lean steak, finely chopped; 250 g (8 oz) lean boneless pork, finely chopped; 60 g/2 oz ($\frac{1}{4}$ cup) chopped bacon or prosciutto; 1 tbsp olive oil; 1 clove garlic, peeled; 1 small onion, finely chopped; 1 tbsp chopped parsley; 1 bay leaf; 1 × 425 g/14 oz can tomatoes; 120 ml/4 fl oz ($\frac{1}{2}$ cup) white wine; 120 ml/4 fl oz ($\frac{1}{2}$ cup) water; 2 tbsp tomato purée (paste); salt and freshly ground black pepper; grated nutmeg; 1 tbsp chopped fresh basil; butter or single (light) cream (optional).

Put steak, pork and bacon or prosciutto, mixed well together, into a saucepan with oil, garlic, onion, parsley and bay leaf. Brown slowly, stirring frequently to prevent meat cooking in lumps. As soon as garlic turns golden, remove it and discard. Add tomatoes (with can juice), wine, water, tomato purée (paste), salt, pepper and nutmeg. Cover and simmer for 1 hour. Add basil and cook 1 minute longer. Remove from heat and discard bay leaf. If liked, add a little butter or a few spoonfuls of cream. Makes sufficient for 500 g/1 lb (4 cups) pasta.
VARIATION
If liked, substitute 250 g/8 oz (1$\frac{1}{3}$ cups) chicken livers for the pork and add an extra 60 g/2 oz ($\frac{1}{4}$ cup) chopped bacon.

Tomato Sauce

Made using fresh or canned tomatoes.

2 tbsp olive oil; 1 small onion, finely chopped; 1 kg/2 lb (4 cups) tomatoes, peeled, seeded and chopped, or 2 × 875 g/1 lb 13 oz cans tomatoes, drained and chopped; $\frac{1}{2}$ tsp salt; $\frac{1}{2}$ tsp sugar or more to taste; $\frac{1}{4}$ tsp black pepper; 2 leaves fresh basil or 1 sprig fresh oregano; 1 bay leaf; 1 tbsp tomato purée (paste).

Heat oil in a saucepan, add onion and cook over a high heat for 5–6 minutes, stirring, until brown. Add tomatoes, salt, sugar, pepper, basil or oregano, bay leaf and tomato purée (paste). Bring to the boil, cover and simmer for 45 minutes, stirring occasionally. Discard herbs before serving. Sauce may be pushed through a sieve to make a smooth purée if desired. Makes 350 ml/12 fl oz (1$\frac{1}{2}$ cups), or sufficient for 500 g/1 lb (4 cups) pasta.

PASTITSO (Pasticcio)

The Greek meat pie made of layers of pasta and savoury meat and topped with a creamy custard sauce. It is cut into squares and served hot or cold.

Pastitso

125 g/4 oz ($\frac{1}{2}$ cup) butter; 2 medium onions, finely chopped; 500 g/1 lb (2 cups) minced (ground) steak; 2 tomatoes, peeled and chopped; 1 tbsp tomato purée (paste); salt and freshly ground black pepper; 90 g/3 oz ($\frac{3}{4}$ cup) grated cheese; 1 × 250 g/8 oz packet pre-cooked lasagne; 1 egg, beaten.
CREAM SAUCE: *60 g/2 oz (4 tbsp) butter; 3 tbsp flour; 600 ml/1 pint (2$\frac{1}{2}$ cups) milk; 3 tbsp single (light) cream (optional); salt and freshly ground white pepper; grated nutmeg.*

Melt butter in frying pan (skillet) and cook onions and minced (ground) steak for 2–3 minutes, stirring. Add tomatoes, tomato purée (paste), salt and pepper and continue cooking over low heat until meat is tender, stirring occasionally. Cover pan if mixture becomes too dry. Remove from heat and stir in 60 g/2 oz ($\frac{1}{2}$ cup) of the cheese.
CREAM SAUCE: Melt butter in a saucepan, blend in flour and cook gently for 2 minutes. Add milk gradually, stirring over a low heat until boiling. Add cream, if using, and season with salt, pepper and nutmeg. Remove sauce from heat.

Place half the lasagne in a well-greased casserole and cover with meat mixture, then remaining lasagne. Blend cream sauce with beaten egg and remaining cheese. Pour over lasagne. Bake in a preheated moderate oven (180°C/350°F, Gas Mark 4) for 40–50 minutes or until top is nicely browned. Serve hot with a green salad. Serves 6.

PASTRY/DOUGH

From crumbly shortcrust and the airy layers of puff and flaky pastry to feathery choux, delicate *pâte sucrée*, tender sour cream or cream cheese pastry, yeast pastry, hot water pastry, strudel and *filo*, pastry (which Americans more commonly call dough) means a world of enjoyment. With skill at your fingertips you can create delicious sweets, puffs, pies and tarts filled with jam, custard, fruit and cream, as well as savoury fillings that make tempting appetizers, snacks and meals.

Most pastries are a mixture of flour and fat, bound with liquid, but variations in ingredients and in ways of mixing and cooking produce different results. A good pastry should be light, tender, crisp and somewhat flaky.

As with most cooking, success in pastry-making is really a matter of practice. Certainly there are those whose delicate touch contributes to the lightness and tenderness of the pastry. But experience has shown that by following a few simple rules, anyone can make good pastry. Start with the simple ones such as shortcrust (basic pie dough), rich shortcrust, sweet flan or sour cream pastry. Master those and you will then be able to make superb quiches and fruit tarts, and will be inspired to go on to other delights.

Commercial Pastries: Nowadays, manufacturers make it easy and foolproof to produce home-baked pastries. Supermarkets carry pastry mixes, packaged *filo*, frozen shortcrust or puff pastry, ready to roll out, even ready-rolled sheets of pastry and stamped-out vol-au-vent cases, ready to bake.

Short Pastries

Most short pastries are made by mixing fat with flour and lightly stirring in just enough liquid to make the mixture hold together. Important points for success are:

● Have ingredients and equipment cool before starting, so that the fat will remain in tiny pieces without melting into the flour.

● Handle the pastry quickly and lightly once the liquid is added to avoid overdevelopment of gluten (elastic strands formed by the flour protein and moisture), which makes pastry tough and causes it to shrink when baked.

● Chill pastry for at least 30 minutes after mixing and before rolling out, and again when it has been shaped, before baking. This relaxes the gluten so that the pastry will be tender and won't shrink when baked. The longer it is chilled after mixing, the better – overnight is ideal – but be sure to remove it from refrigerator at least 1 hour before shaping or you will be obliged to overhandle it.

Flaky Pastries

These pastries are made by folding together layers of pastry dough with butter or other fats in between. When baked, the pastry puffs up into separate thin, crisp 'leaves'.

Important points for success are:

● Have ingredients, equipment and your hands cool before starting, so that the fat will remain in firm layers, separating the pastry layers. Chilling the pastry at intervals during preparation, as described in recipes, is also designed to keep fat layers firm.

● The basic dough for flaky pastries is damper and more elastic than for short pastries. This allows the pastry to stretch when it is folded, and also allows for taking up extra dredging flour during preparation.

● There is a special way of rolling flaky pastries. First beat lightly and evenly with rolling pin from front to back of pastry, then roll out as follows: bring rolling pin down firmly on pastry, give a short, sharp back-and-forth roll, lift pin and repeat.

The idea is to roll pastry thinner without pushing the fat about so that it breaks through surface. Work your way from front to back of pastry with these short, quick rolls but stop just before you get to the back edge so that pastry is not pushed out of shape. If fat does break through, sprinkle it with flour and refrigerate pastry for 10 minutes before continuing.

● Keep corners square and edges straight. Correct the shape by pulling corners out gently rather than pushing sides in.

● Fold pastry exactly in three with edges level. Use a ruler as a guide and mark thirds with a fingertip on a long side before folding.

● Whatever shape you want to make from flaky pastries, always roll them straight along or straight across, keeping the rectangular shape. Rounds, ovals etc. must be cut from the pastry, not shaped by rolling. Cut cleanly with a sharp knife and avoid edges when glazing, so that layers can separate as the pastry rises.

□ **To Line a Flan Ring:** Place a flan ring on a baking tray, or use a loose-bottomed flan tin (fluted pie pan). If the pastry you are using contains sugar or egg, lightly grease sides and base – this is not necessary for plain pastry. Roll pastry out to a circle about 3 mm ($\frac{1}{8}$ in) thick and about 4 cm ($1\frac{1}{2}$ in) bigger than the ring. Lift pastry over rolling pin, then lift and lay pastry over the ring using the rolling pin. Ease pastry carefully into the ring, then, with a floured forefinger or small ball of pastry, press pastry into the angle round the base. Use floured fingertips to press pastry firmly against the sides of the ring, holding a loose ring steady with the other hand while you do so.

Roll across the top of the ring with the rolling pin to trim off surplus pastry. Press pastry gently round the top edge to work it very slightly above the rim of the ring, then work round the top, gently thumbing the pastry a fraction away from the ring. Rest 30 minutes before baking as recipe directs.

To release the baked shell or tart from a flan ring, slide it off the tray on to a serving plate and lift ring off. To release it from a loose-bottomed tin (pan), place tin (pan) on a jar and allow sides to fall down. Slide tart off the base on to a serving plate, or leave on the base to serve.

□ **To Bake Blind:** Flan cases and tart shells are often baked 'blind', meaning without filling. A case or shell may be baked completely if filling is not to be cooked with it, or partially baked to colour and crisp the pastry before adding the filling and finishing the cooking. Care must be taken to see that an empty case or shell doesn't puff up unevenly or buckle as it cooks. Oven temperatures used for baking blind vary with the type of pastry being used (see recipes).

To bake tartlet shells blind: Prick lightly all over base with a fork, bake 6 minutes then check. If any have puffed up, press down gently with a spoon then finish baking.

To bake a larger case/shell blind: Line it with crumpled, light greaseproof (waxed) paper or tissue paper and fill with rice, crusts of bread or dried beans. For partial pre-baking, bake the shell for about 8 minutes or until sides are just coloured. Lift out paper with rice, crusts or beans, return case or shell to oven and bake about 5 minutes more to dry and colour the base. Remove from oven, add filling and finish cooking. If sides of case or shell are overbrowning, protect them with foil.

To pre-bake completely: Bake 10–15 minutes after removing paper and rice, crusts or beans, until case or shell is golden. Remove from oven and cool before filling.

NOTE: To moisture-proof a pastry case or shell which will have a juicy filling, brush inside with lightly beaten egg or egg white or warm jam and place in oven 2–3 minutes to set. **See recipes.**

Plain Shortcrust Pastry

(Pâte Brisée/Basic Pie Dough)
Use for savoury pies, pastries, etc.

180 g/6 oz (1½ cups) flour; pinch salt; 90 g/3 oz (6 tbsp) chilled butter or firm cooking margarine, diced; about 3 tbsp iced water; squeeze lemon juice.

Sift flour and salt into a large bowl. Add diced fat and stir round with a knife until pieces are coated with flour. Rub (cut) fat into flour between thumbs and fingertips, lifting hands above bowl to aerate mixture, until it resembles coarse breadcrumbs. Shake bowl so that any large lumps come to the surface and rub (cut) them in. Mix water and lemon juice. Add 2 tbsp liquid to flour mixture and stir in quickly with a round-ended knife. When dough starts to cling together, use fingers of one hand to gather it into a ball. Sprinkle in more liquid only if necessary to dampen any remaining dry mixture in bowl and use ball of dough to gather it up. The dough should leave the bowl clean.

Place pastry on a lightly floured surface and knead lightly by turning and pressing with floured heel of hand until smooth. Wrap in plastic wrap and chill 30 minutes. Place dough on lightly floured surface and shape with fingers into a round or other shape as required. Lightly flour rolling pin and roll out, lifting and turning dough frequently and lightly flouring work surface as needed to prevent sticking. Chill again after shaping, before baking. Unless otherwise indicated, bake shortcrust pastry in a preheated hot oven (230°C/450°F, Gas Mark 8). Makes sufficient dough to line a 20–23 cm (8–9 in) pie plate or flan ring.

VARIATIONS
● *For a 25 cm (10 in) pastry shell or a two-crust 20–23 cm (8–9 in) pie:* Follow recipe for Plain Shortcrust Pastry, using 250 g/8 oz (2 cups) flour, 125 g/4 oz (½ cup) butter or firm margarine and about 4 tbsp iced water with a squeeze of lemon juice added.

Shortcrust Pastry with Soft Margarine

Solid cooking margarine makes successful pastry but if using soft table margarine, a slightly different method of mixing is needed, since the margarine is too soft to rub (cut) in with the fingertips.

125 g/4 oz (½ cup) soft table margarine; 1 tbsp water; 180 g/6 oz (1½ cups) flour, sifted.

Using a fork, soften margarine with water and 2 tbsp flour. Mash to a paste, then work in remaining flour until you have a smooth ball of dough. Wrap in plastic wrap and refrigerate at least 1 hour. Roll out and use as required. Makes sufficient dough to line a 20 cm (8 in) flan ring or pie plate.

Rich Shortcrust Pastry

(Pâte Brisée à l'oeuf)
This pastry is crisper and more moisture-proof than plain shortcrust. Use it for fruit tarts, quiches and other pies and tarts with rich fillings.

180 g/6 oz (1½ cups) flour; pinch salt; ¼ tsp baking powder; 125 g/4 oz (½ cup) chilled butter, diced; 1 egg yolk; 2 tsp iced water; squeeze lemon juice.

Make pastry in the same way as for Plain Shortcrust Pastry, using egg yolk mixed with water and lemon juice as the liquid. Unless otherwise indicated, bake unsweetened rich shortcrust pastry in a preheated hot oven (220°C/425°F, Gas Mark 7), and sweetened pastry in a preheated moderately hot oven (200°C/400°F, Gas Mark 6). Makes sufficient dough to line a 20–23 cm (8–9 in) pie plate or flan ring.

VARIATIONS

Sweet Rich Shortcrust Pastry: Follow recipe for Rich Shortcrust Pastry, beating 2 tsp caster sugar with egg and water before mixing with dry ingredients.

● *For a 25 cm (10 in) pastry shell or a two-crust 20–23 cm (8–9 in) pie:* Follow recipe for Rich Shortcrust Pastry, using 250 g/8 oz (2 cups) flour, large pinch salt, ½ tsp baking powder, 180 g/6 oz (¾ cup) butter, 1 egg yolk, about 1 tbsp iced water and a squeeze of lemon juice. Use a little more than half the dough for bottom crust, and the remainder for lid. Scraps can be used to decorate the pie if liked.

Shortcrust Pastry in the Food Processor

The food processor makes tender, light pastry in moments. Keep some diced, frozen butter on hand for this recipe.

250 g/8 oz (2 cups) flour; 125 g/4 oz (½ cup) frozen butter, cooking margarine or a mixture of both, diced; ¼ tsp salt; 2 eggs; about 1 tbsp cold water; squeeze lemon juice.

Place flour, butter and salt in food processor with steel blade in place. Process, turning on and off rapidly, until butter is cut into flour and mixture looks like coarse breadcrumbs. Mix eggs with water and lemon juice. With motor running, pour liquid quickly through feed tube. Do not use it all unless necessary – stop pouring as soon as a ball of dough forms round blade. Wrap in plastic wrap and chill for 1 hour before using. Bake as for Rich Shortcrust Pastry. Makes sufficient dough to line 2 × 18–20 cm (7–8 in) pie plates or flan rings.

VARIATION

For sweet pastry, add 75 g/2½ oz (⅓ cup) caster sugar to processor with flour, butter and salt.

Cream Cheese Pastry

A rich, tender pastry for small turnovers and tartlets. Chill well before using and handle carefully.

125 g/4 oz (½ cup) packaged cream cheese; 125 g/4 oz (½ cup) butter; 180 g/6 oz (1½ cups) flour.

Beat cream cheese and butter in a large mixing bowl until soft. Sift in flour and mix to a dough. Wrap in plastic wrap and chill several hours or overnight. (If left overnight, allow to stand at room temperature for about 1 hour before rolling out.) Makes sufficient dough for about 24 small pastries.

Sour Cream Pastry

A rich, melting pastry. As it is very soft, chill well before rolling out. Use for turnovers, individual tarts etc.

280 g/9 oz (2¼ cups) flour; 1 tsp salt; 180 g/6 oz (¾ cup) chilled butter, diced; 1 egg; 120 ml/4 fl oz (½ cup) sour cream.

Sift flour and salt into a large bowl. Add butter and rub (cut) into flour until mixture resembles coarse breadcrumbs. Make a well in centre. Beat egg and sour cream together and pour into well. Stir from centre, gradually incorporating flour to make a soft, pliable dough. Wrap in plastic wrap and chill for 1 hour before using. Unless otherwise indicated, bake sour cream pastry in a preheated moderately hot oven (200°C/400°F, Gas Mark 6). Makes sufficient dough for 12 × 8 cm (3 in) tarts or turnovers.

Biscuit Pastry

This sweet, tender pastry is used for pies, tarts and tartlets and as the base for slices.

125 g/4 oz (½ cup) butter; 125 g/4 oz (½ cup) caster sugar; 1 egg, beaten; 125 g/4 oz (1 cup) plain (all-purpose) flour; 125 g/4 oz (1 cup) self-raising flour.

Cream butter and beat in sugar little by little until mixture is white and fluffy. Beat in egg, then stir in sifted flours. Knead lightly, wrap in plastic wrap and chill about 20 minutes or until firm enough to roll. Makes sufficient for a two-crust 20–23 cm (8–9 in) pie.

Puff Pastry

250 g/8 oz (2 cups) flour; 250 g/8 oz (1 cup) butter; about 150 ml/¼ pint (⅔ cup) iced water; squeeze lemon juice.

Sift flour into a mixing bowl, add 30 g/1 oz (2 tbsp) of the butter, and rub (cut) into flour until mixture resembles coarse breadcrumbs. Add water mixed with lemon juice and stir with a knife, then gather dough together with fingers. Place on a lightly floured surface, knead lightly and shape into a square pat. Wrap in plastic wrap and chill for 1 hour. At

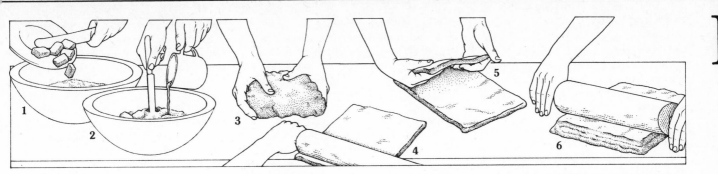

Preparing Rough Puff Pastry

the same time chill remaining butter.

Remove chilled dough and butter from refrigerator; put butter into a loose plastic bag and beat with a rolling pin to make it pliable, then with a floured rolling pin roll it into a 15 cm (6 in) square. Butter and dough should both be firm and of same consistency. Lightly flour work surface and roll out dough to a 25 cm (10 in) square, pulling out corners to make a neat shape. Place butter diagonally on centre of dough and fold the 4 corners in, slightly overlapping, to make an envelope of dough enclosing the butter.

Flour work surface and rolling pin and, working as described under *Flaky Pastries* (page 273), roll dough to a rectangle 1 cm ($\frac{1}{2}$ in) thick. Fold bottom $\frac{1}{3}$ up and top $\frac{1}{3}$ down and seal edges by pressing lightly with rolling pin. This is the first fold. Turn dough round at right angles so that top flap is to your right, as if it were a book. Roll as before to a rectangle 3 times as long as it is wide and about 5 mm ($\frac{1}{4}$ in) thick. Fold into 3, place in a plastic bag and chill about 30 minutes until firm but not hard. Dough has now had 2 folds. Remove dough from refrigerator and roll and fold twice more in the same manner. Chill again for about 30 minutes, then roll and fold twice more (dough has now had 6 folds). Chill again for 30 minutes, and dough is ready for use. Roll out and cut as desired, then chill again for 30 minutes before baking. Unless otherwise indicated, bake puff pastry in a preheated hot oven (230°C/450°F, Gas Mark 8). Makes sufficient dough for 2 × 18 cm (7 in) rounds or 12 small pastries or turnovers.

Flaky Pastry

Easier to make and only a little less delicate and high-rise than Puff Pastry.

250 g/8 oz (2 cups) flour; pinch salt; 90 g/3 oz (6 tbsp) butter; about 150 ml/$\frac{1}{4}$ pint ($\frac{2}{3}$ cup) iced water; 90 g/3 oz (6 tbsp) lard or shortening.

Sift flour and salt into a mixing bowl, add half the butter and rub (cut) in until mixture resembles coarse breadcrumbs **(Fig 1 below)**. Add water, stir in with a knife and gather dough into a ball with your fingers. Knead lightly on a floured work surface until smooth, then with floured hands shape into a rectangular block. Roll out to a rectangle 3 times as long as it is wide and about 5 mm ($\frac{1}{4}$ in) thick **(2)**. Divide lard or shortening in half and work each portion and the remaining butter separately with a wooden spoon until they are of same consistency as dough.

Cut one half of lard or shortening into small pieces and place in rows of about 4, keeping well within the edges, on top $\frac{2}{3}$ of dough **(3)**. Fold bottom (blank) $\frac{1}{3}$ of dough up and top $\frac{1}{3}$ down **(4)** and seal edges by pressing lightly with rolling pin **(5)**. Turn dough round at right angles so that edge of top flap is to your right, as if it were a book. Flour work surface and rolling pin and, working as described under *Flaky Pastries* (page 273), roll dough to a rectangle 5 mm ($\frac{1}{4}$ in) thick **(6)**. Place remaining butter on top $\frac{2}{3}$ as you did the lard or shortening, then fold, turn and roll out again. Repeat, using remaining lard or shortening. Place dough in a plastic bag and chill for at least 30 minutes before using. Rest again after rolling out and cutting, before baking. Unless otherwise indicated, bake flaky pastry in a preheated

hot oven (230°C/450°F, Gas Mark 8). Makes sufficient dough for 2 × 18 cm (7 in) rounds or about 12 small pastries.

Rough Puff Pastry

The simplest of the flaky pastries. Use for sausage rolls, turnovers, etc., where you want crisp, tender layers but not a very high rise.

250 g/8 oz (2 cups) flour; pinch salt; 90 g/3 oz (6 tbsp) butter, diced; 90 g/3 oz (6 tbsp) lard or firm cooking margarine, diced; about 150 ml/$\frac{1}{4}$ pint ($\frac{2}{3}$ cup) iced water; squeeze lemon juice.

Sift flour and salt into a large bowl. Have the fats cool and firm but not hard. Add fats to flour and stir round with a knife until pieces are well coated **(Fig 1 above)**. Mix water and lemon juice and stir into flour with a round-ended knife, without breaking up fat **(2)**. With floured fingers, gently gather mixture into a ball, then place it on a floured work surface. Do not knead; use floured hands to shape it into a rectangular block **(3)**.

Working as described under *Flaky Pastries* (page 273), roll out to a rectangle 1 cm ($\frac{1}{2}$ in) thick **(4)**. Fold bottom $\frac{1}{3}$ up and top $\frac{1}{3}$ down **(5)** and seal edges by pressing lightly with rolling pin. Turn dough round at right angles so that top flap is to your right, as if it were a book. Roll again to a rectangle about 5 mm ($\frac{1}{4}$ in) thick and fold as before **(6)**. Repeat twice more, then place dough in a plastic bag and chill at least 30 minutes. Dough is now ready for use. Rest again after rolling out and cutting, before baking. Unless otherwise indicated, bake rough puff pastry in a preheated hot oven (230°C/450°F, Gas Mark 8). Makes sufficient dough for 2 × 20 cm (8 in) rounds or 16–20 small sausage rolls.

Preparing Flaky Pastry

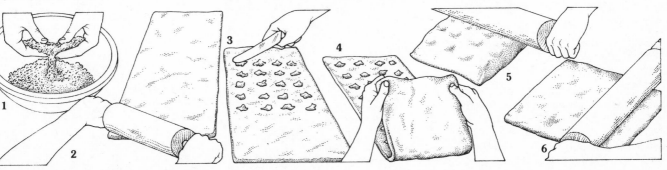

Hot Water Pastry

This pastry is used for raised pies and is the traditional pastry for English cold pies such as pork or veal and ham pie, even when these are made in a mould. It must be used while it is still warm since it becomes brittle when cold.

500 g/1 lb (4 cups) flour; ¾ tsp salt; 250 g/8 oz (1 cup) lard or shortening; 120 ml/4 fl oz (½ cup) plus 2 tbsp water.

Warm flour, then sift with salt into a warm mixing bowl and make a well in centre. Heat lard with water and, when boiling, tip into well and mix with a wooden spoon until smooth. Use at once, keeping dough not being worked in a covered bowl over hot water. Makes sufficient dough for a 20 cm (8 in) covered, raised pie.

Suet Pastry

Suet pastry can be baked, but is usually boiled or steamed to make a soft crust for puddings or for dumplings.

250 g/8 oz (2 cups) self-raising flour; pinch salt; 125 g/4 oz (¾ cup) fresh suet or packaged shredded suet; about 5 tbsp cold water.

Sift flour and salt into a mixing bowl. If using fresh suet, remove any skin and chop fine with a little of the measured flour to prevent it from sticking. Add to flour and stir round with a knife, then add most of the water and stir with knife until dough begins to cling together. Gather into a ball with your fingers. Sprinkle in more water only if necessary to dampen any remaining dry mixture in bowl and use ball of dough to gather it up. Place on a lightly floured work surface and knead lightly by turning and pressing with floured heel of hand until smooth. Roll out and use at once. Makes sufficient dough to line a 1 litre/1¾ pint (4 cup) pudding mould or basin.

VARIATIONS

For an extra light and spongy crust, 60 g/2 oz (½ cup) flour may be replaced by 60 g/2 oz (1 cup) loosely packed fresh white bread-crumbs. For a sweet pudding, 1 tbsp white or brown sugar may be added to the flour.

Pâte Sucrée

(Sweet Flan Pastry)
Pâte Sucrée is fine and crisp, and used for the most delicate sweet tarts.

125 g/4 oz (1 cup) flour; pinch salt; 60 g/2 oz (4 tbsp) butter; 75 g/2½ oz (⅓ cup) caster sugar; 2 egg yolks; 2 drops vanilla essence (extract).

Sift flour and salt on to a work surface and make a well in centre. Place remaining ingredients in well and work them together with the fingertips of one hand. With other hand, use a metal spatula to draw flour

quickly into centre. Mix to a ball of dough. Flour work surface and knead dough lightly by turning and pressing with lightly floured heel of hand until smooth. Wrap in plastic wrap and chill for 1 hour before using. Chill again after shaping, before baking, and prick bottom just before placing in oven. Bake in a preheated moderately hot oven (190°C/375°F, Gas Mark 5) until pastry is a pale biscuit colour. This pastry must not brown or the flavour will be spoilt. Makes sufficient dough to line an 18–20 cm (7–8 in) flan ring (loose-bottomed pie pan), or 18 tiny tartlet moulds, or 6 individual 8 cm (3 in) tartlet tins (pans).

VARIATION

For a 25 cm (10 in) pastry shell: Follow recipe for Pâte Sucrée using 180 g/6 oz (1½ cups) flour, pinch salt, 90 g/3 oz (6 tbsp) butter, 125 g/4 oz (½ cup) caster sugar, 3 egg yolks and 3 drops vanilla essence (extract).

Choux Pastry

Choux Pastry is softer than other pastries and is shaped with a spoon or by squeezing from a piping (pastry) bag. When cooked, it swells into crisp golden shells that are hollow inside. The secret of making shells that will hold their shape is to be sure that the pastry is cooked and dry right through. Place first in a preheated hot oven (230°C/450°F, Gas Mark 8) so that the pastry puffs quickly, then reduce heat to moderate (180°C/350°F, Gas Mark 4) so that pastry will cook without overbrowning. To be fail-safe, leave cooked shells in the turned-off oven with door slightly open for 20 minutes to ensure that they are thoroughly dried out. A well-cooked shell should be golden-brown and firm to the touch and feel very light in the hand.

125 g/4 oz (1 cup) flour; 250 ml/8 fl oz (1 cup) water; 125 g/4 oz (½ cup) butter, cut into pieces; ½ tsp salt; 1 tsp sugar (for sweet puffs); 4 eggs.

Sift flour on to a sheet of greaseproof (waxed) paper. Put water, butter, salt and sugar, if using, into a medium-sized saucepan. Bring slowly to the boil (butter must be melted before water boils).

Preparing Choux Pastry

Immediately remove from heat, tip in flour all at once and stir vigorously with a wooden spatula (**Fig 1 below**). Return to heat and continue stirring until mixture forms a mass, leaves sides of saucepan and begins to film the bottom – this will take only a short time (**2**). Remove from heat and cool a little. Turn mixture into bowl of an electric mixer or leave in saucepan. Beat eggs together and add to dough, a little at a time, beating after each addition until thoroughly incorporated (**3**). Do not add all the egg unless necessary; dough is right when it is as shiny as satin and holds it shape on a spoon. Use warm. Makes sufficient dough for 12 medium-sized éclairs or puffs.

PASTRY CREAM (Crème Pâtissière)

See page 165 for recipe.

PATE BRISEE AND PATE SUCREE

See 274 and left for recipes.

PATE AND TERRINE

Pâtés and terrines are standard features in any French charcuterie, and provide the basis of many a lunch for those travelling in that country.

It is difficult to make a firm distinction between a pâté and a terrine. A fine-textured liver pâté is almost always called a pâté, yet a coarse, meaty product might be called either a *pâté de campagne* or a *terrine maison*.

Originally, a pâté was always enclosed in pastry (dough) and was made with almost any sort of meat or fish. Later, it came to be baked in an earthenware dish (a terrine), which was lined with thinly sliced pork fat to keep the mixture moist.

Most pâtés and terrines contain a good proportion of pork, especially fat belly pork (fresh pork sides). When making a pâté or terrine, if possible choose a particular cut of meat and either mince (grind) it yourself or have it minced (ground) by the butcher, rather than buying ready-minced (ground) meat. Fat is essential to the texture of the pâté or terrine, and enables it to be sliced without crumbling. It also means that a pâté or terrine is served without butter, and with just crusty

French bread or a good wholewheat bread, plus some gherkins or olives or a crisp salad.

A pâté or terrine is sometimes served as a first course; in this case it is usually accompanied by thin, crisp melba toast or warm, freshly made white or brown toast or a selection of savoury crackers. **See recipes.**

Pork and Veal Terrine

500 g (1 lb) (2 cups) minced (ground) pork; 500 g (1 lb) (2 cups) minced (ground) veal; 1 clove garlic, crushed with 1 tsp salt; ½ tsp dried thyme; ½ tsp ground cloves; freshly ground black pepper; grated rind ½ lemon; 1 egg; 120 ml/4 fl oz (½ cup) dry sherry or dry vermouth; thin slices pork back fat or bacon rashers (slices), rind removed; 125 g/4 oz sliced cooked ham, cut into fine strips; 1 bay leaf.

Combine meats, garlic, salt, thyme, cloves, pepper, lemon rind, egg and sherry or vermouth. Mix well. Taste and correct seasoning if necessary. Line a 21 × 11 cm (8½ × 4½ in) terrine or loaf tin (pan) with pork fat or bacon. Spoon half meat mixture into tin (pan), top with ham strips, then spread remaining meat mixture over. Place bay leaf on top. Cover with foil and lid, if using terrine. Stand in roasting tin (pan) filled with water and cook in a preheated moderate oven (180°C/350°F, Gas Mark 4) for about 1½ hours. Cool under heavy weight, then chill. Flavour develops after 1–2 days. Serves 8–10.

Rabbit Terrine
(Terrine de Lapin)

1 rabbit; 125 g (4 oz) lean belly pork (fresh pork sides); 125 g (4 oz) boneless shoulder veal; 1 tsp salt; freshly ground black pepper; 1 tbsp grated onion; ¼ tsp ground allspice; ¼ tsp nutmeg; 2 tbsp brandy; 120 ml/4 fl oz (½ cup) dry white wine; 2 sprigs fresh thyme or marjoram; 1 clove garlic, bruised; thin slices pork fat or bacon rashers (slices), rind removed; 1 bay leaf.

Remove flesh from rabbit, and mince (grind) finely with pork and veal. Season with salt and pepper. Blend in onion, spices, brandy and wine. Bury herbs and bruised garlic in centre of mixture, cover and leave overnight. Line a 21 × 11 cm (8½ × 4½ in) terrine or loaf tin (pan) with thin slices pork fat or bacon. Taste meat mixture and correct seasoning. Remove garlic and herbs. Pack meat mixture into prepared tin (pan) and place bay leaf on top. Cover well with foil and lid, if using terrine. Stand in roasting tin (pan) of water and cook in a preheated moderate oven (180°C/350°F, Gas Mark 4) for about 1½ hours. Cool with weight on top, then chill. Allow to mature 1–2 days before eating. Serves 4–6.

Brandied Chicken Liver Pâté

90 g/3 oz (6 tbsp) butter; 1 onion, chopped; 1 clove garlic, crushed; 250 g/8 oz (1⅓ cups) chicken livers; 1 bay leaf; few sprigs fresh thyme or oregano, or pinch dried herb; 2 tsp brandy; salt and freshly ground black pepper.

Melt 30 g/1 oz (2 tbsp) butter in a frying pan (skillet) and cook onion and garlic over low heat until onion is transparent. Add chicken livers and cook 2–3 minutes, tossing from time to time. Add crumbled bay leaf and thyme or oregano, and cook 1 minute longer. Cool. Chop livers roughly, then pound mixture with wooden spoon or blend in blender. Melt remaining butter and stir into liver mixture with brandy. Season with salt and pepper. Pack into small dish or mould and chill. If desired, unmould before serving. If pâté is to be kept several days, cover with thin film of melted butter. Serves 4.

Chicken Terrine
(Terrine de Poulet)

1 chicken, about 1.2–1.5 kg (2½–3 lb); 2 eggs; 120 ml/4 fl oz (½ cup) single (light) cream; 2 tbsp brandy; salt and freshly ground black pepper; 250 g/8 oz (1 cup) cooked ham, finely chopped; 250 g (8 oz) lean belly pork (fresh pork sides), minced (ground); 250 g (8 oz) boneless shoulder veal, minced (ground); thin slices pork back fat; 20 g/⅔ oz (½ cup) finely chopped fresh herbs (parsley, tarragon, chives).

Remove meat from chicken and cut into strips. Beat eggs with cream, add brandy and season with salt and pepper. Combine with ham and minced (ground) meats. Line a 21 × 11 cm (8½ × 4½ in) terrine or loaf tin (pan) with pork fat. Spread layer of meat mixture on bottom, cover with strips of chicken and sprinkle with herbs. Continue in layers until all ingredients are used, ending with meat mixture. Cover with foil and lid, if using terrine. Stand in roasting tin (pan) of water and cook in a preheated moderately hot oven (200°C/400°F, Gas Mark 6) for about 1 hour. Cool under a weight, then chill. If desired, unmould terrine before serving. Serves 6–8.

PAUPIETTES

Thin slices of meat, fish or poultry, wrapped around a stuffing and braised. A French term, *paupiette* is probably most commonly used with veal; thin slices of beef, rolled around a stuffing and braised, are usually referred to as beef olives.

Veal Paupiettes
(Paupiettes de Veau)

6 thin veal steaks; 1 clove garlic, crushed with ½ tsp salt; 2–3 leaves fresh sage, finely chopped, or pinch dried; 6 slices cooked ham; 6 tbsp fresh white breadcrumbs; 1 tbsp flour; oil; 120 ml/4 fl oz (½ cup) dry white wine; 2 ripe tomatoes, peeled, seeded and chopped; 2 tsp tomato purée (paste); salt and freshly ground black pepper.

Flatten veal steaks, then cut each in half. Mix garlic with sage and rub into one side of each piece of veal. Place half a slice of ham on each piece of veal and top with breadcrumbs. Roll up and secure with wooden toothpicks or tie with fine string. Roll in flour. Heat oil in a frying pan (skillet) and brown veal rolls on all sides. Add wine, tomatoes and tomato purée (paste), and season with salt and pepper. Simmer about 30 minutes, stirring occasionally. Remove toothpicks or string before serving. Serves 6

PAVLOVA

With a crisp meringue outside, delicate marshmallow-like softness inside, filled with cream and topped with fruit, Australia's most famous contribution to the culinary world was named after the great ballerina Anna Pavlova, and is a queen of desserts.

Strawberries and passionfruit are two classic toppings, but any fresh, frozen or canned fruits can be used, or the Pavlova can be topped with lemon cheese or apricot sauce. **See recipes.**

Basic Pavlova

6 egg whites, at room temperature; pinch salt; 500 g/1 lb (2 cups) caster sugar; 1½ tsp vinegar; 1½ tsp vanilla essence (extract); whipped cream for filling; fruit or other topping of your choice.

If you have a gas oven, preheat it to very hot, (Gas Mark 8) before starting to mix pavlova. If you have an electric oven, preheat it to cool (150°C/300°F). Beat egg whites with salt at high speed until soft peaks form. Add sugar, 1 tbsp at a time, beating well after each addition. Stop beating when all sugar has been incorporated and fold in vinegar and vanilla. Pile mixture into a greased 20 cm (8 in) china flan dish (pie plate), and lightly smooth top. Or pile mixture into a greased 20 cm (8 in) loose-bottomed tin (springform pan) and lightly smooth top. Or cover a baking tray with greased foil, mark a 20 cm (8 in) circle on it and pile mixture on to the circle; mould up sides with a spatula and make a slight depression on top. If using a gas oven, turn heat to lowest temperature, put pavlova in and bake 1½ hours or until crisp on top and a pale straw colour. If using an electric oven, put pavlova in and bake 45 minutes, then turn oven off and leave with door shut for 1 hour. When pavlova is cooked, remove from oven and cool

completely. Remove sides of loose-bottomed tin (springform pan), if using. Fill pavlova generously with whipped cream, then with your choice of topping. Serves 6–8.
NOTE: The meringue may be sprinkled with blanched, slivered almonds before baking. They will toast to a golden-brown.

Hazelnut Pavlova

4 egg whites; pinch salt; 350 g/12 oz (1½ cups) caster sugar; 1½ tsp vinegar; 1½ tsp vanilla essence (extract); 125 g/4 oz (1 cup) freshly ground hazelnuts; whipped cream for filling; Chocolate Sauce (page 73) to serve; chopped toasted hazelnuts to decorate.

Beat egg whites with salt at high speed until soft peaks form. Add sugar, 1 tbsp at a time, beating well after each addition. Stop beating when all sugar has been incorporated and fold in vinegar, vanilla and ground hazelnuts. Pile into an oiled and floured 23 cm (9 in) loose-bottomed tin (springform pan) and smooth top lightly. If using an electric oven, bake pavlova in a preheated cool oven (150°C/300°F) for 1 hour, then turn heat off and leave with door shut until cold. If using a gas oven, bake in a preheated cool oven (Gas Mark 2) for 1 hour, then reduce heat to very cool (Gas Mark ½) and bake 30 minutes longer. Turn heat off and leave with door shut until cold. When pavlova is cold, remove sides of tin (pan). The pavlova will collapse slightly. Fill with whipped cream, spoon some of the chocolate sauce over and decorate with chopped hazelnuts. Serve remaining chocolate sauce separately. Serves 6.

PAWPAW

Also known as papaya, this tropical fruit is found in many Pacific countries. When fully ripe, its skin and flesh should be a deep golden-yellow.

The simplest way to enjoy pawpaw is to

peel and halve it, remove the tiny black seeds and cut the flesh into cubes or wedges. Sprinkle with a little lemon juice, chill, and serve as a dessert or breakfast dish.

Pawpaw may be combined with other fruits in a fruit salad – it is particularly good with passionfruit. An attractive and refreshing combination is pawpaw with slices of kiwi fruit, mandarin segments and passionfruit pulp, lightly sweetened and sprinkled with Kirsch, and well chilled before serving as a special dinner party fruit salad.

The juice of pawpaw contains an enzyme, papain, which can be used to break down the fibres of meat and tenderize it. **See recipes.**

Pawpaw Sorbet

Pawpaw sorbet makes an excellent dessert after curries or highly spiced foods.

1 ripe pawpaw, peeled, halved and seeded; 1–3 tbsp lemon juice; 1 egg white; 2 tbsp caster sugar.

Chop pawpaw flesh roughly and blend, a few pieces at a time, or push through sieve, to make a thick, smooth purée. Combine with lemon juice to taste and pour into chilled ice cream tray. Freeze until just starting to set around edges. Whisk egg white until stiff and gradually beat in sugar. Turn pawpaw mixture into chilled bowl and beat until smooth. Fold in egg white. Return to ice cream tray, cover with foil and freeze until firm. Transfer to refrigerator 15–30 minutes before serving. Serves 6–8.

Pawpaw and Mango Whip

1 large ripe mango, peeled, seeded and chopped, or 1 × 425 g/14 oz can mango slices, drained and chopped; 1 small ripe pawpaw, peeled, seeded and chopped; 2 tbsp rum; 1 tbsp lime or lemon juice; 2 tbsp sugar; 250 ml/8 fl oz (1 cup) double (heavy) cream, whipped.

Purée mango and pawpaw in a food processor or blender, or push through a nylon sieve. Transfer to a bowl and stir in rum, juice and sugar. Fold in cream. Cover and chill several hours. Spoon into a serving dish and serve with extra whipped cream and crisp biscuits. Serves 6.

PEACH

A delicious fruit, which may be white or yellow-fleshed, slipstone (the fruit readily separates from the stone) or clingstone (as its name suggests, the fruit clings to the stone). Peaches are at their best and most refreshing eaten perfectly ripe and slightly chilled.

Like many other fruits, the peach is thought to have originated in China and to have been introduced to Europe by way of Persia.

Any surplus of peaches may be made into jam or frozen, but canning or home-bottling is the most popular way of preserving them for year-round enjoyment. Canned peaches may be halved or sliced, in heavy or light syrup or in a fruit nectar; they may be substituted for fresh cooked peaches in most recipes.

Peaches combine nicely with other summer fruits in fruit salad or compote. Sliced fresh peaches, covered with passionfruit pulp, make an elegantly simple and most delicious dessert. And in a different context, peaches highlight the flavour of meat and poultry – serve with grilled (broiled) ham steaks and roast duck.

To peel peaches: Pour boiling water over peaches, leave to stand 1–3 minutes. Skins will loosen and slip off easily. If peaches are really ripe, skins may be rubbed off without boiling water treatment.

Sprinkle peaches with lemon juice to prevent discoloration, if they are not to be cooked or eaten immediately.

☐ **To Poach Peaches:** Peel peaches as above, halve or slice as desired. Prepare syrup, using 125 g/4 oz (½ cup) sugar to 250 ml/8 fl oz (1 cup) water. Add peaches to hot syrup, simmer very gently for 3–5 minutes, cool in syrup. If desired, remove peaches with slotted spoon, reduce syrup over high heat, pour over cooked peaches. Chill. **See recipes.**

Brandied Peaches

Brandied peaches may be served as a dinner party dessert with whipped cream or as an accompaniment to roast duck or ham or grilled (broiled) pork chops.

peaches, peeled, halved and stoned (pitted); sugar; brandy.

Prick peaches all over with fine, sharp needle. Prepare sugar syrup with equal quantities sugar and water, and simmer peaches for 5 minutes. Lift out carefully, pack into wide-mouthed jars and half fill with sugar syrup. Cool, then add brandy to cover peaches completely. Seal jars and store in a cool, dark place for 2–3 months before using.

Peaches in Wine

A striking dessert that is very simple to prepare.

1 ripe peach per person, peeled, stoned (pitted) and sliced; caster sugar if desired; dry red or white or sweet white dessert wine.

Place peach slices in long-stemmed wine glasses. Sprinkle with a little sugar, then fill glasses with wine. Chill 1 hour. Serve with thin, crisp sweet biscuits (cookies).

Right: Lamb in Chilindron Sauce (page 181)

Peaches Aflame

An impressive dinner party dessert.

6 peaches, peeled, halved, stoned (pitted) and poached, or 1 × 411 g/14½ oz can peach halves; ½ tsp arrowroot; 120 ml/4 fl oz (½ cup) brandy; 60 g/2 oz (½ cup) toasted slivered almonds; ice cream to serve.

Pour 120 ml/4 fl oz (½ cup) peach syrup (from poaching or can) into top of chafing dish or pan and bring to the boil. Blend arrowroot with a little cold water, stir into syrup and stir until slightly thickened. Add peaches and baste with syrup until heated through. Warm brandy, ignite and pour over peaches. Top with almonds and serve with ice cream. Serves 6.

Spiced Peaches

Grilled (broiled) peach halves, flavoured with sugar and spice, that go well with ham or tongue.

4 large peaches, peeled, halved and stoned; 3 tbsp brown sugar; 16 whole cloves; sprinkling cinnamon and nutmeg; 45 g/1½ oz (3 tbsp) butter.

Arrange peaches in a heatproof dish. Sprinkle with brown sugar, stud each peach half with 2 cloves and sprinkle with cinnamon and nutmeg. Dot with butter. Cook under a preheated grill (broiler) about 5 minutes. Serves 8 as an accompaniment.

PEANUT

Also known as the groundnut, because, although the flowers of this vine-like plant are borne above ground, the nuts are really edible seeds in pods which form and grow underground.

Peanuts are highly nutritious, being rich in fat and protein, which is why peanut butter is often recommended for children. Peanut oil is a light, almost tasteless oil which can be used for salads or for cooking, and especially for deep-frying.

Peanuts are particularly important in the cooking of many Asian countries. In almost any city from Bangkok to Singapore, you will find satays – five or six small cubes of meat on bamboo skewers, grilled (broiled) quickly over a tiny heap of hot coals and served with a spicy-hot peanut sauce. **See recipes.**

Chocolate Peanut Biscuits

125 g/4 oz (½ cup) butter; 140 g/4½ oz (¾ cup) firmly packed brown sugar; 1 egg; 1 tbsp (unsweetened) cocoa powder; 180 g/6 oz (1½ cups) self-raising flour; 250 g/8 oz (1¼ cups) raw peanuts.

Left: Three-Fruit Marmalade (page 202)

Cream butter with brown sugar, add egg and beat well. Sift cocoa with flour, stir in, then add peanuts. Drop teaspoonsful of mixture on to greased baking trays and bake in a preheated moderate oven (180°C/350°F, Gas Mark 4) for 15 minutes. Makes about 30.

Peanut Crispies

2 egg whites; pinch salt; 180 g/6 oz (¾ cup) sugar; 30 g/1 oz (2 tbsp) butter, melted; ½ tsp vanilla essence (extract); 125 g/4 oz (4 cups) cornflakes; 75 g/2½ oz (¾ cup) desiccated (shredded) coconut; 150 g/5 oz (¾ cup) chopped raw peanuts.

Beat egg whites with salt until stiff. Gradually beat in sugar, then add remaining ingredients and fold in gently but thoroughly. Drop small teaspoons of mixture into patty cases and bake in a preheated moderately hot oven (190°C/375°F, Gas Mark 5) for 20–30 minutes. Makes about 48.

Gado Gado

(Indonesian Vegetable Salad with Peanut Sauce)

½ small cabbage, shredded; 1 small cucumber, finely sliced; 250 g (8 oz) green beans, parboiled; 2 carrots, cut into thin strips; 60 g/2 oz (1 cup) green beansprouts. PEANUT SAUCE: 210 g/7 oz (1 cup) raw peanuts; 120 ml/4 fl oz (½ cup) oil; 1 large onion, sliced; 2 cloves garlic, crushed; 1 tsp chilli powder; ½ tsp shrimp paste or shrimp sauce; 500 ml/18 fl oz (2 cups) Coconut Milk (page 80) or water; ½ tsp brown sugar; ½ tsp grated lemon rind; 1 tbsp vinegar; salt.

Arrange vegetables on salad platter. PEANUT SAUCE: Fry peanuts for 5 minutes in dry pan. Cool. Remove skins, then grind peanuts to a paste. Heat oil in pan and stir-fry onion and garlic with chilli powder and shrimp paste or sauce. Add ground peanuts and coconut milk or water and bring to the boil, stirring constantly. Add remaining ingredients and simmer gently until sauce thickens. Serve at room temperature. Dilute with hot water if too thick. Pour sauce over vegetables or serve separately. Serves 6.

Beef Satay

1 tbsp finely chopped garlic; 2 chillies, finely chopped; 1 tbsp finely chopped onion; 120 ml/4 fl oz (½ cup) Coconut Milk (page 80); 1 tbsp ground coriander; 1 tbsp soy sauce; salt and freshly ground black pepper; 1 kg (2 lb) sirloin or rump (top round) steak, cubed. PEANUT SAUCE: 175 ml/6 fl oz (¾ cup) peanut oil; 2 tbsp dried onion flakes; 1 dried chilli; 1 tbsp lemon juice; 1 tbsp soy sauce; 370 g/12 oz (1 cup) crunchy peanut butter; 1 tbsp sugar; 120–175 ml/4–6 fl oz (½–¾ cup) Coconut Milk (page 80) or water.

Combine all ingredients except steak. Add steak to this marinade and leave 1 hour. PEANUT SAUCE: Heat oil in wok or deep frying pan (skillet). Put onion flakes in a small metal strainer and lower into hot oil. Fry until golden, being careful not to burn. Drain on crumpled paper towels. Fry chilli in oil until puffed and crisp. Remove and drain. Discard stalk and seeds and crumble or chop chilli. Set aside. Combine lemon juice, soy sauce, peanut butter, sugar and coconut milk or water in a saucepan and heat gently, stirring. Remove from heat. When cold, add fried onion and crumbled chilli. Mix thoroughly. Add more liquid if necessary to make a dipping sauce consistency. Thread meat on skewers and grill (broil) over hot coals or under a preheated grill (broiler), brushing occasionally with marinade when turning. Serve hot with sauce. Serves 6.

PEANUT BUTTER

This nutritious paste of ground peanuts is a childhood favourite, and many a peanut-loving adult retains a fondness for it.

Spread on bread, toast or biscuits, peanut butter makes a good snack, and it combines with crisp bacon, celery, dates or raisins for wholesome sandwiches which carry well. Peanut butter cookies and cakes are other ways to enjoy its warm flavour. It is easy to make peanut butter at home in a blender or food processor. **See recipes.**

Peanut Butter

1½–3 tbsp peanut oil; 210 g/7 oz (1 cup) roasted peanuts; salt.

If using a blender, put 1½ tbsp oil into the container and, with motor running, add peanuts through hole in lid. Add more oil as necessary and, if nuts are not already salted, about ½ tsp salt. Process until you have consistency you want, from chunky to smooth. If using a food processor, put peanuts into the container and process, switching on and off, until coarsely chopped. With motor running, add oil through feed tube until you obtain consistency you want. Salt to taste. Makes about 280 g/9 oz (¾ cup).

Peanut Butter Cookies

180 g/6 oz (½ cup) peanut butter; 125 g/4 oz (½ cup) butter; 125 g/4 oz (½ cup) sugar; 90 g/3 oz (½ cup) firmly packed brown sugar; ½ tsp vanilla essence (extract); 1 egg; 150 g/5 oz (1¼ cups) flour; ½ tsp baking powder; ¾ tsp bicarbonate of soda (baking soda); ¼ tsp salt.

Cream peanut butter, butter and sugars together, beat in vanilla and egg. Sift in flour, baking powder, soda and salt and mix to a soft dough. Wrap in plastic wrap and chill for

30 minutes. Roll dough into walnut-size balls and place, well apart, on greased baking trays. Flatten, criss-cross fashion, with a fork dipped in flour. Bake in a preheated moderately hot oven (190°C/375°F, Gas Mark 5) 10–12 minutes until risen and golden-brown. Store in an airtight container. Makes about 35.

VARIATIONS

Peanut Butter and Raisin Cookies: Follow recipe for Peanut Butter Cookies, stirring in 45 g/1½ oz (¼ cup) chopped raisins with the flour.

Orange Peanut Butter Cookies: Follow recipe for Peanut Butter Cookies, substituting 1 tsp finely grated orange rind for the vanilla essence (extract).

Peanut Butter Spice Cake

30 g/1 oz (2 tbsp) butter, softened; 180 g/6 oz (¾ cup) caster sugar; 5 tbsp smooth peanut butter (at room temperature); 1 large egg; 165 g/5½ oz (1⅓ cups) self-raising flour; pinch salt; ½ tsp each ground cinnamon, nutmeg and ginger; ¼ tsp ground cloves; 250 ml/8 fl oz (1 cup) buttermilk.

Cream butter with sugar until light and fluffy, then beat in peanut butter. Add egg and mix well. Sift together flour, salt and spices and fold alternately into creamed mixture with buttermilk, beginning and ending with flour. Turn batter into greased and floured 20 cm (8 in) square cake tin (pan) and place in a preheated moderate oven (180°C/350°F, Gas Mark 4). Bake for 40 minutes or until a skewer inserted in centre comes out clean. Let cake cool in tin (pan) on a wire rack for 10 minutes before turning it out to cool completely. Serve plain, or top with chocolate icing (frosting).

NOTE: If you have no buttermilk, use 250 ml/ 8 fl oz (1 cup) ordinary fresh milk soured with 1 tbsp lemon juice.

Peanut Butter Chews

180 g/6 oz (½ cup) crunchy peanut butter; 3 tbsp honey; 1 tsp vanilla essence (extract); 45 g/1½ oz (½ cup) instant skim milk powder; pinch salt; 3 tbsp icing (confectioners) sugar, sifted; 105 g/3½ oz (½ cup) finely chopped unsalted peanuts.

Mix all ingredients, except chopped peanuts, kneading them together with your hands until well blended. Roll mixture into 2.5 cm (1 in) balls and coat them in peanuts. Store in refrigerator. Makes about 20.

PEAR

The sweet, juicy pear is one of the most versatile of fruits. It may be enjoyed as is or cooked, and it blends as well with wines and liqueurs as it does with other fruits such as raspberries and blackcurrants.

The first pears usually arrive on the market in Britain and America towards the end of summer. A succession of varieties and controlled atmosphere storage allows us to have fresh pears almost all year round. Canned pears can substitute for fresh pears in most recipes.

In England, the best varieties for eating include Williams, Conference, Comice and Laxton. Americans have a wider choice, but the Bartlett pear is particularly good eating in the early part of the season. Seckels and Kiefers are good for cooking and the big yellow-russet Anjou is an excellent all-purpose pear. If you enjoy a tart flavour, try the thin-necked Bosc.

In France, an *eau de vie* (fruit alcohol) is made from pears; a judicious dose may be added to a simple pear dessert for variety.

□ **To Poach Pears:** Choose pears which are still under-ripe, but not too hard. Peel gently with vegetable peeler, rub with lemon juice to prevent browning. Halve lengthways and remove cores with a melon baller or small sharp knife.

Poach in syrup of 1 part sugar to 2 parts water until just tender. A piece of vanilla pod (bean) may be added to the syrup. Remove fruit with slotted spoon and reduce syrup, then pour over fruit.

Poached pears may be served simply with cream or custard, or with a blackcurrant or raspberry purée. **See recipes.**

Pears in Red Wine

6 small pears; 125 g/4 oz (½ cup) sugar; 120 ml/4 fl oz (½ cup) red wine; 120 ml/ 4 fl oz (½ cup) water; strip lemon rind; 1 cinnamon stick.

Peel pears, leaving stalks. Dissolve sugar in wine and water in a saucepan, then add lemon rind and cinnamon and bring to the boil. Boil 1 minute. Arrange pears upright in an ovenproof dish and pour syrup over. Cover and cook in a preheated moderate oven (180°C/350°F, Gas Mark 4) until tender, about 1 hour. If pears are very hard, they may take as long as 2 hours. Arrange pears in serving dish and pour over wine syrup. Serve cold, accompanied by whipped cream if desired. Serves 6.

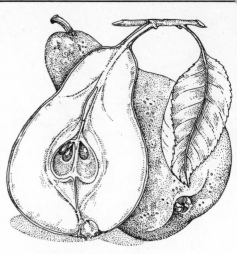

Pears with Sabayon Sauce

6 small pears; 125 g/4 oz (½ cup) sugar; 250 ml/8 fl oz (1 cup) water; 1 vanilla pod (bean); 4 egg yolks; 120 ml/4 fl oz (½ cup) sweet white wine; 75 g/2½ oz (⅓ cup) caster sugar; 1 tbsp Grand Marnier or Cointreau; 1 tbsp slivered almonds, lightly toasted.

Peel pears, leaving stalks. Dissolve sugar in water in a saucepan, add vanilla bean, bring to the boil. Boil 5 minutes. Poach pears gently in syrup until tender, then cool in syrup. Place egg yolks, wine, caster sugar and liqueur in top of double saucepan (double boiler) over simmering water. Beat vigorously with rotary beater until mixture becomes thick and creamy. Do not overcook, nor allow water to boil or mixture will curdle. Drain pears, place in serving dish or dishes, coat with sauce and sprinkle with almonds. Serves 6.

VARIATIONS

Pears with Rum Sabayon Sauce: Poach pears as above and cool. Make sauce using 4 tbsp poaching syrup and 2 tbsp white rum in place of white wine. Sprinkle with blanched julienne (matchsticks) of orange and lemon rind instead of almonds.

Poires Belle Hélène: Peel pears, halve and remove cores. Poach as above and cool. Place in bowls, add a scoop of vanilla ice cream to each and pour hot Chocolate Sauce (see page 73) over.

Pears with Spinach

1 bunch spinach; 1 large ripe pear, peeled and cored; salt and freshly ground black pepper; 1 tbsp single (light) cream (optional).

Trim spinach leaves from stems and rinse well. Cook in large pan, with no additional water, for about 5 minutes. Drain, and squeeze out excess water. Cook pear in water until very soft. Drain. Purée spinach and pear together in a blender. Season with salt and pepper and reheat gently. Blend in cream, if desired, before serving with hot or cold meats. Serves 4–6.

PEAS (GREEN)

Fresh green peas are at their best in early summer. Freshly picked, while still young and small, they have a sweetness and delicacy which are perhaps best appreciated when the peas are served on their own, as a separate course, although early peas also make a good accompaniment to spring lamb or veal. The very tiniest peas are what the French call *petits pois*.

Since about half the weight of the peas is in the pods, allow 1 kg/2 lb (3 cups) fresh peas for 4 servings. Peas may be shelled in advance, but wrap them in a damp cloth or cover them with their pods so they do not lose their moisture. A few pea pods may be cooked with the peas for added flavour, and if they are young and fresh, pea pods can be made into a soup.

Generally, the younger and fresher the peas, the less cooking time they will need. Older peas are still tasty if cooked slowly with additional flavourings, such as ham or herbs. Frozen and canned peas may not equal fresh peas in flavour, but they make up for this in convenience. Their flavour can be improved by treating them in ways similar to those for fresh peas. **See recipes.**

Green Peas

1 kg/2 lb (3 cups) fresh peas, shelled; salt; 1 sprig fresh mint (optional); 30 g/1 oz (2 tbsp) butter.

Drop peas into enough boiling salted water to cover. Add mint and cook for 10–15 minutes until just tender. Drain, refresh under cold water, then return to pan with butter. Shake over low heat until hot and coated with butter. Serve immediately on their own or as a vegetable accompaniment. Serves 4.

VARIATIONS:
Chopped fresh mint or summer savory may be added to peas with butter. 125 g/4 oz (1 cup) sliced sautéed mushrooms may be combined with cooked peas just before serving.

Petits Pois à la Française

(Green Peas, French-style)

1 kg/2 lb (3 cups) fresh peas, shelled; 6 lettuce leaves, or small lettuce heart, shredded; 12 small pickling onions, peeled; 60 g/2 oz (4 tbsp) butter; 2 sprigs each fresh parsley and chervil; 1 tsp sugar; salt; 3 tbsp water.

Place peas in a large saucepan with half lettuce, the onions, butter, herbs, sugar and salt. Cover with remaining lettuce and add water. Cover and cook over gentle heat for 15–20 minutes, shaking pan from time to time, until peas are tender. Remove herbs

and adjust seasoning to taste before serving. Serves 4.

VARIATION
500 g/1 lb (3 cups) frozen peas may be substituted for fresh peas.

Risi e Bisi

(Rice with Peas)

30 g/1 oz (2 tbsp) butter; 1 tbsp olive oil; 1 rasher (slice) lean bacon, rind removed and diced; 2 shallots, chopped; 1.2 litres/ 2 pints (5 cups) chicken stock; 165 g/5½ oz (¾ cup) Italian short-grain rice; 250 g/8 oz (1½ cups) shelled fresh peas or frozen peas; salt; 1 tbsp finely chopped parsley; grated Parmesan cheese to serve.

Heat butter and oil in a large saucepan and cook bacon and shallots about 5 minutes. Add stock and rice, bring to the boil and stir well. If using fresh peas, add with rice; add frozen peas after about 15 minutes. Cook over low heat for 20–25 minutes or until rice is moist and tender. Season with salt, and sprinkle with parsley. Serve with Parmesan offered separately. Serves 4–6.

Pea Purée

250 g/8 oz (1½ cups) shelled fresh peas; pinch sugar; 30 g/1 oz (2 tbsp) butter; 4 tbsp single (light) cream; salt and freshly ground black pepper.

Cook peas in boiling salted water for 15 minutes or until very tender. Drain, then rub through sieve or purée in a blender. Return to saucepan, add sugar and butter and stir until butter is incorporated into purée. Stir in cream, and season with salt and pepper. Serves 4.

Green Pea Soup

30 g/1 oz (2 tbsp) butter; 1 shallot, finely chopped; 1 slice cooked ham, cut into fine strips; 165 g/5½ oz (1 cup) shelled fresh peas; pinch sugar; 875 ml/1 pint 9 fl oz (3½ cups) chicken or veal stock; 1 sprig fresh mint; salt and freshly ground black pepper; 4 tbsp single (light) cream.

Melt butter in a saucepan and cook shallot until soft. Add ham and peas and toss in butter. Add sugar, stock and mint and season with salt and pepper. Simmer until peas are very soft. Remove mint. Rub through a sieve or purée in a blender. Add cream, adjust seasoning and reheat gently. Serves 4.

PECAN

An American nut of the hickory family, rather like a walnut in flavour and appearance; indeed, in many recipes walnuts and pecans are interchangeable.

The name comes from the Indian word for these nuts. Of all the pecan dishes, perhaps the best known is Pecan Pie. **See recipes.**

Pecan Sandwich Spread

60 g/2 oz (½ cup) finely chopped pecans; 30 g/1 oz (¼ cup) finely chopped celery; 45 g/1½ oz (¼ cup) chopped stuffed olives; 1½ tbsp Mayonnaise (page 204).

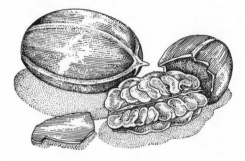

Combine all ingredients. Spread on lightly buttered wholewheat or white bread. Makes about 150 g/5 oz (1 cup), or sufficient for 4 sandwiches.

Southern Pecan Pie

250 g/8 oz (1 cup) sugar; 90 g/3 oz (¼ cup) golden (light corn) syrup; 4 tbsp water; 60 g/2 oz (4 tbsp) butter, melted; 3 eggs, well-beaten; 125 g/4 oz (1 cup) pecan halves; 1 × 23 cm (9 in) unbaked Rich Shortcrust Pastry Shell (page 274).

Mix together sugar, syrup, water and melted butter. Add eggs and pecans and stir well. Pour into pastry (pie) shell. Bake in a preheated moderately hot oven (200°C/ 400°F, Gas Mark 6) for 10 minutes, then reduce heat to moderate (180°C/350°F, Gas Mark 4) and continue baking for about 30 minutes. Serve warm or cold. Serves 8.

Pecan Balls

125 g/4 oz (½ cup) butter, softened; 2 tbsp sugar; 1 tsp vanilla essence (extract); 125 g/4 oz (1 cup) ground or finely chopped pecans; 125 g/4 oz (1 cup) flour, sifted; 70 g/2¼ oz (½ cup) icing (confectioners) sugar.

Cream butter with sugar until fluffy. Mix in vanilla and pecans. Add flour in 2 parts, stirring after each addition until thoroughly blended. Roll into small balls, and place about 5 cm (2 in) apart on ungreased baking trays. Bake in a preheated moderate oven (180°C/350°F, Gas Mark 4) for 12–15 minutes or until pale brown. Sift icing (confectioners) sugar on to flat plate. Roll biscuits in icing (confectioners) sugar as soon as removed from oven. Cool on wire racks. Makes about 20.

Butter Pecan Ice Cream

A toasted-pecan flavoured ice cream.

60 g/2 oz (½ cup) chopped pecans; 60 g/
2 oz (4 tbsp) butter; 1½ tbsp cornflour
(cornstarch); 125 g/4 oz (½ cup) sugar; 2 tbsp
brown sugar; 250 ml/8 fl oz (1 cup) milk;
1 tsp vanilla essence (extract); 250 ml/8 fl oz
(1 cup) double (heavy) cream.

Toss pecans with butter in a frying pan
(skillet) over gentle heat until lightly toasted.
Cool. Mix cornflour (cornstarch) and sugars.
Blend in milk. Pour into a saucepan and
cook until thick, stirring constantly. Remove
from heat and stir in vanilla. Chill. Whip
cream until stiff. Fold in chilled mixture and
pecans. Pour into ice cream tray and freeze.
Serves 4–6.

PECHE MELBA (Peach Melba)

This famous dessert was created by one of the
world's greatest chefs, Auguste Escoffier, to
honour Dame Nellie Melba, after he had
heard her sing in 'Lohengrin'. Melba's per-
formance inspired a dessert of peaches on
vanilla ice cream, served between the wings of
an ice-carved swan and covered with spun
sugar. Later the dish was given its distinctive
flavour by dispensing with the swan and spun
sugar and covering the peaches and ice
cream with fresh raspberry purée. The purée
became known as 'Sauce Melba'.

Today, Pêche Melba is served in great
restaurants all over the world, and remains as
distinctive a dish as it was in Dame Melba's
time.

Pêche Melba

125 g/4 oz (½ cup) sugar; 500 ml/18 fl oz
(2 cups) water; 1 vanilla pod (bean); 4 fresh
peaches, peeled; 500 g/1 lb (3 cups) fresh or
frozen raspberries; 70 g/2¼ oz (½ cup) icing
(confectioners) sugar, sifted; 500 ml/18 fl oz
(2 cups) French Vanilla Ice Cream (page
161).

Place sugar, water and vanilla bean in a
saucepan over medium heat. Stir until
sugar dissolves, then bring to the boil and
simmer 5 minutes. Place peaches in syrup,
cover and poach gently 5–10 minutes or
until just tender. Remove from syrup, drain
and chill, covered. Rub raspberries through a
nylon sieve or purée in a food processor or
blender. Gradually add icing (confectioners)
sugar until sauce thickens. Pile ice cream in a
glass dish, cover top with peaches, whole or
halved according to size, and spoon
raspberry sauce over peaches. Serves 4.

PEPPER

The world's most important spice, grown in
tropical countries such as Indonesia and
India. Highly aromatic and with a pungent,
biting flavour, pepper is used to season all
types of savoury dishes. It can even enter into
sweet recipes, as a spice rather than as a
seasoning, for example in the German biscuits, Pfeffernüsse.

The most commonly available types of
pepper are black or white, both of which may
be found as peppercorns (whole dried berries) or as ground pepper. Like most spices,
the flavour deteriorates after grinding, and
pepper is best if freshly ground. Ideally, there
should always be two pepper grinders, one
for black pepper and one for white; ground
white pepper should be used in pale-
coloured dishes and sauces, where specks of
black would spoil appearance.

Black peppercorns are the dried berries of the
pepper vine (Piper nigrum), picked while still
green and not completely ripe; on drying,
they become dark brown or black. They are
more aromatic than white peppercorns.

White peppercorns are the fully ripe berries,
from which the outer hull is removed before
drying. They are hotter than black
peppercorns.

Green peppercorns are the berries picked
while still green, then preserved in brine. They
are usually available in small cans or jars, and
are soft enough to be ground or mashed to a
paste. Their flavour is much milder than black
or white peppercorns. Green peppercorns
are often used with duck, and in pâtés or as
an alternative to black peppercorns in Pepper
Steak (see opposite).

Pink or red peppercorns come from an
entirely different plant, a tree native to South
America and sometimes referred to as Brazi-
lian pepper tree. Recent research has shown
that many people have allergic reactions to
pink peppercorns, so their use should be
approached with caution. **See recipes.**

Curried Chicken with Green
Peppercorns

4 tbsp vegetable oil; 4 onions, finely
chopped; 1 tbsp green peppercorns, drained
and crushed; 1 slice fresh ginger, finely
chopped; ½ tsp each turmeric and ground
mace; ¼ tsp each ground cloves, coriander
and cinnamon; 10 small chicken thighs, cut
in half; 2 tsp cornflour (cornstarch);
500 ml/18 fl oz (2 cups) chicken stock;
2 apples, peeled, cored and cut into 1 cm
(½ in) cubes; 2 tbsp toasted desiccated
(shredded) coconut to garnish.

Heat oil in a large frying pan (skillet) and
cook onions until softened. Add green
peppercorns and cook for 1 minute, then
add ginger and spices and combine. Add
chicken and brown on all sides. Blend
cornflour (cornstarch) with a little chicken
stock, then combine with remaining stock.
Add to pan and cook, stirring, until

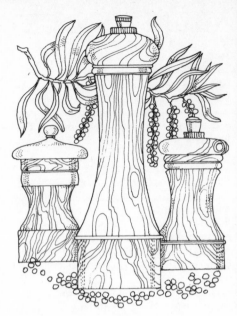

thickened. Reduce and simmer for 5
minutes. Add apples and continue to simmer
for 10 minutes more or until chicken is
tender. Transfer to a heated serving dish,
garnish with toasted coconut and serve with
fluffy boiled rice. Serves 6–8.

Veal and Pepper Loaf

1–2 tbsp black peppercorns; 2 slices white
bread, torn into pieces; 75 g/2½ oz (2 cups)
parsley, stems removed; 3 sticks celery,
chopped; 120 ml/4 fl oz (½ cup) water;
1 kg/2 lb (4 cups) minced (ground) veal; 1
egg, lightly beaten; 1 tsp salt; 6–8 rashers
(slices) bacon, rind removed.

Crush peppercorns in a mortar with a pestle
or in a bowl with end of a rolling pin. Blend
bread in a blender or food processor to
make fine crumbs. Place parsley, celery and
water in the container of the food processor
or blender and blend until ingredients are
chopped but not mushy. Place meat in a
mixing bowl and add peppercorns, parsley
mixture, egg, breadcrumbs and salt. Mix well
with the fingers. Line a 1.5 litre/2½ pint
(6 cup) loaf tin (pan) with bacon rashers
(slices), leaving ends hanging over edge of
tin (pan). Pack meat mixture into tin (pan)
and fold overhanging bacon over meat.
Cover with a lid or foil and bake in a
preheated moderate oven (160°C/325°F,
Gas Mark 3) for 2 hours. Remove from oven,
place a weight on top, and allow to cool,
then chill. Serve with salads. Serves 6–8.

PEPPER STEAK (Steak au Poivre)

There are many versions of steak au poivre.
Here are two, one with crushed black peppercorns, the other with green peppercorns
and a cream sauce.

Pepper Steak

4 pieces rump (top round) or fillet (tenderloin) steak; 1½ tbsp coarsely cracked black peppercorns; olive oil; 15 g/½ oz (1 tbsp) butter; salt; dash Worcestershire sauce; lemon juice; 2 tbsp brandy; chopped fresh parsley and chives.

Trim steaks of excess fat and any gristle. Press pepper into both sides of steaks and leave 30 minutes. Cook in a little oil in heavy frying pan (skillet) until done to your taste. Dot with butter, and season with salt, Worcestershire sauce and lemon juice. Warm brandy, ignite and pour over meat. Sprinkle with herbs and serve immediately, coating steaks with the sauce. Serves 4.

VARIATION

Prepare pepper steak as above. After flaming the steaks with brandy, add 120 ml/4 fl oz (½ cup) single (light) cream, blending in well. Substitute 2 tsp green peppercorns for herbs.

PEPPER (SWEET)

Sweet peppers (also called capsicums) are members of the same large Capsicum family as the hot chilli pepper. Their flesh has a sweet, vigorous flavour, which enlivens salads and many cooked dishes, and their square-ish, hollow shape (the name 'capsicum' means box) makes them perfect for stuffing.

Peppers come in a mosaic of colours – brilliant red, yellow or green. Red peppers are fully ripe ones, and are much sweeter and milder than the unripe green ones; they are also twice as rich in vitamin C.

When buying peppers, avoid any that are wrinkled or have soft spots. They should be smooth, firm and gleaming. Store in the refrigerator crisper and use them within a week or so of purchase.

☐ **Basic Preparation:** The fleshy inner ribs or core and the seeds are discarded before using. Cut the pepper in half lengthways, or cut a lid from the top if you want to keep it whole, and pull out ribs or core and seeds with your fingers. Cut away the stem (unless you are retaining it for its decorative effect in a whole or halved stuffed pepper). Wash under cold running water.

To skin peppers: It is very often worth skinning peppers. It makes their flavour more delicate and changes their texture from crisp to richly soft. Spear whole pepper on a long-handled fork and turn it over a gas flame, or put it close to a very hot grill (broiler), turning until skin is charred all over. Put pepper into a paper bag for 10 minutes to steam, then rub skin off under cold water. Red or yellow peppers are easier to skin than green ones.

To blanch peppers: Some recipes suggest blanching peppers before stuffing, again to give a more delicate flavour. After removing ribs or core and seeds, drop pepper into boiling water for a minute or two, pushing pepper down well under the water. Remove and refresh under cold running water. Drain well and proceed with recipe.

Ways to Use Peppers

● A simple way to cook peppers is to cut them into strips, discarding ribs or core and seeds, and fry in a little oil, perhaps flavoured with garlic. Season with salt and pepper and serve with grilled (broiled) or roasted meat.
● Halved and drizzled with oil, peppers may be grilled (broiled) with meat.
● Sliced into rings, cut into strips or diced they are used raw in many salads.
● Strips of raw pepper may be part of a dish of Crudités (*see Crudités*) to use with a dipping sauce. **See recipes**.

Chilled Pepper Salad

4 large ripe tomatoes, peeled and thickly sliced; 4 peppers (any colour), skinned, cored, seeded and cut into strips; 1 × 50 g/1⅔ oz can flat anchovy fillets; 4 tbsp Vinaigrette Dressing (page 358); freshly ground black pepper; 6–8 black (ripe) olives, halved and stoned (pitted); 3 hard-boiled (hard-cooked) eggs, quartered; chopped parsley or fine strips fresh basil to garnish.

Arrange tomato slices in a shallow dish. Place peppers on top of tomatoes. Drain anchovies; mix their oil with vinaigrette and drizzle this mixture over salad. Season with black pepper. Split anchovy fillets in half lengthways and arrange lattice-fashion on salad. Put an olive half into each square. Chill well. At serving time, arrange eggs round edge and scatter with herbs. Serves 6.

Fettucine and Pepper Salad

250 g (8 oz) fettucine; 2 red or green peppers, skinned, cored, seeded and cut into strips; 125 g/4 oz (1 cup) Gruyère cheese, diced; 6–8 black (ripe) olives; 4 tbsp Mustard Vinaigrette Dressing (page 358); salt and freshly ground black pepper.

Cook fettucine and drain. Mix peppers, cheese and olives in a salad bowl. Mix fettucine with vinaigrette, add to other ingredients and toss lightly. Season and chill 1 hour before serving. Serves 4.

Beef and Peppers in Black Bean Sauce

500 g (1 lb) lean fillet (tenderloin) or rump (top round) steak; 1 tbsp soy sauce; 1 tbsp hoisin sauce (optional); 1 tbsp tomato purée (paste); 1½ tbsp cornflour (cornstarch); 5 tbsp vegetable oil; 1¼ tsp sugar; 2 tbsp Chinese salted black beans; 1 medium red pepper, cored and seeded; 1 medium green pepper, cored and seeded; 1 tsp grated fresh ginger; 3 tbsp dry sherry.

Slice beef thinly across the grain and cut into finger-length strips. Mix soy and hoisin sauces, tomato purée (paste), cornflour (cornstarch), 1 tbsp oil and sugar. Add beef, turn to coat the strips all over, and leave 15 minutes. Meantime, soak beans in cold water for 15 minutes. Cut peppers into 4 cm (1½ in) squares. Heat remaining oil in a frying pan (skillet) or wok over high heat. When it begins to give off a haze, add ginger and drained black beans and stir-fry 30 seconds. Add beef and stir-fry 2 minutes. Add peppers, sprinkle with sherry and stir-fry 1 minute more. Serve at once. Serves 4–6.

Peppers, Onions and Corn

90 g/3 oz (6 tbsp) butter; 3 medium onions, thickly sliced; 2 red or green peppers, cored, seeded and cut into strips; 180 g/6 oz (1 cup) cooked fresh, or drained canned, sweetcorn (whole kernel corn); salt and freshly ground black pepper.

Heat butter and cook onions gently until soft. Add peppers to pan and cook, stirring, on medium heat for 5 minutes. Stir in corn, heat through and season with salt and pepper. Serves 4–6.

Stewed Peppers

(Papriche Stufate)
One of the many Italian dishes starring peppers. Serve hot with grilled (broiled) chops or sausages, or at room temperature as part of an antipasto tray.

120 ml/4 fl oz (½ cup) olive oil; 1 clove garlic, flattened with a heavy knife; 6 green or yellow peppers, cored, seeded and cut into strips; 4 large, ripe tomatoes, peeled and chopped; salt and freshly ground black pepper; 2 tbsp finely chopped parsley to garnish.

Heat oil in a frying pan (skillet) and fry garlic gently until golden-brown, then discard garlic. Add pepper strips and cook gently 5 minutes. Cover with tomatoes and season with salt and pepper. Continue cooking until tomatoes are reduced to a thick sauce. Serve hot or cold, garnished with parsley. Serves 4.

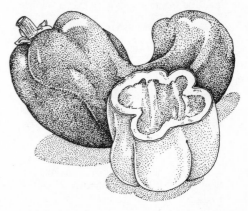

Peppers with Bacon

2 tbsp olive oil; 250 g (8 oz) lean rashers (slices) bacon, rind removed and cut into 4 cm (1½ in) pieces; 1 onion, finely sliced; 2 tbsp water; 4 large, ripe tomatoes, peeled, seeded and chopped; 4 green or yellow peppers, skinned, cored, seeded and cut into strips; salt and freshly ground black pepper.

Heat oil in a frying pan (skillet) over low heat and fry bacon gently until lightly browned. Add onion and water and cook until water evaporates and onion is soft and golden. Add tomatoes and cook over medium heat until soft. Add peppers, salt and pepper and cook until peppers are soft. Serve very hot. Serves 4.

Peppers Stuffed with Pipérade

A marvellous cold dish, filled with a delicious scrambled egg mixture. Serve it for lunch, or as a light supper dish.

2 red peppers, halved, cored and seeded; 3 tbsp olive oil; 125 g/4 oz (½ cup) cooked ham or bacon, chopped; 1 large onion, chopped; 60 g/2 oz (½ cup) chopped green pepper; 1 tomato, peeled, seeded and chopped; salt and freshly ground black pepper; 30 g/1 oz (½ cup) fresh breadcrumbs; 4 tbsp single (light) cream; 3 eggs, beaten; chopped parsley.

Blanch red peppers for a few minutes in boiling water, then drain and cool. Heat 1 tbsp oil in a heavy frying pan (skillet) and lightly brown ham or bacon. Add onion and sauté until soft, adding chopped green pepper halfway through cooking. Stir in tomato and season with salt and pepper. Cover and cook over a low heat for 5 minutes. Allow to cool. Soak breadcrumbs in cream in a small bowl. Add eggs. Heat remaining oil in a heavy frying pan (skillet), add egg mixture and scramble until soft and creamy. Put eggs into a dish and cool. Fold together tomato mixture and scrambled egg and spoon carefully into prepared red pepper shells. Sprinkle tops liberally with chopped parsley before serving. Serves 4.

Stuffed Peppers

4 large red or green peppers; 350 ml/12 fl oz (1½ cups) Fresh Tomato Sauce (page 271). STUFFING: 45 g/1½ oz (3 tbsp) butter; 1 onion, finely chopped; 105 g/3½ oz (½ cup) short-grain rice; 60 g/2 oz (½ cup) mushrooms, chopped; 350 ml/12 fl oz (1½ cups) chicken stock; 125 g/4 oz (½ cup) cooked ham, veal or chicken, finely chopped; salt and freshly ground black pepper.

Cut tops off peppers and scoop out seeds. Blanch in boiling water for 2–3 minutes, see page 285. Pat dry with paper towels and set aside.

STUFFING: Melt 30 g/1 oz (2 tbsp) of the butter in a saucepan and fry onion until softened. Add rice, stir over medium heat for 1–2 minutes, then add mushrooms. Pour stock over, bring to the boil, cover and simmer for 20 minutes or until rice is tender and stock absorbed. Stir in remaining butter and cooked ham, veal or chicken and season with salt and pepper. Put stuffing into peppers and pack them closely together in an ovenproof casserole. Heat tomato sauce and pour over and around peppers. Cover dish with greased foil and cook in a preheated moderate oven (180°C/350°F, Gas Mark 4) for 25–30 minutes or until peppers are tender. Serves 4.

Tomato and Pepper Salad

2 green peppers, cored, seeded and cut into strips; 4 firm tomatoes, sliced; ½ Spanish onion or 6 shallots, finely chopped; 1 bunch fresh coriander or flat-leaved Italian parsley; salt and freshly ground black pepper; 4 tbsp olive oil; 1–2 tbsp wine vinegar.

Put peppers in a serving bowl with tomatoes, onion and coriander or parsley. Season with salt and pepper, pour on oil and vinegar and toss well. Increase amount of oil and vinegar if you wish. Serve as a first course with bread to mop up the juices. Serves 4.

Stuffed Peppers, Piedmont-Style

3 cloves garlic, chopped; 2 large tomatoes, peeled, seeded and diced; 60 g/2 oz (1 cup) fresh breadcrumbs; 3 green or red peppers, skinned, cored, seeded and quartered lengthways; 12 anchovy fillets; 30 g/1 oz (2 tbsp) butter; 4 tbsp olive oil; salt and freshly ground black pepper.

Combine garlic, tomatoes and breadcrumbs and divide among the 12 pepper boat shapes. Place an anchovy fillet on top of each, then a small piece of butter. Put in a greased baking dish. Drizzle oil over and sprinkle with salt and pepper. Bake in a preheated moderate oven (180°C/350°F, Gas Mark 4) for 15–20 minutes; the peppers should not become too soft. Serve cold. Serves 4–6 as part of an antipasto tray and 3–4 as a lunch dish.

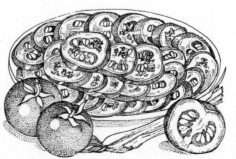

Peperonata
(Peppers with Tomatoes and Onions)

4 tbsp olive oil; 3–4 medium onions, chopped; 2 cloves garlic, sliced; 2 bay leaves; 6 large peppers (any colour or mixed), cored, seeded and cut into thick strips; 500 g/1 lb (2 cups) tomatoes, peeled and quartered; salt and freshly ground black pepper.

Heat oil in a frying pan (skillet) and fry onions, garlic and bay leaves for about 5 minutes, stirring occasionally. Stir in peppers, cover pan and cook gently for about 10 minutes. Add tomatoes, salt and pepper and cook, uncovered and stirring frequently, until most of the liquid has evaporated and mixture is fairly thick. This may take about 30 minutes. Remove bay leaves, season again if necessary and serve cold as antipasto or hot with roast or grilled (broiled) meats. Serves 4–6.

Tabouleh-Stuffed Peppers

140 g/4½ oz (1 cup) burghul (cracked wheat); 8 small green peppers; 150 ml/¼ pint (⅔ cup) olive oil; 120 ml/4 fl oz (½ cup) lemon juice; 10 g/⅓ oz (¼ cup) chopped fresh mint; 10 g/⅓ oz (¼ cup) chopped parsley; 2 tsp salt; freshly ground black pepper; 125 g/4 oz (2 cups) alfalfa sprouts; 125 g/4 oz (1 cup) peeled, seeded and chopped cucumber; 2 tomatoes, chopped; 60 g/2 oz (½ cup) chopped spring onions (scallions).

Soak burghul in water overnight in a glass or ceramic bowl. Drain and squeeze out as much water as possible, then spread out on a tea-towel to dry. Cook peppers in boiling salted water for 5 minutes. Drain and refresh under cold running water. Cut off tops, discard seeds and ribs and let peppers drain. Combine oil, lemon juice, herbs, salt and pepper in a large bowl. Add burghul, then rest of ingredients. Divide mixture among the peppers, mounding it high, and arrange peppers on a serving dish. Serves 8.

PEPPERMINT

One of the many varieties of mint, and one of the most useful herbs in industry. Its leaves yield, on distillation, peppermint oil, which flavours confectionery, ice cream, toothpaste, chewing gum, perfumes, liqueurs and pharmaceutical preparations.

Chocolate and peppermint seem to have a particular affinity – peppermint-flavoured chocolate, or chocolate with a peppermint cream filling, is a delicious accompaniment to after-dinner coffee.

Small bottles of peppermint essence (extract) are available for flavouring cakes, biscuits (cookies) and confectionery. **See recipes.**

P

Peppermint Sticks

125 g/4 oz ($\frac{1}{2}$ cup) butter, melted; 125 g/4 oz ($\frac{1}{2}$ cup) sugar; 90 g/3 oz (1 cup) desiccated (shredded) coconut; 125 g/4 oz (1 cup) flour, sifted; 1 tbsp (unsweetened) cocoa powder; $\frac{1}{2}$ tsp peppermint essence (extract); 1 tsp baking powder; 30 g/1 oz (1 cup) cornflakes, lightly crushed.
PEPPERMINT BUTTER ICING (FROSTING): *90 g/3 oz (6 tbsp) butter; 90 g/3 oz ($\frac{2}{3}$ cup) icing (confectioners) sugar, sifted; peppermint essence (extract).*
DECORATION: *30 g/1 oz (1 square) dark chocolate, melted with 15 g/$\frac{1}{2}$ oz (1 tbsp) butter.*

Cream butter with sugar, then beat in coconut, flour, cocoa powder, peppermint essence (extract) and baking powder. Mix well. Stir in cornflakes. Press into a 30 × 25 cm (12 × 10 in) Swiss roll tin (jelly roll pan); mixture should be nearly 1 cm ($\frac{1}{2}$ in) thick. Bake in a preheated moderate oven (180°C/350°F, Gas Mark 4) for about 20 minutes. Cool.
PEPPERMINT BUTTER ICING (FROSTING): Cream butter until light, then gradually beat in icing (confectioners) sugar. Flavour to taste with peppermint essence (extract). When cake is cold spread roughly with icing (frosting) and drizzle over melted chocolate mixture. Cut into fingers to serve. Makes about 50.

Double Delight Cake

CHOCOLATE ICING (FROSTING): *180 g/6 oz ($\frac{3}{4}$ cup) cream cheese; 125 g/4 oz ($\frac{1}{2}$ cup) butter; $\frac{1}{2}$ tsp vanilla essence (extract); $\frac{1}{2}$ tsp peppermint essence (extract); 850 g/1$\frac{3}{4}$ lb (6 cups) icing (confectioners) sugar, sifted; 4 tbsp hot water; 125 g/4 oz ($\frac{2}{3}$ cup) dark cooking chocolate, melted.*
CAKE: *60 g/2 oz (4 tbsp) butter; 3 eggs; 280 g/9 oz (2$\frac{1}{4}$ cups) flour; 1$\frac{1}{2}$ tsp bicarbonate of soda (baking soda); 1 tsp salt; 175 ml/6 fl oz ($\frac{3}{4}$ cup) milk.*

CHOCOLATE ICING (FROSTING): Beat together cheese, butter and essences (extracts), blending well. Beat in half the icing (confectioners) sugar, then add remaining icing (confectioners) sugar alternately with hot water. Blend in melted chocolate and mix until smooth.
CAKE: Blend butter with 370 g/12 oz (2 cups) of the chocolate frosting. Add eggs, one at a time, and beat for 1 minute. Sift flour, soda and salt, and stir into creamed mixture alternately with milk, beginning and ending with dry ingredients. Spoon into 2 greased and lightly floured 20 cm (8 in) round sandwich tins (layer pans). Bake in a preheated moderate oven (180°C/350°F, Gas Mark 4) for 30–40 minutes. Cool on a wire rack. Sandwich cake together with a little of the remaining icing (frosting) or jam.

Decorate cake by spreading rest of icing (frosting) over top and side.

PERSIMMON

This fruit is a rare treat, because when properly ripe, it is very fragile and soft and needs delicate handling. A ripe persimmon is not unlike a tomato, slightly more orange than red, and almost translucent. Persimmons are most often eaten raw but may be stewed or made into jam.

Another variety of persimmon, called Sharon Fruit, and grown in Israel, is sometimes available. This has an edible skin, no pips and a very sweet flesh; it can be eaten while still firm unlike the ordinary persimmon, which tastes very astringent if not fully ripe and soft.
To eat persimmons: With a small sharp knife, cut around the centre stalk of the persimmon and remove. Scoop out flesh with a small teaspoon. The jelly-like flesh around the seeds is also edible, but the seeds are not.

PESTO ALLA GENOVESE
(Basil, Cheese and Pine Nut Sauce)

This pungent sauce, with its main ingredient basil, is used to flavour pasta dishes by tossing the hot pasta with pesto to taste and enough butter to coat the strands. A little of the sauce is excellent, too, in soups, as well as spooned over poached fish or boiled or baked potatoes. It can be stored, covered with a layer of oil, in a jar in the refrigerator where it will keep for months. For recipe see page 272.

PETITS FOURS

The French name 'Petits fours' is used to describe a variety of small cakes and biscuits (cookies), often highly decorated, which are served after dessert and with coffee. They must be very small and elegant, just the size of one mouthful.

The term, which translates as 'little oven', is thought to have originated because these cakes were baked in a slower oven than big

cakes. Such a difference is no longer relevant; the essential for Petits fours is that they be very small and very attractive.

Petits fours may simply be small-scale versions of the standard range of pâtisserie, such as tiny cream puffs or éclairs, or minuscule fruit tarts. Or they may be based on Almond Paste (see page 7), or on a Genoise Cake (see page 143) cut into attractive shapes, iced and decorated.

PHEASANT

One of the most popular of game birds, often raised commercially. It is a smallish, white-fleshed bird; its flavour can be rather delicate and not very 'gamey', especially if the bird did not grow up in the wild and fatten among grape vines.

An average pheasant weighs about 1 kg (2 lb) and will serve 3–4 persons. For ease of carving, and especially if the bird is stuffed, it is often semi-boned – that is, the drumsticks and wings are left intact, but the thigh bones and main carcase bones are removed – start from the middle of the back and gradually separate flesh from bone around to breast. **See recipes.**

Roast Stuffed Pheasant

1 × 1 kg (2 lb) pheasant; salt and freshly ground black pepper; 4 chicken livers; 60 g/2 oz (4 tbsp) butter; 60 g/2 oz ($\frac{1}{2}$ cup) cooked rice; 1 tbsp juniper berries; 1 tbsp slivered almonds; 2 tbsp strong pheasant or chicken stock; 1 small onion, finely chopped and softened in butter; port or Madeira.

Season pheasant lightly with salt and pepper. Lightly sauté chicken livers in half of the butter. Chop roughly, then mix with rice, juniper berries, almonds, stock and onion. Season with salt and pepper. Spoon stuffing into bird and truss. Rub remaining butter over bird and place, breast down, in roasting tin (pan). Pour a little port or Madeira into tin (pan). Roast in a preheated moderately hot oven (200°C/400°F, Gas Mark 6), basting bird occasionally with pan

287

juices. After 45 minutes, test with skewer through thigh; pheasant is cooked when juices that run out are still faintly pink. If necessary, leave in turned-off oven for 5–10 minutes longer. Serve with Cumberland sauce (see page 91), if desired; alternatively, make sauce with pan juices and pheasant stock. Serves 3–4.

Roast Pheasant

1 × 1 kg (2 lb) pheasant; 2 rashers (slices) bacon, rind removed; 60 g/2 oz (4 tbsp) butter, melted; 120 ml/4 fl oz (½ cup) sherry; 1 tbsp redcurrant jelly; juice ½ lemon; flour.

Truss pheasant, and tie bacon around bird. Rub all over with butter. Roast in a preheated moderate oven (180°C/350°F, Gas Mark 4) for 40 minutes. Meanwhile, combine butter, sherry, jelly and lemon juice. Remove bacon from pheasant. Dredge breast lightly with flour and pour liquid over. Continue roasting a further 15 minutes, basting 2–3 times with pan liquid. Serve this liquid as a sauce. Serves 3–4.

PICKLES

The word 'pickles' usually describes coarsely chopped fruits and vegetables which are preserved in brine or vinegar. Home-made pickles add flavour and variety to all sorts of foods, and with chutneys, belong to the tradition of the English kitchen; the art of making them should not be allowed to die out.

They are, in a way, a legacy from the days of the British Raj in India, when these condiments were a very welcome addition to English food, especially simple cold meats. The British took to these exotic spicy products with open arms, and there was hardly a cookery book of the 19th century which didn't include recipes for relishes, pickles, chutneys and sauces. At the same time, silver cruet sets, filled with glass sauce bottles, were introduced and became a standard utensil on every table.

There is no special equipment needed for pickles, but because of their acidity, be sure to use stoneware, pottery, glass or plastic bowls for brining. Saucepans used should be un-chipped enamel or stainless steel. Use clean, wooden spoons for stirring.

Store pickles in clean glass jars, preferably with glass lids. Plastic-plated metal lids can be used but *never* use metal ones. Glass coffee jars with plastic seals are also good.

A special mixture of spices is prepared as pickling spice, containing many of the necessary spices. **See recipes.**

See also *Chutney.*

Crisp Bread-And-Butter Pickles

90 g/3 oz (¼ cup) coarse salt; 120 ml/4 fl oz (½ cup) water; 1.25 kg/2½ lb (10 cups) very finely sliced cucumbers; 4 medium onions, sliced into rings; 1 large red or green pepper, cored, seeded and sliced; 310 g/10 oz (1¼ cups) sugar; 300 ml/½ pint (1¼ cups) vinegar; ½ tbsp mustard seeds; ¼ tsp turmeric; ¼ tsp whole cloves.

Dissolve salt in water and pour over sliced vegetables. Put some ice on top of cucumbers. Use about 750 ml/1¼ pints (3 cups) crushed ice; it is the ice and salt that give an almost brittle, crisp pickle. Let stand for 3 hours, weighted with a plate. Drain. Combine sugar, vinegar and spices and bring to the boil. Add vegetables and return almost to boiling point. Do not boil. Pack into sterilized jars, fill to overflowing, and seal. Makes 2.25 litres/4 pints (10 cups).

Courgette Pickles

1 kg/2 lb (8 cups) small courgettes (zucchini), finely sliced; 2 medium onions, finely sliced; 75 g/2½ oz (¼ cup) salt; 500 ml/18 fl oz (2 cups) white vinegar; 250 g/8 oz (1 cup) sugar; 1 tsp celery seeds; 1 tsp mustard seeds; 1 tsp turmeric; ½ tsp dry mustard.

Place courgette (zucchini) and onion slices in a crock or bowl. Cover with water and add salt. Let stand for 1 hour, then drain. Mix remaining ingredients in a saucepan and bring to the boil. Pour over courgette (zucchini) and onion. Let stand for 1 hour. Put in pan, bring to the boil and cook for 3 minutes. Pack mixture into hot sterilized jars and seal. Makes 1.5 litres/2½ pints (6 cups).

Cauliflower Pickles

1 medium head cauliflower, broken into florets; 125 g/4 oz (1 cup) tiny white onions, peeled; 90 g/3 oz (⅓ cup) salt; 1.2 litres/2 pints (5 cups) white vinegar; 180 g/6 oz (¾ cup) sugar; 1 tsp turmeric; 1 tbsp mustard seeds; ½ tbsp celery seeds; 1 red chilli.

Mix vegetables with salt and ice cubes, and cover with more ice cubes. Let stand for 3 hours. Drain. Mix remaining ingredients in a large saucepan and bring to the boil, stirring to dissolve sugar. Add cauliflower and onions. Cook for 10 minutes or until tender but not soft. Pack into hot sterilized jars. Reheat liquid to boiling. Pour over vegetables and seal. Makes 1.2–1.5 litres/ 2–2½ pints (5–6 cups).

Chow-Chow

A lovely, golden relish with a mustardy tang.

500 g/1 lb (2 cups) green tomatoes, chopped; 3 small cucumbers, chopped; 1 red or green pepper, cored, seeded and chopped; ½ small cauliflower, chopped; 1 bunch celery, chopped; 500 g/1 lb (4 cups) small white onions, peeled; 250 g/8 oz (1 cup) green beans, cut into short lengths; 1 litre/1¾ pints (4 cups) boiling water; 75 g/2½ oz (¼ cup) salt; 500 ml/18 fl oz (2 cups) cider vinegar; 250 g/8 oz (1 cup) sugar; 2 tbsp celery seeds; 2 tbsp dry mustard; 2 tbsp turmeric; ½ tbsp whole allspice; ½ tbsp pepper; ½ tbsp ground cloves.

Combine vegetables in a large bowl. Cover with boiling water, add salt and let stand for 1 hour. Drain. Rinse well in cold water and drain again. Mix remaining ingredients in a large saucepan and bring to the boil. Add vegetables and cook until tender, stirring frequently. Spoon vegetables into hot, sterilized jars. Fill with cooking liquid and seal. Makes 2.25 litres/4 pints (10 cups).

Dill Cucumber Pickles

25 cucumbers, 8–10 cm (3–4 in) long; 500 ml/18 fl oz (2 cups) cider vinegar; 180 g/6 oz (⅔ cup) salt; 1.2 litres/2 pints (5 cups) water; sprigs fresh dill; cloves garlic, peeled.

Put cucumbers in a large bowl, cover with cold water and let stand overnight. Drain and pack into hot, sterilized jars. Combine vinegar, salt and water in a saucepan and bring to the boil. Pour over the cucumbers. Add 1–2 sprigs of dill and a clove garlic to each jar and seal. Makes about 2 litres/ 3½ pints (8 cups).

Mustard Pickles

(Piccalilli)

750 g/1½ lb (6 cups) small cucumbers, sliced; 250 g/8 oz (1 cup) green tomatoes, diced; 500 g/1 lb (4 cups) small white onions, peeled; 3 green peppers, cored, seeded and diced; ½ cauliflower, cut into small pieces; 75 g/2½ oz (¼ cup) salt; 1.2 litres/2 pints (5 cups) cold water; 60 g/2 oz (½ cup) flour; 3 tbsp dry mustard; 1 tbsp turmeric; 1 litre/ 1¾ pints (4 cups) cider vinegar; 250 g/8 oz (1 cup) sugar.

Put cucumbers, tomatoes, onions, peppers and cauliflower in a large bowl. Mix salt with water, pour over vegetables, cover and let stand for 8 hours or overnight. Drain and rinse under cold running water. Put vegetables in a large saucepan, cover them with fresh cold water and bring to the boil. Drain in a colander once again. Put flour, mustard and turmeric in the pan. Stir in enough vinegar to make a smooth paste, then gradually add remaining vinegar and sugar, stirring well. Bring to the boil, stirring constantly, and cook until thick and smooth. Add vegetables and cook, stirring, until heated through. Spoon into hot, sterilized jars filling them completely and seal. Makes about 2.25 litres/4 pints (10 cups).

Curried Aubergine Pickle

8 dried red chillies; 5 tsp chopped garlic; 4 tsp chopped fresh ginger; 2 tbsp black mustard seeds; 2½ tsp turmeric; 400 ml/⅔ pint (1⅔ cups) oil; 1.5 kg (3 lb) aubergines (eggplant), cubed; 3 tsp salt; 90 g/3 oz (½ cup) firmly packed brown sugar; 175 g/6 fl oz (¾ cup) vinegar; 2 tsp Garam Masala (page 139).

Soak chillies in hot water for 5 minutes. Drain, reserving water. Place chillies, garlic, ginger, mustard seeds and some of the water in which the chillies soaked in a blender or food processor and blend on high speed until puréed. Combine with turmeric. Heat oil and fry blended mixture for a few minutes, then add aubergine (eggplant) cubes. Cover and cook on low heat until aubergine (eggplant) is soft, stirring now and then. Add salt, sugar and vinegar and simmer until thick, stirring frequently to prevent burning. Stir in garam masala. Bottle in sterilized jars. Store covered. Makes about 1 litre/1¾ pints (4 cups).

Red or Green Pepper Relish

You can chop the vegetables for this and other relishes coarse or fine. Use a food processor, if you have one.

12 red or green peppers, or a combination, cored, seeded and chopped; 6 onions, chopped; 6 sticks celery, chopped; 500 ml/18 fl oz (2 cups) cider vinegar; 250 g/8 oz (1 cup) sugar; 1 tbsp salt; ½ tbsp mustard or celery seeds.

Cover vegetables with boiling water, then drain. Put them in a large saucepan, cover with cold water, bring to the boil and drain again. Mix vinegar, sugar, salt and mustard or celery seeds in pan and bring to the boil. Add vegetables and simmer for about 10 minutes. Adjust seasoning if necessary. Spoon vegetables into hot, sterilized jars. Fill to overflowing with cooking liquid and seal. Makes 1.6 litres/2¾ pints (7 cups).

Fresh Dill Pickles

(Kosher Style)

750 ml/1¼ pints (3 cups) vinegar; 750 ml/1¼ pints (3 cups) water; 6 tbsp salt; fresh or dried dill; cloves garlic, sliced; mustard seeds; 30–36 cucumbers, 8–10 cm (3–4 in) long.

Make a brine of the vinegar, water and salt. Bring to the boil. Put a generous layer of dill, ½–1 clove garlic and 1½ tsp mustard seeds in each sterilized 1.2 litre/2 pint (5 cup) jar. Pack cucumbers tightly in jars. When half filled with cucumbers, add another layer of dill and complete packing. Fill jars with boiling brine, leaving 1 cm (½ in) headspace. Put caps on jars, screwing bands tight. Process for 5 minutes in boiling water bath. Pickles will shrivel somewhat after processing, but they will later plump in sealed jar. Makes about 3 × 1.2 litre/2 pint (5 cup) jars.

Mixed Pickles

A sweet and spicy pickle, good with cold meats and toasted cheese or simply with bread and cheese.

6 green tomatoes, chopped; 2 green peppers, cored, seeded and chopped; 1 red pepper, cored, seeded and chopped; 3 onions, chopped; ½ small cabbage, chopped; 2 tbsp salt; ½ tbsp whole cloves; 1 cinnamon stick; ½ tbsp whole allspice; 280 g/9 oz (1½ cups) firmly packed brown sugar; 1 tsp celery seeds; 1 tbsp mustard seeds; 250 ml/8 fl oz (1 cup) cider vinegar.

Sprinkle vegetables with salt, cover and let stand overnight. Cover with cold water, then drain. Tie cloves, cinnamon and allspice in a muslin bag and place with remaining ingredients in a large saucepan. Add vegetables and bring to the boil. Reduce heat and simmer for about 15 minutes. Spoon vegetables into hot, sterilized jars. Remove bag of spices from cooking liquid, fill jars to overflowing with cooking liquid and seal. Makes 2 litres/3½ pints (8 cups).

Celery Relish

This unusual relish is particularly sweet and crunchy.

125 g/4 oz (½ cup) sugar; 2 tsp salt; ½ tsp dry mustard; ¼ tsp ground cloves; ¼ tsp ground allspice; ¼ tsp cinnamon; ¼ tsp celery seeds; 250–350 ml/8–12 fl oz (1–1½ cups) cider vinegar; 2 bunches celery, chopped; 6 large tomatoes, chopped; 1 red pepper, cored, seeded and chopped.

Mix all ingredients well in a large saucepan. Bring to the boil, then reduce heat and simmer until thick, about 1 hour. Spoon vegetables into hot, sterilized jars. Fill to overflowing with cooking liquid, and seal. Makes 2 litres/3½ pints (8 cups).

P

PIE

Although there are exceptions, a pie usually consists of a filling topped with a crust; it may or may not have a bottom crust as well. Fillings range from hearty meats to delicate fruits, and the crust can be made from various kinds of pastry (dough), crumbs, scone dough, meringue or even mashed potato. What they all have in common is that a pie is invariably acclaimed as a treat and a sign of a caring cook. **See recipes.**

One-crust Pies

To make a pie with a top pastry (dough) crust only, prepare filling and, if it is cooked, cool it completely. Place in a pie dish or tart plate just large enough to hold it, mounding it up in the centre to support the crust. If filling is not firm enough to mound, provide support by placing a pie funnel or an upturned egg cup in the centre of the dish before putting in filling.

Roll out pastry (dough) 5 mm (¼ in) thick, and cut a shape about 4 cm (1½ in) larger than top of dish. Cut a strip from the outside edge of this piece, slightly wider than rim of dish. Dampen rim with water and press pastry (dough) strip on to it, cutting ends to fit and dampening them to join. Moisten top of pastry (dough) strip.

Lift remaining pastry (dough) on a lightly floured rolling pin and lay it loosely over dish. Press pastry (dough) lid firmly on to dampened strip. Trim off overhang with a sharp knife, holding up the dish on one hand and cutting with the other, slanting the knife slightly under the rim, as you turn the dish.

If using flaky pastry (paste): With the back of a finger, press round the lid so that it is pushed out slightly beyond the rim of the dish. At the same time, with a knife held horizontally, lightly tap cut edges of pastry (dough) all round. This is called 'knocking up' the pastry (dough) and will give a flaky edge.

Flute the crust by drawing the back of a knife across the edge at 1 cm (½ in) intervals, bringing the knife up and in, while with your other thumb you press the pastry (dough) down just in front of the knife. Pull the pastry (dough) with the knife, do not cut it. Cut a few small slits in pastry (dough) and pierce through centre into pie funnel, if using. Glaze (avoiding cut edges) and bake as directed.

If using short pastry: Press edge of pastry (dough) out so that it is pushed slightly beyond the rim of the dish. Flute edge with your fingers or mark by pressing all round with the tines of a fork. Cut a few small slits in the pastry (dough) and pierce through centre into pie funnel, if using. Glaze and bake as directed in recipe.

Two-crust Pies

A two-crust pie can be made with both top and bottom crusts of short (basic pie dough) or flaky pastry (paste), or it can be made with short pastry beneath and flaky pastry on top.

Divide pastry (dough) into two portions, one a little larger than the other. Roll out larger portion about 3 mm ($\frac{1}{8}$ in) thick, and cut a shape which will line the dish with about 2 cm ($\frac{3}{4}$ in) overhang. Lift pastry (dough) on a lightly floured rolling pin and fit it into the dish, easing it in loosely without stretching it. Use fingertips or a small ball of pastry (dough) dipped in flour, to press crust against the dish so that no air is trapped between.

If filling is very juicy, brush bottom and sides of crust with lightly beaten egg, egg white or, for a sweet pie, melted jam, and allow it to dry for a few minutes. Place filling in dish as described under 'One-crust Pies'.

Roll other portion of pastry (dough) about 5 mm ($\frac{1}{4}$ in) thick to a shape about 2.5 cm (1 in) larger than top of dish. Moisten rim of bottom crust with water. Lift top crust on to a lightly floured rolling pin and lay it loosely over the dish. Press top and bottom crust firmly together. Trim off overhang with a sharp knife, as for One-crust Pies.

With the back of a finger, press round the pastry (dough) lid, so that it is pushed out slightly beyond the rim of the dish. Then 'knock up' the edges as described under 'One-crust Pies'. Cut a few small slits in pastry (dough) and pierce through centre. Glaze and bake as directed in recipe.

Decorating a Pie

Two-crust pies may be decorated with flowers, leaves, tassels or tiny fruits made from the pastry (dough) trimmings. Secure to the crust with beaten egg or egg white, and glaze. Cover decorations with foil if they are browning too much before pie is ready.

Pastry Fruits: Shape several tiny pastry

Decorating a pie

(dough) balls and join to make a cluster of berries; or shape small apples, pears, etc. Poke holes in the tops with a fine skewer and insert pastry (dough) stems or leaves.

Pastry Leaves: Cut pastry (dough) into strips, cut diagonally across into diamonds and trim to leaf shapes. Mark veins with the blunt edge of a knife **(Fig 1 below)** and arrange on pie **(2)**.

Pastry Rose: Cut 3 pastry (dough) strips about 1 × 5 cm ($\frac{1}{2}$ × 2 in). Roll one strip into a cylinder, wrap a second strip loosely round it and pinch base in to open out top; then wrap the third strip round from the opposite side and pinch base in again.

Pastry Tassel: Cut a pastry (dough) strip about 8 × 2.5 cm (3 × 1 in). Cut this strip across like a fringe to about $\frac{2}{3}$ of its width **(3)**, then roll up lengthways, pinching the base together. Place in centre of pie **(4)** and open out the fringe **(5)**.

Lattice-top Pies

A lattice top is a decorative finish to a pie with an attractive filling such as fruit. Roll out dough and cut strips 1–2 cm ($\frac{1}{2}$–$\frac{3}{4}$ in) wide. Arrange the strips on the filling in rows at right angles to each other.

Or weave strips as follows: lay half the strips across the dish, about 2 cm ($\frac{3}{4}$ in) apart. Fold back every second strip halfway. Place a strip at right angles across the unfolded strips. Unfold the doubled strips and fold back the alternate ones. Lay another cross strip about 2 cm ($\frac{3}{4}$ in) from the first. Continue, working towards the edge, then repeat the process, starting from the other side of the centre line. Strips should be loosely arranged, without stretching.

When the whole pie is latticed, dampen the ends of the strips and press them to the bottom crust or to the edge of the dish. Fold edge of bottom crust over ends of strips, or for a one-crust pie, cover ends with a strip of pastry (dough) round the dampened rim of the dish.

Meat Pies

500 g (1 lb) braising steak; 2 tbsp flour; 1 tsp salt; freshly ground black pepper; 120 ml/4 fl oz ($\frac{1}{2}$ cup) water; 1 × 375 g/12 oz packet frozen puff pastry (paste), thawed; beaten egg to glaze.

Trim gristle and fat from steak and cut into thin shreds, then chop finely. Dust with flour, salt and pepper and place in a pudding basin or other heatproof bowl with water. Cover with foil and tie in place with string, or use a snap-on lid. Place in a saucepan with enough boiling water to come halfway up sides of bowl, and simmer for 2 hours or until meat is very tender. Replace water as necessary to maintain level. Allow to cool completely. Roll out dough thin and cut $\frac{3}{4}$ of it into round, oblong or square shapes to fit individual pie tins (pans). Line tins (pans) with dough, and fill about $\frac{3}{4}$ full with meat filling. Cut lids from remaining dough, dampen edges and press into place. Cut a vent in top of each pie for steam to escape. Chill for 15 minutes, then brush with beaten egg. Bake in a preheated moderately hot oven (200°C/400°F, Gas Mark 6) for 25 minutes or until crust is puffed and golden. Serve with Tomato Sauce (see page 272). Makes 4–6 small pies.

Beef and Burgundy Pie

A restaurant favourite, this rich beef filling can be made into one large pie or individual ones, and topped with flaky pastry or a tender scone crust.

2 tbsp oil; 30 g/1 oz (2 tbsp) butter; 60 g (2 oz) pickled (salt) pork, diced; 12 button onions, peeled; 250 g/8 oz (2 cups) button mushrooms; 1 kg (2 lb) shin of beef (fore shank of beef), cubed; 3 tbsp seasoned flour; 1 large onion, chopped; 1 tsp chopped fresh marjoram or $\frac{1}{4}$ tsp dried; 2 tsp chopped fresh thyme or $\frac{1}{2}$ tsp dried; 250 ml/8 fl oz (1 cup) burgundy or other red wine; 250 ml/8 fl oz (1 cup) beef stock (bouillon); salt and freshly ground black pepper; 1 quantity Flaky or Rough Puff Pastry (page 275), or 1 quantity Scone Dough (page 382); beaten egg or milk to glaze.

Heat oil and butter in a large, heavy saucepan or flameproof casserole. Dry pickled pork well and fry until crisp and golden. Remove pork with a slotted spoon and reserve. Brown first button onions, then mushrooms, in fat in pan removing each when done. Toss beef with seasoned flour and brown, a few pieces at a time. Add chopped onion and cook gently until soft,

| 1 | 2 | 3 | 4 | 5 |

then return pork and beef to the saucepan and add herbs, wine and stock (bouillon). Cover and simmer very gently on top of stove, or place in a preheated cool oven (150°C/300°F, Gas Mark 2). Cook until beef is tender, 1½–2½ hours. Add button onions and cook a further 15 minutes, then add mushrooms and cook 10 minutes more. Taste and adjust seasoning. Cool completely.

For pie with pastry (dough) crust: Spoon beef into a pie dish just large enough to hold it, mounded slightly, or into 6 individual pie dishes. Roll out dough and cover dish. Decorate with roses or tassels and leaves made from pastry (dough) trimmings (see page 290). Chill 20 minutes. Cut a few small slits in crust and glaze with beaten egg. Bake in a preheated hot oven (230°C/450°F, Gas Mark 8) for about 10 minutes or until pastry is well risen and beginning to colour, then reduce heat to moderate (180°C/350°F, Gas Mark 4) and continue baking until pastry (dough) is golden-brown and filling heated through, 25–35 minutes more for a large pie, 15–20 minutes more for individual pies. Cover loosely with foil if crust is browning too much.

For pie with scone crust: Spoon filling into pie dish, casserole or 6 individual ramekins, to come 1 cm (½ in) below rim. For a large pie, pat out scone dough to 1 cm (½ in) thick and cut into 12 scones. Place scones close together on top of filling. For small pies, pat out dough, cut 6 rounds to fit ramekins and place on filling. Brush tops with milk. Bake in a preheated very hot oven (240°C/475°F, Gas Mark 9) for 8–10 minutes or until scone crust is well-risen and golden, then reduce heat to moderate (180°C/350°F, Gas Mark 4), cover loosely with foil and continue baking until filling is heated through, 20–30 minutes more. Serves 6.

Fisherman's Pie

500 g (1 lb) fillets white fish; 60 g/2 oz (4 tbsp) butter; 1 tbsp lemon juice; 500 ml/18 fl oz (2 cups) milk; 1 onion, finely chopped; 1 bouquet garni; pinch nutmeg; 3 tbsp flour; 4 tbsp single (light) cream; 45 g/1½ oz (⅓ cup) grated Cheddar cheese; large pinch dry mustard; salt and freshly ground black pepper; 2 tbsp chopped parsley; 90 g/3 oz (½ cup) cooked peas; 3 hard-boiled (hard-cooked) eggs, quartered; 1 quantity Rough Puff or Flaky Pastry (page 275), or 1 × 375 g/12 oz packet frozen puff pastry (paste), thawed; beaten egg to glaze.

Place fish in an ovenproof dish, dot with half the butter and drizzle lemon juice over. Cover with foil and cook in a preheated moderate oven (180°C/350°F, Gas Mark 4) for 20 minutes. Remove any skin or bones

and flake fish, reserving juices. Heat milk in a saucepan with onion, bouquet garni and nutmeg until bubbles form round edge. Remove from heat and stand 5 minutes, then remove bouquet garni. Melt remaining butter in a heavy saucepan, stir in flour and cook on low heat 1 minute. Remove from heat, cool a little and add milk, stirring until smoothly blended. Return to medium heat and stir until boiling. Remove from heat, stir in cream, cheese and mustard and season with salt and pepper. Fold fish and its juices, parsley, peas and eggs into sauce. Cool completely, then spoon into pie dish just large enough to hold it. Cover with pastry (dough) and chill 20 minutes. Cut a few small slits in top and brush with beaten egg. Bake in a preheated hot oven (230°C/450°F, Gas Mark 8) for 10–15 minutes or until crust is well-risen and beginning to brown, then reduce heat to moderate (180°C/350°F, Gas Mark 4) and continue baking until crust is golden-brown and filling is heated through, a further 25–30 minutes. Cover top loosely with foil if pastry is overbrowning. Serves 6.

VARIATIONS
This pie is easy to vary for special occasions. Substitute shelled, cooked prawns (shrimp) or crab, poached scallops or fresh oysters for up to 250 g (8 oz) fish, and use scallop poaching liquid, oyster liquor or white wine in place of 120 ml/4 fl oz (½ cup) of the milk.

Vegetable Pie

500 ml/18 fl oz (2 cups) milk; 1 onion, finely chopped; 1 bouquet garni; pinch nutmeg; 60 g/2 oz (4 tbsp) butter; 3 tbsp flour; 30 g/1 oz (¼ cup) grated mild cheese; large pinch dry mustard; small pinch cayenne; salt and freshly ground black pepper; 560 g/1 lb 2 oz (3 cups) diced or sliced cooked vegetables – beans, peas, carrots, corn, fennel, broccoli, cauliflower, peppers, mushrooms, celery; 1 quantity Rough Puff or Flaky Pastry (page 275) or 1 × 375 g/12 oz packet frozen puff pastry (paste), thawed; beaten egg to glaze.

Heat milk in a saucepan with onion, bouquet garni and nutmeg until bubbles form round edge. Remove from heat and stand 5 minutes, then remove bouquet garni. Melt butter in a heavy saucepan, stir in flour and cook on low heat 1 minute. Remove from heat, cool a little and add milk, stirring until smoothly blended. Return to medium heat and stir until boiling. Remove from heat, stir in cheese, mustard and cayenne and season with salt and pepper. Fold vegetables into sauce and cool completely. Spoon mixture into a pie dish just large enough to hold it. Cover with pastry (dough) and chill for 20 minutes. Cut a few small slits in top and brush with beaten egg. Bake in a preheated

hot oven (230°C/450°F, Gas Mark 8) for 10–15 minutes or until crust is well-risen and beginning to brown, then reduce heat to moderate (180°C/350°F, Gas Mark 4) and continue baking until crust is golden-brown and filling is heated through, a further 25–30 minutes. Cover top loosely with foil if crust is browning too much. Serve very hot. Serves 6.

Savoury Mince Pie

double quantity Savoury Mince (page 217); 1 quantity Shortcrust Pastry (page 274); beaten egg to glaze.

Spoon cool mince (ground meat mixture) into a pie plate or dish which will just hold it, and mound up a little in the centre. Roll out pastry (dough) and cover dish. If you have surplus dough, roll out, cut into triangles and bake with pie for extra servings. Chill 20 minutes. Cut a few small slits in crust and glaze with beaten egg. Bake the pie in a preheated hot oven (220°C/425°F, Gas Mark 7) about 10 minutes or until crust is beginning to colour, then reduce heat to moderate (180°C/350°F, Gas Mark 4) and continue baking until crust is golden-brown and filling heated through, 20–30 minutes more. Cover loosely with foil if crust is overbrowning. Serves 8.

Little Scottish Mutton Pies

These Glasgow favourites were once called 'Tuppenny Struggles' – and wonderful value they were with their generous meat filling and good gravy. Today, we make them more often with lamb than mutton but otherwise they are the same – a perfect example of how delicious simple, old-fashioned recipes can be.

500 g (1 lb) lean, boneless lamb, diced; 1 small onion, grated; ¼ tsp nutmeg; 4 tbsp beef stock; 2 tsp Worcestershire sauce; salt and freshly ground black pepper; 1 quantity Hot Water Pastry (page 276); beaten egg to glaze.

Mix lamb with onion, nutmeg, stock, Worcestershire sauce, salt and pepper. Divide pastry (dough) into 4 even portions. For each pie, take a portion and set aside ⅓ for lid (keep all dough you are not using in a covered bowl over hot water). Have ready a glass jar 8 cm (3 in) in diameter which has been rinsed out with hot water, dried and floured on the outside. Mould dough round jar, fasten on paper collar, fill and cover with pastry lid as described in Individual Raised Pork Pies (page 293). Glaze tops with beaten egg and cut a slit in each for steam to escape. Bake in a preheated moderate oven (180°C/350°F, Gas Mark 4) for 45 minutes, removing paper collars after 20 minutes and covering tops with foil if crusts are browning too much. Serve hot. Makes 4.

Spanish Fish Pie

4 tbsp olive oil; 1 large onion, finely chopped; 750 g (1½ lb) firm fillets white fish; 1 large tomato, peeled, seeded and finely chopped; 1 clove garlic, crushed; 2 tbsp finely chopped parsley; 1½ tsp salt; ½ tsp freshly ground black pepper; 1 tsp grated lemon rind; 45 g/1½ oz (¼ cup) chopped stuffed olives; 3 hard-boiled (hard-cooked) eggs, coarsely chopped; double quantity Rich Shortcrust Pastry (page 274).

Heat 3 tbsp of the oil in a heavy frying pan (skillet) and cook onion until soft and golden. Remove any skin and bones from fish, cut into fingers and add to pan with tomato, garlic, parsley, salt, pepper and lemon rind. Simmer for 10 minutes, stirring gently several times. Check seasoning, then allow to cool. Add olives and eggs. Roll out just over half the pastry (dough) thinly and use to line a 25 cm (10 in) pie plate. Spoon in cold filling. Roll out remaining dough and cover pie. Chill 20 minutes. Cut a few slits in the top for steam to escape and brush with remaining oil. Bake in a preheated moderately hot oven (200°C/400°F, Gas Mark 6) for 25 minutes or until crust is crisp and golden-brown. Serves 4–6.

Bacon and Egg Pie

Plain Shortcrust Pastry made with 250 g/8 oz (2 cups) flour (page 274); 250 g (8 oz) lean rashers (slices) bacon, rind removed and chopped; 4 eggs; 120 ml/4 fl oz (½ cup) single (light) cream; 2½ tbsp chopped parsley; salt and freshly ground black pepper; pinch nutmeg; beaten egg to glaze.

Roll out just over half the pastry (dough) and use to line a 20–23 cm (8–9 in) pie plate. Arrange bacon in pie shell. Break eggs and slip them in on top of bacon. Mix cream with parsley and season with salt, pepper and nutmeg. Pour over eggs. Roll out remaining pastry (dough) to make a lid and cover the pie. Make a slit in the centre and decorate with pastry (dough) leaves made from

trimmings, if liked. Rest in a cool place for 20 minutes, then glaze with beaten egg and bake in a preheated moderately hot oven (200°C/400°F, Gas Mark 6) for about 30 minutes, until golden-brown. Serve warm or cold. Serves 4–5.

Easter Cheese and Spinach Pie

(Torta Pasqualina)
Packaged filo (phyllo) makes this Italian pie easy to make.

250 g/8 oz (12 sheets) filo (phyllo) pastry; 90 g/3 oz (6 tbsp) butter, melted.
FILLING: *2 bunches spinach; 2 tbsp olive oil; 1 medium onion, finely chopped; salt and freshly ground black pepper; 500 g/1 lb (2 cups) Ricotta cheese; 120 ml/4 fl oz (½ cup) single (light) cream or evaporated milk; 30 g/1 oz (2 tbsp) butter; 6 eggs; ½ tsp dried marjoram; 90 g/3 oz (¾ cup) grated Parmesan cheese.*

FILLING: Cut tough white stalks from spinach, rinse leaves well and steam until tender. Drain and chop finely by hand or in a food processor fitted with a steel blade. Press in a sieve to remove any remaining moisture. Heat oil in a heavy saucepan and gently fry onion until soft but not brown. Add spinach and stir together for 1–2 minutes. Season with salt and pepper and set aside. Mash Ricotta in a bowl and stir in cream or evaporated milk and a good pinch of salt.

Line a greased 23–25 cm (9–10 in) pie dish with 6 sheets of filo (phyllo) pastry, brushing each with melted butter. (The filo (phyllo) will stay pliable as you work if you place it between 2 dry tea-towels with a dampened tea-towel on top.) Spread sixth layer of pastry with spinach mixture and spoon Ricotta over top. Make 6 hollows in Ricotta and put a little knob of butter in each. Break an egg into each hollow and season with salt, pepper and marjoram. Sprinkle Parmesan cheese over all. Cover filling with remaining sheets of filo (phyllo), brushing sheets with melted butter. Press edges firmly together and trim excess pastry. Prick top layer of filo (phyllo) with a fork and brush generously with butter. Bake pie in a preheated moderately hot oven (200°C/400°F, Gas Mark 6) for 40 minutes or until the pastry is golden-brown. Serve hot or cold. Serves 6 generously.

Finnish Meat Pie

In Finland, mashed potatoes are often added to the pastry (dough) for savoury pies and the filling may contain a mixture of meats.

PASTRY (DOUGH): *250 g/8 oz (2 cups) flour, sifted; ½ tsp sea salt; 370 g/12 oz (1½ cups) cold mashed potatoes; 125 g/4 oz (½ cup) butter, cut into small pieces; 2–4 tbsp iced*

water; beaten egg to glaze.
FILLING: *1 large onion, finely chopped; 30 g/1 oz (2 tbsp) butter; 500 g/1 lb (2 cups) minced (ground) topside (top round); 250 g/8 oz (1 cup) minced (ground) pork; 250 ml/8 fl oz (1 cup) beef stock; 175 ml/6 fl oz (¾ cup) single (light) cream; 1½ tsp sea salt; freshly ground black pepper; 2 tbsp chopped parsley; 125 g/4 oz (1 cup) cooked brown rice (40 g/1⅓ oz/⅓ cup raw).*

PASTRY (DOUGH): Combine flour, salt and potato in a large bowl. Add butter and rub (cut) into mixture with the fingertips. Add enough iced water to make a firm dough. Wrap in plastic wrap and chill for 30 minutes or longer.
FILLING: Fry onion in butter until soft and golden. Add meats and fry until brown, stirring and breaking up any lumps with a fork. Add stock, cream, salt and pepper and simmer for 15 minutes. Stir in parsley and rice. Check seasoning and allow to cool. Divide pastry (dough) in half and roll out one piece to a rectangle about 25 × 30 cm (10 × 12 in). Place on a greased shallow baking tin (pan) and cover with cold filling, leaving a margin of 2.5 cm (1 in) all around. Dampen edges. Roll out second piece of dough and cover filling, pressing edges firmly to seal. Prick top all over with a fork, glaze with beaten egg and decorate with dough trimmings. Bake in a preheated moderately hot oven (200°C/400°F, Gas Mark 6) for 30 minutes or until crust is crisp and golden-brown. Serve hot, warm or cold. Serves 6–8 as a main course, or 12 as an appetizer.

Raised Pork Pie

A true raised pie is made without a supporting mould, using hot water pastry (dough) which sets, when cool, into a sturdy shell that will stand by itself even before baking. The same pastry (dough) is used for the large cold pies which are called 'raised' but are made in decorative moulds.

1 kg (2 lb) pork, a mixture of lean and fat, cut into 1 cm (½ in) cubes; 1 tsp salt; 1 tbsp chopped mixed fresh herbs, or 1 tbsp chopped parsley mixed with 1 tsp dried herbs; pinch cayenne; freshly ground white pepper; 1 quantity Hot Water Pastry (page 276); beaten egg to glaze.
JELLIED STOCK: *370 g (12 oz) pork bones; 1 onion; 1.5 litres/2½ pints (6 cups) water; salt; 1 bouquet garni; 6 white peppercorns.*

Make jellied stock the day before preparing pie. Place all ingredients in a heavy saucepan, cover and simmer very, very gently for about 4 hours; replenishing water as needed. Strain and allow to cool. Adjust seasoning if necessary. Chill and lift off fat.

Combine pork with salt, herbs, cayenne and plenty of pepper. Set aside. Set aside ⅓

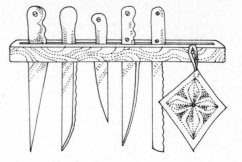

of pastry (dough) for the lid, keeping it covered in a bowl over hot water to prevent it hardening. Flatten remaining dough with your fist, lift it into a loose-sided 20 cm (8 in) pie mould or loose-bottomed tin (springform pan) and press it quickly on to the bottom and sides of the mould, bringing pastry (dough) just above rim. Fill mould to brim with pork filling, doming it slightly to support top crust. Roll out remaining dough and cover pie, pressing top crust on to sides. Trim off overhang (return it to warm bowl), press edge all round to push it out a little and flute with fingers. Cut a hole in centre of pie; decorate with a pastry (dough) rose, placed over hole, and some leaves made from trimmings (see page 290). Glaze pie with beaten egg. Bake in a preheated moderate oven (180°C/350°F, Gas Mark 4) for 2 hours, covering top with a piece of foil if crust is browning too much. Remove from oven and allow to cool in the mould. Warm jellied stock gently until just melted. Remove pastry (dough) rose from pie, place a funnel in the hole and gradually pour in stock to fill pie. Allow to cool and set. To serve, replace pastry (dough) rose, remove sides of mould and lift pie on to a serving platter. Serves 6–8.
VARIATIONS

Veal and Ham Pie: Follow recipe for Pork Pie, but substitute veal bones for pork bones to make the stock and use the following filling instead of pork filling: 750 g (1½ lb) boneless shoulder of veal, cut into 2.5 cm (1 in) cubes; 125 g/4 oz (½ cup) lean cooked ham, cut into small strips; 1 small onion, finely chopped; 2 tsp finely chopped parsley; 1 tsp grated lemon rind; salt and freshly ground black pepper. Arrange veal, ham and onion in layers, scattering with parsley and lemon rind and seasoning with salt and pepper. Dome top slightly. For a variation, hard-boiled (hard-cooked) eggs may be placed end to end when the pie is half-filled, and covered with remaining filling. This gives a slice of egg in the middle of each slice of pie when cut.

Individual Raised Pork Pies: The ingredients given for Raised Pork Pie will make 2 small pies 10–13 cm (4–5 in) in diameter. Prepare jellied stock and filling as directed in recipe. Make Hot Water Pastry and divide in half. For each pie, take half of pastry (dough) and set aside ⅓ for lid (keep all dough you are not using in a covered bowl over hot water). Have ready a large glass jar 10–13 cm (4–5 in) in diameter which has been rinsed out with hot water, dried and floured on the outside. Press dough out to a round, stand jar in the middle and mould dough quickly around it, working it up the sides. Turn jar upside-down with dough on it and continue to mould, pulling dough gently until it is about 10 cm (4 in) in depth. Place a collar of double greaseproof (waxed) paper around the dough and secure it with a paper clip.

Allow dough to cool, then carefully ease jar out of the dough case. Stand case on a baking tray. Spoon in filling, mounding it up. Roll out reserved dough for lid, dampen edges and cover pie, pinching lid on to sides. Make a hole in centre of lid and decorate with a pastry (dough) rose or leaves and berries placed over hole (see page 290). Glaze top with beaten egg and bake in a preheated moderate oven (180°C/350°F, Gas Mark 4) for 1–1½ hours, removing paper collar after 30 minutes and covering top with a piece of foil if necessary to prevent overbrowning. When cool, fill up carefully with stock as for large pie. Makes 2.

Lemon Chiffon Pie

Although it has no top crust, its American origin gives this lovely dessert the name of 'pie' – Americans, a nation of pie-lovers, use the name for open and covered varieties.

CRUMB CRUST: *140 g/4½ oz (1½ cups) fine sweet biscuit (vanilla wafer) crumbs; 75 g/2½ oz (⅓ cup) caster sugar; 75 g/2½ oz (5 tbsp) butter, melted.*
FILLING: *3 tsp gelatine; 4 tbsp cold water; 250 g/8 oz (1 cup) sugar; pinch salt; 1 tsp grated lemon rind; 120 ml/4 fl oz (½ cup) lemon juice; 4 eggs, separated; whipped cream to decorate.*

CRUMB CRUST: Mix crumbs, sugar and butter in a bowl. Turn mixture into a 23 cm (9 in) pie plate and press and pat it out evenly on to the bottom and sides. Bake in a preheated moderate oven (180°C/350°F, Gas Mark 4) for 8–10 minutes. Remove and cool.
FILLING: Soften gelatine in cold water, then stir over simmering water until dissolved. Place 125 g/4 oz (½ cup) of the sugar, the salt, lemon rind and lemon juice in the top of a double saucepan (double boiler) or a heatproof bowl which will fit over a saucepan. Add egg yolks and gelatine mixture, stirring until well blended. Place over simmering water and stir until mixture thickens a little. Pour into a bowl and chill until mixture mounds when dropped from a spoon. Beat egg whites until foamy, then gradually beat in remaining sugar, beating until smooth and shiny. Fold egg whites into lemon mixture. Spread into pie shell and chill until serving time. Decorate with whipped cream. Serves 6–8.
VARIATION

Lime Chiffon Pie: Follow recipe for Lemon Chiffon Pie, using ginger biscuit (gingersnap) crumbs in the crust, and substituting grated lime rind and juice for lemon rind and juice.

Latticed Raisin Pie

250 ml/8 fl oz (1 cup) orange juice; 120 ml/4 fl oz (½ cup) water; 180 g/6 oz (1 cup) seeded raisins; 370 g/12 oz (1½ cups)

sugar; 4 tbsp flour; 3 tbsp lemon juice; large pinch salt; unsweetened Rich Shortcrust Pastry made with 250 g/8 oz (2 cups) flour (page 274).
GLAZE: *lightly beaten egg white; caster sugar.*

Bring orange juice and water to the boil, remove from heat and stir in raisins. Stand 2 hours, then stir in sugar, flour, lemon juice and salt. Return to low heat and stir constantly until boiling and well thickened. Cool completely. Divide pastry (dough) into 2 portions, one a little larger than the other. Roll out larger portion and use to line a 23 cm (9 in) pie plate. Spoon in raisin mixture, mounding it slightly. Roll out remaining dough and cover pie with a lattice top (see page 290). Brush with egg white and sprinkle with caster sugar. Bake in a preheated hot oven (220°C/425°F, Gas Mark 7) for 10 minutes, then reduce heat to moderate (180°C/350°F, Gas Mark 4) and bake 25–30 minutes longer or until top is browned. Serves 6–8.

Brandy Alexander Pie

3 tsp gelatine; 120 ml/4 fl oz (½ cup) cold water; 150 g/5 oz (⅔ cup) sugar; pinch salt; 3 eggs, separated; 4 tbsp brandy; 4 tbsp crème de cacao; 500 ml/18 fl oz (2 cups) double (heavy) cream, whipped; chocolate curls to decorate (page 72).
CRUMB CRUST: *105 g/3½ oz (1¼ cups) sweet biscuit (vanilla wafer) crumbs; 60 g/2 oz (¼ cup) sugar; 75 g/2½ oz (5 tbsp) butter, melted.*

Soften gelatine in cold water in a saucepan. Add half of the sugar, the salt and egg yolks. Stir to blend. Heat over low heat, stirring, until gelatine dissolves and mixture thickens. Do not boil. Remove from heat and stir in brandy and crème de cacao. Chill until mixture starts to thicken slightly.
CRUMB CRUST: Combine all ingredients and press evenly over bottom and sides of a 23 cm (9 in) pie plate. Chill until ready to use. Beat egg whites until stiff. Gradually beat in remaining sugar and fold into the thickened mixture. Fold in half of the whipped cream. Turn into chilled crust and chill for several hours or overnight. Decorate with remaining cream and chocolate curls. Serves 6–8.

PIGEON

A small game bird with a distinctive, almost sweet flavour, which is highlighted by a tangy, sweet-sour sauce. If young and tender, pigeon may be roasted, with a slice of bacon or pork fat or a lump of butter to keep it moist. Alternatively, and especially if it is older, pigeon may be braised or stewed.

Young fledgling pigeons, bred especially for the table, are called squab. They have a more delicate, tender flesh and are better suited to roasting in a very hot oven.

In general, allow one squab or one pigeon per person. If pigeon breasts only are offered, allow 3–4 breasts per person.

PIKELET

This is a version of an old Scottish scone or 'girdle' cake, which is a popular item on the afternoon tea tray. Pikelets can be served warm or cold with butter and honey or jam, or cold with jam and cream. Pikelets can be reheated briefly in a warm oven or under a cool grill (broiler).

Pikelets

125 g/4 oz (1 cup) self-raising flour; ½ tsp salt; 2 tbsp sugar; 1 egg; 250 ml/8 fl oz (1 cup) milk; 30 g/1 oz (2 tbsp) butter, melted; fat for frying.

Sift flour and salt into a bowl. Stir in sugar and make a well in centre. Beat egg, add milk and butter and mix well. Pour into well in dry ingredients all at once and stir to make a smooth batter. Drop scant tablespoonsful of batter on to a hot, greased griddle or shallow frying pan (skillet). Cook until golden, then turn and cook other side until golden. Cool, wrapped in a clean tea-towel or napkin. Serve warm with butter or cold with jam and cream. Makes 25–30 × 8 cm (3 in) pikelets.

PILAF OR PILAFF, PILAU, PILAW

See page 332 for recipe.

PIMENTO

See *Allspice*.

PIMIENTO

Skinned sweet red peppers of a small, elong-ated variety, available canned in oil or brine.

Potato, Prawn and Pimiento Salad

A salad to serve as part of hors d'oeuvre variés or on an antipasto tray.

3 canned pimientos, drained; 4 medium waxy potatoes, cooked and diced; 3 hard-boiled (hard-cooked) eggs, cut into wedges;

125 g/4 oz (⅔ cup) small shelled deveined prawns (shrimp); 1 tbsp finely chopped onion; salt and freshly ground black pepper; 4 tbsp Vinaigrette Dressing (page 358); 5 tbsp Mayonnaise (page 204).

Cut 2 pimientos into squares and reserve the third. Lightly fold together all ingredients, except reserved pimiento and 8–10 of the prawns (shrimp). Spoon into a shallow square or oblong dish. Cut reserved pimiento into strips and garnish salad with strips arranged lattice-fashion, with a prawn (shrimp) in each space. Serves 4–6.

PINEAPPLE

A year-round favourite, doubly welcome in the cold winter months, when its golden sweetness reminds us that sunnier days are not too far away.

Pineapples are grown in tropical and sub-tropical climates, and with modern agricul-tural techniques, fresh pineapples are available at any time of the year. There is also the convenience of canned pineapple – in rings or chunks, crushed or as juice.

Fresh pineapple contains an enzyme, bromeline, similar to papain found in pawpaw, which acts on protein. For this reason, fresh pineapple can never be used in any preparation containing gelatine, or fresh cream. However, the enzyme is destroyed by heat and is not present in canned pineapple.

Fresh pineapple is best served simply, at the end of a rich meal or at breakfast. If fully ripe, it will need very little, if any, sugar. A ripe pineapple should be golden, with a rich sweet perfume and firm yet tender flesh. The green plumes should pull out easily.

Fresh or canned pineapple may also be added to a salad. And rings of pineapple, lightly fried in butter, are a good flavour contrast to hot baked ham, ham steaks or grilled (broiled) pork chops.

☐ **Basic Preparation:** To peel a fresh pineapple, using a sharp stainless steel knife, cut off top and base of pineapple. Hold pineapple firmly with one hand and cut

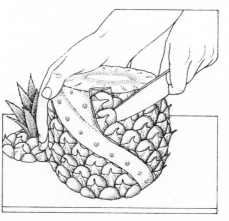

downwards, between eyes, at an angle of 45 degrees (see below). Remove strips of skin between eyes. This method eliminates waste and also gives the pineapple an attractive appearance. **See recipes.**

Pineapple Buttermilk Sherbet

500 ml/18 fl oz (2 cups) buttermilk; 125 g/4 oz (½ cup) sugar; 180 g/6 oz (1 cup) canned crushed pineapple; 1 egg white; 1½ tsp vanilla essence (extract).

Combine buttermilk, sugar and pineapple. Chill in freezer until mushy. Place in a chilled bowl. Add egg white and vanilla and beat mixture until light and fluffy. Pour into ice cream tray and freeze until firm, stirring occasionally. Serves 4.

Pineapple in Kirsch

1 ripe pineapple, peeled; sugar; 2 tbsp Kirsch.

Cut pineapple into quarters lengthways and remove core from each wedge. Cut each wedge into halves or quarters as desired. Arrange on dish, sprinkle with sugar to taste and Kirsch. Chill before serving. Serves 4–6.
VARIATIONS
Other fruits may be added to Pineapple in Kirsch – try strawberries, orange or mandarin segments, fresh grapes, passionfruit, kiwi fruit. Cointreau may be substituted for Kirsch. If warmed and poured over the pineapple just before serving, it may be flamed for presentation.

Pineapple Caribbean

1 small ripe pineapple, peeled; 2 tbsp brown sugar; grated rind 1 orange; pinch cinnamon; pinch nutmeg; 120 ml/4 fl oz (½ cup) orange juice; 30 g/1 oz (2 tbsp) butter; 4 tbsp rum; single (light) cream or ice cream to serve.

Cut pineapple into quarters lengthways and remove core from each wedge. Cut each wedge into slices. Arrange slices in buttered ovenproof dish. Mix brown sugar, orange rind and spices, sprinkle over pineapple then pour over juice. Dot with butter. Bake in preheated moderately hot oven (200°C/400°F, Gas Mark 6) for about 15 minutes. Warm rum, ignite and pour flaming over pineapple at table. Serve with cream or ice cream. Serves 4–6.
VARIATION
1 × 439 g/15½ oz can of pineapple rings, drained, may be substituted for fresh.

Chafing Dish Pineapple

1 ripe pineapple, peeled, cored and diced; 125 g/4 oz (½ cup) butter; 1½ tbsp brown sugar; 5 tbsp rum; 250 ml/8 fl oz (1 cup) single (light) cream.

P

Cook pineapple pieces in butter until golden-brown. Sprinkle with sugar and rum and continue cooking until all liquid is absorbed. Add cream, heat through and serve immediately. Serves 4–6.

Pineapple Whip

1 tbsp gelatine; 4 tbsp cold water; 1 × 439 g/ 15½ oz can pineapple chunks; 1 tbsp grated orange rind; 120 ml/4 fl oz (½ cup) plain yogurt; 1 tbsp honey.

Soften gelatine in cold water in a small saucepan for 5 minutes, then dissolve over gentle heat. Drain juice from pineapple, add enough water to make 350 ml/12 fl oz (1½ cups), then stir in dissolved gelatine. Chill to consistency of unbeaten egg white. Add orange rind, yogurt and honey and beat until thick. Fold in pineapple. Turn into bowl and chill until set. Serves 6–8.

Pineapple Upside-Down Cake

Serve with ice cream or custard.

CARAMEL: 75 g/2½ oz (5 tbsp) butter; 60 g/2 oz (⅓ cup) firmly packed brown sugar.
DECORATION: 3 rings canned pineapple; 6 glacé (candied) cherries; 6 walnut halves.
CAKE: 180 g/6 oz (1½ cups) self-raising flour; ½ tsp salt; 60 g/2 oz (4 tbsp) butter; 180 g/6 oz (¾ cup) caster sugar; 1 egg, well whisked; 120 ml/4 fl oz (½ cup) milk.

CARAMEL: Cream butter with sugar. Spread over bottom and sides of a greased and lined 20 cm (8 in) round cake tin (pan).
DECORATION: Cut through pineapple rings to make 6 thin rings; arrange these on caramel and decorate with cherries and walnuts.
CAKE: Sift flour and salt together 3 times. Cream butter with sugar, then beat in egg until light and fluffy. Stir in sifted flour alternately with milk. Spoon cake mixture carefully on top of the pineapple arrangement in the tin (pan). Bake in preheated moderate oven (180°C/350°F, Gas Mark 4) for 50–60 minutes. Invert on to serving plate immediately cake is removed from oven. Leave for a few minutes then remove tin (pan). Serves 6–8.

PINE NUT

The kernel from the cone of certain types of pine tree, some of which are very common in Mediterranean countries. Naturally, pine nuts often feature in traditional dishes of this region.

In Italy, pine nuts (called *pignoli*) go into the famous sauce, *Pesto alla Genovese* (see page 272). Often a decorative pattern of pine nuts will stud Lebanese kibbi, or toasted pine nuts will be used to garnish a rice pilaf or rice salad. Roasted and salted, pine nuts can be substituted for salted almonds.

Although they are more commonly used in savoury dishes, pine nuts are also made into macaroon-type biscuits (cookies) and sweets (candies). **See recipes.**

Pine Nut Sauce for Fish

60 g/2 oz (4 tbsp) butter; 60 g/2 oz (½ cup) pine nuts, sliced; 2 tbsp lemon juice.

Melt butter over low heat. Add pine nuts and cook gently for 5 minutes or until butter is slightly browned. Add lemon juice and heat. Pour over grilled (broiled) or pan-fried fish fillets. Makes about 175 ml/6 fl oz (¾ cup), sufficient for 4 fillets.

Spinach with Sultanas and Pine Nuts

1 bunch fresh spinach; 2 tbsp olive oil; salt and freshly ground black pepper; 90 g/3 oz (½ cup) sultanas (golden raisins); 60 g/2 oz (4 tbsp) butter; 90 g/3 oz (¾ cup) pine nuts.

Remove stalks and rinse spinach leaves. Pat leaves as dry as possible, then slice into fine shreds. Heat oil in a large frying pan (skillet). Add spinach, salt and pepper and toss over heat until spinach starts to give out juices. Add sultanas (golden raisins) and continue cooking over moderate heat until spinach is tender and juices have evaporated, turning and tossing often. In separate pan, heat butter and cook pine nuts until golden. Add to spinach and serve at once. Serves 4.

PIPERADE

This open-faced omelette is a speciality of the Basque country. It is quick to make if the pipérade mixture (onions, peppers and tomatoes) is made ahead.

Pipérade

2 tbsp oil; 2 onions, finely sliced; 1 red or green pepper, cored, seeded and cut into thin strips; 1 clove garlic, crushed; 2–3 tomatoes, peeled, seeded and sliced; salt and freshly ground black pepper; 15 g/½ oz (1 tbsp) butter; 8 eggs; 2–3 slices cooked ham, cut into strips; 2–3 tbsp chopped parsley.

Heat oil in a frying pan (skillet) and cook onions and pepper gently, covered, until they are tender but not browned. Add garlic and tomatoes, and cook gently about 5 minutes longer. Season with salt and pepper. Remove from pan and keep hot. In the frying pan (skillet) heat butter. Beat eggs with ¼ tsp salt and pepper and add to pan. Cook rapidly, stirring with a fork, to a creamy mass. Remove from pan and top with vegetable mixture, mixing a bit of it delicately into the eggs. Heat strips of ham in frying pan (skillet) and strew over pipérade. Sprinkle with parsley. Serves 4.

PIROSHKI (Pirozhki)

Some say that the Russians were the first to think of the delicious tidbits served with cocktails.

Piroshki, made in tiny cocktail sizes, served piping hot from the oven, make wonderful accompaniments to clear chicken or beef soups, with drinks, or may be served on their own as a first course. Allow at least 3 or 4 for each person.

There are several versions and many varied fillings. Piroshki may be made with yeast dough, shortcrust (basic pie dough), cream cheese pastry or choux pastry (paste), and filled with smoked pork and onion, vegetables, cream cheese or fish. Fried piroshki, filled with meat or cabbage, are a great favourite in Europe. **See recipes.**

Piroshki (with Cream Cheese Pastry)

PASTRY: 125 g/4 oz (½ cup) cream cheese; 125 g/4 oz (½ cup) butter; 180 g/6 oz (1½ cups) flour; beaten egg to glaze.
FILLING: 60 g/2 oz (4 tbsp) butter; 1 onion, chopped; 2–3 rashers (slices) bacon, or 90 g/3 oz speck, rind removed and chopped; salt and freshly ground black pepper.

PASTRY (DOUGH): Beat cream cheese with butter in a mixing bowl. Add sifted flour and mix to a dough. Wrap in greaseproof (waxed) paper and chill overnight or for several hours. (If left overnight, allow to stand at room temperature for 1 hour or so before rolling out.)

FILLING: Melt butter in a frying pan (skillet) and fry onion and bacon or speck until onion is transparent and bacon is crisp. Season with salt and pepper. Roll out pastry (dough) thinly and cut into 5 cm (2 in) rounds with a pastry cutter. Put 1 teaspoonful of filling on to each round, moisten edges with a little beaten egg and fold dough over to form a crescent shape. Seal edges well. Place on lightly greased baking trays. Brush with beaten egg and bake in a preheated moderately hot oven 200°C/400°F, Gas Mark 6) for 10 minutes or until golden brown. Cool slightly. Makes about 24.

Piroshki (with Yeast Dough)

Piroshki freeze well and once thawed, need no more than about 20 minutes reheating, wrapped in foil, in a moderate oven before serving.

30 g/1 oz (2 tbsp) fresh (compressed) yeast; 2½ tbsp sugar; 370 g/12 oz (3 cups) flour; 300 ml/½ pint (1¼ cups) milk; 125 g/4 oz (½ cup) butter; 2 tsp salt; 1 egg yolk, beaten; beaten egg to glaze.
FILLING: *3 large onions, finely chopped; 60 g/2 oz (4 tbsp) butter; 250 g (8 oz) speck or thick rasher (slice) bacon, rind removed and finely chopped; freshly ground white pepper.*

Combine yeast with ½ tbsp of sugar in a small bowl. Stir until yeast becomes liquid. Sprinkle with 1 tsp of flour and leave in a warm place. Meanwhile, heat milk, butter, salt and remaining sugar in a saucepan, stirring occasionally until milk is lukewarm. Sift remaining flour into a large mixing bowl. Make a well in centre and pour in milk mixture, yeast mixture and egg yolk. Stir with a wooden spoon, gradually incorporating flour. Beat dough with your hand for 3 minutes until it is smooth and elastic. Sprinkle with a little flour, cover with damp tea-towel and leave dough to rise in a warm place until dough has doubled in bulk – about 1 hour.
FILLING: Fry onions in butter until golden. Allow to cool. Mix the speck or bacon with onion and season with pepper. Turn dough on to a floured work surface and knead lightly. This is a soft dough. Tear off pieces of dough the size of a large tablespoon. Place 1 teaspoonful of filling in middle of each piece of dough, fold to enclose filling and mould dough into little balls.

Place piroshki on lightly greased baking trays and leave to rise in a warm place for 15 minutes. Brush with beaten egg and bake in a preheated hot oven (230°C/450°F, Gas Mark 8) for 10–15 minutes or until golden. Slide on to a clean tea-towel to keep warm until ready to serve. Makes 60 tiny cocktail, or 30 larger, piroshki.

Fried Piroshki

These dainty fried pastries are made to accompany soups in Russia.

YEAST DOUGH: *15 g/½ oz (1 tbsp) fresh (compressed) yeast; 4 tbsp lukewarm water; ½ tsp sugar; 120 ml/4 fl oz (½ cup) milk; 15 g/½ oz (1 tbsp) butter; 1 tbsp sour cream; 250 g/8 oz (2 cups) flour; ½ tsp salt; 1 egg, beaten; oil for deep-frying.*
FILLING: *1 medium onion, finely chopped; 1 tbsp oil; 250 g/8 oz (1 cup) minced (ground) steak; 250 g/8 oz (1 cup) mixed minced (ground) pork and veal; 2 hard-boiled (hard-cooked) eggs, chopped; 15 g/½ oz (1 tbsp) butter; 2 tbsp stock or water; 1 tsp salt; freshly ground black pepper.*

Combine yeast, water and sugar in a small bowl. Stir and set aside. Place milk, butter and sour cream in saucepan and heat until just warm, stirring occasionally. Sift flour and salt into a large mixing bowl and make a well in centre. Pour in yeast and milk mixtures and beaten egg. Stir with a wooden spoon, gradually incorporating flour. Remove from bowl and knead lightly on a floured work surface. Place dough back in bowl, sprinkle with a little flour, cover and leave to rise in a warm place for about 1 hour or until doubled in bulk.
FILLING: Cook onion in oil until soft; remove to a bowl. Lightly fry meat until brown and crumbly. Combine with onions, hard-boiled (hard-cooked) eggs, butter, stock, salt and pepper. Leave to cool. Turn out dough on to a floured work surface and knead lightly. Roll out thinly and cut into rounds with an 8 cm (3 in) cutter. Place 2 teaspoonsful of filling in centre of each round. Fold over to enclose filling and mould into oval shapes. Stand on a baking tray and keep covered with a clean tea-towel. As soon as all the piroshki have been filled and shaped, deep-fry in hot oil until golden-brown. Drain on paper towels. Serve hot. Makes about 30.
NOTE: Piroshki are best served fresh but may be made ahead and reheated in a moderate oven for 10 minutes.

PISSALADIERE

A wonderful warm, savoury open tart from the south of France. It is often sold in market places where it can be bought, sliced and still hot, with onions, herbs, anchovies and black (ripe) olives spread over pastry (dough) or bread base – an irresistible combination that can easily be prepared at home.

Pissaladière Niçoise

1 × 20 cm (8 in) Shortcrust Pastry Flan Case, baked blind (page 274); 6–8 medium onions, sliced; 4 tbsp oil; 1 bouquet garni; salt and freshly ground black pepper; 2 cloves garlic, crushed; 12–16 anchovy fillets; 8–10 black (ripe) olives.

Put flan case on a baking tray. Cook onions gently in 3 tbsp oil, with bouquet garni, salt and pepper, for about 45 minutes. The onions should almost melt and become a rich golden colour. Stir in garlic after 20 minutes. Transfer onion mixture to pastry case (pie shell), discarding bouquet garni, and make a lattice pattern on top with anchovies and olives. Sprinkle remaining oil on top and bake pissaladière in a preheated moderately hot oven (200°C/400°F, Gas Mark 6) for about 15 minutes or until very hot. If pissaladière is to be a lunch or supper dish, serve with a bowl of tossed green salad. Serves 4–6.
NOTE: The pissaladière can be made using Pizza Dough (see page 299) instead of shortcrust pastry (basic pie dough) if you wish. In this case use a pizza tray and form the dough as for a pizza.

PISTACHIO NUT

Throughout the Middle East you will find street vendors with snacks of salted pistachio nuts. Greek and Lebanese delicatessens in other countries stock them, and often the unsalted nuts as well.

The pistachio needs a hot climate for the small nuts to ripen properly. When ripe, the shell cracks open spontaneously, the nuts are usually salted in the shell. The small, pale green kernels have a unique flavour which is equally appropriate in sweet and savoury dishes. Pistachio nuts are often added to a terrine or to pork sausages; or tossed in butter to garnish a pilaf. Pistachio ice cream is very popular in France and Italy, and chopped pistachios may be included in the filling for Baklava (see page 20). The favourite confections of the Middle East, halva and Turkish delight, often include pistachios, especially the luxury versions. Chopped or sliced, shelled pistachios may decorate desserts, ices and cakes.

PISTOU

The Provençal name for basil and, by extension, it is also the name of the typical soup of Provence – *Soupe au pistou* – in southern France, in which basil is an essential ingredient. This soup is rather similar to the Italian minestrone, with its combination of vegetables and pasta. The basil enrichment added at the end is not too distant from the sauce *Pesto alla Genovese* (see page 272) – which is not really surprising, given the proximity of Provence and Italy and their respective histories.

Right: Beef and Bean Casserole (page 217)

P

Soupe au Pistou

*2 large onions, chopped; 120–250 ml/
4–8 fl oz (½–1 cup) plus 2 tbsp olive oil;
210 g/7 oz (1 cup) dry white beans, soaked
overnight and drained; 500 g/1 lb (2 cups)
green beans, cut into short lengths;
500 g/1 lb (4 cups) courgette (zucchini),
diced; 2 large tomatoes, peeled, seeded and
chopped; 3 potatoes, peeled and diced;
2 litres/3½ pints (8 cups) water; salt and
freshly ground black pepper; 210 g (7 oz)
vermicelli; 5 cloves garlic; about 40 g/1⅓ oz
(1 cup) fresh basil leaves, loosely packed;
5 tbsp grated Parmesan cheese; extra grated
Parmesan cheese to serve (optional).*

Cook onions in 2 tbsp oil in a saucepan until
soft. Add remaining vegetables and cover
with water. Season with salt and pepper.
Bring to the boil, then cover and simmer for
about 1 hour or until white beans are almost
tender. Add vermicelli and continue cooking
until soft.

Meanwhile, pound the garlic and basil to a
paste in a large mortar or bowl. Slowly add
about 120 ml/4 fl oz (½ cup) remaining oil
alternately with cheese. Add additional oil to
obtain a thick but pouring consistency. Taste
soup and adjust seasoning. Pour basil
mixture into soup, or offer it separately. Pass
around a bowl of additional Parmesan if
desired. Serves 8–10.

PITA BREAD

The unleavened bread of the Middle East,
sometimes called peda, Lebanese bread or
pocket bread, because it is flat and hollow
inside, like a pocket. Both white and wholewheat varieties are available.

Pita bread is soft, and can be rolled or
folded around a filling; cubes of grilled
(broiled) meat, or a couple of Falafel (chick
pea croquettes – see page 320), or simply
salad with Tahini Sauce (see page 427). In
the Middle East, it is always served with dips
such as *Hummus bi Tahini* (see page 160) or
Baba Ghannouj (see page 18), and it can also
be folded into a sort of spoon for eating stews
or rice.

In today's kitchen, pita bread finds a place
as a base for a quick pizza: cover it with thin
slices of tomato or thick fresh tomato purée,
add slices of cheese, anchovies, olives and a
sprinkling of oregano and pop into a hot
oven for 5–10 minutes.

Or for an individual *pissaladière à la
minute*: top pita bread with finely sliced
onions, cooked until very soft in oil or butter,
then a lattice of anchovy fillets and black
(ripe) olives, and cook as the quick pizza
above.

*Left: Vermicelli with Tomato and Mussel
Sauce (page 232)*

PIZZA

Probably no other food has had such a quick
rise to fame as the pizza. From Italy, it has
spread to almost every country in the world.
Its power to please lies in the aroma of the
fresh baked yeast crust, the savoury topping,
and its versatility as a snack, first course, or
meal in itself.

The word 'pizza' in Italian actually means
any kind of cake or pie, but the pizza most
familiar is the *Pizza alla Napoletana*, a dish
typical of Naples. It consists of a layer of
dough, rolled or patted to a preferred thickness, and is beautiful to look at topped with
a wonderful fresh tomato sauce or sliced
tomatoes, black (ripe) olives, anchovies, Mozzarella cheese and maybe a sprinkling of oregano leaves. Today, round pizza ovens, with
their glowing coals, are to be found at work,
from the narrow alleyways among the washing of Naples to all over the south and into the
north of Italy as well.

Pizza is traditionally cooked in a round
pan, in a hot oven, until the edges are brown
and crisp and the cheese bubbly and golden.
It is cut into wedges to serve, and eaten with
the fingers. For parties bake pizza in a
rectangular or square tin (pan) which makes it
easier to cut into serving-sized portions.

There are countless varieties of pizza,
ranging from the simplest – just a crust,
tomato sauce and Mozzarella cheese – to the
elaborate Four Seasons Pizza, each section
representing a season of the year. Washed
down with a light wine, pizza makes a
delicious and substantial meal. **See recipes.**

Pizza Dough (1)

If you like a high, fluffy, bread-like crust, use
this dough to make 1 × 30 cm (12 in) pizza.
For a thinner, crisper crust, divide dough roll
or pat out into 2 × 30 cm (12 in) rounds.

*30 g/1 oz (2 tbsp) fresh (compressed) yeast,
or 1½ tsp active dried yeast; 250 ml/8 fl oz
(1 cup) lukewarm water; ½ tsp sugar; 3 tbsp
olive oil; 370 g/12 oz (3 cups) flour; 1½ tsp
salt; freshly ground white pepper.*

Combine fresh (compressed) yeast, water
and sugar in a large bowl. (If using dried
yeast, follow directions on packet.) Set aside
for about 15 minutes or until surface is
foamy. Stir in olive oil. Sift flour and salt over
yeast mixture, season with pepper and blend
with a wooden spoon. Turn dough on to a
lightly floured work surface and knead gently
until smooth and elastic. Place dough in a
large, greased bowl, turning dough to grease
it all over. Cover with a tea-towel and leave in
a warm place for 2 hours, or until doubled in
bulk, light and spongy. Turn on to a lightly
floured work surface, knock (punch) down
and knead 4–5 times. Roll out to a 30 cm
(12 in) round about 1 cm (½ in) thick, or

divide dough in half and roll out into 2
rounds 5 mm (¼ in) thick. Place on a greased
baking tray, cover and leave to rise in a warm
place for about 15 minutes before adding
toppings. Makes 1–2 pizza crusts.
NOTE: After the first rising, pizza dough can
be wrapped in plastic wrap and refrigerated
overnight. The next day, knock (punch)
down, knead lightly, roll out, and allow to
rise for 15 minutes before filling and baking.

Pizza Dough (2)

This recipe makes a dough that can be
successfully reheated. You can make the
pizzas beforehand and reheat them in a cool
oven for 7–10 minutes before serving, or
freeze them until required. The quantity is
enough for 12 individual pizzas, about 12 cm
(5 in) diameter, or 1 large rectangular pizza,
about 35 × 30 cm (14 × 12 in).

*500 g/1 lb (4 cups) flour; 2 tsp salt;
120 ml/4 fl oz (½ cup) lukewarm milk;
30 g/1 oz (2 tbsp) fresh (compressed) yeast,
or 1½ tsp active dried yeast; 1 egg; 2–4 tbsp
olive oil.*

Sift flour and salt into a large, warmed bowl.
Combine a little of milk and fresh
(compressed) yeast and stir until smooth. (If
using dried yeast, follow directions on
packet.) Make a well in centre of flour and
pour in yeast mixture, remaining milk, egg
and 2 tbsp olive oil. Stir with a wooden
spoon to form a dough, adding more olive
oil if required until dough can be shaped into
a ball which comes away cleanly from sides
of bowl. Cover with a tea-towel and leave to
rise in a warm place for about 2 hours or
until doubled in bulk and spongy. Knock
(punch) dough down, knead 4–5 times and
pat out in a greased rectangular baking tray,
or shape into 12 individual round pizzas and
arrange on greased baking trays. Allow
dough to rise in a warm place for 15 minutes
before adding toppings. Makes 1 large or 12
small pizza crusts.

Pizza Sauce

This rich, flavourful tomato sauce is used as
a base for many pizzas. It is spread over the
bread dough before other toppings are
added. Instead of fresh tomatoes, drained
canned whole tomatoes may be used.

*750 g/1½ lb (3 cups) ripe tomatoes, peeled
and chopped; 2 cloves garlic, crushed; 1 tsp
dried oregano; 1 tbsp chopped fresh basil, or
1 tsp dried; 1 bay leaf; 1 tbsp brown sugar;
salt and freshly ground black pepper.*

Place all ingredients in a saucepan and
simmer gently for 30–40 minutes, stirring
often. Taste for seasoning, remove bay leaf
and cool before using. Makes sufficient for
two 30 cm (12 in) rounds, or two 35 × 30 cm
(14 × 12 in) rectangles.

Plum –

Four Seasons Pizza

A choice of four toppings makes this pizza especially colourful and interesting.

½ quantity Pizza Dough (1), patted out to a 30 cm (12 in) round (page 299); 1 quantity Pizza Sauce (page 299).
TOPPING 1: *2 slices cooked ham, cut into strips; 4 medium mushrooms, thinly sliced; salt and freshly ground black pepper.*
TOPPING 2: *4 anchovy fillets, halved; 2 tbsp diced Mozzarella cheese; 2 tsp drained capers.*
TOPPING 3: *4–5 slices salami, cut into strips; 8 black (ripe) olives, stoned (pitted).*
TOPPING 4: *6 prawns (shrimp), shelled and deveined, or 60 g/2 oz (¼ cup) flaked tuna or 1 × 125 g/4 oz can mussels, drained; 4 thin slices Mozzarella cheese.*
TO FINISH: *2 tbsp olive oil; 30 g/1 oz (¼ cup) grated Parmesan cheese.*

Spread cooled sauce over dough and add toppings, a different one for each quarter. Sprinkle olive oil and cheese over whole pizza and bake in a preheated moderately hot oven (200°C/400°F, Gas Mark 6) for 18–20 minutes or until crust is golden and crisp around edges. Serves 6–8.

Salami Pizza

double quantity Pizza Dough (2), patted out to two 35 × 30 cm (14 × 12 in) rectangles or two 30 cm (12 in) rounds (page 299); 4 tbsp olive oil; 60 g/2 oz (½ cup) grated Parmesan cheese; 1 quantity Pizza Sauce (page 299); 1 × 50 g/1⅔ oz can flat anchovy fillets; 125 g/4 oz (½ cup) Italian salami, cut into strips; 12 black (ripe) olives, stoned (pitted) and quartered.

Brush pizza dough with half of the olive oil and sprinkle with half of the Parmesan cheese. Spoon sauce over each, then add anchovy fillets, salami and black olives. Sprinkle with remaining oil and cheese. Bake pizzas in a preheated moderately hot oven (200°C/400°F, Gas Mark 6) for 18–20 minutes or until crust is golden. Serves 12.
VARIATION:
Neapolitan Pizza: Make as for Salami Pizza but replace salami with slices of Mozzarella cheese, and omit Parmesan cheese.

Ham and Mushroom Pizza

double quantity Pizza Dough (2), patted out to two 35 × 30 cm (14 × 12 in) rectangles or two 30 cm (12 in) rounds (page 299); 4 tbsp olive oil; 60 g/2 oz (½ cup) grated Parmesan cheese; 1 quantity Pizza Sauce (page 299); 250 g/8 oz (1 cup) cooked ham, cut into strips; 6–8 mushrooms, finely sliced; salt and freshly ground black pepper.

Brush pizza dough with half olive oil and sprinkle with half of the Parmesan cheese.

Spoon sauce over each pizza and then add ham and mushrooms, seasoning with salt and pepper. Sprinkle remaining olive oil and Parmesan cheese over and bake in a preheated moderately hot oven (200°C/400°F, Gas Mark 6) for 18–20 minutes or until crust is golden and cooked. Serves 12.
VARIATION
Pizza Margherita: Make as for Ham and Mushroom Pizza, substituting 250 g/8 oz (2 cups) diced Mozzarella cheese and 12 leaves fresh basil, finely chopped, for the ham and mushrooms.

PLUM

A round, stone fruit that comes in an abundance of colours, shapes and sizes throughout summer and the early part of autumn. There are large, red-skinned, yellow-fleshed varieties; round, deep crimson blood plums; small, oval, purplish damsons, large prune plums, and sweet greengage plums.

Some varieties of plum are best eaten raw, or combined with other stone fruits, sprinkled with caster sugar and lemon juice and a little brandy and chilled. Others are equally good cooked, or made into a fruit tart; choose the least juicy varieties for a tart.

Spiced pickled plums make a good accompaniment to cold meats. **See recipes.**

Plums in Port

12 plums; 750 ml/1¼ pints (3 cups) water; 250 g/8 oz (1 cup) sugar; 150 ml/¼ pint (⅔ cup) port.
TO SERVE: *Crème Fraîche (page 88) and crisp biscuits (cookies).*

Wash plums. Place water and sugar in a saucepan and bring slowly to the boil, stirring until sugar dissolves. Boil, without stirring, for 5 minutes. Add port and plums and poach gently about 5 minutes or until plums are tender. Remove plums and set aside. Boil the syrup until it is reduced by about ⅓, then pour over the plums. Chill. Serve with Crème Fraîche, and crisp biscuits. Serves 4.

Oven-baked Plums

1 kg (2 lb) plums; 180 g/6 oz (¾ cup) sugar; 4 tbsp water.

Make shallow cut around each plum, then arrange in an ovenproof dish. Sprinkle with sugar and water. Cook in a preheated cool oven (150°C/300°F, Gas Mark 2) for 20–25 minutes or until soft. Serve warm. Serves 6.

Peach and Plum Compote

250 g/8 oz (1 cup) sugar; 250 ml/8 fl oz (1 cup) water; thinly peeled rind 1 orange, cut into fine strips; 1 tbsp lemon juice; about 2 tbsp Cointreau; 4 large ripe peaches, peeled; 4 large ripe plums, peeled.

Dissolve sugar in water in a saucepan over low heat. Bring to the boil, then add orange rind strips and boil 5 minutes. Cool. Add lemon juice and Cointreau to cooled syrup. Place whole fruit in serving bowl and pour over syrup. Cover and chill before serving. Serves 4.

Pickled Plums

An unusual accompaniment to cold meats, especially ham or pork.

370 g/12 oz (1½ cups) sugar; 350 ml/12 fl oz (1½ cups) wine vinegar; 1 small cinnamon stick; 1 tbsp whole cloves; 1 kg (2 lb) plums.

Dissolve sugar in vinegar in a large saucepan over low heat. Bring to the boil and boil for 2–3 minutes, then add cinnamon and cloves. Prick plums in several places with a fine skewer, and add to syrup. Bring to the boil again, skimming off any scum. Lift out plums and place in a bowl. Boil syrup 3–4 minutes, then pour over plums. Leave in a cold place 24 hours. Drain off syrup into a saucepan and bring to the boil. Add plums, return to the boil, then lift out plums. Boil syrup 2 minutes longer, and pour over plums. Cool. Place in sterilized jars and seal. Leave in a cool dark place for 6 weeks before using. Makes about 6 × 250 g (8 oz) jars.

PLUM PUDDING

See *Christmas Pudding.*

POLENTA

A yellow maize or cornmeal grown in northern Italy, where it is regarded as one of the staple foods. Polenta is used in many different ways after it has first been prepared as a rather thick porridge. Polenta is graded according to its texture and can be fine, medium or coarse ground. It is available from most supermarkets, delicatessens and health food stores.

Plain boiled polenta can be grilled (broiled), baked or fried and served with a

300

meat or tomato sauce, or simply with butter and grated cheese. It can be made into gnocchi (see page 145), served in a ring with a chicken liver filling, or with chicken and mushrooms in a casserole. **See recipes.**

Basic Polenta

1.5 litres/2½ pints (6 cups) water; 2 tsp salt; 250 g/8 oz (1½ cups) finely ground polenta (yellow cornmeal); freshly ground black pepper.

Bring water and salt to the boil in a saucepan over medium heat. Slowly pour in polenta (cornmeal), stirring constantly with a wooden spoon until a smooth mixture forms. Lower heat and simmer, stirring frequently, for 20–25 minutes or until polenta (cornmeal) comes away cleanly from sides of pan. Season with pepper. Serves 4.

Polenta in Tomato Sauce

1 quantity Basic Polenta (above); 250 ml/8 fl oz (1 cup) Tomato Sauce (page 272); grated Parmesan cheese.

Turn warm polenta into a greased baking dish. When cool, cut into 5 cm (2 in) squares. Place squares in a lightly greased, shallow ovenproof dish, spoon over tomato sauce and sprinkle generously with grated Parmesan cheese. Bake in a preheated moderately hot oven (190°C/375°F, Gas Mark 5) for 30–40 minutes or until golden-brown. Serves 4.

Polenta Ring with Chicken Livers

1 quantity Basic Polenta (above); 3 rashers (slices) bacon, rind removed and diced; 30 g/1 oz (2 tbsp) butter; 500 g/1 lb (2⅔ cups) chicken livers; 250 g/8 oz (2 cups) mushrooms, sliced; salt and freshly ground black pepper; 3 leaves fresh sage; 4 tbsp dry white wine; finely chopped parsley.

Turn warm polenta into a greased 1 litre/1¾ pint (4 cup) ring tin (pan) and keep warm in a larger pan of hot water while preparing filling. Fry bacon in a frying pan (skillet) until crisp. Add butter, chicken livers and mushrooms and sauté over medium heat about 2 minutes or until chicken livers are just brown. Season with salt and pepper, and add sage and wine. When wine starts to boil, turn down heat and cook for 2–3 minutes. Remove sage leaves. Ease polenta away from edges of ring tin (pan) and turn carefully on to a serving plate. Fill ring with mixture and sprinkle with parsley. Serves 6–8.

Polenta Casserole

1 quantity thick Basic Polenta (above); 500 g/1 lb (4 cups) mushrooms, sliced;
30 g/1 oz (2 tbsp) butter; 750 g/1½ lb (3 cups) diced cooked chicken; 250 ml/8 fl oz (1 cup) Tomato Sauce (page 272); 60 g/2 oz (½ cup) grated Parmesan cheese.

Spread warm polenta in a buttered casserole dish. Sauté mushrooms in butter for 3 minutes and scatter over polenta with the chicken. Coat with sauce and sprinkle with Parmesan cheese. Bake in a preheated moderate oven (180°C/350°F, Gas Mark 4) for 45 minutes. Serves 6.

POMEGRANATE

A late summer fruit, about the size of an apple. Its thick, reddish-golden skin contains a mass of tiny seeds, each enclosed in a capsule of deep pink jelly.

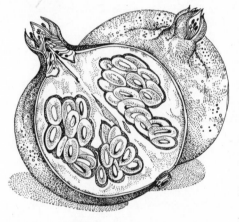

A pomegranate may be halved and squeezed like an orange; its juice is very refreshing and thirst-quenching, and forms the basis for Grenadine syrup. The fleshy seeds may be eaten with a teaspoon, after all the skin and membrane of the pomegranate has been removed. In mediaeval times, pomegranate seeds were sometimes used to decorate a dish of fish or poultry.

POPCORN

A perennial children's favourite for snacks and for birthday parties. It is a special type of dried corn, and may be bought ready-popped, either plain, toffee-coated or candy-coated. Popping your own corn, though, is very simple and much more fun. Automatic popcorn poppers are available, but an ordinary frying pan (skillet) with a lid, or an electric frypan (skillet) will do the same job.
To pop corn: Heat 1–2 tbsp oil in the pan, just enough to film the base, and add enough popcorn to cover half the base of the pan in one layer. Shake over high heat until popping starts, then cover with lid. Shake pan from time to time as long as popping continues (if you remove the lid you will have popcorn all over the room!). When all corn

has popped, toss with melted butter and sprinkle lightly with salt.

POPOVER

First cousin to the Yorkshire pudding, popovers are made with the same basic ingredients, in slightly different proportions, and baked in the same way.

Popovers may be sweet or savoury. They may be eaten with butter and sugar, with honey, jam or golden (light corn) syrup, or they may be split open and filled with a savoury meat, chicken or vegetable mixture. But no matter how they are eaten, they should be served as soon as they come out of the oven, nicely puffed and crisp.

Popovers

125 g/4 oz (1 cup) flour; pinch salt; 2 eggs, beaten with 250 ml/8 fl oz (1 cup) milk; 1 tbsp oil or 15 g/½ oz (1 tbsp) melted butter.

Sift flour and salt into a bowl. Make well in centre and pour in egg mixture. Add oil or melted butter and mix until batter is smooth, then beat well until surface is covered with bubbles. Allow to stand in a cool place for 1 hour. Grease deep bun tins (patty pans) or custard cups well and half fill with batter. Bake in a preheated hot oven (220°C/425°F, Gas Mark 7) for about 40 minutes or until puffed and golden. Serve at once. Makes 8–10.

POPPY SEED

The tiny seed of a poppy plant, used a lot in European and Asian cooking. Although the plant belongs to the same family as the opium poppy, it is non-narcotic but does have some medicinal value – an infusion is said to relieve the pain of toothache.

Poppy seeds are often sprinkled on bread, rolls and savoury biscuits (crackers) before baking, and baking enhances their nutty flavour. In central European countries, such as Austria and Hungary, poppy seeds are combined with sugar and raisins, peel or splice to make a strudel filling. For cakes, they may either be cooked in milk until soft or ground into a sort of flour.

The best poppy seeds are said to come from Holland, and are slate-blue in colour. In some countries, poppy seeds are crushed for their oil (they contain about 50% oil), which may be used as a salad oil. **See recipes.**

Poppy Seed Noodles

noodles, cooked; butter; 1–2 tbsp poppy seeds.

Drain noodles and return to pan. Add butter and poppy seeds and toss well. Serve with goulash, casseroles of meat or poultry.

Poppy Seed Cake

An unusual but delicious cake. Serve as a dessert or as a tea-time treat.

280 g/9 oz (1½ cups) poppy seeds; 6 eggs, separated; 250 g/8 oz (1 cup) sugar; 90 g/3 oz (½ cup) chopped mixed candied peel; 1 tsp ground allspice; whipped cream.

Grind poppy seeds in blender. Beat egg yolks until thick, then gradually add sugar and continue beating until very thick and pale. Stir in peel, allspice and poppy seeds. Beat egg whites until stiff and fold into yolk mixture. Pour mixture into a greased and floured 23 cm (9 in) loose-bottomed tin (springform pan). Bake in a preheated moderate oven (180°C/350°F, Gas Mark 4) for about 50 minutes. Allow cake to cool in tin (pan), then remove sides. Spread top with whipped cream before serving.

PORK

Pork sold in butchers' shops is from young animals and is a tender meat. Good pork should have pale pink, fine-grained flesh, pearly white fat and thin, smooth skin.

As with other meats, there is no international standard butchering technique, so cuts vary from country to country, and even very similar cuts often have quite different names. To further muddy the issue, Americans refer to the thicker roasts of pork as fresh ham. Where feasible we have attempted to give an American alternative to all British cuts suggested.

Please read *Meat* for amount to buy, factors determining tenderness, testing meat for doneness, carving etc. **See recipes.**

Roast Pork

□ Choice Cuts for Roasting:

Leg: A very large roast if left whole, but many butchers sell half legs. In America, referred to as leg of fresh ham. The shank end is easier to cook evenly and to carve if it is boned and tied.

Loin: Can be bone-in or boned and tied. A full loin serves 8–10, but can be cut in two to make smaller roasts.

Rib on the Bone: Consists of 6–8 rib chops in a piece.

Crown Roast: Made from two sets of ribs bent round and tied together to make a circle with the meat inside and the bones outside. The skin and excess fat are removed before tying.

Fillet (Tenderloin): A small, skinless and very tender piece of meat which is usually baked *en croûte*, rather than truly roasted.

Sucking Pig: A whole very young pig, still being milk-fed, hence its name. An impressive party dish.

□ Economical Cuts for Roasting:

Blade (Shoulder Butt): Can be bone-in or boned, rolled and tied. It may be stuffed before being tied.

Hand (Picnic Shoulder): Easier to cook evenly and to carve if it is boned and tied.

Foreloin or Cushion (Center Cut Loin).

Belly or Spring (Fresh Pork Sides): Used as the outer wrapping for a pork and veal-stuffed rolled roast. Belly is a flat and rather fatty cut which gives lots of crackling but has only a thin layer or two of lean meat. It can be slit through the centre and filled with a meaty stuffing for an economical roast.

□ To Roast:

Choice and economical cuts which still have the skin on may be roasted in the same way. Have skin scored by the butcher or score it yourself with a sharp knife, cutting about 3 mm (⅛ in) deep at 1 cm (½ in) intervals. Tie meat into a compact shape if necessary, so that it will cook evenly, and weigh it. Sprinkle skin with cooking salt and rub well in (this makes the crackling crisp). Place pork, skin side up, on a rack in a roasting tin (pan). Roast in a preheated very hot oven (240°C/475°F, Gas Mark 9) until the skin starts to bubble and crisp (about 20–30 minutes), then lower heat to moderate (180°C/350°F, Gas Mark 4) for remainder of cooking time. Do not baste pork or cover dish, or the crackling will lose its crispness. Allow a total roasting time of approximately 30 minutes per 500 g (1 lb), plus an extra 30 minutes. To test for doneness, see *Meat*. Rest for 15–30 minutes in turned-off oven, with door ajar, or other warm place, before carving.

For pork roasts, which have had the skin removed, follow instructions above but omit initial searing to crisp skin. Instead, place pork fatty side up in a preheated hot oven (220°C/425°F, Gas Mark 7) for 10 minutes, then turn heat down to moderate (180°C/350°F, Gas Mark 4) and continue cooking, allowing about 35 minutes per 500 g (1 lb) plus an extra 35 minutes.

CROWN ROAST: Cook in the same manner as other skinless roasts, but allow about 25 minutes per 500 g (1 lb). Stand crown roast directly in the pan, and protect tops of bones with foil to prevent charring.

Grilled (Broiled) Pork

It is best to have pork chops and steaks cut 2–2.5 cm (¾–1 in) thick for grilling (broiling).

□ Choice Cuts for Grilling (Broiling):

Pork Loin Chops or the 'New-style' Cuts: From the loin and chump (rump) area; Medallions, Butterfly steaks.

□ Economical Cuts for Grilling (Broiling):

Leg Chops and Chump Chops: These are inclined to be dry, so need to be marinated before grilling (broiling) or basted very frequently during grilling (broiling).

Spareribs: Delicious barbecued; these are usually pre-baked or simmered to melt away excess fat, and are often marinated and always basted with spicy sauce.

□ To Grill (Broil):

Have meat at room temperature. Use a sharp knife to cut through the skin and fat around the edge at 1 cm (½ in) intervals to prevent buckling. Season with freshly ground pepper and brush with oil or melted butter. Place on a greased rack under a preheated moderate grill (broiler) or over coals. Brush every 2–3 minutes with more oil or melted butter to keep meat moist, and turn 2–3 times. Allow 12–16 minutes, depending on cut and thickness. To test for doneness, see *Meat*.

Pan-fried Pork

This method is suitable for slices of fillet (tenderloin), chops or steaks (any cut) and for the small 'new-style' cuts such as medallions or pork schnitzel cut from the leg. Prepare meat as for grilling (broiling). Use a thick, heavy pan; heat on high heat for a few minutes, add just enough oil, or butter and oil, to coat the base and when it gives off a slight haze, put in the meat. Cook for 30 seconds–1 minute each side until browned, then lower heat to moderate and continue to cook, turning once, until done as desired. To test for doneness, see *Meat*.

If meat is coated with breadcrumbs, cook as described but use a little more fat, enough to come halfway up the pieces.

A pan sauce, such as Quick Mushroom Sauce (see page 369) or those given below, can be made after the meat is removed.

Pan Sauces for Pork

These quantities are enough for 4 large chops or 6–8 small medallions.

Juniper and Herb Sauce Dust pork with flour and pan-fry in butter and oil. Remove meat and keep warm for a few minutes. Pour all but 1 tbsp fat from the pan and add 5 tbsp dry white wine, 5 tbsp beef stock (bouillon), 3 crushed juniper berries and 1 tsp chopped fresh thyme, or ¼ tsp dried thyme. Boil 3 minutes, stirring and scraping up brown bits from pan. Season and pour over pork.

Cider and Cream Sauce Pan-fry pork in a little oil, remove it from pan and keep warm for a few minutes. Pour off fat from pan, add 15 g/½ oz (1 tbsp) butter and melt it. Add 2 tbsp finely chopped shallot and cook gently 2 minutes. Add 5 tbsp cider and boil, stirring and scraping up brown bits from pan, 2–3 minutes. Stir in 4 tbsp single (light) cream, simmer a minute or two longer, season and pour over pork chops or medallions.

Braised or Casseroled Pork

Cuts for braising or casseroling include chops and steaks (any cut) and also diced meat from belly (fresh pork sides) or forequarter.

Pork and Sauerkraut Goulash

Sauerkraut is a good foil for the richness of pork – this is an old Hungarian recipe using canned sauerkraut.

60 g/2 oz (4 tbsp) butter; 1 tbsp oil; 4 onions, finely sliced; 1 kg (2 lb) boneless pork blade (shoulder butt), cut into 2.5 cm (1 in) cubes; 2 tbsp paprika; 1 tbsp tomato purée (paste); 250 ml/8 fl oz (1 cup) water; salt; 1 × 440 g/14 oz can sauerkraut, drained; 1 tsp caraway seeds; 120 ml/4 fl oz (½ cup) single (light) cream; 1 tbsp flour; 1 tsp lemon juice.

Melt butter and oil in a large flameproof casserole and cook onions until golden. Stir in pork and paprika and sauté for 5 minutes. Stir in tomato purée (paste) and water and bring to the boil, stirring. Season with salt, cover and simmer for 30 minutes. Place sauerkraut in a colander and rinse well under cold running water. Drain. Add to casserole with caraway seeds and enough water just to cover. Simmer, covered, for 45 minutes or until pork is just tender. Sour the cream with lemon juice. Combine flour with a little sour cream and stir into goulash. Simmer, stirring constantly, for 10 minutes, then add remaining sour cream and heat through. Adjust seasoning. Serves 4–6.

Mediterranean Style Pork Chops

30 g/1 oz (2 tbsp) butter; 1 tbsp oil; 4 pork chops; salt and freshly ground black pepper; 370 g/12 oz (3 cups) mushrooms, sliced; 2 large green or red peppers, cored, seeded and chopped; 370 g/12 oz (1½ cups) tomatoes, skinned and sliced; 1 tbsp chopped fresh basil; 1 tsp sugar; 250 ml/8 fl oz (1 cup) chicken stock; lemon wedges to garnish.

Melt butter and oil and fry chops quickly until browned on both sides; season and remove from pan. Fry mushrooms and peppers until soft. Add tomatoes, basil, sugar and stock.

Boil for 3 minutes then return chops to pan and simmer, uncovered, for about 30 minutes. The sauce should be thick. Arrange chops on a heated dish with sauce and garnish with lemon wedges. Serves 4.

Pork Chops Lyonnaise

Onions are a feature of Lyonnais cooking, typified by this hearty dish which should be served with lots of mashed potato to absorb the flavoursome juices.

8 pork chops; salt and freshly ground black pepper; 1 kg/2 lb (8 cups) finely chopped onions; 3 tbsp cider vinegar; 3 tbsp dry white wine; 1 sprig fresh thyme or pinch dried.

Trim any excess fat from chops, season them with a little salt and pepper and set aside. Melt a little pork fat in a heavy pan and cook onions gently until starting to turn brown. Remove from pan and keep warm. Melt a little more pork fat if necessary and cook chops about 20 minutes, turning once. Remove to heated serving platter and keep warm. Add vinegar and wine to pan and bring to the boil, scraping up any bits stuck to bottom. Reduce liquid by half, then stir in onions and season with salt, pepper and thyme. Cook, stirring, for 3–4 minutes, then pour around chops. Remove fresh thyme if using. Serve with creamy mashed potatoes. Serves 8.

Spiced Pork Chops with Apple Slices

4 pork loin chops, cut about 2 cm (¾ in) thick; salt and freshly ground black pepper; 1 tbsp oil; 2 cloves garlic, crushed; 1 tbsp Worcestershire sauce; ½ tsp dry mustard; 60 g/2 oz (4 tbsp) butter; 4 apples, cored and thickly sliced.

Use a sharp knife to cut through fat around chops at 2 cm (¾ in) intervals – this is to prevent chops curling during grilling (broiling). Season with salt and pepper. Combine oil, garlic, Worcestershire sauce and mustard and spread over chops. Melt half the butter. Grill (broil) chops as described in introduction, brushing every 2 minutes with melted butter. Meanwhile, fry apple slices gently in remaining butter until golden-brown on both sides. Serve with chops. Serves 4.

Spareribs in Plum Sauce

8–10 meaty pork spareribs (country-style pork ribs); fluffy boiled rice to serve.
MARINADE: 2 tbsp sherry; 1 tbsp light soy sauce; 1 tbsp hoisin sauce; 1 clove garlic, crushed; 2 tsp finely grated fresh ginger.
SAUCE: 1 × 425 g/14 oz can purple plums; 1 tsp chilli sauce; 120 ml/4 fl oz (½ cup) water; 1 tbsp cornflour (cornstarch); 4 tbsp malt vinegar.

Blanch spareribs in boiling water for 2 minutes, then drain and pat dry with paper towels. Arrange spareribs in a shallow dish and prepare marinade.
MARINADE: Combine ingredients, spoon over spareribs and stand 2 hours, turning often, or cover and refrigerate overnight.
SAUCE: Drain plums and measure 175 ml/6 fl oz (¾ cup) syrup into a saucepan. Blend in remaining ingredients. Stone plums, then purée and add to sauce. Bring to the boil, stirring, until thickened. Simmer 5 minutes. Drain spareribs, reserving marinade. Cook spareribs under a preheated hot grill (broiler), on a barbecue, or on a rack in a preheated moderate oven (180°C/350°F, Gas Mark 4), for 25–40 minutes, turning during the cooking. Add any marinade to plum sauce, then pour over spareribs and serve with fluffy boiled rice with a tossed salad. Serves 4–6.

Finnish Karelian Pot

This old Finnish dish is so popular it is sold in cans in Finland. The recipe couldn't be simpler, but the combination of meats and the long, slow cooking gives a unique flavour. In Finland, it would be served with boiled potatoes and tart-sweet lingonberries or cranberries, both available in cans from delicatessens.

500 g (1 lb) lean, boneless pork; 500 g (1 lb) lean, boneless beef; 500 g (1 lb) lean, boneless lamb; 1 tbsp coarse salt; 1 tsp black peppercorns; 3–4 juniper berries (optional); 250 ml/8 fl oz (1 cup) water.

Cut meat into bite-sized cubes and combine. Arrange in layers in a deep, round casserole, sprinkling each layer with a little salt. Add peppercorns, juniper berries and water and cover very tightly. (This amount of water seems small, but juices will come from meat.) Place casserole in a preheated cool oven (150°C/300°F, Gas Mark 2) for 4 hours, or cook in a slow cooker set on low for 6–8 hours. Adjust seasoning, and serve from the casserole or slow cooker. Serves 6–8.

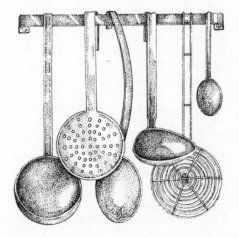

Pork Chops with Pink or Green Peppercorns

4 pork butterfly chops, loin chops or steaks; salt and freshly ground black pepper; 1 tbsp oil; 2 tsp pink or green peppercorns; 1 tbsp French (Dijon) mustard; 120–150 ml/ 4 fl oz–¼ pint (½–⅔ cup) single (light) cream; watercress or parsley to garnish.

Season pork with salt and pepper. Heat oil in a large frying pan (skillet) and fry pork 4–5 minutes on each side. Remove to a heated platter and keep warm. Pour off all but 1 tbsp fat from pan. Add peppercorns and fry for a few seconds, then add mustard and cream. Shake pan or stir with rounded side of a spoon to pick up brown bits on bottom of pan. Continue to cook until sauce thickens. Spoon sauce over pork and garnish with watercress or parsley. Serve with creamy, mashed potatoes or ribbon noodles and a green salad. Serves 4.

NOTE: Many people may be allergic to pink peppercorns so use with caution.

Pork Schnitzels with Lemon

Pork schnitzels look like and can be treated in the same way as veal schnitzels. This is an Italian way of treating tender, thin steaks.

6–8 pork schnitzels; juice 1 lemon; salt and freshly ground black pepper; flour; 30 g/1 oz (2 tbsp) butter; 3 tbsp oil.
TO FINISH: *2 tsp butter; 6–8 slices lemon.*

Season each schnitzel with lemon juice, salt and pepper and let meat stand for 30 minutes. Dry and dust lightly with flour. Heat half the butter and oil in a large frying pan (skillet) and sauté half the steaks for about 3 minutes on each side. Remove to a plate and keep warm. Fry remaining schnitzels, using remaining butter and oil. It is important not to crowd the pan or the meat steams.
TO FINISH: Heat butter in pan and lightly sauté lemon slices. Top schnitzels with lemon, serve with mashed or sautéed potatoes and a salad. Serves 4–6.

Pickled (Salt) Pork

This is a useful cold meat to have on hand for summer eating. Slices of the pork are good mixed with shredded lettuce as a sandwich filling, or diced and added to omelettes. Thin slices top rye bread with a dill pickle and a spot of mustard for open sandwiches. Smear slices with mustard, toss in breadcrumbs and pan-fry or grill (broil) for a hot dish.

1 × 1.5 kg (3 lb) pickled (salt) belly pork (pork sides); 2 carrots, sliced; 1 onion, sliced; 6 black peppercorns; 2 cloves; 2–3 stalks parsley; 3 tbsp wine vinegar.

Soak pork in cold water for 3–4 hours. Drain, put in a saucepan with fresh cold water to cover and add remaining ingredients. Bring to simmering point, skimming off the scum, then cover pan and simmer gently for 1½–2 hours or until very tender. Drain pork, cool slightly and slip out bones. Place in a flat dish, cover with plastic wrap and press with a weight until cold. Chill, then remove to a fresh plate or cover with fresh wrap. Serve in thin slices with hot English mustard and vinegar, or use in any of the ways suggested. Serves 6.

Pork Cheese

For this excellent old-fashioned cold meat dish, fresh or pickled (salt) pork is cooked slowly until it falls from the bone and is pressed in its own juices which form a jelly.

1 fresh or pickled (salt) hand of pork (picnic shoulder); salt and freshly ground black pepper; 4 leaves fresh sage, finely chopped.

If using pickled (salt) pork, soak in water to cover overnight. Drain. Place in a heavy pan with enough fresh water just to cover. Cover and cook over low heat for 4 hours. Drain, reserving liquid, and discard bones. Place meat, including skin, in a bowl and season with salt, if needed, and pepper. Sprinkle sage over pork. Strain a little cooking liquid on to meat in bowl and leave to cool, pressed down with a weight. Chill until set. Turn out and serve with a green salad. Serves 6.

Spareribs with Spiced Barbecue Sauce

2 kg (4 lb) meaty pork spareribs (country-style ribs); fresh coriander or shredded spring onion (scallion) tops to garnish; boiled rice to serve.
BARBECUE SAUCE: *150 g/5 oz (½ cup) tomato purée (paste); 120 ml/4 fl oz (½ cup) olive oil; 4 tbsp red wine vinegar; 1 × 2.5 cm (1 in) piece fresh ginger, chopped; 2 tbsp turmeric; 2 tbsp hoisin sauce; 4 cloves garlic, chopped; 1 tsp hot chilli sauce, or ¼ tsp Tabasco (hot pepper) sauce; salt and freshly ground black pepper.*

Place spareribs in a large saucepan, cover with water and bring to the boil. Reduce heat and simmer 20 minutes. Drain. Make barbecue sauce by whirling all ingredients in a food processor fitted with a steel blade or in a blender about 30 seconds or until well combined, then transfer to a large bowl. Add spareribs, covering them well with sauce, cover bowl and chill overnight. Drain spareribs and place on an oiled rack under a preheated grill (broiler) or over hot coals. Grill (broil), turning once, for 15 minutes or until browned and crisp. Arrange spareribs on a heated platter. If liked strew fresh coriander or shredded spring onion (scallion) tops over spareribs. Serve with boiled rice. Serves 6–8.

Fragrant Pork Balls with Cabbage

Unlike many Chinese dishes, this one can be made beforehand if necessary and gently reheated.

500 g/1 lb (2 cups) minced (ground) pork; 8 spring onions (scallions), finely chopped; 1 tsp grated fresh ginger; 125 g/4 oz (½ cup) drained, chopped water chestnuts (optional); 1 egg, lightly beaten; 3 tbsp dry sherry; 1 tsp salt; ¼ tsp pepper; ½ tsp Chinese five-spice powder; 3 tbsp soy sauce; 1 tbsp cornflour (cornstarch) mixed to a paste with 2 tbsp water; 120 ml/4 fl oz (½ cup) peanut oil; 1 small head cabbage or Chinese cabbage, chopped; 500 ml/18 fl oz (2 cups) water; 2 tsp sugar.

Mix pork with spring onions (scallions), ginger, water chestnuts, egg, 1 tbsp sherry, salt, pepper, five-spice powder and 1 tbsp soy sauce. Wet hands with cornflour (cornstarch) mixture and shape pork mixture into 4 large balls. Heat oil in a wok or deep frying pan (skillet) and fry meatballs until golden-brown on all sides, about 5 minutes. Drain on paper towels and set aside. Reheat oil in wok and fry cabbage, tossing, for 2–3 minutes until coated with oil. Arrange meatballs on top, add water, remaining soy sauce and sherry and sugar and cover pan. Simmer for 1 hour. Serve with plain boiled rice and side dishes of soy sauce and hot mustard. Serves 4.

Barbecued Pork Spareribs

Ask your butcher to cut spareribs (country-style ribs) into individual ribs.

1.5 kg (3 lb) meaty pork spareribs (country-style ribs); 3 tbsp oil; 5 tbsp soy sauce; 5 tbsp water; 2 tbsp hoisin sauce; 1 tsp sugar; 4 slices fresh ginger, shredded; 2 onions, finely sliced; 5 tbsp dry sherry; salt and freshly ground white pepper; 5 tbsp chicken stock.

Blanch spareribs in boiling water for 2 minutes, then drain and pat dry with paper towels. Put ribs and oil into a flameproof casserole. Heat until oil just begins to bubble, then stir-fry for 5 minutes over medium heat, to brown ribs. Add soy sauce, water, hoisin sauce, sugar, ginger and onions. Stir until well blended, turning ribs to coat. Put

casserole into a preheated cool oven (150°C/300°F, Gas Mark 2). Cook for 20 minutes, then stir in sherry and season with salt and pepper. Cook for a further 40 minutes, stirring halfway through. Take dish from oven, remove spareribs and place them side by side on bottom of a baking dish. Return to oven and increase temperature to hot (230°C/450°F, Gas Mark 8). Roast for 12–15 minutes or until crisp and rich golden-brown. Arrange spareribs on a heated platter. Pour chicken stock into casserole dish with onion mixture and stir over moderate heat for 2–3 minutes. Serve in a separate dish. Serves 4–6.

Stir-Fried Pork with Spring Onions

Other vegetables may be substituted for the spring onions (scallions).

310 g (about 10 oz) boneless pork loin or fillet (tenderloin).
MARINADE: *1 clove garlic, crushed; 1 tbsp soy sauce; ½ tbsp sugar; 1 tbsp cornflour (cornstarch).*
TO COOK: *2–3 tbsp oil; 2 tbsp soy sauce; 1 tsp sugar; 6 spring onions (scallions), cut into finger lengths.*

Remove any fat and tough membranes from pork, and cut into slices about 5 mm (¼ in) thick. Using blunt edge of a chopper, or a heavy saucer, pound meat lightly to tenderize and flatten it. Mix marinade ingredients together, pour over pork and allow to stand for 30 minutes. Heat oil in a wok or a large, heavy frying pan (skillet). Fry pork slices on both sides until golden-brown (add a little more oil if necessary to prevent sticking). This should take about 4 minutes altogether. Add soy sauce and sugar. Stir in the spring onions (scallions), quickly mix through pork, then transfer to a heated serving plate and serve at once. This will serve 4–6 as part of a Chinese meal, or 2 as a main course with rice.

Cha Shao Quick Roast Pork

1 kg (2 lb) pork fillet (tenderloin).
MARINADE: *1½ tbsp soy sauce; 1½ tsp red bean curd; 1½ tbsp dry sherry; 1 tbsp hoisin sauce; ½ tsp salt; 1½ tsp sugar or honey; 1 tbsp oil.*

Place pork fillet (tenderloin) in a shallow dish. Combine marinade ingredients, pour over pork and turn meat until well coated with marinade. Leave for 2 hours, turning every 20 minutes. Place pork on a wire rack in a baking dish and roast in a preheated hot oven (220°C/425°F, Gas Mark 7) for 12 minutes, turning halfway through cooking. Remove from oven and cut into 5 mm (¼ in) thick slices. Arrange on a serving platter. Serves 4–6.
NOTE: Red bean curd can be purchased in cans from Chinese grocery stores.

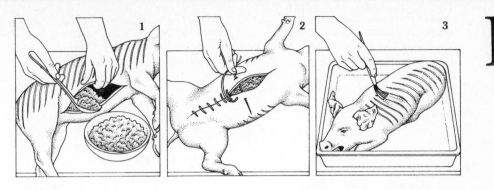

Preparing a Roast Sucking Pig

Island Roast Pork

A good party dish. Serve with rice salad and glazed sweet potatoes.

2.5 kg (5 lb) loin of pork, on the bone or boned, rolled and tied; 1 tbsp light soy sauce; 1½ tsp grated fresh ginger; 1 clove garlic, crushed; 2 tsp salt; 2 tsp oil.

Have skin of pork well scored. Mix soy sauce, ginger, garlic, salt and oil. Rub over pork. Cover and chill overnight. Next day, bring back to room temperature then place pork in a shallow roasting tin (pan). Roast in a preheated very hot oven (240°C/475°F, Gas Mark 9) for 15–20 minutes or until skin is starting to bubble and crisp. Lower heat to moderate (180°C/350°F, Gas Mark 4) and roast for 2 hours. Do not cover pork while roasting. Serves 8–10.

Roast Sucking Pig

Measure your oven and, when ordering the pig, specify the size you require. If necessary ask the butcher to saw it in half across the middle and arrange to have one half cooked in a friend's or neighbour's oven. Also ask the butcher to score the sides of the pig diagonally at 2.5 cm (1 in) intervals from behind the head to the tail.

1 sucking pig, weighing 6–7 kg (12–15 lb); olive oil; 2 onions, finely chopped; 6 shallots, finely chopped; 125 g/4 oz (½ cup) butter; grated rind 1 lemon; 370 g/12 oz (6 cups) fresh white breadcrumbs; 4 tbsp finely chopped mixed fresh herbs (marjoram, parsley, sage and thyme), or 3 tbsp chopped parsley mixed with 1 tbsp mixed dried herbs; salt and freshly ground black pepper; 2 eggs, lightly beaten.
GARNISH: *watercress; baked apples (optional).*

Make stuffing first. Fry onions and shallots in half the butter until soft. Stir in remaining butter then lemon rind, breadcrumbs, herbs, salt, pepper and eggs. Pack loosely into pig **(Fig 1 above)**. Sew up opening, or secure with skewers and lace them with string **(2)**. Cover ears and tail with foil to protect them

from burning. Place pig in a large baking dish, brush with oil and rub with salt **(3)**. Bake in a preheated hot oven (230°C/450°F, Gas Mark 8) for about 45 minutes or until skin starts to crisp, then lower heat to moderate (180°C/350°F, Gas Mark 4) and roast a further 3 hours or until cooked. A small pig of 6 kg (12 lb) will take about 2½ hours. If the pig is cut in half, cooking time will be the same. Check for doneness with a meat thermometer inserted in thickest part of flesh, not touching bone; the pig will be cooked when internal temperature reaches 85°C/185°F. Failing a meat thermometer, pierce thickest part with a skewer and check juice that comes out; when pig is done, it will be quite clear with no tinge of pink. Leave pig in turned-off oven with door ajar for 20 minutes before serving. Place pig on a large platter or board. Serve hot or at room temperature, garnishing platter with watercress and baked apples or other garnish of your choice. If pig is in 2 halves, arrange a watercress garland, secured with toothpicks, over the join. To carve roast sucking pig, please see *Meat*. Serves 12–15.

Potted Hough

1.5 kg (3 lb) shin of beef (foreshank), cut into thick slices; 2 pig's trotters, or 2 veal knuckles, each cut into 3 pieces; 6 black peppercorns; 1 blade mace; 1 bay leaf; 3–4 anchovy fillets, mashed; salt and freshly ground black pepper.
TO SERVE: *cucumber slices; vinegar; hot English mustard; tomatoes; potato salad.*

Put beef, pig's trotters or veal knuckles, peppercorns, mace and bay leaf into a large, heavy saucepan and cover with cold water. Bring to the boil and skim top. Cover and simmer for 3 hours. Cool, then remove meat from broth. Strain broth. Trim away fat and gristle and remove bones from meat. With 2 forks, pull meat apart into fine shreds. Return shredded meat to strained broth and boil uncovered for 20 minutes to reduce. Add anchovies and season with salt and pepper. Boil a further 5 minutes to blend flavours. Pour into 1 large or 2 small bowls which have first been rinsed with cold water. Cover with plastic wrap or a plate and chill until firm. Turn out on to a serving plate and garnish with cucumber slices. Serve the potted hough with vinegar, hot English mustard, tomatoes and a potato salad. Serves 8.

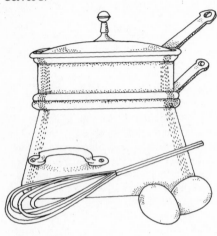

PORRIDGE

This is a relic of the gruel which was a staple item in the daily diet of poor peasants, particularly in the winter months, during many centuries past.

Basically, porridge is a mixture of partially milled grain and water, boiled until thick. Today it is more often a breakfast food, eaten with milk or cream, and maybe sweetened with sugar or honey. It is usually made with rolled oats (see *Oatmeal*), but rolled wheat (wheatmeal) can also be used for porridge. Buckwheat is used in Russia to make a similar kind of porridge, called *kasha* (see *Kasha*), and in those areas of Europe where maize is grown, ground maize is the preferred grain.

Scottish Oatmeal Porridge

500 ml/18 fl oz (2 cups) water; 90 g/3 oz (½ cup) medium ground oatmeal; ¼ tsp salt; milk or single (light) cream to serve.

Bring water to the boil in a heavy saucepan or top of a double saucepan (double boiler). Add oatmeal in a constant stream, stirring continuously. When boiling again, lower heat, cover and simmer very gently for 10 minutes. Add salt and stir. Cover and simmer a further 10 minutes or until oatmeal is well swollen and tender. Serve piping hot in cold soup plates and dip each spoonful into individual bowls of cold milk or single (light) cream before eating. Serves 2.

PORT

A rich, sweet, fortified wine, usually drunk at the end of a meal but sometimes offered as an aperitif. In cooking it is used in a similar fashion to Madeira; for example, as a final enrichment to sauces. A simple sauce for roast duck can be made with pan juices, orange juice and port; Cumberland Sauce (see page 91), served with game and cold meats, calls for port, and a basic brown sauce for roast meat may be varied by the addition of a little port. The once popular dessert of port wine jelly was made with port, redcurrant jelly, a little sugar, gelatine and water. See Port Wine Jelly, page 171.

POTATO

There are numerous varieties of potato but the most readily available from markets or greengrocers depend on consumer demand and growers. Popular varieties change quite rapidly according to their resistance to disease, keeping quality and percentage yield. Growers constantly seek hardier varieties that are acceptable to the consumer and could be described as good all-purpose, old or new potatoes.

It can be difficult to buy potatoes by name so choose different types according to your cooking needs. Potatoes can be new, or old and floury, slightly waxy or very waxy. They are used for different types of dishes or methods of cooking. Your greengrocer will help you choose the right kind for your purpose. Potatoes are economical, filling and most adaptable. They are nutritious, full of flavour and excellent value for money.

Types of Potato

New or Early Potatoes: Tiny new potatoes or slightly bigger ones have creamy pearl, almost transparent skins. Buy them of uniform size for boiling in their skins. They are usually slightly waxy and can be used in salads.
Old and Floury or Mealy Potatoes: These are best for baking in their skins or 'jackets', or for mashing.
Slightly Yellow-fleshed or White-fleshed, Waxy Potatoes: Best for roasting, frying as chips, French fries, matchsticks, shoestring, or game chips; noisette, or sautéed potatoes.
Very Waxy Potatoes: Best for salads.

Do not buy any variety of potato that has green skin or flesh. Potatoes should feel very firm, and have a faint earthy smell. Buy new potatoes in small quantities as you need them because they do not keep well. Store old potatoes in a cool, dark place; they keep particularly well if they are left unwashed, with earth still clinging to the skins.
Instant Mashed Potatoes: This convenience food cannot rival freshly cooked potatoes for flavour, but it can be useful when mashed potato is called for as an ingredient. It can also be used as a quick thickener for soups and stews – simply sprinkle over and stir in.
NOTE: *Potato flour* is a thickening agent used by continental cooks in soups and gravies, and also in baking. **See recipes.**

Boiled New Potatoes

Choose small, new potatoes of uniform size with pearly skins.

500 g (1 lb) new potatoes; 500 ml/18 fl oz (2 cups) water; pinch salt; 2 small sprigs fresh mint (optional); 30 g/1 oz (2 tbsp) butter; 1 tbsp finely chopped fresh mint, parsley or dill.

Scrape skins of potatoes lightly. Bring water to the boil in a saucepan, add potatoes, salt and mint sprigs, if using, and return to a gentle boil. Cover and cook gently for 10–15 minutes, depending on size of potatoes, until tender when tested with a skewer. Drain immediately. Return potatoes to saucepan and shake over low heat until quite dry. Add butter and toss potatoes until each is glistening. Place in heated serving dish and sprinkle with chopped mint, parsley or dill. Serves 4.
NOTE: Omit sprigs of mint in cooking water if garnishing with chopped parsley or dill.

Crispy Olive Potatoes

16 small new potatoes; 60 g/2 oz (4 tbsp) butter, melted; 3 tbsp flour; 1 tsp salt; pinch cayenne; 1 tsp paprika; 90 g/3 oz (½ cup) chopped stuffed olives.

Cook potatoes in boiling salted water until just tender. Drain and peel when cool enough to handle. Toss in melted butter to coat evenly, then coat in flour mixed with salt, cayenne and paprika. Place in a buttered, shallow casserole. Sprinkle with olives and bake in a preheated moderately hot oven (200°C/400°F, Gas Mark 6) for 20 minutes (turn potatoes after first 10 minutes to brown evenly) until piping hot and crispy. Serves 4.

Herbed New Potatoes with Fresh Peas

750 g (1½ lb) new potatoes, scraped; 1¼ tsp salt; 165 g/5½ oz (1 cup) shelled fresh peas; freshly ground black pepper; 2 tbsp shredded fresh mint or basil; 30 g/1 oz (2 tbsp) butter; 4 tbsp single (light) cream; parsley to garnish.

Cook potatoes in boiling water, with salt, until just tender. Ten minutes before potatoes are completely cooked, add peas. When peas are cooked, remove from heat and drain off water. Add pepper, mint or basil, butter and cream and heat a few seconds. Turn into a serving dish and garnish with parsley. Serve immediately. Serves 6.

Sugar-Glazed New Potatoes

500 g (1 lb) new potatoes; 45 g/1½ oz (3 tbsp) butter; 2 tbsp sugar; salt.

Cook potatoes in boiling salted water until just tender. Drain and peel as soon as they are cool enough to handle. Melt butter in a heavy frying pan (skillet) big enough to take potatoes in a single layer. Add sugar and stir over low heat until a light golden-brown. Add potatoes and cook, stirring, until heated through and evenly coated with glaze. Sprinkle with salt and serve at once. Serves 4.

Creamy Mashed Potatoes

Choose old, floury potatoes. When cooked sufficiently the potatoes should break under pressure of a fork but not be mushy. Overcooking or cutting potatoes into small pieces makes them water-soaked and they lose flavour. Always add hot milk for fluffy potatoes as cold makes them sticky.

6 medium potatoes, peeled; salt and freshly ground black pepper; 60 g/ oz (4 tbsp) butter; 120–250 ml/4–8 fl oz ($\frac{1}{2}$–1 cup) hot milk; nutmeg (optional).

Put potatoes into a saucepan with cold water to cover. Add a little salt and bring to the boil. Cook, covered, until potatoes are easily pierced with a skewer, about 20–30 minutes. Drain, return to saucepan and shake pan over a low heat for a few minutes until potatoes are thoroughly dry. Mash with a potato masher or fork **(Fig 1 below)**. Using a wooden spoon beat until very smooth. Add butter to potatoes, then gradually beat in hot milk until potatoes are light and fluffy **(2)**. Season with salt and pepper, and a pinch of nutmeg if liked.

To keep hot: After mashing potatoes push them down well in saucepan, packing tightly. Level top, add butter and spoon about 4 tbsp hot milk over. Cover and leave in a warm place. Before serving beat well, adding more hot milk if necessary. The potatoes will keep for up to 20 minutes. Serves 4–6.
VARIATIONS
Cheese Potatoes: Spread Creamy Mashed Potatoes in a buttered flameproof dish. Sprinkle top generously with grated cheese such as Parmesan, Gruyère or Cheddar and brush with melted butter **(3)**. Or spread with single (light) cream mixed with grated cheese. Place under a preheated hot grill (broiler) until cheese has melted.
Potatoes with Chives or Spring Onions: Fold snipped chives or chopped spring onions (scallions) through Creamy Mashed Potatoes just before serving.
Egg Gratin: Divide hot Creamy Mashed Potatoes among 4 greased individual ramekins and make a depression in each one. Drop an egg into each depression, spoon over a little single (light) cream, or cream mixed with grated cheese. Bake in a preheated moderately hot oven (190°C/375°F, Gas Mark 5) until eggs are set.

Mousseline Potatoes
(Purée of Potatoes)

750 g (1$\frac{1}{2}$ lb) old, floury potatoes, peeled; 30 g/1 oz (2 tbsp) butter; 300 ml/$\frac{1}{2}$ pint (1$\frac{1}{4}$ cups) hot milk; salt and freshly ground black pepper; $\frac{1}{4}$ tsp nutmeg.

Place potatoes in a large saucepan, cover with cold water and bring to the boil. Cook gently for about 20 minutes or until tender. Drain and cool slightly, then return to the pan 2 or 3 at a time and cook over very gentle heat to dry off any moisture. Rub potatoes through a sieve, or process in a food processor using the double-sided steel blade. Return potatoes to the hot pan, place over gentle heat and gradually beat in butter and hot milk. Continue beating until very smooth and soft. Season with salt, pepper and nutmeg and serve immediately. Serves 4.

Baked Jacket Potatoes

In America the Idaho potato is most often chosen for baking. Choose old, floury potatoes for this popular and easy way to serve them.

4 large even-sized baking potatoes; 30 g/1 oz (2 tbsp) butter, quartered.

Scrub potatoes, dry and pierce each 4–6 times with a skewer. Bake directly on the shelf in a preheated moderately hot oven (200°C/400°F, Gas Mark 6) for about 1 hour, depending on size of potatoes. Test by pressing between fingers. When done, cut a cross on top with a pointed knife and squeeze gently to open. Top with butter. Serves 4.
NOTE: The above method produces crisp skin. If softer skin is required rub all over the surface of potatoes with oil before baking.
Toppings: Add a dollop of sour cream and sprinkle with snipped chives; crumble crisp fried bacon over sour cream topping. Sprinkle with crisp bacon and grated cheese; top with butter, grated orange rind and chopped mint.

Preparing creamy Cheese Potatoes

Potatoes Czarina

Baked potatoes are scooped out, seasoned, reheated in the jackets and topped with caviar. An unexpected but superb combination which may be served for lunch with a crisp salad, or as a first course before a simple main dish.

6 large baking potatoes; 30 g/1 oz (2 tbsp) butter; 175 ml/6 fl oz ($\frac{3}{4}$ cup) sour cream; 2 tbsp snipped chives or finely chopped spring onions (scallions); 1 tbsp finely chopped parsley or fresh dill; $\frac{1}{2}$ tsp nutmeg; salt and freshly ground black pepper; 125 g/4 oz (1 cup) caviar or lumpfish roe, chilled.

Scrub potatoes, dry and pierce each 4–6 times. Bake in a preheated moderately hot oven (200°C/400°F, Gas Mark 6) for about 1 hour or until tender when pressed between the fingers. Cut a lid from top of each potato and scoop out pulp with a sharp spoon, being careful not to pierce skins. Place potato shells in turned-off oven to keep warm. Put flesh in a saucepan over low heat and add butter, sour cream, chives or shallots, parsley or dill, nutmeg, salt and pepper. Stir thoroughly with a wooden spoon, mashing pulp and blending ingredients until mixture is piping hot. Arrange potato shells on a heated platter, stuff with seasoned potato, and top each serving with a spoonful of caviar. Serves 6.
VARIATION
Potatoes can be topped with crisp cooked bacon.

Roast Potatoes

Choose potatoes of medium and uniform size. They should be old and slightly waxy for best results. Potatoes that are too small tend to dry out during roasting.

6 medium potatoes, peeled; salt; oil for roasting.

Place potatoes in a saucepan, cover with cold water and bring to the boil. Boil for 5 minutes. Drain and dry well on paper towels. Run the tines of a fork over surface of potatoes and sprinkle very lightly with salt.

Put enough oil into a baking dish to come 1 cm (½ in) up the sides. Heat oil, then put in potatoes and roast in a preheated moderately hot oven (200°C/400°F, Gas Mark 6) for 40–50 minutes or until golden and crusty, turning and basting occasionally. Drain on crumpled paper towels and serve hot. Serves 4–6.

NOTE: If you would like to roast potatoes at the same time as a joint of meat, prepare as above then place in the roasting pan alongside the joint during the last 45 minutes to 1 hour of cooking time, turning and basting the potatoes with pan juices 3 or 4 times.

Potato Chips (French Fries)

French fried potatoes, the popular 'pommes frites' of France, have become equally well liked as potato chips in many other countries. Choose old, dry, slightly waxy potatoes for best results, and cut into uniform lengths and thickness. Soak the potatoes in cold water before frying to help get rid of some of the starch released when the potatoes are cut. Dry the potatoes well before immersing in hot oil; damp potatoes take longer to cook and become greasy. Care should always be taken when deep-frying to lower the food gently into the hot oil to avoid splashing or overflowing. Do not have the frying container more than half full of oil or the oil will overflow when the chips (French fries) are added.

4 large even-sized potatoes, peeled; oil for deep-frying; salt.

Cut potatoes into 5 cm (2 in) lengths, 1 cm (½ in) wide. Soak for 30 minutes in ice-cold water. Drain and dry well with paper towels. Place enough oil in a deep heavy pan to come not more than halfway up the sides and heat gently to 145°C/300°F or until a bread cube placed in the hot oil turns brown in less than 1 minute. Put potatoes in a frying basket and lower into hot oil. Cook until soft but not brown, about 4–5 minutes. Lift out. Increase the temperature of the oil to 190°C/375°F, or until a bread cube turns brown in 30 seconds. Gently lower chips into hot oil and cook until brown and crisp, about 1–2 minutes. Drain on crumpled paper towels, sprinkle with salt and serve immediately. Serves 4.

VARIATIONS

Matchstick Potatoes: Cut potatoes into strips the size of matchsticks and proceed as for Potato Chips, frying once only in oil (190°C/375°F) for about 1–2 minutes until crisp and golden.

Shoestring Potatoes: Cut potatoes into strips not more than 5 mm (¼ in) thick and proceed as for Potato Chips, frying once only in oil (190°C/375°F) for about 2–3 minutes.

Game Chips

Game chips are the classic accompaniment for game and sometimes served at Christmas with the festive roast turkey. Game chips should be of uniform shape, thickness and diameter, resembling fine wafers of potato.

2 large potatoes, peeled; oil for deep-frying; salt.

Shape potatoes into thick cylinders so each slice will be approximately the same diameter. Slice very fine. Soak slices in ice-cold water for 20 minutes, then drain and dry thoroughly. Heat oil to 190°C/375°F or until a bread cube turns brown in 30 seconds. Place ¼ of potatoes at a time in a frying basket and lower gently into hot oil. Keep slices moving about so that they do not stick together. After 1–2 minutes, slices will float to the surface when they are nearly cooked. When golden and crisp, remove and drain on crumpled paper towels. Sprinkle with salt and serve immediately on a folded napkin. Serves 4.

VARIATION

Straw Potatoes: Cut potatoes into sticks 3 mm (⅛ in) thick, then into very thin matchsticks, 3 mm (⅛ in) wide. Soak, dry and fry as for Game Chips.

Pommes de Terre Noisette

(Noisette Potatoes)
Slightly waxy, yellow or white-fleshed old potatoes are best for this method.

1 kg (2 lb) potatoes, peeled; 60 g/2 oz (4 tbsp) butter; salt.

Using a melon baller scoop out balls of potato. Keep in cold water until all potatoes have been prepared. Drain and place in a saucepan with fresh cold water to cover. Bring to the boil and simmer for 2 minutes. Drain and dry thoroughly on paper towels. Heat butter in a frying pan (skillet) and sauté

potatoes, shaking pan occasionally, until they are golden-brown all over. Season with salt. Serve with meat, poultry or fish. Serves 4–6.

Sauté Potatoes

Potatoes for this dish should be old and slightly waxy.

1 kg (2 lb) potatoes; salt; 60 g/2 oz (4 tbsp) butter; 1 tbsp oil.

Preparing Sauté Potatoes

Place potatoes in a large saucepan. Cover with cold water and add salt. Cover, bring to the boil and simmer for 15–20 minutes or until just tender. Drain, then peel when cool enough to handle. Cut into thick slices. Heat butter and oil in a heavy frying pan (skillet) and when foaming add potatoes. Cook briskly, shaking pan and turning potatoes continually. They should never be left to fry. The constant turning gives outside of potatoes a crumbly texture, characteristic of this dish. Sprinkle with salt and serve immediately without draining potatoes. Sauté potatoes make an ideal accompaniment to fish, chicken or steak. Serves 4–6.

Scalloped Potatoes

1 kg (2 lb) old potatoes, peeled and finely sliced; 1 clove garlic, halved; 90 g/3 oz (6 tbsp) butter; salt and freshly ground white pepper; 250 ml/8 fl oz (1 cup) milk; nutmeg; 60 g (2 oz) Gruyère cheese, finely sliced.

Dry potato slices thoroughly. Rub a shallow ovenproof dish with cut sides of garlic and smear with 30 g/1 oz (2 tbsp) butter. Carefully arrange potato slices in layers in the dish, seasoning each layer with salt and pepper. Scald milk (see page 215) and add a little nutmeg, salt and pepper. Arrange cheese on top of potatoes. Carefully pour over milk and add rest of butter, cut into small pieces. Bake in a preheated moderate oven (180°C/350°F, Gas Mark 4) for 40–45 minutes or until tender and golden. Cut into wedges and serve from the dish as an accompaniment to fish, meat or poultry. Serves 6–8.

P

Savoury Potato Cakes

These cakes go well with a fresh green salad.

750 g (1½ lb) potatoes, peeled; 60 g/2 oz (4 tbsp) butter; salt and freshly ground black pepper; 4 rashers (slices) bacon, rind removed and finely chopped; 3 tbsp flour; lard or extra butter, if needed, for frying.

Cook potatoes in boiling salted water until tender. Drain well, return to heat for a minute or so to dry off, and mash until smooth with butter, salt and pepper. Cook bacon in a heavy frying pan (skillet) over a medium heat, without extra fat, for 5 minutes. Remove bacon with a slotted spoon. Beat flour into potatoes and mix in bacon. Pat out on a well-floured work surface until about 5 mm (¼ in) thick. Cut into rounds with a floured pastry cutter. Heat bacon fat in frying pan (skillet), adding a little lard or butter if needed. Add potato cakes and cook over a medium-high heat for about 2 minutes on each side, until golden-brown. Serve at once. Serves 4.

Potato Croquettes

1 quantity Duchess Potatoes (page 310); oil for deep-frying.
COATING: flour; egg; breadcrumbs.

Roll potato mixture into small balls or barrel shapes. Coat with flour, then beaten egg and finally breadcrumbs. Deep-fry for 5–6 minutes and drain on paper towels. If preferred, mould potato mixture into flat cakes, coat with flour, egg and breadcrumbs and shallow-fry in a small amount of butter. Serves 6–8.

Gratin Dauphinois

The mountain province of Dauphine in France produces excellent potatoes which are used in 'gratins'. The addition of cheese does not play any part in the genuine Gratin Dauphinois but is particularly good when the Gratin is served with a baked ham.

1 kg (2 lb) potatoes, peeled; 1 clove garlic, crushed; salt and freshly ground black pepper; nutmeg; 125 g/4 oz (1 cup) Gruyère or Emmenthal cheese, grated (optional); 250 ml/8 fl oz (1 cup) single (light) cream; 30 g/1 oz (2 tbsp) butter.

Slice potatoes thinly. Rub garlic around inside of an ovenproof dish, then butter it well. Arrange potato slices in concentric circles in dish, seasoning each with salt, pepper and nutmeg and sprinkling with grated cheese if using. Pour cream over layers, scatter butter, which has been cut into small pieces, over top and sprinkle with remaining cheese. Bake in a preheated moderate oven (180°C/350°F, Gas Mark 4) for 1 hour or until potatoes are tender and top golden and crisp. Serves 6–8.

Pan Haggerty

This traditional dish from northern England combines potatoes, onions and cheese. It is hearty enough for a main course if you add a green vegetable or salad.

4 tbsp oil; 1 kg (2 lb) potatoes, peeled and finely sliced; 500 g (1 lb) onions, finely sliced; 125 g/4 oz (1 cup) well-flavoured Cheddar cheese, grated; salt and freshly ground black pepper; butter; finely chopped parsley.

You will need a large frying pan (skillet) with a heavy base and a well-fitting lid for this dish. Heat oil in the pan and put in layers of potatoes, onions and cheese, seasoning each layer with salt and pepper and beginning and ending with potatoes. Put lid on pan and cook over gentle heat until underside is crisp and brown and vegetables are tender, about 20–30 minutes. Dot top of potatoes with butter and place pan under a preheated hot grill (broiler) for a few minutes until top is browned. Serve on a heated platter, cut in wedges like a pie and sprinkled with parsley. Serves 6–8.

Sour Cream Potato Cakes

3 large boiled potatoes, coarsely grated – enough to make 370 g/12 oz (2 cups); 1 tsp salt; freshly ground black pepper; 2 tbsp snipped chives or finely chopped shallots; 125 g/4 oz (1 cup) flour, sifted; about 250 ml/8 fl oz (1 cup) sour cream; 60 g/2 oz (4 tbsp) butter; chopped parsley or chives.

Combine grated potatoes with salt, pepper, chives or shallots and flour in a large bowl. Stir in enough sour cream to make a soft dough, about the same consistency as scone dough. Roll or pat out on a lightly floured work surface to a thickness of about 1 cm (½ in). Cut into rounds with a floured 5 cm (2 in) scone cutter. Heat butter in a large, heavy frying pan (skillet) and brown potato cakes for about 3 minutes on each side. Serve at once, sprinkled with a little parsley or chives. Serves 6.

Potatoes Anna

This is a round 'cake' of thinly sliced potatoes, which is turned out and cut into wedges for serving. In Europe a special Anna tin (pan) is available, but you can get good results using a small, heavy frying pan (skillet). Choose a frying pan (skillet) without a wooden handle, since it must be able to go into the oven. Potatoes should be the same size, to give even rounds.

1 kg (2 lb) old potatoes, peeled and finely sliced; 90 g/3 oz (6 tbsp) butter; salt and freshly ground black pepper.

Dry potato slices well. Rub frying pan (skillet) generously with butter and arrange a layer of potatoes in neat, overlapping circles. Season with salt and pepper and dot with small pieces of butter. Arrange another layer of potato slices on top, with more seasoning and butter, and continue until potatoes and butter are used up. Place pan on top of stove over low heat, cover with buttered greaseproof (waxed) paper and a lid, and cook gently for 20 minutes. Remove lid and paper, transfer pan to a preheated moderate oven (180°C/350°F, Gas Mark 4). Continue cooking for 30–40 minutes or until potatoes are brown and crusty on the bottom and cooked through when tested with a skewer. Rest for 1–2 minutes, then invert potatoes on to a heated platter. Cut in wedges to serve. Serves 6–8.

Potatoes in White Wine with Anchovies

6 large, old potatoes; 4 tbsp dry white wine; 2 tbsp wine vinegar; 5 tbsp olive oil; freshly ground black pepper; 2 × 50 g/1⅔ oz cans rolled anchovy fillets, drained; coriander leaves or flat parsley to garnish.

Place potatoes in a saucepan, cover with cold water and bring to the boil. Simmer until tender. Drain and peel when cool enough to handle. Cut into thick slices. Sprinkle with wine and cool to room temperature. Combine vinegar, olive oil and pepper and pour over potatoes. Scatter anchovies over potatoes and garnish with coriander leaves. Serves 6–8.

Rösti

Rösti is the national Swiss potato dish made in the shape of a thick, crispy, golden-brown cake. Sometimes the Rösti is flavoured with crisp bacon and sometimes with onion. It is cut in ample wedges and served with all meat dishes or with fried eggs for breakfast.

1.5 kg (3 lb) old potatoes; $\frac{1}{2}$ tsp salt; 125 g (4 oz) speck or smoked (country-cured) bacon, diced; 30 g/1 oz (2 tbsp) butter.

Place potatoes in a saucepan and cover with cold salted water. Bring to the boil and cook for about 10 minutes. Drain and peel when cool enough to handle. Grate potatoes. Fry speck or bacon in half the butter in a heavy frying pan (skillet). Cook gently until bacon fat is transparent. Spread potatoes in frying pan (skillet) to form a thick cake. Cook over a low heat for about 10 minutes. Slip a knife or spatula under potato cake occasionally to ensure underside is not becoming too brown. Turn cake out on to a large plate. Add remaining butter to pan and when foam has subsided slide potato cake back into it. Cook over a gentle heat for 8 minutes, making sure it does not become too brown. Turn out on to a large heated dish and serve. Serves 6.
NOTES: The Rösti can be browned quickly on both sides over a high heat and then placed in a preheated moderate oven (180°C/ 350°F, Gas Mark 4) for 20 minutes to finish cooking.

Hot Potato Salad

2 rashers (slices) streaky bacon, rind removed; 1 onion, chopped; 1 tbsp flour; 4 tbsp white vinegar; 120 ml/4 fl oz ($\frac{1}{2}$ cup) water; $\frac{1}{4}$ tsp salt; 1 tsp sugar; freshly ground black pepper; 2 tbsp prepared mild mustard; 4 medium potatoes, peeled, cooked and sliced; chopped parsley.

Fry bacon until crisp. Remove from pan with tongs, crumble and set aside. Cook onion in bacon fat until soft and lightly browned. Blend in flour, then stir in bacon, vinegar, water, salt, sugar, pepper and mustard. Bring to the boil, stirring well. Add potatoes, tossing to coat lightly, and heat through. Sprinkle with parsley and serve hot, or let cool, store in refrigerator and reheat before serving. Serves 4.

Preparing Duchess Potatoes

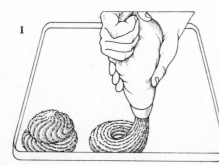

Creamy Potato Salad with Ham

This may be served as a first course at dinner, or as the main course for lunch.

500 g (1 lb) new potatoes; 3 tbsp oil; 1 tbsp vinegar; 1 small onion, finely chopped; salt and freshly ground black pepper; 120 ml/ 4 fl oz ($\frac{1}{2}$ cup) Mayonnaise (page 204); 120 ml/4 fl oz ($\frac{1}{2}$ cup) sour cream; 3 thick slices cooked ham or tongue, cut into julienne (matchstick) strips; chopped parsley; 1–2 canned pimientos, drained and cut into strips (optional).

Cook potatoes in boiling salted water until just tender. Peel while hot and cut into thick slices. Put oil, vinegar and onion in a bowl, beat until thick and season with salt and pepper. Add warm potatoes, folding them into dressing. Allow to cool. Combine mayonnaise and sour cream in another bowl and lightly fold into potatoes. Turn into a salad bowl. Arrange ham or tongue on top of potatoes. Sprinkle with chopped parsley to serve, and, if liked, arrange strips of red pimiento over the salad. This salad is best served at room temperature. Serves 4.

Potato Salad

1 kg (2 lb) potatoes; 120 ml/4 fl oz ($\frac{1}{2}$ cup) Vinaigrette Dressing (page 358); 1 tbsp snipped chives to garnish.

If using tiny new potatoes, scrape skins with a small sharp knife, plunge them into boiling salted water and cook until tender. If using large older potatoes, cover with cold salted water, bring to the boil and simmer until tender, then peel and cut into large dice. The potatoes should be moistened with vinaigrette while still warm. To serve, pile into a bowl and garnish with snipped chives. Serves 4–6.

Duchess Potatoes

1 kg (2 lb) medium, old potatoes, peeled and quartered; 30 g/1 oz (2 tbsp) butter; 1 tsp salt; pinch white pepper; pinch nutmeg; 2 whole eggs; 2 egg yolks.

Cook potatoes in lightly salted boiling water to cover until they are soft. Drain well, then return to the pan and shake over low heat for a few minutes to dry them. Force through

a sieve into a hot saucepan, or push through potato ricer. Beat with a wooden spoon until very smooth. Add butter, salt, pepper, nutmeg and lightly beaten eggs and egg yolks. Mix thoroughly. If made ahead of time, brush surface with a little butter to prevent a crust from forming. When ready to use reheat over low heat, stirring constantly. Pipe mixture through a piping nozzle to make a border around heatproof platters, and brown under grill (broiler). Or pipe into rosettes on a greased baking tray and brown in a preheated very hot oven (220°C/425°F, Gas Mark 7) to serve as a vegetable **(Fig 1 and 2 below left)**. Serves 6–8.

POULTRY

The name given to all domesticated fowl, i.e., chicken, duck, goose, turkey.
See individual entries.

PRALINE

A confection of caramelized sugar and almonds, crushed or ground to a fine powder. Equal quantities of sugar and whole almonds are used. Sometimes about half the almonds are replaced by hazelnuts, but the method remains the same.
Praline may be sprinkled on ice cream, a cold or hot soufflé or custard; added to a butter cream or a crème pâtissière, used to fill cakes and cream puffs; or used to decorate the top and sides of large cakes.
Praline keeps well in an airtight container; it may also be stored frozen. **See recipes**.

Praline

250 g/8 oz (1 cup) sugar; 250 g/8 oz (1$\frac{1}{2}$ cups) whole unblanched almonds.

Cook sugar and almonds in a heavy-based saucepan over low heat until sugar melts, turning nuts over to brown evenly. Continue cooking until sugar has become nut brown in colour. Pour into an oiled tin (pan) or plate. Allow to become quite cold and hard, then break into small pieces and crush with a rolling pin, or grind in a blender or nut mill. Store in airtight container. Makes about 370 g/12 oz (1$\frac{1}{2}$ cups).

Crème Anglaise au Praline

A rich and creamy stirred custard, with a generous topping of praline, is one of the most delectable creams. Serve with poached fruit – pears in burgundy, fresh strawberries or raspberries, fresh or poached whole or halved peaches.

2 tbsp sugar; 4 egg yolks; 1 tbsp cornflour (cornstarch); 250 ml/8 fl oz (1 cup) single (light) cream; 150 ml/$\frac{1}{4}$ pint ($\frac{2}{3}$ cup) milk; 5 tbsp Praline (above).

Beat sugar with egg yolks until thick and light coloured. Stir in cornflour (cornstarch). Bring cream and milk to the boil. Pour a little on to beaten yolks, stirring all the time, then return yolk mixture to saucepan. Cook over a gentle heat, stirring constantly with a wooden spoon, until custard thickens and coats back of spoon thinly. Be sure to stir into corners and all over bottom of pan to prevent custard catching and burning. Remove from heat and beat for 2 minutes to help custard cool, then pour into a serving dish. Cool and chill. Just before serving coat top evenly with praline. Serves 6.

PRAWN/SHRIMP

Small clawless crustaceans, possibly the most popular of all seafoods. Prawns, and their relatives scampi and shrimp, are a delicacy enjoyed by people all over the world.

In America, prawns are usually referred to as shrimp, except in the case of the very large crustaceans the British call Dublin Bay prawns. In America you may see these referred to as Pacific prawns, but they are more commonly called jumbo shrimp.

Cooked prawns are used in some recipes but in most cases it is best to use fresh green or raw prawns. The delicate flesh of prawns does not stand up to being cooked twice – it will toughen and lose much flavour.

□ **To Buy:** Whether green or freshly boiled, prawns should be whole and undamaged. The heads should be firm and unbroken and the tails unsquashed and intact. Green prawns should be washed and free of any mud, and the flesh firm and translucent. The colour of cooked prawns varies according to the variety. Some are rich red while others turn a pale pink. Green or cooked prawns should each be stored by the fishmonger with plenty of crushed ice mixed through them; they should be reminiscent of the sea, with a mild, prawny smell.

□ **To Boil:** Wash thoroughly, then put into a large container of briskly boiling sea-water, or fresh water with 2 tsp salt added to it for each 1 kg/2 lb (4 cups) prawns. Too much salt will toughen the prawns. Boil for 2–3 minutes or until the prawns rise to the surface. Remove immediately, cool quickly in fresh cold water, drain and mix with crushed ice. Or, if you prefer, eat them while still warm with plenty of freshly ground black pepper, brown bread and butter and lemon juice.

□ **To Clean:** Remove the head, shell, legs and tail (unless recipe specifies otherwise). Remove the black vein, which may be gritty, particularly in large prawns, by slitting along the back and pulling it out.

Frozen and Canned Prawns

Choose untorn, well wrapped packs without clumps of ice on the package. Prawns coated with breadcrumbs and frozen ready for cook-ing do not have to be thawed before frying. Use frozen or canned prawns in sauces, fillings and stuffings.

See also Garlic Prawns (page 140) and Prawn Curry (page 93). **See recipes.**

Prawn Cocktail

120 ml/4 fl oz ($\frac{1}{2}$ cup) fresh tomato purée; 2 drops Tabasco (hot pepper) sauce; $\frac{1}{2}$ tsp lemon juice; 2–3 tbsp single (light) cream; shredded lettuce; 1 kg/2 lb (4 cups) medium prawns (shrimp), cooked, shelled and deveined; thin buttered brown bread; 4 lemon wedges.

Combine tomato purée, Tabasco (hot pepper) sauce, lemon juice and cream. Place shredded lettuce in 4 individual dishes, arrange prawns (shrimp) on top and spoon sauce over. Serve with triangles of buttered bread and wedges of lemon. Serves 4.

Orange, Avocado and Prawn Salad

This luxury salad would make a good main course for a small dinner party, yet takes only 10 minutes or so to put together. Serve hot rolls or crusty bread with the salad.

2 ripe avocados, peeled, stoned and sliced lengthways; 2 large oranges; 500 g/1 lb (2 cups) prawns (shrimp), cooked, shelled and deveined; 4 sticks celery, chopped; 1 tbsp snipped chives; 1 head lettuce; 8–10 walnut halves.
FRENCH DRESSING: *2 tbsp lemon juice; 6 tbsp olive oil; 1 tsp chopped fresh oregano, or pinch dried; salt and freshly ground black pepper.*

Mix all ingredients for dressing together by shaking in a screw-top container. Pour half over sliced avocados. Peel oranges, removing outside membrane, and cut between membranes to remove skinless segments. Combine prawns (shrimp), oranges, celery and chives. Line a large bowl with lettuce leaves. Place prawn (shrimp) mixture in centre and arrange avocado slices and walnut halves over it. At the table, pour remaining dressing over salad and toss lightly to combine. Serves 4.

Prawn and Grapefruit Salad

1 kg/2 lb (4 cups) prawns (shrimp), cooked, shelled and deveined; lettuce leaves; 60 g/2 oz ($\frac{1}{2}$ cup) julienne (matchstick) strips celery; 60 g/2 oz ($\frac{1}{2}$ cup) julienne (matchstick) strips red pepper; 30 g/1 oz ($\frac{1}{4}$ cup) julienne (matchstick) strips spring onions (scallions); 2 tbsp lime or lemon juice; salt and freshly ground black pepper; 175 ml/6 fl oz ($\frac{3}{4}$ cup) Mayonnaise (page 204); 2 tbsp chopped parsley; 2 grapefruit, segmented; 16 whole cherry tomatoes, or 4 small tomatoes, quartered.

Chill prawns (shrimp) until ready to serve. Arrange lettuce leaves on 4 small serving plates and top with prawns (shrimp). Sprinkle over celery, red pepper and spring onions (scallions), reserving some for garnish. Season with lime or lemon juice, salt and pepper. Thin mayonnaise carefully with a little boiling water to make a light coating consistency. Spoon over salad. Sprinkle with reserved vegetables and parsley, then arrange grapefruit segments and tomatoes around top. Serves 4.

Sugar-Roasted Prawns

12 large green (uncooked) Dublin Bay prawns (jumbo shrimp); peanut oil; 4 thin slices fresh ginger, finely chopped; 4 spring onions (scallions), with some green tops, finely chopped; 120 ml/4 fl oz ($\frac{1}{2}$ cup) chicken stock; $\frac{1}{2}$ tsp salt; $\frac{1}{2}$ tsp chilli powder; 125 g/4 oz ($\frac{1}{2}$ cup) sugar; 2 tsp sesame oil; coriander sprigs or shredded spring onions (scallions) to garnish.

Remove legs and feelers from prawns (shrimp), leaving on heads and shells. Heat enough peanut oil in a wok or large, heavy frying pan (skillet) to come to a depth of 5 cm (2 in). Cook prawns (shrimp) in hot oil for 3–4 minutes or until they turn pink. Drain prawns (shrimp). Pour off oil from pan to leave only a thin film. Stir-fry ginger and spring onions (scallions) until the aroma is released, about 30 seconds, then pour in chicken stock and add salt, chilli powder and sugar. Cook over very high heat, so liquid

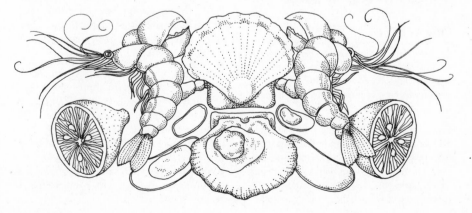

reduces rapidly. When mixture starts to caramelize, turn heat to low and add prawns (shrimp), stirring and turning them over in caramel so they are well coated. Sprinkle with sesame oil, and stir through. Serve at once, garnished with coriander sprigs or shredded spring onions (scallions). Serves 4.

Cold Prawns in Dill Sauce

1 kg/2 lb (4 cups) green (uncooked) medium prawns (shrimp); 120 ml/4 fl oz (½ cup) lemon juice; 1 tsp dried dill; 1 small onion, grated; 2 tsp sugar; 1 tsp salt; ¼ tsp ground allspice; thinly sliced buttered rye bread to serve.
GARNISH: *sprigs fresh dill; lemon wedges.*

Cook prawns (shrimp) in boiling salted water to cover. As soon as they turn pink, drain, reserving 175 ml/6 fl oz (¾ cup) pf the liquid. Mix liquid with lemon juice, dill, onion, sugar, salt and allspice. Shell prawns (shrimp), leaving on tail segments, and devein. Place in a bowl and pour sauce over. Cover and chill overnight. To serve, arrange in an attractive bowl and garnish with dill sprigs and lemon wedges. Serve with buttered rye bread. Serves 4–6.

Prawn and Mushroom Vol-au-Vent

8 × 8 cm (3 in) vol-au-vent cases, bought or home-made (page 464); 60 g/2 oz (½ cup) button mushrooms, sliced; 45 g/1½ oz (3 tbsp) butter; 250 g/8 oz (1 cup) shelled, cooked prawns (shrimp), deveined; 500 ml/18 fl oz (2 cups) hot Béchamel Sauce (page 368); 1 tbsp chopped parsley; 2–3 drops Tabasco (hot pepper) sauce; 2–3 tbsp lemon juice; salt and freshly ground black pepper; sprigs parsley to garnish.

Heat vol-au-vent in a preheated moderate oven (180°C/350°F, Gas Mark 4) for 5–10 minutes. Meanwhile, gently fry mushrooms in butter for 1 minute, then stir in prawns (shrimp) and heat through. Add to the hot sauce with chopped parsley, Tabasco (hot pepper) sauce, lemon juice, salt and pepper. Spoon sauce into warm vol-au-vent. Garnish each with a sprig of parsley. Serves 8.

Prawn Cutlets

12 green (uncooked) Dublin Bay prawns (jumbo shrimp); 2 eggs; 1 tbsp soy sauce; salt; cornflour (cornstarch); fine dry breadcrumbs; oil for deep-frying; lemon wedges to garnish.

Shell prawns (shrimp), leaving tails intact, and devein. Using a sharp knife, slit prawns (shrimp) down back, being careful not to cut right through. Beat eggs with soy sauce and salt. Dip prawns (shrimp) in cornflour (cornstarch) to coat lightly, then into egg

mixture and lastly in breadcrumbs. Press cut sides of prawns (shrimp) gently with palm of hand to flatten. Deep-fry 'cutlets' in hot oil until golden, about 5 minutes, taking care not to overcrowd the pan. Drain on paper towels and serve immediately, garnished with lemon wedges. Serves 2–4.

Potted Prawns

180 g/6 oz (¾ cup) butter; 500 g/1 lb (2 cups) green (uncooked) prawns (shrimp), shelled, deveined and chopped; ¼ tsp ground mace; ¼ tsp nutmeg; pinch cayenne; 1 tsp ground mixed spice (ground allspice); freshly ground black pepper.

Melt butter in a large frying pan (skillet) and add prawns (shrimp), mace, nutmeg, cayenne, mixed spice (allspice) and pepper. Toss in butter for a few minutes until cooked. Spoon prawns (shrimp) and butter into a

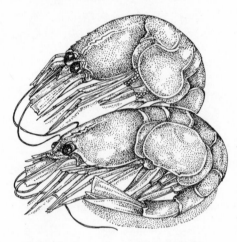

small soufflé dish or 6 individual pots. Press down lightly, then cover with foil and chill overnight. Serve with Melba Toast (see page 212). Serves 6.

Dublin Bay Prawns in Shell with Tomato Sauce

1 kg/2 lb (5½ cups) green (uncooked) Dublin Bay prawns (jumbo shrimp); 2 tbsp oil; 2 tbsp Chinese rice wine or dry sherry; 1 tsp sesame oil.
SAUCE: *1½ tbsp tomato ketchup; 1 tbsp chilli sauce; pinch salt; ¼ tsp sugar; 2 tbsp chicken stock; 1 tbsp shredded fresh ginger; ½ tsp cornflour (cornstarch); 2 tsp water.*

If prawns (shrimp) are very large, cut each in half. Rinse lightly and dry thoroughly. Heat a wok or frying pan (skillet), add oil and stir-fry prawns (shrimp) until a good red colour, 2 minutes. Sprinkle with wine or sherry.
SAUCE: Combine ingredients in a bowl, add to prawns (shrimp), cover and bring to the boil. Reduce heat and simmer gently for 3–4 minutes. Add sesame oil for a final touch and serve hot. Serves 4.

NOTE: You may shell the prawns (shrimp), removing heads but leaving tail shells intact, and devein before cooking.

Braised Prawns with Mange Tout

750 g/1½ lb (3 cups) green (uncooked) prawns (shrimp), shelled and deveined; 1 tbsp Chinese rice wine or dry sherry; 1 tsp cornflour (cornstarch); 1 tsp soy sauce; 125 g/4 oz (1 cup) mange tout (snow peas); 5–6 tbsp oil.
SEASONING: *1 tsp salt; ½ tsp sugar; 1 tsp soy sauce.*

If prawns (shrimp) are large, cut in half. Put into a bowl with wine or sherry, cornflour (cornstarch) and soy sauce. Mix well, then cover and chill for at least 30 minutes. String mange tout (snow peas), if necessary. Mix all ingredients for seasoning together. Heat 4 tbsp oil in a wok or frying pan (skillet) and cook prawns (shrimp), stirring over a high heat until colour changes. Remove. Add further 1–2 tbsp oil to wok and stir-fry mange tout (snow peas) for 2 minutes. Return prawns (shrimp) to wok and add seasoning. Toss until heated through, and serve immediately. Serves 4.

Scandinavian Prawns

250 ml/8 fl oz (1 cup) dry white wine; 2 tbsp fresh chopped dill or 2 tsp dried; 2 sticks celery, chopped; 1 tsp salt; 750 g/1½ lb (3 cups) green (uncooked) prawns (shrimp); sour cream or Mayonnaise (page 204) to serve.

Place wine, dill, celery and salt in a saucepan and bring to the boil. Drop in prawns (shrimp). Stir until prawns (shrimp) take on a pink tinge, then cover and simmer gently for 2–3 minutes. Allow to cool in the liquid. Shell and devein. Serve chilled, with a bowl of sour cream or mayonnaise. Fresh dill may be snipped over prawns (shrimp) to garnish. Serves 4–6 as a main course with rice, or 8–10 as an appetizer without rice.

Prawn Bisque

250 g/8 oz (1 cup) cooked prawns (shrimp); 30 g/1 oz (2 tbsp) butter; 1 tbsp flour; 1 litre/1¾ pints (4 cups) Fish Stock (page 414) or water; ¼ tsp paprika; ¼ tsp salt; 120 ml/4 fl oz (½ cup) single (light) cream; 2 tbsp dry sherry; salt and freshly ground black pepper.
GARNISH: *1 tbsp chopped parsley; 1 tbsp snipped chives.*

Shell and devein prawns (shrimp), reserving heads and shells. Melt butter in a saucepan and sauté heads and shells for 5 minutes. Sprinkle with flour and pound well with a wooden spoon. Add fish stock or water, paprika and salt. Bring to the boil and

P

simmer for 10 minutes, then strain. Reserve a few prawns (shrimp) for garnish and place remaining prawns (shrimp) and strained stock in blender or food processor. Blend or process until smooth. Heat gently, stirring continuously, then add cream, sherry, salt and pepper. Do not let soup boil. Serve immediately, garnished with reserved prawns (shrimp), chopped, and parsley and chives. Serves 6.

NOTE: If you do not have a blender or food processor, chop prawns (shrimp) very finely before adding to strained stock.

Devilled Barbecued Prawns

1 kg/2 lb (4 cups) green (uncooked) prawns (shrimp); 30 g/1 oz (2 tbsp) butter; 1 small green pepper, cored, seeded and diced; 1 tbsp French (Dijon) mustard; 1 tsp Worcestershire sauce; few drops Tabasco (hot pepper) sauce; 1 tbsp mango chutney; 1 tsp tomato purée (paste); 2 tsp barbecue sauce; 2 shallots, chopped; $\frac{1}{4}$ tsp cayenne; salt and freshly ground black pepper; 120 ml/4 fl oz ($\frac{1}{2}$ cup) single (light) cream.

Shell prawns (shrimp), leaving heads on, and devein. Melt butter in a saucepan and sauté green pepper for 1 minute. Add remaining ingredients, except cream and prawns (shrimp) and cook, stirring, over low heat for 1–2 minutes or until amalgamated. Remove from heat and stir in cream. Barbecue or grill (broil) prawns (shrimp), brushing liberally with sauce during cooking. Serve with rice, or without as an appetizer. Serves 4–6.

PROFITEROLE

Profiteroles are small choux pastry puffs with a sweet or savoury filling. They make superb party savouries or glamorous desserts or can star at afternoon tea. Tiny profiteroles, filled or unfilled, are an elegant accompaniment to clear soup. **See recipes**.

Cocktail-size Profiteroles (to serve with drinks or to accompany soup) Make mounds about 2 cm ($\frac{3}{4}$ in) in diameter, and bake 10 minutes in a preheated hot oven (230°C/450°F, Gas Mark 8), then for about 10 minutes more at moderate (180°C/350°F, Gas Mark 4). Dry out in turned-off oven 20 minutes.

Tiny Unfilled Puffs (to accompany soup) Make dots of pastry by squeezing it from a piping (pastry) bag fitted with a plain 5 mm ($\frac{1}{4}$ in) nozzle and cutting off in 5 mm ($\frac{1}{4}$ in) lengths. Bake in a preheated moderate oven (180°C/ 350°F, Gas Mark 4) for about 10 minutes or until crisp and brown.

Cream Puffs Make mounds about 4 cm ($1\frac{1}{2}$ in) in diameter and bake 10 minutes in a preheated hot oven (230°C/450°F, Gas Mark 8), then 20–25 minutes at moderate (180°C/350°F, Gas Mark 4). Cover loosely with a sheet of foil if puffs brown too much

before they feel firm and light in the hand. Slit sides and return to turned-off oven with door ajar for 30 minutes to dry out.

NOTE: Crème Pâtissière fillings may be added to sweet Profiteroles 1–2 hours ahead of time, but whipped cream fillings should not be added more than 30 minutes ahead or profiteroles may go soggy.

Cold fillings which do not contain cream may be added 1–2 hours ahead of time; those with cream should not be added more than 30 minutes ahead, or profiteroles may go soggy. Hot fillings may be added at the last minute and the filled profiteroles placed in the oven for a few minutes if necessary to ensure that they are very hot. Or, for cocktail-sized profiteroles, the filling may be put in cold and heated in the shells, in one layer on a baking tray, in a preheated moderate oven (180°C/350°F, Gas Mark 4) for about 20–25 minutes.

Fill with one of the following, to serve cold with drinks or soup.

● Softened pâté.

● Mashed salmon or finely chopped cooked ham, chicken or prawns (shrimp), mixed with enough Mayonnaise (see page 204) to bind.

● Softened blue cheese mashed with a little cream.

● Caviar mixed with a little sour cream and onion juice.

● Chopped roast beef mixed with enough Béarnaise Sauce (see page 370) to bind.

● Avocado mashed with a little cream cheese, lemon juice and seasonings.

● Finely chopped smoked salmon or other flaked, smoked fish mixed with cream cheese and seasoned with pepper and lemon juice.

Fill with one of the following to serve hot with drinks or in cream-puff-sized shells as a first course.

● Chopped cooked spinach, flaked crab, chopped prawns (shrimp) or asparagus, mixed with Mornay Sauce (see page 368).

● Chopped cooked chicken, ham, brains, sweetbreads or seafood, fried mushrooms or Duxelles (see page 231) mixed with Béchamel or Velouté Sauce (see page 368).

● Sautéed chicken livers and shallots in a

sauce made in the pan with single (light) cream and a little sherry, thickened with cornflour (cornstarch). See also Choux Pastry page 276.

Basic Profiteroles

1 quantity sweetened or unsweetened Choux Pastry (page 276); 1 egg; pinch salt.

Using a piping (pastry) bag with a 1 cm ($\frac{1}{2}$ in) plain nozzle, pipe choux pastry into small, high mounds, well apart, on a lightly greased baking tray. Pipe each mound with one steady pressure, and release pressure before lifting bag away, to avoid a long tail. Alternatively, take spoonfuls of the pastry and push off on to baking tray. Do not try to change shape of choux pastry when putting it out, or it will rise in bumpy shapes instead of round ones. For 5 cm (2 in) profiteroles, make mounds about 3 cm ($1\frac{1}{4}$ in) in diameter. Beat egg with salt and brush over pastry mounds, pushing down tails with a damp finger. Egg glaze may be omitted if the puffs are to be iced (frosted).

Bake in a preheated hot oven (230°C/ 450°F, Gas Mark 8) for 10 minutes, then reduce heat to moderate (180°C/350°F, Gas Mark 4) and bake 15–20 minutes more or until profiteroles are golden-brown, firm and light in the hand. If pastry is becoming too brown before it is cooked through, cover loosely with a sheet of foil. Make a slit or hole with the point of a knife in the side of each profiterole. Return to turned-off oven and leave with door ajar for 20 minutes to ensure that puffs are thoroughly dried out (this is the secret of puffs that will hold their shape without collapsing). Cool on a wire rack. Fill by piping filling through the holes in the sides, or by carefully cutting off tops with a serrated knife, spooning in filling and replacing lids. Unfilled profiteroles will keep in an airtight container for 1–2 weeks. Makes about 16 × 5 cm (2 in) profiteroles.

Profiteroles au Chocolat
(Chocolate Profiteroles)

16 × 5 cm (2 in) Profiteroles (above); 120 ml/4 fl oz ($\frac{1}{2}$ cup) double (heavy) cream, whipped with 2 tsp icing (confectioners) sugar and a few drops vanilla essence (extract), or 175 ml/6 fl oz ($\frac{3}{4}$ cup) Crème Pâtissière (page 165); sifted icing (confectioners) sugar.

HOT CHOCOLATE SAUCE: *180 g/6 oz (1 cup) dark chocolate; 6 tbsp water; 1 tbsp rum or brandy (optional).*

Fill profiteroles with whipped cream or crème pâtissière. Pile them into a serving dish and sift a little icing (confectioners) sugar over the top.

HOT CHOCOLATE SAUCE: Break chocolate into pieces and place in a heatproof bowl with water and rum or brandy, if using. Set bowl over a saucepan of simmering water and stir until chocolate melts. Cook 1 minute longer, then pour into a heated jug and serve with profiteroles. Serves 6–8.

VARIATION

Chocolate Profiteroles for Afternoon Tea: Fill profiteroles as described, then dip tops into Chocolate Glaze (see page 73). Place on a wire rack to set. Omit chocolate sauce.

Profiteroles à l'Orange

(Orange Profiteroles)

3 sugar cubes; 1 orange; 120 ml/4 fl oz (½ cup) double (heavy) cream; 2 tsp brandy (optional); 16 × 5 cm (2 in) Profiteroles (page 313); 90 g/3 oz (6 tbsp) caster sugar.

Rub sugar cubes over rind of orange until sugar is saturated with orange oils. Squeeze juice from half the orange, and pound sugar cubes with 2 tsp of the juice until dissolved. Whip cream with this orange syrup and brandy. Use to fill profiteroles. To make toffee topping, place caster sugar in a small, heavy saucepan and cook slowly, tilting pan frequently from side to side so that sugar heats evenly, until it melts and caramelizes to a golden-brown. Dip base of saucepan in cold water to stop further cooking. Dip top of each profiterole in toffee and place on a wire rack to set. Serves 6–8.

Profiteroles Pralinées

(Praline Profiteroles)

120 ml/4 fl oz (½ cup) double (heavy) cream; 4 tbsp Crème Pâtissière (page 165); 2 tbsp Praline (page 310); 16 × 5 cm (2 in) Profiteroles (page 313); icing (confectioners) sugar.

Whip cream and mix with crème pâtissière and praline. Fill profiteroles and sift a little icing (confectioners) sugar over tops. Serves 6–8.

Coffee Profiteroles

1 tsp instant coffee powder; 2 tsp hot water; 120 ml/4 fl oz (½ cup) double (heavy) cream; 2 tsp icing (confectioners) sugar, sifted; 2 tsp brandy or whisky (optional); 16 × 5 cm (2 in) Profiteroles (page 313); 1 quantity Coffee Glacé Icing (page 164).

Dissolve coffee in hot water and allow to cool. Whip cream with icing (confectioners) sugar, coffee, and brandy or whisky, if using. Fill profiteroles and top with coffee glacé icing. Serves 6–8.

Filled Cream Puffs

250 ml/8 fl oz (1 cup) double (heavy) cream; icing (confectioners) sugar, sifted; few drops vanilla essence (extract); 12 Cream Puffs (page 313).

Whip cream with 1 tbsp icing (confectioners) sugar and vanilla. Fill shells and sift more icing (confectioners) sugar over the tops. Makes 12.

PROSCIUTTO

The general Italian term for ham, although it has come to refer more particularly to raw, uncooked ham (*prosciutto crudo*).

Prosciutto is made throughout Italy (and the same method is followed in many other countries), but the prosciutto of Parma has the highest reputation. It is traditionally prepared in the cold months of the year; legs of pork (ham) are salted, then allowed to dry for about 6 months. The hams are never smoked.

A good prosciutto should be a deep, rosy pink colour, with a thin edge of white fat; it should be quite firm and dry. It is usually cut in paper-thin slices, since it contains very little moisture and its flavour is quite intense. It is often served as antipasto or hors d'oeuvre, either by itself or accompanied by fresh ripe figs or melon. It may also be used with pasta, in which case thicker slices are required.

See also *Ham.*

Prosciutto con Melone

(Raw Ham with Melon)

1 ripe melon, chilled; 6–8 paper-thin slices prosciutto.

Seed and cut melon into 6–8 slices. Serve each portion of melon with a slice of prosciutto draped over it. Serves 6–8.

PRUNE

Any kind of dried plum. Certain varieties of plums are particularly suitable for drying. Prunes should be black and shiny, with a moist dark, sweet flesh. They may often be eaten or used for cooking without any preliminary soaking, but soaking will soften them and reduce cooking time. Red or white wine may be used to give a slightly different flavour, and soaking in weak tea is said to enhance the prunes' flavour.

A simple dish of stewed prunes may be offered for breakfast or as a dessert, and many more elaborate desserts are based on prunes. Halved prunes may be added to a plain cake, a steamed pudding or a custard in place of raisins or sultanas (golden raisins), and the inclusion of nicely-plumped prunes in a winter fruit salad makes a welcome change.

The rich flavour of prunes also combines well with meats such as pork and rabbit. In Germany, prunes are often associated with goose – for example, in a stuffing with apples; with goose giblets; with haricot (navy) beans or lentils, to accompany goose or duck.

Stoned (pitted) dessert prunes may be stuffed with a whole almond or walnut, with marzipan or fondant, or with ground walnuts, sweetened with sugar or honey. **See recipes.**

Pork with Prunes

500 g/1 lb (2⅔ cups) large dessert prunes; 350 ml/12 fl oz (1½ cups) white wine; 6 thick pork chops, trimmed of rind and excess fat; flour; salt and freshly ground black pepper; 30 g/1 oz (2 tbsp) butter; 1 tbsp redcurrant jelly; 250 ml/8 fl oz (1 cup) single (light) cream; squeeze lemon juice.

Soak prunes overnight in wine. Next day, drain off 4 tbsp wine and reserve. Simmer prunes very gently in remaining wine until soft. Remove stones. Lightly flour chops and season with salt and pepper. Brown on both sides in butter, then add reserved wine, cover and simmer gently about 40 minutes. Drain prunes, and add liquid to pan. Cook for about 3 minutes, then remove chops to heated serving dish. Arrange prunes with chops. Reduce pan liquid, then add redcurrant jelly and gradually stir in cream. Adjust seasoning, add lemon juice and pour sauce over chops. Serves 6.

Prune Mousse

500 g/1 lb (2⅔ cups) prunes, stoned (pitted); grated rind and juice 1 orange; grated rind and juice 1 lemon; 1 tbsp port; 3 tsp gelatine; 2 egg whites; 125 g/4 oz (½ cup) caster sugar; whipped cream to decorate.

Cook prunes in water to cover until tender. Purée in a blender or through sieve. If necessary, add a little water to make 350 g/12 oz (1½ cups) purée. Set aside 4 tbsp orange juice. Add remaining juices, rinds and port to purée. Soften gelatine in reserved juice, then dissolve over gentle heat. Add to purée and chill until starting to thicken. Beat egg whites until stiff, and gradually beat in sugar. Fold meringue into prune mixture. Spoon into individual dishes or large serving bowl and chill at least 1 hour. Decorate with whipped cream. Serves 6.

Prune Hors d'oeuvre

large dessert prunes; walnut or pecan halves; rashers (slices) lean bacon, rind removed.

Soak prunes in boiling water or hot tea for 15 minutes, if desired. Drain, remove stones and stuff with nuts. Wrap in bacon and secure with wooden toothpicks. Grill (broil), turning frequently, or bake in a preheated moderately hot oven (200°C/400°F, Gas Mark 6) until bacon is crisp, about 7–10 minutes. Drain on paper towels. Serve hot.

Right: Herb Quiche (page 324) and Mushrooms in Pastry Cases (page 229)

Prune Tart

750 ml/1¼ pints (3 cups) boiling water; 1 tsp tea leaves; 500 g/1 lb (2⅔ cups) large dessert prunes; 1 quantity Rich Shortcrust Pastry (page 274); 1 egg; 120 ml/4 fl oz (½ cup) single (light) cream; 1 tsp cornflour (cornstarch); 60 g/2 oz (¼ cup) caster sugar; 2 tbsp Grand Marnier or Cointreau; 30 g/1 oz (2 tbsp) butter.

Pour boiling water over tea and leave to steep for 5 minutes then drain. Soak prunes in weak tea for 4 hours. Drain and remove stones. Roll out pastry (dough) to about 5 mm (¼ in) thick. Line 23 cm (9 in) tart tin (pan) and arrange prunes on base. Bake in a preheated moderately hot oven (200°C/400°F, Gas Mark 6) for about 15 minutes. Meanwhile, beat egg with cream, cornflour (cornstarch), caster sugar and liqueur. Pour mixture over prunes, dot with butter and bake for 10–15 minutes longer. Serve warm or cold with whipped cream. Serves 6–8.

PUDDINGS

See Desserts and Puddings.

PUFF PASTRY

See page 274 for recipe.

PUFTALOON (Fried Scone)

It seems that puftaloons are peculiar to Australia where, traditionally, they are eaten hot with golden (light corn) syrup or treacle. Puftaloons are a type of scone dough, fried in hot dripping or vegetable cooking oil.

Puftaloons

250 g/8 oz (2 cups) self-raising flour; ½ tsp salt; 30 g/1 oz (2 tbsp) butter; 150 ml/¼ pint (⅔ cup) milk; oil for deep-frying.

Sift flour and salt together. Rub (cut) in butter. Make a well in centre and mix in milk, adding more milk if necessary to make a soft dough. Knead lightly, then roll out on a floured work surface to 1 cm (½ in) thickness. Cut into rounds with a 4 cm (1½ in) cutter. Heat oil in a saucepan or deep frying pan (skillet) and fry scones, turning once, until puffed and golden and cooked through. Drain on paper towels and serve hot. Makes about 12.

PULSES: DRIED BEANS, PEAS AND LENTILS

Dried beans, peas and lentils are classified as 'pulses', a word taken from the Latin 'puls' or

Left: Home Preserves – a selection of jams (page 166), Jellies (page 171), Chutneys (page 76), Pickles (page 288 and Mincemeat (page 217)

'pottage'. There are hundreds of varieties of pulses with differing flavours and textures, but they are all regarded as a good source of protein.

Pulses are readily available from supermarkets, health food stores and delicatessens. They can be stored for up to 1 year in airtight containers, but longer storage will harden them. Buy pulses that are clean and of uniform size and quality. Most are available ready-wrapped, but some can be purchased loose.

Pulses make delicious soups, salads, or main course dishes. They are economical, easy to prepare and help stretch the menu.

Dried Beans

Haricot or White Beans: Smooth, oval beans of which there are more than one variety. Each is virtually interchangeable with another in most recipes. Haricot beans are used in soups, baked bean dishes, stews, with meats and in salads. Varieties of haricot or white beans include:

Navy beans: Excellent in dishes such as Boston Baked Beans.

Flageolets: Used with lamb dishes in France.

Soissons: Often considered to be the finest haricot beans and used to great effect in the superb *cassoulet* dishes of France.

Cannellini: The Italian variety of haricot beans and slightly fatter than their French and English equivalents. Cannellini are delicious in soups as well as many dishes from Tuscany, including Beans with Tuna, served chilled with a garlicky dressing.

Butter Beans: Also known as Lima Beans, and can be large or small. Use the large beans in soups and purées, and the small butter beans in dishes instead of haricot beans or in their own right. Either large or small butter beans are delicious in salads.

Borlotti Beans: Pinky-brown, black-speckled beans used in Italian soup-stews, and sometimes mixed with pasta.

Chick Peas: Also known as Spanish beans, *garbanzo* or *ceci* peas. They are not strictly speaking, peas. Their nutty flavour and crisp texture are perfect in salads, soups, stews and in many other dishes such as *Hummus bi Tahini* (see page 160), a delicious Middle Eastern spread.

Dried chick peas may need soaking for up to 10 hours before cooking, and sometimes need 5–6 hours of gentle simmering to become completely tender. Chick peas can also be purchased canned, which eliminates the soaking and long cooking processes. Simply drain, rinse and use as required.

Red Kidney Beans: Kidney-shaped as their name suggests, and are probably most often associated with Chilli Con Carne (see page 72), or salads. They are also the major component in *frijoles refritos* (Refried Beans), one of the basic dishes of Mexico.

Broad Beans or *Fava Beans:* These are

strongly flavoured beans that form the basis of the Middle Eastern dish *Falafel*, little bean patties flavoured with herbs, garlic and onion (see page 320).

Mung Beans: These can be cooked as for other dried beans, but are probably best used after sprouting, in salads and Chinese dishes (see *Bean Sprouts*).

Black-eyed Peas or Beans: Creamy white beans which derive their name from the little black eye or spot in the centre. Often served in southern U.S.A. with pork and cornbread. Black-eyed peas are the essential ingredient in 'Hopping John' – a mixture of beans, brown rice, bacon and oil.

Soy Beans: Highly nutritious, containing complete protein, and used extensively as food and for oil, particularly in places where other sources of complete protein are scarce. Soy bean curds or *tofu* are used in Oriental dishes as a meat substitute. *Tofu* is a rather bland substance that readily takes on other flavours from other ingredients in the dish. Soy sauce is made from fermented soy beans. The distinctive flavour of soy beans blends well when used with other beans in recipes.

☐ **Basic Preparation:** When buying in bulk discard any broken or defective beans. Rinse well, until the water runs clear. Packaged beans usually need rinsing only. Most beans need soaking to restore the water lost during drying. The soaking water may be used in most recipes. Soak beans by one of the two methods below:

Quick soaking: Put beans in a large saucepan, add cold water to cover and bring to the boil. Cover pan and cook for 2 minutes; remove from heat. Let stand for 1 hour, then cook according to recipe.

Overnight soaking: Put beans in a large bowl, cover with cold water and soak for 6–8 hours but no longer or they may ferment.

☐ **To Cook:** Cook beans in the soaking water or fresh water to cover. Cover the saucepan, bring to the boil, reduce heat and simmer for the time stated in the recipe or for 1½–2 hours (except chick peas which take longer – up to 5–6 hours). Red kidney beans should boil rapidly for the first 10 minutes of cooking to ensure harmful toxins are destroyed. Stir occasionally, being careful not to break the beans. When ready, they should be tender and hold their shape. Sugar, salt or acids (this includes tomatoes) added to the beans during simmering will toughen them, so add after beans are tender.

If beans are to be used for soups or in baked dishes, they should be cooked until they are just barely tender. Add flavourings such as onion, carrot, celery, bouquet garni, bay leaf, garlic or bacon bones.

Most dried beans are also available precooked in cans, which precludes the soaking and long slow cooking. Drain, rinse and use according to recipe.

Dried Peas

Split Peas: Usually sold packaged, skinned and split; they may be bright green or golden yellow, and are often used in soups. Rinse thoroughly and soak in cold water overnight unless otherwise specified on the packet or in the recipe.

Lentils

Red, Brown and Green Lentils: These need less cooking and preparation than dried peas and beans. The small red lentil needs no pre-soaking and becomes tender after about 20 minutes cooking. The brown and green lentils take a little longer to cook. Lentils are excellent in purées and soups.

In Germany, brown lentils accompany roast duck and in France, when cooked with garlic and flavoured with lemon juice, lentil purée is eaten with pickled (salt) pork. Some lentils can be used in salads.

Dhal: This is the Hindi word for pulses, and most packages labelled '*dhal*' contain a mixture of lentils with some dried beans and peas. Dhal is also a delicious spiced purée served with Indian curries, and most take about 45 minutes to cook. **See recipes.**

Boston Baked Beans

430 g/14 oz (2 cups) small white haricot (navy) beans, soaked in water overnight; 125 g (4 oz) pickled (salt) pork or speck, cut into 2.5 cm (1 in) strips; 2 tsp dry mustard; 90 g/3 oz (½ cup) firmly packed brown sugar; 125 g/4 oz (⅓ cup) dark treacle (molasses); 1 tsp salt.

Drain beans, reserving liquid. Place ⅓ of salt pork or speck in bottom of an ovenproof casserole and add drained beans. Blend together mustard, brown sugar and treacle (molasses) with bean liquid and pour over beans. Cut several gashes in remaining salt pork or speck and place on top of beans. Cover and bake in a preheated very cool oven (120°C/250°F, Gas Mark ½) for about 6 hours, adding extra water as needed. Uncover for final hour of cooking so pork will brown and crisp. Season. Serves 6–8.

Beans with Tuna

165 g/5½ oz (¾ cup) dried haricot (navy) or cannellini beans, soaked in water overnight and drained; 120 ml/4 fl oz (½ cup) olive oil; juice 1 lemon; 2 cloves garlic, crushed; salt and freshly ground black pepper; 1 onion, finely sliced; 1 × 200 g/7 oz can solid pack tuna, drained and flaked; chopped parsley.

Place beans in a saucepan and cover with fresh cold water. Bring to the boil, then cover and simmer 2½ hours or until tender. Drain. Mix together olive oil, lemon juice, garlic, salt and pepper and add to hot beans. Stir in onion. Cover and chill for several hours. Fold in tuna, sprinkle with parsley and serve in individual bowls. Serves 4.

Cassoulet

125 g (4 oz) bacon; 750 g (1½ lb) pork spareribs (country-style ribs); 500 g/1 lb (2½ cups) dried white haricot (navy) beans, soaked in water overnight and drained; 1 onion, halved; 1 bouquet garni; 2 cloves garlic, lightly crushed; 500 g (1 lb) breast or shoulder of lamb, boned; 500 g (1 lb) garlic-flavoured boiling sausage such as clobassi; 45 g/1½ oz (¾ cup) fresh breadcrumbs.

Trim rind from bacon and also any rind from pork. Dice bacon. Place beans in a heavy saucepan with bacon, onion, bouquet garni and garlic. Cover with water, bring to the boil and simmer for 1¼ hours. Meanwhile, roast pork spareribs and lamb in a preheated moderate oven (160°C/325°F, Gas Mark 3) for 30 minutes. Add whole sausage to beans and simmer for a further 15 minutes. When beans are almost cooked, drain off and reserve liquid, discarding onion, bouquet garni and garlic. Place half the beans in a deep casserole. On top place sausage, thickly sliced, then lamb and pork, cut into serving-sized pieces. Cover with the remaining beans and moisten with 250 ml/8 fl oz (1 cup) of reserved liquid. Sprinkle breadcrumbs on top. Bake in a very cool oven (120°C/250°F, Gas Mark ½) for 1½ hours, adding more liquid if dish becomes too dry. The breadcrumbs should form a fine golden crust on top by the end of cooking. Serves 6.

Quick Barbecued Baked Beans

2 tbsp dark treacle (molasses); 2 tbsp prepared spicy mustard; juice ½ lemon; 2 tsp Worcestershire sauce; 2 × 420 g/14 oz cans baked beans in tomato sauce; 500 g (1 lb) frankfurters, thickly sliced.

Combine treacle (molasses), mustard, lemon juice and Worcestershire sauce in a saucepan and heat gently. Add beans and frankfurters and simmer for about 10 minutes, or place in a casserole, top with frankfurters and bake in a preheated moderate oven (180°C/350°F, Gas Mark 4) for about 30 minutes. Serves 4–6.

Pasta with Beans

210 g/7 oz (1 cup) dried haricot (navy) or borlotti beans; 1.10 litres/1 pint 18 fl oz (4½ cups) cold water; 370 g (12 oz) macaroni; 3 tbsp olive oil; 1 large onion, chopped; 2 large carrots, sliced; 125 g/4 oz (1 cup) chopped celery; 1 clove garlic, crushed; 500 g/1 lb (2 cups) peeled, chopped tomatoes; 1 tsp chopped fresh sage; 1 tsp chopped fresh oregano; salt and freshly ground black pepper; chopped parsley; grated Parmesan cheese.

Soak beans in water overnight. Next day, put beans and water into a large saucepan. Bring to the boil, then reduce heat, cover and simmer 2–3 hours or until beans are tender. Stir during cooking. Drain, reserving 600 ml/1 pint (2½ cups) liquid. Cook macaroni according to directions on packet. Drain. Heat oil in a large heavy saucepan and sauté onion, carrots, celery and garlic until soft but not coloured. Add tomatoes, sage, oregano, salt and pepper. Cover and cook over a gentle heat for 20 minutes. Add beans, macaroni and 350 ml/12 fl oz (1½ cups) reserved bean liquid. Bring to the boil, then cover and simmer for 35–40 minutes, stirring occasionally, and adding more bean liquid if necessary. Adjust seasoning. Turn into a serving bowl or casserole and sprinkle with parsley and Parmesan. Serves 8.

Chick Peas in Garlic Oil

210 g/7 oz (1 cup) dried or 2 × 375 g/12 oz cans chick peas (garbanzos); 120 ml/ 4 fl oz (½ cup) olive oil; 4 cloves garlic, crushed; salt and freshly ground black pepper; juice 1 lemon; 3 tbsp chopped parsley.

If using dried peas, cover with cold water and bring to the boil, then turn off heat. Cover and leave for 1 hour. Drain, cover with fresh cold water and cook, covered, over low heat for 2–3 hours or until tender. Add a little more water if necessary to prevent sticking. Drain. If using canned peas, drain and rinse in a sieve under cold water before cooking. Heat oil in a frying pan (skillet) and sauté garlic and chick peas on medium heat until lightly browned, stirring gently from time to time. Season with salt, pepper and lemon juice. Stir in half the parsley. Serve hot or at room temperature, sprinkled with remaining parsley. Serves 6–8 as a first course.

Chick Pea Salad

210 g/7 oz (1 cup) dried or 2 × 375 g/12 oz cans chick peas (garbanzos); 2 small onions,

1 halved and 1 sliced into rings; 1 bay leaf; 1 clove garlic; 1 tsp salt; 1 orange; 2 sticks celery, sliced; ½ green or red pepper, cored, seeded and sliced.
DRESSING: 1 tbsp vinegar; 3 tbsp oil; pinch dry mustard; salt and freshly ground black pepper.

Soak dried chick peas in water overnight. Next day, drain, place in saucepan, cover with fresh cold water and add halved onion, bay leaf and garlic. Bring to the boil, skimming off any scum that rises to the surface. Cook, covered, on low heat for 2–3 hours or until tender. Drain, discarding flavourings, add salt and leave to cool. If using canned chick peas, drain them and rinse in a sieve under cold water. Holding orange over a bowl to catch all the juice, remove all rind and white pith with a serrated knife. Loosen segments by cutting down each side of membranes. Lift out segments in one piece and remove any seeds. Squeeze core with remaining membrane over segments. This juice may be added to dressing. Mix orange segments, celery, green or red pepper, peas and onion rings. Beat dressing ingredients together until slightly thickened. Pour over salad and toss well. Serves 4.

Spanish Cocido

210 g/7 oz (1 cup) dried chick peas (garbanzos); 4 tbsp olive oil; 1 × 1 kg (2 lb) piece chuck steak or breast of veal; 3–4 large onions, chopped; 2 cloves garlic, crushed; 2 tomatoes, quartered; 4 carrots, sliced; 20 g/⅔ oz (½ cup) chopped parsley; 1 ham bone or ham hock (optional); 2 tsp salt; 2 chorizos (Spanish sausages) or salami, sliced.

Place chick peas in a saucepan, cover with water and bring to the boil. Boil 2 minutes, then remove from heat and soak 1 hour. Drain. Cover with fresh water and simmer 1½ hours. Heat oil in a large saucepan and sear meat over high heat. When brown all over, add onions, garlic, tomatoes, carrots, parsley, ham bone or hock, if using, salt, sausages and chick peas with their cooking water. Bring slowly to the boil then cover and simmer 1½ hours or until chick peas are tender. Add more hot water during cooking if necessary; the peas must be well covered throughout cooking time. To serve, discard ham bone or hock, if using, (return meat to soup, if liked), slice meat and spoon chick pea sauce over. Serves 6.

Garbanzo Spread

This spread is good for sandwiches or as a dip with crackers. Try it in an open-face sandwich with cucumber and tomato slices.

1 × 375 g/12 oz can chick peas (garbanzos); ½ small onion, finely chopped; 1 clove garlic, crushed; 1 tbsp oil; 10 g/⅓ oz (¼ cup) chopped parsley; 1 tsp chopped fresh basil, or ¼ tsp dried; 1 tsp chopped fresh oregano, or ¼ tsp dried; 1 tsp ground cumin; lemon juice; salt and freshly ground black pepper.

Drain chick peas reserving liquid from can, and mash or purée in a food processor. Cook onion and garlic gently in oil until soft. Stir in herbs and cumin and cook 1 minute longer. Remove from heat and mix in chick pea purée and enough of their liquid to give a spreading or dipping consistency, with lemon juice to taste. Season with salt and pepper. Makes 250–370 g/8–12 oz (1–1½ cups).

Chick Pea and Pasta Soup

This soup from Italy is both filling and nutritious.

1 × 375 g/12 oz can chick peas (garbanzos), drained; 1.5 litres/2½ pints (6 cups) chicken or beef stock (bouillon); 2–3 slices pancetta or rashers (slices) streaky bacon, rind removed and finely chopped; 4 tbsp olive oil; 2 cloves garlic, finely chopped; 4 tbsp chopped parsley; salt and freshly ground black pepper; 250 g/8 oz (2 cups) small pasta shells; grated Parmesan or Pecorino cheese.

Place chick peas and stock in a saucepan and simmer gently for 5 minutes. Spoon out about half the chick peas and reduce to a purée with a little of the stock – use a food processor, blender or food mill. Return purée to pan. Fry pancetta or bacon in oil with garlic and parsley until cooked. Add this mixture (known as the soffritto) to chick pea mixture and bring to the boil. Season with salt and pepper. Add pasta and cook until tender. The soup will thicken considerably during this last stage. Serve with cheese sprinkled over. Serves 4–6.

Refried Beans
(Frijoles Refritos)

625 g/1¼ lb (2 cups) dried red kidney beans, soaked in water overnight; salt; 125 g (4 oz) bacon dripping or lard; 1 large onion, finely chopped; 1 clove garlic, crushed; 1 small dried red chilli, seeded and finely chopped, or 1½ tsp Mexican chilli powder.

Boil beans rapidly in soaking liquid for 10 minutes, then reduce heat and cook gently until tender, about 2 hours. Add salt during last 30 minutes cooking time. Drain beans, reserving cooking liquid. Heat half the dripping or lard in a large frying pan (skillet). Add some of the beans and mash into hot fat. Add a little liquid and stir, then mash more beans into pan. Keep on adding beans and liquid until all are used, then stir over medium heat until mixture thickens. Turn into a bowl and clean the frying pan (skillet). Refrigerate bean mixture until required. Heat remaining fat in pan and gently fry onion, garlic and chilli or chilli powder for a few minutes, stirring. Add beans and continue cooking and stirring until beans are dry. Taste and add more salt if necessary. Serves 6–8 as a side dish or as a filling for tacos. NOTE: This dish can be made using canned kidney beans. Omit the first frying. Mash the beans in their liquid, then fry with onion, garlic and chilli until dry.

Bean Salad

1 onion, chopped; 1 tbsp olive oil; 2 cloves garlic, 1 whole and 1 crushed; 1 bay leaf; 1 tsp salt; 1.25 litres/2¼ pints (5¾ cups) water; 310 g/10 oz (1 cup) dried kidney or lima beans, soaked in water overnight and drained; 1 green pepper, cored, seeded and diced; 120 ml/4 fl oz (½ cup) Vinaigrette Dressing (page 358); 3 tbsp chopped parsley; 1 tsp prepared mustard.

Gently fry half the chopped onion in oil in a heavy saucepan until beginning to colour. Add whole garlic clove, bay leaf, salt and water. Add beans, boil rapidly for 10 minutes then simmer until tender, 2–2½ hours. Drain and cool. Remove garlic clove and bay leaf and add green pepper. Mix dressing, crushed garlic, parsley, mustard and remaining onion. Pour over beans and toss well. Chill. Toss again just before serving. Serves 6–8.

Hopping John
(Black-Eyed Peas and Rice)

210 g/7 oz (1 cup) black-eyed peas, soaked in water overnight and drained; 1 smoked pork hock or 1 small piece pickled (salt) pork, or 1 ham bone; 1 large onion, chopped; 210 g/7 oz (1 cup) long-grain rice; salt and freshly ground black pepper.

Rinse peas in cold water and place in a large saucepan with pork, onion and enough water to measure twice depth of peas. Bring to the boil, then cover and simmer for 1 hour or until peas are tender. Remove pork with slotted spoon; discard any bone and gristle and chop meat into small pieces. Drain peas in a sieve placed over a bowl. Add enough water to liquid, if necessary, to measure 500 ml/18 fl oz (2 cups). Return chopped meat, peas and liquid to saucepan, bring to the boil and add rice. Reduce heat, simmer, covered, until rice is tender and liquid is absorbed. Stir in salt and pepper and spoon into a heated serving bowl. Serves 6.

Falafel

(Bean Croquettes)
This is a deliciously spicy appetizer from the Middle East. The fava or broad beans used in falafel need long soaking to help the skins slip off more easily.

210 g/7 oz (1 cup) dried fava or broad beans; 210 g/7 oz (1 cup) dried chick peas (garbanzos); 1 medium onion, chopped; 2 cloves garlic, chopped; 20 g/⅔ oz (½ cup) finely chopped parsley; pinch chilli powder; 1 tsp ground coriander; ½ tsp ground cumin; 1 tsp bicarbonate of soda (baking soda); salt and freshly ground black pepper; oil for deep-frying.

Soak fava or broad beans in water to cover for 48 hours, changing water twice each day. It is best to cover beans and refrigerate during soaking process to prevent fermentation. Soak chick peas in cold water for 12–15 hours. Drain beans and peas. Remove skins from beans by squeezing each firmly in the fingers until the seed pops out of its skin. You may have to slit the skin of some beans with the point of a sharp knife and then squeeze. Leave skin on chick peas. Combine beans and peas with onion and garlic and process in a food processor in 2 batches, or push through a food mill twice. Add parsley, chilli powder, coriander, cumin and soda and season with salt and pepper. Knead well and leave for 30 minutes. Shape a tablespoonful of the mixture into a ball and flatten into a thick patty, 4 cm (1½ in) in diameter. Repeat until all mixture is used. Deep-fry in hot oil, 6–8 at a time, for 5–6 minutes, turning to brown evenly. Drain on paper towels. Serve hot as an appetizer or in split pita bread with Tahini Sauce (see page 427). Makes about 30.

Soy Bean and Cheese Scramble

2 × 220 g/7½ oz cans soy beans; 5 tbsp olive oil; 1 large red or green pepper, cored, seeded and chopped; 8–10 spring onions (scallions), chopped (including green tops); 2 cloves garlic, crushed; 1 small fresh chilli, chopped, or pinch chilli powder; 2 large, ripe tomatoes, peeled, seeded and roughly chopped; 250 g/8 oz (1⅓ cups) feta cheese, diced; 8–10 soft black (ripe) olives, stoned (pitted) and halved; salt; chopped parsley.

Drain beans in a colander and rinse well under cold running water. Heat oil in a large, heavy frying pan (skillet) and gently fry pepper, spring onions (scallions), garlic and chilli until vegetables are soft but not brown. Add beans and tomatoes and simmer for 2–3 minutes or until mixture is piping hot. Stir in cheese and olives and continue stirring gently until cheese starts to melt. Taste for seasoning, and add salt as required. Turn into a heated dish and sprinkle with parsley. Serves 6.
NOTE: This is a highly seasoned dish. If you prefer a blander flavour, omit chilli and olives and use Cheddar cheese instead of feta.

DRIED PEAS
Pea with Ham Soup

500 g/1 lb (2 cups) split green peas, soaked in water overnight and drained; 2 litres/3½ pints (8 cups) water; 1 ham bone; salt and freshly ground black pepper; 4 bratwurst sausages, or 6 frankfurters (optional).

Place peas, water and ham bone in a large saucepan and bring to the boil. Season with salt and pepper, reduce heat and simmer 30 minutes. Remove ham bone and cut off meat. Chop meat and set aside. Strain soup through a sieve, return to pan and reheat. Heat sausages or frankfurters, if using, in hot water, then drain and slice. Add to soup with ham. Adjust seasoning. Serves 6.

Kichadi

2 cloves; very small piece cinnamon stick; cardamom seeds from 3 pods; 1 tsp turmeric; 2 tsp ground fenugreek seeds; 4 tbsp oil; 2 onions, chopped; 1 green pepper, cored, seeded and diced; 430 g/14 oz (2 cups) brown rice; 1.5 litres/2½ pints (6 cups) water; 1 tsp salt; 250 g/8 oz (1 cup) yellow split peas.

Sauté all the spices in 2 tbsp oil in a large, heavy saucepan. Add onions and green pepper and cook, stirring, until onions are soft. Stir in rice and continue to cook for about 5 minutes or until rice begins to turn white. Add water and salt and bring to the boil. Cover and cook on low heat for 20 minutes. Sauté yellow split peas in remaining oil. Add split peas to rice and continue cooking for 30 minutes. Makes about 1 kg/2 lb (6 cups).

LENTILS
Sausages with Lentils

3 rashers (slices) bacon, rind removed and halved; 6 large pork sausages; 250 g/8 oz (1 cup) lentils; 2 onions, each studded with 3 cloves; 1 bouquet garni; salt and freshly ground black pepper.
GARNISH (optional); 6 spring onions (scallions), chopped; chopped parsley.

Place bacon in a large saucepan over low heat and cook until fat melts. Add sausages to pan and fry, turning occasionally, until evenly browned. Add lentils, onions, bouquet garni, salt and pepper. Pour in sufficient water just to cover the ingredients. Bring to the boil, then cover and simmer gently for 30–40 minutes or until lentils are tender and liquid has been absorbed. Remove bouquet garni and onions and serve hot, garnished with spring onions (scallions) and parsley, if desired. Serves 6.

Lentils with Mint

250 g/8 oz (1 cup) brown lentils; salt and freshly ground black pepper; 1 clove garlic, crushed; 150 ml/¼ pint (⅔ cup) plain yogurt; ½ bunch watercress, stalks removed, or 20 g/⅔ oz (½ cup) chopped parsley; 1½ tbsp chopped fresh mint; 2 tomatoes, peeled, seeded and diced.

Place lentils in a saucepan with enough fresh cold water to cover. Bring to the boil slowly and simmer 15 minutes or until just tender but not mushy. Drain lentils, reserving liquid. Stir in salt, pepper and garlic. Measure 120 ml/4 fl oz (½ cup) lentil liquid and mix it with yogurt. Stir into lentil mixture. Just before serving, lightly mix watercress or parsley into lentils. Finally add mint and tomatoes. Serve as a salad, or use to fill small pita (peda) breads. May be served with cold meats – for non-vegetarians – or with other vegetable dishes. Serves 4.

Mediterranean Lentil Stew

Lentils do not need soaking before cooking. Mixed with vegetables they make a delicious stew.

2 tbsp oil; 2 onions, chopped; 1 clove garlic, crushed; 2 sticks celery, sliced; 4 small courgettes (zucchini), sliced; 4 tomatoes, peeled and quartered; 900 ml/1½ pints (3¾ cups) water or stock; 1 tsp ground coriander; salt and freshly ground black pepper; 250 g/8 oz (1 cup) brown lentils; 2 tbsp chopped coriander or parsley (optional).

Heat oil in a large saucepan. Add onions, garlic, celery and courgettes (zucchini) and fry gently for 5 minutes or until lightly browned, stirring frequently. Add tomatoes, water or stock, ground coriander, salt and pepper. Bring to the boil. Add lentils, then cover and simmer for 1 hour or until lentils are tender. Alternatively, transfer ingredients to a casserole, cover and bake in a preheated moderate oven (180°C/350°F, Gas Mark 4) for 1½–2 hours. Sprinkle with chopped coriander or parsley before serving. Serve hot. Serves 4.

Lentil Salad

500 g/1 lb (2 cups) brown lentils; 1 large onion, studded with 2 cloves; 1 bay leaf; 1 tsp salt; 3 cloves garlic, bruised; 1 strip orange rind; 20 g/⅔ oz (½ cup) chopped parsley; 125 g/4 oz (1 cup) finely chopped spring onions (scallions) 120 ml/4 fl oz (½ cup) olive oil; 1 tsp red wine vinegar; 1 tbsp lemon juice.
GARNISH: *2 rashers (slices) bacon, grilled (broiled) until crisp and crumbled; 2 hard-boiled (hard-cooked) eggs, chopped; 10 g/⅓ oz (¼ cup) chopped parsley; 12–15 black (ripe) olives.*

Cover lentils with cold water in a saucepan and bring slowly to the boil, then remove from heat, cover and stand 1 hour. Drain and return to pan. Cover again with cold water to come 5 cm (2 in) above lentils. Add onion, bay leaf, salt, garlic and orange rind. Bring to the boil, then cover and simmer until just tender, about 20–30 minutes. Drain and discard flavouring ingredients. Cool. Put lentils into a bowl and toss gently with parsley, spring onions (scallions), oil, vinegar and lemon juice. Cover and stand for 1 hour. Fold bacon gently through lentils. Spoon salad into a serving dish and garnish with chopped eggs and parsley and black (ripe) olives. Serves 8.

Cauliflower and Lentil Curry

125 g/4 oz (½ cup) red or brown lentils; 2 onions, finely chopped; 60 g/2 oz (4 tbsp) butter or ghee; ½ tsp chilli powder, or to taste; ¼ tsp turmeric; ½ tsp curry powder; 2 tbsp desiccated (shredded) coconut; 1 medium cauliflower, cut into florets; 1 tsp salt; 250 ml/8 fl oz (1 cup) water; juice 1 lemon.

Place lentils in a saucepan, cover with fresh cold water and simmer gently for about 20 minutes or until almost tender. Drain. Fry onions in butter or ghee until soft. Add spices and coconut and cook gently, stirring, for 3 minutes. Add cauliflower, salt, lentils and water. Cover tightly and cook on low heat for 15–20 minutes or until cauliflower and lentils are soft. Stir in lemon juice. Taste and add more salt if needed. Serve as a main course with rice, pappadams and 1–2 side dishes, or as an accompaniment to a meat curry. Serves 4 as a main course, 6 as an accompaniment.

Dhal (Red Lentils)

250 g/8 oz (1 cup) red lentils; ½ tsp chilli powder; 1 tsp salt; 1 tsp turmeric; 1.10 litres/ 1 pint 18 fl oz (4½ cups) boiling water; 3 tomatoes, quartered; 2 onions, finely chopped; 30 g/1 oz (2 tbsp) butter; 2 tsp grated fresh ginger.

Put lentils, chilli, salt and turmeric into a saucepan with boiling water, and cook until tender. Purée lentils in a blender or push through a sieve. Fry tomatoes and onions in butter until golden. Add to lentils with ginger and cook for 5 minutes. Dhal should have the consistency of a thick sauce and is best eaten with boiled rice. Serves 4–6.

PUMPKIN

To trick-or-treat children at Hallowe'en, this vegetable is perhaps more of a joy than something to be eaten. Historically, pumpkin is from the most ancient of vegetable families, the gourds, which were eaten in soups in Europe well before America and its pumpkins were discovered. There are many varieties of pumpkin, of all shapes and sizes. Some are available almost throughout the entire year; others wait for the first frosts before being harvested, when they are said to keep better and to have a sweeter flesh.

Pumpkin has a sweetish, nutty flavour which may be enhanced with herbs, cheese or spices, as in the traditional Pumpkin Pie. A dash of grated nutmeg is good with mashed pumpkin, too.

Whole pumpkins may be stuffed with bread, cheese, cream and seasonings and baked in the oven for a couple of hours; if the mixture is more liquid, the result is thick pumpkin soup in its own tureen.

Pumpkin Soup – whether cooked in the pumpkin or not – is always a winter favourite; in some Asian countries it is made with coconut milk and flavoured with coriander and spring onions (scallions).

□ **To Cook:** It may be boiled, steamed or baked. Steaming is usually preferable to boiling, unless the pumpkin is to be mashed afterwards, since the pumpkin will keep its shape better and not become waterlogged. Pumpkin is generally peeled before cooking, although the skin of some varieties is edible when young. **See recipes.**

BAKED PUMPKIN Cook with the roast meat, if the tin (pan) is large enough. Roll pumpkin pieces in meat drippings, arrange around meat and cook for 30–45 minutes. Otherwise, cook in a separate tin (pan) with 1–2 tbsp oil or dripping.

BOILED PUMPKIN Cook pieces of pumpkin, not too small, in boiling salted water until tender. Drain, dry briefly over heat then toss with butter and chopped fresh parsley. Alternatively, mash with butter and seasoning to taste.

Pumpkin is often mashed with potato, which can absorb some of the excess moisture from the pumpkin. The pumpkin needs less cooking time, and should be added about 5 minutes after the potato.

STEAMED PUMPKIN Place even-sized pieces of pumpkin in steaming basket and steam until tender, about 10–15 minutes.

Pumpkin Soup

750 g/1½ lb (4½ cups) peeled, seeded and chopped pumpkin; 60 g/2 oz (½ cup) finely chopped onion; 90 g/3 oz (6 tbsp) butter; 750 ml/1¼ pints (3 cups) water; 250 ml/ 8 fl oz (1 cup) milk; 2 tbsp flour; salt and freshly ground white pepper; 1 egg yolk (optional).

Cook pumpkin and onion in 60 g/2 oz (4 tbsp) butter in a saucepan for 10 minutes, stirring constantly. Add water and cook gently until pumpkin is very tender. Push through sieve or purée in blender or food processor with a little of the milk. Melt remaining butter in clean pan and stir in flour, then pumpkin purée and remaining milk, stirring constantly until well blended. Season with salt and pepper. Simmer 20 minutes. If desired, take out a little soup, blend with egg yolk and stir into remaining soup, just before serving. Serves 4–6.
VARIATION
Add a little grated fresh ginger with onion.

Pumpkin Gratin

500 g/1 lb (3 cups) pumpkin, peeled, seeded and chopped; 2 tbsp rice; 175 ml/6 fl oz (¾ cup) water; salt and freshly ground black pepper; 4 tbsp single (light) cream; nutmeg; 3 tbsp grated cheese.

Place pumpkin in a saucepan with rice and water. Season lightly with salt and pepper. Bring to the boil, then cover, reduce heat and cook for 12–15 minutes, by which time pumpkin and rice should be tender and water absorbed. Mash pumpkin and rice, or purée in blender. Add cream, nutmeg and extra seasoning if required. Turn into buttered, shallow ovenproof dish. Sprinkle with cheese and place in a preheated moderately hot oven (200°C/400°F, Gas Mark 6) to warm through and brown surface. Serves 6.

Pumpkin Pie

1 kg/2 lb (6 cups) pumpkin, peeled, seeded and chopped; ½ tsp salt; 140 g/4½ oz (¾ cup) firmly packed brown sugar; 90 g/3 oz (½ cup) sultanas (golden raisins); 1 tsp cinnamon; ½ tsp nutmeg; 1 tbsp flour; grated rind and juice 1 lemon; Rich Shortcrust Pastry for a two-crust pie made using 250 g/8 oz (2 cups) flour (page 274); 30 g/1 oz (2 tbsp) butter; beaten egg white or milk; caster sugar.

Place pumpkin in a saucepan, cover with boiling water, add salt and cook for 5 minutes. Drain. Combine pumpkin with brown sugar, sultanas (golden raisins), spices, flour, lemon juice and rind. Line greased 23 cm (9 in) pie plate with just over half pastry (dough). Add pumpkin filling and dot with butter. With remaining dough, make lid for pie, or cut pastry (dough) into strips and arrange as lattice. Cut small steam vents in lid. Brush dough with egg white or milk and sprinkle with caster sugar. Bake in a preheated moderately hot oven (200°C/400°F, Gas Mark 6) for 30 minutes, then reduce heat to moderate (180°C/350°F, Gas Mark 4) and bake for further 40 minutes or until pastry (crust) is crisp and golden. Serves 6–8.

Pumpkin Pie (American Style)

The traditional American recipe made without the top crust.

310 g/10 oz (2 cups) cooked, mashed pumpkin; 2 eggs, lightly beaten; 350 ml/12 fl oz (1½ cups) evaporated milk; 125 g/4 oz (½ cup) sugar; 1 tsp cinnamon; ½ tsp ground ginger; ¼ tsp ground cloves; ½ tsp salt; 1 quantity Rich Shortcrust Pastry (page 274).

Combine pumpkin with eggs, milk, sugar, spices and salt, blending well. Roll out pastry (dough) and use to line 23 cm (9 in) pie

plate. Fill with pumpkin mixture. Bake in a preheated moderately hot oven (200°C/400°F, Gas Mark 6) for 40 minutes. Serve warm or cool, with cream. Serves 6–8.

PUNCH

Originally, punch was a drink based on rum and flavoured with lemon juice and cinnamon. Today, it is a beverage made in large quantities, usually containing fruit or fruit juice but not necessarily made with alcohol. A bowl of punch is useful at large parties when it is not possible to offer a range of different drinks. **See recipes.**

Wassail Bowl

The Wassail bowl, symbolizing good cheer, is a traditional drink whose origins go back to Anglo-Saxon times.'

12 small red apples; 500 ml/18 fl oz (2 cups) water; 1 tsp freshly grated nutmeg; 2 tsp ground ginger; 1 cinnamon stick; 6 whole cloves; 6 whole allspice; 4 coriander seeds; 1 kg/2 lb (4 cups) sugar; 2.5 litres/4½ pints (10 cups) ale; 2 bottles sherry or Madeira; 12 eggs, separated; 250 ml/8 fl oz (1 cup) brandy.

Prick apples all over and bake them in a preheated moderate oven (180°C/350°F, Gas Mark 4) for 40–50 minutes or until soft. Mix water, spices and sugar in a large saucepan and bring to the boil, stirring until sugar is dissolved. Simmer for 10 minutes, then add ale and sherry or Madeira and heat, do not boil. Beat egg yolks until thick and pale. Whisk egg whites to a firm snow and fold into yolks. Slowly strain half the spiced mixture over the eggs, stirring constantly. Pour into a warmed punch bowl. Bring the remaining spiced mixture almost to boiling point and strain it into the bowl. Add brandy, stir to combine and add apples. Serve hot in punch cups. Serves 25–30.

Champagne Cup

4 tbsp brandy; 4 tbsp Curaçao; 1 × 750 ml/1¼ pint bottle champagne (3 cups); soda (carbonated) water; fresh grapes, strawberries or sliced fresh peaches to garnish.

Pour brandy, Curaçao and champagne over ice in large punch bowl and mix well. Add soda (carbonated) water as desired just before serving, and garnish with fresh fruit. Quantities may be doubled if desired. Serves 6–8.

Rum Punch

FOR EACH DRINK: *crushed ice; 4 tbsp rum; juice ½ lime; 1 tsp sugar; mint sprigs to garnish.*

Half-fill a tall glass with ice and add rum, lime juice and sugar. Stir, and serve garnished with mint sprigs.

Tea Punch

(Alcoholic)

3 tbsp tea leaves; 1.2 litres/2 pints (5 cups) boiling water; 1.2 litres/2 pints (5 cups) sweet white wine (Sauternes, Barsac); 120 ml/4 fl oz (½ cup) lemon juice; ice cubes; fresh fruit to garnish (orange and lemon slices, strawberries or cherries, sliced peaches, pineapple chunks).

Steep tea leaves in boiling water for 5 minutes. Add wine and lemon juice and strain over ice in a punch bowl. Float fruit on top and stand for 10 minutes before serving. Serves 10.

Tea Punch

(Non-alcoholic)

3 tbsp lemon juice; 175 ml/6 fl oz (¾ cup) orange juice; 350 ml/12 fl oz (1½ cups) apricot juice; 1 × 750 ml/1¼ pint bottle ginger ale (3 cups); 350 ml/12 fl oz (1½ cups) strong tea; 3 tbsp sugar; ice cubes; mint sprigs to garnish.

Have fruit juices and ginger ale well chilled. Strain tea into a large jug and stir in sugar, lemon and orange juice and apricot juice. Add ginger ale, stirring gently. Serve over ice cubes in tall glasses, garnishing each drink with a sprig of fresh mint. Serves 8.

PURI

An Indian deep-fried unleavened bread made from *atta* or *roti* flour (available from health food shops and good delicatessens).

Puri

370 g/12 oz (3 cups) atta or roti flour; 1 tsp salt; 1 tbsp ghee or peanut oil; 250 ml/8 fl oz (1 cup) lukewarm water; oil for deep-frying.

Place flour in a bowl, reserving 60 g/2 oz (½ cup). Add salt to flour. Rub (cut) in ghee or add oil. Make a well in the centre and add water all at once, mixing with one hand to form a dough. Knead dough for at least 10 minutes. Wrap in plastic wrap and chill for 1 hour. Shape dough into 14–16 small balls about the size of a large walnut. Roll each one into a thin round about 10 cm (4 in) diameter using reserved flour for dusting the work surface. In a deep frying pan (skillet) heat about 2.5 cm (1 in) oil until a faint haze rises from the surface. Fry puris one at a time, pressing on the edges with an egg slice to encourage them to puff. When risen, turn to cook the other side. Drain on crumpled paper towels and serve hot. Makes about 14–16.

Q

QUAIL

A small game bird, which has been adapted to commercial production. The bird is white-fleshed, and has a faint gamey taste. Quail is usually very tender, and should be cooked quickly in a hot oven or grilled (broiled) over hot coals; because the flesh is rather dry, a piece of pork fat or fatty bacon is placed on the breast or wrapped around the bird.

Quail can be eaten with a knife and fork, but it is easier to eat wings and drumsticks in the fingers; for this reason, finger bowls should always be offered when quail are served. Allow 1 to 2 quail per person for a main course; if serving as an entrée, before the main course, one quail per person is sufficient.

☐ **To Cook:** Season inside lightly with salt and pepper. Rub with butter, place a piece of pork fat or bacon on breast and truss securely. Roast, breast side up, in a preheated moderately hot oven (200°C/400°F, Gas Mark 6) for 10–12 minutes or until juices run clear when thigh is pricked with a fine skewer. Remove trussing string and serve each quail on a round of fried bread.

Quail can be stuffed before roasting; choose a rice stuffing or a walnut and celery stuffing. **See recipes**.

Quail with Grapes

6 quail; salt and freshly ground black pepper; 60 g/2 oz (4 tbsp) butter; 120 ml/4 fl oz (½ cup) dry white wine; juice ½ lemon; 60 g/2 oz (½ cup) white grapes, stalks removed.

Season quail lightly with salt and pepper. Heat butter in a shallow flameproof casserole and cook quail until lightly browned all over. Add wine and lemon juice, cover and cook over low heat for about 15 minutes. Add grapes and cook for about 5 minutes longer. Reduce sauce over high heat if necessary. Serves 6 as a first course, 3–4 as a main course.

Minute Quail

8 quail; salt and freshly ground black pepper; 60 g/2 oz (4 tbsp) butter; 3 shallots, finely chopped; 3 thin slices prosciutto, cut into strips; 250 ml/8 fl oz (1 cup) chicken stock.

Split quail down back, open out flat and remove any small bones from inside. Season with salt and pepper. Heat butter in a shallow flameproof casserole and cook quail for 4–5 minutes on one side. Turn, add shallots and ham to casserole and cook a further 4–5 minutes. Remove quail to heated plate. Deglaze pan with stock and boil to reduce by about half. Pour over quail and serve immediately. Serves 4–6.

NOTE: Quail may be cooked in 2 or 3 lots, if necessary.

Grilled Quail

In this recipe the quail are marinated with herbs in oil, which helps ensure that they do not dry out during grilling (broiling). Take care not to overcook the quail.

8 quail; 120 ml/4 fl oz (½ cup) olive oil; 2 tbsp dried oregano or marjoram; 4 bay leaves, crumbled; salt and freshly ground black pepper; lemon wedges to serve.

Split quail down back and open out flat. Flatten with blade of cleaver. Place in a large shallow dish and sprinkle with olive oil, herbs, salt and pepper. Cover and marinate 2–3 hours, turning quail once or twice. Grill (broil) over hot coals, or under a preheated grill (broiler) for 10–15 minutes or until just cooked and brown. Serve with lemon wedges. Serves 4–6.

QUEEN OF PUDDINGS

This is an elaborate version of baked bread custard.

Queen of Puddings

125 g/4 oz (2 cups) fresh breadcrumbs, white or brown; 2 tbsp vanilla sugar; grated rind 1 lemon; 600 ml/1 pint (2½ cups) milk; 60 g/2 oz (4 tbsp) butter; 4 eggs, separated; 2 tbsp berry jam, or jelly; 125 g/4 oz (½ cup) caster sugar.

Mix breadcrumbs, vanilla sugar and lemon rind. Heat milk and butter almost to boiling, pour over breadcrumb mixture and allow to stand for 10 minutes. Beat in egg yolks. Pour into a greased shallow ovenproof dish. Bake in preheated moderate oven (180°C/350°F, Gas Mark 4) for about 30 minutes or until just firm. Warm jam or jelly and spread evenly over custard without breaking surface. Beat egg whites until stiff. Add half caster sugar and whisk again until glossy. Fold in remaining caster sugar, reserving 1 tsp. Pile meringue on to custard and sprinkle with reserved caster sugar. Return to oven to bake for about 15 minutes or until meringue is slightly browned and crisp. Serve hot. Serves 6.

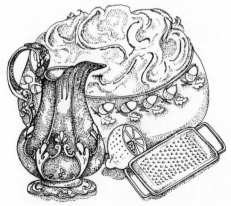

QUENELLE

An ethereal souffléed dumpling, poached in water or stock. Quenelles are made from a mousseline mixture or from a purée of fish, shellfish, veal or chicken beaten into a panada of choux pastry. Panada-type quenelles, though light, tender and a little easier to handle, are less delicate than the mousseline type.

Quenelles are a classic garnish for elegant soups and for certain dishes presented in the grand manner. However, quenelles are usually served with a good sauce nowadays, as a superb entrée or lunch dish in their own right. **See recipes**.

Quenelles
(Mousseline Type)

1 quantity Mousseline mixture (page 223); butter; hot water or stock; sauce (see recipe).

Prepare mousseline mixture of your choice, using fish, shellfish or chicken, or you may use 500 g (1 lb) very lean veal in the same way as chicken. Chill mixture well.

To shape each quenelle, dip 2 spoons into very hot water, scoop out some mixture on one spoon and round it off with inverted bowl of second spoon. Dip second spoon again into hot water, slip it under quenelle and, holding spoons just above surface of a buttered large, deep flameproof dish, slide quenelle off. It should be a neat egg shape. Use small or large spoons depending on size quenelles you want to make; they will swell to almost double their original size when cooked. Shape remaining mixture in same way, placing quenelles a little apart in dish.

Place dish on stove and gently pour round quenelles enough hot water or stock to cover them. Use fish stock for fish quenelles, chicken for others. Bring to just below simmering point (liquid should quiver, but no bubbles rise) and poach over low heat for 10–15 minutes or until quenelles are firm and roll over easily. Remove with a slotted spoon and drain on a tea-towel. They may be served at once, or can be covered and stored in refrigerator for up to 24 hours. To reheat quenelles, return them to buttered

baking dish, cover with hot water or stock and poach very gently for 6–8 minutes or until heated through.

Serve 2–3 small quenelles in each bowl of soup, or 2–3 of the size shaped with a dessertspoon or small tablespoon for an entrée. Mask entrée quenelles with a good sauce such as Velouté, Beurre Blanc or Sauce Suprême (see *Sauces*). Quenelles can be placed on a bed of mushroom or other vegetable purée before sauce is added, and top can be sprinkled with buttered breadcrumbs or grated cheese and browned under a preheated moderate grill (broiler). Makes about 15 entrée quenelles.

Quenelles
(Panada Type)

1 quantity Choux Pastry (page 276); 500 g/1 lb (2 cups) finely minced (ground) shellfish or fresh fish, or finely minced (ground) and sieved chicken or veal; salt and freshly ground white pepper; nutmeg; 2–6 tbsp chilled single (light) cream; butter; hot water or stock; sauce (see recipe above).

Mix together choux pastry, fish or meat; $\frac{1}{2}$ tsp salt; $\frac{1}{4}$ tsp pepper and a large pinch of nutmeg. Chill mixture thoroughly, then beat in chilled cream little by little, using only sufficient to make a mixture firm enough to hold its shape on a spoon. Adjust seasoning. Shape, poach and serve the quenelles in the same manner as for mousseline-type quenelles. Makes about 15 entrée quenelles.

QUICHE

An open-faced tart with a savoury custard filling, thought to have originated in Lorraine, a province of eastern France. It was originally made with bread dough, but short pastry (basic pie dough) has been substituted in modern recipes.

There should be a lot of creamy filling in very little pastry (dough). The pastry (dough) should be rolled out as thinly as possible. Today it is made in a metal flan ring, with straight sides (although many use one with fluted edges), which can stand on a baking tray. The tart can then be slid on to a plate for

serving. Some flan rings have a metal base that lifts out for easy removal of the quiche.

Most widely known is *Quiche Lorraine*, which traditionally contains only eggs, single (light) cream or milk, and bacon or ham. However, there are many other popular fillings including cheese, tomatoes and onions, crab, smoked salmon, mushrooms or other vegetables, combined with a rich savoury custard, poured into the pastry (pie) shell and baked until puffed and brown.

Miniature quiches make delicious hot hors d'oeuvre.

Quiche lends itself to advance preparation. The flan ring, lined with pastry (dough) may be prepared well ahead of time and chilled, the filling prepared and stored in the refrigerator. Half an hour before serving, the filling is placed in the flan, the custard poured in and the quiche baked in a preheated moderately hot oven (190°C/375°F, Gas Mark 5) for about 30 minutes until a knife inserted in the centre comes out clean. Serve as soon as possible, but if guests are not ready, leave the quiche in the turned-off oven, door ajar, and it will stay puffed and brown for about 10 minutes.

A cold quiche is good picnic fare or makes a quick and satisfying snack. **See recipes**.

Herb Quiche

30 g/1 oz (2 tbsp) butter; 8 shallots, finely chopped; 2 eggs; 250 ml/8 fl oz (1 cup) single (light) cream; 1 tbsp snipped chives; 1 tbsp chopped watercress; 1 tbsp chopped parsley; salt and freshly ground black pepper; 1 × 20 cm (8 in) Shortcrust Pastry Flan Case (page 274).

Melt butter in a frying pan (skillet) and sauté shallots lightly. Beat together eggs and cream, and stir in shallots, herbs, salt and pepper. Pour into flan case. Bake in a preheated moderately hot oven (190°C/375°F, Gas Mark 5), for 30–40 minutes or until filling is set. Serves 4–6.

Quiche Lorraine

While the classic Quiche Lorraine contains no cheese, this is a popular variation that is accepted by many.

3–4 rashers (slices) bacon, rind removed; 3 thin slices Swiss or Gruyère cheese; 1 × 20–23 cm (8–9 in) Shortcrust Pastry Flan Case (page 274); 2 eggs; 1 tsp flour; pinch nutmeg; $\frac{1}{2}$ tsp salt; pinch cayenne; 120 ml/4 fl oz ($\frac{1}{2}$ cup) single (light) cream; 120 ml/4 fl oz ($\frac{1}{2}$ cup) milk; 1 tbsp melted butter; watercress or parsley to garnish.

Grill (broil) bacon until crisp. Drain and crumble into bite-sized pieces. Cut cheese same size as bacon. Place bacon and cheese in flan case in layers. Beat together eggs, flour, nutmeg, salt, cayenne, cream and milk,

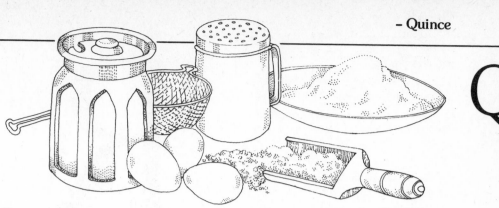

only until combined. (Overbeating causes bubbles on top.) Stir in melted butter. Strain over bacon and cheese. Bake in a preheated moderately hot oven (200°C/400°F, Gas Mark 6) for 10 minutes, then reduce heat to moderate (180°C/350°F, Gas Mark 4), and bake for a further 20 minutes or until a knife inserted in filling comes out clean. Garnish with watercress and serve warm with tossed salad. Serves 4–6.

Herbed Tomato Quiche

350 ml/12 fl oz (1½ cups) single (light) cream; 2 eggs; 2 egg yolks; 2 tbsp tomato purée (paste); salt and freshly ground black pepper; 4 tbsp grated Swiss or Gruyère cheese; 1 × 25 cm (10 in) Shortcrust Pastry Flan Case (page 274); 2 tomatoes, cut into 1 cm (½ in) slices; 2 tbsp chopped parsley; 1 tbsp chopped fresh mixed herbs (lemon thyme, oregano, basil, chives); 3 tbsp grated Parmesan cheese; 2 tsp butter.

Combine cream, eggs, egg yolks, tomato purée (paste), salt and pepper and beat lightly. Add 2 tbsp Swiss cheese. Spoon custard into flan case. Arrange tomato slices on top, sprinkle with salt, pepper and herbs and top with remaining Swiss and Parmesan cheeses. Dot with small pieces of butter. Bake on top shelf of a preheated moderately hot oven (190°C/375°F, Gas Mark 5) for 25–30 minutes or until filling is set and top is golden. Remove quiche from pan and let it cool on a wire rack. Serves 6–8.

Roquefort Quiche

90 g/3 oz (¾ cup) Roquefort cheese, crumbled; 180 g/6 oz (¾ cup) cream cheese; 2 eggs; 150 ml/¼ pint (⅔ cup) single (light) cream; salt and freshly ground black pepper; pinch nutmeg; 1 × 20–23 cm (8–9 in) Shortcrust Pastry Flan Case (page 274).

Beat cheeses with eggs and beat in cream gradually. Season with salt, pepper and nutmeg. Spoon into flan case. Bake in a preheated hot oven (200°C/400°F, Gas Mark 6) for 10 minutes, then reduce heat to moderate (180°C/350°F, Gas Mark 4) and bake for a further 20 minutes. Serves 4–6.

Seafood Quiche

180 g/6 oz (¾ cup) frozen and thawed, or canned, crab, drained and flaked, or cooked shelled prawns (shrimp); 1 tbsp finely chopped shallots; 1 tbsp finely chopped parsley; 1 tbsp dry sherry or vermouth; 1 × 20–23 cm (8–9 in) Shortcrust Pastry Flan Case (page 274); 2 eggs, lightly beaten; 250 ml/8 fl oz (1 cup) single (light) cream, or 120 ml/4 fl oz (½ cup) cream and 120 ml/4 fl oz (½ cup) milk; pinch nutmeg; pinch salt; pinch white pepper.

Remove any bony tissue from crab. Combine seafood with shallots, parsley and sherry or vermouth. Chill, covered, for 1 hour. Sprinkle seafood mixture over bottom of flan case. Combine eggs, cream, nutmeg, salt and pepper. Strain over seafood mixture in flan. Bake quiche in a preheated moderately hot oven (200°C/400°F, Gas Mark 6) for 10 minutes, then reduce heat to moderate (180°C/350°F, Gas Mark 4) and bake for a further 15 minutes or until filling is set and golden. Serve hot or warm. Serves 4–6.

Leek Quiche

30 g/1 oz (2 tbsp) plus 2 tsp butter; 4 tbsp water; ½ tsp salt; 250 g (8 oz) sliced leeks; 2 eggs; 60–120 ml/2–4 fl oz (¼–½ cup) single (light) cream; 120 ml/4 fl oz (½ cup) milk; pinch nutmeg; pinch pepper; 30 g/1 oz (¼ cup) grated Swiss cheese; 1 × 20–23 cm (8–9 in) Shortcrust Pastry Flan Case (page 274); 1–2 slices Swiss cheese, cut into triangles.

Heat 30 g/1 oz (2 tbsp) butter with water and salt in a heavy saucepan. Add leeks, cover and cook 6–8 minutes or until liquid in pan has almost evaporated. Lower heat and cook gently until leeks are soft. Drain. Beat eggs, cream, milk, nutmeg and pepper until just combined. Add leeks and grated Swiss cheese. Pour into flan case and arrange cheese triangles in pattern on top. Dot with small pieces of remaining butter. Bake in a preheated moderately hot oven (200°C/400°F, Gas Mark 6) for 10 minutes, then reduce heat to moderate (180°C/350°F, Gas Mark 4) and bake for a further 20 minutes or until filling is set. Serves 4–6.

Spinach Quiche

500 g (1 lb) spinach; 30 g/1 oz (2 tbsp) butter; 1 small onion, finely chopped; 2 eggs; 1 egg yolk; 250 ml/8 fl oz (1 cup) single (light) cream; salt and freshly ground black pepper; 1 tsp chopped fresh oregano, or pinch nutmeg; 1 × 20–23 cm (8–9 in) Shortcrust Pastry Flan Case, baked blind (page 274).

Remove tough stalks from spinach, rinse well under cold running water and shake off excess. Place in a saucepan, cover tightly and simmer for 4–5 minutes. Drain spinach, pressing well to remove all liquid. Chop finely. Melt butter in a frying pan (skillet), and cook onion until soft but not coloured. Add spinach. Cook over a high heat for 2–3 minutes to remove any remaining moisture, then place in a bowl and allow to cool. Beat eggs and egg yolk together, add cream and mix well. Season with salt and pepper. Add spinach mixture and stir in oregano or nutmeg. Pour into flan case. Bake in a preheated moderately hot oven (190°C/375°F, Gas Mark 5) for 30 minutes or until golden. Serves 4–6.

QUINCE

Looking rather like an ungainly, over-sized pear, the tart-flavoured quince is not eaten raw, but makes a lovely dessert when cooked with sugar.

The quince is rich in pectin, and can be made into a beautiful, deep pink jelly (see page 171). The cooked, sweetened pulp can be dried, to yield a thick, jelly-like paste; this is especially popular in Spain, where it is called *membrillo*. Quinces are best if picked before they are fully ripe, then left to mature in a warm place. The fruit is ripe when it is yellow and strongly perfumed. **See recipes.**

Quince Compote

250 g/8 oz (1 cup) sugar; 500 ml/18 fl oz (2 cups) water; juice ½ lemon; 1 kg/2 lb (5 cups) quinces, peeled, cored and thickly sliced (retain cores and peelings).

Combine sugar, water and lemon juice in a saucepan. Add quince cores and peelings and simmer for 30 minutes. Strain syrup, return to pan and bring back to the boil. Poach quince slices until soft. Serve hot or cold, with cream or yogurt. Serves 8.

Quince Snow

2 large quinces, peeled, cored and thinly sliced; 2 egg whites; about 60 g/2 oz (¼ cup) caster sugar.

Cook quinces in a very little water until quite soft. Purée through sieve or in blender and cool. Beat egg whites until stiff. Gradually fold in quince purée and sugar to taste until smooth and well mixed. Chill. Serve with cream or custard, if desired. Serves 4.

Spiced Quinces

Pickled or spiced quinces make an excellent and unusual accompaniment to cold meats.

4 large quinces, peeled, cored and cut into chunks; salt; sugar; wine vinegar; coriander seeds.

Place quinces in a saucepan, cover with cold water, add salt and bring to the boil. Boil for 10 minutes, then drain, reserving liquid. To each 250 ml/8 fl oz (1 cup) of liquid, add 500 g/1 lb (2 cups) sugar, 4 tbsp vinegar and ½ tsp coriander seeds. Bring to the boil, stirring to dissolve sugar. Add fruit and simmer until tender. Cool. Next day drain off syrup and bring to the boil. Pack quinces into sterilized jars, pour over boiling syrup and seal while still warm. Serve with ham, pork, mutton and turkey.

Quince Paste

(Quince Cheese)
A delicious sweetmeat made from the reduced and sweetened purée of quince, so slowly cooked that it becomes a rich deep amethyst colour. Serve it with cheese, particularly the fresh soft cheeses, or cut it into squares, roll in sugar and serve with coffee.

6 quinces; 120 ml/4 fl oz (½ cup) water; white sugar.

Rub quinces with a cloth to remove the down. Put them whole and unpeeled into a preheated moderate oven (180°C/350°F, Gas Mark 4), and cook until tender, about 3 hours. Alternatively, quarter them (do not peel), remove seeds and steam them in the 120 ml/4 fl oz (½ cup) water. When quinces are cool, slice them (without peeling) into a bowl, discarding cores and any bruised or hard pieces. Put sliced fruit through a food mill or sieve. Weigh purée and add an equal weight of white sugar. Heat in a heavy pan until sugar has dissolved, then boil, stirring nearly all the time, until mixture begins to candy and come away from bottom as well as sides of pan. (The boiling paste erupts and spits so take care.) Turn off heat and continue stirring until boiling has ceased. Fill shallow rectangular earthenware or tin dishes, or one dish, with cheese and leave overnight for mixture to get quite cold.

Next day put these moulds into coolest possible oven until cheese has dried out and is quite firm, about 3–4 hours, although it may take longer. Turn out slabs of paste and cut into portions you are likely to use at one time. Wrap them in greaseproof (waxed) paper or plastic wrap or foil, and store in tins in a dry place.
NOTE: For the cheese board, the quince cheese may be cut into small pieces. For sweetmeats, coat pieces in caster sugar and set in tiny paper cups.

RABBIT

A wonderfully versatile meat, blending equally well with red or white wine in sauces, with herbs and spices, and with mushrooms and prunes.

Rabbit represents good value, and since it is very lean, it is valuable in diets where cholesterol content should be minimized. A whole rabbit usually weighs around 1 kg (2 lb) and will serve 4–5 persons. Very small, young rabbits are sometimes available in spring; these have a milder flavour and are very tender. Some shops sell rabbit pieces, so that you can buy the choicest part of the rabbit, the loin section, and avoid the bony rib section.

Rabbit flesh does tend to be dry, so it is best cooked with liquid, such as wine or stock. Cooking time will depend on the age of the rabbit; older rabbits may need up to 1½ hours cooking, while young rabbits will be cooked in less than 30 minutes.

Many recipes call for a rabbit to be jointed. Cutting up a rabbit is similar to cutting up a chicken: separate the rabbit at leg joints, to give 2 thighs **(Fig 1 opposite)**; cut the loin into 1 or 2 sections through the backbone **(2)**, and cut the rib cage section in 2, along the backbone **(3). See recipes.**

Sauté of Rabbit with Herbs

1 rabbit, jointed; 2 tbsp oil; 1 tbsp finely chopped onion or shallot; salt and freshly ground black pepper; 2 tsp Herbes de Provence (see below); 120 ml/4 fl oz (½ cup) white wine.

Slowly brown rabbit pieces on all sides in oil in a flameproof casserole. Add onion or shallot and cook 1 minute longer. Season with salt and pepper, sprinkle over herbs and add wine. Bring to the boil, stirring, then cover and simmer until rabbit is tender, about 1–1½ hours. Add more wine or stock during cooking if necessary. Adjust seasoning before serving. Serves 4.
NOTE: Herbes de Provence is a mixture of dried thyme, rosemary, marjoram, fennel seeds and savory.

Sauté of Rabbit with Red Wine

Bacon, red wine and garlic combine with rabbit to make a rich and tasty dish.

2 rabbits, jointed; seasoned flour; 1 tbsp oil; 30 g/1 oz (2 tbsp) butter; 125 g (4 oz) bacon, rind removed and cut into small strips; 175 ml/6 fl oz (¾ cup) red wine; 1 clove garlic, crushed; 3 tbsp fresh tomato purée; salt and freshly ground black pepper; chopped fresh parsley.

Lightly dust rabbit pieces with seasoned flour, then brown all over in oil and butter in a flameproof casserole. Remove rabbit from pan. Add bacon and fry 2 minutes. Add wine, bring to the boil and reduce a little. Stir in garlic and tomato purée, season with salt and pepper and return rabbit to pan. Simmer, covered, for about 1–1½ hours or until rabbit is tender. Adjust seasoning, and sprinkle with chopped parsley before serving. Serves 6.

Rabbit with Mustard

1 rabbit, jointed; seasoned flour; 6 small onions, quartered; 1 tbsp oil; 30 g/1 oz (2 tbsp) butter; 125 g (4 oz) streaky bacon, rind removed and diced; 500 ml/18 fl oz (2 cups) stock; salt and freshly ground black pepper; 2 tbsp French (Dijon) mustard; 1 bouquet garni; 120 ml/4 fl oz (½ cup) single (light) cream; chopped fresh parsley.

Lightly dust rabbit pieces with seasoned flour. Cook onions in oil and butter in a flameproof casserole for 3 minutes. Remove and add rabbit and bacon. Brown rabbit on all sides. Pour in stock, season with salt and pepper and add mustard and bouquet garni. Return onions to pan and simmer, covered, for about 1–1½ hours or until rabbit is tender. Remove rabbit to heated dish. Discard bouquet garni; reduce sauce by fast boiling if necessary. Add cream and parsley, and adjust seasoning. Pour sauce over rabbit and serve with boiled or mashed potatoes. Serves 4.

Rabbit and Pistachio Terrine

750 g/1½ lb (3 cups) boneless rabbit meat, minced (ground); 500 g/1 lb (2 cups) sausage meat; 4 rashers (slices) bacon, rind removed and finely chopped; 150 g/5 oz (2½ cups) fresh white breadcrumbs; 1 small onion, finely chopped; 1 clove garlic, crushed; ½ tsp dried thyme; 2 tbsp Pernod; 1 tsp salt; freshly ground black pepper; 1 egg, beaten; 60 g/2 oz (½ cup) chopped, shelled pistachio nuts or walnuts; 250 g (8 oz) rashers (slices) streaky bacon, rind removed.

Place rabbit meat in a large bowl with sausage meat, chopped bacon and breadcrumbs. Add remaining ingredients,

Jointing a rabbit

except bacon rashers (slices) and blend together thoroughly with a wooden spoon. Line a 2.5 litre/4½ pint (10 cup) terrine or loaf tin (pan) with some of the bacon rashers (slices), covering bottom and sides. Spoon rabbit mixture into tin (pan) and level top. Cut remaining bacon into thin strips and arrange on top of mixture in a lattice design. Cover tightly with foil or a lid. Bake in a preheated moderate oven (180°C/350°F, Gas Mark 4) for 1½ hours. Take from oven, remove lid and place a weight on top. Leave until cool, then refrigerate until required. Allow to mellow for 30 minutes at room temperature before serving. Serve in slices with tiny gherkins and crunchy French bread. Serves 10–12.

NOTE: Pernod gives a subtle aniseed flavour to the terrine, and is available in quarter-size bottles.

Rabbit with Green Olives

1 tbsp olive oil; 125 g (4 oz) pickled (salt) pork, diced; 3 onions, thickly sliced; 2 sticks celery, thickly sliced; 1 rabbit, jointed; 1 tbsp flour; 500 ml/18 fl oz (2 cups) hot chicken stock; 1 bay leaf; 1 sprig fresh rosemary, or ½ tsp dried; salt and freshly ground black pepper; 8 green olives, stoned (pitted); 1 tbsp capers (optional).

Put oil, pork, onions and celery into a large flameproof casserole and heat gently, stirring occasionally, until fat runs from pork. Add rabbit and fry gently, turning, until lightly browned on all sides, about 10 minutes. Sprinkle in flour and stir for 1 minute. Stir in hot stock, bay leaf, rosemary, salt and pepper. Bring to the boil, then cover tightly, reduce heat and simmer for 45 minutes to 1½ hours or until rabbit is tender. Add olives and capers, and simmer a further 10 minutes. Discard bay leaf. Serves 4.

RADISH

One of the delights of summer is a bowl of rosy-pink radishes, fresh and crisp, to be eaten simply with butter, salt and crusty bread, in the French manner. Offer them at the start of a meal, since they are said to stimulate the appetite. Sliced radishes are often added to mixed salads, and small whole

radishes make an attractive garnish, cut decoratively or simply trimmed.

Radishes are best eaten when very young; older ones and those which have grown too slowly, are sometimes too hot-tasting to enjoy. Growing your own is the best way to ensure your radishes are fresh, and they are, perhaps, the easiest of all vegetables to grow. *To make radish roses:* Wash small round radishes, remove all but the smallest leaf and trim off the roots. Using a sharp, thin-bladed vegetable knife, cut a small slice from root and then cut 4 slices around radish from root and almost to stem. Chill in iced water until 'petals' open.
To make radish fans: Wash radishes and trim off leaves and root. Put each radish into a wooden spoon and, holding it firmly on the work surface, cut across into thin slices – the sides of the spoon will stop the knife from going all the way through. Chill in iced water until slices open into a fan.

Radish and Courgette Salad

1 bunch radishes, cut into julienne (matchsticks); 125 g/4 oz (1 cup) small courgettes (zucchini), cut into julienne (matchsticks); salt and freshly ground black pepper; 120 ml/4 fl oz (½ cup) Vinaigrette Dressing (page 358); 1 tbsp very finely chopped fresh dill or parsley.

Season radishes and courgettes (zucchini) lightly with salt and pepper, then toss with vinaigrette and dill or parsley. Serve chilled. Serves 4–6.

RAGOUT

The French term *ragoût* usually describes a dish of meat, fish or poultry cooked with vegetables and liquid, although a dish of spring vegetables, such as peas, carrots, onions and potatoes, can also be called a *ragoût.*

The similar Italian term *ragù* usually describes the rich tomato and meat sauce, namely *Ragù alla Bolognese* that is served with piping hot pasta.

Ragout of Lamb with Turnips

2 tbsp oil; 1 kg (2 lb) lamb shoulder, boned and cubed; 1 tbsp flour; 4 onions, quartered; 1 bouquet garni; 1 clove garlic, crushed; 250 ml/8 fl oz (1 cup) stock or water; 500 g (1 lb) small white turnips, peeled and quartered; 30 g/1 oz (2 tbsp) butter; salt and freshly ground black pepper; 6–8 small potatoes, peeled.

Heat oil in a frying pan (skillet) and brown lamb cubes all over. Transfer to a flameproof casserole. Sprinkle flour over lamb and cook, stirring, until lightly browned. Add onions, bouquet garni, garlic and stock or water and bring rapidly to the boil, stirring. Cover and

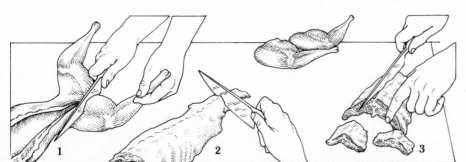

leave to simmer gently. Meanwhile, slowly brown turnips in butter in same pan as used for lamb. Add to casserole, and season with salt and pepper. Continue to simmer, covered, over gentle heat, or cook in a preheated moderate oven (180°C/350°F, Gas Mark 4) for about 1½ hours. Add potatoes and cook for a further 20–30 minutes or until potatoes and lamb are tender. Remove bouquet garni. Serves 6.

RAISINS

Dried grapes of different varieties; they are dried in the sun or artificially, which makes their skins wrinkle, the flavour change and the sugar content increase.

Raisins make nutritious snacks eaten on their own; they are indispensable in fruit cakes, Christmas puddings and mincemeat, delicious in breads, biscuits (cookies) and cakes, and in a sauce to accompany some meats such as ham or in a stuffing for poultry, veal or pork.

When using raisins in a cake mixture, dust them lightly with some of the flour specified in the recipe, then fold them into the batter, scattering well. The flour helps prevent them clumping together.

Raisins may be plumped if necessary, by soaking in hot water for 10 minutes or overnight in fruit juice in the refrigerator. Drain well and use according to your recipe.

Do not buy raisins in large quantities; it is best to keep a small stock on hand, stored in an airtight container – in the refrigerator or freezer, if storing more than a week or two. The seedless golden raisins of U.S.A. are those recognized in Britain as sultanas (see page 419). **See recipes.**

Raisin Sauce

125 g/4 oz (⅔ cup) raisins; 500 ml/18 fl oz (2 cups) water; 180 g/6 oz (1 cup) firmly packed brown sugar; 1½ tbsp cornflour (cornstarch); ¼ tsp ground ginger; 2 tbsp cider vinegar.

Simmer raisins in water for 5 minutes. Combine brown sugar, cornflour (cornstarch), ginger and vinegar, add to pan and cook, stirring, until thickened. Serve hot or cold with ham steaks or tongue. Makes about 600 ml/1 pint (2½ cups).

Raisin Ham with Cheese Sauce

90 g/3 oz (½ cup) raisins; 120 ml/4 fl oz (½ cup) water; 1 tbsp horseradish relish; 8 thin slices cooked ham; 180 g/6 oz (1½ cups) cooked rice; 30 g/1 oz (2 tbsp) butter; 2 tbsp flour; 500 ml/18 fl oz (2 cups) milk; ½ tsp salt; pinch cayenne; 125 g/4 oz (1 cup) grated Cheddar cheese; parsley to garnish.

Bring raisins and water to the boil in covered saucepan. Reduce heat, simmer 10 minutes, then cool. Drain raisins and chop finely. Mix with half the horseradish and spread over each ham slice. Roll up. Spread rice in a greased shallow ovenproof dish and arrange ham rolls on top. Melt butter in a saucepan, stir in flour and cook for 2 minutes without browning. Gradually stir in milk and bring to the boil, stirring. Simmer until thickened. Add salt, cayenne, remaining horseradish and grated cheese. Stir until cheese melts, then pour sauce over ham rolls. Bake in a preheated moderate oven (180°C/350°F, Gas Mark 4) for 20 minutes. Serve hot, garnished with parsley. Serves 4.

Raisin and Nut Stuffing

180 g/6 oz (3 cups) fresh breadcrumbs; 90 g/3 oz (½ cup) raisins; 75 g/2½ oz (⅔ cup) chopped nuts; 2 tbsp chopped parsley; 60–75 g/2–2½ oz (4–5 tbsp) butter, softened; salt and freshly ground black pepper; 1 egg.

Mix all ingredients together well and use as a stuffing for poultry, veal or pork. Makes about 500 g/1 lb (4 cups).

Raisin and Walnut Loaf

250 g/8 oz (2 cups) self-raising flour; pinch salt; 60 g/2 oz (4 tbsp) butter; 60 g/2 oz (¼ cup) sugar; 125 g/4 oz (⅔ cup) raisins, roughly chopped; 125 g/4 oz (1 cup) chopped walnuts; 1 egg, beaten; 1 tbsp golden (light corn) syrup; 120 ml/4 fl oz (½ cup) buttermilk.
TOPPING: *1 tbsp sugar; 2 tbsp chopped walnuts; little buttermilk.*

Sift flour and salt into a mixing bowl. Rub (cut) in butter, then add sugar, raisins, walnuts and egg and mix until well combined. Stir syrup into buttermilk. Add to dry ingredients and beat well. Spoon into a greased 21 × 11 cm (8 × 4½ in) loaf tin (pan). Level top with a spatula.
TOPPING: Mix sugar and walnuts. Brush loaf with buttermilk, and sprinkle sugar and nuts over top. Press gently with a spatula to make

sure topping sticks to loaf. Bake in a preheated moderate oven (180°C/350°F, Gas Mark 4) for 45–50 minutes or until quite firm to touch. Cool in tin (pan) for 5 minutes, then turn out on to a wire rack.

Raisin Marmalade Cake

250 g/8 oz (2 cups) self-raising flour; 125 g/4 oz (½ cup) butter; 140 g/4½ oz (¾ cup) firmly packed brown sugar; 90 g/3 oz (½ cup) raisins; 2 eggs, beaten; 6 tbsp thick cut marmalade.

Sift flour into a bowl and rub (cut) in butter. Add sugar and raisins and mix well. Gradually add eggs and beat well. The mixture should be fairly stiff, but if necessary add 1 tbsp milk. Put ⅔ of mixture into a greased and lined 15 cm (6 in) square cake tin (pan). Smooth top and spread 2 tbsp of marmalade over it. Spread over half remaining cake mixture, add another 2 tbsp marmalade and then rest of cake mixture. Top with remaining marmalade. Bake in a preheated moderate oven (180°C/350°F, Gas Mark 4) for 1 hour 25 minutes or until golden-brown and well risen. Cool on a wire rack. When cold cut cake into squares to serve.

Veal with Raisins

90 g/3 oz (6 tbsp) butter; 1.5 kg (3 lb) breast of veal, boned and cubed; 3 tbsp hot dry sherry or vermouth; 90 g/3 oz (½ cup) raisins; 125 g/4 oz (1 cup) mushrooms, sliced; 1 tbsp tomato purée (paste); 3 tbsp flour; 350 ml/12 fl oz (1½ cups) beef stock (bouillon); 1 bay leaf; 250 ml/8 fl oz (1 cup) sour cream; 1 tbsp redcurrant jelly; salt; pinch cayenne; 1 tsp ground coriander.

Melt butter over moderate heat in a flameproof casserole and brown meat quickly. Pour hot sherry or vermouth over meat. Add raisins and cook briskly for 2–3 minutes, stirring. Mix in mushrooms, tomato purée (paste) and flour. When well blended add the beef stock and bay leaf. Stir until boiling. Cover, reduce heat and cook gently for about 1 hour or until veal is tender. Remove veal using a slotted spoon and keep warm. Whisk sour cream into cooking liquid with redcurrant jelly, salt, cayenne and coriander. Return veal and simmer very gently for 10–15 minutes. Discard bay leaf. Serve with buttered noodles and a tossed salad. Serves 6.

RASPBERRY

Raspberries are among the most delicious of summer fruits, but their season is all too short.

Fortunately, frozen raspberries can be found throughout the year, and although their appearance and flavour might not equal

R

those of the fresh fruits, they can be profitably used in a raspberry sauce (sieve them to remove the tiny seeds).

Fresh raspberries can be served simply with sugar, cream, or a soft, creamy, fresh cheese such as *mascarpone*, but they combine superbly with other fruits, either fresh or cooked. Fill small melon halves with raspberries, or a pineapple shell with pineapple chunks and raspberries; toss with peaches or pears.

If you have an excess of raspberries, they may be made into jam or jelly (unlike strawberry jam, raspberry jam sets well). Alternatively freeze whole or make into purée and freeze in small containers. Frozen purée can be kept for about 6 months. It should be thawed in the refrigerator and stirred well before use. **See recipes.**

Raspberry Sauce

A versatile sauce that can be poured over ice cream, plain yogurt or fresh cream cheese, over orange segments, sliced poached pears or peaches. Serve as sauce with lemon ice cream; use to make a raspberry bavarois; serve with a cream-filled sponge cake or roll; drizzle over a trifle; spread on crêpes before rolling; combine with thick cream for a raspberry fool or use in Pêche Melba (*see* page 284).

250 g/8 oz (1½ cups) raspberries; 60–125 g/ 2–4 oz sugar (¼–½ cup) sugar; squeeze lemon juice.

Purée raspberries with sugar in blender, then strain through sieve to remove seeds. Or push fruit through sieve to purée and stir in caster sugar to taste. Add lemon juice to sharpen flavour. Makes about 350 ml/ 12 fl oz (1½ cups).

Clear Raspberry Sauce

150 g/5 oz (1 cup) fresh or frozen raspberries; 175 ml/6 fl oz (¾ cup) water; 3 tbsp sugar; 2 tsp cornflour (cornstarch) dissolved in 1 tbsp water.

Place raspberries in a saucepan with water and sugar and bring to the boil. Add

cornflour (cornstarch) paste and cook the sauce, stirring, until it thickens. Push through a sieve and allow to cool. Makes 350 ml/ 12 fl oz (1½ cups).

NOTE: If fresh or frozen raspberries are not available, use canned raspberries with their juice instead of water and sugar.

Classic Raspberry Mousse

125 g/4 oz (½ cup) sugar; 175 ml/6 fl oz (¾ cup) water; 500 g/1 lb (3 cups) raspberries; 1 tbsp gelatine; 2 tbsp orange juice; 120 ml/4 fl oz (½ cup) double (heavy) cream, whipped; 3 egg whites.

Dissolve sugar in water in a saucepan. Add raspberries and cook gently for about 3 minutes or until juice is starting to run out. Press through sieve, and allow purée to cool. Soften gelatine in orange juice, then dissolve over low heat. Stir into purée, then fold in whipped cream. Beat egg whites until stiff and fold lightly into raspberry mixture. Pour into serving bowl and chill until set. Serve with additional whipped cream, if desired. Serves 6.

Raspberry Sorbet

Making sorbets is easier if you have a small, electrically-powered machine known as a sorbetière. The paddles of the machine keep the mixture in motion as it freezes, thus preventing the formation of large ice crystals. However, sorbets can be made very successfully without such a machine, as long as the mixture is whisked every half hour or so while freezing.

500 g/1 lb (3 cups) raspberries; juice 2 oranges; juice 1 lemon; 350 g/12 oz (1½ cups) caster sugar.

Place raspberries in blender with juices and blend to a purée. (Alternatively, push through sieve.) Sieve purée to remove seeds, then add sugar and whisk until sugar has dissolved. If desired, sharpen taste with a little more lemon juice. Pour into container of sorbetière and freeze (or freeze in a shallow dish or ice cream trays and whisk frequently). Allow sorbet to ripen (mellow) in refrigerator for 30 minutes or so before serving. Serves 6–8.

RATATOUILLE

Summer vegetables were never combined better than in this colourful French medley, so popular in Provence.

Ratatouille is a most versatile dish. It may be eaten cold, with cold meats or hard-boiled (hard-cooked) eggs, or simply with bread, as a dip. Or it may be eaten hot, as an accompaniment to grilled (broiled) or roast lamb, pork chops or steaks (although lamb seems best suited to the accompaniment of this robust,

garlicky flavour). A plain omelette is enhanced by ratatouille; a quick and easy lunch or supper dish is made by breaking eggs into hollows in a pan of hot ratatouille, and covering the pan until the eggs are set.

□ **To Prepare:** The easy way to make ratatouille is simply to layer prepared vegetables in a pan, starting with sliced onions, then aubergines (eggplant), peppers, courgettes (zucchini) and tomatoes. Season each layer with salt and pepper and a drizzle of olive oil, tuck a few whole garlic cloves between the layers and cook over low heat for about 1 hour. Remove lid towards the end of cooking to allow excess liquid to evaporate. Proportions of each vegetable are not too important in this method, nor does it matter if there are no courgettes (zucchini), but there must be tomatoes.

Ratatouille

2 medium aubergines (eggplant), cubed; salt; 2 large onions, finely chopped; 120 ml/ 4 fl oz (½ cup) olive oil; 2 peppers, cored, seeded and cut into fine strips; 4 courgettes (zucchini), cut into 5 mm (¼ in) slices; 2 cloves garlic, crushed; freshly ground black pepper; 4 ripe tomatoes, peeled, seeded and quartered; finely chopped parsley.

Place aubergine (eggplant) cubes in a colander, sprinkle with coarse salt and leave for 30 minutes. Drain and pat dry with paper towels. Cook onions in oil in a large saucepan until soft and golden. Add aubergine (eggplant) cubes, and cook 2 minutes longer. Add peppers, courgette (zucchini) and garlic, season with pepper, cover and cook gently for about 15 minutes. Add tomatoes and cook about 5 minutes longer. Serve warm or chilled, sprinkled with finely chopped parsley. Ratatouille keeps well in the refrigerator for 3–4 days. Store covered. Serves 4–6.

RED CABBAGE

See Cabbage.

REDCURRANT

A fruit that seems to be even more elusive than the raspberry, but there is some consolation in the knowledge that frozen redcurrants are not too difficult to find, and their delicious, tangy flavour can be preserved in redcurrant jelly. Redcurrants are often combined with other summer berry fruits, such as raspberries, in fruit salads, compotes and in Summer Pudding (see page 421). Cooked in syrup, redcurrants can flavour a plain yogurt or accompany fresh cream cheese.

Redcurrant jelly is one of the most useful ingredients of any pantry. It can be melted and used to glaze red fruits in tarts or on cakes. Many sauces, including Cumberland Sauce (see page 91), call for redcurrant jelly. **See recipes.**

Redcurrants with Raspberry Juice

250 g/8 oz (2 cups) redcurrants; 75 g/2½ oz (½ cup) raspberries; 125 g/4 oz (½ cup) vanilla sugar; juice ½ lemon.

Place redcurrants in serving dish. Sieve raspberries, or purée in a blender and then sieve to remove seeds. Pour over redcurrants. Sprinkle with sugar, then lemon juice. Allow to macerate for at least 3 hours. Serve chilled. Serves 2–3.

Redcurrant Jelly

This jelly is not as firm as most commercial jellies, but is very good for making Cumberland and other sauces. Redcurrant jelly should be melted over gentle heat, or in a bowl over hot water, before mixing with other ingredients for a sauce. It is sometimes necessary to sieve the melted jelly to remove any remaining jelly globules.

1 kg/2 lb (8 cups) redcurrants; 1 kg/2 lb (4 cups) caster sugar.

Place fruit in large saucepan and mix with sugar. Bring to the boil and boil, stirring constantly, for 8 minutes, carefully removing all scum as it rises. Strain through a fine sieve. Spoon resulting jelly into small jars. Seal when cold. Makes about 8 × 120 ml/ 4 fl oz (½ cup) jars.

Redcurrant Sauce

A good accompaniment to duck or goose.

2 tbsp redcurrant jelly; 2 tbsp prepared mustard; pinch cayenne; juice 1 lemon; 4 tbsp port.

Melt redcurrant jelly, and sieve if necessary to remove lumps. Add remaining ingredients and simmer gently 5 minutes. Serve immediately. Makes about 120 ml/4 fl oz (½ cup).

REMOULADE SAUCE

This classic, mayonnaise-based sauce is served with cold seafood, particularly lobster and crab, with poultry and cold meats.

See page 205 for recipe.

RHUBARB

This is available all year round.

Rhubarb is always eaten cooked, and can also be used for jams and jellies, either on its own or mixed with other fruits. It blends beautifully with other fruits, particularly apples and strawberries. It is also delicious with citrus flavourings, and with spices, especially ginger. A simple compote of rhubarb with plain yogurt makes a light, refreshing dessert or breakfast dish.

☐ **Basic Preparation:** Simply remove and discard the leaves, trim the root end and cut the stalks into convenient-sized pieces.
☐ **To Cook:** Cook rhubarb on top of the stove or in the oven, but use very little water, since the rhubarb will give out moisture and shrink as it cooks. Take care not to overcook, or the rhubarb will lose its bright red colour.

Cooked rhubarb may be puréed and used in the same way as strawberry or raspberry purée, or combined with double (heavy) cream or custard to make a Rhubarb Fool. **See recipes.**

Rhubarb Crumble

250 g/8 oz (1 cup) sugar; 120 ml/4 fl oz (½ cup) water; 750 g/1½ lb (4 cups) rhubarb, cut into short pieces; 1 tsp grated orange rind.
CRUMBLE TOPPING: *125 g/4 oz (1 cup) flour; 60 g/2 oz (4 tbsp) butter; 60 g/2 oz (¼ cup) sugar; pinch cinnamon.*

Dissolve sugar in water over heat to make a syrup. Bring to the boil, then add rhubarb and orange rind. Cover and simmer for 5 minutes or until rhubarb is tender but not mushy. Turn into greased ovenproof dish. CRUMBLE TOPPING: Sift flour into a bowl and rub (cut) in butter until mixture resembles crumbs. Mix in sugar and cinnamon. Sprinkle topping over fruit. Bake in a preheated moderate oven (180°C/350°F,

Gas Mark 4) for 30 minutes or until crumble is golden-brown. Serves 6.
VARIATIONS
Substitute 250 g/8 oz (2 cups) sliced apple for 370 g/12 oz (2 cups) rhubarb, or add a little sliced preserved ginger to rhubarb.

Baked Rhubarb and Orange Sponge

1 bunch rhubarb, trimmed and chopped; 45 g/1½ oz (¼ cup) firmly packed brown sugar; 2 tsp grated orange rind; 3 tbsp warmed honey; 60 g/2 oz (4 tbsp) butter; 60 g/2 oz (¼ cup) caster sugar; 1 egg, lightly beaten; 90 g/3 oz (¾ cup) self-raising flour, sifted; 5 tbsp milk.

Place rhubarb in buttered ovenproof dish, sprinkle with brown sugar and half the orange rind, and pour over honey. Cream butter with remaining orange rind and caster sugar until light and fluffy. Beat in egg, then fold in sifted flour alternately with milk. Spread over rhubarb. Bake in a preheated moderately hot oven (190°C/375°F, Gas Mark 5) for about 40 minutes or until golden. Serve hot, with custard or single (light) cream. Serves 6.

Rhubarb Fool

1 bunch rhubarb, trimmed and cut into 5 cm (2 in) lengths; 60 g/2 oz (⅓ cup) firmly packed brown sugar; grated rind 1 orange; 250 ml/8 fl oz (1 cup) double (heavy) cream; 2 tsp Pernod.

Place rhubarb in a saucepan with sugar, orange rind and a little water and simmer gently until just tender. Drain, then push through a sieve or purée in a blender. Cool. Lightly whip cream and fold into cooled purée with Pernod. Serve cold in individual dishes, with sponge fingers (lady fingers) or thin, crisp biscuits (cookies). Serves 4.

RICE

Learn to cook this great staple perfectly and you have the base for hundreds of splendid hot or cold savoury dishes, sustaining puddings and interesting accompaniments to meat, seafood and poultry.

There are many varieties of rice and it is important to choose the right kind for your purpose.

Types of Grain

Rice may be short-, medium- or long-grain.

Short-grain Rice: Best for puddings because it clings together when cooked to give a creamy texture. Short- or medium-grain rice is also the traditional choice for Chinese fried rice or other dishes, since clinging grains are best for eating with chopsticks, though long-grain rice can be used.

Italian *arborio* rice is a short- to medium-grain variety, with large, round grains; it is available at Italian groceries or speciality delicatessens and often labelled *risotti* rice. It is ideal for risotto because it will absorb a great deal of liquid without disintegrating, to give the characteristic texture – soft, moist but not sticky – of this dish.

Medium-grain Rice: Suitable for savoury dishes where the rice should be in distinct grains but holding together – e.g. rice rings, moulds and croquettes. If medium-grain is not available, use long-grain for rice rings and moulds, short-grain for croquettes.

Long-grain Rice: Cooks to give the separate, fluffy grains required for plain boiled rice and for most savoury dishes, stuffings and rice salads.

Basmati rice from Pakistan is a superb, light-textured long-grain rice, with a wonderful aromatic flavour. It is expensive but worth it for dishes like Indian Ghee Rice, pilaf, pilau and Biryani (see page 35).

Types of Rice

White (polished) Rice: This has been hulled and had the bran coating removed. It is tender and easily digested, and is remarkable in its ability to complement, contrast or provide a vehicle for the flavours and textures of many other foods.

Brown Rice: This has been hulled but has not lost its bran coating. It is more nutritious and rather more filling than white rice, and has a nutty taste and slightly chewy texture. Brown rice is particularly good in vegetable dishes or used as a stuffing, and is an excellent binder for meat loaves. It takes longer to cook than white rice (about 40 minutes).

Parboiled Rice: Long-grain polished rice which has been treated before milling with a steam pressure process; this forces some of the bran's nutrients into the grain so that it retains more food value than ordinary white rice. It is not washed before cooking as the steam process has removed surface starch. Since the steam has also hardened it, it takes longer to cook than ordinary white rice (20–25 minutes) and absorbs more liquid ($2\frac{1}{2}$ parts water to 1 part rice). Apart from its nutritive value, the advantage of parboiled rice is that it is almost foolproof in giving beautifully fluffy, separate grains and it has a good nutty flavour.

Quick-cooking or 'Instant' Rice: This has been cooked, then dehydrated. It usually needs only 4–6 minutes' heating in boiling water; follow directions on the pack and be careful not to overcook.

Wild Rice: The seed of a grass related to the rice family. It is very expensive but a great treat – its rare, nutty flavour is the perfect complement to poultry and game. For economy, cooked wild rice can be combined with cooked brown or white rice.

Buying, Storing and Reheating Rice

Buy only as much as you expect to use within a month. It may develop weevils if held for too long. Store all rice airtight in a cool, dry place.

Servings: One cup of raw rice weighs about 210 g/7 oz, and will swell to about 3 cups when cooked, enough for 6–7 servings of plain boiled rice as an accompaniment.

Cooked rice will remain in good condition in a covered container in the refrigerator for 5–6 days. To reheat, place in a sieve or colander and run hot water through it, then stand colander over a saucepan about $\frac{1}{3}$ full of boiling water, cover with a cloth and steam 10–15 minutes. Or spread out in a baking dish, sprinkle with a little milk and dot with butter, cover with a cloth, or foil with a few holes poked in it, and place in a preheated very cool oven (120°C/250°F, Gas Mark $\frac{1}{2}$) until heated through.

Rice can be frozen, though this changes the texture a little and is seldom worthwhile since it is almost as quick to cook rice freshly as to thaw it. Thaw by placing in a sieve and running hot water through it, then steaming over boiling water as described above. Do not freeze rice in liquid, e.g. in a soup, as it goes mushy. **See recipes**.

Boiled Rice

210 g/7 oz (1 cup) rice; 2 litres/$3\frac{1}{2}$ pints (8 cups) water; 2 tsp salt; 1 slice lemon (optional).

Rinse rice in a sieve under cold running water until the water runs clear. Bring measured water to the boil in a large saucepan and add salt. Lemon slice may be added to help keep rice white. Slowly sprinkle in rice through your fingers so that water does not go off the boil. Stir once, then cook uncovered, keeping water at a brisk boil, until rice is tender but still firm. Test by lifting out a grain or two and biting it. The rice is cooked when it is soft but slightly resistant to the teeth; this is called *al dente*. Basmati rice will take 7–10 minutes, other long-grain rice about 12 minutes, short-grain rice a little longer. Start testing a few minutes ahead of time. Drain rice in a sieve or colander and run cold, then hot, water through it to separate grains and wash out any remaining starch.

For very dry, fluffy grains, boil a little water in the saucepan, place colander of boiled rice over it, cover with a cloth and leave to steam for 5–10 minutes; or spread rice out in a baking dish, dot with butter, cover dish with a cloth, or foil with a few holes in it, and place in a preheated very cool oven (120°C/250°F, Gas Mark $\frac{1}{2}$) for 10–15 minutes. Makes 370 g/12 oz (3 cups).

VARIATION

Boiled Brown Rice: If possible soak brown rice in cold water for 20 minutes before cooking as above. Brown rice will take 40 minutes or longer to cook and may need a little more water added.

Steamed Rice

This method retains more of the flavour of the rice.

210 g/7 oz (1 cup) rice; 500 ml/18 fl oz (2 cups) water; $\frac{1}{2}$ tsp salt.

Rinse rice in a sieve under cold running water until the water runs clear. Bring measured water and salt to the boil in a heavy saucepan. Slowly sprinkle in rice through your fingers so that water does not go off the boil. Stir once, then cover with a well-fitting lid and turn heat very low (if necessary use an asbestos mat). Do not lift lid until last few minutes of cooking. Cook very gently for 10–15 minutes or until a test grain is tender but still firm when bitten. Remove from heat and fork up lightly. For very dry, fluffy grains, set the rice aside, still covered, for 5 minutes before forking up. Makes 370 g/12 oz (3 cups).

Chinese-Style Rice

For Chinese fried rice, cook rice this way, spread it out in a shallow dish, cover and refrigerate overnight before using.

430 g/14 oz (2 cups) rice; ½ tsp salt.

Rinse rice in a sieve under cold running water until the water runs clear. Place rice in a heavy saucepan and add salt and enough water to come about 2 cm (¾ in) above level of rice. Bring to the boil, then lower heat to medium and continue cooking until water has almost evaporated and steam holes appear in rice. Reduce heat to very low, cover with tight-fitting lid and steam 15–20 minutes or until rice is tender. Do not lift lid until last few minutes of cooking. Set aside, still covered, for 5 minutes, then fork up lightly. Makes about 750 g/1½ lb (6 cups).

Wild Rice

250 g/8 oz (1 cup) wild rice; salt.

Cover rice with cold salted water in a saucepan. Bring to the boil, skim any foreign particles from top and drain. Bring 750 ml/1¼ pints (3 cups) fresh water to the boil, add 1 tsp salt and stir in rice slowly. Cook without stirring for about 30 minutes or until grains are tender, adding a little more boiling water if necessary. Fluff up with a fork before serving. Makes about 500 g/1 lb (3 cups).

Rice Ring or Mould

butter; Boiled or Steamed Rice (page 331).

Generously butter a ring mould, or dariole or other individual moulds. Drain boiled rice well but do not run water through it. Pack hot rice firmly into moulds, rest in a warm place 3–4 minutes, then place a heated serving plate over each mould and invert it and plate together. Rap sharply on table to release rice and lift mould off carefully.

Indian Ghee Rice

Serve with a curry, grilled (broiled) spiced chicken or pork, lamb or chicken satays. To get the best flavour, onions must be allowed to cook gently for a long time. Do not stir rice once it has come to the boil.

60 g/2 oz (4 tbsp) ghee; 1 onion, finely sliced; 1 tsp turmeric; 430 g/14 oz (2 cups) long-grain rice, preferably Basmati; 875 ml/1 pint 9 fl oz (3½ cups) boiling chicken stock; 8 black peppercorns; 2 whole cloves; 4 cardamom pods; 1 tsp salt; 1 cinnamon stick; 165 g/5½ oz (1 cup) hot cooked peas.

Heat ghee in a heavy saucepan, add half the onion and fry gently until golden-brown. Make sure onion is well cooked but do not allow to burn. Add turmeric and cook,

stirring, for 1 minute. Add rice and fry 5–10 minutes, stirring constantly, until it is golden. Add boiling stock with peppercorns, cloves, cardamom, salt, cinnamon and remaining onion. Bring to the boil, stirring from time to time, then turn heat down very low, cover pan tightly and cook gently 10–20 minutes or until rice is tender and liquid is absorbed. Turn off heat and leave covered until serving time, then remove lid and fluff rice up with a fork. Serve garnished with peas. Serves 4–6.

VARIATION

Curried Rice: Follow recipe for Indian Ghee Rice, adding 2 tsp curry powder with the turmeric.

Basic Rice Pilaf

Pilaf can be an accompaniment, or can be a whole meal with fish, poultry, meat and vegetables added.

430 g/14 oz (2 cups) long-grain rice; 30 g/1 oz (2 tbsp) butter; 1 onion, finely chopped; salt and freshly ground black pepper; 1 litre/1¾ pints (4 cups) boiling stock.

Rinse rice in a sieve under cold running water until water runs clear. Drain thoroughly. Melt butter in a heavy saucepan, add onion and cook gently until soft and golden. Stir in rice, season with salt and pepper and cook, stirring frequently, until rice becomes translucent. Pour in boiling stock and bring to the boil again, then lower heat, cover tightly and cook very gently for about 20 minutes or until all liquid is absorbed and rice is tender (small holes will appear on the surface). Remove lid and cook uncovered for 1–2 minutes. Fluff up with a fork before serving. Serves 8–10 as an accompaniment.

VARIATIONS

Cashew and Sultana Pilaf: Follow recipe for Basic Rice Pilaf. Fry 60 g/2 oz (½ cup) cashew nuts and 60 g/2 oz (⅓ cup) sultanas (golden raisins) in a little ghee or butter until golden. Fork through finished pilaf.

Mushroom Pilaf: Follow recipe for Basic Rice Pilaf, but add 125 g/4 oz (1 cup) mushrooms, sautéed in 30 g/1 oz (2 tbsp) butter, to the pilaf with the stock.

Main-Dish Pilaf: Follow recipe for Basic Rice Pilaf and fold through the finished pilaf 250 g/8 oz (1 cup) diced cooked chicken, flaked fish, shellfish, roast lamb or other meat, 180 g/6 oz (1 cup) cooked or raw vegetables and 2 tbsp toasted almond halves. For vegetables, use sliced sautéed mushrooms, diced celery or pepper, diced cooked carrot, lightly cooked cauliflower or broccoli florets, cooked peas or beans. Serves 4–6.

Fried Rice

Try to get Chinese rice wine – the best is Shaosing, a yellow rice wine. It is available

from good Chinese supply shops.

8–10 dried Chinese mushrooms; salt; 6 tbsp oil; 3 eggs; 6 spring onions (scallions), chopped; 125 g (4 oz) barbecued pork or ham, cut into small slices; 250 g/8 oz (1 cup) shelled small cooked prawns (shrimp); 500 g/1 lb (4 cups) cooked Chinese-Style Rice, refrigerated overnight; 90 g/3 oz (½ cup) cooked peas.
SEASONING: *2 tbsp Chinese rice wine or dry sherry; 4 tbsp chicken stock; 2 tsp soy sauce.*

Soak mushrooms in water to cover for 30 minutes, then drain. Simmer gently in salted water for 5 minutes. Drain. Remove stalks, slice mushrooms thinly and set aside. Heat 2 tbsp of the oil in a wok or frying pan (skillet). Beat eggs with a pinch of salt and add to pan. Cook until firm, stirring so that cooked egg is broken into small pieces. Remove from pan and set aside.

Heat wok or pan and add remaining oil. When hot add spring onions (scallions), meat, prawns (shrimp) and mushrooms. Fry for a few seconds, then add rice, tossing to mix and heat through. Season with salt, and add peas and cooked egg. Combine seasoning ingredients and sprinkle over rice. Mix well and serve. Serves 6.

Saffron Rice

This superb rice is one of the most useful of all recipes. It makes a simple but stylish accompaniment to poultry, meat or seafood that is spicy – Indian, South East Asian, etc. Saffron is expensive but makes the subtle difference. Use a heavy saucepan or an iron casserole for absolutely carefree cooking.

½ tsp crumbled saffron; 310 g/10 oz (1½ cups) Basmati or other long-grain rice; 15 g/½ oz (1 tbsp) butter; 1 tbsp oil; 1 small onion, finely chopped; 750 ml/1¼ pints (3 cups) boiling chicken stock or water; salt.

Soak saffron in enough warm water barely to cover. Rinse rice in a sieve under cold running water until water runs clear. Drain thoroughly. Heat butter and oil in a deep saucepan and cook onion until soft without colouring. Add rice and cook for a further few minutes, stirring all the time until rice is well coated with butter and oil. Pour on stock or water, and add saffron with water in which it was soaked and a large pinch of salt (or less if your stock is salty). Stir once, then cover tightly and cook gently for 15–20 minutes or until rice is tender and liquid has been absorbed. Remove lid and stand for a few minutes to let steam escape. Fluff up with a fork and serve. Serves 8.

Right: Veal Samarkand (page 457) and Mediterranean Style Pork Chops (page 303)

Ham Rice Salad

Good for picnics and summer luncheons. The salad can be varied by using chicken, seafood, salami or other cold meat instead of ham, and other vegetables such as sliced celery, pepper or radish.

750 g/1½ lb (6 cups) Steamed Rice (page 331), cooled to room temperature; 250 g/8 oz (1 cup) cooked ham, sliced 1 cm (½ in) thick and diced; 165 g/5½ oz (1 cup) cooked green peas; 40 g/1⅓ oz (1 cup) chopped spring onions (scallions), including green tops; salt and freshly ground black pepper; 120 ml/4 fl oz (½ cup) Mayonnaise (page 204).
DRESSING: *2 tsp French (Dijon) mustard; 120 ml/4 fl oz (½ cup) olive oil; 4 tbsp good vinegar; 1 clove garlic, crushed; salt and freshly ground black pepper.*

Beat dressing ingredients together well, or shake in a jar. Mix rice with dressing, then add ham, peas, parsley and spring onions (scallions), and season with salt and pepper, if necessary. Lastly, add the mayonnaise. Serves 8.
NOTE: Make ahead and store in refrigerator.

Prawn Jambalaya

This colourful Creole dish derives from Spanish Paella. Like paella, Jambalaya is a complete meal in itself.

210 g/7 oz (1 cup) long-grain rice; 2 thick rashers (slices) streaky bacon, rind removed and cut into strips; 1 tbsp oil or butter; 1 large onion, finely chopped; 2 cloves garlic, crushed; 2 tender sticks celery, sliced; 1 large green pepper, cored, seeded and cut into strips; 350–500 ml/12–18 fl oz (1½–2 cups) boiling chicken stock; 250 g/8 oz (1 cup) drained canned tomatoes, coarsely chopped; 2 tsp chopped fresh thyme, or ½ tsp dried; pinch cayenne; 125 g (4 oz) cooked ham, thickly sliced and cut into small strips; salt and freshly ground black pepper; 500 g/1 lb (2 cups) medium green (uncooked) prawns (shrimp), shelled and deveined; 2 tbsp finely chopped parsley.

Rinse rice in a sieve under cold running water until water runs clear. Drain well. Fry bacon in a large, flameproof casserole until crisp. Remove with a slotted spoon and set aside. Add oil or butter to bacon fat in pan and gently cook onion and garlic until soft but not brown. Add celery and green pepper and cook about 3 minutes or until slightly wilted. Add rice and cook, stirring frequently, about 5 minutes or until rice becomes translucent. Add 350 ml/12 fl oz (1½ cups)

Left: Peperonata (page 286) and Fried Marinated Fish (page 124)

boiling stock with tomatoes, thyme, cayenne, ham, salt and pepper. (Remember that ham may make mixture a little saltier as it cooks.)

Bring to the boil and stir once, then cover tightly and place in a preheated moderate oven (160°C/325°F, Gas Mark 3). Cook 10 minutes. Add prawns (shrimp), pushing them down beneath the surface. Cover again and cook a further 10–15 minutes or until rice is tender and liquid is absorbed. Check once or twice during this time and if rice appears dry, add a few more spoonfuls of boiling stock. Add parsley and fork through. Serve Jambalaya straight from the casserole or on a heated serving dish. Serves 6.
VARIATION
Chicken Jambalaya: Follow recipe for Prawn Jambalaya, but substitute 3 chicken fillets (skinned, boned half-breasts), each cut crossways in half and sautéed 5 minutes in a little butter, for the prawns (shrimp).

Brown Rice Pudding

A pudding so nourishing and satisfying that it would take only soup and a side salad to complete the meal.

370 g/12 oz (3 cups) Boiled Brown Rice (page 331); 750 ml/1¼ pints (3 cups) milk; 3 eggs, beaten; 90 g/3 oz (½ cup) firmly packed brown sugar; ½ tsp mixed spice (ground allspice); 90 g/3 oz (½ cup) mixed dried fruit.
TO SERVE: *brown sugar; sour cream.*

Mix rice with remaining ingredients. Spoon pudding into a greased shallow ovenproof dish. Bake in a preheated moderate oven (180°C/350°F, Gas Mark 4) for 30 minutes. Remove from oven and sprinkle a little more brown sugar evenly over top. Return to oven and bake 10 minutes more. Serve warm with sour cream slightly sweetened with brown sugar. Serves 6–8.

Saffron Pilau

A marvellous dish for a party, barbecue or large luncheon. It goes beautifully with cold roast beef or other meats, hot or cold chicken or grilled (broiled) meat. It is good hot or cold and looks magnificent piled into a big dish. It is also excellent heaped into tomato cases, or moulded into a ring and filled with a savoury mixture. It is a failproof recipe – adding the liquid gradually ensures that the rice will not go soggy.

3 tbsp oil; 2 onions, finely sliced; ½ tsp crumbled saffron; 430 g/14 oz (2 cups) long-grain rice; 875 ml/1 pint 9 fl oz (3½ cups) boiling chicken stock; 8 black peppercorns; 2 whole cloves; 4 cardamom pods, bruised; 1 cinnamon stick; 2 tsp salt; 90 g/3 oz (½ cup) sultanas (golden raisins) or raisins; 60 g/2 oz (½ cup) halved, toasted almonds; 6 hard-boiled (hard-cooked) eggs, halved (optional).

Heat oil in a heavy saucepan and gently fry onions until a pale golden colour. Make sure onions are soft but do not allow to burn; this will take quite a while. Add saffron and cook for 1 minute, stirring. Add rice and fry gently, stirring constantly, for 5 minutes until all rice is coated with oil and golden. Add 400 ml/⅔ pint (1⅔ cups) boiling chicken stock, with peppercorns, cloves, cardamom, cinnamon and salt (reduce if stock is salty). Bring to the boil, then cover and simmer gently for 20–25 minutes or until rice is tender, adding more stock as it is absorbed. Add sultanas (golden raisins) or raisins, cover and allow to plump. Turn off heat and keep covered until ready to serve. A few minutes before serving, uncover pan to allow steam to escape, fluff up rice with a fork and add almonds. Turn on to a large heated serving dish. For a main dish, garnish with eggs. Serves 8–10.
NOTE: 1 tsp turmeric may be substituted for the saffron. It gives good colour but not the same flavour.
VARIATIONS
Pilau-stuffed Tomatoes: Peel 12 firm tomatoes, scoop out centres with a teaspoon, salt inside and turn upside-down on paper towels for 10 minutes to drain. Brush tomatoes lightly with oil, then pile hot Saffron Pilau into the centres and place in a baking dish. Heat in a preheated moderate oven (180°C/350°F, Gas Mark 4) for 10 minutes.
Pilau Ring: Pack Saffron Pilau firmly into an oiled 1.6 litre/2¾ pint (7 cup) ring mould. Rest in a warm place 3–4 minutes, then put a heated platter over the mould and invert. Tap mould to release rice, and remove mould. If liked, fill centre with cooked mushrooms and peas, sautéed chicken livers tossed in a little single (light) cream or any other savoury filling.
Saffron Rice Salad: Prepare Saffron Pilau or Saffron Rice. Combine 2 tbsp vinegar, 2 tsp prepared mustard (Dijon is best) and 6 tbsp oil. Season with salt and pepper and beat with a fork until thick. Toss through rice. To this basic rice salad you can add 250 g/8 oz (1 cup) diced cooked chicken, 60 g/2 oz (½ cup) chopped green peppers and some chopped parsley. Shelled prawns (shrimp) and sliced canned water chestnuts for a crispy contrast make another good combination. For a creamy salad, fold in a little Mayonnaise (see page 204).

Green Rice

Rice combined with fresh green herbs and vegetables, cream and cheese makes a colourful and complete accompaniment to meat or fish or it could be an interesting part of a meatless meal.

120 ml/4 fl oz (½ cup) olive oil; 60 g/2 oz (½ cup) chopped green pepper; 370 g/12 oz

335

(3 cups) Boiled or Steamed Rice (page 331); 700 g/1 lb (3 cups) chopped cooked spinach; 30 g/1 oz (¾ cup) chopped parsley; 20 g/⅔ oz (½ cup) snipped chives; 1 tsp salt; ¼ tsp pepper; 120 ml/4 fl oz (½ cup) single (light) cream; 250 g/8 oz (2 cups) grated Parmesan cheese.

Heat oil in a large saucepan and sauté green pepper for 5 minutes. Stir in rice, spinach, parsley, chives, salt and pepper and toss together until hot. Remove from heat and toss with cream and 125 g/4 oz (1 cup) of cheese. Turn into a heated serving dish and sprinkle remaining cheese on top. Serves 8.

Buttered Rice

This is a good way of using leftover cooked rice. It can be an accompaniment or a meal in itself, depending on what you add to the basic recipe.

60 g/2 oz (4 tbsp) butter; 250 g/8 oz (2 cups) Steamed Rice (page 331); flavouring (see below).

Melt butter in a heavy saucepan, stir in rice and mix well, tossing lightly over gentle heat. Or heat through in a preheated moderate oven (160°C/325°F, Gas Mark 3), shaking dish occasionally, until thoroughly heated through. After buttering rice and before heating, any of the following may be added: sliced mushrooms; strips of canned pimiento; diced celery or pepper; any cooked vegetables; cooked prawns (shrimp), scallops or mussels; chopped parsley or mixed herbs; Pesto alla Genovese (see page 272); chopped spring onion (scallion); desiccated (shredded) coconut and grated fresh ginger. Serves 4.

Khichri

An Indian dish of split peas and rice, a combination which produces a good quality protein essential for a vegetarian meal.

430 g/14 oz (2 cups) long-grain rice; 4 tbsp oil; 4 small onions, sliced; 125 g/4 oz (½ cup) yellow split peas, soaked overnight and drained; 1½ tsp salt; 1 tsp ground cumin; 1 tsp Garam Masala (page 139); 1 clove garlic, crushed; 1 cm (½ in) slice fresh ginger, peeled and finely chopped; 875 ml/ 1 pint 9 fl oz (3½ cups) water.

Soak rice in water to cover for 3 minutes, then drain well. Heat oil in a heavy saucepan and add half the onions. Cook over a moderate heat for 5–10 minutes or until crisp and golden. Lift out onions and drain on paper towels. Keep hot. Add remaining onions to oil and cook gently until soft. Add rice, split peas, salt, cumin, garam masala, garlic and ginger. Reduce heat to moderately low and cook mixture, stirring constantly, for 7–10 minutes or until rice and peas are

coated with oil. Add water. Bring to the boil and cook over moderate heat, stirring, for 4 minutes. Cover pan with foil and tight-fitting lid and simmer gently for 25 minutes. Serve on a heated serving dish, garnished with reserved fried onions. Serves 4–6.

RILLETTES

Better known in English as potted pork, this French dish is basically a pork spread, flavoured with herbs, spices, onions and garlic. Rillettes are most commonly made with pork, but may also be made with goose, rabbit, turkey or duck, although each of these will include some pork.

Pork rillettes are made from belly pork (fresh pork sides), one of the most economical of pork cuts, but also one of the most fatty. This fat is essential to the rillettes, so don't be dismayed by the quantity.

Rillettes are eaten with plain (unbuttered) bread or toast, often accompanied by pickled gherkins. They may be served as a first course, or simply as something to nibble on with drinks.

Rillettes

1 kg (2 lb) boneless belly pork (fresh pork sides), rind removed and cut into small cubes; 1 large clove garlic, bruised; 1 sprig fresh thyme; salt and freshly ground black pepper; 4 tbsp water; ¼ tsp ground cloves; ¼ tsp nutmeg; ½ tsp cinnamon.

Place pork cubes in large, heavy saucepan with garlic, thyme and a little salt and pepper. Add water to prevent mixture sticking. Cook over very gentle heat for about 2 hours or until pork is extremely tender. Drain in a sieve. Discard garlic and thyme, and set fat aside. Using 2 forks, tear pork into shreds. Taste and season as desired with salt, pepper and spices; rillettes should be well seasoned. Return pork mixture to saucepan with a little of the reserved fat and heat, stirring well to mix seasonings through meat. Pack into small pots. Cover surface of each with layer of pork fat then cover with foil. Store in refrigerator. Remove 1–2 hours before serving. Covered with fat, rillettes will keep in the refrigerator for several weeks. Serves 4–6.

RISOTTO

A rice-based dish from the northern provinces of Italy, where rice is to the people of northern Italy what pasta is to those of the south.

The best risotto is made from Piedmontese or arborio rice (see Rice), a small round grain either white or pale yellow which is able to absorb liquid and stand up to long, slow cooking without becoming soft and mushy. A

perfect risotto should be a creamy mass, with each grain having a slightly resistant core to the bite. It can be served plain, flavoured simply with butter and cheese, or more elaborately with such ingredients as mushrooms, tomatoes, meat, poultry, seafood or chicken livers, to name a few.

Risotto is usually served as a dish on its own with grated Parmesan cheese passed separately. One exception to this rule is Risotto Milanese which is served as an accompaniment to Osso Buco Milanese (see page 257). **See recipes**.

Risotto Milanese

125 g/4 oz (½ cup) butter; 1 small onion, finely chopped; 30 g/1 oz (¼ cup) beef marrow, sliced (optional); 430 g/14 oz (2 cups) Italian risotto rice or short-grain rice; 120 ml/4 fl oz (½ cup) dry white wine; 1–1.2 litres/1¾–2 pints (4–5 cups) hot chicken stock; ¼ tsp saffron powder dissolved in 1 tbsp hot water; 60 g/2 oz (½ cup) grated Parmesan cheese.

Melt 60 g/2 oz (4 tbsp) of the butter in a heavy saucepan and fry onion gently until soft. Add beef marrow, if using. Stir in rice until it is well coated with butter. Pour in wine and cook over medium heat until wine has nearly evaporated. Stir in 250 ml/8 fl oz (1 cup) of hot stock. Simmer, stirring occasionally, for 10 minutes and gradually add about 500 ml/18 fl oz (2 cups) more stock. Continue simmering, stirring, for a further 5–10 minutes, gradually adding remaining stock, by which time the rice should have absorbed all the liquid. Do not let rice dry out. Stir in dissolved saffron and add remaining butter and Parmesan cheese. Serve immediately as an accompaniment to Osso Buco Milanese or on its own with extra butter and grated Parmesan cheese. Serves 4.

Risotto

125 g/4 oz (½ cup) butter; 1 onion, chopped; 1 clove garlic; 2 tbsp finely chopped parsley;

R

650 g/1⅓ lb (3 cups) Italian arborio rice; 2 litres/3½ pints (8 cups) boiling chicken stock; salt and freshly ground black pepper; 4–6 tbsp grated Parmesan cheese; extra grated Parmesan cheese to serve.

Melt 60 g/2 oz (4 tbsp) of the butter in a large heavy saucepan and sauté onion and whole garlic clove. When onion is soft and golden add parsley. Cook over a low heat for a few minutes, then discard garlic and add rice. Fry for 5 minutes, stirring constantly, then add 250 ml/8 fl oz (1 cup) boiling stock and cook gently until it is absorbed. Continue cooking gently, adding stock 250 ml/8 fl oz (1 cup) at a time and stirring occasionally, for 20–30 minutes or until rice is tender and all liquid is absorbed. Season with salt and pepper, stir in remaining butter and the cheese and leave risotto over low heat for a few minutes before serving. Serve with plenty of extra grated Parmesan cheese handed separately. Serves 6.

VARIATIONS

Risotto with Mushrooms: Make Risotto as above, adding 2 rashers (slices) bacon, rind removed and finely chopped, with the onion, and 250 g/8 oz (2 cups) mushrooms, sliced, with the parsley. Use only 60 g/2 oz (4 tbsp) butter for frying the onion: do not add more with the cheese.

NOTE: Risotto may be prepared in this way using other vegetables such as tomatoes or courgettes (zucchini). Shelled prawns (shrimp), mussels, chicken meat or chopped sautéed chicken livers may also be added with the mushrooms.

Risotto with Prawns: Make Risotto as above and keep hot. Melt 90 g/3 oz (6 tbsp) butter in a frying pan (skillet) and sauté 1 clove garlic and 1 kg (2 lb) green (uncooked) prawns (shrimp), shelled and deveined, for 5–8 minutes or until prawns (shrimp) are cooked. Discard garlic, then season prawns (shrimp) with salt and pepper. Add to risotto and fold together.

RISSOLE

Strictly speaking, rissoles ought to be made with finely minced (ground) meat, fish or poultry, wrapped in thin shortcrust (basic pie dough) or puff pastry (paste) to form little turnovers, before being deep-fried. Or the pastry (dough) might be coated with egg and breadcrumbs or crushed vermicelli before frying. In the past, they were then served hot, often to accompany cocktails.

Today rissoles have become more informal; the pastry (dough) is usually omitted and egg and breadcrumbs used instead. They are larger and more likely to be served at lunch or family meals. Nevertheless, they remain a delicious way of stretching the budget. **See recipes.**

Chicken Rissoles

1 × 375 g/12 oz packet frozen puff pastry (paste), thawed; 1 quantity Chicken Croquette mixture (page 90); 1 egg, beaten; oil for deep-frying; parsley sprigs to garnish.

Roll out pastry (dough) to about 3 mm (⅛ in) thick. Cut it into 6 cm (2½ in) rounds or squares. Place 1 tsp of croquette mixture in centre of each round or square. Brush edges lightly with water and fold dough over, pressing edges together. Be careful not to fill pastries too much, and seal edges firmly so that none of the filling escapes. Brush tops with beaten egg. Deep-fry in hot oil for 1–2 minutes or until golden-brown. Drain on paper towels. Serve immediately, garnished with parsley sprigs. Makes about 24.

Rissoles with Mushrooms

RISSOLES: 4 tbsp oil; 1 onion, finely chopped; 4 slices bread, cubed; 4 tbsp milk; 750 g/1½ lb (3 cups) minced (ground) steak; 2 eggs, lightly beaten; 2 tbsp tomato purée (paste); ½ tsp salt; ½ tsp white pepper; 60 g/2 oz (½ cup) flour; dry breadcrumbs.
SAUCE: 45 g/1½ oz (3 tbsp) butter; 6–8 mushrooms, finely sliced; 2 tbsp flour; 2 tsp paprika; 250 ml/8 fl oz (1 cup) beef stock (bouillon); 120 ml/4 fl oz (½ cup) sour cream.

RISSOLES: Heat 2 tbsp oil and gently fry onion until soft. Soak bread cubes in milk 10 minutes. Put steak, 1 egg, tomato purée (paste), salt and pepper in a bowl and blend well together. Add onion and soaked bread cubes and blend again. Shape mixture into 8 rissoles. Dip in flour, then in remaining egg and coat with breadcrumbs. Heat remaining oil and fry rissoles until well browned on each side. Drain and keep warm.
SAUCE: Melt butter in a saucepan and gently fry mushrooms for 2 minutes. Blend in flour and paprika, then stir in stock (bouillon). Cook gently until boiling, stirring constantly. Remove from heat, stir in sour cream and serve immediately with rissoles. Serves 4.

Cooked Meat Rissoles

250 g (8 oz) cooked meat, minced (ground); 60 g/2 oz (½ cup) plus 2 tbsp flour; 2 tbsp fresh breadcrumbs; 2 tbsp chopped parsley; ½ tsp dried thyme; salt and freshly ground black pepper; 150 ml/¼ pint (⅔ cup) stock; 1 egg, beaten; 60 g/2 oz (½ cup) dry breadcrumbs; oil for frying.

In a saucepan mix together minced (ground) meat, 2 tbsp flour, fresh breadcrumbs, parsley, thyme, salt, pepper and stock. Stir over gentle heat until mixture becomes thick. Allow to cool. Shape into flat cakes. Dip in remaining flour, then beaten egg and coat

with dry breadcrumbs. Shallow-fry in hot oil until golden-brown on both sides. Serves 2.
NOTE: Use leftover roast beef, lamb or chicken, corned beef, cooked ham, or well drained and flaked canned tuna or salmon.

ROCK CAKE

A batch of Rock Cakes is quickly and easily made and a family favourite for picnics, lunch-boxes or as a quick snack with morning coffee or afternoon tea. Eat them warm or cold, buttered or plain.

Rock Cakes

250 g/8 oz (2 cups) self-raising flour; 90 g/3 oz (6 tbsp) butter; 125 g/4 oz (½ cup) sugar; ½ tsp mixed spice (ground allspice); 2 tbsp currants; 2 tbsp sultanas (golden raisins); 2 tbsp chopped mixed candied peel; 1 egg; 4–5 tbsp milk.

Sift flour into a bowl and rub (cut) in butter until mixture resembles crumbs. Add sugar, spice and fruits and mix in well. Beat egg and add milk. Mix with dry ingredients to a stiff dough. Place tablespoonfuls of mixture in little rough heaps on lightly greased baking trays. Bake in a preheated moderately hot oven (200°C/400°F, Gas Mark 6) for 10–15 minutes or until golden-brown. Makes about 24.

ROCKEFELLER OYSTERS

This recipe was created at Antoine's, one of the long-established and famous restaurants of New Orleans.

Rockefeller Oysters

125 g/4 oz (½ cup) butter; 6 tbsp finely chopped fresh spinach; 3 tbsp finely chopped onion; 3 tbsp finely chopped parsley; 3 tbsp finely chopped celery; 5 tbsp fresh breadcrumbs; dash Tabasco (hot pepper) sauce; about ½ tsp salt; 36 freshly opened oysters, on the half shell; rock salt.

Melt butter in a saucepan and add all ingredients except oysters and rock salt. Cook, stirring constantly, for 15 minutes or until soft. Press through sieve or purée in blender. Cool. Place a layer of rock salt in shallow ovenproof dishes and arrange oysters in half-shells on top. Place a spoonful of sauce on top of each oyster. Cook under a preheated medium grill (broiler) until sauce begins to brown. Serve immediately. Serves 6.

ROE

Both the milt (soft roe) of male fish and the eggs (hard roe) of female fish are delicacies. Soft Roes on Toast, once a popular savoury course for the end of a formal dinner, make a splendid snack. Smoked roe is served like pâté with toast or brown bread and butter, and the salted, dried, pressed roe of the grey mullet, known in Greece as *tarama*, is used to make Taramasalata (see page 428).

The salted roe of the sturgeon is, of course, that great luxury, caviar; red salmon roe (keta), also costly, is used in the same way. Salted lumpfish roe, coloured orange or black, is a less expensive substitute and is commonly available.

Soft Roes on Toast

250 g (8 oz) fresh or canned soft roes; seasoned flour; 60 g/2 oz (4 tbsp) butter; salt and freshly ground black pepper; pinch cayenne; lemon juice; 2 slices hot buttered toast; lemon wedges to serve.

If using fresh roes, poach gently in salted water to cover for 3–4 minutes. Drain fresh or canned roes and remove any dark vein. Dry roes well and dust with seasoned flour. Heat butter and, when foaming, add roes. Brown on both sides, then season with salt, pepper, cayenne and a little lemon juice. Arrange roes on toast, pour seasoned butter over and serve hot, with lemon. Serves 2.

ROLLMOP

See Herring.

ROSEMARY

The herb of remembrance, which grows wild in the countries of southern Europe but is cultivated in the north and in other parts of the world. It grows quite happily in pots in a warm dry place in many gardens.

A sprig of rosemary or its crushed leaves impart a unique aromatic fragrance reminiscent of dry summer hillsides around the Mediterranean shores. The special flavour of rosemary has a great affinity with lamb, veal and pork.

Place a sprig under the rack when roasting or grilling (broiling), or insert a few leaves with some slivers of garlic under the skin before roasting meat. Scent butter with rosemary and in it quickly sauté some tomatoes or mushrooms, or use to toss new potatoes, or courgettes (zucchini).

Rosemary is best used fresh but dried rosemary is especially good to flavour sugar for an unusual touch in puddings and creams, or sprinkled over plain butter cakes. **See recipes.**

Rosemary Butter

125 g/4 oz (½ cup) butter; 2 tsp lemon juice; 2 tsp finely chopped fresh rosemary, or 1 tsp dried; salt and freshly ground black pepper.

Cream butter until softened, then beat in lemon juice. Add rosemary, beat well and season with salt and pepper. Shape into a long roll, chill and slice as required. Makes 125 g/4 oz (½ cup).

Veal Rosemary

2 tbsp oil; 30 g/1 oz (2 tbsp) butter; 750 g (1½ lb) boned veal shoulder, cubed; 1 onion, chopped; 2 tbsp flour; 1 tbsp chopped fresh rosemary, or 1 tsp dried; 500 g/1 lb (2 cups) peeled and chopped tomatoes; 120 ml/4 fl oz (½ cup) dry white wine; 250 ml/8 fl oz (1 cup) chicken stock; salt and freshly ground black pepper; 125 g/4 oz (1 cup) mushrooms, sliced.

Heat oil and butter in a flameproof casserole, add veal and onion and cook until browned

(do this in 2 batches if necessary to avoid overcrowding pan). Stir in flour and rosemary and cook until flour coats meat. Add tomatoes, wine and stock, and bring to the boil, stirring constantly. Season with salt and pepper. Add mushrooms. Cover and cook in a preheated moderate oven (160°C/325°F, Gas Mark 3) for 1 hour or until veal is tender. Serve with buttered rice or creamy mashed potatoes and a green salad. Serves 4–6.

Rosemary Chicken in Cream

30 g/1 oz (¼ cup) flour; ½ tsp salt; ½ tsp white pepper; 2 tsp chopped fresh rosemary, or 1 tsp dried; 4 large half-breasts of chicken; 500 ml/18 fl oz (2 cups) single (light) cream; 2 tbsp chopped parsley.

Season flour with salt, pepper and rosemary and use to coat chicken pieces. Put in a lightly buttered shallow baking dish and carefully pour over cream. Bake in a preheated moderate oven (160°C/325°F, Gas Mark 3) for 30–40 minutes or until chicken is tender, turning after first 15–20 minutes of cooking. Remove pieces to a serving platter and keep warm. Reheat cream sauce, thinning if necessary with a little extra cream or hot milk: the sauce should be a coating consistency. Pour over chicken and sprinkle with parsley. Serves 4.

Rosemary Soda Bread

250 g/8 oz (2 cups) wholewheat flour; 250 g/8 oz (2 cups) plain (all-purpose) flour; 2 tsp sugar; 1 tsp bicarbonate of soda (baking soda); ¾ tsp baking powder; 90 g/3 oz (6 tbsp) butter; 20 g/⅔ oz (½ cup) chopped parsley; 1 tbsp snipped chives; 1 tbsp chopped fresh rosemary or 1 tsp dried; 500 ml/18 fl oz (2 cups) buttermilk.

Sift flours, salt, sugar, soda and baking powder into a large bowl. Rub (cut) in butter until mixture resembles breadcrumbs. Stir in herbs, then buttermilk until dough forms a ball. Knead very lightly until smooth. Place on a greased baking tray and form into a 20 cm (8 in) round. Using a sharp, floured knife cut a cross 1 cm (½ in) deep in the top. Bake in a preheated moderately hot oven (190°C/375°F, Gas Mark 5) for 40–50 minutes or until loaf sounds hollow when tapped on bottom. Serve warm or at room temperature, sliced, with plenty of butter and a sharp Cheddar if liked.

Rosemary Sugar

500 g/1 lb (2 cups) sugar; 2 sprigs fresh rosemary, or 2 tsp dried.

Combine sugar and rosemary in an airtight jar and shake well. Leave for 24 hours. Shake again and store for at least a week

before using. Delicious in puddings, creams or sprinkled over hot cakes or biscuits (cookies). Makes 500 g/1 lb (2 cups).

Spinach Rosemary

500 g (1 lb) spinach; 1 tbsp finely chopped parsley; 4 shallots, finely chopped; 60 g/2 oz (4 tbsp) butter; salt; ¼ tsp white pepper; 1 sprig fresh rosemary, or ½ tsp dried.

Place spinach in a large heavy saucepan and add parsley, shallots, butter, salt, pepper and rosemary. Cover pan and cook over a low heat for 5–10 minutes. Shake pan occasionally to prevent spinach sticking. Serves 4.

ROSE WATER

A fragrant essence (extract) distilled from rose petals, with a history as romantic as its name. Rose water has been used for thousands of years in countries of the Middle East, India and the Balkans, not only in the kitchen but also as a cosmetic ingredient and as purification water during religious ceremonies.

Rose water may be used as a flavouring instead of vanilla or almond essence (extract), and lends its exotic perfume to many creams, sweet dishes and drinks. **See recipes**.

Rose Water Syrup

500 g/1 lb (2 cups) sugar; 250 ml/8 fl oz (1 cup) water; strained juice ½ lemon; few drops pink food colouring; 5 tbsp rose water.

Put sugar and water in a heavy saucepan and stir over gentle heat until sugar has dissolved. Bring to the boil and add lemon juice. Boil, without stirring, for 10 minutes, skimming when necessary. Add enough food colouring to syrup to tint it a deep pink. Stir in rose water and boil for a further 3 minutes. Cool, then bottle and seal. Serve over cracked ice, using 2–3 tbsp per glass. Top each serving with iced water and float a rose petal on top. Makes about 600 ml/1 pint (2½ cups) syrup.

Persian Cream

1 tbsp gelatine; 4 tbsp cold water; 350 ml/12 fl oz (1½ cups) milk; 75 g/2½ oz
(⅓ cup) sugar; 2 eggs, separated; 1 tbsp rose water.
TO SERVE: *250–310 g/8–10 oz (2 cups) partially frozen or well chilled fresh berry fruits; whipped cream; 2 tsp rose water.*

Sprinkle gelatine over cold water and allow to soften. Heat milk and sugar in a heavy saucepan or top of a double saucepan (double boiler). Beat egg yolks and add to warm milk and sugar, off the heat. Stir over very low heat, or over hot water, until custard begins to thicken. Add softened gelatine and stir until dissolved. Allow to cool, then stir in rose water. Beat egg whites until stiff and fold into custard mixture. Chill for at least 4 hours. Serve with partially frozen or fresh berry fruits, and whipped cream flavoured with rose water. Serves 6.

Gulab Jamun

4 tbsp full cream milk powder; 1½ tbsp self-raising flour; pinch bicarbonate of soda (baking soda); ¼ tsp ground cardamom; 15 g/½ oz (1 tbsp) ghee or softened butter; about 2 tbsp water; ghee or oil for frying.
SYRUP: *250 g/8 oz (1 cup) sugar; 500 ml/18 fl oz (2 cups) water; 3 cardamom pods, bruised; 3 tbsp rose water.*

Sift milk powder, flour, soda and ground cardamom into a large bowl. Rub (cut) in butter or ghee, and add sufficient water to make a firm but pliable dough. Shape into balls the size of small walnuts. Fry slowly over gentle heat in hot ghee or oil, turning until well browned. Drain on paper towels.
SYRUP: In a large heavy saucepan combine sugar, water and cardamom pods and heat until sugar dissolves, stirring occasionally. Put fried gulab jamun into syrup and simmer for 30 minutes or until almost double in size and soft and spongy. Cool slightly, then add rose water and cool completely. Serve at room temperature or slightly chilled. Makes about 10.

Almond Cream

45 g/1½ oz (¼ cup) ground rice; 750 ml/1¼ pints (3 cups) milk; pinch salt; 60 g/2 oz (¼ cup) sugar; 90 g/3 oz (¾ cup) ground almonds; 2 tbsp rose water.
DECORATION: *toasted slivered almonds; pomegranate seeds (optional).*

Make a thin paste from ground rice and 4 tbsp milk. Place remaining milk in a saucepan and bring to the boil. Stir in ground rice paste, salt and sugar. Cook, stirring constantly, over medium heat until mixture begins to bubble. Lower heat and simmer for 5 minutes, stirring often. Stir in ground almonds, blending well. Remove from heat and allow to cool a little, stirring occasionally. Stir in rose water and pour into
serving dish. Chill at least 3 hours. Serve decorated with toasted slivered almonds and pomegranate seeds. Serves 6.

Iced Melon and Peaches

1 large ripe honeydew melon; 125 g/4 oz (½ cup) caster sugar; 4 ripe peaches, peeled, stoned (pitted) and sliced; juice 1 lemon; 3 tbsp rose water; crushed ice to serve.

Halve melon, remove seeds and dice flesh or scoop into balls. Sprinkle with sugar. Coat peach slices in lemon juice to prevent discoloration. Add peaches and lemon juice to melon balls, stirring gently. Mix in rose water. Cover bowl and chill for 3 hours. Serve piled into individual glasses and topped with ice. Serves 6–8.

ROUGH PUFF PASTRY

See page 275 for recipe.

ROUILLE

This peppery-hot sauce is a traditional accompaniment to Bouillabaisse (see page 396) and other Mediterranean fish soups.

Rouille

2 cloves garlic; 1 red pepper, skinned, cored, seeded and roughly chopped; 1 dried red chilli, soaked in warm water until soft; 1 × 5 cm (2 in) slice French bread, soaked in water or Fish Stock (page 414) and squeezed to remove excess liquid; 2 tbsp olive oil; 120 ml/4 fl oz (½ cup) hot Fish Stock; salt and freshly ground black pepper.

Pound garlic, pepper, chilli and bread to a smooth paste in a mortar with a pestle. Gradually add olive oil, blending until thick and smooth. Stir in hot fish stock, and season with salt and pepper. Serve separately with fish soups and stews. Rouille may also be made using a blender; add extra 2 tbsp water or stock when blending garlic, peppers and bread. Makes about 250 ml/8 fl oz (1 cup).

ROULADE

The French word for 'roll' applies to different cuts of meat or minced (ground) meat mixtures rolled around a filling; to a galantine when shaped as a roll, or to thin slices of bread or pastry (dough) when rolled around a filling.

Deliciously light roulades can be made from a soufflé-type mixture that is cooked in a Swiss roll tin (jelly roll pan), spread with a filling either savoury or sweet, rolled and served hot or cold. They can be made in advance and reheated successfully – perfect for entertaining.

Appropriate roulades such as Smoked Mackerel, Smoked Salmon or Prawn Roulades can be served as hors d'oeuvre or for any course of a meal, or try a Chocolate Roll (see page 73) with coffee.

Method for Soufflé-type Mixture

Preparing the tin (pan): Choose a Swiss roll tin (jelly roll pan) 25 × 38 × 2.5 cm 10 × 15 × 1 in). Oil the tin (pan) lightly and line with greaseproof (waxed) paper, leaving an overhang of 5 cm (2 in) at each end. Grease the paper, dust lightly with sifted flour and shake out excess. Add mixture and spread evenly **(Fig 1 opposite)**.

To test when cooked: The top should be golden-brown and firm and a fine skewer inserted in the centre of the roulade should come out clean.

Turning out: Have ready a slightly dampened, clean tea-towel, covered with greaseproof (waxed) paper. Quickly turn out the roulade from the tin (pan) on to the lined tea-towel. Immediately and carefully peel the paper lining from the roulade, trim the crusty ends **(2)**, fill and roll up, or roll up and allow to cool before filling, according to your recipe.

Filling and rolling: Spread the prepared filling quickly and lightly over the surface. Immediately roll up as for a Swiss roll (jelly roll), using the tea-towel as a guide. Grasp the corners of the edge nearest you, lift the paper and cloth and the roulade will fall into a roll as you lift and remove them **(3)**. Roll on to a serving platter, seam side down, and serve hot or cold as directed. **See recipes.**

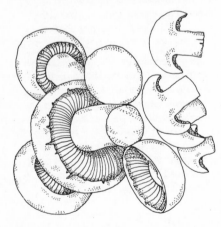

Mushroom Roulade

Serve this superb roulade as a first course at a dinner party. It can be made ahead and reheated: make roulade, cool and store in refrigerator covered loosely with oiled foil. Remove from refrigerator 1½ hours before serving time and heat in a preheated cool oven (150°C/300°F, Gas Mark 2) for 30 minutes, removing foil for last 5 minutes.

90 g/3 oz (6 tbsp) butter; 60 g/2 oz (½ cup) flour; 500 ml/18 fl oz (2 cups) warm milk; 1 tsp salt; ½ tsp white pepper; 1 tbsp brandy; 1 tbsp sour cream; 4 eggs, separated; parsley

sprigs to garnish.
MUSHROOM FILLING: *125 g/4 oz (½ cup) butter; 250 g/8 oz (2 cups) button mushrooms, sliced; 2 tsp lemon juice; 4 tbsp flour; 250 ml/8 fl oz (1 cup) warm milk; ½ tsp salt; freshly ground black pepper; ¼ tsp nutmeg; 120 ml/4 fl oz (½ cup) single (light) cream; 2 tbsp finely chopped parsley.*

Prepare and line a Swiss roll tin (jelly roll pan) 25 × 38 × 2.5 cm (10 × 15 × 1 in), see opposite. Melt butter in a heavy saucepan, blend in flour over low heat and cook, stirring, for 1 minute. Remove from heat, cool a little and add warm milk all at once, stirring until smooth. Return to moderate heat and stir constantly until boiling. Remove from heat and stir in salt, pepper, brandy and sour cream. Whisk in egg yolks one at a time. Beat egg whites until they stand in soft peaks and fold into egg yolk mixture. Spoon into prepared tin (pan), spreading evenly with a spatula. Bake in a preheated moderate oven (160°C/325°F, Gas Mark 3) for about 40 minutes or until golden on top.
MUSHROOM FILLING: Melt half the butter in a saucepan, add mushrooms and sauté quickly. Sprinkle with lemon juice. Remove mushrooms with a slotted spoon. Melt remaining butter in same saucepan, stir in flour and cook over low heat for 1 minute. Remove from heat, cool a little, then add milk all at once and stir, off heat, until smooth. Return to medium heat and stir constantly until boiling. Stir in salt, pepper, nutmeg, cream and parsley. Reserve 6–8 mushroom slices for garnish, and add remainder to saucepan. Cover pan and keep warm over gentle heat until roulade is ready. Turn out roulade. Gently peel off lining paper and trim crusty edges. Spread with hot filling. Roll up (see above) and transfer to an ovenproof platter. Reheat in a moderate oven (180°C/350°F, Gas Mark 4) for 5–10 minutes. Garnish with reserved mushroom slices and parsley sprigs. Serve sliced. Serves 6.

Red Caviar Roulade

90 g/3 oz (6 tbsp) butter; 60 g/2 oz (½ cup) flour; 500 ml/18 fl oz (2 cups) warm milk; 1 tsp salt; ¾ tsp pepper; 1 tbsp brandy; 1 tbsp sour cream; 4 eggs, separated.
CAVIAR FILLING: *125 g/4 oz (½ cup) Philadelphia cream cheese; 1 tbsp lemon juice; 2 tbsp sour cream; freshly ground black pepper; 120 ml/4 fl oz (½ cup) double (heavy) cream, whipped; 1 × 100 g/3½ oz jar red caviar or lumpfish roe.*
GARNISH: *sour cream; caviar.*

Prepare and line a Swiss roll tin (jelly roll pan) 25 × 38 × 2.5 cm (10 × 15 × 1 in), see opposite. Melt butter in a large heavy saucepan, blend in flour over low heat and

cook for 1 minute, stirring. Remove from heat, cool a little, and add milk all at once. Stir until smooth, then return to a medium heat and cook, stirring constantly, until sauce boils. Remove from heat and stir in salt, pepper, brandy and sour cream. Whisk in egg yolks, one at a time. Beat egg whites until they stand in soft peaks and fold into yolk mixture. Spoon into prepared tin (pan), spreading evenly with a spatula. Bake in a preheated moderate oven (160°C/325°F, Gas Mark 3) for 30–35 minutes or until golden on top. Turn out roulade (see left), roll up and allow to cool.
CAVIAR FILLING: Soften cream cheese and beat in lemon juice and sour cream. Season with pepper and fold in whipped cream and caviar. At serving time, unroll roulade, spread with filling and roll up again (see left). Serve cut in thin slices, each garnished with a spoonful of sour cream and a teaspoon of caviar. Serves 8.

Stuffed Beef Roll

500–750 g (1–1½ lb) topside (top round) steak, cut as 1 slice about 1 cm (½ in) thick; salt and freshly ground black pepper; 4 thin slices cooked ham; 3 small hard-boiled (hard-cooked) eggs; 30 g/1 oz (2 tbsp) butter; 2 tbsp oil; 2 leaves fresh sage or ½ tsp dried; 120 ml/4 fl oz (½ cup) dry white wine.

Flatten meat using a meat mallet or broad side of a cleaver. Season well with salt and pepper. Place ham slices, slightly overlapping, down centre, then top with whole hard-boiled (hard-cooked) eggs. Carefully roll up meat, tucking in ends. Tie securely with white string. Heat butter and oil in a flameproof casserole dish just large enough to hold roll without leaving too much space around it. Brown roll all over. Add sage and wine. Cover and simmer very gently for 2–2½ hours or until meat is tender. Serve sliced with pan juices poured over. Accompany beef roll with a selection of vegetables. Serves 6.

Ham Stuffed Beef Rolls

6 thin slices topside (top round) steak, halved to give 12 pieces; 12 thin slices cooked ham; 2 sticks celery, finely chopped; 1 small carrot, finely chopped; salt and freshly ground black pepper; 60 g/2 oz (½ cup) flour; 60 g/2 oz (¼ cup) ham or bacon fat, finely chopped; 1 clove garlic, finely chopped; 1 medium onion, finely chopped; 2 tbsp oil; 120 ml/4 fl oz (½ cup) dry white wine; 2 × 425 g/14 oz cans tomatoes; 1 bay leaf; 1 whole clove; 2 tbsp finely chopped parsley.

Flatten steak pieces as thin as possible. Top each with a slice of ham and sprinkle with half the celery and the carrot. Season with salt and pepper. Roll up slices and tie each little roll with white string. Dust lightly with flour. Combine ham or bacon fat, remaining celery, garlic and onion. Heat oil in a flameproof casserole wide enough to take rolls in one layer. Add chopped mixture and cook, stirring, for 1 minute. Add beef rolls and brown quickly on all sides. Pour in wine and stir over medium heat until it has almost evaporated. Add tomatoes, bay leaf, clove, salt and pepper. Bring to the boil, then cover and simmer over very gentle heat for about 1 hour or until beef is tender. Stir occasionally. Transfer rolls to a heated serving platter, remove string and pour sauce over through a sieve. Sprinkle with chopped parsley. Serves 6.

Polpettone (Meat Roll)

An excellent Italian dish, equally good hot or cold.

1 kg/2 lb (4 cups) very finely minced (ground) veal, beef or pork or a combination of these; 4 eggs; 2 cloves garlic, crushed; 1 onion, very finely chopped; 20 g/⅔ oz (½ cup) finely chopped parsley; salt and freshly ground black pepper; 2 hard-boiled (hard-cooked) eggs, chopped; 60 g/2 oz (¼ cup) cooked ham, chopped; 60 g/2 oz (½ cup) Gruyère cheese, grated; about 120 ml/4 fl oz (½ cup) water or stock.

Combine meat, eggs, garlic, onion, parsley, salt and pepper and mix well. Knead mixture until it adheres well together. Flour your hands and a board. Turn mixture on to board and knead again, then flatten mixture. Put hard-boiled (hard-cooked) eggs, ham and cheese down centre, then carefully roll meat into a large sausage shape. Place in a well greased baking dish and cover roll with greased greaseproof (waxed) paper. Cook in a preheated cool oven (150°C/300°F, Gas Mark 2) for about 1½ hours. Add a little stock or water during cooking if necessary to keep roll moist. Serves 8.

Smoked Mackerel Roulades

1 × 500 g (1 lb) smoked mackerel, skinned and boned (approx 2 cups); 120 ml/4 fl oz (½ cup) sour cream; 2 tsp horseradish cream; juice ½ lemon; freshly ground black pepper; about 12 very thin slices buttered brown bread, crusts removed; watercress to garnish.

Flake mackerel and mix with sour cream, horseradish cream, lemon juice and pepper. Cover and chill for several hours. Spread mixture thinly over bread slices and roll up firmly, securing with toothpicks if necessary. Cover and chill for 1 hour before serving, garnished with watercress sprigs. Makes 12.
VARIATION
Smoked Salmon Roulades: Use 125 g/4 oz (½ cup) chopped smoked salmon instead of

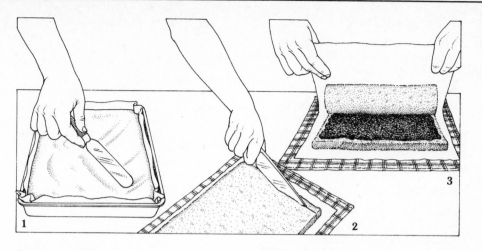

Making a soufflé-type roulade

the mackerel and mix with 120 ml/4 fl oz (½ cup) sour cream, lemon juice and black pepper. Add some finely chopped white pickled onions if liked. Proceed as above.

Walnut Roll

3 tbsp fine cake crumbs or fresh bread-crumbs; 3 eggs, separated; 125 g/4 oz (½ cup) caster sugar; 60 g/2 oz (½ cup) ground walnuts; 30 g/1 oz (¼ cup) self-raising flour; 250 ml/8 fl oz (1 cup) double (heavy) cream, whipped and sweetened with 1 tbsp icing (confectioners) sugar; extra sifted icing (confectioners) sugar.

Butter a Swiss roll tin (jelly roll pan) 25 × 38 × 2.5 cm (10 × 15 × 1 in) and line with buttered greaseproof (waxed) paper allowing 5 cm (2 in) overhang at each end. Sprinkle with the cake crumbs or breadcrumbs, coating surface evenly, then tip out any excess crumbs. Beat egg whites until holding stiff peaks. Beat yolks with caster sugar until mixture is light and creamy. Gently fold in walnuts and sifted flour alternately with stiffly beaten egg whites. Spread in prepared tin (pan). Bake in a preheated moderate oven (180°C/350°F, Gas Mark 4) for about 15 minutes or until cake springs back when centre is lightly touched. Turn out on to a clean tea-towel sprinkled with caster sugar, remove paper, trim cake and roll up (see page 340), and allow to cool. Unroll the cake, spread with sweetened whipped cream and re-roll (see page 340). Roll on to a serving platter seam side down and dust lightly with icing (confectioners) sugar. Serve sliced. Serves 8.

RUM

This distilled spirit is one of the products of the sugar industry. In the kitchen its use is mainly in desserts, although it may also be used in meat dishes, especially those of Caribbean origin or inspiration.

Light rum – whether clear or caramel-coloured – is preferred in cooking.

In French cooking, rum is a very common ingredient of desserts. A rum syrup may be brushed over a sponge before filling; babas and savarins are steeped in rum syrup. Fruits, such as pineapples, bananas and apples, take nicely to a touch of rum, and rum can alternate with brandy in flambé desserts. A sweet soufflé omelette may be flavoured with rum, or a rum sabayon spooned over carefully poached fruits.

Chocolate is one of the best partners to rum, whether as a chocolate cake with a rum cream filling, or chocolate truffles with a hint of rum. **See recipes**.

Baked Stuffed Apples

6 large cooking apples, peeled and cored; 90 g/3 oz (½ cup) chopped glacé (candied) fruit (apricots, cherries, pineapple); 45 g/1½ oz (¼ cup) sultanas (golden raisins); 4 tbsp rum; 1 tbsp sugar; 30 g/1 oz (2 tbsp) butter.

Extract some of the inside of the apples and chop. Mix with glacé (candied) fruit, sultanas (golden raisins) and rum. Fill apples with this mixture, sprinkle with sugar and dot with butter. Bake in a preheated hot oven (200°C/400°F, Gas Mark 6) for about 35 minutes, sprinkling with water from time to time. Serve warm, with single (light) cream if desired. Serves 6.

Ricotta Cheese with Sugar and Rum

500 g/1 lb (2 cups) Ricotta cheese; 2 tbsp sour cream; 125 g/4 oz (½ cup) caster sugar; 4 eggs, separated; 6 tbsp rum; Amaretti biscuits (cookies) to serve (page 6).

Beat Ricotta with sour cream, then mix in sugar. Add egg yolks one at a time, beating until mixture is light and creamy, then stir in rum. Beat egg whites until stiff and fold into mixture. Spoon into 6 individual glasses. Chill for several hours before serving, accompanied by Amaretti biscuits (cookies). Serves 6.

Bananas with Rum

6 bananas; 120 ml/4 fl oz ($\frac{1}{2}$ cup) rum;
60 g/2 oz ($\frac{1}{2}$ cup) dry breadcrumbs; 60 g/2 oz
(4 tbsp) butter; 3 tbsp redcurrant jelly.

Macerate bananas in rum for 1 hour. Drain, reserving rum. Roll bananas in breadcrumbs and fry in butter until golden. Meanwhile, heat rum with redcurrant jelly, stirring until thick and smooth. Spoon sauce over bananas to serve. Serves 4.

Rum Balls

60 g/2 oz (1 cup) stale cake crumbs; 4 tbsp caster sugar; 125 g/4 oz (1 cup) ground almonds; 1 tbsp (unsweetened) cocoa powder; 2–3 tbsp rum; grated chocolate or chocolate vermicelli (sprinkles).

Combine cake crumbs, sugar, ground almonds, cocoa and enough rum to bind mixture together. Form into small balls, roll in grated chocolate or chocolate sprinkles and place in tiny paper cases. Serve with after-dinner coffee. Makes about 50 × 2.5 cm (1 in) balls.

Rum Mousse

3 egg yolks; 125 g/4 oz ($\frac{1}{2}$ cup) caster sugar;
2 tsp gelatine; 4 tbsp water; 250 ml/8 fl oz (1 cup) double (heavy) cream; 120 ml/4 fl oz ($\frac{1}{2}$ cup) rum; grated chocolate.

Beat egg yolks with sugar until light. Sprinkle gelatine over water and leave to soften, then dissolve over hot water. Add dissolved gelatine to egg mixture and beat well. Whip cream until stiff and fold into egg mixture. Stir in rum. Pour into serving bowl and sprinkle with grated chocolate. Chill thoroughly before serving, with additional whipped cream if desired. Serves 6.

RUM BABA

See Baba (au Rhum).

RUSKS

Pieces of bread which have been dried out in the oven, a process which produces a good nutty flavour as well as a crisp texture, transforming stale bread into something quite desirable. One of Italy's favourite nibbles, remembered with nostalgia by many travellers, consists of oven-dried slices of an especially made, slightly sweet, anise-flavoured bread. Another type of rusk, produced commercially for teething babies, is made by slowly baking fingers of bread dough until they are hard; *grissini*, the thin, crisp, Italian-style bread sticks, are made in the same way.

☐ **To Bake:** Cut sliced, crustless bread of any kind into fingers or other shapes such as small triangles, rounds or squares. Arrange in one layer on an ungreased baking tray and place in a preheated cool oven (150°C/300°F, Gas Mark 2) until they are completely dried, crisp and several shades deeper in colour. The time needed will depend on the type and thickness of the bread. Check frequently, turning the pieces over when the upper side is crisp and rearranging them as necessary to colour evenly. Do not allow to become too dark or the flavour will be spoiled. Rusks may curl as they dry; if you want to keep them flat, put a wire rack upside-down on top of them. Cool rusks on a wire rack and store in an airtight container.

Use, cold or slightly rewarmed, within a week or two; after that, the rusks will gradually get a 'tired' flavour.

You can use rusks in most of the ways you would use bread or toast. Serve them buttered or with peanut butter or honey or as snacks for hungry children. **See recipes.**

Pane d'Anise
(Anise Bread)

These nutty rusks, gently anise-flavoured, are traditionally dipped into a glass of red or rosé wine. They're lovely with coffee, too. Serve plain, buttered or with cheese.

125 g/4 oz ($\frac{1}{2}$ cup) butter; 250 g/8 oz (1 cup) sugar; 2 tbsp Pernod; 1 tsp crushed aniseed; 1$\frac{1}{2}$ tbsp brandy or whisky; 3 eggs; 370 g/12 oz (3 cups) flour; 2 tsp baking powder; 125 g/4 oz (1 cup) coarsely chopped almonds, walnuts or pecans.

Cream butter with sugar until fluffy, then beat in Pernod, aniseed and brandy or whisky followed by eggs, one at a time. Sift flour and baking powder together and fold in with nuts. Scrape mixture on to a piece of plastic wrap, wrap and chill for 2 hours. Divide dough into 4 and keep each piece chilled until ready to shape (the dough will be sticky). Put one piece of dough on to one half of a well-greased baking tray and, with wet hands, shape it into a long loaf 5 cm (2 in) wide and 1 cm ($\frac{1}{2}$ in) thick. Form remaining pieces of dough into loaves in same manner, putting 2 loaves on each tray. Bake in a preheated moderately hot oven (190°C/375°F, Gas Mark 5) for 20 minutes or until pale gold. Cool on trays. Cut loaves diagonally into 2 cm ($\frac{3}{4}$ in) slices. Arrange slices, cut side down, close together, in one layer on baking trays. Toast in a preheated moderately hot oven (190°C/375°F, Gas Mark 5) until they are dry, about 10 minutes. Cool on wire racks and store in an airtight container. Makes about 48.

Crisp Wholewheat Sticks

Serve these with drinks or as a snack at any time. They're good for a packed lunch, too – add cheese, radishes and celery sticks.

6 × 2 cm ($\frac{3}{4}$ in) thick slices day-old wholewheat bread, crusts removed; 1 clove garlic, crushed; 1$\frac{1}{2}$ tbsp oil; salt; 1 tbsp poppy seeds.

Cut each slice of bread into 4 fingers. Mix garlic into oil, brush over bread sticks and sprinkle lightly on all sides with salt, then poppy seeds. Arrange, well apart, on baking trays. Bake in a preheated moderate oven (180°C/350°F, Gas Mark 4) for 20–25 minutes, turning once or twice to brown evenly. Cool on a wire rack and store in an airtight container. Serve cold or warm. Makes 24.

VARIATION

Herbed Wholewheat Sticks: Omit garlic and use melted butter instead of oil. Mix butter with $\frac{1}{2}$ shallot, very finely chopped, and 1 tbsp chopped, mixed fresh herbs, or 1 tsp dried herbs chopped with 1 tbsp parsley. Sprinkle with sesame seeds instead of poppy seeds.

Crisp Bread Shells

A variation on the rusk theme, these easy little shells can be filled with any hot savoury mixture to serve as appetizers.

Use sliced fresh white or wholewheat bread, shaping it into tiny bite-sized cornucopias or make the slightly larger flower shapes.

sliced fresh bread, crusts removed; oil or melted butter.

TO SHAPE CORNUCOPIAS: Brush one side of each bread slice with oil or melted butter and cut into 4 squares. Roll each square from one corner, oiled side out, to make a cornucopia shape, and fasten the overlapping opposite corners with a wooden toothpick. Place shells on a baking tray and bake in a preheated moderate oven (180°C/350°F, Gas Mark 4) until crisp and golden, about 15 minutes. Remove toothpicks, cool on a wire rack and store in an airtight container.

TO SHAPE FLOWERS: Brush one side of each bread slice with oil or melted butter. Press, oiled side down, into bun tins (patty pans). Press well down to fit pans, and corners of bread will sit up to form a pretty flower cup. Bake in a preheated moderate oven (180°C/350°F, Gas Mark 4) until crisp and golden, 15–20 minutes. Remove from pans, cool on a wire rack and store in an airtight container.

TO SERVE: When appetizers are required, fill shells with any hot, savoury mixture (see Hot filled Hors d'Oeuvre, page 160). Place on baking trays and heat through for 10–15 minutes in a preheated moderate oven (180°C/350°F, Gas Mark 4).

RUTABAGA

See Turnip.

S

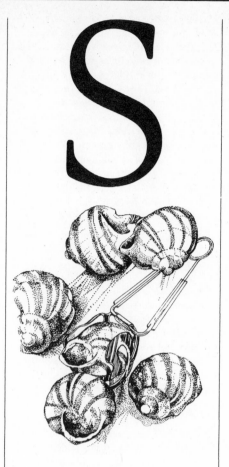

SABAYON SAUCE

A lovely sweet sauce flavoured with wine or fruit juice. Serve cold with poached fresh fruits or fruit jellies, or hot with hot sponge or fruit puddings or warm poached fruits.

Sabayon Sauce (Hot)

3 egg yolks; 75 g/2½ oz (⅓ cup) caster sugar; pinch arrowroot; 120 ml/4 fl oz (½ cup) white wine, sweet sherry or fruit juice.

Beat yolks with sugar and arrowroot in a heatproof bowl until very pale and thick. Add wine, sherry or juice and whisk vigorously. Place bowl over a saucepan of simmering water and continue whisking vigorously until sauce thickens. Do not allow water to get hotter than a simmer, or let water touch bowl. Remove from heat and beat for another few minutes. Serve immediately. Makes about 350 ml/12 fl oz (1½ cups).

VARIATION

Cold Sabayon Sauce: Proceed as above, using an extra egg yolk. After removing from the heat and beating for a few minutes, place bowl over ice and continue whisking until sauce is thoroughly chilled.

SACHER TORTE

Lawsuits have been fought over the right to call a cake by this name. This recipe is close to the one served at the Hotel Sacher in Vienna.

Sacher Torte

180 g/6 oz (1 cup) cooking chocolate; 150 g/5 oz (½ cup plus 2 tbsp) butter; 370 g/12 oz (1½ cups) caster sugar; 2 tbsp rum; 1 tbsp water; 5 eggs, separated; 180 g/6 oz (1½ cups) flour; apricot jam.
CHOCOLATE GLAZE: *90 g/3 oz (½ cup) chocolate, chopped; 175 ml/6 fl oz (¾ cup) single (light) cream; 310 g/10 oz (1¼ cups) caster sugar; 1 tsp golden (light corn) syrup; 1 egg; 1 tsp vanilla essence (extract).*

Melt chocolate in a small heatproof bowl over simmering water, then cool. Cream butter with sugar until light and fluffy. Stir rum and water into cooled chocolate and add to creamed mixture, beating well. Add egg yolks one at a time, beating well after each addition. Fold in sifted flour. Beat egg whites until stiff, and fold through cake mixture lightly until just incorporated. Divide mixture between 2 greased, lined and floured 20 cm (8 in) sandwich tins (layer cake pans). Bake in a preheated moderate oven (180°C/350°F, Gas Mark 4) for 40–45 minutes or until a fine skewer inserted in centre comes out clean. Cool on wire racks. When cold sandwich together with warmed and sieved apricot jam.
CHOCOLATE GLAZE: Combine chocolate,

cream, sugar and syrup in a small heavy saucepan. Stir constantly over low heat until chocolate and sugar melt. Increase heat to medium and cook, without stirring, for 5 minutes or to soft ball stage (mixture forms a soft ball when a little is dropped into cold water). Lightly beat egg and stir in 4 tbsp of chocolate and cream mixture. Return this to remaining chocolate mixture in pan and cook over low heat, stirring constantly, for 3–4 minutes or until glaze coats back of spoon thickly. Remove from heat and add vanilla. Cool to room temperature before using. Place cake on a wire rack over a baking tray. Pour glaze on to cake and smooth with a palette knife. When glaze stops dripping, transfer cake to a serving plate and refrigerate for 3 hours. Remove from refrigerator 30 minutes before serving.

SAFFRON

One of the most common spices of mediaeval cookery, saffron is now too expensive to be used with such abandon, although it is an essential ingredient of the Provençal bouillabaisse, the Milanese risotto and Spanish rice dishes, such as the traditional paella. It is also widely used in Indian cookery, especially in rice dishes and biryani.

Saffron comes from the orange stigmas of a type of crocus flower. The plant is native to Asia and parts of Europe, but was also grown extensively in England at one time, and has given its name to the town of Saffron Walden.

Saffron is available either as the dried stigmas or as a powder. The former may be ground, crumbled or used whole before being mixed with the hot stock or liquid called for in a recipe, while the powder is simply infused in the liquid. **See recipes.**

Mussels in Saffron Sauce

½ tsp saffron threads, crumbled; 4 tbsp warm water; 1 kg (2 lb) mussels, cleaned (see Mussels); 1 small onion, chopped; 1 bay leaf; 3 sprigs parsley; 1 sprig thyme; 3–4 fennel seeds; 150 ml/¼ pint (⅔ cup) water; 250 ml/8 fl oz (1 cup) Béchamel Sauce (page 368); 1 tbsp cooked, finely chopped spinach; 30 g/1 oz (½ cup) fresh breadcrumbs; 30 g/1 oz (2 tbsp) butter, cut into small pieces.

Soak saffron in 4 tbsp warm water for 1–2 hours. Place prepared mussels in a wide flameproof casserole and add onion, bay leaf, parsley, thyme, fennel seeds and 150 ml/¼ pint (⅔ cup) water. Cover and cook over high heat for about 5 minutes, shaking pan occasionally. Remove mussels as soon as they are open, and discard shells. Strain cooking liquid and add 250 ml/8 fl oz (1 cup) to Béchamel, stirring over very low heat. Discard any remaining cooking liquid.

Stir in saffron threads and their soaking liquid, spinach and shelled mussels. Turn mixture into a flameproof gratin dish, sprinkle with breadcrumbs and dot with butter. Cook under a preheated high grill (broiler) for about 5 minutes or until crumbs are crisp and golden. Serve immediately with crusty French bread. Serves 2.

Spanish Rice Soup

$\frac{1}{2}$ tsp saffron threads, crumbled; 4 tbsp warm water; 90 g/3 oz (6 tbsp) butter; 2 large onions, chopped; 210–310 g/7–10 oz (1–1$\frac{1}{2}$ cups) long-grain rice; $\frac{1}{2}$ tsp white pepper; 2 litres/3$\frac{1}{2}$ pints (8 cups) hot chicken stock.

Soak saffron threads in measured water for 1–2 hours. Melt butter in a large heavy saucepan and sauté onions for 5 minutes. Lower heat, add rice and stir until grains are coated with butter and translucent. Season with pepper and add half the stock. Cover and cook over low heat for 25 minutes. Add remaining stock, saffron threads and liquid and cook, uncovered, for a further 10 minutes. Serves 6–8.

Cornish Saffron Cake

$\frac{1}{2}$ tsp saffron threads, crumbled; 4 tbsp warm water; 500 g/1 lb (4 cups) flour; $\frac{1}{2}$ tsp salt; 125 g/4 oz ($\frac{1}{2}$ cup) butter; 30 g/1 oz (2 tbsp) fresh (compressed) yeast; 175 ml/6 fl oz ($\frac{3}{4}$ cup) warm milk; 60 g/2 oz ($\frac{1}{4}$ cup) caster sugar; 2 eggs, beaten; 140 g/4$\frac{1}{2}$ oz ($\frac{3}{4}$ cup) sultanas (golden raisins); 2 tbsp chopped mixed candied peel; 2 tbsp milk.

Soak saffron in measured warm water for 1–2 hours. Sift flour and salt together, add butter and rub (cut) in until mixture resembles crumbs. Dissolve yeast in warm milk, stir in saffron threads and their soaking liquid and add to flour mixture with sugar and eggs. Beat until smooth and elastic. Put into a clean, greased bowl and turn dough over so it is greased lightly all over. Cover bowl with a cloth and leave to rise in a warm place for about 45–50 minutes or until doubled in bulk.

Mix in sultanas (golden raisins) and peel and turn dough into a greased 20 cm (8 in) deep cake tin (pan). Set aside in a warm place to prove for about 15–20 minutes or until dough reaches the top of the tin (pan).

Brush cake with milk and bake in a preheated moderately hot oven (200°C/400°F, Gas Mark 6) for 45–50 minutes. Cool on a wire rack and serve warm or cold with cream. Serves 8.

SAGE

An easily-grown, perennial herb with a strong, pungent and slightly bitter flavour. The leaves may be dried, but for best flavour use young,

fresh sage leaves. Always use sage sparingly; too much can completely overpower a dish.

Sage is common in both English and European cuisine. In Britain it is used as a flavouring in stuffings, especially the traditional Sage and Onion Stuffing for roast duck. It is also one of the components of mixed herbs, and it is used to flavour cheese (e.g. Sage Derby) and breads. **See recipes.**

Veal Chops with Sage and White Wine

4 veal loin chops, 2 cm ($\frac{3}{4}$ in) thick; 30 g/1 oz ($\frac{1}{4}$ cup) flour; 3 tbsp oil; 12 leaves dried or fresh sage; salt and freshly ground black pepper; 120 ml/4 fl oz ($\frac{1}{2}$ cup) dry white wine; 30 g/1 oz (2 tbsp) butter.

Lightly coat chops in flour. Heat oil in a frying pan (skillet) and add chops and sage. Brown chops on both sides for about 8–10 minutes, turning 2 or 3 times. Remove chops to warmed plate when cooked and season with salt and pepper. Tilt pan and drain off excess oil. Add wine to pan and deglaze, scraping up any residue. Boil until almost completely evaporated, then reduce heat and mix in butter. Return chops to pan to warm through. Serves 4.

Sage and Onion Stuffing

4 leaves fresh sage; 2 mild onions, finely chopped; 125 g/4 oz (2 cups) fresh breadcrumbs; grated rind $\frac{1}{2}$ lemon; 2–3 tbsp melted butter; salt and freshly ground black pepper.

Blanch sage leaves in boiling water for 5 minutes, then drain and chop finely. Combine sage, onions, breadcrumbs, lemon rind, melted butter, salt and pepper. If necessary, add a little stock to bind mixture. Sufficient to stuff 1 large duckling.

Roast Pork with Sage

1 × 2 kg (4 lb) boned pork loin (loin roast), in one piece, and trimmed of rind and excess fat; 6 young leaves fresh sage; 1 bay leaf; $\frac{1}{2}$ tsp dried thyme; 2 tsp salt; olive oil; 2–3 cloves garlic, halved.

Prepare meat the day before cooking. Make small cuts in meat and insert sage leaves. Crumble bay leaf, mix with dried thyme and salt and rub mixture over pork. Drizzle 2–3 tbsp olive oil over pork and place halved garlic cloves on top. Cover and leave for at least 12 hours. Next day, place meat in roasting tin (pan) with garlic underneath, and drizzle a little more oil over meat. Roast in preheated moderate oven (160°C/325°F, Gas Mark 3) for about 2 hours, basting from time to time with pan juices, until juices from meat run clear. Remove to heated plate. If desired, deglaze tin (pan) with a little white or rosé wine and serve pan juices with meat. Serves 8.

SAGO

The tiny grains of sago are made from a type of paste, derived from the sago palm, which grows in tropical regions.

Sago is basically a carbohydrate with little distinct flavour of its own. Like other starchy products, however, it can absorb liquids and act as a thickener. It is sometimes used to thicken soups, but its principal use is in desserts. **See recipes.**

Lemon Sago

180 g/6 oz (1 cup) sago; 750 ml/1$\frac{1}{4}$ pints (3 cups) water; grated rind 2 lemons; juice 3 lemons; 3 tbsp golden (light corn) syrup; 3 tbsp sugar.

Soak sago in water for 30 minutes, then add remaining ingredients and pour into a saucepan. Bring to the boil, stirring, and simmer until quite thick. Pour into a mould. Cool and chill. Serve with cream or custard. Serves 6.

Sago Pudding

2 tbsp sago; 750 ml/1$\frac{1}{4}$ pints (3 cups) milk; 60 g/2 oz ($\frac{1}{4}$ cup) sugar; 3 eggs; $\frac{1}{2}$ tsp vanilla essence (extract).

Simmer sago in milk until grains have swelled, then pour into bowl and cool. Beat in sugar, eggs and vanilla. Pour into buttered ovenproof dish. Place dish in tin (pan) of hot water and bake in a preheated moderate oven (180°C/350°F, Gas Mark 4) for about 1 hour. Serve warm or chill in the refrigerator before serving. Serves 4–6.

SALAD

There are few edible foods that cannot be used in salads. The first salad that springs to mind is perhaps the simple green, tossed salad so beloved of the epicurean French.

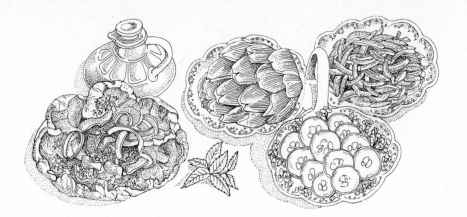

The English used to favour mixed salads, the most popular being lettuce with tomatoes, cucumber and probably beetroot, dressed with vinaigrette or salad dressing. The Americans introduced fruit to green salads. Today, the whole world, from the super chefs of great kitchens, to imaginative home cooks in search of good, healthy, fresh-tasting meals, have taken to salad-making like ducks to water.

Fresh vegetables are the richest and cheapest source of the numerous vitamins and minerals essential to our health. With the herbs, meats, fish, eggs, cheese and oil that are mixed with these, a salad can be a complete balanced meal.

To make the most of salads buy only young, tender, fresh greens, vegetables and fruits. Use imagination with the additional foods. The other golden rule is that the dressing should be added at the last moment (there are, of course, exceptions). Also, a salad looks fluffier and more bouncy when just prepared; it seems to settle on standing and lose its light, freshly-made look.

Included in this section are salads that have become classics, salads that you will find on restaurant menus, and many that are made in homes for family meals and for entertaining. The foods that go to make many salads have been listed and the 'dressings' that add distinction to salads. For other salads see the Index, because many delicious salads are distributed throughout the book. **See also recipes.**

Salad Greens

Selection and care: Greens must be very fresh and unwilted. Buy or pick only enough for a day or two. Discard any tough or dry outer leaves and wash them as you require them. Don't break up the heads before storing them in the refrigerator; separate the leaves and wash them as required. Salad greens need careful washing in cold water, as sand hides in their crevices.

It is very important to dry salad greens thoroughly. Fold the wet leaves in a tea-towel and shake them gently over the sink. When the leaves are dry, break them up, wrap in a dry tea-towel and return to the refrigerator until time to make the salad. A most useful gadget, looking like a hand-operated spin dryer, is a plastic salad dryer; it really makes a splendid job of drying salad greens, without bruising or crushing tender leaves.

Types of Salad Greens

Cabbage: The main varieties used for salads are Savoy, Dutch, head and red cabbages. Discard the outside wilted leaves before slicing. Cabbage has a strong distinctive flavour. See also *Cabbage.*

Chicory (Belgian Endive or Witloof): Tightly clustered white leaves, with yellow, tender tips. The leaves can be used whole or sliced. Chicory has a slightly tangy taste. See also *Chicory.*

Endive, Curly (Chicory): Tightly curled bunchy head. The leaves graduate from dark green to yellow-green at the heart. Use the crisp young leaves and centre stalk. Endive has a slightly bitter taste. See also *Endive, Curly.*

Escarole: Slightly curly, rich green outer leaves, with a fresh yellow heart. Use only the tender centre leaves for salad. The flavour is slightly bitter. See also *Escarole.*

Lettuce: The iceberg lettuce, with its firm heart and crisp outer leaves, is the basis of many salads. Round (bibb) lettuce, with its small soft leaves, is a favourite with home gardeners. Look also for other varieties such as cos (romaine) and Webb's Wonder. Flavours are mild. See also *Lettuce.*

Parsley, Italian: This has a flatter and larger leaf than the more common, tightly curled parsley, and a slightly stronger flavour.

Spinach, English: Dark green leaves on slim stalks, with reddish, fibrous roots. Use when very fresh. Don't confuse spinach with silverbeet, which has larger, tougher leaves; only the very young tender leaves of silverbeet are suitable for salads. Spinach has a mild flavour. See also *Spinach.*

Spring onions (scallions): Sometimes called green onions. Remove outside leaves and root base. Cut off tough green leaves. They have a fresh onion flavour. See also *Onion.*

Types of Salad Vegetables

Avocado: Once a great favourite with the Aztecs, this pear-shaped fruit, with its rich buttery flesh, is greatly appreciated for its delicate but distinctive flavour. There are many varieties and they are found the year round. The perfect partner for cold seafood, avocado is equally good combined with a green salad or served alone with Vinaigrette Dressing (see page 358). See also *Avocado.*

Bean Sprouts: Sprouted mung beans are crisp and crunchy and enjoyed in many salads. The sprouted bean or the shoot (minus the bean) is used. Other shoots like alfalfa are also popular in salads. See also *Bean Sprouts.*

Beans, Green: Small whole beans or long slender runner (snake) beans make an interesting fresh salad. Just top and tail them. If very young, they do not need stringing. Blanch in boiling salted water for 5 minutes, then drain and rinse in cold water to preserve their bright green colour and crisp texture. Season with a little grated nutmeg and toss in a garlic-flavoured Vinaigrette Dressing (see page 358). Scatter snipped fresh chives and chopped parsley over the top. A few mashed anchovies added to the dressing give an excellent flavour to a bean salad. See also *Beans, Green.*

Cabbage, Chinese (Stem lettuce): Shaped much like a large cos (romaine) lettuce, with long, thin, mild-flavoured leaves. The leaves are green-edged and nearly white in the centre. See also *Cabbage.*

Carrots: Carrots for salads must be young and crisp; either grate them or cut into julienne (matchstick) strips. They combine well with all salad vegetables. See also *Carrot.*

Cauliflower: Just as good in salads as it is eaten as a hot vegetable. Break off florets, cutting away the tough stems, and cook in boiling salted water for a few minutes. Then drain and rinse under cold running water. Try it combined with celery, ham and a mustard-flavoured Vinaigrette Dressing (see page 358), served chilled, sprinkled with a few chopped fresh herbs. See also *Cauliflower.*

Chicory, Italian: Long, dark green, smooth stems with leaves resembling spinach. The leaves can be cooked like spinach and the stalks sliced and added to salads.

Courgettes (Zucchini): These small, dark green marrows, which are particularly favoured by Southern Europeans, combine beautifully with quartered tomatoes and peppers. Blanch them in boiling salted water and refresh in ice-cold water before using. Add them to a green salad or toss with mushroom slices, some oregano and a garlic-flavoured Vinaigrette Dressing (see page 358). Excellent with terrines and cold meats. See also *Zucchini*.

Cucumber: The perfect summer salad vegetable, with its cool distinctive taste. It combines perfectly with salad dressings, and is delicious with sour cream to which a little grated fresh ginger and fresh garlic may be added. It is not necessary to remove the skin when cucumber is sliced thinly. Lightly salt the slices, placed in a colander, and allow to stand for about 30 minutes to extract indigestible juices. Drain and rinse well with cold water. Toss in a little Vinaigrette Dressing (see page 358) and scatter with a few freshly snipped chives or finely chopped dill. See also *Cucumber*.

Fennel: One of the nine herbs the early Anglo-Saxons believed guarded against evil. The other kind of fennel – the vegetable Florence fennel – with its white celery-like stem is the one used for salads. Sliced thinly, its distinctive aniseed flavour mixes well with salad greens and tomatoes. Its feathery leaves, when finely chopped, given an aromatic flavour to cream sauces for fish. See also *Fennel*.

Garlic: This pungent bulb is a necessity in today's kitchen. Before using, remove the thin, papery skin surrounding each clove. A cut clove rubbed around a salad bowl gives a lift to a simple green salad. Rubbed with some olive oil on slices of French bread (in France called *chapons*), and then tossed with the greens it imparts its full aromatic flavour to a green salad. A touch of garlic, for many, is an indispensable part of a salad. See also *Garlic*.

Mushrooms: Small button mushrooms are best for salads. They are good eaten raw, and may be left whole or thinly sliced. It's not necessary to peel them: just wipe with a cloth, dipped in water and a little lemon juice. Toss in a light Vinaigrette Dressing (see page 358), with plenty of freshly chopped parsley. See also *Mushroom*.

Peppers, Green and Red: These glossy vegetables are, perhaps, the most beautiful of all salad ingredients. Their sweet peppery flavour is greatly appreciated in rice salads, potato salads and the delicious Provençal ratatouille and Salade Niçoise. See also *Pepper (Sweet)*.

Radish: These are sold in tightly clustered bunches. Ideal for salads or served whole with hard-boiled (hard-cooked) eggs, olives and cherry tomatoes. See also *Radish*.

Tomatoes: Choose firm, red tomatoes. These can be peeled, if liked, and sliced or quartered and tossed in a good dressing; excellent, too, with chopped basil, oregano or parsley. Tomatoes are often added to other salad vegetables to make a mixed salad. Alternatively, scoop out centres and fill with diced cucumber, or a rice or seafood salad.

Watercress, and Mustard and Cress: These herbs are now available from nurseries and speciality kitchen shops for the home gardener. Watercress is bought in tight bunches, and its small, attractive sprigs, with their slightly bitter, peppery taste, make a perfect salad ingredient. Cut off tough stems, tie the dark leafy heads into bunches and stand in ice-cold water to keep them crisp and fresh. Dress them with a mustard-flavoured Vinaigrette Dressing (see page 358).

Mustard and cress is bought already sprouted in punnets. Snip off tops only and sprinkle over salads. See also *Cress*.

Other Salad Ingredients

Anchovies: A little goes a long way. These distinctively flavoured fish are featured in Caesar Salad (see page 52), and Salad Niçoise (see page 238). See also *Anchovy*.

Cheese: Wedges, cubes, slivers, julienne (matchstick) strips, and finger-sized sticks of all kinds of cheese can add richness and flavour to a salad. Blue cheese is often crumbled into a dressing; Parmesan or Pecorino is grated and sprinkled over some salads. Soft cream and Ricotta cheeses make great luncheon salads: sprinkle mounds of cheese with snipped chives, chopped spring onions (scallions) and dust with paprika; accompany with a few salad greens and tomatoes. See also *Cheese*.

Croûtons, Pasta, Potatoes, or Rice: These provide a pleasant contrast to the crispness of vegetables, and add substance to a salad. See also *Croûte and Croûton, Pasta, Potato* and *Rice*.

Eggs, Hard-boiled (hard-cooked): Chopped or quartered eggs are most suitable for a substantial salad; grated or sieved, they can give an attractive mimosa effect to a green salad. Particularly good with strong or bitter greens like endive, chicory, or escarole – eggs seem to round them off. See also *Egg*.

Fish, Meats and Poultry: These add substance to a salad, and are the base on which to build a 'meal-in-itself' salad. Leftover meats, if a little dry, may be marinated in a good dressing. Often meats, poultry and seafood are cooked especially for salad-making and canned varieties are also often featured in salads.

Herbs, fresh: Tossed with a green salad or mixed in with the dressing, herbs give that distinctive taste to a salad. *Fines herbes*, beloved of the French, is the great classic mixture, and is made, traditionally, with chopped parsley, chives, tarragon and chervil; but any combination of these can be used. Use basil in tomato salads; chives with cheese; dill is good with fish and cucumber; Chinese parsley with chicken (particularly if the dressing is Oriental), and ordinary parsley goes with just about all salads.

See also *Herbs*, and individual entries for the different herbs.

Nuts: Soft yet crunchy walnuts or pecans, roughly chopped, can be particularly good as an accent in a winter salad of tart greens. See also individual entries.

Olives, Green, Black (Ripe) or Stuffed: Stone (pit) and slice. Use sparingly in a green salad; they are more appropriate for a mixed concoction or a composed salad (in which case leave them whole). Olives may also be used simply to garnish a salad. See also *Olive*.

Pimiento: Bright red, canned pimiento adds a bright touch to many salads. Drain before using. See also *Pimiento*.

Types of Salads

Green Salad, Tossed: Often called a French salad, this mixture of crisp greens, torn into bite-sized pieces only, is tossed in a light Vinaigrette Dressing (see page 358) at the last moment and liberally sprinkled with chopped parsley and other herbs. It is a classic accompaniment to French roast chicken. It is often served with, or after, a main course, particularly if there are no green vegetables with the dish.

Green salads can be made up of plain lettuce, cos (romaine), or iceberg lettuce, depending on the season, or be a mixture of salad greens and vegetables, such as watercress, sliced cucumber and spring onions (scallions). Chicory (endive) can also be added in season. Tomato and beetroot etc., are not included in a true French tossed green salad.

Mixed Salad, Tossed: A green salad with other additions, e.g. tomatoes, cheese etc., that can make it a light meal in itself. The dressing (see *Salad Dressings*) may be a standard Vinaigrette or varied with herbs or canned anchovy fillets.

Composed Salad: The ingredients are arranged attractively in a bowl, and a little dressing is spooned over. The diner takes portions of salad and helps himself to additional dressing.

Substantial Salad: Often based on rice, macaroni or other pasta, or potatoes with crispy, crunchy salad greens and vegetables.

The dressings used can be as varied as the ingredients.

Vegetable Salad, Cooked: Cooked vegetables may be marinated in a dressing and served as a salad or as part of an hors d'oeuvre tray. Choose young, tender ones and do not overcook them: they should still be a little crisp inside.

Starter Salad: A light salad, refreshing to the palate and not too filling. Particularly popular is a salad based on eggs or fish. Sometimes a selection of salads is presented as hors d'oeuvre, in little white oblong or oval dishes; they are a feature in French and Italian restaurants, particularly for lunch.

Light Meal Salads: When a salad has protein in the form of egg, fish, cheese or meat, plus vegetables, it makes a delicious complete meal. Simply add crusty bread and a glass of light wine.

Side Salad: This is where a salad comes truly into its own, as an accompaniment to a more grand dish. Instead of only serving hot vegetables with cooked meats etc., serve a salad either alone or as well.

The salad should be vegetable based but can vary from a simple tossed salad to a composed salad – take your pick. Dress it carefully with a delicate dressing just before serving, using your imagination to choose an appropriate dressing.

Mixed Green Salad with Chapons

Chapons are slices of French bread (flavoured liberally with garlic, a good olive oil and pepper) which are tossed with a salad of mixed greens to add a distinct garlic flavour. This method is more traditional than rubbing the bowl with a garlic clove.

selection of salad greens (lettuce, curly endive (chicory), spinach, spring onions (scallions), parsley and watercress); 1 cucumber; 2 cloves garlic, crushed; 3–4 tbsp olive oil; freshly ground black pepper; 6 slices French bread; Vinaigrette Dressing (page 358).

Rinse, dry and chill salad greens. Tear into bite-sized pieces. Peel cucumber leaving a little green colour on the flesh. Cut in half lengthways and scoop out seeds with a spoon. Cut into 5 cm (2 in) lengths. Put garlic in a small bowl with olive oil and a good grinding of black pepper. Mix well, then brush on slices of French bread. Add to bowl with salad greens and cucumber, and just before serving toss with a little vinaigrette dressing. Serves 4.

Green Salad

lettuce, or selection of salad greens; 5 tbsp Vinaigrette Dressing (page 358); garlic (optional); chopped mixed fresh herbs (thyme, chives, mint and parsley).

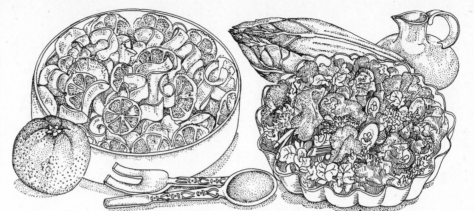

If lettuce leaves are large, pull rather than cut them apart. Wash well, spin-dry in a salad basket or clean cloth (see Salad Greens, page 345). Make sure this is thoroughly done. If lettuce is at all limp, put it into refrigerator (in salad drawer or hydrator) until crisp. Tear into bite-sized pieces and put into a salad bowl with other greens. Watercress should be well rinsed in the bunch under cold running water, then shaken to get rid of moisture. Carefully pick over and remove some of the stalk; use sprigs only. Watercress gives a slightly peppery taste to salads.

Garlic may be used to flavour a green salad, but use it cautiously. Either rub bowl with a peeled clove or, better still, rub a clove well over a crust of French or ordinary bread. Having put salad into bowl, bury this *chapon*, as it is called, among leaves (not forgetting to remove it before serving the salad at the table).

Add vinaigrette dressing by sprinkling it over leaves, tossing lightly to make them glisten. A green salad should be dressed at the last moment, otherwise leaves will wilt and be unappetizing. For a large amount of salad, you will find it easier to mix it with its dressing in a really big bowl, and then to transfer it to your salad bowl.

To make salad the Italian way: sprinkle in enough oil on its own, tossing leaves all the time to make them glisten. Mix vinegar ($\frac{1}{3}$ of the quantity of oil used) and seasoning together, and sprinkle over greens. For a stronger flavour, crush garlic with a little salt and add to this dressing. Stir once or twice before serving salad, so that dressing is evenly distributed. Before serving, sprinkle the salad with chopped herbs and parsley. Serves 4–6.

NOTE: 5 tbsp of vinaigrette is usually enough for one lettuce plus a selection of other greens.

Chicory and Orange Salad

2 oranges; 3 heads chicory (endive), cut diagonally into 5 mm ($\frac{1}{4}$ in) slices; 2 carrots, grated.

VINAIGRETTE DRESSING: *2 tbsp olive oil; 1 tbsp walnut oil; 1 tbsp vinegar; 1 tsp French (Dijon) mustard; pinch sugar; salt and freshly ground black pepper.*

Remove peel and pith from oranges and cut between membrane to remove segments. Combine chicory slices, orange segments and carrot in a salad bowl.
VINAIGRETTE DRESSING: Whisk together ingredients. Add to salad and toss well. Serves 4–6.

Salade Périgordine

1 head lettuce; 4–6 tomatoes, cut into wedges; 4 hard-boiled (hard-cooked) eggs, chopped; 9–10 walnuts, roughly chopped; 3 rashers (slices) streaky bacon, rind removed and cut into strips.
DRESSING: *1$\frac{1}{2}$ tbsp wine vinegar; 1 tsp lemon juice; 5 tbsp walnut, sunflower or corn oil; $\frac{1}{2}$ tsp sugar; $\frac{1}{2}$ tsp French (Dijon) mustard; 1 clove garlic, crushed; salt and freshly ground black pepper.*

Put lettuce leaves, tomato wedges, chopped eggs and walnuts in a large salad bowl and mix gently. Fry bacon, without extra fat, over moderate heat until crisp.
DRESSING: Combine ingredients in a screw-top jar and shake well. Add dressing to salad and toss thoroughly. Drain bacon, stir into salad and serve immediately. Serves 4.

Spinach and Walnut Salad

30 g/1 oz ($\frac{1}{4}$ cup) chopped walnuts; 3 spring onions (scallions), finely chopped; $\frac{1}{2}$ bunch young spinach leaves, torn into pieces; 2 tsp white wine vinegar; 2 tbsp walnut or olive oil; salt and freshly ground black pepper.

Put walnuts, spring onions (scallions) and spinach in a salad bowl. Cover and chill for 1 hour. Combine vinegar, oil, salt and pepper in a screw-top jar and shake well. When ready to serve, pour dressing over salad, toss well to coat the leaves and serve immediately. Serves 4.

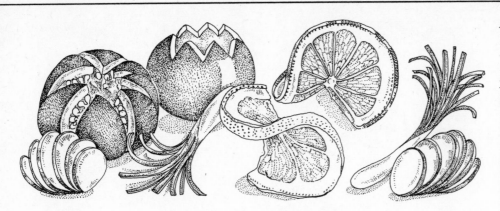

Lettuce Wedges with Cream Dressing

1 firm, medium head lettuce; ½ tsp prepared English mustard; 1 tsp sugar; 2 tsp wine vinegar; ½ tsp dried tarragon; 1 clove garlic, crushed; 1 hard-boiled (hard-cooked) egg, separated; 120 ml/4 fl oz (½ cup) single (light) cream; salt and freshly ground black pepper; snipped chives or chopped parsley to garnish.

Remove outside leaves of lettuce, and cut away core at bottom. Cut lettuce into 6 wedges, and arrange on a large platter or 6 individual plates. Mix together mustard, sugar, vinegar, tarragon, garlic and egg yolk. Stir in cream and season with salt and pepper. Spoon this dressing over lettuce wedges. Chop egg white and sprinkle over lettuce with chives or parsley. Serves 6.

NOTE: Make dressing just before serving, or vinegar will sour cream and make the dressing too thick.

Chicken Waldorf

4 half-breasts of chicken, or skinless, boneless fillets; 250 ml/8 fl oz (1 cup) apple cider; salt and freshly ground black pepper; 2 eating apples, cut into thin wedges; juice 1 lemon; 6–8 spring onions (scallions), shredded; 3 sticks tender celery, cut into julienne (matchstick) strips; 60 g/2 oz (½ cup) walnut pieces; parsley to garnish.
WALNUT SAUCE: *1 egg, lightly beaten; ½ tbsp sugar; 2 tsp flour; ½ tsp dry mustard; 120 ml/4 fl oz (½ cup) single (light) cream; 30 g/1 oz (¼ cup) finely chopped walnuts; little extra cream; salt and freshly ground black pepper.*

Carefully remove skin and bones from chicken breasts. Poach breasts or fillets in cider, seasoned with salt and pepper, about 8 minutes. Cool in liquid. Lift out chicken and cut breasts diagonally into 3 even-shaped fillets. Lay on a large dish, cover with plastic wrap and refrigerate until required. Strain liquid and reserve for sauce. Coat apple wedges with lemon juice.
WALNUT SAUCE: Place reserved chicken cooking liquid in a stainless steel or enamel

saucepan and boil to reduce to 120 ml/4 fl oz (½ cup). Remove from heat and stir in egg, sugar, flour and mustard. Whisk in cream. Return to medium heat and bring to the boil, whisking constantly. Strain through fine sieve and add walnuts. Cool to room temperature, and thin to desired consistency with extra cream. Season with salt and pepper.

One hour before serving, arrange salad on a large platter as follows: place apple wedges down centre and strew over spring onions (scallions) and celery, leaving a few for garnish. Arrange chicken breasts over vegetables. Spoon some walnut sauce over chicken, top with walnut pieces and strew with remaining celery and spring onions (scallions). Serve remaining sauce separately. Garnish with parsley. Serves 6.

Cathay Salad

125 g/4 oz (1 cup) bean sprouts; ¼ bunch spring onions (scallions), finely chopped; 1 avocado, peeled, stoned (pitted) and finely sliced; 250 g/8 oz (1 cup) prawns (shrimp), cooked, shelled and deveined; 2 chicken breasts, poached, skinned, boned and finely sliced; 125 g/4 oz (1 cup) button mushrooms, finely sliced; watercress or round (bibb) lettuce.
MUSTARD AND GINGER DRESSING: *1 tbsp lemon juice; 3 tbsp safflower oil; 1 clove garlic, crushed; ½ tsp grated fresh ginger; 1 tsp tarragon-flavoured mustard or plain French (Dijon) mustard; 1 tbsp single (light) cream.*

Combine bean sprouts, spring onions (scallions), avocado, prawns (shrimp), chicken and mushrooms. Place in a chilled bowl on a bed of watercress or lettuce.
MUSTARD AND GINGER DRESSING: Combine all ingredients in a jar and shake well. Toss salad lightly in dressing just before serving. Serves 2–3.

Curried Pecan Chicken Salad

3 half-breasts of chicken; 1 carrot, sliced; 1 onion, sliced; 7 sticks celery, sliced; salt; 3 medium crisp red apples, cored and diced;

juice 1 lemon; 45 g/1½ oz (⅓ cup) pecan halves or walnuts; 1 tbsp oil; 2 tsp curry powder; 1 small onion, chopped; 120 ml/4 fl oz (½ cup) Mayonnaise (page 204); lettuce leaves to serve.

Poach chicken breasts in enough water to cover, with carrot, sliced onion, 1 celery stick and a little salt for 8 minutes or until tender. Drain and cool. Discard skin and bones and dice meat. Sprinkle apples with lemon juice. Place in a bowl with chicken, pecan halves and remaining celery. Heat oil in a frying pan (skillet), add curry powder and chopped onion and cook gently about 5 minutes. Add to mayonnaise. Toss chicken salad with well-seasoned mayonnaise and chill. Serve piled up on crisp lettuce leaves. Serves 6 as a first course or 4 as a main course.

Oriental Salad

1 head lettuce or a mixture of young spinach, watercress or various kinds of lettuce – whatever is leafy and interesting at the greengrocers; 125 g/4 oz (1 cup) mung bean sprouts; 125 g/4 oz (½ cup) thinly sliced water chestnuts; 30 g/1 oz (¼ cup) slivered toasted almonds.
ORIENTAL DRESSING: *30 g/1 oz (¼ cup) chopped spring onions (scallions); 1 tsp chopped fresh coriander; 10 g/⅓ oz (¼ cup) chopped parsley; 1 tsp grated fresh ginger; 1 tbsp soy sauce; 250 ml/8 fl oz (1 cup) single (light) cream; 1 tsp lemon juice; 2 tbsp Mayonnaise (page 204).*

Rinse and dry lettuce or other greens and refrigerate until crisp. Tear into serving pieces, place in salad bowl and scatter bean sprouts and water chestnuts over.
ORIENTAL DRESSING: Mix all dressing ingredients together and drizzle over salad. Scatter almonds on top and toss lightly. Serve immediately. Serves 6–8.

Duck and Pawpaw Salad

This salad may be made very successfully with cold turkey and is a good salad for those days after Christmas.

500 g (1 lb) cooked duck, turkey or chicken meat, sliced; jellied turkey or duck juices (if available); 1 good-sized ripe pawpaw, peeled, seeded and finely sliced; juice ½ lemon; 60 g/2 oz (½ cup) walnut pieces; curly endive (chicory) or soft round (bibb) lettuce to serve.
DRESSING: *2 tbsp walnut oil; 2 tbsp safflower oil; 2 tbsp finely snipped chives; salt and freshly ground black pepper.*

Moisten meat with any jellied meat juices. Sprinkle pawpaw slices with lemon juice. Stand 10 minutes, then drain, reserving juice. Toast walnuts lightly in a preheated moderate oven (180°C/350°F, Gas Mark 4).

DRESSING: Combine 2 tbsp of the reserved pawpaw juice with oil, chives, salt and pepper. Shake well to combine. Line a salad bowl or dish with endive (chicory) or lettuce and arrange meat and pawpaw on it. Spoon over dressing and garnish with walnut pieces. Serves 4.

Chicken Citrus Salad

1 cucumber, peeled and seeded; 4 half-breasts of chicken, poached, skinned, boned and cut into small pieces; 2 sticks tender celery, finely sliced; 1 small green pepper, cored, seeded and finely sliced; 1 grapefruit, segmented; combination of round (bibb) or iceberg lettuce and watercress.
DRESSING: *5 tbsp Mayonnaise (page 204); 5 tbsp Vinaigrette Dressing (page 358); 1 tsp mild French (Dijon) mustard; ½ small onion, grated; 1 tsp finely chopped chives; salt and freshly ground black pepper.*
GARNISH: *1 tbsp finely chopped parsley; 2 tsp capers.*

Cut cucumber into balls with a melon baller. Place in a bowl with chicken, celery, green pepper and grapefruit.
DRESSING: Whisk all ingredients together until well blended. Pour over salad and toss carefully. Serve in a chilled salad bowl on a bed of lettuce and watercress. Garnish with parsley and capers. Serves 2.

Roast Beef Salad

500 g (1 lb) cold roast beef, cut into strips; 4 medium tomatoes, cut into wedges; 1 celery heart, finely sliced; 75 g/2½ oz (½ cup) stuffed olives; watercress; lettuce.
BLUE CHEESE DRESSING: *2 tbsp single (light) cream; 1 tbsp red wine vinegar; 2 tbsp oil; freshly ground black pepper; 60 g/2 oz (½ cup) blue cheese (preferably French Roquefort), crumbled.*

Combine beef with tomatoes, celery and olives. Place on a bed of watercress and lettuce.
BLUE CHEESE DRESSING: Shake together cream, vinegar, oil and pepper in a jar until well combined. Carefully stir in crumbled cheese just before the dressing is used. Spoon over salad. Serves 4.

Mexican Salad

½ Savoy cabbage, finely sliced; 1 bunch watercress; young nasturtium leaves, or mustard and cress; 1 avocado, peeled, stoned (pitted) and sliced; 4 rashers (slices) lean bacon, rind removed, grilled (broiled) until crisp and crumbled; 1 chilli, seeded and finely chopped; 1 half-breast of chicken, poached, skinned, boned and sliced; 6 small radishes, sliced; 1 red pepper, cored, seeded and sliced.

ANCHOVY DRESSING: *2 anchovy fillets; milk; 1 tbsp wine vinegar; 3 tbsp olive oil; 1 clove garlic, crushed; 1 tsp finely chopped fresh oregano, or pinch dried; freshly ground black pepper.*

Combine cabbage in a large bowl with watercress and nasturtium leaves, avocado, bacon, chilli, chicken, radishes and pepper.
ANCHOVY DRESSING: Soak anchovies in milk for 10 minutes. Drain and pat dry. Mash them to a paste and blend in vinegar and oil. Add garlic and oregano, and season with pepper. Spoon dressing over salad and toss very carefully. Serves 4–6.

Tuna Pasta Salad

370 g/12 oz (3 cups) green tagliatelle noodles; 1 × 200 g/7 oz can tuna fish, drained; 2 small onions, finely sliced; 2 ripe tomatoes, peeled and quartered; 2 hard-boiled (hard-cooked) eggs, quartered; 10 black (ripe) olives, stoned (pitted); chopped parsley.
DRESSING: *1 tbsp tarragon vinegar; 1 tbsp sherry; salt and freshly ground black pepper; 2 tbsp chopped spring onions (scallions); 2 tbsp chopped parsley; 4 tbsp olive oil.*

Cook pasta in boiling salted water until 'al dente', or tender but still firm. Drain well and cool. Flake tuna lightly with a fork (be careful as tuna can easily become mushy). Mix with pasta, onions, tomatoes, eggs and olives.
DRESSING: Combine vinegar, sherry, salt, pepper, spring onions (scallions) and parsley in a bowl. Add oil in a stream, beating dressing until it is well combined. Pour dressing over salad and toss gently. Sprinkle with parsley. Serves 4.

Fettucini and Pepper Salad

250 g (8 oz) fettucini noodles; 2 red or green peppers, halved, cored and seeded; 125 g/4 oz (1 cup) Gruyére cheese, diced; 6–8 walnuts, chopped.
DRESSING: *4 tbsp olive oil; 1 tbsp walnut oil; 1 tbsp vinegar; 1 tsp French (Dijon) mustard; salt and freshly ground black pepper.*

Cook noodles in boiling salted water for 8–10 minutes or until 'al dente' or tender but still firm. Drain. Grill (broil) peppers, cut sides down, under a preheated high grill (broiler) until skins blacken and blister. When cool enough to handle, pull off thin outer skin and cut flesh into long, even strips. Mix pepper strips with cheese and walnuts in a salad bowl.
DRESSING: Combine all ingredients for dressing. Add to noodles, mix lightly and toss with salad. Chill for at least 1 hour before serving. Serves 4.

Italian Ham Salad

125 g/4 oz (1 cup) pasta shells; 125 g (4 oz) cooked ham, sliced and shredded; 6–8 black (ripe) olives, halved and stoned (pitted); 2–3 tbsp thick Mayonnaise (page 204); 1 tsp French (Dijon) mustard.

Cook pasta shells in boiling salted water for about 10 minutes or until 'al dente' or just tender. Drain and refresh under cold running water. Mix ham with olives and pasta. Add mayonnaise to mustard and stir enough into salad to bind. Serves 4.

Penne, Tuna and Olive Salad

Penne is the name for pen-nib shaped lengths of hollow pasta.

250 g (8 oz) penne; 1 large red or green pepper, cored, seeded and finely shredded; 1 medium onion, finely sliced; 4 tender sticks celery, finely sliced; 10 g/⅓ oz (¼ cup) finely chopped parsley; 10 black (ripe) olives, halved and stoned (pitted); lettuce leaves; 1 × 200 g/7 oz can tuna in oil, drained; 2 ripe tomatoes, quartered; sprigs parsley or watercress to garnish.
TARRAGON DRESSING: *1 clove garlic, crushed; ½ tsp salt; freshly ground black pepper; 2 tsp French (Dijon) mustard; 1 tbsp wine vinegar; 3 tbsp olive oil; 1 tsp chopped fresh tarragon, or ¼ tsp dried.*

Cook penne in boiling salted water until 'al dente' or tender but still firm.
DRESSING: Place ingredients in a screw-top jar and shake until creamy and well blended.

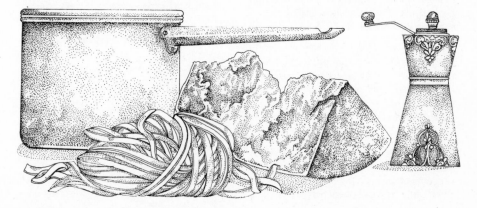

Drain penne and rinse under hot running water. Place in a bowl, toss with dressing and leave to cool. Add pepper, onion, celery, parsley and olives and toss again. Line a serving bowl with lettuce leaves and pile salad in middle. Separate tuna into chunks and arrange on top of salad with tomato quarters. Garnish with sprigs of parsley or watercress and serve at room temperature. Serves 6–8.

Seafood Salad

Any combination of seafood may be used in this salad, and rice, boiled for 14 minutes, may be substituted for the pasta.

125 g (4 oz) penne or other short tubular pasta; 1 tbsp curry powder; 500 g (1 lb) fresh mussels, scrubbed and steamed open; 250 g/8 oz (1 cup) cooked prawns (shrimp), shelled and deveined; 1 × 200 g/7 oz can tuna in oil, drained and flaked; 1 celery heart, or 1 head fennel, finely sliced; 1 red and 1 yellow or green pepper, cored, seeded and finely sliced; 75 g/2½ oz (½ cup) black (ripe) olives, stoned (pitted); salt and freshly ground black pepper.
CURRY AND HERB-FLAVOURED DRESSING: *1 tbsp red or white wine vinegar; 3 tbsp olive oil; 1 tbsp finely chopped fresh herbs (thyme, parsley, chives, oregano, basil); 1 tsp French (Dijon) mustard; 1 tbsp sour cream; ½ tsp curry powder; salt and freshly ground black pepper.*

Cook pasta in boiling salted water, flavoured with curry powder, until 'al dente' or tender but still firm to the bite. Drain well and cool. Remove mussels from their shells. In a salad bowl, combine pasta, mussels, prawns (shrimp) tuna, celery or fennel, peppers and olives. Season with salt and plenty of pepper.
CURRY AND HERB-FLAVOURED DRESSING: Whisk all ingredients together until well blended. Toss salad with dressing just before serving. Serves 4–6.
NOTE: This salad may be served on a bed of crisp curly endive (chicory).

Roquefort Salad

You can buy small portions of the lovely ewe's milk cheese of France. While it is a little expensive, this is an excellent way of enjoying its unique taste.

selection of salad greens (lettuce, chicory, endive); 1 clove garlic, halved; salt; 4 tbsp olive oil; 1 tbsp cider vinegar; 1½ tbsp fresh lemon juice; ¼ tsp freshly ground black pepper; 60 g/2 oz (½ cup) crumbled Roquefort cheese.

Rinse and dry greens, and crisp in refrigerator. Place greens in a salad bowl that has been rubbed with garlic. Add salt, oil, vinegar, lemon juice, pepper and Roquefort. Toss lightly. Serve at once. Serves 6.

Nut and Cheese Salad

3 tbsp Vinaigrette Dressing (page 358); 1 head lettuce, crisped and torn into pieces; 1 head chicory (endive) or tender sprigs curly endive (chicory); 2 tbsp chopped walnuts; 125 g/4 oz (1 cup) Gruyère cheese, diced.

Make vinaigrette in the salad bowl. Add lettuce, chicory (endive), cut in chunky pieces or leaves left whole if tiny, or endive (chicory), nuts and cheese. Just before serving toss lightly with dressing. Serves 4.

Fennel, Pear and Watercress Salad

Serve this salad in a large flattish dish.

2 tbsp wine vinegar; 1 tbsp French (Dijon) mustard; 1 tsp finely grated fresh ginger; salt and freshly ground black pepper; crushed garlic to taste; 4 tbsp olive oil; 1 tbsp walnut oil; 1 bunch watercress; 1 head fennel, finely sliced; 4 ripe pears, peeled, cored and sliced.

Place vinegar in a bowl with mustard, ginger, salt, pepper and garlic. Using a fork, gradually beat in olive and walnut oils until a thick dressing is formed. Place remaining ingredients in a serving dish, pour over dressing and toss together gently before serving. Serves 6–8.

Watercress and Violet Salad

1 bunch violets; 2 tbsp olive oil; 2 tsp wine vinegar; 1 tsp Grand Marnier; 1 bunch watercress; 2 tbsp chopped pecans.

Snip stems off violets. Place olive oil, vinegar and Grand Marnier in a screw-top jar and shake well to blend. Place watercress in salad bowl, top with violets and nuts, add dressing, toss and serve. Serves 6.

Beetroot Salad with Horseradish Sauce

370 g/12 oz (2 cups) diced cooked beetroot; 250 ml/8 fl oz (1 cup) sour cream; 2 tbsp single (light) cream; 2 tbsp lemon juice; 2 tbsp grated onion; 2 tbsp drained, grated, pickled horseradish; 1 tsp salt; 250 g/8 oz (2 cups) peeled and diced apple; 125 g/4 oz (1 cup) diced tender celery; few spring onions (scallions), cut into fine julienne (matchstick) strips, or snipped chives to garnish.

Combine diced beetroot with sour cream, cream, lemon juice, onion, horseradish and salt. Add diced apple and celery, then toss. Cover and chill for 1 hour before serving. Garnish with julienne of spring onions (scallions) or snipped chives. Serves 6–8.

Radish and Red Lettuce Salad

The red Italian lettuce (actually a type of chicory) called radiccio is called for in this recipe, but round (bibb) lettuce can be used instead.

2–3 heads red leaf lettuce or other soft-leaved lettuce, torn into bite-sized pieces; 8 radishes, finely sliced; 4 tbsp Vinaigrette Dressing made with lime juice (page 358); coarsely ground black pepper.

Combine lettuce and radishes in a bowl, drizzle dressing over and toss salad well. Divide salad between two salad bowls and sprinkle each serving with pepper. Serves 2.

Courgette Salad

4 tbsp olive oil; 4 spring onions (scallions), finely chopped; 500 g (1 lb) courgettes (zucchini), thinly sliced; 1 tsp paprika; ¼ tsp sugar; 1 tsp dill seeds or chopped fresh dill; 2 tbsp red or white wine vinegar; salt and freshly ground black pepper; chopped fresh dill to garnish.

Heat olive oil in a deep frying pan (skillet), add spring onions (scallions) and courgettes (zucchini) and sauté over gentle heat for 2–3 minutes or until courgettes (zucchini) are tender but still crisp. Add paprika, sugar, dill seeds or fresh dill, vinegar, salt and pepper. Toss through and cook 1 minute longer. Cool, then chill before serving, garnished with extra chopped fresh dill. Serves 4.

Spinach Salad with Yogurt

500 g (1 lb) fresh spinach, stems removed; 120 ml/4 fl oz (½ cup) plain yogurt; 1 clove garlic, crushed; salt and freshly ground black pepper.

Chop spinach roughly, then cook in covered saucepan, without any water except that which clings to leaves after washing, for about 5 minutes. Drain and cool, then squeeze out excess liquid. Combine yogurt and garlic and mix with spinach. Season with salt and pepper. Serves 4.

New Potato Salad

1 kg (2 lb) new potatoes; salt.
DRESSING: *2 tbsp vinegar; 1 tbsp French (Dijon) mustard; freshly ground black pepper; 6 tbsp olive oil; 10 g/⅓ oz (¼ cup) chopped mixed fresh herbs (parsley, chives, oregano and mint).*

Boil potatoes in their skins in boiling salted water until tender.
DRESSING: Place vinegar, mustard and pepper in a small bowl and gradually whisk in olive oil until thick. Stir in herbs and pour into salad bowl. Drain potatoes, then peel and chop. While potatoes are still warm, toss in dressing. Do not chill. Serves 6–8.

Right: Pissaladière Niçoise (page 296)
Overleaf: Preparation of Tortellini using Egg Pasta (page 267)

Avocado Salad

1 head round (bibb) lettuce; 1 avocado, peeled, stoned (pitted) and sliced.
DRESSING: *1 tbsp white wine vinegar; salt and freshly ground black pepper; 2 tbsp olive oil; few poppy seeds.*

DRESSING: Whisk vinegar, salt, pepper and oil together until well blended, then add poppy seeds. Pour dressing over lettuce and toss well. Add avocado and toss again gently, but avoid breaking avocado. Serves 4.

Curried Potato Salad

500 g (1 lb) small new potatoes; 120 ml/4 fl oz (½ cup) Vinaigrette Dressing (page 358); 120 ml/4 fl oz (½ cup) thick Mayonnaise (page 204).
CURRY MIXTURE: *1 shallot, or ½ small onion, sliced; 2 tbsp olive oil; 1 tbsp curry powder; 1 tsp paprika; 2 tsp tomato purée (paste); 120 ml/4 fl oz (½ cup) water; 1 slice lemon; 2 tsp apricot jam or redcurrant jelly.*

CURRY MIXTURE: In a small pan, quickly soften shallot or onion in oil, then add curry powder and paprika and cook for 1 minute stirring well. Add tomato purée (paste) mixed with water, lemon and ham or jelly. Cover and simmer for 7–10 minutes, then strain. Keep mixture in a small jar until wanted.

Boil potatoes in their skins. Drain, peel and toss them in dressing while still hot. Add enough curry mixture to flavour mayonnaise to taste. Put potatoes in a serving dish and coat with mayonnaise. Serves 4.

Polish Potato Salad

750 g (1½ lb) new potatoes; 2 tbsp white wine; 1 raw beetroot, peeled and finely grated; 1 tbsp grated horseradish; 3 tbsp Mayonnaise (page 204); pinch dry mustard; salt and freshly ground black pepper; 120 ml/4 fl oz (½ cup) plain yogurt.

Cook potatoes in their skins until tender, then peel while still hot and sprinkle with white wine. Allow to cool. Mix beetroot with horseradish and add to mayonnaise. Mix mustard, salt and pepper into yogurt and add this to beetroot mixture. Spoon this dressing over the potatoes and serve. Serves 4–6.

Russian Ham Salad

250 g (8 oz) cooked ham, thickly sliced and cubed; 3 large potatoes, cooked, peeled and cubed; 1 large crisp apple, cored and cubed; 4 sticks celery, finely chopped; 1 large dill pickle, or 4–5 gherkins, finely chopped; 250 ml/8 fl oz (1 cup) Mayonnaise

Preceding Page: Raised Pork Pie (page 292)
Left: Neapolitan Pizza (page 300)

(page 204); 2 tbsp chopped parsley; ½ tsp dried tarragon; salt; 1 small head lettuce.
GARNISH: *slices cooked beetroot; cubes unpeeled apple; onion rings.*

Place ham, potatoes, apple, celery and pickle in a bowl. Mix mayonnaise with parsley and tarragon, add to bowl and toss lightly. Taste and season with salt as required. Line a serving bowl with lettuce leaves and spoon salad into the middle. Garnish with beetroot, apple and onion rings and chill until serving time. Serves 4–6.

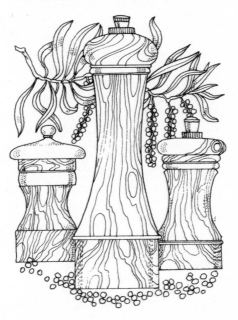

German Salad

4 medium potatoes; 2 frankfurters; 250 g (8 oz) Polish clobassi or kransky sausage; 4 ripe tomatoes, peeled and cut into wedges; ¼ small cabbage, finely shredded – about 370 g/12 oz (2 cups).
DRESSING: *1 tbsp red wine vinegar; ½ tsp sugar; pinch salt; pinch nutmeg; 1 large clove garlic, crushed; 1 tbsp German (mild) or French (Dijon) mustard; 4 tbsp salad oil; 1 tbsp snipped chives; 1 tbsp chopped parsley.*

Boil potatoes in their skins.
DRESSING: Mix together vinegar, sugar, salt, nutmeg, garlic and mustard. Gradually beat in oil, then stir in chives and parsley. Drain potatoes and peel when cool enough to handle. Cut into cubes, place in a large bowl, and pour dressing over while they are still warm. Cover frankfurters and clobassi with cold water, bring to the boil and simmer for 3 minutes. Allow to cool in the water, then drain and skin. Cut frankfurters into diagonal slices and clobassi into bite-sized cubes. Add frankfurters, clobassi, tomatoes and cabbage to bowl of potatoes, and mix lightly together with your hands. Taste and adjust seasoning. Serves 4.

German Potato Salad

For this salad marinate potato slices in boiling stock, then fold in sour cream or mayonnaise before serving.

6 medium potatoes; 1 onion, finely chopped; 300 ml/½ pint (1¼ cups) chicken stock; 4 tbsp white vinegar; 5 tbsp salad oil; 2 tsp prepared mustard; salt and freshly ground white pepper; 120 ml/4 fl oz (½ cup) sour cream; parsley or other fresh herbs to garnish.

Boil potatoes in their skins until just tender. Drain. Peel potatoes while still hot and cut into slices. Place in a bowl with onion. Bring stock to the boil with vinegar, and while boiling pour over potatoes. Leave to marinate until almost all liquid is absorbed, about 20–30 minutes. Pour off any excess liquid, then gently fold in oil mixed with mustard. Taste, and season with salt and pepper if necessary. Lastly, fold in sour cream. Serve at room temperature, garnished with parsley or other fresh herbs. Serves 8–10.

Potato and Ham Salad

500 g (1 lb) new or waxy potatoes; 6 sticks celery, cut into julienne (matchstick) strips; 120 ml/4 fl oz (½ cup) double (heavy) cream; salt and freshly ground white pepper; 1 tbsp lemon juice; 1 thick slice cooked ham, cut into thin strips; 2 tbsp chopped mixed fresh herbs (parsley, chives, mint, chervil).

Boil potatoes in their skins in salted water until just tender. Drain and, when cool, peel and cut into thick slices. Add celery. Whip cream until thick, season well with salt and pepper and stir in lemon juice. Add to potato and celery and mix gently but thoroughly. Arrange in a salad bowl. Sprinkle ham strips and herbs over salad. Chill. Serves 4.

Rice Salad

210 g/7 oz (1 cup) long-grain rice; 90 g/3 oz (¾ cup) button mushrooms, sliced; 1 cucumber, peeled, seeded and diced; 6 crisp radishes, finely sliced; 3 slices fresh or canned pineapple, diced; salt and freshly ground black pepper; 2 ripe tomatoes, quartered, to garnish.
DRESSING: *1 clove garlic, crushed; 1 tsp dry mustard; ½ tsp salt; 2 tbsp wine vinegar; 6 tbsp olive oil; 20 g/⅔ oz (½ cup) finely chopped parsley.*

Cook rice in plenty of boiling salted water for 15 minutes. Drain well. Mix with remaining ingredients except tomatoes.
DRESSING: Combine ingredients, pour over rice salad and mix together. Cover and chill until needed. At serving time, bring to room temperature, adjust seasoning, and garnish with tomatoes. Serves 4.

Persian Rice Salad

A rather different rice salad to serve with roast lamb, kebabs or curries.

370 g/12 oz (1¾ cups) long-grain rice; 2 slices fresh ginger, finely chopped; 1 tsp ground coriander; 1 tsp ground cumin; ½ tsp nutmeg; 6 spring onions (scallions), finely chopped (including some green tops); 90 g/3 oz (½ cup) each raisins and sultanas (golden raisins), soaked in boiling water for 5 minutes and drained; 1 tbsp grated orange rind; 6 ripe apricots, stoned (pitted) and finely sliced; 60 g/2 oz (½ cup) toasted pine nuts; about 120 ml/4 fl oz (½ cup) olive oil; salt and freshly ground black pepper.
GARNISH: *fresh or canned apricot halves; pine nuts.*

Cook rice in plenty of boiling salted water for 15 minutes. Drain well. Place warm rice in a large bowl and add remaining ingredients, seasoning with salt and pepper. You need just enough oil to moisten rice without making it mushy, so add it gradually. Serve salad warm or at room temperature, garnished with apricot halves and pine nuts. Serves 6–8.

Spanish Salad

355 g/11½ oz (1⅔ cups) long-grain rice; ½ tsp saffron powder or good pinch crumbled saffron; 4 green peppers; 75 g/2½ oz (½ cup) each black (ripe) and green olives, stoned (pitted); 1 × 200 g/7 oz can tuna, drained and flaked; 250 g/8 oz (1 cup) cooked prawns (shrimp), shelled and deveined; 3 rashers (slices) bacon, rind removed, grilled (broiled) until crisp and crumbled; salt and freshly ground black pepper; soft round (bibb) lettuce.
DRESSING: *1 tbsp lemon juice; 4 tbsp olive oil; salt and freshly ground black pepper; grated rind ½ lemon; 1 clove garlic, crushed; 1 tbsp chopped fresh basil.*

Cook rice in plenty of boiling salted water, with saffron, for 15 minutes. Drain. Char peppers all over under a preheated grill

(broiler), place in a paper bag to steam for 10 minutes then rub off skins under cold running water. Remove skins, core and seeds and cut into strips. Add to rice with olives, tuna, prawns (shrimp) and bacon. Season salad with salt and pepper while rice is still warm.
DRESSING: Combine all ingredients in a screw-top jar and shake well. Pour over salad and toss. Serve cold on a bed of lettuce. Serves 4.

Rice, Prawn and Almond Salad

105 g/3½ oz (½ cup) long-grain rice; 1 large onion, finely chopped; 30 g/1 oz (2 tbsp) butter; 250 g/8 oz (1 cup) prawns (shrimp), cooked, shelled, deveined and chopped; 60 g/2 oz (½ cup) almonds, blanched and slivered; 120 ml/4 fl oz (½ cup) Vinaigrette Dressing (page 358).

Cook rice in plenty of boiling salted water for 15 minutes. Drain well. Cook onion in butter until soft. Add to rice with prawns (shrimp) and almonds. Stir in dressing. Serve salad in a bowl or hors d'oeuvre dish. Serves 4.

Italian Rice Salad

105 g/3½ oz (½ cup) long-grain rice; 6–8 button mushrooms, quartered; 2 tbsp water; squeeze lemon juice; 4 firm, ripe tomatoes, peeled, seeded and cut into thin wedges; 4–6 black (ripe) olives, halved and stoned (pitted); salt and freshly ground black pepper; 2–3 tbsp Vinaigrette Dressing (made with dry white wine instead of vinegar, page 358).

Cook rice in plenty of boiling salted water for 15 minutes. Drain well and dry. Cook mushrooms in water with lemon juice for 2–3 minutes. Cook quickly, uncovered, so that liquid is well reduced by the time mushrooms are cooked; shake pan and stir well. Add mushrooms to rice with tomatoes and olives. Mix with a fork, season well and moisten with dressing. Serves 4.

Provençal Salad

A richly flavoured salad combining the flavours and colours of the Mediterranean.

1 head round (bibb) lettuce; 4 hard-boiled (hard-cooked) eggs, quartered; 1 × 200 g/ 7 oz can tuna, drained and flaked; 8 small new potatoes, cooked, peeled and sliced; 1 green, yellow or red pepper, cored, seeded and sliced; 2 tbsp black (ripe) olives, stoned (pitted); 6 ripe egg tomatoes, or 4 ripe tomatoes, quartered; 3 anchovy fillets, finely chopped; 1 tbsp grated Parmesan cheese.
DRESSING: *1 tbsp wine vinegar (preferably red); 3 tbsp good olive oil; 1 clove garlic, crushed; 1 tsp mustard flavoured with Provençal herbs, or French (Dijon) mustard;*

1 sprig fresh thyme, finely chopped (if available); salt and freshly ground black pepper.

Make a bed of lettuce leaves in a salad bowl. On this, arrange hard-boiled (hard-cooked) eggs, tuna, potatoes, pepper, olives, tomatoes and anchovy fillets. Chill. Sprinkle with cheese.
DRESSING: Shake ingredients in a screw-top jar until well combined. Spoon dressing over salad just before serving and toss at the table. Serves 4.

Green Bean Salad

Use tender, plump stringless beans or runner (snake) beans for this salad. Serve as a first course or as an accompaniment to meats.

750 g (1½ lb) young green beans; salt and freshly ground black pepper; 2–3 tbsp wine vinegar; ½ tsp French (Dijon) mustard; 6–8 tbsp olive oil; lettuce leaves; 6–8 spring onions (scallions), shredded; 2 tbsp finely chopped parsley.

Cook green beans in boiling salted water until they are barely tender. Meanwhile, beat together vinegar, mustard and oil and season with salt and pepper. Drain beans and toss immediately while still warm in dressing. Chill. When ready to serve, line a salad bowl or rectangular hors d'oeuvre dish with lettuce leaves. Add bean salad and sprinkle with spring onions (scallions) and parsley. Serves 4–6.

Bacon and Egg Lentil Salad

500 g/1 lb (2 cups) red or brown lentils; 1 large onion, studded with 2 cloves; 1 bay leaf; 1 tbsp salt; 3 cloves garlic, bruised; 1 strip orange rind; 20 g/⅔ oz (½ cup) chopped parsley; 125 g/4 oz (1 cup) finely chopped spring onions (scallions) including some green tops; 120 ml/4 fl oz (½ cup) olive oil; 1 tsp red wine vinegar; 1 tbsp lemon juice; freshly ground black pepper; 2 rashers (slices) bacon, rind removed, grilled (broiled) until crisp and crumbled.
GARNISH: *2 hard-boiled (hard-cooked) eggs, finely chopped; 10 g/⅓ oz (¼ cup) chopped parsley; 12–15 black (ripe) olives.*

Place lentils in a saucepan and cover with cold water. Bring slowly to the boil, then remove from heat, cover and stand for 1 hour. Drain and cover with fresh cold water to come 5 cm (2 in) above lentils. Add onion stuck with cloves, bay leaf, salt, garlic and orange rind. Bring to the boil, then cover and simmer until just tender, about 20–30 minutes. Drain and cool. Remove flavouring ingredients and discard them. Put lentils into a bowl and toss gently with parsley, spring onions (scallions), oil, vinegar and lemon juice. Let stand, covered, for 1 hour. Taste and adjust seasoning if necessary. Cover and keep cool but not refrigerated until ready to serve. Toss bacon gently through lentils. Spoon salad into a serving dish and garnish with eggs, parsley and olives. Serves 8.

Three Bean Salad

340 g/11 oz (1 cup) dried red kidney beans; 210 g/7 oz (1 cup) dried haricot (navy) beans; 180 g/6 oz (1 cup) dried butter beans; 1.5 litres/2½ pints (6 cups) chicken stock; 3 bay leaves; 3 sprigs parsley; 1 onion, halved; 3 whole cloves; 18 black peppercorns; 3 tsp salt; 1 red pepper, cored, seeded and diced; 6 spring onions (scallions), sliced; 175 ml/6 fl oz (¾ cup) Vinaigrette Dressing (page 358); chopped parsley to garnish.

Soak kidney, haricot (navy) and butter beans separately overnight in water to cover. Next day drain and put in separate saucepans. Put 500 ml/18 fl oz (2 cups) stock, 1 bay leaf, 1 parsley sprig, ⅓ onion, 1 clove, 6 peppercorns and 1 tsp salt in each pan and bring to the boil. Simmer until beans are tender, about 1¼ hours for kidney beans and 1½ hours for haricot (navy) and butter beans. Drain, removing seasonings, and chill. Combine all beans, diced pepper and spring onions (scallions) in a large serving bowl. Toss with vinaigrette dressing and sprinkle with chopped parsley. Serves 6–8.

Broccoli Salad

2–3 heads broccoli; salt; 120 ml/4 fl oz (½ cup) dry white wine; 4 tbsp olive oil; 5 shallots, chopped; 2 tbsp chopped parsley; 2 cloves garlic, crushed; juice 2 lemons; 2 tsp fresh thyme or ½ tsp dried; 1 tbsp black peppercorns.

Pull off leaves from broccoli, cut off tough base of stems, and pare stems with a vegetable peeler. Cook in boiling salted water for 10 minutes. Rinse under cold water and drain. Cut into 5 cm (2 in) pieces. Put wine, oil, shallots, parsley, garlic, lemon juice, thyme and peppercorns in a saucepan, cover and simmer for 20 minutes. Add broccoli and cook, uncovered, for 2 minutes more (broccoli should still be slightly crisp). Adjust seasoning and pour into a dish. Serve at room temperature or chilled. Serves 6.

Aubergine Salad

1 large aubergine (eggplant).
DRESSING: *2 cloves garlic, chopped; 4 tbsp red wine vinegar; 5 tbsp olive oil; 5 tbsp vegetable oil; 15 g/½ oz (⅓ cup) chopped fresh parsley; chopped fresh dill; salt and freshly ground black pepper.*
GARNISH: *1 onion, chopped; 1 small red pepper, cored, seeded and diced.*

Bake aubergine (eggplant) wrapped in foil, in a preheated moderately hot oven

(200°C/400°F, Gas Mark 6) for 40 minutes or until it is tender. Unwrap and let it cool on a wire rack. Peel and dice flesh, and arrange it in a serving dish.
DRESSING: In a food processor fitted with a steel blade or in a blender, purée garlic, vinegar, oils, parsley, dill, salt and pepper until smooth. Toss aubergine (eggplant) with dressing, and garnish salad with onion and pepper. Chill salad, covered, for 2 hours, and serve with Italian bread. Serves 4–6.

Coleslaw with Sour Cream

½ medium cabbage, finely shredded; 4 tbsp Mayonnaise (page 204); 1 tbsp French (Dijon) mustard; 2 tbsp chopped celery; dash Tabasco (hot pepper) sauce; 175 ml/6 fl oz (¾ cup) sour cream; ½ red pepper, cored, seeded and finely sliced; ½ green pepper, cored, seeded and finely sliced; 3–4 tbsp finely chopped spring onions (scallions).

Put cabbage in a large salad bowl. Combine remaining ingredients, pour over cabbage, toss thoroughly and chill well before serving. Serves 6.

Waldorf Coleslaw

1 small cabbage, shredded; 4 spring onions (scallions), chopped (including some green tops); 2 sticks celery, chopped; 1 green pepper, cored, seeded and chopped; 1 tart eating apple, cored and chopped; 90 g/3 oz (½ cup) sultanas (golden raisins); 120 ml/ 4 fl oz (½ cup) Mayonnaise (page 204) or sour cream; 60 g/2 oz (½ cup) walnut pieces.
DRESSING: *1 tbsp wine vinegar; salt and freshly ground black pepper; 2 tsp French (Dijon) mustard; 2½ tbsp oil.*

Put cabbage, spring onions (scallions), celery, green pepper and apple into salad bowl and add sultanas (golden raisins). Whisk together dressing ingredients. Add to bowl and mix lightly. Cover and refrigerate for 2–3 hours. At serving time, add mayonnaise or sour cream, sprinkle with walnuts and toss. Serves 8.

Mixed Coleslaw

¼ red cabbage, finely shredded; ¼ white cabbage, finely shredded; ½ red pepper, cored, seeded and finely sliced; ½ bunch radishes, sliced; 120 ml/4 fl oz (½ cup) Vinaigrette Dressing (page 358); chopped parsley to garnish.

Bring a large saucepan of water to the boil and add red cabbage. Stir vigorously for 1 minute, then drain immediately in a colander. Rinse cabbage under cold running water to set colour and cool. Leave to drain, then pat red cabbage with a cloth to dry. Put in a large salad bowl with white cabbage, red pepper and radishes. Toss well with dressing

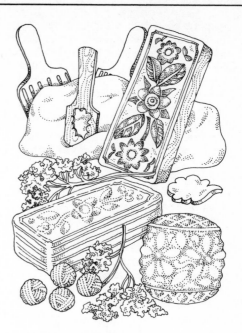

S

and sprinkle salad with parsley before serving. Serves 8.
VARIATION
Creamy Mixed Slaw: Prepare as above, but add 120 ml/4 fl oz (½ cup) sour cream or Mayonnaise (see page 204) with the dressing).

SALAD DRESSINGS

The sauce for a salad may be a simple dressing of oil and vinegar, a creamy, thick mayonnaise, or it may be one of the imaginative variations of these two great basics. Whether simple or intricate, all good dressings have one thing in common: they must be made with the freshest and choicest ingredients available.

Vinaigrette Dressing (oil, lemon juice, vinegar, herbs) can be varied in a multitude of ways, by changing the herbs used, or using different oils and vinegars. And the best quality oil and vinegar you can afford, the freshest eggs you can find, and garden herbs freshly picked, will make a world of difference to the quality of the dressings you make.

Among the oils, there's olive oil, or a wide choice of nut oils (walnut, almond, or peanut), or those made from seeds (sunflower, safflower or sesame) – all have their uses. Like wine, it's worth shopping around for the one that really suits your palate.

Vinegars, too, should be explored. A harsh vinegar will still taste harsh in a dressing. Look for the different flavours – tarragon, wine, or cider.

Vinaigrette or French Dressing

The most widely used dressing in the world is the basic oil-and-vinegar dressing of France – a mixture of good olive oil, wine vinegar, salt and freshly ground black pepper. Add a dollop of good prepared French (Dijon) mustard, if you like it, or a little hot powdered English mustard. Fresh herbs in season are added to suit the food the dressing is going to flavour and season. Garlic is used by those who like the flavour, and features in more robust salads. Be sure the salad greens are perfectly dry, so that the dressing will adhere to the leaves.

The usual proportion of oil to vinegar is three parts to one, but this can be varied to suit your own taste. Some salads call for a dressing where the oil is only lightly spiked with vinegar. If you find the one in three proportion too oily, add salt rather than increase the vinegar to cut the oiliness.

A squeeze of lemon juice is sometimes added at the last moment. Cider vinegar, red wine vinegar or any of the flavoured vinegars, such as tarragon, are excellent.

The choice of oil can vary. A good olive oil is the choice of many. Walnut oil has a distinctive taste and is good on tender green salads; it can also be used in combination with olive oil. The polyunsaturated oils are increasing in popularity. **See recipes.**

See also *Mayonnaise* and *Green Goddess Dressing*.

Vinaigrette Dressing

2 tbsp good vinegar; ¼ tsp salt; 1 tsp French (Dijon) mustard; freshly ground black pepper; 6 tbsp olive oil; pinch caster sugar (optional).

Put vinegar into a small bowl with salt, mustard and pepper. Mix well with a fork or balloon whisk, then slowly add oil, beating until mixture thickens slightly. If dressing tastes sharp, add more oil or a pinch of caster sugar. If dressing is too oily for your taste, add more salt – this cuts oiliness. An alternative method is to combine all ingredients in a screw-top jar and shake well until mixture thickens. The main drawback to this method is the tendency to re-use the jar over and over, even adding little quantities of dressing left over. Makes about 175 ml/ 6 fl oz (¾ cup).

VARIATIONS

Garlic Vinaigrette Dressing: There are several ways to add garlic to your dressing. If you like a pungent dressing, crush 1–2 cloves garlic to a paste with salt, add vinegar, mustard and pepper and then oil. You can chop garlic and add it to the finished dressing for a more rustic salad. For a more delicate flavour, bruise peeled garlic clove and steep in the vinegar for 1–2 hours. The vinegar brings out a more delicate flavour of the garlic, while oil brings out the stronger flavour.

Mustard Vinaigrette Dressing: Increase the amount of French (Dijon) mustard to taste, or add 1 tsp English mustard instead.

French Herb Vinaigrette Dressing: When adding herbs it is best to sprinkle half of the

freshly chopped herbs over the salad, and add the remaining herbs to the dressing. Tarragon, basil, chives and parsley add their own distinctive flavour. They may be used separately or in combination. 1–2 tbsp chopped fresh herbs is sufficient for this quantity of Vinaigrette.

Fines Herbes Vinaigrette

1 tbsp tarragon vinegar; 4 tbsp dry red wine; 1 tsp French (Dijon) mustard; 1 tsp salt; 1 tsp paprika; ½ tsp freshly ground black pepper; 1 tsp finely chopped fresh basil, marjoram or oregano; 20 g/⅔ oz (½ cup) chopped parsley; 2 cloves garlic, crushed; 120 ml/4 fl oz (½ cup) olive oil.

Combine all ingredients and beat well with fork or whisk, or shake well in a screw-top jar. Use over salad greens or sliced tomatoes, or as a dressing for lightly cooked vegetables. Makes 250 ml/8 fl oz (1 cup).

Green Mayonnaise

60 g/2 oz (1 cup) fresh watercress; 2 leaves spinach; 10 g/⅓ oz (¼ cup) fresh tarragon, chervil or parsley; 1 tsp lemon juice; 250 ml/ 8 fl oz (1 cup) Mayonnaise (page 204).

Simmer greens in unsalted water 2 minutes. Drain and rinse in cold water. Press out water, then pound in mortar until greens are reduced to a pulp, or purée in blender. Add lemon juice and combine mixture with mayonnaise. Use with vegetable or fish salads. Makes 350 ml/12 fl oz (1½ cups).

Yogurt Mayonnaise

This is sometimes referred to as eggless mayonnaise. It is the one to use when on a low cholesterol or slimming diet.

3 tsp French (Dijon) mustard; 1½ tbsp olive oil; 175 ml/6 fl oz (¾ cup) low fat plain yogurt; 1 tbsp lemon juice; salt and freshly ground white pepper.

Place mustard in a mixing bowl. Add oil gradually, beating vigorously with a fork or whisk. Blend in yogurt. Add remaining ingredients until mixture is smooth. Refrigerate until required. Makes 250 ml/8 fl oz (1 cup).

Sauce Verte

This very green, herby sauce is a favourite in France and Italy. It is served with chilled seafood, hot boiled beef and some salads, or can be folded through 250 g/8 oz (2 cups) cooked rice to make an interesting rice salad.

40 g/1⅓ oz (1 cup) parsley; 1 tbsp chopped onion; 30 g/1 oz (¼ cup) capers; ½ × 50 g/1⅔ oz can anchovy fillets, drained; 1–2 cloves garlic; 2 small sour gherkins; 1 small boiled potato, or 1 slice white bread, softened in water and drained; 120 ml/4 fl oz

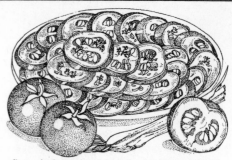

(½ cup) olive oil; salt and freshly ground black pepper; 1 tbsp wine vinegar.

Chop together very finely (or chop in blender or food processor fitted with steel blade), first parsley, then onion, capers, anchovies, garlic and gherkins. Add potato or bread and mix until a coarse, dry, green paste is formed. Place mixture in a bowl and work in just enough oil (about 1 tsp) to form a slightly thinner but smooth paste. Add salt and pepper. Continue to add remaining oil slowly, mixing constantly until paste is of a smooth consistency. Add vinegar and mix thoroughly. Makes 350 ml/12 fl oz (1½ cups).

Buttermilk Dressing

250 ml/8 fl oz (1 cup) buttermilk; 3 tbsp lemon or lime juice; ½ tsp French (Dijon) mustard; ½ tsp paprika; salt and freshly ground white pepper; pinch sugar.

Combine all ingredients in a screw-top jar and shake well. Good with egg and cheese salads. Makes about 300 ml/½ pint (1¼ cups).

Sour Cream and Horseradish Sauce

Serve with cold smoked fish or cold beef.

250 ml/8 fl oz (1 cup) single (light) cream soured with 1 tsp lemon juice, or plain yogurt; 6 spring onions (scallions), chopped; 2 tbsp grated horseradish; 1 tsp French (Dijon) mustard; salt and freshly ground black pepper.

Combine all ingredients in a bowl, mixing thoroughly. Makes 350 ml/12 fl oz (1½ cups).

Old-Fashioned Cooked Salad Dressing

Use this in the same way as Mayonnaise, and use the same variations (see page 204).

1 tbsp sugar; 1½ tbsp flour; 1 tsp salt; 2 tsp dry mustard; 2 egg yolks; 60 g/2 oz (4 tbsp) butter, melted; 350 ml/12 fl oz (1½ cups) milk; 5 tbsp vinegar; dash paprika (optional).

Combine dry ingredients in top of double saucepan (double boiler) or a heatproof bowl which will fit over a saucepan. Add egg yolks, butter and milk and blend well. Gradually stir in vinegar. Cook over simmering water, stirring constantly, until thick. Add paprika if desired. Makes about 500 ml/18 fl oz (2 cups).

SALMON

Fresh salmon is considered one of the great fish delicacies of the world; it is beautifully coloured, the pale pink flesh is both firm and succulent, the flavour unique.

Salmon are caught in the northern hemisphere, and many people consider the very best are those from the rivers of Scotland and Ireland. Excellent varieties are also caught in Norway, Canada and along the North American West Coast. In northern Europe, fresh salmon can be purchased whole or in steaks. There is no substitute for fresh salmon, cooked to perfection, but sometimes frozen steaks are available from good speciality delicatessens and fishmongers in those parts of the world where it is not available fresh.

Canned Salmon: Probably the most familiar type, and enormous amounts are processed every year. One of the most sought-after varieties is sockeye salmon, considered outstanding for canning because of its rich red and very firm flesh.

Smoked Salmon: A superb delicacy. Wafer-thin slices of smoked salmon may be served with lemon wedges and brown bread and butter, with cream cheese and bagels, or on rye bread with sour cream. Smoked salmon lends a touch of luxury to homely scrambled egg, transforming it into a dish for a prince – try it for a special brunch with fine champagne. Choose smoked salmon that has pale pink-gold flesh and is as fresh as possible. A dark red or a deep orange colour usually means a dye or over-cured fish. It may be bought freshly sliced from a whole side of salmon, or ready sliced and vacuum-packed. Smoked salmon is also available canned or in pieces in jars.

Salmon Trout are closely related to trout but feed in the sea and spawn in fresh water. They are found in northern Europe and combine the beautiful flavour and pink-coloured flesh of salmon with the texture of trout. They may be prepared and served in the same way as salmon. **See recipes.**

Poached Salmon

Probably the finest way to serve fresh salmon. May be served hot or cold.

1 × 1 kg (2 lb) salmon steak; 1.1 litres/1 pint 18 fl oz (4½ cups) water; juice ½ lemon; 250 ml/8 fl oz (1 cup) white wine; 1 tsp salt; 6 black peppercorns; 1 bouquet garni (sprig thyme, bay leaf, sprig parsley and stick celery).

Tie fish into shape carefully with white tape, but not tightly as the fish swells during cooking, or wrap in muslin. Place in a shallow flameproof dish. Combine remaining ingredients in a saucepan and bring to just below simmering point. Pour this court bouillon over fish and bring just to the boil. Reduce heat to low, cover dish and poach (the liquid should just shiver throughout cooking – do not let it boil or the delicate flesh will spoil). Continue poaching for 20–30 minutes or until fish flakes easily when tested with a fine skewer. Drain fish, remove skin and serve with parsley, buttered new potatoes and Hollandaise Sauce (see page 369). Serves 6–8.

NOTE: If fish is to be served cold, allow to cool in liquid before skinning. Serve with potato and cucumber salads and Mayonnaise (see page 204) or sour cream.

Grilled Salmon Steaks

4 salmon steaks, cut 2 cm (¾ in) thick; 2 tbsp freshly ground black pepper; juice ½ lemon; 60 g/2 oz (4 tbsp) Maître d'Hôtel Butter (page 49).

Put fish in a glass or earthenware dish. Combine remaining ingredients, except maître d'hôtel butter, and pour over fish. Leave to marinate for about 1 hour, turning steaks several times. Drain fish and place on oiled grill (broiler) rack. Cook under a preheated grill (broiler) for 5 minutes on each side and then a further 2 minutes on each side. Spread ⅓ of maître d'hôtel butter on a warm dish – butter should soften not melt. Remove skin and centre bone from steaks, arrange on prepared dish and place ¼ remaining maître d'hôtel butter on top of each steak. Serves 4.

Smoked Salmon Open Sandwiches

sprigs fresh dill, cress or lettuce leaves; 2 slices rye or black bread; butter; 4–6 slices smoked salmon; 2 slices lemon to garnish; 2 tbsp sour cream.

Place chilled dill, cress or lettuce on buttered rye or black bread. Fold slices smoked salmon and place on top. Garnish with lemon slices and top with sour cream. Serves 1–2.

Scrambled Egg with Smoked Salmon

For a special brunch, serve this elegant dish with hot croissants or champagne.

6 eggs; salt and freshly ground black pepper; 60 g/2 oz (4 tbsp) butter; 125 g (4 oz) smoked salmon, flaked; 3 tbsp single (light) cream; 4 tbsp Mayonnaise (page 204) or double (heavy) cream; 2 tsp snipped fresh dill; 4 slices smoked salmon; sprigs fresh dill to garnish.

Beat eggs and season with salt and pepper. Cook gently in butter, stirring, until set. Fold in flaked smoked salmon and single (light) cream. Allow to cool a little. Serve piled on a dish, with mayonnaise or double (heavy) cream spooned over and sprinkled with snipped dill. Fold slices of smoked salmon and garnish dish with these and sprigs of fresh dill. Serves 4.

Salmon and Potato Bake

A lunch or supper dish to serve with a green salad.

60 g/2 oz (4 tbsp) butter; 3 tbsp flour; ½ tsp salt; freshly ground black pepper; 500 ml/18 fl oz (2 cups) milk; 1 × 440 g (14 oz) can salmon, drained; 750 g (1½ lb) sliced cooked potatoes; 120 ml/4 fl oz (½ cup) Mayonnaise (page 204); 125 g/4 oz (1 cup) grated Cheddar cheese; 1 tsp Worcestershire sauce; ½ tsp French (Dijon) mustard; paprika.

Melt butter in a saucepan and blend in flour, salt and pepper. Gradually add milk off heat, then cook, stirring constantly, until thickened. Remove any bones and skin from salmon and flake. Stir into sauce. Arrange in alternate layers with potatoes in a shallow ovenproof dish. Combine mayonnaise, 60 g/2 oz (½ cup) cheese, Worcestershire sauce and mustard. Spread over salmon mixture. Top with remaining grated cheese and sprinkle with paprika. Bake in a preheated moderate oven (180°C/350°F, Gas Mark 4) for about 30 minutes until golden. Serves 4.

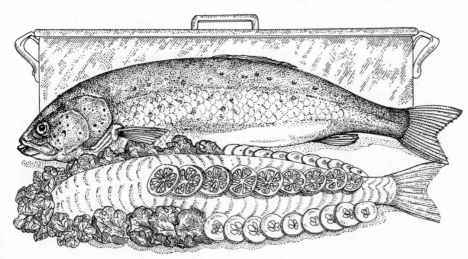

Smoked Salmon with Cucumber

120 ml/4 fl oz (½ cup) sour cream; 2 tbsp cider vinegar; 1 tbsp snipped chives; ½ tsp snipped fresh dill; ½ tsp salt; ¼ tsp pepper; 2 medium cucumbers, peeled and finely sliced; 6 slices pumpernickel bread; butter; 125 g (4 oz) smoked salmon, sliced.

Mix sour cream, vinegar, chives, dill, salt and pepper. Pour over cucumbers and mix. Cover and chill for 2–3 hours. Spread pumpernickel with butter and put a slice of smoked salmon on each piece. Top with cucumber mixture and serve as an appetizer. Serves 6.

Salmon Cakes

500 g/1 lb (2 cups) mashed potatoes; 60 g/2 oz (4 tbsp) butter; 1 tbsp finely chopped onion or chives; 1 × 220 g (7 oz) can salmon or tuna, drained; 1 tsp lemon juice; salt and freshly ground black pepper; 30 g/1 oz (¼ cup) flour; 1 egg, beaten; 30 g/1 oz (½ cup) dry breadcrumbs; oil or butter for frying.

Beat mashed potatoes with butter and onion. Remove any bones and skin from fish and flake. Combine with potatoes and lemon juice, and season with salt and pepper. Form into 6 small cakes. Dip in flour, then egg, then in breadcrumbs. Fry in a little oil or butter until nicely browned. Serve with Sauce Tartare (see page 205), if liked. Serves 4.

Salmon Puffs

1 × 440 g (14 oz) can salmon, drained; 30 g/1 oz (½ cup) fresh white breadcrumbs; 2 tbsp grated onion; 1 tbsp lemon juice; 30 g/1 oz (2 tbsp) butter, melted; salt and freshly ground black pepper; 1 egg; 120 ml/4 fl oz (½ cup) milk; sour cream; snipped chives.

Remove any bones and skin from fish and flake. Combine salmon, breadcrumbs, onion, lemon juice, butter, salt and pepper. Beat egg and add milk. Stir into salmon mixture. Place in 4–6 well-greased individual ramekin dishes. Set dishes in a baking tin (pan) with

water to come halfway up the sides and bake in a preheated moderate oven (180°C/ 350°F, Gas Mark 4) for about 45 minutes or until set and golden. Top each with a spoonful of sour cream and sprinkle with snipped chives. Serves 4.

Salmon Soufflé

1 × 220 g (7 oz) can salmon; milk; 60 g/2 oz (4 tbsp) butter; 30 g/1 oz (¼ cup) flour; ¼ tsp dry mustard; salt; cayenne; 6 eggs, separated; 1 tbsp chopped parsley.

Drain salmon, reserving liquid. Remove any bones and skin from fish and flake. Add enough milk to reserved liquid to make 250 ml/8 fl oz (1 cup). Melt butter in a saucepan and blend in flour, mustard, salt and cayenne. Gradually add milk mixture and cook over medium heat, stirring constantly, until it boils and thickens. Beat egg yolks until pale and thick. Stir a little of the hot sauce into yolks, then add to remaining sauce in pan. Remove from heat. Fold in salmon and parsley. Beat egg whites until they hold soft peaks. Stir 1 tbsp of beaten egg whites into salmon and parsley mixture then gently and quickly fold in remaining whites. Pour into a well-greased 1.5 litre/2½ pint (6 cup) soufflé dish (see *Soufflé* for preparation of dish). Bake in a preheated moderate oven (180°C/350°F, Gas Mark 4) for 45 minutes or until firm. Serve immediately. Serves 4.

Salmon Potato Salad

1 × 440 g (14 oz) can salmon, drained; 125 g/4 oz (1 cup) sliced celery; 370 g/12 oz (1½ cups) cubed cooked potatoes; 60 g/2 oz (½ cup) peeled, seeded and cubed cucumber; salt and freshly ground black pepper; 1 tbsp horseradish relish; 1 tbsp grated onion; 175 ml/6 fl oz (¾ cup) Mayonnaise (page 204).

Remove any bones and skin from fish and flake. Add celery, potatoes, cucumber, salt and pepper. Cover and chill 1–2 hours. Combine horseradish, grated onion and mayonnaise and fold gently through salad just before serving. Serves 4.

Italian Salmon Salad

150 g/5 oz (1¼ cups) pasta bows; 1 × 220 g (7 oz) can salmon, drained and flaked; 1 red pepper, cored, seeded and diced; ½ cucumber, finely diced; 10 black (ripe) olives, stoned (pitted); 120 ml/4 fl oz (½ cup) Vinaigrette Dressing (page 358); watercress to garnish.

Cook pasta in boiling water until 'al dente'. Drain thoroughly and leave to cool. Mix flaked salmon with the pepper, cucumber, olives and pasta. Pour over the dressing and toss lightly. Arrange in a serving dish and garnish with sprigs of watercress. Serves 4.

Salmon Pâté

1 × 220 g (7 oz) can salmon; 2 tsp anchovy essence (extract) or paste; 90 g/3 oz (6 tbsp) butter, softened; juice ½ lemon; 1 tbsp Worcestershire sauce; freshly ground black pepper.

Drain and remove bones and skin from salmon. Place in a bowl with remaining ingredients, mashing well with a fork to form a paste. Pack pâté into a small bowl and serve immediately, or chill in the refrigerator. Makes 250 g/8 oz (1 cup).

Salmon Kedgeree

210 g/7 oz (1 cup) long-grain rice; 1 × 440 g (14 oz) can salmon; 60 g/2 oz (4 tbsp) butter; 2 hard-boiled (hard-cooked) eggs, finely chopped; 2–3 tbsp single (light) cream; salt and freshly ground black pepper; pinch cayenne; 1 tbsp chopped parsley.

Cook rice in boiling salted water until tender, drain well. Keep hot over boiling water or in a cool oven. Remove bones and skin from salmon and flake gently. Melt butter in a saucepan, add salmon, eggs, cream, salt and pepper and stir until hot. Combine fish mixture with hot rice and add parsley. Turn into a serving dish and serve. Serves 5–6.

Smoked Salmon and Dill Dip

250 g/8 oz (1 cup) cream cheese, softened; 5 tbsp single (light) cream; 2 tbsp lemon juice; 1 tbsp grated horseradish; 90 g/3 oz (½ cup) smoked salmon, finely chopped; 1 tbsp snipped fresh dill, or 1 tbsp chopped parsley mixed with ½ tsp dill seeds; salt and freshly ground black pepper; cayenne; sprigs fresh dill or parsley to garnish.

Stir cream cheese with a wooden spoon until smooth, then stir in sour cream, lemon juice and horseradish and combine thoroughly. Fold in smoked salmon, dill, salt, pepper and cayenne. Spoon into a serving bowl and garnish with sprigs of dill or parsley. Makes about 370 g/12 oz (1½ cups).

S

Salmon Delight

*1 × 220 g/7 oz can (1 cup) salmon, drained;
250 g (8 oz) flat noodles, tagliatelle or
macaroni; 90 g/3 oz (6 tbsp) butter; 6 spring
onions (scallions), finely chopped (including
some green tops); 3 ripe tomatoes, peeled
and chopped; salt and freshly ground black
pepper; grated cheese (optional).*

Remove skin and bones from salmon, and
separate into large flakes. Cook noodles in
boiling salted water until tender. Drain. Heat
butter in a large, heavy saucepan and gently
fry spring onions (scallions) for 2–3 minutes
or until they soften. Add tomatoes and stir
for another minute. Add noodles and
salmon and toss gently together for a few
minutes until heated through. Season with
salt and pepper. Spoon on to a serving
platter and, if wished, sprinkle with grated
Parmesan or Cheddar cheese. Serves 4.

SALSIFY

A white-skinned root vegetable, sometimes
called oyster plant because its flavour is akin
to that of oysters.

□ **Basic Preparation:** Wash the roots, then
thinly peel; drop them into a bowl of acidulated water to prevent discoloration.

Salsify may be served in white or cream
sauce, or tossed in butter and parsley, or fried
in a light batter, but the vegetable must be pre-
cooked before proceeding with any of these
preparations.

□ **To Pre-Cook:** Simply drop the prepared
vegetable, cut into lengths of about 5 cm
(2 in), into boiling salted water and cook for
20–25 minutes. Drain, then finish as desired.
Scorzonera (Black Salsify) has a brownish-
black skin, otherwise it closely resembles
salsify in flavour and texture. Prepare and use
the same way as white-skinned salsify.

Buttered Salsify

*1 kg (2 lb) salsify roots; 60 g/2 oz (4 tbsp)
butter; salt and freshly ground black pepper;
finely chopped parsley.*

Prepare salsify as described above, and pre-
cook in boiling salted water. Drain. Heat
butter in frying pan (skillet) and cook salsify
for about 10 minutes, turning often, until
golden. Season with salt and pepper and
toss with chopped parsley. Serves 6.

SAMBAL

See Curry.

SAMOSAS

These Indian savouries are semi-circular pastries filled with minced (ground) lamb, subtly
flavoured with spices and herbs. They are

deep-fried until golden and crisp and are
wonderful with pre-dinner drinks.

Samosas

PASTRY (DOUGH): *125 g/4 oz (1 cup) flour;
½ tsp salt; 15 g/½ oz (1 tbsp) ghee or butter;
3–4 tbsp lukewarm water; milk; oil for deep-
frying.*
FILLING: *15 g/½ oz (1 tbsp) ghee; 2.5 cm (1 in)
piece fresh ginger, grated; 2 onions,
chopped; 2 tbsp chopped fresh mint; 2 tsp
curry paste or powder; 1 tsp salt; 250 g/8 oz
(1 cup) minced (ground) lamb; ½ tsp saffron,
crumbled; 250 ml/8 fl oz (1 cup) hot water;
1 tomato, peeled and chopped; juice
½ lemon; ½ tsp Garam Masala (page 139).*

PASTRY (DOUGH): Sift flour and salt into a
bowl. Rub (cut) in ghee or butter with
fingertips. Add water and knead to form a
stiff dough. Cover bowl with a cloth and
leave the pastry (dough) to stand while
preparing filling.
FILLING: Heat ghee and gently fry ginger, half
the onions and the mint until onions are soft
and golden. Stir in curry paste or powder
and salt and fry for 2–3 minutes. Add lamb
and cook for 5 minutes, stirring frequently.
Meanwhile, soak saffron in hot water. Stir
into meat mixture with tomato. Bring to the
boil, then turn heat very low and cook,
uncovered, for 30–40 minutes, stirring
occasionally. The meat should be tender and
moisture evaporated. Add lemon juice and
garam masala. Allow to cool then mix in
remaining onions.

Divide dough into 14–16 even-sized
pieces. Shape each into a ball and roll out on
a lightly floured board as thinly as possible,
keeping the shape round. Cut each round in
half and moisten edges with milk. Place a
small spoonful of filling on one side of each
half-round and fold other side over. Press
edges together and trim with a fluted cutter if
liked. Heat oil in a heavy pan and deep-fry
samosas, a few at a time, until golden-brown.
Drain on crumpled paper towels. Serve hot.

A bowl of mint or coriander chutney may be
offered for dipping. Makes about 30.

SANDWICHES

Some sandwiches are famous – the Hero, the
Shooter's Sandwich, the Club Sandwich,
the thin, perfect, cucumber sandwiches of
English tea tables – and there are many
others that make a satisfying, nourishing light
meal. Some are designed for rugged appetites; and at the other extreme, Mrs. Beeton
gave instructions for making small tea sandwiches to be eaten with gloved fingers! **See
recipes.**

To keep fresh: They will keep in excellent
condition for up to 24 hours if wrapped in the
following way: stack them 3–4 at a time, place
a lettuce leaf on top and wrap closely in
plastic wrap. Wrap packages in a damp tea-
towel, then slip the whole parcel into a plastic
bag and close tightly. Store in the refrigerator
or in a cool place. Leave sandwiches whole
with crusts on, and trim and cut up just before
serving.

To freeze: They may be frozen for a week or
two but great care must be taken to prevent
sogginess or drying out. Fillings that are
rather high in fat, such as cheese, canned fish
or meat, work best. Do not include mayonnaise, cooked egg white, jellies, fresh fruits or
vegetables with a high water content such as
cucumber, lettuce, celery, tomato, apple,
banana or pineapple.

Butter the bread liberally, being sure to go
right to the edges, make sandwiches and
wrap closely in plastic wrap, 3–4 sandwiches
at a time or in quantities required for school
lunches etc. An extra slice or crust of bread at
each end of the package will help to prevent
drying out. Leave crusts on and sandwiches
whole, if possible, or in large pieces. Over-
wrap in foil or plastic.

Thaw in wrappings – about 2–3 hours; an
inner parcel may be taken frozen in a lunch-
box.

See also Danish Open Sandwiches.

Party Sandwiches

Ribbon Sandwiches Make these with three layers of buttered bread (the middle slice buttered on both sides) with filling in between. Alternate white and brown bread, if you wish. Some good combinations are:

● Sardine mashed with a little chopped parsley and lemon juice on one layer, cream cheese with chopped chives or spring onions (scallions) on the other.

● Thin cucumber slices on one layer, peanut butter or cream cheese on the other.

● Chopped cooked chicken on one layer, cream cheese mixed with chopped celery and walnuts on the other.

● Finely chopped smoked salmon or drained, canned salmon seasoned well with freshly ground black pepper on one layer, cream cheese and chopped capers on the other.

Pinwheel Sandwiches Cut the crusts from an unsliced sandwich loaf and cut loaf lengthways into slices. Butter, then spread with any desired filling and roll up each slice from end to end. Wrap tightly in plastic wrap and leave at least 1 hour. Slice across to serve.

Rolled Sandwiches Remove crusts from fresh sliced white or brown bread and roll lightly with a rolling pin. Butter right to edge and spread with cream cheese, mayonnaise or a home-made spread, or cover with a thin slice of ham, salami or cheese. Place a thin stick of celery, dill pickle, cucumber or an asparagus spear on one edge and roll up, pressing lightly to seal. Lay sandwiches, seam side down, close together on plastic wrap and wrap tightly. Leave at least 1 hour before using.

Lunch-box Sandwiches

These fillings make nourishing sandwiches that carry well.

● Finely chopped green pepper and radish, or grated carrot and bean sprouts on wholewheat bread spread with devilled ham and mayonnaise.

● Raisins, dates or mixed dried fruits, sprinkled with a little mixed spice and a few drops of lemon juice, on wholewheat bread spread with cream cheese.

● Hummus, bean sprouts and thinly sliced cucumber, on wholewheat bread or spread thickly inside pita bread. Finely chopped spring onion (scallion), celery or pepper, or grated raw beetroot or carrot can be added.

● Well-drained, flaked tuna mixed with finely chopped spring onion (scallion), celery and green pepper, a little chopped mango chutney, a dash of soy sauce and enough mayonnaise to bind.

● Drained, mashed baked beans mixed with crumbled crisp-fried bacon. Spread on wholewheat or rye bread, spread with mayonnaise. Thinly sliced cheese may be added.

● Peanut butter and thinly sliced cucumber (leave the skin on for extra crunch).

● Peanut butter, grated carrot and raisins.

● Diced cooked ham or chicken (or both) mixed with mayonnaise, chopped tomato, radish and spring onion (scallion).

● Hard-boiled (hard-cooked) egg, chopped and bound with cream cheese thinned with cream or mayonnaise, and seasoned with salt, pepper and paprika.

● Devilled egg: mix 2 chopped hard-boiled (hard-cooked) eggs with 1 tsp Worcestershire sauce, $\frac{1}{4}$ tsp French (Dijon) mustard, 1 tsp chutney, $\frac{1}{2}$ tsp curry powder, salt, cayenne and 1 tbsp melted butter. Layer with lettuce on brown bread.

● Cream cheese, chopped almonds and bean sprouts.

● Cream cheese, marmalade, raisins and chopped peanuts.

● Cottage cheese, chopped chives and bean sprouts or shredded spinach leaves.

● Cream cheese, grated orange rind and walnut pieces.

● Sliced corned beef (which may be canned) on rye bread, which has been spread with a mixture of softened cream cheese, a little

French (Dijon) mustard and bottled horseradish to taste. Pack a few dill pickles with the sandwich.

● Shredded cabbage and grated carrot, chopped spring onions (scallions) and bean sprouts, seasoned with salt and pepper and bound with mayonnaise. Nice on caraway-seed rye bread.

● Cold cooked or canned fish (or fish fingers), flaked and mixed with a little chopped spring onions (scallions), celery and cucumber, and bound with tartare sauce. Use brown bread for this.

● Liverwurst mixed with a little grated nutmeg, a spoonful of mayonnaise and chopped chives and parsley, layered with lettuce in white bread.

Filled Rolls for Picnics or Lunch-boxes

Use crusty or soft rolls, long or round. Split, pull out some of the crumb if you wish, butter and fill generously. Some especially successful ideas:

● A cold sausage or hamburger (better still if it's put in while hot so that the juices flavour the bread). Add crisp fried or raw onion, fresh herbs, mustard, tomato ketchup or chutney.

● Finely chopped tomato, onion, courgette (zucchini), cucumber and mint or basil, seasoned with salt and pepper and drained in a sieve before filling the roll.

● Liverwurst, crisp-cooked crumbled bacon, chopped tomato, lettuce and thinly sliced cucumber.

● Feta cheese, sliced olives, chopped tomato and bean sprouts.

● Drained flaked tuna, hard-boiled (hard-cooked) egg, chopped spring onions (scallions), bean sprouts and mayonnaise.

● Corned beef and well-drained coleslaw.

● Potato salad and ham, bacon or salami.

● Don't butter the roll but sprinkle the inside with olive oil and spread with tomato purée (paste). Fill with grated cheese mixed with two or three of the following: chopped spring onions (scallions), chopped green pepper, mashed anchovies, strips of ham or salami, drained tuna, sliced olives, capers, sliced mushrooms, fresh chopped herbs or dried herbs re-chopped with parsley. If desired, wrap in foil and heat before taking on a picnic.

Pita Sandwiches Pita or pocket bread with a generous filling makes an excellent portable meal. Use any combination of meat, cheese, fish or vegetables, such as the following:

● Tabouleh with sliced roast beef or lamb, tomatoes and shredded lettuce.

● Sliced cooked chicken with mayonnaise, chopped celery and spring onions (scallions), cooked peas and diced, cooked carrot.

● Garbanzo Spread (see page 319) with sliced cucumber and tomato.

HOME-MADE SANDWICH SPREADS AND FILLINGS

These nutritious spreads are good on bread or crispbread.

Savoury Tomato Spread

Lovely alone or with chicken, cold meat or fish fillings.

1 onion, finely chopped; 15 g/$\frac{1}{2}$ oz (1 tbsp) butter; 3 tomatoes, peeled and chopped; 2 tbsp grated cheese; 2 tsp chopped mixed fresh thyme, sage and marjoram, or $\frac{1}{2}$ tsp dried mixed herbs with 2 tsp chopped parsley; about 30 g/1 oz ($\frac{1}{2}$ cup) fresh breadcrumbs; salt and freshly ground black pepper.

Gently fry onion in butter until soft. Add tomatoes and cook until thick. Stir in cheese and herbs and remove from heat. Add enough breadcrumbs to give a spreading consistency and season with salt and pepper. Store, covered, in refrigerator. Keeps 1 week to 10 days. Makes about 350 g/12 oz (1$\frac{1}{2}$ cups).

Piquant Sardine Spread

1 × 105 g/3½ oz can sardines, drained and mashed; 2 spring onions (scallions), finely chopped; 5 tbsp Mayonnaise (page 204); 2 tsp French (Dijon) mustard; ½ tsp curry powder; 2 hard-boiled (hard-cooked) eggs, finely chopped; 1 tbsp lemon juice; salt and freshly ground black pepper.

Mix all ingredients together well. Store, covered, in refrigerator. Keeps 4–5 days. Makes about 250 g/8 oz (1 cup).

Peanut Butter, Bacon and Carrot Spread

Layer with paper-thin, well-drained tomato slices and lettuce leaves.

180 g/6 oz (½ cup) peanut butter; 60 g/2 oz (½ cup) grated carrot; 2 rashers (slices) bacon, rind removed, grilled (broiled) until crisp and crumbled; about 2 tbsp Mayonnaise (page 204).

Mix peanut butter, carrot and bacon until well blended and add enough mayonnaise to give a spreading consistency. Store, covered, in refrigerator. Keeps 1 week. Makes about 310 g/10 oz (1¼ cups).

Apricot and Nut Spread

140 g/4½ oz (¾ cup) diced dried apricots; 45 g/1½ oz (¼ cup) firmly packed brown sugar; 120 ml/4 fl oz (½ cup) orange juice; 60 g/2 oz (½ cup) finely chopped almonds, walnuts or 105 g/3½ oz (½ cup) peanuts; 2 tbsp currants.

Simmer apricots with brown sugar and orange juice until mixture is soft and liquid has evaporated, about 35 minutes. Watch carefully and stir often to ensure that the mixture does not scorch. Remove from heat and mash with a fork, then stir in nuts and currants. Store, covered, in refrigerator. Keeps several weeks. Makes about 250 g/8 oz (1 cup).

HEARTY SANDWICHES

Great sandwiches for substantial snacking or meals on the run.

The Reuben

The name tells us that we owe the Reuben to the traditions of Jewish cookery. Anyone who knows New York's delicatessens will remember hot sandwiches like this.

1 large, thick slice rye bread; 1 tbsp Thousand Island Dressing (page 205); sauerkraut, rinsed in cold water and squeezed dry; 2 thin slices corned beef; 1 slice Swiss cheese.

Toast bread on one side, then spread other side with dressing. Cover with a generous layer of sauerkraut and top with corned beef then with cheese. Cook under a preheated grill (broiler) until filling is heated through and cheese melted. Serves 1.

Omelette in a Roll

This makes wonderful cocktail food, too, cut across into slices. Flavour the omelette well.

1 oval-shaped soft bread roll, plain or wholewheat; butter.
OMELETTE: *2 eggs; 3 tsp water; ½ tsp salt; freshly ground black pepper; flavouring (see below); 2 tsp butter.*

Slice top from roll, pull out most of the crumb, and butter inside of shell.
OMELETTE: Beat eggs, water, salt and pepper lightly together with a fork. Stir in chosen flavouring. Heat butter in an omelette pan or small frying pan (skillet), and when foam has subsided, pour in egg mixture. Cook over fairly high heat, pulling mixture from edge toward centre with a fork or spatula, so that uncooked mixture runs underneath. When omelette is set underneath but top is still quite moist remove from heat. Flip over ⅓ of

omelette toward centre, then turn over again so that it is folded in 3. Roll out into bread shell, put lid on and wrap tightly in plastic wrap or foil. Leave at least 1 hour before eating. Rolls can be refrigerated if you want to leave them overnight, but bring back to room temperature or warm gently in oven before eating. Serves 1.
FLAVOURINGS: 1 tbsp chopped mixed fresh herbs, or 1 tsp mixed dried herbs chopped with 1 tbsp parsley; 2 tbsp grated well-flavoured cheese mixed with 2 tsp flaked crab, salmon or smoked fish; 1 spring onion (scallion), chopped, with a grating of cheese; 2 tbsp finely chopped cooked ham with 1 spring onion (scallion), chopped, and a little chutney.

Club Sandwich

3 slices white bread; butter; Mayonnaise (page 204); 4 thin slices cooked chicken breast; salt and freshly ground black pepper; 4 thin slices firm, ripe tomato; 3 rashers (slices) bacon, rind removed and fried crisp; stuffed olive to garnish; dill pickles to serve.

Toast bread on both sides. Spread one side of each slice with butter and mayonnaise. Cover one slice with chicken, season with salt and pepper and top with second slice of toast, buttered side up. Cover with tomato and bacon, season and place third slice of toast on top, buttered side down. Cut diagonally in half and garnish with an olive secured with a toothpick. Serve with a few dill pickles. Serves 1.

Shooter's Sandwich

1 long loaf crusty bread, such as Italian bread; 1 thick rump (top round) steak, about 310 g (10 oz); salt and freshly ground black pepper; English or French (Dijon) mustard; 2–3 dill pickles, thinly sliced.

Cut loaf in half lengthways and remove some of the crumb. Grill (broil) steak until medium-rare. Slice across thinly and pile, while hot, into bottom of loaf. Drizzle over any juices that have escaped while slicing. Season with salt, pepper and mustard and top with sliced dill pickle. Put top of loaf on and tie with string. Wrap tightly in foil or plastic wrap and put a heavy weight on top. Leave for about 6 hours. Cut across into thick slices to serve. Serves 4.

The Hero

2 crusty bread sticks (small baguettes); butter; 4–6 lettuce leaves; 180 g (6 oz) cooked ham, thinly sliced; 60 g (2 oz) Gruyère, Jarlsberg or other cheese, thinly sliced; 2 firm, ripe tomatoes; 2 thin slices onion, separated into rings; salt and freshly ground black pepper; sliced stuffed olives or dill pickles (optional).

Cut bread sticks in half lengthways, pull out some of the crumb and butter insides. Fill with layers of lettuce, ham, cheese, tomatoes and onion rings. Season with salt and pepper and add sliced stuffed olives or dill pickles, if desired. Place tops on and tie ends and middles with string. Wrap tightly in foil or plastic wrap and leave 1 hour or longer. Cut across into pieces to serve. Serves 4–6.

An Englishman's Bacon Sandwich

English aficionados of the bacon sandwich have it this way.

3–4 rashers (slices) bacon, rind removed; 2 slices white bread; butter; HP sauce.

Fry bacon until crisp and drain on a paper towel. Butter the bread. Pile bacon on one slice, sprinkle with HP sauce and top with second slice. Serve at once. Serves 1.

363

The Submarine or Poor Boy

The Submarine or Poor Boy is a close relation of The Hero. It can be hot or cold.

1 long French loaf, or 2 small Italian loaves or bread sticks; 4 tbsp olive oil; 180 g (6 oz) Swiss or other cheese, thinly sliced; 4 firm, ripe tomatoes, thinly sliced; 180 g (6 oz) salami, thinly sliced; 1 × 50 g/1⅔ oz can anchovy fillets, drained and halved lengthways; 2–3 canned pimientos, drained and halved or quartered; freshly ground black pepper; chopped parsley; green or black (ripe) olives to garnish.

Cut loaf or loaves in half lengthways and remove some of the crumb. Brush insides of bread with oil. Place cheese slices, overlapping, on one half of the bread, and top with overlapping slices of tomato then salami. Arrange anchovies and pimientos alternately on top, grind a little black pepper over and sprinkle generously with parsley. Put other pieces of bread on top, tie at intervals with string and wrap tightly in foil. Place in refrigerator with a weight on top and leave for several hours, or overnight. To serve cold, unwrap and cut across in thick slices. To serve hot, place the wrapped bread in a preheated moderate oven (180°C/350°F, Gas Mark 4) for 15 minutes. Unwrap and cut across in thick slices. Serve garnished with olives. Serves 4–6.
NOTE: The Submarine may also be served open-faced. Divide the filling evenly between top and bottom halves of bread, making the final topping cheese. Place under a preheated grill (broiler) until cheese is bubbling.
VARIATIONS
Roast Beef Submarine: Follow recipe for The Submarine, but spread bread with butter instead of olive oil and fill with layers of thinly sliced roast beef and tomatoes or mushrooms. Season with salt, pepper and French (Dijon) mustard. For a hot sandwich, smear the beef with leftover gravy.
Ham and Pineapple Submarine: Follow recipe for The Submarine, but spread bread with butter and a little mustard instead of olive oil and fill with layers of thinly sliced cooked ham and pineapple sprinkled with chopped green peppers, toasted almonds and spring onions (scallions).

The BLT (Bacon, Lettuce and Tomato Sandwich)

3–4 rashers (slices) bacon, rind removed; 2 slices white bread; 2 tbsp Mayonnaise (page 204); 4 large slices tomato; salt; 1 crisp lettuce leaf.

Fry bacon until crisp and drain on a paper towel. Toast bread and spread each slice with mayonnaise. Pile tomatoes on one slice, salt and top with bacon, lettuce and second

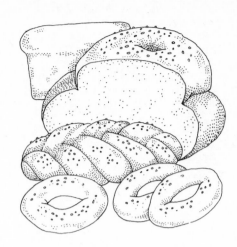

slice of toast, mayonnaise side down. Serve immediately. Serves 1.

Steak Sandwich

A minute steak is a small steak cut thin for quick cooking. A cube steak is a small, thin steak which has been tenderized by breaking some of the meat fibres under pressure. It has a waffle-like surface.

1 onion, thinly sliced; 1 tbsp oil; 1 minute or cube steak; 2 slices white or wholewheat bread; butter; salt and freshly ground black pepper; dash Worcestershire sauce.

Fry onion in oil until lightly browned. Remove onion with a slotted spoon and keep warm. Heat pan until oil begins to give off a slight haze, then add steak and brown for about 2 minutes on each side. Meantime, toast and butter bread. Place steak on one slice of toast, season with salt, pepper and Worcestershire sauce, pile onion on top and cover with second slice of toast. Serve immediately. Serves 1.

Bratwurst Rolls

These little warm rolls with their herby, mustardy sausage stuffing are superb for an outdoor wedding or any casual party.

25 long, soft bread rolls; 250 g/8 oz (1 cup) butter, melted; 12 spring onions (scallions), finely chopped; 20 g/⅔ oz (½ cup) chopped mixed fresh herbs, or 20 g/⅔ oz (½ cup) chopped parsley with 1 tbsp mixed dried herbs; 25 hot grilled (broiled) bratwurst or similar sausages; French (Dijon) mustard; salt and freshly ground black pepper.

Slit open rolls lengthways and pull out some of the crumb from each piece. Brush insides with butter and sprinkle with chopped spring onions (scallions) and herbs. Split sausages lengthways, spread insides with mustard and

put back together. Place a sausage in each hollowed roll (trim to fit if necessary), season with salt and pepper and press roll back together. Wrap rolls, in batches of 6–8, tightly in foil and leave overnight in refrigerator. When rolls are required, heat packages straight from refrigerator in a preheated moderate oven (180°C/350°F, Gas Mark 4) for 20 minutes. Unwrap and pile up in a basket or serving dish. Makes 25.
NOTE: If you are going to have the wedding feast away from home, take the hot rolls in their foil wrapping. They will carry perfectly and remain pleasantly warm.

TEA AND COCKTAIL SANDWICHES

Small sandwiches that can be eaten in 2 or 3 bites are some of the nicest things to serve on a tea table or offer with drinks. They can be made an hour or two ahead of time, arranged on a plate and covered with a damp cloth until required.

Cucumber Sandwiches

cucumber, finely sliced; salt; thin slices fresh white bread; butter; freshly ground white pepper.

Sprinkle cucumber slices with salt. Leave on a tilted plate 20 minutes to allow juice to escape, then drain on paper towels. Butter bread and make sandwiches with cucumber, seasoned with salt and white pepper. Remove crusts and cut into small triangles.

Watercress Sandwiches

thin slices brown bread; butter; chopped watercress; salt; lemon juice.

Butter bread generously and make sandwiches with watercress seasoned with salt and a few drops of lemon juice. Roll each sandwich lightly with a rolling pin. Remove crusts and cut sandwiches into small triangles.

Ham and Watercress Fingers

120 ml/4 fl oz (½ cup) thick Mayonnaise (page 204); 2 tbsp finely chopped green olives; 1 tbsp finely chopped gherkins; 1 tbsp chopped parsley; 1 tbsp chopped spring onion (scallion); 2 tsp French (Dijon) mustard; salt and freshly ground black pepper; 14 thin slices pumpernickel or rye bread; 150 g (5 oz) cooked ham, thinly sliced; watercress leaves.

Combine mayonnaise, olives, gherkins, parsley, spring onion (scallion), mustard, salt and pepper. Spread bread with mayonnaise mixture. Top half the slices with ham, then watercress. Cover with remaining slices, mayonnaise side down, and press lightly together. Remove crusts and cut each sandwich into 3 fingers. Makes 21.

Cream Cheese and Herb Sandwiches

125 g/4 oz (½ cup) cream cheese; 3 tsp lemon juice; salt and freshly ground black pepper; 10 g/⅓ oz (¼ cup) chopped parsley; 10 g/⅓ oz (¼ cup) chopped mixed fresh herbs (chives, thyme, oregano, a little sage); 1 tbsp finely chopped chives or spring onion (scallion); butter; 12 thin slices white or brown bread.

Soften cream cheese, then mash well with lemon juice, salt and pepper. Mix in herbs. Butter bread and make sandwiches with cheese and herb mixture. Remove crusts and cut into fingers or small triangles. Makes 18 fingers, 24 small triangles.

Chicken and Avocado Triangles

These look and taste luxurious, but really make one avocado and a little chicken go a long way.

6 slices white bread; 6 slices brown bread; butter; 1 ripe avocado, peeled and stoned (pitted); 2 tsp lemon juice; salt and freshly ground black pepper; 370 g/12 oz (1½ cups) chopped, cooked chicken meat; 2 tbsp Mayonnaise (page 204); finely chopped parsley to garnish.

Butter bread lightly. Mash avocado with lemon juice, and season with salt and pepper. Combine chicken and mayonnaise. Spread white bread with a layer of avocado, then chicken. Top with brown bread. Trim crusts and cut each sandwich into 4 triangles. Arrange on a platter and garnish with a little finely chopped parsley. Serves 4.

SARDINE

The true sardine is a Mediterranean fish, of the same family as herring, anchovy and pilchard. In the summer it migrates to cooler Atlantic waters, off the French and Portuguese coasts; the canning of sardines is an important industry in these regions.

Sardines, anchovies and similar small fish called sardines in other parts of the world, are usually around 12–15 cm (5–6 in) in length.

☐ **Basic Preparation:** Because the bones are soft enough to eat, the fish need little preparation before cooking – simply cut away the head from the body and gently pull out the insides and the backbone if you wish. Wash and pat dry with paper towels. The sardines can now be coated in flour and fried, or grilled (broiled) or barbecued in a hinged wire fish grill over hot coals.

Fresh sardines are very popular in Mediterranean countries. They are usually fried, but may also be stuffed with a garlic-flavoured spinach mixture, as in Provence, or with a mixture of capers, olives, sultanas (golden raisins) and pine nuts, as in Sicily.

Sardines are also available salted or canned in oil. Salted sardines are prepared in the same way as salted anchovies – they must be thoroughly cleaned and washed, then packed in a jar with fresh olive oil. They can then be used in the same ways as canned sardines – in salads, especially with tomatoes and hard-boiled (hard-cooked) eggs; in sandwiches, and in cocktail savouries. **See recipes.**

Hors d'Oeuvre of Canned Sardines

● Arrange whole canned sardines on a dish, dress with lemon juice and olive oil, and sprinkle with very finely chopped spring onion (scallion), a few onion rings or sieved hard-boiled (hard-cooked) egg yolk.
● Dress whole canned sardines with a Fresh Herb Vinaigrette Dressing (see page 358), made with lemon juice, and sprinkle over lots of chopped parsley.

Sardine Canapés

● Spread toast rectangles with Garlic Butter (see page 140). Slip an onion ring over each canned sardine and place on toasts. Decorate with finely chopped hard-boiled (hard-cooked) egg and chives, or with strips of canned pimiento, or sliced stuffed olives.
● Remove bones from 1 × 120 g/4 oz can sardines. Mash, then season with lemon juice and grated onion. Bind with a little mayonnaise and pile on buttered toast rounds. Serve as is, or top each with a small square of cheese and grill (broil) until melted. Serve hot.
● Spread toast rectangles with Garlic Butter (see page 140). Arrange slices of hard-boiled (hard-cooked) egg on toast. Top with a small sardine and a little Green Mayonnaise (see page 358).

Fried Fresh Sardines

500 g (1 lb) fresh sardines, cleaned; 3–4 tbsp seasoned flour; oil for frying; lemon wedges to serve.

Roll sardines in seasoned flour to coat. Heat 2.5 cm (1 in) oil in a frying pan (skillet) and fry sardines until golden. (Sardines may need to be cooked in several batches.) Remove with a slotted spoon. Reheat oil, return sardines to pan and fry for 30 seconds to crisp coating. Drain on paper towels and serve immediately, with lemon wedges. Serves 4.

Lemon Grilled Sardines

24 fresh sardines or anchovies, cleaned; salt and freshly ground black pepper; juice 1 lemon; 4 tbsp oil; 3 lemons, quartered, to garnish.

Place sardines or anchovies in a bowl, season lightly with salt and pepper and add lemon juice and oil. Mix lightly so that each sardine is well coated. Arrange on rack of grill (broiler) and cook under a preheated hot grill (broiler) for 2–3 minutes on each side. Arrange fish on a heated serving platter and garnish with lemon quarters. Serves 2–3.

Gratin of Fresh Sardines

1 lemon; few sprigs fresh fennel or thyme; 500 g (1 lb) fresh sardines, cleaned; salt and freshly ground black pepper; 120 ml/4 fl oz (½ cup) dry white wine; 1 tbsp olive oil; 30 g/1 oz (½ cup) fresh white breadcrumbs; 1 tbsp finely chopped parsley.

Squeeze juice from ½ lemon; cut other ½ into thin slices. Lay herbs and lemon slices on bottom of oiled shallow ovenproof dish. Arrange sardines on top and season well with salt and pepper. Sprinkle over lemon juice, white wine and oil. Combine breadcrumbs and parsley and scatter over sardines. Cook in a preheated moderately hot oven (200°C/400°F, Gas Mark 6) for 10–15 minutes, basting with pan juices from time to time. Serves 4.

Baked Sardines

500 g (1 lb) fresh sardines or anchovies, cleaned; salt and freshly ground black pepper; 3 tbsp lemon juice; 2 tbsp chopped parsley; 2 cloves garlic, crushed; 60 g/2 oz (1 cup) fresh breadcrumbs; 30 g/1 oz (2 tbsp) butter.

Arrange fish in an oiled flameproof dish large enough to hold fish in one layer. Season lightly with salt and pepper and sprinkle with lemon juice. Sauté parsley, garlic and breadcrumbs in butter in a frying pan (skillet) over high heat, then spread over fish. Heat dish for 1 minute on top of stove over medium heat, then place it in a preheated very hot oven (230°C/450°F, Gas Mark 8). Cook for 10–12 minutes or until fish is golden and breadcrumbs crisp. Serves 4.

Sicilian Baked Sardines

1 kg (2 lb) fresh sardines or anchovies, cleaned; 120 ml/4 fl oz (½ cup) olive oil; 125 g/4 oz (2 cups) fresh breadcrumbs; 20 g/⅔ oz (½ cup) chopped parsley; 1 small onion, finely chopped; 3 tbsp pine nuts; grated rind and juice 1 lemon; salt and freshly ground black pepper; 2 bay leaves.

Cut heads off sardines or anchovies if preferred. Split open down belly, turn skin up on a board and press firmly down backbone. Turn again and lift out backbone. Rinse quickly in salted water and dry well on paper towels. Heat oil in pan and toss 90 g/3 oz (1½ cups) breadcrumbs until crisp. Place fried crumbs in a bowl. Add parsley, onion, pine nuts, lemon rind, salt and pepper. Mix ingredients lightly together. Put a little of this stuffing into each fish and roll sides together round it. Arrange sardines in one layer in an oiled ovenproof dish. Tear bay leaves into pieces and sprinkle on top with any remaining stuffing. Top with remaining breadcrumbs. Bake in a preheated moderate oven (180°C/350°F, Gas Mark 4), 30 minutes. Squeeze lemon juice over and serve immediately. Serves 6.

SASHIMI

A highly regarded Japanese dish, consisting of slices of raw fish garnished with slivers of cabbage, white radish or other vegetables, and always accompanied by *wasabi*, a hot, green horseradish paste, and soy sauce for dipping. The fish selected for sashimi must be very fresh, ideally caught and eaten on the same day.

Sashimi

750 g (1½ lb) very fresh tuna, bream or mackerel; 250 g/8 oz (2 cups) shredded daikon (giant white radish available from Oriental greengrocers); 1 carrot, shredded; 6 spring onions (scallions), shredded; 6 mange tout (snow peas); 6 cooked, unshelled Dublin Bay prawns (jumbo shrimp); 1 tbsp wasabi (available in cans from Oriental groceries); 6 lemon wedges; 1 tbsp grated fresh ginger; shoyu (Japanese light soy sauce).

Fillet fish, removing all skin and bones, and cut into thin slices. Arrange daikon, carrot and spring onions (scallions) in mounds on a serving platter, together with mange tout (snow peas). Arrange fish and prawns (shrimp) in centre of platter. Mix wasabi to a thick paste with a little water and place on platter, with lemon wedges and ginger. To serve, pour shoyu into individual bowls, then allow each diner to add wasabi and ginger to his own bowl of shoyu according to taste. The fish and vegetables are then dipped into this sauce before eating. Serves 6.

SATAY (SATE)

Visitors to Malaysia and Singapore never forget the satay – grilled (broiled) skewered meat, poultry or fish. Satay vendors, with their charcoal braziers, are part of the charm of the city streets, and the smell of grilled (broiled) meats and spices is irresistible.

Beef, pork, lamb, poultry and seafood are all suitable for satay. Small cubes of meat are marinated in a spicy mixture, then threaded on bamboo or wooden skewers and grilled (broiled) over charcoal. They can also be cooked successfully under a domestic grill (broiler).

Bamboo or wooden skewers should be well soaked in water for at least 2 hours before using to prevent them burning.

Serve small satays as a first course or more substantial ones as a main course, accompanied by rice and salad. **See recipes.**

See also *Peanut*.

Malaysian Satay Sauce

4–8 dried chillies, soaked and drained; 8 spring onions (scallions), chopped; 1 clove garlic, crushed; 4 macadamia nuts, chopped; 1 small strip lemon rind, chopped; 105 g/3½ oz (½ cup) raw peanuts; 2 tbsp oil; 250 ml/8 fl oz (1 cup) Coconut Milk (page 80); 2 tsp tamarind pulp soaked in 4 tbsp water for 10 minutes; 1 tsp brown sugar; salt.

Pound chillies, spring onions (scallions), garlic, macadamia nuts and lemon rind, or grind finely in a food processor. Lightly roast peanuts in a dry, heavy frying pan (skillet), then chop or pound coarsely. Heat oil in a saucepan and gently fry chilli mixture for 5 minutes, stirring frequently. Add coconut milk and bring slowly to the boil, stirring constantly. Strain tamarind over a bowl, squeezing out and reserving as much water as possible. Discard tamarind. Add tamarind water to sauce with brown sugar, roasted peanuts and salt. Simmer gently for 2–3 minutes. Serve sauce at room temperature. Makes about 500 ml/18 fl oz (2 cups).

NOTE: Tamarind pulp is available from health food or Asian grocery stores. If not available use 2 tsp lemon juice.

Quick Peanut Sauce

3 tbsp peanut butter; ½ tsp sugar; ½ tsp Tabasco (hot pepper) sauce; 30 g/1 oz (2 tbsp) butter; 1 clove garlic, crushed; juice ½ lemon; 1–2 tbsp light soy sauce; 4 tbsp single (light) cream.

Combine all ingredients, except cream, in a heavy saucepan. Cook over low heat, stirring constantly, until thick. Remove from heat and gradually stir in cream. Serve poured over pork, beef, lamb or chicken satays or use as a dipping sauce. Makes about 120 ml/4 fl oz (½ cup).

Mild Peanut Sauce

6 tbsp smooth or crunchy peanut butter; 250 ml/8 fl oz (1 cup) water; ¾ tsp garlic salt; 2 tsp brown sugar; 2 tbsp light soy sauce; lemon juice; ½ tsp anchovy paste or essence (extract), optional; Coconut Milk (page 80) or water.

Combine peanut butter and water in a saucepan and stir over a gentle heat until mixed. Remove from heat and add all other ingredients, adding enough coconut milk or water to make the paste a thick, pouring consistency. Adjust seasoning and add more salt and lemon juice if necessary. Makes about 250 ml/8 fl oz (1 cup).

Prawn Satay

3 tbsp lemon juice; 120 ml/4 fl oz (½ cup) thick Coconut Milk (page 80); ½ tsp sambal ulek (see Note below); ½ tsp dried shrimp paste (trasi); 1 tbsp dark soy sauce; 1 tsp dark brown sugar; finely grated rind 1 lemon; 2 cloves garlic, crushed with ½ tsp salt; 750 g/1½ lb (3 cups) green (uncooked) prawns (shrimp), shelled and deveined; oil.

Combine lemon juice, coconut milk, sambal ulek, trasi, soy sauce, brown sugar, lemon rind and garlic in a glass or earthenware bowl. Stir until sugar dissolves. Add prawns (shrimp) and stir. Cover and marinate for 2–3 hours in the refrigerator. Drain prawns

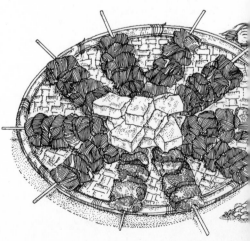

(shrimp), reserving marinade. Thread prawns (shrimp) on bamboo skewers (previously soaked in water to prevent burning), allowing 3–4 prawns (shrimp) per skewer. Brush with oil and grill (broil) over hot coals for about 5 minutes or under a preheated grill (broiler) until prawns (shrimp) are lightly browned. Simmer reserved marinade for 1 minute, stirring, and serve as a sauce. Serves 4.

NOTE: Sambal ulek and trasi are available from health food shops and Asian delicatessens.

Spicy Chicken Satay

1 kg (2 lb) chicken breast, skinned and boned, or chicken fillets; 1 tbsp tamarind pulp soaked in 4 tbsp water for 10 minutes; 1 tbsp ground coriander; 1 tsp ground cumin; ½ tsp ground fennel; 8 spring onions (scallions), chopped; 2 cloves garlic, crushed; 1 strip lemon rind; 2.5 cm (1 in) fresh ginger, chopped; ½ tsp salt; 1 tsp turmeric; 2 tsp brown sugar; 4 tbsp oil; sprigs fresh coriander to garnish.

Cut chicken into pieces 2 cm (¾ in) square. Strain tamarind over a bowl, squeezing out and reserving as much water as possible. Discard tamarind. Place tamarind water in an earthenware or glass bowl and add the remaining ingredients, except oil and fresh coriander. Add chicken, cover and refrigerate overnight. Drain chicken pieces and thread on to bamboo skewers (previously soaked in water for 2 hours). Cook over charcoal or under a preheated medium grill (broiler), brushing frequently with oil, for 5–10 minutes or until golden-brown. Garnish with coriander. Serve with Malaysian Satay Sauce (opposite). Serves 6–8.

NOTE: If tamarind pulp is not available, use 2 tsp lemon juice.

Indonesian Satay

1 tbsp peanut oil; juice 1 lemon; 1 clove garlic, crushed; 1 tbsp dark soy sauce or

Indonesian soy sauce (ketjap manis); 500 g (1 lb) pork fillet (tenderloin), cut into 2 cm (¾ in) cubes.

Combine peanut oil, lemon juice, garlic and soy sauce. Marinate pork cubes in this mixture, turning occasionally, for 2–4 hours. Drain, reserving marinade. Thread cubes on to bamboo skewers (previously soaked in water for 2 hours), allowing 3–4 cubes per skewer. Cook under a preheated grill (broiler) for 10–15 minutes or until well done, basting with reserved marinade. Serve hot with Quick Peanut Sauce or Malaysian Satay Sauce (opposite). Serves 12 as a first course, 6 as a main course.

Malayan Beef Satay

1 kg (2 lb) steak, eye of blade or rump (top round), cut into 2 cm (¾ in) cubes; 5 tbsp light soy sauce; 5 tbsp peanut oil; 2 onions, finely chopped; 2 cloves garlic, crushed; 3 tbsp toasted sesame seeds; 2 tsp ground cumin; 1 tsp lemon juice; salt and freshly ground black pepper.

Put steak cubes into an earthenware bowl. Combine soy sauce, peanut oil, onions, garlic and sesame seeds, pour over meat and leave to marinate at least 3 hours, turning from time to time. Drain meat, reserving marinade. Thread meat cubes on to small bamboo skewers (previously soaked in water for 2 hours), allowing 4–5 cubes per skewer. Mix cumin and lemon juice together and brush over meat. Cook over hot coals of a barbecue or under a preheated grill (broiler), basting with marinade and turning frequently. Grill (broil) 6–8 minutes for rare, 8–10 minutes for medium, 10–12 minutes for well-done. Season. Serves 6–8.

Singapore Beef Satay

750 g (1½ lb) rump (top round) steak; 2 tsp turmeric; 2 tsp ground cumin; 2 tsp ground fennel; finely grated rind ½ lemon; ½ tsp salt; 1 tbsp sugar; 4 tbsp thick Coconut Milk (page 80).

Trim fat from steak and cut fat into small pieces. Cut beef into 2 cm (¾ in) cubes. Combine turmeric, cumin, fennel, lemon rind, salt, sugar and coconut milk in an earthenware or glass bowl. Stir to dissolve sugar. Add beef cubes and mix well, then cover and leave to marinate for 1–2 hours. Thread meat cubes on bamboo skewers (previously soaked in water for 2 hours) with 2–3 little pieces of fat on each skewer between some of the meat cubes. Put about 5–6 pieces of meat on each skewer. Grill (broil) over hot coals or under a preheated grill (broiler) for 8–10 minutes or until beef is tender and brown on all sides. Serve immediately with Peanut Sauce or Malaysian Satay Sauce (opposite). Serves 6.

SAUCES

A good sauce can add distinction to everyday foods – as nice for family meals as for special occasions. It is reassuring to know that there are really only three main categories: *white*, *brown* and *emulsion sauces*.

When you become proficient at the basic recipes, you can make virtually any sauce recipe you come across. Also, there are the myriad pan sauces which fit perfectly into today's life-style – light, quick and foolproof to make; and simple fruit sauces, made from puréed and sweetened fruit.

Remember that a sauce should have body but must never be so thick that it sits heavily on the food. A *pouring* or *flowing* sauce should run freely off a spoon, a *coating* sauce should be just dense enough to cling to the food but not to blanket it thickly. Be ready to add a little more liquid if your sauce is too heavy.

□ **To Store:** Most sauces to be served separately with food can be prepared ahead and reheated when needed. Place hot sauce in a heatproof sauce container. Cover with plastic wrap, placed directly on the surface of the sauce, then with a lid. When cool, store in the refrigerator. To reheat, remove plastic wrap, place sauce container in a pan of hot water and stir over very gentle heat until sauce is hot.

Emulsion sauces, such as Hollandaise and Béarnaise must *not* be heated beyond luke-warm (it is quite correct to serve them at this temperature) or else they will separate; place the sauce container in a pan of warm water off the heat and stir until smooth.

Types of Sauces

Sauces based on a Roux: The basis of many sauces is a *roux*, a cooked mixture of fat and flour. The longer it is cooked, the darker the colour becomes and the nuttier the flavour. A white or golden (blond) roux is used for the lighter-coloured sauces, and a brown one for the dark sauces. It is important for a smooth result to cook the roux slowly, stirring, until it is the desired colour. When the liquid is added, the sauce must be stirred or whisked constantly until boiling so that it will thicken evenly without lumps.

WHITE SAUCES

These are light in colour, usually creamy white or a light straw colour, delicate in taste and smooth as satin. This smooth texture is achieved by a well-made roux and the liquid being carefully added.

The two main white sauces are Béchamel and Velouté. Béchamel is made with butter, flour and milk, flavoured with aromatic vegetables and herbs; Velouté is made with butter, flour and white stock – fish, chicken or veal according to what food it is to accompany. A knob of butter is sometimes

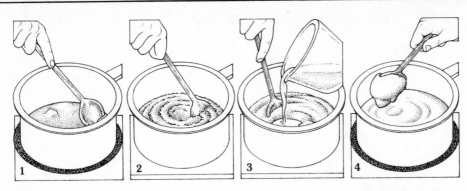

Making a Béchamel Sauce

swirled into the sauce at the last moment for extra richness. A Velouté sauce may also be enriched with egg yolks and cream.

Béchamel Sauce

250 ml/8 fl oz (1 cup) milk; ½ bay leaf; 1 slice onion; 5 black peppercorns; 1 small piece celery; 1 blade mace; 30 g/1 oz (2 tbsp) butter; 1½ tbsp flour; salt and freshly ground white pepper; nutmeg.

Heat milk with bay leaf, onion, peppercorns, celery and mace in a small heavy saucepan until bubbles form round edge. Remove from heat, cover and let stand 20 minutes. Strain and reserve. Wipe out saucepan. Melt butter in it **(Fig 1 above)**. Stir in flour **(2)**. Stir over low heat 1 minute. Remove from heat and cool a little, then add strained milk and stir until smooth **(3)**. Return to medium heat and stir constantly until boiling. Lower heat and cook very gently 5 minutes, stirring. Season with salt, pepper and nutmeg. Makes about 300 ml/½ pint (1¼ cups).
NOTE: This recipe makes a coating sauce – the right consistency for covering food in the dish in which it is to be served **(4)**. For a flowing sauce to be served separately, follow the recipe but use only 1 tbsp flour. For panada thickness (used to bind croquettes and as a soufflé base), follow the recipe but use 3 tbsp flour.
VARIATIONS

Mornay (Cheese) Sauce: To 1 quantity Béchamel Sauce, add 30 g/1 oz (¼ cup) grated Parmesan, Gruyère or sharp Cheddar cheese and a pinch of dry mustard. Stir over low heat just until cheese has melted. Use to coat fish, vegetables, chicken or eggs. To make a dish into a gratin, pour sauce over and place under a preheated hot grill (broiler) or in a hot oven until top is golden-brown (sprinkle first with a little more cheese and/or breadcrumbs tossed in butter if you wish).
Cream Sauce: To 1 quantity Béchamel Sauce add 2 tbsp single (light) cream. Bring to the boil, stirring, then add a few drops lemon juice. Use for food that is served

creamed – eggs, chicken, vegetables, veal.
Caper Sauce: To 1 quantity Cream Sauce add 1½ tbsp capers and 1 tbsp chopped parsley. Serve with hot ox (beef) tongue, lamb tongues, and grilled (broiled) or poached fish.
Curry Cream Sauce: Fry 1 chopped onion in 15 g/½ oz (1 tbsp) butter. Add 1 tbsp curry powder and fry, stirring, 1 minute. Add to 1 quantity Cream Sauce and simmer gently 5–10 minutes. A little desiccated (shredded) coconut may be fried with the curry powder if desired. Adjust seasoning, adding a few extra drops lemon juice if necessary. Serve on hard-boiled (hard-cooked) eggs or mix with 370 g/12 oz (1½ cups) chopped cooked chicken, turkey or lamb or 1 × 440 g (14 oz) can salmon or tuna, and reheat.
Parsley Sauce: To 1 quantity Béchamel Sauce, add 2 tbsp finely chopped parsley and a few drops lemon juice. Serve on boiled potatoes or with tripe, tongue, poached chicken or fish.
Mustard Sauce: To 1 quantity Béchamel Sauce, add 2 tsp dry mustard blended with 1 tsp vinegar, or 1 tbsp French (Dijon) mustard. Serve with boiled meats such as corned beef or with hot poached Continental sausage such as rookwurst.
Onion Sauce: Boil 4 finely chopped white onions in water to cover until tender. Drain and stir into 1 quantity Béchamel Sauce. Stir in 1 tsp single (light) cream and heat gently. Sliced hard-boiled (hard-cooked) eggs, coated with this sauce and sprinkled with parsley, become Oeufs à la Tripe, a breakfast or luncheon dish. Use also with corned beef and other boiled meats.
White or Melted Butter Sauce: Make Béchamel Sauce as above without flavouring the milk first. White sauce can be nice on foods with pronounced flavour such as cauliflower or smoked fish, and can be used as the base for Mornay, Onion and other well-flavoured sauces. For more delicately flavoured foods or as the base for sauces such as Cream Sauce or Parsley Sauce, Béchamel is better.

Velouté Sauce

Serve on vegetables, chicken, meat and fish, and as the basis for many variations.

30 g/1 oz (2 tbsp) butter; 2 tbsp flour; 350 ml/12 fl oz (1½ cups) warm stock (chicken, veal or fish, according to dish for which sauce will be used); salt and freshly ground white pepper; few drops lemon juice; 1 egg yolk; 1 tbsp single (light) cream.

Melt butter in a heavy saucepan and stir in flour. Stir over low heat until straw-coloured. Remove from heat and cool a little, then add hot stock and stir until smooth. Return to medium heat and stir constantly until boiling. Lower heat and cook very gently 15 minutes, stirring frequently. Season with salt, pepper and lemon juice. Stir egg yolk into cream in a small bowl (this is called the liaison). Stir in a little of the hot sauce, then stir this mixture back into sauce. Cook, stirring, until sauce is glossy and a little thicker, but do not boil. Makes about 350 ml/12 fl oz (1½ cups).
VARIATIONS

Poulette Sauce: To 1 quantity Velouté Sauce made with chicken stock, add ½ tsp lemon juice and 2 tsp chopped parsley. Good on broad (fava) beans or other green vegetables, brains or chicken.
Sour Cream Sauce: Follow recipe for Velouté Sauce using fish or veal stock. Omit egg yolk and cream liaison and add 5 tbsp sour cream. Excellent with seafood or veal.
Bercy Sauce: Boil 1 finely chopped shallot in 4 tbsp white wine until liquid has almost evaporated. Stir in 1 quantity Velouté Sauce made with fish or chicken stock, 1 tsp lemon juice and 2 tsp chopped parsley and reheat. Serve with seafood or chicken.
Sauce Suprême: Follow recipe for Velouté Sauce, using strong chicken stock as the liquid and 3 egg yolks with 120 ml/4 fl oz (½ cup) single (light) cream as the liaison. Use this rich sauce to coat Sautéed Suprêmes of Chicken (see page 421) and mousselines of chicken, veal or ham (see *Mousseline*).

BROWN SAUCE

The basic brown sauce is a simplified version of the elaborate *Sauce Espagnole* of classic cuisine, but is still a fine luxury sauce. It and its variations are served with grilled (broiled) and sautéed red meat, and also with browned poultry and game.

Brown Sauce

60 g/2 oz (4 tbsp) clarified butter, or 3 tbsp oil; 1 small onion, diced; 1 small carrot, diced; 1 small piece celery, diced; 1 tbsp flour; 600 ml/1 pint (2½ cups) warm brown stock (bouillon); 1 tbsp tomato purée (paste); 1 bouquet garni; 5 black peppercorns; 4 tbsp dry sherry; mushroom trimmings (optional); salt and freshly ground black pepper.

Heat clarified butter or oil in a heavy saucepan, add diced vegetables (called a mirepoix) and cook on low heat, stirring occasionally, until vegetables shrivel slightly without colouring. Stir in flour and continue to cook very slowly, stirring, until roux is hazelnut brown. Remove from heat and cool a little, then add 350 ml/12 fl oz (1½ cups) of the stock and stir until blended. Stir in tomato purée (paste) and add bouquet garni, peppercorns, sherry and mushroom trimmings if using. Return to medium heat and stir until boiling. Half-cover with a lid and simmer 25 minutes. Add half the remaining stock, return sauce to boil and skim. Simmer for further 5 minutes. Add remaining stock, boil up and skim again. The addition of cool stock accelerates the rising of fat and scum and helps to clear sauce. If pan is tilted slightly the scum and fat will rise on one side only and can be easily removed. Simmer 5 minutes more. Adjust seasoning. Strain, pressing vegetables through sieve to extract juice. Makes about 500 ml/18 fl oz (2 cups).

NOTE: This sauce can be stored in the refrigerator as described in introduction (page 367), for 1 week. If you want to keep it longer, bring to the boil and return to refrigerator in a clean container.

VARIATIONS

Burgundy Sauce: Follow recipe for Brown Sauce but substitute 120 ml/4 fl oz (½ cup) dry red wine for the sherry. Serve with steak, roast beef and game.

Madeira or Marsala Sauce: Follow recipe for Brown Sauce but substitute 4 tbsp Madeira or Marsala for the sherry. Serve with Beef Wellington, ham, or with grilled (broiled) or sautéed kidneys or liver.

Chasseur Sauce: Gently cook 2 finely chopped shallots in 15 g/½ oz (1 tbsp) butter until soft but not coloured. Turn heat up, add 60 g/2 oz (½ cup) sliced mushrooms and shake until just coloured. Add 120 ml/4 fl oz (½ cup) white wine and boil until reduced to a few tablespoons of liquid. Stir in 1 tsp tomato purée (paste) and 250 ml/8 fl oz (1 cup) Brown Sauce and simmer 2–3 minutes. Serve with steaks, cutlets and roasts.

PAN SAUCES

The preceding Brown Sauce, though well worth making for special occasions, is too time-consuming for regular use by most of today's busy cooks. Fortunately, it is easy to make simple and excellent pan sauces in minutes, to enhance meats, chicken or fish.
See also *Suprême of Chicken*.

Marsala and Lemon Sauce

For veal steaks.

3 tbsp Marsala; 1 tbsp lemon juice; 4 tbsp single (light) cream; salt and freshly ground black pepper.

Dust veal steaks with flour and sauté in butter until lightly browned on both sides. Pour over Marsala and let it bubble for a few minutes until it looks syrupy. Add lemon juice and cream. Stir well, scraping up veal juices from pan. Season with salt and pepper and simmer 1 minute longer. Serves 4.

Lemon and Parsley Sauce

For chicken or fish.

30 g/1 oz (2 tbsp) butter; 2 tbsp lemon juice; 1 tbsp chopped parsley; salt and freshly ground black pepper.

Cook chicken pieces or fish fillets or steaks in a little oil and butter, then remove to a heated dish. Slowly pour off fat from pan, then add butter and heat until foaming, stirring and scraping up brown bits from pan. Add lemon juice and parsley. Taste, and season with salt (if needed) and pepper. Spoon over chicken or fish. Serves 2–4.

Quick Mushroom Sauce

For hamburgers, steak or pork chops.

butter; 125 g/4 oz (1 cup) thickly sliced or quartered mushrooms; 1 tsp cornflour (cornstarch), optional; 150 ml/¼ pint (⅔ cup) light (single) cream or stock; 1–2 tbsp lemon juice; salt and freshly ground black pepper.

Cook meat in a little oil and butter, then remove to a heated dish. Add butter to pan if necessary to make about 2 tbsp fat and heat on high heat until foaming. Add mushrooms and cook undisturbed about 45 seconds, then turn over and cook other sides a further 45 seconds. Sprinkle with cornflour (cornstarch) if using, and stir a few moments. Add cream or stock and bring to the boil, stirring and scraping up brown bits from bottom of pan. Cook 1 minute. Add lemon juice, salt and pepper. Spoon sauce over meat or serve separately. Serves 4.

Wine or Vermouth Sauce

For steak or hamburgers.

120 ml/4 fl oz (½ cup) red or white wine or dry vermouth; salt and freshly ground black

pepper; 30 g/1 oz (2 tbsp) butter, cut into pieces.

Cook steaks or hamburgers in a little oil and butter, then remove to a hot dish. Slowly pour off fat from pan. Add wine or vermouth and bring to the boil over high heat, stirring and scraping up brown bits from bottom of pan. When liquid is reduced by about half, season with salt and pepper and remove from heat. Add butter pieces. Do not stir but swirl butter in by swinging pan in a circular motion. Pour over meat and serve immediately. Serves 4.

EMULSION SAUCES

These luscious egg and butter sauces are thickened by the emulsifying action of egg yolk when it is whisked with other ingredients. A wire whisk is a worthwhile investment if you are making these sauces by hand – it really does make the difference in blending them smoothly together. Egg and butter sauces can also be made, effortlessly and speedily, in a blender or food processor. Note that these are warm, not hot, sauces; if overheated they will curdle. **See recipes**.

Hollandaise Sauce

Marvellous with asparagus and fish.

2 egg yolks; 1 tbsp water; lemon juice; 125 g/4 oz (½ cup) unsalted butter, cut into small pieces; small pinch salt.

Heat about 2.5 cm (1 in) water in the bottom of a double saucepan (double boiler) or a saucepan over which a heatproof bowl will fit. Bring just to simmering point. Place egg yolks, water and 1 tsp lemon juice in top of double saucepan (double boiler) or bowl, place over gently simmering water (which must not touch bottom of upper container) and whisk until yolks thicken slightly. This stage is called a sabayon and is reached when you begin to see bottom of bowl between strokes and mixture clings to whisk when it is raised from bowl. Now add butter, a piece at a time, slipping it through your fingers to soften it slightly. Whisk all the time, incorporating each piece of butter thoroughly before adding next piece. When all butter has been added and sauce is thick and creamy, add salt and a little more lemon juice. The sauce should have a delicate lemon flavour but should not be too sharp. Makes about 175 ml/6 fl oz (¾ cup).

NOTE: If the sauce refuses to thicken or curdles (probably because it has got too hot), do not worry, there is a remedy. Rinse out another mixing bowl with hot water, then put in 1 tsp lemon juice and 1 tbsp of the sauce. Beat with a wire whisk until they thicken together, then beat in the rest of the sauce a little at a time, whisking each addition well until quite smooth before adding the next.

VARIATIONS

Hollandaise with Egg Whites: Fold 2 egg whites, beaten until they hold soft peaks, into 1 quantity Hollandaise Sauce just before serving. This makes a lighter sauce and gives more servings. Serve with fish, asparagus or eggs.

Sauce Mousseline: Fold 120 ml/4 fl oz (½ cup) single (light) cream, lightly whipped, into 1 quantity Hollandaise Sauce just before serving. Serve with mousselines of shellfish and chicken (see *Mousseline*), sautéed veal, chicken, asparagus or artichokes.

Sauce Vin Blanc: Place 120 ml/4 fl oz (½ cup) Fish Stock (see page 414 or use cooking liquor from poaching fish) and 4 tbsp dry white wine in a saucepan and boil rapidly until reduced to 2 tbsp. Follow recipe for Hollandaise Sauce using this reduced liquid in place of the lemon juice and water. Serve on poached fish.

Béarnaise Sauce

Serve with grilled (broiled) steak, tournedos or roast beef, also with shellfish and some vegetables (green peas with Béarnaise are delicious).

4 tbsp white wine vinegar; 1 shallot, chopped; 4 black peppercorns; 1 bay leaf; ¼ tsp dried tarragon; 1 sprig fresh thyme, or pinch dried; 2 egg yolks; 125 g/4 oz (½ cup) butter, cut into small pieces; salt and freshly ground white pepper; 1 tsp finely chopped fresh tarragon or parsley (optional).

Put vinegar, shallot, peppercorns, bay leaf, dried tarragon and thyme into a small saucepan and boil until reduced to 1 tbsp liquid. Strain, pressing to extract all flavour. Place reduced flavoured vinegar and egg yolks in the top of a double saucepan (double boiler) or in a heatproof bowl that will fit over a saucepan. Bring 2.5 cm (1 in) water just to simmering point in bottom of double saucepan (double boiler) or saucepan, place container with egg yolks over water (which must not touch container) and whisk until yolks thicken slightly. This stage is called a sabayon and is reached

when you begin to see bottom of bowl between strokes and mixture clings to whisk when it is raised from bowl. Now add butter, a piece at a time, slipping it through your fingers to soften it slightly. Whisk continuously, incorporating each piece of butter thoroughly before adding next piece. When all butter has been added and sauce is thickened and creamy, season lightly with salt and pepper and fold in tarragon or parsley, if using. Makes 175 ml/6 fl oz (¾ cup).

NOTE: If sauce refuses to thicken or curdles, this can be remedied as described for Hollandaise Sauce.

VARIATIONS

Paloise Sauce: Follow recipe for Béarnaise Sauce but substitute 2 tbsp chopped fresh mint (including stalks) for dried tarragon and thyme for making reduced flavoured vinegar, and 1 tsp shredded fresh mint for chopped fresh tarragon or parsley to fold through finished sauce. Serve with roast or grilled (broiled) lamb.

Sauce Choron: Stir 1–1½ tbsp tomato purée (paste) into 1 quantity Bearnaise Sauce. Serve with grilled (broiled) or sautéed veal or lamb.

HOT BUTTER SAUCES

These superbly simple sauces depend on the wonderful fragrance and flavour of butter.

Beurre Blanc

Beurre Blanc, light and creamy, goes back to Escoffier and beyond but is newly popular as a sauce of the Nouvelle Cuisine. It is easy to make with a wire whisk – an essential tool to achieve the liaison between liquid and butter which gives the sauce body. Serve with mousselines (see page 223) or quenelles (see page 324), shellfish, poached or grilled (broiled) fish, chicken, eggs and vegetables such as broccoli, cauliflower or artichokes.

250 ml/8 fl oz (1 cup) poaching liquid (Court Bouillon, page 85) from fish or shellfish, or 250 ml/8 fl oz (1 cup) dry white wine with good squeeze lemon juice added; 1 tbsp finely chopped shallot; 250 ml/8 fl oz (1 cup) chilled butter, cut into large dice; salt and freshly ground white pepper.

Put poaching liquid, or wine and lemon juice, into a small, heavy saucepan, add shallot and boil until reduced to about 2 tbsp liquid. Remove from heat and whisk in 2 pieces of chilled butter. Return to very low heat and continue whisking in butter one piece at a time. The sauce will thicken to consistency of pouring cream. As soon as all butter has been added, remove from heat and whisk in salt and pepper. Makes about 175 ml/6 fl oz (¾ cup).

NOTE: The reduction of liquid and shallot can be prepared ahead and reheated when

needed, but do not try to hold or reheat the completed sauce – it is quite correct to serve it warm rather than hot.

Beurre Noisette

(Brown Butter)

'Noisette' means hazelnut, the golden-brown colour of this sauce. Beurre Noisette is excellent on fish, sweetbreads, eggs and vegetables.

90 g/3 oz (6 tbsp) butter; 1 tbsp lemon juice.

Heat butter slowly in a small frying pan (skillet), shaking pan occasionally to ensure even browning. When butter is golden-brown add any herbs etc., remove from heat and stir in lemon juice. Pour over food while still frothing. Serve very hot. Makes about 120 ml/4 fl oz (½ cup).

Beurre Noir

(Black Butter)

Despite the name the butter is cooked until it is brown, not black. Beurre noir is the classic sauce to serve on brains and is also good with fish, chicken, vegetables and eggs.

90 g/3 oz (6 tbsp) butter; 1 tbsp chopped parsley; 1 tbsp drained capers (optional, but always used for brains); 1 tbsp vinegar.

Heat butter slowly in a small frying pan (skillet), shaking pan occasionally to ensure even browning, until it is nut-brown. Stir in parsley and capers, if using, remove from heat and add vinegar. Pour over food while still frothing. Serve very hot. Makes about 120 ml/4 fl oz (½ cup).

OTHER USEFUL SAUCES

A selection of easy-to-prepare savoury sauces to add variety to everyday dishes.

Smooth Tomato Sauce

An excellent sauce for pasta, gnocchi, grilled (broiled) meats and green vegetables.

3 tbsp olive oil; 1 onion, finely chopped; 1 carrot, finely chopped; 1 stick celery, finely chopped; 2 cloves garlic, crushed; 1 sprig fresh marjoram, finely chopped, or ½ tsp dried; few sprigs parsley, finely chopped; 1 kg/2 lb (4 cups) ripe tomatoes, chopped; salt and freshly ground black pepper; ½ tsp sugar.

Heat olive oil in a saucepan and add onion, carrot, celery, garlic, marjoram and parsley. Cook over low heat until golden. Add tomatoes and season with salt, pepper and sugar. Simmer until tomatoes have turned almost to a purée. Push through a sieve, or blend in a blender or food processor and then sieve. Makes about 500 ml/18 fl oz (2 cups).

Right: Mange Tout (Snow Peas) page 388

Mushroom Sauce

60 g/2 oz (½ cup) mushrooms, preferably flat ones, chopped or sliced; 2 shallots, finely chopped; 45 g/1½ oz (3 tbsp) butter; 2 tsp flour; 300 ml/½ pint (1¼ cups) warm chicken stock; 2 tbsp single (light) cream; 1 tbsp chopped fresh mixed herbs or parsley; salt and freshly ground black pepper; few drops lemon juice.

Gently cook mushrooms and shallots in half the butter in a saucepan until soft. Add remaining butter and melt it, then stir in flour. Cook gently 1 minute. Remove from heat and add stock, stirring until smoothly blended. Return to medium heat and stir until boiling. Reduce heat, simmer 2 minutes, then add cream and herbs and simmer 1 minute longer. Season with salt, pepper and lemon juice. Makes about 300 ml/½ pint (1¼ cups).

Balinese Curry Sauce

This fragrant curry sauce is one of the most adaptable of bases. Chicken, pork, beef or lamb, cut into bite-sized pieces, can be cooked gently in it. For a vegetable curry add cabbage, green beans, aubergine (eggplant), cauliflower, potato. It is also a good base for leftover cooked poultry or meats – just heat gently in the sauce.

120 ml/4 fl oz (½ cup) water; 1 tsp turmeric; 4 curry leaves, or pinch curry powder; 2.5 cm (1 in) piece fresh ginger; 1 tsp ground coriander, or 1 tbsp chopped fresh coriander; ½ tsp grated lemon rind; 1–2 chillies, seeded (or to taste); 4 spring onions (scallions), chopped (including some green tops); 2 cloves garlic; 45 g/1½ oz (3 tbsp) butter; 1 tsp salt; 350 ml/12 fl oz (1½ cups) Coconut Milk (page 80); 2 macadamia nuts or 4 cashew nuts, crushed; 1 tsp sugar.

Put water, turmeric, curry leaves or powder, ginger, coriander, lemon rind, chillies, spring onions (scallions) and garlic into a blender or food processor fitted with a steel blade and process until smooth. If making by hand, pound all these ingredients, except water, in a mortar, then mix in water. Heat butter in a wok or small frying pan (skillet), add spring onion (scallion) mixture and cook briskly, stirring, 5 minutes. Stir in salt and coconut milk, then crushed nuts and sugar.

Vegetables, hard-boiled (hard-cooked) eggs or diced cooked meat may now be added and simmered in the sauce for 15 minutes or until vegetables are done. Raw chicken pieces or diced meat should be cooked gently for about 45 minutes or until tender. Serves 4.

Left: Three Bean Salad (page 357)

Beer or Cider Sauce with Sultanas

45 g/1½ oz (¼ cup) firmly packed brown sugar; 1 tbsp cornflour (cornstarch); large pinch salt; 250 ml/8 fl oz (1 cup) cider or beer; 45 g/1½ oz (¼ cup) sultanas (golden raisins); 8 cloves; 8 cm (3 in) cinnamon stick; 15 g/½ oz (1 tbsp) butter.

Mix brown sugar, cornflour (cornstarch) and salt in a small, heavy saucepan. Stir in cider or beer and add sultanas (golden raisins). Tie spices in a bag and add them. Boil gently 10 minutes, stirring often. Remove spice bag and swirl in butter. Serve immediately. Makes about 250 ml/8 fl oz (1 cup).

Devil Sauce

Devil Sauce is a hot, spicy mixture used to coat foods for grilling (broiling). Devilled chicken joints or small, split chickens, thick lamb or pork chops, fish fillets or fish steaks are all delicious. Devilling is also an excellent way to use cooked meat or poultry. Use the following for uncooked chicken, lamb or pork chops.

DRY DEVIL MIXTURE: *1 tsp salt; 2 tsp sugar; 1 tsp freshly ground black pepper; 1 tsp ground ginger; 1 tsp dry mustard; ½ tsp curry powder; 30 g/1 oz (2 tbsp) butter, melted, for grilling (broiling).*
SAUCE: *2 tbsp tomato relish; 1 tbsp Worcestershire sauce; 1 tbsp soy sauce; 1 tbsp fruit chutney; dash Tabasco (hot pepper) sauce; 30 g/1 oz (2 tbsp) butter; shredded spring onions (scallions) to garnish.*

Mix ingredients for dry devil mixture and rub into surface of chicken or meat. Leave at least 1 hour. Brush food with melted butter for grilling (broiling) and cook under a preheated grill (broiler) until browned on both sides.
SAUCE: Add sauce ingredients to remaining butter for grilling (broiling) and heat gently. Spoon over browned chicken or meat and continue cooking, basting frequently with juices in grill (broiler) pan, until done to your liking. Juices and sauce remaining in pan may be diluted with hot stock or vegetable water and spooned over for serving. Garnish with shredded spring onions (scallions). Makes sufficient for 4 large chicken joints.
VARIATIONS
Devil Sauce for Fish: Mix together all the ingredients for dry devil mixture, plus butter for grilling (broiling) and sauce ingredients. Spread over surface of fish and leave 1 hour. Place in well-heated, greased grill (broiler) pan under a preheated hot grill (broiler) and cook on one side only for fillets or small steaks, or turning once for thick steaks. Garnish with shredded spring onions (scallions). Sufficient for 4–8 fish fillets or 4 fish steaks.
Devil Sauce for Cooked Meat or Chicken: Cut

meat into thick slices; slash chicken flesh at intervals. Mix together all ingredients for dry devil mixture, plus butter for grilling (broiling) and sauce ingredients. Spread over surface, working well in. Leave at least 2 hours. Brown quickly under a preheated grill (broiler), basting several times with remaining mixture. Garnish with shredded spring onions (scallions). Makes sufficient for 4 servings.

Plum Sauce

2 large onions, finely chopped; 90 g/3 oz (6 tbsp) butter; 500 g (1 lb) plums, stoned (pitted); 350 ml/12 fl oz (1½ cups) dry red wine; 1 tbsp sugar; salt and freshly ground black pepper.

Cook onion slowly in butter until soft but not brown. Simmer plums with 250 ml/8 fl oz (1 cup) wine for 10 minutes, then add onions with their butter and season with sugar, salt and pepper. Simmer 10 minutes longer. Add remaining red wine, cover and simmer 40 minutes. Serve hot or warm. Makes about 750 ml/1¼ pints (3 cups).

DESSERT SAUCES

Sweet sauces can be served with a variety of desserts – fresh fruit, ice cream, steamed or milk puddings.

Quick Apricot Sauce

500 g/1 lb (1⅓ cups) apricot jam; 120 ml/4 fl oz (½ cup) water; 2 tbsp sugar; squeeze lemon juice; 2 tbsp Kirsch or Grand Marnier; 30 g/1 oz (¼ cup) toasted, slivered almonds.

Boil jam, water and sugar together slowly for 10 minutes, stirring frequently. Rub through a sieve and add lemon juice and liqueur. Serve warm, adding almonds at last minute. Makes about 500 ml/18 fl oz (2 cups).

Dipping Sauce for Fruit

Arrange a selection of prepared fresh fruits on individual plates and place a small bowl of this sauce on each.

250 ml/8 fl oz (1 cup) sour cream; 22 g/¾ oz (¼ cup) desiccated (shredded) coconut; 2 tbsp chopped walnuts; 2 tbsp sieved apricot jam; 2 tsp finely chopped preserved ginger; 1 tbsp rum or brandy (optional).

Mix all ingredients together. Serves 4.

Lemon Sauce

Serve with a lemon-flavoured sponge pudding.

2 tsp cornflour (cornstarch); 300 ml/½ pint (1¼ cups) water; 3 tbsp lemon juice; 1 tbsp sugar; 1 tbsp golden (light corn) syrup; 1 tsp butter.

Blend cornflour (cornstarch) with a little of the water. Put all remaining ingredients into a small, heavy saucepan and bring to the boil, stirring. Stir in blended cornflour (cornstarch) and bring to the boil again, stirring constantly. Makes about 350 ml/12 fl oz (1½ cups).

Sweet White Sauce

A simple, old-fashioned sauce, very good with steamed pudding.

1 tbsp cornflour (cornstarch); 250 ml/8 fl oz (1 cup) milk; 1 tbsp sugar; ½ tsp vanilla essence (extract).

Blend cornflour (cornstarch) with a little of the milk. Put remaining milk and s ar into a small, heavy saucepan and bring to the boil, stirring. Stir in blended cornflour (cornstarch) and bring to the boil again, stirring constantly. Simmer gently 3 minutes, then add vanilla. Makes 250 ml/8 fl oz (1 cup).

Simple Fruit Sauces

Any canned or stewed fruit, soft fresh fruit or frozen berries, etc., can be made into a sauce.

fresh or canned fruit; 1 tbsp arrowroot or cornflour (cornstarch); sugar; lemon juice; 1–2 tbsp brandy, rum, sherry or liqueur (optional).

Purée fruit in a blender or food processor or rub through a sieve. Add syrup if using canned or stewed fruit. Thicken, if necessary, by blending arrowroot or cornflour (cornstarch) with a little juice or water, heating puréed fruit to boiling point and stirring in enough blended arrowroot or cornflour (cornstarch) to give desired thickness. Sweeten with sugar and sharpen the flavour with lemon juice. Add brandy, rum, sherry or liqueur to taste, if desired. Serve hot or cold.

SAUERKRAUT

Called *choucroute* in French, this is basically shredded cabbage fermented with salt, and flavoured with juniper berries. This fermentation has been used for centuries as a method of preserving cabbage, an important consideration during the long, snow-bound months of winter in northern Europe.

Bulk sauerkraut is sometimes available from big barrels, but more often sauerkraut is bought in jars, canned or in vacuum-packs. If the sauerkraut is packed in brine, it should be washed and thoroughly drained before use. **See recipes.**

Knackwurst with Sauerkraut

2 onions, finely chopped; 30 g/1 oz (2 tbsp) butter; 1 tbsp oil; 1 kg (2 lb) sauerkraut, rinsed if necessary; 2 cooking apples, peeled, cored and sliced; 1 tbsp brown sugar; 1 tsp dry mustard; 120 ml/4 fl oz (½ cup) dry white wine; salt and freshly ground black pepper; 500 g (1 lb) knackwurst sausage or Polish clobassi.

Fry onions in butter and oil in a frying pan (skillet) until transparent. Toss sauerkraut with fork to separate, then add to pan with apples, sugar, mustard and wine. Season with salt and pepper. Spread out in large greased shallow ovenproof dish. Place sausage in pan of cold water, bring to the boil then drain. Cut into thick diagonal slices and arrange on top of sauerkraut mixture. Cover with foil and bake in a preheated moderate oven (180°C/350°F, Gas Mark 4) for 20–30 minutes or until heated through. Serve accompanied by mustard and dill pickles. Serves 6.

Choucroute Soup

500 g (1 lb) sauerkraut; 2 medium potatoes, peeled and diced; 2 rashers (slices) bacon, rind removed; 6 juniper berries; 1 bay leaf; salt and freshly ground black pepper; 2 tsp sugar; 1.2 litres/2 pints (5 cups) stock or water; 2–3 smoked frankfurters, cut into short lengths; 4 tbsp single (light) cream.

Place sauerkraut in a large saucepan with potatoes, bacon, juniper berries, bay leaf, salt, pepper and sugar. Add stock or water and simmer about 1 hour. Push through a sieve or purée using a food mill. Return to pan, add frankfurters and cook for a further 15 minutes. Adjust seasoning, and stir in cream just before serving. Serves 6–8.

Juniper Sauerkraut

1 onion, finely chopped; 1 apple, peeled, cored and chopped; 1 clove garlic, crushed;
60 g/2 oz (4 tbsp) butter; 6 juniper berries, crushed; 500 g (1 lb) sauerkraut; 1 tsp celery seeds; 250 ml/8 fl oz (1 cup) stock; 250 ml/8 fl oz (1 cup) plain yogurt or sour cream.

Cook onion, apple and garlic in butter in a flameproof casserole over low heat until soft. Add juniper berries, sauerkraut, celery seed and stock and simmer for 2–3 minutes. Cover, reduce heat to very low and cook for 45–60 minutes, or cook in a preheated cool oven (150°C/300°F, Gas Mark 2). Stir in yogurt or sour cream just before serving. Serve hot as an accompaniment to grilled (broiled) pork chops or sausages. Serves 6.

SAUERBRATEN

A dish of marinated, spiced beef or pork, pot-roasted to melting tenderness is one of Germany's most celebrated dishes.

Sauerbraten

1 × 3 kg (6 lb) boned and rolled topside (top round) of beef or fresh silverside (bottom round of beef); 120 ml/4 fl oz (½ cup) red wine vinegar; 350 ml/12 fl oz (1½ cups) red wine; 10 black peppercorns; 1 tsp salt; 1 bay leaf; 6 cloves; 2 cloves garlic; 2 strips lemon rind; 1 onion, sliced; ¼ tsp nutmeg; 3 sticks celery, chopped; 2 carrots, chopped; 3 sprigs parsley; 500 ml/18 fl oz (2 cups) beef stock; 3 tbsp cornflour (cornstarch); 120 ml/4 fl oz (½ cup) sour cream.

Place beef in a large china or glass bowl. Combine vinegar, red wine, peppercorns, salt, bay leaf, cloves, garlic, lemon rind, onion, nutmeg, celery, carrots and parsley. Add to beef, cover and refrigerate for 3 days, turning occasionally. Remove meat and reserve marinade. Dry meat well with paper towels. Bring marinade to the boil in a saucepan. Reduce heat and leave to simmer while the meat is cooking; it will be used to baste the meat. Heat a heavy flameproof casserole, add meat, fat side down, and brown well on all sides over moderate heat. Pour off excess fat. Add 250 ml/8 fl oz (1 cup) beef stock, then cover and simmer over very low heat for 3–3½ hours or until meat is tender. Baste occasionally with remaining stock and the hot marinade until all the marinade has been added. Remove meat to a hot platter. Strain cooking liquid, pressing vegetables through the sieve. Remove fat from surface and return to casserole. Thicken with cornflour (cornstarch) mixed with a little water. Add sour cream. The sauce should be served separately from the meat. Serves 8–10.
NOTE: If liked, the gravy may be thickened with 45 g/1½ oz (½ cup) broken ginger nuts (gingersnaps) and 45 g/1½ oz (¼ cup) raisins or currants added for sweetness.

SAUSAGE

Salame, saucisson, wurst – the simple sausage speaks many languages. The art of sausage-making can be traced back many centuries, and sausages have probably been made for as long as the pig has been slaughtered.

The skill and ingenuity of these early sausage-makers is still in evidence today, with different towns and regions still producing their own particular and traditional types of sausage.

Types of Sausage

Fresh Sausages: These may be made of pork or beef, and are seasoned or spiced. The meat may be very finely ground and combined with cereal or some other 'filler', or the sausage may contain meat only. Most fresh Continental sausages are of this latter type. Very finely ground meat, usually pork or beef, or a mixture of both, is also sold in a solid pack. Cereals and seasonings are added (in strictly controlled proportions) to give the characteristic sausage flavour. Use sausage meat to make your own skinless sausages, to extend dishes using minced (ground) beef, or to make stuffings, patties, sausage rolls or Scotch eggs.

Raw Sausages: Also called air-dried sausages, these are typified by the Italian *salame*. These are generally made of pork, or a mixture of pork and beef. The meat is minced (ground) and salted, in the same way as a ham is salted, flavourings and spices are added and the sausages are hung up to dry for several months. Salami type sausages are marvellous in salads; as part of an hors d'oeuvre; combined with fresh melon or figs; on savouries and open sandwiches. They should be quite firm when bought, and should be sliced very thinly.

Cooked Sausages: There is an enormous range of cooked sausages, some of which are also smoked. Polish *clobassi* is one of these, as is the Italian *mortadella*, and many German sausages – *frankfurter, bierwurst, presswurst.* These may be eaten as they are, with a salad and perhaps mustards and pickles, or potato salad and dill cucumbers. Or they may be simmered in stock or water for about 10–20 minutes, depending on size, and eaten hot with starchy vegetables such as mashed potatoes, sauerkraut, cooked lentils, haricot (navy) beans or red cabbage.

Soft Sausages: These include all forms of liver sausage, which is eaten as it is, on bread or biscuits. German *mettwurst* is another soft, spreading sausage.

Black Puddings: Also known as *boudins* in France, or blood sausages, these are made with pigs' blood, onions and seasonings. These may be cooked by simmering or frying, and are usually accompanied by mashed potato, onions and fried apple rings.

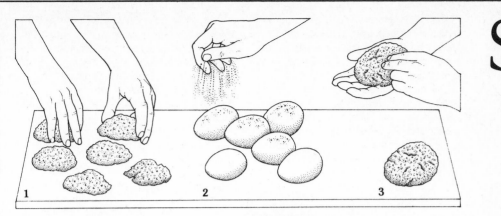

Shaping Scotch Eggs

Andouilles and Andouillettes: French names for smoked and salted sausages made from pork tripe.

☐ **To Cook Fresh Sausages:** Fresh sausages may be grilled (broiled) or fried, and if desired cooking may be preceded by parboiling. Prick the sausages lightly with a sharp-pronged fork or the point of a knife, in order to prevent them bursting. Parboiling also helps to prevent bursting.

When frying sausages, it is rarely necessary to add any fat except just enough to prevent them from sticking. If sausages give out a lot of fat during cooking, drain this off.

When barbecuing sausages, thread them on long skewers to make them easy to turn. **See recipes.**

Risotto with Italian Sausage

2 tbsp finely chopped onion; 45 g/1½ oz (3 tbsp) butter; 2 tbsp oil; 430 g/14 oz (2 cups) long-grain rice; 1 litre/1¾ pints (4 cups) boiling chicken stock; 370 g (12 oz) Italian sausage; 4 tbsp dry white wine; salt and freshly ground black pepper; 3 tbsp grated Parmesan cheese.

Gently fry onion in 30 g/1 oz (2 tbsp) butter and the oil in a saucepan until translucent. Add rice and stir until well coated. Add 120 ml/4 fl oz (½ cup) stock, stirring. As stock is absorbed, add another 120 ml/4 fl oz (½ cup) stock and mix in. Continue adding stock in this way until it is all added and rice is tender. Meanwhile, cook sausage in frying pan (skillet) with wine. Allow wine to evaporate, then cook sausages in their fat for 12–15 minutes. Remove and set aside. When rice is cooked, add salt and pepper. Stir in remaining butter and Parmesan and mix thoroughly. Turn on to heated serving dish. Pour all but 2 tbsp fat from frying pan (skillet) in which sausages cooked. Add about 2 tbsp water and deglaze frying pan (skillet) over high heat, scraping any residue from bottom. Return sausages to pan to heat through, then arrange on risotto and pour pan liquid over. Serve at once. Serves 4.

Scotch Eggs

500 g/1 lb (2 cups) sausage meat; few drops Tabasco (hot pepper) sauce; few drops Worcestershire sauce; 6 hard-boiled (hard-cooked) eggs; 60 g/2 oz (½ cup) flour; salt and freshly ground black pepper; 1 egg, beaten; dry breadcrumbs; oil for deep-frying.

Mix sausage meat with sauces. Divide into 6 equal portions **(Fig 1 above)**. Dust eggs lightly with flour seasoned with salt and pepper **(2)**, then cover each egg with sausage mixture, pressing and moulding on well **(3)**. Brush with beaten egg and roll in breadcrumbs. Chill for at least 1 hour. Deep-fry eggs in hot oil until golden-brown. Drain on paper towels. Cool and chill. Serve cold with salads. Makes 6.

Sausages with Onion Gravy

8 sausages; 60 g/2 oz (4 tbsp) butter; 6 onions, sliced; 2 tbsp flour; 1 tsp dry mustard; 250 ml/8 fl oz (1 cup) beef stock; 175 ml/6 fl oz (¾ cup) flat beer; 1 tsp sugar; 1 tsp chopped fresh thyme, or ¼ tsp dried; salt and freshly ground black pepper.

Prick sausages, place in a saucepan and cover with cold water. Bring to the boil and simmer for 10 minutes. Drain. Peel off skin. Melt butter in a saucepan and sauté onions until softened. Stir in flour and dry mustard and cook for 1 minute. Stir in remaining ingredients, except sausages, bring to the boil, reduce heat and simmer for 15 minutes. Add sausages and continue to simmer for further 5 minutes or until heated through. Serves 4.

German Bean Soup

210 g/7 oz (1 cup) haricot (navy) beans, soaked overnight and drained; freshly ground black pepper; 1 tbsp finely chopped parsley; 2 bay leaves; salt; 1 tbsp oil; 2 medium carrots, sliced; 500 ml/18 fl oz (2 cups) stock; 1 large cabbage leaf; 2 medium leeks, cut into 5 cm (2 in) pieces; pinch nutmeg; 250 g (8 oz) German bratwurst or frankfurters, thickly sliced.

Cover beans with fresh cold water and bring to the boil. Add pepper, parsley and bay leaves and simmer gently for 1 hour or until beans are tender, adding salt towards the end of cooking. Drain and discard bay leaves. Heat oil in a saucepan, add carrots and cook gently for 10 minutes. Add stock, cabbage leaf, leeks and cooked beans. Adjust seasoning and add nutmeg. Cook over moderate heat for 15 minutes, then add sliced sausage and simmer 15 minutes longer. Serves 8–10.

Italian Salad with Cheese and Salami

1 head lettuce, torn into pieces; 2 firm, ripe tomatoes, seeded and cut into wedges; 4 anchovy fillets, chopped; salt and freshly ground black pepper; 2 tbsp wine vinegar; 5 tbsp olive oil; pinch dried oregano; 125 g (4 oz) Italian salami (Milano or Veneto), thinly sliced and cut into strips; 125 g (4 oz) Mozzarella cheese, cut into strips.

Place lettuce leaves in bowl with tomatoes. Add anchovy fillets, salt and pepper to vinegar, then gradually whisk in oil. Add oregano. Taste and add more oil or vinegar if desired. Pour dressing over lettuce and tomato and toss lightly. Arrange salami and cheese around top of salad, and serve immediately with crusty bread. Serves 4.

Frankfurter and Cabbage Salad

4 frankfurters; 4 slices cooked ham, cut into fine strips; 4 ripe tomatoes, peeled, seeded and diced; 1 red or green pepper, cored, seeded and cut into strips; 120 ml/4 fl oz ($\frac{1}{2}$ cup) Vinaigrette Dressing (page 358); $\frac{1}{4}$ tsp paprika; 1 tsp tomato purée (paste); 1 tsp French (Dijon) mustard; $\frac{1}{2}$ small white cabbage, finely shredded; 3–4 tbsp oil; salt and freshly ground black pepper; 1 tbsp white wine vinegar.

Poach frankfurters, drain, cool and slice thickly. Place frankfurters, ham, tomatoes and pepper in large bowl. Combine dressing with paprika, tomato purée (paste) and mustard. Toss frankfurter mixture with this dressing. Arrange salad on $\frac{1}{2}$ of large platter. Toss cabbage with oil, salt and pepper, then add vinegar and toss again. Arrange cabbage salad next to frankfurter salad. Serves 4.

Sausages with Peppers and Wine

500 g (1 lb) chorizo or similar pork sausages; 1 tbsp olive oil; 4 tbsp water; 3 shallots, finely chopped; 1 small red or green pepper, cored, seeded and finely chopped; 1 rasher (slice) bacon, rind removed and diced; 120 ml/4 fl oz ($\frac{1}{2}$ cup) white wine; 1 tbsp Madeira; salt and freshly ground black pepper.

Gently fry sausages in oil until browned all over. Transfer to ovenproof dish. Add water and complete cooking in a preheated moderate oven (180°C/350°F, Gas Mark 4). In pan in which sausages were browned, cook shallots, pepper and bacon for 2–3 minutes. Add wine and Madeira and bring to boil, then simmer for 10–15 minutes or until sausages are ready. Season sauce with salt and pepper and serve with hot sausages Serves 3–4.

Bean and Sausage Platter

8 Italian pork sausages; 2 tbsp olive oil; 150 ml/5 fl oz ($\frac{1}{2}$ cup) fresh tomato purée or Fresh Tomato Sauce (page 271); 120 ml/4 fl oz ($\frac{1}{2}$ cup) water; salt and freshly ground black pepper; 430 g/14 oz (2 cups) dried haricot (navy) beans, soaked and cooked in water until tender, or 750 g/1$\frac{1}{2}$ lb (4 cups) drained canned haricot (navy) beans.

Prick sausages, place in frying pan (skillet) and cover with cold water. Slowly bring to the boil, then drain. In same pan, cook sausages in oil until cooked through and well coloured on all sides. Remove and keep warm. Add tomato purée or sauce to pan and cook for 1–2 minutes. Add water and simmer gently 10 minutes. Season with salt and pepper. Add beans, stir well to mix and reheat for 5 minutes. Return sausages to pan to heat through. Arrange beans on heated serving platter and top with sausages. Serve immediately. Serves 6–8.

Sausages with Apples

500 g (1 lb) pork sausages; 4 apples, cored and sliced; 30 g/1 oz (2 tbsp) butter; 120 ml/4 fl oz ($\frac{1}{2}$ cup) dry cider or white wine; 1 tbsp brandy; 120 ml/4 fl oz ($\frac{1}{2}$ cup) single (light) cream; salt and freshly ground black pepper.

Prick sausages and fry over moderate heat. In another pan, cook apples in butter until golden. Remove from pan and keep warm.

Add cider or wine to pan, bring to the boil and reduce slightly, then add brandy and cream. Reduce heat and stir well. Reduce over high heat if thicker sauce required. Season well with salt and pepper and pour sauce over sausages and apples. Serve immediately. Serves 3–4.

Sausage Rolls

1 × 375 g/12 oz packet frozen puff pastry (paste), thawed; 500 g/1 lb (2 cups) sausage meat; salt and pepper; 1 egg, beaten.

Roll pastry (dough) out thinly and divide into 2 strips about 10 cm (4 in) wide. Trim edges. Form sausage meat into 2 neat rolls and place each roll on a strip of pastry (dough). Brush edges lightly with egg, fold pastry (dough) over sausage meat and seal it to opposite edge. Cut each roll into 12 sections. Rinse baking tray with cold water, place sausage rolls on tray and make 2 diagonal slashes in top of each roll. Brush tops with remaining egg. Chill 20 minutes. Bake in a preheated hot oven (230°C/450°F, Gas Mark 8) for 10 minutes, then reduce heat to moderate (180°C/350°F, Gas Mark 4) and cook 10 minutes longer. Serve hot. Makes 24.
NOTE: If made in advance, cool rolls on a wire rack, then, when needed, reheat for 5–8 minutes in a preheated moderate oven (180°C/350°F, Gas Mark 4).

Glazed Pork Sausages

For a change from plain fried sausages.

8 pork sausages; 60 g/2 oz ($\frac{1}{3}$ cup) firmly packed brown sugar; 500 ml/18 fl oz (2 cups) water; 1 tbsp vinegar.

Put all ingredients into a large frying pan (skillet) and simmer gently until water has evaporated. Tilt pan back and forth to roll sausages and coat them with light glaze that has formed on bottom. Serve immediately with hot boiled rice mixed with chopped pepper, pineapple and spring onions (scallions). Serves 4.

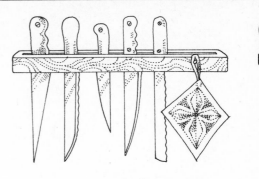

Toad-in-the-Hole

125 g/4 oz (1 cup) flour; $\frac{1}{4}$ tsp salt; 1 egg; 300 ml/$\frac{1}{2}$ pint (1$\frac{1}{4}$ cups) milk; 500 g (1 lb) sausages; 30 g/1 oz (2 tbsp) dripping or lard.

Sift flour and salt into a bowl. Make well in centre, add egg and milk and gradually mix to a smooth batter. Set aside for 30 minutes. Fry sausages in fat in flameproof baking dish for 5 minutes until brown on all sides. Pour batter over sausages and bake in a preheated moderately hot oven (200°C/400°F, Gas Mark 6) for about 30 minutes. Serves 4.

Chick Peas with Tomatoes and Sausages

310 g/10 oz (1$\frac{1}{2}$ cups) dried chick peas, soaked overnight and drained; 250 g (8 oz) pork sausages; 150 g/5 oz (generous $\frac{1}{2}$ cup) bacon, diced; 1 large onion, finely chopped; 2 cloves garlic, chopped; 1 large green pepper, cored, seeded and diced; 4 large ripe tomatoes, peeled, seeded and chopped; nutmeg or cinnamon; $\frac{1}{4}$ tsp dried thyme; salt and freshly ground black pepper.

Place chick peas in saucepan and add fresh cold water to cover. Simmer, covered, for about 1 hour. Prick sausages and brown in frying pan (skillet). Remove and cut into 2.5 cm (1 in) pieces. Set aside. Blanch bacon in boiling water for 1 minute, then drain. Brown bacon, onion, garlic and green pepper in fat from sausages in frying pan (skillet), stirring from time to time. Add tomatoes, spice, thyme, salt and pepper. Cover and cook over low heat for 10 minutes. Fold in sausage pieces. Drain chick peas, reserving 500 ml/18 fl oz (2 cups) liquid. Turn into greased ovenproof baking dish and cover with tomato and sausage mixture. Moisten with reserved liquid. Cover and bake in a preheated moderately hot oven (190°C/375°F, Gas Mark 5) for about 1$\frac{1}{2}$ hours, stirring from time to time. Serve in wide soup plates. Serves 4–6.

Baked Sausage, Cabbage and Apples

500 g/1 lb (2 cups) sausage meat; 1 small onion, finely chopped; 3 tbsp vinegar; 2 tbsp brown sugar; salt and freshly ground black pepper; $\frac{1}{2}$ small cabbage, finely shredded; 3 medium cooking apples, peeled, cored and thinly sliced; nutmeg.

Shape sausage meat into 8 flat patties and brown quickly on both sides in a greased frying pan (skillet). Remove patties. Add onion to fat in pan and brown lightly. Add vinegar, sugar, $\frac{1}{2}$ tsp salt and a grinding of pepper, and remove from heat. Arrange alternate layers of cabbage and apple in a greased casserole, seasoning each layer with salt, pepper and nutmeg. Place sausage patties in a single layer on top and pour

vinegar mixture over. Cover and bake in a preheated moderate oven (180°C/350°F, Gas Mark 4) for 40 minutes. Uncover and bake 10 minutes longer. Serves 4.

Sausages with Ham and Onion Stuffing

1 kg (2 lb) beef sausages; 60 g/2 oz (4 tbsp) butter; 1 onion, finely chopped; 1 tomato, finely chopped; 180 g/6 oz ($\frac{3}{4}$ cup) cooked ham, finely chopped; 60 g/2 oz (1 cup) loosely packed fresh breadcrumbs; 1 clove garlic, crushed; 1 tbsp tomato ketchup or barbecue sauce; few drops Tabasco (hot pepper) sauce; salt and freshly ground black pepper.

Prick sausages, place in a saucepan and cover with cold water. Bring to the boil, simmer 5 minutes and drain. Heat butter in a frying pan (skillet) and fry onion 3 minutes. Add tomato and cook 5 minutes longer. Stir in ham, breadcrumbs, garlic, sauces, salt and pepper. Split sausages open lengthways. Fill with stuffing. Barbecue or grill (broil) until sausages are browned and filling is hot. Serves 6–8.

Curried Sausages

8 sausages; 1 large onion, chopped; 30 g/1 oz diced celery; 1 cooking apple, peeled, cored and diced; 1 clove garlic, crushed; 1–2 tbsp curry powder; 2 tbsp flour; 2 tbsp tomato purée (paste); 500 ml/18 fl oz (2 cups) chicken stock; salt and freshly ground black pepper.

Prick sausages, place in a baking dish and bake in a preheated moderate oven (160°C/325°F, Gas Mark 3) for 15–20 minutes or until well cooked. Drain sausages, reserving 3 tbsp of fat. Place fat in a saucepan and fry onion, celery, apple and garlic until soft. Add curry powder and fry 2 minutes. Blend in flour and tomato purée (paste), then add stock gradually, stirring until boiling. Season with salt and pepper. Add sausages to sauce and simmer until heated through. Serves 4.

Sausage and Corn Picnic Loaf

1 day-old Vienna bread loaf; butter; 3 tbsp oil; 2 onions, finely chopped; 500 g/1 lb (2 cups) sausage meat; 1 large tomato, finely chopped; 1 × 300 g/10 oz can cream-style corn; 1 egg, lightly beaten; salt and freshly ground black pepper; 1 clove garlic, crushed.

Cut one end off bread and pull out some of the crumb. Reserve crumb. Lightly butter inside of loaf. Heat 2 tbsp oil and fry onions until lightly browned. Add sausage and cook, stirring and breaking down lumps with 2 forks until meat changes colour. Remove from heat and stir in reserved breadcrumbs,

tomato, corn, egg, salt and pepper. Pack mixture tightly into loaf, replace end piece and place loaf on a large sheet of foil. Cut 3 slashes across top, brush with remaining oil mixed with garlic, and bring sides of foil up, folding together across top. Bake in a preheated moderate oven (180°C/350°F, Gas Mark 4) for 30 minutes. Unfold foil and bake uncovered 10 minutes longer. Enclose again in foil for carrying. Serves 6–8.

Sausage Roll in Flaky Pastry

2 large onions, thinly sliced; 30 g/1 oz (2 tbsp) butter; 2 tsp brandy, whisky or Calvados; 2 tsp chopped fresh thyme, or $\frac{1}{2}$ tsp dried; $\frac{1}{2}$ tsp chopped fresh sage, or pinch dried; large pinch nutmeg; small pinch ground cloves; about $\frac{1}{2}$ tsp salt (depending on seasoning of sausage meat); freshly ground black pepper; 750 g/1$\frac{1}{2}$ lb (3 cups) sausage meat; 1 quantity Flaky Pastry (page 275), or 1 × 375g/12 oz packet frozen puff pastry (paste), thawed; 1 egg yolk, lightly beaten.

Cook onions gently in butter until soft but not brown. Set aside. Knead liquor, herbs, spices, salt and pepper into sausage meat. Roll meat between 2 sheets of floured plastic wrap to a rectangle about 1 cm ($\frac{1}{2}$ in) thick. Peel off top sheet of wrap and spread meat evenly with onions. Using bottom sheet of wrap to help, roll up meat like a Swiss roll (jelly roll). Lift into a greased shallow baking tin (pan), seam side down, and bake in a preheated moderate oven (160°C/325°F, Gas Mark 3) for 30 minutes, turning occasionally. Remove from oven and cool. Increase temperature to hot (230°C/450°F, Gas Mark 8). Roll out pastry (dough) to a sheet large enough to wrap round the meat. Place meat on pastry (dough) and wrap it round, brushing a little egg yolk on to seam and pressing it together. Place seam side down on baking tray and chill 20 minutes. Cut a few slashes in pastry (dough) and brush with egg yolk. Bake in hot oven for 10–15 minutes or until pastry (dough) is lightly coloured. Reduce heat to moderate (180°C/350°F, Gas Mark 4) and bake 15 minutes longer or until pastry (dough) is golden-brown and meat is heated through. Serve hot or warm. Serves 6.

SAUSAGE ROLLS

See page 376 for recipe.

SAVARIN

A wonderful liqueur-soaked yeast cake, said to have been invented by the great French chef Brillat-Savarin. He used a yeast dough similar to that used for the earlier Rum Baba (see page 18), but omitted the raisins in the mixture, changed the shape and the name, and introduced it to Paris where it became a triumph.

A savarin is baked in a special savarin ring mould. The syrup is usually flavoured with Kirsch, and the centre can be filled with whipped cream, custard or a fruit filling. A savarin is usually glazed, and can be decorated with almonds, glacé (candied) fruits or fresh berry fruits.

Savarin

250 g/8 oz (2 cups) flour; $\frac{1}{4}$ tsp salt; 15 g/$\frac{1}{2}$ oz (1 tbsp) fresh (compressed) yeast; 3 tsp sugar; 120 ml/4 fl oz ($\frac{1}{2}$ cup) warm milk; 2 large eggs; 125 g/4 oz ($\frac{1}{2}$ cup) butter, softened; 120 ml/4 fl oz ($\frac{1}{2}$ cup) Apricot Glaze (page 11); 150 g/5 oz (1 cup) fruit – strawberries, raspberries, cherries, blackberries etc – sprinkled with 2 tbsp Kirsch and 1 tbsp sugar.
SYRUP: *250 ml/8 fl oz (1 cup) water; 250 g/8 oz (1 cup) sugar; 2.5 cm (1 in) piece vanilla pod (bean); 4 tbsp Kirsch.*

Sift flour and salt into a large warmed bowl. In a small bowl cream yeast with sugar, then add warm milk. Make a well in centre of flour and add yeast mixture. Sprinkle a little flour from sides over top, cover with a cloth and leave in a warm place for 15 minutes for yeast to sponge. Beat eggs into butter and add to yeast mixture. Beat vigorously using the hand until all flour is incorporated and the dough is smooth and elastic. Cover with a cloth and leave dough to rise in a warm place until doubled in bulk. This will take

30–40 minutes. Spoon dough into a well-greased 23 cm (9 in) savarin mould or ring tin (pan). Allow to rise in a warm place until dough reaches top of tin (pan). Bake in a preheated moderately hot oven (200°C/400°F, Gas Mark 6) for about 20 minutes or until golden-brown and beginning to shrink a little from sides of mould.

SYRUP: Combine water, sugar and vanilla bean in a saucepan. Stir over medium heat until sugar dissolves. Bring to the boil and boil for 10 minutes. Discard vanilla. Stir in Kirsch. Remove savarin from oven and cool in tin (pan) for 5 minutes. Turn out on to a cake rack and place a dish under rack to catch any syrup if it runs off cake. Prick savarin with a fine skewer all over and while still hot spoon warm syrup over, a little at a time, until all syrup has been absorbed. Allow savarin to cool. Carefully slide on to a serving dish, brush lightly with apricot glaze and fill centre with fruit or one of the fillings suggested below. Serves 6–8.
NOTE: The centre of the savarin may be filled with 500 ml/18 fl oz (2 cups) whipped cream flavoured with Kirsch; 500 ml/18 fl oz (2 cups) Crème Pâtissière (see page 165) flavoured with vanilla and Kirsch; or a macédoine of fresh fruits such as cherries, pears, apricots and pineapple sprinkled with sugar and Kirsch.

SCALOPPINE

The Italian name for the thinly beaten veal steak that the French call *escalope*; the tiny ones, *escalopines* in French, become *piccate* in Italy. Italian cooks use *scaloppine* to make exquisite quick dishes, both simple and sumptuous. For description and basic preparation, see *Escalope.* **See recipes.**

Scaloppine Passetto

4 large scaloppini; 1 tbsp flour; 8 slices prosciutto or ham deluxe; 8 thin slices Mozzarella cheese; $\frac{1}{2}$ tsp dried sage; salt and freshly ground black pepper; butter; 60 g/2 oz ($\frac{1}{2}$ cup) grated Parmesan cheese.

Cut each scaloppine in half. Sprinkle with flour and place between 2 sheets of plastic wrap. Flatten with a cutlet bat, rolling pin or flat side of a meat mallet. Place a slice of prosciutto, then Mozzarella cheese on each steak and sprinkle with sage, salt and pepper. Roll up each steak and secure with a wooden toothpick. Heat enough butter in a frying pan (skillet) to cover bottom generously. Quickly sauté veal rolls in 2 lots, until they are well browned on all sides. Place rolls in an ovenproof dish and sprinkle with Parmesan cheese and a little melted butter. Bake in a preheated moderately hot oven (190°C/375°F, Gas Mark 5) for 10 minutes and serve piping hot. Serves 4.

Saltimbocca

The name means 'jump in the mouth': it is so quick to cook, it jumps into the pan and then into the mouth.

6 large scaloppini, halved and beaten flat; 12 slices prosciutto; 12 leaves fresh sage; 75 g/2$\frac{1}{2}$ oz (5 tbsp) butter; salt and freshly ground black pepper; 120 ml/4 fl oz ($\frac{1}{2}$ cup) dry white wine.

Cover each slice of veal with a slice of prosciutto and place a sage leaf on each. Secure with wooden toothpicks. Heat 60 g/2 oz (4 tbsp) butter in a frying pan (skillet), add veal slices when foam subsides and brown quickly, about 2 minutes on each side. Season very lightly with salt and generously with pepper. Arrange slices, ham side up, on a heated serving dish. Remove toothpicks and keep saltimbocca warm. Add wine to pan and boil 1–2 minutes, stirring and scraping up brown bits with a wooden spoon. Season with salt and pepper. Remove from heat and swirl in remaining butter. Pour sauce over meat and serve immediately. Serves 6.

Scaloppine with Marsala

(Scaloppine alla Marsala)
A famous Sicilian treatment of scaloppine.

4 large scaloppini, halved and beaten flat; salt and freshly ground black pepper; 2 eggs, beaten; 3 tbsp flour; 45 g/1$\frac{1}{2}$ oz (3 tbsp) butter; 120 ml/4 fl oz ($\frac{1}{2}$ cup) dry Marsala or sherry; 120 ml/4 fl oz ($\frac{1}{2}$ cup) beef stock or consommé.

Season scaloppini with salt and pepper, dip in beaten egg and coat with flour. Heat about 30 g/1 oz (2 tbsp) butter in a frying pan (skillet) – use enough butter to cover bottom of pan completely – and brown meat, taking care not to burn, for about 5 minutes on each side. When well browned, add Marsala and swirl liquid round so that it will be thickened by flour and butter. Remove scaloppini to heated plates. Add stock and remaining butter to frying pan, scraping brown bits from bottom and sides. Swirl to make gravy and pour over meat. Serves 4.

Piccata in Tomato Cream Sauce

(Piccata con Pomodoro)

18 piccata, beaten flat; salt and freshly ground black pepper; flour; 125 g/4 oz ($\frac{1}{2}$ cup) butter; 120 ml/4 fl oz ($\frac{1}{2}$ cup) dry white wine; 120 ml/4 fl oz ($\frac{1}{2}$ cup) brown stock; 1 tbsp chopped shallot; 4 ripe tomatoes, peeled, seeded and chopped; pinch sugar; 250 ml/8 fl oz (1 cup) single (light) cream; 2 tbsp lemon juice.

Season piccata with salt and pepper and dust with flour. Reserve about 15 g/$\frac{1}{2}$ oz

(1 tbsp) butter and heat remainder in a frying pan (skillet) over fairly high heat. Brown veal, a few slices at a time, about 2 minutes on each side. Remove slices to a heated serving platter and keep hot. Add wine and stock to pan and boil together rapidly until reduced by half. Add shallot and tomatoes, season with sugar, salt and pepper and cook about 5 minutes. Add cream, reduce heat slightly and simmer 5 minutes longer. Remove from heat, add lemon juice and swirl in reserved butter bit by bit. Pour sauce over piccata and serve immediately. Serves 6.

Piccata with Parsley and Lemon
(Piccata al prezzemolo e limone)

18 piccata, beaten flat; salt and freshly ground black pepper; flour; 125 g/4 oz (½ cup) butter; 5 tbsp lemon juice; 2 tbsp chopped parsley.

Season piccata with salt and pepper and dust with flour. Set aside 15 g/1 oz (1 tbsp) butter and heat remainder in a large, heavy frying pan (skillet). Brown veal, a few pieces at a time, about 2 minutes each side. Transfer them to a heated serving platter and keep warm. Add lemon juice and parsley to pan, remove from heat and swirl in reserved butter bit by bit. Pour over veal and serve immediately. Serves 6.

SCALLOP

A shellfish, also known by its French name, *coquille St. Jacques*, belonging to a group of bivalve molluscs, the most familiar species having scalloped, fan-shaped shells that are both beautiful and symbolic. The exquisite scallop design has been used in paintings through the ages (notably Botticelli's 'The Birth of Venus'). The shell has long been a symbol of Christianity and a badge of the Pilgrims.

Scallops are usually purchased shucked or split, the edible flesh (white adductor muscle and orange coral or roe) removed from the shells. They can be bought fresh or frozen and usually require little preparation except

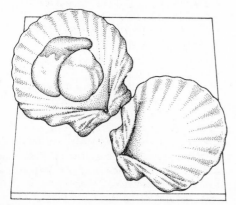

the removal of any small brown parts that may be left after cleaning.

Scallops have a delicate, subtle flavour, admirably suited to simple dishes. They should be cooked for short periods only and can be baked, poached, grilled (broiled) or fried in many ways.

Try scallops fried or baked in the oven in butter with chopped parsley, garlic and lemon juice, or sautéed and served with a little port and single (light) cream stirred in to make a sauce. **See recipes.**

Scallop Chowder

1 litre/1¾ pints (4 cups) milk; 350 ml/12 fl oz (1½ cups) single (light) cream; 60 g/2 oz (4 tbsp) butter; 2 tsp sugar; 1 tsp Worcestershire sauce; ½ tsp salt; ¼ tsp white pepper; 500 g (1 lb) scallops, very finely chopped; lemon juice; paprika; 2 tbsp finely chopped parsley.

Combine milk, cream, butter, sugar, Worcestershire sauce, salt and pepper in a heatproof bowl or top of a double saucepan (double boiler). Heat over simmering water, stirring. Add scallops and simmer for 5 minutes. Season with lemon juice. Serve sprinkled with paprika and chopped parsley. Serves 4–6.

Scallops with Garlic Butter Sauce

500 g (1 lb) scallops; seasoned flour; 75 g/2½ oz (5 tbsp) butter; 1 tbsp olive oil; 1 small clove garlic, finely chopped; 2 tbsp finely chopped parsley; lemon wedges to garnish.

Remove any brown parts from scallops but keep coral. Dust with seasoned flour, shaking well to remove any excess. Melt 15 g/½ oz (1 tbsp) butter with the oil in a sauté pan. When foam subsides, sauté scallops for 3–4 minutes or until light golden. Transfer to a heated dish and keep warm. Clarify remaining butter by melting it slowly and skimming off foam. Spoon clear butter into a container and discard milky solids left at bottom. Return clarified butter to pan and heat until it sizzles without colouring. Remove from heat and stir in garlic. Pour over scallops and serve at once, sprinkled with chopped parsley and garnished with lemon wedges. Serves 4.

Scallops in Green Sauce

500 g (1 lb) scallops; 120 ml/4 fl oz (½ cup) dry vermouth; ½ onion, chopped; 1 sprig parsley; 1 bay leaf; salt and freshly ground black pepper.
GREEN SAUCE: *3–4 spinach leaves; about 250 ml/8 fl oz (1 cup) Mayonnaise (page 204); 10 g/⅓ oz (¼ cup) finely chopped parsley; 3 tbsp snipped chives; 1 tbsp finely*
chopped fresh dill, or ½ tsp dried.
TO SERVE: *lettuce leaves, chopped parsley.*

Remove any brown parts from scallops but retain coral. Heat vermouth with onion, parsley sprig, bay leaf, salt and pepper in a saucepan. Add scallops and simmer gently for 3–4 minutes or until tender, shaking pan occasionally. Drain and cool.
GREEN SAUCE: Steam spinach in a covered saucepan for 1 minute only, then rinse in cold water. Press out water and chop spinach finely. Blend 250 ml/8 fl oz (1 cup) mayonnaise with parsley, spinach, chives and dill. Add extra mayonnaise to taste, if necessary. To serve, place scallops in a bowl lined with lettuce leaves, cover with sauce and garnish with a sprinkling of parsley. Alternatively, set lettuce leaves in 4 individual dishes (scallop shells look nice). Divide scallops between shells and top with green sauce and parsley. Serves 4.

Curried Scallops

1 kg (2 lb) scallops; 90 g/3 oz (6 tbsp) plus 2 tsp butter; 3–4 shallots, chopped; 2 tsp curry powder; 500 ml/18 fl oz (2 cups) dry white wine; 1 bouquet garni (2 sprigs parsley, 1 bay leaf and 2 sprigs fresh thyme); 2 tsp flour; 120 ml/4 fl oz (½ cup) single (light) cream; salt and freshly ground black pepper; finely chopped parsley.

Remove any brown parts from scallops, keeping coral. Melt 90 g/3 oz (6 tbsp) butter in a heavy saucepan over a medium heat and add shallots and curry powder. Stir for 1 minute. Add wine, scallops and bouquet garni and bring to the boil. Reduce heat and poach for 5 minutes. Using a slotted spoon, transfer scallops to a serving dish, or 6 individual scallop shells or dishes, and keep warm. Reduce cooking liquid to 350 ml/12 fl oz (1½ cups) by rapid boiling, and discard bouquet garni. Make a beurre manié by blending 2 tsp butter with flour. Gradually stir into stock in small pieces, and bring to boiling point. Reduce heat, add cream, season with salt and pepper and cook gently, stirring, for a few minutes. Do not allow to boil. Pour sauce over scallops and sprinkle with parsley. Serves 6.

Scallops under a Roof

750 g (1½ lb) scallops; 2 shallots, finely chopped; 1 bouquet garni (2 sprigs parsley, 2 sprigs fresh thyme, 1 bay leaf); ½ tsp salt; freshly ground white pepper; 120 ml/4 fl oz (½ cup) dry white wine; 60 g/2 oz (4 tbsp) butter; 2 tbsp flour; 4 tbsp single (light) cream; 1 tsp grated lemon rind; 1 × 375 g/12 oz packet frozen puff pastry (paste), thawed; 1 egg, beaten.

Remove any brown parts from scallops, keeping coral. Place in a saucepan with shallots, bouquet garni, salt, pepper and wine. Add enough water to come just to top of scallops and simmer for 2 minutes. Drain, reserving 175 ml/6 fl oz ($\frac{3}{4}$ cup) of the cooking liquid. Strain liquid. If scallops are large, halve them. Melt butter in saucepan, stir in flour and cook for 1 minute over a low heat. Remove from heat and cool a little, then add warm scallop liquid and stir until smooth. Return to a medium heat and bring just to the boil, stirring constantly. Stir in cream and lemon rind, adjust seasoning and fold in scallops. Divide mixture among 6 scallop shells or small ovenproof dishes, cover with foil and chill. Roll out pastry (dough) thinly and cut 6 rounds large enough to cover shells, with an overlap of about 1 cm ($\frac{1}{2}$ in) all round. Remove foil from shells and brush edges with beaten egg. Fit pastry (dough) lids over top and cut off surplus pastry (dough). Press edges firmly to seal. Cut 2 small slits in top of each lid and chill for 30 minutes. Brush with beaten egg. Place shells on a baking tray and bake in a preheated hot oven (230°C/450°F, Gas Mark 8) for 10 minutes or until the pastry (dough) is crisp and golden-brown. Serves 6.

Precious Jade Cocktail

Fascinating presentation makes this seafood cocktail the highlight of the meal. Offer a choice of 2 interesting sauces.

2 cucumbers; 370 g/12 oz (1½ cups) cooked prawns (shrimp); 250 g (8 oz) scallops; 4 tbsp dry white wine; 4 tbsp water; salt and freshly ground black pepper; 1 tbsp lemon juice; 3 tbsp oil; fresh dill, parsley or watercress to garnish.
FRESH TOMATO SAUCE: *2 ripe tomatoes, peeled, seeded and finely chopped; 175 ml/6 fl oz (¾ cup) double (heavy) cream, lightly whipped; 2 tbsp grated horseradish; salt and freshly ground black pepper.*
CURRIED MAYONNAISE: *250 ml/8 fl oz (1 cup) Mayonnaise (page 204); 2 spring onions (scallions), finely chopped; 2 tsp chutney; 2 tsp curry powder; salt and freshly ground black pepper; 1 egg white.*

Lightly peel cucumbers, leaving a little pale green, then, with a swivel-bladed potato peeler, shave off thin ribbons of flesh. Drop them into iced water, which will make them curl into pretty shapes. Shell prawns (shrimp), leaving tails intact, and devein. Remove any brown parts from scallops, keeping coral. Poach for 2 minutes in wine and water seasoned with a little salt and pepper. Drain. Whisk together lemon juice, oil, salt and pepper and pour over scallops, turning to coat them with this dressing. Drain cucumber and arrange in middle of 6 individual serving plates. Arrange prawns (shrimp) and scallops on each dish. Garnish with dill, parsley or watercress.

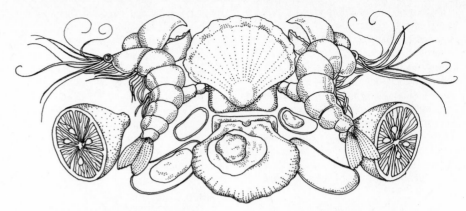

FRESH TOMATO SAUCE: Fold tomatoes into cream, with horseradish, salt and pepper to taste.
CURRIED MAYONNAISE: Mix mayonnaise with spring onions (scallions), chutney, curry powder, salt and pepper. Beat egg white until it forms soft peaks, and fold in. Pass sauces separately, so each guest may choose which he or she prefers. Serves 6.

Scallops Beurre Blanc

500 g (1 lb) scallops; salt and freshly ground white pepper; 250 ml/8 fl oz (1 cup) white wine; little lemon juice; 1 tbsp chopped shallot; 125 g/4 oz (½ cup) butter, cut into pieces; 8–10 chives to garnish.

Remove any brown parts from scallops, keeping coral. Season with salt and pepper. Poach scallops in wine and lemon juice for about 1 minute. Remove scallops and keep warm. Add shallot to poaching liquid and boil to reduce to about 5 tbsp. Over a gentle heat, add butter a little at a time, whisking it in to make a sauce (the consistency of pouring cream). Season sauce with salt and pepper and spoon on to 4 heated entrée plates. Arrange scallops on top and garnish with matchstick lengths of chives. Serves 4.

Scallops with Avocados

The combination of lightly poached scallops and avocado is perfect for a light luncheon followed by a green salad.

250 g (8 oz) scallops; white wine; 1 canned pimiento, cut into strips; 2 ripe avocados, chilled, halved and stoned (pitted); chopped parsley; lemon wedges.
VINAIGRETTE DRESSING: *1 tbsp lemon juice; 1 small clove garlic, crushed with a little salt; 4 tbsp olive oil; salt and freshly ground black pepper; dash Tabasco (hot pepper) sauce.*

Remove any brown parts from scallops, keeping coral. Poach gently in a little wine and water, about 5 minutes. Drain. Mix all ingredients for dressing in a small bowl and pour over scallops. Add pimiento. Cover and chill for at least 1 hour. Scoop out some of the avocado flesh and add to seafood

mixture. Blend lightly. Spoon some marinated seafood into each avocado half and sprinkle with chopped parsley. Serve with wedges of lemon. Serves 4.

Scallops à la Parisienne

In this dish, the scallops sit on a bed of mushroom duxelles and are covered with a creamy sauce made from the scallop liquid.

500 g (1 lb) scallops; 30 g/1 oz (2 tbsp) butter; 4 tbsp fresh breadcrumbs.
COURT BOUILLON: *1 small stick celery, sliced; ½ small carrot, sliced; ½ small onion, sliced; 1 bouquet garni (2 sprigs parsley, 1 bay leaf, 1 sprig fresh thyme and a few black peppercorns); 120 ml/4 fl oz (½ cup) dry white wine; 175 ml/6 fl oz (¾ cup) water.*
MUSHROOM DUXELLES: *30 g/1 oz (2 tbsp) butter; 1 shallot, finely chopped; 125 g/4 oz (1 cup) mushrooms, finely chopped; salt and freshly ground black pepper.*
VELOUTE SAUCE: *30 g/1 oz (2 tbsp) butter; 1 tbsp flour; salt and freshly ground white pepper; 1 egg yolk; 1 tbsp single (light) cream.*
GARNISH: *parsley, lemon wedges.*

Remove any brown parts from scallops, keeping coral.
COURT BOUILLON: Place all ingredients in a saucepan and bring to the boil. Simmer gently for 20 minutes. Add scallops and poach for 3–4 minutes. Remove scallops and strain liquid. Reserve 175 ml/6 fl oz (¾ cup) liquid for sauce.
MUSHROOM DUXELLES: Melt butter in a saucepan and add shallot. Cook for 1 minute, then add mushrooms. Season with salt and pepper and cook for a further 3 minutes. Spoon mixture into 4 scallop shells. Arrange scallops on duxelles.
VELOUTE SAUCE: Melt butter in a saucepan and stir in flour. Cook for 1 minute, then add reserved scallop liquid gradually, stirring all the time. Season with salt and pepper and allow sauce to cook gently for 10 minutes. Combine egg yolk with cream and stir into sauce. Stir for 1 minute over gentle heat but do not allow sauce to boil. Remove sauce from heat and spoon over scallops. Melt

butter in a small pan and toss breadcrumbs in it until they are golden and crisp. Sprinkle over sauce. Place in a preheated moderately hot oven (200°C/400°F, Gas Mark 6) or under a preheated grill (broiler) to heat through until golden. Serve piping hot, garnished with parsley and lemon wedges. Serves 6.

Scallops in White Wine Sauce

500 g (1 lb) scallops; 250 ml/8 fl oz (1 cup) dry white wine; salt and freshly ground white pepper; 2 shallots, halved; 120 ml/4 fl oz (½ cup) water; 60 g/2 oz (4 tbsp) butter; 2 tsp flour; 120 ml/4 fl oz (½ cup) single (light) cream; 60 g/2 oz (1 cup) fresh breadcrumbs.

Remove any brown parts from scallops, keeping coral. Put wine in saucepan with salt, pepper, shallots and water. Add scallops, bring to the simmer and poach for 1 minute. Drain scallops and cut large ones in 2 or 3 slices. Strain cooking liquid and reduce by boiling over medium heat to 120 ml/4 fl oz (½ cup). Melt 45 g/1½ oz (3 tbsp) butter in a saucepan, add flour and blend until smooth. Add reduced poaching liquid, then cream, stirring until sauce boils. Spoon a little sauce over bottom of 4 scallop shells or ovenproof ramekins, divide scallops among shells and cover with remaining sauce. Sprinkle with breadcrumbs. Put a piece of remaining butter on top of each and brown quickly under a preheated grill (broiler). Serves 4.

Scallops Portugaise

1 kg (2 lb) scallops.
COURT BOUILLON: *500 ml/18 fl oz (2 cups) dry white wine; 1 carrot, sliced; 1 onion, sliced; 12 black peppercorns; 1 sprig parsley.*
SAUCE PORTUGAISE: *120 ml/4 fl oz (½ cup) milk; 90 g/3 oz (6 tbsp) butter; 3 tbsp flour; salt and freshly ground black pepper; 4 tbsp single (light) cream; 2 tomatoes, peeled, seeded and chopped.*

Trim any brown parts from scallops, keeping coral.
COURT BOUILLON: Place all ingredients in a large saucepan, bring to the boil and add scallops. Poach for 1–2 minutes, then lift out with a slotted spoon. Cut scallops horizontally in half if they are large. Boil cooking liquid over a high heat until reduced to about 175 ml/6 fl oz (¾ cup). Strain and use to make the sauce.
SAUCE PORTUGAISE: Mix milk with reduced cooking liquid. Melt butter in saucepan, stir in flour and cook for 1 minute over low heat. Remove from heat, cool a little and add milk mixture all at once. Stir until smooth. Return to medium heat and stir until boiling. Season with salt and pepper, reduce heat, then stir in cream and tomatoes. Fold scallops into

sauce. Serve on rice or noodles or in puff pastry (paste) vol-au-vent cases. Serves 6 as a main course, 8 as a first course.

Curried Scallops with Mushrooms

250 g (8 oz) scallops; 3 tbsp stock; 1 tbsp dry breadcrumbs; ½ tsp curry powder; ½ tsp dried oregano; dash Worcestershire sauce; dash Tabasco (hot pepper) sauce; salt and freshly ground black pepper; 3 mushrooms, finely chopped; 2 shallots, finely chopped; 1 clove garlic, crushed with a little salt; 45 g/1½ oz (3 tbsp) butter; 1 tbsp peanut oil; 1 tbsp brandy or Cognac; chopped parsley or finely snipped fresh dill to garnish.

Remove any brown parts from scallops, keeping coral. Place in a bowl with stock, breadcrumbs, curry powder, oregano, sauces, salt and pepper and toss until well coated. Sauté mushrooms, shallots and garlic in butter and oil over a moderate heat for about 3 minutes or until softened without colouring. Add scallops and brandy and stir-fry for 1–2 minutes. Serve scallop mixture over cooked rice in individual dishes or with toast points, sprinkling each serving with parsley or dill. Serves 2.

Baked Scallops

500 g (1 lb) scallops; 2 tbsp chopped parsley; 1 clove garlic, chopped; 1 onion, finely chopped; pinch ground cloves; little nutmeg; salt and freshly ground black pepper; 4 tbsp fresh breadcrumbs; 2 tbsp olive oil.

Remove any brown parts from scallops but retain coral. Finely dice white flesh and coral and mix with parsley, garlic, onion, spices, salt and pepper. Fill scallop shells or small individual ovenproof dishes with scallop mixture. Sprinkle with breadcrumbs and olive oil and place on a baking tray. Bake in a preheated hot oven (220°C/425°F, Gas Mark 7) for 5–10 minutes or until lightly browned. Serve immediately. Serves 4.

Sautéed Scallops

This recipe can be used as a filling for vol-au-vent cases or crêpes, or served over rice or on its own with crusty bread to mop up the juices.

60 g/2 oz (4 tbsp) butter; 6 shallots, chopped; 1 stick celery, diced; 1 carrot, diced; 2 bay leaves; 4 tbsp dry sherry; 500 g (1 lb) scallops; 1 tbsp chopped fresh dill or fennel; salt and freshly ground black pepper; sprigs fresh dill or fennel to garnish.

Melt 30 g/1 oz (2 tbsp) butter in a saucepan and fry shallots, celery, carrot and bay leaves for 3–5 minutes. Add sherry, cover and simmer gently for 10 minutes or until vegetables are soft but not mushy. Remove bay leaves. Remove any brown parts from

scallops, keeping coral. Sauté scallops and dill or fennel in remaining butter in a frying pan (skillet) for 2 minutes. Season with salt and pepper. Add scallops and pan juices to vegetables and serve as above, garnished with sprigs of dill or fennel. Serves 6.

Scallops Newburg

500 g (1 lb) scallops; 60 g/2 oz (4 tbsp) butter; 1 sprig fresh thyme; 1 sprig parsley; 2 tbsp brandy; 2 tbsp Madeira or sweet sherry; 250 ml/8 fl oz (1 cup) single (light) cream; 2 egg yolks; 30 g/1 oz (½ cup) fresh breadcrumbs; 2 tbsp grated Parmesan cheese.

Remove any brown parts from scallops, keeping coral. Melt butter in a saucepan, add scallops, herbs, brandy and Madeira or sherry, cover and simmer for 1 minute. Blend cream with egg yolks in a double saucepan (double boiler) and thicken over a low heat, stirring constantly. Arrange scallop mixture in a flameproof dish. Pour cream sauce over scallops and sprinkle with a mixture of breadcrumbs and cheese. Place under a preheated grill (broiler) until top is golden-brown. Serves 4.

SCAMPI

See *Prawn/Shrimp*.

SCHNITZEL

A favourite in Germany and Austria, schnitzel is the same thin cut of veal as the French *escalope* and the Italian *scaloppine*. The Viennese version, *Wienerschnitzel*, is found on menus all over the world. **See recipes.**

Vienna Schnitzel

(Wienerschnitzel)
Some cooks coat their schnitzels with fine fresh breadcrumbs, some with dry crumbs. In either case, the crumbs should be sieved first so that the coating will cook to an even golden-brown – if crumbs are of uneven size, some will darken too much. The crumbed schnitzels are left 20–30 minutes before frying to allow the egg to harden so that the coating will stay on when cooked. It should puff up in a few places, but never fall away from the veal. Schnitzels can be fried in butter, butter and oil, vegetable shortening or lard.

4 large or 8 small schnitzels, beaten flat to about 3 mm ($\frac{1}{8}$ in) thick; juice 1 lemon (optional); 2 eggs; 2 tbsp cold water; 4 tbsp vegetable oil; seasoned flour; fine, sieved fresh or dry breadcrumbs; 60 g/2 oz (4 tbsp) butter; 4 thin lemon wedges to garnish.

If desired, marinate schnitzels in lemon juice for 30 minutes before coating. Beat eggs with water, and beat in 2 tbsp oil if liked – the oil is supposed to hold breading on securely and help make it crisp. Dry each schnitzel well, then coat on both sides with seasoned flour and pat off excess. Dip into egg mixture, allow excess to drip off then dip into breadcrumbs, firming them on with your hand. Chill 30 minutes. Heat remaining oil in a large frying pan (skillet), add butter and when foam begins to subside, add schnitzels; do not overcrowd pan, cook them in 2 batches if necessary. Cook 2–4 minutes on each side until golden-brown. Put finished schnitzels, uncovered, into a cool oven to keep hot while the rest are being fried. Arrange schnitzels on a heated serving platter and garnish with lemon wedges. Serve immediately. Serves 4.

VARIATIONS

Holstein Schnitzel: Follow recipe for Vienna Schnitzel. Garnish each schnitzel with a fried egg topped with 2 crossed anchovy fillets, and sprinkle with a few capers.

Cheese Schnitzel: Follow recipe for Vienna Schnitzel, but use 45 g/1$\frac{1}{2}$ oz ($\frac{3}{4}$ cup) breadcrumbs mixed with 60 g/2 oz ($\frac{1}{2}$ cup) grated Parmesan cheese instead of plain breadcrumbs to coat them. Before serving, sprinkle with a little grated cheese and some paprika, and garnish with a slice of lemon.

Almond Schnitzel: Follow recipe for Vienna Schnitzel. Garnish each schnitzel with slivered almonds fried in butter.

Plain Schnitzel

(Naturschnitzel)

Purists say that a true Naturschnitzel should be floured on one side only, the floured side being browned first, since if both sides are floured the second one will be soggy.

4 large or 8 small schnitzels, beaten flat to about 5 mm ($\frac{1}{4}$ in) thick; seasoned flour; butter; 120 ml/4 fl oz ($\frac{1}{2}$ cup) beef stock or veal stock; salt and freshly ground black pepper; lemon juice.

Flour schnitzels on one side and pat off excess. Brown both sides slowly (floured side first) in hot butter. Keep finished schnitzels hot in a cool oven while you make the sauce. Add 30 g/1 oz (2 tbsp) butter to pan and when it begins to bubble up, add stock and stir and scrape up brown bits from bottom of pan. Season with salt, pepper and lemon juice. Bring to the boil and pour over the hot schnitzels. Serve immediately. Serves 4.

SCONES

The fragrance of freshly baked scones promises a treat that is never out of style. These most popular of quick breads can be mixed and baked in 15 minutes to enjoy with tea or coffee, or to provide hot savoury snacks or even the basis of a casual meal. Hot scones with cream and a good berry jam make that delight known the world over as Devonshire Cream Tea. The original West of England version uses clotted cream, but whipped cream does very well. **See recipes**.

Scones

370 g/12 oz (3 cups) self-raising flour; 1 tsp salt; 60 g/2 oz (4 tbsp) butter; 250 ml/8 fl oz (1 cup) milk.

Sift flour and salt into a bowl **(Fig 1 below)**. Rub (cut) in butter. Add nearly all the milk at once and mix in quickly with a knife **(2)**. Add remaining milk only if necessary to mix to a soft dough. Turn on to a floured board and knead by turning and pressing with heel of hand 3 or 4 times. Pat out to a round 2 cm ($\frac{3}{4}$ in) thick and cut into 4 cm (1$\frac{1}{2}$ in) rounds with a floured cutter **(3)**. Place scones close together on a lightly greased baking tray. Brush tops with a little milk **(4)** and bake in the top of a preheated hot oven (230°C/450°F, Gas Mark 8) for 10–15 minutes or until well risen and golden. For soft scones, wrap in a tea-towel as soon as they come from oven. For crusty scones, do not wrap, cool on a wire rack. Serve warm with butter or with jam and cream. Makes 12.

VARIATIONS

Fruit Scones: Follow recipe for Scones, but stir in 1 tbsp sugar and 90 g/3 oz ($\frac{1}{2}$ cup) sultanas (golden raisins) or other dried fruit after rubbing (cutting) in butter. A little grated orange or lemon rind, or mixed spice (ground allspice), may also be added.

Cheese Scones: Follow recipe for Scones, but stir in 45 g/1$\frac{1}{2}$ oz ($\frac{1}{3}$ cup) grated well-flavoured cheese, $\frac{1}{4}$ tsp dry mustard and a good grinding of black pepper or a pinch of cayenne after rubbing (cutting) in butter. Bake scones in a preheated hot oven (220°C/425°F, Gas Mark 7) for about 10 minutes.

Making Scones

Cheese-topped Scone Loaf: Prepare dough as for Cheese Scones, place on a lightly greased baking sheet, and shape into a round or rectangular loaf 2.5 cm (1 in) thick. Mix together 45 g/1$\frac{1}{2}$ oz (3 tbsp) softened butter, a pinch of salt, 60 g/2 oz ($\frac{1}{2}$ cup) grated cheese, and a pinch each of cayenne, dry mustard and nutmeg. Spread mixture over loaf. Sprinkle with a little paprika and bake in a preheated hot oven (220°C/425°F, Gas Mark 7) for 12–18 minutes. Cool on a wire rack. Serve cut in slices and buttered.

Herb Scones: Follow recipe for Scones, but add 1 tbsp chopped mixed fresh herbs, or 1 tsp dried herbs with 1 tbsp chopped parsley, 2 tsp finely chopped shallot and 1 tsp sugar after rubbing (cutting) in butter. Serve with morning coffee or as a savoury alternative at tea time.

Crusted Orange Scones: Follow Scones recipe, but add 1 tbsp sugar after rubbing (cutting) in butter, and use 4 tbsp orange juice and 175 ml/6 fl oz ($\frac{3}{4}$ cup) milk for the liquid. Press a piece of loaf sugar dipped in orange juice on top of each scone before baking.

Spiced Fruit Pinwheels: Prepare dough as for Scones. Roll out to a rectangle 5 mm ($\frac{1}{4}$ in) thick, brush with melted butter and sprinkle with sugar and cinnamon. Sprinkle with mixed dried fruit, roll up and cut into 2 cm ($\frac{3}{4}$ in) thick slices. Place, cut sides up, in a greased, shallow baking tin (pan) and bake in a preheated hot oven (220°C/425°F, Gas Mark 7) for 10–12 minutes or until browned.

Wholewheat Scones

250 g/8 oz (2 cups) self-raising flour; $\frac{1}{2}$ tsp salt; 180 g/6 oz (1$\frac{1}{2}$ cups) wholewheat flour; 3 tsp baking powder; 90 g/3 oz (6 tbsp) butter; 300 ml/$\frac{1}{2}$ pint (1$\frac{1}{4}$ cups) milk.

Sift self-raising flour and salt into a mixing bowl. Stir in wholewheat flour and baking powder. Rub (cut) in butter, then make well in centre and add sufficient milk to mix to a soft but not sticky dough. Turn on to a lightly floured board and knead gently. Pat out into a round shape, 2–2.5 cm ($\frac{3}{4}$–1 in) thick. Place on floured baking tray and mark into 8–12 triangles with a sharp, floured knife. Bake in a preheated moderately hot oven (200°C/400°F, Gas Mark 6) for 25–30

minutes or until firm to touch. Cool on wire rack. Break into triangles, split in half and spread with butter or serve with whipped cream and home-made jam. Makes 8–12.
NOTE: Variations given for Scones (opposite) may be used for Wholewheat Scones.

Pumpkin Scones

60 g/2 oz (4 tbsp) butter; 2 tbsp caster sugar; 180 g/6 oz (¾ cup) cold cooked, mashed pumpkin, well drained; 1 egg, beaten; 120 ml/4 fl oz (½ cup) milk; 310 g/10 oz (2½ cups) self-raising flour, sifted; ½ tsp cinnamon; ½ tsp nutmeg; little milk to glaze.

Cream butter with sugar. Add pumpkin and mix well. Add egg, then stir in milk a little at a time. Add flour and spices and mix to a soft dough. Turn out on to a floured board and knead lightly, then roll out to about 2 cm (¾ in) thickness. Cut into rounds with a floured scone cutter. Place rounds on a greased baking tray, brush tops with milk and bake in a preheated moderately hot oven (200°C/400°F, Gas Mark 6) for 15–20 minutes or until golden-brown on top and cooked through. Serve hot, split and buttered. Makes about 20.

Savoury Scone Ring

SCONE MIXTURE: *250 g/8 oz (2 cups) self-raising flour; 1 tsp salt; pinch cayenne; 60 g/2 oz (4 tbsp) butter; 60 g/2 oz (½ cup) grated cheese; 1 egg, lightly beaten; 175 ml/6 fl oz (¾ cup) milk.*
FILLING: *125 g (4 oz) salami, luncheon sausage or corned beef, finely diced; 2–3 gherkins, finely diced; 2 tsp melted butter; 2 tsp finely chopped parsley; 1 small onion, finely chopped; 30 g/1 oz (¼ cup) grated cheese; 1 tbsp tomato ketchup; 1 tsp French (Dijon) mustard; salt and freshly ground black pepper.*

Sift flour, salt and cayenne into a bowl. Rub (cut) in butter and stir in cheese. Mix egg and milk; reserve about 1 tbsp and stir remainder into flour mixture with a knife. Pat dough out to a rectangle about 20 × 30 cm (8 × 12 in).
FILLING: Mix ingredients together and spread over dough. Roll up from a long side and form into a ring, pressing ends together to join. Cut ⅔ of the way through ring at 3 cm (1¼ in) intervals and spread slices a little apart. Brush with reserved egg and milk. Place on a greased baking tray and bake in a preheated moderately hot oven (190°C/375°F, Gas Mark 5) for 30–35 minutes. Serve scone ring warm. Makes 10 slices.

Fruit and Nut Tea Ring

SCONE MIXTURE: *250 g/8 oz (2 cups) self-raising flour; pinch salt; 60 g/2 oz (4 tbsp) butter; 60 g/2 oz (¼ cup) sugar; 90 g/3 oz*

(½ cup) finely chopped dates or raisins; 1 egg yolk; 175 ml/6 fl oz (¾ cup) milk.
FILLING: *30 g/1 oz (2 tbsp) butter, melted; 60 g/2 oz (⅓ cup) firmly packed brown sugar; 30 g/1 oz (¼ cup) finely chopped walnuts; 1 tsp cinnamon.*
GLAZE: *egg white; white sugar.*

Sift flour and salt into a bowl. Rub (cut) in butter and stir in sugar and dates or raisins. Mix egg yolk and milk and stir in quickly with a knife. Pat out dough to a rectangle 2 cm (¾ in) thick.
FILLING: Mix ingredients and spread over. Roll up from a long side and form into a ring, pressing ends together to join. Cut ⅔ of the way through ring at 3 cm (1¼ in) intervals and spread slices a little apart. Brush with egg white and sprinkle with sugar. Place on a greased baking tray. Bake in a preheated hot oven (220°C/425°F, Gas Mark 7) for 20–25 minutes. Serve warm. Makes 10 slices.

Crusted Steak Squares

750 g/1½ lb (3 cups) minced (ground) steak; 30 g/1 oz (¼ cup) diced green or red pepper; 1 small onion, finely chopped; 125 g/4 oz (1 cup) finely chopped mushrooms; 60 g/2 oz (½ cup) grated cheese; 1 tbsp tomato ketchup; 2 tsp Worcestershire sauce; 30 g/1 oz (½ cup) fresh breadcrumbs; 1 egg; 1 tsp salt; ½ tsp freshly ground black pepper; double quantity Scone Dough (opposite); milk to glaze.

Mix steak with vegetables, cheese, sauces, breadcrumbs, egg, salt and pepper. Press into bottom of a greased, shallow square or rectangular baking dish to make a layer about 2 cm (¾ in) thick. Pat out scone dough to size of dish and place on meat mixture. Brush with milk and bake in a preheated hot oven (220°C/425°F, Gas Mark 7) for 10 minutes. Reduce heat to moderate (180°C/350°F, Gas Mark 4) and continue baking 20–25 minutes. Cut into squares to serve. Serves 8.

SCOTCH EGG

See page 375 for recipe.

SEA URCHIN

A small sea creature, with a hard, spiny shell, found on rocky coastal shores. Despite their ferocious appearance, sea urchins are edible, and must be prised from the rocks. Wearing strong gloves, cut them horizontally across the middle with kitchen shears. Drain them, and scoop out the orange-pink coral, which is the only edible part. The coral is usually scooped out and eaten raw, with a dash of lemon juice if desired, and fresh crusty bread.

SEMOLINA

A cereal obtained from wheat grains in the middle stages of flour-milling when the bran, wheat germ and endosperm (the floury part of the grain) are separated. The first millings of the creamy-coloured endosperm is known as semolina.

Semolina, called semolina flour in America, can be purchased fine, medium or coarse ground, and is used to make some types of gnocchi (see page 145), as well as breads, puddings and cakes, the latter two particularly in the Middle East and India. Semolina made from hard durum wheat is used commercially for pasta, and flour-coated coarse semolina grains make cous-cous, an integral part of substantial stews and some desserts in North Africa. Couscous is available from Middle Eastern and Greek grocery stores (see also page 85). Buy semo-lina ready packed or in bulk from super-markets, delicatessens or health food shops. **See recipes**.

Indian Halva

125 g/4 oz (½ cup) sugar; 300 ml/½ pint (1¼ cups) plus 1 tsp water; 8 cardamom pods, bruised; ¼ tsp saffron threads; 125 g/4 oz (½ cup) ghee; 140 g/4½ oz (¾ cup) semolina (semolina flour); 30 g/1 oz (¼ cup) blanched pistachio nuts, shredded; 30 g/1 oz (¼ cup) slivered almonds.

Dissolve sugar in 300 ml/½ pint (1¼ cups) water, with cardamom pods, and boil for 5 minutes. Remove from heat and cool, then strain, reserving cardamom pods. Heat saffron in a spoon over a direct heat, then pound in a small bowl with remaining water to a paste. Stir into strained syrup. Heat ghee in a saucepan and stir in semolina. Cook over a gentle heat until semolina thickens and mixture is creamy. Add syrup and stir over high heat until mixture is thoroughly incorporated. Remove seeds from cardamoms and crush seeds with a rolling pin. Stir into semolina mixture with

pistachios and almonds. Serve warm, piled into individual sweet dishes, or spread out into a thick oblong and leave to cool completely before cutting into diamonds or squares. Serves 8–10.
NOTE: $\frac{1}{4}$ tsp powdered saffron may be used in place of saffron threads. Dissolve in 1 tsp water and stir into strained syrup.

Greek Walnut Cake

250 g/8 oz (1 cup) butter; 250 g/8 oz (1 cup) caster sugar; 1 tsp grated orange rind; 4 eggs, separated; 125 g/4 oz (1 cup) flour; 180 g/6 oz (1 cup) fine semolina (semolina flour); 4 tsp baking powder; 1 tsp cinnamon; 120 ml/4 fl oz ($\frac{1}{2}$ cup) milk; 250 g/8 oz (2 cups) coarsely grated walnuts.
SYRUP: *250 g/8 oz (1 cup) sugar; 250 ml/8 fl oz (1 cup) water; 2 whole cloves; 5 cm (2 in) cinnamon stick; 1 tbsp lemon juice; thin strip lemon rind.*

Cream butter with sugar and orange rind until light and fluffy. Add egg yolks, beating well after each addition. Sift flour, semolina, baking powder and cinnamon. Fold into creamed mixture alternately with milk, and add walnuts, mixing gently. Beat egg whites until stiff and fold into mixture. Pour into a well-greased 33 × 23 × 5 cm (13 × 9 × 2 in) baking dish. Bake in a preheated moderate oven (180°C/350°F, Gas Mark 4) for 45 minutes or until a fine skewer inserted in centre comes out clean.
SYRUP: Combine ingredients in a heavy saucepan and stir over medium heat until sugar dissolves. Bring to the boil and boil over moderately high heat for 10 minutes. Strain. Remove cake from oven and pour hot syrup over cake while still in dish. Allow to cool in dish. When cold cut into square or diamond shapes.

Semolina Cake

125 g/4 oz ($\frac{1}{2}$ cup) butter; 125 g/4 oz ($\frac{1}{2}$ cup) caster sugar; 1 tbsp grated orange rind; 2 eggs; 2 tbsp brandy; 180 g/6 oz (1 cup) semolina (semolina flour); 1 tsp baking powder; 125 g/4 oz (1 cup) ground almonds.
SYRUP: *125 g/4 oz ($\frac{1}{2}$ cup) sugar; 300 ml/$\frac{1}{2}$ pint (1$\frac{1}{4}$ cups) orange juice; 3 tbsp Grand Marnier, Cointreau or brandy.*

Cream butter with sugar and orange rind until light and fluffy. Beat in eggs one at a time, beating thoroughly after each addition. Stir in brandy. Combine semolina, baking powder and almonds and fold lightly into egg mixture. Turn into greased and lined 20 cm (8 in) round cake tin (pan). Place in a preheated moderately hot oven (200°C/400°F, Gas Mark 6), then lower heat to moderate (180°C/350°F, Gas Mark 4) and bake for 30 minutes or until golden on top and a fine skewer inserted in centre comes out clean.

SYRUP: Place sugar and juice in a heavy saucepan, bring to the boil, stirring occasionally, and boil briskly for 5 minutes. Cool slightly, then stir in spirits. Leave cake in tin (pan) and pour syrup over, then return to oven and bake for a further 15 minutes. Remove from oven and allow cake to cool in tin (pan). Turn out for serving, sliced, on its own or accompanied by whipped cream flavoured with 1 tsp grated orange rind.

Greek Halva

250 g/8 oz (1 cup) sugar; 600 ml/1 pint (2$\frac{1}{2}$ cups) water; 125 g/4 oz ($\frac{1}{2}$ cup) butter; 180 g/6 oz (1 cup) coarse semolina (semolina flour); 2 tbsp pine nuts or raw peanuts; 1 tsp cinnamon; extra cinnamon to sprinkle.

Dissolve sugar in water and bring to the boil. Boil for 5 minutes, then set aside. Melt butter in a heavy saucepan and stir in semolina and nuts. Stir constantly over moderate heat for 10–15 minutes or until semolina is golden-brown. Remove from heat. Reheat sugar syrup to boiling and pour into semolina, off the heat, stirring constantly. Add cinnamon and stir over low heat until smooth and bubbling. Cook very gently for 2 minutes. Turn off heat, cover pan with a clean folded tea-towel and put lid on. Leave for 15 minutes. Spread halva in a Swiss roll tin (jelly roll pan). Decorate top using tines of a fork to make a criss-cross pattern. Sprinkle with cinnamon and leave until cool. Cut into 5 cm (2 in) diamond shapes to serve. Makes about 20 pieces.

Semolina Shortbread

125 g/4 oz ($\frac{1}{2}$ cup) ghee; 125 g/4 oz ($\frac{1}{2}$ cup) sugar; 180 g/6 oz (1 cup) semolina (semolina flour), sifted; 30 g/1 oz ($\frac{1}{4}$ cup) flour, sifted; 1 tsp ground cardamom.

Cream ghee with sugar until light. Add semolina, flour and cardamom and mix well. Leave for 30 minutes. Take a scant tablespoonful of mixture, roll into a ball, flatten slightly and put on an ungreased baking tray. Repeat with remaining mixture, leaving a little space around biscuits. Bake in a preheated cool oven (150°C/300°F, Gas Mark 2) for about 30 minutes or until pale golden. Cool on a wire rack. Makes about 24.

Semolina Pudding

575 ml/19 fl oz (2$\frac{1}{4}$ cups) milk; 3 tbsp semolina (semolina flour) – coarse or fine; 15 g/$\frac{1}{2}$ oz (1 tbsp) butter; 1 egg, separated; pinch nutmeg, or $\frac{1}{2}$ tsp grated lemon rind; 1 tbsp sugar; caster sugar to sprinkle.

Heat milk, stir in semolina and cook over gentle heat, stirring occasionally, for 5–6 minutes. Remove from heat and beat in butter, egg yolk, nutmeg or lemon rind and sugar. Whisk egg white until stiff and fold into mixture. Turn into a well-buttered 1 litre/1$\frac{3}{4}$ pint (4 cup) ovenproof dish and sprinkle top with caster sugar. Bake in a preheated moderate oven (180°C/350°F, Gas Mark 4) for 15–20 minutes or until top is lightly browned and slightly puffy. Serves 4.

SESAME

The seeds of this plant have a multitude of uses. Their nutty flavour and crunchy texture are always appreciated, whether sprinkled on cooked vegetables or salads, scattered over breads and biscuits (cookies), or thickly mixed with toffee in sticky sweets (candies).

Sesame seeds have a high oil content, and contain protein and minerals. They are crushed to yield either a pale-coloured, almost flavourless oil which may be used for cooking or salads (it contains a high proportion of unsaturated oils), or a quite different, darker, more viscous and strongly flavoured oil, frequently used in Chinese cooking. This latter oil is sold as 'Oriental' or 'Chinese' sesame oil.

Sesame seeds may also be crushed to produce a thick, oily paste known as *tahini*, which is very widely used in the Middle East (see page 427).

Ways to Use

Toasting, or frying in butter, brings out the flavour of sesame seeds.
● Lightly cooked carrot sticks are delicious when tossed with butter and sesame seeds.
● Fried sesame seeds may be added to mashed potato or sprinkled on a cauliflower au gratin.
● Plain yogurt may be topped with honey and toasted sesame seeds, or they may be mixed into a fruit salad.
● A simple sweet is made by cooking honey to a toffee and adding an equal amount of sesame seeds. **See recipes.**

Sesame Chicken with Rice Noodles

This soup/stew from China's Fukien province is said to rejuvenate the body.

750 g (1$\frac{1}{2}$ lb) chicken joints (thighs, breasts); 250 g (8 oz) Chinese rice noodles; 1 tbsp Oriental sesame oil; 2 tbsp vegetable oil; 1 tbsp shredded fresh ginger; 120 ml/4 fl oz ($\frac{1}{2}$ cup) Chinese rice wine or dry sherry;

750 ml/1¼ pints (3 cups) chicken stock; 1 tsp sugar; 1 tsp salt; 1 small bunch spinach, chopped.

With a cleaver or heavy knife, chop chicken into bite-sized pieces. Soak noodles in warm water to cover for 5 minutes, then drain in a colander. Heat sesame oil with vegetable oil in a wok until it forms a haze. Add ginger and stir-fry for 30 seconds, then add chicken and stir-fry until pieces are golden, about 3 minutes. Add wine, bring to the boil and add stock, sugar and salt. Simmer for 30 minutes or until chicken is tender. Stir in noodles and cook 5 minutes. Stir in spinach, remove wok from heat and stand a few minutes. Ladle mixture into heated bowls. Serves 3–4.

Grilled Sesame Chicken Breasts

1 tbsp oil; 4 tbsp soy sauce; 4 tbsp dry white wine; 1 tsp dried tarragon; 1 tsp dry mustard; 4 boned half-breasts of chicken; sesame seeds to coat.

Combine oil, soy sauce, wine, tarragon and mustard. Marinate chicken in this mixture for 2–3 hours. Grill (broil) chicken breasts gently under a preheated grill (broiler) for 4 minutes each side, basting with a little marinade from time to time. Remove from heat, brush all over with marinade and roll in sesame seeds. Return to grill (broiler) to brown sesame seeds. Serves 4.

Sesame Seed Salad

1 head lettuce, torn into pieces; 75 g/2½ oz (½ cup) stoned (pitted) black (ripe) olives; 2 large ripe tomatoes; 2 tbsp sesame seeds; 15 g/½ oz (1 tbsp) butter; 4 tbsp Vinaigrette Dressing (page 358).

Place lettuce in bowl with olives and tomatoes (cut in wedges). Gently fry sesame seeds in butter until golden. Add to salad and toss with dressing. Serves 4–6.

Sesame Oat Fingers

75 g/2½ oz (¾ cup) rolled oats; 45 g/1½ oz (¼ cup) sesame seeds; 125 g/4 oz (⅔ cup) firmly packed brown sugar; 60 g/2 oz (¾ cup) desiccated (shredded) coconut; 1 tsp salt; 125 g/4 oz (½ cup) butter, melted.

Combine rolled oats, sesame seeds, sugar, coconut and salt. Add melted butter and mix well. Press mixture into a greased shallow tin (pan). Bake in a preheated moderately hot oven (190°C/375°F, Gas Mark 5) for about 30 minutes. Cut into fingers when cold. Makes about 20.

Greek Sesame Rings

250 g/8 oz (1 cup) unsalted butter; 250 g/8 oz (1 cup) caster sugar; 3 eggs;

4 tbsp milk; 1 tsp vanilla essence (extract); ½ tsp grated orange rind; ½ tsp cinnamon; ½ tsp nutmeg; 625 g/1¼ lb (5 cups) flour, sifted; 3 tsp baking powder; 90–180 g/ 3–6 oz (½–1 cup) sesame seeds.

Cream butter with sugar until light. Add 2 eggs, one at a time, beating well after each addition. Lightly beat remaining egg. Take out 1 tbsp egg, add to milk and set aside. Add remainder of egg to creamed mixture with vanilla and orange rind. Sift spices with flour and baking powder, and add to mixture gradually to form smooth dough. Knead for several minutes, then chill dough in refrigerator for 1 hour. To shape biscuits (cookies), take a piece of dough and roll into a thick rope about 1 cm (½ in) in diameter. Form into rings or figure-eight shapes, brush tops with reserved egg-milk mixture and dip into sesame seeds. Place on greased baking trays. Bake in a preheated moderate oven (180°C/350°F, Gas Mark 4) for 25 minutes or until just lightly coloured. Cool slightly on trays before transferring to wire racks. Store in airtight containers. Makes about 60.

SHALLOT AND SPRING ONION

These members of the onion family are both known by each other's name in different parts of the world.

Shallot: The true shallot is often considered the queen of all the onions. Its flavour is intense without being too pungent. Shallots usually grow in clusters, though they can be single, and have long stems and a purplish flesh; the skins can vary from a greyish to copper colour. The shallot is much used in the cooking of northern France to flavour sauces, or in steak, fish or vegetable dishes.
Spring Onion (Scallion): Two types of fresh spring onion are available. The first is slim and bulbless, except for a tiny bulge above the root, and is sold complete with its long, tubular green leaves. It may also be called green onion. In America it is called a scallion. Both the white and green parts are used. It is mild, and delicious in salads and their dress-

ings. Spring onion is also used to great effect in soups, sauces, savoury butters, casseroles, omelettes and other egg dishes, and in many Chinese dishes as both ingredient and garnish.

The second type of spring onion, called Welsh Onion in America, has a shiny, round white bulb about the size of a walnut, on a long, green stem. This onion is excellent sliced into salads, glazed whole in butter or used to give a delicious onion flavour to soups, stews, sauces, fish, meat or poultry dishes.

SHASLIK

See *Kebab*.

SHELLFISH

See *Crab*, *Lobster* and *Prawn/Shrimp*.

SHEPHERD'S PIE

A great homely dish, invented to use up leftover roast lamb but so good in its own right that it's worth cooking more lamb than you need for the first meal just to make sure you have enough left over for a Shepherd's Pie.

Shepherd's Pie

370 g (12 oz) cooked boneless lamb, weighed after trimming off skin, gristle and larger pieces of fat; 30 g/1 oz (2 tbsp) bacon dripping or butter; 1 onion, chopped; 250 ml/8 fl oz (1 cup) leftover gravy, or 1½ tbsp flour and 250 ml/8 fl oz (1 cup) warm beef stock; salt and freshly ground black pepper; 1 tsp Worcestershire sauce; 500 g (1 lb) potatoes, peeled; 30 g/1 oz (2 tbsp) butter; 2 tbsp hot milk.

Mince (grind) lamb or chop it very fine. Melt dripping or butter in a saucepan and fry onion gently until golden, about 5 minutes. Stir in gravy and bring to simmering point. Or stir flour into onions, cook 1 minute, remove from heat and cool a little. Add stock slowly, stirring until smoothly blended, then return to heat and stir until boiling. Add lamb, salt, pepper and Worcestershire sauce. Cover and simmer gently 30 minutes. Meanwhile, cook potatoes until tender. Drain well, dry off over low heat and mash with butter and hot milk. Transfer meat mixture to a pie dish. Spread potato over and rough up surface with a fork. Place under a preheated moderate grill (broiler) until top is golden-brown. Serve at once. Serves 4–6.
VARIATION
Cottage Pie: This is another name for Shepherd's Pie; some cooks use it when the dish has been varied by using beef instead of lamb or by adding diced, cooked vegetables to the filling.

SHERBET

See Ices, Sorbets, Granite and Sherbets.

SHERRY

A fortified wine, usually offered as a pre-dinner drink. It is available in varying degrees of sweetness, dry sherry being the least sweet and sweet sherry the sweetest.

Sherry is often added to a dish at the last minute rather than being used in its cooking. Many soups and sauces benefit from a dash of sherry just before serving.

Rich fruit cakes can be enhanced with sherry, preferably the sweet type. Soak the prepared fruit overnight in sherry, and when the cake comes out of the oven sprinkle a little sherry over. Sweet sherry is also sprinkled over plain cake when used to prepare a trifle, and impromptu desserts can be quickly made with cake, sherry, fresh or stewed fruit and cream. **See recipes.**

Sherried Mushroom Soup

370 g/12 oz (3 cups) mushrooms; 90 g/3 oz (6 tbsp) butter; 2 tbsp flour; 1 litre/1¾ pints (4 cups) warm milk; 1 egg yolk; 4 tbsp dry sherry; salt and freshly ground black pepper.

Slice mushroom caps; finely chop stems. Gently fry in butter until soft. Sprinkle with flour and cook over low heat, stirring, for 4 minutes. Stir in milk. Simmer soup 10 minutes, stirring occasionally. Mix egg yolk with sherry and add to soup. Season with salt and pepper. Heat carefully, stirring constantly. Do not let soup boil. Serves 4.

Sherried Veal with Cream

1 kg (2 lb) boneless veal shoulder or leg, cubed; 60 g/2 oz (4 tbsp) butter; 2 tbsp dry sherry; 2 small onions, finely chopped; 2 tbsp flour; 1 clove garlic, crushed; 3 tomatoes, peeled, seeded and roughly chopped; 1 tbsp tomato purée (paste); 120 ml/4 fl oz (½ cup) veal or chicken stock; 120 ml/4 fl oz (½ cup) single (light) cream; 1 tsp lemon juice; salt

and freshly ground black pepper; 1 bay leaf; chopped chives.

Brown veal in butter in heavy saucepan. Pour in sherry, allow to bubble a little, then remove veal and set aside. Add onions to pan and cook 2 minutes. Sprinkle with flour and stir well, then add garlic and tomatoes and cook for 3 minutes. Remove from heat and stir in tomato purée (paste) and stock. Return to low heat and bring to the boil, stirring. Carefully blend in cream, soured with lemon juice, and season with salt and pepper. Add bay leaf and return veal to pan. Cook over very gentle heat for 45 minutes, or in a preheated moderate oven (180°C/350°F, Gas Mark 4) for 1–1½ hours. Remove bay leaf before serving, sprinkled with chopped chives. Accompany with buttered noodles. Serves 6.

Spanish Chicken in Sherry

1.5 kg (3 lb) chicken joints (thighs and drumsticks or a mixture); about 600 ml/ 1 pint (2½ cups) medium-sweet sherry; 125 g/4 oz (½ cup) butter; tiny white onions, or 4 onions, quartered; 1 × 820 g/1¾ lb can tomatoes; 2 bay leaves; salt and freshly ground black pepper; 90 g/3 oz (½ cup) stuffed olives, sliced.

Place chicken in a deep glass or plastic bowl and pour over enough sherry to cover. Refrigerate, covered, for 2–3 hours or longer. Drain chicken, reserving sherry. Heat butter in a large flameproof casserole and brown chicken pieces on both sides over medium heat. (This will be easier to do if you brown just a few pieces at a time.) Return all chicken to casserole and add onions, tomatoes with their juice, bay leaves and enough reserved sherry to cover ingredients. Season with salt and pepper. Cover casserole and simmer for 30 minutes. Allow to cool, then refrigerate overnight. Next day, bring casserole to room temperature and bake, uncovered, in a preheated moderate oven (180°C/350°F, Gas Mark 4) for 40 minutes or until chicken is tender and sauce

reduced. Stir olives into casserole and cook for a further 2–3 minutes to heat through. Discard bay leaves. Serve with rice or noodles and a mixed salad. Serves 6.

Sherry Sultana Cake

500 g/1 lb (2⅔ cups) sultanas (golden raisins); 175 ml/6 fl oz (¾ cup) water; 4 tbsp sweet sherry; 250 g/8 oz (1 cup) butter; 250 g/8 oz (1 cup) sugar; 2 tsp cornflour (cornstarch) mixed with 120 ml/4 fl oz (½ cup) cold water; 3 eggs; 180 g/6 oz (1½ cups) plain (all-purpose) flour; 180 g/6 oz (1½ cups) self-raising flour; pinch salt; 30 g/1 oz (¼ cup) blanched almonds.

Simmer sultanas (golden raisins) in water and sherry until all liquid is absorbed. Cool. Cream butter with sugar until light and fluffy. Add cornflour (cornstarch) mixture and beat well. Add eggs one at a time, beating well after each addition. Sift flours with salt and fold into creamed mixture. Lastly, fold in sultanas (golden raisins). Turn into 20 cm (8 in) round or square cake tin (pan) lined with greaseproof (waxed) paper. Arrange blanched almonds on top. Bake in preheated cool oven (150°C/300°F, Gas Mark 2) for 1–1½ hours or until a skewer inserted in centre comes out clean. Allow to cool in tin (pan).

SHISH KEBAB

See Kebab.

SHORTBREAD

Eaten all year round but especially at New Year, Scottish Shortbread is famous all over the world, but how many people really know how to make it the Scottish way? The dough must be kneaded for about 15 minutes until it becomes smooth and very buttery before it is pressed into a tin (pan) or ring and decorated. If you do as the Scots do, you will have a superb shortbread, crisp yet tender. If making ahead, recrisp in a moderate oven (180°C/350°F, Gas Mark 4) for 15 minutes.

Shortbread

250 g/8 oz (1 cup) butter; 125 g/4 oz (½ cup) caster sugar; 500 g/1 lb (4 cups) flour.

Cream butter until it resembles whipped cream, then add sugar gradually, beating until mixture is light and fluffy. Work in flour gradually, then knead dough for about 15 minutes or until very smooth. Divide dough into 2 pieces and press into 2 × 20 cm (8 in) flan rings standing on baking trays, or sandwich tins (layer cake pans). With the heel of the hand push dough out until mixture is very smooth, then smooth over surface with a palette knife. Remove flan ring

and crimp edges by pressing edge of dough with the finger and then pinching edge together. If using a sandwich tin (layer cake pan), fork edge for decoration. Prick surface of shortbread with a fork. (This is done to release moisture as it cooks, making shortbread crisp.) Bake in centre of a preheated moderate oven (180°C/350°F, Gas Mark 4) for 10 minutes, then reduce temperature to cool (150°C/300°F, Gas Mark 2) and bake shortbread for a further 40 minutes.

SHORTCAKE

American shortcake is a luscious dessert consisting of a tender, scone-like cake which is split, filled and topped with fruit and cream, and served warm. Rounds of rich pastry (dough) can also be layered with cream and fruit or lemon cheese to make a Continental-style afternoon tea or dessert shortcake. **See recipes.**

American Strawberry Shortcake

250 g/8 oz (2 cups) flour; 60 g/2 oz ($\frac{1}{4}$ cup) caster sugar; 2 tsp baking powder; $\frac{1}{2}$ tsp salt; 125 g/4 oz ($\frac{1}{2}$ cup) butter; 1 egg; 120 ml/4 fl oz ($\frac{1}{2}$ cup) milk; 1 tbsp butter, melted.
FILLING: 500 g (1 lb) strawberries; 125 g/4 oz ($\frac{1}{2}$ cup) sugar; 250 ml/8 fl oz (1 cup) double (heavy) cream; 2 tbsp icing (confectioners) sugar, sifted.

Make filling first. Reserve a few of the best strawberries, unhulled, to decorate. Hull remainder and divide in half. Slice one lot in halves, place in a bowl and toss with 60 g/2 oz ($\frac{1}{4}$ cup) sugar. Crush other half of strawberries with remaining sugar. Whip cream with icing (confectioners) sugar until soft peaks form. Refrigerate filling.

Sift flour, sugar, baking powder and salt into a bowl. Cut butter into mixture with 2 knives until size of small peas. Break egg into a bowl and add 120 ml/4 fl oz ($\frac{1}{2}$ cup) milk; mix lightly. Make a well in centre of flour mixture, add milk and egg all at once and mix quickly with a fork until moistened. Turn mixture into a greased 20 cm (8 in) sandwich tin (layer cake pan) and smooth top. Bake in a preheated hot oven (220°C/425°F, Gas Mark 7) for 25–30 minutes or until a skewer inserted in centre comes out clean.

To serve, immediately turn shortcake out on to a wire rack and split into 2 layers. Place bottom layer, cut side up, on a serving plate and brush with melted butter. Spoon on half of crushed and sliced strawberries, put other layer of cake on and top with remaining strawberries. Pile cream in centre and decorate with reserved whole strawberries. Serve shortcake immediately while still warm. Serves 8.

Continental Strawberry Shortcake

SHORTCAKE PASTRY (DOUGH): 250 g/8 oz (2 cups) flour; pinch salt; 180 g/6 oz ($\frac{3}{4}$ cup) butter; 5 tbsp icing (confectioners) sugar, sifted; 2 egg yolks; few drops vanilla essence (extract).
FILLING: 500 g (1 lb) strawberries; 250 ml/ 8 fl oz (1 cup) double (heavy) cream; 2 tbsp icing (confectioners) sugar, sifted; few drops vanilla essence (extract).

Sift flour and salt on to work surface and make a well in centre. Place remaining pastry (dough) ingredients in well and work together with fingertips of one hand. With other hand, use a metal spatula to draw flour quickly into centre to make a smooth dough. Shape into a ball, wrap in plastic wrap and chill 30 minutes. Divide dough in half and roll or pat out into 2 × 23 cm (9 in) rounds, about 5 mm ($\frac{1}{4}$ in) thick. Place rounds on lightly greased baking trays. Prick all over with a fork and crimp edges with fingers and thumb. Bake in a preheated moderately hot oven (190°C/375°F, Gas Mark 5) for 15–20 minutes or until shortcake is a pale biscuit colour. Do not allow to brown. Remove from oven and, while shortcake is warm, cut one round into 8 segments. Cool shortcake on a wire rack. Reserve 8 unhulled strawberries for decoration; hull and slice remainder. Whip cream with icing (confectioners) sugar and vanilla. Reserve $\frac{1}{3}$ of cream for decoration and mix remainder with sliced strawberries. Place whole shortcake on a serving plate and cover with strawberry and cream mixture. Smooth over and arrange 8 shortcake segments on top. Dust with extra sifted icing (confectioners) sugar and decorate with rosettes of cream topped with reserved whole strawberries. Leave 1 hour before serving. Serves 8.

Danish Raspberry Shortcake

$\frac{1}{2}$ quantity Shortcake Pastry (above).
TOPPING: 500 g/1 lb (3 cups) raspberries; 4 tbsp redcurrant jelly; 1 tbsp water; 120 ml/4 fl oz ($\frac{1}{2}$ cup) double (heavy) cream.

Wrap pastry (dough) in plastic wrap and chill 30 minutes. Roll or pat out to an 18–20 cm (7–8 in) round and crimp edges. Place on a

lightly greased baking tray. Bake in a preheated moderately hot oven (190°C/ 375°F, Gas Mark 5) for 15–20 minutes or until shortcake is a pale biscuit colour; do not allow to brown. Remove from oven and cool on a wire rack. Place shortcake on a serving plate and cover with raspberries. Rub redcurrant jelly through a sieve into a small, heavy saucepan. Add water and heat slowly to boiling point, stirring, then boil until thick enough to coat a spoon lightly and last drops are sticky as they fall from spoon. Brush warm glaze over raspberries. When quite cold, whip cream, and, using a piping (pastry) bag with a 1 cm ($\frac{1}{2}$ in) star nozzle, pipe a border round top of shortcake. Serves 6.

SHORT CRUST (SHORTCRUST)

See Pastry.

SHORT SOUP

Also known as Wonton Soup, a speciality found on Chinese menus throughout the world. Wonton are the little meat-filled dumplings wrapped in a square of pasta – short as opposed to the long strands of pasta that go into Long Soup, hence the name. The wonton wrappers are available from most Chinese grocery suppliers, or ask at the local Chinese restaurant.

Short Soup

SOUP: 1.5 litres/2$\frac{1}{2}$ pints (6 cups) chicken stock; 3 spring onions (scallions), finely chopped; $\frac{1}{2}$ tsp sesame oil.
WONTONS: 370 g/12 oz (1$\frac{1}{2}$ cups) minced (ground) pork; 2 tbsp chopped water chestnuts; 3–4 green (uncooked) prawns (shrimp), shelled, deveined and chopped (optional); 1 tbsp soy sauce; $\frac{1}{2}$ tsp Oriental sesame oil; 1 tsp grated fresh ginger; 24 wonton wrappers; 1 egg, beaten; salt.

Place all soup ingredients in a saucepan and bring to the boil. Reduce heat and simmer 3 minutes.
WONTONS: Combine pork with water chestnuts, prawns (shrimp), soy sauce, sesame oil and grated ginger, mixing well. Place 1 teaspoon filling slightly below centre of each

wonton wrapper. Brush around edges of wrapper with lightly beaten egg. Fold wrapper diagonally in half to form a triangle. Press edges to seal, and press out any air pockets around filling. Brush a dab of egg on front of right corner of each triangle and on back of left corner. With a twisting action, bring 2 moistened surfaces together. Pinch to seal. Drop wontons into vigorously boiling salted water and cook until they float to top, about 5–7 minutes. Drain. Place 4 wontons in bottom of each soup bowl and pour hot soup over. Serves 6.

SHRIMP

See Prawn/Shrimp.

SIENA CAKE

This 'flat' cake with a nougat-like texture, rich with candied peel, toasted nuts and spices is a particular speciality of the town of Siena, Italy.

Siena Cake

105 g/3½ oz (⅔ cup) hazelnuts, toasted, skinned and chopped; 90 g/3 oz (¾ cup) coarsely chopped, blanched almonds; 180 g/6 oz (1 cup) finely chopped candied peel; 30 g/1 oz (¼ cup) unsweetened cocoa powder; 60 g/2 oz (½ cup) plain (all-purpose) flour; ½ tsp ground cinnamon; ¼ tsp ground nutmeg; 125 g/4 oz (½ cup) sugar; 125 g/4 oz (⅓ cup) clear honey.
TOPPING: *2 tbsp icing (confectioners) sugar; 1 tsp ground cinnamon.*

Mix together hazelnuts, almonds, candied peel, cocoa, flour and spices. Put sugar and honey into a small pan, heat gently until sugar dissolves, then boil steadily until a sugar thermometer registers 115°C (240°F) or until a little of the mixture dropped into a cup of cold water forms a soft ball. Take off the heat immediately and stir in nut mixture. Turn into a lined and greased 20 cm (8 in) flan ring or sandwich tin (layer cake pan), spread evenly and press down firmly. Bake in a cool oven (150°C/300°F, Gas Mark 2) for 30–35 minutes. Allow to cool then turn out and sprinkle the top liberally with the icing (confectioners) sugar sifted with cinnamon. Cut into small wedges before serving. Serves 8–12.

SILVERSIDE

See Beef.

SIRLOIN

See Beef.

SMØRREBRØD

See Danish Open Sandwiches.

SNAIL

A small land mollusc, very popular in France, where it is called *escargot*, and found in all wine-growing areas. Snails are also a favourite dish in other Mediterranean countries.

Outside France, it is more common to buy snails, already prepared and cooked, in cans. The large shells are usually sold with the cans, so that the snails can be returned to their shells with a garlic butter before heating. This is the most common way of serving snails in France. Alow about 6–8 per person.

Escargots à la Bourguignonne
(Snails with Garlic Butter)

125 g/4 oz (½ cup) butter; 2 tbsp finely chopped spring onions (scallions); 1–2 cloves garlic, crushed; 2 tbsp finely chopped parsley; salt and freshly ground black pepper; 24 snail shells; 24 canned snails.

Cream butter well, then beat in spring onions (scallions), garlic, parsley, salt and pepper. Put a little garlic butter in each snail shell, then add a snail, and fill shells with remaining butter mixture. Place snails in special plates (with indentations for shells, so that they stay upright and butter does not spill). Bake in a preheated hot oven (230°C/450°F, Gas Mark 8) for about 7 minutes or until butter sizzles. Serve hot, with plenty of crusty bread. Serves 4.

SNOW PEA/MANGE TOUT

Known as *mange tout* in Europe and parts of England, because all of the pea is edible, this delicately-flavoured vegetable is one of the easiest to prepare and cook.
□ **Basic Preparation:** Simply top and tail them, removing strings at the same time, as though they were young beans.
□ **To Cook:** Snow peas are best when lightly cooked to retain some of their crispness. They can be quickly cooked in boiling water, then tossed in butter, or steamed.

Braised Snow Peas

2 tbsp oil; 500 g/1 lb (4 cups) mange tout (snow peas), trimmed and strung; ½ tsp salt; 2 tbsp stock or water; ½ tsp sugar; 2 tsp light soy sauce.

Heat oil in a wok or frying pan (skillet), add peas and stir-fry for 30 seconds without browning. Add remaining ingredients, stir to coat peas and cook 1 minute longer. Peas should be tender but still crisp. Serve immediately. Serves 6.

SORREL

This plant is sometimes considered a herb, sometimes a vegetable. In appearance it is rather like English spinach but its flavour is lemony and fairly sharp, even bitter, although not unpleasant. It is because of its strong flavour that it is often used sparingly, like a herb.

Sorrel is a spring and summer plant, very easy to grow – the leaves should be picked often and while they are young and fresh. They may be added to other greens in a salad, or cooked like spinach and finished with cream or butter. In France, a handful of sorrel is often added to spinach; in this way, the sharpness of its taste is offset by the mild flavour of the spinach.

Cooked, squeezed dry and puréed, sorrel can be combined with fresh cheese and hard-boiled (hard-cooked) egg yolks, to refill the egg whites. Delicious soups are also made with sorrel and other greens, or with potato, cooked in chicken stock and finished with single (light) cream. A hot purée of sorrel, with or without spinach, goes well with pork or veal, and sorrel makes a classic accompaniment to salmon – indeed, it goes well with any fish. **See recipes.**

Fish with Sorrel

Poached fish fillets coated in a creamy sorrel and spinach sauce.

12 small fish fillets, about 100 g (3½ oz) each, skinned; salt and freshly ground black pepper; 90 g/3 oz (6 tbsp) butter; 3 tbsp finely chopped shallot; 1 clove garlic; 1 bouquet garni (4 sprigs each fresh parsley and tarragon, and 1 sprig fresh thyme); 500 ml/18 fl oz (2 cups) dry white wine; 150 g/5 oz (⅔ cup) sorrel, chopped; 150 g/5 oz (⅔ cup) spinach, chopped; 4 sticks tender celery, finely chopped; 2 tsp chopped parsley; 2 tsp chopped chives; 1 tbsp flour; 1 tsp prepared mustard; 120 ml/4 fl oz (½ cup) single (light) cream; lemon juice.

Season fish fillets lightly and fold in 2, skinned side in. Heat 30 g/1 oz (2 tbsp) butter in a saucepan and cook shallot until soft. Add garlic, bouquet garni and wine. Bring to the boil and simmer until reduced by about half. Strain and set aside. Heat remaining butter in a frying pan (skillet). Add sorrel, spinach, celery and herbs and cook for 5 minutes. Sprinkle with flour and stir well, then pour on reduced wine. Bring to the boil, stirring constantly, and simmer gently 10 minutes. Add fish fillets, cover and cook over very low heat for 5–7 minutes. Carefully remove fish to heated plates. Blend mustard and cream, and add to sauce with lemon juice to taste. Adjust seasoning. Pour sauce over fish and serve immediately. Serves 6.

Right: Spinach and Walnut Salad (page 347)

Sorrel Soup

1 small onion, finely chopped; 45 g/1½ oz (3 tbsp) butter; 2 medium potatoes, peeled and diced; 1 litre/1¾ pints (4 cups) chicken stock; salt and freshly ground black pepper; 90 g (3 oz) sorrel leaves; pinch sugar; pinch nutmeg; 3–4 tbsp single (light) cream.

Cook onion in butter in a saucepan until soft. Add potatoes and chicken stock, season with salt and pepper and simmer until potatoes are soft. Place sorrel leaves in blender with potato soup and blend until smooth. (Do this in several lots.) Reheat gently, then add sugar and nutmeg, stir in cream and adjust seasoning. If desired, serve sprinkled with chopped chives or small croûtons. Serves 4.

SORBET

See Ices, Sorbets, Granite and Sherbets.

SOUFFLE

Highly renowned as a creation of French cuisine, a soufflé is one of the lightest, most delectable and useful dishes in a cook's repertoire. Any chef worth his salt can whip up a soufflé on command.

To make a soufflé you need eggs, milk, butter and flour. You make a sauce, add egg yolks then fold in beaten egg whites, bake in the oven and, *voilà* – a light-as-air soufflé. For flavour you can add grated cheese, chopped cooked chicken, seafood, ham or vegetables – the range is limitless. If you want a sweet soufflé, sugar and vanilla essence (extract) are a natural choice. Liqueurs like Grand Marnier, or Cognac, fruits, fresh or candied and, of course, that great favourite chocolate, make a sweet soufflé one of the most popular dishes on restaurant menus.

A word of reassurance; a soufflé is not as difficult to make as many people think. The soufflé gained a reputation for being difficult in the days of wood-burning stoves. With today's excellent thermostatically-controlled ovens, baking a perfect soufflé is assured.

☐ **Basic Preparation:** Success with soufflés is simply a matter of following basic rules:

A soufflé does have to be eaten as soon as it's ready. During baking, the air trapped in the whites expands and the soufflé puffs up, but because of its delicate structure it will not hold up for more than a few minutes.

The flavourings are added in different ways. Cooked chicken, seafood and vegetables are often chopped finely, almost to a purée; cheese may be grated. These are folded into the basic sauce before adding egg

Left: Rabbit with Green Olives (page 327) and Stuffed Tomatoes (page 437)

whites. Sometimes the food is cut into thin slices and folded into the finished mixture, and for some soufflés, whole, lightly-cooked food is added, like a poached egg, or strawberries.

Eggs should be at room temperature. The main point to watch when making a soufflé is that the egg whites are beaten correctly. The whites must have no trace of yolk, and the bowl and beaters must be dry and free of grease. Beat the whites until foamy, add cream of tartar or salt (as indicated in recipe) and beat to a velvety snow. Test by gathering a little mixture on the beater and holding it upright; at the right consistency, the beaten whites will stand on the beater in a firm peak with a slightly drooping top.

It is the air beaten into the egg whites that makes the soufflé expand and rise, so it is important to fold them into the sauce as lightly as possible. Have the sauce warm. (If you have made it ahead, stand the bowl in warm water.) Stir a big spoonful of the whites into the base mixture to lighten it, then scoop the rest of the whites on to the surface and fold in, by cutting down through the mixture with a large metal spoon or rubber spatula. Folding in the whites should only take a minute or so. The mixture will blend a little more as you turn it into the soufflé dish.

Cooking Times: A soufflé made with about 350 ml/12 fl oz (1½ cups) sauce and 3–4 eggs in a 1.2–1.5 litre/2–2½ pint (5–6 cup) soufflé dish, will take about 30 minutes to cook in a preheated moderately hot oven (190°C/375°F, Gas Mark 5). It will rise well above the rim of the dish. At this stage the centre will be creamy, as some people prefer. For a well-cooked soufflé, leave for a further 5 minutes in the oven.

A soufflé made with 5–6 eggs requires a 1.75–2 litre/3–3½ pint (7–8 cup) dish, and will take 40–45 minutes to cook.

To prepare a soufflé dish: For a savoury soufflé, grease the dish and dust with fine dry breadcrumbs or a mixture of breadcrumbs and finely grated Parmesan cheese. For a sweet soufflé, grease, then dust the dish with a little caster sugar. Remove excess crumbs or sugar by turning the dish upside-down and tapping lightly on the table.

For a high cold soufflé, to stand above the rim of the dish, cut a strip of foil or grease-proof (waxed) paper wide enough to be doubled and come 8 cm (3 in) above the dish and long enough to fit around the dish with an overlap of 8–10 cm (3–4 in). Fold over to make a double strip. If a smooth effect on the soufflé is desired, brush one side of the strip with oil. Tie the strip around the dish, oiled side in and fold at the bottom, so that it stands like a collar above the edge.

Cold Dessert Soufflé: The charm of a cold soufflé, apart from its delectable flavour and airy texture, is its spectacular appearance.

The size of the soufflé dish determines the height of the finished soufflé. Sizes vary from individual serving dishes through 12, 15, 18 cm (5, 6, 7 in) diameter and larger. They are usually made with straight sides in oven-proof earthenware, and invariably have a fluted outside and indented rim.

A 3-egg soufflé is made in a 15 cm (6 in) dish, while a larger 6-egg Sweet Sherry Soufflé (see page 392) is made in a large 18 cm (7 in) dish. **See recipes.**

Cheese Soufflé

45 g/1½ oz (3 tbsp) butter; 3 tbsp flour; 250 ml/8 fl oz (1 cup) warm milk; 60 g/2 oz (½ cup) grated Gruyère, Emmenthal or similar Swiss cheese; 1 tbsp grated Parmesan cheese; ½ tsp salt; freshly ground black pepper; pinch cayenne; pinch nutmeg; 4 egg yolks; 5 egg whites; ½ tsp cream of tartar.

Prepare a 1.2–1.5 litre/2–2½ pint (5–6 cup) soufflé dish or 4 individual 250 ml/8 fl oz (1 cup) soufflé dishes, (see left). Place a baking tray on a shelf in the centre of a preheated moderately hot oven (200°C/400°F, Gas Mark 6). Melt butter in a saucepan, stir in flour and cook over low heat for 1 minute. Remove from heat, cool a little, and blend in milk, stirring until smooth. Return to heat and stir until boiling, then take from heat and stir in cheeses, salt, pepper, cayenne and nutmeg. Beat in egg yolks, one at a time. Whisk egg whites with cream of tartar until stiff but not brittle (see Basic Preparation) and fold into cheese mixture. Pour mixture into prepared soufflé dish, tap bottom of dish lightly on work surface to expel any large air pockets, and smooth top of soufflé. Quickly run a spoon around the top of the mixture about 2.5 cm (1 in) from the edge to make soufflé rise evenly in a 'crown'. Immediately place dish on baking tray in oven, close door gently, and turn oven down to moderately hot (190°C/375°F, Gas Mark 5). Bake soufflé about 24 minutes (18 minutes for small soufflés) until it is well puffed up, golden-brown on top and just firm. Have a heated serving platter ready and a warmed serving spoon and fork. Place soufflé dish on platter, and take immediately to table. To serve, pierce top lightly with spoon and fork held vertically, and spread soufflé apart. Include some crust and some creamy centre with each serving. Serves 4.

VARIATIONS

Herb Soufflé: Follow recipe for Cheese Soufflé, folding in 1 shallot, finely chopped, and 1 tbsp finely chopped fresh herbs, such as chives, parsley, marjoram, oregano, in any combination, with the cheese and seasonings. Bake as above.

Cheese and Mushroom Soufflé: Follow recipe for Cheese Soufflé. Sauté 6–8 mushrooms, sliced, in a little butter. Half fill prepared soufflé dish with soufflé mixture, scatter over mushrooms and fill with remaining mixture. Top with mixture of grated Parmesan cheese and breadcrumbs and bake as on page 391.

Spinach Soufflé: Follow recipe for Cheese Soufflé but use 2 tbsp grated Swiss cheese, 1 tbsp grated Parmesan and 90 g (3 oz) finely chopped cooked spinach as the flavouring. Measure the spinach after cooking, squeezing dry and chopping.

Chicken Soufflé

3–4 shallots, chopped; 60 g/2 oz (4 tbsp) butter; 2 tbsp flour; 350 ml/12 fl oz (1½ cups) warm milk; ½ tsp dried marjoram; 1 tsp chopped parsley; salt and freshly ground black pepper; 4 egg yolks; 180 g/6 oz (¾ cup) chopped cooked chicken meat; 5 egg whites.

Prepare a 1.5 litre/2½ pint (6 cup) soufflé dish (see page 391). Place a baking tray on a shelf in the centre of a preheated moderately hot oven (200°C/400°F, Gas Mark 6). Cook shallots in butter in a large pan for 1–2 minutes. Add flour and cook, stirring, for a few minutes. Remove from heat and add warm milk, herbs, salt and pepper. Return to heat, bring slowly to the boil and boil for 2 minutes, stirring constantly. Remove sauce from heat and cool slightly. Beat in egg yolks one at a time. Add chicken. Beat egg whites with pinch of salt until stiff. Lightly fold into chicken mixture, then pour into prepared dish. Immediately place dish on baking tray, close oven door, and turn oven down to moderately hot (190°C/375°F, Gas Mark 5). Bake soufflé for about 35 minutes. Serves 4.
VARIATIONS
Replace chicken with 180 g/6 oz (¾ cup) of any of the following: canned tuna, drained and flaked; diced cooked lobster, prawns (shrimp) or crab; finely chopped cooked brains or sweetbreads.

Vanilla Soufflé

45 g/1½ oz (3 tbsp) butter; 1 tbsp flour; 250 ml/8 fl oz (1 cup) warm milk; ¼ tsp salt; 125 g/4 oz (½ cup) sugar; piece vanilla pod (bean); 4 egg yolks; 5 egg whites.

Making a Vanilla Soufflé

Prepare a 1.5 litre/2½ pint (6 cup) soufflé dish (see page 391), and sprinkle inside with sugar **(Fig 1 below)**. Melt butter in a saucepan, blend in flour and cook 1 minute. Remove from heat and gradually add milk. Add salt, sugar and vanilla bean. Return to heat and cook, stirring constantly, until thick and smooth. Allow to cool. Remove vanilla bean. Beat in egg yolks one at a time **(2)**. Beat egg whites until stiff and fold into vanilla mixture **(3)**. Pour into prepared dish and run a spoon around top about 2.5 cm (1 in) from edge **(4)**. Stand dish in roasting tin (pan) of hot water and bake in a preheated moderately hot oven 190°C/375°F, Gas Mark 5) for 15 minutes. Reduce heat to moderate (180°C/350°F, Gas Mark 4) and cook further 25 minutes. Serve immediately with fruit sauce **(5)**. Serves 6.
VARIATIONS
Chocolate Soufflé: Chop 60 g/2 oz (⅓ cup) cooking chocolate finely and melt over hot water. Add to Vanilla Soufflé mixture before egg yolks, then proceed as above.
Coffee Soufflé: Follow recipe for Vanilla Soufflé, but substitute 120 ml/4 fl oz (½ cup) strong black coffee for 120 ml/4 fl oz (½ cup) of the milk.
Almond Soufflé: Follow recipe for Vanilla Soufflé, but add 60 g/2 oz (½ cup) ground almonds before the egg yolks and substitute ¼ tsp almond essence (extract) for the vanilla. Sprinkle with slivered almonds before baking.

Iced Vanilla Soufflé

1 vanilla pod (bean), or ½ tsp vanilla essence (extract); 500 ml/18 fl oz (2 cups) milk; 3 eggs, separated; 75 g/2½ oz (⅓ cup) sugar; 1 tbsp gelatine; 2–3 tbsp water; 120 ml/4 fl oz (½ cup) double (heavy) cream, whipped; 250 g (8 oz) strawberries, hulled; caster sugar to taste; dash Kirsch; shaved chocolate or whipped cream to decorate.

Prepare a 1.2 litre/2 pint (5 cup) soufflé dish (see page 391). Split vanilla bean and scald with milk (see page 215). Cream egg yolks with sugar and pour on milk. Return to pan and stir over low heat, without boiling, until thick. Strain, cool and add vanilla if

using. Soften gelatine in water, then dissolve over hot water and add to custard. Stir over ice until beginning to set. Fold in cream. Stiffly beat egg whites and fold in. Put a small tall oiled jam jar or bottle in centre of prepared dish. Pour mixture into dish. Chill until set. Before serving remove jar and fill centre of soufflé with whole or sliced sugared strawberries flavoured with Kirsch. Carefully peel off collar and decorate sides with shaved chocolate or whipped cream. Serves 5–6.

Sweet Sherry Soufflé

1 tbsp gelatine; 120 ml/4 fl oz (½ cup) cold water; 350 ml/12 fl oz (1½ cups) sweet sherry; 6 eggs, separated; 180 g/6 oz (¾ cup) caster sugar; 300 ml/½ pint (1¼ cups) double (heavy) cream, whipped; 1 scant tbsp lemon juice; 9–10 Savoy or sponge finger biscuits (lady fingers); extra whipped cream to decorate.

Prepare a 1.75–2 litre/3–3½ pint (7–8 cup) soufflé dish (see page 391). Soften gelatine in cold water for 5 minutes, then dissolve over hot water. Stir in sherry and cool, then chill for 30 minutes or until mixture begins to thicken. Meanwhile, beat egg yolks until frothy. Add 60 g/2 oz (¼ cup) sugar gradually and beat until mixture is thick and lemon coloured. Add sherry mixture to egg yolks and combine well. Fold in whipped cream. Beat egg whites until foamy. Add remaining sugar gradually, beating constantly, then add lemon juice and beat until mixture is stiff but not dry. Fold into sherry mixture gently but thoroughly. Spoon about half mixture into dish and stand biscuits at equal intervals round edge, pushing them down to the bottom. Spoon in remaining mixture. Chill until firm. Remove collar from dish and serve decorated with rosettes of whipped cream. Serves 12.

Strawberry Soufflé

250 g (8 oz) strawberries, hulled; 1 tbsp gelatine; 4 tbsp cold water; 4 eggs, separated; 180 g/6 oz (¾ cup) caster sugar; 300 ml/½ pint (1¼ cups) double (heavy) cream, whipped; pinch salt; few drops red food colouring.

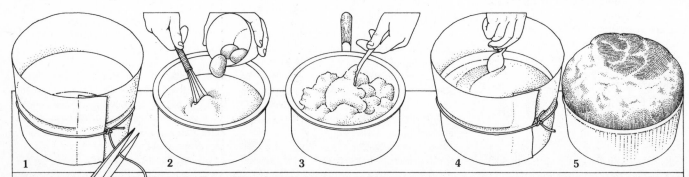

1   2   3   4   5

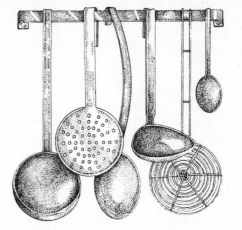

Prepare a 1.25–1.5 litre/2–2½ pint (5–6 cup) soufflé dish or 6 individual 250 ml/ 8 fl oz (1 cup) dishes (see page 391). Sieve strawberries or blend to a purée. Soften gelatine in cold water, then dissolve over hot water. Put egg yolks with 125 g/4 oz (½ cup) sugar in top of double saucepan (double boiler) and cook over simmering water, stirring constantly, until slightly thickened. Stir in gelatine and cool, stirring occasionally. When cold mix in strawberry purée. Fold in cream. Beat egg whites with salt until they hold soft peaks. Gradually add remaining sugar and continue beating until mixture is shiny and holds a definite peak. Fold into strawberry mixture very gently and add a few drops of red food colouring. Pour into the prepared dish or dishes and chill until firm. Remove paper collar before serving. Serves 6.

Liqueur Soufflé
(Bénédictine or Grand Marnier)

5 eggs, separated; 125 g/4 oz (½ cup) caster sugar; 175 ml/6 fl oz (¾ cup) brandy; 120 ml/4 fl oz (½ cup) sherry; 1 tbsp lemon juice; 1 tbsp Bénédictine or Grand Marnier; 1½ tbsp gelatine; 120 ml/4 fl oz (½ cup) water; 300 ml/½ pint (1¼ cups) double (heavy) cream, whipped.

Prepare a 1.5–1.75 litre/2½–3 pint (6–7 cup) soufflé dish (see page 391). Beat egg yolks with sugar until thick and light. Stir in brandy, sherry, lemon juice and liqueur. Soften gelatine in water, then dissolve over hot water and add to mixture. Fold in cream. Stiffly beat egg whites and fold in. Pour into prepared dish and chill until firm. Remove collar before serving. Serves 8–10.

SOUPS

Originally, soup was basic sustenance – a pot of warming nourishment that brought the family together. Soup was a meal in itself: with a generous chunk of bread and a warm hearth to enjoy it by, it revived many a flagging body and spirit. These hearty soups are still with us today: Scotch Broth, Minestrone, Bouillabaisse, Pea and Ham Bone, chowder and many more.

More sophisticated concepts of dining have altered the role of soup. Restaurant chefs have created lighter and more delicate soups for their customers; fond mothers have created soups to nourish a sick and ailing child or more robust ones for the family; hostesses have sought soups to star at a dinner party. Whether you want to make a soup that is a meal in itself, a first course for a family meal, a luxury one for a dinner party, or a chilled soup to tempt jaded appetites on a hot summer day, you will be able to find a recipe, for there is a soup for almost any occasion.

Although soup does not necessarily need to be made from stock, it is good to have stock either in the refrigerator or the freezer ready to turn into soup with freshly-cooked vegetables. See *Stock* for stocks used in soup-making.

Stock cubes can be used but they tend to be salty and give a 'sameness' to soups.

Canned consommé is quite expensive, whereas home-made stock is usually made from ingredients which are very cheap or would otherwise be discarded, and a home-made stock, when made correctly, is nutritious in itself. Canned consommé does have its place, though. When time is short, it is a comforting thought to go to the cupboard and make a lovely soup with this as a base. A touch of sherry, a few herbs, a handful of diced or julienne (matchstick) vegetables, and you have a delicious soup. **See recipes**.

Soups can be divided into several categories – Consommé and Clear Soups; Cream Soups, usually made with softened vegetables as the base; Fish Soups; nutritious Pulse Soups made from dried beans, peas or lentils; Quick Soups that take only minutes to prepare; Hearty Soups which are often served as a complete meal; and Chilled Soups, refreshing to serve on a hot summer's day.

CONSOMME AND CLEAR SOUPS
The term 'consommé' is generally used these days to describe any clear soup. A good consommé starts with a good rich bouillon, clear of fat, then made crystal-clear, and any existing fat cleared by clarification. Beaten egg whites and lean minced (ground) beef, or, in the case of chicken bouillon, egg whites and chicken backs, are added to the simmering bouillon. As the egg whites and meat cook, they attract and hold the tiny particles of fat and other matter that cloud the soup. When this mass of solids is discarded you have a sparkling, clear consommé. Serve with a garnish and, if liked, a dash of sherry or Madeira, and you have the perfect start to a meal.

Consommé Double

1.5 litres/2½ pints (6 cups) cold brown stock (bouillon); 2 egg whites, lightly beaten; 2 egg shells; 250 g/8 oz (1 cup) finely minced (ground) lean beef; 4 tbsp dry flor sherry.

To clarify consommé: remove any fat from stock (bouillon), then place in a saucepan with egg whites, egg shells and beef. Bring slowly to the boil, whisking occasionally with a wire whisk. Allow liquid to rise in pan as it reaches boiling point, then draw pan aside. Boil up carefully once more, taking care not to break crust which will form on top. Draw pan aside, lower heat and then simmer soup

very gently for 30 minutes. This slow simmering will extract all flavour from meat. Strain through a colander lined with butter muslin (cheesecloth), holding back egg white crust with a spoon and then sliding it out on to cloth. The consommé should now be clear. If not, filter it again through egg white on cloth into a clean bowl. Return to heat and add sherry (see below). Serves 6.
NOTE: A little sherry can make a consommé but too much can break it. Use a good dry flor sherry – 1–2 tsp for each serving according to your taste.
VARIATION
Consommé Royale: Break up 2 eggs with a whisk or fork but do not make them frothy. Add 4 tbsp single (light) cream and season with salt and white pepper. Pour into a small mould or cup and steam or poach this custard for 20 minutes or until set. Allow to cool completely, then turn out and slice into strips or cut into shapes. Add to the hot Consommé just before serving.

Spiced Tomato Consommé

1 medium onion, finely chopped; 30 g/1 oz (2 tbsp) butter; 2 litres/3½ pints (8 cups) strong chicken stock; 1 × 425 g/14 oz can tomatoes; 1 large bouquet garni containing strip lemon rind; salt and freshly ground black pepper; 120 ml/4 fl oz (½ cup) dry sherry; 1 tbsp arrowroot; 2 tbsp water or stock; lemon juice.
GARNISH: *single (light) cream; chopped chives.*

Soften onion in butter in a saucepan, and add stock, tomatoes and bouquet garni. Season with salt and pepper. Cover and simmer for 40 minutes, then rub through a sieve. Rinse out pan, add sherry and boil to reduce by half. Stir in sieved soup. Dissolve arrowroot in water or stock and add to soup. Bring to the boil, stirring until thickened. Add a few drops of lemon juice. Adjust seasoning, and serve with a spoonful of cream swirled into each cup and a sprinkling of chopped chives. Serves 8.

Golden Consommé with Melon

1 small cantaloup melon, halved and seeded; 250 ml/8 fl oz (1 cup) canned chicken consommé; 250 ml/8 fl oz (1 cup) tomato juice; pinch nutmeg; salt and freshly ground black pepper; 2 tsp gelatine; 250 ml/8 fl oz (1 cup) strained orange juice.

Scoop out balls from melon with a melon baller (or peel and cut into small dice). Put into a covered container and refrigerate until serving time. Place chicken consommé and tomato juice in a saucepan, and season with nutmeg, salt and pepper. Sprinkle gelatine over and leave 10 minutes to soften. Heat gently, until hot but not boiling. Turn into a bowl and cool, then stir in orange juice. Cover and chill. To serve, divide melon balls among 6 soup bowls and ladle chilled soup over them. Serves 6.

Borsch Julienne

1 litre/1¾ pints (4 cups) strong beef stock (bouillon); 4 beetroot, peeled and grated; 250 ml/8 fl oz (1 cup) red wine; 2 tbsp tomato purée (paste); 1 bay leaf; 3 egg whites, beaten; 1 beetroot, cooked, peeled and cut into fine julienne (matchstick) strips; 175 ml/6 fl oz (¾ cup) sour cream; grated rind 1 lemon; salt; pinch cayenne.

Put stock (bouillon) into a saucepan. Add grated beetroot, wine, tomato purée (paste), bay leaf and egg whites. Cook over moderate heat, whisking constantly, until mixture comes to the boil, then draw aside and leave for 10 minutes. Strain through a fine damp cloth and place in refrigerator until cold. Add fine julienne of beetroot. Season sour cream with lemon rind, salt and cayenne. Serve soup in bowls and offer cream separately. Serves 6.

CREAM SOUPS

These delicious soups are made with the simplest of ingredients, and their tender, melting qualities appeal to many people who are quite indifferent about eating vegetables.

Cooking the chopped vegetables in a little butter until soft is an important step in making cream soups, but care has to be taken not to brown the vegetables or the colour and flavour of the finished soup will be spoilt. The easiest way to soften the vegetables is to melt the butter in the saucepan, add the vegetables and toss well; then place on top a double circle of greaseproof (waxed) paper, pushing it well down over the vegetables, cover the saucepan and cook over very gentle heat for about 15 minutes, shaking the saucepan occasionally.

The addition of single (light) cream gives a very smooth texture to the finished purée, but do not overdo it. With cream especially, it's no use imagining that if a little is good, more will

be better. Too much 'softens' the flavour of the vegetables and, of course, adds to the calories. Use about 2–3 tsp single (light) cream or plain yogurt to each plate of soup.

Green Velvet Soup

2 large, dark green cucumbers; 600 ml/ 1 pint (2½ cups) chicken stock; 30 g/1 oz (2 tbsp) butter; 1½ tbsp flour; 250 ml/8 fl oz (1 cup) warm milk; 1 tsp chopped fresh dill, or ¼ tsp dried; salt and freshly ground white pepper; 4 tbsp single (light) cream; snipped fresh dill or chives to garnish.

Peel cucumbers thinly, so that green beneath skin is left on. Halve lengthways, scoop out seeds and cut into pieces. Purée in a food processor or blender until smooth, adding a little stock to help if necessary. Pour into a jug, add remaining stock and set aside. Melt butter in a large saucepan, stir in flour and cook gently for 1 minute. Remove from heat,

cool a little, and stir in milk. Blend smoothly together, then return to heat and stir until boiling. Add cucumber mixture, dill, salt and pepper. Stir in cream. Reheat gently until piping hot. Serve in heated bowls, garnished with dill or chives. Serves 6.

Walnut Soup

125 g/4 oz (1 cup) peeled walnuts, chopped (see Note); 1 clove garlic, crushed; 1 litre/1¾ pints (4 cups) beef stock (bouillon) or chicken stock; 175 ml/6 fl oz (¾ cup) single (light) cream; salt and freshly ground black pepper.

Using a mortar and pestle, food processor or blender, process walnuts with garlic and a little of the stock until quite smooth. Add to remaining stock. Heat cream to boiling point in a large saucepan, then reduce heat and stir in walnut mixture. Heat gently and season. Serve hot or chilled. Serves 6.
NOTE: Peeled walnuts are the secret of this beautiful soup. Peeled walnuts can be

bought in cans or at a good Chinese grocer. If you have to prepare them yourself, cover the walnuts with water, bring slowly to the boil, simmer for a few minutes, then drain and peel.

Danablu Soup

150 g/5 oz (1¼ cups) Danablu (Danish blue cheese); 30 g/1 oz (2 tbsp) butter; 2 tbsp flour; 1 litre/1¾ pints (4 cups) chicken stock; 250 ml/8 fl oz (1 cup) single (light) cream. GARNISH: 175 ml/6 fl oz (¾ cup) double (heavy) cream, whipped; 3 tbsp chopped parsley.

Mash cheese with a fork. Melt butter in a saucepan, add flour and cook for 1 minute, stirring. Gradually stir in stock and cook, stirring constantly, until slightly thickened. Beat together mashed cheese and cream, and add to soup, beating with a wire whisk. Bring to the boil. Serve in soup plates or small bowls. Garnish each with a spoonful of whipped cream, sprinkled with chopped parsley. Serves 6–8.

Creamy Onion Soup

125 g/4 oz (½ cup) butter; 4 large white onions, finely sliced; 1 clove garlic, crushed; 500 ml/18 fl oz (2 cups) chicken stock; 500 ml/18 fl oz (2 cups) milk; 180 g (6 oz) very thin, raw vermicelli or noodles, broken into very small pieces; 3 egg yolks, beaten; 120 ml/4 fl oz (½ cup) single (light) cream; pinch nutmeg; salt and freshly ground white pepper; 60 g/2 oz (½ cup) grated Cheddar cheese; chopped parsley to garnish.

Heat butter in a large, heavy saucepan and gently cook onions and garlic until very soft but not brown. This will take at least 20 minutes, and they should be stirred often to prevent sticking. Push mixture through a sieve, or purée in a blender or food processor. Return to saucepan, add stock and milk and bring to the boil. Add vermicelli and simmer gently until vermicelli is cooked, about 5 minutes. Pour a little hot soup into egg yolks and stir well, then add to remaining soup. Cook over a very low heat, stirring constantly with a whisk, until thickened. Add cream, nutmeg, salt and pepper, and stir in cheese. Do not allow to boil. Serve in hot soup bowls, sprinkled with a little chopped parsley. Serves 4–6.

Cream of Cauliflower Soup

An excellent winter soup, this is good chilled as well as hot.

1 litre/1¾ pints (4 cups) water; 1 small cauliflower, broken into small florets; 60 g/2 oz (4 tbsp) butter; 3 tbsp flour; 500 ml/18 fl oz (2 cups) chicken stock; ¼ tsp nutmeg; salt and freshly ground white pepper; 2 egg yolks; 5 tbsp single (light) cream; finely chopped parsley or snipped fresh dill to garnish.

Bring water to the boil in a saucepan. Drop in cauliflower florets and cook for about 10 minutes. Drain, reserving cooking liquid. Reserve about 310 g/10 oz (2 cups) cooked florets, and sieve or purée remainder with 250 ml/8 fl oz (1 cup) reserved liquid in a blender or food processor. Melt butter in a saucepan, blend in flour and cook, stirring, until a pale straw colour. Remove from heat and add remaining reserved cooking liquid and stock, stirring until mixture is smooth. Add cauliflower purée, return to heat and stir until boiling. Simmer for about 15 minutes, stirring occasionally. Add reserved cauliflower florets, nutmeg, salt and pepper and simmer for a further 5 minutes. Beat egg yolks with cream. Stir in a ladle of hot soup, then add this mixture to remaining soup, stirring. Heat gently without boiling, then pour into a heated tureen or bowls and sprinkle with parsley. Or chill and serve sprinkled with parsley or dill. Serves 6.

Potage Cressonière

(Watercress Soup)

60 g/2 oz (4 tbsp) butter; 1 clove garlic, chopped; 1 onion, chopped; 2 potatoes, peeled and thinly sliced; 1 tbsp salt; $\frac{1}{4}$ tsp black pepper; 250 ml/8 fl oz (1 cup) water; 1 bunch watercress; 500 ml/18 fl oz (2 cups) milk; 2 egg yolks; 120 ml/4 fl oz ($\frac{1}{2}$ cup) single (light) cream.

Heat butter in a large saucepan. Add garlic and onions and cook, covered, until tender, about 5 minutes. Add potatoes, salt, pepper and water. Cover and bring to the boil. Reduce heat and simmer 15 minutes or until potatoes are almost tender. Discard thick hairy stems from watercress. Cut remaining watercress stems into short lengths. Coarsely chop leaves. Add all the watercress stems, half the leaves and all the milk to potato mixture and continue cooking 15 minutes. Purée in blender or food processor. Return to saucepan and reheat. Beat together egg yolks and cream. Add a ladle full of hot soup, mix well, and stir into remaining soup. Cook gently, stirring constantly, until slightly thickened. Garnish with remaining watercress leaves and serve immediately. Serves 4–6.

Cream of Broccoli Soup

1 onion, sliced; 1 carrot, sliced; 1 small stick celery with leaves, sliced; 1 clove garlic; 120 ml/4 fl oz ($\frac{1}{2}$ cup) water; 370 g/12 oz (2 cups) coarsely chopped cooked broccoli; 1 tsp salt; generous pinch cayenne; 60 g

(2 oz) cooked macaroni; 500 ml/18 fl oz (2 cups) chicken stock; 120 ml/4 fl oz ($\frac{1}{2}$ cup) single (light) cream; sour cream to serve.

Place onion, carrot, celery, garlic and water in a saucepan, bring to the boil and simmer, covered, for 10 minutes. Add broccoli, salt, cayenne and macaroni. Purée in a blender or food processor. With motor running, add stock and cream. Alternatively, sieve broccoli mixture and stir in stock and cream. Chill and serve topped with sour cream. Serves 4–6.

Fresh Mushroom Cream Soup

Raw mushrooms are puréed, then merely reheated giving a true fresh mushroom taste.

1.2 litres/2 pints (5 cups) chicken stock; 1 clove garlic, crushed; 250 g (8 oz) large mushrooms; 60 g/2 oz (4 tbsp) butter; 1 egg yolk; 120 ml/4 fl oz ($\frac{1}{2}$ cup) single (light) cream; 2 button mushrooms, thinly sliced; Croûtons (page 90) to serve.

Heat stock and garlic. Roughly chop large mushrooms. Place about $\frac{1}{3}$ in a blender or food processor with $\frac{1}{3}$ of the butter and stock. Purée until smooth then transfer to a saucepan. Purée remaining mushrooms, butter and stock in 2 batches. Heat mixture gently until very hot, season with salt and pepper. Beat egg yolk with cream until blended. Stir in a little hot soup then pour this mixture back into the saucepan. Heat gently, stirring, until soup becomes glossy and thickens slightly. Do not boil. Serve immediately, garnished with mushroom slices. Pass croûtons around separately. Serves 6.

Cream of Tomato Soup

5–6 medium, ripe tomatoes, peeled and chopped; 1 tbsp chopped onion; $\frac{1}{2}$ tsp celery seeds; $\frac{1}{2}$ bay leaf; 2 cloves; 60 g/2 oz (4 tbsp) butter; 30 g/1 oz ($\frac{1}{4}$ cup) flour; 750 ml/ 1$\frac{1}{4}$ pints (3 cups) warm milk; 1$\frac{1}{2}$ tsp salt; freshly ground black pepper; 2 tbsp tomato purée (paste).

Place tomatoes in saucepan with onion, celery seeds, bay leaf and cloves and simmer gently for 15 minutes or until tomatoes are very soft. Stir occasionally. Meanwhile, melt butter in another saucepan, add flour and cook for 1 minute, stirring. Add milk and cook, stirring vigorously with a whisk, until thickened and smooth. Season with salt and pepper and add tomato purée (paste). Press tomato mixture through a sieve. There should be about 500 ml/18 fl oz (2 cups). Reheat fresh tomato purée, then gradually add to soup base, stirring. If mixture curdles, whisk until smooth. Serves 6.

Cream of Carrot Soup

(Potage Crécy)

30 g/1 oz (2 tbsp) butter; 4 medium carrots, sliced; 1 onion, sliced; 750 ml/1$\frac{1}{4}$ pints (3 cups) hot chicken stock or water; salt; generous pinch cayenne; 6 tbsp single (light) cream; chopped parsley to garnish.

Melt butter in a saucepan, add carrots and onion and cook gently until softened, about 10 minutes. Add 500 ml/18 fl oz (2 cups) chicken stock or water and bring to the boil. Reduce heat, cover and simmer for 10 minutes. Rub through a sieve or purée in a blender. Return soup to pan and heat gently with remaining stock. Season with salt and cayenne, then swirl in cream. Sprinkle with chopped parsley before serving. Serves 4.

FISH SOUPS

Not eaten as much as they should be – a fish soup can be a very welcome addition to our menu – whether as a hearty chowder, a light delicate bisque, or a luxury soup like Oyster Chowder.

Home-made fish stock is no trouble to make – and what is more the ingredients are virtually free! Your fish merchant will often give you the bones and skins of the fish he has been filleting or will sell you a couple of bream or snapper heads for very little. They will make an excellent foundation for many different soups.

See also Stock.

Scottish-Style Fish Soup

This is a bit like an American chowder, more of a stew than a soup.

2 slices pickled (salt) pork, rind removed and cut into strips; 30 g/1 oz (2 tbsp) butter; 1 large onion, finely chopped; 3–4 medium potatoes, peeled and sliced; 600 ml/1 pint (2$\frac{1}{2}$ cups) water; 500 g (1 lb) smoked haddock; 500 ml/18 fl oz (2 cups) milk; salt and freshly ground white pepper; finely chopped parsley to garnish.

Fry strips of pork in a saucepan until fat runs out. Add butter and onion and cook for about 5 minutes. Add potatoes and water. Bring to the boil and simmer for 10–15

minutes. Meanwhile, cook smoked haddock separately in milk. When just tender, remove from pan and, when cool enough to handle, break into flakes, removing bones. Add to vegetable mixture with milk and cook for a further 5 minutes. Season well with salt and pepper and sprinkle lavishly with chopped parsley to serve. Serves 4–6.

Oyster Chowder

2 medium potatoes, peeled and diced; 1 carrot, finely chopped; 2 sticks celery, chopped; 1.5 litres/2½ pints (6 cups) milk; 1 tbsp chopped onion; salt and freshly ground black pepper; 2 tbsp flour; 60 g/2 oz (4 tbsp) butter; 24 fresh oysters, removed from shells; 2 tbsp chopped parsley.

Cook potatoes, carrot and celery in a small amount of boiling salted water in a large saucepan until tender. Drain. Add milk, onion, salt and pepper to vegetables and bring to the boil. Cream flour with half the butter to make a paste and add, in small pieces, to boiling mixture. Cook, stirring, until thickened. Cook oysters, with their liquid, in remaining butter until edges curl. Add to soup, ladle into warmed soup bowls and serve immediately, sprinkled with parsley. Serves 4–6.

Fish Chowder

4 fish heads, or bones from 4 fish (any kind saved when fish were cooked for a meal); 500 ml/18 fl oz (2 cups) water; 1 small onion, chopped; 1 clove garlic, crushed; 2 tbsp chopped green pepper; 2 tbsp butter or olive oil; 500 g/1 lb (2 cups) chopped peeled ripe tomatoes; 2 potatoes, peeled and finely diced; 60 g/2 oz (½ cup) chopped celery; 1 bay leaf; 1 tsp salt; pinch freshly ground black pepper; 250 g (8 oz) fish fillet, cut into strips; 1 tbsp chopped parsley.

Rinse heads or bones and simmer in water 10 minutes. Strain broth and discard bones. Sauté onion, garlic and green pepper in butter or oil until onion is transparent. Add reserved broth, tomatoes, potatoes, celery, bay leaf, salt and pepper. Simmer until

potatoes are tender. Add fish strips and parsley and cook gently 5–8 minutes. Discard bay leaf. Serves 4.

Maryland Crab Bisque

1 onion, finely chopped; 60 g/2 oz (4 tbsp) butter; 500 g/1 lb (2 cups) crabmeat, picked over to remove bits of shell and cartilage; ½ tsp salt; freshly ground black pepper; 750 ml/1¼ pints (3 cups) milk; 250 ml/8 fl oz (1 cup) single (light) cream; 2 tbsp Scotch whisky; a few drops Tabasco (hot pepper) sauce; chopped chives to garnish.

Sauté onion in butter until transparent. Stir in crabmeat, salt and pepper and cook over low heat 5 minutes, stirring occasionally. Scald milk (see page 215), add to crab and cook 5–10 minutes. Add cream and, when mixture is piping hot, stir in whisky and Tabasco (hot pepper) sauce. Serve immediately, with chopped chives. Serves 6.

Italian Clam Soup

4 tbsp olive oil; 1 onion, chopped; 1 clove garlic; 3 anchovy fillets, chopped; 1 tbsp chopped parsley; 120 ml/4 fl oz (½ cup) dry red wine; 1 tbsp tomato purée (paste); 350 ml/12 fl oz (1½ cups) warm water; ½ tsp salt; ½ tsp freshly ground black pepper; 1 × 290 g/9 oz can clams, drained; 1 tsp chopped fresh oregano; 8 thin slices Italian bread, fried in olive oil.

Heat oil in a large saucepan, add onion and garlic and fry until brown. Discard garlic. Add anchovies, parsley and wine to oil and cook 5 minutes. Stir in tomato purée (paste), water, salt and pepper and cook 3–4 minutes. Add clams and oregano and cook 2 minutes longer. Place 2 slices fried bread in each soup dish and pour hot soup over them. Serves 4.

Bouillabaisse

3 tbsp olive oil; 1 onion, chopped; 2 tbsp chopped celery leaves; 1–2 cloves garlic, crushed; good pinch saffron powder; 4 tomatoes, peeled and chopped; 500 ml/

18 fl oz (2 cups) water; 175 ml/6 fl oz (¾ cup) dry white wine; salt and freshly ground black pepper; pinch cayenne; 1.5 kg (3 lb) mixed seafood, such as fish steaks or fillets, cubed; shelled cooked prawns (shrimp) and lobster (optional); squeeze lemon juice; chopped parsley to garnish.

Heat oil in a heavy saucepan, add onion and cook until translucent. Add celery leaves, garlic and saffron, then tomatoes. Cook, stirring occasionally, until reduced to a pulp. Add water and wine. Season with salt, pepper and cayenne. Simmer for 5 minutes. If too thick, add a little more water. Add raw seafood and cook gently; the fish will take about 5–8 minutes, but cooked prawns (shrimp) and lobster only need to be heated through. Squeeze lemon juice over and serve garnished with chopped parsley. Serves 4–6.

DRIED BEAN, PEA AND LENTIL SOUPS

Dried beans, peas and lentils make nourishing and inexpensive soups. Although the proteins they contain lack some of the essential amino acids, this can be rectified by serving cheese, milk or eggs separately, or adding a little meat to the soup.

Beans vary in cooking time according to variety and age, and are usually soaked in water overnight before cooking. If you have forgotten to soak them, a quick method to tenderize them for cooking is to cover with cold water, bring to the boil and simmer for 2 minutes. Remove from heat and let stand, tightly covered, for 1 hour; this is the equivalent of 8 hours' soaking. Or you can use canned beans.

Remember that beans, peas or lentils will expand 2½ times after cooking.

See also *Pulses: Dried Beans, Peas and Lentils.*

Haricot Bean Soup

210 g/7 oz (1 cup) dried haricot (navy) beans, soaked overnight and drained; 1.2 litres/2 pints (5 cups) water; 1 bouquet garni; 1 medium onion; 1 clove garlic; 4–5 sticks celery, finely chopped; 2 leeks (white part only), or 2 onions, finely chopped; 60 g/2 oz (4 tbsp) butter; 4 large tomatoes, chopped; salt; 2 egg yolks; Garlic Croûtons (page 90) to serve.

Cook beans in the 1.2 litres/2 pints (5 cups) water with bouquet garni, whole onion and garlic until tender, about 1 hour. Cook celery and leeks or onions in half the butter until soft but not coloured. Add tomatoes and cook gently for about 10 minutes. Discard onion, garlic and bouquet garni from beans. Combine beans and liquid with vegetables and rub through a sieve or purée in a blender. Return to pan. Season with salt and bring to the boil, stirring. Beat egg yolks with 2 tbsp hot soup. Add to remaining soup with rest of the butter. Reheat but do not allow to boil. Serve with croûtons fried in garlic-flavoured oil. Serves 6–8.

Italian Bean Soup

210 g/7 oz (1 cup) dried haricot (navy) beans, soaked overnight and drained; 1 bouquet garni; salt; 1 tbsp oil; 60 g (2 oz) pickled (salt) pork or bacon, finely chopped; 1 onion, finely chopped; 1 stick celery, finely chopped; 1 clove garlic, crushed; 2 tomatoes, peeled and chopped; 1 tsp salt; freshly ground black pepper; 2 litres/3½ pints (8 cups) hot water; 125 g/4 oz (1 cup) elbow macaroni; grated Parmesan cheese to serve.

Place beans in a large saucepan with fresh water to cover. Add bouquet garni, cover and simmer until tender, about 1 hour. Season with salt at end of cooking time. Drain. Heat oil in saucepan, add pork, onion, celery and garlic and sauté until golden. Add tomatoes with salt, pepper, hot water and cooked beans. Simmer for 5 minutes. Add elbow macaroni and cook a further 8–10 minutes or until macaroni is tender, adding more water if necessary. Serve hot with Parmesan. Serves 6–8.

Yellow Split Pea Soup

500 g/1 lb (2 cups) yellow split peas; 2.5 litres/4 pints (10 cups) water; 1 ham hock; 3 onions, chopped; 2 carrots, diced; handful celery leaves; few parsley stalks; 2 bay leaves: 1 tsp chopped fresh summer savory (if available); salt and freshly ground black pepper; Croûtons (page 90) to serve.

Soak split peas overnight in the water. Next day, put in a large pan and add remaining ingredients. Bring slowly to the boil, cover and simmer gently for 2–3 hours or until peas are very tender. It may be necessary to add more water during cooking to maintain right consistency. To serve, remove hock, celery leaves, parsley and bay leaves and adjust seasoning. Take any meat from hock, chop and return it to the soup. Serve with croûtons. Serves 8–10.

Dhal Soup

60 g/2 oz (4 tbsp) ghee or butter; 1 medium onion, finely chopped; 2 cloves garlic, crushed; 1 tbsp ground coriander; 5 cm (2 in) cinnamon stick; 1 tsp turmeric; 1 tsp ground cumin; ½ tsp ground fenugreek; ¼ tsp chilli powder (or to taste); 250 g/8 oz (1 cup) red lentils; 1.5 litres/2½ pints (6 cups) water; 2 tbsp tomato purée (paste); salt; lemon juice; Croûtons (page 90) to serve.

Heat ghee or butter in saucepan and gently fry onion and garlic until golden. Add spices and cook for 2 minutes, stirring constantly. Add lentils and water with tomato purée (paste) and salt. Simmer, covered, for 30 minutes. Remove cinnamon stick. With a wooden spoon, mash some lentils against side of pan, so you have a thickened soup with some whole lentils in it, or purée in a blender until smooth. Add lemon juice, adjust seasoning and serve with croûtons. Serves 6.

Lentil and Lemon Soup

250 g/8 oz (1 cup) red lentils; 1.5 litres/ 2½ pints (6 cups) water; salt and freshly ground black pepper; 3 rashers (slices) streaky bacon, rind removed and diced; 3 potatoes, peeled and diced; 1 tbsp lemon juice.

Put lentils into a large saucepan with the water, and add a large pinch each of salt and pepper and the bacon. Bring to the boil, then reduce heat and simmer, covered, for 1½ hours or until lentils are soft. Add diced potatoes and simmer for 20 minutes longer or until potatoes are soft. Mix well so potatoes thicken soup, then add lemon juice. Serve very hot. Serves 6.

Pea Soup

A Canadian recipe, good with crisp, butter-fried croûtons.

250 g/8 oz (1 cup) yellow split peas; 1.5 litres/2½ pints (6 cups) cold water; 250 g (8 oz) pickled (salt) pork, finely chopped; 1 large onion, chopped; 2 sticks celery, chopped; 2 medium carrots, chopped; 10 g/⅓ oz (¼ cup) chopped parsley; salt and freshly ground black pepper; ½ tsp ground allspice; Croûtons (page 90) to serve.

Soak peas overnight in water to cover. Next day, boil in soaking water for 10 minutes and drain. Return peas to saucepan and add the cold water and remaining ingredients. Cover pan and simmer over very low heat for 2–3 hours or until peas have become a mush.

Adjust seasoning, ladle into warmed soup bowls and serve with croûtons. Serves 6.

QUICKLY-MADE SOUPS

There are times when you want to supplement a meal with another course, or decide at the last minute to make a soup. Here are some soups that can be made in minutes even without home-made stock.

Italian Egg Drop Soup

In many different parts of the world, egg is added to clear broth to make a light, nourishing soup. This Italian version has a fluffy, creamy texture – with cheese for extra flavour.

1.5 litres/2½ pints (6 cups) beef stock (bouillon) or chicken stock; salt and freshly ground black pepper; 3 eggs, separated; 4 tbsp grated Parmesan cheese; nutmeg.

Heat stock (bouillon) in a large saucepan and season with salt and pepper. Beat egg whites until they form soft peaks; beat yolks lightly. Combine whites and yolks with cheese and a few gratings of nutmeg. When soup boils, stir in egg mixture, then remove from heat and serve immediately. Pass a basket of crusty bread. Serves 6.

Clear Soup with Ravioli

1.75 litres/3 pints (7 cups) beef stock (bouillon); 120 ml/4 fl oz (½ cup) dry white wine or vermouth; 3 tbsp tomato purée (paste); 1 bay leaf; salt and freshly ground black pepper; 24–30 frozen ravioli (about ½ × 500 g/1 lb packet); grated Parmesan cheese to serve.

Place stock (bouillon), wine or vermouth, tomato purée (paste) and bay leaf in a large saucepan and mix together. Heat until soup boils, then season with salt and pepper. Add ravioli to pan and simmer until tender, about 20 minutes. Remove bay leaf and ladle soup into bowls. Sprinkle with a little grated Parmesan cheese and serve with extra Parmesan. Serves 6.

Meatball and Spinach Soup

SOUP: *2 litres/3½ pints (8 cups) beef stock (bouillon) or chicken stock; 2 leeks, or 8 spring onions (scallions), finely sliced; 1 tsp finely chopped fresh ginger; 2 tbsp Chinese rice wine or medium dry sherry; 6 tender spinach leaves, finely sliced; salt and freshly ground black pepper.*
MEATBALLS: *250 g/8 oz (1 cup) lean minced (ground) beef; 4 spring onions (scallions), finely chopped; 1 tsp finely chopped fresh ginger; ½ tsp salt; 1 tbsp cornflour (cornstarch); 1 tbsp light soy sauce; 1 egg.*

Place soup ingredients in a large saucepan. Bring to the boil and simmer for 5 minutes.

MEATBALLS: Mix ingredients and form into small, marble-sized balls. Drop into simmering soup and cook a further 6–8 minutes or until meatballs are cooked through. Serves 6.

Zuppa alla Pavese

A simple chicken broth is enriched with egg, Parmesan cheese and toasted bread to become a soup fit for a king; this soup was served to King Francis I of France by an enterprising Italian farmer's wife. His Royal Highness enjoyed it so much he declared: 'What you have given me is a king's soup!'

90 g/3 oz (6 tbsp) butter; 6 thick slices Vienna bread; 6 eggs; salt; 60 g/2 oz (½ cup) grated Parmesan cheese; 1.5 litres/2½ pints (6 cups) boiling chicken stock.

Melt butter in a frying pan (skillet) and sauté bread until golden. Place bread slices in heated soup bowls. Carefully break an egg into each bowl. Sprinkle each with a little salt and grated cheese. Very carefully ladle 250 ml/8 fl oz (1 cup) of boiling stock into each bowl. Keep stock over heat while working so that it remains hot enough to poach eggs in the bowls. Serve immediately. Serves 6.

Quick Vegetable Soup

You can use any combination of vegetables for this soup, whatever is on hand.

2 tbsp oil; 2 cloves garlic, crushed or finely chopped; 3 onions, chopped; 1 leek, sliced; 250 g (8 oz) streaky bacon, rind removed and diced; ½ bunch broccoli, sliced; 2 carrots, diced; 2 white turnips, diced; 4 potatoes, peeled and diced; ½ Savoy cabbage, shredded; 250 g/8 oz (1 cup) green beans, cut diagonally into 2 cm (¾ in) slices; 2.2 litres/4 pints (9 cups) hot water; salt and freshly ground black pepper; chopped parsley.

Heat oil in a large saucepan, add garlic, onions, leek and bacon and cook very gently until onion is soft but not brown. Add remaining vegetables and cook, stirring occasionally, for 10 minutes. Add hot water, bring to the boil, then lower heat and season with salt and pepper. (The bacon may be salty.) Simmer until vegetables are tender – about 20 minutes. Lastly add some chopped parsley. Serve with fresh crusty bread. Serves 8–10.

Soup of a Thousand Infants

This Portuguese soup gets its charming name from the egg, herbs and breadcrumb drops whisked through it.

1 litre/1¾ pints (4 cups) chicken stock; 1 egg, lightly beaten; 45 g/1½ oz (¾ cup) fine fresh breadcrumbs (process in a blender, then push through a sieve); 10 g/⅓ oz (¼ cup) finely chopped parsley; 1 tsp chopped fresh thyme, or ¼ tsp dried; juice ½ lemon; salt and freshly ground black pepper.

Bring stock to the boil in a saucepan. Meanwhile, mix together egg, breadcrumbs, parsley and thyme. Drop mixture by spoonfuls into boiling stock, beating constantly with a wire whisk. Stir in lemon juice, season with salt and pepper to taste and serve at once. Serves 4.

Ten Minute Tomato Soup

750 g/1½ lb (3 cups) tomatoes, peeled and chopped; 1 clove garlic, crushed; 2 tbsp chopped parsley; 3 tbsp olive oil; 750 ml/1¼ pints (3 cups) chicken stock; salt and freshly ground black pepper; pinch sugar.

Place tomatoes in saucepan with garlic, parsley and olive oil. Cook gently for about 5 minutes. Add stock, salt, pepper and sugar and cook for a further 5 minutes. This soup can be eaten hot or chilled. Serves 4–6.

Beetroot Soup

3 beetroot, peeled and shredded; ½ onion, finely chopped; 1 litre/1¾ pints (4 cups) chicken stock; 2 tomatoes, peeled, seeded and chopped; pinch nutmeg; salt and freshly ground black pepper; 1–2 sweet and sour gherkins, chopped; sour cream to serve (optional).

Place beetroot in a heavy saucepan with onion and 175 ml/6 fl oz (¾ cup) chicken stock. Cover and cook gently for 5 minutes. Add tomatoes with remaining heated stock and bring to the boil. Season with nutmeg and – only if necessary – salt and pepper. Add gherkins. Serve with a swirl of sour cream on each portion, if liked. Serves 6.

HEARTY SOUPS

Some soups are almost a meal in themselves. It is a mistake to serve such soups as part of a substantial three-course meal. Their role is quite different. Serve them for weekend lunches or suppers, followed by a crisp green salad and a piece of fruit, and you have a nourishing and satisfying meal.

Mutton Broth

750 g/(1½ lb) scrag neck (neck slice) of mutton or lamb; 2 litres/3½ pints (8 cups) water or white stock; 1 tbsp salt; 60 g/2 oz (½ cup) chopped celery; 2 carrots, diced; 1 parsnip, diced; 2 onions, diced; freshly ground black pepper; chopped parsley.

Remove as much fat as possible from mutton or lamb, and cut meat into small pieces. Cover the meat and bones with the water or stock and bring slowly to the boil. Remove scum, then add salt and simmer for 1 hour. Add diced vegetables and pepper. Continue cooking gently, covered, for another hour. Remove bones, cut any pieces of meat off bones and return these to broth. Skim to remove any fat, using absorbent paper towels if necessary, adjust seasoning to taste and serve sprinkled with parsley. Serves 8.

Portuguese Chicken Soup with Mint

1 roasting chicken, or 2 kg (4 lb) chicken pieces; 1 large onion, finely chopped; 1 tsp salt; 2 litres/3½ pints (8 cups) water, stock or vegetable cooking liquid; 3 tbsp rice; 5 tbsp lemon juice; 6 tbsp chopped fresh mint.
TO SERVE: *sprigs fresh mint; lemon slices.*

Put chicken or pieces, onion and salt in a very large saucepan. Add water, stock or vegetable cooking liquid and bring slowly to the boil. Simmer for about 1 hour for a whole chicken, less for chicken pieces. They should be tender without being overcooked. Using a slotted spoon remove chicken to a plate and allow to cool. Add rice to broth and simmer for about 20 minutes. Meanwhile, skin and bone chicken and cut flesh into thin strips. Add chicken to broth with lemon juice and mint. Reheat gently and serve in heated bowls over sprigs of mint. Garnish each serving with lemon slices. Serves 6–8.

Cauliflower and Ham Soup Parmesan

60 g/2 oz (4 tbsp) butter; 4 potatoes; peeled and sliced; 1 large carrot, roughly chopped; 1 large onion, sliced; 1 stick celery, chopped; 4 medium tomatoes, peeled and chopped; 4 sprigs parsley; 1 small cauliflower, or ½ large cauliflower, separated into florets; 90 g/3 oz (⅓ cup) cooked ham, chopped; 1 tbsp chopped fresh basil; 1.5 litres/2½ pints (6 cups) boiling water; salt and freshly

ground black pepper; 250 ml/8 fl oz (1 cup) single (light) cream; 125 g/4 oz (1 cup) grated Parmesan cheese; Croûtons (page 90) to serve.

Heat butter in a large heavy saucepan and gently fry potatoes, carrot, onion and celery for a few minutes, stirring. (Do not let vegetables brown.) Add tomatoes, parsley, cauliflower, ham and basil. Stir well, then add boiling water, salt and pepper. Simmer, covered, until vegetables are very tender, about 30 minutes. Purée soup in a blender or food processor (this might need to be done in batches) and return to saucepan. Stir in cream, reheat to boiling, and adjust seasoning. Serve in heated bowls, sprinkled with grated cheese. Pass croûtons separately. Serves 6.

Meat and Vegetable Soup

1 tbsp oil; 30 g/1 oz (2 tbsp) butter; 1 kg (2 lb) meaty soup bones; 2 onions, chopped; 2 carrots, chopped; ½ turnip, chopped; 1 ripe tomato, peeled and chopped; 2 sticks celery, chopped; 20 g/⅔ oz (½ cup) parsley sprigs; 2 tsp brown sugar; 3 beef stock cubes (6 beef bouillon cubes), crumbled (optional); 2 litres/3½ pints (8 cups) water; salt and freshly ground black pepper; 125 g/4 oz (¾ cup) shelled peas (fresh or frozen); 2 tbsp chopped parsley; toast points to serve.

Heat oil and butter in a large, heavy saucepan. Add bones and brown over medium heat. Remove bones. Add chopped vegetables and cook for 5 minutes, stirring several times. Add parsley sprigs, sugar, stock (bouillon) cubes and water. Season lightly with salt and pepper, return bones to pan and simmer gently, covered, for 2½ hours. Take bones out, remove meat and dice. Return the meat to saucepan with peas. Simmer uncovered until peas are tender, about 10 minutes for fresh peas or 3 minutes

for frozen. Adjust seasoning and stir in chopped parsley. Serve soup with toast points. Serves 8–10.

Chicken Corn Soup

1 chicken, cut into pieces; 2 litres/3½ pints (8 cups) water; 1 tbsp salt; ¼ tsp saffron powder; 125 g (4 oz) noodles; 370 g/12 oz (2 cups) fresh corn kernels, cut from cob; freshly ground black pepper; chopped parsley; 2 hard-boiled (hard-cooked) eggs, chopped.

Cover chicken with water in a saucepan, add salt and saffron and bring to the boil. Lower heat, cover and simmer until tender, about 2 hours. Remove chicken from stock and take meat from skin and bones. Chop meat and return to stock. Bring back to the boil. Add noodles and corn and cook until noodles are tender. Season with salt and pepper, and stir in a little parsley and the eggs. Serves 6.

Herbed Pumpkin Soup

60 g/2 oz (4 tbsp) butter; 1 large onion, finely chopped; 1.5 kg/3 lb (8 cups) pumpkin, peeled, seeded and chopped; 1 tbsp flour; 1.2 litres/2 pints (5 cups) boiling water; 1 chicken stock cube (2 chicken bouillon cubes); 250 ml/8 fl oz (1 cup) hot milk; 15 g/½ oz (1 tbsp) butter, or 3 tbsp single (light) cream; salt and freshly ground black pepper; nutmeg; 2 tbsp chopped mixed fresh herbs (parsley with a little oregano, thyme); Croûtons (page 90) to garnish.

Melt butter in a heavy saucepan and add onion and pumpkin. Cover and cook over a low heat about 10 minutes. Sprinkle flour over vegetables and cook over moderate heat for about 5 minutes, stirring frequently. Combine water and stock cube (bouillon cubes), add to pan and simmer, covered, until tender. Cool slightly, then sieve, or purée in blender with a little milk. Gradually stir in hot milk and simmer gently for about 5 minutes. Just before serving, and for a richer soup, swirl in butter or cream. Season with salt, pepper and a little nutmeg, and stir in herbs. Serve hot, garnished with croûtons. Serves 6.

Pot Herb Soup

1 leek, sliced; 165 g/5½ oz (1 cup) shelled fresh green peas; 750 ml/1¼ pints (3 cups) chicken stock; 6 sprigs fresh chives; 6 sprigs fresh chervil; 6 sprigs fresh parsley; 30 g/1 oz (2 tbsp) butter; 1 tbsp flour; 120 ml/4 fl oz (½ cup) milk; salt and freshly ground black pepper; 2 shallots, finely chopped; 2 egg yolks; 4 tbsp single (light) cream.

Cook leek and peas in 600 ml/1 pint (2½ cups) stock until tender. Meanwhile, finely chop chives, chervil and parsley. Melt

butter in a saucepan, add flour and cook for 1 minute, stirring. Bring milk and remaining stock to the boil, then add to butter-flour mixture, stirring vigorously with a whisk. Season with salt and pepper. Add leek and peas with liquid in which they were cooked, shallots and herbs and mix well. Beat egg yolks with cream and add to soup. Cook gently, stirring constantly until thickened, but do not let boil. Adjust seasoning to taste and serve hot. Serves 6.

Potato Soup with Gruyère and Parmesan Cheese

4 large potatoes, peeled and diced; 750 ml/1¼ pints (3 cups) chicken stock; 350 ml/12 fl oz (1½ cups) milk, scalded; pinch nutmeg; salt and freshly ground white pepper; 90 g/3 oz (⅔ cup) grated Gruyère or Emmenthal cheese; 45 g/1½ oz (⅓ cup) grated Parmesan cheese.

Cook potatoes in boiling stock for about 20 minutes or until very tender. Purée potatoes and stock in a blender or rub through a sieve until very smooth. Stir in milk, nutmeg, salt and pepper and simmer until heated through. Divide soup among 4 flameproof bowls and sprinkle each with 2 tbsp of Gruyère then 1 tbsp of Parmesan. Place under preheated grill (broiler) for 2 minutes or until cheese is bubbling. Serves 4.

Lyons Velvet

(Onion Soup Lyonnaise)

45 g/1½ oz (3 tbsp) butter; 1 tbsp oil; 750 g (1½ lb) finely sliced onions; 1 tsp salt; 2 tbsp flour; 1.5 litres/2½ pints (6 cups) boiling beef stock (bouillon); 120 ml/4 fl oz (½ cup) dry white wine or dry vermouth; freshly ground black pepper; 4 eggs; 150 g/5 oz (1¼ cups) Swiss cheese, finely grated; 2 tbsp brandy; 6 slices dry, crustless toast to serve.

Heat butter and oil in a large, heavy saucepan and cook onions gently for 25–30 minutes or until very soft, stirring occasionally. Be careful not to let them burn. Sprinkle salt and flour into pan and stir over medium heat for 2 minutes. Remove from heat and blend in boiling stock (bouillon). Add wine and pepper and strain soup into a large earthenware bowl. (Save the onions to use in a meat loaf, scrambled eggs etc.) Tip soup back into pan and reheat. Beat eggs until light, in bowl that has been heated with soup, and stir in cheese. When soup is boiling, pour slowly into bowl, beating all the time. The boiling liquid will partially cook eggs, and soup will turn thick and creamy. Still beating, add brandy and stir into soup. Have ready slices of dry toast in 6 deep, heated bowls, and ladle soup over. Serve immediately. Serves 6.

French Onion Soup

45 g/1½ oz (3 tbsp) butter; 1 tbsp oil; 4–5 onions, finely sliced; 1 tbsp salt; 2 tbsp flour; 2 litres/3½ pints (8 cups) boiling beef stock (bouillon); 120 ml/4 fl oz (½ cup) dry white wine or dry vermouth; freshly ground black pepper; 2 tbsp brandy (optional).
GARNISH: *slices French bread; 125 g/4 oz (1 cup) grated Swiss cheese, or 60 g/2 oz (½ cup) grated Parmesan cheese.*

Melt butter in large heavy saucepan, add oil and cook onions gently for 20–30 minutes, stirring occasionally. Be careful not to burn onions. Sprinkle in salt and flour and stir over moderate heat 3 minutes. Remove from heat and blend in boiling stock (bouillon). Add wine. Season with pepper. Return to heat, cover and simmer for 30–40 minutes, skimming occasionally.
GARNISH: Put bread in one layer in shallow baking tin (pan). Bake in a preheated moderate oven (160°C/325°F, Gas Mark 3) for about 30 minutes or until crisp and lightly coloured.

Just before serving soup, adjust seasoning and stir in brandy. Pour into heated soup tureen or soup cups over bread slices. Serve cheese separately. Serves 6–8.
VARIATION
French Onion Soup Gratinée: Follow recipe for French Onion Soup. Put prepared bread into a soup tureen and top with 125 g (4 oz) Swiss cheese, cut into fine slivers. Pour boiling soup over. Sprinkle 3 tbsp grated Parmesan cheese over and put under a preheated hot grill (broiler) until cheese melts and browns lightly. Serve immediately.

Leek and Potato Soup

(Potage Bonne Femme)

30 g/1 oz (2 tbsp) butter; 2 leeks, finely sliced; salt and freshly ground white pepper; 2 medium potatoes, peeled and diced; 750 ml/1¼ pints (3 cups) chicken stock; 250 ml/8 fl oz (1 cup) hot milk; little extra butter; Croûtons (page 90) or chopped parsley to garnish.

Melt butter in a heavy saucepan, add leeks and cook over a low heat until soft but not brown. Season with a little salt and pepper, then add potatoes. Stir in chicken stock. Cover and simmer gently for about 30 minutes or until potato is tender. Blend in hot milk and a little extra butter. Adjust seasoning. Serve hot garnished with croûtons or chopped parsley. Serves 6.

Goulash Soup

Make this hearty soup the day before eating.

60 g (2 oz) speck or bacon, cut into strips; 1 large onion, finely chopped; 1½ tbsp paprika; 500 g (1 lb) shin of beef (beef foreshank),

cubed; 1 tsp salt; freshly ground black pepper; 2 tbsp vinegar; 1 tbsp tomato purée (paste); 1 tbsp caraway seeds (optional); 1 clove garlic, crushed; ½ tsp dried marjoram; 2 litres/3½ pints (8 cups) beef stock (bouillon); 3 medium potatoes, peeled and diced.

Heat speck or bacon strips in a large pan until fat runs. If speck is very lean, add a little oil. Add onion and cook with speck until it is golden. Sprinkle with paprika and stir for 1 minute, then add meat and brown lightly. Stir in salt, pepper, vinegar and tomato purée (paste). Simmer for 3–4 minutes, then add caraway seeds, garlic, marjoram and stock. Bring to the boil, cover and simmer over a very low heat for 45 minutes or until meat is almost tender. Add potatoes and cook for a further 20 minutes or until potato is tender. Adjust seasoning before serving. Serves 6.

CHILLED SOUPS

These seem to have a special charm on hot summer days – and, of course, they have the added bonus for the cook in that they can be prepared in the morning, left in the refrigerator ready to be served . . . and should the weather turn chilly, most of them can be heated gently.

Take care when seasoning cold soups – they may need a little extra salt before serving and, if a cream soup, don't have it too thick; it should be of a pleasantly flowing consistency.

Cream of Curried Pea Soup

165 g/5½ oz (1 cup) shelled fresh or frozen peas; 1 onion, sliced; 1 carrot, sliced; 1 stick celery with leaves, sliced; 1 potato, peeled and sliced; 1 clove garlic; 1 tsp salt; 1 tsp curry powder; 750 ml/1¼ pints (3 cups) chicken stock; 250 ml/8 fl oz (1 cup) single (light) cream; whipped cream to serve.

Place vegetables, garlic, salt, curry powder and 250 ml/8 fl oz (1 cup) stock in a saucepan and bring to the boil. Cover, reduce heat and simmer for 15 minutes. Sieve or purée in a blender, then stir in remaining stock and cream. Chill, and serve topped with whipped cream. Serves 6.

Vichyssoise

60 g/2 oz (4 tbsp) butter; 4 leeks or onions, finely sliced; salt and freshly ground white pepper; 4 medium potatoes, peeled and diced; 1.5 litres/2½ pints (6 cups) chicken stock; 500 ml/18 fl oz (2 cups) hot milk; 250 ml/8 fl oz (1 cup) single (light) cream.

Melt butter in a saucepan, add leeks or onions and cook over a low heat until soft but not brown. Season with a little salt and pepper, and add potatoes. Stir in stock. Cover and simmer for about 30 minutes or until potato is tender. Blend in hot milk. Allow soup to cool, then sieve or purée in a blender or food processor. Chill. Stir in cream. Serves 6–8.

Cucumber Buttermilk Soup

2 small cucumbers, peeled, seeded and diced; 750 ml/1¼ pints (3 cups) buttermilk; salt and freshly ground black pepper; dash Tabasco (hot pepper) sauce.

Place cucumbers in a bowl, cover with ice cubes and soak for about 2 hours. Drain cucumbers thoroughly. Add buttermilk, seasoning and Tabasco (hot pepper) sauce. Chill well. Serves 4.

Iced Lebanese Soup

1 large green cucumber, peeled, seeded and diced; salt and freshly ground black pepper; 120 ml/4 fl oz (½ cup) strong chicken stock; 120 ml/4 fl oz (½ cup) tomato juice; 750 ml/1¼ pints (3 cups) plain yogurt;

120 ml/4 fl oz (½ cup) single (light) cream; 600 g/1 lb 3 oz (2⅓ cups) small cooked prawns (shrimp), shelled and deveined; 1 clove garlic, halved.
GARNISH: *1 tbsp chopped fresh mint; 1 hard-boiled (hard-cooked) egg, finely chopped.*

Place cucumber on a plate set at a slight tilt (put a wooden spoon under one side) and sprinkle lightly with salt. Leave aside for salt to draw out some juice from cucumber. Mix stock, tomato juice and yogurt together until well combined and smooth, and stir in cream. Rinse cucumber, drain well and add to soup with prawns (shrimp). Season with salt and pepper and chill thoroughly. Adjust seasoning again just before serving. Rub chilled soup bowls or tureen with cut clove of garlic, ladle soup in and sprinkle with chopped mint and hard-boiled (hard-cooked) egg. Serves 6.

Balkan Chlodnik

2 large beetroot; 500 ml/18 fl oz (2 cups) chicken stock; 250 g/8 oz (1 cup) cooked prawns (shrimp), shelled, deveined and chopped; 3 hard-boiled (hard-cooked) eggs, chopped; 1 cucumber, peeled, seeded and chopped; 1 lemon, thinly sliced; ½ tbsp snipped chives; 1 tbsp chopped fresh dill or parsley; 250 ml/8 fl oz (1 cup) single (light) cream; 2 tsp lemon juice; 250 ml/8 fl oz (1 cup) beer; salt and freshly ground black pepper; chopped fresh dill or parsley to garnish.

Cook beetroot in boiling salted water to cover until tender. Drain. Peel and chop beetroot, and combine with chicken stock in a large bowl. Add remaining ingredients, stir well and chill. At serving time, place an ice cube in 6 bowls and ladle chilled soup into bowls. Sprinkle with chopped dill or parsley. Serves 6.

Chilled Curried Courgette Soup

90 g/3 oz (6 tbsp) butter; 750 g/1½ lb (4 cups) courgettes (zucchini), chopped; 125 g/4 oz (1 cup) chopped spring onions (scallions); 2 tsp curry powder; 1 tbsp ground cumin; 500 ml/18 fl oz (2 cups) chicken stock; 750 ml/1¼ pints (3 cups) buttermilk; salt and freshly ground black pepper
GARNISH: ½ *carrot;* ½ *courgette (zucchini); 2 radishes.*

Melt butter in a large saucepan and add courgettes (zucchini) and shallots. Cover and cook over a low heat for 10 minutes, shaking pan occasionally and checking that vegetables do not colour. Add spices and cook for 2 minutes, stirring, then stir in stock. Purée mixture in a blender or food processor. Pour into a large bowl, stir in buttermilk and season with salt and pepper.

Chill for 4 hours. For garnish, slice vegetables thinly on a slant. Chill in iced water for at least 1 hour, then pat dry. Divide soup among chilled bowls, and garnish with vegetables. Serves 6.

Cold Vegetable Soup

4 tomatoes, peeled and chopped; 1 cucumber, peeled and diced; 1 onion, finely chopped; 1 red or green pepper, cored, seeded and chopped; 2 cloves garlic, finely chopped; 30 g/1 oz (½ cup) fresh white breadcrumbs; 1 tbsp red wine vinegar; 750 ml/1¼ pints (3 cups) chicken stock; 2 tbsp olive oil; leaves fresh basil or sprigs coriander (Chinese parsley); salt and freshly ground black pepper; 120 ml/4 fl oz (½ cup) single (light) cream.

Mix together tomatoes, cucumber, onion, pepper, garlic and breadcrumbs. Add vinegar, stock, oil, and 3 basil leaves or a few sprigs coriander. Season with salt and pepper. Cover and marinate for 12 hours or overnight in refrigerator. Purée in a blender or food processor and strain through a sieve. Stir in cream and adjust seasoning. Serve very cold, topped with thin strips of basil or chopped coriander. Serves 4–6.

Beetroot and Orange Soup

4–5 beetroot, peeled and grated; 1 tsp salt; 1 tsp dried thyme; ¼ tsp pepper; 1 bay leaf; 1.5 litres/2½ pints (6 cups) water; 500 ml/18 fl oz (2 cups) canned tomato juice; 250 ml/8 fl oz (1 cup) orange juice; 2 tbsp gelatine.
GARNISH: *sour cream; 2 tbsp snipped chives.*

Combine grated beetroot, salt, thyme, pepper, bay leaf and water in a large saucepan. Bring to the boil and simmer 20 minutes. Strain mixture into a large bowl, pressing hard on solids. Reserve 180 g/6 oz (1 cup) cooked grated beetroot. Heat tomato juice in saucepan and stir in beetroot

liquid, orange juice and reserved grated beetroot. Take out 175 ml/6 fl oz (¾ cup) liquid and sprinkle gelatine over it. When spongy, stir into hot liquid until dissolved. Transfer mixture to a large bowl and cool, then chill, covered. Break up with a fork. Serve in chilled bowls, garnished with sour cream and chives. Serves 8.

Cold Tomato Soup

750 ml/1¼ pints (3 cups) tomato juice; 2 tbsp tomato purée (paste); 1 × 425 g/14 oz can tomatoes, chopped with their juice; 4 spring onions (scallions) chopped; 2 sticks celery, chopped; 1 tsp curry powder; freshly ground black pepper; grated rind ½ lemon; 2 tbsp lemon juice; 2 tsp sugar; 1 tsp chopped fresh thyme, or pinch dried; 120 ml/4 fl oz (½ cup) single (light) cream, soured with 1 tsp lemon juice; chopped parsley.

Mix together all ingredients except sour cream and parsley. Chill well, covered. To serve, spoon chilled soup into 6 bowls, swirl a little sour cream into each and sprinkle with chopped parsley. If liked, 1–2 ice cubes may be put into each bowl before adding soup. Serves 6.

Rød Grød Med Fløde

(Fruit Soup with Cream)

2 × 450 g/14 oz cans rhubarb; 1 litre/1¾ pints (4 cups) water; 4 tbsp lemon juice; 2 tbsp arrowroot or cornflour (cornstarch); sour cream to serve.

Sieve rhubarb, and its syrup, or purée in a blender or food processor. Mix purée with water and lemon juice in a saucepan and bring to the boil. Mix arrowroot or cornflour (cornstarch) with a little water to make a thin paste. Stir in a little hot soup, then pour this back into saucepan, stirring constantly until soup boils and thickens. Cover and allow to cool, then place in refrigerator. Serve chilled, with sour cream. Serves 8.

Chilled Cucumber Soup

30 g/1 oz (2 tbsp) butter; 1 small onion, chopped; 1 large green cucumber, seeded and diced; 90 g/3 oz (1 cup) watercress sprigs or shredded outside leaves of lettuce; 1 medium potato, peeled and diced; 500 ml/18 fl oz (2 cups) chicken stock; 2 sprigs parsley; ½ tsp salt; ¼ tsp pepper; ¼ tsp dry mustard; 250 ml/8 fl oz (1 cup) single (light) cream.
GARNISH: *chopped chives; diced cucumber; diced radish.*

Melt butter in saucepan and cook onion gently until soft but not brown. Add all remaining ingredients except cream and bring to the boil. Simmer until potatoes are tender, about 15 minutes. Sieve or purée soup in blender or food processor. Adjust seasoning and chill, covered, until required. Before serving, stir in cream and sprinkle with chopped chives, cucumber and radish. Serves 6.

Iced Pepper Soup

A nutritious, refreshing soup that can be made in a few seconds. Use red or green peppers.

2 large peppers, cored, seeded and diced; 500 ml/18 fl oz (2 cups) chicken stock; 2 tbsp lemon juice; salt and freshly ground black pepper; 2 cloves garlic, chopped; ¼ tsp Worcestershire sauce; sour cream to serve.

Place peppers in blender or food processor with 250 ml/8 fl oz (1 cup) stock, lemon juice, salt, pepper, garlic and Worcestershire sauce. Purée until fairly smooth, then add remaining stock. Adjust seasoning. Chill well. Serve topped with sour cream. Serves 2–3.

Chilled Pumpkin Soup

1 onion, sliced; 60 g/2 oz (4 tbsp) butter; 750 g/1½ lb (4 cups) pumpkin, peeled, seeded and chopped; 4 thin slices lemon, seeds removed; 4 tbsp flour; 1.5 litres/2½ pints (6 cups) warm chicken stock; salt and freshly ground white pepper; 250 ml/8 fl oz (1 cup) single (light) cream; lemon juice.

Cook onion gently in butter in large saucepan until soft. Stir in pumpkin and lemon slices, sprinkle with flour and stir over low heat for 3 minutes. Remove from heat and cool a little, then add chicken stock, stirring until smoothly blended. Return to heat and stir until boiling. Season lightly with salt and pepper and simmer, partially covered with a lid, for 1 hour. Discard lemon slices. Purée mixture in a blender and pour into a bowl. Allow to cool, then chill, covered, for at least 4 hours. Stir in chilled cream and lemon juice, and adjust seasoning. Serves 6–8.

Iced Spinach Soup

1 onion, finely chopped; 1 clove garlic, crushed; 30 g/1 oz (2 tbsp) butter; 1 × 250 g/8 oz can spinach, drained, or 1 × 250 g/8 oz packet frozen spinach, thawed; 1 litre/1¾ pints (4 cups) chicken stock; salt and freshly ground black pepper; 250 ml/8 fl oz (1 cup) single (light) cream; snipped chives to garnish.

Sauté onion and garlic in butter until transparent. Add spinach, chicken stock, salt and pepper. Bring to the boil and simmer for about 8 minutes. Chill. Just before serving, adjust seasoning and add cream. To garnish, sprinkle with snipped chives. Serves 4–6.
NOTE: When fresh spinach is available, use it instead of canned. Rinse 1 bunch spinach, remove white stalks and roughly chop leaves. Place in large saucepan, cover and steam, in water left on leaves after rinsing, about 5 minutes, shaking pan to prevent burning. Drain well, then chop spinach or purée in a blender or food processor.

Apple Vichyssoise

4½ large tart-flavoured apples, peeled and cored; 1.5 litres/2½ pints (6 cups) chicken stock; 250 ml/8 fl oz (1 cup) single (light) cream; salt and freshly ground white pepper; pinch sugar; lemon juice.

Chop 4 of the apples roughly and cook in chicken stock for about 20 minutes or until very tender. Sieve or purée in a blender. Cool and chill. Stir in cream, and season with salt, pepper, sugar and lemon juice. Make garnish by cutting remaining ½ apple into fine matchstick-sized strips. This should be done at the last moment so it will not discolour. Sprinkle on top of soup and serve. Serves 6.

Cold Curried Cream of Aubergine Soup

125 g/4 oz (½ cup) butter; 1 medium onion, chopped; 1 tbsp curry powder; 1 large or 2 small aubergines (eggplant), about 625 g (1¼ lb) total weight, peeled and cut into 1 cm (½ in) cubes; 1.2 litres/2 pints (5 cups) chicken stock; 175 ml/6 fl oz (¾ cup) single (light) cream; salt and freshly ground white pepper; leaves fresh coriander or parsley to garnish.

Melt butter and cook onion gently until softened. Stir in curry powder and stir over low heat for 2 minutes. Add aubergine (eggplant) cubes and chicken stock and bring to the boil, then cover and simmer gently for 45 minutes or until aubergine (eggplant) is very soft. Sieve or purée mixture in a blender or food processor. Add cream, salt and pepper. Cool then chill, covered, for at least 3 hours. Divide soup among 6 chilled bowls and sprinkle each with a few leaves of coriander or parsley. Serves 6.

Chilled Melon Soup

1 large cantaloup melon, peeled, seeded and diced; 20 g/⅔ oz (4 tsp) butter; 1 tbsp sugar; grated rind and juice ½ lemon; ¼ tsp ground ginger; ¼ tsp nutmeg; ¼ tsp salt; 350 ml/12 fl oz (1½ cups) water; 120 ml/4 fl oz (½ cup) sweet white wine; few sprigs fresh mint and melon balls to garnish.

Place diced melon in a saucepan and add butter, sugar, lemon rind and juice, ginger, nutmeg and salt. Cook over gentle heat, stirring occasionally, until melon becomes soft and pulpy, about 10 minutes. Sieve or purée mixture in a blender. Stir in water and wine and chill for at least 3 hours. Adjust seasoning, and serve garnished with mint and melon balls. Serves 4.

SOYA (SOY) BEAN

See Pulses: Dried Beans, Peas and Lentils.

SOY SAUCE

The pungent, salty brown sauce that is essential to Chinese, Japanese and South-East Asian cooking. The best is brewed from naturally fermented soya beans and can be distinguished by the thick head of foam, like that on stout, which forms and remains for some time if the bottle is vigorously shaken.

Different types of soy sauce are available. *Chinese soy sauce* can be dark or light; both types are used in cooking and the light sauce, which is the thinner and saltier of the two, is also used as a table condiment.

Japanese soy sauce (shoyu), lighter again, should always be used in Japanese dishes. It is used as an ingredient and as a dip at the table.

Indonesian soy sauce (ketjap manis) is thick and sweet with a salty tang.

All types of soy sauce are available from Oriental food stores. When a recipe calls for 'soy sauce' without further qualification, it is usually best to use a light Chinese or Japanese one.

SPAGHETTI

See *Pasta*.

SPARERIBS

There are two types of pork spareribs. The first are cut from the belly area, giving meaty slices with layers of fat and lean and some small, cross-cut bones; the second are the rib bones, together with what little meat joins them after outer cuts have been removed. These are often known as country-style pork ribs in America.

Beef spareribs, often called short ribs, are cut from the lower end of the set of ribs. They have a fairly high proportion of bone but are quite meaty.

Spareribs may be sold in individual slices or joined in a set. They are good barbecued or grilled (broiled), often served with a spicy American-style or Chinese sauce; the spareribs are usually pre-baked or boiled in order to melt off excess fat.

Many people like to eat spareribs in the fingers, so be sure to supply plenty of paper napkins. Ribs can also be baked, and pork spareribs are braised for wonderful, hearty Middle European dishes with sauerkraut, apples and sometimes potatoes, dumplings, sausages or other meats. **See recipes**.

Spareribs with Sauerkraut

2 kg (4 lb) pork spareribs (country-style pork ribs); 1 × 820 g/1¾ lb can sauerkraut, drained; 1 large onion, finely chopped; 2 tsp caraway seeds (optional); dry white wine; 1 large apple, peeled, cored and sliced; 6–8 medium new potatoes; 1 kg (2 lb) knackwurst, frankfurters, thickly sliced cooked ham, smoked pork chops or a mixture; salt.

Cut spareribs into individual portions. Rinse sauerkraut under cold running water, drain

and squeeze dry in a cloth. Heat a large, heavy flameproof casserole and brown spareribs slowly in their own fat. Remove ribs. Add onion and sauerkraut and brown in fat remaining in pot. Return ribs to casserole, burying them in sauerkraut. Add caraway seeds, if using, and enough white wine just to cover. Cover tightly, bring to simmering point and place in a preheated moderate oven (180°C/350°F, Gas Mark 4). Cook for 1½ hours. Add apple, potatoes and meats, burying them in sauerkraut. Cover again and cook 1 hour longer or until meats are very tender. Alternatively, the dish can be cooked 40 minutes longer, cooled and reheated next day for about 1 hour in a moderate oven. Add salt before serving. Serves 6–8.

Baked Spareribs with Raisins

1 kg (2 lb) pork spareribs (country-style pork ribs) or beef spareribs (short ribs); 2 tsp salt; ¼ tsp pepper; 1 onion, finely chopped; 60 g/2 oz (½ cup) finely chopped celery; 60 g/2 oz (4 tbsp) butter; 1 egg;

175 ml/6 fl oz (¾ cup) water; 370 g/12 oz (6 cups) fresh bread cubes; 180 g/6 oz (1 cup) raisins; ¼ tsp dried sage; ¼ tsp dried thyme or marjoram.

Cut spareribs into individual portions. Place in saucepan, cover with water and add 1 tsp salt and the pepper. Bring to the boil and simmer gently for 45 minutes–1 hour. Drain and pat dry with paper towels. Sauté onion and celery in butter until soft. Beat egg and water in a large bowl, then stir in bread cubes, raisins, herbs, remaining salt and cooked onion mixture. Mix thoroughly and spread in large baking tin (pan). Put spareribs on top and bake in a preheated moderate oven (180°C/350°F, Gas Mark 4) about 1–1½ hours or until crisp and tender. Serves 4.

SPECULAAS

These are special crisp biscuits (cookies) rich in butter and flavoured with brown sugar,

spices and rum made especially for Saint Nicholas' Eve in Holland. Sometimes the biscuits are in the shape of small rectangles sprinkled with almonds and sometimes the biscuit mixture is pressed into elaborate moulds in the shape of men and women or even of Saint Nicholas himself.

Speculaas

370 g/12 oz (3 cups) flour; 4 tsp baking powder; 1 tbsp cinnamon; 1 tsp ground cloves; 1 tsp nutmeg; ½ tsp ground aniseed; ½ tsp salt; ½ tsp ground ginger or white pepper; 250 g/8 oz (1 cup) butter; 280 g/9 oz (1⅓ cups) firmly packed brown sugar; 3 tbsp rum or brandy; 1 egg white to glaze; 125 g/4 oz (1 cup) slivered blanched almonds to decorate.

Sift together flour, baking powder, cinnamon, cloves, nutmeg, ground aniseed, salt and ginger or pepper. Beat butter with brown sugar until mixture is light and fluffy. Stir in rum or brandy. Gradually add flour mixture, stirring until well combined, then form dough into a ball. Knead dough on a board sprinkled with about 4 tbsp sifted flour. Roll out dough into a rectangle about 5 mm (¼ in) thick. With a sharp knife or cutter cut dough into 6 × 3 cm (2½ × 1½ in) rectangles. Place on a buttered baking tray, brush with lightly beaten egg white and decorate with slivered almonds. Bake in a preheated moderately hot oven (190°C/375°F, Gas Mark 5) for 12 minutes or until browned and firm. Cool speculaas on a wire rack and store in an airtight tin. Makes about 40.

SPICE

The word covers a wide variety of aromatic and pungent seasonings used to flavour savoury and sweet dishes. There are hot spices, sweet spices and spicy-sweet spices. They are not gathered from any one part of a plant or tree but from whichever part is most aromatic and most pungent: for example, cinnamon bark is exactly that, and vanilla beans are the pods of a type of orchid. Seeds, buds, berries, roots and pods all provide spices with which we are familiar.

The addition of spices to vinegars for salad dressings, to fresh or dried fruits, or to creams and custards, gives a remarkably subtle aroma and flavour to simple dishes. Delicious home-made preserves, such as pickled onions or eggs, use pickling spices to flavour the preserving vinegar.

Characteristic spices impart vastly different flavours and aromas to the foods of Asia, China and the Middle East, yet they are indispensable, too, when baking our homely cakes, breads and biscuits (cookies).

Spices lose their value as a flavouring agent if they are stale, so purchase in very small quantities and store away from the light in small airtight containers. Use them as soon as possible after purchase.

Pickling Spice: Usually made from mustard seeds, bay leaf, allspice, cinnamon stick, coriander seeds and black peppercorns. Sometimes fresh ginger, chilli and mace are added. The proportions vary in different recipes but excellent mixtures of pickling spice can be bought ready-packaged by spice companies.

Middle East Spice Mix (Baharat): This is the ground spice mix used in the Gulf States and generally throughout the Middle East. It may be made up and used to flavour meatballs or kebabs, and many Middle Eastern sauces, soups, curries and seafood dishes. **See recipes**.

See also individual names of spices; *Garam Masala* and Spiced Pickled Onions (page 252).

Spice Cake

60 g/2 oz ($\frac{1}{4}$ cup) sugar; 140–180 g/4$\frac{1}{2}$–6 oz ($\frac{3}{4}$–1 cup) mixed fruit; 2 tsp mixed spice (ground allspice); 90 g/3 oz (6 tbsp) butter; 175 ml/6 fl oz ($\frac{3}{4}$ cup) water; 250 g/8 oz (2 cups) self-raising flour, sifted; 1 tbsp treacle (molasses) or golden (light corn) syrup; 1$\frac{1}{2}$ tsp bicarbonate of soda (baking soda); 2–3 tbsp warm milk.

Place sugar, mixed fruit, spice, butter and water in a saucepan and heat gently, stirring, until sugar dissolves. Bring to the boil and simmer for 5 minutes. Remove from heat and cool slightly. Fold in flour with treacle (molasses) or syrup and soda dissolved in warm milk. Pour into a greased and lined 18 cm (7 in) round cake tin (pan). Bake in a preheated moderate oven (180°C/350°F, Gas Mark 4) for 1 hour. Turn out and cool on a wire rack.

Pfeffernusse

(Spice Biscuits)
These spicy-flavoured biscuits (cookies) keep for up to 6 weeks in an airtight container.

500 g/1 lb (4 cups) flour; 1 tsp baking powder; 1 tsp ground cloves; 1 tsp ground allspice; a grinding of black pepper; 1 tsp cinnamon; 250 g/8 oz ($\frac{2}{3}$ cup) honey; 370 g/12 oz (1 cup) golden (light corn) syrup; 180 g/6 oz ($\frac{3}{4}$ cup) sugar; 30 g/1 oz (2 tbsp) butter; 15 g/$\frac{1}{2}$ oz (1 tbsp) lard.

Sift together flour, baking powder, cloves, allspice, pepper and cinnamon. Place honey, syrup and sugar in a large, heavy saucepan. Stir over low heat until sugar dissolves, then bring to the boil, without stirring. Reduce heat to low and simmer for 5 minutes. Remove from heat, and stir in butter and lard. Add flour mixture, $\frac{1}{4}$ at a time, beating well until smooth. Place teaspoonfuls of

mixture on 2 greased baking trays, leaving about 2.5 cm (1 in) between each biscuit (cookie). Bake in a preheated moderately hot oven (200°C/400°F, Gas Mark 6) for 10–15 minutes or until light brown. Cool on a wire rack. Makes about 30.

Spiced Apples

1.75 kg/4 lb (8 cups) sugar; 1 tsp salt; 1.2 litres/2 pints (5 cups) white vinegar; 12 cloves; 10 cm (4 in) cinnamon stick; 1 tsp whole allspice; 1.5 kg (3 lb) small firm apples, weighed after peeling, coring and slicing.

Combine sugar, salt, vinegar and spices tied in a muslin bag in a large heavy saucepan. Bring to the boil. Add sliced apples and simmer very gently until tender. Discard spice bag. Using a slotted spoon, lift out apple slices and pack in sterilized jars. Boil syrup steadily until thick and pour over the fruit. Seal jars and store in a cool dark place. Makes about 4 × 500 g/1 lb (2 cups) jars.

Spiced Prunes

500 g/1 lb (2$\frac{2}{3}$ cups) dessert prunes; 350 ml/12 fl oz (1$\frac{1}{2}$ cups) cold tea; 250 g/8 oz (1 cup) sugar; 500 ml/18 fl oz (2 cups) mild white vinegar; 4 cloves; 8 cm (3 in) cinnamon stick.

Put prunes in a bowl, cover with cold tea and soak overnight. Combine sugar, vinegar and spices tied in a muslin bag in a heavy saucepan. Bring to the boil and boil steadily for 15 minutes. Remove from heat and discard spice bag. Pour prunes and tea into another pan and simmer for about 15 minutes or until soft. Drain, reserving 250 ml/8 fl oz (1 cup) tea, and pack prunes into sterilized jars. Add reserved tea to spiced vinegar and pour over prunes. Seal jars and store in a cool, dark place. Leave for 24 hours before using. Makes about 3 × 250 g/8 oz (1 cup) jars.

Spicy Fruit Nuts

oil for frying; 250 g/8 oz (2 cups) raw cashews; 250 g/8 oz (2 cups) blanched

almonds; 850 g/1$\frac{3}{4}$ lb (4 cups) raw peanuts; 1 tbsp salt; 2 tsp Garam Masala (page 139); 2 tsp chilli powder.*

Heat oil in a deep frying pan (skillet) and fry nuts, in batches of about 150 g/5 oz (1 cup) at a time, over medium heat until golden-brown and crisp. Drain on crumpled paper towels. Place fried nuts in a bowl and add salt, garam masala and chilli powder. Mix well to coat nuts thoroughly. Cool completely before storing in an airtight container. Makes 6 × 250 g/8 oz (1 cup) jars.

Spiced Canned Peaches

2 × 425 g/14 oz cans peach halves; 250 g/8 oz (1 cup) sugar; 175 ml/6 fl oz ($\frac{3}{4}$ cup) cider vinegar; 1 tbsp cloves; 1 tbsp whole allspice; 10 cm (4 in) cinnamon stick.

Drain syrup from peach halves into a heavy saucepan. Add sugar, vinegar, and spices tied in a muslin bag. Boil for 10 minutes, then add peaches and cook for 5 minutes or until peaches are heated through. Remove spice bag. Pack peaches in hot sterilized jars and fill with hot syrup. Seal and store in a cool, dark place. Makes about 4 × 250 g/8 oz (1 cup) jars.

Buttered Spiced Beetroot

8 small whole beetroot, cooked and peeled, or 1 × 425 g/14 oz can baby beetroot, drained; 60 g/2 oz (4 tbsp) butter; pinch salt; freshly ground black pepper; $\frac{1}{2}$ tsp cinnamon; $\frac{1}{4}$ tsp ground ginger; 45 g/1$\frac{1}{2}$ oz ($\frac{1}{4}$ cup) firmly packed brown sugar; juice 1 lemon.

Dice beetroot. Combine remaining ingredients in a saucepan, and stir over gentle heat until butter melts. Add beetroot and stir until heated through. Serve hot with pork, ham steaks or hamburgers. Serves 4.

Hot Spiced Wine Punch

A warming punch for a winter party.

2 bottles burgundy or claret; thinly pared rind 1 small orange; thinly pared rind 1 lemon; 8 cm (3 in) cinnamon stick; $\frac{1}{2}$ whole nutmeg, crushed; 6 cloves; 2 tbsp sugar (or more to taste).

Combine all ingredients in a large saucepan. Bring to just under boiling point, then turn off heat and stand for 10 minutes. Strain into mugs and serve hot. Serves 10–12.
NOTE: If you prefer a sweeter drink, stir in more sugar before serving.

Spiced Beef Loaf

1 kg/2 lb (4 cups) finely minced (ground) steak; 90 g (3 oz) bacon rashers (slices), rind removed and finely chopped; $\frac{1}{2}$ tsp dried basil; $\frac{1}{2}$ tsp ground allspice; $\frac{1}{2}$ tsp salt; 6 black peppercorns, crushed; 1 clove garlic, crushed; 2 tbsp port, sherry or red wine; 2 tsp red wine vinegar.

Combine all ingredients in a large bowl and mix very thoroughly. Cover, refrigerate and leave at least 3 hours or overnight. Pack into a 21 × 15 cm (8½ × 6 in) loaf tin (pan). Stand tin (pan) in a baking dish filled with enough water to come halfway up sides and cook in a preheated moderate oven (160°C/325°F, Gas Mark 3) for about 1½ hours. If top of loaf begins to brown too much, cover loosely with foil. Leave to cool in tin (pan). To turn out, run a knife around edges and invert tin (pan) on to a serving platter. Cut in thin slices and serve with spiced fruit, chutney or a mustardy sauce. Serves 6–8.

Baharat

3 tbsp black peppercorns; 1½ tbsp coriander seeds; 1½ tbsp crumbled cinnamon stick or cassia; 1½ tbsp whole cloves; 2 tbsp cumin seeds; 1 tsp cardamom seeds; 1 whole nutmeg; 3 tbsp paprika.

Place peppercorns, coriander seeds, cinnamon stick or cassia, cloves and cumin and cardamom seeds in a blender and grind to a powder. Grate nutmeg and blend into spices with paprika. Store in airtight jar.

Honey Spiced Sponge Roll

3 eggs; 125 g/4 oz (½ cup) caster sugar; generous 60 g/2 oz (½ cup) arrowroot; 1 tbsp flour; ½ tsp cinnamon; 1 tsp mixed spice (ground allspice); 1 tsp cream of tartar; ½ tsp bicarbonate of soda (baking soda); 1 tbsp honey (at room temperature).
HONEY CREAM FILLING: 90 g/3 oz (6 tbsp) butter; 2 tbsp honey; 1 tbsp water.

Beat eggs until thick. Gradually add sugar and continue beating until mixture is thick and will hold its shape, about 10 minutes. Sift together 3 times the arrowroot, flour, cinnamon, mixed spice (ground allspice), cream of tartar and soda. Lightly fold into egg mixture, then add honey, mixing gently until evenly distributed. Turn into greased and lined 30 × 25 cm (12 × 10 in) Swiss roll tin (jelly roll pan) and gently shake to spread mixture evenly. Bake in a preheated moderately hot oven (190°C/375°F, Gas Mark 5) for 15–20 minutes. Turn out on to a tea-towel which has been lightly dusted with caster sugar. Quickly peel off lining paper and trim edges. Roll up immediately in tea-towel from a short side. Allow to cool.
HONEY CREAM FILLING: Beat butter until light, then add honey 1 tablespoon at a time. Add water and continue beating until mixture is smooth and creamy. Unroll cake and spread filling over. Roll up again. (If serving as dessert, roll cake beginning with wider side, and cut into diagonal slices.) Serves 8.

Cinnamon Layered Cake

370 g/12 oz (1½ cups) sugar; 60 g/2 oz (½ cup) mixed chopped nuts; 1 tbsp cinnamon; 125 g/4 oz (½ cup) butter; 2 eggs; 1 tsp vanilla essence (extract); 1 tbsp lemon juice; 250 g/8 oz (2 cups) flour; ½ tsp baking powder; ½ tsp bicarbonate of soda (baking soda); ¼ tsp salt; 250 ml/8 fl oz (1 cup) sour cream.

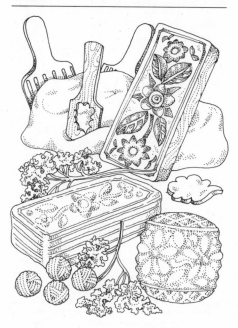

Combine 125 g/4 oz (½ cup) sugar with the nuts and cinnamon and set aside. Cream butter with remaining sugar until light and fluffy. Add eggs, vanilla and lemon juice, beating well. Sift flour with baking powder, soda and salt and add alternately to butter mixture with sour cream. Pour half the batter into a greased and bottom-lined 23 cm (9 in) square cake tin (pan). Sprinkle with half the cinnamon mixture and over it spread remaining batter. Sprinkle rest of cinnamon mixture on top. Bake in a preheated moderate oven (180°C/350°F, Gas Mark 4) for 35–40 minutes or until a skewer inserted in centre comes out clean. Serve warm on its own or with whipped cream flavoured with cinnamon.

SPINACH

Spinach is a delectable green vegetable, and is widely used in cookery. It can serve as an excellent accompanying vegetable, as a bed for other foods, such as eggs and fish, as the basis of a soufflé, tart filling, mould, salad or stuffing, or as a partner to other vegetables, pasta, rice, cheese, meats, seafood and poultry in a score of savoury dishes. Spinach in a dish often gives it the name 'Florentine' (*alla Florentina* in Italian), a tribute to the skill with which the Italians raise this vegetable, and the imagination with which they use it.

Choose spinach which is a bright, intense green and unwilted. The ends of the stems should be unwithered. Since it shrinks greatly in cooking, allow 250 g (8 oz) raw spinach per person. Cut stems short and store unwashed in a plastic bag in the refrigerator crisper until required. Stems can be stored separately, then boiled and served with cheese sauce as a vegetable in their own right.

□ **Basic Preparation:** If spinach is young and tender, cut off stems at base of leaves. If it is more mature, fold each leaf inward and pull off stem toward the tip. Wash, immediately before cooking, by plunging up and down in several changes of cold water until there is no grit to be seen in the bottom of the sink or bowl. Shake to remove most of the water.

□ **To Cook:** Unless it is to be served *en branche* (whole), chop coarsely. Drop into a heavy saucepan, season with salt, pepper and grated nutmeg and cover tightly. Do not add water. Cook on low heat, lifting the lid and stirring frequently until steam has formed and spinach has begun to wilt, then cook covered 1–2 minutes more. Spinach is cooked when it is wilted and tender.

Drain in a colander, refresh under cold running water, then squeeze well to remove as much moisture as possible. This preparation may be carried out ahead of time and the spinach refrigerated, covered, until required. It can be reheated gently in butter to be served as a vegetable, or used as directed in recipes. **See recipes**.

Spinach en Branche

1 kg (2 lb) spinach; 30 g/1 oz (2 tbsp) butter; salt and freshly ground black pepper; nutmeg; lemon juice.

Cook spinach as described above, leaving leaves whole, and press dry. Melt butter in a wide, heavy saucepan, add spinach and heat gently, separating leaves gently with a fork. Season with salt, pepper, nutmeg and a few drops of lemon juice and serve very hot. Serves 4.

Italian Spinach

1 large bunch spinach, coarsely shredded; 30 g/1 oz (2 tbsp) butter; 1 tbsp olive oil; 1 clove garlic, finely chopped; salt; ¼ tsp cayenne; coarsely grated Parmesan cheese.

Place spinach in large saucepan and cook, covered, for 2–3 minutes – toss or turn spinach over occasionally to speed cooking. Drain well. Heat 15 g/½ oz (1 tbsp) butter and olive oil in a frying pan (skillet). Add garlic, salt, cayenne and spinach and toss lightly. Place in a flameproof serving dish and sprinkle with cheese and remaining butter, melted. Brown quickly under a preheated hot grill (broiler). Serves 4.

Purée of Spinach

1 kg (2 lb) spinach, cooked and squeezed dry; 45 g/1½ oz (3 tbsp) butter; salt and freshly ground black pepper; nutmeg; lemon juice; triangular Croûtes, page 90 (optional).

Sieve spinach or purée in a food mill or food processor. Melt butter in a saucepan, add spinach purée and stir on low heat until all surplus moisture has been driven off. Season with salt, pepper, nutmeg and a few drops of lemon juice, and serve domed up in a heated dish, surrounded by triangular croûtes, if desired. Serves 4.

Spinach and Rice

(Spanakaryzo)
A Greek way with spinach.

210 g/7 oz (1 cup) rice; 1 medium onion, finely chopped; 5 tbsp olive oil; 500 ml/18 fl oz (2 cups) boiling water; 1½ tsp salt; 500 g (1 lb) spinach, cut into strips.

Sauté rice and onion in olive oil, stirring occasionally, for 15 minutes. Add boiling water and salt. Cover and simmer for 10 minutes. Add spinach and mix thoroughly. Cover and continue to cook, stirring occasionally, for 15 minutes. Serves 4.

Spinach and Herb Terrine

625 g/1¼ lb (2½ cups) minced (ground) pork; 1 kg (2 lb) spinach; 3 rashers (slices) bacon, rind removed and diced; 125 g/4 oz (½ cup) diced cooked ham; 125 g/4 oz (½ cup) diced cooked tongue; 4 eggs, beaten; 1 onion, chopped; 2 cloves garlic, crushed; 3 tbsp finely chopped parsley; 1 tbsp chopped fresh basil; 1 tbsp chopped fresh chervil; ½ tsp chopped fresh rosemary; 2 tsp salt; ¼ tsp cayenne; freshly ground black pepper; 30 g/1 oz (2 tbsp) butter; 125 g/4 oz (⅔ cup) chicken livers, cut into 1 cm (½ in) pieces; 120 ml/4 fl oz (½ cup) single (light) cream; 250 g (8 oz) fresh pork back fat, cut into thin strips.

Place minced (ground) pork in a bowl. Cook spinach 2 minutes and drain. Chop finely and add to pork with bacon, ham, tongue, eggs, onion, garlic, herbs, salt, cayenne and pepper. Mix well. Melt butter in a saucepan. Add chicken livers and cook until lightly browned. Stir into pork with cream. Place pork fat strips on a board and stretch with back of a knife until they are 3 mm (⅛ in) thick. Use most of the strips to line a 1.5 litre/2½ pint (6 cup) terrine. Spoon pork and spinach mixture into terrine. Use all the mixture, even if it comes above sides of terrine – it will shrink as it cooks. Cover top with remaining pork strips, tucking them into sides of mixture. Cover with foil, or seal a lid with a flour-and-water paste made from 125 g/4 oz (1 cup) flour mixed with 4 tbsp

water. Place terrine in a baking dish of hot water and bake in a preheated moderate oven (180°C/350°F, Gas Mark 4) for 1½ hours. Take from oven, remove lid and place a weight on top. Leave until cool and set. Serve in thin slices. Serves 8–10.
NOTE: If no chervil is available, use extra parsley.

Spinach and Bacon Salad

6 rashers (slices) streaky bacon, rind removed and cut into strips; 1 tsp olive oil; 500 g (1 lb) young spinach, rinsed, dried and chilled.
DRESSING: *3 tbsp olive oil; 1 tbsp wine vinegar; pinch sugar; salt and freshly ground black pepper.*

Fry bacon in olive oil until golden.
DRESSING: Whisk all ingredients together. Toss spinach with dressing in a salad bowl. Pour hot bacon and fat over salad and serve at once. Serves 6.

Cream of Spinach Soup

1.5 litres/2½ pints (6 cups) chicken stock; 2 medium potatoes, peeled and sliced; 2 medium onions, sliced; 1 medium bunch spinach; good pinch nutmeg; salt and freshly ground black pepper; 120 ml/4 fl oz (½ cup) single (light) cream or evaporated milk.

Bring stock to the boil in a large saucepan. Add potatoes and onions, cover and cook for 20 minutes. Reserve 1 spinach leaf for garnish, and roughly chop remainder. Add to pan and cook for another 10 minutes, uncovered. Purée soup in a blender or food processor, return to saucepan and season with nutmeg, salt and pepper. Thin with a little water if necessary, stir in cream or evaporated milk and reheat to boiling. Serve in heated bowls, garnished with reserved spinach, finely shredded. Serves 6.

SPONGE CAKE

See Cakes.

SPRING ONION

See Shallot and Spring Onion.

SPRING ROLL

Variations of spring roll exist throughout South-East Asia, their popularity extending to many countries of the Pacific. Spring rolls may be large or small, eaten as snack food or as part of a meal, their fillings differing from region to region. However, all share some characteristics: wafer-thin wrappers encasing a delectable filling, each one, whether large or small, being rolled up and deep-fried until crisp and golden.

Spring rolls are usually served with a dipping sauce, which again varies from region to region. **See recipes.**

Spring Roll Wrappers

250 g/8 oz (2 cups) flour; ¼ tsp salt; 1 egg, beaten; about 120 ml/4 fl oz (½ cup) water.

Sift flour and salt into a large bowl. Add beaten egg and sufficient water to mix to a stiff dough. Add a little extra flour if dough is too soft and sticky. Turn dough on to a lightly floured surface and knead well. Halve dough and wrap one half in plastic wrap. Roll out other half to wafer-thin thickness. Using a sharp knife trim edges to form a 40 cm (16 in) square. Cut into 20 cm (8 in) squares or size required. Place on a baking tray and cover with a slightly damp cloth until ready to use. Roll out and cut other half of dough the same way. Makes 8 × 20 cm (8 in) spring roll wrappers or 32 × 10 cm (4 in) wrappers.

Spring Rolls

(Chinese)

250 g (8 oz) pork fillet (tenderloin), shredded; 1 tbsp dry sherry; ¾ tsp salt; 1 tsp cornflour (cornstarch); 120 ml/4 fl oz (½ cup) oil; 60 g/2 oz (½ cup) shredded leek or spring onions (scallions); 250 g/8 oz (1 cup) shredded canned bamboo shoot; 30 g (1 oz) dried Chinese mushrooms, soaked in warm water for 30 minutes, drained and finely shredded; 125 g/4 oz (2 cups) bean sprouts; 2 tbsp soy sauce; 8 × 20 cm (8 in) Spring Roll Wrappers (above); beaten egg to seal; oil for deep-frying.

Mix together pork, dry sherry, ½ tsp salt and cornflour (cornstarch). Heat half the oil and sauté pork mixture for about 2 minutes. Remove from pan and place in a bowl. Add remaining oil to pan and sauté leek or spring onions (scallions), shredded bamboo shoot, mushrooms and bean sprouts for about 2 minutes. Remove from pan and place in bowl with pork mixture. Add remaining salt and soy sauce and mix all ingredients together. Allow filling to cool before using. Place 2 tbsp of filling on lower half of each spring roll wrapper. Brush left and right edges with beaten egg. Fold bottom edge up, left and right edges over, and roll up. Brush top edge with egg and press to seal. Heat oil to 185°C/360°F or until a bread cube turns golden-brown in 60 seconds. Deep-fry rolls until crisp and golden, about 5–8 minutes. Drain on crumpled paper towels and serve immediately. Makes 8.

Right: A selection of Lunch-box Sandwich Fillings (page 362)

Singapore Chinese Spring Rolls

6 dried Chinese mushrooms, soaked in warm water for 30 minutes and drained; 3 tbsp peanut oil; 1 tbsp sesame oil; 1 clove garlic, crushed; ½ tsp finely grated fresh ginger; 250 g (8 oz) boneless pork, finely chopped; 250 g/8 oz (1 cup) green (uncooked) prawns (shrimp), shelled, deveined and chopped; 150 g/5 oz (2 cups) finely shredded Chinese cabbage (bok choy); 125 g/4 oz (1 cup) shredded giant white radish; 12 water chestnuts, chopped; 250 g/8 oz (1 cup) chopped canned bamboo shoot; 125 g/4 oz (2 cups) bean sprouts; 6 spring onions (scallions), finely chopped; 1 tbsp light soy sauce; 1 tbsp oyster sauce; ½ tsp salt; 3 tsp cornflour (cornstarch); 16 × 20 cm (8 in) Spring Roll Wrappers (page 406); beaten egg to seal; oil for deep-frying.

Remove stems from mushrooms, and finely chop caps. Heat peanut and sesame oils in a wok or large frying pan (skillet) and fry garlic and ginger for a few seconds. Add pork, increase heat and stir-fry until it changes colour. Add prawns (shrimp) and stir-fry about 1 minute. Mix in vegetables, sauces and salt. Mix cornflour (cornstarch) to a thin paste with a little cold water. Tilt pan so liquid gathers at one edge and add cornflour (cornstarch) paste to liquid, stirring until thickened. Stir through mixture. Remove from heat and cool completely. Put 2 tbsp of filling on lower half of each wrapper. Brush left and right edges with beaten egg. Fold bottom edge up, left and right edges over, and roll up. Brush top edge with egg and press firmly to seal. Heat oil to 185°C/360°F or until a bread cube turns golden-brown in 60 seconds. Deep-fry rolls until crisp and golden, about 5–8 minutes. Drain on crumpled paper towels and serve immediately, with chilli sauce for dipping. Makes 16.

Chicken Spring Rolls

(Vietnamese)

30 g (1 oz) transparent noodles, cooked in water for 10 minutes, drained and cut into 2.5 cm (1 in) pieces; 250 g/8 oz (1 cup) chicken breast meat, skinned and cut into thin strips; 1 tbsp dried wood ears (mushrooms, available from Chinese and Asian grocery stores), soaked in warm water for 30 minutes, drained and finely chopped; 2 spring onions (scallions), finely chopped; 125 g/4 oz (½ cup) crabmeat; ½ tsp black pepper; 8 × 20 cm (8 in) Spring Roll Wrappers (page 406), each cut in half to

Left: Plain, Wholewheat and Cheese Scones (page 382)

form 2 rectangles; beaten egg to seal; oil for deep-frying; shredded spring onions (scallions) to garnish.
NUOC CHAM SAUCE: *2 cloves garlic, crushed; 1 fresh red chilli; 5 tsp sugar; juice and pulp ¼ lime or lemon; 5 tbsp nuoc man (fish sauce available from Asian grocery stores); 5 tbsp water.*

Combine noodles, chicken, mushrooms, spring onions (scallions), crabmeat and pepper. Place 3–4 tsp of filling on lower half of each spring roll wrapper. Brush left and right edges with beaten egg. Fold bottom edge up, left and right edges over, and roll up. Brush top edge with egg and press to seal. Set aside while making sauce.
NUOC CHAM SAUCE: Pound garlic, chilli and sugar using a pestle and mortar, or mash with back of a spoon. Add lime or lemon juice and pulp, then fish sauce and water. Mix well to combine ingredients. Heat oil to 185°C/360°F or until a bread cube turns golden-brown in 60 seconds. Deep-fry rolls for 3–4 minutes or until crisp and golden. Drain on paper towels and serve immediately, garnished with shredded spring onions (scallions). Serve with nuoc cham sauce. Makes 16.

SPROUTS, BRUSSELS

See Brussels Sprouts.

SPUMONE

An Italian moulded ice cream, usually consisting of an outer coating of ice cream, and a filling of whipped cream, contrasting flavoured ice cream or liqueur-soaked fruits, and served sliced. A delicious and less elaborate version is based on a Zabaglione mixture (see *Zabaglione*).
To assemble: Soften the ice cream to be used for the outer layer and spoon about ¾ of it into the base and sides of a chilled metal mould. The layer should be about 2 cm (¾ in) thick. Cover the mould and freeze until solid. Remove from freezer, spoon in the filling and top with the remaining ¼ of ice cream (softened). Cover securely and freeze.
To unmould: Remove from freezer, rub the mould with a cold damp cloth, uncover and invert on to a chilled serving platter. If the spumone sticks, a hot cloth rubbed over the mould should help to release the cream.

Decorate with whipped cream, fruit and nuts if desired. **See recipes.**

Chestnut Spumone

500 ml/18 fl oz (2 cups) double (heavy) cream; 1 litre/1¾ pints (4 cups) vanilla ice cream, softened; 180 g/6 oz (¾ cup) canned sweetened chestnut purée, chilled; 4 tbsp

Pernod or other anise-flavoured liqueur, chilled.
DECORATION *(optional): 250 ml/8 fl oz (1 cup) double (heavy) cream, whipped; 1 tbsp strong black coffee.*

Place cream in a bowl and freeze for about 1 hour or until mushy. Line bottom and sides of a 2 litre/3½ pint (8 cup) metal mould with 750 ml/1¼ pints (3 cups) softened vanilla ice cream. Cover with foil and freeze. Whip partly frozen cream and fold in chestnut purée and liqueur. Place chestnut cream mixture in freezer and freeze for about 2 hours, stirring every 30 minutes. Remove mould lined with ice cream, uncover and fill centre with chestnut cream mixture. Spread remaining softened vanilla ice cream over top. Cover mould and freeze for at least 4 hours. Unmould on to a chilled serving platter just before serving and decorate with whipped cream flavoured with coffee if desired. Serves 6–8.

Spumone Coppelia

750 ml/1¼ pints (3 cups) Chocolate Ice Cream, softened (page 161); 1.2 litres/2 pints (5 cups) hazelnut ice cream, softened (see below); 30 g/1 oz (¼ cup) whole hazelnuts; whipped cream to decorate.

Line bottom and sides of a 2 litre/3½ pint (8 cup) chilled loaf tin (pan) with 500 ml/18 fl oz (2 cups) chocolate ice cream. Cover tin (pan) with foil and freeze. When frozen, fill centre with hazelnut ice cream, then cover with remaining softened chocolate ice cream. Cover tin (pan) and freeze for at least 3 hours. Unmould on to a chilled serving platter, decorate top with hazelnuts and rosettes of whipped cream. Serve sliced. Serves 8–10.
NOTE: Make hazelnut ice cream by combining 1.2 litres/2 pints (5 cups) slightly softened vanilla ice cream (see page 161) with 125 g/4 oz (1 cup) finely ground hazelnuts.

Spumone Zabaglione

3 egg yolks; 2 tsp water; 3 tbsp caster sugar; 120 ml/4 fl oz (½ cup) Marsala or similar sweet wine; 175 ml/6 fl oz (¾ cup) double (heavy) cream.

Combine egg yolks, water, sugar and wine in top of a double saucepan (double boiler) or heatproof bowl. Whisk until lukewarm over a pan of hot, not boiling, water, then remove from heat and continue beating until mixture is foamy and slightly thickened. Whip cream until it holds soft peaks and fold into egg mixture. Pour into a 1 litre/1¾ pint (4 cup) mould, cover with foil and freeze for 3–4 hours. Unmould on to a chilled serving platter, and cut into wedges. Serves 4.

SQUAB

See *Pigeon*.

SQUASH

The American name for certain members of the gourd family – usually known as marrows in England.

Squash originated in America, but British and European growers have been experimenting with them in recent years, so while you may not always find them at your local greengrocer's, adventurous gardeners may wish to grow their own.

There are two sorts of squash – winter and summer. Winter squashes, which usually have hard-shelled skins, are allowed to ripen on the plants, and are stored until required. This category includes the butternut squash (also called butternut pumpkin) and acorn squash. For preparation and cooking see *Pumpkin*.

Summer squash are eaten young and immature, like courgettes (zucchini). The best known variety of summer squash is the custard marrow or squash (patty pan squash).

When buying summer squash, look for small, firm, unblemished ones whose skins have a sheen. Store in the refrigerator crisper and use within a day or two.

□ **Basic Preparation:** Wash the squash and lightly trim the stem end and, if necessary, any little brown mark at the other end. Leave whole, halve or slice according to the recipe. Peel larger custard (patty pan) squash thinly.

It is not usually necessary to peel small, young squash.

Squash beyond the baby stage may have developed slightly bitter juices: to remove this, 'dégorge' (see *Aubergine/Eggplant*) by sprinkling salt on cut surfaces and leaving in a colander to drain for 20 minutes. Rinse under cold running water and pat dry with paper towels before using.

□ **To Cook:** Squash may be boiled, steamed or sautéed. **See also recipes.**

BOILED SQUASH For firm-tender squash, drop slices into a generous amount of fast-boiling

Preparing Squid

salted water and boil for 4–8 minutes. Drain in a colander and run cold water over squash to stop cooking and set the colour. Reheat gently in butter when required, and season with pepper and lemon juice.

STEAMED SQUASH This is a good way to cook custard (patty pan) squash. Leave whole or cut up. Cook, tightly covered, in about 1 cm ($\frac{1}{2}$ in) of salted water, or in a steamer over boiling water, until tender. Time will depend on size of squash pieces. Serve with butter, pepper and lemon juice, or a sauce such as Mornay or Poulette (see page 368) or Fresh Tomato (see page 271).

SAUTEED SQUASH Slice thickly and dégorge as described under Basic Preparation. Heat enough butter to cover bottom of a frying pan (skillet) generously, and when foaming add squash. Cook, stirring and tossing frequently, for 3–4 minutes or until just tender.

A few serving suggestions:

● Add shredded shallots to sautéed squash.
● Sprinkle with chopped fresh herbs, or dried herbs with chopped parsley, before serving.
● Add fresh breadcrumbs (about 45 g/1$\frac{1}{2}$ oz ($\frac{3}{4}$ cup) to 500 g/1 lb (2$\frac{1}{2}$ cups) squash), as you sauté the squash.
● Sprinkle with grated cheese or crumbled crisply fried bacon before serving.

See also *Marrow*.

Baked Stuffed Custard Squash

4 custard (patty pan) squash, about 10 cm (4 in) across, or 2 larger ones, steamed.
STUFFING:*2 rashers (slices) streaky bacon, rind removed and chopped; 30 g/1 oz (2 tbsp) butter; 1 small onion, chopped; 90 g/3 oz ($\frac{3}{4}$ cup) mushrooms, chopped; 2 tbsp chopped green or red pepper; 1 tomato, peeled, seeded and chopped; 125 g/4 oz (1 cup) cooked rice; salt and freshly ground black pepper.*

Cut a lid off each steamed squash and scoop out some flesh with a sharp spoon, discarding any large seeds. Chop this flesh and drain in a sieve. Turn squash shells upside-down to drain.

STUFFING:Gently fry bacon in a dry frying pan (skillet) until fat runs. Add butter and fry onion, mushrooms and pepper until soft.

Stir in tomato and rice and season with salt and pepper. Fill squash with stuffing, replace lids and place in a buttered ovenproof dish. Brush squash with melted butter and bake in a preheated moderate oven (180°C/350°F, Gas Mark 4) for 20–30 minutes until tender. Serves 4.

SQUASH, FRUIT

Fresh fruit squash is deliciously refreshing, topped with iced water and soda (carbonated) water. It is made with sweetened fruit pulp and/or juice, usually from oranges or lemons.

Commercial squash is sold in concentrated form to which water is added for serving. The components of the drink are usually specified on the label by law and may consist solely of chemicals.

Orange Squash

6 (or more) oranges; 750 g/1$\frac{1}{2}$ lb (3 cups) sugar; 750 ml/1$\frac{1}{4}$ pints (3 cups) water; 30 g/1 oz (2 tbsp) citric acid.

Lightly grate rind from the oranges and squeeze out juice. There should be 500 ml/18 fl oz (2 cups) juice, so if necessary squeeze more oranges. Add grated rind to sugar and water in a saucepan and heat until sugar dissolves. Add orange juice and citric acid, mix well and bottle. If you wish to keep squash longer than a week, use special ginger beer preserving bottles available from kitchenware shops and sterilize in simmering water for 30 minutes. Serve topped with crushed ice, iced water or soda (carbonated) water and float a thin slice of orange on top of each glass. Makes 1.5 litres /2$\frac{1}{2}$ pints (6 cups).

SQUID (CALAMARI)

The fine delicate flavour of squid has been known for many centuries to people living around the Mediterranean. Squid are related to the octopus and cuttlefish, but the flesh is more tender and sweet; they are all cephalopods.

In Europe, squid is often sold ready-cleaned, but in Britain and America, this job will usually be up to you. Americans can also buy frozen, canned and even dried squid. When buying fresh squid, choose those with firm flesh that is white and almost translucent. The edible parts are the tentacles and the sac-like body.

See also *Fritto Misto*.

□ **Basic Preparation:** Pull out the head and tentacles from the body (**Fig 1 opposite**). Remove the eyes, ink sac and parrot-like beak at the base of the tentacles and discard. Cut the fins off the body (**2**). Remove the skin (**3**) by rubbing it off the body and tentacles with

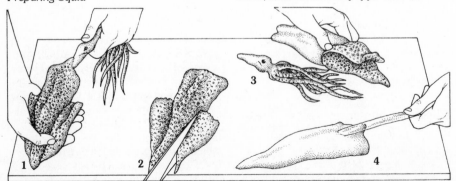

your fingers (dip your fingers in salt to act as an abrasive). Remove any remaining yellow-ish deposit and the long internal quill-like bone (4), which resembles hard cellophane. Wash the squid thoroughly in cold running water and dry well before using.

☐ **To Cook:** Squid can be fried, baked, grilled (broiled) or stewed but, as with all seafood, must not be overcooked or the flesh will become tough. **See also recipes**.

PAN-FRIED SQUID Cut prepared squid into thin slices. Place in a dish with oil, salt and freshly ground black pepper and let stand 1 hour, turning occasionally. Heat a heavy frying pan (skillet), drop in squid slices and cook gently for 3–4 minutes, adding a little more oil if necessary. Serve with lemon wedges.

GRILLED (BROILED) SQUID Cut prepared squid into pieces. Place in a dish with oil, salt and freshly ground black pepper to taste and let stand 1 hour, turning occasionally. Place squid under a preheated grill (broiler) and cook 4–5 minutes on each side, brushing occasionally with oil. Serve with lemon wedges.

SQUID FRIED IN PIQUANT SAUCE Pan-fry squid as above with the addition of 3 cloves garlic, peeled and ½ fresh chilli or ¼ tsp chilli powder. When tender, remove garlic and chilli. Combine 1 tbsp each of breadcrumbs, chopped parsley and butter and toss over squid, stirring over a high heat for 1 minute. Serve with lemon wedges.

Stuffed Baby Squid

12–18 baby squid, cleaned; 1 clove garlic; 4 anchovy fillets; 3–4 sprigs parsley; 2 eggs, lightly beaten; 60 g/2 oz (1 cup) fresh breadcrumbs; salt and freshly ground black pepper; 2–3 tsp olive oil; lemon wedges to serve.

Cut tentacles from squid and chop them as fine as possible with garlic, anchovies and parsley. This may be done in a blender, food processor or mincer (grinder). Combine eggs, breadcrumbs, salt, pepper and olive oil and work to a paste. Add anchovy mixture. Stuff squid bodies with mixture and sew up openings with strong thread. Sprinkle with salt and pepper and brush with oil. Cook under a preheated moderate grill (broiler) for 15 minutes, turning occasionally and basting with oil. Serve very hot, with lemon wedges to garnish. Serves 6.

VARIATION

Squid in Tomato Sauce: Make stuffing as above, using tentacles from 6 large squid, cleaned. Spoon stuffing into 6 squid. Heat 2 tbsp olive oil in a heavy shallow pan and fry 1 medium onion, finely chopped, and 2 cloves garlic, crushed, until soft. Stir in 1 × 425 g/14 oz can tomatoes, season well with salt and freshly ground black pepper, simmer for 15 minutes. Add squid, cover and simmer gently for 1–1¼ hours. Serves 6.

Baby Squid with Parsley

When you can get tiny squid or cuttlefish, try them this way. Do not overcook or they will become tough.

1 kg (2 lb) baby squid, cleaned; 4 tbsp olive oil; 2 cloves garlic, bruised; salt and freshly ground black pepper; 20 g/⅔ oz (½ cup) chopped parsley; juice ½ lemon; triangular Croûtes (page 90) to serve.

Cut squid into rings, or lengthways into 4. If liked, the tentacles may also be cooked. Heat oil gently with garlic cloves until they begin to brown; discard garlic. Add squid, season with salt and pepper and cook over a brisk heat for 1–2 minutes. Sprinkle with parsley and lemon juice and serve very hot, with triangular croûtes. Serves 4.

Calamari

(Fried Squid)

This is a dish often found in Italian restaurants, and is one of the simplest but most delicious ways of serving squid. Serve as a starter or as a main course with a selection of salads.

500 g (1 lb) squid, cleaned; 1 egg; 120 ml/4 fl oz (½ cup) milk; flour; salt and freshly ground black pepper; 60 g/2 oz (½ cup) fine, dry breadcrumbs; oil for deep-frying.

Cut squid tentacles into pieces about 8 cm (3 in) long, and cut body into rings. Beat egg with milk in a shallow dish. Dredge squid in flour, seasoned with salt and pepper, then dip in egg mixture, and roll in breadcrumbs. Heat 8–10 cm (3–4 in) of oil in a deep-fryer to 200°C/400°F. Fry squid in oil until golden, about 2 minutes. This should be done in several batches; do not overcrowd the pan. Drain on paper towels, sprinkle with salt and serve with Sauce Tartare (see page 205). Serves 6.

Deep-Fried Squid

4–6 squid, cleaned; 60 g/2 oz (½ cup) flour; salt and freshly ground black pepper; oil for deep-frying; lemon wedges to serve.

Cut squid tentacles into pieces about 8 cm (3 in) long, and cut body into rings. Season flour with salt and pepper and roll squid pieces in it. Heat oil in a deep-fryer to 185°C/360°F or until a bread cube turns golden-brown in 40 seconds. Deep-fry squid for 2–3 minutes or until golden-brown. If necessary fry in several batches to avoid overcrowding pan. Drain on paper towels and serve immediately, with lemon wedges. Serves 4–6.

STEAK DIANE

A superb dish of tender fillet (tenderloin)

S

steak, flamed in brandy and sherry, the delicious pan juices forming the sauce. Steak Diane is a popular restaurant dish, well worth trying at home when you are dining *à deux*. Have all the ingredients ready before you begin cooking as this will take only a minute or two. Make the dish for two people only as no more than two steaks can be successfully sautéed at one time in the average sauté or frying pan (skillet).

Steak Diane

2 × 1 cm (½ in) thick pieces fillet (tenderloin) steak; salt and freshly ground black pepper; 60 g/2 oz (4 tbsp) butter; 1 clove garlic, crushed; 1 tbsp Worcestershire sauce; 1 tbsp brandy; 2 tbsp dry sherry; 1 tbsp finely chopped parsley.

Trim all fat from steak and beat to flatten until 5 mm (¼ in) thick. Season with salt and pepper. Heat butter in a large frying pan (skillet) and when it is foaming add steaks. Sauté for about 40 seconds (rare) or for about 1 minute (medium) on each side. Add garlic and allow it to cook for 30 seconds. Stir in the Worcestershire sauce. Heat brandy and sherry until warm, set alight and pour over steaks. Shake pan until flames die down. Remove steaks to a heated serving dish and sprinkle with parsley. Give sauce a good stir and pour it sizzling hot over steaks. Serve immediately. Serves 2.

STEAK TARTARE

The classic raw beef mixture that is popular in much of Europe. Traditionally, it is served topped with a raw egg yolk for the diner to mix through the beef, and with small bowls of chopped onion and capers. Steak Tartare also makes excellent appetizers and cocktail or larger open-faced sandwiches. Beef for Steak Tartare should not be minced (ground), but scraped with a metal spoon or chopped in a food processor to give very fine-textured, juicy meat.

411

Steak Tartare

*500 g (1 lb) lean rump (top round) steak;
$\frac{1}{4}$ tsp dry mustard; dash Worcestershire
sauce; few drops Tabasco (hot pepper)
sauce; salt and freshly ground black pepper;
chopped parsley; 4 egg yolks.*
TO SERVE: *finely chopped onion; capers.*

Scrape meat with edge of a metal spoon
until it becomes a fine mince (ground meat),
discarding any fat or gristle as you go. To
prepare in a food processor, remove all fat
and gristle first, cut lean meat into pieces and
process, using steel blade, until almost
smooth. Lightly mix steak with mustard,
Worcestershire sauce, Tabasco (hot pepper)
sauce, salt and pepper. Shape into 4 patties
and place on individual serving plates. Cover
surface of meat with chopped parsley,
pressing it on lightly, and mark a trellis
pattern with a knife. Chill well before serving.
At serving time, make an indentation in top
of each patty with a soup spoon and place a
raw egg yolk in it. Serve with separate bowls
of chopped onion and capers. Serves 4.
VARIATIONS
Steak Tartare Balls: Follow recipe for Steak
Tartare, but mix 1 egg yolk, 1 tsp grated
onion, 2 tbsp finely chopped capers and
1 tbsp finely chopped parsley through meat
with seasonings. Roll mixture lightly into
2.5 cm (1 in) balls and roll in finely chopped
parsley. Chill well before serving. Makes
about 40.

STEAK AND KIDNEY PUDDING/PIE

The perennial favourite, Steak and Kidney
Pudding or Pie, with rich, thick peppery
gravy, has travelled far beyond its origins in
Sussex, and can be found on the tables of
English-speaking people across the world. It
is good, hearty fare, ideal for serving on cold
winter nights, and remains a nourishing,
economical dish for family and friends.

The basic steak and kidney mixture can be
steamed in a suet crust, when it is called Steak
and Kidney Pudding, or it can be baked with a
puff or flaky pastry crust. Many people also
enjoy steak and kidney topped with a sponge
mixture, or with some parsley dumplings
steamed with the meat during the last half
hour of cooking.

A few bottled oysters or sliced mushrooms
make a superb addition to steak and kidney,
enriching the dish sufficiently for serving at
even the smartest of dinner parties. **See
recipes.**

Basic Steak and Kidney

*1 kg (2 lb) chuck or blade steak, cut into
2.5 cm (1 in) cubes; $\frac{1}{2}$–1 calf's kidney, or 2–3
sheep's kidneys, cored and chopped; 1 tbsp
flour; 1 tsp salt; 1 tsp black pepper; $\frac{1}{2}$ tsp*

*mixed dried herbs; 120 ml/4 fl oz ($\frac{1}{2}$ cup)
water; 2 tsp Worcestershire sauce (optional);
$\frac{1}{4}$ tsp nutmeg (optional).*

Sprinkle meats with flour, salt, pepper and
herbs. Spoon into a heavy saucepan and
pour water over. Cover tightly and simmer
very gently over low heat for about 2 hours,
or cook in a preheated moderate oven
(160°C/325°F, Gas Mark 3) for about $2\frac{1}{2}$
hours or until meat is tender. If necessary
add a little more water. When cooked, stir in
Worcestershire sauce and nutmeg, if using.
Serves 4–6.
NOTE: Steak and kidney may be steamed.
Combine the ingredients in a pudding basin
(heatproof mixing bowl). Cover with 2
thicknesses of greased greaseproof (waxed)
paper or foil and tie with string. Put into a
large saucepan with boiling water coming
halfway up sides of basin (bowl). Steam for
$3\frac{1}{2}$–4 hours or until meat is tender,
replenishing water in pan as it evaporates
with more boiling water.
VARIATION
Steak and Kidney with Dumplings: Follow
recipe for Basic Steak and Kidney. About 30
minutes before cooking is finished, add 6–8
Fluffy Herb Dumplings (see page 111).
Cover casserole or saucepan and cook
further 20–30 minutes or until dumplings
are swollen and tender. Do not lift lid of pan
during first 20 minutes of cooking.

Steak and Kidney Pudding

*1 quantity Suet Pastry (page 276); 1 quan-
tity uncooked Basic Steak and Kidney
(left).*

Roll out about $\frac{2}{3}$ of suet pastry (dough) on a
lightly floured work surface to make a round
30 cm (12 in) in diameter and about 5 mm
($\frac{1}{4}$ in) thick. Use to line a 1 litre/$1\frac{3}{4}$ pint
pudding basin (4 cup heatproof mixing
bowl), draping dough loosely over a rolling
pin to help lift it into basin (bowl). Gently
press dough into basin (bowl), being careful
not to stretch or tear it. Roll out remaining
dough into a round about 18–20 cm (7–8 in)
diameter. Spoon uncooked steak and
kidney mixture into prepared basin (bowl),
filling it to within 1 cm ($\frac{1}{2}$ in) of top. Mound
meat a little in centre. Trim excess dough
from rim of basin and brush dough rim with
cold water. Place round of dough on top,
trim off excess and crimp edges all around
rim to seal tightly.

Place a lightly greased round of double
thickness greaseproof (waxed) paper or
single thickness foil over top of pudding,
turning edges down all around to a depth of
about 5 cm (2 in). Dip a clean tea-towel in
cold water and wring it dry. Spread it flat,
sprinkle with flour and shake to remove
excess. Place towel over top of pudding,
floured side down, and tie securely with

string about 4–5 cm ($1\frac{1}{2}$–2 in) under rim.
Knot 4 corners of cloth over top. Place basin
(bowl) in a large pan of fast boiling water to
come $\frac{3}{4}$ up sides of basin (bowl). Cover and
boil steadily over moderate heat for $3\frac{1}{2}$–4
hours. As water evaporates pour in more
boiling water to maintain level. To serve,
remove towel and paper or foil and pin a
folded napkin round basin (bowl). Serve the
pudding straight from the basin (bowl).
Serves 4–6.
NOTE: If the pudding seems a little dry after
cutting, pour in a small amount of boiling
water to augment the gravy.

Steak and Kidney Pie

*1 quantity Basic Steak and Kidney, cooked
and cooled (left); 1 × 375 g (12 oz) packet
frozen puff pastry (paste), thawed; egg yolk,
beaten with a little water to glaze.*

Spoon cooked steak and kidney mixture into
a round or oval pie dish just large enough to
hold it, mounding it up in the centre. Allow
to cool. Roll out pastry (dough) on lightly
floured board to 2.5 cm (1 in) larger all
round than top of dish. Cut off a strip of
dough all round, 2.5 cm (1 in) wide, and
place strip on edge of dish. Brush with a little
egg glaze and cover with dough round or
oval. Press on to strip to seal and trim edge.
Cut an air vent in centre of dough lid.
Decorate with a pastry (dough) rose and
leaves (see page 290). Chill 30 minutes.
Brush with egg glaze and bake in a
preheated moderately hot oven
(200°C/400°F, Gas Mark 6) for 20–30
minutes. Reduce heat to moderate
(180°C/350°F, Gas Mark 4) and bake
further 30–40 minutes. It may be necessary
to cover crust with foil to prevent overbrowning. Serves 4–6.
VARIATIONS
Steak and Kidney Pie with Oysters: Follow
recipe for Steak and Kidney Pie. After
cooking, carefully insert a funnel into centre
vent and push in 1 × 105 g/$3\frac{1}{2}$ oz can oysters,
drained (you may have to halve them first).
Steak and Kidney Pie with Mushrooms:
Add 125 g/4 oz (1 cup) mushrooms, sliced,
to Basic Steak and Kidney mixture before
cooking.

Steak and Kidney Sponge

This light and tender sponge topping absorbs the delicious flavours of the filling.

1 quantity Basic Steak and Kidney, steamed (page 412); 125 g/4 oz (1 cup) self-raising flour; ½ tsp salt; 2 eggs, separated; 250 ml/8 fl oz (1 cup) milk; 60 g/2 oz (4 tbsp) butter, melted.

After steaming steak and kidney mixture, leave basin (bowl) standing in saucepan of hot water while you prepare topping. Sift flour and salt into a bowl and make a well in centre. Beat egg yolks and stir in milk. Pour into flour mixture, add butter and stir until smooth. Beat egg whites until stiff and fold into mixture. Spoon sponge mixture carefully over steak and kidney mixture in basin (bowl) so meat is completely covered. Add more boiling water to saucepan to come halfway up sides of basin (bowl) if necessary. Put lid on saucepan and boil steadily for about 20 minutes. Serve immediately, with a napkin tied around basin. Serves 4–6.

NOTE: Steak and kidney may be cooked in a saucepan or casserole, as described in basic recipe, if preferred. Turn into basin (bowl) and proceed as above.

STEAMED PUDDING

See Desserts and Puddings.

STEAMBOAT

A spectacular Chinese meal of meats and seafood cooked at the table by the diners themselves. The name refers to the traditional cooking vessel, a Mongolian fire pot whose base holds hot coals (available from Chinese grocery stores). A fondue set may be substituted. The pot of simmering stock is set in the centre of the table with the foods and sauces arranged round it. Guests use small strainers to lift their choice of food into the stock, and when cooked, it is plucked out of the strainer with chopsticks, dipped into sauce and eaten. After the meat and seafood are eaten, noodles and vegetables are cooked in the remaining stock and served in soup bowls as a last course.

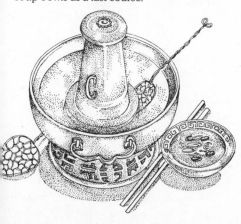

Steamboat

STOCK: *1 kg (2 lb) chicken soup bones; 2.5 litres/4½ pints (10 cups) water; 4 slices fresh ginger; 5 spring onions (scallions), coarsely chopped; 2 cloves garlic, bruised; 1 tsp salt; 4 black peppercorns.*

MEATS AND SEAFOOD: *4 chicken fillets (skinless, boneless half-breasts); 250 g (8 oz) pork fillet (tenderloin); 250 g (8 oz) fillet of beef (tenderloin); 250 g (8 oz) chicken livers, lamb or calf liver; 250 g (8 oz) firm-fleshed white fish fillets, skinned and any bones removed.*

NOODLES AND VEGETABLES: *500 g/1 lb (6 cups) Chinese cabbage (bok choy), cut into 8 cm (3 in) strips; 250 g (8 oz) transparent noodles (rice vermicelli), soaked in boiling water for 30 minutes and drained; 500 g/1 lb (2½ cups) fresh, crisp spinach, shredded; handful mange tout (snow peas) if available; 125 g/4 oz (½ cup) bean curd, thickly sliced.*

To make stock, simmer all ingredients together in a saucepan for 2–3 hours. Strain, cool, then chill. Skim fat from surface.

MEATS AND SEAFOOD: Remove any fat from chicken breasts and pull out white tendon which runs down underside of each half-breast. Remove gristle and fat from pork and beef. Remove sinews and membrane from livers.

Wrap all meats and fish separately in plastic wrap and place in freezer to become firm before slicing. Slice meats and fish as thinly as possible into pieces about 8 × 2 cm (3 × ¾ in), keeping slices in order as they are cut. Arrange on plates and cover.

NOODLES AND VEGETABLES: Drop cabbage into boiling water for 1 minute, then drain and refresh under cold water. If you are using a fire pot, light about 20 heat beads in a fireplace or barbecue and burn about 15 minutes until a white ash forms on surface. Transfer with tongs to grate of fire pot, pushing them well in.

Meantime, bring prepared stock to the boil. If using a fondue set, light burner and set pot over it. Pour stock into pot and place on a thick board in centre of table. Arrange meats, fish and sauces round it, garnishing plates with a little green of spinach or cabbage. Provide a plate, a strainer, chopsticks, a soup bowl and spoon for each guest. Guests now cook and eat meats and fish as described left. When they have done so, drop prepared noodles, vegetables and bean curd into pot, adding a little more stock or water if necessary. Cook for 1 minute, then ladle into soup bowls. Serves 6–8.

SAUCES: Choose from soy sauce, Chinese chilli sauce, hoisin sauce, Chinese barbecue sauce, Chinese lemon sauce (all available at Chinese stores) or one of the following: soy sauce mixed with a little chilli sauce; soy sauce with a little chilli sauce and Chinese sesame oil.

STOCK

The importance of stock cannot be over-estimated in flavouring sauces, casseroles and soups, gravies and many other savoury dishes. Stock is not hard to make; it is simply the flavourful liquid obtained from simmering together the bones, trimmings and flesh of meat, chicken or fish with vegetables, seasonings and water. The liquid is then strained through a fine strainer or cheesecloth and chilled, so that the fat which rises to the top can easily be removed. Slow cooking and skimming the surface of the stock when it first comes to the boil are important, because they help give a clear stock.

The success of good stock depends on its distinctive flavour. Whether beef, chicken or fish, it should taste of that food, and only a few vegetables should be cooked with the meat and bones so that their flavour does not intrude. Make sure the butcher gives you beef bones for beef stock (bouillon) – lamb does not give the same richness. Lamb or mutton stock has its place, and excellent Scottish soups are made from them, but beef and lamb together do not combine well.

Veal is used for white stock, and the Chinese make a light stock with pork bones or a combination of pork and chicken. Each meat with its bones has a use.

Stock will keep in the refrigerator for 1 week, if protected by the layer of fat that would otherwise be removed, or 6 months in a freezer. Particles of meat or vegetables in the stock will reduce the storage time, so care should be taken when straining. It is a good idea, especially if you make a lot of soup, to make a large pot of stock and refrigerate or freeze it for later use.

Although not all soups are made from stock, carefully made stock is so essential to good cooking, that it's well worth making. The ingredients are cheap and easily obtainable. Consider the pressure cooker and crock-pot (electric slow cooker) as modern aids to stock-making. Basic stocks are referred to in the recipes throughout this book and this section tells you how to make them.

Stock or bouillon cubes, canned beef or chicken consommé may be used to replace stock in recipes. These tend to have a 'sameness' about them, though, that reflects in the dishes in which they are used. They do have their place, however.

To clarify stock: Remove fat from cold stock, then place stock in a saucepan with 2 egg whites, lightly beaten, and the 2 egg shells. Bring slowly to the boil, whisking occasionally with an egg whisk. Allow the liquid to rise in the pan as it reaches boiling point, then lower heat and simmer gently for 20 minutes.

Preparing Chicken Stock

You will find that as the egg whites cook they attract and hold any remaining particles of fat and residue that might cloud the stock. Strain through a colander, lined with butter muslin (cheesecloth), and you have a clear liquid ready to use as the basis of many delicious soups. **See recipes.**

Brown Stock For this you use the same ingredients and method as for Beef Stock (see recipes) but the bones and vegetables are first browned to give a richer colour to the stock. Place the bones in a roasting tin (pan) with the carrot and onion, and roast in a preheated moderately hot oven (200°C/400°F, Gas Mark 6) until a good, rich brown colour; place them in a large saucepan.

Rinse out the roasting tin (pan) with a little water, scraping any brown sediment from the bottom, add to the bones and proceed with the recipe for Beef Stock.

White Stock This is made as for Chicken Stock (see below) but veal bones (knuckle is ideal) are used in place of the chicken, or half veal and half chicken. If using veal bones, save the bone from a shoulder or ask the butcher for a veal knuckle, sawn in two to fit your saucepan.

Chicken Stock

This stock is used for white sauce as well as soups.

500 g (1 lb) chicken bones (carcase, backs or wings); about 1.5 litres/2½ pints (6 cups) cold water (enough to cover bones); 1 tsp salt; 1 carrot, halved; 1 tsp black peppercorns; 1 bouquet garni (1 stick celery, 3 sprigs parsley, 1 sprig fresh thyme, 1 bay leaf).

Place bones in a large, heavy saucepan and add remaining ingredients (**Fig 1 above**). Bring to the boil, carefully skimming surface (**2**). Cover pan and simmer very gently for 3–4 hours. Strain through a fine sieve and cool (**3**). Refrigerate until needed, then remove fat which has risen to top of stock, leaving flavoured jelly underneath (**4**). This stock keeps for a week in refrigerator. Makes about 1 litre/1¾ pints (4 cups).

NOTE: Use fresh bones for clear, well-flavoured stock. Your poultry supplier often has a bag of bone pieces (carcases, wing tips,

etc.) at a very reasonable price, or you may use necks and backs. Giblets, if available, may also be added to the stock, except the chicken liver, which is inclined to give a bitter taste.

Beef Stock

This stock (bouillon) is used in brown sauces and soups. Clarified, it is also used in clear soups.

1 kg (2 lb) beef bones (marrow bones or rib bones or a combination); 500 g (1 lb) shin (fore shank) of beef, chopped; 1 carrot, thickly sliced; 1 onion, thickly sliced; 2 tsp salt; about 3 litres/5½ pints (12 cups) cold water (enough to cover bones); 1 tsp black peppercorns; 1 bouquet garni (2 sticks celery, 4 sprigs parsley, 1 sprig fresh thyme, 1 bay leaf).

Put bones into a large saucepan, then add remaining ingredients. Bring slowly to the boil, skimming surface well, then simmer very gently, half-covered, for 4–5 hours (very slow simmering for a long time is secret of well-flavoured stock). Strain through a fine sieve, cool, then chill. Remove surface fat before using. Makes about 2.5 litres/4 pints (10 cups).

Fish Stock

This stock is used in many fish sauces and soups, and can be frozen or will keep well in the refrigerator for a week.

1 fish head and bones (total weight 500 g/1 lb); 1.2 litres/2 pints (5 cups) cold water; 250 ml/8 fl oz (1 cup) white wine, or juice 1 lemon with enough water to make 250 ml/8 fl oz (1 cup); 1 tsp white peppercorns; 1 bouquet garni (1 stick celery, 3 sprigs parsley, 1 sprig fresh thyme, 1 bay leaf).

Place all ingredients in a large saucepan and bring to the boil. Skim surface, then simmer gently for 20 minutes. Strain through a fine sieve or cheesecloth. Makes about 1.2 litres/2 pints (5 cups).

Chinese-Style Stock

A stock which combines chicken with pork bones gives a very delicate flavour which is characteristic of Chinese soups. Pork rib

bones are good ones to use, and your butcher will save these for you if you give a little notice.

500 g (1 lb) chicken bones; 500 g (1 lb) pork bones; 1 carrot, halved; 1 onion, halved; 1 slice fresh ginger; 2 spring onions (scallions), chopped; 1 tsp salt; 1 tsp white peppercorns; 1.2 litres/2 pints (5 cups) water (or enough to cover bones).

Put bones into a deep saucepan and add remaining ingredients. Bring to the boil, skimming surface, then simmer very gently for 2–3 hours. Strain and cool, then chill until needed. Makes about 1 litre/1¾ pints (4 cups).

STOLLEN

One of the most popular German fruit breads. Various Stollen are made for Christmas, a time of great rejoicing, and the most famous was developed in Dresden. Its rather dry dough holds together the lovely fruit and nut treats of Christmas – almonds, raisins, currants and brightly coloured glacé (candied) fruits. It is customary to bake two at a time – one for the household and one to give away. Stollen improves on keeping and once it becomes over-dry, it is almost as good to eat cut into slices and toasted back to freshness.

Stollen

2 strips candied angelica, cut into 1 cm (½ in) dice; 60 g/2 oz (⅓ cup) raisins; 90 g/3 oz (½ cup) currants; 125 g/4 oz (½ cup) glacé (candied) cherries, halved; 125 g/4 oz (⅔ cup) chopped mixed candied peel; 5 tbsp rum; 625 g/1¼ lb (5 cups) flour; large pinch salt; 5 tbsp warm milk; 45 g/1½ oz (3 tbsp) fresh (compressed) yeast; 180 g/6 oz (¾ cup) butter; 125 g/4 oz (½ cup) caster sugar; 2 eggs, lightly beaten; 60 g/2 oz (½ cup) blanched slivered almonds.
TO FINISH: *melted butter; caster sugar; sifted icing (confectioners) sugar.*

Place angelica, raisins, currants, cherries and peel in a bowl and pour rum over. Toss well and allow to stand for 2 hours or preferably overnight. Sift flour and salt into a bowl. Place warm milk in another bowl, add yeast and butter and stir until yeast is dissolved. Mix in sugar and eggs. Make a well in centre of flour, pour in yeast mixture and mix until smooth, commencing with a wooden spoon and then finishing off with the hand. When dough leaves sides of bowl, turn on to a lightly floured board and knead until smooth and elastic – this may take 10–15 minutes. Place dough into a clean greased bowl, cover with a damp cloth and leave to rise in a warm place until doubled in bulk, 50 minutes–1 hour.

When risen, knock (punch) dough down

and shape into a square. Drain rum-soaked fruits, dry well on paper towels and toss in a little flour. Spoon into middle of dough square with almonds. Fold dough over fruits, and knead fruits lightly into dough. Return to greased bowl, cover and leave in a warm place to rise for 30–45 minutes. Knock (punch) down dough and turn on to floured board. Halve dough. Roll out each portion into an oval about 2 cm (¾ in) thick. Brush with melted butter, and sprinkle with a little caster sugar. Fold into three lengthways, overlapping centre with each edge by about 2.5 cm (1 in). Press edges gently to keep in place. Lightly flour hands, taper ends slightly and pat sides to mound stollen in centre. The finished loaf should be about 8 cm (3 in) wide. Place on a greased baking tray. Repeat with second portion of dough. Brush with a little butter and let rise in a warm place for about 1 hour or until doubled in bulk. Bake in a preheated moderately hot oven (190°C/375°F, Gas Mark 5) for about 45 minutes or until golden-brown and crusty. Cool on a wire rack. Dust heavily with sifted icing (confectioners) sugar before slicing and buttering. Makes 2.

STRAWBERRY

Once called 'strayberry' because it propagates itself by runners, the strawberry was known to epicures in Roman times. Today's varieties are no doubt much changed but let us be thankful for those experiments which have given us a berry not only beautiful in shape and colour but delicately perfumed and refreshing.

Nothing compares with the flavour and fragrance of ripe strawberries. They have enough natural sweetness not to need sugar but this is really a matter of choice. They are wonderful on their own but take to other ingredients extremely kindly – cream, a sprinkling of red wine or orange juice, fresh cream cheese and, oddly enough, freshly ground black pepper. And when the time is ripe for an old-fashioned Loving Cup, fill 2 wine glasses with chilled demi-sec champagne, place a dish of sugar-strewn strawberries close by – and the rest is up to you. **See recipes.**

Strawberries Sarah Bernhardt

500 g (1 lb) strawberries, hulled; 3 tbsp caster sugar; 5 tbsp Cointreau; vanilla ice cream; 2 slices glacé (candied) pineapple, finely sliced. CREAM: 250 ml/8 fl oz (1 cup) double (heavy) cream; sugar; 1 tbsp Cointreau.

Place strawberries in a bowl, reserving 6 of the best for decoration. Sprinkle with caster sugar and Cointreau and chill for a few hours, covered. Place a scoop of vanilla ice cream in 6 individual dishes, sprinkle with

glacé (candied) pineapple and spoon over strawberries. Mask dessert with whipped cream, which has been sweetened and flavoured with Cointreau. Decorate each portion with a whole strawberry. Serves 6.

Strawberries Romanoff

8 pieces lump sugar (sugar cubes); 2 oranges; 6 tbsp Curaçao; 500 g (1 lb) strawberries, hulled; 250 ml/8 fl oz (1 cup) Crème Chantilly (page 88).

Rub lumps of sugar over skins of oranges until they are well impregnated with flavour of rind. Crush sugar and mix with Curaçao. Add strawberries and macerate in a covered container in refrigerator until serving time. Arrange strawberries in a bowl in a pyramid shape. Put crème chantilly into a piping (pastry) bag with a rose nozzle and decorate strawberries. Serves 6.

Venetian Strawberries

Believe it or not, the pepper enhances the strawberries' delicate flavour.

500 g (1 lb) strawberries, hulled; 4 tbsp caster sugar; freshly ground black pepper; 250 ml/8 fl oz (1 cup) demi-sec champagne.

Place strawberries in a bowl. Sprinkle with sugar and allow to stand for 10 minutes. Grind some black pepper over them, then pour over champagne. Stir carefully to combine the flavours. Serves 6.

Strawberries in the Snow

500 g (1 lb) strawberries, hulled and sliced; 125 g/4 oz (½ cup) caster sugar; 2 tbsp Kirsch (optional); 4 egg whites; 250 ml/8 fl oz (1 cup) double (heavy) cream.

Sprinkle strawberries with 1 tbsp caster sugar and the Kirsch. Allow to macerate for 15 minutes. Beat egg whites stiffly and gradually beat in remaining sugar. Whip cream stiffly. Fold egg whites into cream, then gently and

carefully mix with macerated strawberries. Spoon into a large bowl or individual dishes and serve chilled. Serves 6.

Strawberries Wilhemine

strawberries; Kirsch; caster sugar; orange juice; Crème Chantilly (page 88) to serve.

Macerate some fine large strawberries in Kirsch, caster sugar and orange juice. Serve with crème chantilly.

Strawberry Fool

Next to strawberries, sugar and cream, this must be the easiest and one of the nicest strawberry desserts.

strawberries – enough to make 250 ml/8 fl oz (2 cups) purée – hulled; 60 g/2 oz (¼ cup) caster sugar; 250 ml/8 fl oz (1 cup) double (heavy) cream.

Crush strawberries or purée in a blender. Sweeten with sugar. Whip cream until thick and fold into purée. Serve well chilled. Serves 4–6.

Baked Strawberry Soufflés

250 g (8 oz) strawberries, hulled and sliced; 125 g/4 oz (½ cup) plus 2 tbsp sugar; 2 tbsp Kirsch; 5 egg whites; whipped cream to serve.

Sprinkle sliced strawberries with 2 tbsp sugar and the Kirsch, and macerate for 1 hour. Butter 6 small soufflé dishes and use 2 tbsp sugar to coat sides and bottom. Beat egg whites until stiff, then gradually beat in remaining sugar to form a stiff meringue. Drain strawberries and fold through meringue, then spoon into dishes. Stand in a baking tin (pan) and add enough hot water to come halfway up sides of dishes. Bake in a preheated moderate oven (180°C/350°F, Gas Mark 4) for 15–18 minutes or until puffed and lightly browned. Serve at once, with whipped cream. Serves 6.

Strawberries à la Ritz

500 g (1 lb) strawberries, hulled; sugar; 250 g/8 oz (1½ cups) raspberries; 175 ml/6 fl oz (¾ cup) double (heavy) cream; candied violets or slivers candied angelica to decorate.

Place ⅔ of the strawberries in a glass serving bowl and sprinkle with sugar to taste. Sieve remaining strawberries with raspberries or purée in a blender or food processor. Spoon purée over whole strawberries and chill until serving time. When ready to serve, whip cream and spread over fruit, masking it completely. Decorate with candied violets or slivers of angelica. Serves 4.
NOTE: If fresh raspberries are not available, use frozen raspberries.

STROGANOFF

This superb dish of strips of fillet (tenderloin) of beef, lightly sautéed and finished off with sour cream, was said to have been created for a Russian Count (Stroganoff) as a light after-theatre supper dish. There are several schools of thought on how it was made and served. One is that it contained beef, seasonings, a touch of tomato purée (paste), sour cream and, just before serving, a hint of grated raw onion, and was served with straw potatoes as texture contrast. The accompaniment had to be ready at the same time as the Stroganoff, which should only take 15 minutes from start to finish. Triangles of hot buttered toast are another acceptable accompaniment.

A second popular version includes sautéed onions and mushrooms and is often served at dinner parties, accompanied by rice.

The two versions are given below, the first just right for two. For those who have come to enjoy onions and mushrooms in their Stroganoff as a main course, the quantities have been increased to cater for four.

It is not recommended you make Stroganoff for a crowd; the large quantity of meat tends to weep and alter the freshness of the dish. The exception is, of course, when being made in a professional kitchen with very large sauté pans. **See recipes.**

Beef Stroganoff (1)

370 g (12 oz) fillet (tenderloin) steak, in one piece; salt and freshly ground black pepper; 2 tsp flour; 30 g/1 oz (2 tbsp) butter; 2 tsp tomato purée (paste); 5 tbsp sour cream; 1 tsp grated onion.

Carefully trim away any fat and sinews from steak. Cut into slices about 5 mm (¼ in) thick, and then into strips about 5 cm (2 in) long and 5 mm (¼ in) wide. Season well with salt and pepper and toss in flour. Heat butter in a heavy frying pan (skillet). When foam subsides, add beef strips. Fry briskly over high heat for 3–4 minutes, keeping pieces of meat on the move by shaking pan. When meat is brown, lower heat and add tomato purée (paste) and sour cream. Stir to get up brown crusty bits from bottom of pan and to coat meat with creamy sauce. Adjust seasoning. Transfer to a small saucepan and place in a larger saucepan of boiling water to keep warm and mellow for about 5 minutes. Just before serving, stir in grated onion. Serve on heated plates with buttered toast points or crisp straw potatoes. Serves 2.

Beef Stroganoff (2)

750 g (1½ lb) fillet (tenderloin) steak, in one piece; salt and freshly ground black pepper; 1 tbsp flour; 60 g/2 oz (4 tbsp) butter; 2 medium onions, finely sliced into rings; 250 g/8 oz (2 cups) button mushrooms, finely sliced; 1 tbsp tomato purée (paste); 5 tbsp sour cream.

Prepare strips of steak as in *Beef Stroganoff (1)*. Season well with salt and pepper and toss in flour. Heat 30 g/1 oz (2 tbsp) of the butter in a heavy frying pan (skillet) and fry onion rings until just coloured, about 10 minutes. Remove to a plate with a slotted spoon. Add mushrooms to pan and fry for a few minutes or until softened. Remove to plate with onions. Add remaining butter to pan and heat. Fry beef strips over high heat for 3–4 minutes, shaking pan to keep pieces of meat on the move. Return onions and mushrooms to pan and shake over medium heat for 1 minute to heat through. Season generously with salt and pepper. Add tomato purée (paste) and sour cream and cook a few minutes longer, stirring gently to combine ingredients. Serve at once, or keep warm by transferring mixture to a saucepan and standing in a pan of hot water for 10 minutes with the lid on. Serve with straw potatoes, buttered noodles or boiled rice. Serves 4 as a main course or 6 as a first course.

STRUDEL

A delicate filled pastry which is usually associated with Austrian cooking, but is claimed as a speciality also by other parts of the former Austro-Hungarian Empire.

True strudel pastry is fascinating but time-consuming to make. Filo (phyllo) pastry sheets or puff pastry (paste), rolled as thin as possible, can be substituted with good results. **See recipes.**

See also Quick Apple Strudel (page 10).

Strudel Pastry

Strudel pastry should be made with high-gluten bread flour so that it will be strong enough to be stretched without tearing. The process of gently pulling and stretching the dough to paper thinness is easier if 2 people work from opposite sides. Have the strudel filling ready before stretching dough – once stretched, it should be used within 5 minutes or it will become brittle.

180 g/6 oz (1½ cups) bread flour; ¼ tsp salt; 1 egg; 120 ml/4 fl oz (½ cup) lukewarm water; 2 tbsp white vinegar; 2 tbsp vegetable oil; melted butter.

Sift flour and salt into a bowl. Beat egg until frothy, stir in water, vinegar and oil and add to flour. Mix with a wooden spoon until smooth, then turn dough out on to a lightly floured work surface. Knead thoroughly, scraping dough off surface as necessary with a knife. As you knead, keep lifting dough and slapping it down hard on the surface. It will be sticky at first but as you continue it will become elastic, smooth and shiny, leaving the hands clean. Kneading will take about 15 minutes and dough should be beaten 100–150 times. Shape it into a ball and cover with a warm bowl. Leave 20 minutes. Meantime, cover a table with a cloth that hangs over edges. Flour cloth well. Brush top of dough with melted butter and lift it on to the floured cloth. Roll out to 3 mm (⅛ in) thickness. Now slip your closed fists, thumbs tucked in and palms downward, under dough. Working from centre, lift and pull it out gently by pulling your hands apart. Work toward edges and move round table so that dough is evenly stretched on all sides. If dry patches appear in dough, brush with melted butter to keep them supple. If dough tears, pinch it together. When dough is as thin as paper, brush generously all over with melted butter and trim off thick edges with scissors. This quantity of dough will make one large strudel to serve 10–12. Fill and bake as directed in recipe.

Apple Strudel

6 large cooking apples, peeled, cored and thinly sliced; 125 g/4 oz (½ cup) caster sugar; 1½ tsp cinnamon; 90 g/3 oz (½ cup) sultanas (golden raisins); 2 tsp grated lemon rind; 1 quantity Strudel Pastry (see left); melted butter; 60 g/2 oz (1 cup) fresh breadcrumbs fried in butter.

Mix apples, sugar, cinnamon, sultanas (golden raisins) and lemon rind together and set aside. Brush stretched-out strudel pastry (dough) with melted butter and sprinkle with fried breadcrumbs. Spoon apple mixture in an 8–10 cm (3–4 in) wide line alone one side, to within 5 cm (2 in) of the edges. Fold edges of pastry (dough) over filling, and roll up, starting from filling end, by lifting the cloth to make the dough roll over and over on itself. Lift strudel on to a greased baking tray, curving it into a horseshoe if too long for the tray. Brush with more melted butter. Bake in a preheated hot oven (230°C/450°F, Gas Mark 8) for 10 minutes, then reduce heat to moderately hot (200°C/400°F, Gas Mark 6) and bake a further 20 minutes or until strudel is crisp and brown. Brush several more times with melted butter while cooking, and again after removing from oven. Serve warm, cut into wide diagonal slices. Serves 10–12.

NOTE: Strudel should be served freshly baked, as the pastry toughens when cold. However, it can be frozen unbaked and then baked straight from the freezer. Remove from freezer wrapping and place on a greased baking tray. Bake as directed in recipe, but allow an extra 15–20 minutes' baking time after reducing heat to

S

moderately hot (200°C/400°F, Gas Mark 6).
Test by inserting a fine skewer into the
centre; tip should be hot when withdrawn.
Cover strudel loosely with foil if pastry
(dough) is overbrowning before filling is
cooked through.

Cheese Strudel

*1 quantity Strudel Pastry (see opposite);
60 g/2 oz (1 cup) fresh breadcrumbs fried in
butter; melted butter.*
*FILLING: 60 g/2 oz (4 tbsp) butter; grated rind
1 lemon; 75 g/2½ oz (⅓ cup) caster sugar;
370 g/12 oz (1½ cups) creamed cottage
cheese; 2 tsp flour; 1 egg; 90 g/3 oz (½ cup)
sultanas (golden raisins), soaked in 2 tbsp
rum or brandy.*

To make filling, cream butter with lemon rind
and sugar, beating until mixture resembles
whipped cream. Rub cottage cheese through
a sieve, or purée in a food processor until
smooth. Using a wooden spoon, work
cheese and flour into butter mixture. Beat in
egg, and stir in fruit. Sprinkle stretched-out
strudel dough with breadcrumbs, then spoon
filling in a line along one long side to within
5 cm (2 in) of the edges. Fold edges of
dough over filling and brush with melted
butter. Roll up, starting from filling end, by
lifting cloth to make dough roll over and over
on itself. With the last roll, roll strudel on to a
greased baking tray; curve it into a horseshoe if too long for tray. Brush with more
melted butter. Bake in a preheated
moderately hot oven (200°C/400°F, Gas
Mark 6) for 20 minutes, then reduce heat to
moderate (180°C/350°F, Gas Mark 4) and
bake a further 10 minutes. Brush several
more times with melted butter while cooking.
Strudel is done when pastry (dough) is as
crisp as parchment and golden-brown. Serve
warm. Strudel can be made ahead and rewarmed in a cool oven. Serves 8.

Savoury Fish or Chicken Strudels

These strudels are made with filo (phyllo)
pastry. The recipe makes 2 strudels which
will cut into 5 servings each – nice for a
luncheon or small buffet party. These
strudels can be frozen.

*90 g/3 oz (6 tbsp) butter; 6 shallots, finely
chopped; 4 tbsp flour; 500 ml/18 fl oz
(2 cups) warm milk; salt and freshly ground
white pepper; ¼ tsp nutmeg; 6 hard-boiled
(hard-cooked) eggs, coarsely chopped;
750 g (1½ lb) fish fillets, poached, drained
and flaked, or 500 g/1 lb (2 cups) chopped
cooked chicken meat; 10 g/⅓ oz (¼ cup) finely
chopped parsley; 60 g/2 oz (½ cup) grated
cheese; ½ tsp French (Dijon) mustard;
340 g/11 oz (16 sheets) filo (phyllo) pastry;
melted butter.*

Melt butter in a heavy saucepan, add shallots
and cook gently for 3 minutes. Stir in flour
and cook for 1 minute. Remove from heat,
cool a little and add warm milk, stirring until
smoothly blended. Return to heat and stir
until boiling. Season to taste with salt,
pepper and nutmeg. Allow to cool, then mix
with chopped eggs, fish or chicken, parsley,
cheese and mustard.

Make one strudel at a time. Remove 8
sheets filo (phyllo) from packet, unfold on to
a dry tea-towel and cover with another dry
tea-towel, then a damp one and set aside.
Take one of the remaining 8 sheets of filo
(phyllo), place on a dry tea-towel and brush
with melted butter. Top with another sheet,
butter it, and so on with the remaining
sheets. Spoon half the filling in a line along
one long side of stacked pastry to within
5 cm (2 in) of edges. Fold edges of pastry
over filling and brush with melted butter.
Using the tea-towel to help, gently roll up
strudel from filling end. With the last roll, roll
strudel on to a greased baking tray. Brush
with melted butter. Make another strudel in
the same way. Bake the strudels in a
preheated moderately hot oven (200°C/
400°F, Gas Mark 6) for 20 minutes, then
reduce heat to moderate (180°C/
350°F, Gas Mark 4) and bake a further 10
minutes. Brush several more times with
melted butter while cooking. Strudel is done
when pastry is as crisp as parchment and
golden-brown. Serve hot, in wide slices.

Strudels can be made ahead and reheated
in a preheated moderate oven (180°C/
350°F, Gas Mark 4), covering loosely with
foil if tops are overbrowning. Serves 10.

STUFFING

Stuffings are made with a wide variety of
ingredients – breadcrumbs, sausage and
other minced (ground) meats, fruit, and rice.
As well as adding an interesting flavour, a
stuffing can help the cook by holding the food
in shape, keeping it moist and making it go
further.

It is important to mix and handle stuffings
lightly so as not to compact them, and to
leave room for the stuffings to expand during
cooking and stay light. If some stuffing is left
over after filling food, cook it separately in a
greased baking dish.

It is best to cook onion and garlic lightly
before adding them to a stuffing, as this
improves the flavour and aids digestion. You
should also pre-cook pork or sausage meat
until it changes colour, to make sure that it
will cook through. Always stuff poultry just
before cooking; this is a safety measure.

Make fresh breadcrumbs for stuffings,
using bread 2–4 days old, by pulling it apart
very lightly with your fingers or with two forks.
Do not put bread through a mincer (grinder)
as the stuffing will be too compact. Of course,
if you have a blender or food processor,
beautiful crumbs can be made in a trice. **See
recipes.**

Basic Breadcrumb Stuffing

*1 small onion, chopped; 1 stick celery with
leaves, chopped; 90 g/3 oz (6 tbsp) butter;
1–2 tsp poultry seasoning or dried sage; ½ tsp
salt; freshly ground black pepper; 2 tbsp
chopped parsley (optional); 310 g/10 oz
(5 cups) stale bread cubes or crumbs; water,
milk or giblet broth (optional).*

Sauté onion and celery in butter until soft but
not brown. Combine with poultry seasoning
or sage, salt, pepper, parsley and bread
cubes or crumbs. If a moist dressing is
desired, add enough liquid barely to moisten
crumbs. Makes sufficient for 2 chickens or 1
small turkey.

VARIATIONS

Breadcrumb Chestnut Stuffing: Follow recipe
for Basic Breadcrumb Stuffing, reducing
quantity of breadcrumbs to 210 g/7 oz
(3½ cups), and adding 125 g/4 oz (1 cup)
boiled, coarsely chopped chestnuts. To
prepare chestnuts, cut a cross in flat side of
each shell. Boil in water to cover 20 minutes
or until tender. Shell, peel and chop.
(Alternatively use canned chestnuts.)
Mushroom Stuffing: Cook 250 g/8 oz
(2 cups) sliced mushrooms in butter with
chopped onion, then proceed as for Basic
Breadcrumb Stuffing.
Sausage Stuffing: Crumble 125–180 g/
4–6 oz (½–¾ cup) sausage meat and brown in
a frying pan (skillet). Remove sausage and
sauté onion and celery in part sausage fat

and part butter. Add all to crumbs and proceed as for Basic Breadcrumb Stuffing.

Apple, Prune and Nut Stuffing

90 g/3 oz (6 tbsp) butter; 1 onion, finely chopped; 2 cooking apples, peeled, cored and finely diced; 250 g/8 oz (4 cups) cubed day-old bread; 180 g/6 oz (1 cup) chopped stoned prunes; 30 g/1 oz ($\frac{1}{4}$ cup) chopped walnuts; 60 g/2 oz ($\frac{1}{2}$ cup) pine nuts; 20 g/$\frac{2}{3}$ oz ($\frac{1}{2}$ cup) chopped parsley; 1 tsp chopped fresh sage, or pinch dried; salt and freshly ground black pepper.

Melt butter in a heavy frying pan (skillet) and sauté onion until soft and golden. Add apples to pan and cook for 3–4 minutes or until apple is soft. Meanwhile, lightly toast bread cubes in a preheated moderate oven (160°C/325°F, Gas Mark 3) for 10 minutes or until crisp. Remove apples and onion with a slotted spoon and place in a bowl with prunes. In same pan, lightly fry walnuts and pine nuts until golden. Combine nuts with apple mixture and bread cubes, and fold through parsley and sage. Season with salt and pepper, and use at once. Makes sufficient for a goose or large duckling.

Mushroom Rice Stuffing

2 rashers (slices) streaky bacon, rind removed and chopped; 30 g/1 oz (2 tbsp) butter; 1 tbsp finely chopped onion; 90 g/3 oz ($\frac{3}{4}$ cup) mushrooms, finely chopped; 125 g/4 oz (1 cup) cooked rice; 1 tbsp chopped parsley; 2 tbsp chopped mixed fresh herbs, or 1 tsp dried; salt and freshly ground black pepper; lemon juice.

Gently fry bacon over medium heat until fat runs. Add butter, onion and mushrooms and fry until soft. Stir in rice, parsley and herbs, and season with salt, pepper and lemon juice. Makes sufficient to stuff 4 tomatoes or peppers, or 1 large fish or marrow (squash).

Ham and Spinach Stuffing

$\frac{1}{2}$ bunch spinach; salt and freshly ground black pepper; nutmeg; 250 g/8 oz (1 cup) finely chopped cooked ham; 1 small onion, finely chopped; 30 g/1 oz (2 tbsp) butter; 60 g/2 oz (1 cup) fresh breadcrumbs.

Place spinach in a heavy saucepan with a

little salt, pepper and nutmeg. Cover pan and cook for 3–4 minutes until softened, shaking occasionally to prevent sticking. Drain well and, when cool enough to handle, squeeze out as much water as possible with your hands. Chop spinach finely and place in a bowl with ham. Season with salt and pepper. Cook onion gently in butter until soft and golden. Add to spinach and ham with a pinch of nutmeg and the breadcrumbs and mix ingredients lightly together with a fork. Adjust seasoning. Makes sufficient to stuff a shoulder of veal for roasting or a breast of veal for braising.

Sausage or Meat Stuffing

Use for turkey, chicken and veal.

1 medium onion, finely chopped; 15 g/$\frac{1}{2}$ oz (1 tbsp) butter; 500 g/1 lb (2 cups) minced (ground) pork or sausage meat; 1 tbsp chopped parsley; 1 tsp dried sage; good pinch ground mace; 60 g/2 oz (1 cup) fresh white breadcrumbs; salt and freshly ground black pepper.

Cook onion in butter until soft, then add meat and cook, stirring and breaking down lumps with a fork, until meat changes colour. Remove from heat and lightly mix in remaining ingredients. Cool before using. Makes sufficient to stuff breast of 1 × 6 kg (12 lb) turkey, or 2 chickens or 2 boned shoulders of veal.

Herb Stuffing

Use for fish, poultry or meat.

1 small onion, finely chopped; 30 g/1 oz (2 tbsp) butter; 125 g/4 oz (2 cups) fresh breadcrumbs; 1 tbsp chopped fresh herbs, or 1 tsp dried (see Note); 2 tbsp chopped parsley; 1 tsp grated lemon rind; $\frac{1}{2}$ tsp salt; freshly ground black pepper; 1 egg, beaten; stock or water.

Cook onion gently in butter until golden. In a bowl, mix together breadcrumbs, herbs, parsley, lemon rind, salt and a generous amount of pepper. Add onion and butter, egg, and enough stock or water to moisten

stuffing very lightly. Do not overmix, just stir through with a fork. Makes sufficient to stuff a chicken, a large whole fish, or a shoulder of lamb.
NOTE: Use sage or savory for duck or goose; lemon thyme for fish, chicken or veal; mint for lamb.

Baltimore Oyster Stuffing

2 tbsp bacon fat; 1 tbsp chopped parsley; 2 tsp snipped chives; 310 g/10 oz (5 cups) stale bread cubes or crumbs; 1 tsp chopped fresh marjoram or thyme; 1 tsp salt; freshly ground black pepper; 25 canned oysters, drained.

Melt bacon fat, add parsley and chives and cook until wilted. Add herb mixture to bread with marjoram, salt and pepper. Lightly mix in oysters. If stuffing seems too dry, moisten with a little oyster liquor. Makes sufficient for 2 chickens or 1 × 3 kg (6 lb) turkey.

Mandarin Stuffing for Goose

250 g/8 oz (2 cups) chestnuts; 60 g/2 oz (4 tbsp) butter; 60 g/2 oz ($\frac{1}{2}$ cup) diced celery with leaves; 3 mandarins; 1 × 250 g (8 oz) packet prepared bread stuffing; $\frac{1}{2}$ tsp poultry seasoning; 370 g/12 oz (3 cups) cooked rice; 120 ml/4 fl oz ($\frac{1}{2}$ cup) stock or water.

Cut a cross in flat side of each chestnut. Boil in water to cover for 20 minutes or until tender. Shell, peel and chop. There should be about 125 g/4 oz (1 cup). Melt butter in a frying pan (skillet), add celery and cook over medium heat about 10 minutes. Meanwhile, peel the mandarins, removing white membranes. Cut segments in half and remove seeds. Combine mandarins, bread stuffing, chestnuts, poultry seasoning, rice and stock. Add cooked celery and butter and mix together lightly with a fork. Makes sufficient for 1 × 4.5 kg (9 lb) goose.
NOTE: Canned chestnuts may be used instead of fresh. Just drain and chop.

Peach and Rosemary Stuffing

60 g/2 oz (1 cup) fresh white breadcrumbs; 1 tsp chopped fresh rosemary, or $\frac{1}{2}$ tsp dried; 4 canned peach halves, chopped; $\frac{1}{2}$ egg, beaten; salt and freshly ground black pepper.

Combine all ingredients. Makes sufficient to stuff a 2 kg (4$\frac{1}{2}$ lb) boned shoulder of lamb.

Potato and Parsley Stuffing

Use as a stuffing for duck or chicken. For a goose or small turkey, double the quantities.

1 tbsp beef dripping; 1 onion, chopped; 250 g/8 oz (1 cup) pork sausage meat; 250 g/8 oz (1 cup) freshly mashed potatoes; salt and freshly ground black pepper; 20 g/$\frac{2}{3}$ oz ($\frac{1}{2}$ cup) chopped parsley.

Melt dripping in a frying pan (skillet) and fry onion until pale golden. Stir in sausage meat, breaking it up as it cooks and browns. Remove pan from heat and mix in potatoes, salt, pepper and parsley. Cool before using. Makes sufficient for a chicken or duckling.

Rice Stuffing with Herbs

Use as a stuffing for vegetables. It is also excellent as a stuffing for a roasting chicken.

250 g/8 oz (1⅓ cups) long-grain rice; 45 g/1½ oz (3 tbsp) butter; 1 onion, chopped; 4 rashers (slices) streaky bacon, rind removed and chopped; salt and freshly ground black pepper; 6 tbsp chopped mixed fresh herbs (chervil, tarragon, dill, mint, parsley and chives).

Cook rice in boiling salted water until almost tender; drain. Melt butter in a frying pan (skillet) and cook onion until translucent. Add bacon and fry, stirring, until lightly coloured. Remove from heat and stir in rice, salt and pepper. Stir in herbs. Makes about 750 g/1½ lb (3 cups).

SUCCOTASH

Americans learned to make succotash from the Indians, who cooked corn and beans in a pot together. Serve succotash hot, well seasoned with plenty of pepper, as a side dish for roast pork, poultry or beef, or with ham steaks.

Succotash

180 g/6 oz (1 cup) canned baby broad (lima) beans, drained; 180 g/6 oz (1 cup) canned sweetcorn (whole kernel corn), drained; salt; ½ tsp black pepper; pinch cayenne; ½ tsp sugar; 30 g/1 oz (2 tbsp) butter; chopped parsley.

Rinse beans and corn under cold running water. Place in a saucepan with salt, pepper, cayenne, sugar and butter. Heat very gently, stirring now and again, until piping hot. Sprinkle with chopped parsley to serve. Serves 4.

SUCKING PIG

See Pork.

SUET

The firm, white fat around lamb and beef kidneys. Beef suet is the kind you will usually find, and is the one to use when a recipe calls for suet. It can be bought in solid form from the butcher, or grated and packaged, usually with a little added flour, ready for use. To prepare butcher's suet, chill it first to make it firmer, then remove membrane and grate or chop fine.

Boiled Plum Pudding

This is not as heavy as the usual pudding and has no spices, but develops a marvellous flavour after two weeks' maturation.

150 g/5 oz (scant 1 cup) raisins, coarsely chopped; 125 g/4 oz (⅔ cup) stoned dates, coarsely chopped; 150 g/5 oz (scant 1 cup) sultanas (golden raisins); 125 g/4 oz (⅔ cup) currants; 90 g/3 oz (½ cup) chopped mixed candied peel; 4 tbsp brandy; 500 g/1 lb (4 cups) self-raising flour; 1 tsp salt; 250 g/8 oz (1 cup) beef suet, grated; 250 g/8 oz (1 cup) caster sugar; 180 g/ 6 oz (½ cup) black treacle (molasses); 350 ml/12 fl oz (1½ cups) water; extra brandy to serve.

Soak fruit and peel in brandy overnight. Sift flour and salt into a large mixing bowl. Rub (cut) suet into flour until mixture resembles crumbs. Stir in sugar, brandy-soaked fruit and treacle (molasses) mixed with water. Mix thoroughly to a firm batter. Rinse a large pudding cloth in boiling water, remove (using rubber gloves) and wring out well. Sift flour over and shake off any excess. Turn pudding mixture into centre of cloth and gather cloth firmly around pudding. Secure cloth tightly with string. Tie ends of pudding cloth around a wooden spoon and rest wooden spoon on edges of saucepan to prevent pudding touching bottom of pan. Pour boiling water into pan to cover pudding and place a lid on top. Steam for 1 hour. By this time, pudding will have taken shape and wooden spoon may be removed. Steam for a further 2½ hours. Hang pudding in a dark, dry place for at least 2 weeks to mature. On day it is to be eaten, steam pudding for a further 1–1½ hours. Unwrap and turn on to a heated platter. Heat some brandy, set alight and pour flaming over pudding, taking it immediately to the table. Serve with vanilla ice cream, whipped cream or Hard Sauce (see page 154). Serves 8–10.
NOTE: Do not worry if a little mould forms on the cloth while the pudding is maturing. Just wipe it off if possible and boil the pudding as instructed in the recipe. Never, never place the pudding in a clean cloth. This will let the water in as soon as you boil it, ruining your pudding.

Shaping Boiled Plum Pudding

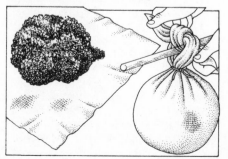

SUKIYAKI

Perhaps Japan's most famous dish: beef and vegetables cooked with soy sauce and saké at the table. An electric frypan (skillet) is ideal for the purpose. The cooking time is brief and the food is cooked and eaten in several batches. To cut the beef into paper-thin slices, wrap first in plastic wrap and place in freezer until firm enough to slice easily.

Sukiyaki

2 onions, finely sliced; 6 spring onions (scallions) cut into 5 cm (2 in) lengths; 1 aubergine (eggplant), finely sliced; 125 g/4 oz (1½ cups) Chinese cabbage (bok choy), cut into 6 cm (2½ in) strips; 6 dried mushrooms, soaked in warm water for 30 minutes, drained, stalks removed and sliced; 125 g/4 oz (2 cups) bean sprouts; 1 × 225 g/ 7½ oz can bamboo shoots, drained and cut into wedges; 1 kg (2 lb) beef fillet (tenderloin), cut into paper-thin slices; 60 g/2 oz (¼ cup) beef suet, chopped; light soy sauce; sugar to taste; 1–2 tbsp saké or dry sherry; 250 ml/8 fl oz (1 cup) beef stock; 125 g/4 oz (½ cup) bean curd; 60 g (2 oz) rice vermicelli, cut into 10 cm (4 in) lengths.
TO SERVE: *eggs; soy sauce; boiled rice.*

Arrange vegetables and beef in separate rows on a platter. Heat a large iron pan or electric frypan (skillet). Rub with some suet, then fry fat for 5 minutes or until pan is well greased. Remove any pieces of suet. Sauté batch of onions and spring onions (scallions) for 5 minutes, stirring frequently. Add batch of remaining vegetables, soy sauce and sugar and wine, then moisten with stock. Add some bean curd and cook over high heat for 5 minutes, stirring frequently. Push all ingredients to side of pan, add batch of beef and cook, stirring, for 3 minutes, adding some vermicelli for the last minute. Guests help themselves from the pan, to which more meat and vegetables are added for second helpings. Before cooking second helping add more suet. Traditionally, each diner breaks a raw egg into his bowl, beats it lightly with chopsticks, adds a little soy sauce if liked, and then dips hot food in it before eating, but some prefer to omit this step. Serve with boiled rice. Serves 6–8.

SULTANA

A variety of seedless white grape once grown only in Smyrna, Turkey. Today sultanas are grown in many parts of the world where they are dried either naturally in the sun or artificially. In North America seedless white raisins or sultanas are called golden raisins.

Sultanas are nutritious and delicious eaten as a snack on their own. Children love to find a little packet of sultanas in their school lunch-boxes or mixed with a little salad of grated carrot and cheese. Sultanas also appear in many cakes, biscuits (cookies), puddings and in some savoury dishes, particularly those containing rice. **See recipes.**

See also *Fruit, Dried and Candied.*

Sultana Rice

500 ml/18 fl oz (2 cups) water; 1 tsp salt; 1 slice lemon; 45 g/1½ oz (¼ cup) sultanas (golden raisins); 210 g/7 oz (1 cup) long-grain rice; 2 tbsp chopped parsley.

Place water in saucepan and bring to the boil. Add salt, lemon slice and sultanas (golden raisins) and sprinkle in rice. Return to the boil and stir once or twice, then turn heat as low as possible, cover pan and steam gently for 20–25 minutes. Do not lift lid or stir during steaming time. Remove from heat, fork through rice to allow steam to escape and fold in parsley. Serve with pork, poultry, ham and veal dishes. Serves 4.

Turkish Sultana Compote

370 g/12 oz (2 cups) sultanas (golden raisins); 120 ml/4 fl oz (½ cup) warm water; 180 g/6 oz (½ cup) honey; grated rind 1 lemon; 60 g/2 oz (½ cup) pine nuts; 250 ml/8 fl oz (1 cup) plain yogurt to serve.

Soak sultanas (golden raisins) in cold water to cover for 1 hour. Drain. Boil together warm water and honey for 2–3 minutes. Stir in sultanas (golden raisins) and lemon rind. Simmer over gentle heat for 10 minutes, skimming with slotted spoon if necessary. Stir in pine nuts. Chill thoroughly before serving with yogurt. Serves 4–6.

Sultana and Cashew Pilau

60 g/2 oz (4 tbsp) ghee; 1 onion, finely chopped; 430 g/14 oz (2 cups) long-grain rice; salt and freshly ground black pepper; 1 litre/1¾ pints (4 cups) boiling chicken stock;

60 g/2 oz (½ cup) cashew nuts; 90 g/3 oz (½ cup) sultanas (golden raisins).

Melt 30 g/1 oz (2 tbsp) ghee in a heavy saucepan, add onion and cook gently until golden. Stir in rice, season with salt and pepper and cook gently until rice becomes coated with ghee and turns translucent. Pour boiling stock over rice, stir once and return to the boil. Lower heat, cover and simmer very gently for about 20 minutes or until liquid is absorbed and rice is tender. Remove lid and cook for 2 minutes more. Heat remaining ghee and fry cashews and sultanas (golden raisins) for 2–3 minutes, stirring constantly. Turn contents of pan into rice and fork through. Serves 8–10.

Sultana Bread

370 g/12 oz (3 cups) flour; 3 tsp baking powder; 180 g/6 oz (¾ cup) butter; 180 g/6 oz (¾ cup) caster sugar; 225 g/7½ oz (1¼ cups) sultanas (golden raisins); 3 eggs; 1 tsp vanilla essence (extract); about 120 ml/4 fl oz (½ cup) milk.

Sift flour and baking powder into a large mixing bowl. Rub (cut) in butter with fingertips, then add sugar and sultanas (golden raisins). Make a well in centre. Lightly mix eggs and vanilla and pour into well. Mix with a fork to a soft dough, adding milk as necessary. Spoon into a greased and lined 23 × 12 cm (9 × 5 in) loaf tin (pan), spreading evenly. Bake in a preheated moderate oven (180°C/350°F, Gas Mark 4) for 1½ hours. Reduce temperature to 160°C/325°F, Gas Mark 3 after baking for 1 hour if loaf is getting too brown. When done, a skewer inserted in centre will come out clean. Serve sliced and buttered.

Sultana Cake

This cake is beautifully moist and will keep for up to 10 days when stored in an airtight container.

250 g/8 oz (1 cup) butter; 250 g/8 oz (1 cup) sugar; 3 eggs; 150 ml/¼ pint (⅔ cup) milk; 280 g/9 oz (1½ cups) sultanas (golden raisins); 3 tbsp almonds, blanched and chopped; 3 tbsp chopped mixed candied peel; 370 g/12 oz (3 cups) flour; 1½ tsp baking powder.

Beat butter with sugar until light and fluffy. Add eggs and mix well. Stir in milk gradually, then add sultanas (golden raisins), almonds and peel. Fold in flour and baking powder sifted together. Spoon into a greased and bottom-lined 20 cm (8 in) round or square cake tin (pan). Bake in a preheated moderate oven (160°C/325°F, Gas Mark 3) for about 1½ hours or until a skewer inserted in centre comes out clean. Leave to cool on a wire rack.

Sultana Spice Cake

180 g/6 oz (1 cup) firmly packed brown sugar; 180 g/6 oz (1 cup) sultanas (golden raisins); 300 ml/½ pint (1¼ cups) water; 125 g/4 oz (½ cup) butter; 1 tsp cinnamon; ½ tsp nutmeg; ½ tsp ground allspice; 250 g/8 oz (2 cups) flour; 1 tsp bicarbonate of soda (baking soda); 1 tsp baking powder; ½ tsp salt.

Combine sugar, sultanas (golden raisins), water, butter and spices in a heavy saucepan. Bring to the boil and boil for 5 minutes. Allow to become completely cold. Sift flour, soda, baking powder and salt, and stir into boiled mixture. Pour into a greased and lined 21 × 15 cm (8½ × 6 in) loaf tin (pan) or a 20 cm (8 in) ring tin (pan). Bake in a preheated moderate oven (180°C/350°F, Gas Mark 4) for 50–60 minutes or until a skewer inserted in centre comes out clean. Turn out on to a wire rack, carefully remove lining paper and cool.

Sultana Fingers

125 g/4 oz (½ cup) butter; 180 g/6 oz (1 cup) sultanas (golden raisins); 125 g/4 oz (½ cup) sugar; 1 egg, lightly beaten; 1 tsp vanilla essence (extract); 250 g/8 oz (3 cups) digestive biscuits (vanilla wafers), finely crushed; 30 g/1 oz (¼ cup) crushed mixed nuts.
CHOCOLATE ICING (FROSTING): *140 g/4½ oz (1 cup) icing (confectioners) sugar; 2 tbsp unsweetened cocoa powder; 30 g/1 oz (2 tbsp) butter, melted; 1 tbsp hot water; ½ tsp vanilla essence (extract).*

Place butter, sultanas (golden raisins) and sugar in a large saucepan and bring slowly to the boil, stirring to dissolve sugar. Remove from heat and cool slightly, then add egg and vanilla essence (extract), beating well. Add biscuit (wafer) crumbs and blend thoroughly. Press mixture into a well-greased 28 × 19 cm (11 × 7½ in) Swiss roll tin (jelly roll pan).
CHOCOLATE ICING (FROSTING): Sift icing (confectioners) sugar and cocoa together, add remaining ingredients and mix well until smooth and glossy. When biscuit (cookie) mixture is cold, spread with icing (frosting) and sprinkle with chopped nuts. Leave until icing (frosting) is set then cut into 2.5 cm (1 in) fingers before serving. Makes about 20.

Sultana Sesame Biscuits

125 g/4 oz (½ cup) butter; 125 g/4 oz (½ cup) sugar; 1 egg; 1 tsp cinnamon; 90 g/3 oz (½ cup) toasted sesame seeds; 90 g/3 oz (½ cup) sultanas (golden raisins); 125 g/4 oz (1 cup) wholewheat flour, sifted.

Cream butter with sugar until light and fluffy. Add egg and beat well. Stir in remaining ingredients and blend well. Spread mixture in a greased 28 × 19 cm (11 × 7½ in) Swiss roll tin (jelly roll pan). Bake in a preheated moderate oven (180°C/350°F, Gas Mark 4) for 20 minutes. Remove from oven, cut into fingers and allow to cool in tin (pan). Makes 24.

SUMMER PUDDING

One of the loveliest fruit puddings of the world is English Summer Pudding. Humble white bread is used as a container for the delicious berry fruits of summer.

Summer Pudding

½ loaf sliced white bread, slightly stale, crusts removed; 500 g (1 lb) strawberries, hulled; 500 g/1 lb (3 cups) raspberries or other berry fruit of your choice (fresh or frozen); 180 g/6 oz (¾ cup) sugar; double (heavy) cream to serve.

Use most of bread slices to line bottom and sides of a greased 1.5–2 litre/2½–3½ pint pudding basin (6–8 cup heatproof mixing bowl). Cut slices to fit basin (bowl) and overlap bread to ensure there are no spaces through which fruit juice can escape. Place fruit in a saucepan with just water clinging to it from rinsing. (Frozen fruit is not rinsed.) Sprinkle sugar over. Cover and cook very gently for 3 minutes or until sugar has dissolved. Leave to cool. Fill bread-lined basin (bowl) with fruit, adding enough fruit juice to soak surrounding bread. Reserve remaining juice. Cover top of pudding with more bread slices cut to fit, place a plate on top and weight with a couple of cans. Chill overnight. Unmould pudding on to a deep serving platter, pour reserved juice over and serve with thick cream. Serves 6–8.
NOTE: You may omit the strawberries and substitute other berry fruits if you wish.
VARIATION
Individual Summer Puddings: Line 6 × 250 ml/8 fl oz (1 cup) individual soufflé dishes with bread (you may need to use more bread than in above recipe) and proceed as above. Weight each dish with small plates, saucers or several thicknesses of foil with a can on top. Chill overnight. Serve as above. Serves 6.

SUNDAE

A concoction of ice cream and sauce, syrup, fruit, whipped cream, chopped nuts, grated chocolate – the combinations limited only by your imagination and degree of nonchalance about digestion or waistline. The name and the dish are attributed to the ingenuity of an American, who complied with a law forbidding the sale of ice cream sodas on a Sunday, by simply omitting the soda (carbonated) water and calling the new dish after the day.

Serve a sundae in a long, shallow dish, in a tall glass or, for a grand effect, in a brandy balloon. **See recipes.**

Banana Split

2–3 scoops vanilla ice cream; 1 banana, halved lengthways; Hot Chocolate Sauce (page 73); whipped cream; chopped nuts; 1 glacé (candied) cherry; 1 cream wafer biscuit (vanilla wafer).

Arrange ice cream along a shallow dish. Place half banana on each side of ice cream. Spoon over chocolate sauce, decorate with whipped cream and nuts and top with a cherry. Serve at once, with a wafer cream biscuit (vanilla wafer). Serves 1.

Triple Strawberry Sundae

4–6 strawberries; 120 ml/4 fl oz (½ cup) whipped cream; 1 scoop strawberry ice cream; 2 scoops vanilla or chocolate ice cream; 1 langue de chat or other crisp finger biscuit (lady finger).
STRAWBERRY SAUCE: 6–8 strawberries, hulled; 1 tbsp caster sugar.

To make sauce, mash strawberries with caster sugar. Chill well.
    Reserve one large, perfect, unhulled strawberry for decoration. Take out about 2 tbsp whipped cream and set aside for decoration. Hull and slice remaining strawberries and fold into remaining cream. Arrange 1 scoop each strawberry and vanilla ice cream in a dish or glass. Pile strawberry and cream mixture on top, then remaining scoop of vanilla ice cream. Spoon sauce over and decorate with reserved cream and strawberry. Serve with a langue de chat or sponge finger (lady finger). Serves 1.

Hot Marshmallow Sundae

3 scoops coffee or chocolate ice cream; 2 halves canned or fresh pears or peaches, or 4 halves apricots; 175 ml/6 fl oz (¾ cup) hot

Marshmallow Sauce (page 204); slivered, toasted almonds.

Arrange ice cream and fruit in a dish or glass. Pour over hot sauce and scatter with almonds. Serve immediately. Serves 1.

SUPREME OF CHICKEN
(Suprême de Volaille)

A boneless, skinless half-breast of chicken, often sold in poultry shops as a 'chicken fillet'.
    Supremes are very versatile, easy to cook for one or for a stylish dinner party.
☐ **Basic Preparation:** Cut and pull out the white tendon that runs down the underside of the meat. Trim edges neatly, then flatten and shape the supremes with your hands. To beat a supreme flat, place it between 2 sheets of greased greaseproof (waxed) paper and beat gently with a cutlet bat, rolling pin or the flat side of a meat mallet, to a thickness of 5 mm (¼ in). **See recipes.**

Sautéed Supremes of Chicken

4 supremes chicken; seasoned flour; 2 tbsp oil; 60 g/2 oz (4 tbsp) butter; lemon wedges or pan sauce of your choice (see page 422).

Turn the supremes in seasoned flour and pat off excess. Heat oil in a frying pan (skillet), add butter and, just as it begins to turn brown, add supremes, flat side down. Sauté on moderately high heat for 3 minutes, turn and sauté other side for 2 minutes. Press chicken with your finger. If it feels springy, it is ready. If still soft and yielding, cook 1 minute longer and check again. Be careful not to overcook; if cooked until there is no springiness, supremes are overdone and will be tough and dry. Remove to a heated serving dish and serve with lemon wedges, or keep hot a minute or two while making one of the pan sauces on the next page or one of the Pan Sauces on page 369. Serves 2–4.

White-Cooked Supremes of Chicken

4 supremes chicken; ½ tsp lemon juice; salt and freshly ground white pepper; 60 g/2 oz (4 tbsp) butter; 1 quantity hot Sauce Suprême, Poulette, Bercy, Mushroom or other sauce of your choice to serve (see Sauces); bouquet of fresh watercress or parsley sprigs to garnish.

Rub supremes with lemon juice and season lightly with salt and pepper. Heat butter in a flameproof casserole or baking dish large enough to take supremes in one layer. When butter is foaming, add supremes and turn over quickly so that they are coated with butter. Lay a piece of buttered greaseproof (waxed) paper over chicken, cover dish and place in a preheated moderately hot oven (200°C/400°F, Gas Mark 6). Cook for 6 minutes, then press chicken with your finger. If it feels springy, it is ready. If still soft and yielding, cover, cook 1 minute longer and check again. Be careful not to overcook. If cooked until there is no springiness, supremes are overdone and will be tough and dry. Remove supremes to a heated serving platter and mask with sauce. Garnish with a bouquet of watercress or parsley and serve immediately. Serves 2–4.

NOTE: If preferred, supremes can be served with any of the pan sauces below, using the butter and juices remaining in the dish.

PAN SAUCES TO SERVE WITH SUPREMES OF CHICKEN

Fines Herbes Sauce

30 g/1 oz (2 tbsp) butter; 2 tsp lemon juice; 2 tbsp finely chopped mixed herbs (parsley, chives, tarragon, chervil).

After removing supremes, add butter to pan in which they were sautéed and heat. When foaming, add lemon juice and herbs. Remove from heat, swirl sauce in pan to combine and pour over supremes.

Shallot and Wine Sauce

1 tbsp finely chopped shallots; 4 tbsp port or Madeira; 120 ml/4 fl oz (½ cup) brown beef stock; salt and freshly ground white pepper; 1 tbsp chopped parsley.

After removing supremes, add shallots to fat remaining in pan and sauté on moderate heat for 1 minute. Stir in port or Madeira and beef stock and boil on high heat until reduced by half. Season with salt and pepper, stir in chopped parsley and pour over supremes; serve immediately.

Mushroom Cream Sauce

30 g/1 oz (2 tbsp) butter; 1 small leek or onion, finely chopped; 8 button mushrooms, thinly sliced; 5 tbsp single (light) cream; salt and freshly ground white pepper.

After removing supremes, add butter to pan in which they were sautéed and heat. When foaming, add leek or onion and mushrooms. Sauté on fairly high heat, stirring once or twice, for 3 minutes. Stir in cream and boil until sauce thickens. Season to taste with salt and pepper and spoon over supremes.

Cognac Cream Sauce

2 tbsp cognac; 5 tbsp cream or Crème Fraîche (page 88); 1 tbsp dry sherry; salt and freshly ground white pepper.

Cook supremes only 2 minutes on each side. Leave them in the pan, pour cognac over and set alight. When flames subside, add cream or crème fraîche and dry sherry. Allow to boil, season to taste with salt and pepper. Remove supremes to a heated platter and pour sauce over. Serve immediately.

SWEDE/TURNIP

See Turnip and Swede.

SWEET AND SOUR SAUCE

This famous Chinese sauce varies a little from region to region. It is often cooked as part of a dish such as Sweet and Sour Pork, but the sauce below can be prepared separately to use as a dip for meatballs, fried wonton and other hot hors d'oeuvre. **See recipes.**

Sweet and Sour Sauce for Dipping

3 tbsp soy sauce; 3 tbsp sugar; 3 tbsp vinegar; 2 tbsp tomato ketchup; 2 tbsp dry sherry; 1½ tbsp cornflour (cornstarch) mixed with 8 tbsp cold water.

Mix all ingredients, except cornflour (cornstarch) and water, in a small saucepan and bring to the boil. Stir cornflour (cornstarch) mixture again and pour into boiling liquid. Cook, stirring constantly, until sauce clears and thickens. Makes about 350 ml/12 fl oz (1½ cups).

Sweet and Sour Pork

750 g (1½ lb) fairly lean boneless pork, cut into 2 cm (¾ in) cubes; ½ tsp salt; 1 tbsp soy sauce; 1 tbsp cornflour (cornstarch); 4 tbsp water; 1 egg, beaten; 1 medium onion; oil; 1 green or red pepper, cored, seeded and cut into strips.
SAUCE: 2½ tbsp sugar; 2 tbsp vinegar; 2 tsp cornflour (cornstarch); 1½ tbsp soy sauce; 1 tbsp sherry; 1½ tbsp fresh tomato purée; 5 tbsp water.

Sprinkle pork cubes with salt and rub meat between your hands to work salt in, then sprinkle with soy sauce and leave for 1 hour, turning meat over several times. Mix cornflour (cornstarch) with water and beat in egg to make a batter. Add pork and mix well to coat pieces. Cut onion downward into quarters, then eighths and separate into petals. Mix sauce ingredients together and set aside. Deep-fry pork in hot oil for about 3 minutes. Drain and keep pork hot in a cool oven. Heat 2 tbsp oil in a wok or frying pan (skillet) and stir-fry onion for 1 minute, then add pepper and stir-fry 1 minute longer. Lower heat, stir sauce mixture and pour in. Stir until sauce is clear and thickened. Add pork to pan and turn pieces gently in sauce for 30 seconds. Serve immediately with boiled or steamed rice. Serves 4–6.

SWEETBREADS

These are considered a delicacy by a great many people, and classic French cuisine includes a number of famous dishes based on sweetbreads.

They are an animal's pancreas and thymus glands, usually taken from a calf. In appearance and texture, sweetbreads are very similar to brains and, like the latter, they must be given special soaking and blanching treatments before cooking.

Once prepared, sweetbreads may be cooked whole or sliced, pan-fried or coated in breadcrumbs and fried. They may also be braised, whole, with aromatic vegetables, herbs and wine and served with a rich mushroom sauce or a delicate creamy sauce.

□ **Basic Preparation:** Soak sweetbreads in cold water for several hours, changing water frequently (**Fig 1 below**). This will allow the blood and impurities to seep out. Then blanch by placing them in a large pan of fresh cold water, bringing it slowly to the boil and boiling for 2 minutes (**2**). Drain and rinse them well under cold running water. The sweetbreads can then be trimmed of pieces of cartilage, ducts and skin (**3**). If they are to be sliced, they should be pressed between two plates or boards.

Once prepared, sweetbreads can be stored in the refrigerator for a day before they are cooked as desired. **See recipes.**

Sweetbreads with Poulette Sauce

500 g (1 lb) prepared sweetbreads; 1 onion, sliced; 1 carrot, sliced; 1 bouquet garni; veal or chicken stock; 45 g/1½ oz (3 tbsp) butter; 2 tbsp flour; 1 egg yolk; 5 tbsp single (light) cream; squeeze lemon juice; 1 tbsp finely chopped parsley; salt and freshly ground black pepper.

Place sweetbreads in saucepan with onion, carrot, bouquet garni and stock just to cover. Bring to the boil and simmer for about 45 minutes. Strain off 350–500 ml/12–18 fl oz (1½–2 cups) stock and reserve. Slice sweetbreads thickly and keep warm. Melt the butter in a clean saucepan, stir in flour and cook for a few seconds, then pour on reserved stock and bring to the boil, stirring constantly. Cook until sauce is of coating consistency. Beat egg yolk with cream, add to sauce and reheat without boiling. Add lemon juice, parsley, salt and pepper. Serve sweetbreads with sauce. Serves 6.

Sautéed Sweetbreads

500 g (1 lb) prepared sweetbreads, thickly sliced; salt and freshly ground white pepper; flour; 30 g/1 oz (2 tbsp) butter; 120 ml/ 4 fl oz (½ cup) strong veal or chicken stock; finely chopped parsley.

Season sweetbreads lightly with salt and pepper and lightly coat with flour. Sauté in foaming butter for 3–4 minutes each side, then remove to warmed plate. Deglaze pan with stock, reduce as desired and pour over sweetbreads. Sprinkle with parsley. Serves 6.

SWEETCORN

See Corn.

SWEET POTATO

Not a true potato but the tuber of a large, leafy plant which can be grown in any warm climate. Sweet potatoes can be either white, or orange-fleshed, and take the shape of a large, fat sausage. Despite the name, sweet potatoes are quite different from potatoes in taste and texture. However, they can be cooked in the same ways as potatoes, such as oven-baked in their skin, or boiled and peeled, then tossed in butter, or mashed. **See recipes.**

Candied Sweet Potatoes

1 kg (2 lb) sweet potatoes; salt; 90 g/3 oz (6 tbsp) butter; 90 g/3 oz (½ cup) lightly packed brown sugar; 4 tbsp water.

Cook sweet potatoes in boiling salted water until tender but still firm. Peel, then cut into halves or quarters. Heat butter, sugar and water in a heavy saucepan to simmering point. Add potatoes and cook on top of stove over very low heat, turning occasionally, for about 15 minutes or until potatoes are delicately golden-brown. Serves 6.

Glazed Sweet Potatoes

1 kg (2 lb) sweet potatoes, peeled and cut into even-sized pieces; salt; 60 g/2 oz (4 tbsp) butter; 1 tbsp oil; 1 tbsp honey; pinch ground ginger.

Drop sweet potatoes into pan of boiling salted water and simmer 5 minutes. Drain. Melt half butter with oil in baking dish and stir in honey and ginger. Add sweet potatoes and toss in honey mixture. Dot with remaining butter. Bake in a preheated moderate oven (180°C/350°F, Gas Mark 4) for 40 minutes or until tender. Brush potatoes with glaze in pan and turn occasionally during cooking. Serves 6.

SWISS ROLL/JELLY ROLL

This impressive rolled sponge cake is baked

Preparing Sweetbreads

in a shallow baking tin (pan), spread with jam and rolled while still hot, or rolled, cooled and then unrolled and spread with warm jam.

Some Swiss rolls (jelly rolls) are also flavoured with spices and honey, and, of course, there is the famous Chocolate Roll.

See also Chocolate Roll (page 73) and Honey Spiced Sponge Roll (page 405).

Swiss Roll

90 g/3 oz (¾ cup) self-raising flour; pinch salt; 3 eggs; 125 g/4 oz (½ cup) caster sugar; 1 tbsp hot water; 3–4 tbsp jam or lemon cheese; caster sugar.

Grease a 30 × 25 cm (12 × 10 in) Swiss roll tin (jelly roll pan) and line with greased greaseproof (waxed) paper, or make a paper case this size using thick greaseproof (waxed) paper (see page 74). Sift flour with salt. Place eggs and sugar in a heatproof bowl and stand over a pan of gently simmering, not boiling, water. Whisk together until mixture is very thick and creamy, about 10 minutes. If using an electric mixer whisking over hot water is not necessary. Remove bowl from water and continue whisking mixture until cool. Fold in flour as lightly as possible with a metal spoon. Lastly, fold in hot water. Pour into prepared tin (pan), shake into corners and spread evenly using a metal spatula. Bake in a preheated hot oven (220°C/425°F, Gas Mark 7) for 7–12 minutes or until pale golden and springy. Do not overcook as it makes rolling up difficult.

Quickly turn out the sponge on to a tea-towel well sprinkled with caster sugar. Carefully strip off lining paper. Trim off crisp edges with a sharp knife. Roll in towel and cool. Unroll sponge. Place jar of jam or lemon cheese in hot water and when warm spread jam or cheese over sponge, taking it almost to edges. Lifting edges of sugared tea-towel nearest you, roll sponge into a neat firm roll. Stand roll on a wire rack with join underneath. Leave until cold, away from any draughts. Sprinkle with a little more caster sugar before serving. Serves 8.

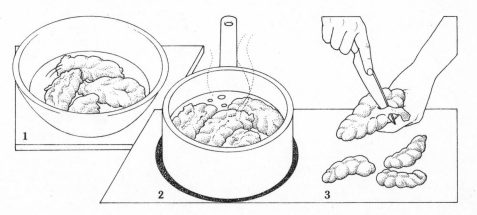

T

TABASCO SAUCE

An orange-red fiery liquid made from hot red peppers and known by its trade name 'Tabasco'. Tabasco sauce, known as hot pepper sauce in America, should always be used with discretion – 1 or 2 drops is often enough. Use in soups, cocktails and barbecue sauces, salad dressings, savoury butters, tomato juice, chilli dishes, and some egg or fish dishes. A drop added to scrambled eggs, fish cakes or salmon mornay enhances the flavour.

Spicy Avocado Sauce

1 large avocado, halved and stoned (pitted); 1 tbsp lemon juice; 3 drops Tabasco (hot pepper) sauce; salt and freshly ground black pepper; 1 tomato, peeled, seeded and chopped; 10 g/⅓ oz (¼ cup) finely chopped parsley; ½ tsp ground coriander; 1 tbsp oil; 1 tbsp white vinegar.

Scoop flesh from avocado into a bowl. Add lemon juice and mash roughly. Mix in Tabasco (hot pepper) sauce, salt, pepper and tomato. Blend to a smooth purée or push through a sieve, then beat in parsley, coriander, oil and vinegar. Cover and refrigerate for 1 hour. Serve with poultry or fish, or as a dipping sauce for meatballs. Makes about 350 ml/12 fl oz (1½ cups).

TABOULEH (Tabbouli, Tabbouleh)

One of the most popular dishes from the Middle East, and Lebanon in particular. Burghul (or cracked wheat), on which the salad is based, gives a delicious nutty flavour that appeals to most people. Plenty of fresh mint and parsley is mixed through and lemon juice imparts a refreshing tang. Serve Tabouleh with flat pita bread as part of an hors d'oeuvre tray or traditional *mezze* of the Middle East, or use as an accompaniment to grilled (broiled) or barbecued lamb or chicken.

Tabouleh

140 g/4½ oz (1 cup) burghul (cracked wheat); 2 large tomatoes, peeled and chopped; 3 tbsp finely chopped spring onions (scallions); salt and freshly ground black pepper; 40–60 g/1⅓–2 oz (1–1½ cups) finely chopped fresh parsley; 20 g/⅔ oz (½ cup) finely chopped fresh mint; 3–4 tbsp olive oil; 3–4 tbsp lemon juice; lettuce leaves to serve.

Soak burghul (cracked wheat) in cold water to cover for about 2 hours. Drain, squeeze out as much water as possible (use your hands to do this) and spread on a clean tea-towel or paper towels to dry. Put burghul (cracked wheat) in a bowl. Add tomatoes and spring onions (scallions) and season with salt and pepper. Add parsley, mint, oil and lemon juice and mix well. Adjust seasoning – salad should taste fresh and lemony. Serve on lettuce leaves on a flat platter or piled in a bowl. Serves 6.

VARIATION

Tabouleh Stuffed Tomatoes: Make Tabouleh, omitting tomatoes. Remove tops from 6 tomatoes and scoop out flesh, leaving shell. Sprinkle tomatoes with salt, turn upside-down and leave to drain for about 30 minutes. Dry with paper towels. Mix chopped tomato flesh with tabouleh and use to fill centres of tomatoes. Arrange on a platter with any leftover tabouleh spooned down the centre.

TABLET

A Scottish version of fudge. Take care to stir gently or the mixture will become grainy before it has caramelized thoroughly.

Tablet

300 ml/½ pint (1¼ cups) milk; 1 kg/2 lb (4 cups) sugar; 60 g/2 oz (4 tbsp) butter; 1 × 400 g/13 oz can sweetened condensed milk; ¼ tsp vanilla essence (extract); walnut halves to decorate.

Combine milk, sugar and butter in a heavy saucepan. Stir over low heat until sugar dissolves, about 20 minutes, then stir in condensed milk and bring to the boil. Boil steadily over medium heat for about 25 minutes or until dark golden-brown. Add vanilla and stir well. Remove from heat and allow to cool for a few minutes. Beat with a wooden spoon or hand-held electric beater for about 10 minutes or until mixture is thick. Pour into a well-greased 28 × 19 cm (11 × 7½ in) Swiss roll tin (jelly roll pan). Place walnut halves on top, mark into pieces with a knife and leave to cool. When set, break into squares as marked. Makes about 60 pieces.

TACO

A tortilla (Mexican corn pancake), folded or rolled round a filling and often fried crisp. It can be filled with a savoury filling before rolling and then fried, or fried first with fillings added afterwards. Crisp taco shells are available in packages. Tacos are eaten at all hours of the day in Mexico, and they have become a popular 'fast food' in other countries. They are good for a party because you can put out the fillings and sauce and let each guest assemble his own. **See recipes**.

See also *Tortilla*.

Right: Siena Cake (page 388)

Tacos

10–12 packaged taco shells or soft tortillas.
FILLING: *1 tbsp oil; 1 clove garlic, crushed; 1 medium onion, finely chopped; 500 g/1 lb (2 cups) lean minced (ground) beef; 1 tsp Mexican chilli powder; 1 tsp ground cumin; 2 tbsp tomato purée (paste); 120 ml/4 fl oz (½ cup) water; salt and freshly ground black pepper; 2 tbsp chopped fresh coriander or parsley.*
SAUCE: *120 ml/4 fl oz (½ cup) fresh tomato purée; 1 small onion, grated; 1 tsp chopped fresh oregano, or ¼ tsp dried; 1 tsp salt; 2 tsp vinegar; pinch sugar; 1 small fresh or dried chilli, seeded and finely chopped.*
TOPPINGS: *125 g/4 oz (1 cup) grated, well-flavoured cheese; 60 g/2 oz (1 cup) shredded lettuce; 125 g/4 oz (1 cup) finely chopped onions; 2 medium tomatoes, chopped; 1 ripe avocado, peeled, stoned (pitted) and diced (optional, but delicious).*

Heat taco shells according to packet instructions, or fold soft tortillas in half and fry in a little hot oil until crisp.
FILLING: Heat oil in a large saucepan and fry garlic and onion until softened, about 4 minutes. Add minced (ground) beef, and stir over medium heat until it turns brown and crumbly. Add chilli powder, cumin, tomato purée (paste), water, salt and pepper. Cook gently, covered, for 10 minutes. Stir in coriander or parsley and adjust seasoning.
SAUCE: Combine all ingredients in a saucepan and simmer for 3 minutes. Set taco shells on a platter, with filling, toppings and sauce in separate bowls. About 2 tbsp of meat filling is placed in every taco, then toppings and sauce are added according to taste. Tacos are eaten in the hand, so be sure to provide plenty of paper napkins! Serves 5–10.
NOTE: For vegetarian tacos, use refried beans (see page 319) as the filling instead of meat or create meatless fillings of your choice.

Salad Tacos

210 g/7 oz (1 cup) cooked or canned red kidney beans, drained; 1 head lettuce, torn into bite-sized pieces; 1 avocado, peeled, stoned (pitted), and cubed; ½ green pepper, cored, seeded and diced; 2 tomatoes, chopped; 1 tsp chopped fresh oregano; 8 taco shells; 60 g/2 oz (½ cup) grated Cheddar cheese.
MARINADE: *½ tsp dry mustard; ½ tsp ground cumin; 2 tbsp wine vinegar; 4 tbsp oil; ¼ tsp salt.*
FRENCH DRESSING: *1 tbsp vinegar; 3 tbsp oil; 1 clove garlic, crushed; pinch sugar.*

Beat marinade ingredients together with a fork. Chill kidney beans in marinade for 2–3 hours. Combine dressing ingredients. Add

Left: Deep-fried Szechuan Fish (page 124)

lettuce, avocado, green pepper, tomatoes and oregano. Drain beans, add to salad and toss lightly. Crisp taco shells as directed on packet. Spoon salad into tacos. Sprinkle cheese over top and serve immediately. Serves 4.

TAHINI (Tahina)

A paste made from toasted sesame seeds, widely used in the Middle East where it is made into delicious creamy sauces and salad dressings, is used to flavour cakes and biscuits (cookies) and is an essential ingredient in the wonderful garlicky chick-pea dip, Hummus bi Tahini (see page 160). **See recipes.**

Yogurt and Tahini Salad

1 small head lettuce, torn into pieces; 2 small carrots, very finely sliced; 1 cucumber, thinly peeled and diced; 2 sticks celery, sliced; 3–4 spring onions (scallions), diagonally sliced into 2.5 cm (1 in) lengths; 30 g/1 oz (¼ cup) roasted cashew nuts; 2 tbsp grated Cheddar or crumbled blue cheese; 30 g/1 oz (½ cup) alfalfa sprouts.
DRESSING: *250 ml/8 fl oz (1 cup) plain yogurt; 120 ml/4 fl oz (½ cup) tahini; 1 clove garlic, crushed; 1 tbsp lemon juice; salt; 1 tbsp chopped parsley.*

Put vegetables into a salad bowl and mix lightly.
DRESSING: Whisk together all ingredients except parsley; fold parsley in lightly. Spoon dressing over salad, sprinkle on cashews and cheese and top with alfalfa. Serves 4–6.

Tahini Sauce

2 cloves garlic; 120 ml/4 fl oz (½ cup) tahini; 60–120 ml/2–4 fl oz (¼–½ cup) cold water; 120 ml/4 fl oz (½ cup) lemon juice; salt.

Place garlic and tahini in blender or food processor and process to crush garlic. Add water and lemon juice alternately, a little at a time, until desired consistency is reached. Add salt to taste. If mixing by hand, crush garlic with salt in a mixing bowl, and gradually beat in tahini. Mix in water and lemon juice alternately until mixture is desired consistency. Makes about 300 ml/½ pint (1¼ cups).

TAMALE

A Mexican speciality: a hearty snack made by spreading cornmeal dough on a corn husk, covering it with a sweet or savoury filling, then rolling it up inside the husk and steaming it. Canned tamales can be found in some good food stores.

Tamale Pie

A savoury Mexican-style pie with a cornbread crust. Yellow cornmeal (polenta) is used in place of the Mexican cornmeal (*masa*).

750 g/1½ lb (3 cups) minced (ground) steak; 1 large onion, chopped; 1 green pepper, cored, seeded and chopped; 1 × 425 g/ 14 oz can tomatoes; 1 × 310 g/10 oz can sweetcorn kernels (whole kernel corn), drained; 90 g/3 oz (½ cup) stoned (pitted) black (ripe) olives; 1 tbsp sugar; 1 tsp salt and 2–3 tsp Mexican chilli powder, or 1 × 50 g/ 1⅔ oz packet commercial chilli seasoning mix.
CRUST: *150 g/5 oz (1 cup) yellow cornmeal (polenta); 1 tsp salt; 600 ml/1 pint (2½ cups) cold water; 60 g/2 oz (½ cup) grated Cheddar cheese.*

Brown minced (ground) beef in a dry frying pan (skillet), stirring and breaking down lumps with 2 forks, until crumbly. Add onion, green pepper, tomatoes with their juice (snipping into pieces with scissors as you add them), corn, olives and seasonings. Turn mixture into a pie or other ovenproof dish and spread evenly.
CRUST: Mix cornmeal (polenta), salt and water in a heavy saucepan and cook, stirring, for 15 minutes or until thick. Spread mixture over meat mixture. It may sink, but will rise during baking. Bake in a preheated moderate oven (180°C/350°F, Gas Mark 4) for about 40 minutes or until topping is firm. Sprinkle with grated cheese and bake 5 minutes longer. Serves 6–8.

TAMARILLO (Tree Tomato)

A glossy, plum-red fruit the size and shape of a large egg. There are also yellow and purplish varieties. Tamarillos, natives of South America, have juicy, slightly acid flesh. Raw tamarillos may be used for fruit salads or on fruit platters, or arranged in slices or wedges on a cheese board to accompany soft creamy cheeses. The puréed flesh is used as an ingredient in sweet and savoury dishes, and the sliced fruit as a garnish.
☐ **Basic Preparation:** Raw tamarillos need no preparation beyond washing. The skin and seeds can be eaten, but as the skin can be bitter, you may prefer to peel the fruit with a knife, or by covering with boiling water for 1 minute, then slipping the skins off.
To prepare tamarillo purée: Blanch the fruit, remove skin, then rub flesh through a sieve.
Creamy Tamarillo Sauce Heat 125 g/4 oz (½ cup) sugar, and 120 ml/4 fl oz (½ cup) each of water and wine together, stirring until sugar has dissolved. Bring to the boil, and boil for 5 minutes. Add purée from 6 tamarillos and simmer until reduced and a little thickened. Stir in 1 tsp lemon juice and 2 tsp brandy. Cool and chill. At serving time, whip 120 ml/4 fl oz (½ cup) double (heavy) cream until it just holds its shape and fold into tamarillo mixture. Makes about 350 ml/ 12 fl oz (1½ cups).

TANDOORI CHICKEN

A great and famous dish of northern India, named after the tandoor (clay oven) in which the spiced chicken is baked. Tandoori chicken came into India from across the North West Frontier and beyond, from the Turks and the descendants of Genghis Khan – a fascinating example of the way in which food interlocks with history.

When cooked in the traditional way, the chicken is threaded on a spit and baked in the tandoor over hot coals, but it can be cooked on an electric rotisserie or on a rack set in a roasting tin (pan), and finished on the barbecue if you wish.

Tandoori Chicken

1 × 1.5 kg (3 lb) chicken.
YOGURT MASALA: *3–4 cloves garlic, chopped; 2.5 cm (1 in) piece fresh ginger, chopped; 1 tsp cumin seeds; pinch nutmeg; 1½ tsp salt; 175 ml/6 fl oz (¾ cup) plain yogurt; 1 tbsp peanut oil; 1 tbsp tomato ketchup; 2 tsp lemon juice; 2–3 drops red food colouring.*
LEMON SPICE SAUCE: *½ tsp pepper; ¼ tsp ground cardamom; 1 tbsp peanut oil; 2 tsp lemon juice.*
TO SERVE: *onion rings; radishes; red or green pepper; chillies; flat bread.*

Remove chicken skin but leave chicken whole. Cut 2 slits about 1 cm (½ in) deep in thighs and breast.
YOGURT MASALA: Put all ingredients in a blender and purée, or grind garlic, ginger, cumin seeds, nutmeg and salt to a paste with a mortar and pestle or end of a rolling pin in a bowl, then mix in remaining ingredients. Spread masala over chicken, rubbing well in, and refrigerate overnight. Next day, bring chicken to room temperature, then place on a rotisserie over a pan, or on a rack in a shallow roasting tin (pan). Pour over remaining masala. Bake in a preheated moderately hot oven (200°C/400°F, Gas Mark 6) for 15 minutes, then reduce heat to moderate (180°C/350°F, Gas Mark 4) and

bake 1 hour more, basting frequently with pan juices.
LEMON SPICE SAUCE: Mix together ingredients. Remove chicken from oven and cut into 6 pieces. Coat chicken pieces with any remaining masala and sprinkle with lemon spice sauce. Return to a moderately hot oven (200°C/400°F, Gas Mark 6) for 10–15 minutes, or cook under a preheated grill (broiler) or over hot coals until dark reddish-brown and crisp. Serve chicken on a large heated platter, with onion rings, radishes, sliced green or red pepper and, for those who appreciate something hot, a few chillies. Pass a flat bread such as Chapatis (see page 62). Serves 3–4.

TANGERINE

See Mandarin and Tangerine.

TAPIOCA

A product extracted from the roots of the cassava plant; it forms into small balls during processing.

It is a starchy product, and thus sometimes used for thickening, but more commonly it is used in desserts, like sago. Tapioca pudding is made by substituting tapioca for sago in the recipe for Sago Pudding (see page 344). It is a great favourite with young children.

Tapioca Almond Cream

250 g/8 oz (2 cups) ground almonds; 1.5 litres/2½ pints (6 cups) water; pinch salt; 90 g/3 oz (½ cup) tapioca; 2 eggs, separated; sugar; 4 tbsp double (heavy) cream, whipped.

Pound ground almonds in a mortar, gradually adding enough water to produce a smooth, thick liquid. Turn into colander lined with a clean tea-towel and placed over a large bowl. Wring and squeeze to extract almond milk. Repeat with remaining water. Alternatively, blend briefly in a blender, then squeeze out almond milk. Pour almond milk into saucepan, bring to the boil, add salt and sprinkle over tapioca. Cook over low heat, whisking constantly, until tapioca is clear and mixture has thickened. Beat in egg yolks off heat, and add sugar to taste. Beat egg whites until stiff, and fold into mixture with cream. Serves 8.

TARAMASALATA

A splendid Greek dip made from tarama, the smoked, dried roe of the grey mullet. Tarama is available in cans. Serve taramasalata as an hors d'oeuvre with olives and crusty bread, pita bread or fresh vegetables such as pepper strips, celery and carrot sticks and radishes for dipping.

Taramasalata

4 thick slices day-old white bread, crusts removed; 120 ml/4 fl oz (½ cup) milk; 125 g/4 oz (½ cup) tarama; 1 small onion, grated; 1 clove garlic, crushed; 4 tbsp lemon juice; 175 ml/6 fl oz (¾ cup) olive oil; freshly ground white pepper.

Soak bread in milk for 5 minutes, then squeeze dry, discarding milk. Mash bread until smooth with a mortar and pestle or with back of a wooden spoon in a bowl. Beat in tarama little by little, then onion, garlic and lemon juice. Mixture should be a smooth paste. Now add olive oil little by little, beating it in with a whisk or rotary beater and making sure that each addition is absorbed before adding more. Taramasalata should be thick and creamy; it will firm more on chilling. Taste and beat in a little more lemon juice if required. Chill well before serving. Makes about 350 ml/12 fl oz (1½ cups).
VARIATION

Blender Taramasalata: Taramasalata is beautifully simple to make in a blender or food processor. For this method, the onion and garlic need only be chopped. Place soaked and squeezed bread and all other ingredients except oil in container of blender or processor and process until smooth. Then, with motor running, add oil gradually through feed tube, making sure each addition is absorbed before adding more. Taste and add a little more lemon juice if required. Chill well before serving.

TARRAGON

A profuse-growing summer herb. Its long, slender leaves are often used to decorate a cold dish, such as jellied chicken, but its role in the kitchen goes far beyond that of a mere garnish.

Tarragon is one of the four fresh herbs found in *fines herbes* (the others being chives, chervil and parsley). Tarragon lends its tang to Béarnaise Sauce (see page 370), and does wonders for chicken in any form. It can be used in salads and salad dressings, either as the fresh herb or in the form of tarragon vinegar. Tarragon may be added to pâtés, especially chicken pâté, to soups and to seafood dishes, hot or cold.

Dried tarragon is more pungent than the fresh, and for many dishes it is advisable to add dried tarragon as well as fresh. **See recipes.**

Tarragon Vinegar Fill a glass jar or bottle with fresh tarragon leaves, add good quality wine vinegar to cover and leave to infuse for 2 weeks. Strain and bottle, adding a sprig fresh tarragon to each bottle if desired. If fresh tarragon is unavailable, use 1–2 tbsp dried tarragon to each 500 ml/18 fl oz (2 cups) wine vinegar.

Tarragon Butter

Serve on grilled (broiled) meats, fish and chicken.

125 g/4 oz (½ cup) butter; 1 tbsp lemon juice; 2–3 tbsp finely chopped fresh tarragon, or mixture of fresh and dried tarragon; salt and freshly ground black pepper.

Cream butter until soft, then gradually beat in lemon juice. Blend in tarragon, and season with salt and pepper. Form into a log. Chill and slice into rounds when firm. Makes enough for 8 pieces of meat, fish or chicken.

Chicken Breasts with Tarragon

6 chicken half-breasts or fillets, boned; 60 g/2 oz (4 tbsp) butter; salt and freshly ground black pepper; 1 tsp dried tarragon; 120 ml/4 fl oz (½ cup) chicken stock; 120 ml/4 fl oz (½ cup) single (light) cream; 1 tbsp chopped fresh tarragon.

Trim chicken if necessary. Cook in frying pan (skillet) in foaming butter for 3–4 minutes each side. Season with salt and pepper and sprinkle with tarragon after turning. When both sides are browned, turn once more and cook for a further 2–3 minutes. Remove and keep warm. Deglaze pan with stock, and boil to reduce by half. Stir in cream and chopped fresh tarragon. Reduce over heat if desired. Pour sauce over chicken and serve immediately. Serves 6.

Tournedos with Tarragon

6 fillet (tenderloin) steaks, about 2.5 cm (1 in) thick; 45 g/1½ oz (3 tbsp) butter; salt and freshly ground black pepper; 2 tbsp Madeira or port; 1 tbsp chopped fresh tarragon.

Cook steaks in heavy frying pan (skillet) in about 15 g/½ oz (1 tbsp) butter for 2–3 minutes each side. Season cooked side with salt and pepper after turning. When little drops of red juice appear on surface of meat, pour over Madeira or port. Allow it to bubble

for about 30 seconds, then stir in tarragon and remaining butter. Serve immediately. Serves 6.

NOTE: Cooked in this way, steaks will be rare. If medium steaks are desired, turn steaks a second time and cook for 2–3 minutes before adding Madeira.

TARTARE SAUCE

See page 205 for recipe.

TARTS AND TARTLETS

The combinations of food, both sweet and savoury, that can be presented in an open pastry (pie) shell are almost endless. There is hardly an occasion from afternoon tea or cocktails to a lunch or dinner party, picnic or family meal, when one would not be welcome.

The terms 'tart' and 'flan' are virtually interchangeable. The French lean toward the former, the English toward the latter, while Americans often call a filled pastry shell an open pie.

□ **To Shape Tart Shells:** For directions on lining large or individual-sized flan rings, see Pastry.

To line individual plain tartlet tins (pans): For the tiny, saucer-shaped tartlet tins (pans) that are joined in a set of 12, roll pastry (dough) thin and, using a round cutter, stamp out rounds a little larger than the top of the tins (pans). If using pastry (dough) containing sugar or eggs, grease tins (pans) lightly. Fit rounds into tins (pans), pressing lightly to ensure that no air remains between pastry (dough) and tin (pan). Prick shells before baking.

To line individual fancy tartlet tins (pans): Place the tins (pans) close together. If using pastry (dough) containing sugar or eggs, grease tins (pans) lightly. Roll pastry (dough) thin, lift on the rolling pin and lay it loosely over all the tins (pans) together. Shape a small piece of pastry (dough) into a ball, dip it in flour and use it to press pastry (dough) into the tins (pans). Flour rolling pin and roll over tins (pans) to remove surplus pastry (dough). Fold trimmings together and roll out to use again. Take each tin (pan), press edges up lightly with the thumb and prick pastry (dough) bottom before baking until dried out and pale golden.

To bake unfilled tart shells: See directions for baking blind under Pastry. **See recipes.**
See also Flan and Quiche.

SAVOURY TARTS

Savoury tarts can be created from store-cupboard ingredients – eggs, milk, cheese, vegetables, even leftover meat and fish.

Basque Tart

1 large onion, finely chopped; 2 cloves garlic, crushed; 30 g/1 oz (2 tbsp) butter; 3 large tomatoes, peeled, seeded and chopped; 1 small red pepper and 1 small green pepper, cored, seeded and cut into short strips; 60 g (2 oz) cooked ham or prosciutto, cut into strips; 1 tsp tomato purée (paste); 2 eggs, beaten; 120 ml/4 fl oz (½ cup) single (light) cream; 60 g/2 oz (1 cup) fresh breadcrumbs; 1 tbsp grated Parmesan cheese; salt and freshly ground black pepper; 1 × 23 cm (9 in) Plain Shortcrust Pastry Tart Shell (page 274).

Cook onion and garlic in butter until soft but not browned. Remove from heat and add tomatoes. Blanch peppers in boiling water for 5 minutes and drain. Add peppers, ham, tomato purée (paste), eggs, cream, breadcrumbs, cheese, salt and pepper to tomato mixture and mix lightly. Turn into tart shell and bake in a preheated moderately hot oven (190°C/375°F, Gas Mark 5) for about 40 minutes or until filling is set and pastry (crust) golden. Serves 4–6.

Cheese Soufflé Tart

This tart should be served while the filling is still puffed up.

3 rashers (slices) streaky bacon, rind removed and finely chopped; 1 onion, finely chopped; 1 × 20–23 cm (8–9 in) Rich Shortcrust Pastry Tart Shell, partially baked blind (page 274); 30 g/1 oz (2 tbsp) butter; 2 tbsp flour; 150 ml/¼ pint (⅔ cup) warm milk; salt and freshly ground black pepper; pinch dry mustard; 60 g/2 oz (½ cup) Gruyère cheese, grated; 2 eggs, separated.

Fry bacon gently in a dry frying pan (skillet) until fat runs. Add onion and cook until golden-brown. Spread onion and bacon on bottom of tart shell. Melt butter in saucepan, add flour and stir on low heat for 1 minute. Remove from heat, cool a little and add milk, stirring until smoothly blended. Season with salt, pepper and mustard. Return to heat and stir until boiling, then remove from heat, stir in cheese and beat in egg yolks one at a time. Beat egg whites until they hold soft peaks and fold into cheese mixture. Turn mixture into tart shell and bake in a preheated moderately hot oven (200°C/400°F, Gas Mark 6) for 20 minutes or until filling is puffed and golden. Serves 4–6.

Tomato and Cheese Tart

A treat to take on a picnic or, baked in a 20 cm (8 in) shallow square tin (pan) and cut into squares, to serve with drinks.

3–4 firm, ripe tomatoes, cut into 1 cm ($\frac{1}{2}$ in) thick slices; 370 g (12 oz) Gruyère cheese, finely sliced; 1 × 23 cm (9 in) Plain Shortcrust Pastry Tart Shell, partially baked blind (page 274); 2 shallots, finely chopped; 4–5 leaves fresh basil, cut into fine ribbons, or $\frac{1}{2}$ tsp dried; salt and freshly ground black pepper; 2 tbsp grated Parmesan cheese; 30 g/1 oz (2 tbsp) butter, melted.

Sprinkle tomato slices with salt and place on a rack for about 30 minutes to drain. Arrange cheese slices, overlapping, in a layer in tart shell. Scatter chopped shallot and basil over and place drained tomato slices on top to cover cheese completely. Season with salt and pepper, sprinkle with Parmesan cheese and drizzle melted butter over. Bake in a preheated moderately hot oven (190°C/375°F, Gas Mark 5) for about 25 minutes or until lightly coloured. Serve warm. Serves 4–6 or makes 16 × 5 cm (2 in) squares.

Spanish Tarts

Make in 10 cm (4 in) rings for a first course, or in tartlet tins (pans) for party savouries.

Rich Shortcrust Pastry made with 180 g/6 oz (1$\frac{1}{2}$ cups) flour (page 274); 1 kg (2 lb) spinach, chopped; salt and freshly ground black pepper; nutmeg; 30 g/1 oz (2 tbsp) butter; 2 onions, finely chopped; 2 tbsp flour; 250 ml/8 fl oz (1 cup) warm milk; 60 g/2 oz ($\frac{1}{2}$ cup) grated Swiss cheese; 1 tsp lemon juice; $\frac{1}{2}$ tsp paprika; 30 g/1 oz ($\frac{1}{2}$ cup) fresh breadcrumbs.

Roll out pastry (dough) and use to line 4 × 10 cm (4 in) flan rings or 16–18 × 5 cm (2 in) tartlet tins (pans). Prick well, chill 30 minutes, then bake blind (see page 273) in a preheated moderately hot oven (200°C/ 400°F, Gas Mark, 6) until golden. Cool in tins (pans). Pack spinach into a saucepan and season with salt, pepper and nutmeg. Cover tightly and cook, in water that clings to leaves after rinsing, 5–6 minutes or until soft. Drain well and, when cool enough to handle, squeeze out as much moisture as possible. Chop spinach finely.

Melt butter in saucepan and cook onions gently until soft but not brown. Add flour and stir over low heat 1 minute. Remove from heat and cool slightly, then add milk, stirring until smoothly blended. Return to heat and stir until boiling. Season with salt, pepper and a little nutmeg. Fold in spinach. Remove from heat and stir in 30 g/1 oz ($\frac{1}{4}$ cup) cheese and the lemon juice. Adjust seasoning. Fill tart shells with mixture. Mix remaining cheese, paprika and breadcrumbs and

sprinkle over the tops. Place under a preheated grill (broiler) or in a preheated moderately hot oven (200°C/400°F, Gas Mark 6), until tops are browned. Serve hot or warm. Makes 4 entrée tarts, 16–18 party savouries.

FRUIT TARTS

The French are masters at the art of producing a fine fruit tart. Attractively arranged fruit in a crisp pastry case (pie shell), the most delectable tarts are made with fresh fruit, served warm from the oven.

Glazed Apple Tart

3 large dessert apples, peeled, halved and cored; 1 × 23 cm (9 in) Sweet Rich Shortcrust Pastry Tart Shell, partially baked blind (page 274); 30 g/1 oz (2 tbsp) butter, melted; 60 g/2 oz ($\frac{1}{4}$ cup) sugar.
GLAZE: *90 g/3 oz ($\frac{1}{4}$ cup) sieved apricot jam; 1 tbsp water.*

Put each apple half, cut side down, on a board and cut across into very thin slices, keeping shape of half intact. Arrange halves in tart shell, fanning slices out somewhat. Brush with melted butter, sprinkle with sugar and bake in a preheated moderately hot oven (190°C/375°F, Gas Mark 5), 5 minutes. Brush again with butter and bake 5 minutes more or until pastry is browned and apples tender. Cool 10 minutes in flan ring or pie pan. If using flan ring, remove sides and place tart on a wire rack. Stir apricot jam and water over low heat until boiling and glaze hangs in heavy drops from spoon. Brush over apples. Serve lukewarm. Serves 6–8.

French Fruit Tart

(Tarte aux Fruites)
This tart has the tempting, glamorous look of the tarts seen in those superb French pâtisseries.

1 × 20 cm (8 in) Pâte Sucrée Tart Shell, baked blind (page 276); $\frac{1}{2}$ quantity Crème Pâtissière (page 165); few mixed fruits (strawberries, grapes, cherries, mandarin or orange segments, apricots or pears); 90 g/3 oz ($\frac{1}{4}$ cup) sieved apricot jam; 1 tbsp water; squeeze lemon juice.

Fill cooled tart shell with crème pâtissière. Have prepared fruit ready and arrange over cream in a decorative fashion, in concentric circles, in any order. The cream should be completely covered with fruit. Make glaze by heating apricot jam, water and lemon juice together, stirring, until mixture hangs in heavy drops from spoon. Brush over fruit while still warm. Put in refrigerator to set glaze until ready to serve. Serves 6.
NOTE: For best results this tart should be put together 1–2 hours before serving. Have the tart shell baked, the crème pâtissière and the glaze at the ready (it will have to be reheated) and then settle down to create a work of art.

Plum Tart

PASTRY (DOUGH): *125 g/4 oz (1 cup) flour; 60 g/2 oz (4 tbsp) butter; 1 tbsp caster sugar; 30 g/1 oz ($\frac{1}{4}$ cup) ground almonds; $\frac{1}{2}$ egg, beaten; little grated lemon rind; 2 tsp rum.*
FILLING: *60 g/2 oz ($\frac{1}{2}$ cup) ground almonds; 125 g/4 oz ($\frac{1}{2}$ cup) sugar; 1.5 kg (3 lb) ripe plums, slit open and stoned (pitted); 3 tbsp icing (confectioners) sugar; $\frac{1}{2}$ tsp cinnamon.*

To make pastry (dough), work all ingredients together. Roll into a ball, wrap in plastic wrap and refrigerate for 1 hour before using. When chilled, roll out on a floured work surface and use to line a 25 cm (10 in) flan tin with a removable base (loose bottomed pie pan). Chill tart shell for 30 minutes.
FILLING: Sprinkle tart shell with ground almonds and 1 tbsp sugar. Arrange plums, cut side up, in circles, packing them tightly and reversing direction of fruit with each circle. Sprinkle with remaining sugar. Place on a baking tray and bake on lowest rack in a preheated moderate oven (180°C/350°F, Gas Mark 4) for 1 hour or until plums are soft. Cool a few minutes, then remove flan ring (pie pan) and allow to stand until just warm. Combine icing (confectioners) sugar and cinnamon and sift over plums before serving. Serves 8.

Tart Tatin

This luscious dessert of caramelized apples on a pastry (pie) crust appears on the menu of nearly every French restaurant. Golden

T

Delicious apples must be used. To make this tart you need a heavy, round flameproof dish – a cast-iron frying pan (skillet) with a screw-on handle is one idea, a small paella pan another.

PASTRY (DOUGH): *125 g/4 oz (1 cup) flour; 2 tsp caster sugar; 90 g/3 oz (6 tbsp) butter, cut into small dice; 1 egg yolk; 1 tbsp cold water.*
FILLING: *125 g/4 oz (½ cup) butter; 325 g/ 10½ oz (1⅓ cups) sugar; 10 large ripe Golden Delicious apples, peeled, cored and cut into thin slices.*

To make pastry (dough), sift flour and sugar into a bowl, make a well in the centre and place butter, egg yolk and water in well. Mix quickly with a fork to form a dough. Roll in plastic wrap and chill 1 hour. To make this pastry (dough) with an electric beater, cream sugar with butter and incorporate egg and water. Mix for a few seconds, then add flour all at once. Do not beat any more when dough is formed. Chill before using.
FILLING: Place butter and sugar in a 23 cm (9 in) round flameproof dish. Allow butter to melt on a gentle heat. Remove from heat and arrange apples, cut side up, in circles in dish, packing them very tightly together. Return to heat and cook gently until butter and sugar form a pale caramel. This will take about 15 minutes. Do not allow caramel to become dark.

While the apples are cooking carefully roll out dough to a 28 cm (11 in) round. Remove dish from heat and cover apples with dough round, pushing edges inside dish. Place on a baking tray and bake in a preheated moderately hot oven (190°C/375°F, Gas Mark 5) for 45 minutes, covering loosely with foil if pastry (shell) is browning too much. Stand for 10 minutes before inverting tart on to a heated dish. Serve tart warm, with lightly whipped cream if desired. Serves 8.

Fruit Tartlets

These fruit-filled glazed tartlets may be made with any fruits in season.

1 quantity Pâte Sucrée (page 276); 500 g (1 lb) fresh fruit in season (see recipe).
GLAZE: *370 g/12 oz (1 cup) sieved jam (use apricot for pale fruits and redcurrant for red fruits); 3 tbsp water; 1 tbsp lemon juice.*

Roll out pastry (dough) thinly and use to line 6 individual 8 cm (3 in) tartlet tins (pans). Chill. Prick bottom of each tartlet with a fork, chill 20 minutes and then bake blind (see page 273) in a preheated moderately hot oven (190°C/375°F, Gas Mark 5) for 8–10 minutes or until pastry (dough) is a pale biscuit colour. Do not allow to brown. Allow to cool.
TO PREPARE FRUITS FOR TARTS:
Strawberries: Wash, dry carefully and hull.

They can be left whole if small, or sliced or halved.
Apricots: Poach in a light syrup – 125 g/4 oz (½ cup) sugar dissolved in 250 ml/8 fl oz (1 cup) water – until just tender. Drain. Slit and remove stones. Small fruits may be used whole, larger fruits sliced or halved. Good quality canned fruit may also be used.
Peaches and Plums: Prepare in the same way as apricots.
Grapes: Wash, halve if desired and seed if necessary (see *Grapes*).
Pears: If using ripe pears, peel, slice finely and arrange in the tartlet shells. Brush with a little lemon juice to prevent discolouring. If the pears are not quite ripe, peel and poach in a light syrup until tender. Drain before slicing.
Rhubarb: Use young rhubarb; wash well and cut into 4 cm (1½ in) lengths. Poach in a light syrup and drain well.
Mandarins: Peel, remove outside skin with a sharp knife and cut between membranes to separate skinless segments. Dry segments on paper towels before using.
Cherries: Wash, then remove stones with a cherry stoner, or halve cherries and lift stones out with a small sharp knife. Dry before placing in tartlet shells.
GLAZE: Heat all ingredients over gentle heat, stirring until glaze hangs in heavy drops from spoon. Brush tartlet shells with hot glaze. Pile fruit into tartlet shells and brush fruit carefully with glaze until it glistens. Allow to set. Makes 6.

Individual Pear Tarts

An example of the French way with fruit tarts. The fruit is arranged in a design that shows its lovely shape, over a layer of crème pâtissière.

1 quantity Biscuit Pastry (page 274); 2 firm ripe pears, peeled, halved and cored; lemon juice; 60 g/2 oz (¼ cup) sugar; 120 ml/4 fl oz (½ cup) water; 1 strip lemon rind; ½ quantity Crème Pâtissière (page 165).

Roll out pastry (dough) and use to line 4 × 10 cm (4 in) loose-bottomed flan rings or pie pans. Chill 30 minutes, then bake blind

(see page 273) in a preheated moderate oven (180°C/350°F, Gas Mark 4) for 8 minutes. Remove lining paper and rice or beans, return to oven and bake 5–10 minutes more or until shells are golden. Remove from oven and cool. Brush each pear half with lemon juice as it is prepared, to prevent discoloration. Put sugar, water and lemon rind into a heavy saucepan and bring to the boil. Add pears, cover tightly and poach gently (just below a simmer) for 8–10 minutes or until pears are just tender. Remove saucepan from heat and cool pears in syrup for 20 minutes. Remove them and drain on a cloth. Spread a layer of crème pâtissière in each tart shell. Place each pear half, cut side down, on a board and cut lengthways into slices. Arrange each half over crème pâtissière in a tart shell, fanning slices out. Boil down remaining poaching syrup until it is sticky, and brush over pears. Warm the tarts slightly in a very cool oven (120°C/250°F, Gas Mark ½) before serving. Serves 4.

Hot Apple Tarts

(Tartes Fines Chaudes Aux Pommes)
The French way of making fruit tarts that look as beautiful as they taste is quite traditional. This is an up-to-date version from a top Paris restaurant.

1 × 375 g/12 oz packet frozen puff pastry (paste), thawed; 4–6 eating apples, peeled and cored; 125 g/4 oz (½ cup) caster sugar; 125 g/4 oz (½ cup) butter; little warmed honey; Crème Fraîche (page 88) to serve.

Roll out pastry (dough) thinly on a floured work surface. With a 15 cm (6 in) round cutter or saucer, cut out 6 rounds. Turn rounds over on to a dampened baking tray and chill for 30 minutes. Slice apples downward very thinly. Arrange on pastry (dough) rounds in overlapping rows. Sprinkle with sugar and dot with butter. Bake in a preheated hot oven (220°C/425°F, Gas Mark 7) for 20–25 minutes or until apples and pastry (crusts) are golden. Brush tops with honey, and serve warm with chilled crème fraîche. Serves 6.

OTHER SWEET TARTS

To serve as dessert or at afternoon tea.

Cream Cheese Tart

*1 quantity Pâte Sucrée (page 276);
125 g/4 oz (½ cup) unsalted butter, softened;
125 g/4 oz (½ cup) caster sugar; 250 g/8 oz
(1 cup) cream cheese, softened; 2 eggs,
beaten; nutmeg; icing (confectioners) sugar.*

Roll out pastry (dough) and use to line a
20 cm (8 in) flan ring or pie pan. Chill 20
minutes. Cream butter with sugar until light
and fluffy. Add cheese, beating until light and
fluffy. Beat in eggs little by little. Spread
mixture in tart shell and sprinkle with
nutmeg. Bake in a preheated moderately hot
oven (190°C/375°F, Gas Mark 5) for 30
minutes or until filling is puffed and golden
and pastry (crust) a pale gold. Protect sides
with crumpled foil if pastry (crust) is
browning too much. Sift icing (confectioners) sugar over surface and serve warm
or cold. Serves 6.

Brown Sugar Tart

*double quantity Pâte Sucrée (page 276);
370 g/12 oz (2 cups) firmly packed brown
sugar; 250 ml/8 fl oz (1 cup) single (light)
cream; 30 g/1 oz (2 tbsp) butter; ¼ tsp vanilla
essence (extract); pinch salt; 2 eggs, beaten.*

Use ⅔ dough to line a 23 cm (9 in) flan ring or
pie pan. Place brown sugar and cream in a
saucepan and bring to the boil, stirring.
Simmer gently for about 15 minutes.
Remove pan from heat and stir in butter,
vanilla and salt. Let mixture cool to
lukewarm. Add eggs and beat until well
blended. Pour into tart shell. Roll out
remaining ⅓ dough, then cut into strips.
Arrange strips lattice-fashion over tart,
pressing lightly at ends to join them to sides.
Bake in a preheated moderately hot oven
(200°C/400°F, Gas Mark 6) for about
20–25 minutes or until pastry (crust) is
cooked. Cool on a wire rack. Serves 6–8.

Neenish Tarts

PASTRY (DOUGH): *125 g/4 oz (½ cup) butter;
125 g/4 oz (½ cup) sugar; ½ tsp almond*
essence (extract); 1 egg; 250 g/8 oz (2 cups)
flour, sifted; 1 tsp baking powder; pinch salt.
FILLING: *90 g/3 oz (6 tbsp) butter; 60 g/2 oz
(½ cup) sifted icing (confectioners) sugar;
3 tbsp sweetened condensed milk; 1 tbsp
lemon juice.*
ICING (FROSTING): *140 g/4½ oz (1 cup) icing
(confectioners) sugar; drop vanilla essence
(extract); 1 tbsp unsweetened cocoa powder;
1 tsp butter.*

To make pastry (dough), cream butter with
sugar and almond essence (extract) until
light and fluffy. Add egg and beat well. Stir in
flour, baking powder and salt. Knead lightly,
then form into a ball, wrap in plastic wrap
and chill for 30 minutes. Roll out and cut
into 24 × 6 cm (2½ in) rounds. Fit into
greased bun tins (patty pans), prick lightly
and chill 20 minutes. Bake in a preheated
moderate oven (180°C/350°F, Gas Mark 4)
for 10–15 minutes or until a pale biscuit
colour. Cool on wire racks.
FILLING: Beat butter until fluffy, then beat in
icing (confectioners) sugar, condensed milk
and lemon juice. Spoon into cooled tarts,
smooth with palette knife and leave to set.
ICING (FROSTING): Sift icing (confectioners)
sugar into a small heatproof bowl, add 1 tbsp
hot water and heat over gently simmering
water. Stir in vanilla and when icing (frosting)
will coat back of a spoon use immediately to
ice (frost) one half of each tart. Add cocoa
and butter to remaining white icing (frosting)
in bowl. Stand over simmering water and stir
until butter melts and icing (frosting) is
smooth and glossy (you may have to beat in
a little more hot water). Use at once to ice
(frost) other halves. Makes 24.

Jam Tarts

*½ quantity Biscuit Pastry (page 274); 12 tsp
jam (apricot, raspberry, strawberry,
blackberry).*

Roll out pastry (dough) thinly and use to line
12 shallow tartlet tins (pans). Prick bases and
put 1 tsp of jam into each. Roll trimmings
and cut narrow strips to make pastry (dough)
crosses on top of jam, if liked; press ends on
to edges. Chill 20 minutes, then bake in a
preheated moderate oven (180°C/350°F,
Gas Mark 4) for 15 minutes. Makes 12.

Lemon Cheese Tarts

*½ quantity Biscuit Pastry (page 274); lemon
cheese (page 186); whipped cream
(optional).*

Roll out pastry (dough) thinly and use to line
12 shallow tartlet tins (pans). Prick bases and
chill 20 minutes, then bake blind in a
preheated moderate oven (180°C/350°F,
Gas Mark 4) for about 15 minutes or until
pastry (dough) is golden. Remove from tins
(pans) and cool on a wire rack. Fill each tart
shell with lemon cheese and top with a dab
of whipped cream, if liked. Serve within 20
minutes. Makes 12.

TEACAKE

In England, traditional teacakes are large
round baked buns of yeast dough, irresistible
when served hot, split, toasted and buttered.
See recipes.

See also *Yeast Cookery* and *Cinnamon*.

Apple Teacake

*1 egg, separated; 125 g/4 oz (½ cup) caster
sugar; 120 ml/4 fl oz (½ cup) milk; ½ tsp
vanilla essence (extract); 30 g/1 oz (2 tbsp)
butter, melted; 125 g/4 oz (1 cup) self-raising
flour, sifted; 1 apple, peeled, cored and thinly
sliced.*
TOPPING: *melted butter; ½ tsp cinnamon
mixed with 1 tbsp sugar.*

Whisk egg white until stiff and gradually beat
in sugar, then egg yolk. Stir in milk, vanilla
and melted butter. Fold flour carefully into
mixture. Pour into a greased 18 cm (7 in)
sandwich tin (layer cake pan) and arrange
apple slices on top of batter. Bake in a
preheated moderately hot oven
(190°C/375°F, Gas Mark 5) for 20–25
minutes. While still hot, brush with melted
butter and sprinkle with cinnamon and
sugar. Serve warm or cold.

Yorkshire Teacakes

*15 g/½ oz (1 tbsp) fresh (compressed) yeast;
300 ml/½ pint (1¼ cups) warm milk;
500 g/1 lb (4 cups) flour; 1 tsp salt;
45 g/1½ oz (3 tbsp) lard or butter; 1½ tbsp
caster sugar; 140 g/4½ oz (¾ cup) currants;
2 tbsp chopped mixed candied peel; milk to
glaze.*

Dissolve yeast in warm milk and leave in a
warm place for about 10 minutes or until
mixture becomes frothy. Sift flour and salt
into a large bowl and rub (cut) in lard or
butter. Stir in sugar, currants and peel. Add
milk and yeast mixture and mix to a firm
dough (you may need to add a little more
flour). Turn dough on to a lightly floured
work surface and knead until smooth and
elastic – about 10 minutes. Form into a ball,
return to clean, very lightly oiled bowl and

T

turn dough round to coat lightly with oil. Cover with a tea-towel and leave to rise in a warm place for about 1 hour or until dough has doubled in bulk.

Turn on to a floured surface, knock (punch) down dough and knead until smooth. Divide into 6 pieces. Shape each into a ball, then roll out to a round 15–18 cm (6–7 in) in diameter. Place teacakes on 2–3 greased baking trays, brush tops with milk and cover with oiled plastic wrap. Allow to rise in a warm place for about 40 minutes or until almost doubled in size. Bake in a preheated moderately hot oven (200°C/400°F, Gas Mark 6) for about 20 minutes or until well risen and golden-brown. Cool on a wire rack. Serve warm or toasted, split open and spread with plenty of butter. Makes 6.

Honey Teacake

300 ml/$\frac{1}{2}$ pint (1$\frac{1}{4}$ cups) sour cream; 140 g/4$\frac{1}{2}$ oz ($\frac{3}{4}$ cup) firmly packed brown sugar; 1 egg; 280 g/9 oz (2$\frac{1}{4}$ cups) wholewheat flour, sifted; 1 tsp bicarbonate of soda (baking soda); 3 tbsp warmed honey; 60 g/2 oz ($\frac{1}{2}$ cup) chopped mixed nuts.
TOPPING: *1 tbsp caster sugar; $\frac{1}{4}$ tsp nutmeg; 2 tsp butter, softened.*

Beat together sour cream, sugar and egg, then stir in flour and soda. Mix well. Beat in warmed honey and chopped nuts. Spoon mixture into a well-greased 20 cm (8 in) round cake tin (pan) and bake in a preheated cool oven (150°C/300°F, Gas Mark 2) for about 1$\frac{1}{2}$ hours. Turn on to a wire rack. Mix topping ingredients and brush over top of loaf. Serve warm or cold, sliced, either buttered or plain.

TERIYAKI

The splendid Japanese dish of marinated, grilled (broiled) and glazed beef or chicken. It can be cooked on a table-top barbecue, on a griddle or in an electric frypan (skillet).

Beef Teriyaki

6–8 slices fillet (tenderloin) steak, each about 5 mm ($\frac{1}{4}$ in) thick; oil.
SAUCE: *1 clove garlic; $\frac{1}{2}$ tsp sugar; $\frac{1}{2}$ tsp grated fresh ginger; 120 ml/4 fl oz ($\frac{1}{2}$ cup) Japanese soy sauce; 120 ml/4 fl oz ($\frac{1}{2}$ cup) mirin (sweet saké) or dry sherry.*
GLAZE: *2 tsp sugar; 3 tbsp water; 1 tsp cornflour (cornstarch) mixed with 1 tbsp cold water.*
GARNISH: *1 tbsp dry mustard; sprigs fresh coriander or parsley.*

Trim any fat and gristle from steaks.
SAUCE: Crush garlic with sugar, then mix with remaining ingredients. Dip both sides of each steak into sauce, then remove from sauce and set aside for 30 minutes.

GLAZE: Put 3 tbsp sauce into a small saucepan and add sugar and water. Bring to the boil. Stir cornflour (cornstarch) mixture again, and stir into saucepan. Stir until mixture boils and becomes clear; set aside. For garnish, mix mustard with enough hot water to make a thick paste; set aside.

Heat grill (broiler) or griddle, brush with oil and cook steak at high heat for about 1 minute each side or until lightly browned. This will give medium-rare steak. For well-done meat, cook 1 minute more. To serve, slice each steak into strips and assemble again into original shape. Heat glaze to boiling point and spoon over steaks. Garnish each plate with a dab of mustard and a sprig of coriander or parsley. Serves 6 as part of a Japanese meal, 4 as a main course.
VARIATION
Chicken Teriyaki: Follow recipe for *Beef Teriyaki*, but substitute 4–6 half-breasts of chicken, boned but with skin left on, for the steaks. After marinating, grill (broil) skin side up for 2–3 minutes or until a light golden-brown. Dip again into sauce and grill (broil) other side 2–3 minutes, then dip a third time into sauce and grill (broil) skin side up until a rich brown. Cut into strips and reassemble to serve. Glaze and garnish as for *Beef Teriyaki* before serving.

TERRINE

See Pâté and Terrine.

THYME

Whether fresh or dried, the herb thyme is indispensable in the kitchen. It is one of the elements of the classic *bouquet garni* and a 'must' in stocks and stews. It goes into wine marinades for meat and poultry, into hearty, one-dish soups, and is particularly good with rabbit.

Branches of thyme may be dried, but since the herb is perennial it is often easier to use sprigs of fresh thyme. Dried thyme, however, is more convenient if the recipe calls for crumbled thyme – for example for a stuffing or to add to a meatball mixture. **See recipes.**

Sauce Marchand de Vin

This sauce should be made in the same pan as the one used to cook steaks. Pour off excess fat before starting sauce.

2 tbsp finely chopped onion; 60 g/2 oz (4 tbsp) butter; 5 tbsp red wine; 1 clove garlic, crushed; 1 sprig fresh thyme; $\frac{1}{2}$ tsp French (Dijon) mustard; salt and freshly ground black pepper.

Cook onion in 15 g/$\frac{1}{2}$ oz (1 tbsp) butter in frying pan (skillet) for 2 minutes over high heat. Add wine, garlic and thyme, and boil to reduce to 3–4 tbsp. Remove from heat. Whisk in remaining butter, cut into small pieces, then add mustard, salt and pepper. Stir in any juices which have run out of steaks. Remove thyme from sauce. Arrange steaks on heated plates, and strain sauce over them and serve immediately. Makes enough for 2 steaks.

Papeton d'Aubergines

This was a dish created in the 15th Century in Avignon by the French papal chef – thus the corruption of French and Italian words.

1.5 kg (3 lb) aubergines (eggplant), peeled and finely sliced; salt; about 120 ml/4 fl oz ($\frac{1}{2}$ cup) olive oil; freshly ground black pepper; 2–3 sprigs fresh thyme; 5 eggs; 60 g/2 oz ($\frac{1}{2}$ cup) grated cheese.

Place aubergine (eggplant), slices in a large colander, sprinkle with salt and leave to dégorge for about 1 hour. Drain and pat dry with paper towels. Heat a little olive oil in a frying pan (skillet), and quickly brown aubergine (eggplant) slices, 3–4 at a time, on both sides. Add more oil to pan as needed. Purée aubergine (eggplant) through food mill or in blender. Season with salt and pepper and add thyme leaves. Add eggs one at a time, beating well. Pour mixture into greased 1.5 litre/2$\frac{1}{2}$ pint (6 cup) soufflé dish, and bake in a preheated moderately hot oven (200°C/400°F, Gas Mark 6) for 10–15 minutes or until a crust forms on top. Sprinkle with grated cheese, reduce oven temperature to moderate (180°C/350°F, Gas Mark 4) and cook for 25–30 minutes longer. Serve warm with grilled (broiled) or roast lamb or beef. Serves 6–8.

TIMBALE

The name given to a deep round mould, usually small, made from metal, earthenware or ovenproof china, with either straight or sloping sides. It also applies to the dish prepared in the mould.

A timbale is made with a delicious creamy custard mixture of fish, poultry, meat or vegetables which is steamed, resulting in a texture resembling that of a soufflé. It is usually served with a sauce.

A timbale provides an elegant method for using leftover ingredients, and also makes a superb first course for a dinner party. **See recipes**.

Courgette Timbale

A rather moist mixture reminiscent of the soft centre in a soufflé and an excellent first course or luncheon dish.

1 kg (2 lb) courgettes (zucchini), grated; salt; 4 medium onions, minced; 45 g/1½ oz (3 tbsp) butter; 1 tbsp oil; 125 g/4 oz (1 cup) grated mixed Parmesan and Gruyère cheeses; 250 ml/8 fl oz (1 cup) single (light) cream; 8 large eggs, well beaten; freshly ground white pepper to taste.
GARNISH: *60 g/2 oz (4 tbsp) butter; 60 g/2 oz (1 cup) fresh white breadcrumbs; 4 tbsp chopped parsley.*

Sprinkle grated courgettes (zucchini) with salt and leave for 30 minutes to drain. Dry well with paper towels. Cook onions gently in butter and oil until translucent. Increase heat to medium, stir in courgettes (zucchini) and cook about 5 minutes, stirring frequently. Cover pan and cook over low heat 2–3 minutes longer or until courgettes (zucchini) are tender. Remove from heat and cool. Add cheese to mixture and stir in cream. Mix in beaten eggs, salt and pepper. Carefully pour into a greased and bottom-lined 1.5 litre/2½ pint (6 cup) mould or 6 individual 250 ml/8 fl oz (1 cup) moulds. Set mould in a baking dish filled with enough water to come about ⅔ the way up the sides of mould. Bake on middle shelf of a preheated moderate oven (180°C/350°F, Gas Mark 4) for 35–40 minutes or until set. Test with a thin-bladed knife inserted in centre – it should come out clean and look slightly buttery when custard is ready. Remove from heat and from water bath. Rest timbale for 15 minutes before unmoulding.
GARNISH: Melt butter in a small frying pan (skillet), stir in breadcrumbs and sauté until golden-brown. Remove from heat and stir in parsley. Run a thin knife around edge of mould and invert timbale on to serving plate. Sprinkle with parsley and breadcrumb garnish and serve immediately. Serves 6.
NOTE: If using individual moulds, bake for 20–25 minutes, depending on their depth.

VARIATION

Broccoli Timbale: Follow recipe for Courgette Timbale, using 370–500 g/12 oz–1 lb (2½–3 cups) cooked, well drained and puréed broccoli instead of courgettes (zucchini). Serve with Hollandaise Sauce, if desired (see page 369).

Timbales of Smoked Salmon

A stunning new way to present smoked salmon for a very special dinner. Crème fraîche makes a delicate filling.

125 g (4 oz) smoked salmon, thinly sliced; 120 ml/4 fl oz (½ cup) Crème Fraîche, chilled (page 88); 2 tbsp red caviar; pinch cayenne, or dash Tabasco (hot pepper) sauce.
FRESH TOMATO PUREE: *4 ripe tomatoes, peeled, seeded and chopped; salt and freshly ground black pepper.*
GARNISH: *snipped chives or fresh dill; whole chives or sprigs fresh dill.*

Rinse 4 individual soufflé dishes or other small moulds and line bottoms with dampened greaseproof (waxed) paper. Line with smoked salmon slices, trimming them level with rims. Chop trimmings finely. Beat crème fraîche until soft peaks form, and fold in chopped salmon, caviar and cayenne or Tabasco (hot pepper) sauce. Fill moulds with mixture. Cover and chill overnight.
FRESH TOMATO PUREE: Mash tomato flesh with a fork or purée in a food processor fitted with the steel blade, then rub purée through a fine sieve. Season with salt and pepper and chill. Run a thin knife around inside of each mould. Invert a serving plate over each, hold plate and mould firmly together and turn them over. Rap plate sharply on table to release timbale, and lift mould and lining paper off carefully. Spoon tomato purée in a cordon around each timbale and sprinkle with snipped chives or dill. Garnish each plate with chives or dill. Serves 4.

Fish Timbales

500 g/1 lb (2 cups) boned and very finely chopped cooked fish; ¼ tsp salt; pinch paprika; ½ tsp grated lemon rind; 2 tsp lemon juice; 120 ml/4 fl oz (½ cup) double (heavy) cream; 3 egg whites; Sauce Tartare (page 205) to serve.

Combine fish, salt, paprika, lemon rind and lemon juice. Whip cream until it holds stiff peaks and fold into fish mixture. Whisk egg whites until stiff and fold in gently. Spoon into a greased and bottom-lined 1 litre/1¾ pint (4 cup) mould or 4 × 250 ml/8 fl oz (1 cup) individual moulds. Set in a baking dish with hot water to come ¾ of the way up sides of mould. Bake in a preheated moderate oven (180°C/350°F, Gas Mark 4) for 30–40 minutes, depending on depth of moulds. Test with a thin-bladed knife inserted in centre – it should come out clean when timbales are ready. Remove from heat and from water bath. Unmould on to serving plates and serve with tartare sauce. Serves 4.

Chicken Timbales

500 g/1 lb (2 cups) minced (ground) cooked chicken; 175 ml/6 fl oz (¾ cup) single (light) cream; ¼ tsp salt; ¼ tsp paprika; 4 egg whites; 1 small canned pimiento, drained and cut into strips; Velouté Sauce (page 368) to serve.

Combine minced (ground) chicken, cream, salt and paprika and blend well. Whisk egg whites until stiff peaks form and fold into chicken mixture. Line 6 greased 250 ml/8 fl oz (1 cup) moulds with strips of pimiento and spoon in chicken mixture. Set in a baking dish with hot water to come ¾ of the way up the sides of the moulds. Bake in a preheated moderate oven (180°C/350°F, Gas Mark 4) for 20–25 minutes or until set. Test with a thin-bladed knife inserted in centre – it should come out clean when timbales are ready. Remove from heat and from water bath. Unmould and serve with velouté sauce. Serves 6.

VARIATION

Ham Timbales: Follow recipe for Chicken Timbales using a mixture of minced (ground) cooked chicken and minced (ground) cooked ham instead of all chicken. Serve with Sauce Suprême (see page 368), if liked.

TIPSY CAKE

A dessert resembling trifle, made from firm sponge cake either whole or in two layers.

Tipsy Cake

2 × 18 cm (7 in) Whisked Sponge or Sponge Sandwich layers (page 53); 175 ml/6 fl oz (¾ cup) sweet white wine, sherry or brandy; 180 g/6 oz (½ cup) warm apricot jam; 60 g/2 oz (½ cup) split, blanched almonds.
DECORATION: *250 ml/8 fl oz (1 cup) double (heavy) cream, whipped and sweetened with 1 tbsp sifted icing (confectioners) sugar; 30 g/1 oz (¼ cup) toasted slivered almonds.*

Prepare each sponge layer separately. Slowly spoon wine, sherry or brandy on cake to moisten evenly. Brush with warm jam and put layers together. Chill for 2–3 hours or overnight. Stud cake with almonds and decorate with whipped cream and toasted slivered almonds. Serves 8–10.

TISANE

A herbal tea or infusion, sometimes sweetened with honey but rarely drunk with milk. Almost any herb can be used to make an infusion, together with the flowers of some plants.

Some tisanes have health-giving reputations. Camomile tea is an old remedy for upset stomachs (Mrs Rabbit gave it to Peter Rabbit after he had gorged himself in the vegetable garden).

Peppermint tea is recommended as a prevention against colds. Angelica tea is said to help digestion. When caffeine is not allowed in the diet, herbal teas are often advised instead. Many have a soothing effect, such as linden flower (*tilleul*) tea.

A tisane may be made from either fresh or dried herbs or flowers. Little sachets of herbs or flowers for infusions may also be bought; these look like tea bags but must be left to infuse for much longer.

Rosemary Tea Pour boiling water over a fresh sprig of rosemary in a cup. Cover, and leave to infuse for 5 minutes. For more than one person, use several sprigs rosemary in a teapot.

Peppermint Tea Put a handful of fresh peppermint leaves in a china or earthenware teapot, pour over boiling water and leave to infuse for 5 minutes. Sweeten to taste with a little honey and add a squeeze of fresh lemon juice.

TOFFEE (Taffy, Toffy)

A very popular sweetmeat of ancient origin, that was probably once made with black treacle (molasses) flavoured with rum. Today the basic recipe contains sugar, water and sometimes butter. It is boiled at a high temperature (this varies according to the type of toffee) to give the texture required after cooling.

Tips when making toffee:
● Always use a large heavy-based pan and oil the sides.
● Use a sugar thermometer for best results.
● Do not stir unless the recipe specifies this.
● Reduce the heat to a low simmer after the toffee has reached a temperature of 127°C/260°F.
● When the toffee reaches the required temperature, pour the mixture immediately into an oiled tin (pan).
● Cool at an even room temperature, and when it is lukewarm, mark into squares with an oiled knife. **See recipes**.

Simple Toffee

500 g/1 lb (2 cups) sugar; 175 ml/6 fl oz (¾ cup) cold water; 1 tbsp vinegar.

Place all ingredients in a heavy 2 litre/3½ pint (8 cup) saucepan. Stir over medium heat until sugar has dissolved. Bring to the boil, without stirring, and cook until syrup is golden-brown. Remove from heat and allow bubbles to settle. Pour into small paper cases (standing in metal pans), or pour into an oiled 18 cm (7 in) square shallow tin (pan) and mark into squares with an oiled knife. Makes about 50 × 2.5 cm (1 in) pieces.

Treacle Toffee

370 g/12 oz (2 cups) demerara (brown) sugar; 120 ml/4 fl oz (½ cup) water; 90 g/3 oz (6 tbsp) butter; pinch cream of tartar; 125 g/4 oz (⅓ cup) black treacle (molasses); 125 g/4 oz (⅓ cup) golden (light corn) syrup.

Dissolve sugar in water in a heavy 2 litre/3½ pint (8 cup) saucepan over low heat. Add remaining ingredients and bring back to the boil, without stirring. Boil to soft-crack stage, or 132°C/270°F if using a sugar thermometer. To test when soft-crack stage is reached, drop ½ tsp toffee syrup into 250 ml/8 fl oz (1 cup) cold water. Work it with your fingers: hard separate threads that bend when removed from water should form.

Pour toffee into an oiled 18 cm (7 in) square shallow tin (pan). Cool for 5 minutes, then mark into squares with an oiled knife and leave to set. When cold, break into squares and wrap in waxed paper. Makes about 50 × 2.5 cm (1 in) pieces.

Toffee Apples

8 medium apples; 500 g/1 lb (2 cups) sugar; 150 ml/¼ pint (⅔ cup) water; 2 tsp vinegar; pinch cream of tartar; red food colouring (optional).

Push a wooden butcher's skewer into each apple. Place sugar, water, vinegar and cream of tartar in a deep, heavy saucepan. Stir over gentle heat until sugar has dissolved, then cover and bring to the boil. Remove lid and boil syrup rapidly, without stirring, for about 15 minutes or until temperature reaches 150°C/300°F, or hard-crack stage. To test when hard-crack stage is reached, drop ½ tsp toffee syrup in 250 ml/8 fl oz (1 cup) cold water. Work it with your fingers for 1–2 seconds: if toffee makes brittle threads that stay brittle out of the water, it is ready. Remove from heat and colour syrup with red food colouring, if liked. Twirl apples quickly in toffee mixture until well coated. Place on a greased baking tray until hard. Makes 8.

VARIATION
Toffee Sprinkles: Cook toffee as for Toffee Apples. Set paper cases in bun tins (patty pans) and ¾ fill with toffee. Sprinkle with hundreds and thousands (colored sprinkles) or desiccated (shredded) coconut. Makes about 10.

TOMATO

Indispensable as the fresh tomato is for eating either raw or cooked, it is only the beginning of this great fruit's usefulness to the cook. The tomato takes so well to being canned, puréed and concentrated that these forms are considered equal in status to the fresh product – indeed, they are sometimes the first choice for their rich colour and deep flavour, especially when fresh tomatoes are a little out of season and may lack flavour. Tomato juice, tomato ketchup, tomato relish or chutney find a place in most kitchens, and are used both to accompany food and ingredients in many recipes.

The tomato comes in a number of varieties from the large, ridged ones (which usually have especially good flavour), through smooth red globes to egg tomatoes, just right for lunch-boxes. There are also yellow varieties. Tiny cherry tomatoes (sometimes called 'Tom Thumb'), now widely available, are brilliant for garnishing. They can be used in salads and, dipped first into gin then into coarse salt, make a sensational nibble to have with drinks.

☐ **To Buy:** The very best fresh tomato is one that has been sun-ripened on the bush, but those available commercially have usually been picked at the stage where they are mature but still green or just beginning to redden. They are often fully ripe by the time they reach the shop.

Tomatoes to be eaten raw or cooked whole or with a stuffing should be bright-coloured but firm, with smooth, tight skins and no soft spots. Tomatoes which are a little beyond this stage and are very soft but still sound are usually cheaper and are excellent for cooking.

☐ **To Store:** Remove from any plastic wrapping and store ripe tomatoes in a cool, dark place; refrigerate (in a plastic bag in the crisper) only if you have more than you can use immediately, and remove half an hour before serving for fullest flavour. Store under-ripe tomatoes in good light but not in sunlight, and they will redden well in a day or two. You can speed the process by keeping them in a closed paper bag with a ripe apple.

□ Basic Preparation:

To peel: Cover tomatoes with boiling water, count to 10 (**Fig 1 below**), then remove and place them under cold running water (**2**). Make a tiny slit in the skin at the base and strip the skin off toward the stem end (**3**).

If the skin does not come away easily, drop tomatoes back into boiling water for a few seconds more, then place under cold running water again. After peeling, use the point of a knife to cut out the blossom at the stem end. Use peeled tomatoes in casseroles, sauces, salads and for garnish.

To seed: Cut tomatoes in half crossways; squeeze them in the palm of your hand, giving a little shake as you do so, over a sieve set over a bowl. Scrape out any remaining seeds with a teaspoon or grapefruit knife, and discard the seeds. Use the liquid in the bowl for the dish you are making, or add it to a stock or sauce.

To season: The correct basic seasoning for tomatoes is salt, pepper and just a touch of sugar to bring out the flavour. A little sugar added to dressings for tomato salads or to dishes using cooked tomatoes will give the fullest flavour. **See recipes.**

Basic Tomato Sauce

This is a good sauce to make in quantity and freeze – the recipe can easily be doubled. Use it as the basis of a superb home-made soup, so different from the canned variety; serve it with sausages or hamburgers, grilled (broiled) meats, fish or chicken; heat it with mussels, prawns (shrimp) or canned fish and serve over rice or noodles; cover frankfurters with it, top with cheese and bake; stir into browned minced (ground) beef and serve with mashed potato. In this recipe, grated carrot has the same slight sweetening effect as sugar; it enhances the delicious tomato flavour of the sauce.

1 large onion, finely chopped; 2 cloves garlic, crushed; 2 rashers (slices) streaky bacon, rind removed and chopped; 30 g/1 oz (2 tbsp) butter; 1 large carrot, grated; 1 kg/2 lb (4 cups) ripe, red tomatoes, peeled, seeded and chopped, or 1 × 820 g/1¾ lb can tomatoes; 120 ml/4 fl oz (½ cup) dry white or red wine, or 4 tbsp sherry; 1 bouquet garni; salt and freshly ground black pepper.

Cook onion, garlic and bacon gently in butter until onion is soft. Add remaining ingredients, chopping canned tomatoes and removing as many seeds as possible. Simmer, partly covered, for 45 minutes, stirring frequently. Add a little more water if needed. Sauce should be thick, but can be thinned as you wish with beef or chicken stock when you use it. Remove bouquet garni, adjust seasoning and store, covered, in refrigerator or freezer. Makes about 4 × 250 g/8 oz (1 cup) jars.

Tomato Meatball Soup

1 tbsp soy sauce; 1 tbsp sherry; 1 spring onion (scallion), chopped; ½ tsp grated fresh ginger; 1 egg, beaten; 2 tbsp cornflour (cornstarch); 250 g/8 oz (1 cup) minced (ground) lean pork or beef; 1 litre/1¾ pints (4 cups) stock; 1 leek, thinly sliced; 4 medium, ripe tomatoes, peeled and diced; 1 tsp peanut oil; chopped fresh coriander or spring onions (scallions) to garnish.

Mix soy sauce, sherry, spring onions (scallions), ginger, egg and cornflour (cornstarch) with minced (ground) meat and set aside. Place stock in large saucepan and add leek and tomatoes. Bring to the boil and simmer for a few minutes. Add oil, then drop teaspoonfuls of meat mixture into simmering soup. Cover and cook gently for 5–8 minutes. Serve sprinkled with fresh coriander or spring onions (scallions). Serves 4.

NOTE: When tomatoes are expensive, use 1 × 425 g/14 oz can tomatoes. Chop the tomatoes and measure juice to replace some of the stock.

Tomato Soup with Fresh Basil Paste

Make the basil paste in the summer when the fresh herb is available, and keep it, covered with oil, in the refrigerator for the winter months.

1 tsp olive oil; 1 medium carrot, sliced; 1 small leek (white part only), sliced; 1 clove garlic, crushed; 1 sprig fresh thyme, or small pinch dried; ½ bay leaf; 3 ripe tomatoes, chopped; 1 tbsp tomato purée (paste); 1.2 litres/2 pints (5 cups) chicken stock; 1 tsp salt; freshly ground black pepper.
BASIL PASTE: *2 handfuls fresh basil leaves; 2 tsp olive oil.*

Heat olive oil in a large heavy saucepan, add carrot, leek and garlic and cook gently for 5 minutes. Stir in thyme, bay leaf, tomatoes and tomato purée (paste), then the stock. Heat until simmering. Season with salt and

Peeling Tomatoes

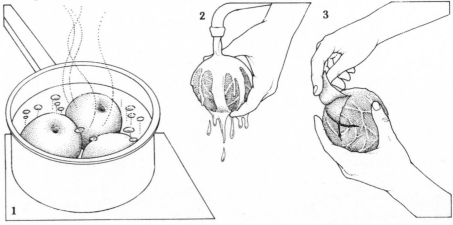

pepper, and simmer, half covered, for 20 minutes.

BASIL PASTE: Put basil leaves and olive oil in a blender or food processor fitted with steel blade and blend to a paste. Rub soup through a sieve and return to saucepan (or purée in a blender or food processor and strain back into pan). Reheat and serve, swirling a small dollop of basil paste into each serving. Serves 6.

Creamy Tomato Soup (Hot or Cold)

250 ml/8 fl oz (1 cup) Basic Tomato Sauce; 750 ml/1¼ pints (3 cups) chicken stock; 250 ml/8 fl oz (1 cup) single (light) cream; salt and freshly ground black pepper; snipped chives, fresh basil or nutmeg, to serve.

Purée sauce in a blender until it is very smooth, or rub it through a sieve. Combine with stock and, if soup is to be served cold, stir in cream and chill. If soup is to be served hot, bring cream to the boil and stir in tomato mixture gradually. Adjust seasoning. Serve scattered with chives or basil, or grate a little nutmeg over each serving. Serves 4.

Hot Vegetable Salad with Basil

120 ml/4 fl oz (½ cup) olive oil; 750 g (1½ lb) courgettes (zucchini), sliced diagonally; 8 spring onions (scallions), sliced (including green tops); 6 sticks celery, sliced; 1 large green pepper, cored, seeded and cut into squares; 2 large carrots, sliced diagonally; 2 tsp salt; 1 tsp pepper; 2 tbsp chopped fresh basil; 3 large tomatoes, peeled, seeded and roughly chopped; 2 tbsp wine vinegar; sprigs fresh basil to garnish.

Heat oil in a large, heavy frying pan (skillet) and add all vegetables except tomatoes. Season with salt and pepper. Cover and cook over low heat for 5 minutes, stirring occasionally. Remove lid and cook for 4–5 minutes more or until vegetables are tender but still crisp. Stir in basil and tomatoes and cook another minute, stirring. Sprinkle with vinegar, toss lightly to combine, and spoon

on to a heated serving platter. Garnish with sprigs of fresh basil. Serves 6.
NOTE: Leftover salad is delicious served chilled.

Julienne-Topped Tomatoes

A mixture of crunchy julienne vegetables gives tomatoes an elegant look for a dinner party. You can prepare the topping the day before.

8 medium tomatoes.
TOPPING: *2 sticks celery, cut into julienne (matchstick) strips; 1 large carrot, cut into julienne (matchstick) strips; 45 g/1½ oz (3 tbsp) butter; 60 g/2 oz (1 cup) fresh breadcrumbs.*

Drop celery and carrot strips into boiling salted water and cook gently for about 3 minutes or until crisp-tender. Drain. Melt 30 g/1 oz (2 tbsp) butter in a frying pan (skillet), add crumbs and toss over medium heat until well coated and slightly crisp. Cut tops off tomatoes and arrange in a greased ovenproof dish. Top each with buttered crumbs. Heat in a preheated moderate oven (180°C/350°F, Gas Mark 4) for 10 minutes. (If you have the oven very hot for another dish, put dish of tomatoes on a shelf in coolest part of oven and lay a piece of foil loosely over it.) Meanwhile, toss celery and carrot in remaining butter over low heat. Top each tomato with a spoonful of vegetables and serve immediately. Serves 8.

Buttered Tomatoes with Basil

6 small tomatoes, peeled and cored; 30 g/1 oz (2 tbsp) butter, melted; salt and freshly ground black pepper; fresh basil, cut into fine ribbons, or chopped parsley.

Arrange tomatoes in a buttered baking dish, blossom ends down. Brush with melted butter, and sprinkle with salt and pepper. Bake in a preheated moderately hot oven (190°C/375°F, Gas Mark 5) for 10–15 minutes or until slightly softened and heated through. Brush with melted butter and sprinkle lightly with salt every 5 minutes. Serve at once, sprinkled with basil or parsley. Serves 6.

Tomates à la Provençale

(Tomatoes, Provençal-Style)
Tomatoes and garlic are the basis for most dishes from Provence – in fact, tomatoes are referred to as 'pommes d'amour' there. If you're a garlic lover, once you eat tomatoes cooked in this way, you won't eat them simply grilled (broiled) again. Tomates à la Provençale is often served in France as a first course, with plenty of the light, crusty French bread to mop up the garlicky oil.

6 large ripe tomatoes, halved; salt and freshly ground black pepper; olive oil; 3 cloves garlic (more if desired), finely chopped; finely chopped parsley.

Squeeze tomato halves gently to remove seeds and juice. Season lightly with salt and pepper. Heat oil in a heavy frying pan (skillet) to a depth of about 1 cm (½ in). Add tomatoes, cut sides up, with garlic. Cover and cook gently until tender, about 20 minutes. Remove to a heated serving dish, pour over cooking oil and sprinkle with chopped parsley. Serve hot with crusty bread, as an accompaniment to grills (broils) or as a separate vegetable dish. Serves 6.

Anchovy-Stuffed Tomatoes

6–8 even-sized tomatoes; 30 g/1 oz (2 tbsp) butter; 2 shallots, chopped; 3 tbsp fresh white breadcrumbs; 6 anchovy fillets; grated cheese; butter.

Slice stem ends off tomatoes. Carefully scoop out seeds and discard. Remove and chop some of the pulp. Melt butter in a frying pan (skillet) and gently fry shallots until soft. Remove with a slotted spoon, and fry breadcrumbs until golden. Mash anchovy fillets and mix with shallots, tomato pulp and fried breadcrumbs. Fill tomatoes with mixture and sprinkle with grated cheese. Bake in a preheated moderate oven (180°C/350°F, Gas Mark 4) for 10–15 minutes. Dot with butter before serving. Serves 6–8.

Tomates Garnis

6 medium, firm, ripe tomatoes; salt; sugar; 60 g/2 oz (4 tbsp) butter; 250 g/8 oz (1½ cups) hot freshly cooked peas.

Cut tops off tomatoes and carefully scoop out seeds. Sprinkle insides with salt and a touch of sugar, then turn upside-down to drain for 30 minutes. Pat insides dry with paper towels. Put ½ tsp butter into each tomato and arrange in a buttered baking dish. Melt remaining butter, reserve 1 tbsp

and mix rest with peas. Fill tomatoes with peas and brush skins with reserved butter. Bake in a preheated moderately hot oven (190°C/375°F, Gas Mark 5) for 10 minutes, brushing skins again with butter after 5 minutes. Serves 6.

Tomatoes au Gratin

4 ripe tomatoes, thickly sliced; salt and freshly ground black pepper; 60 g/2 oz (1 cup) fresh breadcrumbs; 30 g/1 oz (¼ cup) grated Parmesan cheese; 4 tbsp oil.

Arrange tomato slices, overlapping, in a lightly oiled flameproof dish. Season generously with salt and pepper, sprinkle with breadcrumbs, then cheese, and finally oil. Cook under a preheated medium grill (broiler) for 5–6 minutes or until tomatoes are tender and surface is lightly browned. Serve from dish. Serves 4.
VARIATION
Tomatoes and Aubergine au Gratin: Follow recipe for Tomatoes au Gratin, but before grilling (broiling), interleave overlapping slices of tomatoes in the dish with 8 slices of aubergine (eggplant) which have been dusted with flour and very quickly browned in oil over a fairly high heat.

Tomatoes Baked with Herbs

A most versatile yet simple dish, adding a touch of colour and robust flavour to roast chicken or a mixed grill (English Mixed Grill).

6 ripe tomatoes; salt and freshly ground black pepper; 1–2 cloves garlic, chopped; 2 tbsp chopped fresh herbs (basil, parsley, thyme); 45 g/1½ oz (¾ cup) fresh breadcrumbs (optional); 30 g/1 oz (2 tbsp) butter.

Cut tops off tomatoes and season generously with salt and pepper. Sprinkle each with garlic and herbs and top with breadcrumbs (if using). Put a generous dot of butter on top of each tomato. Arrange in a buttered gratin dish and bake in a preheated moderate oven (180°C/350°F, Gas Mark 4) for 10 minutes. Serve from dish. Serves 4–6.

Stuffed Tomatoes

4 large tomatoes, halved; salt and freshly ground black pepper; 60 g/2 oz (1 cup) fresh breadcrumbs; 1 onion, grated; 1 clove garlic, crushed; 60 g/2 oz (½ cup) mushrooms, finely chopped; 1 tsp sugar; 1 tbsp chopped parsley; few leaves fresh basil, cut into fine ribbons, or ¼ tsp dried basil; 2 tbsp olive oil; 4 black (ripe) olives to garnish.

Squeeze or scoop pulp from tomato halves. Season them with salt and pepper and turn upside-down on a plate to drain while preparing stuffing. Chop tomato pulp and mix with breadcrumbs, onion, garlic, mushrooms, sugar, parsley and basil. Season with salt and pepper and mix thoroughly. Pile into tomato halves. Arrange in a well oiled ovenproof dish and sprinkle a little olive oil over each. Bake in a preheated moderate oven (180°C/350°F, Gas Mark 4) for about 30 minutes or until tender but still firm. Serve hot, garnished with olives. Serves 4.

Tomato and Onion Savoury

An excellent old-fashioned accompaniment to bake in the oven with a roast. It is good with barbecued chops or sausages, too.

4 ripe tomatoes, peeled and sliced; 2 onions, finely sliced; 90 g/3 oz (1½ cups) fresh breadcrumbs; 30 g/1 oz (2 tbsp) butter, melted; sugar; salt and freshly ground black pepper.

Arrange tomatoes, onions and breadcrumbs mixed with butter in layers in a shallow ovenproof dish, seasoning tomato layers with a little sugar, salt and pepper, and finishing with a layer of crumbs. Bake in a preheated moderate oven (180°C/350°F, Gas Mark 4) for 45 minutes or until vegetables are soft and top browned. Serves 6.
VARIATION
Herbed Tomato Savoury: Follow recipe for Tomato and Onion Savoury, but sprinkle tomato layers with 2 tsp chopped fresh mixed herbs, or ½ tsp dried herbs mixed with 2 tsp chopped parsley.

Tomatoes with Yogurt

This refreshing salad is a good one for weight-watchers to remember.

120 ml/4 fl oz (½ cup) plain yogurt; 1 tbsp Mayonnaise (page 204); 2 tsp chopped fresh dill, or pinch dried; 2 tsp lemon juice; good pinch dry mustard; salt and freshly ground black pepper; 3 large, ripe tomatoes, peeled and sliced.

Place yogurt in a bowl and stir in mayonnaise, dill, lemon juice, mustard, salt and pepper. Allow to stand for 30 minutes to blend flavours. Arrange tomato slices, in overlapping rows, on a serving platter, and spoon yogurt dressing over just before serving. Serves 6.

Sliced Tomatoes with Basil

One of the simplest and best ways to feast on tomatoes in summer when they and basil are in season.

4 ripe tomatoes, thickly sliced; 2 tsp wine vinegar; ½ tsp French (Dijon) mustard; salt and freshly ground black pepper; pinch sugar; 1½ tbsp olive oil; 2 tbsp fresh basil leaves, cut into fine ribbons.

Place tomato slices in a shallow dish. Mix vinegar with mustard, salt, pepper and sugar

in a small bowl, and beat in oil little by little to make a thick dressing. Spoon over tomatoes and scatter with basil. Serves 4.

Philippine Tomato Salad

A dish showing the Filipino love of sharp flavours, so refreshing in a hot climate.

500 g (1 lb) ripe, red tomatoes, thinly sliced; 4 spring onions (scallions), finely chopped (including some green tops); 1 tbsp lime or lemon juice; ½ tsp grated fresh ginger; salt and freshly ground black pepper.

Arrange tomato slices, in overlapping concentric circles, on a large platter. Sprinkle with remaining ingredients and serve immediately. Serves 4.

Luncheon Tomatoes

Tomatoes filled with a delicious salad can be a main dish or an accompaniment to cold meats.

6 ripe tomatoes; 120 ml/4 fl oz (½ cup) plain yogurt; 4 tbsp Mayonnaise (page 204); 1 small cucumber, diced; 2 spring onions (scallions) finely chopped (including some green tops); 1 stick celery, diced; ½ green or red pepper, cored, seeded and diced; 3 hard-boiled (hard-cooked) eggs, chopped; salt and freshly ground black pepper.

Have ingredients chilled. Cut a slice from the top of each tomato and carefully scoop out most of the pulp and seeds, leaving a shell about 1 cm (½ in) thick. Salt shells lightly inside and turn upside-down to drain. (Reserve scooped-out pulp and seeds for a stew, soup, casserole etc.) Mix yogurt and mayonnaise, and fold in cucumber, spring onions (scallions), celery, pepper and eggs. Season with salt and pepper. Spoon mixture into tomato shells, mounding it up. Serves 6.
VARIATIONS
Instead of hard-boiled (hard-cooked) eggs, use 250 g/8 oz (1 cup) chopped cooked

ham or corned beef, or 1 × 99 g/3 oz can tuna fish or salmon, drained and flaked.

Tomato Relish

Home-made tomato relish is lovely with cold meats, grilled (broiled) chops or cheese, or on sandwiches.

1.5 kg (3 lb) very ripe tomatoes; 500 g/1 lb (4 cups) onions, chopped; 500 g/1 lb (2 cups) sugar; 600 ml/1 pint (2½ cups) malt vinegar; 1 tbsp flour; 1 tbsp curry powder; pinch cayenne; 1 tbsp dry mustard; 1 tbsp salt.

Peel tomatoes and chop over a bowl, to save juice. Measure 175 ml/6 fl oz (¾ cup) juice. Put tomatoes, onions, sugar and vinegar into a saucepan and simmer, uncovered, until mixture is thick. Blend remaining ingredients with reserved tomato juice and stir in. Stir until boiling, then simmer 5 minutes. Bottle in clean, warm jars and seal when cool. Makes about 8 × 250 g/8 oz (1 cup) jars.

Storecupboard Tomato Sauce

A sweet, sharp sauce to serve with hot meats, pies, pasties and sausage rolls.

3 kg/6 lb (12 cups) very ripe tomatoes, chopped; 2 medium cooking apples, peeled, cored and sliced; 2 large onions, sliced; 2 cloves garlic, chopped; 250 g/8 oz (1 cup) sugar; 1 tbsp salt; 1 chilli; 2 tsp ground cloves; 2 tsp black peppercorns; 1 tsp curry powder; 600 ml/1 pint (2½ cups) malt vinegar.

Put all ingredients into a large, heavy saucepan, cover tightly and simmer for 2 hours. Rub through a coarse sieve, and bottle in clean, warm jars. Seal when cool. Makes about 6 × 250 g/8 oz (1 cup) jars.

Tomato Ketchup

4 kg/8 lb (16 cups) ripe tomatoes, chopped; 2 cloves garlic, chopped; 500 g/1 lb (4 cups) onions, chopped; 460 g/15 oz (2½ cups) firmly packed brown sugar; 8 whole cloves; 2 tbsp coarse salt; pinch cayenne; 1 tsp cinnamon; ½ tsp ground ginger; 900 ml/1½ pints (3¾ cups) vinegar.

Put all ingredients in a heavy saucepan. Bring to the boil slowly, then simmer until tomatoes and onions are very soft. Stir from time to time with a wooden spoon to prevent burning. Strain mixture through a nylon sieve, bottle in clean, warm bottles and cork. This sauce keeps well for a long time. Makes about 6 × 300 ml/½ pint (1¼ cup) bottles.

Fresh Tomato Juice

Nothing matches the flavour of home-made juice. When tomatoes are cheap, make this in double or triple quantities and keep tightly covered in the refrigerator.

12 medium, ripe tomatoes, chopped; 120 ml/4 fl oz (½ cup) water; 1 medium onion, sliced; 2 sticks celery (with leaves), sliced; 1 bay leaf; 3 sprigs parsley.
SEASONING: 1–2 tsp salt; freshly ground black pepper; 1 tsp Worcestershire sauce; 1 tsp sugar.

Place tomatoes in a saucepan with water, onion, celery, bay leaf and parsley. Simmer for 15 minutes. Strain and add seasoning ingredients to taste. Chill well before serving. Serves 4–6.

TONGUE

Smooth, richly flavoured tongue, sold fresh, salted or smoked, is one of the best of cold meats and is excellent served hot with a piquant sauce. Cooked, sliced tongue can be crumbed and fried or used in savoury dishes.

Ox (beef), calf and lamb tongues are available; pig (pork) tongue is available with the head. Whatever the variety, smaller tongues are usually better than larger; for prime texture, an ox (beef) tongue should be under 1.5 kg (3 lb). Fresh or salted tongues should be soft to the touch, smoked tongue should be firm but not hard.

☐ **Basic Preparation:** If salted or smoked tongue has been heavily salted (ask the butcher), it must be blanched before cooking. Cover with cold water, bring very slowly to the boil and drain.

☐ **To Cook:** Place tongue (fresh, salted or smoked) in a saucepan and cover with cold water. For 1 ox (beef) tongue or 6–8 lamb tongues, add 6 whole allspice, 6 whole cloves, 6 black peppercorns, a bouquet garni, 1 sliced onion, 1 sliced carrot and 1 sliced stick celery. Add 1½ tsp salt if cooking fresh tongue. Bring slowly to the boil, skim the surface and simmer, for about 3 hours for ox (beef) tongue and 1–1½ hours for lamb tongues.

The boiled tongue is cooked when one of the small bones near the root end can be easily pulled out. Cool in liquid until cool enough to handle, then take tongue out, remove remaining bones and trim off root. Slit underside of skin and remove. Skin should come off easily if you push thumbs underneath it to ease edges, then peel off **(See opposite)**. Tongue is then finished as the recipe directs.

To carve: Cut ox (beef) or calf tongue into slices straight across starting from the thickest part. Toward the thin end, change direction to carve diagonal slices. Carve lamb tongues in long diagonal slices. Carve pressed tongue in thin slices across the top.

Braised Tongue with Sour Cream

1 onion, chopped; 1 carrot, chopped; 1 stick celery, chopped; 1 fresh ox (beef) tongue,

cooked; 125 g/4 oz (½ cup) butter, melted; 120–250 ml/4–8 fl oz (½–1 cup) cooking liquid from tongue; 250 ml/8 fl oz (1 cup) sour cream; salt and freshly ground pepper.

To braise tongue, place vegetables in a large roasting pan. Place tongue on top and pour over melted butter. Cook uncovered in a preheated moderate oven (180°C/350°F, Gas Mark 4) for 45 minutes–1 hour or until tongue is nicely browned. Baste every 10 minutes with pan juices, adding a little of the liquid in which tongue was cooked if juices are evaporating.

Remove tongue to a heated platter. Rub contents of roasting pan through a sieve and return to pan. Boil down, stirring if necessary, until thick. Stir in sour cream and heat to just under boiling point. Season with salt and pepper and serve over tongue. Serves 6.

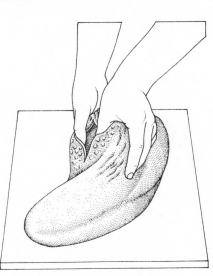

Pressed Tongue

1 fresh, salted or smoked ox (beef) tongue, freshly cooked; sauce of your choice (see below and right) to serve.

After trimming and skinning tongue, curl it while still warm into an 18 cm (7 in) soufflé dish or cake tin (pan). Place on top a plate which will just fit inside the dish or tin (pan), then put a heavy weight, at least 3 kg (7 lb), on the plate. Chill overnight.

Run a knife round the edge and unmould tongue on to a serving plate. Serve in thin slices with Cumberland Sauce (page 91), Rémoulade Sauce (page 205) or one of the following sauces. Serves 6–8.

Apple and Horseradish Sauce

3 cooking apples, peeled, cored and sliced; 2 tbsp water; 2 tbsp sugar; 1 strip lemon rind; 2 tbsp grated horseradish.

Put apples into a heavy saucepan with water, sugar and lemon rind. Cover and cook

gently to a pulp. Cool, remove lemon rind and mash. Stir in horseradish. Makes about 350 ml/12 fl oz (1½ cups).

Spiced Mustard Sauce

2 tbsp brown sugar; 3 tbsp cider or white wine vinegar; 4 tbsp olive oil; 1 tsp prepared English mustard; ½ tsp salt; freshly ground black pepper; pinch ground cloves.

Mix ingredients. Makes about 150 ml/ ¼ pint (⅔ cup).

Crumbed Tongue

8–10 × 1 cm (½ in) thick slices cooked tongue; seasoned flour; 2 eggs beaten; 2 tbsp cold water; 60 g/2 oz (1 cup) fresh breadcrumbs; 2 tbsp oil; 60 g/2 oz (4 tbsp) butter; Rémoulade Sauce (page 205) to serve.

Turn slices of tongue in seasoned flour and pat off excess. Mix egg and water and coat slices with mixture, then with breadcrumbs. Chill for 20 minutes. Fry in oil and butter, turning once, until golden-brown. Drain on crumpled paper towels and serve with Rémoulade Sauce. Serves 4.

Ox Tongue au Gratin

1 fresh or salted, cooked ox (beef) tongue; 3 onions, sliced; 90 g/3 oz (6 tbsp) butter; 1 tbsp flour; 120 ml/4 fl oz (½ cup) dry white wine; 120 ml/4 fl oz (½ cup) beef stock (bouillon); 8–10 mushrooms, sliced; 60 g/2 oz (1 cup) fresh breadcrumbs.

Cut tongue into 1 cm (½ in) thick slices and arrange the slices in a shallow ovenproof dish. Cook onions gently in ½ the butter until soft. Sprinkle in flour, blend thoroughly and stir in wine and stock. Simmer until thickened and spread over tongue. Heat remaining butter, add mushrooms and breadcrumbs and toss until coated with butter. Top dish with mixture and place in a preheated moderately hot oven (200°C/ 400°F, Gas Mark 6) for 15–20 minutes, or under a preheated grill (broiler) until top is crisp and golden. Serves 6.

TORTE

The German word for an open tart or rich cake, containing such ingredients as ground nuts, spices, fruit, chocolate and cream. Some tortes are a cake-like mixture, baked in a pastry case (pie shell); some have many layers interspersed with butter cream.

Many tortes are made with little or no flour, ground nuts taking its place and whisked eggs providing aeration and structure. **See recipes.**

See also *Sacher Torte, Linzer Torte* and *Black Forest Cherry Torte.*

Hazelnut Torte

*6 eggs, separated; 1 whole egg; 180 g/6 oz
(¾ cup) caster sugar; 125 g/4 oz (1 cup)
ground hazelnuts; 45 g/1½ oz (¾ cup) fresh
white breadcrumbs; 1 tsp flour.*
FILLING: *350 ml/12 fl oz (1½ cups) double
(heavy) cream; 1 tsp caster sugar; 1 tsp
vanilla essence (extract); 60 g/2 oz (½ cup)
ground hazelnuts.*

Beat egg yolks and whole egg together until
thick and pale yellow. Gradually beat in
125 g/4 oz (½ cup) sugar, then nuts and
breadcrumbs. Continue to beat until mixture
forms a dense, moist mass. Whisk egg whites
in another bowl until they begin to foam,
then gradually add remaining sugar.
Continue to whisk until whites form stiff
glossy peaks. Mix about half the egg whites
into hazelnut mixture, sprinkle flour over and
fold in remaining egg whites. Pour into a
buttered and floured 25 cm (10 in) spring-
release cake tin (springform pan). Bake in a
preheated cool oven (150°C/300°F, Gas
Mark 2) for 35–45 minutes or until cake
shrinks away slightly from sides of tin (pan).
Remove from oven, release spring on tin
(pan) and remove sides. Allow cake to cool.
FILLING: Whip cream and add sugar and
vanilla. Slice cake into 2 layers and sandwich
back together with ⅓ cream. Using a spatula,
cover top and sides of cake with remaining
cream, and scatter ground hazelnuts over
top and sides. Serves 10.

Griestorte

*3 eggs, separated; 125 g/4 oz (½ cup) caster
sugar; grated rind and juice ½ lemon;
60 g/2 oz (⅓ cup) fine ground semolina
(semolina flour); 2 tbsp ground almonds;
150 ml/¼ pint (⅔ cup) double (heavy) cream,
whipped; 250 g/8 oz (1½ cups) raspberries or
strawberries, sprinkled with 1 tbsp caster
sugar.*

Beat egg yolks with sugar over a pan of hot
water until thick and mousse-like. Remove
from heat, add lemon rind and juice and
continue beating until very thick and pale.
Stir in semolina and ground almonds. Whisk
egg whites until stiff peaks form, then fold

into mixture. Turn at once into a greased
and bottom-lined 20 cm (8 in) cake tin (pan)
that has been dusted with caster sugar and
flour. Bake in a preheated moderate oven
(180°C/350°F, Gas Mark 4) for 30–40
minutes or until cake shrinks a little from
sides of tin (pan). Cool on a wire rack. When
cold, split cake into 2 layers and fill with
whipped cream. Cover top of cake with
raspberries or strawberries. Serves 8.

Mocha Torte

*2 × 90 g/3 oz packets (about 18) sponge
fingers (lady fingers); 1 litre/1¾ pints (4 cups)
double (heavy) cream; 3 tbsp drinking
chocolate powder (sweetened cocoa); 1 tsp
instant coffee powder; 250 ml/8 fl oz (1 cup)
sweet sherry.*
DECORATION: *250 ml/8 fl oz (1 cup) double
(heavy) cream (optional); 100 g (3½ oz) bar
milk chocolate (sweet chocolate).*

Cut sponge fingers in half diagonally to give
2 pointed wedges from each biscuit. Whip
cream with drinking chocolate and instant
coffee until it just begins to hold its shape.
Pour sherry into a shallow dish. Dip sponge
finger halves, one at a time, in sherry, quickly,
to prevent them becoming soggy, and
arrange one layer, cartwheel fashion, on
bottom of greased and bottom-lined 28 cm
(11 in) spring-release tin (springform pan).
Top with ⅓ whipped cream. Repeat with
another layer of sherried sponge fingers,
then cream, and repeat again. You will have
3 layers each of biscuits and cream. Cover
with foil and refrigerate overnight. Remove
sides of tin (pan) and place on a large
serving plate.
DECORATION: Lightly whip well chilled cream
until it holds its shape, and pipe rosettes
around edge of cake. Using a swivel-bladed
vegetable peeler, shave curls of chocolate
from narrow edge of bar of chocolate and
strew over cream, between cream rosettes.
Serve cut into wedges. Serves 12.

Caramel Almond Torte

*3 eggs, separated; 125 g/4 oz (½ cup) caster
sugar; ½ tsp vanilla essence (extract); 4 tbsp*

*Caramel Syrup (page 56); 6 tbsp flour; ½ tsp
baking powder; ½ tsp salt; ¼ tsp cream of
tartar; 60 g/2 oz (½ cup) chopped toasted
almonds.*
TOPPING: *250 ml/8 fl oz (1 cup) double
(heavy) cream, whipped with 1 tbsp brown
sugar; few whole toasted almonds.*

Beat egg yolks until thick, pale and creamy,
then beat in 60 g/2 oz (¼ cup) sugar and the
vanilla. Gradually add caramel syrup and
beat until well blended. Sift flour, baking
powder and salt over mixture and gently fold
in. Whisk egg whites until foamy, add cream
of tartar and whisk until whites hold their
shape. Gradually whisk in remaining sugar,
and continue whisking until whites are a stiff
snow. Fold whites into yolk mixture with
chopped almonds. Pour into a lightly
greased 23 cm (9 in) spring-release cake tin
(springform pan). Bake in a preheated
moderate oven (180°C/350°F, Gas Mark 4)
for 25 minutes or until golden-brown on top
and beginning to shrink away slightly from
sides of tin (pan). Remove sides of tin (pan)
and cool on a wire rack. Top with whipped
cream and almonds to serve. Serves 8.

Coffee and Nut Dobostorte

*4 eggs; 180 g/6 oz (¾ cup) caster sugar;
150 g/5 oz (1¼ cups) flour.*
BUTTER CREAM: *75 g/2½ oz (⅓ cup) sugar;
120 ml/4 fl oz (½ cup) water; 3 egg yolks;
250 g/8 oz (1 cup) unsalted butter, creamed;
60 g/2 oz (½ cup) ground hazelnuts; 1 tbsp
coffee essence (extract).*
CARAMEL: *150 g/5 oz (⅔ cup) sugar; 5 tbsp
water.*
DECORATION: *60 g/2 oz (½ cup) ground
hazelnuts; 8 whole hazelnuts.*

Grease 3 baking trays and dust lightly with
flour, shaking off excess. Using a cake tin
(pan) or plate as a guide, mark 5 × 20 cm
(8 in) circles on trays, 2 circles on 2 of the
trays and one on the third tray. Whisk eggs
with sugar in a heatproof bowl over a
saucepan of very hot water (double boiler)
off the heat until mixture is thick and
mousse-like. Remove from saucepan and
continue whisking until bowl is cold. Using a
metal spoon, fold in sifted flour, lightly and
thoroughly. Divide mixture into 5 portions
and spread inside each circle on prepared
baking trays. Bake in a preheated
moderately hot oven (190°C/375°F, Gas
Mark 5) for 5–8 minutes or until pale
golden-brown. Remove from oven. Using a
sharp knife, trim rounds if necessary. Cool
on wire racks.
BUTTER CREAM: Dissolve sugar in water,
stirring, over medium heat. Bring to the boil
and boil for 5–6 minutes, without stirring,
until syrup reaches thread stage. (To test,
drop ½ tsp syrup into 250 ml/8 fl oz (1 cup) of
ice cold water: it should form threads.) Pour

on to egg yolks and whisk until thick and mousse-like. Gradually beat in creamed butter, ground hazelnuts and coffee essence (extract). Place one round of cake on an oiled baking tray ready to coat with caramel. CARAMEL: Combine sugar and water in a heavy saucepan over very low heat and stir until sugar dissolves. Increase heat, bring to the boil and boil steadily, without stirring, until mixture is a rich dark brown. Pour at once over round of cake. Cool a few minutes until on point of setting, then mark into 8 portions with an oiled knife and trim around edges. To assemble torte, sandwich cake rounds together with ½ butter cream, placing caramel-covered round on top. Spread sides of cake with ½ remaining butter cream, and press ground hazelnuts on to sides. Using rest of butter cream, pipe a rosette on each portion and top with hazelnuts. Serves 8.

Malakoff Torte

A rich, luscious torte made of sponge fingers (lady fingers) dipped in rum syrup and layered with almond coffee butter cream.

18 sponge fingers (lady fingers); 250 ml/ 8 fl oz (1 cup) water; 250 ml/8 fl oz (1 cup) rum; 1 tbsp sugar; toasted hazelnuts to decorate; Crème Chantilly to serve (page 88).
COFFEE CREAM: *280 g/9 oz (1 cup plus 2 tbsp) butter; 75 g/2½ oz (⅓ cup) sugar; 4½ tbsp ground almonds; 1½ tbsp strong black coffee; 5 tbsp double (heavy) cream.*

First make coffee cream. Beat butter until soft and creamy, then gradually add sugar, beating until soft and fluffy. Fold in almonds, and gradually stir in coffee and cream until mixture is smooth and light. Split sponge fingers in half diagonally to give 2 pointed wedges from each biscuit. Combine water, rum and sugar in a shallow dish. Dip sponge finger halves in this mixture, quickly to prevent them from becoming soggy, and arrange one layer, cartwheel fashion, on bottom of greased and bottom-lined 25 cm (10 in) spring-release tin (springform pan). Spread with half of the coffee cream. Repeat layers and finish with a third layer of sponge fingers. Chill for at least 3 hours or preferably overnight. Turn out on to a serving plate and decorate with toasted hazelnuts. Serve with crème chantilly. The torte may also be decorated with rosettes of cream and whole hazelnuts. Serves 12.

TORTILLA

The national bread of Mexico, a tortilla is a thin, flat cake made with cornmeal, from white corn, called *masa*. Tortillas are cooked on a griddle without browning, so they are quite soft, and may be eaten like this or fried briefly in oil to crisp them.

Tortillas may be used as a plate or scoop for other food, or stuffed with a filling and rolled up. They are also the basis for other dishes: a Mexican family might start the day with freshly-made soft tortillas, then eat more tortillas at every meal of the day to accompany meat or as *tacos* or *enchiladas*.

Tortilla is also the Spanish name for omelette. See also *Tacos, Enchiladas* and Spanish Omelette (page 250).

TOURNEDOS

The French name for a small thick steak cut from the centre of a beef fillet (tenderloin); trim fillet (tenderloin) of all fat and gristle **(Fig 1 below)** and remove outer sinew **(2)**. A tournedos should be about 5 cm (2 in) thick when it is ready for cooking **(3)**, but if it comes from the area toward the narrower end of the fillet (tenderloin), it may be cut thicker and flattened with the hand to make it a little wider. Shape it with your hands into a neat circular shape, and tie string round it to keep the shape, before cooking it.

A tournedos can be grilled (broiled) but is usually pan-fried, and is often served on a fried bread croûte (see page 90), to catch the juices. It can be garnished in many ways to make luxury dishes which take their names from the garnish.

In America tournedos are sometimes known as *filets mignons*.

Tournedos

1 tbsp oil; 30 g/1 oz (2 tbsp) butter; 4 tournedos; 4 round Croûtes (white bread sautéed in clarified butter, see page 90); salt and freshly ground black pepper; sauce or garnish of your choice (see right).

Heat a large, heavy frying pan (skillet) until a drop of water flicked on to the surface will bounce and sizzle. Add oil and heat, then add butter and, when just turning brown, put in tournedos. Sear for 2 minutes on each side. Reduce heat to moderately low and continue to cook, turning once, about 5 minutes more for rare, 7 minutes for medium-done. Remove strings from tournedos and place each on a hot croûte set on a heated plate. Season with salt and

pepper. Garnish as desired and serve immediately. Serves 4.
VARIATIONS
Tournedos Rossini: Place a slice of foie gras on each tournedos and spoon 175 ml/6 fl oz (¾ cup) hot Madeira Sauce (see page 369) over them. Top each with a slice of truffle.
Tournedos Parisienne: Garnish each plate with asparagus tips and Noisette Potatoes (see page 308), and spoon 175 ml/6 fl oz (¾ cup) warm Béarnaise Sauce (see page 370) over them.
Tournedos Chasseur: Spoon 175 ml/6 fl oz (¾ cup) hot Sauce Chasseur (see page 369) over tournedos and sprinkle with finely chopped parsley.

TREACLE

A by-product of sugar refining; it is the fluid left after sugar cane has been processed.

There are two types of treacle: *black treacle*, which closely resembles molasses but is sweeter, and *light treacle*, better known as golden (light corn) syrup (see page 146). Light treacle is used in the filling for the nursery favourite Treacle Tart. Black treacle enhances the flavour or rich fruit cakes, puddings and gingerbreads. It can also be used in barbecue sauces, or indeed in almost any recipe calling for molasses.

Treacle is obtainable from most good supermarkets, health food shops and delicatessens. **See recipes.**

See also Rich Ginger Cake (page 144).

Rich Treacle Tart

1 quantity Plain Shortcrust Pastry (page 274); 90 g/3 oz (1½ cups) fresh bread or plain cake crumbs; 370 g/12 oz (1 cup) golden (light corn) syrup; 1 egg, beaten; grated rind and juice ½ lemon.

Roll out pastry (dough) and use to line a 20 cm (8 in) pie plate. Combine remaining ingredients and pour into pastry case (pie shell). Use any remaining pastry (dough) to decorate the tart with a lattice design. Bake in a preheated moderately hot oven (200°C/ 400°F, Gas Mark 6) for 10 minutes, then reduce heat to moderate (180°C/350°F, Gas Mark 4) and bake for a further 20 minutes. Allow to cool, during which time filling will set. Serves 6.

Preparing Tournedos

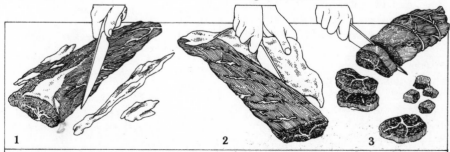

1 2 3

Trifle –

Old-Fashioned Ginger Cake

250 g/8 oz (2 cups) flour; 1 tsp mixed spice (ground allspice); 2 tsp ground ginger; 1 tsp bicarbonate of soda (baking soda); 125 g/4 oz (½ cup) butter; 60 g/2 oz (⅓ cup) firmly packed brown sugar; 2 tbsp black treacle (molasses); 180 g/6 oz (½ cup) golden (light corn) syrup; 2 eggs, beaten; 120 ml/4 fl oz (½ cup) milk.

Sift flour, spice, ginger and soda into a bowl. Combine butter, sugar, treacle (molasses) and syrup in a small heavy saucepan. Heat gently until melted and dissolved, then allow to cool. Stir into dry ingredients with eggs and milk and beat thoroughly until smooth. Pour into a greased and lined 18 cm (7 in) square cake tin (pan). Bake in a preheated cool oven (150°C/300°F, Gas Mark 2) for 1¼–1½ hours or until a skewer inserted in centre comes out clean. Cool in tin (pan) for 15 minutes, then turn out.

Treacle Scones

250 g/8 oz (2 cups) self-raising flour; 1 tsp baking powder; 1 tsp mixed spice (ground allspice); pinch salt; 60 g/2 oz (4 tbsp) butter; 1½ tbsp caster sugar; 2 tbsp sultanas (golden raisins), optional; 1 tbsp black treacle (molasses); about 150 ml/¼ pint (⅔ cup) milk.

Sift flour, baking powder, spice and salt into a bowl. Rub (cut) in butter until mixture resembles fine breadcrumbs. Stir in sugar and sultanas (golden raisins), if using. Gently heat treacle (molasses) in a small saucepan and mix thoroughly with half the milk. Add to dry ingredients with enough of the remaining milk to make a soft dough. Turn dough on to a floured work surface and flatten out to about 2 cm (¾ in) thick. Cut into rounds or squares using a floured scone cutter or sharp knife. Place on a lightly greased baking tray. Bake in a preheated hot oven (230°C/450°F, Gas Mark 8) for 10–12 minutes or until well risen and golden-brown. Cool on a wire rack. Makes about 12.

Bara Brith

250 g/8 oz (2 cups) self-raising flour; pinch salt; 1 tsp mixed spice (ground allspice); 60 g/2 oz (4 tbsp) butter; 75 g/2½ oz (⅓ cup) sugar; grated rind 1 lemon; 140 g/4½ oz (¾ cup) sultanas (golden raisins); 90 g/3 oz (¼ cup) black treacle (molasses); 1 egg, beaten; ½ tsp bicarbonate of soda (baking soda); 120 ml/4 fl oz (½ cup) milk.

Sift flour, salt and spice into a bowl. Rub (cut) in butter until mixture resembles fine breadcrumbs. Stir in sugar, lemon rind and sultanas (golden raisins). Add treacle (molasses) and egg. Dissolve soda in milk, add to flour mixture and mix until well blended. Turn into a greased and lined

21 × 15 cm (8½ × 6 in) loaf tin (pan). Bake in a preheated moderate oven (180°C/350°F, Gas Mark 4) for about 1¼ hours or until a skewer inserted in centre comes out clean. Turn on to a wire rack to cool. Wrap in foil and store for 24 hours before serving.

TRIFLE

English trifle is similar to tipsy cake. It contains sponge cake, soaked in a combination of good sweet sherry and brandy, rich egg custard, cream, nuts and jam. Although not traditional, some people like to add fresh or canned fruit to the sponge cake base.

Trifle

2 × 18 cm (7 in) Sponge Sandwich layers, made the day before (page 53); strawberry or raspberry jam; 120 ml/4 fl oz (½ cup) sweet sherry; 2 tbsp brandy; about 250 ml/8 fl oz (1 cup) Crème Anglaise (page 97); 250–350 ml/8–12 fl oz (1–1½ cups) Crème Chantilly (page 88); 60 g/2 oz (½ cup) almonds, blanched and split.
DECORATION: *6 glacé (candied) cherries, halved; candied angelica, rinsed in warm water to remove sugar coating and cut into strips; 60 g/2 oz (½ cup) roughly crushed macaroons (optional).*

Cut sponge into 3.5 cm (1½ in) pieces and spread each piece lightly with jam. Pile into a serving dish and sprinkle with sherry and brandy. Allow to soak while making the crème anglaise. Pour hot custard over soaked cake, cover and chill overnight. Cover trifle thickly with crème chantilly, piling it up in decorative swirls. Sprinkle almonds over, and decorate with glacé (candied) cherries, strips of angelica and crushed macaroons. Serves 8–10.

TRIPE

The lining of the stomach of cattle or sheep, but particularly the former. These animals actually have four different stomachs, so tripe is available either quite smooth or honeycombed. Tripe is nearly always sold blanched and partly cooked, but it still needs further long, slow cooking. This is usually preceded by a second blanching, in order to freshen the flavour. One of the classic accompaniments to tripe is onions. **See recipes.**

Tripe and Onions in Parsley Sauce

1 kg (2 lb) tripe, cut into squares; 350 ml/ 12 fl oz (1½ cups) water; 5 onions, sliced; 1 tsp salt.
PARSLEY SAUCE: *60 g/2 oz (4 tbsp) butter; 2 tbsp flour; 250 ml/8 fl oz (1 cup) milk; salt and freshly ground black pepper; 2 tbsp chopped parsley.*

Place tripe in a large saucepan, cover with cold water and bring to the boil. Boil for 5 minutes, then drain and discard water. Add measured water, bring to the boil, cover and simmer for 1 hour. Add onions and salt and continue to cook until tripe is tender – about 1 further hour. Take care not to overcook. When tender, drain off liquid and reserve 250 ml/8 fl oz (1 cup) for the sauce.
PARSLEY SAUCE: Melt butter in a clean saucepan and add flour. Cook without browning for 2 minutes. Remove from heat and stir in reserved liquid from tripe and milk. Return to heat and cook, stirring, until sauce thickens. Season with salt and pepper. Add parsley, tripe and onions. Serves 6.

Tripes à la Lyonnaise

1 kg (2 lb) tripe; 1 tsp salt; 4 large onions, finely sliced; 1 clove garlic, chopped; 60 g/2 oz (4 tbsp) butter; salt and freshly ground white pepper; 350 ml/12 fl oz (1½ cups) dry white wine; 2 tbsp lemon juice; 1 tbsp chopped parsley to garnish.

Place piece of tripe in large saucepan, cover with water and bring to the boil. Drain off water, and add fresh water just to cover. Add salt, bring to the boil and simmer gently until tender, about 1 hour. Drain tripe and cut into thin strips about 5 cm (2 in) long. Fry onions and garlic in 30 g/1 oz (2 tbsp) butter until golden. Add remaining butter with tripe and cook for a further 5 minutes. Season with salt and pepper, and stir in wine. Cook over high heat for 1 minute, then reduce heat, cover and simmer gently for 1 hour. Add lemon juice, and sprinkle with parsley before serving. Serves 6.

Casserole of Tripe

500 g (1 lb) tripe; 1 knuckle veal, split; 2 rashers (slices) lean bacon, rind removed and cut into squares; 1 large onion, sliced; 3–4 carrots, quartered; 30 g/1 oz (2 tbsp) butter; 1 clove garlic, chopped; 1 tbsp chopped parsley; 250 ml/8 fl oz (1 cup) dry white wine; salt and freshly ground black pepper.

Place tripe and veal knuckle in a saucepan, cover with cold water and bring to the boil. Drain off water. Fry bacon, onion and carrots in butter for about 5 minutes. Cut tripe into small squares, and place on top of vegetables with knuckle. Sprinkle with garlic and parsley, add wine, and bring just to the boil. Cover tightly and cook very gently for 2–2½ hours. Remove veal knuckle and season casserole with salt and pepper to taste before serving. Serves 4.

Right: Potato and Parsley Stuffing (page 418) and Rice Stuffing with Herbs (page 419)

TROUT

The flavour of this freshwater fish is so delicate and the texture so fine it is regarded as one of the great fish of the world.

Trout are caught in mountain streams and lakes, and many fishermen consider the best method of cooking them is to dip them in flour and sauté each side in butter or bacon fat, with as little time as possible between catching and eating.

Indeed, they are absolutely delicious treated this way, but not everyone has the opportunity to fish for trout. Most people rely on the fishmonger to supply fresh trout. These are produced especially for the market at trout farms, and their quality is excellent. They are also available frozen, and can be purchased from good supermarkets and delicatessens.

Smoked trout is also considered a superb delicacy. Serve skinned and filleted with thin brown bread and butter, a twist of lemon and a grinding of black pepper. Smoked trout is available at good delicatessens.

☐ **Basic Preparation:**

To clean fresh trout: Split the fish along the belly from the vent to the head. Remove the gills, entrails and stomach lining, leaving the head and tail intact. Rinse well in cold running water to remove all trace of blood. Dry well with paper towels.

To prepare cleaned fresh trout: Simply rinse lightly in cold water and pat dry with paper towels.

To prepare frozen trout: Allow fish to thaw according to instructions on the packet. Rinse lightly in cold water and pat dry with paper towels.

To fillet smoked or cooked trout: Cut the fish down the lateral line along the side. Hold the knife against the backbone and, with a fork, ease the flesh from the rib cage and backbone. Slide the 2 fillets off the fish to each side of it. Lift up the tail and slide the knife under the backbone, lifting it up and easing off the flesh. Discard the tail, backbone and head, leaving 4 fillets ready to eat.

☐ **To Cook:** Trout can be grilled (broiled), baked, poached, barbecued or pan-fried. Be careful not to overcook or the flesh will be dry and powdery, losing much flavour. The flesh should be moist and flake easily when sufficiently cooked. Leave the head on and when done the eye will be quite white and opaque. **See also recipes.**

BAKED TROUT Season the trout cavity with freshly ground black pepper and salt. Put in a buttered shallow ovenproof dish, dot with butter, pour over 4 tbsp white wine, cover with foil and bake in a preheated moderate oven

Left: Taramasalata (page 428) and Savoury Tuna Spread (page 449)

(180°C/350°F, Gas Mark 4) for 15–20 minutes.

POACHED TROUT Lower trout into boiling court bouillon (see page 85) and cook for 5 minutes. If serving hot, transfer drained trout to a heated platter and pour over a little melted butter. If trout is to be served cold, allow to cool in court bouillon and remove skin just before serving.

BARBECUED TROUT Season trout with salt and freshly ground black pepper, place a knob of butter or bacon fat in the cavity, spread fish with softened butter. Wrap in foil and cook over or in coals for 10–15 minutes.

GRILLED (BROILED) TROUT Wrap each trout with a very thin bacon rasher (slice). Place under a preheated moderate grill (broiler) and grill (broil) for about 5 minutes on each side or until the bacon is crisp and trout is cooked.

PAN-FRIED TROUT For 2 trout, melt 30 g/1 oz (2 tbsp) butter and 2 tsp oil in a large, heavy-based frying pan (skillet). Dip the fish lightly in seasoned flour and place in the pan when the butter stops foaming. Fry over moderate heat for 4–5 minutes on each side or until the eye is white and opaque and the flesh easily penetrated with a fine skewer.

Trout Meunière

2 trout, cleaned; milk; seasoned flour; 90 g/3 oz (6 tbsp) butter; 2 tbsp oil; 1 lemon, sliced; squeeze lemon juice; salt and freshly ground black pepper; chopped parsley to garnish.

Dip trout in milk, then dust lightly with seasoned flour and shake off any excess. Melt 60 g/2 oz (4 tbsp) butter and the oil in a large frying pan (skillet). When butter foams, add trout and cook for about 6 minutes on each side or until golden-brown and flesh flakes easily when tested with a fine skewer. Transfer to a heated serving dish and place a few slices of lemon on each fish. Heat remaining butter in frying pan (skillet) and when it foams add lemon juice. Season with salt and pepper and pour sizzling butter over fish. Garnish with chopped parsley. Serves 2.

VARIATION

Trout Amandine: Cook trout as for Trout Meunière. Remove to a serving platter and keep warm. Heat 60 g/2 oz (4 tbsp) butter in a pan and gently fry 30 g/1 oz ($\frac{1}{4}$ cup) blanched, slivered almonds until golden-brown. Add 1 tbsp lemon juice, salt and pepper. Pour over hot fish and serve at once.

Trout Nantua

500 ml/18 fl oz (2 cups) water; 120 ml/4 fl oz ($\frac{1}{2}$ cup) white wine; 1 bay leaf; 2 sprigs parsley; 6 black peppercorns; salt; juice $\frac{1}{2}$ lemon; 4 trout, cleaned.
SAUCE: *150 ml/$\frac{1}{4}$ pint ($\frac{2}{3}$ cup) Mayonnaise*

(page 204); 5 tbsp tomato juice; dash Tabasco (hot pepper) sauce; salt and freshly ground black pepper; 60 g (2 oz) cooked shelled prawns (shrimp), deveined.
GARNISH: *1 cucumber, finely sliced; watercress sprigs.*

Combine water, wine, bay leaf, parsley, peppercorns, salt and lemon juice in a large frying pan (skillet). Bring to the boil, then reduce heat and place trout side by side in simmering liquid. Poach trout very gently for 5–8 minutes or until flesh will flake easily when tested with a fine skewer. Allow to cool in the liquid. Drain trout, and skin and fillet fish.
SAUCE: Combine mayonnaise, tomato juice, Tabasco (hot pepper) sauce, salt, pepper and prawns (shrimp) and spoon over fish. Garnish with cucumber slices and watercress sprigs. Serve with thin triangles of brown bread and butter. Serves 4.

Smoked Trout with Horseradish Cream

2 smoked trout; slices or wedges lemon or lime; citrus leaves or fresh dill; 2 tbsp grated horseradish; 250 ml/8 fl oz (1 cup) sour cream; salt and freshly ground black pepper; thin brown bread and butter sandwiches.

With a sharp knife, slit trout skin along back and belly, and cut through skin just behind head and in front of tail on both sides. Carefully peel off skin and place whole trout on a serving platter or board. Garnish with lemon or lime and a spray of citrus leaves or dill. Mix horseradish and sour cream, and season with salt and pepper. Place in a bowl. To serve, cut through flesh along back and down centre, and loosen and lift off blocks of trout. When first side is served, turn over and repeat with other side. Serve with horseradish cream, freshly ground black pepper, and small brown bread and butter sandwiches. Serves 6–8.

Grilled Trout with Herbs

4 trout, cleaned; salt and freshly ground black pepper; lemon juice; 4 tbsp chopped mixed fresh herbs (parsley, chives, marjoram and basil); flour; 60 g/2 oz (4 tbsp) butter, melted.
SAUCE: *30 g/1 oz (2 tbsp) butter; 1 tbsp hot water; squeeze lemon juice.*

Season trout inside and out with salt, pepper and lemon juice. Place 1 tbsp chopped herbs inside each cavity. Sprinkle fish with a little flour, patting it in with the fingers. (This improves colour and also helps to keep fish moist.) Place melted butter in grill (broiler) tray, add fish and turn fish over in butter to coat on all sides. Cook under a preheated high grill (broiler) for 5–8 minutes, without turning, until skin is crispy and flesh flakes easily when tested with a fine skewer. The underside will also be cooked at this stage. Place fish on a heated serving platter. Add butter for sauce to grill (broiler) tray with hot water and lemon juice. Swirl this around to heat through, then pour over fish and serve at once. Serves 4.

Trout Del Nera

4 trout, cleaned; 2–3 tbsp olive oil; salt and freshly ground black pepper; 20 g/⅔ oz (½ cup) chopped parsley; few sprigs fresh rosemary, chopped; sprigs fresh herbs to garnish; 4 lemon wedges to serve.

Arrange trout on greased preheated grill (broiler) tray or pan, brush with oil and season with salt and pepper. Combine chopped herbs and sprinkle half over fish. Cook under a preheated high grill (broiler) for about 5–8 minutes, brushing occasionally with oil. Season with salt and pepper and sprinkle over remaining chopped herbs. Grill (broil) a further 1 minute or until fish flakes easily when tested with a fine skewer. Just before serving, trickle over a little more olive oil. Garnish with herb sprigs and serve with lemon wedges. Serves 4.

Baked Trout Rio

4 trout, cleaned; 2–3 tbsp lemon juice; salt and freshly ground black pepper; 1 clove garlic, crushed; 250 ml/8 fl oz (1 cup) dry white wine; 2 tbsp chopped parsley; 2 tbsp snipped chives; 2 tbsp dry breadcrumbs; 2 tbsp finely ground nuts; 60 g/2 oz (4 tbsp) butter, melted.

Season trout inside and out with lemon juice, salt and pepper, and place a little garlic inside each cavity. Arrange in a buttered baking dish just large enough to hold them in one layer. Pour wine over trout and sprinkle with parsley and chives. Mix breadcrumbs and nuts together and scatter over top, then pour over melted butter. Bake in a preheated moderately hot oven (200°C/400°F, Gas Mark 6) for 10–15 minutes or until fish flakes easily when

tested with a fine skewer. Serve trout straight from baking dish. Serves 4.

Smoked Trout Pâté

2 smoked trout, skinned and filleted; 250 ml/8 fl oz (1 cup) sour cream; 250 g/8 oz (1 cup) Ricotta cheese; juice ½ lemon; salt and freshly ground black pepper; Melba Toast to serve (page 212).

Flake trout and place in a blender with sour cream and Ricotta cheese. Blend until smooth. Or mash with a fork or process in a food processor and push through a sieve. The mixture should be very smooth. Stir in lemon juice, salt and pepper. Pack into a 750 ml/1¼ pint (3 cup) soufflé dish or 6 × 120 ml/4 fl oz (½ cup) individual pots. Cover and chill overnight. Serve with Melba toast. Serves 6.

Trout in Cream Sauce

30 g/1 oz (¼ cup) flour; salt and freshly ground black pepper; 4 trout, cleaned; 60 g/2 oz (4 tbsp) butter, melted; 175 ml/6 fl oz (¾ cup) single (light) cream; 1 tbsp snipped chives.

Season flour with salt and pepper and dust trout lightly, shaking off any excess flour. Brush a small baking dish with melted butter and place trout in dish. Brush fish with remaining butter to coat well. Bake in a preheated moderately hot oven (200°C/400°F, Gas Mark 6) for 7–10 minutes or until skin is brown and crisp, basting occasionally with butter in dish. Meanwhile, season cream with salt and pepper and bring to the boil. Continue boiling for about 3 minutes or until thickened slightly. Remove from heat and stir in chives. Place trout on a heated serving platter and pour over hot cream sauce. Serve immediately. Serves 4.

TRUFFLE

One of nature's best-kept secrets, the truffle has resisted exploitation by modern agriculture. It is an edible fungus which grows

underground, usually near oak trees, in many parts of the world. Not all truffles, however, have the same quality. The most esteemed are the black truffles from the Périgord in France, closely followed by the white truffles found in the Piedmont area of northern Italy.

The harvest takes place around late autumn, with the aid of specially trained pigs or dogs who sniff out the elusive truffles. Some truffles are used fresh, particularly for Christmas specialities such as roast truffled turkey, truffled *boudin blanc* (white pudding), or truffled goose liver pâté; others go into manufactured foods or are canned for year-round use.

Outside France and Italy, truffles usually come in cans – either as a whole small truffle, truffle pieces or peelings, or truffle juice. Canned truffles or truffle pieces may be used in any recipe calling for truffles and truffle juice may be used in a sauce. Even the peelings can be used to add flavour to a sauce, but should be removed before serving.

In almost all dishes, it is best to add the truffle to whatever it is intended to perfume and then leave for several hours, at least, to allow the perfume of the truffle to permeate the food.

Ways to Use Truffles

Use a small truffle to advantage in a terrine or pâté; with a loin of pork for roasting; when slipped under the skin of a plump chicken before gently poaching; or when added to a flavoursome brown Madeira sauce and served with perfectly cooked beef fillet (tenderloin) or a warm, poached chicken liver mousse. **See recipes.**

Chicken Breasts with Truffle Sauce

1 × 30 g/1 oz can truffle pieces; 4 tbsp port or Madeira; 6 chicken fillets (skinless, boneless half-breasts); salt and freshly ground black pepper; about 60 g/2 oz (½ cup) flour; 90 g/3 oz (6 tbsp) clarified butter (page 49); 1 tbsp chopped shallot; 120 ml/4 fl oz (½ cup) chicken stock.

Mix truffle pieces and juice with port or Madeira, and leave to stand for 30 minutes. Season chicken with salt and pepper and lightly coat with flour. Cook chicken in hot clarified butter in a frying pan (skillet) for about 3 minutes each side or until springy to touch. Remove to a heated dish. Add shallot to pan and cook for about 1 minute. Stir in stock and truffle mixture, bring to the boil and reduce over high heat until slightly thickened and syrupy. Pour sauce over chicken and serve immediately. Serves 6.

Truffled Loin of Pork

1 × 1 kg (2 lb) boned pork loin (pork loin blade roast), rind removed (bone and rind reserved); salt and freshly ground black

pepper; 1 × 60 g/2 oz can truffle pieces, or 1 whole small truffle, chopped; 1 small clove garlic, sliced; 500 ml/18 fl oz (2 cups) chicken stock; 120 ml/4 fl oz (½ cup) dry white wine.

Spread meat flat and season with salt and pepper. Drain can of truffle pieces, if using, and reserve liquid. Place pieces of truffle at intervals along meat, together with slivers of garlic. Roll up meat neatly and tie securely with fine string. Leave for 1 hour, then place in baking dish with bones, trimmings and rind cut into strips. Roast in a preheated moderate oven (160°C/325°F, Gas Mark 3) for 30 minutes, then add stock, wine and liquid from truffle can, if available. Cover and leave to cook for 2–2½ hours longer. Remove pork and set aside to cool. Drain off liquid. Chill pork and liquid. Next day, remove layer of fat from jellied liquid. Slice pork and arrange on a serving platter, surrounded by chopped jelly. Serves 6.

TRUFFLE, CHOCOLATE

This is a rich, luscious, cocoa-covered ball, which earns its name from its similarity to the real truffle, fresh from the earth. Chocolate Truffles are perfect to serve with after-dinner coffee.

Chocolate Truffles

150 g/5 oz (5 squares) dark chocolate; 5 tbsp double (heavy) cream; 30 g/1 oz (2 tbsp) unsalted butter; rum or brandy (optional); sifted unsweetened cocoa powder.

Melt chocolate in a heatproof bowl placed over a pan of hot water. Bring cream to the boil in a pan, add to chocolate and mix well. Refrigerate overnight. Next day, heat mixture gently over hot water again; when melted, gradually blend in butter and flavour with a little rum or brandy if desired. Remove from heat and cool. Chill until firm. Form into small balls, and roll in cocoa. Store in refrigerator, but remove about 1 hour before serving. Makes about 24.

TUILES

Crisp curled wafer biscuits (cookies), very thin and delicious as petits fours with coffee or as an accompaniment to ice creams. After baking, the pliable mixture is draped over a rolling pin to cool, which gives the characteristic tuile shape. Handle the mixture quickly and lightly at this point as it cools and crisps quickly. Bake in batches of no more than 4 at a time for ease of handling. Tuiles can be flavoured with almonds, orange or lemon rind or vanilla essence (extract). Store in airtight containers.

Tuiles d'Amandes

2 egg whites; 125 g/4 oz (½ cup) caster sugar; 60 g/2 oz (½ cup) flour, sifted; ½ tsp vanilla essence (extract); 30 g/1 oz (¼ cup) blanched, slivered almonds; 60 g/2 oz (4 tbsp) butter, melted and cooled.

Beat egg whites until stiff and gradually beat in sugar. Gently fold in flour, vanilla, almonds and butter. Spread 3–4 tsp of mixture to form flat rounds or ovals, well separated from each other, on greased baking trays. Bake in a preheated moderately hot oven (190°C/375°F, Gas Mark 5) for 4–5 minutes or until golden. Remove from heat and, using a spatula, lift off carefully. Quickly drape over a rolling pin to cool. When cold, store in an airtight container. Makes 10–16 according to size required.
VARIATIONS
Tuiles à la Vanille: Follow recipe for Tuiles d'Amandes, omitting slivered almonds and increasing vanilla essence (extract) to ¾ tsp.
Tuiles à l'Orange: Follow recipe for Tuiles d'Amandes, omitting slivered almonds and vanilla and using 2 tsp finely grated orange rind instead (or lemon rind for lemon-flavoured Tuiles).

TUNA

Tuna is usually purchased in cans, but fresh tuna is available in fish markets in some parts of the world. It has dark flesh, which turns pink when cooked, and is usually sold in steaks. Fresh tuna should be skinned before serving; it can be grilled (broiled), sautéed, baked or poached or, sliced paper-thin, eaten raw in Japanese Sashimi (see page 366).

Canned tuna is sold packed in oil or brine, in solid-pack style (large pieces), chunk style (smaller pieces) and sandwich or salad style (flaked). Various manufacturers also can it with flavourings such as onion, tomato or curry etc. It is one of the best items to have on the emergency shelf. A can or two of tuna can be turned quickly into appetizers to serve with drinks, a hearty soup, a first course or main dish or, of course, into substantial salads and sandwiches.
☐ **To Cook:** Fresh tuna is often marinated before cooking and must be well basted while grilling (broiling) or baking. For grilling (broiling), baking or poaching use steaks about 4 cm (1½ in) thick; for pan-frying use thinner ones, about 2 cm (¾ in) thick, or slice the tuna thinly into escalopes, flour lightly and fry 2–3 minutes on each side. In general, it is best to leave the skin on the steaks for cooking, to hold them in shape, but peel it off before serving as it is unattractively dark and can have a strong flavour. **See recipes.**
Tuna Spreads
The spreads on page 449 can be used for sandwiches, or can be piled on toasted French bread and grilled (broiled) to make hot canapés. **See recipes.**

Tuna Brochettes

1 kg (2 lb) tuna steaks, cut 2 cm (¾ in) thick; 120 ml/4 fl oz (½ cup) olive oil; 4 tbsp lemon juice; 1 tsp salt; freshly ground black pepper; 2 sticks French bread, cut into 1 cm (½ in) slices; bay leaves.

Remove skin from tuna and cut meat into bite-sized pieces. Mix oil, lemon juice, salt and pepper, add tuna and marinate it for 1 hour, turning pieces gently once or twice. Thread a slice of bread on to a small bamboo or flat metal skewer, add a piece of fish and a bay leaf, and repeat until skewer contains 3 pieces of fish, 3 bay leaves and 4 pieces of bread. Do not push ingredients too close together. Repeat with more skewers and remaining bread, tuna and bay leaves. Brush filled skewers with marinade and cook under a preheated high grill (broiler) for about 10 minutes or until browned, turning and basting with marinade frequently. Serves 6.
NOTE: Soak bamboo skewers in hot water for 2 hours before using, to prevent charring.

Fresh Tuna with Coriander

4 tuna steaks, cut about 2 cm (¾ in) thick; 250 ml/8 fl oz (1 cup) dry white wine; seasoned flour; 2 tbsp oil; 30 g/1 oz (2 tbsp) butter; salt and freshly ground black pepper; 2 tsp lemon juice; 2 tbsp chopped fresh coriander leaves.

Marinate tuna in white wine for 2 hours. Drain, reserving wine. Dry steaks and dust lightly with seasoned flour. Heat oil in a frying pan (skillet), add butter and, when just turning brown, put steaks in. Sauté 3–5 minutes on each side. Remove tuna to heated plates, peel off skin and keep warm. Add reserved wine to pan and boil over high heat for 30 seconds, stirring in brown bits from pan. Remove from heat, season with salt and pepper and stir in lemon juice and coriander. Pour over fish and serve immediately. Serves 4.

Vitello Tonnato

(Veal with Tuna Sauce)
The famous and superb Italian summer dish of veal masked with a creamy tuna sauce. Serve with a green salad.

1 × 2 kg (4 lb) boned veal leg roast, rolled and tied; 6 anchovy fillets, chopped; 1 onion, sliced; 2 sticks celery, sliced; 2 carrots, sliced; 2 sprigs parsley; 2 cloves; salt and freshly ground black pepper; 2–3 bay leaves; 250 ml/8 fl oz (1 cup) dry white wine (optional); lemon slices to garnish.
TUNA SAUCE: *1 × 200 g/7 oz can tuna in oil, drained; 6 anchovy fillets; 1 tsp capers; 2 tbsp lemon juice; freshly ground black pepper; 120 ml/4 fl oz (½ cup) Mayonnaise (page 204).*

With a sharp-pointed knife make holes in surface of meat and insert pieces of anchovy. Place meat in a flameproof casserole with onion, celery, carrots, parsley, cloves, salt and pepper. Put bay leaves on top of meat. Pour in wine if using and sufficient water to cover meat. Bring slowly to the boil, then reduce heat, cover and simmer for 1½–2 hours. When veal is tender, remove string and allow to cool in the stock.
TUNA SAUCE: Pound tuna with anchovy fillets, capers and lemon juice, or purée in a food processor until smooth. Season with pepper. Combine with mayonnaise. Add a little of the veal stock if sauce is too thick.

Drain veal well when cold, put into an earthenware or glass bowl and cover with tuna sauce. Cover and marinate overnight. A few hours before serving, remove veal from sauce and slice thinly. Arrange slices on serving platter and spoon over sauce thinned with a little more veal stock or olive oil. Chill again until ready to serve. Garnish with sliced lemon. Serves 8.

Fresh Tuna with Peas, Tuscan Style

Tuscan cooks sauté thin slices of tuna and serve them in a superbly simple wine sauce with peas. Serve in deep plates with lots of bread to mop up the sauce.

4 tbsp olive oil; 1 clove garlic, crushed; 1 small onion, finely chopped; 500 g (1 lb) tuna fillets, skinned and thinly sliced; 4 tbsp dry white wine; 2 tsp tomato purée (paste); salt and freshly ground black pepper; 250 g/8 oz (1½ cups) cooked green peas; 2 tsp finely chopped parsley.

Heat oil in a large frying pan (skillet) and brown garlic and onion gently. Push vegetables to side of pan. Add tuna and brown lightly. Add wine and tomato purée (paste), and salt and pepper. Cover and cook on very low heat for 10–15 minutes. Add peas, heat through for a few minutes and serve very hot, sprinkled with finely chopped parsley. Serves 4–6.

Italian Tuna with Haricot Beans and Tomatoes

150 g/5 oz (¾ cup) dried haricot (navy) beans, soaked overnight and drained; 4 tbsp olive oil; 1 clove garlic, sliced; 3 large ripe tomatoes, peeled and chopped; 1 × 200 g/7 oz can tuna in oil, drained and broken into chunks; 1 tsp chopped fresh basil, or ½ tsp dried; salt and freshly ground black pepper.

Cook beans in fresh water to cover until tender. Drain. Heat oil in a large saucepan and brown garlic. Discard garlic and add tomatoes. Salt lightly and cook for 10 minutes. Stir in beans and tuna, sprinkle with basil and pepper and simmer 10 minutes. Serve very hot. Serves 6.

Hot Tuna and Potato Salad

4 medium potatoes, peeled, cooked and cut into chunks; 45 g/1½ oz (⅓ cup) sliced celery; 1 medium onion, chopped; 75 g/2½ oz (½ cup) cooked peas; 1 × 200 g/7 oz can tuna in oil; 4 rashers (slices) streaky bacon, rind removed; 3 tbsp sugar; 6 tbsp vinegar; 2 tbsp water; ½ tsp celery seeds; 1 egg, beaten; salt and freshly ground black pepper.

Put potatoes, celery, onion, peas and tuna with its oil into a shallow casserole. Put bacon into a cold frying pan (skillet) and cook slowly until crisp. Remove bacon and reserve. Add sugar, vinegar, water and celery seeds to bacon fat in pan and simmer 5 minutes. Stir a little of the hot mixture into egg, then stir this back into pan. Pour over potato and tuna mixture. Season with salt and pepper, mix lightly and level surface. Crumble bacon over top. Bake, uncovered, in a preheated moderate oven (180°C/350°F, Gas Mark 4) for about 15 minutes or until heated through. Serves 6.

Tuna and Apple Salad

1 large red apple, cored and finely sliced; 1 tbsp lemon juice; 60 g/2 oz (½ cup) thinly sliced celery; 1 × 200 g/7 oz can tuna in oil, drained and broken into chunks; salt and freshly ground black pepper; 4 tbsp Mayonnaise (page 204); 4 tbsp sour cream; lettuce leaves.

Toss apple slices in lemon juice and place in a bowl with celery and tuna. Season with salt and pepper, add mayonnaise and sour cream and mix lightly. Serve on a bed of lettuce. Serves 2 as a light luncheon, 4 as a first course.

Tuna Mornay

60 g/2 oz (4 tbsp) plus 2 tsp butter; 2 tbsp flour; 2 tsp dry mustard; 350 ml/12 fl oz (1½ cups) milk; salt and freshly ground black pepper; 60 g/2 oz (½ cup) grated cheese; 2 × 200 g/7 oz cans tuna in oil, drained and broken into chunks; 20 g/⅔ oz (⅓ cup) fresh breadcrumbs.

Melt 60 g/2 oz (4 tbsp) butter in a saucepan, blend in flour and cook over a gentle heat for 1 minute. Add mustard, then milk, stirring until sauce thickens. Season with salt and pepper and add 2 tbsp grated cheese. Fold in tuna and turn into a greased flameproof dish. Top with remaining cheese mixed with breadcrumbs and dot with remaining butter. Place under a preheated grill (broiler) until bubbly and golden. Serves 4.

Brandade of Tuna and Beans

A sturdy French provincial dish to serve with only a green salad and crusty bread.

210 g/7 oz (1 cup) dried haricot (navy) beans, soaked overnight and drained; 1 × 200 g/7 oz can tuna in oil, drained; 90 g/3 oz (¾ cup) grated mature (sharp) Cheddar cheese; 60 g/2 oz (4 tbsp) butter; 1 clove garlic, crushed; salt and freshly ground black pepper; 3 tbsp fine dry breadcrumbs.

Cook beans in fresh water to cover until very tender. Drain and mash beans thoroughly with a fork. Mash tuna into beans. Beat in cheese, half the butter, the garlic, salt and pepper. This can all be done in a food processor – brandade should have a firm texture. Pile mixture in a shallow, buttered baking dish. Sprinkle with breadcrumbs and dot with remaining butter. Bake in a preheated moderately hot oven (200°C/400°F, Gas Mark 6) for 25 minutes or until browned. Serve warm. Serves 4.

Tuna with Peas

2 × 200 g/7 oz cans tuna in oil; 1 onion, finely chopped; 2 tbsp tomato purée (paste); 1 tbsp chopped parsley; 500 g/1 lb (3 cups) green peas; salt and freshly ground black pepper; pinch sugar; freshly cooked pasta or rice to serve.

Drain oil from cans of tuna into a large saucepan. Heat oil and sauté onion over a medium heat until soft. Stir in tomato purée (paste), parsley, peas and water barely to cover peas. Season with salt, pepper and sugar. Cover and cook for 10 minutes. Add tuna, broken into chunks, and simmer for 3 minutes more. Serve over freshly cooked pasta tossed with butter and Parmesan cheese, or with rice, noodles or crusty bread and butter. Serves 6.

Tuna Marks

2 × 200 g/7 oz cans tuna in oil; 15 g/½ oz (1 tbsp) butter; 60 g/2 oz (½ cup) chopped spring onions (scallions), including some green tops; 125 g/4 oz (½ cup) sliced canned water chestnuts; 2 tsp grated fresh ginger; 1 tsp soy sauce; 500 ml/18 fl oz (2 cups) sour cream; hot boiled rice to serve; shredded spring onions (scallions) to garnish.

Drain oil from tuna cans into a frying pan (skillet). Add butter and heat, then add spring onions (scallions) and cook gently until soft. Break tuna into large flakes, add with remaining ingredients and heat through. Serve on rice, scattered with shredded spring onions (scallions). Serves 4.

Tuna and Vegetable Plate with Sour Cream Dressing

If you have cans of tuna and asparagus in the cupboard, this attractive luncheon dish can be prepared in a flash.

2 × 200 g/7 oz cans tuna in oil, drained and broken into chunks; 1 × 340 g/11 oz can asparagus spears, drained and chilled; 250 g/8 oz (2 cups) button mushrooms, sliced; 5 tbsp olive oil; 2 tbsp white wine vinegar; ¼ tsp salt; ¼ tsp dry mustard; crisp lettuce leaves; 1 cucumber, finely sliced; 2 ripe tomatoes, peeled and cut into wedges. SOUR CREAM DRESSING: 120 ml/4 fl oz (½ cup Mayonnaise (page 204); 120 ml/4 fl oz (½ cup) sour cream; 1 tbsp anchovy paste; 2 tbsp finely chopped parsley; 2 tsp chopped capers; salt and freshly ground black pepper.

Place tuna in a shallow dish with separate piles of asparagus and mushrooms. Combine oil, vinegar, salt and mustard and pour over tuna and vegetables. Cover and chill for 1 hour.
SOUR CREAM DRESSING: Combine all ingredients. To arrange salad, cover bottom of an oval platter with lettuce leaves. Place tuna in middle of platter and mushrooms at either end. Fill in sides with a decorative pattern of asparagus spears, cucumber slices and tomato wedges. Serve the dressing separately. Serves 4–6.
VARIATION
Canned butter (fava) or haricot (navy) beans can be used in place of asparagus.

Taiba

(Algerian Chilled Tuna with Red Pepper)
The original recipe has enough chilli to make it quite fiery – suit yourself about the amount you use.

2 red chillies, or to taste, seeded and chopped; 1 small red pepper, halved, cored and seeded; 6 ripe tomatoes, peeled, seeded and chopped; 4 tbsp olive oil; 4 cloves garlic, crushed; 2 tbsp tomato purée (paste); 3 × 200 g/7 oz cans tuna in oil, drained and coarsely flaked; ½ tsp ground coriander; salt and freshly ground black pepper.

When preparing chillies, work under cold running water, and wash your hands immediately afterwards. Grill (broil) pepper halves, skin side up, under a preheated high grill (broiler) until skin blisters and blackens, then rub skin off under running water. Chop finely. Heat oil in saucepan and add vegetables, garlic and tomato purée (paste). Stir over moderate heat 5 minutes. Add tuna, coriander, salt and pepper. Simmer on low heat, stirring gently once or twice, for 5 minutes or until liquid has evaporated. Let taiba cool, then chill, covered, for 2 hours or overnight. Serve with crusty bread. Serves 6.

Nutty Tuna Spread

1 × 185 g/6 oz can flaked (sandwich) tuna; 125 g/4 oz (1 cup) finely chopped walnuts; 1 tsp lemon juice; Mayonnaise (page 204) or softened cream cheese; salt; freshly ground black pepper.

Mix undrained tuna with walnuts and lemon juice, and stir in enough mayonnaise or softened cream cheese to bind. Season to taste. Makes about 500 g/1 lb (2 cups).

Savoury Tuna Spread

1 × 185 g/6 oz can flaked (sandwich) tuna, drained; 2 tbsp finely chopped celery; 1 tbsp finely chopped spring onion (scallion); 2 tbsp finely chopped cucumber; 3 tbsp Mayonnaise (page 204); dash Worcestershire sauce; dash Tabasco (hot pepper) sauce.

Mix all ingredients together. Makes about 750 g/1½ lb (3 cups).

TURKEY

Turkey breeding has changed over the years, and the present-day bird has more tender breast meat in proportion to dark meat than the same-sized bird of years ago.

Turkeys are available now from a small 2.5 kg (5 lb) up to a giant 12.5 kg (26 lb).

A good turkey is compact, with pearly-white skin and a broad plump breast.

A 3–4 kg (6–8 lb) turkey, unstuffed weight, will serve 8–10 people.

A 4–6 kg (8–12 lb) bird will serve 10–14 people.

A 6–8 kg (12–16 lb) bird will serve 14–16 people.

Most turkeys are purchased frozen, and they will take up to 3 days to thaw in the refrigerator. It is most important that the bird is properly thawed before it is stuffed and cooked, also that the stuffing is added just before roasting. Make the stuffing the day before, as well as the stock so it is ready for making the gravy.

To stuff a turkey: A turkey is usually stuffed with 2 different stuffings – one in the crop and one in the main body cavity. When the turkey is cooked, the stuffing in the crop is carved into slices, so everyone gets a piece of stuffing surrounded by white breast meat and crispy skin. The stuffing from the main body cavity is spooned around the carved meat. Be careful to stuff the crop lightly as the stuffing will expand during cooking, and too much may cause the skin to split, spoiling the appearance of the turkey.

To truss a turkey: See Roast Stuffed Turkey, page 450.

☐ **To Roast:** One important point to remember – if you are cooking a very large turkey, do make sure beforehand that your oven is large enough to hold it.

Roasting Times: An unstuffed turkey takes 20–30 minutes less overall to cook than a stuffed one. The times given on the next page are for stuffed turkeys. Since ovens vary and the shape of your bird can make a difference, check frequently after suggested cooking time is two-thirds over. Roast in a moderate preheated oven (160°C/325°F, Gas Mark 3).

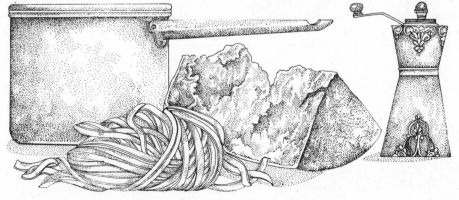

Ready-to-cook Weight	Cooking Time
3–4 kg (6–8 lb)	3–3½ hours
4–6 kg (8–12 lb)	3½–4 hours
6–8 kg (12–16 lb)	4–6 hours

To tell when cooked: If a meat thermometer pushed into the thickest part of the thigh registers 90°C/190°F, the turkey is cooked.

If you don't own a thermometer, pierce the thickest part of the thigh with a fork or fine skewer. If the fork goes in easily and the juice which runs out is clear, the turkey is cooked. If the juice has a pink tinge, further cooking is required.

Rest turkey for 15 minutes in the turned-off oven, with door ajar, while making the gravy. This resting period allows the meat to firm up and makes carving easier.

☐ **To Carve:** First make sure your carving knife is razor-sharp. Remove the trussing strings and skewers and set the bird on a large board or serving plate (a board is easier to carve on). Holding the bird steady with a carving fork, place a long-bladed sharp knife between the thigh and body of the bird and cut through the joint **(Fig 1 right)**. Remove the leg by pressing it outward with the knife blade, while bending it back with the fork. Separate the thigh and drumstick, and slice off the dark meat **(2)**. Repeat with the other leg. Remove the wings and cut into two if desired **(3)**. Carve down the breast on each side with straight, even strokes **(4)**.

Carve the stuffing in the crop, including some of the white breast meat, into thin slices; remove stuffing from the body cavity with a spoon.

☐ **To Serve:** The white meat is usually arranged in overlapping slices at one end of a heated platter, with slices of dark meat at the other.

ROAST TURKEY PORTIONS

To roast a half-turkey or turkey breast, place it, skin side up, on a greased rack in a roasting tin (pan). Spread with softened butter and roast, uncovered, in a preheated moderate oven (160°C/325°F, Gas Mark 3), basting with pan juices every 15 minutes, until juices run clear when the thickest part of the meat is pierced with a fine skewer, or a meat thermometer inserted into the thickest part, away from bone, reads 90°C/190°F. The time will depend on the size and shape of the portion but, as a guide, allow about 30 minutes per 500 g (1 lb). Rest for 15 minutes in the turned-off oven with door ajar, while making the gravy as described in the recipe for Roast Stuffed Turkey (right).

If you want to serve stuffing with turkey portions, prepare it and spread it in a buttered ovenproof dish. Moisten with a spoonful or two of the pan juices from the turkey and bake it in the oven with the turkey for the last 45 minutes of cooking. **See recipes.**

Turkey à la King Follow recipe for Chicken à la King (see page 70), substituting cooked

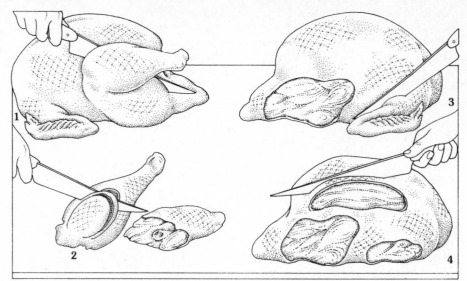

turkey for chicken.

Devilled Turkey Devilled cooked turkey drumsticks or other joints, cut into pieces of suitable size, are a traditional and splendid Boxing Day dish. Follow directions for cooked meat or chicken under recipe for Devil Sauce (see page 373).

Roast Stuffed Turkey

1 × 6 kg (12 lb) turkey with giblets; 1 quantity Sausage or Meat Stuffing (page 418); 1 quantity Chestnut Stuffing (page 66); 60 g/2 oz (4 tbsp) butter, softened; salt and freshly ground black pepper; 2 tbsp flour. GIBLET STOCK: 900 ml/1½ pints (3¾ cups) chicken stock; 1 slice onion; 1 slice carrot; small piece celery.

Thaw turkey completely if frozen, and remove bag of giblets from cavity. Wipe cavity of turkey with damp paper towels. Spoon sausage or meat stuffing into the crop, being careful not to pack it too tightly, and press outside of breast to mould stuffing to a good shape. Bring neck flap over stuffing to the back and secure it with a poultry pin or small skewer. Spoon chestnut stuffing into body cavity. Shape bird nicely with both hands. Place turkey on its back, legs towards you. Place centre of a piece of string below breast at neck end, bring ends down over wings then down underneath bird. Cross string underneath, then bring it forward and up to tie ends of drumsticks and parson's nose together. Wipe bird with a paper towel and spread butter over, being sure to cover breast and legs. Grind a little black pepper over. Place turkey on a rack in a large roasting tin (pan), propping up legs with crumpled foil if necessary. Cover pan with a tent of greased foil. Roast in a preheated moderate oven (160°C/325°F, Gas Mark 3) for 4–4½ hours or until done (see left). Baste every 25 minutes with

Carving a turkey

juices in tin (pan), unless you have a self-basting turkey. Remove foil for last 30 minutes to allow turkey to brown.
GIBLET STOCK: While turkey is roasting, put giblets into a saucepan with stock, onion, carrot and celery. Cover and simmer for 45 minutes or until giblets are tender. Strain and reserve 750 ml/1¼ pints (3 cups) for the gravy. The diced heart and gizzard may be added to the gravy if desired.

Remove turkey to a heated serving platter or carving board and allow to rest in a warm place for 20 minutes while making gravy and finishing vegetables. Pour off all but about 3 tbsp of turkey drippings from roasting tin (pan). Put tin (pan) on medium heat, sprinkle in flour and stir briskly to prevent lumps from forming. Cook, stirring all the time, until browned. Stir in reserved giblet stock, scraping up all good brown bits on bottom of tin (pan). Bring to the boil and simmer 2 minutes. Season with salt and pepper and strain. Stir in diced heart and gizzard, if using. Serves 14.

Turkey Hash

60 g/2 oz (4 tbsp) butter; 1 onion, chopped; 500 g (1 lb) cubed cooked turkey; 370 g (12 oz) cubed cooked potatoes; 120 ml/4 fl oz (½ cup) leftover gravy or single (light) cream, or a mixture of both; salt and freshly ground black pepper; 1 tbsp finely chopped parsley.

Heat butter in a large frying pan (skillet) and fry onion until golden-brown. Stir in turkey and potatoes and cook, pressing down with a spatula to form a flat cake, for 3–4 minutes. Lower heat, pour in gravy or cream, and season with salt and pepper. Cook for a further 10 minutes. Serve cut into wedges, sprinkled with chopped parsley. Serves 4–6.

Turkey Pie

60 g/2 oz (4 tbsp) butter; 1½ tbsp flour; 250 ml/8 fl oz (1 cup) warm turkey stock (made from carcase) or chicken stock; 4 tbsp single (light) cream; salt and freshly ground black pepper; 2 tsp lemon juice; 12 button onions; 500 g (1 lb) cubed cooked turkey; 165 g/5½ oz (1 cup) cooked peas; 1 quantity Plain Shortcrust Pastry (page 274), or 1 × 375 g/12 oz packet frozen puff pastry (paste), thawed.

Melt 30 g/1 oz (2 tbsp) butter in a saucepan, add flour and stir over low heat 2 minutes. Remove from heat, cool a little and add stock, stirring until smoothly blended. Return to heat and stir until boiling. Stir in cream, salt, pepper and lemon juice. Remove from heat and cool. Cook onions in remaining butter until lightly browned. Arrange turkey in a layer in a pie dish, cover with onions with their butter, then peas, and pour sauce over. Roll out pastry (dough) and use to cover dish. Cut slits in dough lid to allow steam to escape. Chill 20 minutes, then bake in a preheated hot oven (230°C/450°F, Gas Mark 8) for 10 minutes. Reduce heat to moderate (180°C/350°F, Gas Mark 4) and bake for a further 20 minutes, covering loosely with foil if crust is browning too much. Serves 4–6.

TURKISH DELIGHT

A jelly-type sweet (candy) most popular in the Middle East, delicious served with coffee when guests call. Flavour with citrus juices, rose water or peppermint; add chopped nuts; colour delicately with a few drops of food colouring and roll each morsel in sifted icing (confectioners) sugar. Turkish delight makes a lovely gift from your kitchen.

Turkish Delight

2 tbsp gelatine; 250 ml/8 fl oz (1 cup) water; 1 lemon; 1 orange; 750 g/1½ lb (3 cups) sugar; 90 g/3 oz (⅔ cup) cornflour (cornstarch); red or green food colouring; sifted icing (confectioners) sugar.

Sprinkle gelatine over 4 tbsp of the water and set aside to soften. Peel lemon and orange thinly, without any white pith. Squeeze and strain juice. Place lemon and orange rinds and juice in a deep, heavy saucepan with sugar and 150 ml/¼ pint (⅔ cup) water. Bring slowly to the boil, stirring to dissolve sugar before boiling point is reached. Boil steadily without stirring for 4–5 minutes until a sugar thermometer registers 105°C/221°F, or when ½ tsp of syrup dropped into a cup of cold water forms long threads. Mix cornflour (cornstarch) with remaining cold water and add to syrup with softened gelatine. Simmer until clear and

gelatine has dissolved, stirring occasionally. Add a few drops of food colouring, and strain into a lightly oiled 18 cm (7 in) shallow tin (pan). Leave to set overnight. Next day, cut into squares and roll in sifted icing (confectioners) sugar. Package in layers separated with wax paper lightly dusted with sifted icing (confectioners) sugar. Makes about 50 × 2.5 cm (1 in) squares.

VARIATIONS

60 g/2 oz (½ cup) chopped nuts – almonds, pistachios, walnuts – may be added before pouring mixture into tins (pans).

Crème de Menthe Turkish Delight: Follow the recipe for Turkish Delight, but omit the orange and lemon rinds and juice, and instead flavour with ½ tsp oil of peppermint and colour with green food colouring.

Rose Water Turkish Delight: Follow the recipe for Turkish Delight, but omit the orange and lemon rinds and juice, and instead flavour with 2 tbsp rose water and tint pink with red food colouring. Add 60 g/2 oz (½ cup) chopped pistachio nuts before pouring into prepared tins (pans).

TURMERIC

One of the principal spices of India, and an ingredient in most commercial curry powders. The powder is obtained from the dried root of a plant of the ginger family.

The most obvious characteristic of turmeric is its colour – ranging from brilliant yellow to deep gold. It may be used as a fabric dye as well as for colouring and flavouring foods, such as curries and Indian rice dishes, as well as chutneys and pickles.

Turmeric can be used instead of saffron to give a yellow colour although the flavour is quite different. It goes into almost all vegetable curries in India, and many other vegetarian dishes. Indonesian curries, too, often call for turmeric.

Like all aromatic spices, turmeric loses its pungency if stored too long; it should be bought in small quantities, and replaced when its aroma fades. **See recipes.**

Mixed Vegetable Curry

Brussels sprouts, chokos or cabbage could replace any of the vegetables suggested in this recipe.

120 ml/4 fl oz (½ cup) oil; ½ tsp mustard seeds; 2 tsp turmeric; 6–8 curry leaves (optional); 2 cloves garlic, crushed; 2 cm (¾ in) piece fresh ginger, grated; pinch chilli powder; ½ small cauliflower, broken into florets; 250 g/8 oz (1 cup) green beans, cut into short lengths; 1 carrot, finely sliced; 6 leaves spinach, torn into pieces; salt.

Heat oil in large saucepan and fry mustard seeds, turmeric, curry leaves (if using), garlic, ginger and chilli for a moment or two. Add

cauliflower, beans and carrot and fry over medium heat, stirring, until vegetables are half cooked and still crisp. Add spinach and fry for a further 5 minutes. Add salt, cover and simmer over a low heat for 2–3 minutes. Serves 4.

Indian Lamb Kebabs

1 kg (2 lb) boneless leg of lamb, cut into cubes; 1 small clove garlic; 1 tsp salt; 1 tsp finely grated fresh ginger; ½ tsp black pepper; ½ tsp turmeric; ½ tsp ground coriander; ½ tsp ground cumin; ½ tsp crushed dried curry leaves; ½ tsp crushed dried oregano; 2 tsp soy sauce; 2 tsp sesame oil; 2 tsp lemon juice; 1 tbsp peanut oil.

Place lamb cubes in large bowl. Crush garlic with salt, and combine with remaining ingredients. Pour over lamb and stir well to ensure that each piece is covered with mixture. Cover well and refrigerate for at least 3 hours. Drain meat and thread on to small skewers. Cook under a preheated grill (broiler) or over hot coals until nicely browned on all sides. Serve hot with boiled rice and Indian side dishes if desired. Serves 6.

TURNIP AND SWEDE (Rutabaga, Neep and Swedish Turnip)

These root vegetables grow wild in parts of eastern Europe and Siberia but are widely cultivated in many other countries.

Turnip: It can be either round or long; has white flesh and is at its best when young and small. The round ones should be no bigger than tennis balls and the long ones about the size of a medium carrot. The green tops when very young and fresh can be prepared the same way as spinach. Buy turnips when young, and choose firm, heavy roots with no soft spots. Most turnips are peeled and cubed or sliced before cooking, with some exceptions such as the classic accompaniment to roast duckling – glazed whole baby turnips. Turnips are also delicious with ham, turkey and boiled lamb.

Swede: Also known as Swedish turnip, rutabaga in the U.S.A., and neep in Scotland. Swede has a pale yellow flesh, with a firm dense texture. The flavour is slightly milder

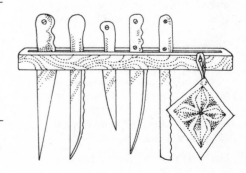

than that of a turnip and it can grow much larger without much impairment to taste and texture. Choose swedes that are heavy, with no soft spots, holes or bruising. Peel thickly and cut into dice or slices according to your recipe. They are delicious boiled then mashed with butter; roasted around a joint of lamb, beef or pork; used in soups or stews, or combined with other ingredients such as cheese or bacon. **See recipes**.

Roast Turnips or Swedes

500 g (1 lb) turnips or swedes (rutabagas), peeled and cut into 2.5 cm (1 in) pieces; dripping, lard or oil.

Drop turnips or swedes (rutabagas) into boiling water and cook for about 4 minutes. Drain and dry the pieces on paper towels. Have ready an ovenproof dish with enough hot dripping, lard or oil to come 1 cm ($\frac{1}{2}$ in) up sides. Put in dried vegetables and roast in top part of a preheated moderate oven (180°C/350°F, Gas Mark 4) for about 40 minutes or until crisp and tender. Turn pieces several times during roasting. Serves 4.

Glazed Baby Turnips

500 g (1 lb) small whole baby turnips, peeled; 2 tsp caster sugar; 60 g/2 oz (4 tbsp) butter.

Cook turnips in boiling salted water until just tender. Drain off all but 2 tbsp of liquid. Add sugar and cook over low heat until dissolved. Stir in butter, increase heat and cook until sugar and butter mixture begins to brown. Keep shaking pan so turnips are thoroughly coated in mixture, making sure it does not burn. Serve with roast duckling. Serves 4–6.

Turnip Casserole

560 g (1 lb 2 oz) diced cooked turnips or swedes (rutabagas), or a combination of both; 90 g/3 oz (6 tbsp) butter; 1 tbsp sugar; $\frac{1}{2}$ tsp salt; freshly ground black pepper; 60 g/2 oz (1 cup) fresh breadcrumbs; 125 g/4 oz (1 cup) Gruyère cheese, diced.

Mash turnips or swedes (rutabagas) and

combine with 60 g/2 oz (4 tbsp) butter, the sugar, salt, pepper, 45 g/1½ oz ($\frac{3}{4}$ cup) of the breadcrumbs and the cheese. Turn into a buttered 1 litre/1$\frac{3}{4}$ pint (4 cup) ovenproof dish, top with remaining breadcrumbs and pour over remaining butter, melted. Bake in a preheated moderate oven (180°C/350°F, Gas Mark 4) until top is browned, about 20 minutes. Serves 4–6.

Turnips in Sour Cream

4 turnips, peeled and diced; 2 tsp caraway seeds; 4 tbsp single (light) cream; $\frac{1}{2}$ tsp lemon juice; paprika; additional lemon juice.

Cook turnips in boiling salted water, with caraway seeds, for 5 minutes. Drain off water, then add cream soured with $\frac{1}{2}$ tsp lemon juice. Heat through gently for a few minutes. Sprinkle with paprika and a little lemon juice and serve hot. Serves 4.

Mashed Swedes

500 g (1 lb) swedes (rutabagas), peeled and cubed; 2 medium potatoes, peeled and cubed; 30 g/1 oz (2 tbsp) butter; 4 tbsp single (light) cream; salt and freshly ground black pepper.

Put swedes (rutabagas) and potatoes in a saucepan of cold salted water, bring to the boil and boil until tender. Drain, and mash well, purée in a food processor or push through a sieve. Return purée to the cleaned saucepan and place over low heat. Beat in butter and cream, season with salt and plenty of black pepper to taste and serve very hot. Serves 4–6.

TURNOVER

A square or circle of pastry (dough) folded over a filling. It is quicker and easier to make than a pie, is portable and is a treat for many occasions. Serve turnovers, sweet or savoury as a main course or dessert.

Use plain or sweet shortcrust pastry (basic pie dough), cream cheese or sour cream pastry (dough), commercial or home-made flaky pastry (paste) or, speediest of all, frozen

ready-rolled sheets of puff pastry (paste). Turnovers can be baked or deep-fried. **See recipes**.

Basic Turnovers

Fillings must be completely cold when the pastry is folded around them.

1 quantity Plain or Sweet Shortcrust Pastry, Cream Cheese Pastry, Sour Cream Pastry or Rough Puff Pastry (pages 274–275), or 1 × 375 g/12 oz packet frozen puff pastry (paste), thawed; filling of your choice (see recipe); lightly beaten egg or egg white; caster sugar (for sweet turnovers only).

Roll out dough 5 mm ($\frac{1}{4}$ in) thick and cut into squares or circles of desired size. Mound chosen cold filling in centre of one half of each piece of pastry (dough) – a triangular half for squares. Do not overfill; use about 1$\frac{1}{2}$ tbsp filling for 10 cm (4 in) turnovers, 1 tbsp filling for 8 cm (3 in) turnovers. Brush edges with beaten egg or egg white, fold other half over and press edges to seal. If using rough puff or puff pastry (paste), lightly tap cut edges with back of a knife horizontally, while pressing edges together. If using shortcrust (basic pie dough), cream cheese or sour cream pastry (dough), press round sealed edges with tines of a fork or point of a teaspoon for a decorative effect. Place turnovers on greased baking trays and chill 20 minutes. Brush savoury turnovers with beaten egg; sweet ones with beaten egg white, then sprinkle over caster sugar.

Cut 2 or 3 slits in tops to allow steam to escape and bake in a preheated oven until pastry (dough) is golden-brown. Bake shortcrust (basic pie dough), rough puff or puff pastry (paste) turnovers at 230°C/450°F, Gas Mark 8 and cream cheese or sour cream pastry (dough) turnovers at 200°C/400°F, Gas Mark 6.

Turnovers may also be deep-fried. Shape as described above, but do not cut slits in pastry (dough). Chill 20 minutes. Heat oil in a deep-fryer until a small piece of pastry (dough) will brown in 1 minute. Place turnovers in a frying basket, fry until golden (about 5 minutes), then drain on crumpled paper towels and serve hot. Makes about 12.

SAVOURY FILLINGS FOR BASIC TURNOVERS
Cheese and Tomato: Peel, seed and chop 2 large tomatoes and mix with 1 tbsp fresh breadcrumbs, 4 tbsp grated cheese, 1 tbsp grated onion, 1 egg, salt and pepper.
Savoury Mince: Chop 1 small onion and fry, without extra fat, with 250 g/8 oz (1 cup) minced (ground) beef, breaking the meat down with a fork. When meat has changed colour, sprinkle with 2 tsp flour and stir until brown. Add 4 tbsp water or beef stock (bouillon), $\frac{1}{4}$ tsp Worcestershire sauce, 1 tsp tomato ketchup, salt and pepper. Stir until

thickened. 2 tsp chopped parsley or other fresh herbs, a pinch dried herbs, or ½ small carrot, grated, may be added. Cover and simmer for 10 minutes, then cool.

Cooked or Canned Fish, Meat or Chicken: Flake or chop finely and mix with your choice of chopped tomato, celery, herbs, green pepper, grated onion, mustard or grated lemon rind. Add just enough chutney, single (light) cream, plain yogurt, mayonnaise, gravy or any suitable sauce you may have to moisten slightly. Season well with salt and pepper. Half a thick slice of the softer type of Continental sausage, spread with French (Dijon) mustard, is excellent too, or for tiny party turnovers, rolled stuffed anchovy seasoned with pepper and a few drops of lemon juice, is delicious.

Vegetable: Sliced mushrooms or chopped cooked vegetables are good mixed with chopped herbs or grated cheese, seasoned well with salt and freshly ground black pepper. Moisten slightly, as for meat fillings, if needed.

SWEET FILLINGS FOR BASIC TURNOVERS

Fruit: Use apples or pears, stewed or thinly sliced and sprinkled with sugar and lemon juice; or use berries or other fresh or canned fruits. Drain canned fruits well.

Dried Fruit: Use fruit mincemeat or raisins, sultanas (golden raisins) or mixed dried fruit, sprinkled with brown sugar and lemon juice.

Cream Cheese or Ricotta: Use cream cheese, or Ricotta cheese mixed with a little single (light) cream. Sweeten with brown or white sugar, then add your choice of flavourings: ground cinnamon, cardamom or mixed spice (ground allspice), brandy or rum, chopped dried or glacé (candied) fruits, grated orange or lemon rind.

Jam or Lemon Cheese: Use a good berry jam, apricot jam (which may be mixed with slivered almonds), marmalade sprinkled with cinnamon or a few drops of orange liqueur, or lemon cheese.

Pork Turnovers

60 g/2 oz (4 tbsp) butter; 1 large onion, finely chopped; 2 tbsp flour; 175 ml/6 fl oz (¾ cup) warm milk; 4 tbsp single (light) cream; 250 g/8 oz (1 cup) finely chopped cooked pork; 1 cooking apple, peeled, cored and chopped; grated rind 1 lemon; 1 tbsp lemon juice; ½ tsp crumbled dried rosemary; salt and freshly ground black pepper; Plain Short-crust Pastry made with 250 g/8 oz (2 cups) flour (page 274); beaten egg to glaze.

Melt butter in a saucepan and cook onion gently until soft. Add flour, stir over low heat 1 minute and remove from heat. Cool a little, then add milk, stirring until smoothly blended. Return to heat and stir until boiling. Add cream, pork, apple, lemon rind, lemon juice, rosemary, salt and pepper and mix

well. Cool completely. Roll out dough 5 mm (¼ in) thick and cut into 8 × 10 cm (4 in) rounds. Divide filling among rounds, mounding it on one half of each and leaving a margin for sealing. Brush edges with beaten egg and fold other halves over, pressing edges to seal and crimping with fingers and thumb. Chill 20 minutes. Cut 2 slits in top of each turnover and glaze with beaten egg. Place on a greased baking tray and bake in a preheated hot oven (230°C/450°F, Gas Mark 8) for 15 minutes or until golden-brown. Makes 8.

Sausage and Apple Turnovers

3 thick beef or pork sausages; 15 g/½ oz (1 tbsp) bacon fat or butter; 1 large cooking apple, peeled, cored and finely chopped; nutmeg; 3 tsp currants; 2 tsp lemon juice; Rich Shortcrust Pastry made with 250 g/8 oz (2 cups) flour (page 274); salt and freshly ground black pepper; beaten egg to glaze.

Prick sausages all over, cover with cold water and bring to the boil. Simmer 3 minutes, then drain, cool and skin. Heat bacon fat or butter in a frying pan (skillet) and fry sausages until brown on all sides. Set aside to cool. Mix apple with nutmeg, currants and lemon juice. Roll out dough and cut 6 × 15 cm (6 in) rounds. Divide apple mixture among rounds, placing it on one side only and leaving a margin for sealing. Cut sausages in half and place on apple mixture. Season with salt and pepper. Brush edges of dough rounds with beaten egg and fold over, pressing edges to seal and crimping with fingers and thumb. Chill for 20 minutes. Brush tops with egg and cut 2 or 3 small slits in each turnover for steam to escape. Place on a greased baking tray and bake in a preheated hot oven (220°C/425°F, Gas Mark 7) for 10 minutes, then lower heat to moderate (180°C/350°F, Gas Mark 4) and bake 20 minutes longer, covering turnovers with foil if pastry (dough) is browning too much. Makes 6.

Apricot Turnovers

PASTRY (DOUGH): *180 g/6 oz (1½ cups) flour; 90 g/3 oz (6 tbsp) butter; 1 tsp grated lemon rind; 45 g/1½ oz (⅓ cup) ground almonds; 1 egg, beaten; 1 egg white; caster sugar to glaze.*
FILLING: *125 g/4 oz (⅔ cup) dried apricots; 1 cinnamon stick; 60 g/2 oz (¼ cup) sugar; 2 tsp brandy or Grand Marnier.*

To make pastry (dough) sift flour into a bowl and rub (cut) in butter until mixture resembles crumbs. Stir in lemon rind and almonds. Add whole egg and 1–2 tsp cold water, if necessary, to make a soft dough. Wrap in plastic wrap and chill 1 hour.
FILLING: Simmer apricots with cinnamon stick in water to cover until very soft. Add

sugar, stir to dissolve and simmer for 10–15 minutes longer or until liquid has almost evaporated. Remove from heat, remove cinnamon stick, stir in brandy and cool completely. Roll out dough and cut 6 × 10 cm (4 in) rounds. Put a spoonful of filling on one side of each round, leaving a margin for sealing, and brush edges with egg white. Fold other sides over, pressing to seal, and mark edges with point of a teaspoon. Brush with egg white, sprinkle with caster sugar and cut 2 small slits in top of each turnover. Chill for 20 minutes, then place on a greased baking tray and bake in a preheated moderately hot oven (200°C/400°F, Gas Mark 6) for 15 minutes or until golden-brown. Serve warm, to accompany coffee, or with whipped cream as a dessert. Serves 6.

TZATZIKI

A refreshing Greek yogurt and cucumber dip to serve with triangles of toasted Lebanese bread, Melba toast, slices of French bread or crisp raw vegetables. Tzatziki is also used as a sauce to complement fried or grilled (broiled) fish, lamb kebabs or barbecued meats; or fold diced green pepper, celery, tomato and spring onions (scallions) through, garnish with fresh coriander or olives and serve as a salad.

Tzatziki

370 ml/12 fl oz (1½ cups) plain yogurt; 1 medium green cucumber; 1 tbsp lemon juice; 1 large clove garlic, crushed; salt and freshly ground black pepper; 1 tbsp chopped fresh mint.

Line a sieve with a double thickness of cheesecloth (or use a disposable cloth). Place over a bowl, spoon yogurt in and let it drain for 2 hours. Meantime, peel cucumber thinly with a vegetable peeler so that some of the green under the skin is left. Cut lengthways in half, scoop out seeds and grate flesh, or chop very fine. Place in a sieve and leave 20 minutes to drain off excess juice. Combine drained yogurt, cucumber, lemon juice and garlic in a bowl and season with salt and pepper. Fold in half the mint and sprinkle the rest over the top. Makes about 500 ml/18 fl oz (2 cups).

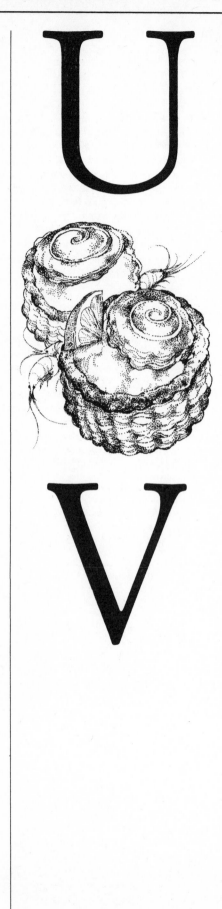

UPSIDE-DOWN CAKE

The Americans are credited with inventing cakes whose decorative, caramelized fruit topping is baked underneath the cake layer. The important point about all upside-down cakes is that the bottom of the cake tin (pan) should be completely covered with a butter and sugar mixture which forms a caramel, and this base is then completely covered with fruit. **See recipes**.

See also Pineapple Upside-Down Cake (page 295).

Fruit Upside-Down Cake

Use well-drained canned, poached or soft fresh fruit such as stoned plums or apricots, or berries. The cake layer in this recipe is light and short.

FRUIT LAYER: *180 g (6 oz) well-drained canned or poached fruit (apples, pears, peaches, cherries) or prepared, soft, fresh fruit; 30 g/1 oz (2 tbsp) butter; 3 tbsp caster sugar.*
CAKE: *60 g/2 oz (4 tbsp) butter; 60 g/2 oz ($\frac{1}{4}$ cup) caster sugar; 1 egg; 60 g/2 oz ($\frac{1}{2}$ cup) self-raising flour, sifted.*

FRUIT LAYER: Leave berries whole; halve or slice other fruit. Melt butter in an 18 cm (7 in) round sandwich tin (layer cake pan). Sprinkle evenly with sugar, and arrange fruit on caramel mixture in a decorative pattern.
CAKE: Cream butter with sugar, then add egg and beat well. Fold in flour. Spoon cake mixture over fruit, being careful not to disturb arrangement. Bake in a preheated moderate oven (180°C/350°F, Gas Mark 4) for 30 minutes or until cake is cooked. Turn out, leaving fruit side up. Serve warm with cream, ice cream or custard, or cold with coffee.

Prune and Apricot Upside-Down Cake

FRUIT LAYER: *30 g/1 oz (2 tbsp) butter; 4 tbsp brown sugar; 12 prunes, stoned (pitted); 12 dried apricots; 4 glacé (candied), herries; 8 blanched almonds.*
CAKE: *60 g/2 oz (4 tbsp) butter; 60 g/2 oz ($\frac{1}{4}$ cup) sugar; few drops vanilla essence (extract); 1 egg, beaten; 125 g/4 oz (1 cup) self-raising flour; pinch salt; 2$\frac{1}{2}$ tbsp milk.*

FRUIT LAYER: Melt butter in an 18 cm (7 in) square cake tin (pan). Sprinkle evenly with sugar, and arrange prunes, apricots, cherries and almonds on caramel mixture in an attractive pattern.
CAKE: Cream butter with sugar until light and fluffy. Add vanilla and egg and mix well. Sift flour with salt and fold in alternately with milk. Spoon cake mixture carefully over fruit, taking care not to disturb arrangement. Bake in a preheated moderate oven (180°C/350°F, Gas Mark 4) for 25 minutes or until cake is cooked. Turn out, leaving fruit side up. For a dessert, serve warm with cream; cool if serving as a cake.

VACHERIN

A luscious meringue dessert usually made into a case or basket to hold a filling of fruits, creams or ice creams. Sometimes the base is a disc of sweet pastry (dough) or almond paste with the meringue piped on in rings one on top of the other around the edge. The filling is then piled into the centre. Vacherins can also be assembled with discs of meringue layered with filling. **See recipes**.

Vacherin Melba

VACHERIN MERINGUE CASE: *4 egg whites; 250 g/8 oz (1 cup) caster sugar; $\frac{1}{2}$ tsp vanilla essence (extract).*
FILLING: *750 ml/1$\frac{1}{4}$ pints (3 cups) vanilla ice cream; 180 g/6 oz (1 cup) sliced canned or fresh peaches; 75 g/2$\frac{1}{2}$ oz ($\frac{1}{2}$ cup) fresh, frozen or canned raspberries, puréed.*

To make the meringue case, cut a round of greaseproof (waxed) paper 20 cm (8 in) in diameter, place on a greased baking tray and spray with non-stick cooking spray. Whisk egg whites and sugar together until very thick and glossy. Fold in vanilla. Put mixture in a piping (pastry) bag with a plain 1 cm ($\frac{1}{2}$ in) nozzle. Pipe (or spread) layer of meringue over paper round, then pipe several rings around edge, one on top of the other, to form a case. Bake in a preheated cool oven (150°C/300°F, Gas Mark 2) for 35–40 minutes or until crisp and pale golden. Turn off oven and allow to cool completely in oven with door open. Just before serving, fill meringue case with softened ice cream. Arrange peach slices on top and pour raspberry purée over peaches. Serve immediately. Serves 8.
VARIATION
Vacherin Chantilly with Fruits: Make meringue case as above. Just before serving, whip 500 ml/18 fl oz (2 cups) double (heavy) cream and fold in 2 tbsp Grand Marnier and 1 tbsp sifted icing (confectioners) sugar. Put a layer of fresh fruit, such as strawberries, or sliced peaches, bananas, apricots or grapes (or a mixture of fruits), in meringue case. Pile whipped cream on top and decorate with a little more fruit. If using peaches or bananas, sprinkle slices with lemon juice to prevent discoloration. Serve immediately.

Mocha Vacherin

VACHERIN MERINGUE CASE: *4 egg whites; 250 g/8 oz (1 cup) caster sugar; $\frac{1}{2}$ tsp cinnamon; 90 g/3 oz ($\frac{3}{4}$ cup) ground hazelnuts.*
MOCHA SAUCE: *125 g/4 oz ($\frac{1}{2}$ cup) sugar;*

V

175 ml/6 fl oz (¾ cup) water; 1 tbsp instant coffee powder; 2 tbsp boiling water; 1 tbsp rum.
FILLING: ½ tsp instant coffee powder; 1 tbsp brown sugar; 1 tbsp hot water; 150 ml/¼ pint (⅔ cup) double (heavy) cream.
DECORATION: sifted icing (confectioners) sugar; 120 ml/4 fl oz (½ cup) double (heavy) cream, whipped; whole hazelnuts.

Cut 2 rounds of greaseproof (waxed) paper 20 cm (8 in) in diameter. Place on a greased baking tray and spray with non-stick cooking spray. Whisk egg whites until stiff. Add 1 tbsp caster sugar and beat 30 seconds longer. Sift remaining sugar with cinnamon and fold into egg whites with ground hazelnuts. Spread or pipe meringue over the 2 paper rounds. Bake in a preheated cool oven (140°C/275°F, Gas Mark 1) for 1–1¼ hours. Turn off oven and allow to cool completely in oven with door open.
MOCHA SAUCE: Dissolve sugar in 120 ml/4 fl oz (½ cup) of the water over low heat. Increase heat and boil without stirring until syrup is rich golden-brown. Remove from heat and carefully stir in remaining cold water. Return to low heat and stir until caramel dissolves. Pour into a heatproof bowl and allow to cool. As syrup cools and begins to thicken, stir in instant coffee, dissolved in boiling water, and rum. When cold, the mocha sauce should be thick and syrupy.
FILLING: Mix coffee and brown sugar with hot water and allow to cool. Whip cream and, as it begins to thicken, add coffee and brown sugar mixture. Continue beating until cream holds soft peaks. Sandwich 2 meringue rounds with filling. Dust top of gâteau with sifted icing (confectioners) sugar and pipe rosettes of cream around edge. Decorate rosettes with whole hazelnuts. Serve with mocha sauce. Serves 8.

VANILLA

Vanilla beans can truly be called fragrant; their aroma is one of the most pleasant of all flavourings. The vanilla bean is actually the pod of a climbing orchid native to Central America, and was first brought to Europe from Mexico. This explains why British and European cooks call them pods, while Americans call them beans. The flavour of vanilla is available in the form of beans, in vanilla essence (extract) and in the tiny sachets of vanilla sugar. The essential flavouring of vanilla can be synthesized, and both imitation vanilla essence (extract) and sugar flavoured with imitation vanilla are to be found; neither of these, however, is a proper substitute for real vanilla.

Vanilla finds its niche in the realm of desserts, and is also used as a flavouring for chocolate. In cakes, creams, custards, ice creams and sauces, vanilla is a vital ingredient. Poaching in a vanilla-flavoured syrup highlights the flavour of many fruits, especially apricots and pears. For custards and custard-based desserts, a piece of vanilla bean is left to infuse in the hot milk. This piece of vanilla bean may be washed, dried and re-used. Store it in a jar of sugar or caster sugar, where it will gradually impart its flavour to the sugar; this vanilla-flavoured sugar can be used whenever a vanilla flavour is called for.
Vanilla Sugar The easiest way to make vanilla sugar is simply to bury pieces of vanilla bean in a jar of sugar. A more strongly flavoured vanilla sugar can be made by blending a whole vanilla bean, cut into short sections, with 250 g/8 oz (1 cup) sugar. Sieve before use. Store airtight. **See recipes.**

Syrup for Poaching Fruits

250 g/8 oz (1 cup) sugar; 350 ml/12 fl oz (1½ cups) water; 2.5 cm (1 in) piece vanilla pod (bean), split lengthways.

Dissolve sugar in water, then add vanilla pod (bean) and bring to the boil. Simmer gently for 5–10 minutes. Remove vanilla pod (bean). Add fruit as desired (apricots, pears, peaches, cherries, etc.) and poach gently until tender. Cool in syrup. Makes about 575 ml/19 fl oz (2¼ cups).

Baked Apricots

1 kg (2 lb) ripe apricots, halved and stoned; 2 tbsp vanilla sugar (see above); 60–120 ml/2–4 fl oz (¼–½ cup) water.

Arrange apricots in an ovenproof baking dish. Sprinkle with vanilla sugar and water (if apricots are very ripe, very little water will be required). Bake in a preheated cool oven (150°C/300°F, Gas Mark 2) for about 1 hour or until apricots are soft. Serve hot. Serves 6.

Vanilla Biscuits

125 g/4 oz (½ cup) butter or margarine; 4 tbsp caster sugar; 1 tsp vanilla essence (extract); 125 g/4 oz (1 cup) flour; ½ tsp baking powder; blanched almond halves or glacé (candied) cherries to decorate.

Melt butter or margarine and cook until it browns slightly. Cool over cold water, then add sugar and cream until light. Beat in vanilla. Gradually work in flour sifted with baking powder. Using floured hands, shape into small balls and flatten them slightly. Top each with almond or cherry. Place on lightly greased baking tray. Bake in a preheated moderately hot oven (190°C/375°F, Gas Mark 5) for 12–15 minutes or until crisp and golden. Makes about 50 biscuits (cookies).

Rich Vanilla Custard

5 cm (2 in) piece vanilla pod (bean); 500 ml/18 fl oz (2 cups) hot milk; 1 egg; 2 egg yolks; 2 tbsp sugar; 15 g/½ oz (1 tbsp) butter.

Infuse vanilla pod (bean) in hot milk in heavy saucepan for 5–10 minutes, then remove. Beat egg, egg yolks and sugar together, pour on milk and mix well. Return to saucepan with butter and cook over low heat, stirring constantly, until thick. Remove from heat and beat with rotary beater until slightly cooled. Pour into a bowl or jug and cool. Makes about 575 ml/19 fl oz (2¼ cups).

Strawberries in Vanilla Syrup

500 g (1 lb) strawberries, hulled; juice 1 lemon; 370 g/12 oz (1½ cups) sugar; ½ vanilla pod (bean), split lengthways; 250 ml/8 fl oz (1 cup) water.

Sprinkle strawberries with lemon juice and about 125 g/4 oz (½ cup) sugar. Leave to macerate for 30 minutes. Meanwhile, make a syrup with remaining sugar, vanilla pod (bean) and water. Poach strawberries in this syrup over very low heat for about 5 minutes. Cool, then chill for 5–6 hours. Serves 6.

Vanilla Crescents

150 g/5 oz (1¼ cups) flour; pinch salt; 150 g/5 oz (½ cup plus 2 tbsp) unsalted butter, softened; 30 g/1 oz (¼ cup) icing (confectioners) sugar, sifted; 2 egg yolks; 1 tsp vanilla essence (extract); 150 g/5 oz (1¼ cups) ground almonds, preferably unblanched; extra icing (confectioners) sugar.

Sift flour with salt on to a work surface. Make a well in centre and put in butter, sugar, egg yolks and vanilla. Sprinkle ground almonds on to flour. Work ingredients in centre with fingertips of one hand until they are well blended. With other hand, use a metal spatula to draw dry ingredients quickly into centre, and mix to a ball of dough. Knead dough lightly, wrap in plastic wrap and chill 1 hour. Pinch off walnut-sized pieces of dough, roll into balls, then roll under your hand to form little cylinders and bend into crescents. Place on a lightly greased baking tray. Bake in a preheated moderate oven (180°C/350°F, Gas Mark 4) for 10–12 minutes or until lightly coloured. Remove to a wire rack, placing a sheet of greaseproof (waxed) paper underneath. Dredge biscuits heavily with sifted icing (confectioners) sugar while they are still warm. Makes about 75.

VARIETY MEATS

An American term referring to the parts of an animal left over after cutting up a carcase. See *Offal*.

VEAL

Since it comes from young animals, veal (calf meat) is tender and its flavour is delicate. Milk-fed veal, is very pale. Grass-fed veal is a little more pink but should not be red. Good veal is fine-grained and smooth, with only a thin edge of white satiny fat. The bones are large in proportion to the size and should be bluish white.

Veal has only a small amount of external fat and little internal fat, so care must be taken to guard against dryness when cooking. It should be cooked with low to moderate heat, either by a moist-heat method (stewing, braising, pot-roasting) or, for roasting or grilling (broiling), with plenty of additional fat provided by very frequent basting and perhaps a covering of streaky bacon for a roast. The two exceptions to the moderate heat rule are pan-fried cutlets or chops which are browned quickly to seal them but then cooked gently until done, and the very thin slices called escalopes (scaloppini), which are sautéed briefly on medium to high heat.

Please read *Meat* for amount to buy, factors determining tenderness, testing meat for doneness, carving, etc. As with other meats, there is no international butchering technique, so cuts vary from country to country and even very similar cuts often have quite different names. Where feasible, we have attempted to give an American alternative to all British cuts suggested.

Roast Veal

☐ **The Choice Cuts for Roasting:**

Leg: May be cut into 2 or more roasting

Boning and stuffing a breast of veal: Using a small sharp knife, remove skin then lift back natural flap to expose rib bones (Fig 1 right). Cut bones away from meat (2). continuing until all bones have been removed (3). Spread breast with stuffing then roll and tie or secure with skewers (4).

pieces, on or off the bone.
Cushion (round roast): A boneless leg roast.
Rump: Boneless.
Loin: The most succulent cut, which may be on the bone or boned, rolled and tied.
Fillet (tenderloin): Small, boneless and fatless, the most tender cut of all.

☐ **Other Cuts for Roasting:**

Shoulder: On the bone or boned and rolled.
Forequarter Roasts: Boned and rolled breast, and foreloin rib, sold on or off the bone.

☐ **To Roast:** Choice and other cuts are roasted in the same way. Weigh the veal roast and place it on a rack in a roasting tin (pan). Smear the surface of the meat with butter and lay rindless rashers (slices) of streaky bacon or strips of fresh pork fat over the top. Place in a preheated moderate oven (160°C/325°F, Gas Mark 3) and roast for about 45 minutes per 500 g (1 lb), basting with pan juices and extra butter, if necessary, every 15 minutes. Since underdone veal is indigestible and unpleasant, it should always be well-done. To test for doneness, use a meat thermometer or pierce with a fine skewer; juices should run clear. Rest for 15–20 minutes in a warm place, before carving.

Grilled (Broiled) Veal

Veal is rarely grilled (broiled) since it lends itself better to other methods of cooking. However, some cuts can be grilled (broiled), as long as they receive constant brushing with oil or melted butter to prevent the close-grained texture of veal becoming dry and tough. Veal should always be served well-done.

☐ **The Choice Cuts for Grilling (Broiling):**

Loin Chops: These may include a piece of kidney.
Cutlets: Rib chops.

NOTE: Both chops from the loin and those from the rib are sometimes called 'cutlets'.

☐ **To Grill (Broil):** Have chops cut 2 cm (¾ in) thick and at room temperature. Cut through edge in several places to prevent buckling. Roll up tails of chops and secure with poultry pins or small skewers. Season on both sides with freshly ground black pepper and brush with oil or melted butter. To give a golden finish, dust with a little flour. Place on a greased rack under a preheated grill (broiler) and cook under moderate heat, brushing every 2 minutes with oil or melted butter.

Turn the chops 2 or 3 times during grilling (broiling). Chops will take 12–14 minutes; they are cooked when the thickest part of the meat releases clear juice when pierced with a fine skewer.

Sautéed Veal

This method is suitable for loin chops, cutlets and leg or fillet (tenderloin) steaks, cut about 2 cm (¾ in) thick, and for the thin delicate slices called escalopes or scaloppini.

To cook escalopes, see *Escalope* and *Scaloppine*.

☐ **To Sauté:** Have meat at room temperature and prepare it as for grilling (broiling). Heat enough oil to cover the bottom of a heavy frying pan (skillet) generously. Add an equal quantity of butter, and add meat when foaming subsides. Cook 30 seconds–1 minute on each side or until browned, then lower heat and continue to cook gently, turning once, until cooked through – when the meat feels firm if pressed, or when beads of juice are clear if meat is pierced with a fine skewer.

PAN SAUCES FOR SAUTEED VEAL

Serve sautéed veal chops, steaks or escalopes (scaloppini) with lemon wedges, or with one of the following quickly made pan sauces. Quantities are sufficient for 4 large chops or escalopes (scaloppini).

Sour Cream and Caper Sauce After sautéing veal, remove it to a heated platter and keep warm. Add 175 ml/6 fl oz (¾ cup) sour cream to the pan, stir in 2 tsp French (Dijon) mustard and bring to the boil, stirring in all the brown bits from the pan. Season with salt and pepper and stir in 2 tsp drained capers. Spoon over the veal and top each chop or steak with 2 crossed halves of anchovy fillet.

Cream and Lemon Sauce After sautéing veal, remove it to a heated platter and keep warm. Add 120 ml/4 fl oz (½ cup) single (light) cream and 2 tbsp lemon juice to the pan and boil 1 minute, stirring in all the brown bits from the pan. Season with salt and pepper and spoon over the veal.

Port and Mushroom Sauce While veal is cooking, gently cook 125 g/4 oz (1 cup) sliced mushrooms in a separate, covered saucepan with 1 tbsp each butter and lemon juice.

When veal is done, remove to a heated platter and keep warm. Add 1 tbsp finely chopped shallots to the pan and fry, stirring 1

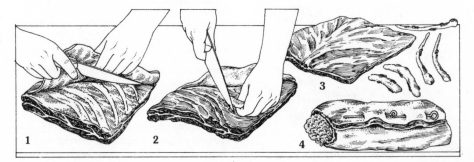

minute, then stir in 4 tbsp port and 120 ml/4 fl oz ($\frac{1}{2}$ cup) dry white wine and boil on high heat 2 minutes. Add mushrooms with their juice, season to taste and spoon over veal.

Ham Sauce After sautéing veal, remove it to a heated platter and keep warm. Add 2 tbsp finely chopped shallot and 60 g (2 oz) cooked ham, cut into thin strips, to the pan. Fry 2 minutes, then stir in 120 ml/4 fl oz ($\frac{1}{2}$ cup) veal or chicken stock and 2 tsp wine vinegar. Boil, stirring in all the brown bits from the pan, for a minute or so, then season with salt and freshly ground black pepper. Remove from heat and swirl in a knob of butter and 1 tbsp chopped parsley. Spoon over veal.

Apple and Onion Sauce Dust veal with seasoned flour before sautéing as usual in oil and butter. Remove veal to a heated platter and keep warm. Add 30 g/1 oz (2 tbsp) butter to the pan and when it is foaming, add 1 sliced onion and 1 sliced apple. Fry until golden. Add 120 ml/4 fl oz ($\frac{1}{2}$ cup) dry white wine, or 120 ml/4 fl oz ($\frac{1}{2}$ cup) chicken stock and 2 tsp wine vinegar, and boil 1 minute, stirring gently. Season with salt and pepper and spoon over veal.

Pan-fried Crumbed Veal

The most famous example of veal cooked this way is Wienerschnitzel (see page 381), but thicker veal steaks and cutlets are juicy and delicious when fried with a crisp crumb coating. Coat meat with egg and bread-crumbs. In a heavy frying pan (skillet) heat enough butter and oil to come halfway up the pieces of veal. When foam subsides arrange the pieces in one layer without crowding the pan. Cook over moderate heat until golden-brown then turn and cook other side, 12–15 minutes in all. Drain on crumpled paper towels and serve immediately.

Braised or Casseroled Veal

Braising (pot-roasting) in a covered casserole with aromatic vegetables is an excellent way to cook a large piece of veal for maximum juiciness and flavour. **See recipes.**

See also *Blanquette, Escalope, Osso Buco Milanese, Scaloppine, Schnitzel.*

Veal Birds

8 veal escalopes (scaloppini), about 10 × 15 cm (4 × 6 in); flour; 60 g/2 oz (4 tbsp) butter; 120 ml/4 fl oz ($\frac{1}{2}$ cup) chicken stock; 120 ml/4 fl oz ($\frac{1}{2}$ cup) dry white wine; 1 bouquet garni; salt and freshly ground black pepper; 4 tbsp single (light) cream; chopped parsley to garnish.
STUFFING: *30 g/1 oz (2 tbsp) butter; 1 small onion, finely chopped; 125 g/4 oz (1 cup) mushrooms, finely chopped; 90 g/3 oz (1$\frac{1}{2}$ cups) fresh white breadcrumbs; 2 tbsp chopped parsley; finely grated rind and juice 1 lemon.*

To make the stuffing, melt butter in a frying

pan (skillet), add onion and fry until golden. Stir in mushrooms and cook 1 minute. Remove pan from heat, stir in remaining stuffing ingredients and allow to cool. If escalopes (scaloppini) are not already beaten out, pound them between 2 sheets of plastic wrap until very thin. Place stuffing along one end of each escalope (scaloppini), roll up securely and tie with thread. Roll in flour until evenly coated. Melt butter in a flameproof casserole, put in rolls and brown quickly on all sides. Pour in stock and wine and bring to the boil, stirring constantly. Lower heat, and add bouquet garni, salt and pepper. Cover and simmer gently for 30–40 minutes or until meat is tender. Remove bouquet garni, stir in cream just before serving, sprinkled with chopped parsley. Serve with creamy mashed potatoes. Serves 4.

Veal and Ham Birds with Hazelnut Sauce

8 veal escalopes (scaloppini); 8 thin slices cooked ham; 2 tbsp finely chopped parsley; 2 cloves garlic, crushed; 90 g/3 oz (6 tbsp) butter; 60 g/2 oz ($\frac{1}{2}$ cup) chopped hazelnuts or walnuts; 1 large onion, finely chopped; 120 ml/4 fl oz ($\frac{1}{2}$ cup) white wine; $\frac{1}{2}$ tsp cinnamon; salt and freshly ground black pepper; 2–3 tbsp sour cream.

If escalopes (scaloppini) are not already beaten out, pound between 2 sheets of plastic wrap until very thin. Place a slice of ham on each slice of veal, and sprinkle with parsley and garlic. Tuck sides in, and make into neat rolls, securing with white thread or fine string. Heat butter in a large, heavy frying pan (skillet) and gently brown rolls on all sides. Remove, and arrange side by side in a casserole just large enough to take them comfortably. Add hazelnuts and onion to butter remaining in frying pan (skillet) and fry until onion is soft and golden. Add wine, cinnamon, salt and pepper. Stir well to get up any brown bits from bottom of pan, and pour over veal rolls. Cover casserole and

bake in a preheated moderate oven (180°C/350°F, Gas Mark 4) for 20–25 minutes or until veal is tender. Take rolls out, remove strings and arrange on a heated serving platter. Stir sour cream into juices in casserole, and return to oven for a minute to heat through. Adjust seasoning and pour over rolls. Serves 4.

Veal Breast with Spinach Stuffing

In Italy, veal is served in a number of interesting ways. This economical cut of veal is most delicious with its spinach and rice stuffing.

1 × 1.5–2 kg (3–4 lb) boned breast of veal, cut with a pocket; salt and freshly ground black pepper; 45 g/1$\frac{1}{2}$ oz (3 tbsp) butter; 1 medium onion, chopped; 250 g/8 oz (2 cups) mushrooms, chopped; 500 g (1 lb) spinach; $\frac{1}{2}$ tsp chopped fresh rosemary or basil; 125 g/4 oz (1 cup) cooked rice; 1 egg, lightly beaten; 4 slices pickled (salt) pork or pork back fat; 1 tbsp flour; 250 ml/8 fl oz (1 cup) chicken or veal stock.

Season veal with salt and pepper. Heat butter, add onion and fry until transparent. Add mushrooms and cook, stirring often, for about 3 minutes. Meanwhile, wash spinach and cook, tightly covered, for 3–4 minutes. There is no need to add water; spinach will cook in water which clings to leaves. Drain and, when cool enough to handle, squeeze as dry as possible, then chop. Mix spinach, onion and mushrooms with herbs, salt, pepper, rice and egg. Use mixture to fill pocket in veal and close with metal skewers. Place meat on a rack in a roasting tin (pan). Arrange slices of pickled (salt) pork or fat over veal and add enough water to tin (pan) to cover bottom by about 1 cm ($\frac{1}{2}$ in). Cover with foil and bake in a preheated moderate oven (180°C/350°F, Gas Mark 4) for 2 hours. Uncover and bake 30 minutes longer. Remove meat to a heated plate and keep warm while you prepare gravy. Add flour to tin (pan) and allow to brown a little over a gentle heat, then add stock and stir into a smooth gravy. Serves 6–8.

Breast of Veal Samarkand

1 × 1.5 kg (3 lb) breast of veal; 3 tbsp oil; 3 tbsp flour; 3 tbsp dry sherry; 90 g/3 oz ($\frac{1}{2}$ cup) sultanas (golden raisins); 1 tbsp tomato purée (paste); 350 ml/12 fl oz (1$\frac{1}{2}$ cups) beef stock (bouillon); 2 tbsp redcurrant jelly; 1 tsp salt; pinch cayenne; 2 tsp ground cumin; 250 ml/8 fl oz (1 cup) sour cream; chopped parsley to garnish.

Remove meat from bones and cut into bite-sized pieces. Heat oil in a flameproof casserole and quickly brown meat on all sides. Sprinkle flour over meat and cook gently for a few minutes, stirring. Pour in sherry and stir well, getting up any brown bits from the bottom. Add sultanas (golden raisins), tomato purée (paste) and stock. Stir, bring to the boil and add redcurrant jelly, salt, cayenne and cumin. Cover casserole tightly, reduce heat and simmer gently for 1 hour or until meat is tender. Stir in most of the sour cream and heat through. Adjust seasoning to taste. Spoon into a heated serving bowl and serve sprinkled with parsley and a swirl of sour cream. Serves 6–8.

Veal Cutlets Modena-Style

6 veal cutlets (loin chops), 2.5 cm (1 in) thick; 1 egg; salt; 30 g/1 oz ($\frac{1}{4}$ cup) flour; dry breadcrumbs; 125 g/4 oz ($\frac{1}{2}$ cup) butter; 1 tbsp olive oil; 1 medium onion, finely chopped; 2 tbsp Marsala; 2 tsp tomato purée (paste); 120 ml/4 fl oz ($\frac{1}{2}$ cup) white stock (chicken or veal); freshly ground black pepper.

Fold tail end inside each cutlet and secure with a small skewer. Beat egg with a pinch of salt on a plate. Dip cutlets (chops) in flour, then egg, and coat with breadcrumbs. Heat butter with oil in a heavy sauté pan or frying pan (skillet). Add cutlets and brown well on both sides. Add onion and fry until it begins to brown. Pour on Marsala and cook until it evaporates to 1 tbsp. Stir in tomato purée (paste), stock, salt and pepper, and continue cooking for 15–20 minutes or until cutlets (chops) are tender when tested with a skewer. Remove skewers from cutlets (chops). Arrange cutlets on a heated serving dish and spoon pan juices over. Serves 6.

Veal Pot Roast

2 tbsp oil; 30 g/1 oz (2 tbsp) butter; 1 × 2.5 kg (5 lb) shoulder of veal, boned, rolled and tied; 125 g/4 oz (1 cup) diced onions; 1 large carrot, sliced; 125 g/4 oz (1 cup) diced celery; 1 bay leaf; 10 black peppercorns; 1 clove garlic, crushed; 1 tsp salt; $\frac{1}{4}$ tsp paprika; 120 ml/4 fl oz ($\frac{1}{2}$ cup) dry white wine; 1 tbsp Beurre Manié (page 35).

Heat oil in a large heavy, flameproof casserole, add butter and, when turning brown, add meat. Brown it on all sides. Lift

meat out. Add all remaining ingredients, except wine and beurre manié, to casserole and cook for 1–2 minutes over moderate heat, stirring, until onion begins to soften. Set a rack over vegetables and put meat on it. Pour over wine and add enough water to cover vegetables. Cover casserole tightly and place in a preheated moderate oven (160°C/325°F, Gas Mark 3). Cook for $2\frac{1}{2}$ hours or until tender. Uncover and cook a further 20 minutes. Remove meat to a heated platter. Remove rack and, on moderate heat on top of stove, whisk beurre manié little by little into gravy. Stir until smooth and cook gently 5 minutes. Discard bay leaf. Serve gravy with sliced meat. Serves 8.

Veal Foyot

2 large onions, finely chopped; 30 g/1 oz (2 tbsp) butter; 120 ml/4 fl oz ($\frac{1}{2}$ cup) dry white wine; 120 ml/4 fl oz ($\frac{1}{2}$ cup) beef stock (bouillon); salt and freshly ground white pepper; 1 × 2–2.5 kg (4–5 lb) veal leg roast; 125 g/4 oz (1 cup) Gruyère cheese, finely grated; 30 g/1 oz ($\frac{1}{2}$ cup) fresh breadcrumbs; 60 g/2 oz (4 tbsp) butter, melted.

Cook onions gently in 30 g/1 oz (2 tbsp) butter until soft but not browned. Add wine and stock and boil 2 minutes; season with salt and pepper. Place veal in a greased roasting tin (pan) and brush well with wine mixture. Rub with salt and pepper. Mix grated cheese and breadcrumbs and use to coat meat, pressing it on firmly with your hands. Drizzle gently with melted butter, being careful not to disturb coating. Pour remaining wine mixture into tin (pan), round meat but not over it. Place in a preheated moderate oven (180°C/350°F, Gas Mark 4), and cook for 3 hours, basting very gently once or twice with pan juices – do not disturb coating. If liquid in pan is drying out, add a little more hot water. Rest veal for 20 minutes in turned-off oven with door ajar, then lift carefully on to a heated serving platter. Bring pan juices quickly to the boil on top of the stove and pour into a heated gravy boat. To serve, carve veal across joint into thick slices, and serve on heated plates

with a little sauce spooned over. Veal Foyot should be served unaccompanied, and followed by a salad. Serves 8.

Veal Braised with Vermouth

1 kg (2 lb) boneless lean veal, cut into 4 cm ($1\frac{1}{2}$ in) cubes; 60 g/2 oz (4 tbsp) butter; 4 medium onions, thinly sliced; 2 tbsp flour; 120 ml/4 fl oz ($\frac{1}{2}$ cup) dry white wine; 4 tbsp dry vermouth; 600 ml/1 pint ($2\frac{1}{2}$ cups) chicken or veal stock; salt and freshly ground black pepper; 1 bouquet garni; 250 g/8 oz (2 cups) button mushrooms; 1 egg yolk; 1 tsp lemon juice; 120 ml/4 fl oz ($\frac{1}{2}$ cup) single (light) cream; 1 tbsp chopped parsley.
TO SERVE: *hot buttered rice; 2 tbsp grated Parmesan cheese.*

Brown veal cubes in butter in a wide, heavy saucepan, deep sauté pan or flameproof casserole. Add onions and cook until they colour lightly, then stir in flour and cook, stirring gently, 2 minutes. Add wine, vermouth and enough of the stock barely to cover meat, and stir until simmering. Season with salt and pepper and add bouquet garni. Cover and simmer 40 minutes. Add mushrooms and cook 10 minutes longer or until veal is tender. Beat egg yolk and lemon juice with cream, stir in a little hot liquid from veal, then stir this back into pan. Cook gently, stirring, until liquid thickens a little more and becomes glossy; do not allow to boil. Adjust seasoning and discard bouquet garni. Serve veal scattered with parsley, on a bed of hot buttered rice with 2 tbsp grated Parmesan cheese folded through it. Serves 6–8.

Braised Veal Shoulder with Spinach and Mushroom Stuffing

1 × 2 kg (4 lb) boned shoulder of veal; 1 tbsp French (Dijon) mustard; 3 tbsp oil; 60 g/2 oz (4 tbsp) butter; 2 carrots, sliced; 2 medium onions, sliced; 1 bouquet garni; 250 ml/8 fl oz (1 cup) dry white wine; 250 ml/8 fl oz (1 cup) chicken or veal stock; salt and freshly ground black pepper.
STUFFING: *500 g (1 lb) spinach; 2 tbsp finely chopped shallots; 30 g/1 oz (2 tbsp) butter; 250 g/8 oz (2 cups) mushrooms, thinly sliced; 5 tbsp single (light) cream; 30 g/1 oz ($\frac{1}{2}$ cup) fresh breadcrumbs; 90 g/3 oz (scant $\frac{1}{2}$ cup) cooked ham, diced; 30 g/1 oz ($\frac{1}{4}$ cup) grated Parmesan cheese; 1 egg, beaten; 1 tbsp chopped parsley; salt and freshly ground black pepper; nutmeg.*

Lay veal flat, slice part way through thickest part of meat and open it out. Spread cut surface of meat with mustard, and set aside.
STUFFING: Cook washed spinach, with only water that clings to leaves, in a tightly covered saucepan for 3–4 minutes. Drain,

squeeze out as much moisture as possible and chop fine. Cook shallots gently in butter for 3 minutes, then add mushrooms and cook 5 minutes more, stirring several times. Remove from heat and mix in spinach and remaining ingredients for stuffing.

Spread stuffing over meat. Roll up and tie firmly with string at intervals along its length to make a plump sausage shape. Heat oil and butter in a heavy, flameproof casserole and brown meat roll on all sides. Remove meat. Add carrots and onions to casserole and brown them lightly. Add bouquet garni, wine and stock and bring to the boil, stirring and scraping bottom of casserole to mix in brown bits. Place meat on bed of vegetables. Cover tightly and cook in a preheated moderate oven (180°C/350°F, Gas Mark 4) for 2 hours or until veal is tender, turning it after first hour.

Remove meat to a warm place and rest for 15 minutes, then remove strings and carve across into thick slices. Arrange veal down a heated serving platter. Bring pan juices to the boil, adjust seasoning, discard bouquet garni, and spoon a little over veal. Serve remainder in a sauce boat. Serves 8.

Sautéed Veal with Lemon and Rosemary

4 veal cutlets (chops) or 8 small escalopes (scaloppini); 2 tbsp olive oil; 60 g/2 oz (4 tbsp) butter; 8 paper-thin slices lemon; ½ tsp chopped fresh rosemary, or pinch dried; 4 tbsp dry white wine; salt and freshly ground black pepper.

Sauté veal in oil and half the butter, adding lemon slices to pan for the last 5 minutes of cooking. Remove veal to a heated platter, arrange lemon slices on top and keep warm. Add remaining butter to pan and, when it is frothing, add rosemary and wine. Bring to the boil, stirring in all brown bits from pan. Season with salt and pepper and spoon over veal. Serves 4.

Veal and Vegetable Casserole

90 g/3 oz (6 tbsp) butter; 750 g (1½ lb) boned shoulder of veal, cut into 5 cm (2 in) long strips; 2 large onions, sliced; 1 clove garlic, chopped; 3 carrots, cut into sticks; 60 g/2 oz (½ cup) sliced celery; 2 tbsp flour; 500 ml/18 fl oz (2 cups) chicken stock; 4 tomatoes, peeled and cut into chunks; 1 green pepper, cored, seeded and cut into strips; salt and freshly ground black pepper; paprika; 250 g (8 oz) sliced, cooked green beans.

Heat butter in a flameproof casserole and brown veal. Remove meat. Add onions and garlic to casserole and cook gently until soft. Add carrots and celery and cook a few minutes longer, then stir in flour and cook 2

minutes more. Gradually blend in stock, stirring until sauce is smooth, and bring to the boil. Add tomatoes and green pepper and season with salt, pepper and paprika. Return veal to casserole, cover and cook in a preheated moderate oven (160°C/325°F, Gas Mark 3) for 1½ hours or until the veal is tender. Remove lid of casserole, add beans and push down into sauce. Leave in oven for 5 minutes to heat beans through. Serve with mashed potato. Serves 4–6.

Veal Chops Stuffed with Cheese

6 veal chops; 125 g (4 oz) Fontina, Gouda or Jarlsberg cheese, thinly sliced; salt and freshly ground white pepper; flour; beaten egg; dry breadcrumbs; 90 g/3 oz (6 tbsp) butter.

Slit each chop horizontally almost to bone to make a pocket. Stuff pockets with slices of cheese. Lay chops flat and press edges together, then seal by beating with heel of a heavy kitchen knife. Season chops on both sides with salt and pepper, dust with flour and coat with egg and breadcrumbs. Heat butter. Fry chops over moderate heat for 10–15 minutes or until golden-brown on both sides and cooked through. Serves 6.

Veal Patties with Sour Cream Sauce

*500 g/1 lb (2 cups) minced (ground) veal; 30 g/1 oz (½ cup) fresh breadcrumbs; 1 tsp grated lemon rind; 1 tsp chopped fresh marjoram, or ¼ tsp dried; ½ tsp chopped fresh rosemary, or ¼ tsp dried; 1 tsp salt; ½ tsp pepper; 2 tbsp sour cream; 1 egg; flour; 45 g/1½ oz (3 tbsp) butter.
SAUCE: 15 g/½ oz (1 tbsp) butter; 1 onion, finely chopped; 250 ml/8 fl oz (1 cup) sour cream; salt and freshly ground black pepper; pinch nutmeg.*

Mix veal, breadcrumbs, lemon rind, herbs, salt, pepper, sour cream and egg. Shape into 8 patties about 2 cm (¾ in) thick and flour lightly. Heat butter in a heavy frying pan (skillet) and brown patties on both sides, then turn heat low and cook gently for about 5 minutes more on each side. Remove to a heated platter and keep warm.

SAUCE: Add butter and onion to pan and cook until onion is lightly browned. Add sour cream and heat slowly, stirring in all brown bits from pan. Do not allow to boil. Season with salt, pepper and nutmeg, and spoon over patties. Serves 4.

Veal in White Wine

*3 tbsp oil; 1.5 kg (3 lb) boneless lean veal, cut into bite-sized cubes; 1 large onion, finely chopped; 120 ml/4 fl oz (½ cup) fresh tomato purée; 1 tbsp flour; 500 ml/18 fl oz (2 cups) chicken stock; 250 ml/8 fl oz (1 cup) dry white wine; 1 clove garlic, crushed; 1 bay leaf; ½ tsp dried thyme; ½ tsp dried rosemary; salt and freshly ground black pepper; chopped parsley to garnish.
VEGETABLE ADDITION: 125 g/4 oz (½ cup) butter; 12 small white onions; 1 tbsp sugar; 12 small mushroom caps; 3 large tomatoes, peeled, quartered and seeded.*

Heat oil in a deep, heavy saucepan and brown veal cubes on all sides over moderate heat. Add onion and fresh tomato purée, and stir together for 2 minutes. Mix flour with a little stock, and add to pan with remaining stock and white wine. Add garlic, bay leaf, thyme and rosemary, and season generously with salt and pepper. Stir until boiling, then reduce heat, cover, and simmer for 1 hour. Meanwhile, heat half the butter in a heavy frying pan (skillet) and slowly brown onions over medium heat. Sprinkle with sugar and stir until onions are glazed. Remove onions to a plate. Heat remaining butter in same pan. Add mushroom caps and toss until coated with butter. Remove. Add onions, mushrooms and tomatoes to veal and simmer for a further 30 minutes or until meat is tender. Adjust seasoning, discard bay leaf and spoon into a serving dish. Sprinkle with parsley and serve. Serves 8.

VEGETABLES

See individual entries.

VELOUTE SAUCE

See page 368 for recipe.

VENISON

Venison is the meat from several species of deer, which may be raised commercially or hunted as game, as in parts of northern Europe. Venison meat is very lean, and joints for roasting may need to be larded or covered with a fine sheet of pork fat. The farm-raised venison is milder in flavour, moister and often younger than game venison, and if cooked quickly and carefully does not need to be larded. Also, it does not need to be hung or marinated.

As with beef, the forequarter cuts of venison are best used in casseroles. The saddle, or both sides of the loin, is roasted while the leg may either be roasted or cut into steaks. Venison steaks should be pan-fried and served fairly rare; overcooked, they are too dry. Marinating steaks in a basic wine-oil marinade helps counteract this dryness.

Traditional vegetable accompaniments to venison include chestnuts, potatoes, Brussels sprouts and lentils. Sauces for venison are usually based on red wine, and redcurrant jelly may also accompany venison. **See recipes**.

Venison Casserole

1 kg (2 lb) boned shoulder venison, sinews removed and cubed; about 2 tbsp flour; 2 onions, chopped; 2 tomatoes, peeled, seeded and chopped; 1 bouquet garni; small piece cinnamon stick; 5 pickled walnuts, sliced; salt and freshly ground black pepper; 1 tsp Angostura bitters; 175 ml/6 fl oz ($\frac{3}{4}$ cup) dry red wine.

Coat meat cubes lightly in flour and place in a greased ovenproof casserole. Arrange onions and tomatoes on top, add bouquet garni, cinnamon and walnuts, and season with salt and pepper. Stir bitters into wine and add to casserole. Cover tightly and cook in a preheated moderate oven (180°C/350°F, Gas Mark 4) for about 2 hours. Discard bouquet garni. Serves 4–6.

Roast Saddle of Venison

1 × 3.5–4 kg (7–8 lb) saddle of venison; $\frac{1}{2}$ tsp dried thyme; salt and freshly ground black pepper; 8–10 thin slices pickled (salt) pork; 120 ml/4 fl oz ($\frac{1}{2}$ cup) fresh orange juice; 3 tbsp redcurrant jelly; 2 tbsp brandy.

Wipe venison with a damp cloth. Rub well with thyme, salt and pepper. Place on rack in roasting tin (pan) and cover with pork slices. Roast in a preheated hot oven (230°C/450°F, Gas Mark 8) for about 45–60 minutes (venison is more tender if quite rare). Remove pickled pork, transfer venison to heated plate and keep warm. Skim off excess fat from roasting tin (pan), place tin (pan) on heat and add orange juice, scraping up any residue from bottom of pan. Add redcurrant jelly, stirring constantly. Bring to the boil, pour in warmed brandy and flame. Serve immediately with venison. Serves 8.

VERMOUTH

Vermouth is an aperitif wine, made by infusing selected herbs and spices in a base wine then fortifying the resultant wine with distilled spirits. There are many brands of vermouth, each with slightly different infusion mixtures, but most brands include a dry white, sweet white and sweet red vermouth.

Because their flavour is more concentrated than that of a table wine, vermouths are particularly useful when finishing a sauce, mixing a forcemeat stuffing or assembling the meats for a pâté or terrine – they flavour without making the mixture too liquid.

Simple and delicious sauces can be made quickly by deglazing a pan in which meat, chicken, scallops or prawns (shrimp) have been pan-fried; try deglazing with dry white vermouth for seafood or veal escalopes (scaloppini), with red vermouth for chicken breasts. Sweet vermouths can enhance the flavour of fresh summer fruit, lightly chilled, and red vermouth can substitute for red wine and some of the sugar when poaching fruits such as prunes or pears. Fresh or poached fruit may also be treated to a sabayon sauce, based on vermouth. **See recipes**.

Pears in Vermouth

500 ml/18 fl oz (2 cups) sweet red vermouth; 250 g/8 oz (1 cup) sugar; 120 ml/4 fl oz ($\frac{1}{2}$ cup) orange juice; 1 tsp grated orange rind; 6–8 pears, peeled, halved and cored; 1 lemon, halved.

Combine vermouth, sugar, and orange juice and rind in a saucepan. Bring to the boil, stirring to dissolve sugar, and simmer gently for 5 minutes. Rub pears with lemon to prevent browning. Drop pears into simmering syrup, and simmer 8–10 minutes longer or until tender. Cool in syrup, then remove. Reduce syrup to 250 ml/8 fl oz (1 cup) by rapid boiling and pour over pears. Cool then chill. Serve chilled, with sweetened whipped cream flavoured with orange liqueur if desired. Serves 6–8.

Veal Escalopes with Mushrooms

12 small, thin veal escalopes (scaloppini), trimmed; 60 g/2 oz (4 tbsp) butter; 1 tbsp oil; 3 tbsp chopped shallots; 4 tbsp dry vermouth; 120 ml/4 fl oz ($\frac{1}{2}$ cup) stock; 1 tbsp cornflour (cornstarch) mixed with 2 tsp water; 250 ml/8 fl oz (1 cup) single (light) cream; salt and freshly ground black pepper; 250 g/8 oz (2 cups) mushrooms, sliced.

Fry veal escalopes (scaloppini) in 30 g/1 oz (2 tbsp) of the butter and oil over moderately high heat for about 4 minutes each side. (It is preferable to cook veal in 3–4 batches, using a proportion of butter and oil for each batch.) Remove escalopes (scaloppini) to heated dish when cooked. Pour off some of the oil/butter mixture, leaving 2 tbsp. Add shallot and cook gently for 1 minute. Add vermouth and stock and scrape up residue from bottom of pan. Reduce over high heat to about 3 tbsp. Blend cornflour (cornstarch) mixture with cream; add to pan. Boil, stirring until thickened. Season with salt and pepper, and remove from heat. In a separate pan, fry mushrooms in remaining butter for 4–5 minutes. Season, then add to cream sauce. Simmer for 1 minute. Season escalopes (scaloppini) lightly with salt and pepper, and add to sauce in pan. Cover and warm through for 4–5 minutes, basting veal with sauce occasionally. To serve, arrange veal on heated dish and spoon sauce over. Serves 4–6.

VERTE SAUCE

See page 358 for recipe.

VICTORIA SPONGE

A classic sponge sandwich (layer cake) layered with jam, the top lightly dusted with caster sugar. It keeps well, and was a great favourite at tea parties in Victorian times. The success of the cake depends on the air beaten into the mixture.

Victoria Sponge

250 g/8 oz (2 cups) self-raising flour; pinch salt; 250 g/8 oz (1 cup) butter; $\frac{1}{2}$ tsp vanilla essence (extract); 250 g/8 oz (1 cup) caster sugar; 4 eggs, beaten; jam; caster sugar to dust.

Sift flour with salt. Cream butter and vanilla thoroughly, then beat in sugar by degrees until light and fluffy. Gradually beat in eggs until thoroughly combined. Be careful not to add eggs too quickly or mixture will curdle and texture of cake will be affected. Fold in flour. Spoon mixture into 2 × 20 cm (8 in) sandwich tins (layer cake pans) that have been greased, bottom-lined with greased greaseproof (waxed) paper and dusted with flour. Bake in a preheated moderately hot oven (190°C/375°F, Gas Mark 5) for 40–45 minutes or until cakes have shrunk slightly from sides of tins (pans). Turn on to a wire rack to cool. When cold, sandwich together with a good jam of your choice and dust top with caster sugar.

Right: Stuffed Zucchini (page 486)

VICHYSSOISE

One of the specialities created by the great French chef Louis Diat for the old Ritz-Carlton in New York. Vichyssoise now appears on restaurant menus throughout the world and is made in many homes. It had its origins in the simple leek and potato soup, *Potage Bonne Femme* of France, which when put through a mouli became *Potage Parmentier*. Both of these soups are served hot.

Casting around for a new cold soup to entice his clientele, Diat remembered how his mother used to cool her potage by adding cold rich milk to it. A cup of cream, an extra straining, a sprinkling of chives *et voilà!* he had his new soup. Diat named it after Vichy, the famous spa located near his boyhood home, as a tribute to the fine cooking of the region.

For recipe see page 400.

VINAIGRETTE

The classic vinaigrette or French dressing is a subtle mixture of good quality olive oil, wine vinegar, salt and pepper. To this basic mixture is sometimes added mustard, fresh herbs or, as in southern France, garlic. Flavourings depend on taste and the types of salad the vinaigrette is to dress. Vinaigrette can also be used as a dressing for cooked, cooled vegetables. Serve vegetable vinaigrette as an hors d'oeuvre, or as an accompaniment to hot or cold meats.

For vinaigrette dressing recipe see page 358.

Vegetable Vinaigrette

500 g (1 lb) vegetables – cauliflower, baby onions, carrots, button mushrooms, courgettes (zucchini), asparagus, green beans, mange tout (snow peas) or mixture.
DRESSING: *3 tbsp oil; 1 tbsp wine vinegar; 1 clove garlic, crushed; ½ tsp French (Dijon) mustard; 1 tbsp finely chopped mixed fresh herbs, or 1 tbsp parsley chopped with 1 tsp dried mixed herbs; salt and freshly ground black pepper.*

Trim vegetables; break cauliflower into florets, cut carrots into sticks. Cook vegetables separately in boiling salted water just until crisp-tender – minutes only for most, 45–50 seconds for mange tout (snow peas). Drain and refresh under cold running water. Make a dressing by combining remaining ingredients. Arrange vegetables on a serving dish, spoon dressing over, cover and marinate 2 hours. Serve slightly chilled. Serves 6.

Left: Rich Treacle Tart (page 441)

VINEGAR

Vinegar is the acid liquid obtained from various fruits and grains after alcoholic and acetous fermentation takes place. Thus wine vinegar is fermented from fresh wine, malt vinegar is made from malt liquor, cider vinegar from cider, and sweet-sour vinegars from rice wine. They vary greatly in strength and flavour according to the grain or fruit from which they are made.

Vinegar is an essential ingredient in salad dressings, mint and horseradish sauces and can be used sparingly instead of lemon juice in hollandaise, béarnaise and mayonnaise sauces. Many marinades for meat and game contain vinegar (the acid has a tenderizing effect), and it is used in pickling of all kinds – fruit, vegetables, meats, fish and eggs.

All vinegars are corrosive so when mixing pickles, or using marinades or any recipes containing vinegar, use utensils made of glass, earthenware, china, or stainless or enamelled steel.

Types of Vinegar
Wine Vinegar: Wine vinegars can be red or white and are sometimes quite strong, but always have a delicious flavour. They can be diluted according to taste with the addition of a little red or white wine as appropriate. The best and purest wine vinegar probably comes from Orléans in France. Use white wine vinegar in mayonnaise and red or white in vinaigrette.
Cider Vinegar: This has a strong, distinctive flavour and is much sharper than wine vinegar. Makes an excellent vinaigrette to use with a fresh tomato salad.
Malt Vinegar: A strong, dark vinegar made from malted barley. The colour does not necessarily denote the strength as it is sometimes coloured with caramel to varying degrees of brown. Use for pickling.
Distilled or White Vinegar: Not as strong as malt vinegar; use for pickling when the vinegar needs to be clear to enhance the colour of the pickle.
Rice Vinegar: Often used in Oriental cooking especially in the Japanese dish Sushi or Vinegared Rice. It has a sweet, delicate flavour.
Flavoured Vinegars: Red or white wine vinegar and distilled white vinegar can be flavoured with spices, herbs, chillies or garlic. These are steeped in the vinegar for some days, and the liquid is then strained and decanted into sterilized bottles for use. Use flavoured vinegars for salad dressings, sauces and vinaigrettes. **See recipes.**

Herb Vinegar

40 g/1⅓ oz (1 cup) fresh herbs (thyme, mint, tarragon, or basil, etc.); 1 litre/1¾ pints (4 cups) red or white wine vinegar.

Pack herbs into jars (use 4 × 250 ml/8 fl oz (1 cup) jars or 2 × 500 ml/18 fl oz (2 cup) jars), fill with vinegar, cover and store at room temperature. Leave for 2–3 weeks, shaking jars once each day. Strain vinegar into sterilized bottles, insert a few sprigs of chosen herb, cover and store. Makes 1 litre/1¾ pints (4 cups).

Garlic Vinegar

8 cloves garlic; 1 tsp salt; 750 ml/1¼ pints (3 cups) white vinegar.

Crush garlic with salt. Heat vinegar to boiling point and pour over garlic. Pour into jars, cool and cover. Leave for 2–3 weeks, shaking occasionally. Strain into sterilized jars, cover and store. Makes 750 ml/1¼ pints (3 cups).

Chilli Vinegar

Add a few drops of this hot vinegar to fresh chutneys that are to accompany curries, or use for a hot spicy salad dressing.

4–6 fresh chillies, or 1 tbsp dried; 500 ml/18 fl oz (2 cups) white vinegar or malt vinegar.

Put chillies into a jar. Bring vinegar to the boil and pour over chillies. Cool, cover and store for 5–6 weeks before use, shaking jar occasionally. Makes 500 ml/18 fl oz (2 cups).

Spiced Vinegar

A good, all-purpose spiced vinegar for use when pickling. Use distilled white vinegar for a clear pickle.

1 litre/1¾ pints (4 cups) vinegar (malt or white); 6 black peppercorns; 6 cloves; 1 cinnamon stick; 5 blades mace; 2 tsp whole allspice.

Place vinegar in saucepan with spices. Bring slowly to boiling point, then remove pan from heat, cover and leave for 2 hours. Strain if desired. Use spiced vinegar cold. Makes 1 litre/1¾ pints (4 cups).

Pickled Eggs in Spiced Vinegar

12 hard-boiled (hard-cooked) eggs.
SPICED VINEGAR: *2.5 cm (1 in) piece fresh ginger, lightly crushed; 1 tbsp white peppercorns; 1 litre/1¾ pints (4 cups) white wine vinegar; 4 chillies.*

Tie ginger and peppercorns in a muslin bag. Bring vinegar to boiling point and add ginger and peppercorns. Lower heat and simmer for 5 minutes. Allow to cool. Shell eggs and pack into sterilized jars. Put 1 or 2 chillies in each jar and fill with spiced vinegar, making certain eggs are covered completely. Cover and store for 3–4 weeks before using. Makes 4 × 250 ml/8 fl oz (1 cup) jars or 2 × 500 ml/18 fl oz (2 cup) jars.

Spiced Oranges

4 medium oranges, each cut into 8 wedges; ¼ tsp bicarbonate of soda (baking soda); 1 tsp whole allspice; 12 cloves; 500 ml/18 fl oz (2 cups) malt vinegar; 8 cm (3 in) cinnamon stick; 2.5 cm (1 in) piece fresh ginger; 500 g/1 lb (2 cups) sugar.

Put oranges into a saucepan and add water to cover and the soda. Bring to the boil and simmer gently for 15 minutes. Place remaining ingredients in another saucepan and bring to the boil, stirring until sugar has dissolved. Drain orange wedges and place in vinegar syrup. Cover and simmer for 20 minutes. Remove orange wedges with a slotted spoon and pack into sterilized hot dry jars. Boil syrup and top up jars. Cover and seal. This pickle will be ready in a week. Makes about 1.5 litres/2½ pints (6 cups).

VINE LEAVES

Probably the most familiar use of vine leaves in cookery is to stuff them with an aromatic mixture of meats or rice. The result is delicious. These little parcels are enjoyed in the Middle East and Mediterranean countries (see *Dolma, Dolmades*). They are served hot or cold, with or without a sauce.

Fresh vine leaves for cooking should be medium light green and not too young. Any leaves from any vine bearing edible grapes are suitable. If you do not have fresh vine leaves, buy those preserved in brine available from good delicatessens.

□ **Basic Preparation** (fresh and preserved vine leaves): Rinse leaves in cold water. Boil a large saucepan of water, drop in leaves and blanch for 3 minutes to soften leaves. Remove with a slotted spoon to a bowl of cold water, drain and dry with paper towels before using. You may have to blanch leaves in several batches.

To stuff vine leaves: Place the leaves shiny side down on a work surface. Trim off stalks. Place filling in centre of each leaf and roll up, turning in sides of leaf to encase filling.

Vine Leaves and Mushrooms

500 g/1 lb (4 cups) mushrooms; 1 clove garlic; 250 g (8 oz) fresh or preserved vine leaves, blanched; olive oil; salt and freshly ground black pepper.

Remove and chop mushroom stems finely with garlic. Place vine leaves in layers in bottom of an oiled flameproof dish. Cover them with a film of olive oil and place over moderate heat until oil is hot. Add mushroom caps, stalk side up, cover dish with a lid or foil and cook in a preheated moderate oven (180°C/350°F, Gas Mark 4) for 20 minutes. Remove from oven. Add chopped stems and garlic, and season with

salt and pepper. Return to oven and cook for a further 10 minutes. Serve hot as a first course. Serves 4.

VOL-AU-VENT

Ever-popular vol-au-vent are tender light cases of puff pastry (paste) containing a filling of seafood, poultry, eggs, ham or vegetables usually bound with a creamy sauce.

Vol-au-vent cases can be bought prepared and ready to be filled at cake shops, supermarkets and delicatessens or frozen, ready to be baked. You may prefer to shape your own cases using either commercial frozen or home-made puff pastry (paste). **See recipes**.

Basic Vol-au-Vent Cases

1 × 375 g/12 oz packet frozen puff pastry (paste), thawed, or 1 quantity Puff Pastry (page 274); beaten egg yolk to glaze.

Roll out chilled pastry (dough) to a thickness of about 5 mm (¼ in). Cut into rounds with a floured cutter to size of your choice (**Fig 1 below**). Arrange half the rounds on a dampened baking tray. Cut centre out of remaining rounds with a slightly smaller cutter to leave a ring of pastry (dough) about 3 cm (1¼ in) wide. Gather trimmings together (do not knead) and roll out to make more vol-au-vent cases. Prick rounds previously placed on tray with a fork and brush edges with water. Carefully place a pastry (dough) ring on top of each round and press gently to seal (**2**). Mark a criss-cross pattern with tip of a sharp knife around tops of rings and brush with a little beaten egg yolk (**3**).

Bake on top shelf of a preheated hot oven (230°C/450°F, Gas Mark 8) for 10 minutes or until well puffed, crisp and golden. Remove any soft dough from inside and cool cases on a wire rack.

One 375 g/12 oz packet frozen pastry (paste) makes 3 × 10 cm (4 in) cases or 9 × 5 cm (2 in) cases. 1 quantity home-made puff pastry (paste) makes 4 × 10 cm (4 in) cases or 12 × 5 cm (2 in) cases.

NOTE: Vol-au-vent cases can be made ahead and stored in an airtight tin. Reheat for 5–6 minutes in a preheated moderate oven (180°C/350°F, Gas Mark 4) when required

Making vol-au-vent cases

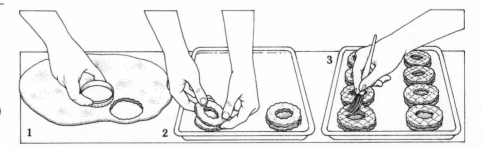

and spoon hot filling into centre.

FILLINGS FOR VOL-AU-VENT

The following quantities are sufficient for 2 × 10 cm (4 in) vol-au-vent cases or 12 × 5 cm (2 in) cases.

Creamed Spinach To 210 g/7 oz (1 cup) cooked, well dried, puréed spinach, add 4 tbsp sour cream, ¼ tsp nutmeg, and 2 tbsp finely chopped shallots fried in 1 tsp butter. Reheat, stirring, before filling cases.

Seafood To 250 g/8 oz (1 cup) cooked shelled prawns (shrimp), crab or fresh bottled oysters, drained, add 120 ml/4 fl oz (½ cup) hot thick Béchamel Sauce (see page 368), 1 tbsp single (light) cream, 2 drops Tabasco (hot pepper) sauce and a squeeze of lemon juice. Season with salt and freshly ground black pepper to taste.

Vol-au-Vent à l'Indienne

45 g/1½ oz (3 tbsp) butter; 1 onion, finely chopped; 1 tsp curry powder; 1 tsp tomato purée (paste); 3 tbsp flour; 500 ml/18 fl oz (2 cups) warm milk; 4 large vol-au-vent cases, about 10 cm (4 in) diameter (left); 1 tsp lemon juice; 4 tbsp single (light) cream; 4 hard-boiled (hard-cooked) eggs, quartered; sprigs parsley to garnish.

Melt butter in a saucepan. Add onion, curry and tomato purée (paste) and cook gently for 4–5 minutes, stirring occasionally. Blend in flour and cook for 1 minute. Remove from heat and add warm milk, stirring until smooth. Return to a low heat and bring to the boil, stirring constantly. Simmer for 5 minutes. Meanwhile, place vol-au-vent cases on a lightly greased baking tray and heat in a preheated moderate oven (180°C/350°F, Gas Mark 4) for 5–6 minutes. Remove sauce from heat and stir in lemon juice and cream. Gently fold in hard-boiled (hard-cooked) eggs. Pile filling into hot vol-au-vent cases and garnish with parsley. Serves 4.

Ham and Egg Vol-au-Vent

4 large vol-au-vent cases, about 10 cm (4 in) diameter (left); 250 g/8 oz (1 cup) diced cooked ham; 2 hard-boiled (hard-cooked) eggs, chopped; 2 shallots, finely chopped; 1 tbsp chopped green pepper; 45 g/1½ oz (3 tbsp) butter; 250 ml/8 fl oz (1 cup) hot Béchamel Sauce (page 368); 1 tsp French

(Dijon) mustard; salt and freshly ground black pepper.

Place vol-au-vent cases on a lightly greased baking tray and heat in a preheated moderate oven (180°C/350°F, Gas Mark 4) for 5–6 minutes. Meanwhile, gently fry ham, eggs, shallots and green pepper in butter until hot. Stir into hot sauce with mustard, salt and pepper. Spoon into hot cases. Serves 4.

Chicken Vol-au-Vent

4 large vol-au-vent cases, about 10 cm (4 in) diameter (opposite); 250 g/8 oz (1 cup) chopped cooked chicken; 6–8 button mushrooms, sliced; 45 g/1½ oz (3 tbsp) butter; ½ tsp Worcestershire sauce; 2 tbsp finely chopped pickled cucumbers; 250 ml/8 fl oz (1 cup) hot Béchamel Sauce (page 368); salt and freshly ground black pepper; 2 tbsp toasted slivered almonds to garnish.

Place vol-au-vent cases on a lightly greased baking tray and heat in a preheated moderate oven (180°C/350°F, Gas Mark 4) for 5–6 minutes. Meanwhile, gently fry chicken and mushrooms in butter until heated through. Stir chicken, mushrooms, Worcestershire sauce and pickles into hot béchamel sauce, and season. Spoon into hot cases and top with almonds. Serves 4.

Scallop Vol-au-Vent

250 ml/8 fl oz (1 cup) dry white wine; 1 bouquet garni; 250 g (8 oz) scallops, thickly sliced, with coral; 4 shallots, finely chopped; 1 tsp crumbled saffron; 250 ml/8 fl oz (1 cup) single (light) cream; 2 tsp arrowroot or cornflour (cornstarch); 1 tbsp dry sherry; 30 g/1 oz (¼ cup) spring onions (scallions) or leeks, cut into julienne (matchstick) strips; salt and freshly ground white pepper; 24 small cocktail-size vol-au-vent cases.

Place wine and bouquet garni in a saucepan and bring to the boil. Add scallops and poach for 1 minute. Remove scallops with a slotted spoon to a plate. Discard bouquet garni. Add chopped shallots to cooking liquid and boil to reduce to about 2 tbsp. Add saffron and cream, reduce heat and simmer for about 3 minutes. Combine arrowroot or cornflour (cornstarch) with sherry and add to sauce. Stir until thickened. Add vegetable julienne, reserving a little for garnish, and cook 1 minute to soften. Season with salt and pepper. Place vol-au-vent cases on a lightly greased baking tray and heat in a preheated moderate oven (180°C/350°F, Gas Mark 4), for 5 minutes. Reheat sauce gently, stir in scallops and spoon into cases. Sprinkle with reserved vegetables. Makes 24.

WAFFLE

Waffles have been known and loved in Europe for hundreds of years, their popularity having extended more recently to America and other parts of the western world. French waffles, or *gaufres*, are made from a light spongy batter and emerge from the specially patterned irons puffed, crisp and golden. They are usually sweet and served piping hot with a flavoured butter cream. Scandinavian waffles are often heart-shaped, honeycomb-patterned and served with lingonberries and sour cream or fresh butter. Belgian waffles are sometimes made with a yeast batter and served with fresh strawberries and a very light fluffy cream. But perhaps more familiar are waffles American-style.

To prepare a waffle iron: Follow the manufacturer's directions for seasoning an electric waffle iron before using.

□ **To Cook:** Heat the waffle iron until the indicator shows it is ready to use. If using a non-electric iron, heat until a splash of water on its surface sizzles dry. Do not grease because most waffle batters contain enough butter not to need it. Put the batter into a jug. Pour enough batter on to the bottom plate to cover about ⅔ of the surface. Close the lid and cook for 3–4 minutes. When the waffle is ready, the steam will have stopped coming from the sides and the top will lift off easily. If it does not, leave for another minute to finish cooking. **See recipes.**

Ways to Serve Waffles

Have savoury waffles at breakfast or brunch with eggs, ham, bacon or sausages; top them with grilled (broiled) tomatoes, kidneys, mushrooms or cheese; or eat for luncheon topped with any creamed vegetable, poultry or ham mixture. Serve sweet waffles at any time with butter and honey or golden (light corn) syrup; jam and whipped cream; ice cream and caramel or chocolate sauce; butter, lemon or orange juice and sugar; whipped cream and fresh or stewed fruits; or as do the Canadians with unique, delicious maple syrup.

Basic Waffle Batter

If serving with savoury foods, omit the sugar.

210 g/7 oz (1¾ cups) flour; 2 tsp baking powder; ½ tsp salt; 1 tbsp sugar; 3 eggs, separated; 350 ml/12 fl oz (1½ cups) milk; 90 g/3 oz (6 tbsp) butter, melted.

Sift flour, baking powder, salt and sugar into a large bowl. Beat egg yolks with milk and melted butter. Make a well in centre of flour mixture, pour in liquid and with just a few swift strokes combine liquid with flour. The batter will still have small lumps. Beat egg whites until stiff peaks form and fold quickly into batter until barely blended. Cook waffles as described above and serve hot. Makes 6–8.

Buttermilk Waffles

250 g/8 oz (2 cups) flour; $\frac{1}{4}$ tsp bicarbonate of soda (baking soda); 1$\frac{1}{2}$ tsp baking powder; 1 tbsp sugar; $\frac{1}{2}$ tsp salt; 2 eggs, separated; 400 ml/$\frac{2}{3}$ pint (1$\frac{2}{3}$ cups) buttermilk; 90 g/3 oz (6 tbsp) butter, melted.

Sift dry ingredients into a bowl. Beat egg yolks with buttermilk and melted butter and combine with dry ingredients. Whisk egg whites until stiff, but not dry, and fold into batter. Cook waffles as described on page 465. Makes 6–8.

Sour Cream Waffles

5 eggs; 125 g/4 oz ($\frac{1}{2}$ cup) caster sugar; 125 g/4 oz (1 cup) flour; 1 tsp baking powder; 1 tsp bicarbonate of soda (baking soda); 1 tsp ground cardamom or ginger; 250 ml/8 fl oz (1 cup) sour cream; 60 g/2 oz (4 tbsp) unsalted butter, melted.

Beat eggs and sugar until mixture falls back into bowl in a ribbon when beater is lifted out. Sift together dry ingredients. Using a large metal spoon, fold half dry ingredients into egg mixture, then sour cream and remaining dry ingredients. Stir in butter lightly. Set aside for 10 minutes before using. Cook waffles as described on page 465. Serve with berry fruits and sour cream. Makes 12.

WALDORF SALAD

Invented for the opening of New York's Waldorf-Astoria Hotel, Waldorf Salad has become a classic, especially good with ham and chicken.

See also Chicken Waldorf (page 348) and Waldorf Coleslaw (page 357).

Waldorf Salad

3 unpeeled green or red apples, cored and diced; 125 g/4 oz (1 cup) diced celery; 175 ml/6 fl oz ($\frac{3}{4}$ cup) Mayonnaise (page 204); salt and freshly ground black pepper; 60 g/2 oz ($\frac{1}{2}$ cup) walnut pieces.

Mix apples and celery in a bowl, add mayonnaise and fold through. Season, add walnuts and fold through. Turn into a salad bowl and serve at once. Serves 6–8.

WALNUT

The walnut has a long history; the Romans considered it the nut of Jupiter, and food fit for the gods. Native to Persia, walnut trees were introduced to Rome by the Greeks, and Roman legionaries carried the nut with them to England, where they soon became established. Later, however, many trees in both Europe and England were cut down to satisfy the demand for walnut furniture.

There are countless uses for walnuts, both sweet and savoury. Try walnuts with a blue vein cheese, especially Roquefort; add walnuts to a salad of cos (romaine) lettuce; make a Waldorf Salad with walnuts, celery, apple and mayonnaise (see left). Walnuts are combined with meat and chicken in Chinese cooking, and can be added to the stuffing for quail or other birds. Ground walnuts form the basis of several Middle Eastern sauces for cold fish or poultry.

Honey and walnuts make a superb combination in biscuits (cookies) and desserts; in Greece, plain yogurt is often drizzled with honey and topped with walnuts. Dates, raisins and other dried fruit go well with walnuts, and delectable caramel and chocolate fudges (see page 138) can be made with walnuts. Young green walnuts are sometimes pickled in a spiced vinegar, after first soaking in brine and may be served with cheese.

To blanch (peel) walnuts: Walnuts are usually used unblanched, but for a few delicate dishes such as Walnut Soup (page 394), the skin should be removed. Cover the shelled nuts with cold water, bring to the boil, reduce heat and simmer a few minutes. Remove from heat. Take nuts one at a time from water and use a sharp knife to peel off as much skin as possible. It is time-consuming.

Compote of Pears and Prunes with Walnuts

750 g (1$\frac{1}{2}$ lb) small pears, peeled; 250 g/8 oz (1$\frac{1}{3}$ cups) prunes; 90 g/3 oz ($\frac{3}{4}$ cup) walnut halves; 350 ml/12 fl oz (1$\frac{1}{2}$ cups) dry red wine; 310 g/10 oz (1$\frac{1}{4}$ cups) sugar; small cinnamon stick; 2 bay leaves.

Place pears, prunes and walnuts in a saucepan, and add wine, sugar, cinnamon and bay leaves. Cook very gently for about 20 minutes or until pears are tender. Cool, then cover and allow to macerate for a day. Remove cinnamon and bay leaves if liked before serving. Serves 6.

Walnut Sauce for Pasta

120 ml/4 fl oz ($\frac{1}{2}$ cup) single (light) cream; 90 g/3 oz ($\frac{3}{4}$ cup) walnut pieces, finely chopped; salt and freshly ground black pepper; grated Parmesan cheese to serve.

Heat cream gently and stir in walnuts. Season well with salt and pepper. Pour sauce over hot cooked pasta, and offer grated Parmesan cheese separately. Makes about 250 ml/8 fl oz (1 cup) sauce or enough for 2 servings of pasta.

Walnut Butter Biscuits

250 g/8 oz (1 cup) butter; 210 g/7 oz (1$\frac{1}{2}$ cups) icing (confectioners) sugar, sifted; 1 egg; 1 tsp vanilla essence (extract);

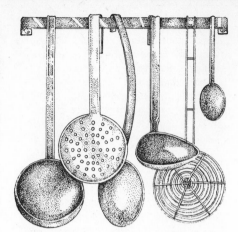

310 g/10 oz (2$\frac{1}{2}$ cups) flour; $\frac{1}{2}$ tsp bicarbonate of soda (baking soda); 1 tsp baking powder; $\frac{1}{4}$ tsp salt; 180 g/6 oz (1$\frac{1}{2}$ cups) finely chopped walnuts; walnut halves to decorate.

Cream butter with icing (confectioners) sugar. Add egg and vanilla and beat well. Sift flour with soda, baking powder and salt. Stir into creamed mixture with chopped nuts. Form mixture into small balls, place on greased baking trays and top each with a walnut half. Bake in a preheated moderately hot oven (190°C/375°F, Gas Mark 5) for 10–12 minutes or until lightly browned. Cool on wire racks. Makes about 36.

Walnut Bread

370 g/12 oz (3 cups) flour; 1 tsp salt; 3 tsp baking powder; 250 g/8 oz (1 cup) caster sugar; 125 g/4 oz (1 cup) walnut pieces; 1 egg, beaten; 250 ml/8 fl oz (1 cup) milk.

Sift flour, salt and baking powder into a bowl. Add sugar and walnuts, then stir in egg and milk. Mix until smooth. Turn into two 21 × 11 cm (8$\frac{1}{2}$ × 4$\frac{1}{2}$ in) greased loaf tins (pans). Bake in a preheated moderate oven (180°C/350°F, Gas Mark 4) for 45 minutes or until a skewer inserted in centre comes out clean. Cool on wire rack. Serve sliced with butter, and cheese if desired. Makes 2.

Maple Walnut Pie

340 g/11 oz (1 cup) maple syrup; 120 ml/4 fl oz ($\frac{1}{2}$ cup) plus 3 tbsp water; 3 tbsp cornflour (cornstarch); 60 g/2 oz (4 tbsp) butter; Sweet Rich Shortcrust Pastry, made with 250 g/8 oz (2 cups) flour (page 274); 125 g/4 oz (1 cup) coarsely chopped walnuts.

Bring maple syrup and 120 ml/4 fl oz ($\frac{1}{2}$ cup) water to the boil and boil for 2 minutes. Mix cornflour (cornstarch) and remaining water together in a small bowl, then add to boiling syrup, stirring constantly. Cook about 2 minutes or until mixture thickens. Remove from heat, stir in butter, and cool quickly by placing pan in refrigerator. Line a 20 cm

(8 in) pie plate with a little more than half the pastry (dough). Pour in cooled syrup mixture and sprinkle walnuts on top. Roll out remaining pastry (dough), and cover pie, crimping edges to seal. Cut a few slashes in centre of lid to allow steam to escape. Bake in centre of a preheated moderately hot oven (200°C/400°F, Gas Mark 6) for 30 minutes. Serve warm or at room temperature with a bowl of whipped cream if liked. Serves 6–8.

Walnut Chocolate Cake

This cake, a speciality from northern Italy, is baked in a shallow tart or pie plate and is about 2.5 cm (1 in) thick when baked.

30 g/1 oz (2 tbsp) butter, melted; 2 tbsp fine dry breadcrumbs; 5 eggs, separated; 150 g/5 oz (⅔ cup) caster sugar; 180 g/6 oz (1½ cups) ground walnuts; 150 g/5 oz (5 squares) dark chocolate, grated; grated rind ½ lemon; 60 g/2 oz (⅓ cup) chopped mixed candied peel; icing (confectioners) sugar, sifted.

Brush melted butter over bottom and sides of a 25 cm (10 in) straight-sided tart or pie plate. Sprinkle breadcrumbs over bottom and sides and shake out excess. Beat egg yolks with sugar until light and fluffy. Add ground walnuts, grated chocolate, lemon rind and peel, and mix thoroughly. Whisk egg whites until stiff peaks form and fold gently into walnut mixture. Pour on to prepared plate. Bake cake in a preheated moderate oven (180°C/350°F, Gas Mark 4) for about 1 hour or until a skewer inserted in centre comes out clean. Turn cake on to a wire rack to cool. Sprinkle sifted icing (confectioners) sugar over top and serve cut in thin wedges.

Cheese and Walnut Rounds

Beautifully flavoured savoury biscuits (crackers) with a crisp, tender shortbread texture.

210 g/7 oz (¾ cup plus 2 tbsp) butter, softened; 180 g/6 oz (1½ cups) grated mature (sharp) Cheddar cheese; 4 tbsp finely chopped walnuts; 2 tsp finely snipped chives; 280 g/9 oz (2¼ cups) flour; 45 g/1½ oz (¼ cup) ground rice; pinch cayenne; ½ tsp salt.

Cream butter and beat in cheese a little at a time. Stir in 2 tbsp walnuts and chives. Sift flour, ground rice, cayenne and salt together and stir into butter mixture. Pinch off pieces of dough and roll into balls about 2.5 cm (1 in) diameter. Flatten between your hands. Place a little apart on greased baking trays, brush lightly with cold water and sprinkle with remaining walnuts. Bake in a preheated moderate oven (180°C/350°F, Gas Mark 4) for about 15 minutes or until lightly browned. Cool on baking tray for 3 minutes, then remove and cool completely on a wire rack. Store in an airtight container and serve cold or slightly warmed. Makes about 60.

Walnut Sauce for Ice Cream

370 g/12 oz (1½ cups) caster sugar; 120 ml/4 fl oz (½ cup) water; 125 g/4 oz (1 cup) walnut pieces; pinch salt; 1 tsp vanilla essence (extract).

Bring sugar and water to the boil, stirring until sugar has dissolved. Boil, without stirring, until thick and syrupy. Add walnuts, salt and vanilla, and cook 2 minutes longer. Serve spooned over vanilla ice cream. Makes about 500 ml/18 fl oz (2 cups).

WATER CHESTNUTS

These crunchy morsels are the bulbs of an aquatic plant. Peeled, canned water chestnuts, whole or sliced, are available in most supermarkets as well as in Chinese food stores, and fresh water chestnuts are sometimes to be found in Chinese greengrocers'. Use a sharp knife to peel the dark skin from fresh water chestnuts before using them. Store peeled, fresh or canned water chestnuts, covered with water, in the refrigerator, changing water daily. They will keep for about a week.

Water chestnuts are frequently used in Chinese cookery, and their delicate flavour and crisp texture are pleasant in salads and hors d'oeuvre, and with other vegetables. **See recipes**.

Chicken Liver and Water Chestnut Appetizers

1 × 230 g/7½ oz can whole water chestnuts, drained; 500 g (1 lb) chicken livers; 250 g (8 oz) bacon rashers (slices), cut thin, rind removed.
FRENCH DRESSING: *1 tbsp wine vinegar; ½ tsp salt; freshly ground black pepper; 3 tbsp vegetable oil.*

Slice water chestnuts thickly if large. Place in a small bowl.
FRENCH DRESSING: Mix vinegar with salt and pepper, and beat in oil with a fork or whisk. Pour over water chestnuts and set aside. Trim membrane and any dark parts from livers and cut in halves or quarters if large. Stretch bacon with back of a knife and cut into pieces about 9 cm (3½ in) long. Wrap a piece of chicken liver and water chestnut in each piece of bacon and secure with a wooden toothpick. Cook under a preheated medium grill (broiler) for 3–4 minutes on each side. Makes about 20.

Stir-Fried Beans and Water Chestnuts

1 tbsp cornflour (cornstarch); 120 ml/4 fl oz (½ cup) chicken stock; 1 tbsp oil (preferably peanut); 500 g (1 lb) green beans, cut into 5 cm (2 in) lengths; 1 tsp sugar; 1 × 230 g/ 7½ oz can water chestnuts, drained and sliced if whole; 1 tbsp dry sherry; light soy sauce; hot steamed rice to serve.

Mix cornflour (cornstarch) with 1 tbsp chicken stock. Heat oil in a wok or heavy frying pan (skillet), add beans and stir-fry on moderate heat for 3 minutes. Stir in sugar, water chestnuts, remaining stock and sherry. Cover and simmer 2 minutes. Add soy sauce to taste. Stir cornflour (cornstarch) mixture again, add to pan and stir until beans are lightly glazed. Serve immediately on hot steamed rice. Serves 4.

Stir-Fried Pork with Water Chestnuts

2 tbsp peanut oil; 1 large clove garlic, sliced; 1 tsp grated fresh ginger; 250 g (8 oz) pork fillet (tenderloin), cut across grain into strips about 8 × 1 cm (3 × ½ in); 1 × 230 g/7½ oz can water chestnuts, drained and sliced if whole; 2 tsp light soy sauce; 1 tsp sugar; 1 tsp Chinese rice wine or 1 tbsp gin; 350 ml/ 12 fl oz (1½ cups) chicken stock; 1 tbsp cornflour (cornstarch); 3 drops Chinese sesame oil; 2 spring onions (scallions), sliced on long diagonal into shreds; hot steamed rice to serve.

Heat a wok or heavy frying pan (skillet), add oil and when it begins to give off a slight

haze, add garlic and ginger and stir-fry for 15 seconds. Add pork and stir-fry until browned, about 5 minutes. Add water chestnuts and stir-fry for 1 minute, then add soy sauce, sugar and wine or gin. Stir for 30 seconds, then add 250 ml/8 fl oz (1 cup) stock, cover and cook on moderate heat for 5 minutes. Mix cornflour (cornstarch) with remaining stock, add and stir until liquid is thickened. Add sesame oil and half the spring onions (scallions), mix well and serve garnished with remaining spring onions (scallions) on hot steamed rice. Serves 4.

WATERCRESS

See Cress.

WATERMELON

See Melon.

WATERZOOI (Waterzootje)

A hearty Flemish dish resembling a soup-stew and made with either chicken and vegetables or fish. Sometimes the liquid is served separately as soup, sometimes the solids are served over rice, and at other times the liquid and solids are served together. Whichever way it is served, Waterzooi is satisfying, warming and delicious. Have plenty of crusty white bread to go with it and a good crisp tossed salad to follow. **See recipes.**

Waterzooi de Poisson
(Flemish Fish Soup)

60 g/2 oz (4 tbsp) butter; 3 sticks celery, chopped; 1 kg (2 lb) mixed fish steaks, skinned and boned; salt and freshly ground black pepper; 175 ml/6 fl oz (¾ cup) dry white wine; ¼ tsp dried thyme; 1 bay leaf; 1 sprig fresh basil; 250 g/8 oz (2 cups) hot boiled rice.

Melt half the butter in a deep, heavy saucepan. Add celery and arrange fish on top. Season well with salt and pepper. Add wine and enough water to cover fish. Sprinkle with herbs and add remaining butter, cut into small pieces. Bring to the boil, reduce heat, cover and simmer gently until fish is cooked, 15–20 minutes depending on thickness of steaks. Put hot rice in 4

bowls, lift fish steaks from soup with an egg slice and place on top of rice. Pour hot cooking liquid over fish or serve it separately in other bowls. Serves 4–6.

Chicken Waterzooi

125 g/4 oz (½ cup) butter; 1 kg (2 lb) boneless chicken meat, cut into large chunks; 6 sticks celery, chopped; 4 sprigs parsley; 4 leeks, sliced; 1 onion, chopped; 1 bay leaf; ¼ tsp nutmeg; 4 black peppercorns; salt; 1.5–2 litres/2½–3½ pints (6–8 cups) chicken stock; 2 tsp lemon juice; 3 egg yolks; 120 ml/4 fl oz (½ cup) single (light) cream; 6 lemon slices to garnish.

Heat butter in a deep, heavy saucepan and brown chicken pieces. Add celery, parsley, leeks, onion, bay leaf, nutmeg, peppercorns and salt. Pour in stock, adding a little extra if necessary to cover chicken, and bring to the boil. Skim surface, then lower heat, cover, and simmer very gently for about 30 minutes or until chicken is tender. Using a slotted spoon, remove chicken and keep warm. Strain liquid into a clean saucepan and add lemon juice. Beat together egg yolks and cream and add to liquid. Cook over a gentle heat, stirring constantly, until soup thickens slightly. Do not let it boil. Return chicken to soup, pour into a heated tureen and float lemon slices on top. Serves 6–8.

WELSH RAREBIT (Rabbit)

Versions of this dish have existed for a long time in England and Scotland as well as Wales. 'Rabbit' seems to be an older version of the name.

Welsh Rarebit

125 g/4 oz (1 cup) grated mature (sharp) cheese; 4 tbsp beer; 4 tbsp milk or single (light) cream; ½ tsp dry mustard; salt; cayenne; 15 g/½ oz (1 tbsp) butter; 1 egg, well beaten; 4 slices buttered toast.

Put cheese, beer and milk or cream into a small saucepan and heat gently, stirring, until cheese melts. Remove from heat and stir in mustard, salt, cayenne, butter and egg. Return to low heat and stir until mixture thickens a little, but do not allow to boil. Pour over toast and serve at once. Serves 4.
VARIATION
Buck Rarebit: Top each serving of Welsh Rarebit with a poached egg.

WHISKY (Whiskey)

Whisky or Scotch is, of course, the national drink of Scotland, and it is hardly surprising that it should find its way into many of the traditional dishes of that country. Scottish grouse might be cooked with whisky; Atholl

Brose is a drink made of honey, oatmeal and whisky; the same basic ingredients, with cream, make a dessert known as Cranachan (see page 242); whisky is sprinkled over strawberries before serving; and whisky can flavour little after-dinner biscuits.

Apart from Scottish fare, whisky can be used for almost any chafing dish recipe. It can replace brandy in fruit cakes, giving a delightfully different flavour; a Christmas pudding can even be served with a whisky butter sauce.

There is also the differently spelt 'whiskey' of Ireland and the bourbon whiskey of America. These can be used in the same way as Scotch or other whiskies for culinary purposes. **See recipes.**

See also Ice Cream, Coffee and Scotch (page 81) and *Irish Coffee.*

Whisky Prawns

4 tbsp olive oil; 60 g/2 oz (4 tbsp) butter; 2 tbsp finely chopped shallots; 1 clove garlic, crushed; 500 g (1 lb) green (uncooked) prawns (shrimp), shelled and deveined; 2 ripe tomatoes, peeled, seeded and diced; salt and freshly ground black pepper; tiny pinch cayenne; 120 ml/4 fl oz (½ cup) whisky; 120 ml/4 fl oz (½ cup) dry white wine; hot steamed rice to serve; 5 tbsp single (light) cream; 1 tsp cornflour (cornstarch) mixed with 1 tbsp milk; 1 egg yolk.

Heat oil in a frying pan (skillet), add butter and, when melted, add shallots and garlic. Cook gently for 3 minutes. Add prawns (shrimp), tomatoes, salt, pepper and cayenne and cook gently, turning over with an egg slice, for 3 minutes or until prawns (shrimp) change colour. Pour over half the whisky, set alight and shake pan until flames die down. Add wine and simmer 3 minutes. Remove prawns (shrimp) to a bed of hot steamed rice and keep warm. Add remaining whisky and cream to pan and heat until boiling, then add cornflour (cornstarch) mixture, stirring until mixture boils again. Stir a little sauce into egg yolk, return to pan and stir for 1 minute without boiling. Adjust seasoning, pour over prawns (shrimp) and serve immediately. Serves 4–6.

Veal Kidneys with Whisky

2 veal kidneys, skinned, cored and cut into 1 cm (½ in) slices; seasoned flour; 90 g/3 oz (6 tbsp) butter; 4 tbsp whisky; 120 ml/4 fl oz (½ cup) single (light) cream; salt and freshly ground black pepper.

Soak kidney slices for 30 minutes in cold water. Drain and dry well on paper towels. Coat in seasoned flour. Heat butter until just beginning to brown, add kidneys and fry on moderate heat just until slices are stiffened and lightly browned on both sides. Remove

W

slices as they are done, and keep them warm. Return all slices to pan. Pour whisky over and set it alight. Shake pan until flames die down, then add cream and simmer gently for 5 minutes. Season with salt and pepper and serve immediately with boiled rice or toast points. Serves 3–4.

Atholl Brose

125 g/4 oz ($\frac{2}{3}$ cup) oatmeal; about 150 ml/ $\frac{1}{4}$ pint ($\frac{2}{3}$ cup) water; 2 tbsp honey; about 1 litre/1$\frac{3}{4}$ pints (4 cups) whisky.

Put oatmeal into a bowl and mix with water until it is a thick paste. Allow to stand for 30 minutes, then drain off liquid, pressing down well with a spoon so that oatmeal is quite dry. Discard oatmeal. Combine liquid and honey, stirring until well blended. Pour into two 750 ml/1$\frac{1}{4}$ pint (3 cup) bottles and fill up with whisky. Cork well. Shake before using. Serves about 25.

Whisky Boiled Fruit Cake

125 g/4 oz ($\frac{1}{2}$ cup) butter or margarine; 250 ml/8 fl oz (1 cup) milk; 250 g/8 oz (1 cup) sugar; 500 g/1 lb (2$\frac{2}{3}$ cups) mixed dried fruit; 1 tsp mixed spice (ground allspice); $\frac{1}{2}$ tsp cinnamon; 4 tbsp whisky; 1 scant tsp bicarbonate of soda (baking soda); 2 eggs, beaten; 125 g/4 oz (1 cup) self-raising flour; 125 g/4 oz (1 cup) plain (all-purpose) flour.

Place butter, milk, sugar, fruit and spices in a saucepan, bring to the boil, cover and simmer for 5 minutes. Cool a little, then stir in whisky and soda and allow to cool completely. Add beaten eggs and mix well. Sift flours together and fold into mixture, then spoon into a greased and bottom-lined 20 cm (8 in) cake tin (pan). Bake in a preheated moderate oven (180°C/350°F, Gas Mark 4) for 1 hour or until a skewer inserted in centre comes out clean. Cool in tin (pan).

WHITEBAIT

Whitebait are tiny fish, the 'fry' or young of sprats (smelts) and herrings and other similar fish. They are eaten whole, usually either fried or in fritters.

Purchase whitebait as fresh as possible from good reliable suppliers and cook on the same day. Allow 125 g (4 oz) whitebait per person. **See recipes.**

Fried Whitebait

60 g/2 oz ($\frac{1}{2}$ cup) flour; salt and freshly ground black pepper; 500 g (1 lb) whitebait; oil for deep-frying; lemon wedges to serve.

Sift flour with salt and pepper and lightly coat whitebait, shaking gently to remove

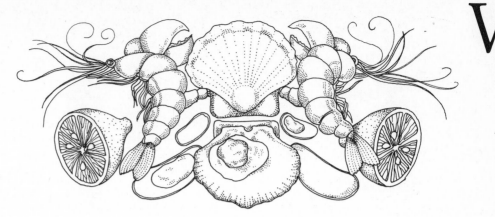

excess flour. Heat oil until just starting to smoke. Fry whitebait for 2–3 minutes. Cook only as many whitebait as will cover bottom of frying basket. Drain on crumpled paper towels. When all are cooked, return all whitebait to frying basket and fry quickly for a few seconds a second time until crisp and golden. Drain on paper towels, and serve with lemon wedges and fingers of brown bread and butter. Serves 4.

Whitebait Fritters

2 eggs; 250 g (8 oz) fresh whitebait, or 2 × 185 g/6 oz cans; salt and freshly ground black pepper; peanut oil for frying; sprigs parsley to garnish; lemon wedges to serve.

Beat eggs, add whitebait and stir until well mixed. Season with salt and pepper. Heat enough oil to cover bottom of frying pan (skillet) with a thin film. Spoon in about 1 tbsp whitebait mixture to make a large fritter. Fry 2 minutes each side or until golden. Garnish with parsley and serve with lemon wedges. Makes 4–6 large fritters.

WHITE SAUCE

See page 367.

WITLOOF

See *Chicory*.

WINE

The reason for cooking with wines is that they give depth and richness to the flavours of food. Now that well-made, inexpensive wines are available in the ingenious casks which enable you to tap off just a glassful, as well as in flagons and bottles, it seems as natural to have wine at hand in the kitchen as to have onions or butter and eggs.

Quick dishes and family meals can benefit as much from wine as can food for special occasions. Add a touch of white wine to a salad dressing or sprinkle a little on the potatoes for potato salad while they are still warm. Add a dash of white wine to the pan juices for basting a chicken. Swirl a glassful round the pan in which you have cooked ham steaks, pork chops, fish or veal; boil for a minute, stirring to pick up all the good brown bits, season and pour over the meat. Make a quick snack of toast with a wine and cheese topping, or a tasty wine-flavoured Savoury Charlotte with ingredients you probably have on the shelf. Poach or bake fruit in wine. Add a little white wine to carrots as they glaze. Use 120 ml/4 fl oz ($\frac{1}{2}$ cup) wine as the liquid for a pot roast; stir a spoonful of red or white wine into gravy or soup; make a quick red wine pan sauce for sausages, kidneys or hamburgers. All these ideas are easy, and all lift everyday eating.

Wines for Cooking

The only firm rule is that the wine you cook with should be one that you would drink. There is no need to sacrifice a fine bottle to the cooking pot, but wine for cooking should always be sound and pleasant to your palate. When it is added toward the end of cooking time or when the dish is cooked for only a short time, the full character of the wine comes through, so it is worth using the best you can. This need not be extravagant since you usually add only a spoonful or so if the cooking time is short.

In general, cook with the wine that you would drink with the food – white wine for white meats, seafood and chicken, red wine for darker meats such as beef, lamb and duck. There are exceptions – Coq au Vin is an example of chicken cooked in red wine, Alsatian Lamb is cooked in white wine. Fruits, vegetables and cheese may go with either red or white wine in different dishes.

If you have leftover table wine to use for cooking, cork the bottle tightly and store it in the refrigerator. It will last 4–5 days before turning vinegary. Use wooden spoons and pans with a non-metal lining when you are cooking with wine, as it readily picks up a metallic taste.

How much to use: Do not think that if a little wine improves a dish, a lot will make it better. Moderation is the key word. Think in terms of a wineglassful – about 120 ml/4 fl oz ($\frac{1}{2}$ cup) – if it will be cooked with other ingredients for some time, a spoonful or two if it will be cooked briefly.

The purpose of the wine is to enhance the flavour of the food, not to dominate it. Follow a recipe or, if you are adding wine to a basic recipe, follow these guidelines and proceed with discretion, tasting often. **See recipes**.

White Wine Cheese Toast

60 g/2 oz (4 tbsp) butter; 1$\frac{1}{2}$ tbsp flour; 250 ml/8 fl oz (1 cup) warm milk; 180 g/6 oz (1$\frac{1}{2}$ cups) grated Gruyère cheese; 120 ml/4 fl oz ($\frac{1}{2}$ cup) dry white wine; 1 clove garlic, crushed; 1 egg, beaten; salt and freshly ground black pepper; nutmeg; 1 loaf French bread.

Melt butter in a small heavy saucepan, add flour and stir over gentle heat for 1 minute. Remove from heat and cool a little, then add milk, stirring until smoothly blended. Return to heat and stir until boiling. Add cheese, wine, garlic, egg, salt, pepper and nutmeg. Stir just until cheese melts, then remove from heat. Slice bread on diagonal into 10–12 thick slices. Toast lightly on one side under a preheated grill (broiler) then spread other side generously with cheese mixture and grill (broil) under medium heat until lightly browned. Serves 6.

Savoury Charlotte

A substantial luncheon or supper dish made from ingredients you probably have on hand.

1 clove garlic, crushed; salt; 60 g/2 oz (4 tbsp) butter, softened; 8 slices stale white bread; 6 eggs; 120 ml/4 fl oz ($\frac{1}{2}$ cup) single (light) cream; 120 ml/4 fl oz ($\frac{1}{2}$ cup) chicken stock; 350 ml/12 fl oz (1$\frac{1}{2}$ cups) dry white wine; 1 tbsp chopped shallot; 250 g/8 oz (2 cups) grated Cheddar cheese; 125 g/4 oz

(1 cup) button mushrooms, sliced, or 1 × 440 g/14 oz can salmon, drained, skin and bones removed and flesh coarsely flaked; white pepper; lemon juice.

Crush garlic with a little salt and beat into butter. Remove crusts from bread and spread slices with garlic butter. Cut into fingers and use to line bottom and sides of a 20 cm (8 in) soufflé dish, placing buttered side against dish. Reserve any leftover fingers for top of charlotte. Beat eggs with cream, and add chicken stock, wine, shallot, cheese and mushrooms or salmon. Season with salt, pepper and lemon juice. Pour gently into bread-lined dish and top with any remaining bread fingers, buttered side out. Bake in a preheated moderate oven (180°C/350°F, Gas Mark 4) for 35–40 minutes or until a knife inserted in centre comes out clean. Serves 6.

Veal Chops Braised with Herbs

1 tbsp oil; 30 g/1 oz (2 tbsp) butter; 4 thick veal chops; salt and freshly ground black pepper; 2 tbsp chopped shallot; 120 ml/4 fl oz ($\frac{1}{2}$ cup) dry white wine or vermouth; 2 tsp chopped fresh basil or tarragon, or $\frac{1}{2}$ tsp dried; 120 ml/4 fl oz ($\frac{1}{2}$ cup) single (light) cream.

Heat oil and butter and brown chops for 3–4 minutes on each side. Season with salt and pepper. Arrange in a single layer in a flameproof casserole. Add shallot to frying pan (skillet) and cook gently 5 minutes. Add wine and basil or tarragon and simmer 3 minutes. Pour over chops. Cover casserole and bake in a preheated moderate oven (180°C/350°F, Gas Mark 4) for 20 minutes or until chops are tender. Lift out chops and place on a heated serving dish. Add cream to casserole and stir over gentle heat until heated through. Pour over veal and serve. Serves 4.

Continental Shepherd's Pie

Tomatoes, cheese and a little red wine make something different of this famous dish.

60 g/2 oz (4 tbsp) butter; 500 g/1 lb (2 cups) potatoes, peeled, cooked and mashed; 1 tbsp single (light) cream; salt and freshly ground black pepper; 2 onions, chopped; 1 clove garlic, crushed; 3 tomatoes, peeled and chopped; 500 g/1 lb (2 cups) cooked lamb or beef, minced (ground); 1 tbsp chopped parsley; 2 tbsp red wine; 60 g/2 oz ($\frac{1}{2}$ cup) grated cheese.

Melt half the butter in a heavy saucepan. Add potatoes, cream, salt and pepper and mix well. Turn potatoes into a bowl and set aside. Heat remaining butter in same saucepan, add onions and garlic and cook gently until soft. Add tomatoes and meat, and stir over moderate heat for 5 minutes.

Add parsley and wine, season with salt and pepper and mix well. Spread half the potatoes in bottom of a greased, shallow ovenproof dish. Cover with meat mixture and top with remaining potatoes. Sprinkle with cheese and bake in a preheated hot oven (220°C/425°F, Gas Mark 7) for 30 minutes. Serves 6.

Dixie Steak

750 g (1$\frac{1}{2}$ lb) braising steak (blade), cut into 2.5 cm (1 in) cubes; $\frac{1}{2}$ tsp curry powder; 1$\frac{1}{2}$ tsp sugar; 1 tbsp flour; salt and freshly ground black pepper; 1 onion, sliced; 1 green or red pepper, cored, seeded and sliced; 250 ml/ 8 fl oz (1 cup) red wine; 250 ml/8 fl oz (1 cup) water.

Place steak cubes in a casserole. Combine curry powder, sugar, flour, salt and pepper and sprinkle over meat. Cover with sliced onion and pepper; mix wine and water and pour over. Cover and cook in a preheated moderately hot oven (190°C/375°F, Gas Mark 5) for 1$\frac{1}{2}$ hours or until meat is tender. Serves 4–6.

Daube à l'Avignonnaise

A daube is a dish of meat cooked very slowly in a flavoursome wine stock. The meat is often larded with pickled (salt) pork or bacon and marinated first for deep, rich flavour. You can make the daube a day ahead, chill and remove fat from the surface, then reheat it gently when wanted.

2 kg (4 lb) boned leg of lamb; 4 cloves garlic; 2 tbsp finely chopped parsley; 125 g (4 oz) bacon or speck; 4 large onions, sliced; 2–3 carrots, chopped; salt and freshly ground black pepper; 1 tsp crumbled dried herbs (thyme, bay leaf, marjoram); 350 ml/12 fl oz (1$\frac{1}{2}$ cups) red wine; 4 tbsp brandy; 4 tbsp olive oil; strip orange rind; 1 tbsp Beurre Manié (page 35), optional.

Cut lamb into large pieces, each weighing about 90 g (3 oz), and cut a small, deep slit in each. Crush 1 clove garlic and mix with parsley. Cut bacon into pieces about the thickness of your little finger and half the length, one for each piece of lamb. Roll these bacon pieces in parsley and garlic mixture and insert a piece of bacon into each piece of lamb. Put meat in a glass or earthenware dish with half the onions, the carrots, salt, pepper and herbs. Pour over red wine and brandy and leave to marinate for 4–5 hours. Cut remaining bacon into squares and put bacon and oil into a heavy flameproof casserole. Cook gently until bacon fat runs, then add remaining onions and brown. Add meat, orange rind and remaining whole garlic cloves. Pour over marinade and simmer until liquid is reduced by $\frac{1}{3}$. Cover very tightly and place in a preheated cool

W

oven (150°C/300°F, Gas Mark 2). Cook for 4–5 hours. If desired, thicken sauce by placing casserole over low heat on top of stove and whisking in beurre manié, a little at a time. Serves 8.

Burgundy Ham

1 canned ham, about 2.5 kg (5 lb); 1 stick celery, sliced; 3 cloves; 1 tsp black peppercorns; 4 sprigs parsley; 2 onions, sliced; 1 sprig fresh thyme, or ¼ tsp dried; 500 ml/18 fl oz (2 cups) red burgundy or other dry red wine; 1½ tsp arrowroot; 1 tbsp redcurrant jelly.

Put ham into a deep casserole with remaining ingredients, except arrowroot and redcurrant jelly. Cover and bake in a preheated cool oven (150°C/300°F, Gas Mark 2) for 1 hour, basting ham several times with pan juices. Place casserole over low heat on top of stove. Mix arrowroot with a little cold water and stir in 120 ml/4 fl oz (½ cup) of cooking liquid. Pour into casserole, add redcurrant jelly and stir until liquid boils. Cover, replace in oven and cook for 15 minutes. Adjust seasoning. Slice ham and arrange on a heated serving platter. Strain sauce and spoon over. Serves 8.

Baked Beef Hash

45 g/1½ oz (3 tbsp) butter; 1 onion, finely chopped; 500 g (1 lb) diced cooked beef; 370 g/12 oz (2 cups) diced cooked potato; 4 tbsp dry red wine; 4 tbsp single (light) cream; 4 tbsp gravy or beef stock (bouillon); ¼ tsp Worcestershire sauce; 2 tbsp chopped parsley; 1 tsp chopped fresh thyme, or ¼ tsp dried; 1 tsp chopped fresh marjoram, or ¼ tsp dried; salt and freshly ground black pepper; paprika; chopped parsley to garnish.

Heat 30 g/1 oz (2 tbsp) of the butter in a frying pan (skillet), add onion and fry until lightly browned. Add beef and half the potatoes and cook, turning over with an egg slice, for 3 minutes. Stir in wine, cream, gravy, Worcestershire sauce and herbs, and season with salt and pepper. Turn mixture into a shallow ovenproof dish. Melt remaining butter in frying pan (skillet), add remaining potatoes and turn them over until they are well coated. Spread potatoes on top of hash and sprinkle with a little paprika. Bake in a preheated moderately hot oven (190°C/375°F, Gas Mark 5) for 20 minutes. Sprinkle with chopped parsley and serve very hot. Serve with vegetables or top with poached eggs. Serves 4.

Rhineland Pork Stew

60 g/2 oz (4 tbsp) butter; 1 large onion, chopped; 2 tbsp flour; 500 ml/18 fl oz (2 cups) stock or water; salt and freshly ground black pepper; 6 cloves; 1 bay leaf; 1 × 425 g/14 oz can tomatoes, drained; 1 kg (2 lb) boneless pork shoulder (shoulder butt), cut into 2.5 cm (1 in) cubes; 4 tbsp white wine.

Melt butter in a large heavy saucepan. Add onion and cook until softened but not browned. Sprinkle flour over onion and cook, stirring for 5 minutes or until flour has turned a golden colour. Add stock or water gradually and stir until smooth and thickened. Add salt, pepper, cloves, bay leaf and tomatoes. Cover and simmer 10 minutes. Add pork and wine and simmer, covered, for 1½ hours or until meat is tender. Discard bay leaf and cloves. Serves 4–6.

Alsatian Lamb

1 small leg of lamb; 350 ml/12 fl oz (1½ cups) dry white wine; 1 clove garlic, crushed; 1 onion, studded with 4 cloves; 1 bay leaf; 3 carrots, sliced; 1 tsp chopped fresh thyme, or ¼ tsp dried; salt and freshly ground black pepper; 250 g (8 oz) long bacon rashers (slices); 250 ml/8 fl oz (1 cup) stock or vegetable water; 1 tsp arrowroot (optional).

Remove excess fat from lamb. Combine wine, garlic, onion, bay leaf, carrots, thyme, salt and pepper in a large bowl. Marinate lamb in wine mixture for 12 hours. Drain, reserving marinade. Wrap lamb in bacon rashers (slices), securing with wooden toothpicks. Place on a rack in a roasting tin (pan) and add about 250 ml/8 fl oz (1 cup) marinade. Place in a preheated hot oven (230°C/450°F, Gas Mark 8) and reduce temperature to moderate (180°C/350°F, Gas Mark 4). Roast lamb for 1–1½ hours or until cooked, basting every 15 minutes with marinade. Remove lamb to a heated platter and leave in turned-off oven with door ajar while you make gravy.

Remove rack from roasting tin (pan) and place tin (pan) on top of stove. Add stock or vegetable water and boil rapidly, stirring often, until liquid is reduced to about 250 ml/8 fl oz (1 cup). If you like, thicken gravy slightly by stirring in arrowroot blended with a little cold water. Strain gravy into a heated sauceboat. Serve lamb with gravy, small boiled potatoes and whole green beans. Serves 4–6.

Poulet au Citron

Chicken with lemon cream sauce is an example of using a good white table wine to add flavour to a sauce.

1 lemon; 105 g/3½ oz (7 tbsp) butter; 2 kg (4 lb) chicken pieces (half-breasts, thighs, drumsticks); 1 tbsp sherry; 120 ml/4 fl oz (½ cup) dry white wine; grated rind 1 orange; salt and freshly ground white pepper; 175 ml/6 fl oz (¾ cup) single (light) cream; little grated cheese.

Grate rind from lemon and set aside. Peel lemon and slice thinly. Heat 90 g/3 oz (6 tbsp) butter in a large frying pan (skillet). When foaming, brown chicken on all sides. Reduce heat, cover pan and cook – shaking the pan and turning chicken every now and then – for 10–15 minutes or until chicken is nearly cooked.

Remove chicken, add sherry and wine to pan. Stir over moderate heat, picking up brown bits from bottom of pan, for a few minutes. Add orange and lemon rinds and season with salt and pepper. Turn heat to high and stir in cream slowly. The sauce should thicken a little. Put back chicken and turn to coat with sauce. Heat through for a few minutes. Arrange on a heated flameproof serving dish, spoon over sauce and sprinkle with cheese. Put a few slices of lemon and remaining butter, in small pieces, on top. Brown under a preheated grill (broiler). Serves 6.

Steak and Walnuts

4 rump (top round) or T-bone steaks; salt and freshly ground black pepper; 1 tbsp brown sugar; 1 tbsp oil; 30 g/1 oz (2 tbsp) butter; 6–8 pickled walnuts; dash Worcestershire sauce; 1 tbsp flour; red wine.

Sprinkle each steak with salt, pepper and a little of the brown sugar. Heat oil and butter and pan-fry steaks until done as you like them. Remove and keep hot. Drain walnuts, reserving liquid, and chop them. Add to pan with Worcestershire sauce and remaining sugar, then stir in flour and cook, stirring, for 2 minutes. Add reserved juice from walnuts and enough red wine to make a thin sauce. Stir until boiling, season with salt and pepper and spoon over steaks. Serves 4.

Poulet Basque

8 chicken pieces (drumsticks, thighs, half-breasts); salt and freshly ground pepper; 3 tbsp oil; 4 large tomatoes, peeled, seeded and coarsely chopped; 1 large green and 1 large red pepper, seeded and cut in julienne (matchstick) strips; 90 g/3 oz (¾ cup) mushrooms, sliced; 180 g/6 oz (¾ cup) cooked ham, diced; 120 ml/4 fl oz (½ cup) dry white wine; 1 tbsp chopped parsley.

Season chicken with salt and pepper and brown in oil, using a large, heavy saucepan. Add tomato, peppers, mushrooms and ham and pour wine over. Cover and simmer 25–30 minutes or until chicken is tender. Arrange chicken pieces on a heated platter and keep warm. Boil sauce until slightly reduced, taste and adjust seasoning and pour over chicken. Sprinkle with parsley and serve. Serves 4.

Chicken and Rice Casserole

1.5 kg (3 lb) chicken pieces (thighs, drumsticks, half-breasts); 60 g/2 oz (½ cup) seasoned flour; 2 tbsp oil; 60 g/2 oz (4 tbsp) butter; 210 g/7 oz (1 cup) long-grain rice; 12 small white onions; 250 g/8 oz (2 cups) mushrooms, halved or quartered if large; 1 × 140 g/4½ oz can pimientos, drained and chopped (optional); 1 clove garlic, chopped; salt and freshly ground black pepper; 1 tsp dried tarragon; 250 ml/8 fl oz (1 cup) hot chicken stock; 120 ml/4 fl oz (½ cup) dry white wine.

Coat chicken pieces in seasoned flour. Heat oil and butter in a large flameproof casserole, and slowly brown chicken on all sides, doing this in several batches if necessary. When all chicken is browned, return it to casserole and add rice and onions. Stir gently for a few minutes, then add mushrooms, pimientos (if using) and garlic. Season with salt and pepper, sprinkle tarragon over and gently pour over stock and wine. Bring to the boil, then cover and bake in a preheated moderately hot oven (190°C/375°F, Gas Mark 5) for about 40 minutes or until chicken and rice are tender. Add a little hot water or more stock, if necessary. Serves 6.

Ham Steaks in White Wine Sauce

60 g/2 oz (4 tbsp) butter; 6 gammon (ham) steaks; 1 tbsp flour; 350 ml/12 fl oz (1½ cups)

dry white wine; 3 tbsp redcurrant jelly; 1 tsp French (Dijon) mustard; salt and freshly ground black pepper.

Heat butter in a frying pan (skillet); when sizzling, brown gammon (ham) steaks, in 2 or 3 batches, for about 2 minutes each side. Remove gammon (ham) and keep warm. Stir flour into pan and cook for 1 minute. Add wine gradually, stirring until sauce boils and thickens. Stir in redcurrant jelly and mustard, season with a very little salt and pepper and simmer for 1 minute. Spoon hot sauce over gammon (ham) steaks to serve. Serves 6.

Beef Casserole for a Crowd

45 g/1½ oz (3 tbsp) butter; 3 onions, thinly sliced; 3 spring onions (scallions), cut into short lengths; 2 carrots, sliced; 1 stick celery, sliced; 2 cloves garlic, crushed; 1 sprig fresh thyme, or pinch dried; 1 sprig fresh rosemary, or pinch dried; 2 bay leaves; few stalks parsley, chopped; 2.5 kg (5 lb) braising steak (blade or chuck steak), cut into 5 cm (2 in) cubes; 2 tsp salt; freshly ground black pepper; 2 tsp paprika; 120 ml/4 fl oz (½ cup) red wine.

Smear butter over bottom and sides of a large casserole, or 2 smaller ones. Put in half the vegetables and herbs, then meat, then remaining vegetables and herbs. Sprinkle with salt, pepper and paprika and pour wine over. Cut a piece of greaseproof (waxed) paper the size of the casserole, butter it and place on top, then cover with a well-fitting lid. Bake in a preheated moderate oven 160°C/325°F, Gas Mark 3) for 3–4 hours or until meat is tender. Serves 12–15.

Pokolbin Veal Paprika

Pokolbin in the Hunter Valley is one of Australia's famous wine-growing areas.

1 small onion, chopped; 30 g/1 oz (2 tbsp) butter; 1 kg (2 lb) lean veal steak, cut into bite-sized cubes; 125 g/4 oz (1 cup) whole button mushrooms; salt and freshly ground white pepper; 1 tbsp paprika; 250 ml/8 fl oz (1 cup) white wine; 1 tbsp cornflour

(cornstarch); 350 ml/12 fl oz (1½ cups) sour cream.

Cook onion gently in butter in a saucepan until transparent. Lift out with a slotted spoon and set aside. Turn heat to high, add veal to pan and brown on all sides. Return onion to pan with mushrooms and sprinkle with salt, pepper and paprika. Add water to cover, cover pan and simmer for 1 hour or until meat is tender. Add a little more water if meat is drying out during this time. Tip contents of pan through a sieve into a bowl, and return liquid to pan. Add wine and boil over high heat until reduced by half. Blend cornflour (cornstarch) with a little cold water and add to pan, stirring until sauce boils and thickens. Return veal and mushrooms, heat through gently and adjust seasoning. Just before serving, stir in sour cream and heat but do not boil. Serve with hot buttered rice or noodles. Serves 6–8.

Veal Casserole

1 kg (2 lb) boneless veal; 60 g (2 oz) bacon, rind removed and diced; 30 g/1 oz (2 tbsp) butter; 4 tbsp flour; 250 ml/8 fl oz (1 cup) hot water or white stock; 250 ml/8 fl oz (1 cup) red wine; salt and freshly ground white pepper; Bouquet Garni (page 40); 24 button onions, peeled; 2 cloves garlic, chopped.

Trim gristle from veal and cut into cubes. Brown with bacon in butter. Sprinkle flour over and stir 2 minutes then stir in hot water or stock and wine. Season with salt and pepper, add bouquet garni, onions and garlic, cover and simmer 2 hours. Adjust seasoning to taste, remove bouquet garni and serve with boiled rice or noodles. Serves 4–6.

Baked Fish with Tomatoes and Mushrooms

1 × 1.5 kg (3 lb) whole fish, cleaned and scaled; 90 g/3 oz (6 tbsp) butter; 30 g/1 oz (¼ cup) chopped onion; 125 g/4 oz (1 cup) chopped mushrooms; 1 tomato, peeled, seeded and chopped; 1 tsp chopped chives;

1 tbsp chopped parsley; 45 g/1½ oz (¾ cup) fresh breadcrumbs; salt and freshly ground black pepper; 1 tbsp lemon juice; 120 ml/4 fl oz (½ cup) dry white wine.

Heat half the butter in a frying pan (skillet), add onion and cook until transparent. Add mushrooms and cook until wilted. Add tomato and simmer 5 minutes. Stir in chives, parsley, breadcrumbs, salt and pepper. Stuff fish loosely with herb mixture and close with skewers and string. Place fish in a baking pan lined with greased foil, and sprinkle with lemon juice, wine, salt and pepper. Dot with remaining butter. Bake, uncovered and basting occasionally, in a preheated moderately hot oven (200°C/400°F, Gas Mark 6) for 30–40 minutes or until the fish flakes easily when tested with a fine skewer. Sprinkle with additional butter and lemon juice. Serves 6.

Fish Fillets with Wine and Onion Sauce

6 fillets white fish, skinned; 3 small onions, thinly sliced; 175 ml/6 fl oz (¾ cup) dry white wine; 2 tbsp lemon juice; 1 bay leaf; 1 tsp salt; 6 black peppercorns; 30 g/1 oz (2 tbsp) butter; 2 tbsp flour; ¼ tsp dry mustard.

Arrange fish on a bed of sliced onion in a buttered shallow ovenproof dish. Add wine, lemon juice, bay leaf, salt and peppercorns. Cover with buttered paper and bake in a preheated moderate oven (180°C/350°F, Gas Mark 4) for 15–20 minutes. Remove fillets to a heatproof serving dish and keep warm. Strain contents of dish into a bowl, rubbing onion through sieve. If necessary, add water to make 250 ml/8 fl oz (1 cup). Melt butter in a small saucepan, add flour and cook for 1 minute. Remove from heat and cool a little, then add mustard and strained liquid, stirring until smoothly blended. Return to heat and stir until boiling. Pour over fillets. Place in a preheated moderately hot oven (200°C/400°F, Gas Mark 6) for 2 minutes if fish has been allowed to cool. Serve immediately. Serves 4.

Oysters in White Wine

1 onion, finely chopped; 4 shallots, finely chopped; 45 g/1½ oz (3 tbsp) butter; 250 ml/8 fl oz (1 cup) dry white wine; salt and freshly ground white pepper; 1 tbsp chopped parsley; 2½ tbsp single (light) cream; squeeze lemon juice; 24 canned oysters, drained; 30 g/1 oz (½ cup) fresh breadcrumbs tossed in 1 tbsp melted butter.

Cook onion and shallots gently in butter until golden. Add wine, salt and pepper and simmer until reduced by half. Remove from heat and stir in parsley, cream and lemon juice. Add oysters. Turn into a flameproof dish and sprinkle with buttered breadcrumbs. Brown under a preheated hot grill (broiler). Serve immediately, with crusty bread to mop up juices. Serves 4 as a first course, 2 as a light meal.

Oeufs Bourguignonne
(Eggs in Red Wine Sauce)

90 g/3 oz (6 tbsp) butter; 3 small onions, finely chopped; 3 tbsp flour; 400 ml/⅔ pint (1⅔ cups) red wine; salt and freshly ground pepper; pinch sugar; 6 large eggs; 6 slices bread, crusts removed.

Melt 30 g/1 oz (2 tbsp) butter in a saucepan and cook onion gently until golden. Add flour and cook, stirring, 5 minutes. Add wine, a little at a time, stirring constantly until smooth, then continue to stir until boiling. Season with salt, pepper and sugar, reduce heat and simmer gently for 15 minutes.

Meanwhile, heat remaining butter in a frying pan (skillet) and fry bread until golden-brown on both sides. Drain on crumpled paper towels, place on heated individual plates and keep warm.

Poach eggs in the red wine sauce, keeping them rather soft. Do this in 2 batches if necessary, keeping cooked eggs hot in a dish in a very cool oven. To serve, place eggs on bread croûtes, spoon sauce over and serve immediately. Serves 6 as a first course, 3 as a luncheon or supper dish.

Red Cabbage with Wine

Excellent with sausages or with roast duck, pork or game.

½ large or 1 small red cabbage, cored and finely shredded; ½ tsp salt; freshly ground black pepper; pinch nutmeg; 1 small onion, finely chopped; 30 g/1 oz (2 tbsp) butter; 2 tsp white wine vinegar; 250 ml/8 fl oz (1 cup) red or white wine; 250 ml/8 fl oz (1 cup) water; 1 large green apple, peeled, cored and diced.

Drop cabbage into boiling water and boil for 10 minutes, then drain and refresh under cold water. Drain well again. Season with salt, pepper and nutmeg and set aside. Cook onion in butter until soft but not brown. Add vinegar, wine, water and cabbage. Cover and simmer 30 minutes. Add apple and cook 25–30 minutes longer, adding a little more water if drying out. Serves 6.

Wine Cream

1 tbsp cornflour (cornstarch); 250 ml/8 fl oz (1 cup) dry white wine; 250 g/8 oz (1 cup) caster sugar; grated rind and juice ½ lemon; grated rind and juice 1 orange; 6 egg yolks; 2 egg whites; sponge fingers (lady fingers) to serve.

Mix cornflour (cornstarch) with 4 tbsp of the wine. Put sugar, remaining wine, lemon and orange rinds and juice, and cornflour (cornstarch) mixture into a saucepan and stir until boiling. Cook for 1 minute, stirring constantly. Beat egg yolks. Add a little of the hot mixture, then stir this back into pan and stir over low heat until thickened. Do not allow to boil. Strain mixture into a bowl, cool and chill. Just before serving, whisk egg whites until they hold soft peaks and fold lightly into custard. Serve with sponge fingers (lady fingers). Serves 6.

WONTON

Wonton, an important part of Chinese cookery, are little packages of savoury food wrapped in squares of fresh noodle dough and deep-fried, steamed or boiled. They are served as appetizers, as part of a meal with a sauce, or floating in a clear broth (see Short Soup).

Wonton skins (wrappers) are the same as those used in Spring Rolls and can be made at home (see page 406) but are available ready-made in some Chinese food stores. There are about 90 wrappers to 500 g (1 lb). Store tightly wrapped in plastic, in the refrigerator or freezer. They will keep for about a week under refrigeration.

Fried Wonton

250 g/8 oz (1 cup) minced (ground) pork; 2 tbsp soy sauce; 1 tsp brown sugar; 1 tsp salt; 250 g (8 oz) frozen spinach, thawed; 40 wonton wrappers; oil for deep-frying.

Combine pork, soy sauce, brown sugar and salt in a bowl and mix well. Squeeze spinach to remove excess water and dry in paper towels to remove as much moisture as possible. Chop very fine. Add to pork mixture and mix thoroughly. Place about ½ tsp of mixture in centre of each wonton wrapper. Dampen edges with water, gather edges and sides together to enclose filling in a little parcel, and press firmly together to seal. Heat oil to moderately hot and deep-fry wonton (a few at a time) for about 5 minutes or until golden-brown. Drain on crumpled paper towels and serve with Chinese Chilli Sauce, or Sweet and Sour Sauce (see page 422). Makes about 40.

WORCESTERSHIRE SAUCE

A spicy, piquant, commercially bottled sauce first made early last century from an old recipe belonging to Mr. Lea and Mr. Perrins. It is a thin, very dark brown sauce and contains among other ingredients soy sauce, vinegar, chilli, anchovies, garlic, fruits and numerous spices.

Use a little Worcestershire sauce to flavour stews, casseroles, meat pies, soups and sauces or sprinkle sparingly over steaks, hamburgers or chops according to individual taste. Try a few drops in iced tomato juice for a starter to the day. **See recipes.**

Devilled Skirt Steak

4 pieces skirt (eye of blade) steak, about 125 g (4 oz) each; 1 medium onion, grated; ½ tsp dry mustard; 1 tbsp vinegar; 1 tbsp Worcestershire sauce; 1 tsp salt; 1 clove garlic, crushed; freshly ground black pepper.

Place steak in a shallow earthenware or glass dish. Spread grated onion on steaks. Combine remaining ingredients, pour over and turn to coat steaks on both sides. Marinate for 2–3 hours, turning frequently. Grill (broil) over hot coals or under a preheated hot grill (broiler) for about 2–3 minutes on each side. Serve immediately. Serves 4.

Creamy Tomato Juice

350 ml/12 fl oz (1½ cups) well chilled tomato juice; 175 ml/6 fl oz (¾ cup) chilled single (light) cream; 1 tsp grated onion; pinch salt; pinch celery salt; 1 tsp Worcestershire sauce; 15 g/½ oz (½ cup) crushed ice; cayenne to garnish.

Combine all ingredients, except cayenne, in a blender jar or hand shaker. Blend or shake until well mixed. Serve immediately, garnished with a shake of cayenne. Serves 4.

Bloody Mary

5 tbsp vodka; 250 ml/8 fl oz (1 cup) chilled tomato juice; 1 tsp lemon juice; 1 tsp Worcestershire sauce; 2 drops Tabasco (hot pepper) sauce; ¼ tsp celery salt; pinch garlic salt; 22 g/¾ oz (¾ cup) crushed ice.

Combine all ingredients in a shaker or the goblet of a blender. Shake or blend until well mixed. Pour without straining into whisky sour glasses and serve. Serves 2.

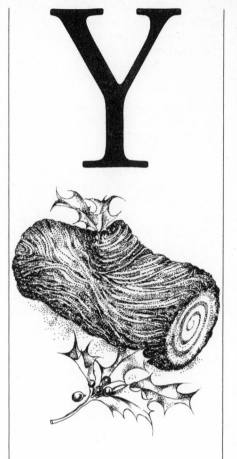

YAKITORI

This immensely popular Japanese dish consists of marinated chicken threaded on bamboo skewers and traditionally cooked over a charcoal grill.

Yakitori

2 whole chicken breasts; 8 chicken livers; 8 spring onions (scallions), cut into short lengths.
MARINADE: *2½ tbsp saké or dry sherry; 2½ tsp soy sauce; 1 clove garlic, crushed; 1½ tsp sugar; 4 slices fresh root ginger, peeled and finely chopped.*
TERIYAKI SAUCE: *120 ml/4 fl oz (½ cup) bottled teriyaki sauce; 2 tbsp saké or dry sherry; 120 ml/4 fl oz (½ cup) chicken stock.*

Combine the marinade ingredients in a small bowl, and the teriyaki sauce ingredients in a flat dish. Bone and skin the chicken breasts and cut into bite-sized pieces. Trim the livers, and cut each one in half. Add the livers to the marinade and leave, covered, in the refrigerator for about 1 hour.

Thread 4 chicken pieces and 3 lengths of spring onion (scallion) alternately on to skewers, beginning and ending with chicken. Thread the chicken livers on to another set of skewers, 4 pieces each. Turn the filled skewers around in the teriyaki mixture, coating all sides. Leave for several hours in teriyaki, turning twice.

Preheat the grill (broiler) and line the rack with foil. Grill (broil) the yakitori for 3 minutes on one side, brushing with teriyaki sauce. Turn and cook the other side, brushing again with teriyaki sauce. Serve at once on individual plates, each person receiving two chicken skewers and one of liver. Serves 4.

YAM

In appearance, yams are rather like sweet potatoes but they taste more like ordinary potatoes when cooked. They are the tubers of a tropical vine which originated in China but is now found throughout the Pacific, the West Indies and Africa. Yams can be baked, boiled or fried.
☐ **To Cook:** Yams may be baked whole, in their skins, but should be peeled before boiling or frying. Yams quickly discolour when peeled, so drop into cold acidulated water (water with a little lemon juice or vinegar added) as soon as peeled. Add a little lemon juice to the water when boiling, too. **See recipes.**

Sweet Yam Soufflé

750 g (1½ lb) yams; 150 g/5 oz (½ cup plus 2 tbsp) butter; ½ tsp salt; ¼ tsp pepper; 2 tbsp

Y

brown sugar; 2 eggs, beaten; 2 tbsp white wine; $\frac{1}{2}$ tsp cinnamon.

Bake yams whole, without peeling, in a preheated hot oven (230°C/450°F, Gas Mark 8) for about 1 hour or until tender. Halve, scoop out flesh, and mash with 125 g/4 oz ($\frac{1}{2}$ cup) butter. Add salt, pepper, sugar, eggs and wine, and beat until fluffy. Pour into a greased ovenproof dish, sprinkle with cinnamon and dot with remaining butter. Bake in a preheated moderate oven (180°C/350°F, Gas Mark 4) for about 45 minutes. Serve warm. Serves 6.

Boiled Yams with Cheese Sauce

500 g (1 lb) yams, peeled and thickly sliced; squeeze lemon juice; 60 g/2 oz (4 tbsp) butter; 2 tbsp flour; 250 ml/8 fl oz (1 cup) hot milk; 125 g/4 oz (1 cup) grated Parmesan cheese; salt and freshly ground black pepper; pinch cayenne.

Cook yams in boiling salted water, with lemon juice, until soft. Drain and set aside. Melt butter in a saucepan, stir in flour and cook for about 1 minute. Add milk and mix well. Bring to the boil, stirring constantly. Add half the cheese, and season with salt, pepper and cayenne. Place yam slices in a greased ovenproof dish, cover with sauce, then sprinkle over remaining cheese. Warm through in a preheated moderately hot oven (200°C/400°F, Gas Mark 6) for 5–10 minutes. Serves 6.

YEAST COOKERY

Cooking with yeast – baking breads, rolls, sweet fruit loaves, spiced buns, festive breads – is one of the joys of the kitchen. It is satisfying and relaxing to knead the dough, shape it and enjoy the warm spicy aroma while it bakes. Yeast is a living organism and needs food, warmth and moisture to grow. These essentials are provided when bread-type doughs are mixed. The yeast starts to work and the carbon dioxide created makes the dough rise and gives breads and buns their characteristic light texture. Be careful the liquid added is only lukewarm because too much heat will kill the yeast. Tackle yeast cookery with confidence and enjoyment; the dough is not delicate like pastry and thorough kneading results in a light even-textured product. You will not need a lot of time for preparation; most of the time is taken by the dough itself when it is set aside to rise or prove.

☐ **To Buy and Store Yeast:**
Fresh or Compressed Yeast: May be purchased from good delicatessens and health food stores. Buy in small amounts or as much as you need for the recipe, keep wrapped in the refrigerator and use within 2–3 days.

Larger amounts of yeast can be divided into packets of 15 g ($\frac{1}{2}$ oz), wrapped in foil, labelled and frozen. These are best used within 3 months of freezing.

Fresh (compressed) yeast should crumble easily, be a pale cream putty colour and have a fresh, pleasant, very faintly alcoholic smell. Do not use yeast if it smells strongly alcoholic or is a dark colour – this means it is stale.

Quantities: 1 tbsp fresh (compressed) yeast equals 15 g/$\frac{1}{2}$ oz; 2 tbsp fresh (compressed) yeast equals 30 g/1 oz.

To sponge fresh (compressed) yeast: Some recipes recommend allowing the yeast to sponge first before mixing into the dry ingredients. Follow the recipe instructions and leave the yeast and liquid in a warm place for about 15 minutes. It is ready when a creamy foam covers the surface. Not all recipes use this method, so read the instructions before proceeding.

Dried Yeast (Active Dry Yeast): Various types of dried yeast are available commercially, their differences being in the way they are used and in the quantities necessary for leavening. Be careful to check the instructions for use on the packet and use only those amounts specified as equivalent to fresh (compressed) yeast when substituting. Too much yeast will spoil the product, making it coarse and sour. Some dried yeasts need to be reactivated before using.

Dried yeast (active dry yeast) is widely available. It is packaged in sachets, cans and, in America, sold in 125 g (4 oz) vacuum-packed jars. Unopened sachets will keep for about 1 year in a cool, dry place.

Dried yeast (active dry yeast) may be substituted in recipes calling for fresh (compressed) yeast. Follow the instructions on the packet, or, as a guide, use 7 g/$\frac{1}{4}$ oz (1$\frac{1}{2}$ tsp) in place of 15 g/$\frac{1}{2}$ oz (1 tbsp) fresh (compressed) yeast. Dried yeast (active dry yeast) may often be added directly to the flour used in recipes since it does not always need to be reactivated before use, but check your sachet. If you need to reactivate the yeast, follow their instructions or, as a guide, combine 7 g/$\frac{1}{4}$ oz (1$\frac{1}{2}$ tsp) dried yeast with 2 tbsp hand-warm water and $\frac{1}{4}$ tsp sugar and leave for 10–15 minutes until frothy on top. Whisk lightly and use as your recipe indicates.

☐ **To Prepare the Dough:** Place dry ingredients in a warm bowl, make a well in the centre and pour in liquids and yeast (unless recipe specifies otherwise). Mix to a soft dough and beat well to develop the gluten in the flour.

Kneading the dough: Not all yeast doughs require kneading but if recipe specifies, turn on to a lightly floured board and knead to a smooth, elastic ball. This will take about 10 minutes. Knead in as little extra flour as possible. The dough will be quite sticky when you first start kneading but will become

smooth and satiny quite quickly. Dough is sufficiently kneaded when the impression of a finger, pressed lightly into it, smooths out quickly.

Rising: Put ball of dough into a clean, very lightly oiled bowl and turn dough over so the surface is lightly greased. Cover bowl with lightly oiled plastic wrap or a damp tea-towel. Set the bowl in a warm place free from draughts for about 1–2 hours or until the dough doubles in bulk. A temperature of about 27°C/80°F is ideal. To test when ready, lightly and quickly press 2 fingers into the top of the dough to a depth of about 1 cm ($\frac{1}{2}$ in). If dents remain the dough is ready. If they fill up, leave for 15 minutes before testing again.

Knocking (punching) down dough: After the first rising the dough is usually knocked (punched) down to expel excess carbon dioxide. Turn the dough on to a lightly floured board, punch your fist into the middle, then knead several times. Shape as required and leave to prove for 30 minutes – 1 hour, depending on size or as recipe states. Before baking test again with fingers, if dents remain, the dough is ready.

☐ **To Bake:** The shaped dough is usually put in a preheated moderately hot oven (200°C/400°F, Gas Mark 6) for the first 15 minutes to kill the yeast and prevent over-proving. When baked the bread or buns will sound hollow when tapped underneath. **See recipes**.

See also *Bread, Baps* and *Stollen.*

Basic Sweet Rich Dough

This basic dough makes many different loaves, rolls and twists of any size or shape you wish. Add spices, fruits, cherries or nuts; brush with melted butter and sprinkle with cinnamon and sugar before baking, or bake, cool and drizzle over some Glacé Icing (see page 164).

560 g/1 lb 2 oz (4$\frac{1}{2}$ cups) flour; large pinch salt; 175–250 ml/6–8 fl oz ($\frac{3}{4}$–1 cup) milk; 125 g/4 oz ($\frac{1}{2}$ cup) butter; 30 g/1 oz (2 tbsp) fresh (compressed) yeast; 125 g/4 oz ($\frac{1}{2}$ cup) caster sugar; 2 eggs, beaten.

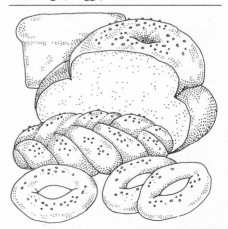

Sift flour with salt into a large bowl (**Fig 1 below**). Heat 175 ml/6 fl oz ($\frac{3}{4}$ cup) of the milk to lukewarm, add butter and allow to melt (**2**), then add to yeast and stir until dissolved (**3**). Mix in sugar and beaten eggs (**4**). Make a well in flour, pour in milk mixture (**5**) and stir until smooth, first with a wooden spoon and then with the hand. Add more warm milk if necessary to make a soft dough. When dough comes away cleanly from sides of bowl, turn on to a floured work surface and knead until smooth and elastic (**6**). Only add a little more flour if dough is too soft to knead. Place dough in a greased bowl and turn dough over so that it is lightly greased. Cover with plastic wrap or a damp cloth and leave to rise in a warm place for 45–50 minutes or until doubled in bulk (**7**). Knock (punch) down dough, pull sides to centre, turn over, then cover and allow to rise again for 30 minutes before shaping and baking.

WAYS TO USE BASIC SWEET RICH DOUGH

Sugarplum Ring: Use $\frac{1}{2}$ the quantity of Basic Sweet Rich Dough. Leave to rise in a warm place until doubled in bulk. Pinch off bits of dough and form into balls about 2.5 cm (1 in) in diameter. Knead balls lightly on a floured work surface. Roll balls of dough in melted butter, then in a mixture of brown sugar and cinnamon and place in a greased 20 cm (8 in) ring tin (pan). Leave a little space between each to allow for rising. Cover with a floured, damp cloth and allow to rise in a warm place until almost doubled in bulk. Sprinkle over chopped walnuts or almonds. Bake in a preheated moderate oven (180°C/350°F, Gas Mark 4) for 30–35 minutes.

Cloverleaf Rolls: Use $\frac{1}{2}$ the quantity of Basic Sweet Rich Dough. Leave to rise in a warm place until doubled in bulk. Shape risen dough into small walnut-sized balls. Grease bun tins (patty pans) and put 3 balls of dough in each. Cover and let rise in a warm place until doubled in bulk, 30–45 minutes. Brush rolls with milk or beaten egg and bake in a preheated moderately hot oven (200°C/400°F, Gas Mark 6) for about 15 minutes. Makes 12–18.

Preparing a Basic Sweet Rich Dough

Crescents: Use $\frac{1}{2}$ the quantity of Basic Sweet Rich Dough. Leave to rise in a warm place until doubled in bulk. Roll out dough to the size of a dinner plate. Spread with softened butter, and sprinkle with poppy seeds or sesame seeds. Cut into 8 wedges, and roll up each wedge from the widest edge towards the point. Stretch the dough gently and shape into a crescent. Place crescents well apart on a greased baking tray. Cover with a cloth and allow to rise in a warm place until the rolls double in size. Brush with a little beaten egg or milk and sprinkle over a few poppy seeds or sesame seeds. Bake in a preheated hot oven (230°C/450°F, Gas Mark 8) for 10–15 minutes or until the rolls are golden. Makes 8.

Greek Easter Bread

It's an old Greek custom to bake eggs in a nest of sweet dough. Use raw eggs, either natural white or brown, or colour them with Easter egg dye obtainable from many Greek delicatessens.

1 quantity Basic Sweet Rich Dough (page 475; 90 g/3 oz ($\frac{1}{2}$ cup) finely chopped mixed candied peel; 30 g/1 oz ($\frac{1}{4}$ cup) chopped almonds; $\frac{1}{2}$ tsp aniseed (optional); 5 eggs; Glacé Icing (page 164); red food colouring; chopped nuts or fruit jellies (small colored candies) to decorate.

After second rising, turn dough on to a floured work surface. Combine peel, almonds and aniseed, if using, and knead into dough. Divide dough in half and roll each half into a long rope about 60 cm (24 in) long. Twist ropes loosely together and shape into a ring on a large greased baking tray. Arrange unshelled eggs in hollows evenly around ring. Cover and leave to rise in a warm place for 30–40 minutes. Bake the ring in a preheated moderately hot oven (190°C/375°F, Gas Mark 5) for 30–35 minutes. Remove to a wire rack to cool. When cool, spread with glacé icing, tinted pale pink, leaving the eggs uncovered. Decorate with nuts or jellies (candies).

Greek Feast Bread

This subtly lemon-flavoured loaf, with its three-in-one design, represents the Holy Trinity. It is decorated with cherries and almonds. This quantity makes one very large bread. If your baking tray is small, use only $\frac{2}{3}$ dough to make the 3 balls, and use the remaining dough for small rolls. If desired, the rolls can be made in the shape of nests and a raw egg in the shell placed on top of each before rising, to be baked with the rolls as in the Greek Easter Bread.

1 quantity Basic Sweet Rich Dough (page 475); 1 tbsp grated lemon rind; 180 g/6 oz (1 cup) sultanas (golden raisins).
DECORATION: *Glacé Icing (page 164); glacé (candied) cherries; whole almonds.*

Prepare dough, adding lemon rind and sultanas (golden raisins) with yeast mixture. Cover dough and leave to rise in a warm place until doubled in bulk, then knock (punch) down and leave to rise again. After the second rising, turn on to a floured work surface and knead lightly. Divide into 3 and roll each portion into a ball. Place on a large greased baking tray in a clover leaf pattern, 1–2.5 cm ($\frac{1}{2}$–1 in) apart. Cover and leave in a warm place to rise again until doubled, about 30 minutes. Bake in a preheated moderately hot oven (190°C/375°F, Gas Mark 5) for about 30 minutes or until lightly browned and a skewer inserted in centre comes out clean. Remove to a wire rack and cover loosely with a tea-towel. Ice when cool, and decorate with cherries and almonds.

Tea Ring

$\frac{1}{2}$ quantity Basic Sweet Rich Dough (page 475); 30 g/1 oz (2 tbsp) softened butter; 60 g/2 oz ($\frac{1}{4}$ cup) caster sugar; 60 g/2 oz ($\frac{1}{3}$ cup) raisins; 2 tsp cinnamon.
DECORATION: *Glacé Icing (page 164); walnut halves; glacé (candied) cherries; candied angelica.*

After second rising, turn dough on to a floured work surface and roll out to an oblong about 1 cm ($\frac{1}{2}$ in) thick. Dot surface with softened butter and sprinkle with sugar, raisins and cinnamon. Roll up dough tightly, beginning at longer side, and seal by pinching edges well together. Curl dough into a ring, joining ends together well, and place on a greased baking tray. Using

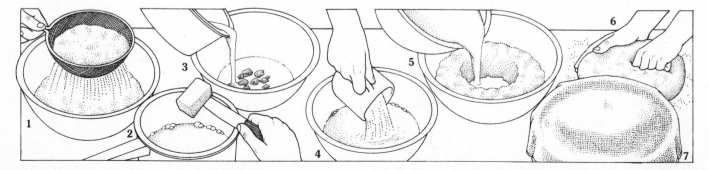

scissors or a sharp knife, snip ring at 2.5 cm (1 in) intervals around outside edge, making each cut or snip ⅔ through dough. Cover with a cloth and leave to rise for 15–20 minutes. Bake tea ring in a preheated moderately hot oven (190°C/375°F, Gas Mark 5) for about 25 minutes or until golden-brown and a skewer inserted in centre comes out clean. Make a thin glacé icing and brush over ring while still warm, then decorate with nuts, cherries and angelica.

Cardamom Braid

½ quantity Basic Sweet Rich Dough (page 475); 1–2 tsp ground cardamom; 1 egg; 2 tsp milk; caster sugar.

Make up Basic Sweet Rich Dough as directed, adding ground cardamom to the flour before sifting. Leave in a warm place until doubled in bulk.

Turn on to a floured surface and knead lightly. Divide into 3 equal portions and shape each piece into a rope about 2.5 cm (1 in) across. Line ropes up on a greased baking tray and, starting from middle, plait loosely towards ends, taking care not to stretch dough. Seal ends by pinching well together. Cover and leave in a warm place to rise until doubled in bulk.

Beat egg and milk then brush over braid. Sprinkle generously with caster sugar and bake in a preheated moderate oven (180°C/350°F, Gas Mark 4) for 30–35 minutes or until brown. Remove to a wire rack and loosely cover with a tea-towel. Cool before slicing.
NOTE: This quantity makes one large braid, you can use it to make two smaller braids if liked.

Hot Cross Buns

A favourite Hot Cross Bun recipe that always works.

500 g/1 lb (4 cups) flour; 1 tsp mixed spice (ground allspice); ½ tsp cinnamon; 1 tsp salt; 60 g/2 oz (4 tbsp) butter; 45 g/1½ oz (¼ cup) currants or sultanas (golden raisins); 45 g/1½ oz (¼ cup) chopped mixed candied peel; 30 g/1 oz (2 tbsp) fresh (compressed) yeast; 125 g/4 oz (½ cup) caster sugar; 120 ml/4 fl oz (½ cup) lukewarm water; 120 ml/4 fl oz (½ cup) lukewarm milk; 1 egg, lightly beaten.
PASTE FOR CROSS: 4 tbsp self-raising flour; 2 tbsp cold water.
GLAZE: ¼ tsp gelatine; 2 tbsp water; 1 tbsp sugar.

Sift flour, mixed spice (ground allspice), cinnamon and salt into a bowl. Rub (cut) in butter, then mix in currants or sultanas (golden raisins) and peel. Make a well in centre. Cream yeast with sugar and add a little warm water to dissolve yeast

completely. Blend remaining water and milk with yeast and add with beaten egg to flour. Mix to form a soft dough. Turn on to a lightly floured work surface and knead until smooth and elastic. Shape into a ball, place in a clean, greased bowl and turn over so that top of dough is greased. Cover and leave to rise in a warm place until doubled in bulk, 1¼–1½ hours. Turn risen dough on to a lightly floured work surface and gently press out to 1 cm (½ in) thick. Divide dough into 16 pieces and shape each into a small ball. Place balls on a greased baking tray, at least 2.5 cm (1 in) apart, or arrange in greased round cake tins (pans). Cover buns with a tea-towel and leave to rise in a warm place for a further 20–30 minutes.

To make paste for cross, combine flour and water and beat to a smooth paste. Put into a greaseproof (waxed) paper funnel or small piping (pastry) bag with a plain nozzle. Using a sharp knife, make a slight indentation in shape of a cross on top of each bun just before baking and pipe prepared paste into cross. Bake in a preheated moderately hot oven (200°C/400°F, Gas Mark 6) for about 15 minutes. Meanwhile, to make glaze, sprinkle gelatine over water in a small saucepan. When softened, dissolve over a low heat. Add sugar and stir until dissolved. Remove from heat. Remove buns from oven and brush with glaze while still hot. Stand buns in a warm place, such as on opened door of turned-off oven. This helps to set glaze. Makes 16.
VARIATION
If liked, omit the paste cross and decorate with a sweet icing (frosting) cross. Mix 140 g/4½ oz (1 cup) sifted icing (confectioners) sugar with enough hot milk to make a firm consistency, about 2 tsp. Put into a piping (pastry) bag with a plain nozzle and carefully pipe crosses on tops of baked warm buns.

Chelsea Buns

1 quantity Basic Sweet Rich Dough (page 475); 60 g/2 oz (4 tbsp) butter, softened; 60 g/2 oz (¼ cup) caster sugar; 180 g/6 oz

(1 cup) currants; 1 tsp mixed spice (ground allspice); extra caster sugar.
GLAZE: 60 g/2 oz (¼ cup) sugar; 5 tbsp water.

After first rising, turn dough on to a floured work surface, knead lightly and roll out to a rectangle about 30 × 23 cm (12 × 9 in). Spread with softened butter, and sprinkle with 1 tbsp sugar. Fold each end over to meet in centre, then fold dough in half and roll out again. Sprinkle with rest of sugar, the currants and spice. Roll up like a Swiss roll (jelly roll). Cut into slices about 4 cm (1½ in) thick. Arrange slices, cut side up and almost touching, in a well greased 20 cm (8 in) sandwich tin (layer cake pan). Cover loosely with a clean tea-towel and leave to rise in a warm place for about 20 minutes. The buns should now be touching. Sprinkle with extra caster sugar. Bake the buns in a preheated moderately hot oven (200°C/400°F, Gas Mark 6) for about 20 minutes. Meanwhile, make glaze. Combine sugar and water in a saucepan and stir over gentle heat until sugar has dissolved. Increase heat and boil, without stirring, for 3 minutes. Remove buns from oven, brush with glaze and return to oven for 30 seconds to dry glaze. Leave to cool before separating buns. Serve warm or cool with plenty of butter. Makes 12.

Cottage Loaf
(Basic Milk Dough)

500 g/1 lb (4 cups) flour; 1 tsp salt; 15 g/½ oz (1 tbsp) fresh (compressed) yeast; 3 tsp sugar; 300 ml/½ pint (1¼ cups) milk; 60 g/2 oz (4 tbsp) butter.

Sift flour and salt into a large mixing bowl. Make a well in centre of flour. Cream yeast with sugar in a small bowl. Heat 120 ml/4 fl oz (½ cup) milk to lukewarm and add to yeast and sugar mixture. Mix until dissolved, then pour into well in flour. Stir in a little of surrounding flour, then cover with a cloth and leave in a warm place for 30 minutes. Melt butter, add remaining milk and warm slightly. Pour into yeast batter in bowl and gradually mix in flour to make a dough. The dough for a cottage loaf should be quite stiff, so add some more flour if necessary.

477

Knead dough, then allow to rise until it is doubled in bulk. Knock (punch) dough down and knead lightly for 10 minutes. Shape ⅔ of dough into a ball and place on greased baking tray. Shape remaining dough into a ball, place on top of other dough, then press a floury finger right down centre of both. Leave to rise until doubled in bulk, about 35 minutes. Brush with milk, sprinkle with a little flour and bake in the centre of a preheated hot oven (230°C/450°F, Gas Mark 8) for 20 minutes. Reduce temperature to moderate (180°C/350°F, Gas Mark 4) and bake for 20–25 minutes more. To test if bread is cooked, knock firmly on base: the bread should sound hollow.

VARIATION

Fruit Loaf: Prepare dough as for Cottage Loaf, using a little more liquid. When dough has doubled in bulk, knock (punch) dough down and knead in 125 g/4 oz (⅔ cup) mixed dried fruit. Cut dough in half, shape and place in 2 well greased 21 × 11 cm (8½ × 4½ in) loaf tins (pans). Cover and leave to rise for 35–40 minutes. Bake loaves in a preheated hot oven (230°C/450°F, Gas Mark 8) for 20 minutes, then reduce heat to moderate (180°C/350°F, Gas Mark 4) and bake for a further 20–25 minutes. Paint loaves with honey or thick milk and sugar syrup as soon as they come out of the oven. Cool on a wire rack. Makes 2.

High Fibre Loaf

625 g/1 lb 6 oz (5 cups) strong wholewheat (wholewheat bread) flour; 125 g/4 oz (2 cups) unprocessed bran; 1½ tsp salt; 1½ tsp sugar; 30 g/1 oz (2 tbsp) fresh (compressed) yeast; 450 ml/¾ pint (2 cups) lukewarm water; 1 tbsp oil.
TOPPING: *2 tbsp cold water; pinch salt; 2 tbsp rolled oats.*

Mix the flour, bran, salt and sugar in a warmed bowl. Blend the yeast with a little of the water, then stir into remaining water. Add to the dry ingredients with the oil and mix to a firm dough. Turn out on to a lightly floured surface and knead for 10 minutes until smooth and elastic. Shape the dough into a ball and place in a bowl, cover with highly oiled plastic wrap and leave in a warm place for 1 hour or until doubled in bulk.

Knead the dough again on a floured surface for 5 minutes then divide in half. Pat each piece of dough out into a rectangle then fold into 3 or roll up like a Swiss (jelly) roll. Place in 2 well-greased 21 × 11 cm (8½ × 4¼ in) loaf tins (pans), shaping to fit into the corners; cover with oiled plastic wrap. Leave in a warm place for 30 minutes until the dough has risen to the tops of the tins (pans).

Mix the cold water and salt together and brush over the tops of the loaves, then sprinkle with rolled oats. Bake in a preheated hot oven (230°C/450°F, Gas Mark 8) for 35–40 minutes, until loaves are well risen, crisp on top and hollow when tapped. Turn out on to a wire rack to cool. Makes 2.

Sourdough Rye Bread

Delicious rye bread made with a sourdough starter. Make the starter first and let it stand at room temperature for 2 days before using. The starter can be refrigerated, where it will keep for 5–6 days. Return to room temperature before using to make bread.

SOURDOUGH STARTER: *7 g/¼ oz (1½ tsp) fresh (compressed) yeast; ½ tsp sugar; 150 ml/ ¼ pint (⅔ cup) lukewarm water; 90 g/3 oz (¾ cup) plain (all-purpose) flour.*
BREAD: *15 g/½ oz (1 tbsp) fresh (compressed) yeast; 2 tsp brown sugar; 310 g/10 oz (2½ cups) plain (all-purpose) flour; 350 ml/12 fl oz (1½ cups) lukewarm water; 250 g/8 oz (2 cups) rye flour; 1 tsp salt; 2 tsp caraway seeds; 1 tbsp salad oil.*

SOURDOUGH STARTER: Cream yeast with sugar, then stir in lukewarm water until dissolved. Sift in flour and mix until smooth. Cover bowl with plastic wrap and leave for 2 days, unrefrigerated, before using.
BREAD: Cream yeast with ½ tsp brown sugar and ½ tsp plain (all-purpose) flour. Mix in 120 ml/4 fl oz (½ cup) lukewarm water until dissolved, and leave in a warm place for about 10 minutes or until surface of mixture is frothy. Sift together remaining plain (all-purpose) flour, rye flour, salt and remaining sugar, returning husks in sieve to bowl. Stir in caraway seeds. Make a well in centre. Combine creamed yeast mixture with remaining lukewarm water, 2 tbsp sourdough starter and oil. Add to well in flour mixture and mix well. If dough is too dry, add extra water. Turn dough on to a lightly floured work surface and knead until smooth and elastic. Halve dough and shape into 2 rounds. Place both rounds side by side in a greased 21 × 15 cm (8½ × 6 in) loaf tin (pan). Cover tin (pan) with a clean cloth and leave to rise in a warm place until dough reaches top edge of tin (pan), about 45 minutes. Brush top of dough with water and bake in a preheated moderately hot oven (200°C/400°F, Gas Mark 6) for 35–40 minutes. Turn out and leave to cool on a wire rack.

Norwegian Sweet Bread

In many parts of the world, beer is added to bread to give extra flavour and richness. This good-tasting Norwegian bread has a full flavour and delicious chewy texture.

30 g/1 oz (2 tbsp) fresh (compressed) yeast; 300 ml/½ pint (1¼ cups) lukewarm milk;
750 g/1½ lb (6 cups) plain (all-purpose) flour; 125 g/4 oz (½ cup) sugar; 3 tsp salt; ½ tsp ground cloves; ½ tsp black pepper; 350 ml/12 fl oz (1½ cups) light beer; 180 g/6 oz (½ cup) golden (light corn) syrup; 250 g/8 oz (2 cups) rye flour; 180 g/6 oz (1 cup) raisins.

Soften yeast in warm milk in a large bowl and let stand for 5 minutes. Beat in 125 g/4 oz (1 cup) plain (all-purpose) flour, the sugar, salt, cloves and pepper. Cover bowl with a tea-towel and stand in a warm place for 40 minutes or until dough is light and bubbly. Add beer and syrup. Beat in rye flour and raisins, and enough of the remaining plain (all-purpose) flour to make a moderately stiff dough. Turn dough out on to a lightly floured work surface and knead until smooth and elastic, 8–10 minutes. Place in a greased bowl, turning dough to grease surface. Cover and allow to rise in a warm place until doubled in bulk, about 1 hour. Knock (punch) dough down and rest for 10 minutes. Divide dough into thirds and shape into 3 round loaves. Place on greased baking trays, cover and let rise until doubled in bulk, 35–40 minutes. Bake in a preheated moderately hot oven (190°C/375°F, Gas Mark 5) for about 40 minutes. Makes 3.

Sally Lunn

These traditional English cakes are named after an 18th-century cake seller.

500 g/1 lb (4 cups) flour; 1 tsp salt; 30 g/1 oz (2 tbsp) fresh (compressed) yeast; 1 tsp sugar; 2 eggs; 1 egg yolk; 250 ml/8 fl oz (1 cup) single (light) cream; 4 tbsp lukewarm water.
GLAZE: *4 tbsp milk; 3 tsp caster sugar.*

Place flour and salt in a large bowl. In a separate bowl, cream yeast with sugar. Beat whole eggs and egg yolk and strain into creamed yeast mixture. Stir in cream and whisk until frothy. Add lukewarm water. Pour yeast mixture into flour and mix to a soft dough, adding a little more water if necessary. Beat well, then cover with lightly oiled plastic wrap and clean tea-towel. Put in a warm place to rise for about 1½ hours or until doubled in bulk.

Turn dough on to a lightly floured work surface and knead lightly. Halve dough and shape into 2 rounds about 20 cm (8 in) in diameter. Put rounds into 2 greased 20 cm (8 in) cake tins (pans). Bake in a preheated moderately hot oven (200°C/400°F, Gas Mark 6) for 20–25 minutes. Combine milk and sugar and heat gently to dissolve sugar. Remove cakes from oven, brush with milk and sugar glaze and return to oven for 30 seconds to dry glaze. Serve warm with butter, or sliced, toasted and buttered. Makes 2.

Right: Fried Wonton (page 473)

Old-Fashioned Penny Buns

625 g/1¼ lb (5 cups) flour; ½ tsp salt; 15 g/½ oz (1 tbsp) fresh (compressed) yeast; 60 g/2 oz (¼ cup) plus ½ tsp sugar; 575 ml/19 fl oz (2¼ cups) lukewarm milk; 90 g/3 oz (6 tbsp) butter; 1 egg, beaten; 90 g/3 oz (½ cup) currants.
GLAZE: *60 g/2 oz (¼ cup) sugar; 120 ml/4 fl oz (½ cup) water.*

Place 310 g/10 oz (2½ cups) flour and the salt in a large bowl. Cream yeast with ½ tsp sugar in a small bowl. Stir in about 120 ml/4 fl oz (½ cup) milk until dissolved. Make a well in flour and pour in yeast mixture. Mix to a soft dough, using a little more milk if necessary, and beat well. Cover with lightly oiled plastic wrap and set aside to rise for 30–40 minutes. Warm remaining milk and melt butter in it. Allow to cool to lukewarm, and add egg. Stir into risen flour mixture together with currants, and remaining flour and sugar. Beat well, then cover bowl with lightly oiled plastic wrap and a clean tea-towel. Set aside to rise in a warm place for about 1½ hours or until doubled in bulk. Turn on to a floured work surface, punch your fist into dough and knead lightly. Shape pieces of dough into small buns and place on a greased baking tray so buns are just touching each other. Cover loosely with a cloth and allow to rise for 15 minutes.

Bake the buns in a preheated moderately hot oven (200°C/400°F, Gas Mark 6) for 15–20 minutes. Meanwhile, make glaze. Put sugar and water in a small saucepan and heat gently, stirring until sugar dissolves. Increase heat and boil for 3 minutes, without stirring. Remove buns from oven, brush with glaze and replace in hot oven for about 30 seconds to dry glaze. Serve warm from oven, with or without butter. Makes about 15.

Berlin Doughnuts

30 g/1 oz (2 tbsp) fresh (compressed) yeast; 4 tbsp lukewarm water; 60 g/2 oz (4 tbsp) butter; 250 ml/8 fl oz (1 cup) milk; 60 g/2 oz (¼ cup) sugar; 2 eggs, beaten; 1 tsp salt; 460 g/15 oz (3¾ cups) flour; 1 tsp grated lemon rind; 1 egg white; raspberry jam; oil for deep-frying; icing (confectioners) sugar.

Dissolve yeast in lukewarm water. Heat butter and milk in a saucepan, stirring until butter has melted. Cool to lukewarm. Combine yeast mixture, butter and milk mixture, sugar, eggs and salt in a large bowl and beat well. Add flour and lemon rind, beating well. Cover bowl with lightly oiled plastic wrap and a tea-towel and let rise in a warm place for about 45 minutes or until doubled in bulk. Turn on to a floured work

Left: Stollen (page 414)

surface and knead lightly. Wrap in plastic wrap and chill 20 minutes. Roll out dough to a thickness of about 1 cm (½ in) and cut into rounds using a 5 cm (2 in) floured cutter. Brush half the rounds with lightly beaten egg white. Push 1 tsp raspberry jam into centres of other rounds. Top jam rounds with rounds brushed with egg white, pinching edges firmly together. Cover loosely with a tea-towel and let rise in a warm place until almost doubled in size, about 20 minutes.

Heat oil in a deep saucepan until a cube of bread dropped into oil turns brown in 60 seconds, or temperature reaches 180°C/350°F. Fry doughnuts a few at a time for 3–5 minutes or until golden-brown, turning once. Drain on crumpled paper towels. Dust with sifted icing (confectioners) sugar and serve warm. Makes about 12.

VARIATION

Ring Doughnuts: Roll out dough and cut into 5 cm (2 in) rounds as above. Omit jam but cut a small circle from the centre of each round. Leave to rise and fry as for Berlin Doughnuts, drain, and coat in caster sugar.

Swedish Coffee Breads

60 g/2 oz (4 tbsp) butter or margarine; 500 g/1 lb (4 cups) flour; 75 g/2½ oz (⅓ cup) sugar; pinch salt; 30 g/1 oz (2 tbsp) fresh (compressed) yeast; 250 ml/8 fl oz (1 cup) lukewarm milk.
TO FINISH: *beaten egg; sugar; chopped nuts; melted butter; cinnamon; currants; sultanas (golden raisins).*

Melt butter and allow to cool. Place flour in a bowl. Add sugar and salt, mix and make a well in centre. In a small bowl, cream yeast in a little of the milk and add to flour with butter and remaining milk. Mix with a spoon until all milk and butter have been absorbed, then cover with a damp cloth and leave to rise in a warm place for 2 hours or until dough has doubled in size. Knock (punch) down and knead dough until soft and smooth. Divide into 3 portions and shape as follows:

Coffee Twist: Take 1 portion of dough and divide it into 3 equal pieces. Roll each piece between floured hands to a long strand. Plait strands together lightly, then cover and allow twist to rise on a baking tray for 45 minutes. Brush with beaten egg, and sprinkle with sugar and chopped nuts. Bake in a preheated moderate oven (180°C/350°F, Gas Mark 4) for 15–20 minutes. Makes 1.

Cinnamon Ring: Roll out second portion of dough as thinly as possible on a floured work surface. Brush with melted butter and sprinkle heavily with sugar and cinnamon. Roll up like a Swiss roll (jelly roll) and join ends together to make a ring. Make sure ends are well sealed. Place ring on a baking tray to rise. Cut almost through dough at 2.5 cm (1 in) intervals with scissors. Turn

leaves of dough thus formed to alternate sides to expose filling. Allow to rise again for 45 minutes. Brush with beaten egg and bake in a preheated moderate oven (180°C/350°F, Gas Mark 4) for 15–20 minutes. Makes 1.

Fruit and Nut Buns: Roll out remaining portion of dough as thinly as possible on floured work surface. Brush with melted butter and sprinkle heavily with sugar, currants, sultanas (golden raisins) and chopped nuts. Roll up like a Swiss roll (jelly roll) and cut into 2.5 cm (1 in) slices to form small buns. Decorate each bun by cutting with scissors in different patterns according to your imagination. Allow to rise on baking tray 45 minutes. Brush with beaten egg and bake in a preheated moderately hot oven (200°C/400°F, Gas Mark 6) for 5–10 minutes. Makes about 12.

Honey Potato Buns

15 g/½ oz (1 tbsp) fresh (compressed) yeast; 4 tbsp lukewarm water or potato cooking water; 3 tbsp milk; 5 tbsp vegetable oil; 180 g/6 oz (½ cup) honey; 90 g/3 oz (½ cup) lukewarm, freshly cooked, sieved potatoes (no milk or seasoning added); 1½ tsp salt; 1 egg, beaten; about 370 g/12 oz (3 cups) flour; melted butter to glaze.

Stir yeast into water in a small bowl until dissolved. In a large bowl, mix milk, oil, honey, potatoes and salt. Add egg, then yeast mixture. Stir in flour, 125 g/4 oz (1 cup) at a time, to make a soft but not sticky dough. Turn out on to a floured work surface and knead until dough is smooth and elastic and small blisters appear just under surface. Wash bowl in warm water, dry and oil lightly. Place dough in it and turn dough about so that it is lightly oiled all over. Cover with oiled plastic wrap and let it rise in a warm place for about 1½ hours or until doubled in bulk. Pat dough out into a rectangle on a floured work surface and cut into 24 even pieces. Roll into balls and place in a greased shallow baking tin (pan) about 35 × 25 cm (14 × 10 in). Cover loosely with a damp cloth and let rise in a warm place until doubled in bulk, about 45 minutes. Brush with melted butter and bake in a preheated hot oven (220°C/425°F, Gas Mark 7) for 12–15 minutes or until golden. Makes 24.

Mix and Drop Rolls

250 ml/8 fl oz (1 cup) lukewarm water; 15 g/½ oz (1 tbsp) fresh (compressed) yeast; 60 g/2 oz (¼ cup) sugar; 1 tsp salt; 1 egg, beaten; 4 tbsp vegetable oil; 370 g/12 oz (3 cups) flour.

Put water into a large bowl and stir in yeast until dissolved. Add sugar, salt and egg. Stir mixture well, then let stand for about 10 minutes until bubbly. Add oil and half the flour and beat with your hand until very smooth, then add remaining flour and beat in. Cover bowl with oiled plastic wrap and leave in a warm place for about 30 minutes or until dough has almost doubled in bulk. Drop dough into greased deep bun tins (muffin pans) so that each cup is half full. Let rise in a warm place until almost doubled in bulk. Bake in a preheated moderately hot oven (200°C/400°F, Gas Mark 6) for 15 minutes or until golden-brown. Makes 24.

VARIATIONS

Flavourings 1: After dough has risen in bowl, divide into 4 parts and place each in a bowl with one of the following: 45 g/1½ oz (¼ cup) drained, crushed pineapple; 4 tbsp chopped raisins; 4 tbsp chopped pecans, walnuts or almonds; 30 g/1 oz (¼ cup) grated cheese; 60 g/2 oz (¼ cup) crumbled crisp-fried bacon; 2 tbsp mixed, chopped fresh herbs, or 2 tsp dried herbs mixed with 2 tbsp chopped parsley; 1 tbsp unsweetened cocoa powder mixed with 1 tbsp sugar; 2 tsp cinnamon or mixed spice (ground allspice). Mix each portion of dough with the added ingredient until well blended. Then spoon into tins (pans), let rise and bake as in the basic recipe.

Flavourings 2: Before putting dough into bun tins (muffin pans), place one of the following ingredients into each greased tin (pan): 1 tsp butter, 1 tsp brown sugar and 3 pecan or walnut halves; 1 tsp butter and 1 tsp desiccated (shredded) coconut; 1 tsp butter and 1 tsp jelly-style jam. Half fill prepared tins (pans) with dough, let rise and bake as in the basic recipe.

Bran Rolls

250 ml/8 fl oz (1 cup) lukewarm water; 30 g/1 oz (2 tbsp) fresh (compressed) yeast; 250 ml/8 fl oz (1 cup) boiling water; 250 g/8 oz (1 cup) butter or margarine; 150 g/5 oz (⅔ cup) sugar; 90 g/3 oz (1 cup) unprocessed bran; 1½ tsp salt; 2 eggs, beaten; 750 g/1½ lb (6 cups) flour.

Put lukewarm water into a large bowl and stir in yeast until dissolved. In another bowl, pour boiling water over butter or margarine, stir in sugar, bran and salt and let stand until lukewarm. Stir eggs into bran mixture. Add yeast mixture and mix well. Stir in flour 125 g/4 oz (1 cup) at a time. Cover bowl with oiled plastic wrap and a cloth and let rise in a warm place until almost doubled in bulk, about 2½ hours. Knock (punch) dough down and drop by spoonfuls into greased bun tins (muffin pans) filling cups half full. Let rise in a warm place until almost doubled in bulk, about 1 hour. Bake in a preheated moderately hot oven (190°C/375°F, Gas Mark 5) for about 15 minutes or until golden. Makes 48.

YOGURT

Yogurt has a long history and an enviable reputation for promoting health and longevity. In the Middle East and India, yogurt is part of the basic daily diet and is frequently used in cooking.

Yogurt is a fermented milk product, with a pleasantly tangy taste and a smooth, refreshing texture. It can be made from cow's milk or goat's milk, full cream or skim. Flavoured yogurts are available commercially, as well as plain yogurts, but the latter is easily prepared at home.

Ways to Use Yogurt

Plain or flavoured yogurt is a delicious, soothing dessert. Plain yogurt may take the place of cream with an apple pie, steamed pudding or fruit salad; topped with honey and walnuts, in Greek fashion, it appeals to young and old; and it complements perfectly fresh berry fruits, such as strawberries and raspberries.

Yogurt accompanies curries and Indian vegetable dishes, Middle Eastern dishes such as lentils and rice, or fried aubergine (eggplant). Meats and vegetables are often cooked in yogurt, and yogurt can serve as the base of a spicy marinade for chicken. Salads can be dressed with yogurt dressing, or the same basic ingredients may be combined as a dip or spread, or even a chilled summer soup. Hot vegetable soups can be enriched with yogurt, and in summer yogurt blended with water and garnished with mint makes a most refreshing and cooling drink (see *Lassi*).

Cooking with yogurt: Yogurt curdles if cooked for a long time, for example in recipes such as meatballs in yogurt, or yogurt soup. To prevent this, the yogurt should be mixed with cornflour (cornstarch) – 1 tsp of cornflour (cornstarch) mixed in a little cold water to every 350 ml/12 fl oz (1½ cups) yogurt – slowly brought to the boil and then allowed to simmer over very low heat, uncovered, for about 10 minutes. Stir constantly with a wooden spoon, in one direction only, while bringing to the boil. **See recipes.**

Home-Made Yogurt

Either fresh or powdered milk may be used, full cream or skim. If you want yogurt of a thick, junket-like consistency, evaporate some of the water from the milk by allowing it to simmer gently for about 20 minutes over low heat. Yogurt needs a 'starter' for fermentation; use 2 tbsp commercial or home-made plain yogurt per 500 ml/18 fl oz (2 cups) milk. Temperature is important for satisfactory fermentation to take place. If you have a thermometer, the milk should reach 45°C/115°F when it is cooled after heating and before the yogurt 'starter' is added. Or test by inserting a finger into the milk for a count of 10 by which time the heat from the milk will 'sting' your finger.

NOTE: Automatic yogurt makers, which keep the mixture at a constant temperature can be used.

Yogurt Cheese

If yogurt is turned into a muslin-lined sieve and left to drain overnight, the result is a soft, creamy sort of cheese, called *labna* in the Middle East. It may be eaten as is, or flavoured with herbs, spices or garlic, or added to salads or vegetable dishes.

For a creamier cheese combine cream with plain yogurt before draining. The resulting soft cream cheese is delicious with fruit and has many other uses:

Ways to Use Yogurt Cream Cheese

● Halve a small ripe melon, remove seeds, fill with a few spoonfuls of Yogurt Cream Cheese and sprinkle with a little brown sugar.
● Curl a few slices of prosciutto and serve with Yogurt Cream Cheese as a first course.
● Mound about 125 g/4 oz (½ cup) Yogurt Cream Cheese on a dessert plate, mask with sweetened cream and surround with any fresh summer fruit, or sliced or halved stewed apricots, plums or peaches.
● Offer a little black pumpernickel bread or Scottish oatcakes with Yogurt Cream Cheese, served in place of a cheese board.

Home-Made Yogurt (1)

500 ml/18 fl oz (2 cups) milk; 2 tbsp plain yogurt.

Heat milk to boiling and when froth starts to rise remove from heat. Pour into a casserole and leave until milk is warm, then beat 2 tbsp milk into yogurt in a small bowl and set aside. Allow remaining milk to cool to a little more than blood heat (45°C/115°F), or test as described left. Remove skin on top of milk and gently mix in yogurt starter, stirring only a few times to blend. Cover casserole with lid, wrap in a blanket or thick cloth and leave undisturbed in a warm place for 8–10 hours or until thickened. Chill for at least 4 hours before using. Makes about 350 ml/ 12 fl oz (1½ cups).

Home-Made Yogurt (2)

500 ml/18 fl oz (2 cups) milk; 30 g/1 oz (¼ cup) full-cream milk powder 2 tbsp plain yogurt.

Set aside 2 tbsp fresh milk and stir milk powder into remainder. Heat gently to boiling point, stirring occasionally to dissolve milk powder. Simmer very gently for 20 minutes (**Fig 1 opposite**). Remove skin from top of milk and pour milk into a small casserole dish (**2**). Leave to cool until a little warmer than blood heat (45°C/115°F), or test as described left (**3**). Beat yogurt into reserved 2 tbsp milk and mix very gently into warm milk, stirring only a few times to blend (**4**). Cover dish with a lid, wrap in a thick cloth or blanket and leave undisturbed in a warm place for 8–10 hours or until thickened. Chill at least 4 hours before using. Makes about 300 ml/½ pint (1¼ cups).

VARIATION

Skim Milk Yogurt: Replace milk powder and fresh milk with 125 g/4 oz (1 cup) skim milk powder and 350 ml/12 fl oz (1½ cups) water. Use low-fat yogurt as a starter.

Yogurt Cream Cheese

500 ml/18 fl oz (2 cups) plain yogurt; 250 ml/8 fl oz (1 cup) single (light) cream.

In a bowl combine yogurt and cream. Pour mixture into a sieve lined with a double thickness of dampened cheesecloth and set over a bowl. Let mixture drain for 8 hours or until whey has drained off and curds are firm. Makes about 370 g/12 oz (1½ cups).

Yogurt Cheese with Fresh Herbs

600 ml/1 pint (2½ cups) plain yogurt; salt and freshly ground black pepper; 1 tbsp sour cream; ½ clove garlic, crushed; 2 tbsp chopped parsley; 2 tsp chopped mixed fresh herbs (oregano, thyme, dill, chives).

Pour yogurt into a colander or sieve lined with muslin or cheesecloth and set over a bowl. Tie it up with a string so that it forms a bag. Lift it out of colander and leave it to drain overnight, tying string to a wooden spoon across a bowl. Next day, tip drained curds from bag into a bowl and beat until smooth, adding a little salt and pepper and the sour cream. Mix garlic with half the herbs and fold in. Form into a round flat shape, or pile into a small dish, and sprinkle over remaining herbs. Chill for 1–2 hours before serving. Serves 4.

Turkish Yogurt Soup

4 tbsp rice; 1.2 litres/2 pints (5 cups) good chicken or beef stock; 1 tbsp cornflour (cornstarch); 500 ml/18 fl oz (2 cups) plain yogurt; 2 egg yolks, beaten; 2 tbsp chopped fresh mint.

Cook rice in stock for 20 minutes. In separate pan, blend cornflour (cornstarch) with a little yogurt, then add remaining yogurt, beating until smooth. Add egg yolks and a few spoonfuls hot stock and whisk. Stir over low heat until thickened, but do not allow to boil. Add yogurt mixture to simmering stock. Cook for a further 2 minutes, stirring constantly. Thin with a little water if necessary. Serve sprinkled with chopped mint. Serves 6.

Quick Yogurt Soup

500 ml/18 fl oz (2 cups) plain yogurt, chilled; 250 ml/8 fl oz (1 cup) tomato juice, chilled;

2 tbsp parsley sprigs; 2 tbsp chopped spring onion (scallion); 1 tbsp fresh mint sprigs; 1 tsp fresh oregano sprigs, or ¼ tsp dried; salt and freshly ground black pepper; 125 g/4 oz (1 cup) finely chopped cucumber; black (ripe) olives and crusty bread to serve.

Put yogurt, tomato juice and herbs into a blender or food processor and process until herbs are finely chopped. Pour into 4 soup bowls and top with cucumber. Serve with olives and crusty bread. Serves 4.

Chicken in Yogurt

1.5 kg (3 lb) chicken joints, skinned; 350 ml/12 fl oz (1½ cups) plain yogurt; 1 large red or green pepper, cored, seeded and finely chopped; 1 tsp paprika; 5 cm (2 in) piece fresh ginger, peeled and grated; 2 green chillies, seeded and crushed; 4 cloves garlic, crushed; 1 tsp salt; 5 tbsp finely chopped parsley or fresh coriander.

Prick chicken all over with very sharp fork and place in a bowl. Combine yogurt with pepper, paprika, ginger, chillies, garlic and salt. Pour over chicken, cover and marinate overnight in refrigerator, turning from time to time. Next day, heat a large pan, add chicken and marinade and stir in parsley. Cover and cook on high heat for 5 minutes, then reduce heat to medium and cook for about 20 minutes or until chicken is tender. Turn chicken over to coat evenly in yogurt mixture, and serve immediately. Serves 6.

Mogul Chicken

Convenient chicken pieces, marinated in yogurt and spices and baked until golden-brown, are delicious hot or cold.

6 half-breasts of chicken; 2 tsp grated lemon rind; 120 ml/4 fl oz (½ cup) plain yogurt; 4 tbsp oil; 1 onion, grated; 2 cloves garlic, crushed; 2 tsp grated fresh ginger; 1 tbsp curry powder; 1 tsp ground cumin; 1 tsp ground coriander; 1 tsp paprika; 8 cm (3 in) cinnamon stick, broken into pieces; 1 tsp salt.

Remove skin from chicken and make 3 or 4 deep diagonal slashes in each piece. Place chicken in one layer in a large shallow baking

Making Home-Made Yogurt (2)

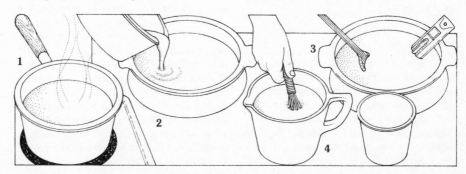

dish. Combine remaining ingredients and spoon over chicken, rubbing it in and coating thoroughly. Cover and refrigerate for 12 hours, turning pieces over and rubbing in marinade several times. Remove dish from refrigerator 1½ hours before serving time. Stand at room temperature for 1 hour, then remove chicken pieces, place a rack in dish and arrange chicken on it, bony side up, in one layer. Place in a preheated moderately hot oven (200°C/400°F, Gas Mark 6) and bake for 15 minutes or until lightly coloured, then turn pieces over and baste with marinade. Bake 10–15 minutes more, basting again after 7 minutes. Chicken is done when it is golden-brown and juices run clear when thickest part of flesh is pierced with a fine skewer. Serve hot or at room temperature. Serves 6.

Yogurt Salad Dressing

250 ml/8 fl oz (1 cup) plain yogurt; 1 tbsp vinegar or lemon juice; 2 tsp grated onion or finely chopped shallot; salt and freshly ground black pepper; chopped fresh herbs as desired.

Whisk together yogurt, vinegar or lemon juice and onion or shallot. Season with salt and pepper and add herbs if desired. Use with green salads, chicken salads, cooked vegetable salads and beetroot. Makes 250 ml/8 fl oz (1 cup).

Onions Baked with Yogurt

120 ml/4 fl oz (½ cup) milk; 60 g/2 oz (4 tbsp) butter; 6 onions, sliced; 3 egg yolks; 250 ml/8 fl oz (1 cup) plain yogurt; salt and freshly ground pepper; 60 g/2 oz (½ cup) grated cheese; 15 g/½ oz (¼ cup) soft wholewheat breadcrumbs or wheat germ.

Put milk, butter and onions into a saucepan, cover and simmer 20 minutes. Drain and lay onions in a greased, shallow ovenproof dish. Mix egg yolks with yogurt, salt and pepper. Pour mixture over onions, covering them, and sprinkle with cheese and breadcrumbs or wheat germ. Bake in a preheated moderate oven (180°C/350°F, Gas Mark 4) for 20 minutes or until topping is set and browned. Serve with grilled (broiled) or roast lamb. Serves 6.

Yogurt Mousse

500 ml/18 fl oz (2 cups) plain yogurt; 4 tbsp brown sugar; grated rind and juice 2 lemons; grated rind and juice ½ orange; 2 tbsp gelatine; 4 tbsp water; 3 egg whites.
TO SERVE: *bananas, lemon juice and brown sugar.*

Put yogurt into a large bowl and beat in sugar, lemon and orange juices and rinds. Soak gelatine in water and dissolve over hot water. Fold gently into yogurt mixture. Whip egg whites until they hold soft peaks, and fold into yogurt mixture. Chill for 2 hours and serve on the same day, the texture changes if kept. Serve with bananas sprinkled with lemon juice and brown sugar. Serves 6.

Yogurt Honey Cakes

750 ml/1¼ pints (3 cups) water; 625 g/1¼ lb (2½ cups) sugar; 1½ tbsp lemon juice; ½ tsp vanilla essence (extract); 250 ml/8 fl oz (1 cup) plain yogurt; 4 tbsp single (light) cream; 2 eggs; 250 g/8 oz (2 cups) plain (all-purpose) flour; 1 tsp bicarbonate of soda (baking soda); 250 g/8 oz (1 cup) butter.
TO SERVE: *honey and whipped cream.*

Mix water, sugar and lemon juice in a saucepan, bring to the boil and simmer 5 minutes. Stir in vanilla and keep syrup hot.

Beat yogurt with cream and eggs until smooth. Sift flour with soda and gradually stir into yogurt mixture. Heat half the butter in a frying pan (skillet) and drop in tablespoonfuls of the batter, spaced well apart. Cook until golden-brown underneath, turn and cook other side. As cakes are cooked, drop into hot sugar syrup, leave 5 minutes then remove to a platter.

When you have used up half the batter, pour off any remaining butter from the pan, wipe it out quickly and repeat the cooking process with remaining butter and remaining batter. Soak in hot syrup as before, remove to platter and allow to cool a little.

Halve cakes, spread with honey and cream. Serve immediately. Makes about 20.

Yogurt Ice Cream

Use a creamy, mild yogurt in preference to a skim milk yogurt.

500 ml/18 fl oz (2 cups) plain yogurt; 125 g/4 oz (½ cup) caster sugar; ½ tsp vanilla essence (extract).

Beat yogurt with sugar and vanilla. Pour mixture into shallow ice cream tray, cover with foil and place in freezer. When about half frozen, remove from freezer and process in blender until smooth. Return to freezer. Allow yogurt ice cream to soften for about 30 minutes in refrigerator before serving. Serve with fresh or cooked fruits. Serves 3–4.

YORKSHIRE PUDDING

The Yorkshire Pudding of England should be crisp, light, well puffed and golden. It is made from a simple batter mixture that is baked in the oven and traditionally served with roast beef. In Yorkshire it is sometimes served separately, before the meat. Yorkshire pudding can be baked in one tin (pan) or in individual bun tins (deep muffin pans). Some people like to place the joint on a trivet and pour the batter directly into the baking dish beneath so the pudding bakes under the meat and catches the drippings as the meat roasts. Have the batter ingredients at room temperature before mixing for maximum rising.

For recipes see page 28.

YULE LOG (Bûche de Noël)

The traditional French Christmas cake is log-shaped, covered with chocolate butter cream (Crème au Beurre) and patterned to represent the bark of a log.

Yule Log

60 g/2 oz (½ cup) flour; ½ tsp baking powder; ¼ tsp salt; 60 g/2 oz (⅓ cup) dark chocolate, chopped; 4 eggs; 180 g/6 oz (¾ cup) caster sugar; 1 tsp vanilla essence (extract); ¼ tsp bicarbonate of soda (baking soda); 2 tbsp cold water; extra caster sugar; 1 quantity Chocolate Crème au Beurre (page 164).

Sift together flour, baking powder and salt. Melt chocolate in a heatproof bowl over a saucepan of hot water. Put eggs into a bowl, add sugar and beat over hot water, or on highest speed of electric mixer, until mixture is very light and thick and greatly increased in volume. Fold sifted flour mixture and vanilla into egg mixture all at once. Stir soda and cold water into melted chocolate and fold quickly and evenly into cake mixture. Turn the mixture into a greased and lined 38 × 25 × 2.5 cm (15 × 10 × 1 in) Swiss roll tin (jelly roll pan). Bake cake in a preheated moderately hot oven (200°C/400°F, Gas Mark 6) for 15 minutes or until cake springs back when centre is lightly touched. Loosen edges and turn on to a tea-towel thickly dusted with caster sugar. Peel off lining paper and trim edges of cake with a sharp knife. Roll immediately in towel and leave to cool on a wire rack for at least 1 hour. When cold, carefully unroll cake and spread with ⅓ of chocolate butter cream. Roll cake once more and cut off one end of cake at an angle. Place roll on plate or board, arrange cut piece of cake alongside to resemble a stump and cover whole 'log' with remaining butter cream. Make a bark-like finish with a fork and chill until serving time.

ZABAGLIONE (Zabaione al Marsala)

The famous Italian dessert, Zabaglione, is a superb mixture of egg yolks, Marsala and sugar whisked to perfection over hot water. Serve in warmed individual glasses accompanied with crisp biscuits (cookies) or sponge fingers (lady fingers), or spoon over fresh strawberries.

Chilled Zabaglione is a delicous variation for those who prefer a cold dessert, or the chilled mixture can be used to fill puffs or éclairs. **See recipes.**

Zabaglione

8 egg yolks; 2 tbsp sugar; 300 ml/½ pint (1¼ cups) Marsala.

Combine egg yolks and sugar in a heatproof bowl or top of a double saucepan (double boiler) and beat together until pale and fluffy. Stir in Marsala and place over hot, but not boiling, water. Whisk constantly over a low heat until mixture is frothy and thick. Be careful it does not boil or it will curdle. As soon as mixture is thick, pour into warmed glasses and serve immediately. Serves 4–6.

Chilled Zabaglione

1 tbsp gelatine; 1–2 tbsp water; 8 egg yolks; 125 g/4 oz (½ cup) sugar; 250 ml/8 fl oz (1 cup) Marsala; ½ tsp vanilla essence (extract); grated rind ½ lemon; ¼ tsp cinnamon; 575 ml/19 fl oz (2¼ cups) double (heavy) cream.

Soften gelatine in water, then dissolve over simmering water. Set aside. Beat egg yolks and sugar in a heatproof bowl or top of a double saucepan (double boiler) until white and fluffy. Stir in Marsala and place over hot, but not boiling, water. Whisk constantly over a low heat until mixture is frothy and thick. Remove from heat, stir in dissolved gelatine and continue beating until mixture is cool. Add vanilla, lemon rind and cinnamon. Place bowl or pan in a larger one containing crushed ice and continue beating until mixture is thoroughly chilled and thick. Whip cream until it holds stiff peaks and fold through ice-cold mixture. Place in individual glasses and chill for 2–3 hours. Serves 6–8.

ZEST

The name given to the outside coloured rind of any citrus fruit, such as lemon, orange, grapefruit and lime. Zest contains essential oils that lend a distinctive flavour to any dish in which it is used.

To remove zest: Scrape surface of fruit with a very fine grater using short sharp strokes; or rub fruit surface with sugar lumps until they become impregnated with citrus oils; or pare very thinly with a vegetable peeler. Make certain you do not include any white pith with the rind as this can make the dish bitter.

See also *Lemon.*

ZUCCHINI (Courgette)

Zucchini are small young members of the marrow family, very popular in Italy and France, where they are known as courgettes. They have a light delicate flavour and the texture, when cooked, should have a slight bite. Choose very young zucchini that are no more than 10 cm (4 in) long so they will be sweet and tender. They should be firm to the touch without any bruising or soft spots. Avoid spongy zucchini – they may be bitter.

□ **Basic Preparation:** Wash the zucchini gently, but do not peel. Trim off stem and any little brown mark at the other end, then cut diagonally into thick or thin slices or long strips, or if small and young enough, leave whole. If slices are to be deep-fried, sprinkle them with salt and leave to drain for 1 hour; use 2 tsp salt for 500 g (1 lb) zucchini. Rinse, drain and pat dry with paper towels.

□ **To Cook:** Boil quickly, uncovered, in a little lightly salted water for 3–4 minutes or until tender, depending on the thickness of the slices. Drain and toss in butter. Be careful not to overcook as zucchini softens a little after draining and the texture should be tender but still crisp.

Or toss in oil or a mixture of oil and butter and gently pan-fry until tender.

Alternatively, grate raw zucchini and toss in butter over gentle heat for 1–2 minutes; stir in a little single (light) cream and a pinch of nutmeg. You can also grate raw zucchini into salads. **See recipes.**

Sautéed Zucchini

750 g (1½ lb) courgettes (zucchini), thinly sliced; salt and freshly ground black pepper; 3 tbsp oil; 1 tbsp chopped parsley; 1 tbsp chopped fresh oregano.

Put courgette (zucchini) slices in a colander, sprinkle with salt and leave for 1 hour. Rinse, drain and dry on paper towels. Heat oil in a large frying pan (skillet). Cook courgette (zucchini) slices until translucent and edges are lightly browned, turning with a spatula to cook uniformly. This should take only 3–4 minutes. Add more oil if needed. Sprinkle with salt, pepper and herbs. Serve with grilled (broiled) meats or poultry. Serves 6.

Buttered Zucchini

salt; 500 g (1 lb) small courgettes (zucchini); 60 g/2 oz (4 tbsp) butter; freshly ground black pepper.

Bring about 5 cm (2 in) of water to the boil in a saucepan and add ¼ tsp salt and courgettes (zucchini). Keep heat fairly high so that water boils briskly, and cook courgettes (zucchini) for about 4 minutes if very small, 6–7 minutes if larger, turning over halfway through with a wooden spoon if water does not cover them. Drain courgettes (zucchini) and cut diagonally into 2 or 3 pieces or leave whole. Melt butter in a saucepan, add courgettes (zucchini) and heat gently, rolling about by tilting pan, until very hot and coated in butter. Season lightly with salt and pepper and serve immediately. Serves 4.

NOTE: You can boil the courgettes (zucchini) ahead of time, cool quickly under cold running water and set aside. Cut into pieces and reheat in butter just before serving.

Grated Buttered Zucchini

500 g (1 lb) courgettes (zucchini); salt; 125 g/4 oz (2 cups) shredded watercress or lettuce; 60 g/2 oz (4 tbsp) butter; freshly ground black pepper; pinch nutmeg.

Grate courgettes (zucchini) on coarse side of a hand grater, or with coarse grating attachment of a food processor. Toss with a little salt and stand for 30 minutes in a colander or sieve to drain. Rinse under cold water and dry using paper towels. Fold watercress or lettuce through courgettes (zucchini). Heat butter and, when foaming, put in vegetables. Toss with 2 forks over medium heat. When very hot, season with salt, pepper and nutmeg. Serve immediately. Serves 4–6.

Deep-Fried Zucchini

500 g (1 lb) courgettes (zucchini), thinly sliced lengthways; 2 tsp salt; 60 g/2 oz (½ cup) flour; freshly ground black pepper; oil for deep-frying.

Place courgettes (zucchini) in a colander, sprinkle with salt and leave to drain for 1 hour. Rinse in cold water, drain and dry well using paper towels. Combine flour and black pepper, and shake courgettes (zucchini) slices lightly in flour mixture. Heat oil in a deep saucepan and deep-fry courgettes (zucchini) for about 1 minute or until golden, crisp and tender. Fry slices in 4 or 5 batches to prevent their sticking together. Drain on crumpled paper towels and serve immediately, with a grinding of black pepper. Serves 4.

Zucchini Soup

15 g/½ oz (1 tbsp) butter; 2 tsp oil; 1 small onion, chopped; 6 medium courgettes (zucchini), thickly sliced; 1 medium potato, peeled and sliced; salt and freshly ground black pepper; ½ tsp dried tarragon (optional); 1 litre/1¾ pints (4 cups) chicken stock; 4 tbsp single (light) cream (optional).

Heat butter and oil in a saucepan, add

prepared vegetables and sprinkle with salt, pepper and tarragon. Cover and cook over a low heat for 10 minutes, shaking pan occasionally and checking that vegetables do not colour. Add stock and simmer, covered, for 10 minutes or until vegetables are soft. Cool, then push through a sieve or purée in a blender or food processor. Reheat soup, adding more seasoning if necessary. For extra richness, 1 tbsp single (light) cream may be added to each serving. Serves 4.

Creamed Zucchini with Rosemary

A delicately flavoured dish, excellent on its own or with veal, chicken or lamb.

750 g (1½ lb) courgettes (zucchini), cut diagonally into 2.5 cm (1 in) slices; 90 g/3 oz (6 tbsp) butter; 120 ml/4 fl oz (½ cup) single (light) cream; 10 cm (4 in) sprig fresh rosemary; salt and freshly ground black pepper.

Drop courgette (zucchini) slices into lightly salted boiling water and cook for 5 minutes. Drain and dry with paper towels. Melt butter in clean saucepan, add courgettes (zucchini), cover and cook very gently for about 5 minutes or until tender. Gently stir occasionally to prevent courgettes (zucchini) from browning or sticking. Stir in cream, sprig of rosemary, season with salt and pepper, and leave to cook for a further 5 minutes. Turn slices frequently to coat with sauce and become flavoured with rosemary. Remove rosemary before serving. Serves 4.

Zucchini Boortha

60 g/2 oz (4 tbsp) ghee or butter; 1 onion, finely chopped; 1 small clove garlic, finely chopped; 1 tsp grated fresh ginger; ½ tsp ground cumin; 3 red or green chillies, seeded and chopped; 500 g (1 lb) courgettes (zucchini), thickly sliced; 30 g/1 oz (2 tbsp) creamed coconut; salt; 1 tsp lemon juice.

Melt ghee or butter in a heavy pan and fry onion, garlic, ginger, cumin and chillies until soft, about 5 minutes. Add courgettes (zucchini) and cook until tender, about 15 minutes, then mash. Add creamed coconut, allow it to melt, then season with salt and lemon juice. Serves 4.

Zucchini à la Grecque

Serve chilled as a first course or with crusty French bread as a light luncheon dish.

8–10 small courgettes (zucchini), cut into 5 mm (¼ in) slices; 1 tbsp chopped fresh tarragon, or 1 tsp dried; 1 tbsp lemon juice; 1 clove garlic, crushed; 1 tbsp finely chopped parsley; 1 tomato, peeled and seeded; pinch dried thyme; salt and freshly ground black pepper; 1 bay leaf; 4 tbsp olive oil; 250 ml/8 fl oz (1 cup) water.

Place all ingredients in a heavy saucepan or flameproof casserole. Cover and bring to the boil. Reduce heat and simmer gently until courgettes (zucchini) are tender but still firm, 5–6 minutes. Cool, then chill. Serves 3–4.

Ricotta Stuffed Zucchini

A delicately flavoured Ricotta cheese filling blends beautifully with courgettes (zucchini). Serve as a first course, for a light luncheon or at supper.

8 plump courgettes (zucchini), about 10–13 cm (4–5 in) long; ½ tsp salt; 1 thick slice white bread, crusts removed; 4 tbsp milk; 125 g/4 oz (½ cup) Ricotta cheese; ½ tsp chopped fresh oregano, or ¼ tsp dried; 1 clove garlic, crushed; 30 g/1 oz (¼ cup) grated Parmesan cheese; 1 egg yolk; freshly ground black pepper.

Drop courgettes (zucchini) into a saucepan of boiling salted water and boil for 3 minutes, then drain. Meanwhile, soak bread in milk and when soft, squeeze it dry. Slice courgettes (zucchini) in half lengthways and, using a teaspoon, scoop out centres to make boat-shapes with shells about 5 mm (¼ in) thick. These provide cases for filling. Finely chop scooped-out courgette (zucchini) flesh and put into a bowl. Add bread, Ricotta, oregano, garlic, Parmesan, egg yolk and pepper and beat thoroughly. The mixture should be fairly soft; if too stiff add a little milk. Fill courgette (zucchini) cases with stuffing. Oil a shallow baking dish and arrange courgette (zucchini) close together in a single layer. Bake in a preheated moderately hot oven (190°C/375°F, Gas Mark 5) for 20–25 minutes or until filling is golden-brown. Serves 4.

Tomatoes and Zucchini

2 tbsp oil; 1 clove garlic, crushed; 500 g (1 lb) courgettes (zucchini), cut into 5 mm (¼ in) slices; 2 tomatoes, peeled, seeded and diced; salt and freshly ground black pepper.
GARNISH: *12 black (ripe) olives, halved and stoned (pitted); finely chopped parsley.*

Heat oil in a heavy frying pan (skillet), add garlic and courgette (zucchini) and cook, stirring frequently, until softened. Add tomatoes and cook until they are soft. Season with salt and pepper. Garnish with olives and parsley. Serve hot or at room temperature. Serves 4.

Herbed Zucchini Salad

500 g (1 lb) courgettes (zucchini); 3 tbsp olive oil; 1 tbsp lemon juice; 1 tbsp chopped parsley; 1 tbsp snipped chives; 2 tbsp chopped fresh basil, oregano or marjoram; salt and freshly ground black pepper.

Cook courgettes (zucchini) in sufficient lightly salted boiling water to cover for 7–8 minutes or until just tender. Drain, then quarter courgettes (zucchini). Combine olive oil and lemon juice, pour over hot courgettes (zucchini) and toss gently to coat thoroughly. Cool and chill. Just before serving, drain off any remaining liquid and add herbs, salt and pepper. Toss gently and serve immediately. Serves 4.

Stuffed Zucchini

6 medium courgettes (zucchini), halved lengthways; 30 g/1 oz (2 tbsp) butter; 250 g/8 oz (1 cup) minced (ground) steak; 1 clove garlic, crushed; 1 tbsp tomato purée (paste); 2 tsp light soy sauce; salt and freshly ground black pepper; 120 ml/4 fl oz (½ cup) water.

Scoop out flesh from courgette (zucchini) halves and chop. Retain courgette (zucchini) shells. Melt butter in a frying pan (skillet) and brown meat with garlic. Stir in tomato purée (paste), soy sauce, salt, pepper and chopped courgette (zucchini) flesh. Cook gently for 5 minutes. Spoon meat mixture into courgette (zucchini) shells and place them in a shallow casserole or gratin dish in one layer. Pour water around courgettes (zucchini). Cover dish with a lid or foil and bake in a preheated moderate oven (180°C/350°F, Gas Mark 4) for 20–30 minutes or until courgettes (zucchini) are tender. Serves 4–6.

Z

Zucchini Bread

3 eggs; 560 g/1 lb 2 oz (2¼ cups) caster sugar; 3 tsp vanilla essence (extract); 250 ml/8 fl oz (1 cup) oil; 250 g/8 oz (2 cups) grated courgettes (zucchini); 370 g/12 oz (3 cups) flour; ¼ tsp baking powder; 1 tsp salt; 1 tsp bicarbonate of soda (baking soda); 3 tsp cinnamon; 125 g/4 oz (1 cup) chopped walnuts.

Beat eggs until li_____ _____ _____ then add sugar, vanilla an_____ mousse-like, wh_____ when poured f_____ courgette (zuc_____ baking powde_____ Fold this into_____ with walnuts_____ bottom-lined _____ (pans). Bak_____ (180°C/35_____ or until a s_____ out clean._____ Makes 2._____

NOTE: Us_____ (zucchini_____

Zucch_____

This ze_____ antipa_____

750 g_____ thin s___ 120 ml/4 fl oz (½ cup)_____ juice; 1 tbsp chopped fresh oregano, o_____ dried; 3 cloves garlic, crushed; ½ tsp salt; 45 g/1½ oz (¼ cup) black (ripe) olives; freshly ground black pepper.

Place courgettes (zucchini) in a shallow dish. Combine olive oil, lemon juice, oregano, garlic and salt, mix well and pour over courgettes (zucchini). Cover, place in a refrigerator and marinate for at least 2 hours. One hour before serving, transfer courgettes (zucchini) to salad plates with a slotted spoon, reserving marinade. Garnish with olives, sprinkle with pepper and drizzle with reserved marinade. Serves 6–8.

Souffléd Stuffed Zucchini

4 large courgettes (zucchini); salt; oil; 350 ml/12 fl oz (1½ cups) Mornay Sauce (page 368); 3 large eggs, separated; pinch cream of tartar; 1 tbsp grated Parmesan cheese; freshly ground black pepper.

Halve courgettes (zucchini) lengthways and scoop out flesh leaving a 1 cm (½ in) thick wall. Salt courgettes (zucchini), stand 15 minutes, rinse and dry. Lightly oil outsides of courgettes (zucchini). Chop flesh fine and combine with mornay sauce and egg yolks. Whisk egg whites with cream of tartar until they hold soft peaks, and fold into sauce. Pile

---

---

mixture into courgette (zucchini) shells. Arrange on a greased baking tray. Place in a preheated moderately hot oven (200°C/400°F, Gas Mark 6), turn heat down immediately to 190°C/375°F, Gas Mark 5 and bake 18 minutes or until filling is puffed and golden-brown and courgettes (zucchini) are tender. Serve immediately on heated plates. Serves 4 as a first course, 8 as a vegetable accompaniment to meat or poultry.

_____ssaka

_____es (zucchini), thickly sliced; _____ oil; 1 large onion, chopped; _____inely chopped; 500 g/1 lb _____ed (ground) lamb or veal; 1 tsp _____opped fresh oregano, or ½ tsp _____/6 fl oz (¾ cup) beef stock; _____d black pepper; brown sugar; _____r; 3 tomatoes, peeled and thickly _____p grated Parmesan cheese; 2 tbsp _____rumbs.

_____g/1 oz (2 tbsp) butter; 2 tbsp flour; _____pint (1¼ cups) warm milk; salt and _____ound black pepper; 90 g/3 oz _____up) feta cheese, crumbled; 2 egg _____aten.

_____urgettes (zucchini) into a colander and _____e liberally with salt. Leave 30 minutes _____n, then rinse and dry slices on paper _____s. Heat oil in a frying pan (skillet) and _____ courgettes (zucchini) until golden on _____sides. Remove courgette (zucchini) slices from pan with a slotted spoon and set aside.

Add onion and garlic to the pan and cook gently until soft. Turn up heat, add meat and cook until it changes colour, stirring and breaking down lumps with a fork. Sprinkle with flour and oregano and stir in, then add beef stock and season to taste with salt and pepper. Cook gently for a few minutes, stirring once or twice. Taste and add a very little brown sugar and vinegar as needed according to your taste.

Make the sauce: melt butter in a saucepan, add flour and cook, stirring, on gentle heat 1 minute. Remove from heat, cool a little and add warm milk, stirring until smoothly blended. Return to heat and stir until boiling. Season with salt and pepper then stir in cheese, remove from heat and whisk in egg yolks. Stir 2 tbsp of this sauce into meat mixture.

Turn meat mixture into a greased, wide but fairly deep ovenproof dish. Arrange tomatoes in a layer on top then courgette (zucchini) slices on tomatoes. Pour cheese sauce over courgettes (zucchini) and sprinkle with Parmesan and breadcrumbs. Bake in a preheated moderately hot oven (190°C/375°F, Gas Mark 5) for about 30 minutes or until top is golden-brown. Serves 6–8.

ZWIEBACK

A twice-baked rusk of German origin made with a sweetened yeast dough usually flavoured with lemon and cinnamon. Zwieback is baked as a loaf, cooled and sliced. The slices are then dried out in the oven to become crisp and golden-brown. They keep well stored in an airtight container.

Serve Zwieback to nibble with sherry or sweet white wine, or top with jam.

Zwieback may also be crushed and used in a crumb crust for unbaked desserts such as some cheesecakes or gelatine mixtures.

Zwieback

30 g/1 oz (2 tbsp) fresh (compressed) yeast; 150 ml/¼ pint (⅔ cup) lukewarm milk; 500 g/1 lb (4 cups) strong (bread) flour; 105 g/3½ oz (7 tbsp) butter, melted and cooled; 75 g/2½ oz (⅓ cup) sugar; grated rind ½ lemon; 1 tsp salt; ½ tsp cinnamon; extra melted butter.

Dissolve yeast in milk and leave until frothy, about 15 minutes. Sift flour into a bowl and make a well in centre. Pour yeast mixture into well and mix in about ¼ of flour. Cover bowl and leave in a warm place for yeast sponge to rise, about 20 minutes. Beat in butter, sugar, lemon rind, salt and cinnamon. Mix to a fairly stiff dough and knead thoroughly for about 10 minutes or until smooth and elastic. Cover bowl with a clean cloth and leave to rise in a warm place until doubled in bulk, about 1½ hours. Turn on to a lightly floured work surface, knock (punch) dough down and knead briefly. Divide into 6 pieces and shape into ovals about 5 cm (2 in) thick. Place on 2 floured baking trays and leave in a warm place for about 30 minutes or until doubled in bulk again. Brush with melted butter and bake in a preheated moderate oven (180°C/350°F, Gas Mark 4) for about 25 minutes or until pale golden. Cool on wire racks. When quite cold, cut into 1 cm (½ in) slices, place on baking trays and bake in a preheated moderate oven (160°C/325°F, Gas Mark 3) for about 20 minutes or until golden-brown on both sides. Makes about 50.

487

RECIPE INDEX

RECIPE INDEX

RECIPE INDEX

RECIPE INDEX

ACKNOWLEDGEMENTS

Photographs by *Bryce Attwell* 24, 60, 77, 132, 169, 207, 261, 263, 401; *Rex Bamber* 21, 351; *Robert Golden* 96, 114, 189, 226, 279, 298, 334, 352, 354, 390, 425; *Melvin Grey* 1, 2–3, 4, 59, 78, 95, 131, 167, 168, 170, 187, 208, 225, 315, 333, 426, 443, 479; *Paul Kemp* 408, 480; *Roger Phillips* 42, 280, 389, 462; *Paul Williams* 149, 243, 372.

Illustrations by *Russell Barnett; Vana Haggarty; Pat Ludlow* and *Sara Silcock.*